Southern
Africa

Malawi
p118

Zambia
p566

Mozambique
p169

Victoria Falls
p549

Zimbabwe
p617

Namibia
p242

Botswana
p42

Swaziland
p530

Lesotho
p97

South Africa
p322

Anthony Ham,
James Bainbridge, Lucy Corne, Mary Fitzpatrick,
Trent Holden, Brendan Sainsbury

PLAN YOUR TRIP

Welcome to Southern
Africa 4
Southern Africa Map 6
Southern Africa's Top 17. . 8
Need to Know 16
If You Like. 18
Month by Month 21
Itineraries 25
Planning a Safari 31
Southern Africa
at a Glance 38

MARK READ/LONELY PLANET ©

SOSSUSVLEI P289

RADEK BOROVKA/SHUTTERSTOCK ©

MAKGADIKGADI PANS
NATIONAL PARK P55

ON THE ROAD

BOTSWANA 42
Gaborone 43
Mokolodi Nature
Reserve 49
Eastern Botswana 50
Francistown. 50
Makgadikgadi &
Nxai Pans 54
Makgadikgadi Pans
National Park 55
Nxai Pans National Park . . 57
Chobe National Park . . . 58
Okavango Delta 65
Maun. 65
Moremi Game Reserve . . . 74
Kalahari 76
Central Kalahari
Game Reserve. 76
Understand Botswana . . 81
Survival Guide. 87

LESOTHO 97
Maseru 100
Northeastern
Highlands. 106
Southern Lesotho. 108
Understand Lesotho . . . 111
Survival Guide. 114

MALAWI 118
Lilongwe. 120
Northern Malawi. 126
Karonga 126
Livingstonia. 128
Central Malawi 136
Nkhotakota 137
Cape Maclear 140
Southern Malawi 144
Liwonde 144
Majete Wildlife Reserve. . 157
Understand Malawi . . . 158
Survival Guide. 162

MOZAMBIQUE 169
Maputo 172
Southern
Mozambique 182
Ponta d'Ouro &
Ponta Malongane 182
Limpopo National Park . . 184
Central Mozambique . . 195
Beira 195
Northern
Mozambique 206
Nampula 206
Mozambique Island 210
Pemba 219
Quirimbas Archipelago . . 224
Understand
Mozambique 228
Survival Guide. 233

NAMIBIA 242
Windhoek. 243
North-Central
Namibia 253
Etosha National Park. . . . 260
Northern Namibia 264
The Caprivi Strip 266
Northwestern
Namibia 269
Damaraland. 269
The Kaokoveld 272
The Skeleton Coast 275
Central Nambia. 277
Swakopmund 277
Walvis Bay 283
Southern Namibia 292
Lüderitz 294
Fish River Canyon 297
Understand Namibia . . 301
Survival Guide. 311

SOUTH AFRICA. . . . 322
Cape Town 323
Western Cape 355

Contents

Winelands 355
The Overberg 364
Garden Route 371
Eastern Cape 382
Garden Route East 382
Sunshine Coast 386
KwaZulu-Natal 404
Durban 406
Zululand 419
Free State 440
Bloemfontein 441
Gauteng 449
Johannesburg 449
Soweto 464
Pretoria 465
Mpumalanga 471
Nelspruit (Mbombela) . . . 471
Kruger National Park . . 476
Limpopo 481
Polokwane 481
Bela-Bela 484
North West Province . . 489
Sun City 491
Northern Cape 495
Kimberley 495
Kgalagadi
Transfrontier Park 501
**Understand
South Africa 505**
Survival Guide 518

SWAZILAND 530
Mbabane 532
Central Swaziland 534
Ezulwini Valley 534
**Northwestern
Swaziland 540**
**Northeastern
Swaziland 541**
Hlane Royal
National Park 541
Mlawula
Nature Reserve 542
Mkhaya Game Reserve . . 543

**Understand
Swaziland 544**
Survival Guide 546

VICTORIA FALLS . . 549
Livingstone 554
Victoria Falls 559

ZAMBIA 566
Lusaka 567
Eastern Zambia 577
South Luangwa
National Park 578
North Luangwa
National Park 584
Southern Zambia 584
Lower Zambezi
National Park 585
Western Zambia 590
Kafue National Park 590
Northern Zambia 596
The Copperbelt 603
Understand Namibia . . 605
Survival Guide 610

ZIMBABWE 617
Harare 619
Northern Zimbabwe . . . 629
Kariba Town 629
Eastern Highlands 633
Mutare 633
Bvumba Mountains 635
Chimanimani 637
**The Midlands
& Southeastern
Zimbabwe 640**
Masvingo 640
Great Zimbabwe 640
Western Zimbabwe 643
Bulawayo 643
**Understand
Zimbabwe 650**
Survival Guide 656

UNDERSTAND

**Southern Africa
Today 662**
History 664
Culture 671
Wildlife 679
**Music in
Southern Africa 695**
Environment 701

SURVIVAL GUIDE

Directory A–Z 714
Transport 727
Health 736
Language 741

Welcome to Southern Africa

An astonishingly diverse region fused by its prolific wildlife, breathtaking landscapes and remnants of ancient culture, Southern Africa is Africa at its most memorable.

Wildlife Watching

Southern Africa has some of Africa's greatest safari destinations: Kruger, Chobe, Etosha, South Luangwa and the Okavango Delta. The sheer number of elephants, lions, leopards, hyenas, rhinos, buffaloes, antelope and myriad other species will quickly overwhelm your camera. Spot them on self-drives, guided wildlife drives or charter flights...and if that's not up close and personal enough, what about the chance to track highly endangered black rhino...on foot? Or the chance to see the fabled black-maned lions of the Kalahari, or the desert elephants of Namibia? Or explore the Caprivi Strip, one of Africa's emerging wildlife destinations, before the rest of the world catches on.

Landscapes

There's famous Table Mountain rising high above Cape Town, that mighty gash hacked out of the earth's surface at Fish River Canyon, and the desertscapes of the Kalahari, but the lonely rural tracks that take you out into an otherwise trackless wilderness are just as memorable. In Namibia, huge slabs of flat-topped granite rise from mists of wind-blown sand and swirling dust. And Zambian floodplains are dotted with acacia trees and flanked by escarpments of dense woodland. Want to see all the landscapes the region has to offer? Put aside a lifetime.

Cultural Experiences

For insight into extraordinary rock art left by ancestors of the San, visit Tsodilo Hills in Botswana and the extensive rock-art galleries in Namibia, South Africa and Zimbabwe. Step back through the centuries in the cultural melting pot of Mozambique Island; stay in a mud hut in Zimbabwe and watch Shona sculptors at work; prop up the bar at a *shebeen* in Soweto; or mingle with Basotho people in Lesotho. Southern Africa has so many different takes on African culture, both ancient and contemporary, that it can be difficult to know where to begin.

Adventure Activities

Namibia is Southern Africa's headquarters for adrenaline-pumping fun, but there's adventure to be had all over the region. Sail by dhow past remote islands off Mozambique's jagged coastline, abseil Livingstonia in Malawi, and try tackling the ferocious rapids down the Zambezi River or bungeeing from a bridge at Victoria Falls. In South Africa, the Garden Route with its old-growth forests offers shark-cage diving, surfing, skydiving, canoeing and kloofing (canyoning). But it's in Swakopmund in Namibia where you'll truly take off, with the stirring juxtaposition of sand dunes and Atlantic Ocean waves providing a splendid backdrop to so many acts of sheer joy.

Why I Love Southern Africa

By Anthony Ham, Writer

Southern Africa ticks all my Africa boxes at once. This is one of the greatest wildlife shows on earth. I love the sight of lions on a kill or black rhinos communing in secret at an Etosha watering hole. Or the possibility of seeing desert elephants and tracking rhinos on foot amid the stirring beauty of Damaraland. Or the chance to learn the wisdom of the ancients in a San community in the Kalahari. And I love the search for Lady Liuwa as hyenas stream across the plain at Liuwa Plain in Zambia. What's not to love?

For more about our writers, see p768

Above: Skeleton Coast (p275), Namibia

Southern Africa

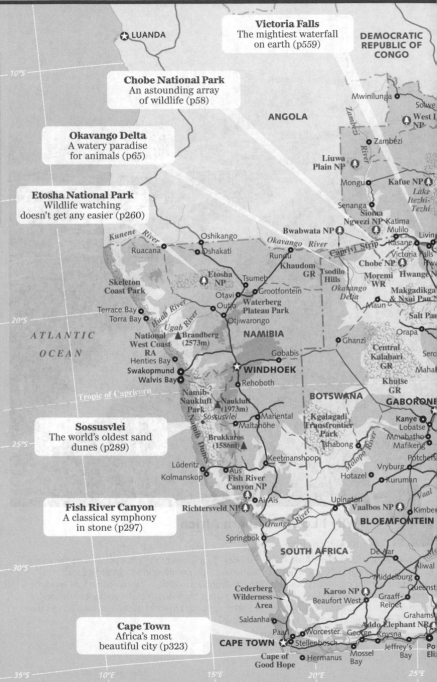

Victoria Falls
The mightiest waterfall
on earth (p559)

Chobe National Park
An astounding array
of wildlife (p58)

Okavango Delta
A watery paradise
for animals (p65)

Etosha National Park
Wildlife watching
doesn't get any easier (p260)

Sossusvlei
The world's oldest sand
dunes (p289)

Fish River Canyon
A classical symphony
in stone (p297)

Cape Town
Africa's most
beautiful city (p323)

DEMOCRATIC
REPUBLIC OF
CONGO

LUANDA

ANGOLA

Mwinilunga
Solwe
West I
NP

Zambezi

Liuwa
Plain NP

Mongu
Kafue NP
Lake
Itezhi-
Tezhi

Senanga
Sioma
Ngwezi NP Katima
Mulilo

Kunene River

Oshikango
Okavango River
Bwabwata NP
Caprivi Strip
Kasane
Livin

Ruacana
Oshakati
Rundu
Khaudom
GR
Tsodilo
Hills

Victoria Falls
Chobe NP
Pw

Etosha
NP
Tsumeb
Moremi
WR
Hwange N

Skeleton
Coast Park

Grootfontein
Okavango
Delta

Makgadikga
& Nxai Pan

Terrace Bay
Otavi
Outjo
Waterberg
Plateau Park
Maun
Salt Par

Torra Bay
Huab River
Ugab River
Otjiwarongo

ATLANTIC

National
West Coast
RA
Brandberg
(2573m)
NAMIBIA
Ghanzi
Orapa

OCEAN

Henties Bay
Swakopmund
Walvis Bay

Gobabis

WINDHOEK
Central
Kalahari
GR
Sero
Maha

Rehoboth

BOTSWANA
Khutse
GR
GABORONE

Tropic of Capricorn

Namib
Naukluft
Park
Naukluft
(1973m)
Mariental
Kgalagadi
Transfrontier
Park
Kanye
Lobatse

Sossusvlei
Maltahöhe
Mmabatho
Mafikeng

Namib Dunes
Brukkaros
(1586m)
Tshabong
Potchel

Keetmanshoop
Molopo River
Vryburg

Lüderitz
Aus
Hotazel
Kuruman

Kolmanskop
Fish River
Canyon NP

Vaal

Richtersveld NP
Ai-Ais
Upington
Vaalbos NP
Kimbe

Orange River
BLOEMFONTEIN

Springbok

SOUTH AFRICA
De Aar

Aliwal

Middelburg
Queenst

Cederberg
Wilderness
Area
Karoo NP
Beaufort West
Graaff-
Reinet

Saldanha
Grahams

Paarl
Worcester
George
Knysna
Addo Elephant NP

CAPE TOWN
Stellenbosch
Jeffrey's
Bay
Po
Elia

Cape of
Good Hope
Hermanus
Mossel
Bay

35°S
10°E
15°E
20°E
25°E

Southern Africa's
Top 17

Victoria Falls

1 The largest, most beautiful and simply the greatest waterfall in the world. As iconic to Africa as 'Dr Livingstone, I presume', thunderous Victoria Falls (p549) will blow your mind and soak your shirt. It's the sheer scale of the falls that is its most impressive feature. A million litres of water a second are funnelled over the 1908m drop, creating a plume of spray that can be seen for kilometres. When you're in Southern Africa this really is a sight that you should move heaven and earth to see.

Okavango Delta

2 The Okavango (p65) in Botswana is an astonishing, beautiful and wild place. Home to wildlife spectacles of rare power and drama, the delta changes with the seasons as flood waters ebb and flow, creating islands, river channels and pathways for animals that move this way and that at the waters' behest. No visit to the delta is complete without drifting in a traditional *mokoro* (dugout canoe). Exclusive and remote lodges are an Okavango speciality, and self-drivers can find outstanding campsites in the heart of the Okavango's Moremi Game Reserve.

Chobe National Park

3 Botswana's Chobe National Park (p58) ranks among the elite of African safari destinations. For a start, there are more elephants here than anywhere else on earth, numbering in the tens of thousands. And they're big – really big. Then you have the iconic landscapes of Savuti with its elephant-eating lions. There's Linyanti, one of the best places on the continent to see the highly endangered African wild dog. And finally the Chobe Riverfront, where most of Africa's charismatic megafauna come to drink.

Fish River Canyon

4 The enormous gash in the surface of the planet in the south of Namibia is an almost implausible landscape, and the canyon's rounded edges and sharp corners create a symphony in stone of gigantic and imposing proportions. Seen most clearly in the morning, Fish River Canyon (p297) is desolate, immense and seemingly carved into the earth by a master builder. The exposed rock and lack of plantlife only adds to the effect and invariably inspires thoughtful reflection and a quiet sense of awe.

Etosha National Park

5 There are few places in Southern Africa that can compete with the wildlife possibilities of extraordinary Etosha National Park (p260) in Namibia. A network of waterholes dispersed among the bush and grasslands surrounding the pan – a blindingly white, flat, saline desert that stretches into the horizon – attracts enormous congregations of animals, with lions and black rhinos highlights among many. A single waterhole can render thousands of sightings over the course of a day. Etosha is simply one of the best places on the planet for wildlife viewing.

The Drakensberg

6 The majestic mountains and foothills of the World Heritage–listed Ukhahlamba-Drakensberg Park (p427) are among South Africa's most awe-inspiring landscapes. Drakensberg means 'Dragon Mountains' in Afrikaans, while the Zulu named the range Quathlamba ('Battlement of Spears'); both convey the area's backdrop of incredible peaks. People have lived here for thousands of years, evidenced by the many San rock-art sites. With its Zulu villages, wilderness areas and good accommodation and eateries, this is the perfect place for photographers, hikers and adventurous travellers.

Kruger National Park

7 Kruger (p476) is one of Africa's great wilderness experiences and the mightiest of the country's national parks – a trip here will sear itself in your mind. Its accessibility, numbers and variety of wildlife, and staggering size and range of activities make Kruger unique and compelling. From wilderness trails and bush walks to mountain biking and remote 4WD trails, there are myriad opportunities to enjoy both the wild and the wildlife. Kruger is definitely one of the finest places to see animals – big and small – in the world.

SIMON EEMAN/SHUTTERSTOCK ©

Kgalagadi Transfrontier Park

8 Kgalagadi (p501) covers almost 40,000 sq km of raw Kalahari in South Africa's Northern Cape and Botswana, roamed by some iconic Kalahari predators. This is an immense land of sizzling sunsets, velvety night skies and rolling red dunes. You might spot black-maned lions napping under thorn trees or purring along the road: the park is a key global centre for spotting big cats, home to about 800 lions, cheetahs and leopards. But there are also brown hyenas, gorgeous gemsboks and all manner of desert-adapted creatures.

Sossusvlei

9 The towering red dunes of Sossusvlei (p289) rank among the most beautiful desert landscapes on earth. They're also one of the more improbable: the sands originated in the Kalahari millions of years ago and are now reclaiming land from the sea. The valley is dotted by hulking dunes, and interspersed with unearthly, dry *vleis* (marshland). Clambering up the face of these constantly moving giants is a uniquely Namibian experience, and as you survey the seemingly endless sand sea that surrounds you, you'll feel as though time itself has slowed.

South Africa's Winelands

10 Whitewashed Cape Dutch architecture dots an endlessly photogenic landscape of rolling hills and vines in neat rows. The Winelands (p355) is the quintessential Cape, where world-class wines are the icing on the proverbial cake. Stellenbosch, Franschhoek and Paarl, the area's holy trinity of wine-tasting towns, host some of the southern hemisphere's oldest, largest and prettiest wine estates. But this is not the only wine region – head to Tulbagh for sparkling wines, the heights of the Cederberg for crisp sauvignon blancs, and Rte 62 for robust reds and port.

Mozambique Island

11 There are no crowds and few cars, but Mozambique Island (p210) is hardly silent. Echoes of its past mix with the squawking of chickens, the sounds of children and the calls of the muezzin to remind you that the island is very much alive. Wander along cobbled streets, past graceful squares rimmed by once-grand churches and stately colonial-era buildings. This Unesco World Heritage Site, with its time-warp atmosphere and backdrop of turquoise seas, is a Mozambique highlight, and not to be missed. Below top: Fort of São Sebastião

Quirimbas Archipelago

12 Idyllic islands amid azure seas, dense mangrove channels opening onto pristine patches of soft sand, dhows silhouetted against the horizon and magical Ibo Island, with its silversmiths, fort and crumbling mansions – the remote Quirimbas Archipelago (p224) in Mozambique is a time and place set apart, accessed with difficulty, and invariably left behind with regret. Whether you dive and snorkel amid corals and fish, wander Ibo's sandy lanes, relax in a luxury lodge or explore on a dhow, the archipelago never fails to enchant.

South Luangwa National Park

13 Stroll single file through Zambia's South Luangwa National Park (p578) with a rifle-carrying scout in the lead, no 4WD engine sounds and no barrier between you and the wildlife, both predators and prey. The focus here is on the little things, including the medicinal uses of native flora and a CSI-like investigation of animal dung. Simply sitting under a tree and looking out over a plain filled with munching grazers is an opportunity for a quasi-meditative immersion in South Luangwa.

Lesotho Lodge Living

14 There are few places where lodge accommodation and village experiences are integrated. A trip to Semonkong (p108) and other similar places in Lesotho provides you with opportunities to stay in historic buildings – generally, former trading posts – and to mingle with locals, head off on guided pony treks and enjoy village life at a *shebeen*. Also on tap are hiking and abseiling, San rock art, dinosaur prints, and wonderful plants and birdlife.

13

14

ATTILA JANDI/SHUTTERSTOCK ©

EVENFH/SHUTTERSTOCK ©

Lake Malawi

15 The emerald jewel in Malawi's crown is undoubtedly its interior sea, Lake Malawi (p141). Fringed by golden beaches, the 'calendar lake' – so-called because it measures 365 miles long and 52 miles wide – offers travellers an underwater palace to swim among brilliantly coloured cichlid fish and desert islands to escape to. The resorts of Chintheche Strip, Nkhata Bay and Cape Maclear also offer a spectrum of great accommodation and activities such as kayaking and windsurfing to ensure you can make the best of it.

Mkhaya Game Reserve

16 Top of the conservation pops, Swaziland's stunning Mkhaya (p543) private reserve was established in 1979 to save the pure Nguni breed of cattle from extinction. It's known, however, for its preservation of both the black and white rhino populations. The reserve is staffed entirely by Swazis from neighbouring communities who run an extremely effective antipoaching unit. That's not all: roan and sable antelopes, *tsessebi* and elephants roam the reserve. A bird hide, too, gives you an opportunity to get up close and personal with rare species.

Great Zimbabwe

17 Clamber around boulders, step past teetering rocks, slip through narrow stone crevices and take in the stunning views as you explore the architectural feat that is Great Zimbabwe (p640). These 11th-century mysterious ruins lend the nation its name and provide evidence that ancient Africa reached a level of civilisation not suspected by earlier scholars. Come for sunset and watch in awe as the sun sinks behind the majestic walls of the greatest medieval city in sub-Saharan Africa.

Need to Know

For more information, see Survival Guide (p713)

Currency
Botswanan pula (P), Lesotho loti (pl maloti, M), Malawian kwacha (MK), Mozambican metical (Mtc), Namibian dollar (N$), South African rand (R), Swazi lilangeni (pl emalangeni, E), Zambian kwacha (ZMW), Zimbabwean bond notes

Language
English, Portuguese (Mozambique), Afrikaans, many African languages

Visas
Mostly either not required or available on arrival; see p724.

Money
ATMs widely available in larger towns and cities. Credit cards accepted in most shops, restaurants and hotels (especially in South Africa, Swaziland, Botswana and Namibia).

Mobile Phones
Local SIM cards available across the region and can be used in unlocked Australian and European phones.

Time
All countries are two hours ahead of GMT/UTC, except for Namibia, which is one hour ahead.

When to Go

Tropical climate, wet and dry seasons
Warm to hot summers, mild winters
Desert, dry climate

Lusaka
GO Apr–Aug

Harare
GO Apr–Oct

Livingstone •
GO Jul–Oct

Windhoek
GO May–Oct

Cape Town
GO Nov–Apr

High Season (Apr–Aug)
➡ Most places bask in sunshine, with comfortable (but often chilly) nights.

➡ Cape Town experiences rain and blustery winds.

➡ High season in Botswana and Namibia begins in June and runs until October.

Shoulder (Feb, Mar, Sep & Oct)
➡ Usually quite comfortable in the central areas.

➡ Great time to visit with good wildlife viewing but fewer tourist numbers.

➡ Rains in Botswana and Namibia make getting off-road difficult, but it's high season in the Kalahari.

Low Season (Nov–Jan)
➡ In the north, plan for inclement weather.

➡ Heat can be oppressive and travel more difficult due to washed-out roads.

➡ Birdwatching and thunderstorms at their best.

Useful Websites

Lonely Planet (www.lonelyplanet.com) Destination information, hotel bookings, traveller forum and more.

Regional Tourism Organisation of Southern Africa (www.retosa.co.za) Promotes tourism in the region.

Zambezi Traveller (www.zambezitraveller.com) Travel info for destinations along the Zambezi River.

Safari Bookings (www.safaribookings.com) Fantastic resource for booking your safari, with expert and traveller reviews.

Expert Africa (www.expert africa.com) A tour operator with extensive online coverage of the region.

Exchange Rates

See p721 for exchange rates. For current exchange rates see www.xe.com.

IMPORTANT NUMBERS

COUNTRY	COUNTRY CODE	EMERGENCY NO.
Botswana	☎267	☎999
Lesotho	☎266	☎112
Malawi	☎265	☎997, 998, 999
Mozambique	☎258	
Namibia	☎264	☎10111
South Africa	☎27	☎112
Swaziland	☎268	☎999
Zambia	☎260	

Daily Costs

Prices vary considerably between countries.

Budget: Less than US$75

➡ Dorm bed: US$10–15

➡ Campsite: US$18–30

➡ Two meals in cheap restaurants: US$10–20

➡ Intercity bus: US$25–100

Midrange: US$75–150

➡ Double room in midrange hotel: US$50–150

➡ Two meals in nice restaurants: US$25–30

➡ Internal flights: US$100–200

Top End: More than US$150

➡ Double room in top-end hotel: from US$150

➡ Per person in high-season lodge: from US$1000

➡ 4WD rental per day: from US$150

➡ Meals in top-end restaurants: US$40–50

Arriving in Southern Africa

OR Tambo International Airport (Johannesburg, South Africa) Regular air connections to Southern African capitals; Gautrain serves central Jo'burg (R145, 20 minutes) and Pretoria (R155, 45 minutes) every 12 to 30 minutes; shuttles and taxis take about one hour to Jo'burg (R400) and Pretoria (R450).

Cape Town International Airport (South Africa) Shuttles (from R180), taxis (from R200) and MyCiTi buses (R70, every 30 minutes) to central Cape Town take about 30 minutes. Shuttles also serve Stellenbosch (from R200, 45 minutes).

Maun Airport (Botswana) No public transport, but the airport is in Maun's town centre and most hotels offer airport pick-up.

Chief Hosea Kutako International Airport (Windhoek, Namibia) Taxis to the centre cost up to N$400 and take between 45 minutes and an hour.

Maputo International Airport (Mozambique) Taxis to Maputo's city centre cost Mtc400 to Mtc600 (10 to 20 minutes).

Getting Around

➡ Southern Africa has a reasonable road and air network within the area, but distances are long, land-based public transport is inconsistent and border crossings can slow things down considerably.

➡ If you're not travelling as part of an organised tour, the two major options are to use patchy public transport, or rent your own 4WD.

For much more on **getting around**, see p730

PLAN YOUR TRIP NEED TO KNOW

If You Like...

Wildlife Safaris

Some of the best wildlife viewing on the continent is at your fingertips. Unique opportunities abound while on safari.

Chobe Riverfront (Botswana) Africa's largest elephants draw near to the water's edge with predators prowling nearby. (p62)

Etosha National Park (Namibia) Incredible wildlife viewing with animals crowding around easily seen waterholes. (p260)

Kgalagadi Transfrontier Park (South Africa) Deep in the Kalahari is one of the world's best places to spot big cats, from cheetahs to black-maned lions. (p501)

Kruger National Park South Africa's famous park has 5000 rhinos alone, and landscapes from woodland to mopane-veld. (p476)

Mana Pools National Park (Zimbabwe) For the wild at heart – you're almost guaranteed to see lions; unguided walks allowed. (p632)

Hwange National Park (Zimbabwe) A vast African classic wilderness with fabulous elephant- and predator-watching. (p647)

Okavango Delta (Botswana) One of the world's largest inland river deltas; the life-sustaining

waters ebb and flow, supporting vast quantities of wildlife. (p65)

South Luangwa National Park (Zambia) Abundant wildlife, wonderful scenery and walking safaris. (p578)

Adventure Activities

Adventure sports thrive in Southern Africa and enthusiasts find ways to raise their heart rate in most countries. Try sandboarding an ancient desert, throwing yourself out of a plane, surfing the Atlantic or shooting down foaming white-water rapids.

Northern Mozambique Sail by dhow past remote islands or venture into trackless bush in the interior. (p206)

Semonkong (Lesotho) Take a plunge on the longest commercially operated single-drop abseil (204m) down the Maletsunyane Falls. (p108)

Swakopmund Namibia's, and indeed Southern Africa's, capital of adventure sports, this is adrenaline-junkie heaven. (p279)

Great Usutu River (Swaziland) White-water rafting in Swaziland including Grade IV rapids, which aren't for the faint-hearted. (p546)

Victoria Falls (Zimbabwe) Tackle the Grade V rapids down the Zambezi River or bungee from Victoria Falls bridge. (p549)

Beaches

Coastal beaches and miles of inland lakeshore mean there are no excuses not to wet your toes. Turquoise waters, coral reefs and sandy beaches are ideal for swimming, snorkelling, diving or just good ol' sunbathing. Mozambique is the pick.

Chizumulu Island A tiny floating paradise with an almost Mediterranean coastline and an uber-chilled beach lodge. (p136)

Ponta d'Ouro (Mozambique) Mozambique's southernmost tip features a long, dune-fringed beach with reliable surf and dolphin spotting. (p182)

Tofo (Mozambique) A long arc of white sand with azure waters, surfing and diving with manta rays. (p188)

Vilankulo (Mozambique) Quiet beaches stretch north and south, with horse riding and views of the distant Bazaruto Archipelago. (p192)

Pomene (Mozambique) A stunning estuarine setting, a wild coastline and rewarding birding

Top: Okavango Delta (p65), Botswana
Bottom: Sandboarding, Swakopmund (p277), Namibia

are among the draws of this often-overlooked spot. (p191)

Wimbi Beach (Mozambique) Hit a beach shack for a sundowner on northern Mozambique's finest municipal strip of sand. (p221)

Muizenberg (South Africa) You could pick any of the Cape Peninsula or Simons Town beaches but this one's as good for families as it is for surfers. (p336)

Cultural Interactions

Experiencing the rich tapestry of Southern African culture will enhance any visit to the region. There are myriad ways of accessing the region's peoples, their traditions and ways of life.

The Kalahari (Botswana) Numerous lodges and camps employ San guides and trackers to take you out onto their ancestral lands and introduce you to their culture. (p76)

Bairro Mafalala (Mozambique) Learn about the rich history and culture of Maputo's Mafalala neighbourhood during a walking tour. (p173)

Mozambique Island (Mozambique) Step back through the centuries in this historical treasure trove and cultural melting pot. (p210)

Kaokoveld (Namibia) Immerse yourself in the world of the Himba, one of Southern Africa's most soulful people. (p272)

Soweto (South Africa) Stay the night in a backpackers or B&B and learn local history from residents over a *shebeen* beer. (p464)

Tengenenge (Zimbabwe) An open-air gallery, showcasing more than 120 Shona sculptors, where you can see the artists at work and stay in a traditional mud hut. (p631)

Hiking

A great way to experience the magic of the region is to hear the crunch of the earth beneath your boots. Here are some of Southern Africa's great hikes.

Chimanimani Mountains (Mozambique) Get to know local culture while hiking through lush, seldom-visited forest areas. (p201)

Drakensberg (South Africa) From day-hikes to week-long treks, the dramatic Drakensberg creates happy hikers. (p427)

Fish River Canyon (Namibia) The best way to get a feel for this massive gash in the earth is to embark on a five-day hike along the valley floor. (p297)

Waterberg Plateau Park (Namibia) Four-day guided and unguided trails are available through pristine wilderness landscape, with the possibility of some rare wildlife sightings. (p257)

Lesotho A country 'made' for hiking. (p97)

Mt Mulanje and the Zomba Plateau (Malawi) The country's best spots for hiking. (p154)

The Wild Coast (South Africa) Strap a pack to your back and take a hike past rugged cliffs, remote beaches and Xhosa villages. (p401)

Landscapes

One of the best things about exploring the region is discovering its array of landscapes: from swirling desert sands and slabs of ancient granite mountain, to jagged coastlines, rock-strewn moonscapes and lush savannah.

Okavango Delta (Botswana) A watery paradise of reed-lined channels whose paths change with each passing year. (p65)

Damaraland (Namibia) One of Southern Africa's most beautiful corners with blood-red mountains, palm valleys, rock art and wonderful wildlife. (p269)

Fish River Canyon (Namibia) The cliche says it's Africa's Grand Canyon and, unlike many cliches, this one's pretty close to the mark. (p297)

Sossusvlei (Namibia) The sand-dune desert you always dreamed of with stunning, sculpted sands all the way to the Atlantic shoreline. (p290)

Drakensberg (South Africa) Awesome peaks and formations, such as the Ampitheatre, are fronted by rolling hills. (p427)

The Wild Coast (South Africa) The green hills dotted with pastel rondavels, rugged cliffs and empty Indian Ocean beaches are unforgettable. (p401)

Mutinondo Wilderness (Zambia) Mutinondo offers soul-stirring landscapes dotted with huge purple-hued inselbergs and laced with meandering rivers. (p598)

Liuwa Plain National Park (Zambia) As close as you'll get in Southern Africa to the Serengeti's wild and vast savannah plains. (p594)

Makgadikgadi Pans National Park (Botswana) Mesmerising and strangely beautiful pancake-flat salt-pan network, larger than any on the planet. (p55)

Off-Road Driving

This is adventure country for 4WD enthusiasts. In many remote places age-old tracks are the only way to navigate through the African wilderness.

Kaokoveld (Namibia) One of the last true wildernesses in Southern Africa, the remote and beguiling Kaokoveld is a serious off-road challenge. (p272)

Khaudum National Park (Namibia) With virtually no signage, and navigation dependent on GPS coordinates and topographic maps, Khaudum is a wildlife and off-road adventure. (p265)

Central Kalahari Game Reserve (Botswana) An off-roader's dream if you're after solitude, desertscapes and the echo of lions roaring in the night. (p76)

Savuti (Botswana) The tracks that connect Savuti to the outside world are some of the sandiest in the country – make it here and you've earned your stripes. (p63)

Makgadikgadi Pans (Botswana) If the notion of exploring 12,000 sq km of disorientating salt pans is your idea of an adventure, then head straight here. (p55)

North Luangwa National Park (Zambia) You'll have to navigate rough tracks while dodging the diverse wildlife just to reach this remote park. (p584)

Richtersveld (South Africa) This wild frontier is a moonlike swatch of land accessible only by 4WD. (p504)

Month by Month

TOP EVENTS

Cape Town Minstrel Carnival, South Africa, January

Maitisong Festival, Botswana, March

National Arts Festival, South Africa, July

Umhlanga Dance, Swaziland, August

Oktoberfest, Namibia, October

January

With Christmas, over the party in the Cape is only just beginning. In the north it's the rainy season, but great for birdwatching, plus high season in the Kalahari.

🎎 Cape Town Minstrel Carnival

The Mother City's most colourful street party, the Cape Town Minstrel Carnival runs for a month from 2 January. With satin-and-sequin-clad minstrel troupes, ribald song-and-dance parades and general revelry, it's the Cape's Mardi Gras. (p340)

February

Rains in the northern part of the region can make travel difficult. Wildlife is hard to spot in the tall grass but it's a great time for birdwatching.

🎎 Gwaza Muthini

This early February celebration in Marracuene, Mozambique, commemorates the colonial resistors who lost their lives in the 1895 Battle of Marracuene. It also marks the start of the *ukanhi* season, a traditional brew made from the fruit of the canhoeiro tree.

☆ Marrabenta Festival

To hear *marrabenta* – Mozambique's national music – at its best, don't miss the annual Marrabenta Festival (www.ccfmoz.com). It's held mostly in Maputo, but also in Beira, Inhambane and several other locations. The timing is set to coincide with Marracuene's Gwaza Muthini commemorations.

🎎 N'cwala

A Ngoni festival held near Chipata in eastern Zambia on 24 February. Food, dance and music are all enjoyed to celebrate the end of the rainy season and pray for a successful harvest.

March

The rains are petering out and the sizzling temperatures are coming to an end. Keep in mind South African school holidays begin in late March: accommodation can be hard to find across the region.

🎎 Enjando Street Festival

The Namibian capital's biggest street party, also known as Mbapira, occurs in March every year. It's also a good excuse for people to dress in extravagant ethnic clothes that bring the streets to life. (p246)

🎎 Maitisong Festival

Botswana's largest performing arts festival is held annually over seven days from mid-March to early April in Gaborone. The festival features an outdoor program of music, theatre, film and dance, with top performing artists from around Africa. (p43)

☆ Ditshwanelo Human Rights Film Festival

Screenings on human rights topics are held at the AV Centre at Maru a Pula School in Gaborone, Botswana, during the festival, and guest speakers are invited to talk about their experiences. (www.ditshwanelo.org.bw)

🎊 Kuomboka Ceremony

Celebrated by the Lozi people of western Zambia to mark the ceremonial journey of the litunga (the Lozi king) from his dry-season palace to his wet-season palace on higher ground at Limulunga. It usually takes place in late March or early April. (p595)

April

The end of the low season in the Delta and surrounding areas – parks have new growth, the rains are finishing and the temperatures are becoming more pleasant but tourist numbers are still down. South African school holidays continue until mid-April.

🎊 Windhoek Karneval

Established in 1953 by a small group of German immigrants, Windhoek's April Karneval is one of the highlights of Namibia's cultural calendar, culminating in the Royal Ball. (p246)

🎊 Maun Festival

A two-day celebration with plenty of music, parades, poetry, theatre, craftwork, dance and food; visual arts also feature. Held in Maun, the festival raises funds for local schools while commemorating northwestern Botswana's rich cultural roots. (p69)

🎊 AfrikaBurn

This subcultural blowout features art installations and themed camps as a corner of the Karoo in South Africa is temporarily turned into a surreal paradise. If you're in the area in April make a beeline here.

☆ Harare International Festival of Arts

A not-to-be-missed event in Zimbabwe, Harare International Festival of Arts features local and international performers in opera, jazz, classical music, funk, theatre and dance. (p621)

May

Beginning of winter and the dry season, and a great time to visit before high-season prices kick in for Botswana and Namibia. Snow may fall on the highlands of South Africa and Lesotho where it is much wetter.

☆ Wild Cinema Festival

This film festival, held in May, showcases the work of local and South African talent at cinemas throughout Windhoek, Namibia.

🎊 Festival Azgo

This Maputo-based extravaganza has become Mozambique's largest arts and culture festival, featuring artists from Mozambique as well as elsewhere in the region. (p173)

June

An excellent month to visit, although high season gets underway in some Namibia and Botswana lodges. Expect cool, dry weather, minimal crowds and choppy seas in Mozambique.

☆ Kweto Siriwala

Ibo Island Day, on 24 June, marks the feast of St John the Baptist and is celebrated as Kweto Siriwala ('to not forget your roots') day in Mozambique's Quirimbas Archipelago. Events include traditional music and dance, and dhow races.

July

High season is underway in Botswana and Namibia – expect warm clear days and ideal conditions; combined with South African school holidays until mid-July, it's busy, so book accommodation in advance.

☆ Lake Malawi International Yachting Marathon

This international event – a gruelling eight-day, 560km race – is the longest freshwater contest in Africa. Starting at Lake Malawi's Club Macacola it ends at the Chintheche Inn. A great time to be on one of the lake's islands.

🏃 Mulanje Porter's Race

Formerly just for porters, the race is now open to anyone with the lungs and legs to make it 25km up the staggeringly steep Mt Mulanje in Malawi. A great spectacle; participation is not for the faint of heart. (p155)

☆ National Arts Festival

Feel South Africa's creative pulse at the country's premier arts festival from late June to early July in studenty Grahamstown. Performers from every conceivable discipline descend on the refined city, hijacking space from squares to sports fields. (p394)

☆ Open of Surfing

The winter months bring big waves to South Africa's Eastern Cape, and Jeffreys Bay holds its international Open of Surfing. Part of the surf-loving town's 10-day Winter Fest in mid-July, the contest attracts more than 10,000 spectators. (p386)

August

Wildlife watching is at its best as water sources become limited in the parks, so it's a popular time for visitors on safari. Temperatures on the rise across the region; most lodges crowded with European visitors.

🎎 Maherero Day

One of Namibia's largest festivals falls on the weekend nearest 26 August. Dressed in traditional garb, the Red Flag Herero people gather in Okahandja for a memorial service to commemorate their chiefs killed in the Khoikhoi and German wars.

☆ Timbilas Festival

Watch Chopi musicians play intricate rhythms on large marimbas, often in orchestras consisting of 20 or more instruments, plus singers and dancers. While the Mozambican festival (www.amizava.org) is not always well organised, the musical tradition is fascinating. It's held in Quissico.

🎎 Umhlanga Dance

A showcase of potential wives for the king: marriageable young Swazi women journey from all over the kingdom, carrying reeds, to help repair the queen mother's home around August or September (dates vary). (p538)

September

Temperatures are rising but it's still a popular time for travel to the region and tourist numbers are high. South African school holidays in late September can jam accommodation.

☆ //Ae//Gams Arts Festival

Windhoek's main arts festival is held in September, and includes troupes of dancers, musicians, poets and performers all competing for various prizes. The best of Namibian food is also on show. (www.face book.com/AeGamsArtsand CulturalFestival)

☆ Kugoma

This festival (www.kugo mashortfilms.wixsite.com/ kugoma) in Mozambique showcases short films from throughout the Southern African region, with many free screenings and discussion forums held in and around Maputo.

☆ Lake of Stars Music Festival

'Glastonbury on the beach': this brilliant three-day Malawian festival bubbles with stellar UK and African bands, and a host of celebrated global DJs. Money raised goes toward the Children in the Wilderness charity. (p161)

☆ Morija Arts & Cultural Festival

This annual five-day event held in September or October in Lesotho showcases the diversity of Sotho culture through dance, music and theatre. (p103)

October

The end of high season in Botswana and Namibia with hot weather throughout, but Windhoek is a magnet for beer drinkers and it's a popular time, especially for German tourists. First rains arrive in the northernmost regions.

🍷 Oktoberfest

Windhoek in Namibia stages its own Oktoberfest – an orgy of food, drink and merrymaking in an event that showcases the best in German beer, usually drunk at tables set up inside large marquees. There's plenty of traditional German dress on display, too. (p246)

November

November is when many locals begin scanning the skies for rain. High season is over and wildlife watching is good, but the build-up to the rains can be unpleasant. Migratory birds fill the skies.

☆ Kirstenbosch Summer Sunset Concerts

Summer music festivals take place in stunning settings across South Africa. In the Western Cape, the choice includes the Kirstenbosch Summer Sunset Concerts in Cape Town's botanic gardens (November to April).

💃 Mafalala Festival

Held annually between late October and late November, this festival (www.iverca.org) showcases Maputo's rich artistic and cultural legacy, focusing especially on the city's lively Mafalala neighbourhood.

December

The rains should be in full swing across central and northern regions. It's high season in Botswana's Kalahari. Expect calm seas (good for diving) along the coast. There's a peak period everywhere over Christmas and New Year.

Itineraries

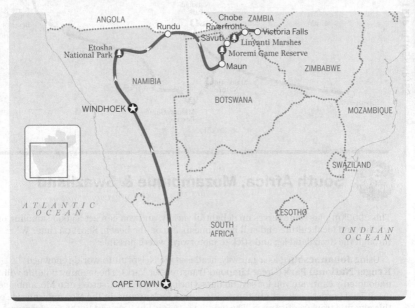

2 WEEKS Southern Africa's Greatest Hits

This sampling of the best of what Southern Africa has to offer is a bit of a whirlwind tour, but it maximises your time in the best way possible by focusing on a few big-ticket destinations. It requires a mix of flying and 4WD adventuring.

Begin in **Cape Town**, Southern Africa's most beautiful city. After a couple of days enjoying its sophisticated charm, fly north to **Windhoek** to enjoy the colonial-era architecture and launch your Namibian journey. Overnight there, pick up your car and drive north the next day to **Etosha National Park** to look for lions, black rhinos and so much more. After a minimum of two nights, drive southeast then northeast to **Rundu**, where you can overnight on the banks of the Okavango River, before continuing on the next day to **Maun** in Botswana. From Maun, an unexciting town with excellent infrastructure, drive northeast through some of Africa's wildest, most beautiful and wildlife-rich country as you traverse the Okavango Delta on your way through **Moremi Game Reserve**, **Savuti**, **Linyanti** and **Chobe Riverfront**, camping at least one night in each. From Chobe Riverfront, it's a short hop across the border into Zimbabwe and on to **Victoria Falls**, arguably the world's greatest waterfalls.

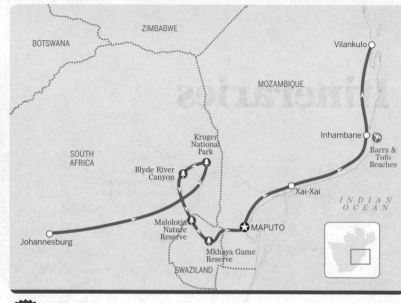

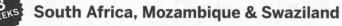

3 WEEKS South Africa, Mozambique & Swaziland

This 2000km-plus route serves up delightful variety, and you can get a good sampling of wildlife and local culture and still have time to laze on the beach. Short on time? Whiz through the Swaziland leg and stick to motorways where possible.

Using **Johannesburg** as a gateway, head east via Nelspruit to world-renowned **Kruger National Park** (Great Limpopo Transfrontier Park). The teeming wildlife will undoubtedly captivate you for several days. One option here is to cross into Mozambique via official border posts within the park, taking a look around in the Mozambican side of this gigantic transfrontier park. The wildlife is sparse but it's a serious bush adventure. Then you could nip across to the coast and do the rest of this itinerary in reverse, making a nice loop back through Swaziland and into South Africa again. Otherwise, if you've time, duck out of Orpen Gate for a look at remote and off-the-tourist-radar **Blyde River Canyon**. This awe-inspiring natural sight has good access points such as the Three Rondavels and Gods Window, and if you're really captivated, consider a 2½-day walk along the valley floor.

Continue south into Swaziland, where you can spend a few days hiking through the grasslands and forests of **Malolotja Nature Reserve** before heading on via Mbabane to the tiny but brilliant **Mkhaya Game Reserve**, noted for its black rhinos. After sampling the fine hospitality and food of this tiny mountain kingdom, it's time to get your feet wet. Head for the border town of Lomahasha in Swaziland and cross into the former Portuguese colony of Mozambique (formalities are straighforward) via the Mozambican border town of Namaacha. Motor down the approximately 50km to culturally intriguing **Maputo** and then head north on the EN1 and, if you're getting desperate for a dip, stop at **Xai-Xai**'s surf-pounded beaches. Continue up the EN1 to **Inhambane**, one of the country's oldest and most charming towns. Beaches close by include legendary **Tofo**, with azure waters, and the more sedate **Barra**. If you've got more steam, trundle a bit further north to **Vilankulo**, the gateway to the tropical paradise of the Bazaruto Archipelago.

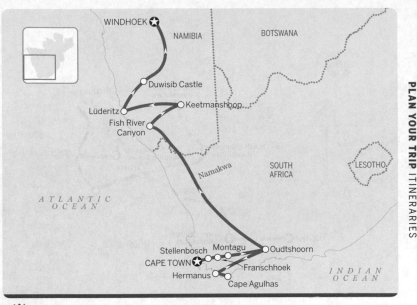

3 WEEKS South Africa & Namibia

For road-trip lovers. Even if you can't squeeze in all of this 3000km-plus journey, you'll come away with an immense appreciation of this remarkable region. Looking to make cuts? Shave some kilometres off the Western Cape loop. A car (4WD useful but not necessary) is definitely your best bet for this mega road trip.

After a few days in **Cape Town**, ogling Table Mountain from various vantage points around town, tear yourself away from this wonderful city and head to the fertile valleys of the Winelands, with a night or two in **Stellenbosch** or **Franschhoek**.

From here, continue east to the artists enclave of **Montagu**, and then via the scenic Rte 62 through the Little Karoo to **Oudtshoorn**, South Africa's ostrich capital. Some possible detours along the way include a trip to **Hermanus** for whale watching if the season is right, or to **Cape Agulhas** for the thrill of standing at Africa's southernmost point.

From Oudtshoorn take the N12 north and then loop back towards Cape Town via the N1, link up with the N7 and head for **Namakwa** to see the fabulous wildflower displays, which are especially good in August and September.

Keep tracking up the N7, cross into Namibia at Vioolsdrif and head to Hobas to see the **Fish River Canyon** – a mighty gash hacked out of the Earth's surface – one of the continent's great natural wonders. The best way to appreciate this work of nature's master builder is a five-day trek along the valley floor.

Further north along the B1, **Keetmanshoop** has some colonial architecture; but don't linger, head west along the B4 to surreal **Lüderitz**, a coastal colonial relic sandwiched between the desert and the Atlantic seaboard. Heading back to the B1, turn north at the C13 and make a beeline for the baroque **Duwisib Castle**, which is well worth exploring. You can stay 300m from the castle on a rustic farm or camp. From there head to Mariental back on the B1, and it's another couple of hours to **Windhoek**, Namibia's small but colourful and cosmopolitan capital city with its bracing highland climate.

PLAN YOUR TRIP ITINERARIES

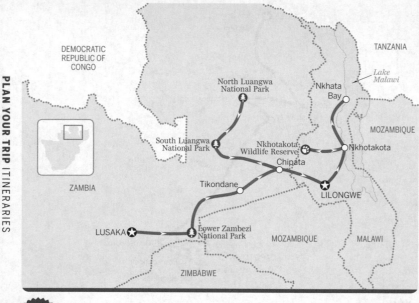

3 WEEKS — Zambia & Malawi

A 2000km route through the Southern African outback. Travelling in Zambia offers a taste of the real Africa, though the dusty roads will become a distant memory once you're lazing by the crystal-clear waters of Lake Malawi.

Start with a few days in Zambia's cosmopolitan capital, **Lusaka**, with its genuine African feel and the country's best nightlife. Then head out on the highway to the stunning **Lower Zambezi National Park**, with its beautiful flood plain that's dotted with acacias and other large trees. There's no public transport to the park, so you'll need your own car to get there, or go on an organised tour.

Hook up with the Great East Rd and head to chaotic **Chipata**. Before you get here, you'll come across **Tikondane**, a small grassroots NGO working with local communities that has decent budget accommodation and meals. At Chipata you can organise a trip to **South Luangwa National Park**, one of the most majestic parks on the continent. Make sure you do a walking safari when you're here – it's one of the best places in Southern Africa to do it. From Chipata you can drive to Mfuwe Gate, or take one of the minibuses that make the trip to Mfuwe village. The really adventurous could try to reach the wild and spectacular **North Luangwa National Park**, but it's important that you seek local advice before doing this; you need to be well prepared.

Return to Chipata, then it's on to Malawi and the town of **Lilongwe**, which is worth a day or two to check out the old town and the local Nature Sanctuary. From Lilongwe strike out north along the M1 to **Nkhata Bay** on Lake Malawi, which is perfect for swimming, kayaking or just lazing about after some hard weeks on the road. Possible detours on the way to or from Nkhata include historic **Nkhotakota**, from where you can organise a trip to the revitalised **Nkhotakota Wildlife Reserve**, where you have a good chance of seeing elephants and roan and sable antelope. There's excellent lodge accommodation available in the park.

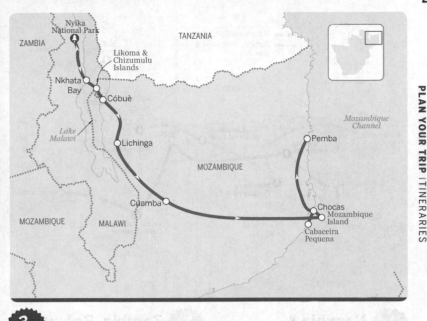

3 WEEKS Malawi & Mozambique

This 1500km Mozambican bush adventure takes you into the heart of one of Southern Africa's most intriguing and diverse countries. Mozambique Island makes a wonderful contrast to the bush, and you can finish on the beach in the tropical island paradise of Quirimbas Archipelago.

Drag yourself out of the crystal waters at **Nkhata Bay** and, if you have time before heading across the lake, make a beeline to the enigmatic **Nyika National Park**. Here, you can briefly forget you're in Africa on a multiday hike among rolling grasslands and a surprisingly cool climate. When you're ready, hop onto the *Ilala* ferry for the blissful **Likoma Island**, where swimming, snorkelling and local cultures are the star attractions. Splash out for a night at Kaya Mawa if you've the pennies – it's one of Africa's finest paradise retreats. Take the ferry over to the Mediterranean-esque **Chizumulu Island**, with its idyllic beaches, and return by dhow (if the waters are calm enough).

From Likoma hop back on the ferry to Metangula and from there take a *chapa* (converted passenger truck or minivan) up towards **Cóbuè**, on the other side of the lakeshore in Mozambique. (Or, take a dhow direct from Likoma to Cóbuè). Stay the night just south of Cóbuè at Nkwichi Lodge, a magnificent bush retreat that is part of an important development and conservation project; it's well worth a splurge. If your budget isn't up to Nkwichi, try one of several backpacker-friendly places in Cóbuè itself.

After exploring the lake area, head south to cool **Lichinga**; surrounded by scenic, rugged terrain, it is the capital of remote Niassa province. Carry on through to Mandimba and on to bustling **Cuamba**, where you can pick up a train all the way through to Nampula. Then jump on a bus to magnificent **Mozambique Island**, with its intriguing architecture and time-warp atmosphere. If you need a beach break after exploring the island, hire a dhow to take you over to **Chocas** and the lovely nearby beach at **Cabaceira Pequena**. The trip finishes up a bit further north at **Pemba**, which is the gateway to the superb Quirimbas Archipelago.

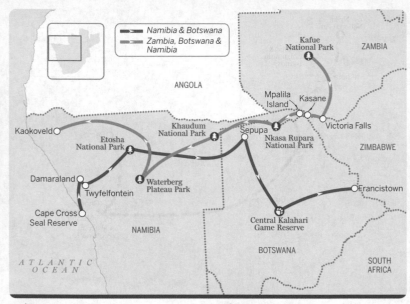

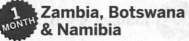

1 MONTH Namibia & Botswana

This itinerary takes you from Namibia's Atlantic coastline to the heart of the Kalahari in Botswana. Although it touches on some of the big attractions, it mostly follows lightly trammelled routes.

Starting on Namibia's Skeleton Coast, a treacherous coastline with shipwrecks and desert wilderness, check out **Cape Cross Seal Reserve**. Travel north into the wonders of **Damaraland**, with wild, open spaces and memorable wildlife, then head for **Twyfelfontein**, one of the most extensive rock-art galleries in Africa. Journey on to **Etosha National Park**, one of Africa's great wildlife-viewing areas. Exit Etosha via Von Lindequist Gate. Track along the B8 into Botswana at the Mahango-Mohembo border crossing. Drive down the west side of the Okavango Panhandle, perhaps stopping in **Sepupa** to do a dugout-canoe trip in the Okavango Panhandle. The last leg of this ambitious trip is the **Central Kalahari Game Reserve** to the southeast, at the heart of Botswana. Enter at the Matswere Gate at the northeastern end: wildlife includes lions and brown hyenas. Finish by exiting the same gate and travelling east to **Francistown**, a busy town with plenty of good places to stay and eat at journey's end.

1 MONTH Zambia, Botswana & Namibia

From Zambia's central savannah plains to Namibia's remote northwest, this route combines wild landscapes, remote trails and brilliant wildlife. You'll need your own vehicle to cover the whole route.

Starting in the magnificent **Kafue National Park** in Zambia – classic wildlife country and one of the largest parks in the world – head south to **Victoria Falls**, a thunderous sight. From here head into **Kasane** in Botswana to see the wildlife-prolific Chobe Riverfront. Charter a boat to **Mpalila Island**, a luxuriously remote retreat in the middle of the Zambezi. From here, head into Namibia's Caprivi Strip, and visit the mini-Okavango of the **Nkasa Rupara National Park** where the rains bring a delta-like feel to the forested islands. Then drive to the untamed wilderness of **Khaudum National Park**, a serious adventure destination. From Khaudum head south through Grootfontein, from where it's worth making a detour to the **Waterberg Plateau Park**. North of Grootfontein the road takes you into Namibia's cultural heartland, the Owambo region, and on into the remote **Kaokoveld**, homeland to the Himba people, and possibly one of the last true wildernesses left in Southern Africa.

Plan Your Trip
Planning a Safari

The unique wildlife and the landscapes they inhabit make for magical safari experiences in Southern Africa. But making the most of this dream journey into the African wilds requires careful planning – here's where we show you how.

Planning Your Trip

Planning your safari can be an enjoyable experience, but there are some important considerations to guide your preparations. These include choosing the best season, deciding what of safari you'd like to undertake, and selecting an operator to get you travelling.

When to Go

Getting around is easier in the dry season (May to October), and in many parks this is when animals are easier to find around waterholes and rivers. Foliage is also less dense, making wildlife spotting simpler. However, as the dry season corresponds in part with the high-travel season, lodges and camps in some areas get crowded and accommodation prices are at a premium.

If you're planning a self-drive safari in northern Namibia, northern Botswana, Zambia and elsewhere, you'll need to watch out for the wet season (December to March), when some tracks become completely submerged and driving is particularly risky.

Apart from these general considerations, the ideal time to make a safari very much depends on which parks and reserves you want to visit and your particular interests. For example, the wet season is the best time for birdwatching in many areas, although some places may be inaccessible during the rains. Wildlife concentrations also vary markedly, depending on the season.

Best Safaris

Best Safari to Spot the Big Five
Kruger National Park (p476), South Africa

Etosha National Park (p260), Namibia

Majete Wildlife Reserve (p157), Malawi

Hwange National Park (p647), Zimbabwe

Best Short Safari
Kruger National Park (p476), South Africa

Chobe National Park (p58), Botswana

Mkhaya Game Reserve (p543), Swaziland

Best Adventure Safari
North Luangwa National Park (p584), Zambia

Central Kalahari Game Reserve (p76), Botswana

Mana Pools National Park (p632), Zimbabwe

Most Remote Safari
Khaudum National Park (p265), Namibia

North Luangwa National Park (p584), Zambia

Liuwa Plain National Park (p594), Zambia

Gorongosa National Park (p199), Mozambique

Best Walking Safari
South Luangwa National Park (p578), Zambia

Mana Pools National Park (p632), Zimbabwe

Kafue National Park (p590), Zambia

Choosing an Operator

Travellers are faced with a boggling array of organised tour options in Southern Africa, and the only problem will be making your selection.

A good operator is the single most important variable for your safari, and it's worth spending time thoroughly researching those you're considering. At the budget level in particular, you may find operators who cut corners so be careful to go with a reputable outfit. There are many high-quality companies that have excellent track records.

Do some legwork (the internet is a good start) before coming to Southern Africa. Get personal recommendations (this can be done on Lonely Planet's Thorn Tree forum: http://lonelyplanet.com/thorntree), and once in the region, talk with as many travellers as you can who have recently returned from a safari or trek with the company you're considering.

Some questions to consider when deciding on which company to choose:

➡ Is the itinerary exactly what you want?

➡ Do you understand the planning and what is expected for each stage of the tour?

➡ Will you be staying in, or near, the park you want to visit?

➡ Is accommodation in a large lodge or an intimate, private camp?

➡ Does the operator have a commitment to responsible tourism?

➡ Does the operator give back to local communities and respect cultures?

➡ What are the numbers like on the tour – how many people will be in your group?

➡ Does the operator have a good reputation?

Be sceptical of price quotes that sound too good to be true, and don't rush into any deals, no matter how good they sound.

Take the time to go through the itinerary in detail, confirming what is expected and planned for each stage of the trip. Be sure that the number of wildlife drives per day and all other specifics appear in the written contract, as well as the starting and ending dates and approximate times.

Safari Operators

Typically most visitors to Southern Africa will book a safari with a specialist tour operator and many local operators do the bulk of their business this way. Operators recommended here enjoyed a good reputation at the time of research, as do many others that couldn't be listed due to space considerations.

The recommendations here provide an overview of some of the best operators who cover at least two countries in the region.

&Beyond (www.andbeyond.com) Stunning lodges and fine safaris in remote locations in Botswana, Namibia, Mozambique and South Africa, mixed with impressive conservation programs.

Africa Adventure Company (p729) This top safari specialist can organise any sort of Southern Africa itinerary.

African Wildlife Safaris (p729) Australia-based company offering trips to South Africa, Botswana, Namibia, Zambia and Zimbabwe.

Barefoot Safaris (☑in South Africa +27 73-462 9232; www.barefoot-safaris.com) Small-group safaris, self-drive, trekking and sailing; covers Zambia, Malawi and surrounding countries.

Dana Tours (www.danatours.net) Combined Mozambique–South Africa–Swaziland itineraries. Offices in Maputo and Nelspruit.

Great Plains Conservation (www.greatplains conservation.com) Among the elite of safari operators, combining a growing portfolio of stunning lodges with cutting-edge conservation work.

Kiboko Safaris (☑01-751226; www.kiboko -safaris.com; Kiboko Town Hotel, Mandala Rd) Excellent budget camping and lodge safaris in Malawi and South Luangwa, Zambia. Also luxury safaris in Malawi.

Land & Lake Safaris (www.landlake.net) A well-regarded Malawi-based operator with trips into Zambia as well.

Mabaruli African Safaris (www.mabaruli.com) Based in Windhoek, this outfit offers cycling safaris as well as a tour that takes in Namibia (Etosha National Park), Botswana (Okavango Delta) and Zambia (Victoria Falls).

Robin Pope Safaris (www.robinpopesafaris.net) This longstanding operator offers excellent safaris in Malawi and Zambia, with some fine walking safaris.

Wilderness Safaris (www.wilderness-safaris.com) Offers a range of tours in all Southern African countries including Botswana, Namibia, South Africa, Zambia and Zimbabwe. In addition to the standard luxury lodge-based tours in remote areas, it offers fly-in safaris and activity-based trips.

We can't emphasise enough the need to check on the current situation with all of the listed companies and any others you may hear about

Self-Drive Safari Operators

Drive Botswana (p733) This excellent operator arranges 4WDs and complete-package self-drive itineraries, including maps, trip notes and bookings for campsites covering Botswana, Mozambique, Namibia, South Africa, Zambia and Zimbabwe.

Safari Drive (p733) Expensive but professional and upmarket company with its own fleet of recent-model vehicles. Prices include all equipment, emergency back-up, detailed route preparation and bookings, satellite phone and free tank of fuel.

Wildlife Specialists

All international companies offering safaris to Southern Africa – and there are many of them – will most likely make wildlife watching the centrepiece of the safari experiences they offer. But there are two UK companies in particular for whom wildlife is their raison d'être, with all of the benefits that brings:

Naturetrek (p729) This company's aim is to get you to where the animals are. It offers specialised wildlife-viewing itineraries.

Wildfoot Travel (p729) High-end wildlife-focused tours to some of the region's best lodges and wildlife areas.

Safari Style

While price can be a major determining factor in safari planning, there are other considerations that are just as important:

Ambience Will you be staying in or near the park? (If you stay well outside the park, you'll miss the good early-morning and evening wildlife-viewing hours.) Are the surroundings atmospheric? Will you be in a large lodge or an intimate private camp?

Equipment Mediocre vehicles and equipment can significantly detract from the overall experience. In remote areas, lack of quality equipment or vehicles and appropriate back-up arrangements can be a safety risk.

Access and activities If you don't relish the idea of spending hours on bumpy roads, consider parks and lodges where you can fly in. To get out of the vehicle and into the bush, target areas offering walking and boat safaris.

Guides A good driver/guide can make or break your safari.

Community commitment Look for operators that do more than just give lip-service to ecotourism principles, and that have a genuine, long-standing commitment to the communities where they work. In addition to being more culturally responsible, they'll also be able to give you a more authentic and enjoyable experience.

Setting the agenda Some drivers feel that they have to whisk you from one good 'sighting' to the next. If you prefer to stay in one strategic place for a while to experience the environment and see what comes by, discuss this with your driver. Going off in wild pursuit of the Big Five (elephant, lion, rhino, leopard, buffalo) means you'll miss the more subtle aspects of your surroundings.

Less is more If you'll be teaming up with others to make a group, find out how many people will be in your vehicle, and try to meet your travelling companions before setting off.

Special interests If birdwatching or other special interests are important, arrange a private safari with a specialised operator.

Resources

Safari Bookings (www.safaribookings.com) Fantastic resource for booking your safari with expert and traveller reviews.

Good Safari Guide (www.goodsafariguide) An independent online resource with a focus on luxury lodges and tented camps.

Types of Safari

As safaris become more crafted to their clientele, the typical image of khaki-clad tourists bush-whacking through the scrub is becoming obsolete. These days a safari can incorporate anything from ballooning over the undulating dunes of the Namib, to scooting along the lush channels of the Okavango in a traditional *mokoro* (dugout canoe). Horse-riding, trekking, birding, fishing, night-drive and camel safaris are all on the agenda. The typical safari is now a highly sophisticated experience that reconnects with that vital sense of adventure.

A BEGINNER'S GUIDE TO TRACKING WILDLIFE

Visitors to Africa are always amazed at the apparent ease with which professional guides locate and spot wildlife. While most of us can't hope to replicate their skills in a brief visit, a few pointers can hone your approach.

Time of day This is possibly the most important factor for determining animal movements and behaviours. Dawn and dusk tend to be the most productive periods for mammals and many birds. They're the coolest parts of the day, and also produce the richest light for photographs. Although the middle of the day is usually too hot for much action, this is when some antelopes feel less vulnerable at a watering hole, and when raptors and reptiles are most obvious.

Weather Prevailing conditions can greatly affect your wildlife-viewing experience. For example, high winds may drive herbivores and birds into cover, so concentrate your search in sheltered areas. Summer thunderstorms are often followed by a flurry of activity as insect colonies and frogs emerge, followed by their predators. Overcast or cool days may prolong activity such as hunting by normally crepuscular predators, and extremely cold winter nights force nocturnal species to stay active at dawn.

Water Most animals drink daily when water is available, so water sources are worthwhile places to invest time, particularly in the dry season. Predators and very large herbivores tend to drink early in the day or at dusk, while antelopes tend to drink from the early morning to midday. On the coast, receding tides are usually followed by the appearance of wading birds and detritus feeders such as crabs.

Food sources Knowing what the different species eat will help you to decide where to spend most of your time. A flowering aloe might not hold much interest at first glance, but knowing that it is irresistible to many species of sunbirds might change your mind. Fruiting trees attract monkeys, while herds of herbivores with their young are a predator's dessert cart.

Habitat Knowing which habitats are preferred by each species is a good beginning, but just as important is knowing where to look in those habitats. Animals aren't merely randomly dispersed within their favoured habitats. Instead, they seek out specific sites to shelter – hollows, trees, caves and high points on plains. Many predators use open grasslands but also gravitate towards available cover, such as large trees, thickets or even grass tussocks. Ecotones – where one habitat merges into another – can be particularly productive because species from both habitats will be present.

Tracks and signs Even when you don't see animals, they leave many signs of their presence. Spoor (tracks), scat (droppings), pellets, nests, scrapes and scent marks provide information about wildlife, and may even help to locate it. Check dirt and sand roads when driving – it won't take long for you to recognise interesting spoor. Elephant footprints are unmistakable, and large predator tracks are fairly obvious. Also, many wild cats and dogs use roads to hunt, so look for where the tracks leave the road – often they mark the point where they began a stalk or sought out a nearby bush for shade.

Equipment Probably the most important piece of equipment you can have is a good pair of binoculars. These help you not only spot wildlife but also correctly identify it (this is essential for birding). Binoculars are also useful for viewing species and behaviours where close approaches are impossible. Field guides, which are pocket-sized books that depict mammals, birds, flowers etc of a specific area with photos or colour illustrations, are also invaluable. These guides also provide important identification pointers and a distribution map for each species.

At the budget end, in addition to the very convenient hop-on, hop-off bus services in South Africa, there are plenty of budget tours and safaris available to take you to the regional highlights. You'll have the most options in Cape Town, Jo'burg, Victoria Falls, Livingstone, Maun, Windhoek and other places frequented by tourists. As with all tours, the range of options is enormous: they can last from two days to three weeks and can involve camping and mucking-in to luxury shuttles between five-star lodges. Vehicles may be private aircraft, Kombi vans, no-frills safari trucks or comfortable buses with air-con and chilled wine in the fridge.

Wildlife watching tops the region's list of attractions and forms the basis of most safaris, and little wonder. To name just a few, Etosha National Park in Namibia, Botswana's Okavango Delta and Chobe National Park, South Africa's Kruger National Park and South Luangwa in Zambia are all packed with animals – in fact, you'll find the greatest density and variety of wildlife in Southern Africa, and some of the best wildlife watching on the continent. The evocative topography is just the icing on the cake.

It's good to keep in mind that although there are safaris catering to most budgets, in countries such as Botswana, most safari experiences are skewed towards the top end of the market. Overall there is a lot more to choose from at the higher end of the price spectrum, where ambience, safari style and the operator's overall focus are important considerations.

Fly-In Safaris

Taking off in a little six-seater aircraft to nip across to the next remote safari camp or designer lodge means you'll be able to maximise your time and cover a selection of parks and reserves to give yourself an idea of the fantastic variety of landscapes on offer.

The biggest temptation will be to cram too much into your itinerary, leaving you rushing from place to place. It's always better to give yourself at least three days in each camp or lodge in order to really avail yourself of the various activities on offer.

While a fly-in safari is never cheap, they are all-inclusive and what you pay should cover the cost of your flight transfers as well as meals, drinks and activities in each camp. Obviously, this all takes some planning and the earlier you can book a fly-in safari the better – many operators advise on at least six to eight months' notice if you want to pick and choose where you stay.

Fly-in safaris are particularly popular and sometimes a necessity in the Delta region of Botswana. Given the country's profile as a top-end safari destination, many tour operators specialise in fly-in safaris or include a fly-in element in their itineraries.

Mobile Safaris

Many visitors to Southern Africa will experience some sort of organised mobile safari – ranging from an all-hands-on-deck 'participation safari', where you might be expected to chip in with camp chores and supply your own sleeping bag and drinks, all the way up to top-class, privately guided trips.

As trips at the lower end of the budget scale can vary enormously in quality, it pays to canvass opinion for good local operators. This can be done on Lonely Planet's Thorn Tree forum (http://thorntree.lonelyplanet.com), or by chatting to other travellers on the ground. Failing this, don't hesitate to ask lots of questions of your tour operator and make your priorities and budget clear from the start.

For those booking through overseas tour operators, try to give as much notice as possible, especially if you want to travel in the high season. This will give you a better chance of booking the camps and lodges of your choice.

Overland Safaris

Given the costs and complex logistics of arranging a big safari, many budget travellers opt for a ride on an overland expedition, run by specialists such as Africa in Focus (www.africa-in-focus.com) and Dragoman (www.dragoman.com). Most of these expeditions are multicountry affairs starting in either Cape Town (South Africa) or Nairobi (Kenya) and covering a combination of countries including Namibia, Botswana, Zimbabwe, Zambia, Malawi and Tanzania.

The subject of overlanding often raises passionate debate among travellers. For

BUSH DRIVING & CAMPING IN SOUTHERN AFRICA

These are road-tested tips to help you plan a safe and successful 4WD expedition.

➡ Invest in a good GPS, but you should still always be able to identify your location on a map.

➡ Stock up on emergency provisions, even on main highways. Fill up whenever you pass a station. For long expeditions, carry extra fuel in metal jerry cans or reserve tanks (off-road driving burns nearly twice as much fuel as highway driving). Carry 5L of water per person per day, as well as plenty of high-calorie, non-perishable emergency food items.

➡ You should have a tow rope, a shovel, an extra fan belt, vehicle fluids, spark plugs, a bailing wire, jump leads, fuses, hoses, a good jack and a wooden plank (to use as a base in sand and salt), several spare tyres and a pump. A good Swiss Army knife or Leatherman-type tool, plus a roll of gaffer (duct) tape, can save your vehicle's life in a pinch.

➡ Essential camping equipment includes a waterproof tent, a three-season sleeping bag (or a warmer bag in the winter), a ground mat, fire-starting supplies, firewood, a basic first-aid kit and a torch (flashlight) with extra batteries.

➡ Natural water sources are vital to local people, stock and wildlife, so please don't use clear streams, springs or waterholes for washing yourself or your gear. Similarly, avoid camping near springs or waterholes lest you frighten the animals and inadvertently prevent them from drinking. Always ask permission before entering or camping near a settlement.

➡ Avoid camping in dry riverbeds, as large animals often use them as thoroughfares, and even when there's not a cloud in the sky, flash floods can roar down them with alarming force.

➡ Keep to obvious vehicle tracks: in this dry climate, damage to the delicate landscape and flora caused by off-road driving may be visible for hundreds of years.

➡ Sand tracks are least likely to bog vehicles in the cool mornings and evenings. Move as quickly as possible and keep the revs up, but avoid sudden acceleration. Shift down gears before deep sandy patches.

➡ When negotiating a straight course through rutted sand, allow the vehicle to wander along the path of least resistance. Anticipate corners and turn the wheel slightly earlier than you would normally, then accelerate gently out of the turn.

➡ Driving in the Kalahari is often through high grass, and the seeds it disperses can quickly foul radiators and cause overheating. If the temperature gauge climbs, remove as much plant material as you can from the grille.

➡ Keep your tyre pressure slightly lower than on sealed roads, but don't forget to re-inflate upon returning to the tarmac.

➡ Avoid travelling at night, when dust and distance may create confusing mirages.

➡ Keep to local speed limits. If the road is corrugated, gradually increase your speed until you find the correct speed – it'll be obvious when the rattling stops.

➡ If you have a tyre blowout, do not hit the brakes. Instead, steer straight ahead as best you can, and let the car slow itself down before you bring it to a complete stop.

➡ In rainy weather, gravel roads can turn to quagmires and desert washes may fill with water. If you're uncertain, get out and check the depth, and only cross when it's safe. Always be on the lookout for animals.

➡ Avoid swerving sharply or braking suddenly on a gravel road or you risk losing control of the vehicle.

➡ In dusty conditions, always switch on your headlights. Overtaking can be extremely dangerous due to your view being obscured by dust kicked up by the car ahead. Flash your high beams at the driver to indicate that you want to overtake. If someone behind you flashes their lights, move as far to the left as possible.

some the massive trucks and concentrated numbers of travellers herded together are everything that's wrong with travel. They take exception to the practice of rumbling into tiny villages to 'gawk' at the locals and then roaring off to party hard in hostels and bush camps throughout the host countries. Often the dynamics of travelling in such large groups (15 to 20 people at least) creates a surprising insularity resulting in a rather reduced experience of the countries you're travelling through.

For others, the overland truck presents an excellent way to get around on a budget and see a variety of parks and reserves while meeting up with people from different walks of life. Whatever your view, bear in mind that you're unlikely to get the best out of any particular African country by racing through on such inflexible itineraries.

Self-Drive Safaris

It's possible to arrange an entire safari from scratch if you hire your own vehicle. This has several advantages over an organised safari, primarily total independence and being able to choose your travelling companions. However, as far as costs go, it's generally true to say that organising your own safari will cost nearly as much as going on a cheap organised safari. Also bear in mind that it's wise to make all your campsite bookings (and pay for them) in advance, which means that you'll need to stick to your itinerary.

Apart from the cost, vehicle breakdowns, accidents, security, weather conditions and local knowledge are also major issues. It's not just about hiring a 4WD, but having the confidence to travel through some pretty rough terrain and handle anything it throws at you. If you don't have 4WD off-roading experience, Africa is

not the place to start! However, if all this doesn't put you off then it can be a great adventure.

Your greatest priority will be finding a properly equipped 4WD, including all the necessary tools you might need in case of a breakdown.

You can find pretty much all the camping essentials you need in major supermarket chains, which have outlets in most cities and some larger towns throughout the region. Camping equipment can also usually be rented through your 4WD-rental company.

Walking & Hiking Safaris

At many national parks, especially in Zambia and Zimbabwe, you can arrange walks of two to three hours in the early morning or late afternoon, with the focus on watching animals rather than covering distance. Following the walk, you'll return to the main camp or lodge.

It's also possible in Namibia to arrange safaris on foot to track black rhinos in the wild. This presents a unique opportunity to see one of Africa's most endangered animals in their native habitat. This type of safari usually takes place on a private concession.

Horse-Riding Safaris

Riding on horseback is a unique way to experience the landscape and its wildlife – Botswana, Namibia, South Africa and, to a lesser extent, Zimbabwe and Mozambique present numerous opportunities to canter among herds of zebras and wildebeest. You'll need to be an experienced rider, though, as most horseback safaris don't take beginners – after all, you need to be able to get yourself out of trouble should you encounter it.

Southern Africa at a Glance

Before delving into some of the best landscapes, wildlife watching and cultural experiences on the continent, remember that together these countries make up a huge area, and even crossing overland between them requires careful planning.

Wildlife regions abound, with South Africa, Botswana and Zambia offering the greatest diversity and numbers. Incredible landscapes just seem to pop up, but Namibia's north, the Kalahari, and South Africa's Drakensberg – to name but a few – are the stuff of legend. Many of the countries offer access to some of the best galleries of San rock art in Africa, while cities such as Cape Town, Windhoek and Maputo provide opportunities to delve deeper into the cultural fabric of the region.

Botswana

Landscape
Wildlife
Lodges

Delta & Desert

Two iconic landscapes, the shifting waters of the Okavango Delta and the vast emptiness of the Kalahari Desert, provide more than merely a backdrop to some of Africa's best wildlife spectacles. These are remote lands of singular beauty.

Wildlife

One of the greatest wildlife shows on earth, from black-maned Kalahari lions to the largest elephant population on the planet. Another highlight involves getting up close and personal with meerkats.

Lodges & Campsites

Botswana has some of the most exclusive lodges in Africa. For self-drivers, campsites are widespread and often outstanding. Together they make up one of the best safari accommodation scenes in Africa.

p42

Lesotho

Adventure
Culture
Wilderness

Adventures

Malealea, Ramabanta and Semonkong wow adventurers. Superb hiking and sturdy Basotho ponies take travellers to another level, as does Southern Africa's highest waterfall.

Cultural Interaction

Traditional Basotho cultural life remains strong, and the art of the San people is present throughout the country; lowland villages produce weavings, and music abounds at Morija Arts & Cultural Festival.

Remote & Rugged

Sehlabathebe National Park is as remote as you can get, Ts'ehlanyane National Park as lush and rugged, while the central highlands afford extraordinary vistas. With so much to see, it's difficult to know how this tiny country crams it all in.

p97

Malawi

The Lake
Walking
Safaris

Diving

If lakes don't get you excited, you've never been to Lake Malawi. Carved out by the Rift Valley, Lake Malawi is a bottle-green paradise swarming with fish and desert islands. It's perfect for diving with crystal clear depths and the most diverse freshwater fish on the planet.

Trekking

The otherworldly landscapes of the soaring Mulanje massif and Zomba Plateau are perfect places to trek, with decent cabins to stay in, well-marked trails and reliable guides.

Reinvigorated Wildlife

Malawi is firmly back on the map with restocked parks throughout the country, reintroduced lions, elephant populations on the move, world-class safari lodges and excellent tour operators.

p118

Mozambique

Beaches
Culture
Adventure

Beaches & Islands

From the pounding surf and windswept dunes of Ponta d'Ouro to the turquoise waters and white sand of the Quirimbas Archipelago, Mozambique offers some of the continent's best beaches

Culture

Mozambique's cultures have returned with full force after years of suppression. Sample this vibrancy in Maputo, with dance, theatre and other cultural offerings.

Bush Adventure

Northern Mozambique is one of the continent's last adventure frontiers, with unspoiled beaches and islands, and trackless bush. Sail on a dhow to uninhabited islands, relax on pristine beaches or experience remote bush in the interior.

p169

Namibia

Adventure
Landscape
Wildlife

Heart Stoppers

Southern Africa's HQ for adrenaline-pumping fun. Shoot down a dune on a sandboard, fling yourself out of an aircraft or go camel-riding. Most adventures begin in Swakopmund.

Canyons & Deserts

Granite monoliths rise from the desert plains through mists of sand and dust. The enormous gash hacked out of the planet at Fish River Canyon should not be missed, nor should Namib-Naukluft National Park, where the swirling sand dunes are mesmerising.

Etosha & Beyond

Etosha National Park has long been renowned as one of Africa's finest parks, and deservedly so. But there are other brilliant places to see wildlife, among them the Caprivi Strip, Okonjima and Erindi.

p242

South Africa

Cuisine
Wildlife
History

Culinary Diversity

Experience Indian-style curries in Durban, hearty meaty fare inland, seafood along the coast and Cape Malay cuisine in and around Cape Town.

Creatures Great & Small

The self-drive safari is South Africa's wildlife-watching trump card. As well as its diverse wildlife, including the Big Five, it has enough birds to keep twitchers happy. And with most parks accessible to most vehicles, it's an easy place to get wild.

Lest We Forget

To understand South Africa, you must understand its recent past. Even small-town museums have an apartheid exhibit, while larger cities have vast spaces dedicated to documenting the country's darkest era.

p322

Swaziland

Handicrafts
Activities
Culture

Handicrafts & Textiles

Outlets such as Manzini Market abound, its handicrafts and textiles supplied by rural sellers, while the Ezulwini and Malkerns Valleys have a well-earned reputation for their craft centres and markets.

Adventures

Choose between Malolotja Nature Reserve's hiking and canopy tours; walks, mountain biking and horse riding in Mlilwane Wildlife Sancturay; Great Usutu River rafting; caving in Gobholo; and tracking black rhinos in Mkhaya.

Famous Festival

Swaziland's ceremonies are famous; among them is the Umhlanga Dance, essentially a debutante ball for Swazi maidens. It's a fascinating spectacle, that goes to the heart of what makes Swaziland tick.

p530

Zambia

Wildlife
Landscapes
Waterfalls

Wildlife Utopia

A wealth of animals and a network of bush camps make Zambia one of Africa's finest wildlife-watching destinations. South Luangwa National Park is the highlight, but there are many more, including Kafue, known for its leopards, and Liuwa Plains National Park.

Wild Africa

Outside Lusaka, almost everywhere in Zambia is bush. Once you're out in the wild, the logistical hassles fade away as the raw beauty of the landscape takes over.

Vic Falls

The world's largest waterfall assaults the senses: get drenched by the spray, fill your ears with its roar and feast your eyes on its magnificence. Raft the rapids, cruise the Zambezi or simply stand awestruck on the sidelines.

p566

Zimbabwe

Wildlife
Adventure
Archaeology

Wild Safaris

It doesn't get much wilder than the parks of Zimbabwe. Hwange is home to one of the largest elephant populations in Africa, while Mana Pools offers unguided walking in a park with predators; recommended only for the bravest of souls.

White-Water Adventures

Zimbabwe is the perfect base for some serious adrenaline rushes. Bungee off Victoria Falls bridge or tame the rapids on the Zambezi River.

Rock Art & Ruins

Landscapes of natural granite boulders in the Matobo National Park are the canvas for ancient rock paintings by the San people, while Great Zimbabwe is the site of the greatest medieval city in sub-Saharan Africa.

p617

On the Road

Malawi
p118

Zambia
p566

Mozambique
p169

Victoria Falls
p549

Zimbabwe
p617

Namibia
p242

Botswana
p42

Swaziland
p530

Lesotho
p97

South Africa
p322

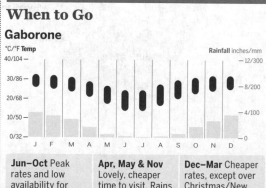

Botswana

♪ 27 / POP 2.183 MILLION

Includes ➜
Gaborone.....................43

Makgadikgadi &
Nxai Pans.....................54

Chobe National
Park..............................58

Okavango Delta...........65

Kalahari.......................76

Best Places to Eat

➜ Courtyard Restaurant (p47)

➜ Cafe Dijo (p47)

➜ Hilary's (p71)

➜ French Connection (p71)

➜ Caravela Portuguese Restaurant (p47)

Best Places to Sleep

➜ Zarafa Camp (p65)

➜ Mombo Camp (p75)

➜ Vumbura Plains Camp (p74)

➜ Sandibe Safari Lodge (p72)

➜ Jao Camp (p73)

➜ Kalahari Plains Camp (p77)

Why Go?

Blessed with some of the greatest wildlife spectacles on earth, Botswana is one of the great safari destinations in Africa. There are more elephants in Botswana than in any other country on earth; the big cats roam free; and you'll find everything from endangered African wild dogs to aquatic antelopes, rhinos making a comeback and abundant birdlife at every turn.

This is also the land of the Okavango Delta and the Kalahari Desert, at once iconic African landscapes and vast stretches of wilderness. Put these landscapes together with the wildlife that inhabits them, and it's difficult to escape the conclusion that this is wild Africa at its best.

Botswana may rank among Africa's most exclusive destinations – accommodation prices at most lodges are once-in-a-lifetime propositions – but self-drive expeditions are also possible. And whichever way you visit, Botswana is a truly extraordinary place.

When to Go

Gaborone

°C/°F Temp · Rainfall inches/mm

Jun–Oct Peak rates and low availability for lodges across the north. Warm days and mild nights.

Apr, May & Nov Lovely, cheaper time to visit. Rains can last into April and some trails are waterlogged.

Dec–Mar Cheaper rates, except over Christmas/New Year. High season in the Kalahari.

GABORONE

POP 234,500

Depending on your perspective, low-key Gaborone (or Gabs to its friends) is either terribly unexciting or one of Africa's more tranquil capital cities. There aren't that many concrete reasons to come here – it's a world of government ministries, shopping malls and a seemingly endless urban sprawl – and most travellers can fly to Maun or cross overland elsewhere. Yet, it can be an interesting place to take the pulse of the nation.

The city is largely a modern creation, with little sense of history to provide interest. Indeed, ask Batswana who were born and raised in Gaborone where they're from, and they may well tell you the name of a family village or cattle post they've never seen. So while the local Batswana may not see Gaborone as a traditional family 'home', they do see it as the place where their future, and that of their nation, is forged.

◎ Sights

Gaborone Game Reserve WILDLIFE RESERVE
(☑318 4492; adult/child/vehicle P10/5/10; ◷6.30am-6.30pm) This reserve was established in 1988 by the Kalahari Conservation Society to give the Gaborone public an opportunity to view Botswana's wildlife in a natural and accessible location. It seems to be working: although the reserve is only 5 sq km, it's the third busiest in the country and boasts wildebeest, elands, gemsboks, kudus, ostriches and warthogs. The birdlife, which includes kingfishers and hornbills, is particularly plentiful and easy to spot from observation areas.

The reserve also has a few picnic sites, a game hide and a small visitor-education centre. All roads in the reserve are accessible by 2WD; guided drives are not offered. The reserve is about 1km east of Broadhurst Mall and can be accessed from Limpopo Dr.

National Museum & Art Gallery MUSEUM
(Map p46; ☑397 4616; 331 Independence Ave) FREE Botswana's National Museum closed in mid-2016 for a much-needed overhaul. Prior to the closure, the collection itself was fairly modest, with plenty of stuffed animals alongside sections on the country's precolonial and colonial history, while the art-gallery section had a similarly unremarkable portfolio of traditional and modern African and European art.

☞ Tours

Africa Insight TOURS
(☑316 0180, 72 654 323; www.africainsight.com; half-/full-day tours P545/1198) This outfit offers half- and full-day No. 1 Ladies' Detective Agency tours endorsed by author Alexander McCall-Smith himself, with more wide-ranging excursions around Gaborone and beyond also possible. Among the latter are 'Predator Weekends' – weekend safaris to Khutse Game Reserve.

Garcin Safaris TOURS
(☑71 668 193, 393 6773; garcinsafaris@info.bw; half-/full-day tours from US$140/220) Resident and Gaborone expert Marilyn Garcin does great tours of the city, including a No. 1 Ladies' Detective Agency–focused jaunt. She also offers recommended safaris around Botswana.

Kaie Tours TOURS
(☑397 3388, 72 261 585; www.kaietours.com) Travel agency offering city tours, day trips in the Gabs hinterland and overnight safaris to Khutse Game Reserve and South Africa's Madikwe Game Reserve.

✯ Festivals & Events

Maitisong Festival PERFORMING ARTS
(☑397 1809; www.maitisong.org; ◷Mar-Apr) Botswana's largest performing-arts festival has been running since 1987 and is held over seven days in late March or early April. It features an outdoor program of music, theatre, film and dance, as well as an indoor program at the Maitisong Cultural Centre and the Memorable Order of Tin Hats (MOTH) Hall. Highlights include top performing artists from around Africa.

⊨ Sleeping

Gaborone primarily caters to domestic and business travellers. Even so, the city has a good range of accommodation to suit most budgets, and unlike most tourist areas there are some reasonable midrange possibilities. Gaborone sprawls for kilometres and no matter where you stay you'll need wheels (either a rental car or taxi) to get anywhere.

★Mokolodi Backpackers HOSTEL $
(☑74 111 164; www.backpackers.co.bw; camping/dm/s P135/235/325, 2-person units/chalets P550/645, 3-person rondavels P750; @☲) This great place, around 14km south of the city centre, is the only accommodation with a real backpacker vibe around Gaborone. It has everything from comfortable rondavels

Botswana Highlights

① **Moremi Game Reserve** (p74) Enjoying the ultimate safari with some of the best wildlife-watching on earth.

② **Okavango Delta** (p65) Gliding gently through the vast unspoiled wilderness in a wooden *mokoro* (dugout canoe).

③ **Chobe National Park** (p58) Getting up close and personal with Africa's largest elephant herds.

④ **Central Kalahari Game Reserve** (p76) Looking for black-maned lions in the heart of the Kalahari Desert.

⑤ **Makgadikgadi Pans National Park** (p55) Watching the wildlife gather by the banks of the Boteti River.

⑥ **Kgalagadi Transfrontier Park** (p79) Exploring the Kalahari's best dune scenery in Botswana's deep south.

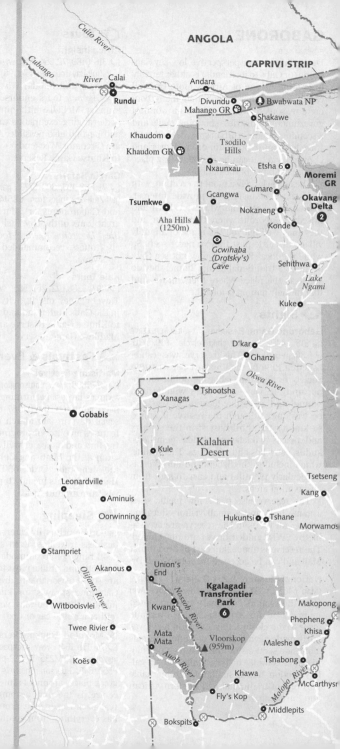

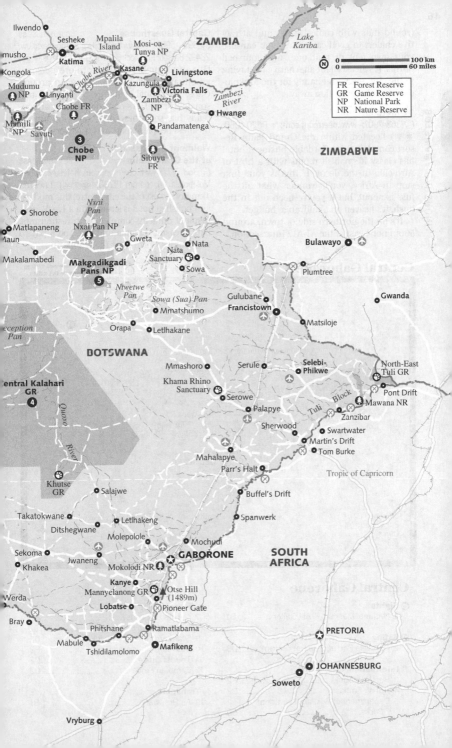

(round huts with conical huts) and attractive chalets to good campsites (you can use your own tent or rent one) and four-bed dorms. It's an excellent alternative to staying in the city centre and handy for the Mokolodi Nature Reserve, 1km away.

★**Metcourt Inn**   HOTEL **$$**
(☑363 7907; www.peermont.com; r P620-1060; ❋☎) Located within the Grand Palm Resort complex, this affordable business hotel has classy if smallish rooms with a hint of Afro-chic in the decor. If this is your first stop in Africa, you'll wonder what all the fuss is about, but if you've been out in the bush, it's heaven on a midrange budget.

It's on the northern side of town, around 500m northeast of the A1-A12 intersection.

Capital Guesthouse   GUESTHOUSE **$$**
(☑391 5905; www.thecapitalguesthouse.co.bw; 28492 Batsadi Rd, Block 3; r P950-1500; ℗❋☎) One of a number of newer, more personal guesthouses and B&Bs opening up around Gabs, the Capital is quietly elegant and reasonably central. It's on a quiet street and already has something of a following among business people, expats and travellers.

**Walmont Ambassador
at the Grand Palm**   HOTEL **$$$**
(☑363 7777; www.peermont.com/hotels/walmont; Molepolole Rd; r from P1700; ❋☎) Located 4km northwest of the city centre, this modern and polished hotel is situated in a Las Vegas–inspired minicity complete with restaurants, bars, a casino, cinema and spa. You'll pay to stay, but it's worth it for the pampering.

Central Gaborone

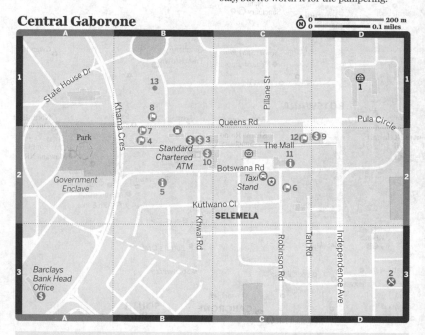

Central Gaborone

◎ **Sights**
1 National Museum & Art Gallery.............D1

✕ **Eating**
2 Caravela Portuguese Restaurant.........D3

ℹ **Information**
3 Barclays Bank B2
4 British Embassy B2
5 Department of Wildlife & National
    Parks.. B2

6 French Embassy....................................C2
7 German Embassy...................................B2
8 South African Embassy.........................B1
9 Standard Chartered Bank....................D2
10 Standard Chartered Bank....................B2
11 Tourist Office..C2
12 Zambian Embassy.................................C2

ℹ **Transport**
13 Air Botswana.. B1

✗ Eating

Gabs has numerous good restaurants aimed at an expat market. The upmarket hotels are another good place to try. For cheap African food, stalls near the bus station (and on the Mall during lunchtime) sell plates of traditional food, such as *mealie pap* (maize-meal porridge) and stew. For self-caterers, there are well-stocked supermarkets across the city.

★ Cafe Dijo   CAFE $$
(☑ 318 0575; Kgale Hill Shopping Mall, Lobatse Rd; mains from P79; ☺ 7am-4pm Mon-Fri, 8am-1pm Sat; 🐾) This classy but casual place is one of our favourite haunts in Gabs. The lunch specials change regularly, but usually include Thai chicken curry, chicken tandoori wraps and excellent salads, alongside toasted ciabatta, wraps and Botswana's best carrot cake. With free wi-fi and great coffee (from filter coffee to Australian iced coffee), you could easily spend hours here.

★ Caravela Portuguese Restaurant   PORTUGUESE $$
(Map p46; ☑ 391 4284; www.thecaravela.com; Mokgosi Close, Extension 4; mains from P79; ☺ noon-2.30pm & 6-10pm) One of Gabs' most popular expat haunts, serving up assured Mediterranean cooking in a pretty garden setting. It's close to the city centre, but in a quiet residential corner, which adds to a real sense of it being for people-in-the-know. Seafood, all manner of platters, and dishes such as Portuguese steaks make this a terrific place to eat.

★ Courtyard Restaurant   AFRICAN, INTERNATIONAL $$
(☑ 392 2487; www.botswanacraft.bw; Western Bypass, off Airport Rd; mains P65-110; ☺ 8am-5pm Mon-Sat) In the garden area out the back of Botswanacraft (p47), this tranquil spot serves up imaginative African cooking (including guinea-fowl pot), with other local staples making a rare appearance. It also serves salads and sandwiches and there's even occasional live music.

Bull & Bush Pub   INTERNATIONAL $$
(Map p49; ☑ 397 5070, 71 212 233; off Sebone Rd; mains P55-126; ☺ noon-10.30pm Mon-Fri, to 11.30pm Sat & Sun) This long-standing South African–run Gabs institution is deservedly popular with expats, tourists and locals alike. Though there's something on the menu for everyone, it's renowned for its thick steaks, pizzas and cold beers. It has some themed nights – Monday is ribs night, Thursday is pizzas – while on any given night, the outdoor beer garden is buzzing with activity.

🛍 Shopping

Botswanacraft   ARTS & CRAFTS
(☑ 392 2487; www.botswanacraft.bw; Western Bypass, off Airport Rd; ☺ 8am-6pm Mon-Fri, to 5pm Sat, 9am-1pm Sun) Botswana's largest and best craft emporium sells traditional souvenirs, including pottery from Gabane and Thamaga, San jewellery and baskets from across the country, at fixed prices. It also has books, jewellery, carvings and textiles, but most of these are from elsewhere in Africa, from Mali to the Congo. There's also the good onsite Courtyard Restaurant.

Exclusive Books   BOOKS
(Map p49; ☑ 370 0130; shop 28A, Riverwalk Mall; ☺ 9am-8pm Mon-Fri, to 5pm Sat, to 2pm Sun) Easily Gaborone's best bookshop, this large outpost of a respected South African chain has literature, nonfiction and travel books, with excellent sections focused on Africa.

Kalahari Quilts   ARTS & CRAFTS
(☑ 72 618 711; www.kalahariquilts.com; unit 7A, Kgale Hill Shopping Mall; ☺ 9am-5pm Mon-Fri, to 2pm Sat) These stunning quilts are made by Batswana women, overseen by the engaging Jenny Healy, and are a unique craft to take home. Each one bears an individual imprint, although all do a good job at capturing the primary-colour-heavy palette of Botswana.

ℹ Information

DANGERS & ANNOYANCES

Gaborone is a safe city by African standards and a welcome respite from the tension on the streets of some South African cities. Crime does happen here (mostly pickpocketing and petty theft, with occasional muggings) although most visitors encounter no problems. Even so, it pays to be careful.

➔ Always take cabs at night, especially if you're a woman or on your own.

➔ Use drivers recommended by hotels and try to keep their phone numbers, as some people have been robbed in unmarked cabs.

➔ The main mall is fine to walk around in during the day but is best avoided after dark.

Traffic

Gridlocked traffic is becoming an increasing problem as more Batswana buy cars and start driving, often for the first time in their lives. Be extremely careful on the road during the last weekend of the month, when everyone gets paid and many people get drunk before getting behind the wheel – a toxic combination.

POLICE STATION

Central police station (Map p46; ☑ 355 1161; Botswana Rd; ☺ 24hr)

BOTSWANA GABORONE

EMERGENCY & IMPORTANT NUMBERS

Country code	267
International access code	00
Emergency	999
Ambulance	997
Fire	998
Police	999

MEDICAL SERVICES

Gaborone Hospital Dental Clinic (395 3777; Segoditshane Way) Part of the Gaborone Private Hospital.

Gaborone Private Hospital (300 1999; Segoditshane Way) For anything serious, head to this reasonably modern, but expensive, hospital, opposite Broadhurst Mall. The best facility in town.

Princess Marina Hospital (Map p49; 355 3221; Notwane Rd; 24hr) Equipped to handle standard medical treatments and emergencies, but shouldn't be your first choice for treatment.

MONEY

Major branches of Standard Chartered and Barclays Banks have foreign-exchange facilities and ATMs and offer cash advances. The few bureaux de change around the city offer quick service at slightly better rates than the banks, but they charge up to 2.75% commission.

American Express (Map p49; Shop 113, 1st fl, Riverside Mall; 9am-5pm Mon-Fri, to 1.30pm Sat)

Barclays Bank (Map p46; The Mall; 8.30am-3.30pm Mon-Fri, 8.15-10.45am Sat)

Barclays Bank Head Office (Map p46; Khama Cres)

Standard Chartered Bank (Map p46; The Mall; 8.30am-3.30pm Mon-Fri, 8.15-11am Sat)

UAE Foreign Exchange (Map p49; 1st fl, Riverwalk Mall; 9am-5pm Mon-Fri, to 1.30pm Sat)

POST

Central post office (Map p46; The Mall; 7.30am-noon & 2-4.30pm Mon-Fri, to 12.30pm Sat)

TOURIST INFORMATION

Tourist office (Botswana Tourism; Map p46; 395 9455; www.botswanatourism. co.bw; Botswana Rd; 7.30am-6pm Mon-Fri, 8am-1pm Sat) Moderately useful collection of brochures; next to the Cresta President Hotel.

ⓘ Getting There & Away

Gabs is well connected to the rest of the country by both road and air, but remember that the focus of the national public transport system is directed at locals rather than tourists – you'll find plenty of connections from Gaborone to Maun, Kasane, Francistown and Ghanzi, but few to the major national parks or other upcountry attractions.

AIR

From **Sir Seretse Khama International Airport** (GBE; 391 4401; www.caab.co.bw), 14km northeast of the centre, **Air Botswana** (Map p46; 368 0900; www.airbotswana.co.bw; Matstitam Rd; 9.30am-5pm Mon-Fri, 8.30-11.30am Sat) operates international services to Harare, Johannesburg and Lusaka, as well as domestic services to Francistown (P1406), Kasane (P2060) and Maun (P1791).

BUS

Please note that minibuses to Johannesburg drop you off in a pretty unsafe area near Park Station; try to have onward transport arranged *immediately* upon arrival.

Domestic buses leave from the main bus terminal (Map p49). To reach Maun or Kasane, you'll need to change in Francistown. Buses operate according to roughly fixed schedules and minibuses leave when full.

DESTINATION	FARE (P)	DURATION (HR)
Francistown	97	6
Ghanzi	155	11
Kanye	24	2
Mochudi	15	1
Palapye	60	4
Serowe	60	5
Thamaga	10	1

ⓘ Getting Around

TO/FROM THE AIRPORT

Taxis rarely turn up at Sir Seretse Khama International Airport; if you do find one, you'll pay around P100 to the centre. The only reliable transport between the airport and town are the courtesy minibuses operated by top-end hotels for their guests. If there's space, nonguests may talk the driver into a lift.

CAR & MOTORCYCLE

Most major international car-rental companies have offices (which may not be staffed after 5pm) at the airport.

LOCAL TRANSPORT

Packed white combis (minibuses), recognisable by their blue number plates, circulate according to set routes and cost P7. They pick up and drop off only at designated lay-bys marked 'bus/taxi stop'. The main city loop passes all the major shopping centres except the Riverwalk Mall and the Kgale Centre, which are on the Tlokweng and Kgale routes respectively. Combis can be hailed either along major roads or from the combi stand (Map p49).

Gaborone

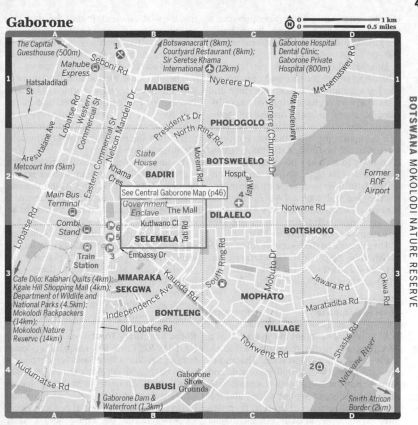

Gaborone

⊗ Eating
1 Bull & Bush Pub B1

⊕ Shopping
2 Exclusive Books D4

ℹ Information
   American Express .... (see 2)
3 Namibian High Commission B3
4 Princess Marina Hospital C2
   UAE Foreign Exchange .... (see 2)
5 US Embassy B3
6 Zimbabwean Embassy B3

TAXI

Taxis, which can be easily identified by their blue number plates, are surprisingly difficult to come by in Gabs. Very few cruise the streets looking for fares, and most seem to be parked around Botswana Road (Map p46) or near the combi stand. You're better off arranging one through your hotel. If you manage to get hold of one, fares (negotiable) are generally P50 to P80 per trip around the city.

Final Bravo Cabs (☑ 312 1785)
Speedy Cabs (☑ 390 0070)

AROUND GABORONE

Mokolodi Nature Reserve

The 30-sq-km private **Mokolodi Nature Reserve** (☑ 316 1955; www.mokolodi.com; per vehicle per day P70, day/night wildlife drives per person P175/250, giraffe/rhino tracking P550/650; ⊙ 7.30am-6pm, often closed Dec–Mar) was established in 1994 and is home to giraffes, elephants, zebras, baboons, warthogs, rhinos, hippos, kudus, impalas, waterbucks and klipspringers. The reserve also protects a few retired cheetahs, leopards, honey badgers, jackals and hyenas, as well as more than 300 species of birds.

Mokolodi also operates a research facility, a breeding centre for rare and endangered species, a community-education centre and a sanctuary for orphaned, injured or confiscated birds and animals. Among the activities on offer is rhino- and giraffe-tracking.

It is important to note that the entire reserve often closes during the rainy season (December to March) – phone ahead before you visit at this time. Visitors are permitted to drive their own vehicles around the reserve (you will need a 4WD in the rainy season), though guided tours by 4WD or on foot are available. If you're self-driving, pick up a map from the reception office.

The entrance to the reserve is 12km south of Gaborone. By public transport, take a bus to Lobatse and get off at the signposted turnoff. From there, it's a 1.5km walk.

**Mokolodi Nature
Reserve Campsite** CAMPGROUND $$
(camping per adult/child P150/75, chalets P680-1400) Spending the night in the reserve is a refreshing and highly recommended alternative to staying in Gaborone. The campsites are secluded and well groomed, and feature braai (barbeque) pits, thatched bush showers (with steaming-hot water) and toilets. If you want to safari in style, there are three- to eight-person chalets in the middle of the reserve; prices increase significantly on weekends. Advance bookings are necessary. If you don't have a vehicle, staff can drive you to the campsite and accommodation areas for P10.

EASTERN BOTSWANA

Khama Rhino Sanctuary

With the rhinos all but disappeared from Botswana, the residents of Serowe banded together in the early 1990s to establish the 43-sq-km **Khama Rhino Sanctuary** (463 0713; www.khamarhinosanctuary.org.bw; adult/child P79/39, vehicle under/over 5 tonnes P97/285; 7am-7pm). Today the sanctuary protects 30 white and four black rhinos – the sanctuary was not originally set up for black rhinos, but when one wandered across the border from Zimbabwe it was the start of a beautiful relationship. Some rhinos have been released

into the wild, especially in the Okavango Delta, joining imports from Botswana's regional neighbours. The sanctuary is also home to wildebeest, impalas, ostriches, brown hyenas, leopards and more than 230 bird species.

The best time for spotting the rhinos is late afternoon or early morning. Malema's Pan, Serwe Pan and the water hole at the bird hide are the most wildlife-rich areas of the sanctuary; these locations are clearly marked on the sanctuary map (P10) available at the park entrance.

Two-hour day/night wildlife drives (day/night P715/836) can take up to four people. Nature walks (P275) and rhino-tracking excursions (P440) can also be arranged. If self-driving, you can also hire a guide to accompany your vehicle for P275.

Staying overnight inside the sanctuary at one of the well-maintained campsites or chalets means you're ideally placed to go rhino watching at the optimum times – just before sunset and just after sunrise.

The office at the entrance sells basic nonperishable foods, cold drinks and firewood. Otherwise, bring your own supplies.

Rhino Sanctuary Trust CAMPGROUND, CHALETS $
(71 348 468, 73 965 655; krst@khamarhinosanctuary.org.bw; Khama Rhino Sanctuary; camping per adult/child 103/51, dm P440, chalets P660-880;) Shady campsites with braai pits are adjacent to clean toilets and (steaming-hot) showers, while there are also some pricey six-person dorms. For a little more comfort, there are rustic four-person chalets and six-person A-frames; both have basic kitchen facilities and private bathrooms. There's also a restaurant, bar and a swimming pool.

If you don't have a vehicle, staff can drive you to the campsite and accommodation areas for a nominal fee.

The entrance gate to the sanctuary is 26km northwest of Serowe along the Serowe–Orapa road (turn left at the poorly signed T-junction about 5km northwest of Serowe). Khama is accessible by any bus or combi heading towards Orapa, with the entrance right next to the road.

Francistown

POP 98,961

Francistown is Botswana's second-largest city and an important regional centre – there's a fair chance you'll overnight here if you're on the way north from South Africa, or driving without haste between Gaborone and Maun. There's not much to catch the eye, but there are places to stay and eat, as well as excellent supermarkets for those heading out into the wilds.

🛌 Sleeping

★ A New Earth Guest Lodge GUESTHOUSE **$**
(📞71 846 622; anewearthguestlodge@gmail.com; Bonatla St; r from P520; P❄🅿📶🏊) Out in the quiet southeastern suburbs of Francistown, this lovely little guesthouse has a family-run feel and rooms decorated in earth tones or with exposed stone walls and down-home furnishings. Patricia, your host, is a delight and reason alone to stay here. It can be a little tricky to find, so ring ahead for directions.

★ Woodlands Stop Over CAMPGROUND, BUNGALOW **$$**
(📞73 325 911, 244 0131; www.woodlandscamping bots.com; off A3, S 21°04.532', E 27°27.507'; camping per adult/child P115/95, s/d P725/865, with shared bathroom P415/610, q P1740; 🏊) A wonderfully tranquil place, 15km north of town off the road to Maun, Woodlands is easily the pick of places to stay around Francistown if you have your own wheels. The budget chalets are tidy, the bungalows are nicely appointed and come with loads of space, while the immaculate campsites are Botswana's cleanest and a wonderful respite from dusty trails.

🍴 Eating

★ Barbara's Bistro INTERNATIONAL **$$**
(📞241 3737; Francistown Sports Club; mains from P75; ⊘noon-2pm & 7-10pm Mon-Sat) Located in the town's eastern outskirts in the sports club, this leafy spot is a fabulous choice. Barbara, the German owner, is a charismatic host and loves nothing better than to sit down and run through the specials. The food is easily Francistown's best – German pork dishes like *eisbein* are recurring themes, while the Karoo lamb is outstanding.

★ Thorn Tree CAFE **$$**
(St Patrick St, Village Mall; breakfast P30-70, mains P55-100; ⊘6am-3pm Mon-Sat; 📶) An oasis of sophistication at the northern end of Francistown, Thorn Tree (no relation to Lonely Planet's famous online bulletin board) does burgers, salads, pizza, pasta, jacket potatoes, fresh fish and great coffee. The outdoor terrace is lovely. Highly recommended.

Savanna INTERNATIONAL **$$**
(St Patrick St, 1st fl, Village Mall; mains P60-154; ⊘noon-10pm Mon-Sat; 📶) This place, upstairs in the Village Mall, serves up the town's best flame-grilled steaks, but it also does fish and

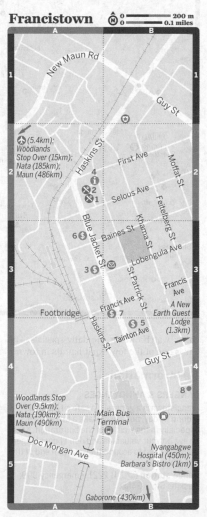

Francistown

🍴 Eating
| 1 Savanna | A2 |
| 2 Thorn Tree | A2 |

ℹ️ Information
3 Barclays Bank	A3
4 Botswana Tourism	A2
5 First National Bank	B4
6 FxA Bureau de Change	A3
7 Standard Chartered Bank	B3

ℹ️ Transport
| 8 Air Botswana | B4 |

Eastern Botswana

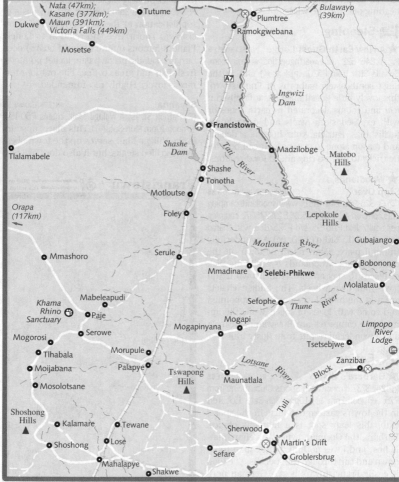

chips; watch out for the daily specials. The bar is one of the few expat haunts in town.

ℹ️ Information

DANGERS & ANNOYANCES

Francistown is a generally a safe city to walk around by day, but always take a taxi at night, especially in the vicinity of the bus station. Keep an eye on your valuables and don't linger longer than you need to around the southern end of the bus station.

Police station (📞 241 2221, emergency 999; Haskins St; ⏰ 24hr)

MEDICAL SERVICES

Nyangabgwe Hospital (📞 211 1000, emergency 997; Marang Rd; ⏰ 24hr)

MONEY

There are plenty of banks along the main street, but most won't change money before 10am when they receive the day's official exchange rates from their head offices.

Barclays Bank (Blue Jacket St; ⏰ 8.30am-3.30pm Mon-Fri, 8.15-10.45am Sat)

First National Bank (⏰ 8.30am-3.30pm Mon-Fri, 8.15-10.30am Sat)

FxA Bureau de Change (Blue Jacket St; ⏰ 8.30am-4.30pm Mon-Fri, to 12.30pm Sat)

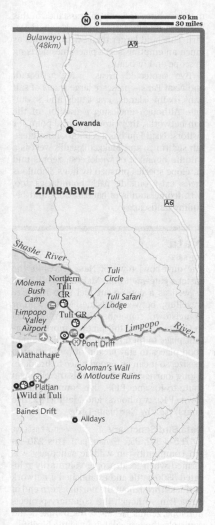

Getting There & Away

AIR
Air Botswana (☑241 2393; www.airbotswa na.co.bw; off St Patrick St, 1st fl, Galo Mall; ⊙7.30am-4.30pm Mon-Fri, 8.30-11.30am Sat) flies once daily between Francistown and Gabs (P1406); you may find cheaper fares online.

BUS
From the **main bus terminal** (Haskins St), located between the train line and Blue Jacket Plaza, buses and combis connect Francistown with the following places.

DESTINATION	FARE (P)	DURATION (HR)
Gaborone	97	6
Kasane	110	7
Maun	105	5
Nata	40	2

CAR & MOTORCYCLE
Engen Petrol Station (Blue Jacket St; ⊙24hr)

Getting Around
Francistown's airport is 5.5km northwest of the city centre. A taxi into town shouldn't cost more than P70.

Tuli Block

Tucked into the nation's right-side pocket, the Tuli Block is one of Botswana's best-kept secrets. This 10km- to 20km-wide swath of freehold farmland extends over 300km along the Limpopo River's northern banks and is made up of a series of private properties, many with a conservation bent. The Block's northern reaches now make up the Northern Tuli Game Reserve. Wildlife is a big attraction, but so too is the landscape, which is unlike anywhere else in Botswana. With its moonscapes of muddy oranges and browns, its kopjes (hills) overlooked by deep-blue sky, it's the sort of Dalí-esque desert environment reminiscent of Arizona or Australia. Yet the barren beauty belies a land rich in life. Elephants, hippos, kudus, wildebeest and impalas, as well as small numbers of lions, cheetahs, leopards and hyenas, circle each other among rocks and kopjes (hills) scattered with artefacts from the Stone Age onwards. More than 350 species of bird have been recorded.

Sleeping & Eating
The office at the entrance sells basic nonperishable foods, cold drinks and firewood. Otherwise, bring your own supplies. There's

Standard Chartered Bank (Blue Jacket St; ⊙8.30am-4.30pm Mon, Tue, Thu & Fri, 9am-4.30pm Wed, 8.30-11am Sat)

POST
Post office (Blue Jacket St; ⊙8am-noon & 2-4.30pm Mon-Fri, 8am-noon Sat)

TOURIST INFORMATION
Tourist office (☑244 0113; www.botswana-tourism.co.bw; St Patrick St, Village Mall; ⊙7.30am-6pm Mon-Fri, 9am-2pm Sat) Moderately useful for brochures and basic local information, but little else.

nowhere to eat in the Tuli Block other than in the camps and lodges themselves. The nearest supplies are to be had in Bobonong or, further away, Selebi-Phikwe or Palapye.

Molema Bush Camp　　CAMPGROUND, CHALETS **$**
(⌨264 5303; www.tulitrails.com; camping per person P125-185, chalets tw/f P500/600) Run by the owners of Tuli Safari Lodge, this campground in the Northern Tuli Game Reserve is one of few real options for self-drive visitors hoping to camp. The sites are shaded and have private ablution blocks, while the simple chalets are comfy and reasonably priced.

★ **Wild at Tuli**　　TENTED CAMP **$$$**
(⌨72 113 688; www.wildattuli.com; Kwa-Tuli Game Reserve; s/d full board US$250/400) This fabulous camp on an island in a branch of the Limpopo River is run by respected conservationists Judi Gounaris and Dr Helena Fitchat, and they bring a winning combination of warmth and conservation knowledge to the experience. Meals are home-cooked and eaten around the communal table and the tents are extremely comfortable.

Tuli Safari Lodge　　LODGE **$$$**
(⌨264 5303; www.tulilodge.com; s/d with full board & wildlife drives US$630/840; ✳☲) In the Northern Tuli Game Reserve, this fine lodge is set in a riverine oasis, surrounded by red-rock country that teems with wildlife. Although at the upper end of the scale for the Tuli Block, the rates are well priced compared to other exclusive private reserves in the country and the standards are high.

❶ Getting There & Away

There are daily flights between Johannesburg and the Limpopo Valley Airport at Polokwane across the border in South Africa, which is convenient for the Mashatu Game Reserve and Tuli Safari Lodge. Flights can sometimes be booked as part of a package with either reserve.

You'll need your own vehicle to reach (and explore) the Tuli Block. Once there, most roads in the Tuli Block are negotiable by 2WD.

MAKGADIKGADI & NXAI PANS

Within striking distance of the water-drowned terrain of the Okavango Delta, Chobe River and Linyanti Marshes lies Makgadikgadi, the largest network of salt pans in the world. Here the country takes on a different hue, forsaking the blues and greens of the delta for the burnished oranges, shim-

mering whites and golden grasslands of this northern manifestation of the Kalahari Desert. This land larger than Switzerland is as much an emptiness as a place, mesmerising in scope and in beauty.

Two protected areas – Makgadikgadi and Nxai Pans – preserve large tracts of salt pans, palm islands, grasslands and savannah. Although enclosing a fraction of the pan networks, they provide a focal point for visitors: Nxai Pan has a reputation for cheetah sightings, and Makgadikgadi's west is a wildlife bonanza of wildebeest, zebras and antelope species pursued by lions. Fabulous areas exist outside park boundaries too, with iconic stands of baobab trees and beguiling landscapes.

Nata

POP 5313

The dust-bowl town of Nata serves as the eastern gateway to the Makgadikgadi Pans, as well as a convenient fuel stop if you're travelling between Kasane, Maun and/or Francistown; remember that there's no fuel in Gweta, making this an even more important place to fill up. Nata has a collection of good places to stay far out of proportion to its size, so it can be a good place to break up a long journey. Regular combis travelling en route to Kasane (P105, five hours), Francistown (P40, two hours) and Maun (P92, five hours) pass by Northgate Lodge.

Nata Bird Sanctuary　　WILDLIFE RESERVE
(⌨71 544 342; P55; ◷7am-7pm) This 230-sq-km community-run wildlife sanctuary was formed when local people voluntarily relocated 3500 cattle and established a network of tracks throughout the northeastern end of Sowa Pan. Although the sanctuary protects antelope, zebras, jackals, foxes, monkeys and squirrels, the principal draw is the birdlife – more than 165 species have been recorded here. It's at its best in the wet season when the sanctuary becomes a haven for Cape and Hottentot teals, white and pink-backed pelicans and greater and lesser flamingos.

★ **Elephant Sands**　　LODGE **$**
(⌨7353 6473; www.elephantsands.com; camping per person P60, s/d/f safari tents & chalets from P600/810/910; ☲☲) Some 52km north of Nata, Elephant Sands, run by Mike and Saskia, is a fabulous place to stay. Excellent and spacious safari tents, some chalets and a few campsites encircle a natural water hole that is always filled with elephants – in the bar,

restaurant and pool area, you'll be as close to wild elephants as it's possible to be.

Nata Lodge LODGE $$
(📞620 0070; www.natalodge.com; camping per adult/child P75/45, d luxury tents/chalets US$110/138; ✳☎) Nata Lodge offers luxury wood-and-thatch chalets, stylish wood-floored safari tents and a good campsite all set amid a verdant oasis of monkey thorn, marula and mokolane palms. When you consider the cost of comparable places elsewhere in Botswana, this place is a steal, although remember that meals (breakfast/dinner start from P75/185) and activities cost extra to the prices quoted here.

Gweta

POP 4689

Gweta, just off the Nata–Maun highway, is a dusty and laid-back crossroads town on the edge of the pans, framed by bushveld and big skies. Given that the petrol station here has been dry for years, the only real reason to stop is to stay overnight, or as your entry point to one of Uncharted Africa's camps further south. The name of the village is derived from the croaking sound made by large bullfrogs, which, incredibly, bury themselves in the pan sand until the rains provide sufficient water for them to emerge and mate. You're quite a distance from anywhere here: Gweta is 205km from Maun, 290km from Francistown, 416km from Kasane and 491km from Ghanzi. Hourly combis travelling to Francistown (P54, three hours) and Maun (P65, four hours) pass along the main road.

Gweta Lodge LODGE $$
(📞76 212 220; www.gwetalodge.com; P80, standard/premium r P700/1100, f P1000; ✳☎☎) In the centre of town, Gweta Lodge is a friendly place that combines a lovely bar and pool area with a range of accommodation options spread around the leafy grounds. The rooms are large and comfortable, the campsites are excellent and activities include half-day/overnight tours of Ntwetwe Pan and its human-habituated meerkats (P650/1150) as well as walking tours of the village (P150).

Planet Baobab LODGE $$
(📞in South Africa +27 11-447 1605; www.unchartedafrica.com; camping per adult/child US$15/8, s/d/q huts from US$165/190/600; ☎☎) About 4km east of Gweta, a huge concrete aardvark marks the turn-off for Planet Baobab.

This inventive lodge forsakes masks and wildlife photos, replaced by a great open-air bar-restaurant (meals P45 to P90) filled with vintage travel posters, metal seats covered in cowhide, beer-bottle chandeliers and the like. Outside, colourfully painted rondavels lie scattered over the gravel.

Makgadikgadi Pans National Park

This 3900-sq-km **park** (per day per non-resident/vehicle P120/50; ⊙6am-6.30pm Apr-Sep, 5.30am-7pm Oct-Mar), the southern section of the Makgadikgadi and Nxai Pans National Park, extends from the Boteti River in the west to the Ntwetwe Pan in the east. The return of water to the Boteti River in recent years has drawn plenty of wildlife, particularly in the dry season from May to October, when the river, even at low levels, is the only source of permanent water in the reserve. The Boteti River has hippos a few kilometres northwest of Khumaga Campsite.

Out in the east of the park, the wildlife is less accustomed to vehicles, but watch for zebras, gemsboks and the occasional predator. Birdlife is especially rich along the Boteti River, from the plague-like red-billed queleas to much rarer African fish-eagles and wattled cranes. Out in the east, you're more likely to see vultures and birds of prey.

Dry season (May to October) is best for driving on the pans, with big wildlife concentrations along the Boteti River later in the season. During the wet season (November to March or April), driving can be perilous but the zebra migration on the eastern pans can be quite a sight.

Fuel is only reliably available in Maun and Nata (*not* Gweta).

THE PANS IN A NUTSHELL

The Sowa (Sua), Nxai and Ntwetwe Pans together make up the 12,000-sq-km Makgadikgadi Pans. While Salar de Unyuni in Bolivia is the biggest single pan in the world, the Makgadikgadi network of parched, white dry lakes is larger. Ancient lakeshore terraces reveal the pans were once part of a 'super lake' of more than 60,000 sq km that reached the Okavango and Chobe Rivers to the far north. However, around 10,000 years ago, climatic changes caused the huge lake to evaporate, leaving only salt behind.

Makgadikgadi & Nxai Pans National Parks

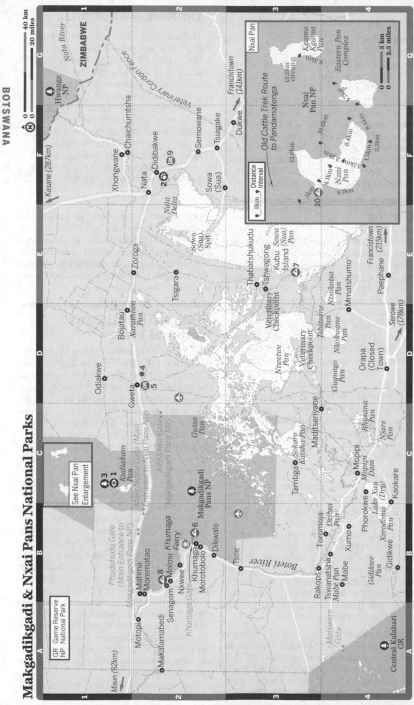

GR Game Reserve
NP National Park

See Nxai Pan Enlargement

Nxai Pan

Old Cattle Trek Route to Pandamatenga

Distance Interval 5km

Kgama Kgama Pan

Eastern Pan Complex

Nxai Pan NP

Nxai Pan

Francistown (215km)

ZIMBABWE

Nata River

Hwange NP

Kasane (287km)

Veterinary Cordon Fence

Chaichumtsha

Xhongwane

Nata

Didibakwe

Semowane

Tsiagake

Dukwe

Francistown (141km)

Sowa (Sua)

Nata Delta

Sowa (Sua) Spit

Zoroga

Tsigara

Bojatau

Xaruthau Pan

Thabatshukudu

Tshwagong

Kubu Island (Sua)

Sowa (Sua) Pan

Veterinary Checkpoint

Ntsikotsa Pan

Mmatshumo

Francistown (215km)

Paephane

Serowe (178km)

See Nxai Pan Enlargement

Kudiakam Pan

Phuduhudu Gate (Main Entrance to Makgadikgadi Pans NP)

Matima

Morematao

Molosi

Nxwee

Khumaga Ferry

Morotobolo

Khumaga Gate

Makxao-Xau Gate (Entrance to Nxai Pans NP)

Makolwane Gate (Main Entrance to Makgadikgadi Pans NP)

Odiakwe

Gweta

Gutsa Pan

Ntwetwe Pan

Veterinary Checkpoint

Tshitame Pan

Nkokwane Pan

Gugpuago Pan

Orapa (Closed Town)

Rysana Pan

Njare Pan

Maditsenyane

Sokoro

Kitsha Pan

Tamtiga

Mopipi

Mopipi Dam

Kaokare

Phorokwe

Xorodomo (Dry)

Lake Xau

Delbut Pan

Toromoja

Rakops

Gidikwe Pan

Tswanatsha Mabe Pan

Mabe

Xumo

Gidikwe Pan

Makgadikgadi Pans NP

Dikwalo

Tsoe

Botlet River

Central Kalahari GR

Matswere Gate

Motopi

Makalamabedi

Senagom

Nxwee

Maun (82km)

Nxai Pan enlargement labels:
Kgama Kgama Pan
Eastern Pan Complex
Nxai Pan NP
Nxai Pan
13.3km circuit
12.6km
10.6km
8.3km
6.4km
9.1km
5.5km
1.5km
8km
14.8km

The main entrance to the park is Phuduhudu Gate (S 20°12.439', E 24°33.346'), 141km west of Nata and 164km east of Maun, 100km south of the Gweta–Maun road. There's another entrance, Khumaga Gate (S 20°28.333', E 24°31.056'), close to Khumaga Campsite, but you'll need to cross the river on a pontoon ferry (☎ 74 002 228; per vehicle P150; ⏰ 6am-6.30pm Apr-Sep, 5.30am-7pm Oct-Mar). Otherwise, there's the little-used XireXawa Gate (S 20°25.384', E 24°7.093') in the far east of the park.

Khumaga Campsite
CAMPGROUND $

(✐ 686 5365; www.sklcamps.com; S 20°27.311', E 24°30.968'; camping per adult/child US$50/25) The Khumaga Campsite sits high above the Boteti River and is an attractive site with good shade, braai pits and an excellent ablutions block with flush toilets and (usually) hot showers. Some readers have complained of night-time noise from the village across the river, but the last time we slept here all we could hear was a frog symphony.

Meno a Kwena
TENTED CAMP $$$

(✐ camp 71 326 089, reservations 686 0981; www.menoakwena.com; s/d US$966/1380) The name means 'Teeth of the Crocodile', and you can indeed see some down by the river from Meno a Kwena's riverbank perch. There are nine luxury tents with safari nostalgia furnishings – gold-plated lamps, heavy wooden chests, Persian rugs – and each faces the Boteti River valley. Excellent food is another feature, as are brilliant sunrise views.

Nxai Pans National Park

This 2578-sq-km park (per day per nonresident/vehicle P120/50; ⏰ 6am-6.30pm Apr-Sep, 5.30am-7pm Oct-Mar) is one of the most accessible places to experience the salt pans that are a Kalahari speciality, although it's more about smaller pans surrounded by grasslands and scrubby vegetation than the vast, salty wastes that you find further south. Wildlife is a highlight here; elephants, giraffes and jackals are pretty much guaranteed, and you have a good chance to see lions and cheetahs as well. The grassy expanse of the park is interesting during the rains, when large animal herds migrate from the south and predators arrive to take advantage of the bounty; it's also impressive when the land is dry and dust clouds migrate over the scrub and umbrella acacias.

The park also occupies an important historical area: crossing the park is the old Pandamatenga Trail, which once connected a series of bore holes and was used until the 1960s for overland cattle drives.

The **main water hole** is good for elephants, jackals and other plains wildlife, while the 12km **Baobab Loop** in the park's northwest has a good combination of sheltering scrub, seasonal water holes and open grasslands. The park's eastern reaches get little traffic and feel wonderfully remote. The pans in the far northeast are often deserted.

Ask at the park entrance for the latest locations of lion and cheetah sightings.

The main entrance to the park is at Makolwane Gate, which is about 140km east of Maun and 60km west of Gweta. Some 35km north of this park gate is an additional entrance (18km north of the Baines' Baobab turn-off), where you may need to sign in.

A 4WD is required to get around the national park. When we visited, the main track from Makolwane Gate to north of the Baines' Baobab turn-off consisted of deep sand and deep ruts – you're unlikely to get stuck but it's a jarring experience.

Two tracks lead from the main track to Baines' Baobabs. When we visited, the longer, northernmost of the two was much easier to traverse, but ask at the park gate.

Baines' Baobabs
LANDMARK

(S 20°06.726', E 24°46.136') In the south of the park are the famous Baines' Baobabs, which were immortalised in paintings by the artist and adventurer Thomas Baines in 1862.

Makgadikgadi & Nxai Pans National Parks

⊙ **Sights**
1 Baines' Baobabs C1
2 Nata Bird Sanctuary F2
3 Nxai Pans National Park C1

⊕ **Activities, Courses & Tours**
4 Uncharted Africa D2

⊟ **Sleeping**
   Baines' Baobab .... (see 1)
5 Gweta Lodge D2
6 Khumaga Campsite B2
7 Kubu Island Campsite E3
8 Meno a Kwena B2
9 Nata Lodge F2
10 Nxai Pan Camp F3
   Planet Baobab .... (see 4)

KUBU ISLAND

Along the southwestern edge of Sowa Pan is a ghostly, baobab-laden rock, entirely surrounded by a sea of salt. In Setswana, *kubu* means 'hippopotamus' (in ancient times this was a real island on a real lake inhabited by hippos). It's not only the name that evokes a more fertile past – the fossilised droppings of water birds that once perched here overlooking the waters still adorn the boulders.

Sprawling **Kubu Island Campsite** (75 494 669; www.kubuisland.com; Lekhubu, S 20°53.460', E 25°49.318'; camping per adult/child P100/50) has 14 sites and is one of Botswana's loveliest. Baobabs are a backdrop to most campsites, many of which have sweeping views of the pan. There are bucket showers and pit toilets. The views from the island are some of the most evocative anywhere on the pans, although there's little wildlife around.

Access to Kubu Island involves negotiating a maze of grassy islets and salty bays. Increased traffic has now made the route considerably clearer, but drivers still need a 4WD and a compass or GPS equipment set with Tracks4Africa. The island can be difficult to reach after rains.

Baines, a self-taught naturalist, artist and cartographer, had originally been a member of David Livingstone's expedition up the Zambezi, but was mistakenly accused of theft by Livingstone's brother and forced to leave the party. Today, a comparison with Baines' paintings reveals that in almost 150 years, only one branch has broken off.

★ **Baines' Baobabs**　　　CAMPGROUND $

(reservations 686 2221; www.xomaesites.com; S 20°08.362', E 24°46.213'; camping per adult/child P400/200) Just three sites sit close to the famed baobabs, and it's a wonderfully evocative site once the daytrippers go home – this is the best place to camp in the park, though wildlife is scarce. There are bucket showers and pit toilets.

Nxai Pan Camp　　　TENTED CAMP $$$

(686 1449; www.kwando.co.bw; s/d US$620/880;) Out in the park's quiet northwestern corner, Nxai Pan Camp has eight rooms done up in an African-modern style, curving in a crescent around an open plain. Inside, smooth linens and indoor and outdoor showers do a good job of pushing the whole rustic-luxury vibe.

CHOBE NATIONAL PARK

Famed for some of the world's largest herds of massive elephants, **Chobe National Park** (per day per non-resident/vehicle P120/50; 6am-6.30pm Apr-Sep, 5.30am-7pm Oct-Mar) in Botswana's far northeastern corner is one of the great wildlife destinations of Africa. In addition to the mighty pachyderms, a full suite of predators and more than 440 recorded bird species are present; watch for roan antelope and the rare oribi antelope.

Chobe was first set aside as a wildlife reserve in the 1930s and became Botswana's first national park in 1968. It encompasses three iconic wildlife areas that all carry a whiff of safari legend: Chobe Riverfront, which supports the park's largest wildlife concentration; the newly accessible and Okavango-like Linyanti Marshes; and the remote and soulful Savuti, with wildlife to rival anywhere.

Whether you're self-driving and camping under the stars, or flying into your luxury lodge, Chobe can be enjoyed by everyone.

To avoid vehicle crowding, the Chobe Riverfront section of the park has a decongestion strategy whereby self-drive daytrippers may visit the park only between 9am and 2.30pm. Visit the park gate as soon as

Chobe National Park

⊚ Sights
1 Gobabis Hill C3
2 Leopard Rock C3
3 Savuti Marshes C3

🛏 Sleeping
4 Chobe Game Lodge F1
5 Duma Tau A3
6 Elephant Sands G4
7 Hyena Pan A3
8 Ihaha Campsite E1
9 Linyanti Campsite B2
10 Ngoma Safari Lodge E1
　 Savute Elephant Camp .... (see 11)
　 Savute Safari Lodge .... (see 11)
11 Savuti Campsite C3
12 Selinda Camp A3
13 Zarafa Camp A3

Chobe National Park

BOTSWANA

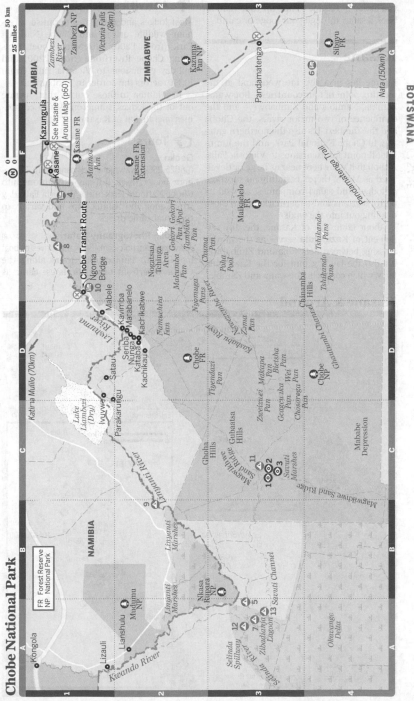

| FR | Forest Reserve |
| NP | National Park |

50 km
25 miles

ZAMBIA

Zambezi River
Zambezi NP
Victoria Falls (8km)

Kazungula
Kazane
See Kasane & Around Map (p60)
Kasane FR

ZIMBABWE

Kazuma Pan NP

Pandamatenga
Sibuyu FR

Nata (150km)

Matinos Pan
Kasane FR Extension

Maikaelelo FR

Chobe Transit Route
Ngoma Bridge

Mabele
Kavimba
Seriba Marabanelo
Nunga
Kataba
Kachikau

Lesikhuma River

Katima Mulilo (70km)

Nogatsaa/Tchinga Area
Mokamba Pan
Gokori Pan Pool
Tumbiko Pan
Chuma Pan
Poha Pool

Tshikando Pans

Pandamatenga Trail

Chobe FR

Kasikibi River
Ngomuga Pans
Zoma Pan
Chinamba Hills
Tshikando Pans

Tiyendazi Pan

Zweizwei Pan
Makapa Pan
Bietsha Pan
Gcgcyuka Pan
Wei Pan
Chosiroega Pan

Ghautuambi Channel Hills
Chobe NP

Furmachiza Pan

BOTSWANA

Ghoha Hills
Gubaatsa Hills

Mahabe Depression

Magwikhwe Sand Ridge

11
1 2
3
Savuti Marshes

Magwikhwe Sand Ridge

Lake Liambezi (Dry)
Ivuywe
Parakarungu
Satau

Linyanti River

9

NAMIBIA

Linyanti Marshes
Mudumu NP
Lianshulu
Lizauli
Kongola

Nkasa Rupara NP

Kwando River

Selinda Spillway
12
7
5
4
Zibadianja Lagoon
13 Savuti Channel

Okavango Delta

you arrive in Kasane to line up your visit, or book a safari through your lodge or camp.

Kasane

POP 15.000

Kasane lies in a riverine woodland at the meeting point of four countries – Botswana, Zambia, Namibia and Zimbabwe – and the confluence of two major rivers, the Chobe and the Zambezi. It's also the northern gateway to Chobe National Park, and the jumping-off point for excursions to Victoria Falls. Although it's nowhere near as large or developed as Maun, there's certainly no shortage of lodges and safari companies, as well as petrol stations and supermarkets for those heading out into the wilds.

About 12km east of Kasane, the tiny settlement of **Kazungula** serves as the border crossing between Botswana and Zimbabwe; it's also the landing pint for the Kazungula ferry, which connects Botswana and Zambia.

🏃 Activities

Most lodges and campsites organise three-hour wildlife drives into Chobe National Park (from P200), three-hour boat trips along Chobe Riverfront (from P200) and full-day excursions to Victoria Falls (from P1350) across the border in Zimbabwe.

In addition to those outfits that operate out of the lodges, numerous safari companies operate out of Kasane.

☞ Tours

Gecko   TOURS

(📞 625 2562; www.oldhousekasane.com) Three-hour boat cruises, full-day expeditions into Chobe National Park and a Victoria Falls day trip. Canoe and fishing trips add variety to the usual game drives.

Pangolin Photography Safaris   SAFARI

(www.pangolinphoto.com; 3hr game drives or boat trips US$120) Photography tours along the Chobe Riverfront using the latest cameras

Kasane & Around

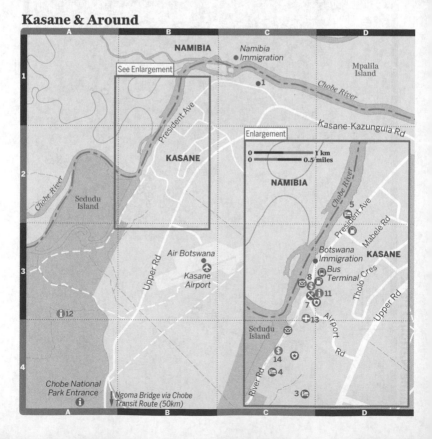

with instruction thrown in; park fees cost extra. Its custom-made boats ensure that everyone has a front-row seat.

🛏 Sleeping

★Senyati Safari Camp
CAMPGROUND, CHALETS **$$**

(📞71 881 306; http://senyatisafaricampbotswana. com; off Kazungula-Nata Rd; camping per adult/ child from P115/63, s/d/f chalets P450/650/800; ❄🍽) Off the main highway south of Kazungula (the turn-off is well signposted 6.8km south of Kazungula, from where it's a further 1.6km off-road), this wonderful spot has comfy chalets and some of northern Botswana's best campsites, each with their own ablutions block. The bar and some of the chalets overlook a water hole where elephants congregate in large numbers nightly.

Old House
GUESTHOUSE **$$**

(📞625 2562; www.oldhousekasane.com; President Ave; s/d P940/1500; ❄🛜🍽) Close to the centre, with a lovely intimate feel, the Old House has attractive rooms adjacent to a quiet garden by the riverbank; rooms on the street side can be noisy with a popular bar across the road. The bar-restaurant is one of Kasane's best, and the rooms are stylish and comfortable without being overdone.

★Chobe Bakwena Lodge
LODGE **$$$**

(📞625 2812; www.chobebakwena.com; s/d all inclusive May-Oct US$490/760, Nov-Apr US$410/ 630) With consistently good reviews from travellers, Bakwena is an excellent place offering the benefits of Chobe River frontage with convenient proximity to Kasane. Chalets, some right on the river, sit high on stilts and there's a prevailing sense of light and space thanks to the ample space and light colour scheme. Service is attentive, adding up to a fine package.

★Chobe Safari Lodge
LODGE **$$$**

(📞625 0336; http://underonebotswanasky. com/camps/chobe-safari-lodge.php; President Ave; camping per adult/child P85/60, r/f from P1265/1675; ❄🍽) One of the more affordable upmarket lodges in Kasane (or Botswana, for that matter), Chobe Safari is excellent

---

Kasane & Around

⊕ Activities, Courses & Tours

   Gecko .... (see 5)
1 Pangolin Photography Safaris C1

⊟ Sleeping

2 Chobe Bakwena Lodge E2
3 Chobe Chilwero Lodge C4
4 Chobe Safari Lodge C4
5 Old House D2
6 Senyati Safari Camp E4

⊗ Eating

7 Coffee & Curry C3
   Hot Bread Shop .... (see 11)
   Old House .... (see 5)

⊕ Information

8 Barclays Bank C3
9 Botswana Immigration (for
    Kazungula Ferry to
    Zambia) F2
10 Botswana Immigration (for
    Zimbabwe) F2
11 Botswana Tourism D3
   Cape to Cairo Bureau de
    Change & Internet .... (see 8)
   Chobe Private Clinic .... (see 5)
12 Department of Wildlife &
    National Parks A3
13 Kasane Hospital C3
14 Open Door Bureau de Change C4

BOTSWANA CHOBE RIVERFRONT

value, especially if you're travelling with kids (family rooms and tents are available). Understated but comfortable rooms are priced according to size and location, though all feature attractive mosquito-netted beds and modern furnishings. Rates are room only, but it's still outstanding value.

✗ Eating

Coffee & Curry   INDIAN $
(☑625 2237; Shop 1AB, Hunters' Africa Mall, off President Ave; mains P45-70; ⊘9am-10pm Mon-Sat, 11am-9pm Sun) Just about everything (except African!) is served at this simple Indian-run place, with a reasonable selection of curries and other Indian dishes, as well as a few pizzas and Southeast Asian–inspired dishes.

Hot Bread Shop   BAKERY $
(Hunters' Africa Mall, off President Ave; ⊘7.30am-7pm) If you're arriving from the bush and craving freshly baked bread, look no further than this fine place up behind the Shell petrol station. It also does a few cakes and pastries.

★Old House   INTERNATIONAL $$
(☑625 2562; www.oldhousekasane.com; President Ave; breakfast P50-80, light meals P40-80, mains P50-115) This open-air bar-restaurant close to the riverbank is every bit as good as the guesthouse it inhabits. The menu contains all the usual suspects such as burgers, toasted sandwiches, salads, steaks and pizzas, with fish and chips not forgotten either. There's also a kids' menu.

ⓘ Information

MEDICAL SERVICES

Chobe Private Clinic (☑625 1555; President Ave) Offers 24-hour emergency services.
Kasane Hospital (☑625 0333; President Ave) Public hospital on the main road.

MONEY

Barclays Bank (Hunters' Africa Mall, off President Ave; ⊘8.30am-3.30pm Mon-Fri, 8.15-10.45am Sat) Offers better exchange rates than the bureaux de change. Be sure to stock up on US dollars (post-1996) if you're heading to Zimbabwe.
Cape to Cairo Bureau de Change & Internet (Hunters' Africa Mall, off President Ave; ⊘8.30am-5pm Mon-Fri, to 4.30pm Sat) Charges 3% commission on cash, 4% on travellers cheques.
Open Door Bureau de Change (President Ave; ⊘8.30am-5pm Mon-Fri, 9am-4.30pm Sat) Next to Choppies Supermarket; charges 2% commission on cash, 3% on travellers cheques.

POLICE STATIONS

Police station (☑625 2444; President Ave; ⊘24hr)

POST

Chobe Post Office (Hunters' Africa Mall, off President Ave; ⊘9am-5pm Mon-Fri, to noon Sat)

TOURIST INFORMATION

Tourist Office (☑625 0555; www.botswana-tourism.co.bw; Hunters' Africa Mall, off President Ave; ⊘7.30am-6pm Mon-Fri, 9am-2pm Sat) Plenty of brochures for lodges and safari companies, and generally helpful, although you're better off visiting the park gate for information on Chobe National Park.
Department of Wildlife & National Parks (DWNP; ☑625 0235; Sedudu Gate) This is the place to pay for your park permit and get information on visiting Chobe National Park.

ⓘ Getting There & Away

AIR

Air Botswana (☑625 0161; www.airbotswana.co.bw) connects Kasane to Maun (P715) and Gaborone (P2060), and has an office at Kasane airport, which is near the centre of town.

CAR & MOTORCYCLE

The direct route between Kasane and Maun is only accessible by 4WD, and may be impassable after heavy rains. There is nowhere along the Kasane–Maun road to buy fuel, food or drinks, or to get vehicle repairs. Most traffic between Kasane and Maun travels via Nata.

LOCAL TRANSPORT

Combis heading to Francistown (P110, seven hours), Maun (P120, six hours) and Nata (P105, five hours) run when full from the Shell petrol station and bus terminal on Mabele Rd.

ⓘ Getting Around

Combis travel regularly between Kasane and Kazungula via the ferry, and continue to the immigration posts for Zambia and Zimbabwe if requested. The standard fare for anywhere around Kasane and Kazungula is about P50.

Chobe Riverfront

The Chobe Riverfront rarely disappoints, with arguably Botswana's densest concentration of wildlife. Although animals are present along the riverfront year-round, the density of wildlife can be overwhelming during the dry season, especially in September and October. Whether you cruise along the river in a motorboat, or drive along the banks in a 4WD, you're almost guaranteed an up-close encounter with some of the largest elephants on the continent.

If you don't have your own wheels, any of the hotels and lodges in Kasane can help you organise a wildlife drive or boat cruise along the river. Two- to three-hour cruises and wildlife drives typically cost around P200, though you will also have to pay separate park fees. As always, shop around, compare prices and choose a trip that suits your needs.

🛏 Sleeping

Ihaha Campsite
CAMPGROUND $

(kwalatesafari@gmail.com; S 17°50.487', E 24°52.754'; camping per adult/child P260/130) Ihaha is the only campsite for self-drivers inside the park along the Chobe Riverfront and it's a wonderful base for watching wildlife. The trees need time to mature and shade can be in short supply at some sites, but the location is excellent – it's by the water's edge 27km from the Northern Gate. There's an ablutions block and braai areas.

Chobe Chilwero Lodge
LODGE $$$

(🖉in South Africa +27 11-438 4650; www.sanctu arylodges.com; Airport Rd; per person low/high season from US$590/990; ❄🗑😹) Chilwero means 'place of high view' in Setswana, and indeed this exclusive lodge boasts panoramic views. Accommodation is in one of 15 elegant bungalows featuring romantic indoor and outdoor showers, private terraced gardens and colonial fixtures adorned with plush linens. The lodge is on expansive grounds that contain a pool, a spa, an outdoor bar and a well-reviewed gourmet restaurant.

Chobe Game Lodge
LODGE $$$

(🖉625 0340, 625 1761; www.chobegamelodge. com; River Rd; s/d Jul-Oct US$1470/2370, per person Apr-Jun & Nov US$995, Jan-Mar & Dec US$795; ❄🗑😹) This highly praised safari lodge is one of the best in the Chobe area. The lodge is constructed in the Moorish style and flaunts high arches, barrel-vaulted ceilings and tiled floors. The individually decorated rooms are elegant yet soothing, and some have views of the Chobe River and Namibian floodplains – the views from the public areas are sublime.

Ngoma Safari Lodge
LODGE $$$

(🖉73 747 880, 620 0109; www.africaalbidatourism. com/safari-lodges/ngoma-safari-lodge; s/d Jun-Oct US$1154/1950; ❄@😹) At the western end of the Chobe Riverfront, close to the Ngoma Bridge border crossing between Botswana and Namibia, this lovely lodge is removed from the clamour close to Kasane. It offers eight stylishly appointed, river-facing suites with thatched roofs on a rise set back from (and high above) the riverbank.

❶ Getting There & Away

From central Kasane, the Northern Gate is about 6km to the southwest. Unlike all other national parks operated by the DWNP, you do not need a campsite reservation to enter, though you will be expected to leave the park prior to closing if you do not have one. All tracks along the riverfront require a 4WD vehicle, and you will not be admitted into the park without one.

You can either exit the park through the Northern Gate by backtracking along the river or via the Ngoma Bridge Gate near the Namibian border. If you exit via Ngoma, you can return to Kasane via the Chobe transit route. (If you're simply bypassing Chobe en route to/from Namibia, you do not have to pay park fees to travel on this road.) Be advised that elephants frequently cross this road, so keep your speed down and do not drive at night.

Savuti

Savuti's flat, wildlife-packed expanses and rocky outcrops, awash with distinctly African colours and vistas, make it one of the most rewarding safari destinations on the continent. With the exception of rhinos, you'll find all of Africa's most charismatic megafauna in residence here or passing through – on one afternoon wildlife drive, we encountered 15 lions and two leopards.

The area, in the southwestern corner of Chobe National Park, contains the remnants of the 'superlake' that once stretched across northern Botswana – the modern landscape has a distinctive harsh and empty feel to it. Because of the roughness of the terrain, the difficulty in reaching the area and the beauty you'll find when you get here, Savuti is an obligatory stop for all 4WD enthusiasts en route between Kasane and Maun.

◉ Sights

Leopard Rock
LANDMARK

The rocky monoliths that rise up from the Savuti sand provide more than welcome aesthetic relief amid the flat-as-flat plains. The outcrops' caves, rocky clefts and sometime-dense undergrowth also represent ideal habitat for leopards. The southernmost of these monoliths (the first you come to if you're driving from Maun or Moremi Game Reserve) is known as Leopard Rock and sightings of the most elusive of Africa's big cats are reasonably common here. A 1.6km-long sandy track encircles the rock.

Gobabis Hill HILL

In the heart of Savuti, Gobabis Hill is home to several sets of 4000-year-old rock art of San origin. The best are the depictions of livestock halfway to the summit on the south side of the rock; park at S 18°35.632', E 24°04.770', from where it's an easy 150m climb up to the paintings.

Savuti Marshes NATURAL FEATURE

For decades since the early 1980s, this vast open area in southern Savuti consisted less of marshes than sweeping open plains, save for occasional inundations during the rainy season. But the area's name again makes sense with the return of water to the Savuti Channel. Once-dry tracks now disappear into standing water that draws predators and prey from all across the region. The marshes lie between the Savuti Channel and the main Savuti–Maun track.

🛏 Sleeping

Savuti Campsite CAMPGROUND $$

(www.sklcamps.com; S 18°34.014', E 24°03.905'; camping per adult/child US$50/20) One of the best campgrounds in Chobe, with five of the seven sites (all with braai pits) overlooking the (usually dry) river – sites one to four could do with more shade, while Paradise camp is our pick. The ablutions block has sit-down flush toilets and showers (usually hot).

★ Savute Elephant Camp LODGE $$$

(☑686 0302; www.belmondsafaris.com; s/d Jun-Oct US$4058/5680; ❄🏊🍴) The premier camp in Savuti is made up of 12 lavishly appointed East African–style linen tents on raised wooden platforms, complete with antique-replica furniture that will appeal to colonial safari nostalgics. The main tent houses a dining room, lounge and bar, and is next to a swimming pool that overlooks a pumped water hole.

★ Savute Under Canvas TENTED CAMP $$$

(☑in South Africa +27 11-809 4300; www.andbeyond.com/savute-under-canvas/; per person Jul-Oct US$725, Apr-Jun & Nov US$590, Feb & Mar US$480) This cross between a tented camp and luxury mobile safari enables you to experience the freedom of camping (sites are moved every few days) with the exclusivity that comes with having a beautifully appointed tent, butler and excellent meals served in between your game drives. Tents

have bathroom facilities, including hot bucket showers. No children under 12.

Savute Safari Lodge LODGE $$$

(☑686 1559; www.desertdelta.com; s/d Jul-Oct US$1230/1890, Apr-Jun & Nov US$675, per person Dec, Jan & Mar US$535; ⊗closed Feb) Next to the former site of the legendary Lloyd's Camp, this upmarket retreat consists of 12 large and contemporary thatched chalets with neutral tones, wooden floors and fairly standard layouts. The main safari lodge has a sitting lounge, elegant dining room, small library and cocktail bar. There's also a breathtaking deck where you can watch the sunset over the bush.

ⓘ Getting There & Away

Chartered flights use the airstrip several kilometres north of the lodges in Savuti. Check with your lodge regarding booking a flight.

Tracks in the Savuti area can be hard slogs – deep sand, hidden troughs to jolt the unwary, and deep corrugations. Many routes around Savuti are often unnavigable from January to March. Many travellers visit Savuti en route between Moremi Game Reserve and Linyanti. All of these routes require a 4WD vehicle.

If driving direct to Savuti from Maun, take the sealed road to Shorobe (40km), then the decent gravel road to Mababe, which is close to Mababe Gate. The road from the gate to Savuti (around 52km) is sandy and slow-going in parts.

If driving from Kasane, the sealed road goes as far as Kachikau, from where a rutted, sandy track leads 41km to Ghoha Gate. After the gate, drive 10.3km along the main track then take the road to the right labelled 'Airstrip' – it avoids the worst of the sand and loops back around onto the main track close to Savuti.

Linyanti Marshes

Hard up against the border with Namibia, the Linyanti River spreads into a 900-sq-km flooded plain that attracts stunning concentrations of wildlife during the dry season. On the Namibian side of the river, this well-watered wildlife paradise is protected by the Mudumu and Nkasa Rupara National Parks, which mirror the 7km of frontage along the northwestern edge of Chobe National Park.

Wildlife trails run along the marsh shoreline and sightings of the marshes' stable populations of elephants, lions, cheetahs and leopards are fairly common, although you'll need to be patient, especially for big cats. The Linyanti region is widely considered one of the best places in Africa for African wild dogs, but sightings are by no means guaranteed. Given that most of the luxury lodges are outside the national park, night drives are another highlight.

From the south, the track from Savuti is a hard slog of deep sand. The track running east towards Kachikau (where it meets the sealed road to Kasane) is only slightly better.

Most guests choose to fly into their camp on a chartered flight from Maun or Kasane. Flights tend to be cheaper from Maun.

Linyanti Campsite CAMPGROUND $
(☑686 5365; www.sklcamps.com; S 18°16.228', E 23°56.163'; camping per adult/child US$50/25) Most of the sites sit on a shady and gentle rise just up from the water's edge, with good views of the marshes costing nothing extra. There are the usual braai pits, hot showers, sit-down flush toilets and, in the dry season, lots of elephants and baboons. Expect hippos to make a lot of noise during the night.

★ Zarafa Camp TENTED CAMP $$$
(☑in South Africa +27 87 354 6591; www. greatplainsconservation.com; s/d mid-Jun–Oct US$4133/5510, rates vary rest of year) 🍴 Make no mistake: this is one of the premier properties anywhere in Africa. As ecofriendly as it's possible to be out here, Zarafa's tented villas are utterly gorgeous – and as we've come to expect from Great Plains, the attention to detail is exemplary.

★ Duma Tau TENTED CAMP $$$
(☑686 0086; www.wilderness-safaris.com; s/d high season US$2050/3450, rates vary rest of year; ❄❄) 🍴 This 10-room camp was rebuilt completely in 2012 with a commitment to sustainability; all of the camp's power comes from solar energy, and waste disposal is state of the art. The raised tents overlook the hippo-filled Zibadianja Lagoon from a mangosteen grove.

Hyena Pan TENTED CAMP $$$
(www.hyenapan.com; s/d all-inclusive high season US$604/930, low season US$448/690) This quietly elegant and relatively affordable camp, an hour's drive from the Khwai airstrip, is an excellent choice. Appealing if simple tents sit close to a water hole that's popular with elephants. All the region's wildlife is possible on the wildlife drives, but a real highlight is the 'Elephant Song' walking trail that takes you up close to the local elephants.

OKAVANGO DELTA

Welcome to one of Africa's most extraordinary places. There is something elemental about the Unesco World Heritage–listed Okavango Delta: the rising and falling of its waters; the daily drama of its wildlife encounters; its soundtrack of lion roars, saw-throated leopard barks and the crazy whoop of a running hyena; and the mysteries concealed by its papyrus reeds swaying gently in the evening breeze. Viewed from above on a flight from Maun, the Okavango is a watery paradise of islands and oxbow waterways. At ground level, the silhouettes of dead trees in the dry season give the delta a hint of the apocalypse.

The stirring counterpoint to Botswana's Kalahari Desert, the Okavango is one of the world's largest inland deltas. The up-to-18,000-sq-km expansion and expiration of the Okavango River means that this mother of waters sustains vast quantities of wildlife that shift with the seasons in this mother of waters.

Generally, the best time to visit the delta is from July to September or October, when the water levels are high and the weather is dry. Tracks can get extremely muddy and trails are often washed out during and after the rains. From January to March, the Moremi Game Reserve can be inaccessible, even with a state-of-the-art 4WD. Bear in mind that several lodges close down for part or all of the rainy season, but others revel in the abundant birdlife. Mosquitoes are prevalent, especially in the wet season (November to March).

Although a few visitors arrive from Chobe National Park and Kasane, Maun is where you'll have the most choice when it comes to organising safaris. Charter flights into the lodges and camps of the delta from Maun are considerably cheaper than those from Kasane.

Maun
POP 60,263

As the main gateway to the Okavango Delta, Maun (mau-uunn) is Botswana's primary tourism hub. With good accommodation and a reliably mad mix of bush pilots, tourists, campers, volunteers and luxury-safari-philes, it's a decent-enough base for a day or two. That said, if your only business in Botswana involves staying in the lodges and tented camps of the delta, you may do little more than hang around the airport. No great loss: the town itself has little going for it – it's strung out over kilometres with not much of a discernible centre – but some of the hotels and camps have riverside vantage points.

Okavango Delta

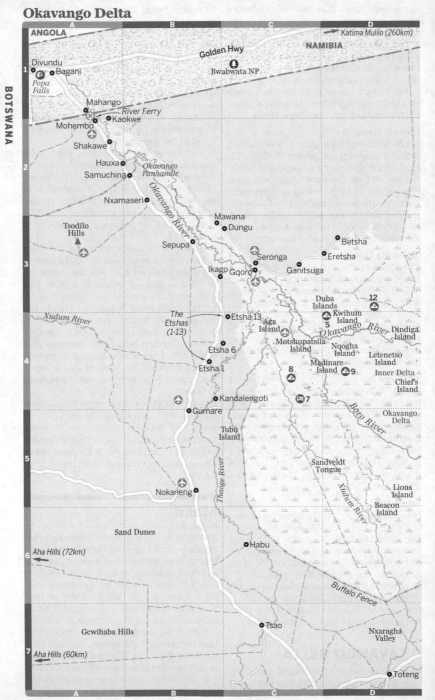

🏃 Activities

Scenic Flights

Flying over the delta in a light plane or helicopter is the experience of a lifetime. Prices can be steep, but the views are unforgettable.

To join a scenic flight you can either contact a charter company or simply ask at the front desk at your accommodation. But plan ahead, as it's unlikely that you'll be able to contact a charter company and join a scenic flight on the same day.

Prices can depend on the length of your flight (usually 45 minutes or one hour) and the number of people on board (planes are generally the three-, five- or seven-seat variety). Sample prices start from P2900/3600 per plane for a 45-/60-minute flight. One alternative to the fixed-wing flights, and one that many travellers prefer since they take the doors off, is a scenic helicopter flight with Helicopter Horizons.

The offices for all air-charter companies in Maun are either in or next to the airport. Bring your passport when making a booking.

Helicopter Horizons　　　SCENIC FLIGHTS
(📞 680 1186; www.helicopterhorizons.com; per person from US$150, min 3 people) A range of helicopter options, all with the passenger doors removed to aid photography. If you're willing to drive out to the buffalo fence and take your flight from there, the 22-minute flight will be almost entirely over the delta, rather than wasting time and money flying there.

Okavango Delta

🟢 Activities, Courses & Tours
　1　Lelobu Safaris E6

🛏 Sleeping
　2　Baine's Camp E5
　3　Chitabe Camp E5
　　　Chitabe Lediba ....(see 3)
　4　Discovery Bed & Breakfast F6
　5　Duba Expedition Camp D4
　6　Gunn's Camp E5
　7　Jao Camp C4
　8　Kwetsani Camp C4
　9　Mombo Camp D4
　10　Nxabega Okavango Camp.................E5
　11　Thamalakane Lodge.........................F6
　12　Vumbura Plains Camp......................D3
　13　Xaranna Camp E5

ℹ Information
　14　Maun General Hospital E6

ℹ Transport
　15　Bus Station E6

You may need to combine this option with a *mokoro* excursion.

Wilderness Air   SCENIC FLIGHTS
(📞 686 0778; www.sefofane.com) Part of Wilderness Safaris. Offers scenic flights and flies in guests to Wilderness Safaris lodges and camps.

Mack Air   SCENIC FLIGHTS
(📞 686 0675; www.mackair.co.bw; Mathiba I St) Offers scenic flights; located around the corner from Wilderness Safaris. It costs P2900/3600 for the whole plane for 45/60 minutes – how much you pay depends on the number of passengers.

Major Blue Air   SCENIC FLIGHTS
(📞 686 5671; www.majorblueair.com; Mathiba I St) One of the better operators for scenic flights.

👉 Tours

Audi Camp Safaris   SAFARI
(📞 686 0599; www.audisafaris.com; Shorobe Rd, Matlapaneng) Well-run safaris into the delta and further afield out of popular Audi Camp.

Ker & Downey   SAFARI
(📞 686 0570; www.kerdowney.com; Mathiba I St) One of Africa's most exclusive tour operators, Ker & Downey is all about pampering and luxury lodges.

Maun

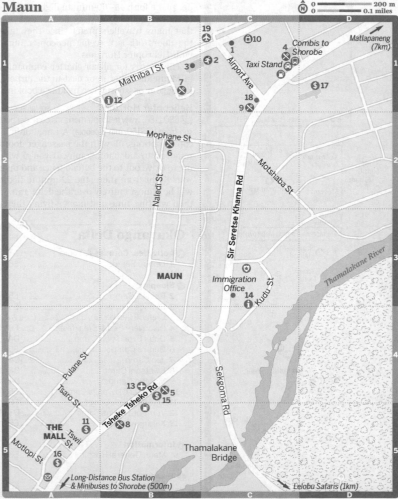

Lelobu Safaris SAFARI
(☑74 511 600; www.botswanabudgetsafaris.com)
A flexible and professional operation (the
name means 'Chameleon' in Setswana) run
by Rebecca and Anton, Lelobu organises
excellent custom-designed itineraries with
a focus on getting you out into the delta,
especially around Chief's Island; reasonable
price tags attached.

Old Bridge Backpackers SAFARI
(☑686 2406; www.maun-backpackers.com;
Shorobe Rd, Matlapaneng) This experienced
budget operation is run from the Old Bridge
Backpackers and we're yet to hear a bad
word about its expeditions.

Wilderness Safaris SAFARI
(☑686 0086; www.wilderness-safaris.com; Mathiba I St) Near the airport, this operator specialises in upmarket safaris and owns many
of Botswana's best camps.

✪ Festivals & Events

Maun Festival CULTURAL
A two-day celebration with plenty of music,
parades, poetry, theatre, craftwork, dance
and food; visual arts also feature. The festival raises funds for local schools while commemorating northwestern Botswana's rich
cultural roots.

⛺ Sleeping

★ Old Bridge Backpackers CAMPGROUND $
(☑686 2406; www.maun-backpackers.com; Hippo Pools, Old Matlapaneng Bridge; camping P80,
dm P150, s/d tents without bathroom P330/400,
s/d tents with bathroom P480/580; @☒) One
of the great boltholes on Southern African
overland trails, 'the Bridge' has a great bar-

at-the-end-of-the-world kind of vibe. Accommodation ranges from dome tents by the
riverbank to well-appointed campsites and
some more private tents.

Audi Camp CAMPGROUND $
(☑686 0599; www.audisafaris.com/audi-camps;
Matlapaneng; camping from P70, s/d tents without bathroom from P160/190, with bathroom
P630/760; @☎☒) Off Shorobe Rd, Audi
Camp is a fantastic campsite that's become
increasingly popular with families, although
independent overlanders will also feel welcome. Management is friendly and helpful,
and there's a wide range of safari activities.
The restaurant does a mean steak. If you
don't have your own tent, the preerected
tents complete with fan are a rustically luxurious option.

Okavango River Lodge CAMPGROUND, CHALET $
(☑686 3707; www.okavango-river-lodge.com; Matlapaneng; camping P100, s/d tents P180/300, s/d/f
chalets P330/460/600) This down-to-earth
spot off Shorobe Rd has a lovely setting on
the riverbank. The owners are friendly and
unpretentious, and pride themselves on
giving travellers useful (and independent)
information on trips through the delta. Between this spot and the Old Bridge Backpackers, you'll find most of Maun's tourist
and expat-oriented nightlife.

★ Kraal Lodging GUESTHOUSE $$
(☑72 320 090; www.thekraallodgingbotswana
.com; exit 6, Disaneng Rd; r P1200-2000; P☀
☎☒) Run by respected film-makers June
and Tim Liversedge, the Kraal is a terrific
place to stay. The attractive thatched ron-
davels are beautifully appointed with just
the right blend of safari prints, earth tones

Maun

◉ Activities, Courses & Tours
Helicopter Horizons .... (see 12)
1 Ker & Downey C1
Mack Air .... (see 3)
2 Major Blue Air C1
Okavango Kopano Mokoro
Community Trust .... (see 12)
Wilderness Air .... (see 3)
3 Wilderness Safaris B1

✕ Eating
4 Choppies C1
5 Delta Deli B4
6 French Connection B2
7 Hilary's B1
8 Shop-Rite Supermarket B5
9 Wax Apple Cafe C1

🛍 Shopping
10 African Arts & Images C1

ℹ Information
11 Barclays Bank A5
12 Botswana Tourism B1
13 Delta Medical Centre B4
14 Department of Wildlife &
National Parks C3
15 Open Door Bureau de Change B4
16 Standard Chartered Bank A5
17 Sunny Bureau de Change D1

ℹ Transport
18 Air Botswana C1
19 Maun Airport C1

BOOKING A MOKORO TRIP

A day trip from Maun into the Eastern Delta usually includes a two- to three-hour return drive in a 4WD to the departure point, two to three hours (perhaps longer each day on a two- or three-day trip) in a *mokoro* (dugout canoe), and two to three hours' hiking. At the start of a *mokoro* trip, ask the poler what he has in mind, and agree to the length of time spent per day in the *mokoro*, out hiking and relaxing at the campsite – bear in mind that travelling by *mokoro* is tiring for the poler.

One of the refreshing things about booking *mokoro* trips is the absence of touts wandering the streets of Maun. That's because all polers operating *mokoro* trips out of Maun are represented by the **Okavango Kopano Mokoro Community Trust** (☑686 4806; www. okmct.org.bw; off Mathiba 1 St; ☺8am-5pm Mon-Fri, to noon Sat). This trust sets daily rates for the polers (P180 per poler per day, plus a P68 daily membership fee for the trust) by which all safari operators have to abide. Other costs include a guide (P200 per day) and a camping fee (P50 per person per night) if your expedition involves an overnight component.

In terms of pricing, catering is an important distinction. 'Self-catering' means you must bring your own food as well as cooking, sleeping and camping equipment. This option is a good way to shave a bit off the price, though most travellers prefer catered trips. It's also easier to get a lower price if you're booking as part of a group or are planning a multiday tour.

A few other things to remember:

➡ Ask the booking agency if you're expected to provide food for the poler (usually you're not, but polers appreciate any leftover cooked or uncooked food).

➡ Bring good walking shoes and long trousers for hiking, a hat and plenty of sunscreen and water.

➡ Water from the delta (despite its unpleasant colour) can be drunk if boiled or purified.

➡ Most campsites are natural, so take out all litter and burn toilet paper.

➡ Bring warm clothes for the evening between about May and September.

➡ Wildlife can be dangerous, so make sure to never swim anywhere without checking with the poler first.

and African handicrafts and artwork. There's a pool, free wi-fi and a barbecue area, and the owners are a mine of information on the region. The same owners run **African Arts & Images** (www.juneliversedge.com; Mathiba I St; ☺8am-5pm Mon-Fri, 9am-5pm Sat & Sun) next to the airport.

Discovery Bed & Breakfast   B&B $$
(☑72 448 298; www.discoverybedandbreakfast. com; Matlapaneng; s/d from US$60/80; ❉) Dutch-run Discovery does a cool job of creating an African-village vibe in the midst of Maun – the owners strive for and achieve 'affordable accommodation with a traditional touch'. The thatched, rondavel-style housing looks pretty bush from the outside and feels as posh as a nice hotel on the inside.

Thamalakane Lodge   LODGE $$$
(☑72 506 184; www.thamalakane-lodge.com; Shorobe Rd; d/f chalets US$238/345; ❉◉❉) With a beautiful setting on a sun-drenched curve of the Thamalakane River, overlooking wading hippos and waving reeds (when

there's enough water), Thamalakane wins in the location stakes, at least for Maun. It has beautiful little stone chalets stuffed with modern amenities and dressed up in safari-chic tones. The lodge is 19km northeast of Maun, off the road to Shorobe.

 Eating

Choppies   SUPERMARKET $
(☑686 2063; www.choppies.co.bw; off Sir Seretse Khama Rd; ☺8am-8pm Mon-Fri, to 6pm Sat & Sun) One of the cheaper supermarkets in Maun. It has slightly less choice than some of the others and we'd buy our meat elsewhere, but you'll save quite a bit if you stock up here on cans and packet food.

Delta Deli   DELI $
(☑686 1413; Tsheko Tsheko Rd; ☺8am-5.30pm Mon-Fri, to 1.30pm Sat) Ask anyone in Maun the best place to buy meat in town for your next barbecue or camping expedition and they're likely to send you here. Part of the Riley's Garage service station set-up, it has

easily the most appealing meat selection we found in Botswana – terrific steaks, marinated cuts and excellent sausages.

French Connection
FRENCH $

(Mophane St; breakfast P40-75, mains P40-95; ⊘8.30am-5pm Mon-Fri, to 2pm Sat) Close to the airport, but on a quiet backstreet, this fine place serves up fresh tastes that might include Turkish pide, Moroccan lamb or Creole fish cakes; the meze platter is especially good. Run by a delightful French owner and driven by a far-ranging passion for new tastes, it's a lovely spot with a shady garden setting.

Shop-Rite Supermarket
SUPERMARKET $

(☑686 0497; Tsheke Tsheko Rd; ⊘8am-6pm Mon-Fri, to 5pm Sat) Shop-Rite is astoundingly well stocked with fresh meat, fruit and vegetables, and a bakery that sells fresh bread, sandwiches and takeaway salads.

Wax Apple Cafe
CAFE $

(☑72 703 663; Airport Ave; breakfast P20-45, light meals P30-45; ⊘7.30am-5pm Mon-Fri, to 2pm Sat; 🛜) Handy for the airport (a 100m walk away) and with a lovely casual atmosphere, Wax Apple is a wonderful addition to Maun's eating scene. Apart from great teas and coffees, it serves tasty baguettes and wraps, with the odd local dish on the short-but-sweet menu. There's also a gift shop with some nice jewellery and paintings. Free wi-fi.

★Hilary's
INTERNATIONAL $$

(breakfast P16-92, light meals P46 56, mains P82; ⊘8am-4pm Mon-Fri, 8.30am-noon Sat; ☑) This homey place offers a choice of wonderfully earthy meals, including homemade bread, homemade lemonade, filter coffee, baked potatoes, soups and sandwiches. It's ideal for vegetarians and anyone sick of greasy sausages and soggy chips.

ℹ️ Information

DANGERS & ANNOYANCES

Maun is an extremely safe destination in which to travel. Petty theft (usually from cars or campsites, but rarely with violence) was an issue until a police crackdown a few years ago. These days you're unlikely to have a problem, but it still pays to be careful – don't leave valuables or bags in parked cars in the city centre and lock them away if you're sleeping in a tent at one of the campsites.

ENTRY & EXIT FORMALITIES

Immigration (⊘9am-4pm Mon-Fri)

MEDICAL SERVICES

Delta Medical Centre (☑686 1411; Tsheke Tsheko Rd) Along the main road; this is the best medical facility in Maun. It offers a 24-hour emergency service.

Maun General Hospital (☑686 0661; Shorobe Rd) About 1km southwest of the town centre.

MedRescue (☑390 1601, 680 0598, 992; www.mri.co.bw) For evacuations in the bush.

MONEY

Barclays Bank (Tsheke Tsheko Rd; ⊘8.30am-3.30pm Mon-Fri, 8.15-10.45am Sat) Has foreign-exchange facilities and offers better rates than the bureaux de change. Barclays charges 2.5% commission for cash/travellers cheques, but no commission for cash advances with Visa and MasterCard.

Open Door Bureau de Change (Tsheke Tsheko Rd; ⊘7.30am-6pm Mon-Fri, 8am-4pm Sat, 9am-4pm Sun)

Standard Chartered Bank (Tsheke Tsheko Rd; ⊘8.30am-3.30pm Mon-Fri, 8.15-11am Sat) Has foreign-exchange facilities and offers better

Matlapaneng

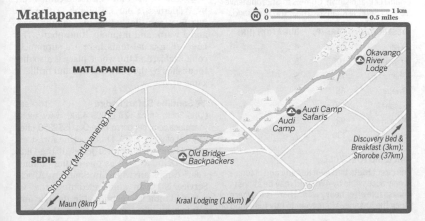

N 0 —————— 1 km
   0 —————— 0.5 miles

MATLAPANENG

Okavango River Lodge

Shorobe (Matlapaneng) Rd

SEDIE

Audi Camp
Audi Camp Safaris

Old Bridge Backpackers

Discovery Bed & Breakfast (3km); Shorobe (37km)

Maun (8km)

Kraal Lodging (1.8km)

rates than the bureaux de change. Standard Chartered charges 3% commission for cash and travellers cheques, but isn't as well set up as Barclays Bank.

Sunny Bureau de Change (Sir Seretse Khama Rd, Ngami Centre; ⊙8am-6pm) Although you will get less favourable exchange rates than at the banks, this is a convenient option if the lines at the banks are particularly long.

POLICE

Police station (☑686 0223; Sir Seretse Khama Rd)

POST

Post office (⊙9am-5pm Mon-Fri, to noon Sat) Near the mall.

TOURIST INFORMATION

Department of Wildlife & National Parks (DWNP) (DWNP; ☑686 1265; Kudu St; ⊙7.30am-4.30pm Mon-Fri, 7.30am-12.45pm & 1.45-4.30pm Sat, 7.30am-12.45pm Sun) To pay national park entry fees and book park campsites not in private hands.

Tourist office (☑686 1056; off Mathiba I St; ⊙7.30am-6pm Mon-Fri, 9am-2pm Sat) Provides information on Maun's many tour companies and lodges.

ℹ Getting There & Away

AIR

Air Botswana (☑686 0391; www.airbotswana. co.bw) has flights to Gaborone (from P1791) and Kasane (from P715). There are also international flights between Maun and Johannesburg (South Africa), Victoria Falls (Zimbabwe) and Livingstone (Zambia).

BUS

The **bus station** (Tsheke Tsheko Rd) for longdistance buses and combis is southwest of the centre. For Gaborone, you'll need to change in Ghanzi or Francistown. Combis to Shorobe leave from Sir Seretse Khama Rd near the taxi stand.

DESTINATION	FARE (P)	DURATION (HR)
D'kar	55	4
Francistown	105	5
Ghanzi	75	5
Gweta	65	4
Kasane	120	6
Nata	92	5
Shakawe	130	7

CAR & MOTORCYCLE

The direct route between Kasane and Maun is only accessible by 4WD and may be almost impassable after heavy rain. There is nowhere along the Kasane–Maun road to buy fuel, food or drinks, or to get vehicle repairs. All other traffic between Kasane and Maun travels via Nata – this route is sealed all the way.

ℹ Getting Around

Maun airport (MUB; ☑686 1559) is close to the town centre, so taxis rarely bother hanging around the terminal when planes arrive. If you've prebooked accommodation at an upmarket hotel or lodge in Maun or the Okavango Delta, make sure it provides a (free) courtesy minibus. Otherwise, walk about 300m down Airport Rd to Sir Seretse Khama Rd and catch a combi (around P40 to P50 for the camps in the Matlapaneng or Sedie districts northeast of the city).

Eastern Delta

The Eastern Delta includes the wetlands between the southern boundary of Moremi Game Reserve and the buffalo fence that crosses the Boro and Santandadibe Rivers, north of Matlapaneng. If you're short of time and/or money, this part of the Okavango Delta remains an affordable and accessible option. From Maun it's easy to arrange a day trip on a *mokoro*, or a two- or three-night *mokoro* trip combined with bush camping.

Then again, the Chitabe concession and surrounding area has been quietly building a reputation as one of the wildlife hotspots of recent times, and a luxury experience is very much a possibility here as well.

🛏 Sleeping

★Chitabe Lediba   TENTED CAMP **$$$**
(☑686 0086; www.wilderness-safaris.com; s/d Jun-Oct US$1950/3280, rates vary rest of year; ❄ ❄) One of the more intimate camps run by Wilderness Safaris, Chitabe Lediba has just five tents (including two family ones) and a warm and intimate atmosphere. The larger-than-usual tents here are supremely comfortable, and the whole place is also distinguished by the warm service and brilliant game drives.

★Sandibe Safari Lodge   LODGE **$$$**
(☑in South Africa +27 11-809 4300; www.andbe yondafrica.com; per person Jun-Oct US$2350, rates vary rest of year; 📶 ❄) This riverine forest retreat is the architectural jewel of the Okavango Delta, as well as one of the premier safari camps anywhere in Southern Africa. Service is warm and welcoming, the accommodation is exceptional in its style and comfort, and the location (next to the famed

Chitabe concession) is one of the best any-where in the delta.

Chitabe Camp TENTED CAMP $$$

(☑686 0086; www.wilderness-safaris.com; s/d Jun-Oct US$1950/3280, rates vary rest of year; ❀❄) Near the Santandadibe River, at the southern edge of Moremi Game Reserve, Chitabe is an island oasis (only accessible by boat or plane). Accommodation at Chitabe Camp is in East African–style luxury tents, which have bathrooms and are built on wooden decks and sheltered beneath the shade of a lush canopy.

❶ Getting There & Away

If you're on a *mokoro* day trip or a multiday bush-camping expedition from Maun, you will be transported to/from the Eastern Delta by 4WD. Transport into the lodges is usually by charter flight and then 4WD and/or *mokoro*.

As with elsewhere in the delta, Wilderness Safaris' camps are serviced by Wilderness Air (p68); Mack Air (p68) is the other most popular charter company. Enquire with your lodge.

Inner Delta

Welcome to the heart of the Okavango, a world inaccessible by roads and inhabited by some of the richest wildlife concentrations on earth. Not surprisingly, these are some of the most exclusive patches of real estate in Botswana, with luxury lodges and tented camps inhabiting some of the delta's prettiest corners. If for whatever reason you

can't stay here, take a scenic flight or, better still, a helicopter sightseeing flight from Maun with Helicopter Horizons (p67).

Roughly defined, the Inner Delta occupies the areas west of Chief's Island and between Chief's Island and the base of the Okavango Panhandle. Most of the water-based camps of the Inner Delta offer *mokoro* trips through the Inner Delta (roughly from June to October or November), with game drives also a possibility. Some lodges that inhabit islands also offer that rare travel experience of arriving by boat (usually after a short 4WD transfer from the nearest airstrip).

🛏 Sleeping

★ Jao Camp LODGE $$$

(☑686 0086; www.wilderness-safaris.com; s/d Jun-Oct US$2700/4700, rates vary rest of year; ❀❄) Part of Wilderness Safaris' portfolio of premier camps, Jao is a special place that combines Asian style (the public areas and the rooms were inspired by a Balinese longhouse) with a very African feel (jackalberry and mangosteen trees, liberal use of thatch). Rooms are uberluxurious and the staff are extremely professional and attentive to your every need.

★ Kwetsani Camp TENTED CAMP $$$

(☑686 0086; www.wilderness-safaris.com; s/d Jun-Oct US$1820/3000, rates vary rest of year; ❄) This highly recommended camp has the usual high levels of comfort, but there are some very special selling points. The recently overhauled rooms, elevated high above the water,

---

OKAVANGO DELTA SEASONS

The Okavango Delta varies greatly with the seasons and understanding how the delta changes over time is important for planning your visit.

November–December Rains begin to fall in the highlands of Angola, in the catchment areas of the Cubango and Cuito Rivers. Down in the delta, waters are receding, despite rains falling in the delta itself and surrounding area. By December, the waters begin to flow down these two rivers towards Botswana.

January–February The waters of the Cubango flow more quickly and near the Okavango River, arriving before the waters of the Cuito. Water levels in the delta remain low.

March–April Continuing rainfall (in good years) adds to the growing volume of water that flows southeast through the Okavango Panhandle and begins to enter the delta proper.

May–June The flooding of the Okavango Delta begins in earnest, and water levels rise across the delta. Depending on the year and its rains, waters may reach further into the southeast via the Boteti River and Selinda Spillway.

July–September The flooding of the delta peaks and the waters reach their southeasternmost limits, a point that can vary considerably from one year to the next.

October Having reached their limits some time in September, the waters begin to evaporate and disappear, and water levels recede towards the northwest.

are simply stunning, while the camp manager, Dan Myburg, is a top-class photographer who can help elevate your photography above the usual even in just a few days.

★**Vumbura Plains Camp** TENTED CAMP **$$$**
(☑686 0086; www.wilderness-safaris.com; s/d Jun-Oct US$2810/4890, rates vary rest of year; ☒) One of Wilderness Safaris' flagship properties, this regally luxurious twin camp is on the Duba Plains in the transition zone between the savannahs and swamps north of the delta. Although divided into north and south sections, with separate eating and other common areas, this is essentially a single lodge. It inhabits the Kwedi Concession and the wildlife viewing is superlative.

★**Duba Expedition Camp** TENTED CAMP **$$$**
(☑in South Africa +27 87 354 6591; www.greatplainsconservation.com; s/d mid-Jun–Oct US$2700/3600, rates vary rest of year) Opened in 2016, this wonderful camp has six tents that are immaculate, large and the sort of canvas home you'll struggle to tear yourself away from. But do so you must, for the wildlife here is some of the best in Africa – this is the homebase area for Dereck and Beverley Joubert and their marvellous wildlife films.

★**Gunn's Camp** TENTED CAMP **$$$**
(☑686 0023; www.underonebotswanasky.com; s/d Jul-Oct US$900/1480, per person Apr-Jun US$560, Nov-Mar US$405) A beautiful option for those wanting the amenities of a high-end safari – expertly cooked meals, attentive service and wonderful views over its island location in the delta – with a more rugged sense of place. The elegant tented rooms are large, lovely and as comfy as you'll find anywhere, but there's more of a feeling of being engaged with the wilderness.

★**Nxabega Okavango Camp** TENTED CAMP **$$$**
(☑in South Africa +27 11-809 4300; www.andbeyond .com; per person Jun-Oct US$1665, Nov-May US$755-1035; ☎☒) In a grove of ebony trees on the flats near the Boro River, this exquisitely designed camp has sweeping views of the delta floodplains. The rooms are magnificent – the private terraces in each are large with lovely swing chairs, each built around water's-edge termite mounds or trees, lending a real sense of intimacy with the landscape.

ℹ Getting There & Away

The only way into and out of the Inner Delta for most visitors is by air. This is an expensive extra, but the pain is alleviated if you look at it as two scenic flights. Chartered flights to the lodges typically cost about US$200 per leg. A *mokoro* or 4WD vehicle will meet your plane and take you to the lodge. If you're flying into one of the camps operated by Wilderness Safaris, Wilderness Air (p68) will be your carrier. For other camps, Mack Air (p68) is one of the most reliable operators. It is possible to book directly with the air-charter company, but it usually makes more sense to make a booking through the safari or lodge company as part of your accommodation booking, not least because it sometimes works out cheaper that way.

Moremi Game Reserve

Moremi Game Reserve (per day per non-resident/vehicle P120/50; ⊙6am-6.30pm Apr-Sep, 5.30am-7pm Oct-Mar), which covers one-third of the Okavango Delta, is home to some of Africa's densest concentrations of wildlife. It's also one of the most accessible corners of the Okavango, with well-maintained trails and accommodation that ranges from luxury lodges to public campsites for self-drivers.

Moremi has a distinctly dual personality, with large areas of dry land rising between vast wetlands. The most prominent 'islands' are Chief's Island, accessible by *mokoro* from the Inner Delta lodges, and Moremi Tongue at the eastern end of the reserve, which is mostly accessible by 4WD. Habitats range from mopane (woodland) and thorn scrub to dry savannah, riparian woodland, grassland, floodplain, marsh and permanent waterways, lagoons and islands.

With the recent reintroduction of rhinos, Moremi is now home to the Big Five (lions, leopards, buffaloes, elephants and rhinos), and notably Africa's largest population of red lechwe. The reserve also protects one of the largest remaining populations of endangered African wild dogs.

The best time to see wildlife in Moremi is the late dry season (July to October), when animals are forced to congregate around permanent water sources, which are accessible to wildlife (and humans). September and October are optimum times for spotting wildlife and birdlife, but these are also the hottest two months. January and February are normally very wet, and as tracks in the reserve are mostly clay, they are frequently impassable during these months.

🛏 Sleeping

★**Xakanaxa Campsite** CAMPGROUND **$**
(Xakanaxa Lediba; kwalatesafari@gmail.com; S 19°10.991, E 23°24.937; camping per adult/child

P260/130) A favourite Moremi campground, Xakanaxa occupies a narrow strip of land surrounded by marshes and lagoons. It's no coincidence that many upmarket lodges are located nearby – the wildlife in the area can be prolific and campers are frequently woken by elephants or serenaded by hippo grunts. Be warned: a young boy was tragically killed by hyenas here in 2000.

Third Bridge Campsite　　CAMPGROUND **$**

(www.xomaesites.com; Third Bridge; S 19°14.340', E 23°21.276'; per adult/child P400/200) The favourite campsite for many self-drivers, Third Bridge has sites away from the main track – set on the edge of a lagoon (watch out for hippos and crocs), it's a beautiful place to pitch. Be wary of baboons and avoid walking on the bridge or sleeping in the open because wildlife – especially lions – use the bridge as a thoroughfare.

★ **Mombo Camp**　　TENTED CAMP **$$$**

(686 0086; www.wilderness-safaris.com; s/d Jun-Oct US$3564/5736, rates vary rest of year;) Ask anyone in Botswana for the country's most exclusive camp and they're likely to nominate Mombo. The surrounding delta scenery is some of the finest in the Okavango and the wildlife watching is almost unrivalled. The rooms are enormous and the entire package – from the service to the comfort levels and attention to detail – never misses a beat.

★ **Baine's Camp**　　TENTED CAMP **$$$**

(in South Africa +27 11-438 4650; www.sanctuaryretreats.com; per person US$750-1530) Five elevated suites overlook a tree line that conceals (but not too much) great wildlife viewing in a shady, woodsy area of the delta close to the southern end of Chief's Island; the outdoor bath tubs are pure indulgence.

★ **Xaranna Camp**　　TENTED CAMP **$$$**

(in South Africa +27 11-809 4300; www.andbeyond.com; per person Jun-Oct US$1770, rates vary rest of year;) Xaranna is a worthy member of the elite group of camps run by &Beyond, which mixes daringly designed luxury accommodation with serious conservation work. Xaranna's large rooms have expansive terraces, private pools and as little to separate you from the delta surrounds as is possible. The food is excellent and the service first-rate.

❶ Information

The village of Khwai has a couple of shops that sell basic supplies. Otherwise, petrol and supplies are only available in Kasane and Maun. If you're self-driving, you'll need to book your campsites many months in advance.

Entry fees to the reserve should be paid for in advance at the DWNP office in Maun (p72),

Moremi Tongue

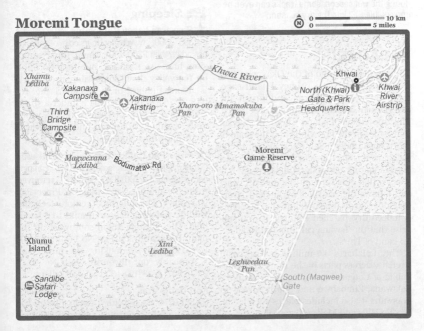

though they can be paid at the gate if you have no other choice. Self-drivers will, however, only be allowed entry to the reserve if they have a confirmed reservation at one of the four public campsites.

North (Khwai) Gate & Park Headquarters (⊙1 April to 30 September 6am-6:30pm; 1 October to 31 March 5.30am-7pm) Pick up your photocopied map of the reserve (they sometimes run out) and pay your park fees here.

❶ Getting There & Away

Chartered flights (and/or 4WD) are usually the only way to reach the luxury lodges of Moremi, with the Khwai River and Xakanaxa strips being regularly used.

If you're driving from Maun, the reserve entrance is at South (Maqwee) Gate, about 99km north of Maun via Shorobe. Take the sealed road to Shorobe, where the road turns into awfully corrugated gravel. Once inside the park, it's about 52km (two hours) from South Gate to Third Bridge along a reasonable track, en route passing through beautiful, wildlife-rich country. It's about 25km (one hour) from Third Bridge to Xakanaxa Lediba, and another 45km (1½ hours) from there to North Gate.

From Kasane and the east, a track links Chobe National Park with the other gate at North (Khwai) Gate.

Check the road conditions with the DWNP offices in Gaborone or Maun, and/or with other drivers, before attempting to drive into Moremi during the wet season; some tracks can even be impassable well into the dry season.

KALAHARI

The parched alter ego of the Okavango Delta, the Kalahari is a primeval landscape, recalling in stone, thorns and brush the earliest memories of the human experience. This impression of a land where time began finds voice in the hot winds and the snap of thorn bush under a San tracker's feet in the Kalahari. It is the timeless roar of a Kalahari lion resonating across the still desert air. It is a valley that cuts through the desert's heart and follows the path left by ancient rivers that long ago disappeared into the dust. This is indeed dry, parched country. It's no surprise that the Tswana call this the Kgalagadi: Land of Thirst.

The Kalahari's 1.2-million-sq-km basin stretches across parts of the Democratic Republic of Congo, Angola, Zambia, Namibia, Botswana, Zimbabwe and South Africa; in Botswana it also includes places such as the Tsodilo Hills and Makgadikgadi Pans.

Central Kalahari Game Reserve

The dry heart of the dry south of a dry continent, the **Central Kalahari Game Reserve** (CKGR; per day per non-resident/vehicle P120/50; ⊙6am-6.30pm Apr-Sep, 5.30am-7pm Oct-Mar) (CKGR) is an awesome place. If remoteness, desert silences and the sound of lions roaring in the night are your thing, this could become one of your favourite places in Africa. Covering 52,800 sq km (about the size of Denmark), it's also one of Africa's largest protected areas. This is big-sky country, home to black-maned Kalahari lions, a full suite of predators and an utterly wonderful sense of the remote.

The park is most easily accessible during the dry season (May to September) when tracks are sandy but easily negotiated by 4WD vehicles. Nights can be bitterly cold at this time and daytime temperatures are relatively mild. During the rainy season (November to March or April), tracks can be muddy and nearly impassable for inexperienced drivers. Watch for grass seeds clogging engines and searing temperatures in October. You will not be permitted into the park without a campsite reservation. Collecting firewood is banned in the CKGR, so bring your own.

🛏 Sleeping

⭐**Passarge Valley Campsites** CAMPGROUND $ (☑395 3360; www.bigfoottours.co.bw; camping per adult/child P200/100) These three campsites have no facilities, but their location on the valley floor (some kilometres apart) is among the best in the Kalahari. Site No 2 (S 21°26.847', E 23°47.694'), under a shady stand of trees in the centre of the valley floor, is simply wonderful and the world is yours and yours alone.

⭐**Piper Pan Campsites** CAMPGROUND $ (☑395 3360; www.bigfoottours.co.bw; camping per adult/child P200/100) Slightly removed from the main circuit, the two Piper Pan sites have a wonderfully remote feel and wildlife watching is good thanks to a water hole. The pans are 26km southwest off the main Letiahau track. Site No 1 (S 21°76.827', E 23°19.843'), overlooking the main pan, is probably our favourite, but No 2 (S 21°76.827', E 23°19.843') is also excellent.

Kori Campsites CAMPGROUND $ (☑381 0774; dwnp@gov.bw; camping per person P30) The four campsites known as Kori sit

THE SAN & THE CKGR

The Central Kalahari Game Reserve (CKGR) was originally established in 1961 as a private reservation for the San in order to protect them from the encroachments of the modern world and to protect their ancestral homelands. But the government of Botswana later changed its mind (primarily, critics say, because diamonds were found within the park's boundaries), and although the southern and western parts of the CKGR are still home to small populations of San, a wave of forced relocations has greatly reduced the population. The future of the San is now one of the biggest political hot potatoes for Botswana's government.

Nearly all of Botswana's and Namibia's San were relocated from their ancestral lands to new government settlements such as New Xade, just outside the CKGR. In 2006 this resettlement program earned the government a reprimand from the UN's Committee on the Elimination of Racial Discrimination. The Botswanan government maintains that its relocation policies have the San's best interests at heart. Development, education and modernisation are its buzzwords. The trouble is, many San actively rejected the government's version of modernisation if it meant giving up their ancestral lands and traditions.

After South Africa's highest court found in favour of the Richtersveld people (relatives of the San) of Northern Cape Province in 2003 – for the first time, the court recognised that indigenous people have both communal land ownership and mineral rights over their territory – the San of Botswana launched a similar appeal. The court case brought by the First People of the Kalahari (FPK) against the government's relocation policies was concluded in May 2006, and approximately 1000 San attached their names to the effort. During the proceedings many San tried to return home to the CKGR, but most were forced off the grounds of the reserve. In December 2006 the high court ruled that the eviction of the San was 'unlawful and unconstitutional'. One justice went so far as to say that not allowing the San to hunt in their homeland 'was tantamount to condemning the residents of the CKGR to death by starvation'.

In 2007 DeBeers sold its stake in the Ghaghoo (formerly Gope) Diamond Mine in the far east of the CKGR to Gem Diamonds, and the mine officially began production in September 2014. A few San have been allowed back into the reserve, although the government continues to drag its heels in fully implementing the court ruling, more than a decade after it was handed down.

on the hill that rises gently from the western edge of Deception Valley. There's plenty of shade and some have partial views of the valley, making any of them a wonderful base. There are braai pits and pit toilets.

Motopi Campsites CAMPGROUND $
(395 3360; www.bigfoottours.co.bw; camping per adult/child P200/100) In the northwestern corner of the reserve, these three campsites are wonderfully isolated from the rest of the reserve. Nearby Motopi Pan is great for wildlife, and lions are common in the surrounding area – we spent hours with one pride here without seeing another vehicle.

★**Deception Valley Lodge** LODGE $$$
(www.dvl.co.za; S 20°59.12', E 23°39.47'; s/d/f all-inclusive Jun-Oct US$789/1214/1821, Nov-May US$660/1016/1525;) Just outside the CKGR's northeastern boundary, this exclusive bush retreat inhabits 150 sq km of privately owned Kalahari bush and has a much more personal feel than many of Botswana's luxury lodges. The eight large chalets (two can be combined into family accommodation) are swathed in lovely earthen hues, while the food is as memorable as the warm, attentive service.

★**Kalahari Plains Camp** TENTED CAMP $$$
(in South Africa +27 11-807 1800; www.wilderness-safaris.com; per person mid-Jan–May US$965, Nov–mid-Jan US$935, Jun-Oct US$650;) If we could choose one place to stay in the CKGR, this would be it. These lovely solar-powered tents inhabit a gorgeous location southeast of Deception Valley and face the setting sun with stunning views. The spacious tents have wooden floors, extremely comfortable beds, 24-hour electricity, yoga mats and a roof terrace (for those wishing to sleep under the stars).

ⓘ Getting There & Away

Airstrips (for chartered flights only) are located near Xade, Xaka and Deception Pan.

A 4WD is essential to get around the reserve, and a compass (or GPS equipment) and petrol reserves are also recommended. Several 4WD tracks lead into the CKGR, but not all are official entrances. Accessible gates:

Matswere Gate (S 21°09.047', E 24°00.445') The main gate, signposted off the sealed B300 just northwest of Rakops.

Southern Gate (S 23°21.388', E 24°36.470') The main gate to Khutse Game Reserve (which abuts the CKGR to the south, with no fence between the two), which is most easily reached via Letlhakeng, 100km to the southeast.

Tsau Gate (S 21°00.081', E 24°47.845') In the reserve's far northwest and the most accessible gate from Maun.

Central Kalahari & Khutse Game Reserves

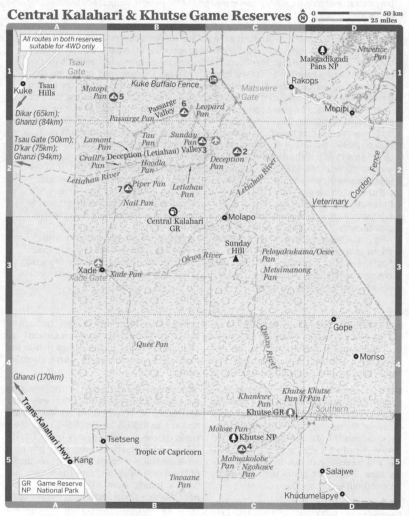

Central Kalahari & Khutse Game Reserves

Sleeping
1 Deception Valley Lodge C1
2 Kalahari Plains Camp C2
3 Kori Campsites B2
4 Moreswe Pan Campsites C5
5 Motopi Campsites B1
6 Passarge Valley Campsites B1
7 Piper Pan Campsites B2

Xade Gate (S 22°20.268', E 23°00.577') The tracks to the gate start near D'kar or Ghanzi and are signposted.

ℹ Getting Around

Unless you're staying at an upmarket lodge in which game drives are included, or have organised your visit on a mobile safari from Maun, you'll need your own fully equipped 4WD to get around.

Khutse Game Reserve

The 2500-sq-km **Khutse Game Reserve** (☑596 0013; per day per nonresident/vehicle P120/50; ⊙6am-6.30pm Apr-Sep, 5.30am-7pm Oct-Mar), which is an extension of the southern boundary of the Central Kalahari Game Reserve (CKGR), is a popular weekend excursion for residents of Gaborone, but it's still deliciously remote and crowds are rare, especially from Sunday to Thursday. It has all the attractions of the Kalahari, including good (if low-density) wildlife watching, well-maintained trails and around 60 mineralised clay pans that once belonged to Africa's largest inland lake. Leopard and lion sightings in particular are possible, while gemsboks and giraffes are also commonly seen.

The name Khutse, which means 'Where One Kneels to Drink' in Sekwena (the local dialect of Setswana), indicates that the area once had water, though today the reserve experiences continual droughts.

The entrance gate and park office are 210km from Gaborone. To Kang it's 363km via Lethlhakeng, or 285km if you take the short cut that heads southwest from Salajwe; only take the latter route if you have sufficient fuel to get you all the way to Kang. From Letlhakeng to the park entrance (100km), the road is graded gravel that is generally fine for 2WD vehicles. A 4WD vehicle is necessary for exploring the reserve.

Khutse boasts several superbly located campsites, all of which are administered by **Big Foot Tours** (☑395 3360; www.bigfoottours. co.bw; camping per adult/child P200/100).

Moreswe Pan Campsites CAMPGROUND $ (☑395 3360; www.bigfoottours.co.bw; camping per adult/child P200/100) Our pick of the campsites in Khutse, these four sites far from civilisation are fine places to rest, and some have terrific, sweeping views over the pan, with the water hole nearby. Each site has a braai pit, bucket showers and a pit toilet. We've stayed in site No 2 and thought it one of the loveliest campsites in the country.

Kgalagadi Transfrontier Park

In 2000 the former Mabuasehube-Gemsbok National Park was combined with South Africa's former Kalahari Gemsbok National Park to create the new **Kgalagadi Transfrontier Park** (dwnp@gov.bw; non-resident adult/vehicle per day P20/4; ⊙6am-7.30pm Jan & Feb, 6.30am-7pm Mar, Sep & Oct, 7am-6.30pm Apr & Aug, 7am-6pm May, 7.30am-6pm Jun & Jul, 5.30am-7.30pm Nov & Dec). The result is a 28,400-sq-km bi-national park that is one of the largest and most pristine arid wilderness areas on the continent. The park is also the only place in Botswana where you'll see the shifting sand dunes that many mistakenly believe to be typical of the Kalahari. This is true desert; in the summer it can reach 45°C, and at night it can drop to -10°C.

Kgalagadi is home to large herds of springboks, gemsboks, elands and wildebeest, as well as a full complement of predators, including lions (official estimates put the lion population of the park at around 450), cheetahs (200), leopards (100), brown hyenas (600) and spotted hyenas (375). More than 250 bird species are present, including several endemic species of larks and bustards.

The best time to visit is from December to May, although the park can be visited year-round. From June to October or November, night-time temperatures can be extremely cold (as low as -10°C) and daytime temperatures are relatively mild. Although October can be very hot (45°C), the best wildlife watching is from October onwards.

◉ Sights

◉ Mabuasehube Section

The eastern Mabuasehube section covers 1800 sq km and is the easiest area of the park to access from the Botswana side of the border. Here, a series of salt pans, separated by classic Kalahari scrub vegetation, makes this section of the park a worthwhile destination in its own right. That said, if you restrict yourself to Mabuasehube and surrounding pans alone, you'll miss the exceptional breadth of Kalahari landscapes that is a feature of this park.

The two largest pans, Mpayathutlwa and Mabuasehube, are also the most beautiful, surrounded as they are by low hills that offer some gorgeous views early in the morning or late in the day. There are 4WD trails that circumnavigate both pans. **Mpayathutlwa Pan**, 12km west of the park gate, has a water hole at the northern end (some of the best views are to be found close to where the trail leads down the hill to the water hole) and two appealing campsites on the western side. **Mabuasehube Pan**, around 10km north of Mpayathutlwa, is similarly superb, with marvellous views from all along the southern edge and parts of the eastern and western sides; the trail heads off into the bush at the northern end, but there is a fine lookout halfway around. Mabuasehube Pan is used as a salt lick by migrating herds in late winter and early spring.

The other, smaller pans – Lesholoago, Monamodi and Bosobogolo – are also worth exploring. On the northern side of **Khiding Pan**, 11km west of Mabuasehube Pan, meerkats are a real possibility if you go quietly.

◉ Two Rivers Section

Although you can reach the Two Rivers section from either Kaa or Mabuasehube, access is still easiest from South Africa. However you get here, the pools of rainwater that collect in the dry beds of the Auob and Nossob Rivers provide the best opportunities for wildlife viewing in the park. Here you'll also come across Kalahari dunes and camel thorn–dotted grasslands.

We recommend spending at least three days in this area of the park, slowly making your way back and forth along the riverbanks and dipping down to the river's edge where possible, but allowing time also for watching and waiting from the shadows as wildlife comes and goes. Look up also into the trees for horizontal branches that might just provide a vantage point for a sleeping leopard.

There's a lot of ground to cover – it's 161km from Two Rivers to Nossob and a further 61km to Polentswa, and this section offers the best wildlife watching – and that's just along the **Nossob River**. Over on the **Auob River**, it's 121km from Two Rivers to Mata Mata, which will take around 2½ hours, or even longer if you stop along the way. And don't neglect the trails that connect the two rivers – lion prides thrive close to river confluences, and this is classic Kalahari lion country.

🛏 Sleeping

Camping in the park is only allowed at designated campsites; those on the Botswana side of the frontier must be booked at the DWNP office in Gaborone (p86) or Maun (p72).

Bookings for huts and chalets on the South African side are recommended from June to September and during all weekends and public and school holidays. Contact South African National Parks (p81).

🛏 Mabuasehube Section

★ Mabuasehube Pan Camp Sites
CAMPGROUND $

(📞 bookings 318 0774; dwnp@gov.bw; camping per person P30) The four campsites that sit above or close to the southern end of Mabuasehube Pan are among the loveliest in the Kalahari, with fabulous, sweeping views of the pan, for the most part uninterrupted. They're all terrific (and have showers and toilets) but Sites No 2 and 3 are our pick – the only, minor drawback here is that they're quite close to one another.

Mpayathutlwa Pan Campsites
CAMPGROUND $

(📞 bookings 318 0774; dwnp@gov.bw; camping per person P30) It's a close-run thing for us to choose between these lovely sites and those of Mabuasehube, around 10km to the north. The Mpayathutlwa sites, on the west side of the pan some 12km west of the park entrance gate, have fine views from their shady, elevated vantage point.

🛏 Two Rivers Section

Twee Rivieren Rest Camp
CAMPGROUND $

(Map p502; www.sanparks.org; camping R265, 2-person cottages from R1045, family cottages/chalets R1275/1635; ❄) The most accessible and popular rest camp on either side of the river, Twee Rivieren features a swimming pool and, unusually for this area, an outdoor bar-restaurant. Rustic chalets have modern amenities, including air-con, hot showers and a full kitchen. This is the only one of the Kgalagadi camps to have 24-hour electricity and a relatively strong mobile phone (cellphone) signal.

★ !Xaus
LODGE $$$

(Map p502; www.xauslodge.co.za; s/d all-inclusive R5707/8780; @❄) If you're after Kgalagadi's most luxurious experience, book a night here. Owned and operated by the local San community, the lodge is a dry, dreamy fantasy in ochre, decorated with wall hangings made by a local women's sewing collective and overlooking an evocative circular pan.

ℹ Information

Campers staying at the Polentswa and Rooiputs campsites can pick up firewood at Two Rivers campsite (Botswana), while petrol and basic food supplies are available at Twee Rivieren (South Africa). In Botswana there are reliable petrol supplies at Hukuntsi and Kang. Maps of the park are available at the park gates. The only mobile-phone reception in the park is at Twee Rivieren.

South African National Parks (☑in South Africa +27 12-428 9111, in South Africa +27 82-233 9111; www.sanparks.org) Your starting point for information and reservations for the South African side of Kgalagadi Transfrontier Park.

❶ Getting There & Away

There is no public transport to the park. The park gates are located in the following places:

➡ Twee Rivieren (South Africa)

➡ Two Rivers (Botswana)

➡ Mabuasehube (Botswana)

➡ Kaa (Botswana)

CAR & MOTORCYCLE

The Two Rivers Section is accessible from the south via Two Rivers and Twee Rivieren, and from the north via Kaa. Access to the Kalahari Gemsbok National Park is via Twee Rivieren. Both are about 53km north of the Bokspits border crossing. The border crossings to Namibia at Union's End and Mata Mata are closed because traffic disturbs the wildlife.

To get to Mabuasehube Gate, most travellers coming from the Botswana side take the sealed road from Kang, southwest to Hukuntsi (108km). Just before Hukuntsi, a potholed road branches left (south) to Lokgwabe (11km). From Lokgwabe, an unsealed road (which was regraded in 2016 but remains sandy in patches) runs south, then east, then south again for 136km to Mabuasehube Gate. The gate is signposted at various points along the way from Lokgwabe. Allow for three hours' driving from Kang to the gate.

To reach Kaa Gate from the Botswana side, make your way to Hukuntsi, pass through the town and take the reasonable unsealed road heading southwest. From Hukuntsi, it's 59km to the small settlement of Zutshwa then a further 73km to the gate. Mabuasehube section is possible from the south (via Tshabong), north (via Tshane) and east (via Werda).

❶ Getting Around

You'll need your own 4WD vehicle for getting around the park, although some of the camps are accessible by 2WD.

Two 4WD trails connect the Two Rivers and Mabuasehube sections of the park, but only the southernmost of the two (which connects Nossob and Bosobogolo Pan, 171km away and 20km southwest of Mabuasehube Gate) is open to the public. The northern Mabuasehube Wilderness 4x4 Trail (155km) must be prebooked through the DWNP in Gaborone (p86) or Maun (p72).

UNDERSTAND BOTSWANA

Botswana Today

Botswana's recent history is a lesson to other African countries. Instead of suffering from Africa's oft-seen resource curse, Botswana has used the ongoing windfall from its diamond mines to build a stable and, for the most part, egalitarian country, one whose economic growth rates have, for decades, been among the highest on earth. This is a place where things work, where education, health and environmental protection are government priorities. Even when faced with one of the most serious challenges confronting Africa in the 20th century – HIV/AIDS – the government broke new ground in making antiretroviral treatment available to all.

The country's dependence on diamonds is, however, also a major concern when looking into Botswana's future; diamonds make up 85% of the country's export earnings and one third of government revenues. As such, the economy remains vulnerable to a fluctuating world economy in 2015 the economy grew by just 1% (which is very low by the country's recent, albeit lofty standards) and unemployment sits at a worrying 20%, prompting the government to announce an economic stimulus package in 2016. Tourism is the big growth industry as the country attempts to diversify an economy that remains, despite some leaner times, one of the strongest in Southern Africa.

On 30 September 2016, Botswana celebrated 50 years as an independent country. We were fortunate enough to join in the celebrations and the outpouring of national pride made it clear that this is one of Africa's most enduring success stories. Yes, much of it wouldn't have been possible without diamonds – the country would be unrecognisable to those who were around 50 years before – but Botswana has used its resources to make a better life for its people, something that can be said about few other resource-rich African nations. But there's more to it than simple good economic management, because this country is very much united. Despite considerable diversity, the project of building a cohesive and peaceful nation has been similarly successful – people here identify themselves first and foremost as Botswanans, with tribal affiliation very much in second place. If this sounds like a given, again, a quick scan of other countries on the continent serves as a reminder that this is so special that it fully deserves the slogan that accompanied the anniversary celebrations – 'Botswana: United and Proud'.

History

First Footprints

To understand Botswana, one must look deep into the past. Here, history extends back through the millenniums to the earliest presence of humanity on the planet, when humans took their first footsteps on the savannahs of southern and eastern Africa. Developing rudimentary tools, these people hunted and gathered across the abundant plains, moving seasonally over grassland and scrub in and around the extensive wetlands that once covered the north of the country.

By the Middle Stone Age, the Boskop, the primary human group in Southern Africa, had progressed into an organised hunting and gathering society. They are thought to be the ancestors of the modern-day San. Archaeological evidence and rock art found in the Tsodilo Hills place these hunter-gatherers in shelters and caves throughout the region from around 17,000 BC. The paintings that gave expression to the natural world in which they lived attest to their increasing level of sophistication – clumsy stone tools gave way to bone, wood and, eventually, iron implements. Better tools meant more efficient hunting, which allowed time for further innovation.

Such progress prompted many of these hunter-gatherers to adopt a pastoral lifestyle – sowing crops and grazing livestock on the exposed pastures of the Okavango Delta and the Makgadikgadi lakes. Some migrated west into central Namibia, and by 70 BC some had even reached the Cape of Good Hope.

Rise of the Tswana

One of the most significant developments in Botswana's human history was the evolution of the three main branches of the Tswana ethnic group in the 14th century. Three brothers – Kwena, Ngwaketse and Ngwato – broke away from their father, Chief Malope, to establish their own followings in Molepolole, Kanye and Serowe respectively. These fractures probably occurred in response to drought and expanding populations eager to strike out in search of new pastures.

The Ngwato clan split further in the late 18th century, following a quarrel between Chief Khama I and his brother Tawana, who subsequently left Serowe and established his chiefdom in the area around Maun. The four major present-day Batswana groups – the Batawana, Bakwena, Bangwaketse and Bangwato – trace their ancestry to these splits and Botswana's demographic make-up owes much to the dispersal of the various groups.

The Boers & the British

While Mzilikazi was wreaking havoc on the Batswana and missionaries were trying to convert the survivors to Christianity, the Boers were pressured by their British neighbours in the Cape. The Boers were farmers from the eastern Cape in Southern Africa, the descendants of Dutch-speaking settlers. In 1836 around 20,000 Boers set out on the Great Trek across the Vaal River into Batswana and Zulu territory and proceeded to set up their own free state ruling the Transvaal – a move ratified by the British in the Sand River Convention of 1852. Effectively, this placed the Batswana under the rule of the so-called new South African Republic, and a period of rebellion and oppression ensued. Following heavy human and territorial losses, the Batswana chiefs petitioned the British government for protection from the Boers.

But Britain had its hands full in Southern Africa and was in no hurry to take on and support a country of uncertain profitability. Instead, it offered to act as arbitrator in the dispute. By 1877, however, animosity against the Boers had escalated to such a dangerous level that the British conceded and annexed the Transvaal – thereby starting the first Boer War. The war continued until the Pretoria Convention of 1881, when the British withdrew from the Transvaal in exchange for Boer allegiance to the British Crown.

With the British out of their way, the Boers once again looked northward into Batswana territory. In 1882 the Boers managed to subdue the towns of Taung and Mafikeng, and proclaimed them the republics of Stellaland and Goshen. They might have gone much further had it not been for the annexation of South West Africa (modern-day Namibia) by the Germans in the 1890s.

With the potential threat of a German-Boer alliance across the Kalahari, which would have put an end to their dreams of expansion into mineral-rich Rhodesia (Zimbabwe), the British started to look seriously at the Batswana petitions for protection. In 1885 they proclaimed a protectorate over their Tswana allies, known as the British Crown Colony of Bechuanaland.

Independence

The extent to which the British subordinated Botswanan interests to those of South Africa during this period became clear in 1950. In a case that caused political controversy in Britain and across the Empire, the British government banned Seretse Khama from the chieftainship of the Ngwato and exiled him for six years. This, as secret documents have since revealed, was in order to appease the South African government, which objected to Khama's marriage to a British woman at a time when racial segregation was enforced in South Africa.

This only increased growing political agitation, and throughout the 1950s and '60s Botswanan political parties started to surface and promote the idea of independence, at the precise historical moment when African colonies elsewhere were seeking their freedom. Following the Sharpeville Massacre in 1960, South African refugees Motsamai Mpho, of the African National Congress (ANC), and Philip Matante, a Johannesburg preacher affiliated with the Pan-African Congress, joined with KT Motsete, a teacher from Malawi, to form the Bechuanaland People's Party (BPP). Its immediate goal was independence.

In 1962 Seretse Khama and Kanye farmer Ketumile 'Quett' Masire formed the moderate Bechuanaland Democratic Party (BDP). The BDP formulated a schedule for independence, drawing on support from local chiefs such as Bathoen II of the Bangwaketse, and traditional Batswana. The BDP also called for the transfer of the capital into Botswana (ie from Mafikeng to Gaborone) and a new nonracial constitution.

The British gratefully accepted the BDP's peaceful plan for transfer of power, and Khama was elected president when general elections were held in 1965. On 30 September 1966, the country – now called the Republic of Botswana – was granted full independence.

In contrast to the situation in so many other newly independent African states, Seretse Khama wisely steered Botswana through its first 14 years of independence. He guaranteed continued freehold over land held by white ranchers, and adopted a strictly neutral stance (at least until near the end of his presidency) towards South Africa and Rhodesia. The reason, of course, was Botswana's economic dependence on the giant to the south, but, that said, Khama refused to exchange ambassadors with South Africa and officially disapproved of apartheid in international circles.

Modern Politics

Sir Seretse Khama died in 1980 (not long after Zimbabwean independence), but his Botswana Democratic Party (BDP), formerly the Bechuanaland Democratic Party, continues to command a substantial majority in the Botswana parliament. Sir Ketumile 'Quett' Masire, who succeeded Khama as president from 1980 to 1998, followed the path laid down by his predecessor and continued to cautiously follow pro-Western policies.

In 1998 President Masire did something very few African leaders seem to manage – he retired in keeping with new constitutional provisions and stepped gracefully off the political stage. His successor and former vicepresident, Festus Mogae, became president and his position was confirmed in elections the following year. With the country in the grip of an HIV/AIDS catastrophe – Botswana had the highest infection rate of any country in the world – Mogae won international acclaim by announcing in 2001 that treatment drugs for HIV/AIDS patients were to be distributed free of charge. Mogae was reelected president in a landslide in 2004.

Festus Mogae handed over the presidency to vicepresident Ian Khama (son of Sir Seretse Khama) on 1 April 2008. Mogae is lauded in global circles for the move. Whatever the international community thought of Mogae, his decision to make Khama president generated concern at home as Khama had not yet been elected as president.

Since assuming power, Khama has cracked down on drinking, demanding earlier curfews at bars). In addition, Khama, a former commander of the Botswana Defence Force, has appointed military and law-enforcement colleagues to government posts traditionally held by civilians, which has caused some concern in civil society. Nonetheless, the BDP with Khama at the helm easily won elections in October 2009.

Khama's government also generated controversy with policies that continue to make life difficult for the San who want to return to the CKGR and with the decision to ban all commercial hunting in Botswana from 2014. Even so, Khama remains popular and he was reelected as president for a second term in 2014. At the same time, the BDP won a clear majority of parliamentary seats and, having controlled Botswana's politics since independence, looked likely to remain in power for some years to come.

People of Botswana

Botswana's population is made up of eight major tribal groupings, although within this broader framework there are 26 tribal groups in all. The Tswana are the most populous, and all citizens of Botswana – regardless of colour, ancestry or tribal affiliation – are known as Batswana (plural) or Motswana (singular). Almost everyone, including members of non-Tswana tribes, communicates in Setswana, a native language, rather than the official language of English.

Tswana

Botswana means 'land of the Tswana' and about 80% of the country's population claims Tswana heritage. The origins of the Tswana are simple enough. As land-owning agriculturalists, the Tswana ethnic group has clearly defined areas of influence. The Bangwato are centred on the Serowe area, the Bakwena in and around Molepolole, and the Bangwaketse near Kanye. A later split in the Bangwato resulted in a fourth group, the Batawana, who are concentrated near Maun in the northwest. Known for being proud, conservative, resourceful and respectful, the Batswana have an ingrained feeling of national identity and an impressive belief in their country. Their history – a series of clever manoeuvres that meant they avoided the worst aspects of colonisation – has nurtured a confidence that is rare in postcolonial Africa.

The importance of the family in Batswana society has made the crisis caused by the HIV/AIDS pandemic particularly damaging. At last count, the country had more than 60,000 AIDS orphans (down from more than 90,000 in 2011), a staggering 2.7% of the population. How the country reacts to this breakdown of traditional family networks is one of the greatest challenges facing its people.

San

The San are Botswana's first inhabitants: they were living in the Kalahari and Tsodilo Hills as far back as 30,000 years ago, as archaeological finds in the Kalahari have demonstrated. Some linguists even credit them with the invention of language. Unlike most other African countries, where the San have perished or disappeared through war and interbreeding, Botswana, along with Namibia, retains the remnants of its San communities – barely 100,000 individuals in total, which may include many with mixed San ancestry. Of these, around 60% live in Botswana (the !Kung, G//ana, G/wi and !xo being the largest groups), where they make up just 3% of Botswana's population, and 35% in Namibia (the Naro, !Xukwe, Hei//kom and Ju/'hoansi), with the remainder scattered throughout South Africa, Angola, Zimbabwe and Zambia.

For a window on the life of the San, join local hunter !Nqate in Craig and Damon Foster's film *The Great Dance* (2000), an inspiring collaborative project that involved the local community at every stage of the filming and editing. And a word on terminology: in Botswana you'll often hear the term 'Basarwa' being used to describe the San, but this is considered by the San to be pejorative as it literally means 'people of the sticks'.

Environment

The Land

Botswana is the geographic heart of sub-Saharan Africa, extending over 1100km from north to south and 960km from east to west, an area of 582,000 sq km. The country is entirely landlocked, and is bordered to the south and southeast by South Africa, across the Limpopo and Molopo Rivers; to the northeast by Zimbabwe; and to the north and west by Namibia.

THE KALAHARI

Around 100 million years ago the supercontinent Gondwanaland dramatically broke up. As the land mass ripped apart, the edges of the African continent rose up, forming the mountain ranges of Southern and central Africa. Over the millennium, water and wind weathered these highlands, carrying the fine dust inland to the Kalahari Basin. At 2.5 million sq km, it's the earth's largest unbroken tract of sand, stretching from northern South Africa to eastern Namibia and Angola, and to Zambia and Zimbabwe in the west.

Depending on who you believe, between 68% and 85% of the country, including the entire central and southwestern regions, is taken up by the Kalahari. The shifting sand dunes that compose a traditional desert are found only in the far southwest, in the Kgalagadi Transfrontier Park. In the northeast are the great salty deserts of the Makgadikgadi Pans; in ancient times part of a vast superlake, they're now the largest (about 12,000 sq km) complex of salt pans in the world and considered to be part of the Kalahari.

In Botswana, large tracts of the Kalahari are protected, with at least five protected areas (listed from north to south):

➡ Nxai Pans National Park (p57)
➡ Makgadikgadi Pans National Park (p55)
➡ Central Kalahari Game Reserve (p76)
➡ Khutse Game Reserve (p79)
➡ Kgalagadi Transfrontier Park (p79)

OKAVANGO DELTA

The Okavango Delta is one of Africa's most extraordinary landscapes, not to mention the antidote to the Kalahari's endless sea of sand. Covering between 13,000 and 18,000 sq km, it snakes into the country from Angola to form a watery paradise of convoluted channels and islands that appear and disappear depending on the water levels. The delta is home to more than 2000 plant species, 450 bird species and 65 fish species, not to mention an estimated 200,000 large mammals.

The delta owes its existence to a tectonic trough in the Kalahari basin, a topographical depression that ensures that the waters of the Okavango River evaporate or are drunk by plants without ever reaching the sea; the delta is extremely flat with no more than a 2m variation in the land's altitude, which means that the waters simply come to a halt. The delta's waters surge and subside at the behest of the rains in far-off Angola, and every year around 11 cu km of water flood into the delta. The flooding is seasonal, beginning in the Angolan highlands in January and February, the waters travelling approximately 1200km in a month. Having reached the delta, the waters disperse across it from March to June, before peaking in July and August – during these months, the water surface area of the delta can be three times that of the nonflooding periods.

Wildlife

Botswana is home to anywhere between 160 and 500 different mammal species, 593 recorded bird species, 150 different reptiles, over 8000 insect and spider species, and more than 3100 types of plants and trees.

BIRDS

Botswana is not only a big wildlife country but also a birding paradise. Between September and March, when the delta is flush with water, you should be able to train the lenses of your binoculars on any number of Botswana's 593 recorded species, including

ENDANGERED SPECIES

According to the International Union for the Conservation of Nature (IUCN), species which are listed as Vulnerable in Botswana include the cheetah, black-footed cat, lion and hippo. In greater trouble and listed as Endangered is the African wild dog, while the black rhino is considered Critically Endangered.

the delta's famous African skimmers, the endangered wattled crane, slaty egrets, African jacanas, bee-eaters, pygmy geese and the shy Pel's fishing owl. You can still see many bird species in the dry season, when it's often easier to spot them around the few remaining water sources.

Most of Botswana's best birding is concentrated in the north of the country around the Okavango Delta, including the Okavango Panhandle, the Chobe Riverfront, the Central Kalahari Game Reserve, Khama Rhino Sanctuary, and the Tuli Block, especially around the Limpopo River.

One especially good site is the Nata Bird Sanctuary, which is home to over a quarter of Botswana's birds. The sanctuary is covered in a sea of pink flamingos, and other migratory birds, during the rainy season from November to March.

Environmental Issues

As a relatively large country with a very low population density, Botswana is one of Africa's most unpolluted and pristine regions. Botswana faces most of the ecological problems experienced elsewhere in Africa, such as land degradation and desertification, deforestation (around 21% of the country is covered by forests), water scarcity and urban sprawl. In addition to these, some major ecological and conservation issues continue to affect the country.

THE FENCE DILEMMA

If you've been stopped at a veterinary checkpoint, or visited the eastern Okavango Delta, you'll be familiar with the country's 3000km of 1.5m-high buffalo fence, officially called the Veterinary Cordon Fence. It's not a single fence but a series of high-tensile steel-wire barriers that run cross-country through some of Botswana's wildest terrain.

The fences were first erected in 1954 to segregate wild buffalo herds from domestic free-range cattle in order to thwart the spread of foot-and-mouth disease. Botswana's beef-farming industry is one of the most important in the country, both economically and in terms of the status conferred upon cattle owners in Batswana society. At the same time, wildlife tourism is a major money earner and the country's international reputation is often tied to its perceived willingness to protect the country's wildlife. Balancing these two significant yet sometimes-conflicting industries is one of the most complicated challenges facing Botswana's government.

POACHING

Poaching is not common in Botswana, and its well-patrolled borders are monitored by the Botswana Defence Force (BDF). What little poaching there is seems to be 'for the pot' – local people supplementing their diets by hunting wild animals – rather than large-scale commercial enterprises.

National Parks & Reserves

All public national parks and reserves in Botswana are run by the **Department of Wildlife & National Parks** (DWNP; Map p46; ☑ 381 0774; dwnp@gov.bw; Millenium Office Park, New Lobatse Rd; ☺7.30am-4.30pm Mon-Fri, 7.30am-12.45pm & 1.45-4.30pm Sat, 7.30am-12.45pm Sun). There are other park offices in Maun (p72) and Kasane (p62), as well as a rarely visited outpost in Kang (☑ 651 7036; off Trans Kalahari Hwy/A2; ☺7.30am-12.45pm & 1.45-4.30pm). There are a few things worth remembering about visiting Botswana's national parks and reserves:

➡ Park fees have long been slated for a significant rise – we thought it would have happened by now, but don't be surprised if they're significantly above those listed here by the time you arrive.

➡ Although there are exceptions (such as the Chobe Riverfront section of Chobe National Park) and it may be possible on rare occasions to get park rangers to bend the rules, no one is allowed into a national park or reserve without an accommodation booking for that park.

➡ It is possible to pay park entrance fees at park entrance gates, after a spell in which places had to be reserved and fees paid in advance at DWNP offices in Gaborone, Maun or Kasane (you'll still see some signs around Botswana to that effect). Even so, you should always try to book and pay in advance.

➡ The gates for each DWNP park are open from 6am to 6.30pm (1 April to 30 September) and from 5.30am to 7pm (1 October to 31 March). It is vital that all visitors be out of the park, or settled into their campsite, outside of these hours. Driving after dark is strictly forbidden (although it is permitted in private concessions).

Camping & Booking

The Department of Wildlife & National Parks runs a small number of campsites (especially in the Central Kalahari Game Reserve and Kgalagadi Transfrontier Park), and reservations for any DWNP campsite can be made up to 12 months in advance at the DWNP offices in Maun (p72) or Gaborone (p86); Chobe National Park bookings are also possible at the Kasane DWNP office (p62). It's at these offices that you can also pay the park entry fees (upon presenting proof of a confirmed campsite reservation).

We recommend that, wherever possible, you make the bookings in person or arrange for someone to do so on your behalf. In theory, the DWNP also allows you to make bookings over the phone or via email, but in practice getting anyone to answer the phone or reply to emails is far more challenging than it should be. If you do manage to make a phone or email booking, insist on receiving (either by fax, email or letter) a receipt with a reference number on it that you must keep and quote if you need to change your reservation.

When making the reservation, you need to tell the DWNP:

➡ the name of the preferred campsite(s) within the park – in order of preference if listing more than one

➡ the number of nights required, and the date of your arrival at and departure from the park and campsite

➡ the number of adults and children camping

➡ the vehicle's number plates and also the country in which the vehicle is registered (this may be waived if you don't yet have a vehicle)

➡ proof of your status if you are not paying 'foreigner' rates.

NATIONAL PARKS – BEST OF BOTSWANA

PARK	FEATURES	ACTIVITIES	BEST TIME
Central Kalahari Game Reserve	52,800 sq km; one of the largest protected areas in the world; semi-arid grassland	wildlife viewing; walking; visiting San villages	year-round
Chobe National Park	11,700 sq km; mosaic of grassland and woodland; high elephant population	wildlife viewing; birdwatching; fishing	Jun-Oct
Kgalagadi Transfrontier Park	38,000 sq km; straddles the South African border; semi-arid grassland	wildlife viewing; birdwatching	year-round
Khutse Game Reserve	2590 sq km; adjoins Central Kalahari Game Reserve; same features	wildlife viewing; walking; visiting San villages	year-round
Makgadikgadi & Nxai Pans NPs	7300 sq km; largest salt pans in the world; migratory zebras and wildebeest; flamingos	wildlife viewing; trekking with San; quad biking	Mar-Jul
Moremi Game Reserve	3800 sq km; grassland, flood plains and swamps; huge wildlife density	wildlife viewing; walking; scenic flights; boating	Jun-Oct
Northern Tuli Game Reserve	collection of private reserves; unique rock formations	wildlife viewing; horse riding; walking; night drives	May-Sep
Khama Rhino Sanctuary	43 sq km; last refuge of Botswana's rhinos	wildlife viewing; birdwatching	May-Oct

Once you have booked it is difficult to change anything, so make sure to plan your trip well and allow enough time to get there and look around. A refund (less a 10% administration charge) is only possible with more than 30 days' notice.

COSTS

Infants and children up to the age of seven are entitled to free entry into the national parks. Foreign adults/children aged eight to seventeen years pay P120/60. Camping/vehicles under 3500kg cost P50 each.

SURVIVAL GUIDE

❶ Directory A–Z

ACCOMMODATION

The story of Botswana's accommodation is a story of extremes. At one end, there are fabulously located campsites for self-drivers (the closest the country comes to budget accommodation outside the main towns). At the other extreme, there are top-end lodges where prices can be eye-wateringly high. In between, you will find some midrange options in the major towns and places such as the Okavango Panhandle, but elsewhere there's very little for the midrange (and nothing for the noncamping budget) traveller.

Prices

The following price ranges refer to a double room with bathroom. Unless otherwise stated, breakfast is included in the price. Upmarket places tend to price in US dollars rather than pula.

$ less than US$50
$$ US$50–100
$$$ more than US$100

Bed Levy & Government Tax

Note that all hotels, lodges, campsites and other forms of accommodation are required by the government to charge a P10 bed levy per person per night. This levy is rarely, if ever, included in quoted accommodation rates.

In addition to the levy, a 12% government tax is levied on hotels and lodges (but not all campsites) and, unlike the levy, is usually included in prices.

Seasons

While most budget and midrange options tend to have a standard room price, many top-end places change their prices according to season. High season is usually from June to November (and may also apply to Christmas, New Year and Easter, depending on the lodge), low season corresponds to the rains (December to March or April) and the shoulder is a short April and May window. The only exception is the Kalahari, where June to November is generally considered to be low season.

Camping

Just about every place of interest, including all major national parks, has a campsite. Once the domain of the Department of Wildlife and National Parks (DWNP), many of the campsites are now privately run. The change in ownership has seen prices rise considerably. In some cases, the companies in question have upgraded the ablutions blocks to have hot and cold showers and flush toilets, and they generally make sure the sites are in good nick. Others do little to maintain their sites, offer cold bucket showers and pit toilets and run inefficient booking systems. All campsites have braai (barbecue) pits.

All campsites *must* be booked in advance and they fill up fast in busy periods, such as during South African school holidays. It is very important to remember that you will not be allowed into almost every park run by the DWNP without a reservation for a campsite.

Camping areas are usually small, often with only two or three places to pitch a tent and/or park a vehicle.

Outside of the parks and reserves, some hotels and lodges also provide camping areas. Most private and hotel/lodge campsites have sit-down toilets, showers (often hot), braai pits and washing areas. One definite attraction is that campers can use the hotel bars and restaurants and splash around the hotel swimming pool for free.

Elsewhere, camping in the wild is permitted outside national parks, reserves, private land and away from government freehold areas. If you want to camp near a village, obtain permission from the village leader or police station and enquire about a suitable site.

Hotels

Every major town has at least one hotel, and the larger towns and tourist areas, such as Gaborone, Maun, Francistown and Kasane, offer several in different price ranges. In general, midrange and top-end travellers are well looked after, but budget travellers will struggle to find anything as cheap as the budget accommodation in Namibia (the really cheap places in Botswana often double as brothels). There's a relatively high demand for hotel rooms in Gaborone, in particular from business travellers, so it pays to book ahead here and also elsewhere in the high season.

BOOK YOUR STAY ONLINE

For more accommodation reviews by Lonely Planet authors, check out hotels. lonelyplanet.com. You'll find independent reviews, as well as recommendations on the best places to stay. Best of all, you can book online.

The range of hotel accommodation available includes rondavels, which are detached rooms or cottages with a private bathroom; B&B-type places, often with a shared bathroom (mostly in Gaborone); motel-style units with a private bathroom and, sometimes, cooking facilities, usually along the highways of eastern Botswana; and luxury hotels in major towns.

Lodges & Tented Camps

Botswana's claim to being Africa's most exclusive destination is built around its luxury lodges (sometimes called 'camps'). You'll find them where there are decent concentrations of wildlife, most notably in Chobe National Park, the Tuli Block, Moremi Game Reserve, all over the Okavango Delta and, to a lesser extent, the parks and reserves of the Kalahari. It's impossible to generalise about them, other than to say that most pride themselves on their isolation, exclusivity, luxury and impeccable service. Most feature permanent or semipermanent luxury tents, a communal dining area overlooking a water hole or other important geographical feature, and a swimming pool.

For many visitors, they're once-in-a-lifetime places with accommodation rates to match – some start at around US$1000/1500 per person per night in the low/high season, but many cost considerably more than that. Usually included in these rates are all meals, some drinks and most wildlife drives and other activities. Most places are only accessible by 4WD transfer or air; the latter will cost an extra US$150 to US$200 per leg.

ACTIVITIES
Hiking

Botswana lags behind neighbours Namibia and Zambia as a hiking destination, although a number of treks are possible.

Walking safaris in the company of an armed guard form part of the available activities at many lodges, and leaving the safety of your vehicle will sharpen your senses and your awareness of your surroundings. Places where such hiking excursions along nature trails are possible include the Okavango Delta, the Central Kalahari Game Reserve (CKGR) and the Makgadikgadi Pans. The treks run out of the luxury lodges of the Makgadikgadi Pans or the CKGR, for example, are a fascinating opportunity to explore the arid environs with San guides, who can point out the hidden details of the landscape and its specially adapted flora and fauna.

You don't need to stay at a luxury lodge or tented camp to explore a small corner of the delta on foot, as many of the *mokoro* expeditions organised from Maun include walking components. Also, a small but growing number of mobile safaris in the delta and Moremi Game Reserve, organised from Maun, involve multiday hikes.

Options are limited for more free-range trekking, but the Tsodilo Hills, where trails lead up to thousands of rock-art sites, are undoubtedly the premier spot. Guides are available from the main campsite in the region. Another possibility is the Tswapong Hills in the country's east, which sees very few tourists. For both, you'll need to be entirely self-sufficient.

Horse Riding

Cantering among herds of zebras and wildebeest is an unforgettable experience, and the horse-riding safaris in Botswana are second to none. You'll need to be an experienced rider as most horseback safaris in Botswana don't take beginners – after all, you need to be able to get yourself out of trouble should you encounter it.

Places where such safaris are possible:

African Animal Adventures (☑733 66 461; www.africananimaladventures.com) Expeditions from Maun.

Grassland Safari Lodge (☑72 104 270; www.grasslandlodge.com; camping P175, chalets per person Nov-May US$308, Jun-Oct US$358) Safaris into the Central Kalahari Game Reserve.

Mashatu Game Reserve (☑in South Africa +27 11-442 2267; www.mashatu.com; chalets/d US$765/1020, luxury tents US$562/750; ❈❋) In the Tuli Block.

Ride Botswana (☑71 671 608, 72 484 354; www.ridebotswana.com) Based in Maun, with expeditions to the delta and Kalahari

Uncharted Africa (☑in South Africa +27 11-447 1605; www.unchartedafrica.com) Out onto the salt pans of Makgadikgadi.

Mokoro Trips

Travelling around the channels of the Okavango Delta in a *mokoro* is a wonderful experience that is not to be missed. The *mokoro* is poled along the waterways by a skilled poler, much like an African gondola. Although you won't be spotting much wildlife from such a low viewpoint, it's a great way to appreciate the delta's birdlife and gain an appreciation, hopefully from a distance, of the formidable bulk of hippos.

Scenic Flights

A scenic flight of fancy in a light aircraft or helicopter high above the Okavango Delta is a thrilling activity. These can be arranged either in Maun directly with the operator or through your accommodation.

CUSTOMS REGULATIONS

Most items from elsewhere in the Southern African Customs Union (SACU) – Namibia, South Africa, Lesotho and Swaziland – may be imported duty free. You may be asked to declare new laptops and cameras, but this is very rarely enforced.

Visitors may bring into Botswana the following amounts of duty-free items: up to 400 cigarettes, 50 cigars or 250g of tobacco; 2L of wine or 1L of beer or spirits; and 50mL of perfume or 250mL of eau de cologne.

The most rigorous searches at customs posts are for fresh meat products – don't buy succulent steaks in South Africa for your camping barbecue and expect them to be allowed in.

There is no restriction on currency, though you may need to declare any pula or foreign currency you have on you when entering or leaving the country. This depends on the border crossing and who is on duty.

DANGERS & ANNOYANCES

Crime is rarely a problem in Botswana, and doesn't usually extend beyond occasional pickpocketing and theft from parked cars. Gaborone is one of Africa's safer cities, but it still pays to take a taxi after dark.

Although police and veterinary roadblocks, bureaucracy and bored officials may be tiresome, they're mostly harmless. Careful scrutiny is rare, but you may have to unpack your luggage for closer inspection at a border or veterinary checkpoint.

Road Safety

Although vehicle traffic is light on most roads outside of the major towns and cities, the most significant concern for most travellers is road safety. Botswana has one of the highest accident rates per capita in the world, and drunk and reckless driving are common, especially at month's end (wage day). Cattle, goats, sheep, donkeys and even elephants are deadly hazards on the road, especially at dusk and after dark when visibility is poor. Never drive at night unless you absolutely have to.

EMBASSIES & COMMISIONS

Most diplomatic missions are in Gaborone. Many more countries (such as Australia and New Zealand) have embassies or consulates in South Africa.

France (Map p46; ☑368 0800; www.ambafrance-bw.org; 761 Robinson Rd, Gaborone; ⊗8am-4pm Mon-Fri)

Germany (Map p46; ☑395 3143; www.gaborone.diplo.de; Queens Rd, Gaborone; ⊗9am-noon Mon-Fri)

Namibia (Map p49; ☑390 2181; namibhc@info.bw; Plot 186, Morara Close, Gaborone; ⊗7.30am-1pm & 2-4.30pm Mon-Fri)

South Africa (Map p46; ☑390 4800; sahcgabs@botsnet.bw; 29 Queens Rd, Gaborone; ⊗8am-noon & 1.30-4.30pm Mon-Fri)

UK (Map p46; ☑395 2841; www.gov.uk/government/world/botswana; Queens Rd, Gaborone; ⊗8am-4.30pm Mon-Thu, to 1pm Fri)

US (Map p49; ☑395 3982; http://botswana.usembassy.gov; Embassy Dr, Government Enclave, Gaborone; ⊗7.30am-5pm Mon-Thu, to 1.30pm Fri)

Zambia (Map p46; ☑395 1951; zamhico@work.co.bw; Plot No 1118, Queens Rd, The Mall,

Gaborone; ⊙ 8.30am-12.30pm & 2-4.30pm Mon-Fri)

Zimbabwe (Map p49; 🗐 391 4495; www. zimgaborone.gov.zw; Plot 8850, Orapa Close, Government Enclave, Gaborone; ⊙ 8am-1pm & 2-4.30pm Mon-Fri)

FOOD

The following price ranges refer to a main course.

$ less than US$10

$$ US$10–20

$$$ more than US$20

GAY & LESBIAN TRAVELLERS

Homosexuality, both gay and lesbian, is illegal in Botswana. Article 164 of Botswana's Penal Code prescribes a maximum seven-year prison term for 'carnal knowledge…against the order of nature', and intolerance has increased in the region over the last few years due to the homophobic statements of leaders in neighbouring Namibia and Zimbabwe. But the situation is more nuanced than it may first appear. Botswana's employment laws forbid workplace discrimination or dismissal on the basis of a person's sexual orientation, and Botswana's former president, Festus Mogae, told the BBC in 2011 that he had, while in office, directed police to neither harass nor arrest gays and lesbians. Gay and lesbian people with whom we spoke in Botswana suggested that the situation, at least in Gaborone, is relatively relaxed and that they were able live quite openly as gays and lesbians.

Even so, given the sensitivity of the subject and the strongly held views of many Batswana, it is advisable to refrain from any overt displays of affection in public.

INTERNET ACCESS

Cyber cafes Common in large and medium-sized towns; connection speeds fluctuate wildly.

Post offices Some post offices, including in Kasane, have a few internet-enabled PCs.

Wireless Reasonably common in midrange and top-end hotels in towns, but very rarely available in safari lodges.

MAPS

The best paper map of Botswana is the *Botswana* (1:1,000,000) map published by Tracks4Africa (www.tracks4africa.co.za). Updated every couple of years using detailed traveller feedback, the map is printed on tear-free, waterproof paper and includes distances *and* estimated travel times. Used in conjunction with Tracks4Africa's unrivalled GPS maps, it's far and away the best mapping product on the market. Even so, be aware that, particularly in the Okavango Delta, last year's trails may this year be underwater, depending on water levels, so these maps should never be a substitute for expert local knowledge.

If for some reason you are unable to get hold of the Tracks4Africa map, the only other maps that we recommend are those published by Shell Oil Botswana and Veronica Roodt. The *Shell Tourist Map of Botswana* (1:1,750,000) is available at major bookshops in Botswana and South Africa.

Probably of more interest are Shell's zoomed-in maps (with varying scales) of the various reserves and other popular areas. These include numerous GPS coordinates for important landmarks and the tracks are superimposed onto satellite images of the area in question. Some are a little out of date, but they're still excellent. Titles include *Okavango Delta*, *Chobe National Park*, *Moremi Game Reserve* and *Kgalagadi Transfrontier Park*.

MONEY

There are ATMs in major towns. Credit cards are accepted in most top-end hotels, but lodges and tour operators require advance payment by bank transfer. Otherwise, bring US dollars in cash.

ATMs

Credit cards can be used in ATMs displaying the appropriate sign, or to obtain cash advances over the counter in many banks – Visa and MasterCard are among the most widely recognised. Transaction fees can be prohibitive and usually apply per transaction rather than by the amount you're withdrawing – take out as much as you can each time. Check also with your bank before leaving home to see if some banks have agreements with your home bank that work out cheaper than others.

You'll find ATMs at all the main bank branches throughout Botswana, including in Gaborone, Maun, Francistown and Kasane, and this is undoubtedly the simplest (and safest) way to handle your money while travelling.

Cash

The unit of currency is the Botswanan pula (P). Pula means 'blessings' or 'rain', the latter of which is as precious as money in this largely desert country. Notes come in denominations of P10, P20, P50 and P100, and coins (thebe, or 'shield') are in denominations of 5t, 10t, 25t, 50t, P1, P2 and P5.

Most common foreign currencies can be exchanged, but not every branch of every bank will do so. Therefore it's best to stick to US dollars, euros, UK pounds and South African rand, which are all easy to change.

Foreign currency, typically US dollars, is also accepted by a number of midrange and top-end hotels, lodges and tour operators. South African rand can also be used on Botswanan combis (minibuses) and buses going to/from South Africa, and to pay for Botswanan vehicle taxes at South Africa–Botswana borders.

Most banks and foreign-exchange offices won't touch Zambian kwacha and (sometimes) Namibian dollars; in border areas you can sometimes pay at some businesses with the latter. To make sure you don't get caught out, buy/sell these currencies at or near the respective borders.

There are five commercial banks in the country with branches in all the main towns and major villages. Although you will get less favourable rates at a bureau de change, they are a convenient option if the lines at the banks are particularly long.

There is no black market in Botswana. Anyone offering to exchange money on the street is doing so illegally and is probably setting you up for a scam, the exception being the guys who change pula for South African rand in front of South Africa–bound minibuses – locals use their services, so they can be trusted.

For current exchange rates, log on to www.xe.com.

Credit/Debit Cards

All major credit cards, especially Visa and MasterCard, but also American Express and Diners Club, are widely accepted in most shops, restaurants and hotels (but only in *some* petrol stations).

Major branches of Barclays Bank and Standard Chartered Bank also deal with cash advances over the counter and don't charge commissions for Visa and MasterCard. Almost every town has at least one branch of Barclays and/or Standard Chartered that offers foreign-exchange facilities, but not all have the authority or technology for cash advances.

Tipping

While tipping isn't obligatory, the government's official policy of promoting upmarket tourism has raised expectations in many hotels and restaurants. A service charge may be added as a matter of course, in which case there's no need to leave a tip. If there is no service charge and the service has been good, leave around 10%.

It is also a good idea to tip the men who watch your car in public car parks and the attendants at service stations who wash your windscreens. A tip of around P10 is appropriate.

Guides and drivers of safari vehicles will also expect a tip, especially if you've spent a number of days under their care.

Most safari companies suggest the following as a rule of thumb:

➜ guides/drivers – US$10 per person per day
➜ *mokoro* trackers and polers – US$5 each per person per day
➜ camp or lodge staff – US$10 per guest per day (usually placed in a communal box)
➜ transfer drivers and porters – US$3

OPENING HOURS

The whole country practically closes down on Sunday.

Banks 8.30am–3.30pm Monday to Friday, 8.15am–10.45am Saturday

National parks 6am–6.30pm April to September, 5.30am–7pm October to March

Post offices 9am–5pm Monday to Friday, 9am–noon Saturday, or 7.30am–noon and 2pm–4.30pm Monday to Friday, 7.30am–12.30pm Saturday

Restaurants 11am–11pm Monday to Saturday; some also open the same hours on Sunday

PUBLIC HOLIDAYS

During official public holidays, all banks, government offices and major businesses are closed. However, hotels, restaurants, bars, smaller shops, petrol stations, museums and national parks and reserves stay open, while border crossings and public transport continue operating as normal. Government offices, banks and some businesses also take the day off after New Year's Day, President's Day, Botswana/Independence Day and Boxing Day.

New Year's Day 1 January

Easter Good Friday, Easter Saturday and Easter Monday (March/April)

Labour Day 1 May

Ascension Day May/June, 40 days after Easter Sunday

Sir Seretse Khama Day 1 July

President's Day Third Friday in July

Botswana/Independence Day 30 September

Christmas Day 25 December

Boxing Day 26 December

TELEPHONE

The operator of Botswana's fixed-line telephone service is Botswana Telecom (BTC; www.btc.bw). Local and domestic calls at peak times start at P40 per minute and rise according to the distance. When deciding when to call, remember that prices drop by up to one-third for local and domestic calls, and 20% for international calls, from 8pm to 7am Monday to Friday, 1pm to midnight Saturday and all day Sunday. These discounts don't apply if you use the operator.

There are no internal area codes in Botswana. The country code for Botswana is 🖉 267 and the international access code is 🖉 00.

Mobile Phones

Botswana has two main mobile-phone networks, Mascom Wireless (www.mascom.bw) and Orange Botswana (www.orange.co.bw), of which Mascom is the largest provider. All providers have dealers in most large and medium-sized towns, where you can buy phones, SIM cards and top up your credit. Government-run Botswana Telecommunications

Corporation (www.btc.bw) runs the beMobile network, but its future was uncertain at the time of writing.

The coverage map for the two main providers is improving with each passing year, but when deciding whether to get a local SIM card, remember that there's simply no mobile coverage across large parts of the country (including much of the Kalahari and Okavango Delta). That said, the main highway system is generally covered.

Most Botswana mobile numbers begin with ⏻71, 72 or 73.

TIME

Botswana is two hours ahead of GMT/UTC, so when it's noon in Botswana, it's 10am in London, 5am in New York, 2am in Los Angeles and 8pm in Sydney (not taking into account daylight-saving time in these countries). There is no daylight-saving time in Botswana.

TOURIST INFORMATION

The Department of Tourism, rebranded in the public sphere as Botswana Tourism (www.botswanatourism.co.bw), has an excellent website and a growing portfolio of tourist offices around the country. These tourist offices don't always have their finger on the pulse, but they can be an extremely useful source of brochures from local hotels, tour operators and other tourist services.

For information on national parks, you're better off contacting the Department of Wildlife and National Parks (p86).

Another useful resource is the **Regional Tourism Organisation of Southern Africa** (⏻ in South Africa +27 11-315 2420; www.retosa.co.za), which promotes tourism throughout Southern Africa, including Botswana.

There are tourist offices in the following places:

➡ Gaborone (p48)
➡ Maun (p72)
➡ Kasane (p62)
➡ Francistown (p53)
➡ **Kang** (⏻ 651 7070; www.botswanatourism.co.bw; Trans Kalahari Hwy/A2; ⏱7.30am-4.30pm Mon-Fri, 9am-2pm Sat)

TRAVELLERS WITH DISABILITIES

People with limited mobility will have a difficult time travelling around Botswana – although there are many disabled people living in the country, facilities are very few and much of the country can be an obstacle course. Along streets and footpaths, kerbs and uneven surfaces will often present problems for wheelchair users, and only a very few upmarket hotels/lodges and restaurants have installed ramps and railings. Also, getting to and around any of the major lodges or camps in the national wildlife

parks will be extremely difficult, given their remote and wild locations.

Make sure to choose the areas you visit carefully, and clearly explain your requirements to the lodge and/or safari operator when making your original enquiry. The swampy environs of the Okavango Delta will be particularly challenging for people who have special needs, although the lodges in the Kalahari and the Makgadikgadi Pans are relatively accessible, providing you are travelling with an able-bodied companion. It is also worth bearing in mind that almost any destination in Botswana will require a long trip in a 4WD and/or a small plane.

Download Lonely Planet's free Accessible Travel guide from http://lptravel.to/Accessible Travel.

VISAS

Most visitors can obtain tourist visas at the international airports and borders (and the nearest police stations in lieu of an immigration official at remote border crossings). Visas on arrival are valid for 30 days – and possibly up to 90 days if requested at the time of entry – and are available for free to passport holders from most Commonwealth countries (but not Ghana, India, Nigeria, Pakistan and Sri Lanka), all EU countries, the USA and countries in the Southern African Customs Union (SACU), ie South Africa, Namibia, Lesotho and Swaziland.

If you hold a passport from any other country, apply for a 30-day tourist visa at an overseas Botswanan embassy or consulate. Where there is no Botswanan representation, try going to a British embassy or consulate.

Tourists are allowed to stay in Botswana for a maximum of 90 days every 12 months, so a 30-day visa may be extended twice. Visas can be extended for free at immigration offices in Gaborone, Francistown, Maun and Kasane. Whether you're required to show an onward ticket and/or sufficient funds at this time depends on the official(s).

Anyone travelling to Botswana from an area infected with yellow fever needs proof of vaccination before they can enter the country.

ⓘ Getting There & Away

Botswana is not the easiest or cheapest place in the world to reach by air, and some travellers prefer to enter the country overland from South Africa or, more recently, Namibia as part of a longer safari.

Flights, tours and rail tickets can be booked online at www.lonelyplanet.com/bookings.

ENTERING BOTSWANA

Entering Botswana is usually straightforward provided you are carrying a valid passport. Visas are available on arrival for most nationalities and are issued in no time. If travelling with children, parents should be aware of the need to carry birth certificates and may require other documents (see p719).

If you're crossing into the country overland and in your own (or rented) vehicle, expect to endure (sometimes quite cursory, sometimes strict) searches for fresh meat, fresh fruit and dairy products, most of which will be confiscated if found. For vehicles rented in South Africa, Namibia or other regional countries, you will need to show a letter from the owner that you have permission to drive the car into Botswana, in addition to all other registration documents.

At all border crossings you must pay P120 (a combination of road levy and third-party insurance) if you're driving your own vehicle. Hassles from officialdom are rare.

For a moderately useful list of the government's entry requirements, see www.botswanatourism.co.bw/entryFormalities.php. The Tracks4Africa *Botswana* map has opening hours for all border crossings.

Passport

All visitors entering Botswana must hold a passport that is valid for at least six months. Also, allow a few empty pages for stamp-happy immigration officials, especially if you plan on crossing over to Zimbabwe and/or Zambia to Victoria Falls.

AIR

Botswana's main airport, Sir Seretse Khama International Airport (p48), is located 11km north of Gaborone. Although it's well served with flights from Jo'burg and Harare, it's seldom used by tourists as an entry point into the country. Other, more popular entry points are **Kasane Airport** (BBK; ☑ 625 0133, 368 8200) and Maun Airport (p72).

The national carrier is **Air Botswana** (BP; ☑ 390 5500; www.airbotswana.co.bw), which flies routes within Southern Africa. Air Botswana has offices in Gaborone, Francistown, Maun, Kasane and Victoria Falls (Zimbabwe). It's generally cheaper to book Air Botswana tickets online than through one of its offices.

In addition to **Air Namibia** (☑ in Maun 686 0391; www.airnamibia.com) and **South African Airways** (☑ in Gaborone 397 2397; www.flysaa.com), which do fly into Botswana, the country is served by a number of special charter flights.

LAND

Botswana has a well-developed road network with easy access from neighbouring countries. All borders are open daily. It is advisable to try to reach the crossings as early in the day as possible to allow time for any potential delays. Remember also that despite the official opening hours, immigration posts at some smaller

border crossings sometimes close for lunch between 12.30pm and 1.45pm. At remote border crossings on the Botswanan side, you may need to get your visa at the nearest police station in lieu of an immigration post.

To/From Namibia

There are five border crossings between Botswana and Namibia:

Gcangwa–Tsumkwe Little-used crossing along a 4WD-only track close to Botswana's Tsodilo Hills.

Kasane–Mpalila Island Crossing this border is only possible for guests who have prebooked accommodation at upmarket lodges on the island.

Mamuno Remote but busy crossing on the road between Ghanzi and Windhoek.

Mohembo Connects Shakawe, Maun and the Okavango Panhandle with northeastern Namibia.

Ngoma Bridge East of Kasane, connecting to Namibia's Caprivi Strip.

Bus

The public-transport options between the two countries are few. Going to Namibia, one option is to catch the daily combi (minibus) from Ghanzi to Mamuno (three hours) and then to cross the border on foot, bearing in mind that this crossing is about 1km long. You will then have to hitch a ride from the Namibian side at least to Gobabis, where you can catch a train or other transport to Windhoek. It's time-consuming and unreliable at best.

Tok Tokkie Shuttle (☑ in Namibia 061-300 743; www.shuttlesnamibia.com) makes the 12-hour Windhoek–Gaborone run, departing Windhoek at 6pm on Wednesday and Friday, and from Gaborone at 1pm on Thursday and Saturday. One-way fares cost N$500 and there's free wi-fi and air-con on board.

Car & Motorcycle

Drivers crossing the border at Mohembo must secure an entry permit for Mahango Game Reserve. This is free if you're transiting, or N$100 per person per day plus N$50 per vehicle per day if you want to drive around the reserve (which is possible in a 2WD).

From Divundu, turn west towards Rundu and then southwest for Windhoek, or east towards Katima Mulilo (Namibia), Kasane (Botswana) and Victoria Falls (Zimbabwe), or take the ferry to Zambia.

To/From South Africa

Gaborone is only 280km as the crow flies from Jo'burg along a good road link.

There are 14 border crossings between South Africa and Botswana. Five of these provide access of sorts from the South African side of the

Kgalagadi Transfrontier Park, five are handy for Gaborone, and the remaining four are good for eastern Botswana and the Tuli Block.

The major crossings:

Bokspits The best South African access to the Kgalagadi Transfontier Park.

Martin's Drift, Zanzibar, Platjan & Pont Drift Eastern Botswana and the Tuli Block from the Northern Transvaal.

Pioneer Gate Connects Gaborone (via Lobatse and Zeerust) with Jo'burg.

Ramatlabama Connects Gaborone with Mafikeng.

Tlokweng Connects Gaborone and Jo'burg via the Madikwe Game Reserve in South Africa.

Bus

Intercape Mainliner (www.intercape.co.za) runs a service from Jo'burg to Gaborone (from SAR420, 6½ hours, one daily); while you need to get off the bus to sort out any necessary visa formalities, you'll rarely be held up for too long at the border. From Gaborone, the Intercape Mainliner runs from the petrol station beside the Mall and tickets should be booked a week or so in advance; this can be done online.

The **Mahube Express** (Map p49; ☑ 396 0488, 74 236 441; www.mahubeexpress.com) runs twice-daily services from Gaborone to Johannesburg's OR Tambo International Airport, leaving the Square Mart close to the city centre at 7am and 2pm. Tickets cost P300.

You can also travel between South Africa and Botswana by combi. From the far (back) end of the bus station in Gaborone, combis leave when full to a number of South African destinations, including Jo'burg (P310/R4100, six to seven hours). Be warned that you'll be dropped at Jo'burg's Park Station, which is not a safe place to linger. Combis also travel from Selebi-Phikwe to the border at Martin's Drift (P52, two hours).

Public transport between the two countries bears South African number plates and/or signs on the door marked 'ZA Cross Border Transport'.

Car & Motorcycle

Most border crossings are clearly marked, but it is vital to note that some crossings over the Limpopo and Molopo Rivers (the latter is in Botswana's south) are drifts (river fords) that cannot be crossed by 2WD in wet weather. In times of very high water, these crossings may be closed to all traffic.

To/from Zimbabwe

There are three land border crossings between Botswana and Zimbabwe.

Kazungula The main crossing point from Kasane to Victoria Falls.

Pandamatenga A little-used backroads crossing off the road between Kasane and Nata.

Ramokgweban–Plumtree Connects Francistown with Bulawayo and Harare.

Bus

Incredibly, there is no public transport between Kasane, the gateway to one of Botswana's major attractions (Chobe National Park), and Victoria Falls. Other than hitching, the only cross-border options are the 'tourist shuttle' minibuses that take about one hour and can be arranged through most hotels, camps and tour operators in Kasane. There is little or no coordination between combi companies in either town, so combis often return from Victoria Falls to Kasane empty. Most combis won't leave Kasane unless they have at least two passengers.

Some hotels and lodges in Kasane also offer private transfers to Livingstone/Victoria Falls (from P1450, two hours). They usually pick up booked passengers from their hotels at around 10am.

From the Zimbabwean side of the border, try Backpackers Bazaar in Victoria Falls. Some hotels and hostels in Zimbabwe will arrange for your transport from the border, but you need to contact them beforehand.

Elsewhere, buses leave early to mid-afternoon from the bus station in Francistown bound for Bulawayo (P80, two hours) and Harare (P150, five hours). For anywhere else in western Zimbabwe, get a connection in Bulawayo.

RIVER
To/from Zambia

Botswana and Zambia share one of the world's shortest international borders: about 750m across the Zambezi River. The only way across the river is by ferry from Kazungula.

At the time of writing there was no cross-border public transport. A combi from Kasane to the border crossing at Kazungula should cost no more than P50. Once there, you'll need to complete the formalities and take the ferry on foot. There is no regular public transport from the Zambian side of the river, although there is one combi that goes to Dambwa, 3km west of Livingstone. If you don't have a vehicle, ask for a lift to Livingstone, Lusaka or points beyond at the ferry terminal or on the ferry itself.

Visas into Zambia cost US$50 per person for most nationalities. You'll also have to pay the Zambian road toll (US$48), carbon tax (ZMW150) and third-party vehicle insurance (ZMW487, valid for one month and payable even if you already have insurance) if you are taking a vehicle into Zambia.

If you're heading to Liuwa National Park and other places in Zambia's far west, consider crossing into Namibia at Ngoma and driving around 70km to the Namibia–Zambia border at Katima Mulilo – although it involves an extra crossing, the roads are much better on the Zambian side.

❶ Getting Around

Botswana's public-transport network is limited.

Car Hiring a vehicle is the best and most practical option.

Air Although domestic air services are fairly frequent and usually reliable, Air Botswana (and charter flights) is not cheap and only a handful of towns are regularly served.

Bus & Combi Public buses and combis (minibuses) are also cheap and reasonably frequent, but are confined to sealed roads between towns.

AIR

Air Botswana (p93) operates a limited number of domestic routes. It's usually much cheaper to purchase tickets online through the Air Botswana website than in person at one of its offices. Sample one-way fares at the time of writing:

Gaborone–Francistown P1406
Gaborone–Kasane P2060
Gaborone–Maun P1791
Kasane–Maun P715

Children aged under two, sitting on the lap of an adult, are charged 10% of the fare and children aged between two and 12 are charged 50% of the fare. Passengers are allowed 20kg of luggage (unofficially, a little more is often permitted if the flight is not full).

Charter Flights

Charter flights are often the best – and sometimes the only – way to reach remote lodges, but they are an expensive extra cost; fares are not usually included in the quoted rates for most lodges.

On average, a one-way fare between Maun and a remote lodge in the Okavango Delta will set you back around US$150 to US$250. These services are now highly regulated and flights must be booked as part of a safari package with a mandatory reservation at one of the lodges. This is essential: you can't simply turn up in these remote locations and expect to find a bed for the night, as many lodges are very small. Likewise, you are not permitted to book accommodation at a remote lodge in the delta without also booking a return airfare at the same time. Packages can be booked through agencies in Maun. Wilderness Air (p68) and Mack Air (p68) are the main companies.

It is very important to note that passengers on charter flights are only allowed 10kg to 15kg (and rarely 20kg) of luggage each; check the exact amount when booking. However, if you have an extra 2kg to 3kg, the pilot will usually only mind if the plane is full of passengers.

If you can't stretch the budget to staying in a remote lodge, you can still book a flight over the delta with one of the scenic flight or helicopter companies in Maun (p67).

BUS & COMBI

Buses and combis regularly travel to all major towns and villages throughout Botswana, but are less frequent in sparsely populated areas such as western Botswana and the Kalahari. Public transport to smaller villages is often nonexistent, unless the village is along a major route.

The extent and frequency of buses and combis also depends on the quantity and quality of roads. For example, there is no public transport along the direct route between Maun and Kasane (ie through Chobe National Park), and services elsewhere can be suspended if roads are flooded. Also bear in mind that there are very few long-distance services, so most people travelling between Gaborone and Kasane or Maun, for example, will need a connection in Francistown.

Buses are usually comfortable and normally leave at a set time, regardless of whether they're full. Finding out the departure times for buses is a matter of asking around the bus station, because schedules are not posted anywhere. Combis leave when full, usually from the same station as buses. Tickets for all public buses and combis cannot be bought in advance; they can only be purchased on board.

CAR & MOTORCYCLE

The best way to travel around Botswana is to hire a vehicle. With your own car you can avoid public transport and organised tours. Remember, however, that distances are long.

You cannot hire motorbikes in Botswana and motorbikes are *not* permitted in national parks and reserves for safety reasons.

Driving Licence

Your home driving licence is valid for six months in Botswana, but if it isn't written in English you must provide a certified translation. In any case, it is advisable to obtain an International Driving Permit (IDP). Your national automobile association can issue this and it is valid for 12 months.

Fuel & Spare Parts

The cost of fuel is relatively expensive in Botswana – at the time of writing it was P7.62 for petrol and P7.35 for diesel – but prices vary according to the remoteness of the petrol station. Petrol stations are open 24 hours in Gaborone, Francistown, Maun, Mahalapye and Palapye; elsewhere, they open from about 7am to 7pm daily.

Hire

To rent a car you must be aged at least 21 (some companies require drivers to be over 25) and have been a licenced driver in your home country for at least two years (sometimes five).

Insurance

Insurance is *strongly* recommended. No matter who you hire your car from, make sure you understand what is included in the price (such as unlimited kilometres, tax and so on) and what your liabilities are. Most local insurance policies do not include cover for damage to windscreens and tyres.

Third-party motor insurance is a minimum requirement in Botswana. However, it is also advisable to take damage (collision) waiver, which costs around P150 extra per day for a 2WD and about P300 per day for a 4WD. Loss (Theft) Waiver is also an extra worth having. For both types of insurance, the excess liability is about P5000 for a 2WD and P10,000 for a 4WD. If you're only going for a short period of time, it may be worth taking out the Super Collision Waiver, which covers absolutely everything, albeit at a price.

Road Conditions

Good sealed roads link most major population centres. The most notable exception is the direct route between Kasane and Maun – a horribly corrugated gravel track – meaning that you'll need to take the long way around via Gweta and Nata. The road from Maun to Shakawe past the Okavango Panhandle is generally reasonable, but beware of potholes.

Tracks with sand, mud, gravel and rocks (and sometimes all four) – normally accessible by 2WD except during exceptional rains – connect most villages and cross a few national parks.

Most other 'roads' are poorly defined – and badly mapped – and should only be attempted by 4WD. In the worst of the wet season (December to February), 4WDs should carry a winch on some tracks (eg through Chobe or Moremi National Parks). A compass or, better, GPS unit with the Tracks4Africa maps loaded is essential for driving by 4WD around the salt pans of the Kalahari or northern Botswana at any time.

Road Rules

To drive a car in Botswana, you must be at least 18 years old. Like most other Southern African countries, traffic keeps to the left side of the road. The national speed limit is 60km/h up to 120km/h on sealed roads; when passing through towns and villages, assume a speed limit of 60km/h, even in the absence of any signs. Mobile police units routinely set up speed cameras along major roads, particularly between Gaborone and Francistown and between Maun and Gweta – on-the-spot fines operate on a sliding scale, but can go as high as P500 if you're 30km/h over the limit and you may be asked to pay on the spot. On gravel roads, limits are set at 60km/h to 80km/h; it's 40km/h in all national parks and reserves.

Other road rules to be aware of:

➡ Sitting on the roof of a moving vehicle is illegal.

➡ Wearing seatbelts (where installed) is compulsory in the front (but not back) seats.

➡ Drink-driving is against the law, and your insurance policy will be invalid if you have an accident while drunk.

➡ Driving without a licence is a serious offence.

➡ If you have an accident causing injury, it must be reported to the authorities within 48 hours. If vehicles have sustained only minor damage and there are no injuries – and all parties agree – you can exchange names and addresses and sort it out later through your insurance companies.

➡ In theory, owners are responsible for keeping their livestock off the road, but in practice animals wander wherever they want. If you hit a domestic animal, your distress (and possible vehicle damage) will be compounded by trying to find the owner and the red tape involved when filing a claim.

➡ Wild animals, including elephants and the estimated three million wild donkeys in Botswana, are a hazard, even along the highways. The Maun–Nata and Nata–Kasane roads are frequently traversed by elephants. The chances of hitting a wild or domestic animal is far, far greater after dark, so driving at night is definitely not recommended.

➡ One common, but minor, annoyance are the so-called buffalo fences (officially called Veterinary Cordon Fences). These are set up to stop the spread of disease from wild animals to livestock. In most cases your vehicle may be searched (they're looking for fresh meat or dairy products) and you may have to walk (and put additional pairs of shoes) through a soda solution and drive your car through soda-treated water.

LOCAL TRANSPORT

Public transport in Botswana is geared towards the needs of the local populace and is confined to main roads between major population centres. Although cheap and reliable, it is of little use to the traveller as most of Botswana's tourist attractions lie off the beaten track.

Combis, recognisable by their blue number plates, circulate according to set routes around major towns; ie Gaborone, Kasane, Maun, Ghanzi, Molepolole, Mahalapye, Palapye, Francistown, Selebi-Phikwe, Lobatse and Kanye. They are very frequent, inexpensive and generally reliable. However, they aren't terribly safe (most drive too fast), especially on long journeys, and they only serve the major towns. They can also be crowded.

Lesotho

POP 2.1 MILLION / ☎266

Includes ➡

Maseru	100
Morija	103
Roma	104
Thaba-Bosiu	104
Northeastern Highlands	106
Semonkong	108
Malealea	109
Mafeteng	110
Quthing	110

Best Places to Eat

➡ Maliba Lodge (p105)

➡ No.7 Restaurant (p100)

➡ Sky Restaurant (p107)

➡ Semonkong Lodge (p108)

Best Places to Sleep

➡ Malealea Lodge (p109)

➡ Maliba Lodge (p105)

➡ Semonkong Lodge (p108)

➡ Sani Mountain Lodge (p108)

➡ Kick4Life Hotel (p100)

Why Go?

Beautiful, culturally rich, safe, affordable and easily accessible from Durban and Johannesburg, mountainous Lesotho (le-*soo*-too) is a vastly underrated travel destination. The contrast with South Africa could not be more striking, with the Basotho people's distinct personality and the altitudinous terrain's topographical extremes. Even a few days in Lesotho's hospitable mountain lodges and trading posts will give you a fresh perspective on Southern Africa.

This is essentially an alpine country, where villagers on horseback in multicoloured balaclavas and blankets greet you round precipitous bends. The hiking and trekking – often on a famed Basotho pony – is world class and the infrastructure of the three stunning national parks continues to improve.

The 1000m-high 'lowlands' offer craft shopping and sights, but don't miss a trip to the southern, central or northeastern highlands, where streams traverse an ancient dinosaur playground. This is genuine adventure travel.

When to Go
Maseru

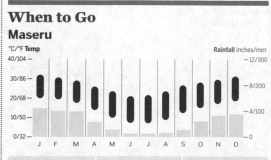

Mar–Apr Purple cosmos flowers in the green meadows and cool autumn temperatures.

Jun–Aug See snow frosting the mountaintops and hit the slopes at Afriski Mountain Resort.

Sep Morija Arts Festival celebrates Sotho culture; peach blossoms colour the landscape.

Lesotho Highlights

1 **Semonkong** (p108), **Malealea** (p109), **Roma** (p104) or **Ramabanta** (p104) Experiencing unique lodge accommodation in these picturesque villages.

2 **Sani Pass** (p107) Absorbing awesome vistas and hiking the challenging wilderness hikes of the northern highlands.

3 **Ts'ehlanyane National Park** (p105) Revelling in the underrated nature and hikes (and luxury lodge) of this wilderness area.

4 **Semonkong to Ketane Falls** (p108) Hiking from through the beautiful Thaba Putsoa mountains to the magnificent Ketane Falls.

5 **Quthing** (p110) Stomping for dinosaur prints in southern Lesotho.

6 **Thaba-Bosiu** (p104) Climbing to Lesotho's most important historical site outside Maseru.

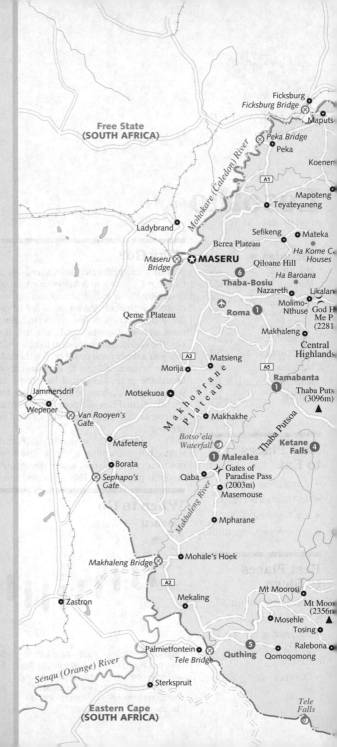

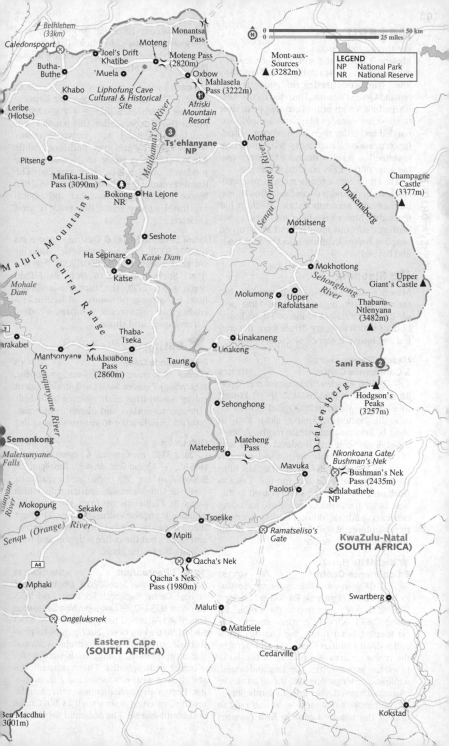

MASERU

POP 430,000 / ELEV 1600M

Maseru is one of the world's more low-key capital cities. It sprawls across Lesotho's lower-lying western edge, rimmed by the Berea and Qeme Plateaus. Founded by the British in 1869 as an administrative post, over the past few decades Maseru has rapidly expanded and today there's a modicum of traffic congestion. A major city-rebuilding programme has hidden many of the once-visible scars of the 1998 political unrest.

The city boasts a temperate climate, well-stocked shops and a decent selection of restaurants and accommodation. While it has few sights, Maseru is where you can get your bearings, sort out logistics and stock up on supplies before heading into the highlands and beyond.

🛏 Sleeping

Maseru's B&B scene is fairly modest, but there is no shortage of choices. Most people kick on to stay at Roma or Thaba-Bosiu, both of which are easy drives from the capital and have a few good sleeping options.

Maseru Backpackers & Conference Centre HOSTEL $

(☏2232 5166; www.lesothodurhamlink.org; Airport Rd; camping/dm/r M90/160/450; P🐾) Linked to a British Anglican NGO and run by locals, this hostel has sparse, clean four- to eight-bed dorms and private rooms. A Basotho-style self-catering rondavel (round hut; M550), with a double, twin and lounge, is right on Maqalika Reservoir. It's 3km from the city centre; look out for the 'Lesotho Durham Link' sign. The main reason to stay here is for the outdoor activities, including canoeing and kayaking on the reservoir, rock climbing, abseiling and archery. Meals are available with notice.

★ Kick4Life Hotel & Conference Centre HOTEL $$

(☏2832 0707; www.kick4life.org; Lesotho Football for Hope Centre, Nightingale Rd; s/d incl breakfast M750/800; P🐾) Attached to the football-focused NGO Kick4Life, this smart, soccer-themed hotel funds the charity's work and its staff includes Kick4Life protégées. In the reception area is a picture of two lucky Lesothan lads meeting the England squad, while soccer strips decorate the 12 attractive rooms, all named after famous footballers.

The terrace's city view is second only to that of the nearby **Lesotho Sun** (www.sun international.com; Hilton Rd; 🐾) bar; it also overlooks the 11-a-side pitch. Transfers to/ from Ladybrand in South Africa are available (per person M150).

Lancer's Inn HOTEL $$

(☏2231 2114; www.lancersinn.co.ls; cnr Kingsway & Pioneer Rd; s/d M925/1025; P🐾) Owned by the Dutch ambassador, this popular central business hotel has renovated rooms with satellite TV and open bathroom, while garden paths meander to pleasant stone rondavels and self-catering chalets. The **Rendezvous** (lunch/dinner mains M60/90; ⏱noon-11.30pm) restaurant, bar and adjoining travel agency make this place a good package.

Avani Lesotho Hotel & Casino HOTEL $$$

(☏2224 3000; www.minorhotels.com; Hilton Rd; s/d incl breakfast from M1800/1900; P🐾) Surveying Maseru from its hilltop perch since 1979, the capital's landmark hotel has a range of rooms and facilities including two restaurants, two bars, a casino, a travel agent and shops.

🍴 Eating

Renaissance Café CAFE $

(Pioneer Mall; mains M70; ⏱7am-9pm Mon-Sat, to 6pm Sun) Pioneer Mall's only independent eatery is a no-frills affair, offering meal deals (Tuesday to Friday) and dishes from breakfasts and sandwiches to stir-fries and grills.

Ouh La La CAFE $

(☏2832 3330; cnr Kingsway & Pioneer Rd; mains M45-80; ⏱7.30am-9pm Mon-Fri, 8am-7pm Sat, 9.30am-4pm Sun; 🐾) Locals and expats mix easily in this streetside garden cafe, which takes its Gallic theme from the adjoining Alliance Française cultural centre. The light menu is mostly sandwiches, crêpes, pastries and salads, but the coffee is decent and wine is available by the glass.

★ No.7 Restaurant INTERNATIONAL $$

(☏2832 0707; www.kick4life.org; Lesotho Football for Hope Centre, Nightingale Rd; mains lunch M60-95, dinner M75-130; ⏱7am-10pm Mon-Sat, to noon Sun; 🐾) Attached to football-focused NGO Kick4Life and its hotel, No.7 pumps its profits back into Kick4Life's charitable work and the team includes young locals training for a career in hospitality. The restaurant is a stylish spot with city views and a menu fusing European sophistication with Basotho touches, offering dishes such as fillet steak and bouillabaisse. The halloumi salad is superb. On the way in, you might pass Kick-4Life program members playing football.

Piri Piri
INTERNATIONAL $$

(Orpen Rd; mains M85-130; ⏱11am-10pm Mon-Sat) This restaurant near the Maseru Sun does Portuguese, Mozambican and South African dishes, including steaks, seafood, *feijoada* (a traditional Portuguese stew) and piri-piri chicken. Choose between romantic, low-lit rooms and a gazebo in the garden.

Regal Restaurant
INDIAN $$

(📱2231 3930; off Kingsway; mains M60-130; ⏱11.30am-2.30pm & 6-9.30pm; 📱) Occupying a Basotho hat–style building, this 1st-floor Indian restaurant is a favourite among businessmen and politicians. Lesotho's only Indian eatery, it serves classics such as korma, madras, rogan josh and vegetable curries. The service is professional, the Hindi music is unobtrusive and you can almost imagine you're in a British curry house.

🔒 Shopping

Pioneer Mall (www.pioneer.co.ls; cnr Pioneer & Mpilo Rds; ⏱9am-6pm Mon-Fri, to 4pm Sat, to 2pm Sun) has banks, an internet cafe, a currency-exchange bureau, a Western Union branch and a pharmacy. If you're looking for a souvenir, head to the Basotho Hat building.

Basotho Hat
ARTS & CRAFTS

(Kingsway; ⏱8am-4.30pm Mon-Fri, to 4.30pm Sat) More expensive than elsewhere, but convenient and well stocked with two floors of quality crafts from across the country. Credit cards are accepted and it's a low-pressure shopping environment.

Collectables
ARTS & CRAFTS

(Pioneer Mall, cnr Pioneer & Mpilo Rds; ⏱9am-6pm Mon-Sat, to 2pm Sun) Souvenirs, sandals and other items including bags by the local Seihati Weavers.

LNDC Centre
MALL

(cnr Kingsway & Pioneer Rd) Has a Shoprite supermarket and cafes.

ℹ Information

INTERNET ACCESS
Head to Pioneer Mall for the best internet access.
999 Internet (Kingsway; per hr M30; ⏱8am-8pm Mon-Fri, to 5pm Sat) A good option opposite the post office.

MEDICAL SERVICES
In an emergency, try contacting your embassy, as most keep lists of recommended practitioners. For anything serious, you'll need to go to South Africa.
Maseru Private Hospital (📱2231 3260; off Pioneer Rd, Ha Thetsane) In the suburb of Ha Thetsane, about 7km south of central Maseru.

MONEY
There are several banks with ATMs on Kingsway. The top-end hotels will do foreign-exchange transactions (at poor rates).
FNB (Kingsway)
Nedbank (Kingsway) Does foreign-exchange transactions Monday to Friday.
Standard Lesotho Bank (Kingsway)

POLICE
Police Station (📱112; cnr Constitution & Linare Rds)

POST
Post Office (cnr Kingsway & Palace Rd)

TOURIST INFORMATION
The **tourist information office** (📱2833 2238; visitlesotho.travel; Pioneer Mall, cnr Pioneer & Mpilo Rds; ⏱9am-6pm Mon-Fri, to 3pm Sat, to 1pm Sun) has lists of tour guides, information on public transport and, when in stock, free Maseru city maps

Tourist offices can also be found at **Maseru Bridge Border Post** (📱2231 2427; ⏱8am-5pm Mon-Fri, 9am-1pm Sat & Sun), **Moshoeshoe I International Airport** (📱2835 0479; ⏱9am-4.30pm Mon-Fri, 10am-4pm Sat & Sun) and the headquarters of the **Lesotho Tourism Development Corporation** (LTDC; 📱2231 2231; cnr Linare Rd & Parliament St; ⏱8am-5pm Mon-Fri).

TRAVEL AGENCIES
There are travel agencies at Pioneer Mall , the LNDC Centre and Lancer's Inn hotel.
Leloli Travel Agency (📱5885 1513; maju@leo.co.ls; Pioneer Mall, cnr Pioneer & Mpilo Rds; ⏱8am-5pm Mon-Fri, 9am-noon Sat) Books flights and Budget hire cars.
Maseru Travel (📱2231 4536; mampek.maserutravel@galileosa.co.za; Maseru Book Centre, Kingsway; ⏱8.30am-5pm Mon-Fri, 9-11am Sat) Represents Budget hire cars, Intercape buses and airlines including South African Airways.
Shoprite Money Market (kiosk, LNDC Centre) The easiest place to buy Greyhound, Intercape, Cityliner, Translux and SA Roadlink bus tickets.

ℹ Getting There & Away

There are three main transport stands to the northeast of the main roundabout:
Sefika taxi rank (Airport Rd) A major stand located behind Sefika Mall with services to nationwide destinations, including Roma, Motsekuoa (for Malealea) and points south.

Maseru

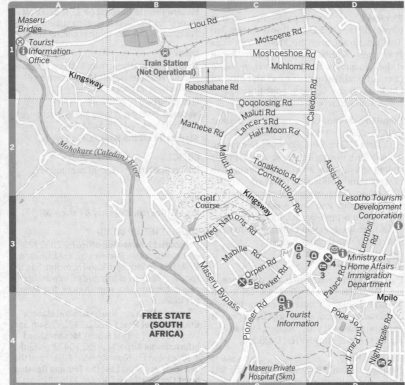

Maseru

Sleeping
1 Avani Lesotho Hotel & Casino	E4
2 Kick4Life Hotel & Conference Centre	D4
3 Lancer's Inn	D3

Eating
No.7 Restaurant	(see 2)
4 Ouh La La	D3
5 Piri Piri	C3
Regal Restaurant	(see 6)
Renaissance Café	(see 8)
Rendezvous	(see 3)

Drinking & Nightlife
Lesotho Sun	(see 1)

Shopping
6 Basotho Hat	C3
Collectables	(see 8)
7 LNDC Centre	D3
8 Pioneer Mall	C4

Motsamai Street taxi rank (cnr Motsamai St & Market Rd) Services to local destinations (including Motsekuoa) and points north such as Maputsoe and Leribe (Hlotse). The rank is behind KFC located on Main North Rd, between Pitso Ground and Setsoto Stadium.

Manonyane bus stop (Market Rd) Shared taxis to Thaba-Bosiu and Semonkong, Leribe and points north. Also Lesotho Freight Service buses to destinations including Leribe and Thaba-Tseka. The stop is located near Pitso Ground.

Buses to Mokhotlong (Stadium Rd) depart from Stadium Rd behind Pitso Ground, while those to **Qacha's Nek** (Main South Rd) depart from next to St James Primary and High Schools on Main Rd South.

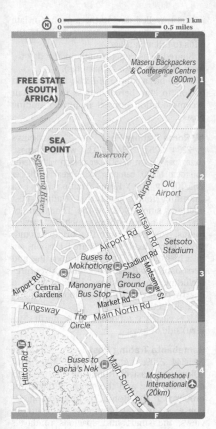

FREE STATE (SOUTH AFRICA)

SEA POINT

Reservoir

Maseru Backpackers & Conference Centre (800m)

Old Airport

Setsoto Stadium

Buses to Mokhotlong

Central Gardens

Manonyane Bus Stop

Pitso Ground

Kingsway

Market Rd

The Circle

Main North Rd

Buses to Qacha's Nek

Moshoeshoe I International (20km)

Airport Rd

Sequnana River

Rantsala Rd

Airport Rd

Mosenai St

Main South Rd

Hilton Rd

AIR

South African Airways (SAA; ☑ 310662; www.flysaa.com; Maseru Book Centre, Kingsway Rd)

CAR & MOTORCYCLE

Avis (☑ 2235 0328; www.avis.co.za; Moshoeshoe I International Airport)

Basotho Car Rental (☑ 2232 4123; www.basothocarrental.com; Camara de Lobos Bldg, Maseru Bridge border post) Competitive rates and airport transfers.

ⓘ Getting Around

Moshoeshoe I International Airport (MSU; ☑ 2235 0777) is 21km south of town, off Main South Rd en route to Morija. Shared taxis to the airport depart from Sefika taxi rank (p101) (behind Sefika Mall). Maseru accommodation, tourist offices and travel agencies can organise private transfers, which cost around M100.

Taxi The standard fare for a seat in a shared 'four-plus-one' travelling around town is M6.50. For a private taxi, try **Superb Taxis** (☑ 2831

9647) – standard fee for a trip around town is M40. **Luxury** (☑ 2232 6211) is another option.

MORIJA

Tiny Morija is the site of the first European mission in Lesotho. It's an important and attractive town with a rich cultural heritage that makes a pleasant stopover or day trip from Maseru. The Morija Museum is the unofficial national museum, and if you're here in late September or early October don't miss the Morija Arts & Culture Festival.

⊙ Sights

Morija Museum & Archives   MUSEUM
(☑ 2236 0308; www.morija.co.ls; M20; ⊙ 8am-5pm Mon-Sat, from 2pm Sun; ℗) This small, considered museum contains ethnographical exhibits, archives from the early mission and scientific artefacts. There's an excellent collection of books for sale, including those by curator Stephen Gill. Staff will guide you to **dinosaur footprints** (M50 per person) in the nearby Makhoarane Mountains, an hour-long return walk.

Maeder House Crafts Centre   ARTS CENTRE
(☑ 5991 1853; ⊙ 11am-4pm Tue-Sat, 1-5pm Sun; ℗) This art studio is near the museum in a missionary house dating back to 1843. Various local artists work and exhibit their art here. If you're staying overnight, the ladies in the adjoining shop can make you a *shweshwe* (printed dyed cotton fabric) shirt. Lesotho's first printing press is in the neighbouring printing works.

🏃 Activities

Pony trekking (one person per hour/half day/day M220/600/880), guided hikes to dinosaur footprints (per person M50) and village sleepovers (per hiker/rider M440/1060 including full board) can be organised through Morija Guest Houses (p104). Reserve a day in advance. An optional packhorse for luggage is M480 extra.

✯ Festivals & Events

Morija Arts & Cultural Festival   CULTURAL
(www.morija.co.ls/festival) This highlight of Lesotho's cultural calendar continues to grow in prestige; an increasing number of attendees make the trip from South Africa each year. The five-day event, held annually in late September or early October, showcases the diversity of Sotho culture through dance,

electronic and jazz music, poetry and theatre. Past highlights have included horse racing, *moraba-raba* (the African equivalent of chess) competitions, and performances by the likes of South Africa's Hugh Masekela and Zimbabwe's Oliver Mtukudzi.

🛏 Sleeping & Eating

★ Morija Guest Houses
GUESTHOUSE $

(📞 6306 5093; www.morijaguesthouses.com; camping M110, r per person with shared bathroom M260-340, breakfast/lunch/dinner M70/130/150; 🅿 🛜) 🍽 At this sterling stone-and-thatch house perched high above the village, guests can choose between cosy rooms in the main building and cottages below. Entertainment from mountain biking to traditional choir and dance performances is offered, making this a top spot to experience the area. Backpackers who arrive by public transport pay R200 per person, regardless of the room.

Lindy's B&B
GUESTHOUSE $

(📞 5885 5309; www.lindysbnb.co.ls; s/d M450/650, with shared bathroom M350/560, breakfast/dinner M75/130; 🅿 🛜) Lindy offers a large, modern stone duplex with two en-suite rooms and a century-old cottage with two more rooms, both ringed by the Makhoarane Mountains.

Cafe Jardin
CAFE $

(mains M40-70; ⊗ 8am-5pm Mon-Sat, from 2pm Sun) The small courtyard tearoom at the Morija Museum serves dishes such as pizzas and chicken and chips. It's busy on weekends and during the Morija festival.

❶ Getting There & Away

Shared taxis run throughout the day to/from Maseru (M25, 45 minutes) and Matsieng (M10, 10 minutes).

ROMA

Nestled amid sandstone cliffs about 35km southeast of Maseru, Roma was established as a mission town in the 1860s. Today it's Lesotho's centre of learning, with the country's only university as well as several seminaries and secondary schools. The beautiful National University of Lesotho campus is worth a wander and boots hanging from phone lines confirm Roma's student credentials. The southern entry/exit to town takes you through a striking gorge landscape and

is best travelled during the morning or late afternoon when the lower sun lights the cliffs to full advantage.

Shared taxis run throughout the day to/from Maseru (M30, 45 minutes).

Roma has a couple of B&Bs, but the main reason to stay hereabouts is the excellent accommodation housed in former trading posts.

★ Roma Trading Post
GUESTHOUSE $

(📞 2234 0267, 2234 0203; www.tradingpost.co.za; per person M350, per person with shared bathroom M200, camping M85, breakfast/dinner M55/100; 🅿 🛜) Roma Trading Post is a charming fourth-generation trading post operated since 1903 by the Thorn family. The attached guesthouse includes garden rooms, rondavels and the original sandstone homestead, with shared kitchen, set in a lush garden. The accommodating and personable staff can organise adventures including pony trekking, hiking, visits to nearby *minwane* (dinosaur footprints) and local attractions.

It is clearly signposted on the north (Maseru) side of town

Ramabanta Trading Post
LODGE $

(📞 5844 2309; s/d M300/600; 🅿) About 40km southeast of Roma, off the tar road to Semonkong and the south, is this sister property to the Roma Trading Post guesthouse. Set in neat grounds with mountain views, the smart and spacious rondavels have a lounge and dining room; three have a kitchenette and the main building features a lounge, bar and restaurant (breakfast M90).

Activities on offer include pony trekking, hiking and village visits. Staying here provides the chance to link up Roma, Ramabanta, Semonkong and other places in the area on overnight hikes and pony treks.

Shared taxis serve Ramabanta from Maseru (M50, two hours), continuing to Semonkong.

THABA-BOSIU

About 25km east of Maseru is the famed and flat-topped Thaba-Bosiu (Mountain at Night), where King Moshoeshoe the Great established his mountain stronghold in 1824. It's regarded as the birthplace of the Basotho nation and, although an unassuming spot, is Lesotho's most important historical site.

HIGHLANDS PARKS & RESERVES

Bokong Nature Reserve (☑2246 0723, 5950 2291; adult/child M10/5, chalets M500; ☺8am-5pm) has perhaps the most dramatic setting of the three northern parks, with stunning vistas over the Lepaqoa Valley from the **visitors centre** (☑5950 2291; adult/child M10/5; ☺8am-4pm), various short walks and a good, rugged two- to three-day hike to Ts'ehlanyane National Park. Bearded vultures, rock shelters and valleyhead fens (wetland areas) are features here.

The impressive Lepaqoa waterfall is worth the trek; in winter it freezes into a craggy column of ice. Guides are available and pony trekking can be arranged. The reserve sits at just over 3000m and gets cold at night, so come prepared. There are basic chalets next to the visitor centre – bring your own food, sleeping bag and stove. Park staff don't recommend camping due to the heavy winds the area tends to receive. Bookings must be made through **Lesotho Northern Parks** (☑in Butha-Buthe 2246 0723).

Bokong lies roughly midway between Leribe (Hlotse) and Katse. Shared taxis from Leribe (M60, two hours) and Katse (M70, 1½ hours) will drop you at the visitors centre, about 2km south of the viewpoint atop the stunning Mafika-Lisiu Pass (3090m). When leaving, you may have to wait a while before a taxi with space passes.

Ts'ehlanyane National Park (☑in Leribe 2246 0723; adult/vehicle M40/10; ☺gate 8am-4.30pm; ℗) is a Lesotho Northern Parks–administered national park that protects a beautiful, 5600-hectare patch of rugged wilderness, including one of Lesotho's only stands of indigenous forest, at a high altitude of 2000m to 3000m. This underrated and underused place is about as far away from it all as you can get and is perfect for hiking.

In addition to day walks, there's a 39km day hike or pony trek to/from Bokong Nature Reserve, covering some of Lesotho's most dramatic terrain. Heading north from Bokong to Ts'ehlanyane is easier as Bokong is higher; the challenging route is also better tackled by pony or horse. Hiking guides can be arranged at Ts'ehlanyane gate (M40 within the park, M450 to Bokong) or Maliba Mountain Lodge.

Community-run pony trekking and horse riding can be arranged through Maliba or the park gate. Book at least 24 hours ahead. Maliba also offers community-run tours of the villages bordering Ts'ehlanyane.

Maliba Lodge (Madiba; ☑in South Africa 031-702 8791; www.maliba-lodge.com; chalet s/d incl full board M2570/3440; ℗☏) offers a range of accommodation in Ts'ehlanyane National Park, but its signature offering is six lavish chalets – Lesotho's plushest accommodation. Each features a four-poster bed, antique furniture, terrace and hot tub facing the mountain range, heated towel racks and sherry by the door. Go for the secluded number 6, the honeymooners' choice.

The origins of Thaba-Bosiu's name are unclear and numerous versions exist. The most interesting is that, to intimidate enemies, magic herbs were placed on a rope, which was wrapped around the mountain. When intruders crossed the rope at night, they were overcome with the drugged sensation that Thaba-Bosiu was 'growing' and it was thus an unconquerable mountain.

Shared taxis to Thaba-Bosiu (M20, 30 minutes) depart from the Manonyane transport stand in Maseru. If you're driving, take the Mafeteng Rd for about 13km and turn left at the Roma turn-off; after about 6km, take the signposted road left. Thaba-Bosiu is 10km further along.

At the mountain's base is a **visitor information centre** (☑2835 7207; ☺8am-5pm Mon-Fri, from 9am Sat, 9am-1pm Sun), where you can organise a guide to walk with you to the top (M40, two hours). Horse riding is also available (M100 per hour; book ahead), as are two-hour walks to see rock paintings (M50).

From the summit, there are good views over the surrounding area, including to Qiloane Hill, which allegedly provided the inspiration for the Basotho hat. Also fascinating to see are the remains of fortifications, Moshoeshoe's grave and parts of his original settlement.

★**Cultural Village**   MUSEUM
(☑5884 0018; www.thababosiu.com; M20; ☺8am-sunset; ℗) Revamped in 2016, the well-maintained cultural village is a highly worthwhile stop. Excellent guided tours of

the complex explain traditional Basotho culture and history, and end with a visit to a statue of the much-revered Moshoeshoe I. There's a restaurant (mains M60 to M160) with a wraparound veranda – a great place for an afternoon drink.

Thaba-Bosiu's accommodation options are within walking distance of each other on the main road. It's a fine alternative to staying in Maseru.

Mmelesi Lodge　　　　　　LODGE **$**
(☑5250 0006; www.mmelesilodge.co.ls; s/d incl breakfast M520/700; P 🛜) Mmelesi Lodge has sandstone chalets in the style of thatched *mokhoro* (traditional Basotho huts), reached along flower-lined paths. The bar often fills with government workers, while the restaurant serves surprisingly good food (mains M50 to M75).

NORTHEASTERN HIGHLANDS

East of Butha-Buthe, the road weaves up dramatically through spectacular mountains – part of the Drakensberg range – with rocky cliffs and rolling hills. South Africa does a good job of marketing its portion of the Drakensberg escarpment, but the raw beauty of the Lesotho section is hard to beat, with stunning highland panoramas, low population density and plenty of winter snow.

All the areas covered in this section are excellent for hiking, but you'll need to be fully equipped with a four-season sleeping bag, waterproof gear, topographical maps and a compass. Trout fishing is reputed to be top notch.

This area has many of the country's worst stretches of main road. In places the asphalt has actually made the road more pot-holey, making for a wild and slow ride in a regular vehicle. Lesotho's mass, Chinese-run roadwork program is another complication, as the work can further slow traffic.

Oxbow

Reached after crossing the dramatic Moteng Pass (2820m), Oxbow consists of a few huts and a couple of lodges nestled amid some wonderful mountain scenery and is an ideal place to get away from the bustle while still enjoying amenities. The area regularly receives snow in winter and boasts a ski

resort. It's also popular with South African trout anglers and birdwatchers.

The daily (except Sunday) bus between Maseru and Mokhotlong will drop you at Oxbow (M120, 4½ hours), passing in both directions in the morning. Shared taxi is a better option for Mokhotlong, as the bus is packed by the time it reaches Oxbow. Taxis run in the morning to Butha-Buthe from Oxbow (M70, 1½ hours) and Afriski Mountain Resort (M90, two hours), with services to Mokhotlong throughout the day. The road follows a series of hairpin turns up the Moteng and Mahlasela Passes, and can be treacherous in snow and ice.

Afriski Mountain Resort　　SKIING, HIKING
(☑086 123 747 54; www.afriski.net; half-/full-day pass M350/450, half-/full-day equipment rental M295/395; ⊙slopes 9am-4pm Jun-Aug) Skiers and snowboarders should make tracks to Afriski Mountain Resort, about 10km from Oxbow via the Mahlasela Pass (3222m), one of Southern Africa's highest road passes. The world-class resort has 3km of slopes, with lessons and packages available.

Try to get here at the very start or very end of the season when the slopes are blissfully empty. Once school holidays begin, it gets extremely busy. In summer, activities including hiking, fly fishing, mountain biking and abseiling are offered.

New Oxbow Lodge　　　　　LODGE **$**
(☑in South Africa 051-933 2247; www.oxbow.co.za; s/d incl breakfast M390/700; P) On the banks of the Malibamat'so River, this incongruous alpine chalet would look more at home in the Alps. It fills during winter with South African skiers and snow oglers; at other times, its eerie isolation and intermittent electricity, compounded by golfball-size hailstones clattering on the deserted games room and bar, bring to mind *The Shining*.

The dated rooms and rondavels have baths (no shower), tea and coffee, gas fire and bedside candles for the black mountain nights. You can dine in the restaurant or bar (mains M40 to M120); room-only accommodation and à la carte meals will likely work out cheaper than half board. A small shop here supplies the basics. June to August (peak season), full-board is compulsory (singles/doubles M990/1630).

Afriski Mountain Resort　　　RESORT **$$**
(☑in South Africa 086 123 747 54; www.afriski.net; dm M265, r per person from M500, self-catering chalets per person M1000; P) The ski resort

offers myriad accommodation options, all comfortable and modern. Book ahead in June and July, especially over the weekend. Prices peak in July and drop outside the June-to-August ski season.

★ **Sky Restaurant** PIZZA, INTERNATIONAL **$$**
(mains M80-130; ⊙7am-9pm; 🛜) Africa's highest restaurant (3010m) overlooks the slopes at Afriski Mountain Resort and reflects the resort's international sheen with its stylish wood finish and big red pizza oven. Lunch choices include pizzas, burgers and steaks, with pasta dishes and Lesotho trout on the dinner menu. There is also a small shop here and, during winter, a lively cafe bar at the foot of the gondola.

Mokhotlong
POP 28.150

From Oxbow, a tarmac road winds its way over a series of 3200m-plus passes and through some superb high-altitude scenery before dropping down to Mokhotlong (Place of the Bald Ibis). The route was the original Roof of Africa Rally course.

Mokhotlong is the main town in eastern Lesotho, albeit a remote outpost with a Wild West feel. There's not much to do other than watch life go by, with locals sporting Basotho blankets passing by on their horses. However, the Senqu (Orange) River – Lesotho's main waterway – has its source near Mokhotlong and the town makes a good base for walks. There are also accommodation options out in the mountain wilds en route to Thaba-Tseka and Oxbow.

Mokhotlong's shared-taxi rank is above the main road near the Pep store. There are a few shared taxis daily to/from Butha-Buthe (M110, three hours), with occasional direct services to Maseru (M170, six hours). A bus runs Monday to Saturday to/from Maseru (M130), departing in each direction by about 6am. Shared taxis to Linakaneng (M40) will drop you by St James Lodge or Molumong Lodge & Pony Trekking Centre; change in Linakaneng for Thaba-Tseka, although there are infrequent services on this rough and little-travelled route. There is a daily shared taxi to Sani Top (M90, two hours), departing Mokhotlong early in the morning.

Petrol and diesel are normally available in Mokhotlong. You need a 4WD vehicle to tackle the road to Thaba-Tseka but you can reach Mokhotlong and travel on to Sani Top in a regular car.

Shops in town sell the basics but it's best to come somewhat equipped. Some guesthouses in Mokhotlong serve evening meals.

Roof of Africa SPORTS
(www.roofofafrica.info) This annual motorbike race is one of the world's toughest off-road endurance events, challenging contestants to ride hundreds of kilometres through the Lesotho highlands. It takes place in late November or early December.

Boikhethelo Guesthouse GUESTHOUSE **$**
(☎6318 8445, 2292 0346; boikhetheloguesthouse@gmail.com; s/d incl breakfast R400/600) A simple, well-run guesthouse with friendly staff and hearty dinners (book ahead). Rooms are in cute thatched cottages with marvellous views.

St James Lodge LODGE **$**
(☑in South Africa 071 672 6801; camping M100, d M500, with shared bathroom R400; P) ✈ This working mission is a humble yet quietly stylish place to stay. The rooms and rondavels offer an electricity-free, self-catering experience, so bring your own food. Pony trekking, scenic walks and Sehonghong River tubing are available, as are guided tours of the church, mission, village and St James' projects. It's 12km southwest of Mokhotlong on the road to Thaba-Tseka.

Grow HOSTEL **$**
(☑5989 8949; www.grow.org.ls; d with shared bathroom M150-200; P) This NGO has an office just off the main road into Mokhotlong; look for it on the left about 2km after the Senqu Hotel. It offers two clean twin rooms, a kitchen and a lounge with intermittent electricity in the neighbouring building. It's happy to accept travellers if volunteers and training groups aren't staying.

Sani Top

Sani Top sits atop the steep Sani Pass, the famous road into Lesotho through the Drakensberg range in KwaZulu-Natal. South Africa's highest mountain pass, it offers stupendous views on clear days and unlimited hiking possibilities.

Besides local hikes, a rugged three- to four-day trek south to Sehlabathebe National Park (p109) is possible. The route follows a remote Drakensberg escarpment edge and should only be attempted if you're well prepared, experienced and in a group of at least four people.

The road to Sani Top is tarred all the way from Butha-Buthe. There is a daily shared taxi from Mokhotlong (M90, two hours), departing early in the morning.

Tour operators run day trips and expeditions up the pass from KwaZulu-Natal. Driving, you'll need a 4WD to get up the pass, but confident drivers (with good brakes) can descend it in a car.

Thabana-Ntlenyana   HIKING
Africa's highest peak south of Mt Kilimanjaro, Thabana-Ntlenyana (3482m) is a popular but long and arduous hike (12km, nine hours). There's a path, but a guide (from M350) would be handy; arrange the night before through Sani Mountain Lodge. It's also possible to do the ascent on horseback.

Hodgson's Peaks   HIKING
Hodgson's Peaks (3256m) is a 6km, five-hour hike up a valley. There are views of KwaZulu-Natal from the summit.

Sani Stone Lodge   LODGE $
(☑5631 0331, 2892 4000; www.sanistonelodge.co.za; camping M90, dm/d M170/500; ℗) About 8km from Sani Top, this Basotho-run lodge offers simple rooms, an en-suite dorm and three cosy rondavels (double M800) with all-important fireplaces. Guided hikes, village visits and pony treks are available, and the bar-restaurant is a welcome sight after a trek in the highlands.

★ Sani Mountain Lodge   LODGE $$$
(☑in South Africa 073 541 8620, in South Africa 078 634 7496; www.sanimountain.co.za; dm/camping M250/95, s/d/tr with half board M1520/2290/3165; ℗) At 2874m, this lodge atop the Sani Pass stakes a claim to 'highest drinking hole in Southern Africa'. Pub trivia aside, cosy rondavels and excellent meals (mains from M55) reward those who make the steep ascent from KwaZulu-Natal. Backpackers doss down the road in modern rooms that hold between two and six people.

In winter, the snow is sometimes deep enough for skiing; pony trekking and village visits can be arranged with notice. A 4WD shuttle (M325) to/from the South African border post is offered to guests staying more than one night.

SOUTHERN LESOTHO

The region south of Morija, across to Sehlabathebe National Park in the southeast, is less developed than the northwest but lingers in the memory banks of all who pass through. The mountain ranges eat up the sky out here, where a velvety orange-pink light pours over rocky peaks and yawning valleys. If you like hiking and pony trekking in rugged isolation, head south.

The road from Quthing to Qacha's Nek is one of Lesotho's most impressive drives, taking you along the winding Senqu (Orange) River gorge and through striking canyon scenery before climbing up onto the escarpment. Another stunner is the road through the interior from Semonkong down to Qacha's Nek. Despite what some maps show, both are tarred all the way to Qacha's Nek.

Semonkong

Semonkong (Place of Smoke), a one-pony town in the rugged Thaba Putsoa range, gets its name from the nearby **Maletsunyane Falls** (204m), which are at their loudest in summer. The town is the starting point for many fine hiking and pony-trekking trails, including the two-day ride via the peaks of the Thaba Putsoa to **Ketane Falls** (122m).

Semonkong is about 110km southeast of Maseru on the tar road to Qacha's Nek; both are a three-hour drive. Shared taxis run all day to/from Maseru (M70) and leave throughout the morning to/from Qacha's Nek (M120). A private taxi to/from Qacha's Nek costs around M250.

If you're heading in from South Africa, it's possible to get a shared taxi from Kokstad in the Eastern Cape, changing at Matatiele.

★ Semonkong Lodge   LODGE $$
(☑2700 6037; www.semonkonglodge.com; camping M100, dm/s/d from M175/560/860; ℗) ◢ Near the Maletsunyane River, this lodge is a model of community tourism and a great place for everyone from families to adventure seekers. If the inviting accommodation, including cosy rondavels with fireplaces, doesn't make you extend your stay in the mountains, fireside feasts in the lodge's Duck & Donkey Tavern (lunch/dinner mains M75/120) surely will.

There's also a kitchen for those who want to self-cater. Staff can arrange all kinds of tours and hikes, employing locals to navigate the villages and steep trails, including extreme fishing expeditions, pony trekking and even pub crawls by donkey. Then there's the world's longest commercially operated, single-drop abseil (204m) down the Maletsunyane Falls.

The lodge is signposted from the town centre, 2km down a gravel road.

Malealea

This remote village has three travel trump cards: its breathtaking mountain scenery, its trading-post lodge and its successful community-based tourism. Many visitors to Lesotho head straight here to sample traditional Basotho life or, as the sign outside town says, to just 'pause and look upon a gateway of paradise'. The area has been inhabited for centuries, as shown by the many **San rock paintings** in the vicinity.

🏃 Activities

Malealea is one of the best places in Lesotho to organise a hike or pony trek in the mountains – you can even rent a mountain bike if you prefer to explore on wheels. Organise activities through Malealea Lodge.

Options range from easy **two-hour pony rides** (one/two/three people M385/550/750) to San rock art or a gorge viewpoint, to **overnight expeditions** (M785/1000/1350 per day) with accommodation in **Basotho village huts** (M110 per hut for one to three people). Multiday routes include Ribaneng Waterfall (two days, one night); Ribaneng and Ketane Waterfalls (four days, three nights); and Ribaneng, Ketane and Semonkong (six days, five nights).

You can hike to spots including **Pitseng Gorge** (three or six hours return), with its gnarly cliffs and swimming holes, and **Botsoela Waterfall** (four hours; five including San rock art). Hiring a guide (M20 per hour) is recommended. Guided overnight hikes are also possible (with/without packhorse M525/175 per day), with accommodation in huts.

Village visits provide a stimulating insight into the local people and their customs. Down the slope from Malealea Lodge are the tiny museum and craft shop, housed in traditional Basotho huts, from where you can wander through the village – solo or with a guide. You can pay **guided visits** (M20 per hour) to the *sangoma* (traditional medicine practitioner; only for the genuinely interested), the village school and the late Mr Musi's reclaimed *donga* (eroded ravine used for small-scale agriculture).

The six-day, 300km-plus **Lesotho Sky** (www.lesothosky.com; ☉ late Sep) mountain-bike race passes through this rugged

DON'T MISS

SEHLABATHEBE NATIONAL PARK

Lesotho's most undervisited national park, **Sehlabathebe National Park** (☏ 2232 6075; per person/vehicle M60/15; ☉ gate 8am-4.30pm) is remote, rugged and beautiful. The rolling grasslands, wildflowers and silence provide complete isolation, with only the prolific birdlife (including the bearded vulture) and the odd rhebok for company. Hiking (and horse riding from Sani Top or the Drakensbergs) is the main way to explore, and angling is possible in the dams and rivers. Come well prepared for the changing elements: this is a summer-rainfall area and thick mist, potentially hazardous to hikers, is common. The winters are clear, but it gets cold at night with occasional light snowfalls.

A daily bus connects Mavuka village, near the park gate, and Qacha's Nek (M100, five hours), leaving Mavuka around 5am and returning at 2pm..

area in late September. Year-round you can hire bikes (half-/full day including guide M150/300 per person). Malealea Lodge can also recommend scenic drives for 4WD and high-clearance 2WD vehicles.

🛏 Sleeping & Eating

★ **Malealea Lodge** LODGE $
(☏ 5018 1341, in South Africa 082 552 4215; www.malealea.com; camping M110, s/d from M450/600, with shared bathroom from M277.50/370; 🅿) 🧺
Offering 'Lesotho in a nutshell', Malealea is a deserving poster child for the mountain kingdom. Every sunset, village choirs and bands perform at the mountaintop lodge. Activities are community run, and a proportion of tourist revenues and donations goes directly to supporting local projects. The views, meanwhile, are stupendous.

Accommodation ranges from campsites and twin 'forest' (backpacker) huts in a pretty wooded setting away from the lodge to simple, cosy en-suite rooms and rondavels. A sense of history pervades the site, which began life in 1905 as a trading post, established by teacher, diamond miner and soldier Mervyn Smith. From 1986 the Jones family ran the store before transforming it into accommodation and integrating it with the surrounding community.

Malealea also offers a bar, hearty meals (breakfast/lunch/dinner for M80/100/135), self-catering facilities and a shop with basic goods. There are now intermittent wi-fi and mobile-phone signals at the lodge. September to December are the busy months.

❶ Getting There & Away

Early-morning shared taxis connect Maseru and Malealea (M100, 2½ hours). Later in the day, catch a shared taxi to the junction town of Motsekuoa (M50, 1½ hours), from where there are connections to Malealea (M40, one hour). Services from Mafeteng and the south also stop in Motsekuoa.

Driving, head south from Maseru on the Mafeteng road (Main Rd South) for 60km to Motsekuoa. Opposite the shared-taxi corner, turn left (east) at the sign for Matelile, Qaba and Malealea Lodge. Ten kilometres further on, take the right fork and continue another 15km. When you reach the signposted turn-off to Malealea, travel about 7km along an unsealed road over the Gates of Paradise Pass (2003m) to the village and lodge.

It's also possible to approach Malealea from the south, via Mpharane and Masemouse, but this gravel road is rough and not suitable for a 2WD car.

Mafeteng

On the scenic main road south of Motsekuoa (the turning for Malealea) is Mafeteng, a scruffy town with a busy main drag. Although not worth a stop, it's the best place to stock up before heading south and there are a few places to sleep and eat if the need arises.

Shared taxis, sprinters (Mercedes minibuses; faster and more expensive than shared taxis) and buses stop in Mafeteng (near Van Rooyen's Gate border crossing) en route between Maseru and Quthing.

Mafeteng Hotel   HOTEL $$
(☑ 2270 0236; s/d incl breakfast M558/716; P ❄) In leafy grounds on the edge of town, Mafeteng Hotel offers worn rooms in a peachy-pink hexagonal building that looks like a displaced air-traffic control tower. There's a bar and meat-oriented restaurant (mains M70 to M100).

From the main road, follow the sign to the National AIDS and HIV Commission, between the roundabout and FNB bank on the south (Mohale's Hoek) side of town.

Mohale's Hoek

Like other towns hereabouts, shabby Mohale's Hoek has little to offer other than a place to overnight, although it does at least boast a decent accommodation option.

Shared taxis, sprinters and buses running between Maseru and Quthing stop in Mohale's Hoek (near Makhaleng Bridge border crossing).

Hotel Mount Maluti   HOTEL $
(☑ 2278 5224; www.hmmlesotho.com; s/d incl breakfast M700/750; P ❄ ❄) Offers dated rooms in cool blocks opening onto pleasant gardens. Its restaurant is a decent lunch stop (mains M70 to M110), serving sandwiches, burgers, pizza and pasta, and the whole shebang is signposted off the main road.

Quthing

POP 20,000

Quthing, the southernmost major town in Lesotho, is also known as Moyeni (Place of the Wind). It was established in 1877, abandoned during the Gun War of 1880 and then rebuilt at the present site. Activity centres on the new part of town, Lower Quthing, with its bustling main road.

The transport stand is in Lower Quthing. Shared taxis serve Maseru (M80, 2½ hours) and Qacha's Nek (M90, 2½ hours), as do faster, more expensive sprinters and slower, cheaper buses. Services to and from the capital are more frequent. Shared taxis run to/from Tele Bridge border post, which is linked by shared taxi to Sterkspruit (South Africa) for onward transport. The gravel road connecting Tele Bridge and the main Quthing–Mohale's Hoek road is passable in a 2WD car.

There are a few basic fast food stands, but you're better off eating at your guesthouse.

Dinosaur Footprints   ARCHAEOLOGICAL SITE
(M15; ⊙ 8am-5pm; P) One of Quthing's main claims to fame is the proliferation of dinosaur footprints in the surrounding area. The most easily accessible are signposted on the left as you leave town heading northeast towards Qacha's Nek. In this building are 230-million-year-old footprints and a craft shop. Children will offer to guide you to more footprints for a small tip.

Masitise Cave House Museum   MUSEUM
(☑ 2700 3259; http://masitisecavehouse.blogspot. co.za; adult/child M10/3; ⊙ 8.30am-5pm Mon-Fri,

to 2pm Sat & Sun; P) Five kilometres west of Quthing is this intriguing section of an old mission, built directly into a San rock shelter in 1866 by Reverend David-Frédéric Ellenberger, a Swiss missionary who was among the first to arrive in Lesotho. There's a cast of a dinosaur footprint in the ceiling, a museum with displays on local culture and history, and San paintings nearby.

To get here, take the signposted turn-off near the Masitise Primary School and follow the road about 1km back past the small red church. At the neighbouring house you can ask for the key from the caretaker, the church pastor. From here, the museum is five minutes further on foot.

Upper Quthing
AREA

On the hill above Lower Quthing, overlooking the Senqu (Orange) River gorge, this former colonial administrative centre has good views and gently dilapidated buildings. Walk or catch a shared taxi up from Lower Quthing to escape the hustle and bustle and have a quiet stroll.

Fuleng Guest House
GUESTHOUSE $

(☏2275 0260; info.fulengguesthouse@gmail.com; s/d from M450/570; P) This hillside guesthouse offers rondavels with a view, a restaurant (breakfast/meals M65/90), cheeky garden gnomes, a rock feature and a friendly local experience. Find it by the main road on the way up to Upper Quthing. Rates are higher if you pay by card.

UNDERSTAND LESOTHO

Lesotho Today

A bloodless coup attempt rocked Lesotho in August 2014, harking worryingly back to 1998, when South African Development Community (SADC) forces had to restore order. Prime Minister Thomas Thabane fled the country and accused the military of trying to overthrow him; following SADC mediation, peaceful general elections took place in February 2015. Thabane's All Basotho Convention lost narrowly and a coalition government was formed by seven other parties.

The Basotho-dominated country did not experience apartheid and, with life revolving around subsistence farming, levels of social inequality and crime are lower than in South Africa. The mountain kingdom does face serious issues though, including unemployment, food shortages, a 23% HIV/AIDS rate and an average life expectancy of 49 years.

History

The Early Days

Lesotho is the homeland of the Basotho – Sotho-Tswana peoples who originally lived in small chiefdoms scattered around the highveld in present-day Free State.

During the 19th century, the Voortrekkers and various other white entrepreneurs began to encroach on Basotho grazing lands. On top of this came the *difaqane* (forced migration in Southern Africa).

Yet the Basotho emerged from this period more united – largely due to Moshoeshoe the Great, a village chief who rallied his people and forged a powerful kingdom. Moshoeshoe first led his own villagers to Butha-Buthe, from where he was able to resist the early incursions of the *difaqane*. He later moved his headquarters to the more easily defended mountain stronghold of Thaba-Bosiu, where he repulsed wave after wave of invaders.

Over the following decades, Moshoeshoe brought various peoples together as part of the loosely federated Basotho state; by the time of his death in 1870, it would have a population exceeding 150,000. He also welcomed Christian missionaries into his territory. In return for some Christianisation of Basotho customs, the missionaries were disposed to defend the rights of 'their' Basotho against Boer and British expansion.

Defending the Territory

In 1843 – in response to continuing Boer incursions – Moshoeshoe allied himself with the British Cape Colony government. While the resulting treaties defined his borders, they did little to stop squabbles with the Boers, who had established themselves in the fertile lowveld west of the Mohokare (Caledon) River. In 1858 tensions peaked with the outbreak of the Orange Free State–Basotho War. Moshoeshoe was ultimately forced to sign away much of his western lowlands.

In 1868 Moshoeshoe again called on the British, this time bypassing the Cape Colony administration and heading straight to the imperial government in London. The British viewed continual war between Orange Free State and Basotholand as bad for their own interests. To resolve the situation, they annexed Basotholand.

The decade after Moshoeshoe's death was marked by squabbles over succession. After briefly changing hands from the British imperial government to the Cape Colony, Basotholand again came under direct British control in 1884. When the Union of South Africa was created in 1910, Basotholand was a British protectorate and was not included. Had the Cape Colony retained control, Lesotho would have become part of South Africa and, later, an apartheid-era homeland.

Independence

During the early 20th century, migrant labour to South Africa increased and the Basotho gained greater autonomy under British administration. In 1955 the council requested internal self-government, with elections to determine its members. Meanwhile, political parties formed: the Basotholand Congress Party (BCP; similar to South Africa's African National Congress) and the conservative Basotholand National Party (BNP), headed by Chief Leabua Jonathan.

The BNP won Lesotho's first general elections in 1965 and made independence from Britain the first item on its agenda. The following year, the Kingdom of Lesotho attained full independence, with Chief Jonathan as prime minister and King Moshoeshoe II as nominal head of state.

Chief Jonathan's rule was unpopular and the BCP won the 1970 election. In response, Jonathan suspended the constitution, arrested and expelled the king, and banned opposition parties. Lesotho effectively became a one-party state.

Coup Decades

A military coup deposed Chief Jonathan in 1986 and restored Moshoeshoe II as head of state. Yet, following ongoing power disputes between the king and coup leader Justin Lekhanya, Moshoeshoe II was deposed and exiled in 1990. His son, Letsie III, assumed the throne, with only ceremonial powers, in 1992.

The '90s were a decade of unrest. A BCP split led prime minister Ntsu Mokhehle to form the breakaway Lesotho Congress for Democracy (LCD) and continue to govern, with the BCP now in opposition. Mokhehle died in 1998 and Pakalitha Mosisili took over the leadership of the LCD. The party subsequently won a landslide victory in elections that were declared reasonably fair by international observers but were widely protested against within Lesotho.

In September 1998 the government called on its Southern African Development Community (SADC) treaty partners – Botswana, South Africa and Zimbabwe – to help it restore order. Rebel elements of the Lesotho army resisted, resulting in heavy fighting and widespread looting in Maseru. The LCD won again in the 2002 elections, but opposition parties gained a significant number of seats.

In 2006, 17 LCD members led by Thomas Thabane, formed the breakaway All Basotho Convention (ABC) party. In the controversial 2007 elections, the LCD retained its majority and national strikes against the government ensued. A two-week curfew was imposed, there was an assassination attempt on Thabane and many people were detained and tortured. In 2009 there was an assassination attempt on Mosisili.

In the hotly contested 2012 elections, Thabane became prime minister after the ABC formed a coalition with other parties including the LCD. Lesotho teetered on the verge of another coup in 2014, when Thabane fled to South Africa, accusing the military of trying to overthrow him. Following SADC mediation, general elections took place in February 2015. Thabane's ABC lost narrowly and a coalition government of seven parties was headed by Pakalitha Mosisili's new party, the Democratic Congress. Mosisili is once again prime minister, with Mothetjoa Metsing of the LCD remaining deputy prime minister.

The Culture

Traditional Basotho culture is flourishing, and colourful celebrations marking milestones, such as birth, puberty, marriage and death, are a central part of village life. While hiking you may see the *lekolulo,* a flutelike instrument played by herd boys; the *thomo,* a stringed instrument played by women; and the *setolo-tolo,* a stringed mouth instrument played by men. Cattle hold an important position in daily life, both as sacrificial animals and as symbols of wealth.

The Basotho believe in a Supreme Being and place a great deal of emphasis on *balimo* (ancestors), who act as intermediaries between people and the capricious forces of nature and the spirit world. Evil is a constant danger, caused by *boloi* (witchcraft; witches can be either male or female) and *thkolosi* (small, mischievous beings, similar to the Xhosa's *tokoloshe*). If these forces are bothering you, visit the nearest *ngaka* (a learned man, part sorcerer and part doctor) who can combat them. Basotho are traditionally buried in a sitting position, facing the rising sun and ready to leap up when called.

LESOTHO LITERATURE

Little Lesothan literature is available in English. However, Thomas Mofolo's *Chaka* (1925), one of the greatest 20th-century African novels, and *Traveller to the East* (1907), the first Sotho novel, have been translated into English. Other authors to look out for include Mpho 'M'atsepo Nthunya, who writes about female experiences in the autobiographical *Singing Away the Hunger* (1996).

People & Economy

Lesotho's main link with South Africa has been the mining industry. For most of the 20th century, Lesotho's main export was labour, with about 60% of males working in South Africa, primarily in mining. In the early 1990s, at least 120,000 Basotho men were employed by South African mines and up to one-third of Lesotho's household income was from wages earned by the miners. When the mining industry was restructured, the number of Lesotho miners was halved and many have returned home to Lesotho to join the ranks of the unemployed.

Chinese-owned textile factories subsequently became the country's major employers and exporters. In recent years, the US economic slowdown and increased competition from countries such as Vietnam and Bangladesh have taken their toll.

Women

Basotho women shouldered a big share of the economic, social and family responsibilities while their husbands and male relatives went to work in the mines in South Africa. As mining jobs disappeared, the textile industry became an important part of Lesotho's economy and about 90% of the new jobs went to women.

Contrary to the trend elsewhere in the region, Basotho women are often better educated than their male counterparts, because many boys in rural areas are forced to tend cattle (or head off to South Africa to work) instead of spending time in the classroom. Lesotho has a high rape rate, due partly to entrenched beliefs in men's sexual entitlement.

Environment

The Drakensberg range is at its most rugged in tiny Lesotho – a 30,355 sq km patch of mountain peaks and highland plateau that is completely surrounded by South Africa. It has the highest lowest point of any country in the world – 1400m, in southern Lesotho's Senqu (Orange) River valley.

Wildlife

Due primarily to its altitude, Lesotho is home to fewer animals than much of the rest of the region. Those you may encounter include rheboks, jackals, mongoose, meerkats, elands and rock hyraxes. However, Lesotho's montane areas are of particular interest for their rare smaller species. Many are found only in the Drakensberg, including the highly threatened Maloti minnow, the African ice rat, several species of lizards and geckos, and the Lesotho river frog.

The country's almost 300 recorded bird species include the lammergeier (bearded vulture) and the southern bald ibis.

Among Lesotho's earliest wild inhabitants were dinosaurs: the small, fast-running Lesothosaurus was named after the country.

National Parks & Protected Areas

In part because land tenure allows communal access to natural resources, less than 1% of Lesotho is protected – the lowest protected-area coverage of any nation in Africa. Sehlabathebe National Park is the main conservation area, known for its isolated wilderness. Other protected areas include Ts'ehlanyane National Park and Bokong Nature Reserve.

Environmental Issues

Environmental discussion in Lesotho centres on the controversial Highlands Water Project. Among the concerns are disruption of traditional communities, flooding of agricultural lands and possible adverse ecological impacts on the Senqu (Orange) River.

Other issues include animal population pressure (resulting in overgrazing) and soil erosion. About 40 million tonnes of topsoil are lost annually, with sobering predictions that there may well be no cultivatable land left by 2040.

On a brighter note, Lesotho and South Africa are working together within the framework of the Maluti-Drakensberg Transfrontier Conservation and Development Project to protect these two alpine areas.

SURVIVAL GUIDE

❶ Directory A–Z

ACCOMMODATION

The best accommodation options, and a highlight of travelling in Lesotho, are the various tourist lodges, which offer excellent digs, good food and a range of activities. Family-run guesthouses of varying quality can be found across the country. Top-end accommodation is scarce – exceptions are a few hotels in Maseru and one superb lodge in Ts'ehlanyane National Park. Camping opportunities abound away from major towns but always ask locally for permission.

ACTIVITIES

Lesotho is a supreme destination for lovers of rugged outdoor adventure. The mountains offer endless opportunities to explore on foot or on a Basotho pony. You'll find guides and maps

---

available at the main lodges. Lesotho is also excellent 4WD country, though you need to be experienced and come well equipped.

Pony Trekking

Pony trekking is one of Lesotho's top drawcards. It's done on sure-footed Basotho ponies, the result of crossbreeding between short Javanese horses and European full mounts. Good places to organise treks include Malealea Lodge (p109), Semonkong Lodge (p108), Ts'ehlanyane National Park (p105) and Bokong Nature Reserve (p105).

Advance booking is recommended and no prior riding experience is necessary. Whatever your experience level, expect to be sore after a day in the saddle. For overnight treks, you'll normally need to bring food (stock up in Maseru), a sleeping bag, a torch (flashlight), water-purification tablets and warm, waterproof clothing. Check Malealea's website for more on the provisions and preparation required.

Fishing

Lesotho is an insider's tip among trout anglers. As in South Africa, the season runs from September to May. There is a small licence fee of M10 and a bag limit of 12 trout over 25cm in length. Only rod and line and artificial nonspinning flies may be used.

The nearest fishing area to Maseru is the Makhaleng River, 2km downstream from Molimo-Nthuse restaurant, about 60km east of Maseru at the foot of God Help Me Pass. You can also access the river from Ramabanta and Malealea.

Hiking

➡ The entire country is ideal for hiking, away from major towns.

➡ The eastern highlands and the Drakensberg crown attract serious hikers.

➡ There are few organised hiking trails – mostly footpaths.

➡ You can walk almost everywhere, accompanied by a compass and the relevant topographical maps.

➡ In all areas, especially the remote eastern highlands, rugged conditions can make walking dangerous if you aren't experienced and prepared. Temperatures can plummet to zero even in summer and thunderstorms and thick fog are common.

➡ Waterproof gear and warm clothes are essential.

➡ In summer, rivers flood and fords can become dangerous; be prepared to change your route or wait until the river subsides.

➡ By the end of the dry season, good water can be scarce, especially in higher areas.

➡ Consider hiring a local guide where possible.

---

❶ PRACTICALITIES

Electricity

Lesotho's electricity is generated at 220V. Plugs have three round prongs as used in South Africa.

Media

The *Sunday Express* (sundayexpress.co.ls) and *Lesotho Times* (www.lestimes.com) carry Lesothan news.

Weights & Measures

Lesotho uses the metric system.

HIKING TIPS

If you're hiking without a guide, you might be hassled for money or 'gifts' by shepherds in remote areas and there's a very slight risk of robbery. Children sometimes beg and throw stones at cars, especially 4WD vehicles, on remote roads.

Lives are lost each year from lightning strikes; keep off high ground during electrical storms and avoid camping in the open. Waterproof clothing is essential for hiking and pony trekking.

DANGERS & ANNOYANCES

Lesotho is generally a very safe country. Travellers should not flaunt valuables anywhere. Be especially vigilant in Maseru; do not walk around at night, as muggings have occurred. Bag-snatching and pickpocketing are the main risks during the day. Occasional political unrest generally affects only the capital; stay off the streets and avoid large crowds.

There are numerous police roadblocks; halt at the first stop sign and wait to be waved forward. Most policemen will quickly check your papers or just wave you on. Some may suggestively tell you how thirsty they are if they see you have drinks.

EMBASSIES & CONSULATES

Embassies and consulates are found in Maseru. Missions in South Africa generally have responsibility for Lesotho. For more listings, visit www.foreign.gov.ls.

French Honorary Consul (☏ 2232 5722; www.ambafrance-rsa.org/-Lesotho-320; Alliance Française, cnr Kingsway & Pioneer Rd)

German Honorary Consul (☏ 2233 2292, 2233 2983; www.southafrica.diplo.de; 70c Maluti Rd)

Netherlands Honorary Consul (☏ 2231 2114; www.dutchembassy.co.za; Lancer's Inn, cnr Kingsway & Pioneer Rd)

South African High Commission (☏ 2222 5800; www.dirco.gov.za; cnr Kingsway & Old School Rd)

US Embassy (☏ 2231 2666; maseru.us embassy.gov; 254 Kingsway)

EMERGENCY & IMPORTANT NUMBERS

Ambulance	☏ 2231 3260, 112
Fire	☏ 112
Police	☏ 5888 1010, 5888 1024, 112

GAY & LESBIAN TRAVELLERS

The country's law does not protect against discrimination based on sexual orientation or gender identity. Gay sexual relationships are taboo, with open displays of affection frowned upon.

INTERNET ACCESS

Web access is available in Maseru and a few accommodation options elsewhere have wi-fi.

MONEY

ATMs are common in Lesotho, but cards are rarely accepted outside the capital.

Moneychangers

➜ Maseru is the only place where you can reliably exchange foreign cash and travellers cheques.

➜ Rand notes are usually available on request.

Tipping

Wages are low, and tipping is expected. The main exceptions are in rural parts of Lesotho, where it's generally the custom to simply round up the bill.

OPENING HOURS

Banks 9am–3.30pm Mon–Fri, 8.30am–noon Sat

Bars noon–midnight

Businesses and shopping 8.30am–6pm Mon–Fri, 8.30am–1pm Sat; many supermarkets also 9am–noon Sun; major shopping centres till 9pm daily

Cafes 8am–5pm

Government offices 8am–12.45pm & 2pm–4.30pm Mon–Fri

Post offices 8am–4.30pm Mon–Fri, 8am–noon Sat

Restaurants 11.30am–3pm & 6–10pm (last orders); many open 3–6pm

POST

Delivery is slow and unreliable.

MALOTI OR RAND?

The South African rand is universally accepted in Lesotho, but even though it's tied to its neighbour's currency, the maloti is not accepted in South Africa. Most ATMs dispense maloti, so don't get caught with a pocketful. If you are spending a short time here before returning to South Africa, stocking up on rand will eliminate the worry of having to spend all your maloti before leaving Lesotho.

LESOTHO GETTING THERE & AWAY

TAP WATER

It's best to purify tap water or use bottled water in Lesotho.

PUBLIC HOLIDAYS

New Year's Day 1 January
Moshoeshoe's Day 11 March
Good Friday March/April
Easter Monday March/April
Workers' Day 1 May
Africa or Heroes' Day 25 May
Ascension Day May/June
King's Birthday 17 July
Independence Day 4 October
Christmas Day 25 December
Boxing Day 26 December

TELEPHONE

→ Lesotho's telephone system works reasonably well in the lowlands, but even landlines are temperamental in the highlands.

→ There are no area codes.

→ Lesotho's eight-digit landline and mobile phone (cell) numbers respectively begin with ☑ 2 and 5 or 6.

→ International calls are expensive.

→ For international reverse-charge calls dial ☑ 109.

→ Mobile phone signals are rare in the highlands and can only be picked up on a few mountain passes.

→ The main mobile phone service providers are Vodacom Lesotho (www.vodacom.co.ls) and Econet Telecom (www.etl.co.ls).

→ Most villages have a Vodacom or Econet booth, selling credit and SIM cards (about M20; bring your passport).

→ The booths generally have a landline, offering calls to Lesotho and South Africa for about M8 per minute.

→ Mobile credit comes in R5 vouchers; international bundles are available.

→ South African SIMs work on roaming.

TIME

→ Lesotho is on SAST (South Africa Standard Time), which is two hours ahead of GMT/UTC.

→ There is no daylight-saving period.

→ Most timetables and businesses use the 24-hour clock.

TOURIST INFORMATION

There is a tourist office in Maseru (p101); elsewhere they are thin on the ground.

Lesotho Tourism Development Corporation (http://visitlesotho.travel)

See Lesotho (www.seelesotho.com)

VISAS

→ Citizens of most Western European countries, the USA and most Commonwealth countries are granted a free entry permit at the border or airport.

→ The standard permitted stay is 30 days.

→ To stay for an extra 14 days, apply at the **Ministry of Home Affairs immigration department** (☑ 2232 5049; www.gov.ls; 2nd flr, Post Office Blg, Kingsway, Maseru).

→ If you ask for longer at the border (or the ministry), it may be granted..

→ Travellers who require a visa can get one at diplomatic missions in Pretoria and elsewhere.

→ If you arrive at the **Maseru Bridge** (☺ 24hrs) border crossing without a visa, with some luck you'll be issued a temporary entry permit to allow you to get to Maseru, where you can apply for a visa at the Ministry of Home Affairs. However, don't count on this, as it depends on border officials' whim.

❶ Getting There & Away

Most people enter Lesotho by road from South Africa. There are 13 border crossings with South Africa and, save for some queues at the Maseru Bridge crossing, getting into the country is generally a pleasant business.

AIR

Airlink (☑ 2235 0418; www.flyairlink.com) has daily flights between Jo'burg and Moshoeshoe I International Airport, 21km south of Maseru (from R1100, one hour). Flying to Bloemfontein airport (130km west of Maseru) is cheaper, as is hiring a car in South Africa.

New local airline **Maluti Sky** (☑ 2231 7733; www.flymalutisky.com) also offers flights between Maseru and Johannesburg.

LAND

Most of the border posts with South Africa can be crossed in a 2WD, though you will need a 4WD to enter at Ramatseliso's Gate or Sani Pass. There is a M30 road toll to pay on entry to the country.

There are no restrictions on bringing your own bicycle.

Border Crossings

All of Lesotho's borders are with South Africa and are straightforward to cross.

The main crossing is at Maseru Bridge, east of Bloemfontein. Queues here are sometimes very long exiting and, on some weekend evenings, entering Lesotho; use other posts if possible.

❶ Getting Around

You can now access most of Lesotho in a 2WD car, but it is still not possible to do a complete circuit without a 4WD, due to rough gravel roads in the east between Mokhotlong and Qacha's Nek. Bus and shared-taxi networks cover the country; taxis do not normally operate to a schedule but leave only when full.

BUS

Buses and shared taxis A good network of buses, minibus shared taxis (known locally as just 'taxis'), sprinters and private or shared car taxis (known as 'four-plus-ones') covers most of the country. Minibus taxis serve the major towns and many smaller spots. Buses (cheaper and slower) and sprinters (faster and more expensive) serve the major towns. There are no classes and service is decidedly no-frills.

Departures Most departures are in the morning (generally, the longer the journey, the earlier the departure).

Northern Lesotho Heading northeast from Maseru by shared taxi, you usually have to change at Maputsoe. The transfer sometimes happens en route into Maputsoe if your vehicle meets another taxi.

Tickets On larger local buses, although you'll be quoted long-distance fares, it's best to just buy a ticket to the next major town. Most passengers will likely get off there, leaving you stuck waiting for the vehicle to fill up again while other buses and shared taxis leave. Buying tickets in stages is only slightly more expensive than buying a direct ticket. It's not necessary (or possible) to reserve a seat in advance.

CAR & MOTORCYCLE

It usually works out cheaper to rent a vehicle in South Africa and drive it over the border. You'll need a permission letter from the rental company to cross the border; some companies charge a fee (around R500) for this.

Lesotho has rental operations in Maseru and Moshoeshoe I International Airport.

Road Conditions

➤ Driving in Lesotho can be challenging, with steep terrain, hairpin turns and inclement weather.

➤ Roads are being built and upgraded, many financed by Chinese mining corporations and the Highlands Water Project.

➤ During roadworks, previously passable gravel and tar roads become impassable to 2WD cars.

➤ A tarred road, passable in a 2WD, runs clockwise from Qacha's Nek to Mokhotlong, with possible onward access to Sani Top.

➤ Stretches of tar and good gravel also give 2WD access to Semonkong (from both the

north and south), Thaba-Tseka (from the north and west) and Ts'ehlanyane National Park.

➤ Apart from issues caused by roadworks, sealed roads in the highlands are generally good, but very steep in places.

➤ Rain will slow you down, and ice and snow in winter can make driving dangerous.

➤ If you're driving an automatic, you'll rely heavily on your brakes to negotiate steep downhill corners.

➤ Away from main roads, there are places where even a 4WD will struggle, such as the road north from Sehlabathebe National Park.

➤ Rough roads and river floodings after summer storms are the biggest problems.

➤ People and animals on the road can also be a hazard.

➤ There are sometimes police or army roadblocks.

Road Rules

➤ Driving is on the left-hand side of the road.

➤ Seatbelts are mandatory for the driver and front-seat passengers.

➤ The main local idiosyncrasy is the 'four-way stop' (crossroad), found even on major roads. All vehicles are required to stop, with those arriving first the first to go (even if they're on a minor cross street).

➤ There are numerous police roadblocks in Lesotho; halt at the first stop sign and wait to be waved forward. Most police officers will quickly check your papers or just wave you on.

➤ 80km/h on main roads; 50km/h in villages.

Signage

Main routes are numbered, beginning with A1 (Main North Rd). Side roads branching off from these have 'B' route numbers.

LOCAL TRANSPORT

Shared Taxi

Minibus shared taxis don't have stellar road-safety records but can sometimes be your only option. They are widely used for short and long routes.

In larger towns you will find 'four-plus-ones' – normal taxis that collect passengers as they go. They are more expensive and more comfortable than minibus taxis, but are often only used for short routes.

Private Taxi

Larger cities have private taxi services. It's best to call in advance rather than hailing a taxi on the street. In Maseru, try Superb Taxis (p103).

Malawi

POP 18,570,321

Includes ➜

Lilongwe...................... 120
Karonga....................... 126
Mzuzu.......................... 131
Nkhata Bay 133
Nkhotakota 137
Cape Maclear............. 140
Liwonde....................... 144
Zomba Plateau............ 147
Blantyre & Limbe........ 149
Mulanje 154

Best Places to Sleep

➜ Kaya Mawa (p135)

➜ Mkulumadzi Lodge (p158)

➜ Mvuu Camp (p146)

➜ Chelinda Lodge (p129)

Best Places to Eat

➜ Casa Rossa (p147)

➜ Huntingdon House (p155)

➜ L'Hostaria (p151)

➜ Mushroom Farm (p128)

Why Go?

Apart from the legendary Malawian friendliness, what captures you first about this vivid country is its geographical diversity. Slicing through the landscape is Africa's third-largest lake: Lake Malawi, a shimmering mass of clear water, its depths swarming with colourful cichlid fish. Be it for diving, snorkelling, kayaking or just chilling, a visit to the lake is a must.

Suspended in the clouds in Malawi's deep south are the dramatic peaks of Mt Mulanje and the mysterious Zomba Plateau, both a hiker's dream, with mist-cowled forests and exotic wildlife. Further north is the otherworldly beauty of the Nyika Plateau, its rolling grasslands resembling the Scottish Highlands.

Malawi was once dismissed as a safari destination, but all that changed with a lion-reintroduction program at Majete Wildlife Reserve, which is now one of a few worthwhile wildlife-watching destinations nationwide.

When to Go
Lilongwe

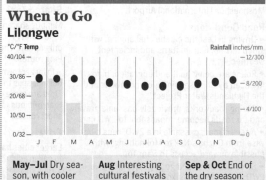

May–Jul Dry season, with cooler temperatures and lush vegetation.

Aug Interesting cultural festivals and good beach weather; the higher areas are chilly.

Sep & Oct End of the dry season: optimum wildlife-watching, but temperatures are high.

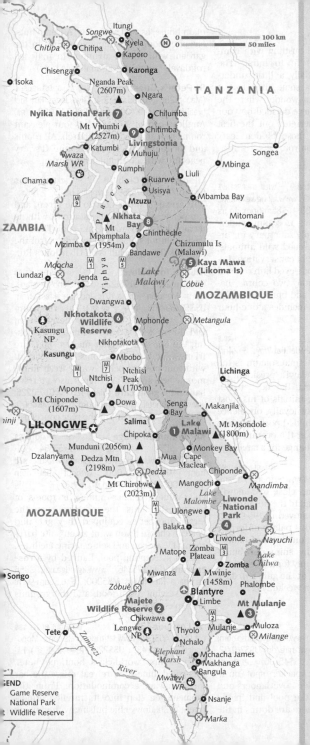

Malawi Highlights

❶ Lake Malawi
(p141) Kayaking across the bottle-green lake from ultra-chilled Cape Maclear to Mumbo Island.

❷ Majete Wildlife Reserve (p157) Searching for reintroduced lions in Malawi's only Big Five park.

❸ Mt Mulanje
(p155) Scrambling up the twisted peaks and admiring the astounding views.

❹ Liwonde National Park (p144) Spotting hippos and crocs on the Shire River and getting up close to elephants.

❺ Kaya Mawa
(p135) Escaping to this dreamy boutique hotel on Likoma Island.

❻ Nkhotakota Wildlife Reserve
(p138) Kayaking past crocs in the Bua River.

❼ Nyika National Park (p129) Cycling the rugged grasslands, home to zebras and antelope.

❽ Nkhata Bay
(p133) Diving among cichlids and feeding fish eagles in northern Malawi's up-and-coming beach town.

❾ Livingstonia
(p128) Heading to the hills to find this atmospheric mission, home to fantastic ecolodges.

LILONGWE

Sprawling, chaotic and bustling with commerce, Lilongwe feels fit to burst. The nation's capital is initially a little underwhelming and it takes some time to get your bearings – you may wonder where the centre is – but once you've decided on your favourite restaurants, ferreted out the best malls and discovered those hidden leafy oases, the place grows on you.

⦿ Sights

Lilongwe Wildlife Centre   WILDLIFE RESERVE
(Map p122; ☑ 0881 788999; www.lilongwewildlife. org; Kenyatta Rd; MK3500; ⦿ 8am-5pm, tours on the hour 9am-4pm) This 1.1-sq-km wilderness area is Malawi's only sanctuary for orphaned, injured and rescued wild animals, and plays an active role in conservation. Local residents include a one-eyed lion rescued from Romania, a python, two cobras, baboons, duikers, servals, and blue and vervet monkeys. The entry fee includes a one-hour tour of the enclosures.

Kamuzu Mausoleum   SHRINE
(Map p122; Capital Hill, Presidential Way; ⦿ 24hr) This marble and granite mausoleum is the final resting place of Malawi's 'president for life', Dr Hastings Kamuzu Banda. Between four pillars bearing the initials of his most prized principles – unity, loyalty, obedience and discipline – is a wrinkled portrait of the 'lion of Malawi'. Guides at the entrance will show you around in exchange for a small tip.

Parliament Building   NOTABLE BUILDING
(Map p122; Presidential Way; ⦿ tours 7.30am-4.30pm Mon-Fri) To get up close to Malawi's movers and shakers, head to the home of the national parliament. It moved in 1994 from Zomba to the ostentatious palace of former president Banda on the outskirts of Lilongwe and now occupies this shiny new building near Capital Hill. Apply for a free guided tour by filling in a form at the gate two days beforehand (and only on weekdays).

🛏 Sleeping

Mabuya Camp   HOSTEL $
(Map p122; ☑ 01-754978; www.mabuyacamp.com; Livingstone Rd; camping/tent hire/dm US$7/9/12, r with/without bathroom US$45/30; P 🛜 🏊) Lilongwe's liveliest backpacker spot buzzes with a mix of travellers, overlanders and volunteers relaxing by the pool and in the large, shady gardens. There are dorms in the

main house, as well as chalets, A-frame huts, en-suite rooms and camping pitches in the garden, with shared ablutions in thatched rondavels (round, traditional-style huts).

St Peter's Guesthouse   GUESTHOUSE $
(Map p125; ☑ 0995 299364; Glyn Jones Rd; incl breakfast dm MK4000, r MK8000-10,000; P) Anglican-owned St Peter's has four pleasant rooms next to a red-brick church. All rooms and the four-bed dorm are en suite. It's very peaceful, with a tranquil, leafy garden.

Lilongwe Golf Club   CAMPGROUND $
(Map p125; ☑ 01-753598; camping US$5; P 🛜 🏊) This tranquil site is next to the green, and campers can use the bar-restaurant with its terrace, kids' playground and pool. There's a basic ablutions block and guards patrol the grounds. The golf club is off Glyn Jones Rd.

Kiboko Town Hotel   GUESTHOUSE $$
(Map p125; ☑ 01-751226; www.kiboko-safaris. com; Mandala Rd; s/d/tr incl breakfast from US$59/69/108; P ⦿ 🍽 @ 🛜) This fresh upstairs guesthouse is right in the centre of Old Town, with a long veranda overlooking the Mandala St craft market. Staff are friendly and the 13 rooms are pleasant, with four-posters, ochre walls, fresh linen, mozzie nets and DSTV. There's also a terrace bar and a great **cafe** (Map p125; ☑ 01-751226; www.kibokohotel.com; Mandala Rd; mains MK4500; ⦿ 7am-5pm; P 🛜 🛗) in the rear courtyard.

Korea Garden Lodge   HOTEL $$
(Map p125; ☑ 01-759774, 01-757854, 01-753467; www.kglodge.net; Tsiranana Rd; s/d from MK25,000/35,000, without bathroom MK18,000/22,000; P 🍽 @ 🛜 🏊) This good-value hotel has numerous rooms of varying standards; the more you pay, the larger and better equipped they get, and you can choose if you want an en-suite bathroom, TV, air-con and self-catering facilities. There's a tempting pool, flanked by a **restaurant** (☑ 01-753467; www.kglodge.net; 3056 Tsiranana Rd; mains MK5000; ⦿ 6.30am-9pm; P 🛜) serving Asian food, and the grounds are replete with plants.

★ Latitude 13°   BOUTIQUE HOTEL $$$
(☑ 0996 403159; www.latitudehotels.com; Mphonongo Rd, Area 43; r US$220; P ⦿ 🍽 @ 🛜) Lilongwe's first world-class boutique hotel, this gated, nine-suite retreat raises the bar for Malawian accommodation. From the moment you step into its rarefied atmosphere of shadowy chic pulsing with glowing

pod lights you're transported right off the African continent.

★Kumbali Country Lodge LODGE $$$

(☑0999 963402; www.kumbalilodge.com; Capital Hill Dairy Farm, Plot 9 & 11, Area 44; s/d incl breakfast from US$200/240; P❋🛜🐕) A short drive from the city centre, on a 650-hectare forest reserve, is a choice of swanky individual thatched chalets (Madonna has stayed here on her controversial visits to Malawi) with beautiful views of nearby Nkhoma Mountain.

✗ Eating

Land & Lake Cafe CAFE $

(Map p125; ☑01-757120; Land & Lake Safaris, Area 3; mains MK3000; ⊗8am-4.30pm Mon-Fri, to 2pm Sat; P🛜🍴) This garden cafe at Land & Lake Safaris' headquarters, off Laws Ave, serves croissants, bagels and English breakfasts, light lunches from quesadillas to spuds, and tempting desserts.

★Ad Lib INTERNATIONAL $$

(Map p125; ☑0994 350630; www.adlibglasgow.com; Mandala Rd; mains MK6000; ⊗9am-late) An adventurous extension of a hip Glaswegian diner chain, this popular local gathering spot has a covered street-front terrace and a jolly red-walled interior with a long bar. The menu gallops enthusiastically across a broad spectrum, including steaks, jerk chicken, fish and chips, wood-smoked meats, nachos, quesadillas, Angus-beef burger (recommended) and southern fried chicken popcorn.

★Koko Bean CAFE $$

(Map p122; ☑0994 263363; Lilongwe Wildlife Centre, Kenyatta Rd; mains MK5000; ⊗8am-5pm) Soundtracked by world music, this breezy urban sanctuary is surrounded by lawns, thatched shelters and a bar overlooking a sprawling jungle gym – perfect for a family visit. Come for breakfasts from French toast to hearty 'hangover' omelettes, with a pot of tea or coffee; sandwiches, wraps and burgers; and pizzas with zingy toppings.

★Ama Khofi CAFE $$

(Map p122; ☑0998 196475; Four Seasons Centre, Presidential Way; mains MK5000; ⊗7.30am-5pm Mon-Sat, 9am-5pm Sun; P🛜🍴) Follow your nose to this delightful Parisian-style garden-centre cafe with wrought-iron chairs, a bubbling fountain and leafy surrounds. The menu has salads, main courses such as beef burgers and roast-beef sandwiches, and

homemade sweet treats that include cakes and ice cream.

🍷 Drinking & Nightlife

Living Room CAFE, BAR

(Map p122; ☑0881 615460; www.facebook.com/thelivingroomlilongwe; mains MK4000, cocktails MK2000; ⊗8am-late) With woodcarvings on its shaded veranda, this tucked-away chill-out den (find it off Mzimba St) offers coffee, cocktails, board games and dishes from steaks to chambo and chips. Check Facebook for details of events, which include live music on Tuesdays and poetry on Wednesdays. The adjoining sports bar, Champions, opens at 11am; Amazon nightclub opens at 7pm on Friday and Saturday.

Chameleon Bar BAR

(Map p122; ☑0888 833114; Four Seasons Centre, Presidential Way; ⊗4-11pm Mon-Wed, to midnight Thu, to 1am Fri & Sat, 2-11pm Sun; 🛜) This Scottish-owned watering hole faces **Buchanan's Grill** (Map p122; ☑0999 463686, 01-772859; www.buchanansgrill.com; Four Seasons Centre, Presidential Way; mains M6000, bar snacks MK4000; ⊗noon-2pm & 6-9pm Mon-Sat, noon 2.30pm Sun) in a leafy compound, with tables outside and a glass bar and purple walls within. It's popular with Malawians and expats both, and Sundays are big here, with live music from 2pm to 9.30pm. Karaoke is offered on the last Thursday of the month and soccer matches are screened.

Harry's Bar BAR

(Map p122; ⊗6pm-late) This hard-to-find wooden shack, located off Mzimba St, dishes up a bubbling atmosphere, live jazz in the garden and revolving entertainment. A Lilongwe institution and a must for any self-respecting hedonist.

☆ Entertainment

Umunthu Theatre THEATRE

(Map p122; ☑01-757979; www.umunthu.com) In a converted warehouse off Paul Kagame Rd, Umunthu puts on regular live music, films, club nights and more, showcasing the best of Malawian talent. A variety show (MK500) takes place on Friday evening.

🛍 Shopping

★Four Seasons Centre MALL

(Map p122; Presidential Way; 🛜) An oasis of fine dining and upmarket shopping, featuring clothing and design boutiques, a bar,

MALAWI LILONGWE

Lilongwe

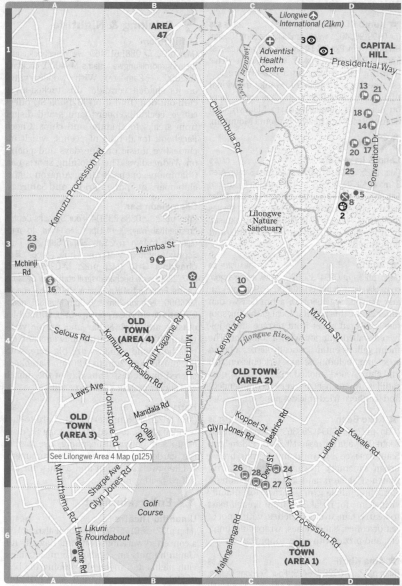

MALAWI LILONGWE

a restful one-stop shop. There's also a play park with a bouncy castle to keep nippers amused.

Lilongwe City Mall   MALL
(Game Complex; Map p125; Kenyatta Rd) The best mall around for shops, fast-food joints, banks and other services, with a central location in Old Town. It also has branches of the mobile networks Airtel and TNM.

a restaurant and a cafe, Four Seasons is a

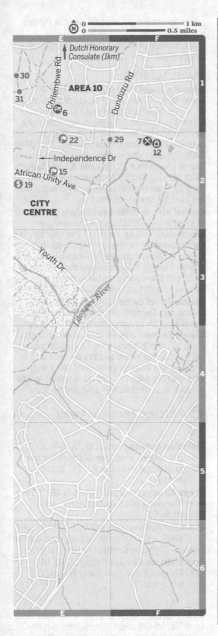

Lilongwe

◎ Sights
1	Kamuzu Mausoleum	D1
2	Lilongwe Wildlife Centre	D3
3	Parliament Building	D1

⊕ Activities, Courses & Tours
4	Adventure Office	A6
5	Central African Wilderness Safaris	D2

⊜ Sleeping
	Mabuya Camp	(see 4)
6	Sunbird Capital Hotel	E1

⊗ Eating
	Ama Khofi	(see 12)
7	Buchanan's Grill	F2
8	Koko Bean	D2

⊜ Drinking & Nightlife
	Chameleon Bar	(see 7)
9	Harry's Bar	B3
10	Living Room	C3

⊛ Entertainment
11	Umunthu Theatre	B3

⊕ Shopping
12	Four Seasons Centre	F2

ⓘ Information
13	British High Commission	D1
14	German Embassy	D2
15	Irish Embassy	E2
16	Money Bureau	A3
17	Mozambican High Commission	D2
18	South African High Commission	D2
19	Standard Bank	E2
20	US Embassy	D2
21	Zambian High Commission	D1
22	Zimbabwean Embassy	E2

ⓘ Transport
23	AXA Coach Terminal	A3
24	Buses to Dar es Salaam & Lusaka	C5
25	Ethiopian Airlines	D2
	Kenya Airways	(see 6)
26	Local Minibus Rank	C5
27	Long Distance Minibuses	C5
28	Main Bus Station	C5
29	Malawian Airlines	F2
30	South African Airways	E1
31	Ultimate Travel	E1

MALAWI LILONGWE

African Habitat   ARTS & CRAFTS
(Map p125; ☏ 01-752363; grabifem@hotmail.com; Old Town Mall; ⊗ 8.30am-5pm Mon-Fri, to 1pm Sat) Excellent for sculpture, woodcarvings, sarongs, cards and jewellery, as well as T-shirts and bags.

Craft Market   MARKET
(Map p125; cnr Mandala & Kamuzu Procession Rds; ⊗ 8am-4pm Mon-Sat) At these stalls outside the Old Town post office, vendors sell everything

from trinket woodcarvings, basketware and jewellery to traditional Malawian chairs.

Baobab Books   BOOKS
(Map p125; ☑ 0999 280858; Uplands House, Kamuzu Procession Rd; ⊙ 8am-4.30pm Mon-Fri, to noon Sat) Excellent secondhand books hop with a wide range of novels, guidebooks, children's books and more. It also has a small cafe.

ℹ Information

IMMIGRATION

Immigration Office (Map p125; ☑ 01-750626; www.immigration.gov.mw; Murray Rd; ⊙ 7.30am-noon & 12.30-4pm Mon-Fri, to noon Sat)

MEDICAL

Adventist Health Centre (Map p122; ☑ 01-771543; ⊙ casualty 24hr) Good for consultations, plus eye and dental problems. Off Presidential Way.

Daeyang Luke Hospital (☑ 01-711395; www.hospital.daeyangmission.org; Area 27; ⊙ casualty 24hr, inpatients 8am-4.30pm Mon-Fri) Recommended private hospital. Off the M1 en route to the airport.

Michiru Pharmacy (Map p125; ☑ 01-754294; Nico Shopping Centre, Kamuzu Procession Rd; ⊙ 8am-5pm Mon-Fri, to 1pm Sat & Sun) Sells antibiotics and malaria pills as well as the usual offerings.

MONEY

Money Bureau (Map p122; ☑ 01-750875; www.fdh.co.mw; Crossroads Complex, Kamuzu Procession Rd; ⊙ 8am-4pm Mon-Fri, to noon Sat) Has good rates.

Standard Bank (Map p122; African Unity Ave, City Centre; ⊙ 8am-3pm Mon-Fri, 9-11am Sat) Change money and get a cash advances on Visa cards. There's a 24-hour ATM that accepts Visa, MasterCard, Cirrus and Maestro.

SAFE TRAVEL

During the day it's fine to walk around most of Old Town and City Centre, although City Centre is quieter at the weekend, so be on your guard then. Malangalanga Rd and the area around the main bus station and market can be dangerous, and walking to Old Town from there is not recommended. Muggers' haunts en route include the Kamuzu Procession Rd bridge between Area 2 and Area 3.

Watch out for your things while at the bus station, and if you arrive after dark take a taxi or minibus to your accommodation. Generally it isn't safe to walk around anywhere in the city after dark. Following a spate of carjackings, many local motorists jump red lights after dark.

Bus tickets should only be bought at the bus station.

Avoid Lilongwe Wildlife Centre after dark due to late-night hyena appearances.

TRAVEL AGENCIES

Ultimate Travel (Map p122; ☑ 01-776000; www.ultimatetravel.mw; President Walmont Hotel, Umodzi Park) offers city tours and nocturnal experiences of Lilongwe nightlife. For a day trip into the surrounding countryside, contact The **Adventure Office** (Map p122; ☑ 0996 347627; www.theadventureoffice.com; Mabuya Camp, Livingstone Rd) or **Land & Lake Safaris** (Map p125; ☑ 01-757120; www.landlake.net; Area 3). Travel agencies are also generally your best bet for tourist information.

Central African Wilderness Safaris (CAWS; Map p122; ☑ 01-771153; www.cawsmw.com; Woodlands Lilongwe, Youth Dr) The country's top safari operator specialises in trips to its high-end lodges in Liwonde and Nyika National Parks; also operates lodges in Lilongwe and the Chintheche Strip, and offers packages to Likoma Island and Zambia's South Luangwa National Park.

Ulendo Travel Group (☑ 01-794555; www.ulendo.net) Decades-old Ulendo is a one-stop travel shop for accommodation and car hire; **Ulendo Airlink** (☑ 01-794638; www.flyulendo.com) has flights head to hard-to-reach spots such as Likoma Island and the national parks; and a variety of expertly tailored tours and safaris in Malawi and Zambia are available. The reliable, specialist staff is a big selling point.

ℹ Getting There & Away

AIR

Ethiopian Airlines (Map p122; ☑ 01-772031; www.ethiopianairlines.com; Mantion Service Station Building, Kenyatta Rd; ⊙ 7.30am-4.30pm Mon-Fri)

Kenya Airways (Map p122; ☑ 01-774227; www.kenya-airways.com; Sunbird Capital Hotel, Chilembwe Rd)

Malawian Airlines (Map p122; ☑ 0992 991097, 01-774605; www.malawian-airlines.com; Golden Peacock Shopping Centre, Presidential Way)

South African Airways (Map p122; ☑ 01-772242; www.flysaa.com; Umodzi Park) Off Chilembwe Rd.

BUS

AXA (Map p122; ☑ 01-820100; www.axacoach.com; City Mall) buses run daily from outside its office to Blantyre (MK11,300, four hours), leaving at 7am, noon and 4.30pm. Buses leave around noon for Mzuzu (MK7000, four hours).

Destinations from the **main bus station** (Map p122; Malangalanga Rd, Area 2) include Mzuzu (MK4000, five hours), Blantyre (MK3500, four hours), Kasungu (MK2500, two hours), Nkhata

Lilongwe Area 4

Lilongwe Area 4

⊕ Activities, Courses & Tours
Land & Lake Safaris...........................(see 6)

🛏 Sleeping
1 Kiboko Town Hotel C3
2 Korea Garden Lodge B4
3 Lilongwe Golf Club D4
4 St Peter's Guesthouse C4

✖ Eating
5 Ad Lib.. C3

Kiboko Town Hotel...........................(see 1)
Korea Garden Restaurant..............(see 2)
6 Land & Lake Cafe A2

🛍 Shopping
7 African Habitat.......................................C1
8 Baobab Books..B2
9 Craft Market...D3
10 Lilongwe City Mall D3

Bay (MK4000, five hours) and Dedza (MK2000, one hour).

Long-distance minibuses (Map p122) depart from the main bus station area to nearby destinations such as Zomba (MK5000, four to five hours), Dedza (MK2000, 45 minutes to one hour), the Zambian border at Mchinji (MK2500, two hours), Mangochi (MK5000, 4½ hours),

Limbe (for Blantyre; MK4000, three to four hours) and Nkhotakota (MK4000, three hours).

Intercape (Map p125; ☎ 0999 403398; www.in tercape.co.za; Kamuzu Procession Rd; ⊗ ticket office 5am-5pm Mon-Fri, to 2pm Sat, to 11am Sun) has modern buses to Jo'burg (MK36,000 to MK43,000, 36 hours), leaving daily from outside its office at 6am and departing Jo'burg daily at 8.30am. Intercape also operates a bus to Mzuzu (MK15,000 to MK23,000, five hours, daily except Friday and Sunday), which waits for the service from Jo'burg to arrive and leaves between 9pm and 11pm.

Kob's Coach Services (✉ in Zambia 260 977794073) leaves for Lusaka (Zambia) on Wednesday and Saturday at 5.30am, arriving at 5pm (MK20,000). **Taqwa Coach Company** (✉ in Zambia +260 977 114825) departs five evenings a week to Dar es Salaam (Tanzania; US$60, 30 hours) via Mzuzu, with onward connections to Nairobi (Kenya). In both cases, get there a good hour early for a decent seat. Both the Lusaka and the Dar es Salaam **services** (Map p122; Devil St) leave from Devil St, adjacent to the main bus station.

CAR

Avis (✉ 01-756105; www.avis.com) and Budget have offices at the **Sunbird Capital Hotel** (Map p122; ✉ 01-773388; www.sunbirdmalawi. com; Chilembwe Rd; s/d incl breakfast from US$142/172; ⓟ ⊜ ✳ @ ⓦ ⊠). Local companies include the following:

Best Car Hire (✉ 01-751097; www.bestcarhire malawi.com)

Chancy Mapples Car Hire (✉ 0888 323287, 0997 615442; www.car-hire-malawi.com)

Sputnik Car Hire (✉ 01-758253; www.sputnik-car-hire.mw)

SS Rent A Car (Map p125; ✉ 01-751478; www. ssrentacar.com; Kamuzu Procession Rd)

❶ Getting Around

LOCAL TRANSPORT

The most useful local minibus route is between Old Town and City centre. The journey should cost around MK200; you can cross the whole city for MK300.

From Old Town, minibuses leave from next to Shoprite. They head north up Kenyatta Rd, and along Youth and Convention or Independence Dr. The minibus stand for the return journey from City Centre is at the northern end of Independence Dr.

You can also catch minibuses to Old Town and City Centre from the main bus station area.

TAXI

The best places to find taxis are at the big hotels and major shopping malls, including outside Old Town Shoprite. The fare between Old Town and City Centre is about MK6000, while a tuktuk should cost under MK4000. Negotiate a price with the driver first.

Mawaso Taxi Service (✉ 0999 161111, 0995 169772) Trips across town, airport pickups and drop-offs, and intercity journeys.

NORTHERN MALAWI

Remote northern Malawi is where ravishing highlands meet hippo-filled swamps, vast mountains loom large over empty beaches, and colonial relics litter pristine islands and hilltop villages. It's Malawi's most sparsely populated region and the first taste many travellers get of this tiny country after making the journey down from East Africa.

Karonga

Dusty little Karonga is the first town you'll come across on the journey down from Tanzania and, while it's unlikely to enrapture you, it suffices for a stop to withdraw some kwacha – and have a close encounter with a 100-million-year-old dinosaur. Karonga has the proud title of Malawi's 'fossil district', with well-preserved remains of dinosaurs and ancient humans. Its most famous discovery is the Malawisaurus (Malawi lizard) – a 9.1m-long, 4.3m-high fossilised dino skeleton found 45km south of town. See an impressive replica at the **Cultural & Museum Centre Karonga** (CMCK; ✉ 01-362579, 0888 515574; www.facebook.com/CMCK.Malawi; MK1000; ⊙8am-4.30pm Mon-Sat, from 2.30pm Sun).

Rooms at the **Sumuka Inn** (✉ 0999 444816; s/d standard MK13,000/18,000, deluxe MK15,000/20,000, executive MK17,500/22,500; ⓟ ✳) are badly in need of renovation – and a good clean – but it remains a friendly and reasonably comfortable stopover. You can have a hot shower here, a fridge of cold Carlsbergs awaits in reception, and the restaurant (mains MK3000) serves cooked breakfasts and basic meals such as chambo.

The **Safari Lodge** (✉ 01-362340; incl breakfast s/d standard MK5500/6500, executive MK9000/11,500) is a fallback option with spacious but basic rooms with tiled floors and a bar where drinkers watch the football.

❶ Getting There & Away

AXA deluxe buses leave Karonga at noon daily for Blantyre (MK12,000, 18 hours), stopping in Mzuzu (MK4000, four hours) and heading down the lakeshore via Salima (MK11,150, 11 hours). Change in Mzuzu for Lilongwe. In the opposite direction, buses leave Blantyre around 5pm and reach Karonga around 11am the following day.

AXA has a **ticket office** (✉ 01-362787; www. axacoach.com) at Karonga bus station, in the market area 500m north of the museum.

Northern Malawi

LEGEND
NP   National Park
WR   Wildlife Reserve

Minibuses run from the bus station to destinations including Mzuzu (MK4000, four hours) via Chitimba (MK2100, 1½ hours), and the Songwe border crossing to Tanzania (MK1200, one hour).

If you've got a 4WD you can cross into northern Zambia via Chitipa in northern Malawi. It's four hours from Karonga to Chitipa on a rough dirt road (there's no public transport, but you might be able to get a lift on a truck). After going through customs it is another 80km or four hours' drive to the Zambian border post at Nakonde.

Livingstonia

Built by Scottish missionaries, Livingstonia feels sanctified, special and otherworldly, with its tree-lined main street graced by crumbling colonial relics. But for the stunning mountain views, there's not much to do in town other than visit the museum, church and sundry historical curios. Experiencing this piece of mountaintop history, and staying at one of the nearby permaculture farms, will be a magical, peaceful chapter in your Malawian journey.

After two failed attempts at establishing a mission at Cape Maclear and at Bandawe (too many people kept dying from malaria), the Free Church of Scotland moved its mission 900m above the lake to the village of Khondowe. Called Livingstonia after Dr David Livingstone, the mission was built under the leadership of Dr Robert Laws in 1894. The town provides a fascinating glimpse of Malawi's colonial past: most of its old stone buildings are still standing, many used by the local university.

◎ Sights

Stone House Museum
MUSEUM

(☑01-368223; MK700; ⊙7.30am-4.30pm) The fascinating museum in Stone House (once the home of Livingstonia founder Dr Robert Laws, and now a national monument) tells the story of the European arrival in Malawi and the first missionaries. Here you can read Dr Laws' letters and books, including the old laws of Nyasaland, and peruse black-and-white photos of early missionary life in Livingstonia.

Manchewe Falls
WATERFALL

This impressive waterfall thunders 125m into the valley below, about 4km from Livingstonia (towards the lake). Follow a small path behind the falls and there's a cave where, so the story goes, local people once hid from slave traders.

Livingstonia Church
CHURCH

(☑01-311344; admission by donation) Dating from 1894, this mission church has a beautiful stained-glass window featuring David Livingstone with his sextant, his medicine chest and his two companions, with Lake Malawi in the background. You can climb the tower for a bird's-eye view of Livingstonia.

🛏 Sleeping & Eating

★ Lukwe EcoCamp
LODGE, CAMPGROUND $

(☑0999 434985; www.lukwe.com; camping US$6, s/d without bathroom US$15/25; P 🛜) 🍃 This serene, tasteful permaculture camp is about helping local farmers and being completely self-sufficient. Comfortable glass-fronted chalets and thatch-covered tents are set in leafy terraced gardens, with private balconies and shared solar- and donkey-boiler-heated showers, composting loos and self-catering kitchen. See the mountain drop into infinity and spy Manchewe Falls from the swing chair.

★ Mushroom Farm
LODGE, CAMPGROUND $

(☑0999 652485; www.themushroomfarmmalawi.com; camping US$5, dm US$8-10, s/d US$30/40, without bathroom from US$15/25; P 🛜) 🍃 Perched on the edge of the Livingstonia escarpment (aka an abyss!), this permaculture ecolodge and campsite is worth the arduous journey for the warm welcome and views that will have you manually closing your jaw. The safari tents, hardwood A-frames and dorms provide charmingly rustic accommodation; better still is the en-suite cob house with cliffside shower.

The bar-restaurant (mains US$5, pre-ordered dinner US$7) offers sweeping views and organic veggie fusion dishes such as tortilla wraps and Asian noodle salad. Activities on offer include yoga, woodcarving, guided day hikes (US$3 per person) to Livingstonia, Manchewe Falls and the Chombe Plateau, and coffee-plantation tours. The off-the-grid facilities include fire-heated shared showers, composting loo, solar-powered electricity and self-catering kitchen.

Hakuna Matata
HOSTEL, CAMPGROUND $

(☑0991 092027, 0882 297779; www.facebook.com/chitimbahakunamatata; camping/dm MK3500/4900, s/d without bathroom MK7000/11,000; P 🛜) At the foot of the mountain in lakeside Chitimba, this beach camp is an excellent launch pad for tackling the ascent to Livingstonia. The whitewashed rooms have mozzie nets and fans, and one room has a private bathroom. Chat to the personable South African host, Willie, in the refreshingly shaded cafe (mains MK2000, pre-ordered dinner MK4000).

ⓘ Getting There & Away

From the main north–south road between Karonga and Mzuzu, the road to Livingstonia (known as the Gorode) turns off at Chitimba, forcing its way up the escarpment. This twisting, ulcerated road is a test for the most steely drivers: a white-knuckle experience of 20 switchbacks and hairpins, with a boulder-strewn, mainly unpaved surface – at times single track – with the mountain abysmally close to you.

Don't attempt this in anything but a 4WD and *never* in rain. You can get a place in a shared pickup truck, which may involve a long wait for the vehicle to fill with passengers, for MK2000 (plus MK1000 per big backpack). The journey takes around 45 minutes, and pickups leave from the small station at the junction of the main M1 road and the Gorode.

Be warned that accidents are not uncommon in the shared pickups. A safer option is to hire a vehicle; organise this through your accommodation or call **Thomas** (☑ 0882 175409; up to 8 passengers MK20,000). Thomas lives in Livingstonia, so you may want to arrange the transfer in advance of your arrival in Chitimba. Alternatively, Willie at Hakuna Matata in Chitimba offers day trips in his bakkie (pickup) to Livingstonia for up to 10 people (US$10 per person, minimum charge US$60) – an easy and recommended option.

You can tackle the 15km trip up the mountain on foot, an ascent of just under 1000m that takes around three hours. Park your car, leave your bags and stock up on iced water at Hakuna Matata. There have been isolated incidents of muggings on the Gorode, so check on the latest situation and hire a guide if you're by yourself or setting off late. Enquire at Hakuna Matata, phone your accommodation or ask at the M1–Gorode junction for guide Stanley Zinyengo Gondwe, who can also arrange porters.

Coming from the south, another way to reach Livingstonia is to drive up the dirt road from Rumphi, for which you'll need a 4WD – that said, it's an easy, dusty and very pretty drive. You can also join this 78km route about halfway along by turning off the M1 at Phwezi. During the rainy season the dust turns to mud and even 4WDs may not make it.

Nyika National Park

It's a rough drive to these beguiling highlands, but Malawi's oldest reserve is worth every bump. Towering over 2000m above sea level, the 3200-sq-km **Nyika National Park** (person/car US$10/3; ☉ 6am-6pm) is eas-

ily one of the country's most magical experiences. Turning burnt amber in the afternoon sun, the highland grass flickers with the stripes of zebras and is punctuated by glittering boulders that look like set dressing from a *Star Trek* movie.

Thanks to the top guides of **Central African Wilderness Safaris** (☑ 0881 085177, 01-771393; www.cawsmw.com), your chances of seeing animals on a morning wildlife drive (US$35 per person) or walk (US$20 per person) are extremely high.

The most exciting wildlife drives, however, are by night, with decent chances of your guide scoping out leopards. The current population of around 100 is one of the region's densest.

Wildlife viewing is good year-round, although in July and August the cold weather means the animals move off the plateau to lower areas. Birdwatching is particularly good between October and April, when migratory birds are on the move.

🛏 Sleeping & Eating

Chelinda Campground　CAMPGROUND $
(☑ 0881 085177, 01-771393; www.cawsmw.com; camping US$15; ⓟ) Set in a secluded site with vistas of the plateau's rolling hills, this camp has permanent security, clean toilets, hot showers, endless firewood and shelters for cooking and eating. Self-caterers should stock up in Mzuzu or Rumphi. There's a small shop at Chelinda for National Parks staff, but provisions are often basic and supplies sporadic.

★**Chelinda Lodge**　LODGE $$$
(☑ 01-771393, 0881 085177; www.cawsmw.com; s/d all-inclusive US$450/700; ⓟ☉◉☎) Sitting on a hillside in a clearing of pine trees, upmarket Chelinda is a traveller's dream. The main building crackles with fires at every turn, complemented by inviting couches, walls adorned with lush wildlife photography, pillars hung with woodcarvings, glittering chandeliers and high beams. Rates include park entrance fees and wildlife-watching activities.

★**Chelinda Camp**　CHALET $$$
(☑ 0881 085177, 01-771393; www.cawsmw.com; s/d all-inclusive US$355/530; ⓟ☎) Nestled into the lee of a valley beside a small lake, this Central African Wilderness Safaris lodge is insanely picturesque. Its bungalows have an unfussy '70s aspect to them and are ideal

Nyika National Park

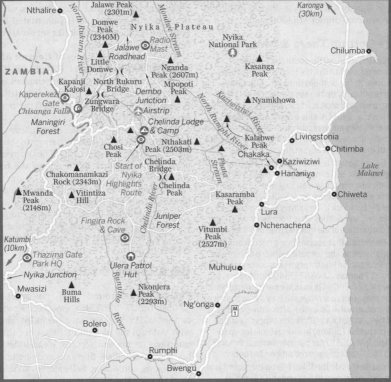

for families, with small kitchen, cosy sitting room and stone fireplace. Rates include park entrance fees and wildlife-watching activities.

❶ Getting There & Away

The main Thazima Gate (pronounced and sometimes spelled Tazima) is 55km northwest of Rumphi – about two hours' drive. Once inside the park, it's another 60km, two-hour drive to Chelinda. Especially from Rumphi to Thazima Gate, the corrugated road is appallingly bumpy; do call to check on its condition in the wet season. Petrol is available at Chelinda but in limited supply, so fill up before you enter the park.

It's possible to bring a mountain bike into Nyika; if you pick up a ride from Rumphi to Thazima, you can cycle the last 60km to Chelinda. An early start is recommended due to the distance.

Unfortunately, getting to Chelinda by public transport is tricky. From Rumphi, a truck or *matola* (pickup; MK3000) heading north to Chitipa could drop you at the turnoff to Chelinda,

16km west of the lodges and campground near the Zambian border. However, that will leave you somewhat stranded, and, when you make it to Chelinda, you will then have the return journey to tackle. On the bright side, taxi services in Mzuzu and Rumphi offer transfers; the main drawback, if the driver is hanging around and taking you back to Rumphi, is that you will have to pay for his or her accommodation.

If you are prepared to wait around, it may be possible to make an ad-hoc arrangement for staff from Chelinda to pick you up when they go shopping in Rumphi or Mzuzu.

Vwaza Marsh Wildlife Reserve

This compact, 1000-sq-km **reserve** (✆0991 912775, 0884 203964; moyoleonard52@gmail.com; person/vehicle US$10/3; ⊙6am-6pm) is home to plentiful wildlife, and ranges from large, flat areas of mopane (woodland) to open swamp and wetlands. The Luwewe River runs through the park, draining the marshland, and joins the South Rukuru River (the reserve's southern border), which flows into Lake Kazuni.

Lake Kazuni Safari Camp offers basic accommodation, and *matolas* run here from Rumphi, but visiting on a tour with the likes of Nkhata Bay Safaris (p133) is the easiest option.

The best time to visit is the dry season; just after the rainy season, the grass is high and you might go away without seeing anything.

If you're travelling by public transport, first get to Rumphi (reached from Mzuzu by minibus for MK2000). From Rumphi, *matolas* (pickups) travel to/from the Kazuni area and you should be able to get a lift to the main gate for around MK1500. Minibuses also ply this route to/from Kazuni village, and can drop you by the bridge, 1km east of the park gate and camp.

By car, head west from Rumphi. Turn left after 10km (Vwaza Marsh Wildlife Reserve is signposted) and continue for about 20km. Where the road swings left over the bridge, go straight on to reach the park gate and camp after 1km.

Lake Kazuni Safari Camp CABIN $

(☑ 0884 203964, 0991 912775; moyoleonard52@gmail.com; camping per site MK7500, r MK10,000; P) The camp's five simple en-suite, thatch-and-brick twin cabanas are perfectly positioned on the lakeshore; the animals are so plentiful that it feels as though you've stepped into a children's picture book. The camp is very basic and guests must bring their own food and drinks, including water; the accommodating staff will be happy to cook you dinner in the camp kitchen.

Mzuzu

Dusty, sprawling Mzuzu is Malawi's third-largest city, northern Malawi's principal town and the region's transport hub. Travellers heading along the M1 – across to Nkhata Bay, Nyika or Viphya, or up to Tanzania – are likely to spend a night or two here. With some good accommodation options, Mzuzu is an appealingly authentic and laid-back spot to experience everyday Malawian life.

Mzuzu has banks, shops, a post office, supermarkets, pharmacies, petrol stations and other facilities, which are especially useful if you've entered Malawi from the north.

Mzuzu Museum MUSEUM

(☑ 0884 201126, 0939 386624; M'Mbelwa Rd; MK500; ☺ 7.30am-noon & 1-4.30pm Mon-Sat; P) The city museum has displays on the people and the land of northern Malawi. Exhibits include traditional hunting implements, musical instruments, and photos of a paramount chief's coronation ceremony. If you're heading up to Livingstonia, there's an interesting exhibition telling the story of the missionaries who established the town.

🛏 Sleeping

★ Macondo Camp GUESTHOUSE $

(☑ 0991 792311; www.macondocamp.com; Chimaliro 4; camping MK3000, dm MK5000, s/d without bathroom MK14,000/17,000, apt MK35,000; P 🖱) Run by Italian couple and serial overlanders Luca and Cecilia, Macondo has cute rooms in the main house, tented chalets with wooden decks overlooking the lawn and banana trees, and an annexe with dorm beds.

Joy's Place HOSTEL $

(☑ 0991 922242, 0998 391358; www.facebook.com/joyinmzuzu; dm US$8, r/tr/q without bathroom US$25/30/35; P 🖱) Popular with the aid-work fraternity, these pleasantly decorated rooms with mozzie nets and bright bedspreads are hidden away in a suburban house. Choose between the eight-bed en-suite dorm and a private room sharing a bathroom with one other room. There's a relaxing lounge and a popular **restaurant** (☑ 0998 391358, 0991 922242; mains MK3500; ☺ 7am-8pm; P 🖱).

Umunthu Camp LODGE $

(☑ 0992 417916, 0881 980019; umunthucamp@gmail.com; dm/r MK5000/12,000; ☺ restaurant 7am-9pm Tue-Sun; P 🖱) The brainchild of South African couple Andries and Farzana, Umunthu has coolly decorated, sparsely furnished rooms and a four-bed dorm with adjoining bathroom. The bar-restaurant (mains MK5000) draws on the resident kitchen garden, serving dishes including pizza, pasta, burgers and steaks. It's behind Shoprite supermarket, signposted from the main drag.

Sunbird Mzuzu HOTEL $$$

(☑ 01-332622; www.sunbirdmalawi.com; Kabunduli Viphya Dr; s/d/ste incl breakfast from US$120/150/240; P ✳ @ 🖱) Easily the city's plushest digs, this large hotel in imposing

MALAWI MZUZU

Mzuzu

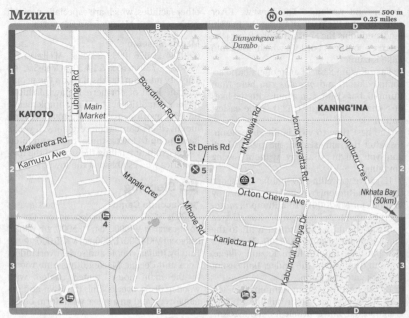

Mzuzu

◎ Sights
1 Mzuzu Museum.....................................C2

🛏 Sleeping
2 Joy's Place...A3
3 Sunbird Mzuzu.....................................C3
4 Umunthu Camp....................................A2

⊗ Eating
Joy's Place....................................(see 2)
5 Soul Kitchen...B2

🛍 Shopping
6 Hardware Market................................B2

grounds has huge rooms with deep-pile carpet, flat-screen DSTV, fridge and views of Mzuzu's golf course. As you'd expect from Sunbird, the service is friendly and efficient and the place is of an international standard.

✗ Eating

Soul Kitchen   MALAWIAN $
(☏0884 957150; St Denis Rd; mains MK2000; ⊘7am-10pm Mon-Sat) Watch Mzuzu go by on Soul Kitchen's shaded stoep with a barbecue smoking away at one end and a view of the city's only traffic light. Barbecued chicken,

chambo, omelette and T-bone steak are on the menu.

★**Macondo Camp**   ITALIAN $$
(☏0991 792311; mains MK4500; ⊘7am-9pm; 🅿🛜) This Italian restaurant offers treats such as homemade pasta made daily, Parmesan flown from Italy and monthly live music on the stoep. Dishes include pizza, steaks, spring rolls and the ever-popular ravioli with blue cheese, which can be accompanied by a good selection of Italian and South African wines. It's at the namesake guesthouse northeast of central Mzuzu.

ⓘ Getting There & Away

AXA buses leave at 5pm for Blantyre (MK8000, 13 hours) via the lakeshore, and at 7am for Karonga (MK4000, four hours). AXA departs at 7pm for Lilongwe (MK7000, four hours).

Minibuses and shared taxis go to Nkhata Bay (MK1500, one to two hours), Karonga (MK4000, four hours), Chitimba (MK2000, 2½ hours), Rumphi (MK2000, one hour) and the Tanzanian border (MK5200, five hours).

If you need to repair your vehicle, there's a well-stocked **Hardware Market** (Boardman Rd), where the many shopkeepers can sell you all manner of parts and recommend mechanics.

Nkhata Bay

Nkhata Bay has an almost Caribbean feel, with its fishing boats buzzing across the green bay, market stalls hawking barbecued fish, and reggae filling the languorous afternoons. There are also loads of activities to enjoy before you hammock flop, be it snorkelling, diving, fish-eagle feeding, kayaking or forest walks.

◉ Sights & Activities

Chikale Beach
BEACH
On the southern side of Nkhata Bay, Chikale Beach is a popular spot for swimming and lazing on the sand, especially at weekends. After church on Sunday, the locals set up a speaker stack and enjoy a few beers.

Monkey Business
KAYAKING
(☑ 0999 437247; monkeybusinesskayaking.blog spot.co.za; Butterfly Space) Monkey Business, at Butterfly Space hostel, can organise paddling excursions personally tailored to your needs – anything from half a day to a few days down the coast.

Aqua Africa
DIVING
(☑ 0999 921418; www.aquaafrica.co.uk) This dependable British-run outfit offers dives for certified divers (from US$50) and numerous courses, including the three- to four-day PADI Open Water course (US$380 including all materials). Colourful cichlid fish, the kind you've probably seen in a dentist's aquarium, swim throughout the lake, but more spectacular are the schools of dolphinfish that are drawn to your torch (flashlight) on night dives.

Nkhata Bay Safaris
TOURS
(☑ 0999 265064; www.nkhatabaysafaris.com; 4-day tour for 2 people camping/chalets US$655/755) Run by a Malawian team headed by Davie, this tour operator offers four- to 10-day trips to Vwaza Marsh Wildlife Reserve, Nyika National Park, Livingstonia and further afield. It can help with local activities, transport and accommodation bookings, and has recently introduced day and overnight wildlife-watching tours to Vwaza and overnight safaris to Nkhotakota Wildlife Reserve (US$275 per person).

🛏 Sleeping

★ Mayoka Village
LODGE $
(☑ 0999 268595, 01-994025; www.mayokavillage beachlodge.com; camping/d US$5/12, chalet s/d US$30/45, f US$50-70, s/d/tr/q without bathroom

US$20/35/45/60; P🛜) 🏄 Cleverly shaped around the rocky topography of a cliff, boutique-style Mayoka cascades down in a series of beautiful bamboo-and-stone chalets. There are myriad romantic nooks for taking in the lake below or grabbing some rays on sunloungers. The waterfront bar-restaurant (mains MK2500) is a beach hideaway serving cocktails and dishes from wraps and burgers to Malawian red-bean stew.

Butterfly Space
HOSTEL $
(☑ 0999 265065, 0999 156335; www.butterfly -space.com; camping/dm MK1500/3000, chalets per person with/without bathroom MK8000/7000; P@🛜) Run by Alice and Josie, inspiring, colourful and socially committed Butterfly is a rare backpackers' oasis. There's a *palapa*-style lounge or spacious beachfront bar to chill in, a private beach, an internet cafe, a media centre, a self-catering block and a restaurant serving authentic Tongan cuisine, as well as sandwiches, chapattis, pasta and burgers (mains MK2000, pre-ordered dinner MK3000).

Aqua Africa
GUESTHOUSE $$
(☑ 0999 921418; www.aquaafrica.co.uk; standard s/tw US$30/40, deluxe s/d incl breakfast US$60/80; ⊙ restaurant 7am-6pm; P❄🛜) With whitewashed rooms featuring polished stone floors, step-in mozzie nets and blue curtains opening onto balconies overlooking the bay, this dive school's four rooms often host its students. The Dive Deck Cafe, complete with wicker loungers and viewing deck, has an excellent menu ranging from full breakfasts to nachos, Cajun chicken, fish burgers and peanut-coated chicken strips (mains MK2500).

Njaya Lodge
LODGE $$
(☑ 01-352342, 0999 948673, 0884 743647; www. njayalodge.com; d, tr & q US$60, cottages US$70, r without bathroom per person US$15; P🛜) Set in terraced gardens bursting with frangipanis and palms, with manicured lawns tumbling down to the spearmint water, Njaya has a range of accommodation from garden chalets on the hillside to striking stone cottages right by the lake. It's a little run-down but in a wonderful secluded location.

🍴 Eating & Drinking

Crest View
MALAWIAN $
(☑ 0881 174804; mains MK2000; ⊙ 6am-9pm; 🅿) Thrifty travellers appreciate this local hangout with football on the TV and a good view

Nkhata Bay

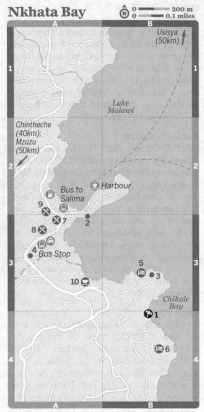

Nkhata Bay

◉ Sights
1 Chikale Beach..B4

✚ Activities, Courses & Tours
2 Aqua Africa...A3
3 Monkey Business...................................B3
4 Nkhata Bay Safaris...............................A3

⊜ Sleeping
Aqua Africa....................................(see 2)
Butterfly Space.............................(see 3)
5 Mayoka Village.......................................B3
6 Njaya Lodge..B4

✖ Eating
7 Crest View...A3
8 Kaya Papaya..A3
9 Peoples Supermarket...........................A2

⊙ Drinking & Nightlife
10 One Love...A3

of the action happening on the main street. *Nsima* (a filling porridge-like dish made from white maize flour and water) with beans, omelettes and other local favourites are on the menu.

Peoples Supermarket　SUPERMARKET $
(⊙ 6.30am-7pm Mon-Fri, to 6pm Sat, 8am-5pm Sun) For self-catering, the Peoples Supermarket on the main drag sells toiletries, biscuits and milk.

One Love　CAFE $
(☑ 0996 955164; www.facebook.com/onelove-handmadeart) At One Love, with an unbeatable view of the bay, Kelvin the Rasta serves cold beers and simple dishes such as chapattis, *nsima* and beans (mains MK1300). He also sells his woodcarvings and drums. Hours are variable, so call ahead before making a special trip.

★ **Kaya Papaya**　THAI $$
(☑ 0888 576489, 0993 688884; mains MK4000; ⊙ 11am-10pm, last food orders 8.45pm; 🖥 ☑) Close to the harbour, with a big upstairs balcony overlooking the main street, Kaya Papaya has an appealing Afro-Asian-fusion chic that's matched by a menu of zesty salads, pizza and Thai fare such as green curry, chicken satay and stir-fries. If you're still hungry, try a banana pancake.

❶ Information

Travellers have been mugged when walking outside the town centre (in particular to and from Chikale Beach and the surrounding lodges at night), so take extra care when walking this route as it's unlit and can be quite deserted. Muggings have subsided thanks to police efforts, but it's best to walk with another guest or a staff member from your lodge after dark.

Most travellers will encounter a fair amount of hassle from Rastas and beach boys offering a bewildering range of services and stimulants. If you're not interested, be polite but firm and they should leave you alone.

❶ Getting There & Away

Most transport leaves from the bus stop in the market area. AXA runs to Karonga via Mzuzu, leaving around 5.30am, and down the lake to Blantyre via Salima, departing around 6.30pm. Minibuses run to Nkhotakota (MK1500, five hours), Chintheche (MK950, one hour) and Mzuzu (MK1000, 1½ hours). There are also regularly departing and less cramped shared taxis (MK1500 to Mzuzu) and a daily bus to Salima (MK8000, nine hours, 5am), which respectively leave from the main bus stop and from outside the Admarc maize store.

To reach Lilongwe the quickest option is to head down the lake to Salima and change; alternatively, travel inland to Mzuzu and pick up a service going south.

Another option is to privately hire a taxi; you can likely share with someone from your accommodation heading in the same direction. Mzuzu costs MK12,000 (MK20,000 return) and Lilongwe MK100,000. **Noba Taxi** (📞 0995 260191) is a trustworthy and well-priced operation.

The *Ilala* (p167) ferry leaves from the **harbour** (📞 0882 870392) and heads north up the lakeshore to Chilumba on Sunday morning. Returning south, it departs Nkhata Bay for Chizumulu and Likoma Islands on Monday evening. Tanzania's Songea ferry crosses from Mbamba Bay (Tanzania) and the MV *Chambo* (p167) ferry sails from Metangula (Mozambique) via Likoma and Chizumulu on Wednesday, returning from Nkhata Bay on Thursday morning. This should mean you can catch the *Chambo* to the islands on Thursday and return to Nkhata Bay on the *Ilala* on Saturday...but there are no guarantees.

Drivers can fill up at the petrol station on the main road.

Likoma Island

Blissful Likoma Island – situated on the Mozambican side of Lake Malawi but part of Malawi – measures 17 sq km and is home to around 9000 people.

Likoma's flat and sandy south is littered with baobabs and offers an uninterrupted panoramic view of Mozambique's wild coast. The island's main drawcards are its abundance of pristine beaches and the attendant snorkelling, diving and water sports, but there's a healthy dose of other activities, both cultural and physical, to fill several days here.

◉ Sights & Activities

Swimming is a must on Likoma and is best on the long stretches of beach in the south. The tropical-fish population has been unaffected by the mainland's overfishing, and the snorkelling is excellent. Snorkels are on hand at the island's accommodation options, which can arrange scuba diving and PADI courses too.

A range of water sports is also available through accommodation, from learning to kitesurf to waterskiing and wakeboarding.

The island's compact but diverse area is perfect for walking and mountain biking;

you can bring bikes across on the ferry or hire them from accommodation.

Cathedral of St Peter CHURCH
(Chipyela; ☉ dawn-dusk) Likoma's huge Anglican cathedral (1911), said to be the same size as Winchester Cathedral, should not be missed. Its stained-glass windows, crumbling masonry and sheer scale are testament to the zeal of its missionary creators' religious conviction.

Climb the tower for spectacular views. If you're lucky you might meet the charming verger, who'll happily give you a tour, and you're welcome to join in the vibrant service on Sunday morning. The cathedral is less than 500m inland (and uphill) from the ferry terminal.

🛏 Sleeping & Eating

★ **Mango Drift** HOSTEL $$
(📞 0999 746122; www.mangodrift.com; camping US$6, tent rental US$1, dm US$8, s/d US$60/70, without bathroom US$25/30; @ 🗢) Far from backpacker hardship, this affordable island idyll is one of Malawi's most luxurious hostels. Its stone chalets are the closest you'll come to boutique this side of US$100, with hibiscus petals scattered on snow-white linen, wicker furniture, sundown verandas and loungers on the sand. The shared toilets and shower block are no less immaculate.

★ **Kaya Mawa** BOUTIQUE HOTEL $$$
(📞 0999 318360; www.kayamawa.com; full board per person from US$415; ✳@🗢) Remember Scaramanga's pad in *The Man with the Golden Gun*? Kaya Mawa, set on an amber-coloured beach lapped by turquoise water, is the ultimate location to live out your inner Bond fantasy. Its cliffside chalets, cleverly moulded around the landscape, are so beautiful you'll never want to leave.

ℹ Getting There & Away

Ulendo Airlink flies daily to Likoma from Lilongwe (adult/child one way US$295/211), with further scheduled departures from several other locations. The second option is to charter a flight; from Lilongwe, the one-way fare is US$365 for adults and US$260 for children, with a minimum of two passengers. Note that this does not give you exclusive use of the aircraft. The third, most affordable option is to check the 'bid to fly' section of Ulendo Airlink's website and make an offer for a seat on one of the listed flights.

The *Ilala* ferry stops at Likoma Island twice a week, usually for three to four hours, so even if you're heading elsewhere, you might be able to nip ashore to have a quick look at the cathedral. Check with the captain before you leave the boat. The ferry sails Nkhotakota–Likoma Island–Chizumulu Island–Nkhata Bay on Saturday, returning south on Monday/Tuesday. Additionally, the *Chambo* ferry sails Metangula (Mozambique)–Likoma Island–Chizumulu Island–Nkhata Bay on Wednesday, returning on Thursday. There's also a Metangula–Likoma MV *Chambo* service on Saturday, which returns on Sunday.

Dhows sail in the morning from Mdamba to Cóbuè (Mozambique). The fare is around MK2000; for a little extra they can pick you up or drop you off at Mango Drift. It is sometimes possible to catch a local boat to Chizumulu Island for around MK1000 per person, or to privately hire a boat with an engine (MK25,000 to MK30,000); ask your accommodation.

The lodges pick guests up from flight and ferry arrivals.

Chizumulu Island

Stretches of azure water and white rocky outcrops give Chizumulu Island – floating around 10km west of the larger Likoma Island – a Mediterranean flavour, while the backdrop of dry scrub is positively antipodean. Few travellers make it to Chizumulu thanks to its remote location and ferry schedules. However, you may stop off on a cruise or on the ferry en route between Likoma and Nkhata Bay.

The *Ilala* ferry stops right outside Wakwenda Retreat. It normally sails Nkhotakota–Likoma Island–Chizumulu Island–Nkhata Bay on Saturday, returning south on Monday/Tuesday. Additionally, the MV *Chambo* ferry sails Metangula (Mozambique)–Likoma Island–Chizumulu Island–Nkhata Bay on Wednesday, returning on Thursday.

This makes it possible to arrive at Chizumulu from Nkhata Bay early on Tuesday morning on the *Ilala,* and return to Nkhata Bay on the Wednesday on the MV *Chambo*. Alternatively, you can arrive at Chizumulu on Thursday on the MV *Chambo,* returning to Nkhata Bay on Saturday on the *Ilala*.

There are now no daily dhow ferries between the two islands, though it's possible to find a local boat over to Likoma for MK1000 per person – if one is heading across (no guarantees). The trip can take anywhere from one to three hours depending on the weather; it's an extremely choppy ride when the wind is blowing, and potentially dangerous if a storm comes up. If you're unsure, ask at Wakwenda Retreat for advice. It's also possible to privately hire a boat with an engine for MK25,000 to MK30,000.

Wakwenda Retreat (☑ SMS only 0999 348415; www.facebook.com/wakwenda; camping/ dm US$5/7, s/d without bathroom US$15/20), sometimes known as Nick's Place, smack bang on a postcard-perfect beach, is utter chill-out material. The bar occupies an outcrop of rocks by the water's edge with multilevel decks, featuring sunloungers and a plunge pool. The campsite is clustered around a massive, hollow baobab tree, which you can camp inside, and there are huts with verandas too.

CENTRAL MALAWI

This small corner of Malawi is chiefly famed for its dazzling white beaches, like the backpacker magnet, Cape Maclear, and for its desert islands like Mumbo and Domwe – both reached by sea kayak or boat. Nkhotakota Wildlife Reserve, its wildlife stocks increased by a major elephant translocation, has fine lodges and good access from the coast. North of here is the Viphya Plateau, a haunting wilderness of mountains, grasslands and mist-shrouded pines. For cultural appeal, meanwhile, you can't beat the Kungoni complex and mission buildings in Mua.

Viphya Plateau

The Viphya Plateau forms the spine of central and northern Malawi, snaking a cool path through the flat scrubland, dusty towns and sunny beaches that reign on either side. Tightly knit forests give way to gentle valleys and rivers, and huge granite domes rise softly from the earth like sleeping beasts. Indigenous woodland bristles with birds and wildflowers, monkeys dart through the trees and antelope can often be seen.

Buses and *matolas* (pickups) can drop off and pick up at the Luwawa Forest Lodge turnoff on the M1; the bus costs MK5000 from Lilongwe. Returning south, *matolas* regularly pass by on the M1 between 8am and 9am.

There's no public transport to Luwawa Lodge, so you'll have to walk from the Luwawa turnoff or call the lodge for a pickup (US$10 per group).

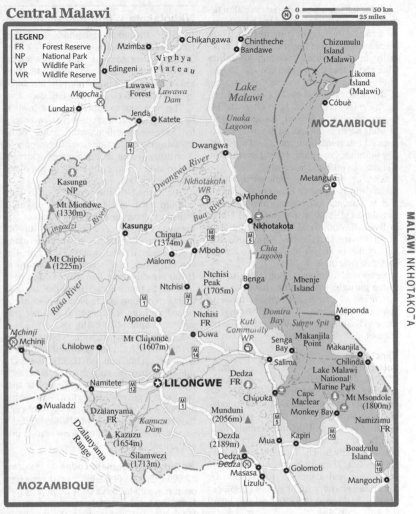

★ **Luwawa**
Forest Lodge LODGE, CAMPGROUND **$$**
(☎ 01-342333, 0999 512645; www.luwawaforest
lodge.net; camping US$8, dm US$14, r without
bathroom per person US$40, chalets incl breakfast/
half-board/full board per person US$80/105/120,
cottages US$120-160; P 🛜) Set at 1585m,
homey Luwawa sits in a clearing of pine
trees, its manicured gardens spilling with
colourful flowers and morning mist. There
are seven chalets and cottages, perfect
for families (as they sleep up to five), with
bunks, bathrooms, self-catering facilities
and swallow-you-up four-posters, as well as
more affordable rooms, dorms and a shaded
camping area.

Nkhotakota

One of the oldest market towns in Africa,
unassuming Nkhotakota had a significant
and sinister part to play in Malawi's history.
In the 1800s the town was home to a huge
slave market, set up by Swahili-Arab trader
Jumbe Salim-bin Abdullah. From here thou-
sands of unfortunate captives were shipped
annually across the lake to Tanzania, before
being forced to march to the coast.

Today the town is strung out over 4km between the busy highway and the lake. If you do arrive on the ferry or stumble from a bus, there are a couple of historical sights – especially the **Livingstone Tree** and **All Saints Church** (☉ dawn-dusk) – and lakeside lodges, but if you can it's better to continue straight to the nearby Nkhotakota Wildlife Reserve.

The *Ilala* ferry stops here en route between Monkey Bay and Likoma Island, heading north to Likoma on Saturday morning and returning from the island on Tuesday morning, before continuing south from Nkhotakota on Tuesday evening.

AXA buses pass through around midnight daily, heading to Blantrye via Salima and to Karonga via Mzuzu. Minibuses go to Salima (MK1500, two hours) and Nkhata Bay (MK3500, five hours). Waiting for a direct service to Lilongwe (MK2200, four hours) may be slower than going to Salima and changing there.

Buses and minibuses stop close to the **Puma garage**: services to Nkhata Bay stop just north of this petrol station; those to Salima and Lilongwe stop to the south; and those to Kasungu stop to the west, at the beginning of the Kasungu road.

Nkhotakota

Pottery Lodge   LODGE $$
(☎ 0999 380105, 0997 189064; www.nkhotakota-pottery-lodge.com; camping/dm US$10/15, s/d from US$36/54; P 🛜) This German-run lodge offers 10 simple garden rooms, each with mozzie net, fan and private veranda overlooking the lake, and a six-bed dorm next to 200m of sandy beach. Superior rooms have kitchenettes. There's a bar-restaurant where live music and dance performances are sometimes staged, with breakfast (US$8 per person), half board (US$20) and full board (US$26) available.

Sitima Inn   HOTEL $$
(☎ 0999 260005; www.sitimainn.com; camping/dm MK4500/7500, s/d incl breakfast from MK30,000/48,750, without bathroom from MK15,000/26,250; P ✳) Within staggering distance of the *Ilala* ferry, this low-slung cream building with art-deco aspirations is quirky to say the least, incorporating old boat materials, car doors and nautical motifs. Despite the faint hint of decline, rooms are mostly neat, pleasantly decorated and houseproud. There are also two basic four-bed dorms and a slightly tacky suite.

Nkhotakota Wildlife Reserve

West of the main lakeshore road lies **Nkhotakota Wildlife Reserve** (☎ 0999 521741; www.african-parks.org; person/car US$10/3; ☉ 6am-6pm), comprising 1800 sq km of rough, inhospitable terrain inhabited by animals from elephants to buffaloes.

The best way to experience the bush is by staying at one of the reserve's two excellent lodges and walking with a guide, or by kayaking down the Bua River from Tongole, your heart in your mouth as crocs upstream slip soundlessly into the murk to come and take a closer look.

The turnoff to the reserve's main gate is 10km north of Nkhotakota town. Public transport along the coast road north of Nkhotakota can you drop you at this turnoff, from where the gate is 10km away along a dirt track. You can walk to the gate, but you can't walk in the park unaccompanied. If you are staying at Bua River Lodge, SMS or email 24 hours ahead (don't call, because mobile reception at the lodge is bad) to be picked up from the turnoff (US$5 per person) or Nkhotakota (US$10).

Ulendo Airlink (p167) offers charter flights to the reserve from Lilongwe and Likoma Island (adult/child one way US$271/194 each; minimum two passengers). The airstrip is near Tongole Wilderness Lodge. Note that you are not guaranteed exclusive use of the aircraft. A more affordable option is to check the 'bid to fly' section of Ulendo Airlink's website and make an offer for a seat on one of the listed flights.

★ Tongole Wilderness Lodge   LODGE $$$
(☎ 0999 055778, 01-209194; www.tongole.com; per person with full board US$435; P 🛜 ✳) 🌿 Built with local materials, this eco-conscious lodge sits at elevation above the Bua River, a well-worn elephant crossing. Its thatched, near-church-high lodge is crowned by a mezzanine walkway leading to an aerial viewpoint – the perfect place to balance a G&T and binoculars. Huge chalets include plunge baths, marble basins, rain showers, wooden decks and wrought-iron doors with widescreen views.

Bua River Lodge   LODGE, CAMPGROUND $$$
(☎ 0995 476887, 0885 181834; www.buariverlodge.com; camping US$10, with full board island/riverside tents US$150/110, hillside r US$85; P) 🌿 Run by likeable Englishman (and Eric Sykes lookalike) John, Bua River – perched

above a beautiful boulder-strewn section of the river – is an adult Neverland. By night, trails lit by solar lanterns deter nosy wildlife and snake their way to safari tents kitted out with alfresco rain showers, African-chic decor, thick duvets and locally carved chairs.

Senga Bay

Sitting at the tip of a broad peninsula jutting into the lake, Senga Bay thrums with music by night; by day, fishing nets dry on the beach, boats are propped up photogenically on the shore and backstreets are vivid with playing kids. The trickle of travellers who pass through may find the fishing and conference town a little workaday, but it's a pleasant spot to break a journey along the lake, with some great accommodation and a more authentic feel than nearby Cape Maclear.

◉ Sights

Lodges and guides can organise activities including windsurfing, snorkelling, boat trips, spotting otters by kayak and learning to dive.

Nonguests can use the beach and facilities at Steps Campsite, but be warned that it gets extremely busy at weekends.

Stuart M Grant
Tropical Fish Farm　　　　　AQUARIUM
(Red Zebra Tours; ✆ 0999 568425; www.lakemalawi.com; Kambiri Point, South Senga Bay) About 10km south of Senga Bay is Stuart Grant's tropical fish farm, which breeds and exports cichlids. If you're interested you can do a half-hour tour of the farm and its several hundred tanks.

🛏 Sleeping & Eating

★ Cool Runnings　　HOSTEL, CAMPGROUND $
(✆ 0999 915173, 01-263398; www.facebook.com/Cool-Runnings-Malawi-183925861628566; camping/safari tents/dm US$5/8/10, fixed trailers per person US$12, r US$35; P 🛜) 🏊 The smiley yellow faces leading to this excellent-value beachside guesthouse say it all. Like a home away from home and run by warm host Sam, Cool Runnings offers accommodation in a cute old house, a fixed trailer, a grassy campsite, a three-bed safari tent, and what could be Malawi's two nicest dorms, each containing two beds.

Steps Campsite　　　　CAMPGROUND $
(✆ 01-263444, 01-263222; captitalres@sunbird malawi.com; camping MK3000, day use MK1500; P) Perfectly situated by the giant boulders

that bookend the golden stretch of beach, this campsite is owned by Sunbird Hotels and benefits from its premier-level service. It's better during the week, as it fills with locals and visitors from Lilongwe over the weekend.

Mufrasa Backpacker Lodge　　LODGE $$
(✆ 0888 919098, 0999 667753; camping MK4000, dm MK5000, r with/without bathroom from MK17,000/12,000; P) This faded banana-and-pastel-green beachfront place has a sandy patio with scattered loungers, a little bar and a Caribbean vibe. Clean rooms have vividly coloured linen, and African art on the walls, and are tantalisingly close to the lull of the surf.

Red Zebra Cafe　　　　　MALAWIAN $
(✆ 0999 212328; mains MK3000; ⊗ 6am-9.30pm; P 🍴) Situated in a garden off the main road, this local eatery serves simple dishes such as chicken, beef and veggie curries, chambo and omelettes. Eat within its colourful interior or alfresco.

❶ Information

Take great care when swimming near the large rocks at the end of the beach at Steps Campsite; there's a surprisingly strong undertow. Flags advise on whether it's safe to swim.

Some beaches here, especially at the bay's southern end, are flat, sheltered and reedy: perfect conditions for bilharzia snails, so check with your accommodation if it's safe to swim.

During the wet season, seek local advice before swimming in the lake at dusk and after dark, as crocs are occasionally at large.

❶ Getting There & Away

From Salima, minibuses and *matolas* (pickups) run to Senga Bay (MK500), dropping you in the main street. If you want a lift all the way to Steps Campsite, negotiate an extra fee with the driver. A private taxi costs MK3500 to MK5000 from Salima, depending on where you want to be dropped.

From Lilongwe, buses (MK1700, two hours) and minibuses (MK1500), the latter departing more frequently but more packed, run to Salima. AXA buses stop at Salima bus station, which has an AXA office, en route up/down the lake between Mzuzu and Blantyre.

If you're travelling to/from Cape Maclear, consider chartering a boat; it's not too expensive if you get a group together (US$220 through Cool Runnings guesthouse). There's also the *Ilala* ferry, which sails to Monkey Bay on Wednesday morning, and heads north from Monkey Bay to

WORTH A TRIP

MUA

Sitting on a hill aglow with flame trees, Mua is a rare treat; its red-brick terracotta-tiled mission seems transplanted from Tuscany, its **church** strangely beautiful. The Roman Catholic mission was established in 1902, and a visit to its sepia-tinted structures is complemented by the excellent **Kungoni Centre of Culture & Art** (☑ 01-262706, 0999 035870; www.kungoni.org; ⊘ 7.30am-4pm Mon-Sat). With the **Chamare Museum** offering gripping insights into the culture of Malawi's various ethnic groups, plus the nearby **Kungoni Art Gallery**, Mua could be an unexpected highlight of your trip. For accommodation, try **Namalikhate Lodge** (☑ 01-262706; www.kungoni.org; camping MK5000, s/d MK17,000/22,000; ⊘ restaurant 7.30am-6.30pm; ℗).

Mua is about 50km south of Salima on the road to Balaka. The Mua Mission is about 2km from the main road and is signposted (the Mua Mission Hospital sign is clearest). The road uphill is quite rough, so call ahead to check on its current condition if you're driving a 2WD.

From the turnoff on the main road, you can catch passing minibuses heading to Salima (MK1200, one hour) and Monkey Bay (MK3000, two hours).

Senga Bay and beyond on Friday. Additionally the weekly MV Chambo (p167) ferry sails to/from Metangula (Mozambique) via Makanjila.

Self-drivers can fuel up at the petrol station.

Monkey Bay

Hidden behind the Cape Maclear headland, sultry Monkey Bay is enchantingly slow: languid locals, a petrol station and a few shops are all that you'll find here. It's backpacker country, with two beachfront traveller joints, and the harbour is the launch pad for the *Ilala* ferry's long journey up the lake. Fish, snorkel or hammock flop – whatever you do, you may need to recalibrate your calendar.

From Lilongwe, buses run to Monkey Bay, usually via Salima and the southern lakeshore (MK3000, four hours). It's probably quicker to catch a minibus to Salima (MK1700, two hours), where you should find a minibus or *matola* (pickup) going direct to Monkey Bay.

From Blantyre, it's easiest to reach Monkey Bay by minibus with a change in Mangochi (total MK6000, five to six hours).

The *Ilala* ferry leaves **Monkey Bay Harbour** (☑ 0881 100018, 0996 784594) on Friday morning and heads up the lake to Senga Bay and points north, arriving back on Wednesday afternoon.

Ulendo Airlink (p167) flies a few days a week to Monkey Bay and the Makokola airstrip, between Monkey Bay and Mangochi, from Lilongwe (adult/child US$220/159), Likoma Island, Liwonde National Park and Majete Wildlife Reserve. Charter flights are also available, as are discounted seats on upcoming departures; check the 'bid to fly' section of Ulendo Airlink's website.

Mufasa Ecolodge HOSTEL, CAMPGROUND $
(☑ 0993 080057; www.facebook.com/Mufasa RusticLodgeBackpackers; camping/tent hire/dm MK3000/3500/5000, s/d without bathroom MK8000/12,000; ℗ 🛜) This traveller's magnet is the main reason to hang around in Monkey Bay, with a sheltered beach bookended by smooth boulders and campsites on the sand or mountainside. Rooms are basic bamboo affairs, but the beach bar is appealing, with lounging cushions, wicker swing chairs and a relaxed vibe. Come dusk expect communal fires, drum circles and backpacker bonhomie.

Norman Carr Cottage BOUTIQUE HOTEL $$$
(☑ 0888 355357, 0999 207506; www.normancarr cottage.com; s/d all-inclusive from US$145/240; ℗ ✳ 🛜 🏊) Balancing simplicity, character and luxury, this beach retreat's six suites and two-bedroom family cottage have massive handmade king-size beds, small living areas and open-air garden showers. The beach and gardens are full of hanging chairs and sun beds and there's a beachside pool and whirlpool – perfect for a Malawian gin and tonic.

Cape Maclear

A long stretch of powder-fine sand bookended by mountains and lapped by dazzling water, Cape Maclear deserves all the hype thrown at it. By day the bay glitters a royal blue, studded with nearby islands and puttering, crayon-coloured fishing boats.

Especially in the early morning, the tideline is a hub of local life, with women washing clothes and their children, while fisherfolk spread out vermilion nets to dry and tourists emerge onto the verandas of nearby beach cabanas. Come afternoon the sleepy lanes ring with music from backstreet gospel choirs, while the evenings fill with reggae from the tinny sound system of that bar under the baobab. Much of the surrounding area is part of **Lake Malawi National Park** (person/car US$10/3), a Unesco World Heritage Site.

🏃 Activities

Water Sports

Cape Maclear Scuba   DIVING
(☑ 0999 952488; www.capemaclearscuba.com; Thumbi View Lodge; casual dive US$50, PADI Open Water course US$400) With a reputation for affordability, this outfit offers casual dives and PADI courses from the toe-dipping Discover Scuba (US$70) to the Advanced Open Water and Dive Master.

Danforth Yachting   SAILING, DIVING
(☑ 0999 960770, 0999 960077; www.danforthyachting.com) Fancy sailing to Likoma and Chizumulu Islands? Book two weeks ahead to charter the *Mufasa* for anything from two days to a fortnight, with rates starting at US$225 per person per night (US$900 minimum), including full board and activities such as snorkelling and fishing. No children under 16.

Kayak Africa   KAYAKING
(☑ 0999 942661, in South Africa 21-783 1955; www.kayakafrica.co.za) For a longer paddle expedition, Kayak Africa is great, as you can arrange to kayak to one of its beautiful camps on Domwe and Mumbo Islands, or even between them. The islands are respectively 5km and 10km offshore, and separated by 7km of lake.

Hiking

There's a range of hikes and walks in the hills. Entry into the national park is US$10, which you can pay at the **Lake Malawi National Park Headquarters** (Otter Point Rd; ☉ 7.30am-noon & 1-5pm Mon-Sat, 10am-noon & 1-4pm Sun) or the nearby gate, and the rate for a Cape Maclear Tour Guides Association guide is US$15 per person. It's better to hire a guide.

The main path starts by the **Missionary Graves** and leads up through woodland to a col below **Nkhunguni Peak**, the highest on the Nankumba peninsula, with great views

over Cape Maclear, the lake and surrounding islands. It's six hours return to the summit; plenty of water and a good sun hat are essential.

Another interesting place to visit on foot is **Mwala Wa Mphini** (Rock of the Tribal Face Scars), which is just off the main dirt road into Cape Maclear, about 5km from the Lake Malawi National Park Headquarters. This huge boulder is covered in lines and patterns that seem to have been gouged by long-forgotten artists but are simply a natural geological formation.

Volunteering

Panda Garden   VOLUNTEERING
(☑ 0993 229822; www.heeedmalawi.net; ☉ 7am-5pm) 🌿 This environmental NGO offers volunteering opportunities such as gardening and bilharzia research on the lake, including identifying host-carrying snail areas (scuba divers welcome).

Billy Riordan Memorial Clinic   MEDICAL
(Otter Point Rd; consultations child/adult US$50/100, out of hours US$60/125; ☉ minor complaints 8am-noon & 2-4pm Mon-Fri, emergency 10am noon & 3-4pm Sat & Sun) Set up by an Irish charity (www.billysmalawiproject.org), and run by medical volunteers and more than 30 local staff.

🛏 Sleeping

★ Funky Cichlid   HOSTEL $
(☑ 0999 969076; www.thefunkycichlid.com; camping/dm US$5/10, s/d without bathroom from US$20/30; ▣ 🛜) With its cheeky logo of a cichlid clad in sunglasses, this backpacker beach resort is Cape Mac's top spot to chill by day and party by night. Cool white-washed rooms and six- to eight-bed dorms

---

❶ CAPE MACLEAR TOUR GUIDES ASSOCIATION

All guides registered with the Cape Maclear Tour Guides Association work to a set price list and circulate at different resorts along the beach on a regular basis, so it's more than likely you'll be *softly* approached by one within an hour or two of arrival. Note that the association excludes entrance fees to **Lake Malawi National Park** from its prices. Most tours and activities have a minimum of three people (you can pay the difference if there are only one or two of you).

Cape Maclear

Cape Maclear

⊙ Sights
1 Lake Malawi National Park A4
2 Missionary Graves A5
3 Mwala Wa Mphini B3

⊙ Activities, Courses & Tours
4 Cape Maclear Scuba A5
5 Danforth Yachting A5
6 Kayak Africa A5
7 Panda Garden A5

⊜ Sleeping
   Cape Maclear EcoLodge ....(see 7)
8 Chembe Eagles Nest A2
9 Domwe Island Adventure Camp A1
10 Funky Cichlid A5
11 Gecko Lounge B4
12 Malambe Camp B4
13 Mgoza Lodge B4
14 Mufasa Ecolodge B3
15 Pumulani A4
   Thumbi View Lodge ....(see 4)
   Tuckaways Lodge ....(see 11)

⊗ Eating
   Gecko Lounge ....(see 11)
   Mgoza Restaurant ....(see 13)
16 Mphipe Lodge A5
17 Thomas's Grocery, Restaurant
   & Bar A5
   Thumbi View Lodge ....(see 4)

in the morning views is a cracking start to the day.

Cape Maclear EcoLodge LODGE $
(☑ 0999 140905; www.heeedmalawi.net; d/f from US$45/75, s/d without bathroom from US$20/35; P ❋ 🛜) Part of a non-profit NGO, these simple rooms open onto little terraces with cane chairs bedecked with colourful cushions, overlooking a leafy garden at the quiet end of the beach. There is a range of rooms, a restaurant and numerous water-based activities on offer, including diving with the on-site operator.

Malambe Camp HOSTEL $
(☑ 0999 258959; www.malambecamp.co.uk; camping/tent hire/dm MK1500/2500/3000, hut without bathroom s/d MK5000/6500; 🛜) This backpacker hit has shaded pitches right on the beach, a spotless ablution block, and a cool cafe-bar with a covered dining area ringed by pot plants and dotted with wicker chairs. Choose from simple huts constructed from reed mats, and an eight-bed reed dorm.

are decorated with funky murals, with well-maintained shared ablutions and packages available including breakfast, full or half board, drinks and water sports.

★ Tuckaways Lodge HOSTEL $
(☑ 0993 405681; www.geckolounge.net; s/d/f without bathroom US$25/40/100; P) Affiliated with the neighbouring Gecko Lounge, this neat and well-maintained compound offers a family room and five twin or double bamboo cabins with walk-in mozzie nets and decks overlooking the beach. Waking up to a waiting flask of tea to enjoy as you take

Gecko Lounge   LODGE $$
(📞 0999 787322; www.geckolounge.net; dm/r/
chalet q US$15/75/90; 🅿️ 🛜) A firm family fa-
vourite and with good reason, Gecko's self-
catering chalets are right on the manicured
beach. Each has a double and a bunk bed,
fridge, fan, tile floor, mozzie nets and pri-
vate veranda, as well as plenty of hammocks
and swing chairs outside. Equally pleasant
are the subdivided eight-bed dorm and the
double and family rooms, replete with Afri-
can decor.

The thatch- and wicker-accented **res-
taurant** (📞 0999 787322; www.geckolounge.net;
mains MK6000; ⊗ 8am-8pm; 🛜 🍴) is popular
for its tasty pizzas and burgers, as well as
being the perfect sundowner spot. You can
also rent kayaks and snorkel gear, making
Gecko a winning beachfront option.

Chembe Eagles Nest   LODGE, CAMPGROUND $$
(📞 0999 966507; www.chembenest.com;
camping US$10, chalets incl breakfast US$85;
🅿️ @ 🛜 🏊) At the far northern end of
Cape Maclear Beach, this lodge sits in an
idyllic spot on a beautiful and very clean,
broad stretch of private beach, strewn with
palm trees and shaded tables, and nestled
against the side of the hills. Chalets have
cool, tiled floors, thatched roofs and granite bathrooms with hot showers; campsites
have power points.

★ **Pumulani**   LODGE ❸❸❸
(📞 01-794491; www.robinpopesafaris.net; per person all-inclusive US$355-470; ⊗ Apr-Jan; 🅿️ ❄️
@ 🛜 🏊) Pumulani is a stylish lakeside lodge
with nature-inspired rooms – think grass
roofs and huge windows to let in the light,
views of the surrounding forest and lake,
and massive wooden terraces from which to
gaze at the clear waters and sweep of gold-
en sand below. The food, served in the open
bar-restaurant, is equally amazing.

★ **Mumbo Island Camp**   CAMPGROUND $$$
(📞 0999 942661, in South Africa 21-783-1955;
www.kayakafrica.co.za; per person all-inclusive
US$260) Situated exclusively on Mumbo
Island, this eco-boutique camp has cha-
lets and a walk-in tent on wooden plat-
forms (with en-suite bucket showers and
eco-loos), tucked beneath trees and above
rocks, with spacious decks and astounding
views. Accommodation rates include boat
transfers, full board, kayaking, snorkelling
and guided hikes.

★ **Domwe Island
Adventure Camp**   CAMPGROUND $$$
(📞 0999 942661, in South Africa 21-783-1955; www.
kayakafrica.co.za; camping US$30, safari tents per
person US$60) 🌿 Domwe is the smaller and
more rustic of Kayak Africa's two neighbouring island lodges, run on solar power and
romantically lit by paraffin lamps. It's self-
catering, with furnished safari tents, kitchen,
shared eco-showers and composting toilets.
It has a bar and a beautiful staggered dining
area, open to the elements and set among
boulders. Food can be provided on request.

🍴 Eating

Thumbi View Lodge   CAFE $
(📞 0998 599005, 0997 463054; www.thumbiview
lodge.com; mains MK3000; ⊗ 7am-8pm) On the
lane opposite Thumbi View's gate, this cafe
serves light meals and snacks such as vegetable curry, spaghetti Bolognese, lasagne,
fish, burgers and toasted sandwiches. Book
by 1pm to join the set dinner, which typically consists of Indian or South African dishes
such as slow-cooked oxtail from the owners'
homeland, in the main lodge.

Mphipe Lodge   ITALIAN $
(📞 0884 997481; www.andiamotrust.org; mains
MK2500; ⊗ 7am-9pm; 🅿️) For a different take
on lake fish, Mphipe serves it in pasta dishes.
Malawian staples such as *kampango* (catfish)
and *nsima* (a porridge-like dish made from
maize flour) are also on the menu. The lodge
funds a children's hospital in Balaka.

Mgoza Restaurant   INTERNATIONAL $
(📞 0995 632105; www.mgozalodge.com; mains
MK2000; ⊗ kitchen 7am-9.15pm, bar to 10pm; 🛜 🍴)
With shaded *palapa* (palm-leaf) shelters in a
garden facing the lake, this is a cool spot to
chat in the friendly bar or take dinner outside.

Located at Mgoza Lodge, the restaurant
serves up great full English breakfasts,
healthy fruit smoothies and, come evening,
fresh fish and great burgers loaded with
fried onions. The garden is an atmospheric
dinner-time setting.

**Thomas's Grocery,
Restaurant & Bar**   MALAWIAN $
(📞 0999 270602, 0999 468383; dishes MK1800;
⊗ 8am-7pm Mon-Sat, bar to 11.30pm daily) This
local gathering place comprises a shop and
a bar with shaded seating and a reggae
soundtrack. Simple dishes such as omelette,
spaghetti, and beans with chapati or *nsima*

are offered, and the shop sells biscuits, toiletries and basic provisions.

❶ Getting There & Away

By public transport, first get to Monkey Bay, from where a *matola* (pickup) to Cape Maclear costs MK1000 and a motorbike costs MK1500. The journey takes about an hour and they drop at the lodges.

Approaching by car on the M10 tar road, the road to Cape Maclear (signposted) turns west off the main drag about 5km before Monkey Bay. The first third of the 18km road to Cape Maclear is badly corrugated, but thereafter it's a smooth, tarred ride.

If you're heading to/from Senga Bay, ask around about chartering a boat. The Cape Maclear Tour Guides Association charges US$300, which, if split between several people, is a good alternative to the long, hard bus ride. Monkey Bay is US$200.

To catch a *matola* or motorbike in Cape Maclear, ask your lodge to call a driver, as there is no official bus station. As usual, *matolas* leave on a fill-up-and-go basis.

SOUTHERN MALAWI

Southern Malawi is home to the country's commercial capital, Blantyre, and incredibly diverse landscapes. These include mist-shrouded Mt Mulanje, Malawi's highest peak, and the Zomba Plateau, a stunning highland area. Safari-lovers can experience luxury and adventure combined in two of the country's best wildlife reserves: Liwonde and Majete, the country's only Big Five Park.

Liwonde

Straddling the Shire River, Liwonde is the main gateway to Liwonde National Park. The river divides the town in two, with the market and most services found on the eastern side, along with the turnoff to the park. If you're unable to stay in the park, it's possible to use Liwonde as a base for a short safari by road or river.

Regular minibuses run along the main road through town to/from Zomba (MK1000, 45 minutes), Limbe (for Blantyre; MK2500, three hours), Mangochi (MK2500, two hours) and the Mozambique border at Nayuchi (MK3000, 2½ to three hours).

There are two petrol stations east of the river en route to the Liwonde National Park turnoff.

Shire Camp LODGE $

(☑ 0999 210532, 0884 629214; camping/dm/r US$5/10/20; ℗) Shire Camp's faded bamboo-and-brick cabanas in varying states of repair have tiled floors, fans, hot-water bathrooms and netted breeze vents. The three-bed ensuite dorm is the best option. Right on the river, the colourful thatched bar-restaurant (mains MK3000) serves basic meals such as chambo, omelettes, burgers and pasta.

The campsite is less appealing, with hard, rocky ground and a basic ablutions block. Shire Camp can take you on a 2½-hour river safari (US$35 per person, two people minimum), which heads into Liwonde National Park. The camp is on the river's west bank. Take the dirt road next to the National Bank; follow the sign to Hippo View Lodge.

Hippo View Lodge HOTEL $$

(☑ 01-542116/8; www.hippoviewlodge.com; incl breakfast s/d superior MK35,000/55,500, deluxe MK48,000/65,500; ℗ ❄ ⧉ ⛱) This 111-room behemoth does its best to banish a lingering feeling of faded grandeur, with rooms in blocks overlooking riverside gardens shaded by palms and a huge baobab. Superior rooms have tiled floor, fridge, phone and plasma-screen TV; it's worth upgrading to the more attractive and modern deluxe rooms, with larger bathrooms and tea and coffee.

Liwonde National Park

Set in 584 sq km of dry savannah and forest alongside the serene Shire River, the relatively small **Liwonde National Park** (www.african-parks.org; person/car US$20/4; ⊙ 6am-6pm) is one of Africa's best spots for river-based wildlife watching, with around 550 elephants, 2000 hippos and innumerable crocs. Animals including black rhinos, buffaloes and sable antelopes are found on dry land, where the terrain rolls from palm-studded flood plains and riverine forests to mopane and acacia woodlands interspersed with candelabra succulents.

The park's excellent lodges offer a fantastic range of wildlife-spotting drives, walks and boat trips.

Njobvu Cultural Village CULTURAL

(☑ 0888 623530; www.njobvuvillage.org; r incl breakfast per person US$16, all-inclusive US$50) 🌿 Near Liwonde National Park's Makanga Gate, Njobvu offers visitors a rare opportunity to stay in a traditional Malawian village,

Southern Malawi

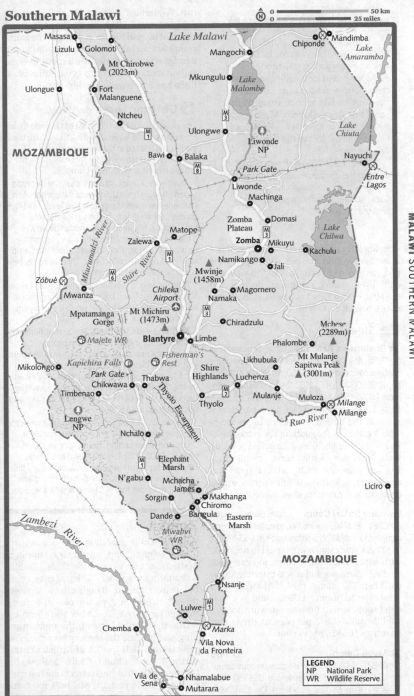

LEGEND
NP   National Park
WR   Wildlife Reserve

LIWONDE RHINO SANCTUARY

The **rhino sanctuary** (01-821219, 01-771393; www.cawsmw.com; US$80) is a fenced-off area within Liwonde National Park, developed for breeding rare black rhinos, and expanded to protect other mammal species from poaching. With a scout from Mvuu Camp or Mvuu Lodge in the park, you can go on a three-hour hike, searching for the rhinos in the 48-sq-km reserve.

In late 2016 10 black rhinos were living in the enclosure, along with populations of Lichtenstein's hartebeest, Cape buffalo, Burchell's zebra, eland and roan antelope.

sleeping in mud-brick huts (with or without a mattress – your choice!). During the day you are invited to take part in the villagers' daily lives, visiting traditional doctors and the village school, and eating local food such as the porridge-like *nsima*.

🛏 Sleeping

★ **Bushman's Baobabs** LODGE, CAMPGROUND $$
(0995 453324, 0884 659901; www.bushmans baobabs.com; camping US$7.50, dm US$15, s US$65-85, d US$90-120, tr/f US$180/240, s/d without bathroom US$25/50; P) 🚗 The former Chinguni Hills Lodge is a fun place to experience a night in the bush and a safari. In an accessible location in the south of the park, Bushman's offers 14-bed dorms, thatched A-frame tents, luxurious en-suite tents, en-suite chalets, and campsites with barbecue spots and a self-catering kitchen. Wildlife drives, walks, and boat and canoe trips are offered.

Liwonde Safari Camp LODGE, CAMPGROUND $$
(0881 813240; www.liwondesafaricamp.com; camping/dm US$10/15, safari tent s/d US$40/60; P) This rustic camp is immersed in the park, with stilted safari tents, dorm and campsite sharing ablutions and a self-catering kitchen. There's a plunge pool, a thatched bar, meals (buffet dinner US$15), and – if you don't spot animals from the viewing decks – wildlife walks (US$5 per person), drives and boat trips (US$25 per person).

★ **Mvuu Camp** LODGE $$$
(01-821219, 01-771393; www.cawsmw.com; camping US$15, chalets all-inclusive s/d US$360/520; P @ 🛜) Run by the excellent Central Afri-

can Wilderness Safaris, Malawi's premier safari operator, Mvuu sits on the river in the realm of myriad hippos and crocs. The camp comprises a main restaurant building and, nearby, scattered chalets with cosy interiors, step-in mozzie nets, comfy beds, immaculate linen and stone-walled bathrooms.

❶ Getting There & Away

The main park gate is 6km east of Liwonde town. From the gate to Mvuu Camp is 28km along the park track (closed in the wet season); a 4WD vehicle is recommended for this route. The park lodges offer transfers from Liwonde.

Another way in for vehicles is via the dirt road (open all year) from Ulongwe, a village between Liwonde town and Mangochi. This leads for 14km through local villages to the park's western boundary. A few kilometres inside the park is a car park and boat jetty, where a watchman hoists a flag to arrange a boat from Mvuu Camp or Mvuu Lodge to collect you. This service is free if you're staying at the camps.

Alternatively, if you book in advance to stay at Mvuu Camp or Mvuu Lodge, you can organise a boat transfer–safari from Hippo View Lodge in Liwonde town for US$80.

For those without wheels, the best option is to get any bus or minibus between Liwonde town and Mangochi and get off at Ulongwe (make sure you say this clearly, or the driver may think you want to go to Lilongwe). In Ulongwe, locals wait by the bus stop and will sometimes take you by bicycle to the park (this takes about an hour and costs around MK4500).

Ulendo Airlink (p167) flies a few days a week to the Liwonde National Park airstrip (near Mvuu Camp and Mvuu Lodge), from Lilongwe (adult/child US$295/211), Likoma Island and Monkey Bay. Charter flights are also available, as are discounted seats on upcoming departures; check the 'bid to fly' section of Ulendo Airlink's website.

Zomba

With its chilly elevation and atmospheric old colonial and missionary buildings nestled in the wooded foothills, Zomba is hauntingly special – like a chapter of the British Empire hanging by a tenuous thread. It has the typical chaos of a dusty market town, but the higher you climb towards the Zomba Plateau, the more stunning and pristine the scenery becomes. The capital from 1891 to 1974 of British Central Africa, Nyasaland and, finally, Malawi, it's home to wide, tree-lined streets and an easy charm. This is perhaps Malawi's most appealing city, and a great base for exploring the plateau to the north.

African Heritage ADVENTURE, CULTURAL

(Luso Lathu Art & Coffee Shop; ☑0999 235823; www.africanheritage.mw; Zomba Gymkhana Club) This craft shop doubles as a tourism hub, offering guided tours, shuttles to the Zomba Plateau (US$10), mountain-bike rental (MK1000 per hour) and a detailed plateau map (MK1000). Half-day tours cover the plateau and historical Zomba, while longer itineraries go further afield to Mt Mulanje, Mua, Lake Chilwa and beyond.

🛏 Sleeping & Eating

Pakachere Backpackers & Creative Centre HOSTEL $

(☑0994 685934, 0882 858089; www.pakachere. com; camping/tent hire/dm US$5/7/10, r/tr US$40/45, r without bathroom US$35; P 🗟) This locally run hostel is nicely decorated, and has craftwork for sale and a bar-restaurant opening onto a garden with thatched seating areas. The spacious rooms are worn but clean, with tiled floors and mozzie nets, and there's six-bed dorm and an en-suite 10-bedder with secure storage space.

★Casa Rossa GUESTHOUSE, CAMPGROUND $$

(☑0991 184211, 0881 366126; www.casarossamw. com; Mountain Rd 5; incl breakfast camping US$5, r US$50-60, without bathroom US$40; P 🗟) Named after its oxblood veranda overlooking town, this Italian-owned guesthouse offers hillside tranquillity and the best restaurant (mains MK3100-8100; ⊙9am-9pm Tue-Sun, residents only Mon; P 🗟) around. Rooms in the old colonial house are simple but comfortable and the campsites in the leafy garden have electricity, fireplace and two barbecues.

★Annie's Lodge LODGE $$

(☑01-527002, 01-951636; www.annieslodge.com; Livingstone Rd; incl breakfast s US$40-70, d US$50-80; P ❄ 🗟) Set in the foothills of the Zomba Plateau, Annie's has a bar-restaurant with an appealing terrace for a sundowner, and black-and-white-brick chalets with green tin roofs, engulfed in palm trees and flowers. The 40-plus rooms are carpeted, clean and welcoming, with DSTV, bathroom and fan or air-con.

❶ Getting There & Away

Zomba is on a main route between Lilongwe and Blantyre. The bus station is in the town centre, off Namiwawa Rd. Minibuses depart every hour or so to Limbe (for Blantyre; MK1500, one hour) and Lilongwe (MK6000, five hours), and head to Liwonde (MK1000, 45 minutes). There are more services in the morning.

Alternatively, you can privately hire a taxi; the fare to Blantyre is MK30,000. Organise it through your accommodation; they may know of another guest or local going in the same direction who can share the ride.

For Mt Mulanje, there is a daily National Bus Company service at 11am to Phalombe (MK1500, 1½ hours), where you can pick up a minibus to Mulanje.

Zomba Plateau

Rising nearly 1800m behind Zomba town, and carpeted in thick stands of pine, the Zomba Plateau is beguilingly pretty. As you ascend the snaking road past wildflowers, stoic locals heaving huge burdens of timber, and roadside strawberry vendors, the place almost feels like alpine France; then a vervet monkey jumps out, a pocket of blue mist envelops your car, and you remember you're in Africa. This gorgeous highland paradise, replete with streams, lakes and tumbling waterfalls, is home to monkeys, bushbucks, and birds including mountain wagtails and Bertram's weavers.

The plateau can be covered on foot, mountain bike or car (4WD only on the back roads), with myriad winding trails that ring and cross the mountain. It's divided in two by the Domasi Valley. The southern half has a tarred road to the top, a hotel, several picnic places, waterfalls and viewpoints, and a network of driveable tracks and hiking paths.

Plateau Stables HORSE RIDING

(☑0993 764600; www.plateaustables.com; per person per hour US$40) Opposite Mulunguzi Dam, this long-running stable offers one- to five-hour plateau excursions on well-kept horses. In the wet season (mid-November to mid-March), phone ahead to check that weather conditions are suitable.

🛏 Sleeping

Ku Chawe
Trout Farm CAMPGROUND, BUNGALOWS $

(P) This campsite is ideally located in the lee of a valley amid a giant gum- and cedar-tree clearing. In late 2016 it was showing signs of not being well maintained and was undergoing a change of management.

Zomba Plateau (Southern Section)

MALAWI ZOMBA PLATEAU

Zomba Plateau (Southern Section)

⊙ Sights
1 Model Hut B3

⊙ Activities, Courses & Tours
2 Plateau Stables B4

⊟ Sleeping
3 Annie's Lodge C4
4 Casa Rossa B4

5 Ku Chawe Trout Farm B3
6 Pakachere Backpackers &
  Creative Centre C4
7 Sunbird Ku Chawe B4
8 Zomba Forest Lodge A4

⊗ Eating
Casa Rossa .... (see 4)

If you're keen to camp on the plateau, En-quire in Zomba or at the nearby **Sunbird Ku Chawe** (☑ 01-773388, 01-514211; www.sunbird malawi.com; incl breakfast s US$127-203, d US$157-233; ⊕❄@🛜) hotel whether the campsite is functional again.

★ **Zomba Forest Lodge**   GUESTHOUSE $$$
(☑ 0997 593325, 0992 802702; www.zomba forestlodge.com; per person with full board US$110; Ⓟ) 🍂 Book at least a day ahead to stay at this four-room guesthouse owned by British-Malawian couple Tom and Petal. Woodcarvings and Tom's artwork decorate the Afro-chic rooms, and candles, paraffin and solar power light the off-the-grid property. Hike up to the plateau or wander the 8-hectare grounds, with its 3.5km of walking trails and indigenous rainforest along the stream.

Blantyre & Limbe

Founded by Scottish missionaries in 1876, and named after the town in South Lanarkshire, Scotland, where explorer David Livingstone was born, Blantyre is Malawi's second-largest city. It's more appealing and cohesive than Lilongwe thanks to its compact size and hilly topography, and though there's not much to do here, it makes a good springboard for exploring Majete Wildlife Reserve and Mt Mulanje.

Attached to the Blantyre's eastern side, **Limbe** is home to a grand old mission church, a minibus station and a golf club. Unlike Blantyre, however, which has seen a finessing of its restaurants and hotels, Limbe has fallen into disrepair over the last couple of decades. You may have to change minibuses here, but it's best to head straight on.

Malawi's commercial and industrial hub, Blantyre has the country's best and most diverse choice of restaurants, a small selection of lively watering holes and a smattering of sights. Add to that tour operators, banks, internet cafes and other practicalities, and Blantyre makes a pleasant stopover.

⊙ Sights & Activities

Mandala House   HISTORIC BUILDING
(Map p152; ☑01-871932; Kaoshiung Rd; ⊙8.30am-4.30pm Mon-Fri, to 12.30pm Sat) This is the oldest building in Malawi, built in 1882 as a home for the managers of the African Lakes Corporation. It's a quietly grand colonial house, encased in wraparound verandas and set in lovely gardens. Inside are the inviting Mandala Cafe (p151),

an eclectic art gallery (p151) and the **Society of Malawi Library & Archive** (Map p152; ☑01-872617; www.societyofmalawi.org; 1st fl, Mandala House, Kaoshiung Rd; ⊙9am-4pm Mon-Fri) **FREE**.

Museum of Malawi   MUSEUM
(Chichiri Museum; Map p150; ☑01-873258; Kasungu Cres; adult/child under 13yr MK500/100; ⊙7.30am-4.30pm) Malawi's interesting national museum has a few gems, including a royal ceremonial stool dating from the 16th century and a display on Gule Wamkulu dances. The museum is between central Blantyre and Limbe, accessed from Moi Rd opposite Chichiri Shopping Mall. Take a minibus headed for Limbe and ask to be let off at the museum.

St Michael and All Angels Church   CHURCH
(CCAP Church; Map p152; www.stmichaelchurchmw.com; ⊙services 6am, 7am, 8.30am, 10.30am & 5pm Sun) This magnificent red-brick Church of Central Africa Presbyterian building was preceded by a simpler structure, built by Scottish missionary Reverend DC Scott in 1882. In 1888 the missionaries started work on a new, more impressive church with elaborate brickwork moulded into arches, buttresses, columns and towers, topped with a grand basilica dome. The church is off Old Chileka Rd.

Blantyre Sports Club   GYM
(Map p152; ☑01-835095, 01-821172; btsportsclub@africa-online.net; day membership adult/child under 18yr MK5500/1000; ⊙6am-10pm, pool & golf course to 5pm) Established in 1896, and

MALAWI BLANTYRE & LIMBE

DON'T MISS

HIKING ON THE ZOMBA PLATEAU

The southern half of the plateau is ideal for hiking. The network of tracks can be confusing, though, so for more help with orientation there's a 3D map of the plateau in the **Model Hut** (⊙8.30am-4.30pm).

The **Potato Path** is the most popular hike at Zomba. It's a direct route from town all the way up to the plateau. To find the path, head up the main road to the plateau and turn right at the firebreak line just past Casa Rossa guesthouse. From here a few paths climb steeply through woodland and converge on the plateau near the Sunbird Ku Chawe hotel (45 minutes).

From near the Sunbird Ku Chawe, the Potato Path goes straight across the southern half of the plateau, sometimes using the park tracks, sometimes using narrow shortcuts, and leads eventually to Old Ngondola village, from where it descends steeply into the Domasi Valley.

Allow two to three hours for the ascent, and about 1½ hours coming down.

Greater Blantyre & Limbe

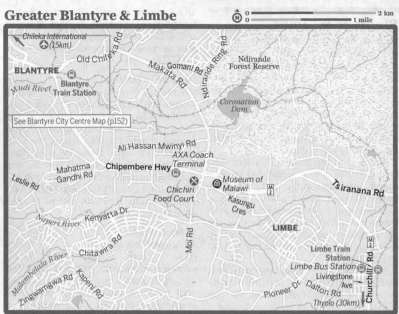

with a faint whiff of colonialism, this is a great place to work up a sweat or keep the kids amused. There's a restaurant and bar, and you can pay supplements to use the pool (adult/child MK2000/1000), gym, and tennis, squash and nine-hole golf courses. It's off Victoria Ave.

🛏 Sleeping

★ Doogles   HOSTEL $

(Map p152; ☎ 0999 186512; www.dooglesma lawi.com; Mulomba Pl; dm US$15, r US$30-45; P@ 🛜 ≋) Doogles is popular with discerning travellers of all stripes, its inviting pool and bar ringed by walls with a cool sunset-safari design. From there, the complex leads to a big TV lounge, lush gardens, super-fresh en-suite rooms with shower, clean six-bed dorms, and thatched en-suite chalets with mozzie nets and fans.

Blantyre Lodge   HOTEL $

(Map p152; ☎ 01-834460; Old Chileka Rd; s/d incl breakfast MK10,500/14,000; P ❋ 🛜) So-so en-suite rooms with grotty bedspreads, TV, bare white walls and a few sticks of furniture. But it's close to the main bus station. Opt for a room out the back, away from the main drag.

Henderson Street
Guest House   GUESTHOUSE $

(Map p152; ☎ 01-823474; 19 Henderson St; incl breakfast s/d standard MK12,000/14,000, executive MK15,000/17,000; P 🛜) Five minutes' walk from the town centre, this old-fashioned place sits in a leafy garden and has a welcoming veranda. The seven rooms are tired but clean and cosy, with a mishmash of old and new furniture, small TV, and tiled bathroom with shower.

Hotel Victoria   HOTEL $$

(Map p152; ☎ 01-823500; www.hotelvictoriamw. com; Lower Sclater Rd; s/d incl breakfast from MK45,000/50,000; P ❋ @ 🛜 ≋) Upmarket Victoria attracts corporate types and aid workers with its pool, marble lobby and air-conditioned restaurant. Eighty rooms enjoy plump pillows, thick carpet, DSTV, writing desk, fridge and less impressive bathroom. Deluxe and larger executive rooms are a big step up, with flat-screen TV, office chair, and bathroom with oval tub and shower. Ask for one away from Victoria Ave.

Kabula Lodge   LODGE $$

(☎ 01-821216; www.kabulalodge.co.mw; Kabula Hill; incl breakfast s/d from US$40/50, without bathroom US$20/30; P ❋ 🛜) Hidden down a dirt road off Michiru Rd, on the crest of a hill northwest of the city centre, friendly Kabula enjoys peace aplenty and scenic mountain views from its breakfast terrace. Executive rooms are equally pleasing, with wrought-iron beds, minimal decor, DSTV, fridge and air-con, but some rooms and shared bathrooms are basic, so ask to see a few.

Malawi Sun Hotel HOTEL **$$$**
(Map p152; ☑ 01-824808; www.malawisunho tel.com; Robins Rd; incl breakfast s/d standard US$100/125, executive US$145/170; 🅿 ⊜ ❋ @ ☎ ☎) This comfortable hotel has a small African-style lounge with mountain views, a tempting swimming pool and a food court. The 73 rooms are decent, with DSTV, comfy beds, fridge, tea and coffee. It's worth upgrading to executive from standard (also called 'ethnic' for their Malawian decorative touches); shoot for a balcony overlooking the hills.

✖ Eating

Food Court FAST FOOD **$**
(Map p152; ☑ 0997 915519; www.malawisunhotel. com; Malawi Sun Hotel, Robins Rd; Blue Savannah mains MK2000; ⊗ 8am-9pm) With striking views of the mountains, this breezy alfresco courtyard is surrounded by a bakery (Bread Basket), a fast-food joint (Blue Savannah) and an ice-cream parlour (Scoops & Shakes), the latter selling iced coffees, milkshakes and ice-cream cones.

Chichiri Food Court FAST FOOD **$**
(Map p150; Chichiri Shopping Mall, Chipembere Hwy) This alfresco food court is popular with families for its play area and bouncy castle. The fast-food outlets here include a pizzeria (Jungle Pepper), ice-cream parlours and fried-chicken joints.

★ L'Hostaria ITALIAN **$$**
(Map p152; ☑ 0888 282828; www.facebook.com/ hostariaMW; Sharpe Rd; mains MK5500; ⊗ noon-2pm & 6.30-9pm Tue-Sun; 🅿 ☎ ⌨) In an atmospheric old house with black-and-white floors and a large veranda overlooking a lawn, L'Hostaria offers Italian recipes and fresh produce that attract local expats in the know. Come for a relaxing evening and wood-fired pizzas, homemade pastas and steaks.

★ Mandala Cafe CAFE **$$**
(Map p152; ☑ 01-871932; Mandala House, Kaoshi ung Rd; mains MK5000-6000; ⊗ 8.30am-4.30pm Mon-Fri, to 12.30pm Sat; 🅿 ☎ ☎) Sit on a breezy stone terrace in the grounds of Mandala House (p149), or inside at this chilled cafe adorned with artworks and guidebooks. Regulars love the Italian cuisine, fillet steak, Thai chicken, freshly brewed coffee, iced tea and gelato. A real oasis.

★ 21 Grill on Hanover STEAK **$$**
(Map p152; ☑ 01-820955; Protea Hotel Ryalls, 2 Hanover Ave; mains MK7000; ⊗ 11am-3pm & 4-10pm Mon-Fri, from 4pm Sat & Sun; 🅿 ❋ ☎ ⌨) Established in 1921, this historical restaurant is one of Malawi's more sophisticated eateries, occupying a library-like room with salmon-coloured seats and ornate carpets. The menu focuses on meat dishes, from South African Karoo lamb curry to flaming Jack Daniel's steak, but it also has a good selection of fish, pasta, salad and decadent desserts.

★ Casa Mia INTERNATIONAL **$$$**
(☑ 01-827871; www.blantyreaccommodation.com; Kabula Hill Rd; mains MK5000-11,000; ⊗ 6.30am-9.30pm; 🅿 ❋ ☎ ⌨) Don your smarts for dinner at this classy guesthouse restaurant. The wine-stacked interior, with its antique Cinzano prints, white tablecloths and expat clientele, is a pleasant environment for dishes ranging from steaks and carbonara to red wine–marinaded Karoo lamb and chambo Thermidor. Lunch on the breezy terrace is more casual.

♬ Drinking & Nightlife

Kwa Haraba CAFE
(Map p152; ☑ 0994 764701, 0993 801564; www. facebook.com/KwaHaraba-138690532886703/; Phekani House; ⊗ 7.30am-5pm Sun-Tue & Thu, to 8pm Wed, to 10pm Fri & Sat) This craft shop and cafe serves fresh juices bursting with goodness and light meals such as feta pizza, ham and cheese pita sandwiches, salads and toasted sandwiches. The wonderful masks, paintings, secondhand paperbacks and fabric make a creative environment. Cocktails and music from 6pm Friday and Saturday, and poetry between 6pm and 7pm Wednesday. Phekani House is off Glyn Jones Ave.

🛍 Shopping

Mandala House ARTS & CRAFTS
(Map p152; ☑ 01-871932; Kaoshiung Rd; ⊗ 8.30am-4.30pm Mon-Fri, to 12.30pm Sat) Situated in Mandala House (p149), the oldest colonial dame in the city, this eclectic gallery features vividly coloured, contemporary work

Blantyre City Centre

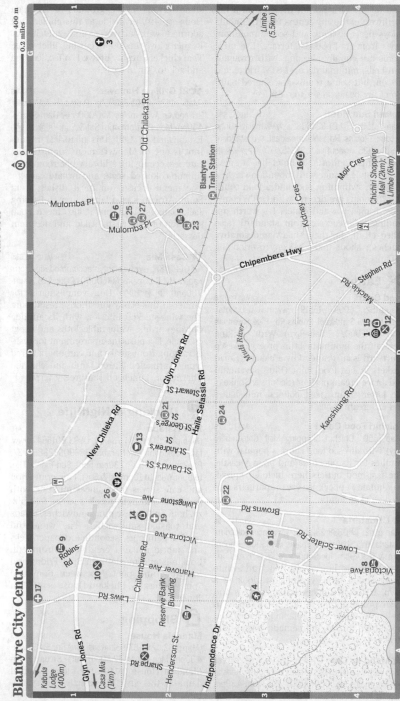

Blantyre City Centre

◉ Sights
1 Mandala House D4
2 Shree Hindu Temple............................... C1
  Society of Malawi Library &
  Archive .... (see 15)
3 St Michael and All Angels Church.......... G1

✪ Activities, Courses & Tours
4 Blantyre Sports Club............................. B3

🛏 Sleeping
5 Blantyre Lodge.. E2
6 Doogles E1
7 Henderson Street Guest House............ A2
8 Hotel Victoria.. D4
9 Malawi Sun Hotel B1

✖ Eating
10 21 Grill on Hanover................................ B1
   Food Court.......................................(see 9)
11 L'Hostaria... A2
12 Mandala Cafe D4

○ Drinking & Nightlife
13 Kwa Haraba.. C2

⊕ Shopping
   Central Africana Bookshop..........(see 16)
14 Craft Stalls.. B2
15 Mandala House.. D4
16 Uta Waleza Centre F3

⊕ Information
17 Blantyre Adventist Hospital................... B1
18 Immigration Office.................................. B3
   Jambo Africa.................................(see 16)
19 One Stop Pharmacy................................ B2
20 Tourist Office B3

⊕ Transport
21 AXA House Coach Terminal C2
22 City Bus Station...................................... C3
23 Intercape E2
24 Mibawa Bus Depot C3
25 National Bus Company........................... E2
26 SS Rent A Car C1
27 Wenela Bus Station................................ E2

by local artists, as well as sculpture, old maps and prints, and huge, carved wooden thrones.

Central Africana Bookshop   BOOKS
(Map p152; ☑ 01-876110; www.centralafricana.com; Uta Waleza Centre, Kidney Cres; ☺ 8am-5pm Mon-Fri, 9am-1pm Sat) This long-running bookshop on two levels has an excellent selection of Africana, ranging from dusty old tomes to coffee-table books, and from novels and guidebooks to a section dedicated to Livingstone.

Uta Waleza Centre   MALL
(Map p152; Kidney Cres) With a few design shops and an excellent bookshop, Uta Waleza is a good place to buy presents and souvenirs.

Craft Stalls   ARTS & CRAFTS
(Map p152; Chilembwe Rd; ☺ 8am-4pm Mon-Sat) There are good craft stalls under an awning next to the salmon-coloured Malawi Savings Bank building. The work on sale is excellent and browsing is refreshingly hassle free.

⊕ Information

IMMIGRATION
Immigration Office (Map p152; ☑ 01-823777; www.immigration.gov.mw; Government Complex, Victoria Ave; ☺ 7.30am-noon & 12.30-4pm

Mon-Fri, to noon Sat) For visa extensions or temporary-residency applications.

MEDICAL SERVICES
Blantyre Adventist Hospital (Map p152; ☑ hospital 01-820006, medical appointments 01-820399; Kabula Hill Rd; ☺ casualty 24hr) This private hospital and medical and dental clinic charges MK5400 for a doctor's consultation and MK2000 for a malaria test. Cash only.

One Stop Pharmacy (Map p152; ☑ 0888 860230, 01-824148; Chilembwe Rd; ☺ 8am-5.30pm Mon-Fri, 9am-2pm Sat) This well-stocked pharmacy sells bilharzia tablets (if you've been swimming in the lake), as well as malaria prophylaxis.

TOURIST INFORMATION
Jambo Africa (Map p152; ☑ 0882 904166, 0111 572709; www.jambo-africa.com; Uta Waleza Centre, Kidney Cres; ☺ 8am-5pm Mon-Fri, 9am-noon Sat) A great one-stop shop for travel tickets, car hire, excursions and accommodation, Jambo owns a park lodge and two self-catering cottages on the lake. It has a second office next to the Shree Hindu Temple (Map p152; ☑ 01-820761; Glyn Jones Rd).

Tourist Office (Map p152; ☑ 01-827066; Government Complex, Victoria Ave; ☺ 7.30am-4.30pm Mon-Fri) In a cottage-like tax building dating to 1939, this small office covers the whole country. It stocks a few leaflets and maps, sells wall maps of Malawi (MK5000), and can offer enthusiastic, though not always particularly helpful, advice.

ℹ Getting There & Away

AIR

Blantyre's **Chileka International Airport** (📞 01-827900) is about 15km north of the city centre. A taxi to the city costs around MK15,000, but agree on a price with the driver first. The price can be negotiated down a bit if you're going from the city to the airport. If your budget doesn't include taxis, frequent local buses between the City Bus Station and Chileka Township pass the airport gate (the fare's around MK2000).

BUS & MINIBUS

Blantyre's main bus station for long-distance buses is **Wenela Bus Station** (Map p152; Mulomba Pl), east of the centre. Companies including **National Bus Company** (Map p152; 📞 0888 561365; Wenela Bus Station, Mulomba Pl) have daily services to Lilongwe (MK3500, four hours), Mzuzu (MK7500, nine to 10 hours), Zomba (MK1500, 1½ to two hours), Mulanje (MK1500, 1½ hours) and Karonga (MK10,500, 14 hours).

AXA buses depart from the **terminal** (Map p150; Chipembere Hwy) next to the Chichiri Shopping Mall, then pick up at the central **office** (Map p152; 📞 01-820411, 01-820100; www. axacoach.com; St George's St; ⊙ ticket office 6am-5pm) en route to Lilongwe (MK11,300). These Super Executive coaches leave in both directions at 7am and 4.30pm. Cheaper Special and Executive buses to/from Mzuzu (Special MK11,550, Executive MK12,600) via Lilongwe (MK6350, MK8100) leave in both directions at 7am and 6pm. Buses taking the lakeshore route to Mzuzu don't work to a fixed schedule but leave when they're full, normally around 5pm. For all services, it's best to book ahead.

Most intercity minibuses leave from **Limbe Bus Station** (Map p150), off Livingstone Ave; it's normally fastest to take a minibus there (MK200, 15 minutes), either from the **Mibawa depot** (Map p152) or the roadside, then pick up a long-distance service. A taxi there costs around MK4000. Routes from Limbe include Zomba (MK1500, one hour), Mulanje (MK1500, 1¼ hours) and Mangochi (for Monkey Bay; MK4000, five hours).

Minibuses to Chikwawa (for Majete Wildlife Reserve; MK1500, 1½ hours) depart from Blantyre's **City Bus Station** (Map p152).

The car park next to Blantyre Lodge is the pickup and drop-off point for long-distance bus companies headed for Jo'burg. **Intercape** (Map p152; 📞 0999 403398; www.intercape.co.za; Blantyre Lodge, Old Chileka Rd) goes to Jo'burg at 8am daily (MK45,000, two days).

CAR

Avis (📞 01-622719), Budget and **SS Rent A Car** (Map p152; 📞 01-822836; www.ssrentacar. com; Glyn Jones Rd) have offices in the city.

Mulanje

Mulanje is famous for both its infinity of emerald-green tea plantations, and the achingly pretty Mt Mulanje – a massif of some 20 peaks reaching over 2500m. The town makes a reasonable base for forays into the massif, with a good lodge and a few eateries along the main road.

A daily National Bus Company bus runs to/from Blantyre (MK1500, 1½ hours), as do regular pretty minibuses to/from Limbe (MK1500, 1½ hours); on the minibus, you may have to change in Thyolo. If you're heading for the border with Mozambique, minibuses and matolas (pickups) run to Muloza (MK800, 30 minutes).

Mulanje Infocentre TOURIST INFORMATION (📞 0888 122645, 01-466466; infomulanje@sdnp. org.mw; Phalombe Rd, Chitakale Trading Centre; ⊙ 8am-5pm Mon-Fri, by appointment Sat & Sun) The best source of information about hiking on Mt Mulanje and beyond, with helpful staff and documentation. They can book the Mulanje forestry huts and organise guides and porters, as well as tours to local waterfalls, tea estates and villages, the latter potentially including a Gule Wamkulu ceremony (with notice).

🛏 Sleeping & Eating

Kokotowa Executive Lodge LODGE $ (📞 01-466743; Chitakale Trading Centre; incl breakfast s/d/tr standard MK10,000/11,500/13,000, executive MK12,000/13,000/15,000; P ❷) Popular for conferences, Kokotowa's 12 rooms (with more coming) are basic but clean, spacious and comfortable, with large beds, plentiful furniture and fans. The whole shebang is arranged around a courtyard with bar, restaurant and secure parking. Find it off the M2, on the Blantyre side of the Chitakale junction; follow the sign for the altogether less impressive Chididi Motel.

Mulanje Motel MOTEL $ (📞 01-466245; M2; r MK5000; P) Mulanje Motel's 18 basic but clean rooms have flowery bedding, fan and functional if frugal bathroom; those in the rear annexe are rather dingy. Around the front courtyard are a restaurant and a bar with pool table.

★ **Kara O'Mula**　　　　　　　LODGE $$
(☑ 01-466515; www.karaomula.com; incl breakfast s/d US$50/65, chalets US$65/75; P 🛜 ⛱) Hidden up a dirt track right beneath Mt Mulanje, this delightful eyrie cloaked in lush vegetation has a swimming pool (fed by fresh water from a small waterfall), a cosy thatched bar, back-up power and a long veranda to savour the wonderful views of mountains and tea estates. It's homey, welcoming and the perfect base from which to hike.

★ **Huntingdon House**　　HISTORIC HOTEL $$$
(☑ 0882 599717, 0993 121854; www.huntingdon-malawi.com; Satemwa Tea and Coffee Estate, Thyolo; per person all-inclusive US$325, self-catering bungalows US$225; P 🚗 🛜) Between Mulanje and Blantyre, this atmospheric colonial homestead, still run by the founding family, offers accommodation among the emerald-green fields of a Shire Highlands tea estate. Book ahead to stay in one of the five rooms, with their coat stands, claw-footed bathtubs and pervasive mood of calm, and enjoy the excellent **restaurant** (1-/2-course lunch MK5500/7000, afternoon tea MK7500, dinner MK12,000; ⊙ noon-8pm; P 🛜 🍴) and **tea tastings** (☑ 01-473500; tastings per person US$10; ⊙ tastings 10.30am-3.30pm Mon-Fri, by appointment Sat & Sun), guided walks and mountain biking.

Mulanje Pepper　　　　　　PIZZA $$
(☑ 0999 826229, 0888 826229; www.junglepepperpizza.com/mulanje; Phalombe Rd, Chitakale Trading Centre; pizzas MK4500-5600; ⊙ 11am-9pm Wed-Mon) Underneath Mulanje Infocentre, the former Pizzeria Basilico (and country cousin of Blantyre's Jungle Pepper) serves an excellent selection of wood-fired pizzas (you can see them rolling the dough before your very eyes), as well as a range of pastas and grills. It has a breezy terrace overlooking the street.

Mt Mulanje

A huge hulk of twisted granite rising majestically from the surrounding plains, Mt Mulanje towers over 3000m high. All over the mountain are dense green valleys and rivers that drop from sheer cliffs to form dazzling waterfalls. The locals call it the 'Island in the Sky', and on misty days (and there are many) it's easy to see why: the massif is shrouded in a cotton-wool haze, its highest peaks bursting through the cloud to touch the heavens.

Some people come to the base of the mountain just for a day visit, but the stunning scenery, easy access, clear paths and well-maintained huts make Mulanje a fine hiking area worthy of a few days. While here, look out for the endemic Mulanje cedar, which can grow up to 40m high. The abundant wildlife also includes klipspringers, duikers, vervet and blue monkeys, rock hyraxes (dassies), black eagles, buzzards, hawks and kestrels.

On the second Saturday in July, the 20-year-old **Mt Mulanje Porters Race** follows a gruelling, rocky route over the country's highest peak. It was originally only for porters and guides, but these days anyone can take the 22km challenge. Contact Mulanje Infocentre (p154) for details.

🛏 Sleeping

Below the Mountain

Likhubula Forest Lodge　　LODGE $
(☑ 0888 773792, 0111 904005; Likhubula; camping MK3500, s/d from MK12,100/14,100; P) This faded but lovely old colonial house has lots of character: a homey kitchen, five clean rooms (two with their own bathroom), a veranda, a communal lounge with rocking chairs, and a nightly fire crackling. The easy charm of the staff and the recommended food make it a memorable place to overnight, with breakfast, half board and full board available.

Thuchila Tourist Lodge　　LODGE $
(☑ 0881 327988; www.facebook.com/thuchilatourist.lodge; camping MK5000, incl breakfast

HIKING ON MT MULANJE

There are about six main routes up and down Mulanje. The three main ascent routes go from Likhubula: the **Chambe Plateau Path** (also called the Skyline Path), the **Chapaluka Path** and the relatively easy **Lichenya Path** (aka the Milk Run). Other routes, more often used for the descent, are Thuchila Hut to Lukulezi Mission, Sombani Hut to Fort Lister Gap, and Minunu Hut to the Lujeri Tea Estate.

Once you're on the massif, a network of paths links the huts and peaks, and many permutations are possible. It takes anything from two to six hours to hike between one hut and the next.

Mt Mulanje

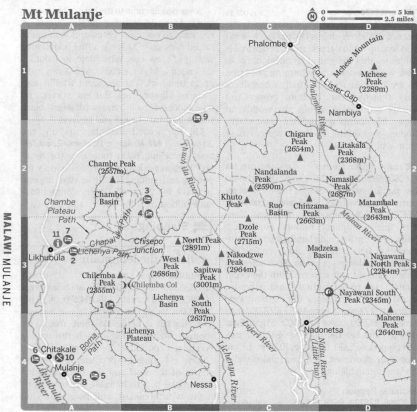

MALAWI MULANJE

Mt Mulanje

Sleeping
1 CCAP Cottage	A3
2 CCAP Guesthouse	A3
3 Chambe Hut	B2
4 France's Cottage	B2
5 Kara O'Mula	A4
6 Kokotowa Executive Lodge	A4
7 Likhubula Forest Lodge	A3
8 Mulanje Motel	A4
9 Thuchila Tourist Lodge	B1

Eating
10 Mulanje Pepper	A4

Information
11 Likhubula Forestry Office	A3
Mulanje Infocentre	(see 10)

s/d MK15,000/17,000, without bathroom from MK6000/7500; P📶) This rustic lodge has an edge-of-the-world feel (maybe it's the caged baboons outside), with lush gardens nestled in the shadow of the massif. There are basic rooms with shared bathroom, while comfortable blue-walled en-suite chalets further up the slope have fridge, fan and a swimming hole below. The bar-restaurant (mains MK2000) serves curries, chambo, *nsima* and the like.

CCAP Guesthouse   GUESTHOUSE $
(📞 0888 863632, 0881 188887; www.ccapblan tyre-synod.org/ccap-likhubula-mulanje.html; Likhubula; camping US$5, dm US$11, s/d/q from US$47/55/93, r without bathroom per person US$16) The CCAP (Church of Central Africa Presbyterian) Mission, after the Likhubula gate, has cosy rooms, four- and 12-bed dorms, and one- and two-bedroom self-catering chalets (number one is homey). The friendly guesthouse among jacaranda trees is a pleasant place to rest after a long hike. Breakfast (US$4), and lunch and dinner (US$6), are available to both guests and nonguests.

On the Mountain

There are eight forestry huts on Mulanje: Chambe, Chisepo, Lichenya, Thuchila, Chinzama, Minunu, Madzeka and Sombani. Each is equipped with benches, tables and open fires with plenty of wood. Some have sleeping platforms (no mattresses); in others you just sleep on the floor. You provide your own food, cooking gear, candles, sleeping bag and stove (although you can cook on the fire). A caretaker chops wood, lights fires and brings water, for which a small tip should be paid. Payments must be made at Likhubula Forestry Office – show your receipt to the hut caretaker.

CCAP Cottage   CHALET $

(☑ 0888 863632, 0881 188887; per person US$8) On the Lichenya Plateau, this basic cottage is a step up from the forestry huts found elsewhere in the mountains, with utensils in the kitchen, plus mattresses and blankets. You can make reservations at the CCAP Guesthouse, from where the cottage is a six-hour walk.

France's Cottage   CHALET $

(☑ 0888 122645; www.mcm.org.mw/mulanje_huts.php; per person camping/cottages MK500/1000) This historical two-bedroom cottage sleeps six and comes with a living room complete with cooking fireplace. There are two single beds and two bunks. It's in the Chambe Basin near the **Chambe Hut** (per person camping/huts MK500/1000). Book through the Mulanje Infocentre or Likhubula Forestry Office – show your receipt to the hut caretaker.

ℹ Information

Hiking on Mt Mulanje is controlled by the **Likhubula Forestry Office** (☑ 0111 904005, 0888 773792; ⊙ 7.30am-4.30pm), at the small village of Likhubula, about 15km north of Mulanje town centre. Entry fees payable at the gate are MK1000 per person, MK500 per vehicle, and MK1000 per day for parking. Register here with Macdonald and the friendly staff, and make reservations for the mountain huts (or call in advance). The office can also advise day-trippers about short hikes on the lower slopes.

Also excellent for information and bookings is the Mulanje Infocentre. Emmie and the knowledgeable staff provide all pertinent information about hiking on the mountain and have a good reference library of books and maps.

Mulanje is a big mountain with notoriously unpredictable weather. After periods of heavy rain streams can become swollen and impassable – do not try to cross them! You should wait until the flood subsides or adjust your route to cross in safety further upstream. Also be aware that much of the mountain's granite surface can become very slippery and dangerous when wet. Even during the dry season, it's not uncommon to get rain, cold winds and thick mists, which make it easy to get lost.Between May and August, periods of low cloud and drizzle (called chiperone) can last several days, and temperatures drop below freezing. Always carry a map, a compass and warm and waterproof clothing in case the weather changes.

Mountain Club of Malawi (☑ 0888 842701, 01-821269; www.mcm.org.mw) Comprehensive source of info on hiking, mountain biking and rock climbing in the massif.

ℹ Getting There & Away

The dirt road to Likhubula turns off the main sealed Blantyre–Mulanje road at Chitakale Trading Centre, about 2km northwest of the centre of Mulanje town – follow the signpost to Phalombe.

If you're coming from Blantyre on the bus, ask to be dropped at Chitakale. From there, you can pick up a *matola* (pickup), minibus (MK1000) or bicycle taxi (MK700) to Likhubula. Alternatively you can walk (11km, two to three hours); it's a pleasant hike with good views of the southwestern face of Mulanje on your right.

Majete Wildlife Reserve

Malawi's only Big Five park, this rugged wilderness of hilly miombo (woodland) and savannah hugs the west bank of the Shire River. Since African Parks took over its management in 2003, things have really been looking up for the once heavily poached reserve. A perimeter fence has been erected, and accommodation and roads have been massively upgraded. With Majete's lion-reintroduction program, the **park** (☑ 0999 521741; www.african-parks.org; person/vehicle US$20/4; ⊙ 6am-6pm) is now a conservation case study and an exciting destination.

Majete lies west of the Shire River, some 70km southwest of Blantyre. Take the M1 to Chikwawa, from where signs will direct you 20km to the reserve along 2WD-accessible roads. By public transport, the nearest you can get is Chikwawa.

Regular minibuses run from Blantyre to Chikwawa (MK1500, 1½ hours). From there, the easiest option is to arrange a transfer with your lodge, but you can privately hire a *matola* (pickup; MK6000 to MK8000).

MALAWI MAJETE WILDLIFE RESERVE

Ulendo Airlink (p167) flies a few days a week between the reserve airstrip, 1.5km west of the gate, and destinations including Lilongwe (adult/child US$341/243) and Likoma Island. Charter flights are also available, as are discounted seats on upcoming departures; check the 'bid to fly' section of Ulendo Airlink's website.

Community Campsite CAMPGROUND **$**
(☑ 0999 521741; www.african-parks.org; camping/tent hire US$10/25, gazebo s/d US$12/15; P) Enabling visitors on a budget to stay in the reserve and fully immerse themselves in the wildlife-viewing activities, this campground has shady places to pitch up, park or sleep on a stilted gazebo under the stars. There's drinkable borehole water, a thatched bar, clean ablution blocks and hot showers, as well as barbecues, cooking utensils and free firewood.

★**Mkulumadzi Lodge** LODGE **$$$**
(☑ 01-794491; www.mkulumadzi.com; per person all-inclusive US$445; P※@🛰🐾) Romantically reached by a suspension bridge over a croc-infested river, this extraordinary lodge is a fusion of African tradition and boutique chic. The eight chalets are artfully blended with the bush, with grass roofs, step-in rain showers and windows offering widescreen views of the Shire River as you flop in a sunken, candlelit bath.

★**Thawale Camp** LODGE **$$$**
(☑ 0999 521741; www.african-parks.org; chalets per person with half board/full board/full board plus activities from US$138/150/180; P) 🍽 Situated around a watering hole frequented by antelopes and warthogs, this upmarket bush camp is about 3km inside the reserve from the main entrance. The standard, luxury and family tented chalets on raised wooden platforms feel safari-ready with their khaki sheets, outside barbecues and private verandas overlooking the floodlit watering hole.

UNDERSTAND MALAWI

Malawi Today

The smiles travellers encounter in 'the warm heart of Africa' belie a country grappling with the disasters of drought, flooding and food shortages. These environmental challenges are set against a background of political corruption, unsustainable population growth and deforestation, and one of the world's highest HIV/AIDS infection rates at about 10%. Going into 2017, leadership difficulties continue to dominate headlines. However, there is good news in the conservation sector, with animal translocations proceeding apace. Among the highlights: 250 elephants are set to be translocated from Majete to Nkhotakota in 2017 and Liwonde's rhino sanctuary continues to conserve endangered black rhinos.

History

The Difaqane ('The Crushing)'

Also known as the *Mfecane,* meaning the 'crushing' or 'scattering', the period between 1815 and about 1840 saw indigenous tribes in Southern Africa involved in internecine, bloody struggles. Much of this can be attributed to one man, Shaka, king of the Zulu tribe. In the early 19th century there were three centralised kingdoms: the Ngwane, Mdwandwe and Mthethwe. In 1869 Shaka, ruler of the Mthethwe, revolutionised military warfare by replacing the throwing spear with a stabbing spear and surrounding his enemy in a tight horseshoe then closing in on them. Very soon widespread massacres spread across Southern Africa, depopulating countries and killing some two million people.

Among those that fled were the Mdwandwe clan, who headed for Mozambique, coercing the local Tonga people to form a cooperative army with them – the Jere-Ngoni. By 1825, blazing their own trail of carnage, the Jere-Ngoni entered Malawi, terrorising the Yao people near the lake and the Tumbuka people to the north, raiding villages, butchering old men and forcibly enlisting young men. The army settled on Lake Malawi and were to remain there until their Mdwandwe chief's death in 1845. This bloody period is remembered as 'The Killing'.

The Dark Days of Slavery

Slavery, and a slave trade, had existed in Africa for many centuries, but in the early 19th century demand from outside Africa increased considerably. Swahili-Arabs, who dominated the trade on the east coast of Africa, pushed into the interior, using powerful local tribes such as the Yao to raid and capture their unfortunate neighbours. Several trading centres were established in Malawi, including Karonga and Nkhotakota – towns that still have a Swahili-Arab influence today.

Livingstone & the First Missionaries

The first Europeans to arrive in Malawi were Portuguese explorers who reached the interior from Mozambique in the early 1600s. Its most famous explorer, though, was David Livingstone from Scotland, whose exploration heralded the arrival of Europeans in a way that was to change Malawi forever.

In 1858, when Livingstone found his route up the Zambezi blocked, he followed a major tributary called the Shire into southern Malawi, reaching Lake Malawi in September 1859 – and providing fodder for thousands of tourist brochures to come by reportedly dubbing it the 'lake of stars'.

Livingstone died in Zambia in 1873. In 1875 a group from the Free Church of Scotland built a new mission at Cape Maclear, which they named Livingstonia, and in 1876 the Established Church of Scotland built a mission in the Shire Highlands, which they called Blantyre. Cape Maclear proved to be malarial, so the mission moved to Bandawe, then finally in 1894 to the high ground of the eastern escarpment. This site was successful; the Livingstonia mission flourished and is still there today.

The Colonial Period

By the 1880s competition among European powers in the area was fierce. In 1889 Britain allowed Cecil Rhodes' British South Africa Company to administer the Shire Highlands, and in 1891 the British Central Africa (BCA) Protectorate was extended to include land along the western side of the lake. In 1907 the BCA Protectorate became the colony of Nyasaland.

Colonial rule brought an end to slave traders and intertribal conflicts, but also introduced a whole new set of problems. As the European settlers' demand for land grew, the hapless local inhabitants found themselves labelled 'squatters' or tenants of a new landlord, and were forced to seek work on the white-settler plantations or to become migrant workers in Northern and Southern Rhodesia (present-day Zambia and Zimbabwe) and South Africa. By the turn of the 19th century some 6000 Africans were leaving the country every year; this had escalated to 150,000 by the 1950s.

Transition & Independence

After WWI the British began allowing the African population a part in administering the country, although it wasn't until the 1950s that Africans were actually allowed to enter the government.

In 1953, in an attempt to boost its sluggish development, Nyasaland was linked with Northern and Southern Rhodesia in the Federation of Rhodesia and Nyasaland. But the federation was opposed by the pro-independence Nyasaland African Congress (NAC) party, led by Dr Hastings Kamuzu Banda. The colonial authorities declared a state of emergency and Banda was jailed.

By mid-1960 Britain was losing interest in its colonies. Banda was released, and he returned to head the now renamed Malawi Congress Party (MCP), which won elections held in 1962. The federation was dissolved, and Nyasaland became the independent country of Malawi in 1964. Two years later, Malawi became a republic and Banda was made president.

Banda: Hero to Villain

Banda swiftly forced members of the opposition into exile, banning political parties, declaring himself 'president for life' and outlawing the foreign press. Miniskirts, women in trousers, long hair for men and other such signs of Western cultural influence were also banned.

Alongside this move towards dictatorship, Banda remained politically conservative, giving political support to apartheid-era South Africa, which, in turn, rewarded Malawi with aid and trade.

With the end of the Cold War in the 1990s, South Africa and the West no longer needed to support Banda, and within the country opposition was swelling. In 1992 the Catholic bishops of Malawi condemned the regime and called for change, and demonstrations, both peaceful and violent, added their weight to the bishops' move. As a final blow, donor countries restricted aid until Banda agreed to relinquish total control.

In June 1993 a referendum was held for the people to choose between a multiparty political system and Banda's autocratic rule. Over 80% of eligible voters took part; those

LOCAL KNOWLEDGE

GULE WAMKULU

Performed at funerals, major celebrations and male initiation ceremonies, Gule Wamkulu or 'Great Dance' is the most popular dance among the Chewa. It can't be performed by just anyone; only members of a secret society, sometimes called the Nyau brotherhood, are allowed to participate. Dancers perform clad in magnificent costumes and brightly painted masks made from cloth, animal skins, wood and straw. Each dancer represents a particular character (there are more than 150 Gule Wamkulu characters): a wild animal, perhaps, or an ancestral spirit, sometimes even a modern object such as a car or a plane. Each character has its own meaning – for example, lions represent strength and power and often appear at the funeral of a chief.

Supported by an entourage of drummers and singers, the dancers achieve a state through which they can summon up the spirits of animals or dead relatives. As the drumbeats quicken, they perform dances and movement with incredible energy and precision. Some of this is pure entertainment, some of it is a means of passing on messages from ancestral spirits, and some of it aims to scare the audience – as a moral lesson or a warning. Through acting out mischievous deeds, the Gule Wamkulu characters are showing the audience, as representatives of the spirit world, how not to behave.

There are both individual and group performances and they take place during the day and at night – when the audience watches from afar. The dance is widespread in central and southern Malawi and is also performed in Zambia's Eastern Province and the Tete province of Mozambique.

voting for a new system won easily, and Banda accepted the result.

The 1990s: Fresh Hope

At Malawi's first full multiparty election in May 1994, the victor was the United Democratic Front (UDF), led by Bakili Muluzi. He quickly closed political prisons, encouraged freedom of speech and print, and initiated free primary-school education; he also undertook several economic reforms with the help of the World Bank and the IMF.

In November 1997 Dr Banda died. His age was unknown, but he was thought to be 99.

In 2002, after failing to pass a bill that would have given him life presidency, Muluzi chose Bingu wa Mutharika as his successor, and in 2004 Mutharika duly won the election. The new leader resigned from the UDF and set up his own party, the Democratic Progressive Party (DPP). A massive famine in 2005 saw Malawi bear the brunt of crop failure and drought in the region. In 2006, under the Highly Indebted Poor Country Initiative, Malawi qualified for debt relief.

Mutharika: Malawi's New Dictator

In 2010 Mutharika expelled his deputy, Joyce Banda, from the party, but he had no choice but to retain her as vice-president as she was elected in 2009 as his running mate. Then in 2011 a diplomatic spat erupted between Mutharika and the UK after a leaked British document accused him of being autocratic. Mutharika hit back, expelling the British High Commissioner; immediately, Malawi's biggest donor froze millions of dollars of aid.

By the end of 2011, Malawi was crippled by soaring fuel prices of up to 150% and terrible shortages that ground the country's already ailing industry to a halt. Foreign exchange was also banned as Mutharika took the inflammatory measure of inflating Malawi's currency on the international markets.

On 5 April 2012 Mutharika suffered a heart attack. In the following days, the army placed a cordon around Joyce Banda's house to assist her constitutional succession to power (lest Mutharika's supporters enact a coup). She was sworn in as Malawi's first female president on 7 April.

Joyce Banda: Unfulfilled Promise

In 2012 Banda took some very brave steps to get her house in order: first, she devalued the kwacha by 40%; next, she sold the US$15 million presidential jet, saving the poor country US$300,000 a year in maintenance and insurance. Meanwhile, she proved herself a shrewd international diplomat; foreign funding to Malawi swiftly resumed, with the IMF agreeing to a donation of US$157 million.

Banda's presidency lasted until 2014, when her predecessor's brother, Peter Mutharika, was voted in. Her two-year term was rocked by the 'cashgate' scandal, which saw international aid temporarily frozen when up to US$100 million disappeared from government coffers. She is reportedly planning to run in the 2019 election.

Culture

Malawi's main ethnic groups are Chewa, dominant in the centre and south; Yao in the south; and Tumbuka in the north. Other groups include the Ngoni (also spelt Angoni), inhabiting parts of the central and northern provinces; the Chipoka (or Phoka) in the central area; the Lambya; the Ngonde (also called the Nyakyusa) in the northern region; and the Tonga, mostly along the lakeshore.

There are small populations of Asian and European people living mainly in the cities and involved in commerce, farming (mainly tea plantations) and tourism. The Indian community is well established, with many businesses owned and run by Indians, while the Chinese population is growing.

Around 83% of Malawians are Christians. Some are Catholic, while many follow indigenous Christian faiths that have been established locally.

Malawi has a significant Muslim population of around 13%, mostly living in the south. Alongside the established churches, many Malawians also follow traditional animist religions.

LAKE OF STARS MUSIC FESTIVAL

One of the region's largest spectacles, this three-day **music festival** features live acts from around Africa and Europe. It takes place in a different lakeshore venue each year, with proceeds benefiting charity. Booking accommodation well in advance is essential, but there are normally camping spots available until the last minute.

The Arts

Literature

Poetry is very popular. The late Steve Chimombo was a leading poet whose collections include *Napolo and Other Poems*. His most highly acclaimed work is a complex poetic drama, *The Rainmaker*. Another returned exile, Jack Mapanje, published his first poetry collection, *Of Chameleons and Gods*, in 1981.

Malawi's most acclaimed novelist is the late Legson Kayira, whose semi-autobiographical *The Looming Shadow* and *I Will Try* earned him acclaim in the 1970s. A later work to look out for is *The Detainee*. Another novelist is Sam Mpasu; also a politician, he served a two-year jail sentence following a corruption scandal in the 2000s. His *Nobody's Friend* was a comment on the secrecy of Malawian politics – it earned him an earlier two-year prison stint in 1975. After his release he wrote *Political Prisoner 3/75* and later became minister for education in the new UDF government.

MALAWI CULTURE

MUST READ: THE BOY WHO HARNESSED THE WIND

When the 2001 drought brought famine, and terrible floods decimated his parents' crops, 14-year-old William Kamkwamba was forced from school. While he was educating himself at his old primary school, one book in particular spoke to him; it was about electricity generation through windmills.

A lightbulb moment flashed. Exhausted from his work in the fields every day, William picked around for scrap and painstakingly began his creation: a four-bladed windmill. Soon neighbours were coming to see him to charge their phones on his windmill.

When news of William's invention spread, people from across the globe offered to help him. He was shortly re-enrolled in college and travelling to America to visit wind farms, and he has since been mentoring children on how to create their own independent electricity sources. *The Boy Who Harnessed The Wind* (by William Kamkwamba and Bryan Mealer) is his amazing story, published in 2009.

Natural Environment

Pint-sized, landlocked Malawi is wedged between Zambia, Tanzania and Mozambique, measuring roughly 900km long and between 80km and 150km wide, with a total area of 118,484 sq km.

Lying in a trough formed by the Rift Valley, Lake Malawi makes up over 75% of Malawi's eastern boundary. West and south of the lake, escarpments rise to high plateaus covering much of the country.

Wildlife

In 2012 Malawi began reintroducing lions at Majete Wildlife Reserve, finally giving the country its 'Big Five' stamp. Many people head for Liwonde National Park, noted for its herds of elephants and myriad hippos. Along with Majete, it's the only park in the country where you might see rhinos.

Elephants are also regularly seen in Nkhotakota Wildlife Reserve, Majete and Nyika National Park. Nyika has the country's largest population of leopards and Nkhotakota has been bolstered by a historic elephant translocation from Liwonde and Majete. Vwaza Marsh Wildlife Reserve is known for its hippos, as well as elephants, buffaloes and antelope, but is currently in poor shape due to unsatisfactory management.

Lake Malawi has more fish species than any other inland body of water in the world, with a total of over 1000, of which more than 350 are endemic. The largest family of fish in the lake is the Cichlidae (cichlids).

For birdwatchers, Malawi is rewarding: over 600 species have been recorded in the country, and birds rarely spotted elsewhere in Southern Africa are easily seen here, including the Böhm's bee-eater, wattled crane and African skimmer.

National Parks

Malawi has five national parks. These are (from north to south) Nyika, Kasungu, Lake Malawi (around Cape Maclear), Liwonde and Lengwe. There are also four wildlife reserves – Vwaza Marsh, Nkhotakota, Mwabvi and Majete – meaning that 16.8% of Malawi's land is protected.

Most parks and reserves cost US$10 per person per day (each 24-hour period), plus US$3 per car per day. Citizens and residents pay less. All fees are payable in kwacha or US dollars.

SURVIVAL GUIDE

ℹ Directory A–Z

ACCOMMODATION

There are generally good selections of backpacker hostels and top-end accommodation but fewer midrange guesthouses and hotels. One tip: consider sharing a bathroom; many budget and midrange options have lovely rooms with a bathroom for every two rooms. Camping offers affordable access to high-end lodges, as many have campsites.

ACTIVITIES
Birdwatching

Malawi is a great destination for birding, with over 600 species recorded here. The best place to start is the national parks. Liwonde is an excellent spot, with particularly good birdlife along the river, and the forests in Nyika are also good. For water birds, Elephant Marsh in Malawi's far south is your surest bet. Land & Lake Safaris (p124) in Lilongwe can organise birdwatching tours around the country.

Cycling

Several lakeshore lodges hire out mountain bikes from about US$10 a day. Great mountain-biking areas include Nyika National Park, with its hilly landscape and good network of dirt tracks, and the Viphya Plateau. These areas' lodges offer rental bikes.

Diving, Snorkelling & Other Water Sports

Lake Malawi's population of colourful fish attracts travellers to come scuba diving. The lake is reckoned by experts to be among the best freshwater diving areas in the world, and one of the cheapest places to learn how to dive. The water is warm and, (depending on the season) visibility and weather conditions are usually good. Places where you can hire scuba gear and take a PADI Open Water course include Nkhata Bay, Cape Maclear, Likoma Island and Senga Bay. If you don't want to dive you can still enjoy the fish: snorkelling gear can be hired from dive centres, and lakeside hotels rent out snorkels.

ℹ SLEEPING PRICE RANGES

The following price ranges refer to an en-suite double room excluding breakfast, in high season.

$ less than MK35,000 (US$50)

$$ MK35,000–MK70,000 (US$50–US$100)

$$$ more than MK70,000 (US$100)

Upmarket lodges along the lake have facilities for waterskiing or windsurfing. You can also go sailing, or join luxurious 'sail safaris' where everything is done for you – Danforth Yachting (p141) and Pumulani (p143) in Cape Maclear on the southern lakeshore can both organise this. Kayaking is available at Cape Maclear and Nkhata Bay and at many of the lodges dotting the lakeshore.

Hiking & Rock Climbing

The main areas for hiking are Mt Mulanje and the Nyika Plateau. Other areas include the Zomba Plateau, and various small peaks around Blantyre. Mulanje is Malawi's main rock-climbing area, with some spectacular routes and Africa's longest vertical rock wall, although local climbers also visit smaller crags and outcrops. Rock climbing can also be arranged in Livingstonia and the Viphya Plateau.

The Mountain Club of Malawi (p157) provides a wealth of information about hiking and climbing on Mt Mulanje.

BUSINESS HOURS

Banks Usually 8am to 3.30pm weekdays.

Bars Noon to 11pm.

Post offices Generally 7.30am to 5pm weekdays, sometimes with a break for lunch. In Blantyre and Lilongwe, they're open Saturday morning too.

Restaurants If they don't serve breakfast, 11am to 10pm.

Shops and offices 8am to noon and 1pm to 5pm weekdays. Many shops also open Saturday morning.

CHILDREN

Child care Easy to arrange informally through your hotel.

Restaurant high chairs Available at many big-city restaurants.

Nappies & Formula Widely available in major cities, but not elsewhere.

Warning Never let your children swim in Lake Malawi from just before dusk into the night. There are many tragic stories about kids who outstayed their welcome and got taken by crocs and hippos, who come out at this time.

EMBASSIES & CONSULATES

Australia Contact the Australian Embassy in Harare, Zimbabwe.

Canada Contact the Canadian High Commission in Maputo, Mozambique.

France Contact the French Embassy in Harare, Zimbabwe.

New Zealand Contact the New Zealand High Commission in Pretoria, South Africa.

The following are in Lilongwe:

British High Commission (Map p122; 01-772400; www.gov.uk; City Centre)

German Embassy (Map p122; 01-772555; www.lilongwe.diplo.de; Convention Dr, City Centre)

Irish Embassy (Map p122; 0888 207543; www.dfa.ie/irish-embassy/malawi; 3rd fl, Arwa House, African Unity Ave, City Centre)

Mozambican High Commission (Map p122; 01-774100; www.minec.gov.mz; Convention Dr, City Centre)

Netherlands Honorary Consulate (0999 960481; https://zimbabwe.nlembassy.org; Heavenly Close, Area 10)

South African High Commission (Map p122; 01-773722; www.dirco.gov.za; Plot 19)

US Embassy (Map p122; 01-773166; lilongwe.usembassy.gov; 16 Kenyatta Rd, City Centre)

Zambian High Commission (Map p122; 01-772590; www.facebook.com/zambiahighcommissionlilongwe; City Centre)

Zimbabwean Embassy (Map p122; 01-774988, 01-774413; www.zimfa.gov.zw; Area 13)

INTERNET ACCESS

Across the country, most accommodation and restaurants catering to foreigners offer wi-fi, generally operated by Skyband (www.skyband.mw). The advantage of this system is that you can buy a voucher (typically MK2000 for 500MB) and use it at multiple locations. The disadvantage is that Skyband hot spots can be hit and miss, so many residents prefer to access the internet on their phone using an Airtel (http://africa.airtel.com) SIM card. TNM (www.tnm.co.mw) SIM cards are not as good for surfing the web. Mobile-phone data typically costs MK5000 for 1GB, valid for 30 days.

Wi-fi is rarely free in budget accommodation but may be in midrange and top-end places. You'll find internet cafes in Lilongwe, Blantyre and most towns.

MONEY

Take some US dollars and a back-up card. ATMs are widespread and credit cards accepted. Power cuts scupper both; keep a reserve supply of cash. For exchange rates see p721.

ℹ EATING PRICE RANGES

The following price ranges refer to a standard main course.

$ less than MK3500 (US$5)

$$ MK3500–MK7000 (US$5–US$10)

$$$ more than MK7000 (US$10)

ATMs

Standard and National Banks are the best bet for foreigners wishing to withdraw cash, and their ATMs accept Visa, MasterCard, Cirrus and Maestro cards. ATMs are found in most cities and towns including Lilongwe, Blantyre, Mzuzu, Karonga, Liwonde, Salima, Mangochi, Zomba and Nkhata Bay. Visa is most widely accepted.

ATMs dispense a maximum of MK40,000 per withdrawal, but you can insert your card three times in a row, thus ending up with MK120,000 (US$168). Your bank at home will charge you for each transaction. Alternatively you can go into the bank and withdraw your card limit in kwacha, although you will have to queue and the tellers are sometimes reluctant.

It's worth taking at least one back-up card, as the banks often experience network problems: for example, sometimes foreign credit cards work in the ATMs but debit cards don't.

Cash

Malawi's unit of currency is the Malawian kwacha (MK). This is divided into 100 tambala (t).

Banknotes include MK1000, MK500, MK200, MK100, MK50, MK20, MK10 and MK5. Coins are MK10, MK5, MK1, 50t, 20t, 10t, 5t, 2t and 1t, although the small tambala coins are virtually worthless.

At big hotels and other places that actually quote in US dollars you can pay in hard currency or kwacha at the prevailing exchange rate. As the US dollar is stronger than the kwacha, you will save money by paying with dollars where possible.

ATMs and card machines generally don't work during the frequent power cuts, so carrying a wad of kwacha, and preferably US dollars too, is wise.

Credit & Debit Cards

You can use Visa cards at some but not all of the large hotels, high-end lodges and top-end restaurants (be warned that this will add a 5% to 10% surcharge to your bill). MasterCard is less commonly accepted.

Inform your bank that you will be travelling in Malawi.

PUBLIC HOLIDAYS

When one of these dates falls on a weekend, normally the following Monday is a public holiday. Islamic holidays are also observed throughout Malawi by the Muslim population.

New Year's Day 1 January
John Chilembwe Day 15 January
Martyrs' Day 3 March
Easter March/April – Good Friday, Holy Saturday and Easter Monday
Labour Day 1 May

Kamuzu Day 14 May
Independence Day 6 July
Mother's Day October, second Monday
Christmas Day 25 December
Boxing Day 26 December

SAFE TRAVEL

Malawi is one of the safest African countries for travellers, but you should still be reasonably cautious and employ common sense.

➡ The cities are most dangerous. Catch taxis and don't wander around at night.

➡ Much of the danger comes from the chaotic roads and unfit vehicles; drive carefully, and bail out if a minibus feels excessively unsafe.

➡ Take care to avoid environmental hazards such as bilharzia and traveller's diarrhoea.

Wildlife

Potential dangers at Lake Malawi include encountering a hippo or crocodile after dusk, when they come up onto beaches. The Shire River is replete with crocodiles, and locals disappear in dugouts on a regular basis, so be careful of dipping your hand in the water while on a river safari. Popular tourist beaches are safe, although, just to be sure, you should seek local advice before diving in. Avoid sheltered, reedy beaches where bilharzia host snails are found. The most dangerous animals in Malawi are the mosquitoes that transmit malaria.

TELEPHONE & MOBILE PHONES

Mobile phones are in use everywhere, and coverage is extensive. The major networks are Airtel and TNM, with 099 and 088 prefixes respectively. TNM has better coverage in rural areas and is popular with locals. Airtel is popular among expats and travellers; it also has good coverage, and works better in the cities, especially for using the internet and social-media apps.

SIM cards are readily available from street vendors for around MK1000. If you need to cut the card to fit your phone, there will invariably be someone nearby ready to whip out his cutter for MK500 or so. You can buy top-up scratchcards from vendors and shops. Cards generally come in maximum denominations of MK1000. Mobile-phone data typically costs MK5000 for 1GB, valid for 30 days.

Emergency & Important Numbers

Country code	☏ 265
International access code	☏ 00
Ambulance	☏ 998
Police	☏ 997
Fire	☏ 999

TIME

Malawi follows Central Africa Time, which is two hours ahead of Greenwich Mean Time (GMT/UTC). There is no daylight saving time.

TOURIST INFORMATION

There are tourist-information offices in Blantyre and Lilongwe, but you're much better off asking for advice from your accommodation or a travel agency. Outside Malawi, tourism promotion is handled by UK-based **Malawi Tourism** (☑ in the UK 0115-972 7250; www.malawitourism.com), which responds to enquiries from all over the world.

VISAS

Most nationalities require a visa, which is issued (in most cases) upon arrival at the airport or major land border.

A one-month single-entry visa costs US$75, six- and 12-month multiple-entry visas cost US$150 and US$250 respectively; a seven-day transit visa costs US$50. Card payments should be possible at the airports, but it would be wise to have the fee handy in cash US dollars. You can apply in advance through your local Malawian embassy, but it is more expensive (US$100 for a single-entry visa).

Check the Malawian Department of Immigration website, www.immigration.gov.mw/visa.html, for more info. At the time of writing, the site advised travellers to apply in advance or, if that was not possible, to obtain a letter of authorisation. However, this directive was not being enforced and was likely to be dropped. There was also discussion of establishing an electronic visa system, so it would be worth checking with your accommodation for updates.

Once in Malawi, travellers with a one-month single-entry visa can apply to extend it to three months total at the immigration offices in Lilongwe, Blantyre and Zomba. This costs MK5000 per month cash. Temporary-residence permits, lasting up to six months and available in Lilongwe and Blantyre, cost US$100.

VOLUNTEERING

There are numerous volunteer opportunities in Malawi. A good initial contact is **Volunteer Abroad** (www.volunteerabroad.com), which has listings of current options. Otherwise, local grass-roots opportunities include the following:

Billy Riordan Memorial Trust (www.billys-malawiproject.org) Has an established clinic in Cape Maclear and provides medical care in the area. The trust needs medical volunteers (doctors, dentists, nurses, lab technicians etc).

Butterfly Space (p133) Involved in a number of projects in Nkhata Bay, as is neighbouring Mayoka Village.

Cool Runnings (p139) Involved in a variety of projects in the Senga Bay area.

Panda Garden (p141) Based in Cape Maclear, Panda Garden is always on the lookout for divers and others to help with bilharzia research in the lake.

Ripple Africa (www.rippleafrica.org) Recruits volunteer teachers, doctors, nurses and environmental workers for projects in the Chintheche district.

Wildlife Action Group (www.wag-malawi.org) Uses volunteers to assist in the management and maintenance of forest reserves near Salima.

ℹ️ Getting There & Away

AIR

There are no direct flights to Malawi from Europe or the United States. The easiest way to reach the country by air is via Kenya, Ethiopia or South Africa.

Lilongwe International Airport (Kamuzu International Airport; LLW; ☑ 0992 991097) A taxi or airport shuttle to/from town costs US$35. It's a standard charge, advertised on a board in the arrivals terminal, and taxi drivers meet incoming flights. You can also arrange a transfer in advance through your accommodation.

Chileka International Airport (Blantyre) A taxi from the airport to the city costs around MK10,000, but agree on a price with the driver first. The price can be negotiated down if you're going from the city to the airport. Frequent local buses between the City Bus Station and Chileka Township also pass the airport gate (around MK2000).

Airports & Airlines

Lilongwe International Airport 25km north of Lilongwe City Centre, handles the majority of international flights, while **Chileka International Airport**, 15km north of central Blantyre, also receives numerous flights.

The country's national carrier relaunched as Malawian Airlines in 2012, when its previous incarnation, Air Malawi, went into liquidation and the government partnered with Ethiopian Airlines.

Ethiopian Airlines (☑ 01-772031; www.ethiopianairlines.com) Flies daily from Addis Ababa (Ethiopia) to both Lilongwe and Blantyre.

Kenya Airways (☑ 01-824524, 01-774227; www.kenya-airways.com) Links both Lilongwe and Blantyre with Nairobi (Kenya) four days a week.

Malawian Airlines Has a decent regional network, with flights heading to Dar es Salaam (Tasmania), Johannesburg (South Africa), Lusaka (Zambia) and Harare (Zimbabwe) from Blantyre and Lilongwe.

Proflight Zambia (☑ 01-700444; www.proflight-zambia.com) Flies Lilongwe to Lusaka (Zambia) six days a week.

South African Airways (☎01-772242, 01-620617; www.flysaa.com) Flies three days weekly between Blantyre and Johannesburg (South Africa), and six days weekly between Lilongwe and Johannesburg (with connections to Durban, Cape Town etc).

LAND

Overland, travellers can enter the country from Zambia, Mozambique or Tanzania. Indeed, Malawi is a popular staging post for overland trucks heading between Nairobi and Cape Town. Most border posts close from 6pm to 7am.

Bus

It's possible to cross into Malawi by bus from Tanzania, Zambia, Zimbabwe and South Africa, and there are direct services from Johannesburg (South Africa), Dar es Salaam (Tanzania), Lusaka (Zambia) and Harare (Zimbabwe) to Blantyre and Lilongwe. When crossing the border you will have to get off the bus to pass through customs and pay for your visa.

Mozambique
South

Take a minibus to the Mozambican border crossing at Zóbuè and then a minibus to Tete, from where buses go to Beira and Maputo. You could also get a Blantyre–Harare bus to drop you at Tete.

Central

There are daily buses from Blantyre to the Mozambican border at Marka; failing that, take a bus to Nsanje and continue by minibus or *matola* (pickup). It's a few kilometres between the border crossings – you can walk or take a bicycle taxi – and you can change money on the Mozambique side. From here pickups go to Mutarara and over the bridge to Vila de Sena.

North

There are three border crossings from Malawi into northern Mozambique: Muloza, from where you can reach Mocuba in Mozambique, and Nayuchi and Chiponde, both of which lead to Cuamba in Mozambique.

Regular buses run from Blantyre, via Mulanje, to Muloza. From here, it's 1km to the Mozambican border crossing, then another few kilometres into Milange. From Milange there's usually a *chapa* (pickup or converted minibus) or truck about every other day in the dry season to Mocuba, where you can find transport on to Quelimane or Nampula.

Further north, minibuses and *matolas* run a few times per day between Mangochi and the border crossing at Chiponde. It's then 7km to the Mozambican border crossing in Mandimba and the best way to get there is by bicycle taxi. Mandimba has a couple of *pensãos* (pensions), and there's at least one vehicle daily, usually a truck, between here and Cuamba.

The third option is to go by minibus from Liwonde to the border at Nayuchi. From Nayuchi, where there are moneychangers, you can walk to Entre Lagos, and then get a *chapa* to Cuamba.

South Africa

A number of bus companies run services from Lilongwe and Blantyre to Johannesburg. The best option is Intercape (p125), which operates daily services between Jo'burg and both Blantyre and Lilongwe, with a service continuing north five days a week from the latter to Mzuzu.

Buses from Lilongwe leave from outside the petrol station on Paul Kagame Rd in Old Town. In Blantyre, most Johannesburg-bound buses depart from the car park outside Blantyre Lodge.

Tanzania

If you're going in stages, Mbeya in southern Tanzania is handy for crossing to/from northern Malawi. Buses and minibuses ply the M1 between Mzuzu and Karonga, from where you can get a minibus or taxi to the Songwe border crossing. It's 200m across the bridge to the Tanzanian border crossing.

Once on the Tanzanian side of the border, minibuses travel 115km north to Mbeya, where you will need to overnight before continuing on the next morning to Dar es Salaam. You can change money with the bicycle-taxi boys, but beware of scams.

Zambia

Four direct Kob's Coach Services (p126) buses per week link Lilongwe and Lusaka (MK20,000, 12 hours), departing from Devil St on Wednesday and Saturday mornings. Regular minibuses run between Lilongwe and Mchinji. From here, it's 12km to the border. Local shared taxis shuttle between Mchinji and the border crossing.

From the Zambian side of the border, shared taxis run to Chipata, about 25km northwest of the crossing, from where you can reach Lusaka or South Luangwa National Park.

LAKE

Dhows sail in the morning from Mdamba on Likoma Island (Malawi) to Cóbuè (Mozambique). If you're planning to visit Mozambique you must get a visa in advance and be sure to get your passport stamped at Malawian immigration in Mdimba.

In the market by the cathedral in Cóbuè there's an immigration office for your entry/exit formalities. Right beside the office are the boatmen.

Mozambique

Operated by the **Malawi Shipping Company** (p237), the *Chambo* connects Metangula

(Mozambique) with Likoma Island, Chizumulu and Nkhata Bay. It leaves Metangula at 5am on Wednesday, and reaches Likoma around 11.30am, Chizumulu around 12.30pm and Nkhata Bay around 2pm.

On the return journey, it leaves at 5am on Thursday, stops in Chizumulu around 7.30am and Likoma around 9am, and departs Likoma around 2pm to reach Metangula around 8pm.

There's also a Saturday service just to/from Likoma, leaving Metangula at 5am and arriving on the island around 11.30am. It returns on Sunday at 1.30pm, arriving in Metangula around 8pm.

The *Chambo* also heads south from Metangula to Chipoka via Makanjila and Senga Bay, leaving at 5am on Monday, passing Senga Bay around 6.30pm and arriving in Chipoka around 9pm. It returns north at 5am on Tuesday, passing Senga Bay around 7am and reaching Metangula around 8pm.

Malawian and Mozambican immigration officers both board the *Chambo* to issue exit/entry stamps and visas. You can check for timetable changes at www.malawitourism.com.

Tanzania

The Tanzanian *Songea* (www.mscl.go.tz) sails south, at 1pm on Thursday, from Itungi via Liuli and Mdamba Bay (all in Tanzania) to Nkhata Bay. A 1st-class ticket from Mdamba Bay to Nkhata Bay costs around US$5.

🛈 Getting Around

AIR

Malawian Airlines (📞 01-827900, 01-774605; www.malawian-airlines.com) The national carrier operates daily flights between Lilongwe and Blantyre (US$50, one hour), a good alternative to the bus. Its booking system isn't always reliable, so it's worth confirming your flight by phone or at an office.

Ulendo Airlink (📞 01-794638; www.flyulendo.com) The aviation wing of Ulendo Travel Group operates scheduled and charter flights on safe twin-prop planes to locations including Likoma Island and all the major wildlife parks. Check the 'bid to fly' section of Ulendo Airlink's website for discounted seats on upcoming flights.

BOAT

The *Ilala* ferry chugs passengers and cargo up and down Lake Malawi once a week in each direction. Travelling between Monkey Bay in the south and Chilumba in the north, it makes nine stops at lakeside villages and towns in between, as well as at Likoma and Chizumulu Islands. Many travellers rate this journey (or a leg of it) as a highlight of the country, although there are occasionally nasty storms. If you're unlucky, be prepared for some pitching and rolling. The boat dates from 1949 and is certainly no cruise liner, so it's better to regard it as a practical method of getting from A to B than an experience in itself.

When the *Ilala* stops at lakeside towns or villages, the water is too shallow for it to come close; the lifeboat is used to ferry passengers ashore. In both directions, the ferry docks at Nkhata Bay for seven hours and traders come aboard, selling food, drinks and newspapers. The whole trip, from one end of the line to the other, takes about three days. You can normally download the latest schedules from Malawi Tourism.

Classes & Reservations

The classes are the exclusive Owner's Cabin, Standard Cabin, Upper Deck, Second and Economy. The standard cabins were once luxurious, and are still in reasonable condition. This class and the upper deck are popular with travellers, due largely to the sociable bar. There are also seats, a shaded area and mattresses for hire on the upper deck. Second and Economy classes are dark, crowded and permeated by engine fumes, and are not recommended.

Cabin and Upper Deck class passengers can dine in the ferry's restaurant, which serves beef curry, peri-peri chicken and the like. Dishes such as beans, rice and vegetables are served from a galley on the economy deck.

Reservations are usually required for Cabin class, and are recommended to ensure a comfortable journey.

BUS

Malawi's best bus company is **AXA Coach Service** (📞 01-820100; www.axacoach.com), with three classes of vehicle: Super Executive, Executive and Special. The former is a luxury nonstop service with air-con, toilet, comfortable reclining seats, USB ports, reading lights, good drivers, snacks, fresh coffee and even an on-board

MALAWI GETTING AROUND

SAMPLE FERRY ROUTES & FARES

Following are sample fares from Nkhata Bay.

DESTINATION	OWNER'S CABIN	STANDARD CABIN	UPPER DECK	2ND	ECONOMY
Nkhotakota	MK25,770	MK19,850	MK12,490	MK7160	MK5120
Monkey Bay	MK44,800	MK34,440	MK20,450	MK11,860	MK8120

magazine. Services operate between Blantyre and Lilongwe twice a day, leaving every morning and afternoon from special departure points in each city (not the main bus stations).

The Executive and Special services are the next in line. These buses have air-con and reclining seats as well as TVs, but they don't have toilets. They ply the route between Blantyre and Karonga via Lilongwe and Mzuzu daily, serving the main towns, with limited stops elsewhere.

Other smaller bus companies, including the National Bus Company, have daily services up and down the lake and between the country's main centres. These are marginally more comfortable than minibuses, but no more efficient, and they generally cost the same.

Minibuses are the most popular option because they leave regularly throughout the day. They operate on a fill-up-and-go basis; you can speed up the process, and buy yourself some comfort, by purchasing two seats. Direct long-distance minibuses are becoming less common; you will likely have to change once or twice on a long-distance journey up the lakeshore or M1. You can still buy a long-distance ticket – the driver should transfer your fare to the connecting service – but it is wiser to only pay as far as the place where you will change minibuses.

In rural areas, the frequency of buses and minibuses drops dramatically – sometimes to nothing. In cases like this, the 'bus' is often a truck or pickup, with people just piled in the back. In Malawi this is called a *matola*.

CAR & MOTORCYCLE

The majority of main routes are sealed, though off the main routes roads are rutted and potholed, making driving slow and dangerous.

Secondary roads are usually graded dirt. Some are well maintained and easy to drive on in a normal car; others are bad, especially after rain, and slow even with a 4WD. Rural routes are not so good, and after heavy rain are often impassable. Several lodges along the lakeshore have poor access roads that need a 4WD. The same goes for the country's national parks and wildlife reserves.

TAXI

You can often share a taxi instead of waiting for the minibus to depart – a safer, more comfortable and faster option.

Privately hiring a taxi will likely work out cheaper than renting a car with a driver, plus removing driving stress and giving you an unofficial guide and interpreter. **High Class Taxi Services** (✆ 0888 100223, 0999 356920; justinchimenya@yahoo.com) in Blantyre and **Mawaso Taxi Service** (✆ 0999 161111, 0995 769772; plizimba@gmail.com) in Lilongwe both offer multiday services.

TRAIN

Central Eastern African Railways (CEAR; ✆ 01-840841; www.cear.mw) operates the following services. The trains are slow and unreliable, so buses and minibuses are a better option. The following journeys cost MK2100 in business class.

Limbe–Balaka via Blantyre (11½ hours) Departs 7am Wednesday, returns 6am Friday.

Balaka–Nayuchi via Liwonde (six hours) Departs 6am Thursday, returns 1.30pm.

Limbe–Makhanga (9¾ hours) Departs 9am Saturday, returns 7am Sunday.

Mozambique

POP 25.3 MILLION

Includes ➡

Maputo	172
Ponta d'Ouro & Ponta Malongane	182
Limpopo National Park	184
Vilankulo	192
Beira	195
Quelimane	203
Nampula	206
Mozambique Island	210
Pemba	219

Best Places to Sleep

➡ Coral Lodge 15.41 (p215)

➡ Nkwichi Lodge (p219)

➡ Ibo Island Lodge (p225)

➡ &Beyond Benguerra (p195)

➡ Montebelo Gorongosa Lodge & Safari (p199)

Best Places to Eat

➡ Cinco Portas (p225)

➡ Rickshaws Cafe (p213)

➡ Café del Río (p202)

➡ Restaurante Maúa (p200)

➡ Green Turtle Restaurant & Beach Bar (p190)

Why Go?

Mozambique beckons with its coastline and swaying palms, its traditions, its cultures, its vibe and its opportunities for adventure. This enigmatic southeast African country is well off most travellers' maps, but it has much to offer those who venture here: long, dune-fringed beaches, turquoise waters abounding in shoals of colourful fish, well-preserved corals, remote archipelagos in the north, pounding surf in the south and graceful dhows with billowing sails. Add to this colonial-style architecture, pulsating nightlife, a fascinating cultural mix and vast tracts of bush. Discovering these attractions is not always easy, but it is unfailingly rewarding. Bring along patience, a tolerance for long bus rides, some travel savvy and a sense of adventure, and jump in for the journey of a lifetime.

When to Go
Maputo

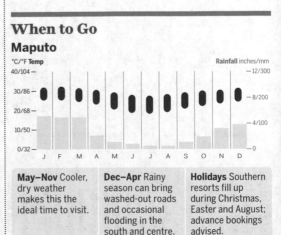

May–Nov Cooler, dry weather makes this the ideal time to visit.

Dec–Apr Rainy season can bring washed-out roads and occasional flooding in the south and centre.

Holidays Southern resorts fill up during Christmas, Easter and August; advance bookings advised.

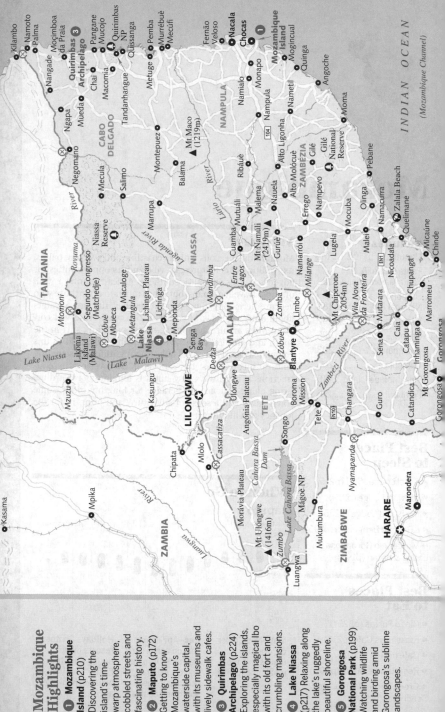

Mozambique Highlights

1 Mozambique Island (p210) Discovering the island's time-warp atmosphere, cobbled streets and fascinating history.

2 Maputo (p172) Getting to know Mozambique's waterside capital, with its museums and lively sidewalk cafes.

3 Quirimbas Archipelago (p224) Exploring the islands, especially magical Ibo with its old fort and crumbling mansions.

4 Lake Niassa (p217) Relaxing along the lake's ruggedly beautiful shoreline.

5 Gorongosa National Park (p199) Watching wildlife and birding amid Gorongosa's sublime landscapes.

6 Chimanimani Mountains (p201)
Hiking and learning about local culture.

7 Inhambane (p186) Wandering the town's quiet streets before relaxing on nearby beaches.

8 Bazaruto Archipelago (p194)
Snorkelling around the islands and enjoying Bazaruto's lodges.

9 Ponta d'Ouro (p182) Diving, dolphin spotting and enjoying the long, windswept beach.

Gweru
Shurugwi
Masvingo
Great Limpopo TP
Gonarezhou NP
Chimanimani NP
Chimanimani
Mt Binga (2436m)
Inchope
Special Reserve
Savane
Dondo
Beira
SOFALA
Sofala
Sofala Bay
Bízi River
E6
E7
E8

Louis Trichardt
Pafuri
Gir'yonco
Kruger NP
Limpopo River
Sevé River
MANICA
Espungabera
Zinave NP
Banhine NP
Massingir
GAZA
Inhassoro
Manyikeni
Vilankulo
8 Bazaruto Archipelago
Mapinhane

Nelspruit
N4
Ermelo
SOUTH AFRICA
Ressano Garcia
Moamba
Magude
Goba
Narraacha
Komatipoort
Chókwè
Massingir
Chidenguele
Xai-Xai
Zongoene
Bilene
Macia
Manjacaze
Morrumbene
Maxixe
Barra
Tofo
7 Inhambane
Lindela
Zavora
Quissico
Inharrime

Tropic of Capricorn

Pomene
Zalala Beach
Massinga
Linga Linga

MAPUTO
MAPUTO
Marracuene
Inhaca Island
Maputo Special Reserve
Ponta Malongane
9 Ponta d'Ouro
Salamanga
Zitundo
Kosi Bay
Kosi Bay
SWAZILAND
MBABANE

LEGEND
NP National Park
TP Transfrontier Park

N
0   200 km
0   100 miles

MAPUTO

With its Mediterranean-style architecture, waterside setting and wide avenues lined with jacaranda and flame trees, Maputo is easily one of Africa's most attractive capitals. It's also the most developed place in Mozambique, with a wide selection of hotels and restaurants, well-stocked supermarkets, shady sidewalk cafes and a lively cultural scene.

The heart of the city is the bustling, low-lying *baixa* (old town), spreading out north and east from the port. A few kilometres away, the seaside Avenida Marginal is lined with new developments on its inland side, while on the sea side life moves at a more leisurely pace.

Maputo is pricier than elsewhere in the country. Yet prices are reasonable and there's enough selection to make it a good destination no matter what your budget. Getting to know the city is a highlight of visiting Mozambique and essential to understanding the country. Don't miss spending time here before heading north.

◉ Sights & Activities

National Art Museum MUSEUM
(Museu Nacional de Arte; ☑21-320264; artemus@tvcabo.co.mz; 1233 Avenida Ho Chi Minh; Mtc20, Sun free; ◷11am-6pm Tue-Fri, 2-6pm Sat & Sun) Half a block west of Avenida Karl Marx, the National Art Museum has an excellent collection of paintings and sculptures by Mozambique's finest contemporary artists, including Malangatana and Alberto Chissano.

Fort FORTRESS
(Fortaleza; Praça 25 de Junho; Mtc20; ◷9.30am-4pm) The old fort was built by the Portuguese in the mid-19th century near the site of an earlier fort. Inside is a garden and a small museum with remnants from the era of early Portuguese forays to the area. The sealed, carved wooden coffin of Ngungunhane – final ruler of the famed kingdom of Gaza – is on display in one of the side rooms.

Praça da Independência PLAZA
This wide and imposing plaza is the gateway from the upper part of town to the *baixa*. It's rimmed by several notable buildings and well worth a stroll.

Iron House HISTORIC BUILDING
(Casa de Ferro; Praça da Independência) This house was designed by Eiffel (or an associate) in the late 19th century as the governor's residence, but its metal-plated exterior proved unsuitable for tropical conditions.

Cathedral of Nossa Senhora da Conceição CATHEDRAL
(Praça da Independência) With its simple but imposing lines and soaring, white spire, this cathedral is one of Maputo's most attractive buildings. It was completed in 1944. Inside, don't miss the altar work, the stained-glass windows and the paintings.

City Hall NOTABLE BUILDING
(Conselho Municipal; Avenida Samora Machel) The hulking, neoclassical City Hall looks down over the *baixa* area from a low hill at the top of Avenida Samora Machel. The building, which was completed in 1947, is still in active use today, so it cannot usually be visited unless you have business in one of the offices inside.

Train Station HISTORIC BUILDING
(Caminho dos Ferros de Moçambique, CFM; Praça dos Trabalhadores) Maputo's landmark train station is one of the city's most imposing buildings. The dome was designed by an associate of Alexandre Gustav Eiffel (of Eiffel Tower fame), although Eiffel himself never set foot in Mozambique. Also impressive are the wrought-iron latticework, pillars and verandas gracing the dark-green exterior. Inside is the **Kulungwana Espaço Artístico** (☑21-333048; www.kulungwana.org.mz; Praça dos Trabalhadores; ◷10am-5pm Tue-Fri, to 3pm Sat & Sun), with a small exhibition of works by local and visiting artists, and sculptures and paintings for sale.

Municipal Market MARKET
(Mercado Municipal; Avenida 25 de Setembro; ◷8am-6pm Mon-Sat, 9am-2pm Sun) With its long rows of vendors, tables piled high with produce, fresh fish and colourful spices, and stalls overflowing with everything from brooms to plastic buckets, the Municipal Market is Maputo's main market and well worth a stroll. Get here early, when everything is still fresh, and before the crowds.

National Money Museum MUSEUM
(Museu da Moeda; Praça 25 de Junho; Mtc20; ◷11am-5pm Tue-Fri, 9am-3.30pm Sat, 2-5pm Sun) Housed in a restored yellow building on the corner of Rua Consiglieri Pedroso, the National Money Museum dates from 1860. Inside are exhibits of local currency, rang-

ing from early barter tokens to modern-day bills.

Natural History Museum MUSEUM
(Museu de História Natural; ☑21-490879; Praça Travessa de Zambezi; Mtc50, Sun free; ⊙9am-3.30pm Tue-Fri, 10am-5pm Sat & Sun) The Natural History Museum, near Hotel Cardoso, is worth a stop simply to see its stately Manueline architecture and its garden with a mural by Malangatana. Inside are some taxidermy specimens accompanied by interactive computer terminals, a small ethnography exhibit and a fascinating display of what is probably the region's only collection of elephant foetuses.

Clube Marítimo de Desportos SWIMMING
(☑21-491373; clubemaritimo@tdm.co.mz; Avenida Marginal; per day Mtc400; ⊙5am-8pm Mon-Fri) For lap swimming, try the 25m pool at Clube Marítimo de Desportos. At weekends, the pool is open for members only.

☞ Tours

★ Bairro Mafalala Walking Tour CULTURAL
(☑82 418 0314, 82 415 1580; www.iverca.org; ⊙3hr tour per person Mtc1000-1500) ✈ This excellent walking tour through Mafalala *bairro* focuses on exploring the area's rich historical and cultural roots. It includes a stop at a local *curandeiro* (healer) and a traditional dance performance. The per-person price varies depending on group size; tours depart off Avenida Marien N'gouabi. Highly recommended.

Maputo a Pé WALKING
(☑82 419 0574; www.facebook.com/Maputo.a.Pe/; tour per person about Mtc2000) These informative and recommended walking tours of Maputo focus on the city's rich historical, architectural and artistic legacies. They're a great way to get an overview of the city and an introduction to its major sights and rich traditions.

☆☆ Festivals & Events

There's almost always an art or music festival happening in Maputo. For upcoming events check with the Centro Cultural Franco-Moçambicano (p179).

Festival Azgo CULTURAL
(www.azgofestival.com; ⊙May) This Maputo-based extravaganza has become Mozambique's largest arts and culture festival,

featuring artists from Mozambique as well as elsewhere in the region.

Marrabenta Festival CULTURAL
(http://ccfmoz.com; ⊙Feb) To hear *marrabenta* – Mozambique's national music – at its best, don't miss the annual Marrabenta Festival. It's held mostly in Maputo but also takes place in Beira, Inhambane and several other locations. The timing is set to coincide with Marracuene's Gwaza Muthini (p21) commemorations.

🛏 Sleeping

If you want to be in the thick of things, choose somewhere in or near the *baixa* (best for budgets too). For sea breezes and tranquillity, head to the upper part of town, around Sommerschield and Polana, or to Avenida Marginal and Costa do Sol.

🛏 Baixa

Base Backpackers HOSTEL $
(☑82 452 6860, 21-302723; thebasebackpackers@gmail.com; 545 Avenida Patrice Lumumba; dm/d Mtc500/1500; @) This scruffy but friendly backpackers is small, but justifiably popular and often full, with a convenient, quiet location on the edge of the *baixa*. It has a kitchen, backyard bar, terrace and braai (barbecue) area with views to the port. Via public transport from Junta, take a 'Museu' *chapa* to the final Museu stop, from where it's a short walk.

Hotel Monte Carlo HOTEL $$
(☑82 300 2006, 21-304048; www.montecarlo.co.mz; 620 Avenida Patrice Lumumba; r Mtc4000-6800; ❄@☎☒) A convenient central location, efficient staff, tidy rooms (some of the higher-priced ones are quite spacious) and a restaurant make this business hotel overall good value.

Residencial Palmeiras BOUTIQUE HOTEL $$
(☑82 306 9200, 21-300199; www.palmeiras-guesthouse.com; 948 Avenida Patrice Lumumba; s/tw/d Mtc3950/4850/4850; ❄☎) This popular place has bright decor, comfortable, good-value rooms (all but one with private bathroom) and a tiny garden. It's near the British High Commission on a quiet but central street, and just a short walk from the *baixa*.

Hotel Cardoso HOTEL $$$
(☑21-491071; www.cardoso-hotel.com; 707 Avenida Mártires de Mueda; s/d from US$290/315;

MOZAMBIQUE MAPUTO

Central Maputo

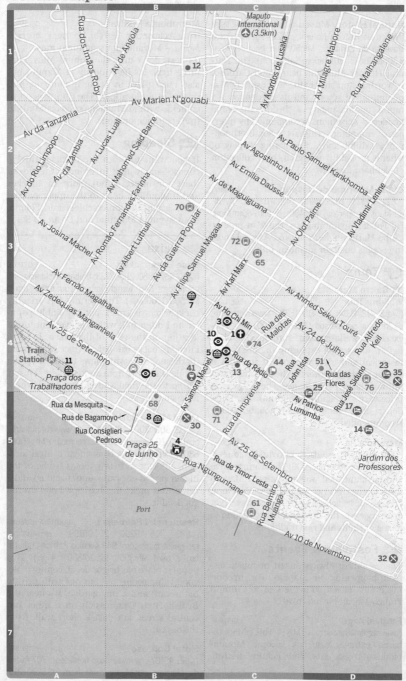

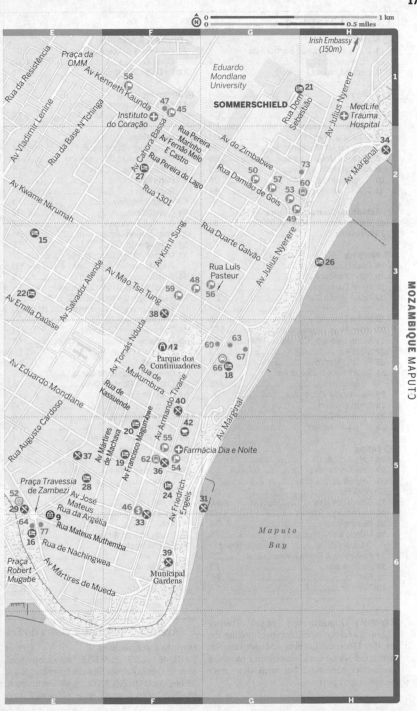

Central Maputo

◎ Sights
1 Cathedral of Nossa Senhora da
  Conceição..C4
2 Centro Cultural Franco-
  Moçambicano...C4
3 City Hall...C4
4 Fort..B5
5 Iron House...C4
  Kulungwana Espaço Artístico.......(see 11)
6 Municipal Market.......................................B4
7 National Art Museum.................................B4
8 National Money Museum..........................B5
9 Natural History Museum...........................E6
10 Praça da Independência...........................C4
11 Train Station...A4

☉ Activities, Courses & Tours
12 Bairro Mafalala Walking Tour..................B1
13 Maputo a Pé..C4

⊜ Sleeping
14 Base Backpackers.......................................D5
15 Fatima's Place...E3
16 Hotel Cardoso...E6
17 Hotel Monte Carlo......................................D5
18 Hotel Polana..G4
19 Hotel Terminus...F5
20 Hoyo-Hoyo Residencial..............................F5
21 Montebelo Indy Congress Hotel............G1
22 Mozaika...E3
23 Pensão Martins...D4
24 Residencial Duqueza de
  Connaught...F5
25 Residencial Palmeiras...............................D5
26 Southern Sun..H3
27 Sundown Guesthouse.................................F2
28 Villa das Mangas..E5

⊗ Eating
29 Café Acacia..E5
30 Café Continental..B5
31 Cais 66..G5
32 Feira Popular...D6
33 Gianni Sorvetaria.......................................F6
34 Marisqueira Sagres...................................H2
35 Mimmo's...D4
36 Mundo's...F5
  O Escorpião....................................(see 32)
37 Pastelaria & Restaurante Cristál..........E5
38 Pizza House...F3
39 Surf...F6
40 Taverna..F4

⊜ Drinking & Nightlife
41 Café-Bar Gil Vicente..................................B4
  Cais 66...(see 31)
42 La Dolce Vita Café-Bar............................F5

⊜ Shopping
43 Feira de Artesanato, Flôres e
  Gastronomia de Maputo....................F4

ⓘ Information
44 British High Commission.........................C4
45 Canadian High Commission...................F1
46 Cotacambios..F5
47 Dana Agency...F1
  Dana Tours......................................(see 47)
48 Dutch Embassy...F3
49 French Embassy..G2
50 German Embassy...G2
51 Immigration Department..........................D4
52 Livro Aberto..E5
53 Malawian High Commission...................G2
  Pizza House Internet Café..........(see 38)
54 Portuguese Embassy..................................F5
55 South African High Commission...........F5
56 Swazi High Commission............................G3
  Tanzanian High Commission.......(see 27)
57 US Embassy...G2
58 Zambian High Commission......................F1
59 Zimbabwean High Commission...........F3

ⓘ Transport
60 Chapas to Costa do Sol.........................H2
61 Chapas to Ponta d'Ouro...........................C6
62 Cheetah Express...F5
63 Europcar..G4
64 Expresso Rent-A-Car.................................E6
65 Greyhound...C3
66 Hotel Polana Taxi Rank............................G4
67 Kenya Airways...G4
68 LAM Central Reservations.......................B5
69 LAM Sales Office..G4
  Luciano Luxury Coach...................(see 71)
  Museu...(see 9)
70 Ponto Final..B3
71 Post Bus Ticketing Office.........................C5
72 Ronil..C3
73 South African Airways..............................H2
74 TAP Air Portugal..C4
  Taxi Rank..(see 36)
75 Taxi Rank..B4
76 Translux...D4
77 Tuk-Tuk Stand..E6

✳@⎙⊠) Opposite the Natural History Museum, and on the clifftop overlooking the bay, this 130-room hotel is a Maputo classic, with good service, well-appointed rooms, a business centre and a bar with views over the water and port area.

⌂Avenida Marginal & Costa do Sol

Maputo Backpackers HOSTEL $
(☎82 467 2230, 21-451213; maputobp@gmail.com; 95 Quarta Avenida (Rua das Palmeiras), Bairro Triunfo; dm/d Mtc750/3200, s/d without bathroom Mtc2100/2500) A small, quiet place well away

from the centre and near Costa do Sol, with a handful of rooms (including eight- and 10-bed dorms) with fans but no nets. *Chapas* to/from town (Mtc7) stop nearby: ask the driver to let you off at 'Escola', which is on Quinta Avenida; walk back one block to Maputo Backpackers. Taxis charge from Mtc300.

Southern Sun   HOTEL $$$
(☑ 21-495050, in South Africa 011-461 9744; www.tsogosun.com/southern-sun-maputo; Avenida Marginal; s/d from US$220/250; ✳ @ ☎ ≋) Set attractively directly on the water (although there's no beach swimming), Southern Sun has comfortable rooms, attentive service, a small gym and a waterside restaurant. The overall ambience is amenable, and the combination of a waterside location and full facilities makes it very good value in its class.

⎙ Sommerschield & Polana

Hoyo-Hoyo Residencial   HOTEL $
(☑ 82 300 9950, 21-490701; www.residencialhoyo hoyo.co.mz; 837 Avenida Francisco Magumbwe; s/d from Mtc2960/3330; ✳ ☎) This solid, no-frills hotel lacks pizzazz, but its 36 small rooms are serviceable and reasonably comfortable, and the ambience is familial.

Pensão Martins   PENSION $
(☑ 21-301429;   pensaomartins@gmail. com; 1098 Avenida 24 de Julho; s/d/tr/ste Mtc2500/3000/3500/4000;   ✳ ≋)   This peach-coloured establishment has a sleepy reception area and bland but mostly spacious rooms in a convenient central location.

Fatima's Place   HOSTEL $
(☑ 21-302994, 82 185 1577; www.mozambique backpackers.com; 1321 Avenida Mao Tse Tung; dm/s/d US$12/40/55, s/d/tr/q with shared bathroom US$35/45/60/75; ☎) In the upper part of town, the long-standing Fatima's has an outdoor kitchen-bar, a small courtyard garden, a mix of rooms and lots of travel info.

Hotel Terminus   HOTEL $$
(☑ 21-491333; www.terminus.co.mz; cnr Avenidas Francisco Magumbwe & Ahmed Sekou Touré; s/d from Mtc3850/6150; ✳ @ ☎ ≋) This three-star establishment in the upper part of town has small but well-appointed rooms with TV, plus good service and facilities, a business centre, a small garden, a tiny pool and a restaurant. It's popular with business travellers and often fully booked.

Sundown Guesthouse   HOTEL $$
(☑ 84 313 7202, 21-497543; www.hotelmaputo. com; 107 Rua 1301, Sommerschield; r US$115; ✳ @ ☎) This popular place offers good-value, well-appointed double-bedded rooms in a small apartment block on a quiet street in the Sommerschield residential area.

Mozaika   BOUTIQUE HOTEL $$
(☑ 84 367 4650, 21-303939; www.mozaika.co.mz; 769 Avenida Agostinho Neto; s/d incl breakfast from Mtc3680/4610, apt Mtc7900; ✳ @ ☎ ≋) This boutique hotel – in a convenient central location – is justifiably popular, with eight small rooms, each decorated with its own theme and set around a small garden courtyard with a tiny pool. There's also a self-catering apartment and a bar.

Residencial Duqueza de Connaught   BOUTIQUE HOTEL $$
(☑ 21-492190, 21-302155; www.duquezadecon naught.com; 290 Avenida Julius Nyerere; s/d Mtc3850/4950; ✳ ☎ ≋) This lovely, quiet, eight-room boutique hotel is in a restored home with polished wood, linen bedding and spotless rooms. Meals can be arranged with notice.

Villa das Mangas   HOTEL $$
(☑ 21-497078; www.villadasmangas.com; 401 Avenida 24 de Julho; s/d from Mtc4982/5680; ✳ ☎ ≋) The pluses at this tidy, whitewashed establishment are its aesthetics and its convenient central location. Rooms – most clustered around the pool in a tiny garden area – are small, with TV and mosquitoes.

Montebelo Indy Congress Hotel   HOTEL $$$
(☑ 21-498765, 21-480505; www.montebelohotels. com; 99 Rua Dom Sebastião, Sommerschield; s/d/ chalets from Mtc7670/8330/15,665; ✳ @ ☎ ≋) This place, in a quiet corner of Sommerschield, has well-appointed rooms and apartments ('chalets') set in expansive, manicured, enclosed gardens. There's a pool with an adjoining children's play area, plus a gym and a good restaurant.

Hotel Polana   HOTEL $$$
(☑ 21-241700, 21-491001; www.serenahotels. com; 1380 Avenida Julius Nyerere; r from US$270; ✳ @ ☎ ≋) In a prime location on the clifftop with uninterrupted views over the sea, the Polana is Maputo's classiest hotel. Rooms are in the elegant main building or in the 'Polana Mar' section closer to the water. There's a large pool set amid lush gardens, a

business centre, and a restaurant with daily breakfast and dinner buffets.

✖️ Eating

✖️ Baixa

Café Continental CAFE $
(cnr Avenidas 25 de & Samora Machel; light meals from Mtc200; ⊘ 6am-10pm) This faded but classic place in the *baixa* is a Maputo landmark, with a large selection of well-prepared pastries, plus light meals, a large seating area, a small street-side terrace and lots of ambience.

Café Acacia CAFE $$
(Jardim dos Professores, Avenida Patrice Lumumba; light meals from Mtc350; ⊘ 7am-9pm; 👶) A tranquil garden setting with a children's play area and bay views, plus tasty pastries and coffees.

✖️ Avenida Marginal & Costa do Sol

Fish Market MARKET $
(Mercado de Peixe; Avenida Marginal; dishes Mtc250-400; ⊘ 9am-9pm Mon-Fri, 8am-11pm Fri-Sun) The lively Fish Market is in a large white building en route to Costa do Sol. Peruse the many creatures that inhabit the nearby waters, or go all the way and choose what you'd like from the main hall and get it grilled at one of the small adjoining restaurants. Cooking prices average about Mtc160 per kilo.

Stalls also offer rice, chips or other accompaniments on order. Waits can be long on weekends. The best time to visit is late afternoon.

Supermarés SUPERMARKET $
(Avenida Marginal, Costa do Sol; ⊘ 9am-7pm Mon-Sat, to 1pm Sun) A large mall with a supermarket, as well as ATMs and many shops.

Restaurante Costa do Sol SEAFOOD $$
(☑ 21-451662; costadosol1908@hotmail.com; Avenida Marginal, Costa do Sol; mains from Mtc400-900; ⊘ noon-11pm Tue-Sun; 🅿️) A Maputo classic dating from 1938, this beachside place – now under new management – draws the crowds on weekend afternoons. There's seating on the large sea-facing porch or indoors, and an array of seafood dishes and grills, with prawns the speciality. It's about 5km from the centre at the northern end of Avenida Marginal.

Cais 66 SEAFOOD $$
(☑ 84 547 5906; Avenida Marginal, at Clube Naval; mains from Mtc400; ⊘ 10am-midnight) Enjoy sushi and snacks on the upstairs deck or seafood grills in the breezy waterside dining area downstairs. It's located at Clube Naval, Maputo's long-standing yacht club.

O Escorpião PORTUGUESE $$
(☑ 21-302180; meals from Mtc400; ⊘ 11.30am-3pm & 6.30-10.30pm Tue-Sun) O Escorpião, in the **Feira Popular** (cnr Avenida 25 de Setembro & Rua Belmiro Muanga; admission Mtc20; ⊘ 11.30am-midnight; 🅿️), close to the entrance, is a classic Portuguese family-style restaurant offering a wide selection of well-prepared Portuguese and Mozambican dishes.

Marisqueira Sagres SEAFOOD $$$
(☑ 21-495201; 4272 Avenida Marginal; seafood mains Mtc500-950; ⊘ 9am-midnight Tue-Sun) This waterside place is popular for dinner and Sunday lunch, with a large menu of well-prepared seafood platters, plus meat grills and continental fare, and a small pool.

✖️ Sommerschield & Polana

Pizza House CAFE $
(☑ 21-485257; 601/607 Avenida Mao Tse Tung; pizzas & light meals Mtc80-400, daily menu Mtc300; ⊘ 6.30am-10.30pm; ❄️) Popular with locals and expats, this place has sidewalk seating, plus reasonably priced Portuguese-style pastries, sandwiches, burgers, grilled chicken and a good-value daily menu.

Surf CAFE $
(Jardim dos Namorados, Avenida Friedrich Engels; snacks & light meals from Mtc150; ⊘ 7.30am-9pm; 👶) This large, amenable place has indoor and garden seating, views from the escarpment over the bay, a children's play area, reasonably priced snacks and light meals, and fast service.

Gianni Sorvetaria GELATERIA $
(www.gianni.co.mz; ground fl, Polana Shopping Centre, cnr Avenidas Julius Nyerere & 24 de Julho; gelato from Mtc90; ⊘ 7am-9pm) Delicious Italian gelato, plus sandwiches and light meals.

Mimmo's PIZZA $
(☑ 21-309491; cnr Avenidas 24 de Julho & Salvador Allende; meals Mtc250-450; ⊘ 11am-11pm) This bustling street-side pizzeria also has pastas, and seafood and meat grills. Service is usually prompt. Check your bill and your change carefully.

Pastelaria & Restaurante Cristál
CAFE $$

(☑84 302 3560, 82 281 5180; restaurantecristal@hotmail.com; 554 Avenida 24 de Julho; snacks/mains from Mtc100/400; ⊙6.30am-11pm) This long-standing place has delicious pastries and breads, light meals, indoor and street-side seating, and a popular, reasonably priced restaurant serving well-prepared local and continental dishes.

Taverna
EUROPEAN $$

(☑84 444 5550, 84 444 5551; 995 Avenida Julius Nyerere; meals Mtc450-700; ⊙noon-3pm & 6-10pm Mon-Fri, noon-3.30pm Sun) Tasty Portuguese cuisine with *fado* music in the background and a large wine selection; it's just up from Avenida Eduardo Mondlane.

Mundo's
BURGERS, PUB $$

(☑84 468 6367, 21-494080; cnr Avenidas Julius Nyerere & Eduardo Mondlane; mains Mtc200-500; ⊙8.30am-10pm; 🛜🅿) Burritos, burgers, pizzas and other hearty fare are served up in large portions on wooden tables set around a street-side veranda and cooled by a misting system in the summer months.

🍸 Drinking & Nightlife

Thursday to Saturday are the main nights; things only get going after 11pm. Cover charges range from Mtc50 to Mtc200.

Cais 66
BAR

(☑21-493204; Clube Naval, Avenida Marginal; ⊙10am-2am) The late-night waterside bar at the yacht club is especially popular with old-timers on Thursday and Friday.

La Dolce Vita Café-Bar
CAFE

(822 Avenida Julius Nyerere; ⊙10am-late Tue-Sun; 🛜) This sleek tapas and late-night place has live music on Thursday evening. By day, try the juices and smoothies.

Café-Bar Gil Vicente
BAR

(43 Avenida Samora Machel; ⊙8pm-late) A popular place with a constantly changing array of groups. Most performances start about 10pm or later.

☆ Entertainment

Centro Cultural Franco-Moçambicano
CULTURAL CENTRE

(☑21-314590; www.ccfmoz.com; Praça da Independência) An excellent place, with art exhibitions, music and dance performances, films, theatre, a craft shop, a cafe and more.

🛍 Shopping

Feira de Artesanato, Flôres e Gastronomia de Maputo
ARTS & CRAFTS

(Parque dos Continuadores, Avenida Mártires de Machava; ⊙9am-5pm) Batiks, woodcarvings and other crafts at stalls spread throughout the Parque dos Continuadores.

ℹ Information

IMMIGRATION

Immigration Department (Serviço Nacional de Migração (Senami); 316 Avenida Ho Chi Minh; ⊙for visa matters 7.30am-2pm Mon-Fri) Just downhill from Avenida Amilcar Cabral. Allow five to seven days for processing visa extensions.

INTERNET ACCESS

Livro Aberto (Maputo Community Library; www.livroaberto.org; Avenida Patrice Lumumba; ⊙8am-4pm Mon-Fri, 9am-4pm Sat; 🛜) There's wi-fi access and places to sit, plus the chance for Portuguese lessons or volunteering at this local community library in Jardim dos Professores.

Pizza House Internet Café (Avenida Mao Tse Tung; per hr Mtc60; ⊙7.30am-10pm Mon-Fri, 9am-5pm Sat; 🛜) Upstairs at Pizza House.

MEDICAL SERVICES

Farmácia Dia e Noite (☑84 505 8238; 764 Avenida Julius Nyerere; ⊙24hr) Opposite the South African High Commission.

Instituto do Coração (☑82 305 3097, 82 327 4800, 21-416347; 1111 Avenida Kenneth Kaunda; ⊙24hr) Western standards and facilities for all ailments (not just cardiac issues); meticals, US dollars and Visa cards accepted.

MedLife Trauma Hospital (☑84 302 0999; 2986 Avenida Julius Nyerere; ⊙24hr) Western standards and facilities; meticals, US dollars and Visa cards accepted.

MONEY

There are 24-hour ATMs all over town, including at the airport. Changing cash is easy. Travellers cheques are not accepted anywhere.

Cotacambios (ground fl, Polana Shopping Centre, cnr Avenida Julius Nyerere & Mao Tse Tung; ⊙9am-9pm Mon-Sat, 10am-8pm Sun) Useful for changing cash out of hours.

SAFE TRAVEL

Although most tourists visit Maputo without mishap, be vigilant and take precautions.
➔ Avoid carrying a bag (thieves may think you have something valuable).
➔ Avoid situations in which you are isolated.
➔ At night, always take a taxi.

➡ Avoid the stretches of Avenida Marginal between Praça Robert Mugabe and the Southern Sun hotel; the access roads leading down to the Marginal from Avenida Friedrich Engels; and the area below the escarpment south of Avenida Patrice Lumumba.

➡ Areas off-limits to pedestrians (no photos) include the eastern footpath on Avenida Julius Nyerere in front of the president's residence and the Ponta Vermelha zone in Maputo's southeastern corner.

TRAVEL AGENCIES

Dana Agency (☑21-484300; eduarda@dana.co.mz; ground fl, 1170 Avenida Kenneth Kaunda) Domestic and international flight bookings.

Dana Tours (☑21-497483; www.danatours.com; 1st fl, 1170 Avenida Kenneth Kaunda) Specialises in travel to the coast, and can also sort you out for destinations throughout Mozambique, plus Swaziland and South Africa. Midrange and up.

Mozaic Travel (☑84 333 2111, 21-451379; www.mozaictravel.com; 1072 Rua Acordo de Nkomati) Excursions around the country, including to Limpopo National Park and Bazaruto Archipelago. Located in Bairro Triunfo, off Avenida Marginal.

❶ Getting There & Away

AIR

Kenya Airways, LAM, South African Airways and TAP Air Portugal have regular flights to Maputo.

Kenya Airways (☑21-495483; www.kenya-airways.com; 333/659 Avenida Barnabé Thawé) On the hill side going down to Avenida Marginal.

LAM Central Reservations (☑82 147, 84 147, 21-468800, 21-326001; www.lam.co.mz; cnr Avenidas 25 de Setembro & Karl Marx) In the *baixa*.

LAM Sales Office (☑21-496101, 21-490590; www.lam.co.mz; cnr Avs Julius Nyerere & Mao Tse Tung)

South African Airways (☑21-488970, 84-488 9700; www.flysaa.com; 520 Avenida do Zimbabwe) In Sommerschield.

TAP Air Portugal (☑21-303927, 21-303928; www.flytap.com; Hotel Pestana Rovuma, 114 Rua da Sé)

BUS

Maputo's main long-distance bus depot for up-country arrivals and departures is **'Junta'** (Terminal Rodovia'ria Interprovincial da Junta; cnr Avenida de Moçambique & Rua Gago Coutinho), about 7km (Mtc300 in a taxi) from the city centre. Time your travels to avoid arriving at night. *Chapas* to Swaziland, South Africa and Namaacha in southern Mozambique also depart from Junta. **Benfica** (Avenida de Moçambique)

is useful for *chapas* to Marracuene. Chapas to Ponta d'Ouro depart from Catembe.

Correios de Moçambique (the postal service) runs buses from Maputo to Beira, Chimoio, Tete, Quelimane and Nampula, departing from its **ticketing office** (☑82 332 5812, 82 312 3103; postbusmoz@correios.co.mz; Avenida Zedequias Manganhela) behind the main post office on Avenida Zedequias Manganhela. In late 2016 the service was suspended due to the political skirmishes in the centre of the country.

Sample prices and travel times for daily routes from Maputo include Inhambane (Mtc600, seven hours), Tofo (Mtc750, 7½ hours), Vilankulo (Mtc900, nine hours) and Beira (Mtc1700, 17 hours). There is twice-weekly service from Junta to Nampula (Mtc3100, 36 hours) and Pemba (Mtc3600), with overnight stops en route, although it's better to do these journeys in stages.

Johannesburg

Departure and ticketing points for express buses to Johannesburg:

Greyhound (☑21-302771, in South Africa 011-611 8000; www.greyhound.co.za; Avenida Karl Marx; ⊗6.30am-7pm Mon-Fri, 6.30am-noon & 6-7pm Sat, 6.30am-7am & 6-7pm Sun) Avenida Karl Marx, just south of Avenida Eduardo Mondlane.

Luciano Luxury Coach (☑84 661 5713, in South Africa 072-278 1921, 083 993 4897; Avenida Zedequías Manganhela) Behind the main post office.

Translux (☑21-303829, 21-303825, in South Africa 086 158 9282; www.translux.co.za; Simara Travel & Tours, 1249 Avenida 24 de Julho; ⊗ticket sales only 7am-5pm Mon-Fri, to 10am Sat & Sun) At Simara Travel & Tours.

Nelspruit

Cheetah Express (☑84-244 2103, in South Africa 013-755 1988; cheetahexpressmaputo@gmail.com; cnr Avenidas Eduardo Mondlane & Julius Nyerere) Daily between Maputo and Nelspruit (Mtc1300 return, no one-way option), departing Maputo at 6am from Avenida Eduardo Mondlane next to Mundo's.

Tofo

Fatima's Place (p177) has a daily shuttle between Maputo and Tofo (Mtc800). With notice, it does pick-ups from other Maputo hotels. If seats are still remaining, it will also stop at Junta to take on additional passengers.

❶ Getting Around

TO/FROM THE AIRPORT

Maputo International Airport (☑21-465827/8; www.aeroportos.co.mz) is 6km northwest of the city centre (Mtc400 to Mtc600 in a taxi).

BUS & CHAPA

Buses have name boards with their destination. City rides cost about Mtc5.

Chapas go everywhere, with the average price for town trips Mtc5 to Mtc7. Most are marked with route start and end points, but you should also listen for the destination called out by the conductor. To get to Junta, look for a *chapa* going to Zimpeto, Zona Verde or Jardim; coming from Junta into town, look for a *chapa* heading to 'Museu'.

Chapas to Costa do Sol (cnr Avenidas Kenneth Kaunda & Julius Nyerere)

Chapas to Ponta d'Ouro (Catembe Ferry Pier, Avenida 10 de Novembro)

Museu *Chapas* to the airport and Junta (Mtc7 from Museu to Junta). *Chapas* marked 'Museu-Benfica' go along Avenida Eduardo Mondlane.

Ponto Final (cnr Avenidas Eduardo Mondlane & Guerra Popular) Terminus for *chapas* running along Avenida Eduardo Mondlane.

Ronil (cnr Avenidas Eduardo Mondlane & Karl Marx) *Chapas* to Junta, Benfica and Matola.

CAR

Park in guarded lots when possible, or tip the young boys on the street to watch your vehicle. There are several options for renting vehicles.

Avis (☑21-321243; www.avis.co.za; Maputo International Airport) At the airport, with offices also in Beira, Nampula and Tete; good deals often available.

Europcar (☑84 302 8330, 21-497338; www.europcar.co.mz; 1418 Avenida Julius Nyerere) Next to Hotel Polana and at the airport. Offices also in Beira, Nampula and Tete.

Expresso Rent-A-Car (☑21-493619; timisay@tropical.co.mz; Avenida Mártires de Mueda) At Hotel Cardoso; 2WD vehicles only.

Sixt (☑82 302 3555, 21-465250; www.sixt.co.mz; Maputo International Airport) Offices also in Beira, Tete, Nampula and Pemba.

TAXI & TUK-TUK

➡ Taxi ranks include the **Hotel Polana taxi rank** (Avenida Julius Nyerere) and those in front of most other top-end hotels. Taxis also park at the **Municipal Market** (Avenida 25 de Setembro) and in front of **Mundo's restaurant** (Avenida Julius Nyerere). Town trips start at Mtc150. From central Maputo to Costa do Sol costs Mtc300 to Mtc400. From Junta to anywhere in the city centre costs Mtc350 to Mtc400.

➡ Tuk-tuks are less expensive than taxis (town trips from Mtc100), although they can be hard to find. Look for them opposite **Hotel Cardoso** (Rua Mateus Muthemba), and on Avenida Julius Nyerere, just up from the South African High Commission.

AROUND MAPUTO

Inhaca Island

Just 7000 years ago – almost yesterday in geological terms – Inhaca Island (Ilha de Inhaca) was part of the Mozambican mainland. Today this wayward chunk of Mozambican coastline lies about 40km offshore from Maputo, and is an enjoyable weekend getaway. It's also an important marine research centre, known in particular for its coral reefs. The reefs are among the most southerly in the world, and since 1976 parts of the island and surrounding waters have been designated a **marine reserve** (Reservas Florestais e Marinhas da Inhaca; ☑21-901090; www.ebmi.uem.mz; adult Mtc200). Over 300 species of bird have also been recorded on the island.

The **Fernando Nhaca Lodge** (☑82 718 8549; d Mtc2000, with shared bathroom Mtc1000) is a good budget place with simple rooms with nets in a private home in Inhaca village. You can arrange meals with the owner or cook your own food. It's about a 15-minute walk from the ferry pier, or Sr Fernando will meet you with his vehicle at the ferry with advance notice (no charge).

The long-standing **Restaurante Lucas** (☑87 611 3006; rlucas.inhaca@gmail.com; mains Mtc400-700; ☺from 7am) is a local-style restaurant and the main place to eat. It's pricey, but the seafood grills are delicious, and the ambience is laid-back. Order in advance if you're in a rush or if you fancy a particular dish. It's about a five-minute walk from the ferry dock.

❶ Getting There & Away

The government ferry *Nyaleti* departs from Maputo's Catembe pier at 7.30am on Tuesday, Thursday, Saturday and Sunday (Mtc400, three hours). Departures from Inhaca are at 3pm. Dana Tours also organises Inhaca excursions.

Marracuene & Macaneta Beach

Macaneta is the closest open-ocean beach to Maputo, with stiff sea breezes and long stretches of dune-fringed coast. It's on a narrow peninsula divided from the mainland by the Nkomati River, and is reached via Marracuene, 35km north of Maputo along the EN1. For sleeping, try **Jay's**

Beach Lodge (⌨ 84 863 0714; www.jaysbeach lodge.co.za; per vehicle for day visitors US$3, camping US$8, chalet d/q US$45/85). About 20km north, and a possible stopping point for self-drivers, is **Blue Anchor Inn** (⌨ 21-900559, 82 325 3050; www.blueanchorinn.com; adult/child Mtc1120/560).

Take any northbound *chapa* (minibus) from Benfica (Mtc50, one hour) to Marracuene, from where it's a 10-minute walk through town to the Nkomati River, crossed by a new bridge. Once over the bridge on the other side, follow the rutted road for about 5km to a junction of sorts, from where you'll find most of the Macaneta places about 5km to 8km further, and signposted. There are unofficial 'shuttle' vehicles that charge Mtc150 return between the river and the beach lodges. Otherwise, there is no public transport; hitching is slow except at weekends. For drivers, a 4WD is essential.

SOUTHERN MOZAMBIQUE

Long, dune-fringed stretches of white sand, heaping plates of prawns, diving and snorkelling, an established tourism infrastructure, and straightforward road and air access from South Africa make Mozambique's southern coast an ideal destination if you're seeking a beach holiday or an easy introduction to the country.

Ponta d'Ouro & Ponta Malongane

The colonial-era town of Ponta d'Ouro has boomed in popularity in recent years and is the first Mozambique stop on many Southern Africa overland itineraries. Its best asset is its excellent beach: long, wide and surf-pounded. Offshore waters host abundant life, including dolphins, whale sharks and – from July to October – whales. Thanks to Ponta d'Ouro's proximity to South Africa, it fills up on holiday weekends. South African rand are accepted almost everywhere.

About 5km north is the quieter and even more beautiful Ponta Malongane, with an expanse of windswept coastline fringed by high, vegetated dunes and patches of coastal forest.

🏃 Activities

Diving

The Tandje Beach Resort compound is the base for several dive operators, and more are in town. Instruction and equipment rental are available at all. Ask about low-season and midweek discounts.

Diving is possible year-round; the best months are November to February and May to September.

Blue Reef Divers   DIVING
(⌨ 082 453 8694; www.brdivers.co.za; Parque de Malongane, Ponta Malongane) This dive operator based at Parque de Malongane offers various packages, with discounts available for advance bookings.

Devocean Diving   DIVING
(⌨ 84 418 2252; www.devoceandiving.com; Ponta d'Ouro) This long-established PADI five-star resort is in the town centre next to the police station. In addition to a range of diving instruction and excursions, it also offers budget accommodation at its popular divers' camp within its large, walled compound.

Dolphin Tours

Dolphins frequent the waters off Ponta d'Ouro, and many visitors come hoping to catch a glimpse of these beautiful creatures. However, remember that they're wild, which means sightings can't be guaranteed. And as studies have shown that human interaction with dolphins can be detrimental to their health, it's best to stick to ethical guidelines such as those produced by National Oceanic and Atmospheric Administration (NOAA) program Dolphin SMART. Advice includes staying at least 45m from dolphins, and never chasing, touching or swimming in close quarters with them.

Prices are about Mtc1350 per person for a two-hour excursion, generally also involving snorkelling near Ponta Malongane and sailing down towards the lighthouse on the Mozambique–South Africa border.

Dolphins can be spotted year-round (although there are no refunds if you don't spot any). Whale sharks are best seen between July and November. Between June and August it's chilly in the boats, so bring a windbreaker. If conditions are stormy or too windy, the boats don't go out. From October/November to February the sea tends to be calmest.

MOZAMBIQUE PONTA D'OURO & PONTA MALONGANE

Dolphin Centre WILDLIFE WATCHING
(Somente Aqua Dolphin Centre; ☑ 21-901189, 84 242 9864; www.thedolphincentre.com; Ponta d'Ouro; dolphin tours adult/child Mtc1350/1200) This place, at the southernmost end of town, is worth visiting, if only to read its information about dolphins. Tours take about two hours, and are preceded by a presentation on these lovely mammals and their environment. The centre also has rooms to rent.

Dolphin Encountours WILDLIFE WATCHING
(☑ 84 330 3859; www.dolphin-encountours.co.za; Ponta d'Ouro) Dolphin Encountours is based in the main square in the town centre, just next to the BCI ATM. It offers a variety of excursions, some for dolphin spotting and some for diving.

🛏 Sleeping

🛏 Ponta d'Ouro

Tandje Beach Resort CAMPGROUND $
(Ponta do Ouro Camp; ☑ 84 597 2660, in South Africa 011-465 3427; reservations@tandjebeach resort.com; Ponta d'Ouro; camping from Mtc500, 2-/4-person bungalows from Mtc2800/5000) In addition to the facilities and budget accommodation of **Scuba Adventures** (☑ 21-900430; www.scubaadventures.co.za; Ponta d'Ouro) dive camp, located on its grounds, Tandje has a shaded, seaside camping area with shared ablutions and basic bungalows, including a few beach-facing ones. It's at the southern end of town.

Coco Rico BUNGALOW $
(☑ 84 875 8029, in South Africa 034-413 2515; www.cocorico.co.za; Ponta d'Ouro; 8-person chalets from Mtc6600; 🛜🍽) About 200m north of the town centre, past the Catholic church, Coco Rico has large, well-equipped, eight-person wooden self-catering chalets just back from the beach.

Motel do Mar Beach Resort HOTEL $$
(☑ 82 764 0380, 21-650000; www.pontadoouro.co.za; Ponta d'Ouro; 4-person chalets with/without sea view US$125/105; 🍽) In a fine seaside location (though not all rooms manage to have full sea views), this motel is a throwback to colonial days. It has a restaurant that does seafood grills, a 1960s ambience and blocks of faded but nevertheless quite pleasant two-storey self-catering chalets.

🛏 Ponta Malongane

Ponta Malongane CAMPGROUND $
(☑ 076 418 2523, in South Africa 082 453 8694; http://brdivers.co.za/malongane-accomodation/; Parque de Malongane, Ponta Malongane; camping adult/child US$10/5, dive-camp tents US$30, 4-person self-catering chalets US$120) This long-running, laid-back place is based in the sprawling, shaded Parque de Malongane. It has various accommodation options, including camping, four-person rondavels (round, traditional-style huts) and chalets, and small, rustic twin-bedded log huts.

**Tartaruga Marítima
Luxury Camp** TENTED CAMP $$
(☑ 84 373 0067, in South Africa 035-340 7013; www.tartaruga.co.za; Ponta Malongane; s/d US$66/100; 🍽) About 2km north of the main Ponta Malongane 'junction', and well signposted, this lovely and tranquil retreat has spacious, comfortable safari-style tents tucked into coastal forest behind the dunes and is just a few minutes' walk from a wonderful stretch of beach. There's no restaurant, but there is a raised lounge-bar and self-catering braai (barbecue) area with ocean views.

🍴 Eating

Café Love CAFE $$
(Ponta d'Ouro; meals Mtc300-500; ⊙ 7am-10pm) Tasty pizzas, pastas, salads and desserts and a changing daily special. Also has a small children's adventure playground. It's along the main road uphill from the market.

Ponta Beach Bar & Fishmonga SEAFOOD $$
(fishmonga@pontainfo.com; Main Sq, Ponta d'Ouro; snacks/mains from Mtc100/250; ⊙ 8am-7pm; 🛜) Directly overlooking the main Ponta d'Ouro beach, this place has a chilled vibe, and a large menu featuring tasty and generously portioned waffles, burgers, seafood grills and more.

Mango Tropical Cafe CAFE $$
(☑ 84 780 6593; mangoshack@hotmail.co.za; Ponta d'Ouro; mains Mtc480; ⊙ 8am-5pm Fri-Wed) This quiet rooftop cafe serves up good smoothies, fresh juices, mezze platters and light seafood meals. It's located on the main road, above the Dolphin Centre.

ⓘ Information

There's a BCI ATM in the small square at the entrance to town.

MOZAMBIQUE PONTA D'OURO & PONTA MALONGANE

ℹ Getting There & Away

PONTA D'OURO
Car

Ponta d'Ouro is 120km south of Maputo. The road is potholed but in decent shape for the first 60km. Thereafter, parts are under renovation, while other sections are soft, deep sand. Allow about three hours in a private vehicle (4WD only), although this time will be reduced once the planned paving between the Kosi Bay border post and Maputo is completed (estimated to be December 2017).

Chapa

Direct *chapas* (minibuses) depart Maputo's Catembe ferry pier by about 6am or earlier on Tuesday and Friday (Mtc200, five hours). Departures from Ponta d'Ouro are on Wednesday and Saturday from in front of the market. Otherwise take the ferry to Catembe, where there are several direct *chapas* daily. From Ponta d'Ouro back to Catembe, there is a *chapa* most weekdays departing at 4am. Arrange with the driver the evening before to pick you up at your hotel.

A bridge is being constructed across Maputo Bay – the estimated completion date is December 2017. Together with the rehabilitation of the road between Maputo and the Kosi Bay border post, it will change all of this information, so ask around before setting off.

From South Africa

The Kosi Bay border crossing is 11km south of Ponta d'Ouro. If the ongoing paving work hasn't reached this section by the time you do, you'll need a 4WD for the sandy track. Most *chapas* from Catembe pass here first, before stopping at Ponta d'Ouro (Mtc50 from the border to Ponta d'Ouro). Coming from South Africa, there's a guarded lot just over the border where you can leave your vehicle in the shade for R40 per day. All the hotels do pick-ups from the border for about US$10 to US$15 per person (minimum two people). Allow about five hours for the drive to/from Durban (South Africa).

PONTA MALONGANE

There's no public transport to Ponta Malongane, though *chapas* between Maputo and Ponta d'Ouro stop at the signposted turnoff, about 5km before Ponta Malongane. To get between Ponta d'Ouro and Ponta Malongane, you can walk along the beach at low tide (7km) or go via the sandy road.

Bilene

This small resort town sits on the large Uembje Lagoon, which is separated from the open sea by a narrow, sandy spit and dunes.

If you're based in Maputo with a car at your disposal, it makes an enjoyable getaway, but if you're touring and want some sand, head further north to the beaches around Inhambane or south to Ponta d'Ouro.

Bilene is 140km north of Maputo and 35km off the main road. A direct bus departs Maputo's Praça dos Combatentes ('Xikelene') at about 6am (Mtc200, five hours). Otherwise go to Maputo's Junta station and have any northbound transport drop you at the Macia junction, from where pickups run throughout the day to/from Bilene (Mtc30, 30 minutes).

Leaving Bilene, there are direct departures daily at 6am to Xipamanine in Maputo, and again at about 11.30am to Maputo's Xikelene. All Bilene departures are from the main junction at the market – at the base of the hill just before the beach. Some transport also departs just uphill from the market, from the BCI roundabout.

Complexo Palmeiras (📞82 304 3720, 282-59019; http://complexopalmeiras.blogspot.com; campsites Mtc180, plus per person Mtc240, 2-/4-person chalets Mtc2800/3000) has camping, basic and poorly ventilated concrete chalets, and dark two-person rondavels. What it lacks in appealing accommodation is compensated for by the beautiful, large, white-sand beach out the front. Bring your own towels. Follow the main road into town to the final T-junction, then go left for about 1km.

The tidy, long-standing **Café O Bilas** (light meals & snacks Mtc140-250; ⊙8am-7pm) next to the petrol station is good for pizzas, hamburgers and other light meals. There's also a rooftop terrace.

Limpopo National Park

Together with South Africa's Kruger National Park and Zimbabwe's Gonarezhou National Park, Limpopo National Park forms part of the Great Limpopo Transfrontier Park, with Kruger and Limpopo linked via two fully functioning border crossings. Most visitors use Limpopo as a transit corridor between Kruger and the coast. There are also several 4WD eco-trails, as well as light hiking and canoeing. All activities can be booked through www.dolimpopo.com.

Poaching is a problem in Limpopo. Wildlife on the Mozambique side can't compare with that in South Africa's Kruger, and it's

MAPUTO SPECIAL RESERVE

This pristine 1040-sq-km wilderness area, about two hours from the capital and formerly known as the Maputo Elephant Reserve, is at the centre of efforts by the Peace Parks Foundation (www.peaceparks.org) to protect the wildlife and ecosystems of the surrounding Maputaland area. Thanks to wildlife-translocation efforts by the Mozambican and South African governments and the Peace Parks Foundation, numbers of animals in the reserve have increased. The reserve's elephant population is currently estimated at about 450, although these are threatened by ongoing poaching. Other species include hippos, giraffes, zebras and impalas.

The main attraction at Maputo Special Reserve is its pristine wilderness feel – it offers a real bush adventure close to the capital. The stunning terrain is another draw, mixing woodland, grassland, dune forest and open beach. It is wild and impenetrable in parts. Due to this, and to the skittishness of some of the wildlife, it's quite possible to visit without seeing many animals.

More of a certainty are the birds: over 300 types have been identified, including fish eagles and many wetland species. The coastline is also an important nesting area for loggerhead and leatherback turtles; peak breeding season is November to January.

Accommodation in the reserve is limited to a rustic, sea-facing **campsite** (camping adult/child Mtc200/100) and a luxury **beach lodge** (☑84 247 6322; www.anvilbay.com; Ponta Chemucane, Maputo Special Reserve; per person with full board US$434; ☎).

Maputo travel agencies operate day and overnight trips to the reserve. Otherwise you'll need your own (4WD) transport. The main entrance (also known as 'Futi Gate' or 'West Gate') is 65km from Catembe along the Ponta d'Ouro road. From here it's 3km to the park gate, and then 35km (about 1½ hours) further along a rough road to the coast and the campground. Further along the Ponta d'Ouro road there's a second, signposted entrance ('Gala Gate' or 'South Gate'), from where it's 22km into the reserve.

The road leading to the park entrances was under rehabilitation in late 2016, and will ultimately be paved from Maputo Special Reserve north to Maputo and south to the Kosi Bay border post. For now a 4WD is necessary both to reach the reserve, and to travel inside the reserve, where some tracks are deep sand.

quite possible to spend time in the park without seeing large animals.

🛏 Sleeping & Eating

Campismo Aguia Pesqueira CAMPGROUND $
(☑84 301 1719; www.limpopopn.gov.mz; camping Mtc210, d chalets Mtc1500) This good park-run campground is set on the edge of the escarpment overlooking Massingir Dam, about 55km from Giriyondo border crossing and about 25km from Massingir. All sites have lovely views over the dam, plus braai facilities. There's a communal kitchen and ablutions, plus several rustic two-bed self-catering chalets, also with views.

Covane Community Lodge LODGE, CAMPGROUND $$
(☑28-951055, 86 958 7864; www.covanecommunitylodge.com; camping Mtc330, hut s/d Mtc925/1850, chalet d Mtc2400) 🍽 This community-owned and commercially run place is about 13km outside Limpopo's Massingir gate on a rise overlooking the dam. It of-

fers lovely, good-value lakeside chalets, plus camping and rustic twin-bedded bush huts.

Machampane Wilderness Camp TENTED CAMP $$$
(☑in South Africa 021-701 7860; www.dolimpopo. com; s/d all-inclusive US$260/350) The upmarket Machampane has five spacious, well-appointed safari tents in a tranquil setting directly overlooking a section of the Machampane River, where you're likely to see hippos plus a variety of smaller wildlife and many birds. Morning and evening guided walks are included.

❶ Getting There & Away

The main park entrance on the Mozambique side is **Massingir Gate** (⊙6am-6pm), about 5km from Massingir town (which has an ATM). It's reached via a signposted turnoff from the EN1 at Macia junction that continues through Chokwé town (where there's also an ATM) on to Massingir. While daily *chapas* go between Maputo's Junta and Massingir (Mtc220), there is no possibility for onward transport within the park, so Limpopo remains primarily a self-drive destination.

To enter Limpopo from South Africa's Kruger park, you'll also need to pay Kruger park-entry fees, and Kruger's gate quota system applies (see www.sanparks.org for information).

The closest petrol stations on the Mozambique side are in Xai-Xai, Chókwè and Massingir. Travelling via Mapai, there is no fuel until Mapinhane.

Xai-Xai

Xai-Xai (pronounced 'shy-shy', and known during colonial times as João Belo) is a long town, stretching for several kilometres along the EN1. It's of little interest to travellers, but the nearby **Xai-Xai Beach** (Praia do Xai-Xai), about 10km from the town centre, has invigorating sea breezes, and it's an agreeable overnight stop if you're driving to or from points further north. Nearby are other lovely beaches, including stunning **Chidenguele**, about 70km north of Xai-Xai and about 5km off the EN1.

The busy 'praça' transport stand is near the old Pôr do Sol complex on the main road at the southern end of town. Buses to Maputo depart from here daily at about 6am (Mtc350, four hours). It's marginally faster to take one of the north–south through buses, although getting a seat can be a challenge. Wait by the Pôr do Sol complex or, better, walk or take a *chapa* (minibus) to the *pontinha* (bridge control post), where all traffic needs to stop. Some through buses also stop at the old Oliveiras depot along the main road at the northern end of town, diagonally opposite the Catholic church.

To Xai-Xai Beach (Mtc5), chapas depart from the praça transport stand, or you can catch them anywhere along the main road. They run at least to the roundabout, about 700m uphill from the beach, and sometimes further.

Complexo Halley   HOTEL $
(☎82 312 5900, 282-35003; complexohalley1@yahoo.com.br; Xai-Xai Beach; d Mtc2500-3000; ✷) This long-standing beachfront hotel is the first place you reach after coming down the beach-access road from town, and it's an appealing choice. It has stiff sea breezes, a seaside esplanade, a good restaurant and pleasant, homey rooms (ask

for one that' faces the sea). All rooms have hot-water bathroom and some have air-con and TV.

On Friday evening there's an all-night disco at the hotel; on Saturday it's across the road at the beachside esplanade.

Reef Resort   BUNGALOW $$
(☎82 972 9867, in South Africa 083 305 1588; www.reefresort.co.za; Xai-Xai Beach; 4-/8-person houses from Mtc6600/11,400) This midsize, low-key self-catering place has chalets of varying sizes, all with lovely decks overlooking the sea. The owners have made efforts to provide access for travellers with disabilities, and several of the chalets are wheelchair friendly. Follow the road from town down to the beach, then go north along the waterside track for about 2km.

Inhambane

With its serene waterside setting, tree-lined avenues, faded colonial-style architecture and mixture of Arabic, Indian and African influences, Inhambane is one of Mozambique's most charming towns and well worth a visit. It has a history that reaches back at least a millennium, making it one of the oldest settlements along the coast. Today Inhambane is the capital of Inhambane province, although it's completely lacking in any sort of bustle or pretence. It is also the gateway to a fine collection of beaches, including Tofo and Barra.

◉ Sights

Museum   MUSEUM
(☎293-20756; cnr Avenida da Vigilância & Rua 1 de Maio; donations welcome; ⊙9am-5pm Tue-Fri, 2-5pm Sat & Sun) **FREE** This tiny museum near the unmissable new mosque is well worth a stop. Its displays include collections of traditional musical instruments, clothing and household items from the surrounding area. Some of them have captions in English.

Cathedral of Nossa Senhora de Conceição   CATHEDRAL
The beautiful old Cathedral of Nossa Senhora de Conceição, dating from the late 18th century, is just northwest of the jetty. It is no longer used for services, and it is not possible to go inside, although the exterior is well worth a look.

Inhambane

Inhambane

◎ Sights
1 Cathedral of Nossa Senhora de
  Conceição..B2
2 Museum..B1
3 Old Mosque..B1

🛏 Sleeping
4 Casa do Capitão....................................A1
5 Hotel África Tropical............................B2
6 Hotel Inhambane..................................B2

✕ Eating
7 Buena Vista Café...................................B2
8 TakeAway Sazaria.................................B2
9 Verdinho's...B2

ℹ Transport
10 Boats & Dhows to Maxixe....................A2
11 Bus Station...C2

Old Mosque   MOSQUE

Along the northern end of the waterfront
road is Inhambane's attractive 'Old Mosque',
dating to 1840.

🛏 Sleeping & Eating

Hotel África Tropical   PENSION **$**

(Sensasol; ☑ 84 641 7312; Rua da Liberdade; r
Mtc1500; ❄) África Tropical has a row of
small, tidy rooms facing a tiny garden. Some
rooms have a double bed, others a double
plus a single; all have fan, net and hot water. Breakfast is extra, and there's a small
restaurant. The hotel's just off Avenida da
Independência.

Hotel Inhambane   HOTEL **$**

(☑ 293-30375; hotelinhambane@sirmotors.com;
Avenida da Independência; s/d/tr Mtc3414/3414/4160;
❄) This centrally located hotel has simple,
mostly clean and mostly spacious rooms
with TV and hot water. There's no food on
site, but several eateries are within easy
walking distance.

Casa do Capitão   HOTEL **$$$**

(☑ 84 026 2302, 293-21408/9; www.hotelcasado
capitao.com; Avenida Maguiguana; r from Mtc9750;
❄ 🛜 ⚑) This low-key hotel is in a fantastic
location, overlooking Inhambane Bay on
two sides. Views are wonderful and rooms
are well appointed. It's the most upmarket
choice in town – a nice treat if you're in

Inhambane on a honeymoon or if you just want pampering.

TakeAway Sazaria
CAFE $

(Avenida da Independência; mains from Mtc100; ⊙8am-5pm Mon-Fri) Tasty, inexpensive soups, *pregos* (steak rolls) and sandwiches to eat there or take away.

Buena Vista Café
AFRICAN $

(Avenida da Independência; meals Mtc200-350; ⊙8am-10pm Tue-Sun) Inexpensive, tasty daily menus and local dishes.

Verdinho's
EUROPEAN $$

(📞84 563 1260; 70 Avenida Acordos de Lusaka; mains Mtc250-450; ⊙8am-10pm Mon-Sat; 🛜) The popular Verdinho's features a large menu including tasty salads, burgers, pizzas, pasta and continental dishes, and seating indoors or at shaded tables outside on the patio, where you can watch the passing scene.

❶ Getting There & Away

AIR
LAM has five flights weekly connecting Inhambane with Maputo, Vilankulo and Johannesburg (from about US$100 one way). Inhambane's airstrip is 5km southeast of town.

BOAT
Small motorised passenger boats operate from sunrise to sundown between Inhambane and Maxixe (Mtc10, 25 minutes). The pier on the Maxixe side is just across the EN1 from the main bus stand. Sailing dhows do the trip more slowly for Mtc5, and one of Inhambane's great morning sights is sitting on the jetty and watching them load up. It's also possible to charter a motorboat (from about Mtc200, 10 minutes).

BUS & CAR
The bus station is behind the market. *Chapas* (minibuses) to Tofo run throughout the day (Mtc15 to Mtc18, one hour). There is a daily direct bus to Maputo, departing at 5.30am (Mtc600, seven hours, 450km). Fatima's Nest in Tofo has a daily shuttle to Maputo (Mtc800) that stops at Inhambane. There's also at least one bus daily in the morning from Inhambane to Vilankulo (Mtc300). For all other southbound and northbound transport, you'll need to head to Maxixe.

Coming from Maputo, a direct bus departs Junta station between 5am and 6am, or take any northbound bus to Maxixe.

There's at least one daily *chapa* to Maxixe (Mtc50) via the shortcut road; the turnoff from the EN1 is at the Agostinho Neto area, 20km south of Maxixe.

Tofo

Thanks to its sheltered azure waters, white sands, easy access and fine diving, the beach at Tofo has long been legendary on the Southern Africa holiday circuit. The magnificent beach runs in a long arc, at the centre of which is a small town with a perpetual party atmosphere. Many people come to Tofo expecting to spend a few days, and instead stay several weeks or more. For something quieter, head around the point to Barra, or further north or south.

🏃 Activities

Tofo is Mozambique's unofficial diving capital. There's a good selection of dive operators, all of which offer instruction and equipment rental.

Tofo Scuba
DIVING

(📞82 826 0140; www.tofoscuba.com) This PADI five-star Gold Palm resort offers a full range of instruction, dives and equipment, and also has nitrox and a heated training pool. It's at the northern end of the beach, with a surf shop and a good cafe adjoining.

Liquid Dive Adventures
DIVING

(📞0846 512 737, 0846 130 316; www.liquid diveadventures.com) This PADI Green Star outfit offers Open Water courses and other instruction plus a full range of diving. It's at the entrance to town: go left at the first Y-intersection, and Liquid Dive Adventures is about 150m up on the left. There's also a small vegetarian restaurant on the premises.

Diversity Scuba
DIVING

(📞82 932 9042, 293-29002; www.diversityscuba. com) In the town centre near the market, this PADI five-star Gold Palm Instructor Development Centre offers the usual array of instruction and dives, and also has Nitrox. Upstairs is a small cafe.

Peri-Peri Divers
DIVING

(📞82 550 5661; www.peri-peridivers.com) A full range of dives and PADI diving instruction, with a focus on personalised, small-group dives. It's next to Albatroz Lodge, just south of the town centre on the small bluff above the beach.

🛏 Sleeping

Wuyani Pariango
HOSTEL $

(📞84 712 8963; www.pariangobeach.com; camping Mtc300, dm Mtc500, r Mtc2500, with shared bathroom Mtc1500-1800; 🛜) This good budget place is in the centre of Tofo, just north of the market and just back from the beach. It has various simple reed-and-thatch rooms in the backyard walled garden plus space to pitch a tent.

Nordin's Lodge   BUNGALOW $
(📱84 520 4777, 293-29009; 2-/4-person chalets Mtc2000/4000) The unassuming Nordin's is at the northern edge of town in a good, shaded location directly on the beach. It has four rustic, dark and rather faded thatched chalets that come with hot water, fridge and self-catering facilities.

Albatroz Lodge   LODGE $
(📱293-29005, 82 255 8450; www.alba trozlodge.com; 2-/4-/6-person chalets Mtc1500/3000/3500; 🏊) Albatroz has large, rustic thatched self-catering cottages in a quiet setting on the bluff overlooking the beach. There's a restaurant and a dive operator next door.

Fatima's Nest   HOSTEL $
(📱82 185 1575; www.mozambiquebackpack ers.com; camping Mtc400, dm Mtc500, s/d/ tr Mtc1600/2200/3200, without bathroom Mtc1000/2000/2600) The long-standing Fatima's, ever popular and now considerably expanded, has camping, dorm beds and a mix of very basic bungalows and rooms, all on low dunes overlooking the beach just north of the town centre. There's also kitchen, bar, pool table and evening beach bonfires.

Casa Na Praia   GUESTHOUSE $$
(📱82 821 5921; www.casanapraiatofo.com; d Mtc5500-8800, tr Mtc4500-10,000) This place in the centre of Tofo beach has accommodation in three buildings: the more luxurious Casa Amarela, with lovely, attached beach-facing rooms with verandas; the cosy Bungalow Africa; and Casa Azul, a cheery white-with-blue trim, colonial-era house. There are semi-open-air bathrooms, each one different, and a very nice, beachside cafe–breakfast area.

Casa do Mar   B&B $$
(📱in South Africa 082 455 7481; www.casa-do-mar.co.za; r US$140; ❄️🛜🏊) This luxury B&B overlooking the main section of Tofo beach has bright, spotless rooms – some with sea views – in a large private home, and a chef who prepares gourmet meals. Breakfast is extra.

Hotel Tofo Mar   HOTEL $$$
(📱82 393 2545; www.hoteltofomar.com; s/d Mtc4080/6300, with sea view from Mtc5640/8700) Situated in a prime location directly on the beach in the town centre, the recently renovated Hotel Tofo Mar has clean, bright rooms and good service. The restaurant-bar area is usually a hive of activity in the evenings.

✕ Eating & Drinking

Beach Baraca   BREAKFAST $
(mains Mtc180-250; ⊙7.30am-8pm) In the central market area, Beach Baraca serves tasty smoothies, good, healthy breakfasts, wraps and sandwiches.

Branko's Bar   PIZZA $
(pizza Mtc190-350) This tiny, unassuming place in the central market area has tasty pizzas, plus seafood and beef cooked on 'hot rocks' at your table. It's usually packed.

Café Happi   CAFE $
(snacks & light meals from Mtc100; ⊙7am-5pm; 🛜) This good veg-only cafe at Liquid Dive Adventures has tasty breakfasts, salads, sandwiches, smoothies and more. It's near the entrance to town: go left at the Y-junction, and it's about 100m further on the left.

What U Want   ITALIAN $$
(mains Mtc300-500) Tasty Italian and Mozambican cuisine, good pizzas and starters like focaccia and bruschetta. It's in the centre of town, just northwest of the market area.

Mr Fresh   SUPERMARKET
(⊙8.30am-6.30pm Mon-Fri, 8am-6pm Sat, 8.30am-5pm Sun) This small place is Tofo's main supermarket. It's near the town entrance: go left at the Y-junction when coming into town, and it's just ahead on the right.

ℹ Information

Tofo On-Line (per minute Mtc3; ⊙9am-6pm; 🛜) In the town centre, just northeast of the market. It also sells tasty apple crumble as well as other snacks.

ℹ Getting There & Away

Chapas (minibuses) run throughout the day along the 22km sealed road between Tofo and Inhambane, departing Tofo from about 5am (Mtc15 to Mtc18 for a large bus, one hour). To Maputo's Junta, there's usually one direct bus daily, departing Tofo by about 5am (Mtc750, 7½

MOZAMBIQUE TOFO

hours). Fatima's Nest also has a daily shuttle to Maputo (Mtc800). Otherwise you'll need to go via Inhambane or Maxixe. If you do this and want to catch an early north/southbound bus, it's possible in theory to sleep in Tofo, but for a more sure connection, stay in Inhambane the night before.

If you leave early from Maputo, it's possible to get to Inhambane in time to continue straight on to Tofo that day, with time to spare.

Tofinho

Perched high up on an escarpment running between a dramatic rocky outcrop and a green point of land is Tofinho, Mozambique's unofficial surfing capital. Its topography and the prevailing winds ensure high-quality surfing from March to September, with the best months being June and July. It's also a chilled beach destination in its own right, and works well in combination with the lively beach town of Tofo, just to the north.

Self-drivers can reach Tofinho by following the road from Inhambane to Tofo, and then taking a sharp right uphill just before the entrance to Tofo. There is no public transport.

Turtle Cove   BUNGALOW, CAMPGROUND **$**
(☑ 82 719 4848; www.turtlecovetofo.com; camping US$10, dm US$15, chalet d US$50; ✱) This is the spot to go if you're interested in chilling out, with Moorish-style stone houses with bathrooms, a few very basic grass huts, camping and a slow restaurant.

Mozambeat Motel   BUNGALOW, CAMPGROUND **$**
(☑ 84 422 3515; www.mozambeat.com; camping US$5, dm US$15, cabin d/tr US$55/70; ☎✱) Partiers will likely enjoy this place. It offers a mix of accommodation, including camping (your tent or theirs), dorm beds, small and simple wooden cabins and larger stone-and-thatch suites, all set around a garden.

Casa John   GUESTHOUSE **$$**
(☑ in South Africa 082 451 7498; www.casajohn. co.za; 2-/3-bedroom houses US$150/225; ✱) Just back from the cliff near the monument, this place has lovely, well-appointed two- and three-bedroom self-catering houses ('Casa John' and 'Casa Amarela') in a breezy setting overlooking the sea.

Barra

Barra sits at the tip of the Barra Peninsula, where the waters of Inhambane Bay mix with those of the Indian Ocean. Many self-drivers prefer Barra's quieter scene and its range of midrange accommodation options, but Tofo is a better bet if you're backpacking or relying on public transport.

Daily *chapas* (minivans) go between Inhambane and Conguiana village along the Barra road. From here, you'll need to sort out a pick-up or walk (it's about 4km to the main hotel area).

The self-catering **Bayview Lodge** (☑ 84 743 3334; www.bayviewlodgemoz.com; 2-/4-/16-person houses from US$95/190/260; ✱) is just back from lovely Barra Beach. There's one large 16-person house (minimum booking for seven people), and several smaller one- and two-bedroom brick cabins. The beach is just a short walk away, and there's a good in-house restaurant on the sand. Turn left at the main junction coming into Barra, from where it's signposted.

Green Turtle Restaurant & Beach Bar (☑ 82 026 0580; mains Mtc450-550) is the closest to gourmet dining that you'll find in the area, with tasty French cuisine – the seafood dishes and desserts are particularly notable – and lovely views. It's on the beach about 2km to the left of Barra junction at Bayview Lodge, and well signposted.

Maxixe

Maxixe (pronounced ma-*sheesh*) is about 450km northeast of Maputo on the EN1 and is convenient as a stopping point for traffic up and down the coast. It's also the place to get off the bus and onto the boat if you're heading to Inhambane, across the bay.

Buses to Maputo (Mtc550, 6½ hours, 450km) depart from the bus stand by the Tribunal (court) from 6am. There are no buses to Beira originating in Maxixe; you'll need to try to get space on one of those coming from Maputo that stop at Maxixe's main bus stand (Mtc1200 from Maxixe to Beira). Thirty-seater buses to Vilanculo originating in Maputo depart Maxixe from about 10am from the main bus stand. Otherwise, *chapas* (minibuses) to Vilanculo (Mtc200, 3½ hours) depart throughout the day from Praça 25 de Setembro (Praça de Vilankulo), a couple of blocks north of the bus stand in front of the Conselho Municipal.

If you're driving to Inhambane, take the shortcut road signposted to the east about 20km south of Maxixe in the Agostinho Neto area.

Stop Residencial   MOTEL $
(☑82 125 2010, 293-30025; stopmaxixe96@ hotmail.com; d/tw/ste Mtc1800/1800/2000; ❉) Tidy, functional rooms with hot-water bathrooms. Most of the rooms are in a low multistorey building just off the EN1 next to Barclays Bank. For bookings, directions and check-in, go to Restaurante Stop next to the ferry.

Restaurante Stop   PORTUGUESE $
(☑293-30025; EN1; mains Mtc200-300; ⊙6am-10pm) Restaurante Stop, on the northern side of the jetty, has prompt service, clean toilets, tasty meals and a shaded dining terrace. It makes a good rest point on the journey north or south.

Massinga & Morrungulo

The bustling district capital of Massinga is a convenient stocking-up point If you're heading to the beach, with numerous shops, a petrol station and a garage. Nearby is beautiful Morrungulo beach. Its long, wide, white sands – stretching seemingly endlessly in both directions – are fringed by a low escarpment topped with dense stands of coconut palms.

Morrungulo is 13km from the main road down a good dirt track that's negotiable with a 2WD. Sporadic *chapas* (minibuses; Mtc25) run from the Massinga transport stand (on the EN1) to Morrungulo village, close to Morrungulo Beach Lodge , and within about 3km of Sylvia Shoal.

About 1.5km north of the junction where the road from the EN1 joins the sandy coastal track is the unassuming **Sylvia Shoal** (☑in South Africa 083 270 7582, in South Africa 071-604 8918; www.sylviashoal.co.za; camping/ barracas US$10/12, chalet d/q US$58/82), with shaded campsites, a handful of self-catering chalets set behind low dunes and a restaurant (during low season open with advance bookings only).

Morrungulo Beach Lodge (☑84 246 7533, 293-70101; www.morrungulo.com; camping adult/child US$10/5, 4-person garden/sea-front chalets US$95/115) has rustic, thatched beachfront and garden self-catering bunga-

lows and campsites on a large, manicured bougainvillea- and palm-studded lawn running down to the beach. The setting – with magnificent views of Morrungulo Bay from the escarpment – is outstanding, although the colonial-era ambience may be a turnoff for some. It's 13km off the EN1, and signposted about 8km north of Massinga.

Pomene

Pomene, the site of a colonial-era beach resort, is known for its fishing and birding, for its striking estuarine setting and especially for its magnificent open-ocean coastline. The area is part of the **Pomene Reserve** (adult/vehicle Mtc400/400), which protects coastal and marine life. The beach here is beautiful, especially up near the point by the lighthouse and the now-derelict Pomene Hotel.

Pomene is on the coast about halfway between Inhambane and Vilankulo, off the EN1. The turnoff is about 11km north of Massinga (which is the best place to stock up) and is signposted immediately after the Morrungulo turnoff. From the turnoff, which is also the end of the tarmac, it's about 55km (1½ to two hours) further along an unpaved road to Pomene village and the main accommodation options, both of which are signposted.

Pomene View   LODGE $
(☑84 465 4572; www.pomeneview.co.za; 5-/6-person chalets US$90/110; ❉) Pomene View, on a rise amid the mangroves and coastal vegetation on the mainland side of the estuary, is small and tranquil, with its own special appeal and wide views. Accommodation is in self-catering brick-and-thatch chalets, and there's a bar and restaurant. From the signposted turnoff north of Massinga, it's about 54km to get here (follow the Pomene View signs).

Pomene Lodge   LODGE, CAMPGROUND $$
(☑in South Africa 076-583 1662, in South Africa 011-023 9901; www.barraresorts.com; camping US$15, water chalet s/d US$100/165; ❉) Pomene Lodge, in a fine setting on a spit of land between the estuary and the sea, has no-frills self-catering reed bungalows just back from the beach, plus a row of faded but spacious and nicer 'water chalets' directly over the estuary. The lodge is a few kilometres from Pomene village. Self-drivers will need a 4WD.

Vilankulo

Vilankulo is the finishing (or starting) point of Mozambique's southern tourism circuit. It's also the gateway for visiting the nearby Bazaruto Archipelago, separated from the mainland by a narrow channel of turquoise sea. During South African holidays, Vilankulo is overrun with pickups and 4WDs, but otherwise it's a quiet, slow-paced town with some lovely nearby beaches.

🏃 Activities

Diving

Diving here is rewarding, and it's possible year-round. The best months are April to September and the worst are December and January, although conditions can vary markedly within these periods. The main sites are well offshore around the Bazaruto Archipelago (about a 45-minute boat ride away).

Odyssea Dive   DIVING
(📱82 781 7130; www.odysseadive.com) This reliable outfit is the main dive outfitter in Vilankulo, offering a range of dives and PADI instruction. It's at the southern end of town, about 500m south of the Old Market on the beach.

Dhow Safaris

Several outfits offer day or overnight dhow safaris around the Bazaruto Archipelago. Besides the recommended Sailaway, Marimba Secret Gardens also organises good day trips to Bazaruto (from US$60 per person) as well as to lovely Santa Carolina Island (from US$70 per person) – all including park fees, lunch and snorkelling equipment. There is officially no camping on the islands in the park; operators running overnight tours camp along the mainland coast.

There are also many independent dhow operators in Vilankulo. If you go with a freelancer, remember that while some are

reliable, others may quote tempting prices, and then ask you to 'renegotiate' things once you're well away from shore. Check with the **tourist information office** (Rua da OMM; ⊙8am-3.30pm Mon-Fri, 9am-1pm Sat) or with your hotel for recommendations and don't pay until you're safely back on land. For non-motorised dhows, allow plenty of extra time to account for wind and water conditions; it can take two to three hours

Vilankulo

🟢 Activities, Courses & Tours
1 Kite Surfing Centre	A1
Odyssea Dive	(see 3)
2 Sailaway	B2

🛌 Sleeping
3 Casa Babi	B4
4 Casa Jules & Zombie Cucumber Backpackers	B3
5 Hotel Dona Ana	B1

🍴 Eating
6 Café Moçambicano	A3
7 Café Zambeziana	B4
8 Kilimanjaro Café	B2
9 Taurus Supermarket	B2

🚌 Transport
| 10 Buses to Maputo | A4 |
| 11 New Market Transport Stand | B2 |

(sometimes longer) under sail from Vilankulo to Magaruque, and much longer to the other islands. For motorised dhows, plan on about five hours' return travel time between Vilankulo and Bazaruto.

Sailaway
DHOW SAFARIS
(293-82385, 82 387 6350; www.sailaway.co.za; per person snorkelling excursion/overnight safari from US$75/260) The recommended Sailaway offers day and overnight island dhow safaris. Check out its website for a sampling of the possibilities. All boats have extra motors, safety and first-aid equipment and communication gear on board. Sailaway's Vilankulo base is on the road paralleling the beach road, about 400m south of the Hotel Dona Ana.

Horse Riding
Mozambique Horse Safari
HORSE RIDING
(84 251 2910; www.mozambiquehorsesafari.com) Mozambique Horse Safari, based in Chibuene, offers rides on the beach, including a fishing-village tour, for riders of all levels. A wonderful experience.

Kite Surfing
Kite Surfing Centre
KITESURFING
(www.kitesurfingcentre.com) Lessons, rentals and – best of all – kite surfing safaris to the islands. It's north of town, next to the signposted Casbah Beach Bar.

🛏 Sleeping
Baobab Beach Backpackers
HOSTEL, CAMPGROUND $
(82 731 5420, 84 413 3057; www.baobabbeach.net; Rua do Palacio, Bairro Desse; camping US$7, dm US$10, bungalow d from US$34, with shared bathroom from US$26) With its waterside setting, chilled vibe and straightforward, good-value bungalows, Baobab Beach is a favourite with the party set. It has a popular, reasonably priced restaurant, and an area for self-catering. It's about 500m south of the Old Market. Walking here from town is fine by day; at night, it's best to take a taxi.

Casa Jules & Zombie Cucumber Backpackers
HOSTEL $
(84 421 2565, 84 686 9870; www.casajules.com; dm Mtc500, s/d from Mtc2500/3000; 🕾) This place just back from the beach road offers a quiet vibe, hammocks, bar, restaurant, tranquil gardens and helpful staff. Accommodation is in dorms or simple, tidy, thatched garden huts (as part of the original Zombie Cucumber Backpackers), or more spacious double and triple rooms up on the hillside at the newer 'Casa Jules'.

Marimba Secret Gardens
BUNGALOW $$
(82 005 3015, 84 048 9098; www.marimba.ch; dm/d/tw US$18/104/110; 🕾) This appealing place is set slightly back from the beach about 25km north of Vilankulo along a bush track. Accommodation is in beautifully designed octagonal bungalows on stilts, and there's a restaurant and evening bonfires. It's a good bet if you're looking for a quiet spot to relax away from Vilankulo's bustle and seeking a chance to get acquainted with local life.

Aguia Negra
LODGE $$
(293-82387, in South Africa 083 289 0036; www.aguianegrahotel.com; s/d/tr/q Mtc2500/4500/5400/7200; 🕾🕾) This is a lovely place, with thatched A-frame chalets set around a spacious, green, grassy compound directly overlooking the sea. Each chalet has an open loft area, and there's a sparkling blue pool and a restaurant. It's about 2km north of the Hotel Dona Ana junction.

Archipelago Resort
RESORT $$
(84 775 8433, 293-84022; www.archipelago-resort.com; 6-person garden/sea-view bungalows from US$170/190; 🕾) This wonderful resort has 18 spacious, well-appointed Indonesian-style self-catering bungalows set in expansive green grounds overlooking the sea. All have large verandas, two bedrooms and two bathrooms downstairs, and a two-bed loft.

Casa Babi
B&B $$$
(84 412 6478, 82 781 7130; www.casababi.com; s/d US$125/170; 🕾🕾) This cosy place has four beach-facing rooms, plus a five-person self-catering chalet in the small garden behind. All rooms are attractively decorated, and each has its own terrace and swing.

Hotel Dona Ana
HISTORIC HOTEL $$$
(293-83200; www.thehoteldonaana.com; Rua da Marginal; s/d from US$170/280; 🕸🕾🕾) The Dona Ana is a throwback to Vilanculo's earlier days, with pastel-pink-and-grey art deco design and a waterside location. Its 52 rooms are bright and pleasant – most are in the main hotel building, and some are in the greener, more tranquil 'Beach Wing' annex.

✕ Eating

Café Moçambicano CAFE $
(Avenida Eduardo Mondlane; pastries from Mtc25)
A good budget bet, with tasty pastries, bread, yoghurt, juice and a small, tidy indoor eating area plus a bakery next door. It's opposite Barclays Bank.

Café Zambeziana CAFE $
(light meals from Mtc250) Immediately to your right when exiting the old market, this local place has tasty but inexpensive grilled chicken and barbecue sandwiches.

Kilimanjaro Café CAFE $
(breakfast Mtc150-200, sandwiches & light meals Mtc250-300; ☺8am-5pm Mon-Sat; 🛜) Salads, sandwiches, pizza, pasta and a changing daily menu plus smoothies and gourmet coffees. It's in the Lexus shopping mall.

Taurus Supermarket SUPERMARKET
(Avenida Eduardo Mondlane; ☺7am-6pm Mon-Sat) Well stocked for self-catering. It's near the end of the tarmac road, diagonally opposite Millennium BIM.

🛍 Shopping

Machilla Magic ARTS & CRAFTS
(☑82 393 3428; www.machillamagic.com; ☺8am-4pm Mon-Fri, to 2pm Sat) This place sells an appealing selection of reasonably priced handicrafts, 95% of which are made from reclaimed or recycled materials. It's on the beach road, about 2.5km north of Hotel Dona Ana.

ℹ Information

SOS Netcare 911 (Nhamacunda Medical Centre; ☑84 378 1911; ☺24hr) This new, well-equipped medical clinic has pharmacy, dentist, laboratory and modern facilities. It can handle minor surgeries and can also assist with arrangements for medical evacuation to South Africa or elsewhere. It's in the Nhamacunda area, about 6km north of town past the beach hotels. It also has an ambulance.

ℹ Getting There & Away

AIR
Offices for all airlines are at the airport, which also has an ATM. The airport turnoff is along the road running to Pambara junction, 1.5km from the main roundabout at the entrance to town. From the turnoff, it is 2km further.

LAM has daily flights to/from Maputo (from about US$150 one way) and **SAAirlink** (☑in South Africa 011-451 7300; www.flyairlink.com)

has daily flights from Johannesburg (about US$150 one way).

BUS
Vilanculo is 20km east of the EN1, down a tarmac access road, with the turnoff at Pambara junction. *Chapas* (minibuses) run between the two throughout the day (Mtc20). Except for large buses to Maputo and *chapas* to Chibuene, all transport departs from the transport stand at the **new market** (Mercado Novo; Avenida Eduardo Mondlane).

Beira (Mtc550 to Mtc600, 10 hours) Buses depart Vilanculo between 4.30am and 6am at least every second day; book the afternoon before.

Chimoio There's no direct bus to Chimoio. You'll need to take a Beira bus as far as Inchope junction (Mtc550 to Mtc600 from Vilankulo), and then get a minibus from there.

Inhassoro (Mtc85, 1½ hours, several daily)

Maputo (Mtc950, nine to 10 hours, usually two daily, departing from 3.30am) Book your ticket with the drivers the afternoon before and verify the time. Departures are from a stop in front of the small red shop one block up from the old market, opposite the tribunal and west of the main road. Coming from Maputo, departures from Junta are at about 5am.

Maxixe (Mtc200, three to four hours) Several minibuses depart each morning to Maxixe (for Inhambane and Tofo). Allow six to seven hours for the entire journey from Vilankulo to Tofo.

Bazaruto Archipelago

The Bazaruto Archipelago has clear, turquoise waters filled with colourful fish, and offers diving, snorkelling and birding. It makes a fine upmarket holiday if you're looking for the quintessential Indian Ocean getaway.

The archipelago consists of five main islands: Bazaruto, Benguera (also spelled Benguerra, and formerly known as Santo António), Magaruque (Santa Isabel), Santa Carolina (Paradise Island or Ilha do Paraíso) and tiny Bangué.

Since 1971 much of the archipelago has been protected as **Bazaruto National Park** (Parque Nacional de Bazaruto; adult Mtc400). You'll see dozens of bird species, including fish eagles and pink flamingos. There are also red duikers, bushbucks, and especially on Benguera, Nile crocodiles. Dolphins swim through the clear waters, along with 2000 types of fish, plus loggerhead, leatherback and green turtles. Most intriguing are the elusive dugongs.

If you have limited funds, try visiting the archipelago on a dhow cruise from Vilankulo, or come in low season, when some lodges offer special deals.

🏃 Activities

Diving

Diving is generally best from about May to September, although it's possible year-round, and visibility can vary greatly even from day to day. Dives, equipment rental and dive-certification courses can be organised at any of the island lodges, or in Vilankulo.

Snorkelling at Santa Carolina island is considered among the best in the archipelago and is possible just offshore. Magaruque is also noted for its fine snorkelling in the crystal-clear shallows just off the beach on the island's southwestern corner.

🛏️ Sleeping & Eating

★ **&Beyond Benguerra**   LODGE **$$$**
(☑ in South Africa 011-809 4300; www.andbeyond.com/benguerra-island/; r per person all-inclusive from US$765; ☎ ☒) ⟋ This is perhaps the most intimate of the archipelago lodges, with lovely, well-spaced beach chalets ('cabanas') and villas ('*casinhas*'), fine beachside dining under the stars and a good selection of activities. The entire lodge is open design, with open air showers, luxury bathtubs with views, and private infinity plunge pools. It's well worth the splurge, if your budget allows.

Azura Benguerra   RESORT **$$$**
(☑ 84 731 0871, in South Africa 011-467 0907; www.azura-retreats.com; r per person all-inclusive from US$655; ☒ ☎ ☒) ⟋ This lovely place is one of the archipelago's most luxurious retreats. Accommodation is in secluded beach villas nestled amid tropical vegetation, with private plunge pools, wonderful cuisine, outdoor showers under the stars, fine views and a selection of activities.

Anantara Bazaruto Island
Resort & Spa   RESORT **$$$**
(☑ 84 304 6670, in South Africa 010-003 8979; bazaruto.anantara.com/; r with full board from US$800; ☒ ☎ ☒) This is the largest and most outfitted lodge in the archipelago. It offers a mix of private villas and beachfront chalets, and a range of activities. While it lacks the laid-back island touch of many of the other places, for some visitors this will be compen-

sated for by the high level of comfort and amenities.

ℹ️ Getting There & Away

SAAirlink flies five times weekly between Johannesburg and Vilankulo, from where you can arrange island helicopter or boat transfers with the lodges. **CR Aviation** (☑ 84 490 9734; www.craviation.co.mz; Vilankulo Airport) has flights connecting Vilankulo with Bazaruto (about US$335 return). **Archipelago Charters** (☑ 84 839 5204, in South Africa 083 378 4242; www.archipelago.co.za) has a helicopter service connecting Vilankulo with Bazaruto, Benguera and Magaruque, and also offers scenic-flight charters.

There are airports on Benguerra Island and Bazaruto Island.

All the top-end lodges arrange speedboat transfers for their guests. Most day visitors reach the islands by dhow from Vilankulo, where there are a number of dhow safari (p192) operators.

CENTRAL MOZAMBIQUE

Central Mozambique – Sofala, Manica, Tete and Zambézia provinces – doesn't draw the tourist crowds, although it's a convenient transit zone. However, ignore it and you'll miss out on some of the country's most intriguing secrets: Mozambique's most accessible national park (Gorongosa), its finest hiking area (Gurúè), its most abundant birdlife (Caia and Marromeu) and its best fishing lake (Cahora Bassa).

Beira

Faded, withered and decidedly rough around the edges, Mozambique's second-largest city seems like a place that's been left behind. Yet even seedy Beira has its highlights. There's **Macuti Beach** (Praia de Macuti; Avenida das FPLM), an unkempt but broad swath of sand commandeered by weekend footballers and haunted by shipwrecks, some glorious if grimy examples of colonial architecture and a few eating surprises if you know where to look.

The heart of the city is the area around the Praça do Município and Praça do Metical. To the north is the old commercial area of the *baixa*, while about 1km east is Praça do Maquinino, the main transport hub. From Praça do Município, tree-lined streets lead south and east through shady Ponta Gêa and on to Macuti Beach.

Beira

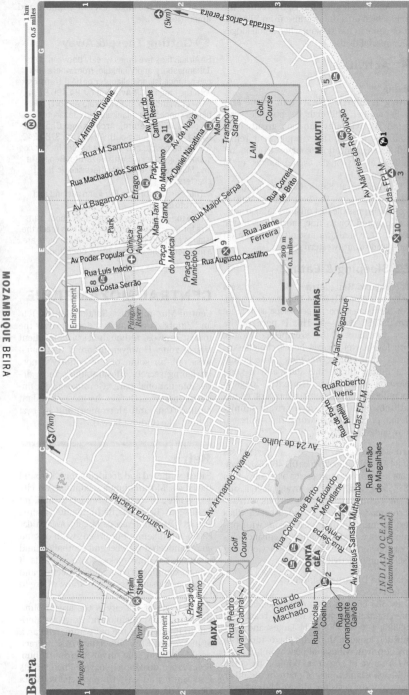

MOZAMBIQUE BEIRA

Beira

⊙ **Sights**
1 Macuti Beach..............................F4

🛌 **Sleeping**
2 Beira Guest House.......................B4
3 Biques.......................................F4
4 Hotel Sena F4
5 Jardim das Velas.........................G4
6 Pensão Moderna.........................B3

7 Royal Guest House......................B3
8 VIP Inn Beira..............................E1

✗ **Eating**
  Biques ....(see 3)
9 Café Riviera...............................E2
10 Clube Náutico E4
11 Restaurante 2 + 1 ....F2
12 Tutto D'Italy...............................B4

🛌 Sleeping

Royal Guest House GUESTHOUSE **$**
(📞23-324030; 1311 Avenida Eduardo Mondlane; r incl breakfast Mtc3000; ❄🛜🧺) This intimate residential-style B&B in the shady Ponta Gêa area has large, characterful rooms with mini fridge, TV and laundry service. No meals (apart from breakfast) are available. There's a pleasant garden and small pool out the back.

Biques CAMPGROUND **$**
(📞84 597 7130, 23-313051; Macuti Beach; camping Mtc200; 🅿) Although it acts primarily as a beach bar and restaurant, ever-popular Biques, set on a breezy rise overlooking Macuti Beach, also offers limited camping space. It's the only camping spot in town and a good place for watching the sunset.

Pensão Moderna PENSION **$**
(📞23-329901; Rua Marques Sá da Bandeira; d/tr Mtc1755/2750) The inaptly named Moderna isn't exactly a bastion of shining modernity these days, but it still serves as a good budget bet, with adequate rooms, most with fan and shared bathroom. It's two blocks south of the cathedral.

Beira Guest House GUESTHOUSE **$$**
(📞82 315 0460; woodgateangola@yahoo.co.uk; Rua Nicolau Coelho; r incl breakfast Mtc3500; ❄🛜🧺) A B&B in an old private home in the residential Ponta Gêa, just off Rua do Comandante Gaivão. The clean rooms come with mosquito nets and swatters. It's good value and friendly, and there's a small garden and pool.

VIP Inn Beira HOTEL **$$**
(📞23-340100; www.viphotels.com; 172 Rua Luís Inácio; s/d incl breakfast from Mtc4100/4400; ❄🛜) All things considered, the VIP is probably your best accommodation bet in Beira's *baixa,* a little oasis of light in an otherwise dark and dingy quarter. The clean, spacious lobby opens a theme that continues upstairs

in rooms that are comfortable, if lacking in wow factor. Bank on a substantial buffet breakfast, a relaxing bar and very helpful staff.

⭐ **Jardim das Velas** HOTEL **$$$**
(📞23-312209; www.jardimdasvelas.wixsite.com; 282 Avenida das FPLM, Makuti Beach; d/q US$105/120; 🅿❄🛜) For a fantastic alternative to the business hotels of Macuti, check into this quiet Mediterranean-style place near the lighthouse. Upstairs arc six spotless, modern doubles with views of the sea, and there are six equally well-equipped four-person family rooms with bunks downstairs. A lush walled garden hosts breakfast and an all-day cafe and snack bar that makes excellent waffles.

Hotel Sena BUSINESS HOTEL **$$$**
(📞23-311070; www.senahotel.net; 189 Avenida Mátires da Revolução; s/d Mtc6500/7800; 🅿❄🛜) A few blocks back from Macuti Beach, the Sena styles itself as a business hotel, though there's a boutique edge to its slick lobby and super-modern rooms. The hotel opened in 2010, but a new wing complete with gym

ℹ **TRAVEL & SECURITY IN CENTRAL MOZAMBIQUE**

Following attacks by Renamo opposition forces on buses in the provinces of Sofala, Manica, Tete and Zambézia in 2016, the public-transport system has been in a state of flux. Some services are suspended, several routes are subject to military convoys (p235) and a couple of bus companies are not operating at all. As a result, transport information for the region is particularly liable to change. Check ahead before travelling in central Mozambique and always review the current security situation before setting out.

MOZAMBIQUE BEIRA

and restaurant was added in 2016. Service is – as you'd expect – businesslike and it offers cheaper deals at weekends.

✗ Eating

Café Riviera
CAFE $

(Praça do Município; mains from Mtc150; ⊙ 7.30am-9pm Mon-Sat, to 7pm Sun) Head to this old-world street-side cafe for caffeine Portuguese style and a *bolo* (cake) as you watch the passing Beira scene – both the pretty and the gritty. It offers all the usual snacks, including chicken and samosas, in an African colonial atmosphere that'll make you feel as though you've slipped into a Graham Greene novel.

★ Biques
INTERNATIONAL $$

(☑ 23-313051, 84 597 7130; Macuti Beach; mains from Mtc400; ⊙ 10am-10pm) Biques (pronounced *beaks*) is a sight for sore eyes if you've just emerged bleary-eyed from the bush. Perched on a rise overlooking a windswept scoop of Macuti Beach, it's long been revered by overlanders for its pizza oven, triple-decker club sandwiches and sweet chocolate brownies. Wash your meal down with a frosty beer (served in a *real* beer glass).

Clube Náutico
SEAFOOD $$

(☑ 23-311720; www.restaurantnautico.com; Avenida das FPLM, Macuti Beach; mains Mtc400-750, plus admission per person Mtc20; ⊙ 8am-10pm; 🏊) This colonial-era swimming and social club is a popular waterside hang-out. Average food and slow service are redeemed by the relaxing beachside setting.

★ Tutto D'Italy
ITALIAN $$$

(☑ 87 427 4569; Rua Vasco Fernando Homen; pasta Mtc400-600, mains Mtc650-850; ⊙ 11am-10pm; 🚸) Top of the list of 'weird epiphanies in Beira' is this fabulous Italian restaurant hidden (there's no sign) in a children's park on the cusp of the Ponta Gêa neighbourhood. All the Italian favourites – antipasti, veal, octopus and pasta dishes – are served here, and all taste as though they've been teleported from Rome or Naples.

Restaurante 2 + 1
AFRICAN $$$

(☑ 23-323434; 100 Rua 7; mains Mtc500-1200; ⊙ 10am-11pm) Get past the cheap 2+1 Takeaway outside and dive into the air-conditioned heaven of this lovely restaurant, a plush, inviting culinary star in the otherwise dilapidated Maquinino neighbourhood. The helpful waiters dress up for work and.the food is (and tastes) equally smart.

This being Beira, the fish is king, though it's often doused with Portuguese flavours.

ℹ Information

Clínica Avicena (☑ 23-327990; Avenida Poder Popular; ⊙ 24hr) Just north of Praça do Metical.

ℹ Getting There & Away

AIR

Beira Airport is 7km northwest of town. There are flights on **LAM** (☑ 23-324142, 23-303112; www.lam.co.mz; 85 Rua Major Serpa Pinto) twice weekly to/from Johannesburg, daily to/from Maputo, and several times weekly to/from Tete, Nampula, Pemba and Lichinga. **SAAirlink** (☑ 23-301569, 23-301570; www.flyairlink.com; Beira Airport) flies several times weekly between Beira and Jo'burg.

BUS & CHAPA

Beira has several transport hubs depending on what bus company you're using, but the main one is in the Praça do Maquinino area, bounded by Avenidas Daniel Napatima and Samora Machel. There's no real order to things; ask locals where to go for buses to your destination.

Because Beira is off the main north–south EN1, an option for northbound or southbound passengers is to go to Inchope, a scruffy junction 130km west of Beira (Mtc130, three hours), where the EN6 joins the EN1, and try your luck with passing Maputo–Nampula buses there. Warning: they are often full and waits can be long.

Chimoio

To Chimoio (Mtc200, three hours), *chapas* (minivans) go throughout the day from the main transport stand in the city centre. For Gorongosa National Park you'll need to change at Inchope.

Maputo

Numerous companies serve Maputo (Mtc1700, 17 hours), including **Etrago** (☑ 82 320 3600; www.etrago.co.mz), departing Tuesday and Thursday at 3pm and Saturday at 3am from Praça do Maquinino in the city centre.

Quelimane

For Quelimane (Mtc700, 10 hours), direct Nagi Investimentos and Maning Nice buses leave daily by 5.30am. Alternatively, some through buses en route to Nampula stop at Nicoadala, from where you can get a *chapa* the remaining 40km.

Vilankulo

To Vilankulo (Mtc550 to Mtc600, 10 hours, daily), there's a direct bus departing by about 4.30am.

ⓘ Getting Around

Chapas to Makuti (Mtc10) depart from the main transport stand.

The **main taxi stand** is at the western edge of Praça do Maquinino. Taxis don't cruise for business, and companies come and go, so ask your hotel for the updated numbers.

A taxi to the airport should cost between Mtc450 and Mtc500.

Car rental can be arranged at Beira Airport with **Sixt** (☑ 23-302651; www.sixt.com; Beira Airport) and **Europcar** (☑ 23-303090; Beira Airport).

Gorongosa National Park

About 170km northwest of Beira is **Gorongosa National Park** (Parque Nacional de Gorongosa; ☑ 82 308 2252; www.gorongosa.org; adult/child per day US$20/10; ⊙ 6am-6pm Apr-Dec), which was gazetted in 1960 and soon made headlines as one of Southern Africa's premier wildlife parks. It was once renowned for its large prides of lions, as well as for its elephants, hippos, buffaloes and rhinos, but the civil war during the 1980s and early 1990s destroyed its infrastructure. Rehabilitation work began in 1995, and in 1998 Gorongosa reopened to visitors.

In recent years the park has received a major boost thanks to assistance from the US-based Carr Foundation, which has joined with the government of Mozambique to fund Gorongosa's long-term restoration and ecotourism development.

The Montebelo lodge is the only option in the park itself, though it should be joined by **Muzimu Tented Camp** (www.gorongosacollection.com) in late 2017.

Gorongosa Adventures Campsite
CAMPGROUND $

(☑ 82 957 1436; gorongosainfo@gmail.com) About 9km outside the main gate, and 500m off the park access road, is this unsignposted, unnamed campsite, which works as an option if you arrive after the park closes (6pm). It has twin-bed permanent tents under bamboo roofs; clean, hot showers; and well-equipped cooking facilities. Make contact in advance to check it's open and to confirm prices.

★ Montebelo Gorongosa Lodge & Safari
LODGE $$

(☑ 82 308 2252; www.gorongosa.org; s/d Mtc3300/4300, bungalow s/d Mtc4125/5125; P❄️🛜🏊) Located at Chitengo park headquarters, Montebelo has lovely comfortable rooms in rondavels or standard blocks. Count on hot water, soap, mosquito nets and night-time coffee. It also offers the opportunity to organise 'fly camps', depositing you deep in the bush with your own tent and guide (US$500 per person for two nights including flight, meals and guide).

ⓘ Getting There & Away

The park turnoff is at Inchope, about 130km west of Beira, from where it's 43km north along reasonable tarmac to Nota village and then 11km east along an all-weather gravel road to the park gate. From the gate it's another 18km to Montebelo Gorongosa Lodge and park HQ.

The park entrance is reachable with a 2WD. *Chapas* (minibuses) heading north from Inchope to Gorongosa town (Vila Gorongosa), about 25km beyond the park turnoff, will drop you at the turnoff, from where you can arrange a pickup with park staff (bookings essential). Pickups are also possible from Beira, Chimoio and Inchope; see www.gorongosa.net for prices.

Chimoio

Chimoio is a gateway city, not just for travellers heading into and out of Zimbabwe (located 100km west) but also for the dual lures of Chimanimani and Penha Longa, the rugged mountainous frontiers that are loaded with DIY, back-to-nature experiences.

🛏 Sleeping

Pink Papaya
HOSTEL $

(☑ 82 555 7310; http://pinkpapaya.atspace.com; cnr Ruas Pigivide & 3 de Fevereiro; dm/s/d/q Mtc500/1000/1300/2000) Pink Papaya is one of the few genuine backpacker hostels in central Mozambique and an excellent orientation point if you've just arrived from Zimbabwe. Located in a salubrious part of town near the governor's mansion, it has helpful management, clean dorm beds and doubles, and a well-equipped kitchen and braai area. Breakfast is available on request.

Residencial Dabhad
PENSION $

(☑ 251-23264; http://dabhad.com; cnr Ruas do Bárue & dos Agricultores; r incl breakfast from Mtc1750; P❄️🛜) The Dabhad offers good value: friendly, basic twin or double rooms have TV, hot water and even mini toothbrushes. No meals apart from breakfast.

★ **Residencial Chinfura**   B&B $$
(☑ 251-22640; Avenida Liberdade; r Mtc2200-3300; 🅿️❄️🛜) In terms of value for money, this is probably the best accommodation option in Chimoio. Located on the edge of the main town behind a guarded entrance, the large rooms are separated from the main house and have their own pleasant terrace and breakfast room. Beds are large, towels are thick, there are coffee-making facilities and the wi-fi is strong.

Hotel Castelo Branco   HOTEL $$$
(☑ 82 522 5960, 251-23934; Rua Sussundenga; s/d incl breakfast Mtc7200/8200; 🅿️❄️🛜🏊) Castelo Branco looks alluring from the outside, but inside it's beige, bare and, frankly, overpriced. Not that you'll be uncomfortable: the hotel's clean and spacious, and the service is good. The place just lacks sparkle. Making up for the lack of character are a small garden, a pleasant pool and a hearty breakfast buffet.

✖ Eating

Banana Split   BURGERS, SNACKS $
(cnr Ruas Pigivide & Dr Araujo de la Cerda; snacks Mtc150-400; ⊙7am-9pm) This new locally run place offers a Mozambican take on fast food, with burgers, wraps, samosas and desserts served in a small, bright four-table cafe or available for takeaway. The daily cakes are delightful.

Restaurante-Bar Jumbo   EUROPEAN $
(Rua do Bárue; mains about Mtc300; ⊙10am-9pm) The basic but reliable Jumbo has grilled chicken and continental dishes. Seating is downstairs in a dark bar or in a cosy wood-panelled room upstairs.

Ponto do Encontro   CAFE $$
(Avenida 25 de Setembro; mains Mtc350-650; ⊙7am-9pm) The aptly named 'meeting point' is one of the town's best meeting and eating places, both as a Portuguese-style cafe (the coffee and pastries are excellent) and as a restaurant. The house special is chicken in mushroom sauce, served with rice and chips. It also has a buffet-style counter at lunchtime.

★ **Restaurante Maúa**   AFRICAN $$$
(Feria Popular, EN6; mains Mtc500-800; ⊙11am-10pm Tue-Sun) Tap any local with taste buds and they'll probably tell you that this place – one of several restaurants in the **Feira Popular** (EN6) complex – serves the best food in Chimoio, possibly even central Mozambique. The menu leans heavily towards Mozambican flavours, with excellent tiger prawns, piri-piri chicken, steak and *matapa* (cassava leaves sauteed with cashews and coconut milk).

ℹ Information

Eco-Micaia Office (☑ 82 303 4285; www.micaia.org) The office of local foundation Eco-Micaia can offer info on Ndzou Camp and the Chimanimani Reserve in general. It's behind the Shoprite supermarket just off the main EN1 highway.

ℹ Getting There & Away

There are three flights weekly on **LAM** (☑ 251-24715; Hotel Inter, Av 25 de Setembro; ⊙8.30am-4.30pm Mon-Fri, 8am-noon Sat) to Maputo, with some flights also stopping in Beira. The tiny airport is 10km from town, and signposted about 5km west of Chimoio along the Manica road.

Most transport leaves from the main bus station, near the train station. Several bus companies operate out of Chimoio, including national stalwarts Maning Nice and Nagi Investimentos. The Nagi office is next to **Shoprite** (EN6; ⊙9am-8pm Mon-Sat, to 3pm Sun) supermarket.

Manica

Little Manica, 70km west of Chimoio, is situated in what was once the heart of the kingdom of Manica and an important gold-trading area. The surrounding region makes good hiking terrain.

All transport departs from the market, diagonally opposite Millennium BIM. *Chapas* (minibuses) run frequently to/from Chimoio (Mtc65, one hour) and to the Zimbabwean border (Mtc25, 30 minutes).

**Chinamapere
Rock Paintings**   ARCHAEOLOGICAL SITE
Depicting animal and human figures, these rock paintings are thousands of years old (exact dates vary) and are thought to have been left by the San people. Locals consider the site sacred. The paintings are located about 5km from town and are signposted ('*pinturas rupestres*').

Geology Museum   MUSEUM
(Museu de Geologia; ☑ 251-24433; ⊙7am-3.30pm Mon-Fri) 🆓 This collection of rocks highlighting the local geology is probably less interesting than the handsome colonial building in which it's housed – it dates from 1883.

The museum is enlivened by a few recently added explanation boards (in Portuguese).

🛏 Sleeping

Manica Lodge   LODGE $
(📞251-62452; Bairro Josina Machel; small/large rondavel d Mtc1700/2200; 🅿❄📶) At the western end of town, about 400m off the main road (the signposted turnoff's just after the immigration office), this agreeable establishment has stone rondavels scattered like hobbit houses around tranquil, manicured gardens. The larger ones are reasonably spacious and have a TV. There's also a good restaurant (mains Mtc300 to Mtc600) and friendly, helpful staff.

Pensão Flamingo   PENSION $
(📞251-62385; EN6; r Mtc1500; ❄) On the main road a few blocks west of Millennium BIM, this small-town resthouse-style place is a cut above your average African roadside digs. Simple, clean rooms come with bathroom, towels and air-con units, plus there's a reasonable restaurant (mains Mtc150 to Mtc350) downstairs.

Chimanimani Mountains

Silhouetted against the horizon on the Zimbabwean border southwest of Chimoio are the surprisingly green and wooded Chimanimani Mountains, with **Mt Binga** (2436m), Mozambique's highest peak, rising up on their eastern edge. Much of the range is encompassed by the **Chimanimani National Reserve** (Reserva Nacional de Chimanimani; adult/vehicle/camping Mtc400/400/200), which is part of the larger Chimanimani Transfrontier Conservation Area (ACTF), together with Chimanimani National Park in Zimbabwe.

It's possible to hike throughout the mountains, but facilities are scant and public transport practically nonexistent. Consequently most visitors come in their own 4WDs, armed with tents and plenty of supplies. Those who come generally make a beeline for Mt Binga, which can be climbed in two days, with one night spent on the mountain – the best starting point is Chikukwa, where guides (essential) and porters can be arranged. Travellers lucky enough to climb Binga often list it as one of their Mozambique highlights.

To reach the main reserve entrance (portão) on the Mussapa Pequeno River via public transport, take a *chapa* (minibus) from Chimoio to Sussundenga (one hour, Mtc45). Once in Sussundenga, you'll need to wait for another vehicle going towards Rotanda. After passing Munhinga, watch for the signposted Chimanimani turnoff. Ask the bus driver to drop you at 'container', from where you'll have to walk 4km along a track through lovely miombo (woodland) to the reserve entrance. From there, it's another 26km to Chikukwa Camp, starting point for the Mt Binga climb.

Drivers should head 15km south of Sussundenga to Munhinga and then branch west towards Rotunda. At 'container' turn south again into the reserve.

Ndzou Camp   CAMPGROUND, HUT $
(📞82 303 4285, 86 779 1665; camping per tent Mtc500, dm Mtc750, rondavel d Mtc2500) 🌿 Ndzou Camp, a joint venture between Eco-Micaia (p200) and the local community, is a basic back-to-nature place in the middle of Moribane Forest Reserve with admirable eco-credentials (solar-powered lighting and recycled rainwater). It offers camping, rondavels and a small family lodge; for the time being, it's the only real non-camping place to stay in the Chimanimani area.

Tete

There are two Tetes: the hot, dusty, frenetic city that greets you with all the subtlety of a microwave oven during the day, and the cool, sedate, infinitely more inviting place that seduces you at sunset.

Straddling the mighty Zambezi, Tete has been an important trade centre and river crossing for centuries. There was a Swahili settlement here long before the Portuguese arrived in the 1530s, and the Europeans quickly established it as a base for ivory and gold marketing. These days the river is forded by two bridges, the impressive Samora Machel suspension bridge, dating from 1973, and a second, more functional road bridge that opened in 2014.

For travellers, Tete is primarily a journey breaker on the way to Malawi or Zambia, or a base to visit the Cahora Bassa dam area.

🛏 Sleeping

Guesthouse Milano   GUESTHOUSE $
(📞84 843 9547; Avenida Independencia No 1727; d Mtc2500; ❄📶🏊) This attractive guesthouse is a dark horse on the accommodation scene,

tucked away on a side street in the city centre. Quiet rooms out the back are large, fresh and well tended, and a small plunge pool decorates an appealing courtyard.

Motel Tete
MOTEL **$**

(☑ 252-22345, 82 588 2040; N103; r from Mtc2500; ⓟ ❈ ⬚ ⬚) If you can handle the slightly out-of-town setting (which has its advantages in hot, hectic Tete), this Tete institution is an excellent option, set off by its location overlooking the river. The 'motel' moniker doesn't do the place justice. Rooms are large and light-filled with all amenities, and there's a handy on-site restaurant and swimming pool.

It's about 15 minutes on foot from Tete town centre along the main road to Changara.

Hotel Inter Tete
BUSINESS HOTEL **$$**

(☑ 251-24200; www.interhotels.co.mz; 18B Avenida 25 de Setembro; r from Mtc6500; ⓟ ❈ ⬚ ⬚) Tete's newest hotel is a large, business-like affair with modern, functional rooms, well-manicured grounds and a few bells and whistles – the gym and spa area are particularly pleasant. The main sticking point is the location, which is a little out in the sticks and fails to capitalise on the city's prime riverside setting.

Villa Habsburg
GUESTHOUSE **$$$**

(☑ 252-20323; www.villahabsburg.com; s/d US$120/200; ❈ ⬚) Possibly the most un-Tete-like of all Tete's accommodation is this lovely B&B in a renovated mansion on the north bank of the river about 1km downriver from the suspension bridge. It has four well-appointed rooms, arty common areas, a cricket-pitch-quality lawn and impressive river views.

✖ Eating

VIP Café
INTERNATIONAL, CAFE **$$**

(cnr Avenidas da Liberdade & Julius Nyerere; mains Mtc180-450; ⊘ 7am-9pm) This clean, air-conditioned restaurant might lack your typical Mozambican feel, but it's the best place to grab a coffee, ice cream, pastry or salad while cooling off.

★ Café del Río
INTERNATIONAL **$$$**

(☑ 84 746 3740; www.cafedelrio.co.za; mains Mtc500-1000; ⊘ 8am-10.30pm Tue-Thu, to midnight Fri & Sat, to 9.30pm Sun) When Tete's heat has melted you to a runny pulp, revive your spirits at Cafe del Rio, a beautiful thatched restaurant furnished like an upmarket African safari lodge that catches gorgeous sunsets over the Zambezi. You can easily while away a whole evening here playing chess, smoking cigars, knocking back cocktails and enjoying steak and the local speciality, *pende* fish.

ⓘ Getting There & Away

AIR

LAM (☑ 252-22056; Avenida 24 de Julho; ⊘ 8.30am-4.30pm Mon-Fri) flies several times weekly to/from Maputo, Beira, Lichinga, Nampula, Quelimane and Johannesburg. There are also international flights to Harare (Zimbabwe) and Lilongwe (Malawi). Tete's **Chingozi Airport** is 6km from town on the Moatize road (Mtc500 in a taxi); take any *chapa* (minibus) heading to Moatize.

BUS & CHAPA

Due to political unrest in late 2016, transport in and out of Tete is in a state of flux. Check on arrival for updates and proceed with caution.

Most long-distance buses to places such as Maputo, Beira and Chimoio depart from the Interprovincial Transport Terminal at Retiro, about 8km south of Tete (Mtc300 in a taxi).

Beira

To/from Beira, services are handled by Nagi Investimentos and Acai; they depart Tete at 6am most days (Mtc700, seven to eight hours), political unrest permitting.

Chimoio

To/from Chimoio (Mtc500, six to seven hours), the first departures in each direction are between 4.30am and 5am, which means that, theoretically, if you're travelling from Chimoio to Blantyre (Malawi) via Tete, you'll be able to make the journey in one long day without overnighting in Tete, after walking across the bridge to catch transport to Zóbuè.

Moatize

For Moatize (Mtc15), *chapas* depart throughout the day from the Moatize bus stand on Rua do Qua in the city centre.

Songo

To Songo (for Cahora Bassa Dam), several pickups daily depart from the old *correios* (post office) building in the lower part of town near the cathedral (Mtc190).

Ulóngwe

To Ulóngwe, there is at least one direct *chapa* departing daily from Mercado da OUA. Otherwise, take any car heading to Zóbuè, get out at the Angónia junction about 15km before Zóbuè and get onward transport from there.

Cahora Bassa Dam & Songo

Songo (150km northwest of Tete) is a purpose-built Mozambican town constructed specifically for builders raising massive Cahora Bassa dam, the fifth-largest dam in the world. The dam is set at the head of a magnificent gorge in the mountains and makes a good day or overnight trip from Tete. It's also a wonderful destination for anglers, and is renowned for its tiger fish.

Chapas (minibuses) run several times daily between Tete and Songo (Mtc150, three to four hours), departing Tete from the old *correios* (post office) building. Once in Songo, it's another 7km down to the dam – you'll have to walk or hitch. Ugezi Tiger Lodge does pick-ups from Tete (US$180 for a car fitting six people).

Hidroeléctrica de Cahora Bassa   DAM
(HCB; ☑ 252-82157, 252-82224, 252-82221) The dam, including the impressive underground turbine rooms, can be visited by advance arrangement only. Contact Hidroeléctrica de Cahora Bassa in Songo – look for the HCB office in the *substação* (substation) and ask for Relações Públicas (Public Relations), or ask at one of the hotels. There's no charge for a visit, and permits are no longer necessary to enter Songo. However, you'll need to get a letter of approval from HCB; allow at least 24 hours.

🛏 Sleeping & Eating

Centro Social do HCB   BUNGALOW $
(☑ 252-82666; r Mtc2500; ✿) This pleasant place in the town centre has clean, comfortable twin-bed rooms set in large, manicured grounds. All rooms have fridge, window screens and private bathroom with hot water. Breakfast is extra.

Songo Hotel by Montebelo   HOTEL $$
(☑ 252-8270407; www.montebelohotels.com; Barrio Norte; s/d/ste Mtc6000/7000/8000; P ✻ ☎ ✿) If you're feeling isolated in Songo, head to one of the Montebelo group's newer acquisitions (formerly Hotel Girassol), a small but select place with pleasant gardens, a pool with sunloungers and modern rooms with flat-screen TV and (usually) wi-fi. The restaurant – all white tablecloths and polished glasses – is equally recommendable.

Ugezi Tiger Lodge   LODGE $$
(☑ 84 599 8410; www.ugezitigerlodge.co.za; camping Mtc600, s/d Mtc2750/5150; P ✻ ✿) Anglers, or anyone wanting an escape to nature, will love this rustic fishing camp perched on a hill overlooking Lake Cahora Bassa. Choose between camping; basic, somewhat faded chalets on the densely vegetated hillside; and a self-catering houseboat. It's all very no-frills, but the morning scenery on the lake at the base of the property (there's no beachfront) is beautiful.

Caia

This village is the main north–south crossing point over the Zambezi River – the 2376m-long Armando Emílio Guebuza Bridge opened in 2009. It's mainly used as a pit stop on the journey between Beira and Quelimane, but there's a forest reserve with overnight accommodation 30km to the south that's one of the best places in Mozambique for birdwatching.

M'phingwe Lodge   LODGE $
(☑ 82 301 6436; www.mphingwe.com; FN1; cabins Mtc900-1250, without bathroom Mtc600-850, cottages Mtc1550-2950) ✔ Located in **Catapu Forest Reserve** (www.dalmann.com; EN1), M'phingwe has six rustic but spotless double cabins (two with shared bathroom) and two family cottages. There's an on-site restaurant with simple, meat-heavy meals plus a network of trails in the adjacent forest offering excellent birdwatching. The complex is 32km south of Caia on the main EN1 road. No camping.

Quelimane

Quelimane is a small city with a scruffy sensibility that acts as a convenient waystation for travellers jockeying between northern and southern Mozambique, or overlanders heading for the border with Malawi. The mainstay of the local economy is the coconut, best enjoyed in a sauce atop your chicken known as *frango à zambeziana*.

🛏 Sleeping & Eating

Hotel Chuabo   HOTEL $
(☑ 24-213182, 24-213181; 232 Avenida Samora Machel; s/d Mtc2975/3150; ✻ ☎) The Chuabo is a Quelimane institution, one of the few hotels anywhere in Mozambique that managed to stay running throughout the war

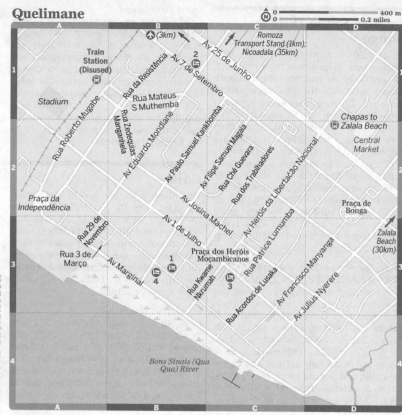

Quelimane

Sleeping
1 Hotel Chuabo...B3
2 Hotel Elite...B1
3 Hotel Flamingo C3
4 Pensão 1 de Julho B3

years. These days the whole place reeks of another era – if you like (unintentional) retro, this is your bag. Drink in the furry carpets, oversized bedrooms, wood-strip walls and – best of all – curvaceous staircase that spirals down six levels.

Pensão 1 de Julho HOTEL **$**
(☏24-213067; cnr Avenidas Samora Machel & Filipe Samuel Magaia; tw Mtc2000, without bathroom Mtc1500; ☀) The 1st of July is distinctly old-fashioned, or maybe those dusty wooden animal carvings were never in fashion – who knows? Near the old cathedral, this faded budget choice has reasonable rooms with fan, sink and bucket shower, and a central location near the river. Skip the food.

Hotel Elite HOTEL **$$**
(☏24-219900; www.elitehotels.com; cnr Avenidas 7 de Setembro & Eduardo Mondlane; r/ste Mtc3900/5600; ☀ ☎ ⊛) Look out, Quelimane: the accommodation bar has been raised! Seeming small and relatively modest, the new Hotel Elite is something of a palace behind its outer skin and not as small as the exterior suggests. The 23 deluxe rooms come with all mod-cons, and a number are equipped with king-sized beds and sofas.

Hotel Flamingo HOTEL **$$**
(☏82 552 7810, 24-215602; www.hotelflamingoquelimane.com; cnr Rua Kwame Nkrumah & Avenida 1 de Julho; incl breakfast s Mtc2000-3200, d Mtc2500-3800; ℗ ☀ ☎ ⊛) This pop-

ular hotel opposite Praça dos Heróis has two levels of motel-style rooms arranged around a central pool and restaurant. It's nothing to look at from the outside but far more salubrious within. The substantial breakfasts come with eggs, chips and baked beans.

❶ Getting There & Away

The transport stand (known locally as 'Romoza') is at the northern end of Avenida Eduardo Mondlane. *Chapas* (minibuses) run frequently to/from **Nicoadala** at the junction with the main road (Mtc50, 45 minutes). Routes south towards Beira were in flux in late 2016 due to political unrest.

BEIRA

To Beira (Mtc700, 10 hours) there's a daily bus leaving between 4am and 5am.

CHIMOIO

To Chimoio (Mtc750, eight hours), a Maning Nice bus departs daily at 3am from its office on Avenida Eduardo Mondlane, about 1km past the Romoza transport stand and on the opposite side of the road.

GURÚÈ

To Gurúè (Mtc350, six hours) there's a bus daily at 4.30am; buy your ticket the day before. Even with a ticket, it's best to show up early at the bus stand to be sure of a seat.

NAMPULA

To Nampula, Nagi Investimentos and Maning Nice buses depart daily at around 4.30am (Mtc700, 10 hours). Several vehicles also run daily to **Mocuba** (Mtc200, two to three hours), from where you can get onward transport to Nampula via Alto Molócuè, or to the Malawi border at Milange.

ZALALA

Chapas to Zalala (Mtc50, one hour) depart Quelimane from next to the central market, at the corner of Avenidas Heróis da Libertação Nacional and 25 de Junho.

Mocuba

The large, lively town of Mocuba is the junction for travel between Quelimane and Nampula or Malawi. It's home to a large market and an impressive 300m-long bridge over the wide, gently flowing Licungo River. Travellers stop here to cool off, fuel up, grab a snack and use the ATM.

Transport to Quelimane (Mtc200, two to three hours) leaves from the market throughout the day. For Nampula (Mtc500), the best bet is to try to get a seat on the Nagi bus from Quelimane, which passes Mocuba from about 7am. There are several vehicles daily in the morning between Mocuba and Milange (Mtc300, four hours), departing from Mocuba's market, though you'll maximise your chances of a lift by walking west past the airstrip to the Milange road junction. Mocuba to Gurúè costs around Mtc250.

Pensão Cruzeiro PENSION $
(☎24-810184; Avenida Eduardo Mondlane; tw/d Mtc1000/1200; P ✳) Bog-standard African resthouse with dark, grubby-looking rooms that do, at least, have running water, air-con and soap.

Padaria e Pasteleria Africa BAKERY $
(Avenida Eduardo Mondlane; snacks from Mtc50; ⊙7am-6pm) Don't judge a book by its cover: this rather bare-looking bakery knocks out super-fresh, melt-in-your-mouth pastries.

Gurúè

Floating like a hazy apparition amid sloping tea plantations, with the solid mass of Mt Namúli (2419m), Mozambique's second-highest peak, standing sentinel in the background, Gurúè is a joy to behold, especially after the long and bumpy journey to get here. Rest assured: every bump is worth it. This is one of Mozambique's primary hiking areas, where you can stroll through tea

ZALALA BEACH

The closest beach to Quelimane is Zalala Beach, about 30km northeast of town. Long and wide, with a row of fringing palms and a large village nearby, it's an ideal day excursion for getting a taste of local Zambézian life. The drive out from Quelimane is bumpy and scenic, through extensive coconut plantations formerly owned by Companhia da Zambézia. For overnighting, try the lovely **Zalala Beach Lodge** (☎24-217055, 84 390 1630; www.zbls.org; s/d US$100/150, with half board US$115/180, with full board US$125/200; P ✳ ☒) 🍴. *Chapas* (minibuses) to Zalala Beach (Mtc50, one hour) depart Quelimane from next to the central market.

MOZAMBIQUE MOCUBA

plantations at sunset, take a picnic to a local waterfall or address the steep (and sacred) slopes of Mt Namúli.

Pensão Gurúè PENSION $

(☎82 579 4512; pensao.gurue@gmail.com; Avenida Eduardo Mondlane; r Mtc2500; ✸) On the main street in the lower part of town, this pension is *the* place in Gurúè, not just for its simple, comfortable rooms but also for its affiliated restaurant downstairs and the fact that it acts as an information portal for the area. Austrian owner Peter has been here for 20 years and knows the area intimately.

❶ Getting There & Away

Transport in Gurúè departs from near the market at the lower end of town.

There's at least one daily bus to Nampula (Mtc350, six hours); otherwise you'll have to do the journey in stages, changing in Nampevo and possibly also Alto Molócuè. Buses leave at 5am or earlier – essential if you're trying to make a connection in Nampevo.

For connections to/from Quelimane, there's a daily direct *chapa* (minibus) departing at 4.30am (Mtc350, six hours); buy tickets the day before. Otherwise there are several vehicles daily to Mocuba (Mtc250, 3½ to four hours), from where you can continue to Quelimane.

There's usually one vehicle daily between Cuamba and Gurúè (Mtc250 to Mtc300, five hours).

WORTH A TRIP

HIKES FROM GURÚÈ

Mt Namúli Rising up from the hills about 15km northeast of Gurúè are the mist-shrouded slopes of **Mt Namúli** (2419m), from which flow the Licungo (Lugela) and Malema Rivers. If you find yourself in the area with time to spare, it makes a scenic but challenging climb for which you'll need a good level of fitness and lack of a fear of heights (as there are several near-vertical spots where you'll need to clamber on all fours).

Cascata Don't worry if you haven't the time or energy to summit Mt Namúli. Equally memorable is the 8km (one way) hike to the *cascata* (waterfall) in the hills north of town. Take a picnic, carry plenty of water and allow an easy day for the excursion. A guide isn't required, as you'll encounter plenty of local villagers and tea pickers along the route.

To get there, head first to the UP4 tea factory (also known as Chá Sambique), which you can see in the distance to the north; ask locals to point out the way and allow about 45 minutes on foot. From UP4 it's approximately another two hours on foot along a winding track through the tea plantations to the falls, which will be to your right. Swimming is possible in the pools above the cascades.

NORTHERN MOZAMBIQUE

With tranquil Lake Niassa to the west, wild Niassa Reserve in the centre and the palm-fringed islands of the Quirimbas Archipelago off the east coast, northern Mozambique is the country's last frontier, a potpourri of mystery, intrigue and adventure. While poor roads and remoteness can make travel here a challenge, it's never boring. However, with natural gas recently discovered in the area, the north may change quickly. Visit soon, before the magic disappears.

Nampula

Anchored by its white cathedral and embellished with a museum, Nampula is worth a brief stopover if you're in the area. Indeed, many travellers find themselves resting up here before pitching north to Pemba or east to Mozambique Island.

❍ Sights & Activities

**Cathedral of
Nossa Senhora de Fátima** CATHEDRAL
(Avenida Eduardo Mondlane) Easily Nampula's most handsome and attention-drawing sight, the creamy white city cathedral dates from the late colonial period: the Portuguese finished building it in 1956. After admiring its twin towers and elegant dome, head inside to see the colourful stained glass and – if you're lucky – catch the choir in full song.

Museu Nacional
de Etnografía   MUSEUM
(National Ethnography Museum; Avenida Eduardo Mondlane; Mtc100; ◎9am-5pm Tue-Fri, 2-5pm Sat & Sun) This museum makes a gallant effort to showcase the life and culture of Mozambique's complicated tribes and ethnic groups, although the end product is a little dusty and lacking in resources. Most interesting are the exhibits dedicated to Makonde culture around the town of Mueda in Cabo Delgado province. Even better, there's a Makonde Collective (p208) selling handmade artefacts out the back.

Complexo Bamboo
Swimming Pool   SWIMMING
(Ribáuè Rd; adult/child Mtc250/150) This leafy complex 7km northwest of Nampula's city centre has a pool and makes a good spot to cool off.

🛏 Sleeping

Ruby Nampula   HOSTEL $
(☑84 206 7756; rubybackpackers@outlook. com; Rua Daniel Napatima; dm/d Mtc750/1850; ⊜) Ruby's has clean dormitories and a couple of private doubles. There's hot water, a self-catering kitchen and a small bar selling snacks and cakes. (There's another Ruby's on Mozambique Island; p212). Once jointly owned, they've recently separated. However, there's still some reciprocity between the two.) The staff are very helpful with onward-travel information – this is a good jumping-off point for Mozambique Island.

Complexo Bamboo   CHALET $
(☑26-216595, 26-217838; bamboo@teledata.mz; Ribáuè Rd; s/d/ste Mtc2350/2750/3750; P❄☀) Well-maintained rooms (the twins are nicer than the doubles) in expansive grounds with a playground make this a good choice for families. All rooms have TV and mini fridge, and there's a popular restaurant. It's about 7km out of town; follow Avenida de Trabalho west from the train station, then right onto Ribáuè Rd; Bamboo is 1.5km down on the left.

Quality Residencial   HOTEL $
(☑26-217872, 26-216871; www.residencialqual ity.com; 953 Avenida de Trabalho; s/d/ste from Mtc2200/2500/2950; P❄⊜) Over a decade old and showing it, the Quality is about 1km from the city centre along the Quelimane road, meaning it's handy for most bus departures (the station's a 10-minute walk with bags). Rooms are a little dark and worn but have various amenities, including kettle and hot water. Service is friendly.

★Hotel Milénio   HOTEL $$
(☑26-218877; 842 Avenida 25 de Setembro; d/ste Mtc3900/4500; ❄@⊜☀) What might look like a standard business hotel has raised the game in Nampula with some useful bonuses, most notably a gym (with proper working machines), a sizeable outdoor pool, well-equipped, surgically clean rooms and, arguably, the best restaurant in town. For what you get, the price is a veritable bargain.

Residencial Primavera   HOTEL $$
(☑26-214600; www.residprimavera.blogspot.ca; Rua 1024; r incl breakfast Mtc3500; ❄⊜☀) Hidden behind the museum, this thoroughly decent new option offers a lot more than its ordinary exterior suggests. Rooms are furnished to a high standard and well stocked with complimentary water, bathroom ablutions, coffee-making equipment and fluffy towels. There's a small, modern breakfast room and a patio hosting a pool and a huddle of gym equipment. Service is professionally friendly.

Nampula Hotel by Montebelo   HOTEL $$
(☑26-216000; www.montebelohotels.com; 326 Avenida Eduardo Mondlane; s/d Mtc3785/4435; P❄⊜) The former Girassol hotel, now rebranded, isn't really one of the Montebelo chain's most inspiring options and is overrated with four stars. The ugly high-rise building (in which the hotel occupies the 4th floor) doesn't help. Rooms are business bland, with TV, mini fridge and beige decor. The restaurant is three floors down on the 1st floor.

🍴 Eating

★Hotel Milénio Restaurant   INDIAN $$
(842 Avenida 25 de Setembro; mains Mtc450-700; ◎12.30-3pm & 6.30-10pm) Equipped with a chef from Mumbai, this sleek restaurant at Hotel Milénio knocks out the best Indian food in northern Mozambique, with excellent meat and vegetarian dishes. Recommended is the lamb biriyani, the *bhuna* and the chicken tikka. All come with lashings of rice and/or naan. Equally spicy are some finely seasoned Mozambican standards. No alcohol served.

MOZAMBIQUE NAMPULA

Nampula

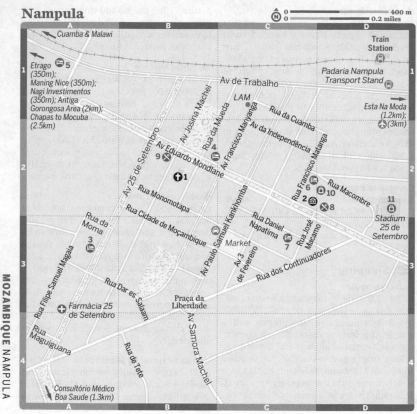

Nampula (map)

- 0 / 400 m
- 0 / 0.2 miles

Cuamba & Malawi

Train Station

Etrago 5 (350m);
Maning Nice (350m);
Nagi Investimentos (350m); Antiga
Gorongosa Area (2km);
Chapas to Mocuba (2.5km)

Padaria Nampula
Transport Stand

Av de Trabalho

LAM

Esta Na Moda (1.2km); (3km)

Av Josina Machel

Rua da Mueda

Av Francisco Manyanga

Rua da Cuamba

Av da Independência

Av 25 de Setembro

Av Eduardo Mondlane 9 4

1

Rua Monomotapa

Rua Cidade de Moçambique

Rua da Moma

3

Rua Filipe Samuel Magaia

Rua Paulo Samuel Kankhomba

Market

Rua Daniel Napatima

Rua José Macamo

Av 3 de Fevereiro

Rua dos Continuadores

Rua Francisco Matanga 6 10

2 8

Rua Macombre

11

Stadium 25 de Setembro

7

Rua Dar es Salaam

Praça da Liberdade

Farmácia 25 de Setembro

Rua Maguiguana

Rua de Tete

Av Samora Machel

Consultório Médico Boa Saude (1.3km)

VIP Cafe
INTERNATIONAL **$$**

(cnr Avenidas Eduardo Mondlane & Josina Machel; snacks from Mtc100, mains Mtc400-600; ⊙7am-10pm) This clean, new, impossibly inviting nook in a glassy shopping centre draws you in with its shiny espresso machine and display case replete with fresh pastries. Cakes aside, there's a full laminated menu of sandwiches, burgers and fuller dishes, some with Lebanese inflections.

Sporting Clube de Nampula
EUROPEAN **$$**

(Avenida Eduardo Mondlane; mains Mtc300-600; ⊙8am-10pm; ⏏) You're practically guaranteed to meet a fellow traveller or expat at this shady post-colonial watering hole next to the ethnography museum. Some just come for beers and conversation at the outdoor bar. Others gravitate to the indoor dining area for *bife a portuguesa* (steak and eggs), grilled fish, *feijoada* (beans and sausages) and a couple of Chinese-influenced plates.

🛍 Shopping

Makonde Collective
ARTS & CRAFTS

(Avenida Eduardo Mondlane; ⊙9am-5pm Tue-Fri, 2-5pm Sat & Sun) *The* place to buy Makonde crafts – primarily the legendary woodcarvings – plus you can see the craftspeople at work. It's located in an open compound behind the ethnology museum.

Sunday Morning Craft Market ARTS & CRAFTS

(stadium; ⊙dawn-noon Sun) Held in the town's large stadium, this market is a good place for crafts. Go early, before things get hot and crowded.

ℹ Information

Consultório Médico Boa Saude (☑84 460 5170, 84 601 5600; Rua dos Viveiros, Bairro Muahivire) One of the better bets if you're ill. Just off Avenida das FPLM.

Nampula

◎ Sights
1 Cathedral of Nossa Senhora de Fátima	B2
2 Museu Nacional de Etnografia	C2

⊕ Sleeping
3 Hotel Milénio	A3
4 Nampula Hotel by Montebelo	B2
5 Quality Residencial	A1
6 Residencial Primavera	C2
7 Ruby Nampula	C3

⊗ Eating
Hotel Milénio Restaurant	(see 3)
8 Sporting Clube de Nampula	D2
9 VIP Cafe	B2

⊕ Shopping
10 Makonde Collective	D2
11 Sunday Morning Craft Market	D2

Farmácia 25 de Setembro (Avenida 25 de Setembro; ☺8am-6pm Mon-Sat, 9am-1pm Sun) Just down from Hotel Milénio.

❶ Getting There & Away

AIR

Nampula Airport is very handily positioned just 4km northeast of the city centre (Mtc200 in a taxi).

There are flights on **LAM** (☑26-213322, 26-212801; Avenida Francisco Manyanga; ☺8am-4pm Mon-Fri, 9.30am-11.30am Sat) to Maputo daily, and to Beira, Lichinga, Quelimane, Tete and Pemba several times weekly. There are also flights to Johannesburg (South Africa), Nairobi (Kenya) and Lilongwe (Malawi).

BUS & CHAPA

Most long-distance buses depart from next to the Petromoc petrol station in the Antiga Gorongosa area (from the train station, follow Avenida de Trabalho west for around 2km). Companies with ticket offices here include **Maning Nice** (☑82 706 2820; Avenida de Trabalho), **Nagi Investimentos** (☑84 955 1669, 84 265 7082; Avenida de Trabalho) and Etrago. Note that Nagi Investimentos services to Pemba and other destinations in Cabo Delgado province leave from another location near the airport roundabout in the east of town. Esta Na Moda ticketing and departures are at a roundabout 1.5km east of the train station. Most services leave at the crack of dawn.

Beira

Nagi Investimentos and Maning Nice both service Beira (Mtc1500 to Mtc1700, 16 hours) daily, departing at 3am.

Cuamba

Nagi Investimentos serves Cuamba (Mtc400, seven hours) daily, leaving at 5am.

Lichinga

Nagi Investimentos serves Lichinga (Mtc1000, 15 hours), leaving Thursday and Saturday at 4am.

Moçimboa da Praia & Mueda

Maning Nice services Moçimboa da Praia (Mtc600, 13 hours, daily), Mueda (Mtc700, daily) and Montepuez (Mtc500, nine hours, daily).

Mocuba

Maning Nice buses run to Mocuba (Mtc500) or you can opt for a cheaper but slower and less comfortable *chapa*.

Mozambique Island

To Mozambique Island (Mtc200, three to four hours) *chapas* depart between 5am and 11am from the transport stand along Avenida do Trabalho just outside the train station. Look for one that's going direct; many go only to Monapo, where you'll need to stand on the roadside and wait for another vehicle. The best connections are found on one of the *tanzaniano chapas*, which depart Nampula between about 7am and 10am, depending on how early they arrive from Mozambique Island, and which continue more or less nonstop to the island. This transport stand is also the place to find *chapas* to Mossuril, Namapa and other points north and east.

Pemba

To Pemba (Mtc500, six to seven hours) your best bet is Nagi Investimentos (daily from between 3am and 5am) or Esta Na Moda, with a daily service leaving at noon.

Quelimane

To Quelimane (Mtc600 to Mtc700, 10 hours), Maning Nice and Nagi Investimentos buses leave daily at 3am and 4am respectively.

TRAIN

A passenger train connects Nampula and Cuamba. It traditionally ran daily (except Monday) in either direction. However, since 2015, due to line rehabilitation and preference being given to freight (mainly coal), it has been reduced to a twice-weekly passenger service leaving Nampula on Saturday and Tuesday at 5am. Hopefully it will revert to its full schedule soon. The spectacular but typically African journey takes 10 to 12 hours. There are theoretically three classes of carriage (executive/1st/2nd Mtc600/400/170), although they might not function on all trips. It's well worth investing in executive if you can.

Tickets can be purchased between 2pm and 5pm on the day before travel (but not earlier).

Boarding starts at 4am. Arrive early and bring plenty of snacks. As with all Mozambican transport, be sure to check ahead for current schedules at the **train station** (☑ 21-344800; www. cdn.co.mz; 1000 Avenida de Trabalho).

ℹ Getting Around

The main **taxi rank** (Avenida Paulo Samuel Kankhomba) is near the market. For car hire, **Sixt** (☑ 82 300 5170, 26-216312; www.sixt. com), **Europcar** (☑ 84 322 3473; www.europcar. com) and several others are at the airport.

Mozambique Island

Dhows shifting silently through shallow seas, bruised colonial buildings withering elegantly in the tropical heat, and the voices of a church choir competing with the muezzin's call to prayer. You'll encounter all this and more within the crowded confines of Mozambique Island, one of the historical highlights of Africa, a fragrant melange of African, Portuguese, Swahili, French and Goan flavours left to mellow in the iridescent waters of the Indian Ocean for centuries.

Half-forgotten until it was recognised as a World Heritage Site in 1991 and still bizarrely overlooked by the average African safari enthusiast, the diminutive island (500m wide by 3km long) protects a romantic cluster of semi-ruined, semi-restored edifices known as Stone Town in its northern half. Further south lies Makuti Town, a crowded collection of dishevelled reed houses that's home to 15,000 Mozambicans.

◎ Sights

While wandering through Stone Town, watch for the restored, ochre-toned **BIM building** (Avenida Amilcar Cabral) and the ornate **colonial administration offices** overlooking the gardens east of the **hospital**, itself an impressive neoclassical building. A few blocks north of the market is the recently restored **Hindu temple** and, on the island's western edge, a fairly modern **mosque** (Rua da Solidariedade) painted an unmissable shade of green.

Mozambique Island

0 _____ 200 m
0 _____ 0.1 miles

Mozambique Island

⊙ Sights
1 BIM......................................A4
2 Chapel of Nossa Senhora de
   Baluarte...B1
3 Fort of São Sebastião.......................B1
4 Hindu Temple..............................A4
5 Hospital.....................................A5
6 Igreja da Misericórdia....................A3
7 Mosque......................................A5
   Museu de Arte Sacra....................(see 6)
8 Palace & Chapel of São Paulo..............A3

⊙ Activities, Courses & Tours
9 Genito Magic Tour...........................A4
10 Ilha Blue.......................................A3

⊙ Sleeping
11 Amakuthini...................................A5
12 Casa das Ondas............................B2
13 Casa de Yasmin............................B2

14 Jardim dos Aloés.........................A3
15 Mooxeleliya................................B3
16 O Escondidinho...........................A4
17 Patio dos Quintalinhos.................A5
18 Pousada Ilha de Moçambique.......B2
19 Ruby Backpacker.........................A3
20 Villa Sands.................................A4

⊗ Eating
21 Bar Flôr de Rosa.........................A4
22 Café-Bar Áncora d'Ouro...............A3
23 Karibu..A3
24 Relíquias....................................A3
25 Rickshaws Cafe...........................A5
26 Sara's Place................................A5

⊙ Transport
27 Dhows to Cabaceira Grande..............A4
28 Transport Stand..........................B7

Palace & Chapel of São Paulo   MUSEUM
(Palácio de São Paulo; [☏26-610081; adult/child Mtc100/50; ⊙8am-4.30pm) This imposing terracotta edifice – the former governor's residence and now a museum – dates from 1610. The interior hosts the recently refurbished **Museu de Artes Decorativas**, which gives a remarkable glimpse of what upper-class life must have been like during the island's 18th-century heyday. In addition to household items from Portugal, Arabia, India and China, there are many pieces of original furniture, including an important collection of beautifully ornamented Indo-Portuguese pieces carved by Goan craftsmen.

In the chapel, don't miss the altar and the pulpit, the latter of which was made in the 17th century by Chinese artists in Goa (India). On the ground floor is the small but fascinating **Maritime Museum**, with gold coins, ship compasses, Chinese porcelain and other items recovered from local shipwrecks.

One ticket covers both museums as well as the Museu de Arte Sacra next door. Tours are guided and available in several languages, including Portuguese and English.

Fort of São Sebastião   FORTRESS
(adult/child Mtc100/50; ⊙8am-4.30pm) The island's northern end is dominated by the massive Fort of São Sebastião – the oldest complete fort still standing in sub-Saharan Africa and, arguably, the finest military building on the continent. Construction

began in 1558 and took 62 years. The fort has withstood numerous Dutch, British and Omani bids to diminish it. While the structure remains in a pretty unkempt state, with little explanatory information, it size and aura, along with the views from its battlements, are awe-inspiring.

Just beyond the fort, at the island's tip and accessed via the fort entrance, is the tiny **Chapel of Nossa Senhora de Baluarte**, built in 1522 and the oldest European building in the southern hemisphere.

Igreja da Misericórdia   CHURCH
(Church of Mercy) With a distinctive white facade, this church is best viewed while sitting at a table in the Café-Bar Áncora d'Ouro opposite. The original church was destroyed during a Dutch raid in 1607; the current structure dates from the 17th century.

Museu de Arte Sacra   MUSEUM
(Museum of Sacred Art) Containing religious ornaments, paintings and carvings, this museum is housed in the former hospital of the Holy House of Mercy, a religious guild that assisted the poor and sick in several Portuguese colonies from the early 1500s onwards. Entry is included in your São Paulo palace (p211) ticket and you'll get the same multilingual guide.

🏃 Activities

Strong tidal flows make it dangerous to swim around Mozambique Island's northern and southern ends. The cleanest of the island's patches of sand is Nancaramo Beach, next to the fort. For beautiful, clean sand, head across Mossuril Bay to Chocas and Cabaceira Pequena (p214), or to the beach on Goa Island.

Ilha Blue
TOURS

(☑84 396 9438; www.ilhablue.com; Avenida dos Heróis) 🏄 Run by an expat British-Australian couple, this professional, community-involved tour company offers cycling, snorkelling, kayaking and dhow safaris, all led by local guides. It shares digs with a clothes shop called Orera Orera in Stone Town.

Genito Magic Tour
TOURS

(☑84 546 4817; www.genitomagictour.com; Avenida dos Heróis) 🏄 Under the tutelage of Unesco-recognised guide Genito, aka 'Harry Potter', you can arrange tours of Makuti Town (US$8) and/or Stone Town and the fort (US$8). Also available are fishing with local fisherfolk and dhow excursions to local islands (with snorkelling). Genito's based at Magic Internet Cafe in Stone Town.

🛏 Sleeping

Ruby Backpacker
HOSTEL $

(☑84 866 0200; ruby.backpackers@gmail.com; Travessa da Sé; dm/d Mtc650/1550; @🤶) Located in a renovated 400-year-old house, the island's only backpackers is a good one. It has dorm beds upstairs and downstairs, twin and double rooms, a self-catering kitchen, hot showers, a bar, a fantastic rooftop terrace, bicycle rental, laundry service, a travellers' noticeboard and lots of information about onward travel.

Mooxeleliya
GUESTHOUSE $

(☑82 454 3290, 26-610076; flora204@hot mail.com; d incl breakfast with/without air-con Mtc2500/2000) Mooxeleliya (the Makua name translates roughly as, 'Did you rest well?') has five simple but spacious, high-ceilinged rooms upstairs and two darker, three- to four-person, family-style rooms downstairs. There's a small cooking area with fridge and a communal TV/sitting area. It's just down from the Misericórdia church.

Casa das Ondas
GUESTHOUSE $

(☑82 569 2888, 82 438 6400; Rua dos Combatentes; incl breakfast r Mtc2300, with shared bathroom Mtc1700; 🧼🤶) A Dutch-Mozambican-run guesthouse with three very characterful rooms that reflect the hybrid personality of Mozambique Island. Rooms are spacious

and recently renovated; only one has a private bathroom. It's just to the left of the cinema.

Casuarina Camping
CAMPGROUND $

(☑84 616 8764; casuarina.camping@gmail.com; camping Mtc250, d from Mtc2000, with shared bathroom from Mtc1000; 🤶) On the mainland opposite Mozambique Island, a two-minute walk from the bridge (to your right, coming from the island), Casuarina has a well-maintained campground on a small, clean beach, plus simple bungalow-style rooms and ablution blocks with bucket showers. The seemingly basic restaurant is lauded by those in the know, especially for its pizza (made in a real oven).

Casa de Yasmin
GUESTHOUSE $

(☑82 676 8850, 26-610073; Rua dos Combatentes; r/ste Mtc1500/2500; 🧼) This family house at the island's northern end has a quintet of clean but view-less downstairs rooms (each with bathroom and air-con) and a larger upstairs suite with a glimpse of the sea. It's the white house to the right of the cinema. There's no sign.

Pousada Ilha de Moçambique
HOTEL $

(☑26-610101; Rua dos Combatentes; s/d incl breakfast from Mtc2600/2800; 🧼) In a good setting at the island's northern tip in the shadow of the fort and opposite a beach, this place has a governmental, utilitarian feel despite a recent renovation. The 22 boring rooms hold no surprises, except perhaps the large windows and sea views. There's a restaurant.

Amakuthini
GUESTHOUSE $

(Casa de Luís; ☑82 436 7570, 82 540 7622; dm Mtc500, d incl breakfast Mtc1200) For total cultural immersion, head to this authentic but rough-around-the edges place in Makuti Town, the scruffy neighbourhood of reed houses where the locals live. It has an eight-bed dorm and several small, dark rooms with fan in a tiny garden behind the family house. All beds have nets.

★ O Escondidinho
HOTEL $$

(☑26-610078; www.oescondidinho.net; Avenida dos Heróis; s/d Mtc3900/4400, with outside bathroom Mtc2500/3300; 🧼🧼) In a sturdy but genteel old trading house in Stone Town, you can recline like a colonial lord in atmospheric high-ceilinged rooms furnished with four-poster beds draped with mosquito nets. Seven of the 10 rooms have large bathrooms and there are more refinements downstairs, with a flower-embellished garden and small pool overlooked by one of the town's best restaurants.

Villa Sands
BOUTIQUE HOTEL **$$**

(☑82 744 7178; www.villasands.com; Rua dos Trabalhadores; d from Mtc7000; ❋ ⓢ ⌨) Imagine a cross between Swedish and Mozambican design (if you can) and you've imagined Villa Sands, which mixes sleek, minimalist Scandinavian lines with more elaborate African accents: think gilded mirrors and wood-beamed roofs. Bright boutique-style rooms overlook the water; the upstairs ones have views and their own pool, and there's also a restaurant (meals from Mtc600) and rooftop terrace.

Excursions, including diving trips, can be organised.

Patio dos Quintalinhos
GUESTHOUSE **$$**

(Casa de Gabriele; ☑26-610090, 82 419 7610; www.patiodosquintalinhos.com; Rua do Celeiro; incl breakfast d US$73, with shared bathroom US$45, ste/q from US$78/90; ℗ @ ⓢ ⌨) Opposite the green mosque, Quintalinhos has a handful of comfortable, creatively designed rooms set around a small courtyard, including one with a loft, and a suite with skylight and private rooftop balcony with views to the water. There's also a rooftop terrace, a pool and secure parking. Staff can help with bicycle rental and excursions.

★ Jardim dos Aloés
B&B **$$$**

(☑87 827 4645; www.jardim-dos-aloes.com; Rua Presidente Kaunda; r incl breakfast Mtc10,500-11,200; ❋ ⓢ) ◗ These three exquisite suites are relatively new on the island scene and have upped the ante, mixing retro decor (record players, antique phones) and interesting books with elements of the island's past and present. It's a beautiful melange of hammocks, terraces and alcoves hidden behind high walls in the heart of Stone Town.

✖ Eating

Sara's Place
AFRICAN **$**

(Avenida 25 de Junho; mains Mtc150-300; ⊙8am-10pm) Inhabiting a reed house in the square opposite the hospital, Sara's is a confirmed local favourite – small and scruffy, but salt-of-the-earth – where you can taste chicken and fish served with the unique island speciality *matapa de siri siri* (seaweed with coconut milk).

MATAPA DE SIRI SIRI

Word on the street says you haven't really been to Mozambique Island until you've tasted *matapa de siri siri*. This local take on a popular Mozambican dish takes the standard *matapa* recipe – ground cassava leaves slow-cooked with garlic, onion, coconut milk and cashews – and substitutes the cassava leaves with a local seaweed. For good measure, prawns are sometimes added to the mix. *Matapa de siri siri* has a soft, stew-like consistency not unlike sautéed spinach and works well as a starter served with bread, but it can also be used as a side dish. It's not only fragrant but also highly nutritious, and it's only available in its classic homemade form on Mozambique Island.

Café-Bar Áncora d'Ouro
CAFE **$**

(☑26-610006; Barrio do Museu; snacks from Mtc200; ⊙8am-9pm Thu-Tue) This lovely cafe evokes the faded charm of colonial Mozambique, with old black-and-white prints adorning the walls and hefty tomes on the tables. There's no better place to relax with coffee and a muffin (or waffles) as you listen to the choir across the square and watch kids chase tyres. It's opposite the Misericórdia church.

★ Rickshaws Cafe
INTERNATIONAL **$$**

(☑82 678 0098; Rua dos Trabalhadores; mains Mtc495-610; ⊙7am-11pm) The new kids on the block have nabbed a beautiful sunset location on the island's western side where you can sit alfresco and relish food from a menu that mixes Mozambican favourites with fish tacos, pizza, brownies and burgers. It's American run, and the name harks back to a method of transport once popular on the island.

★ Karibu
SEAFOOD **$$**

(☑84 380 2518; Barrio do Museu; mains Mtc400-800; ⊙11am-3pm & 6-9.15pm Tue-Sun) This excellent new restaurant in Stone Town specialises in the island's seafood bounty. Tuna, prawns, marlin and lobster are all done to perfection here, overseen by the hands-on Portuguese owner. Choose from the chalkboard menu and sit alfresco in front of artfully arranged antiques in the window.

MOZAMBIQUE MOZAMBIQUE ISLAND

Relíquias FUSION $$

(☑ 82 525 2318; Avenida da República; mains Mtc190-600; ⊗10am-10pm Tue-Sun) This popular if unexciting spot does all the local standards, including seafood, hot chicken, prawn or goat curries, and *matapa* (cooked cassava leaves with peanut sauce) and coconut rice. Seating is indoors or out the back overlooking the water. There's a *menu ecónomico* for Mtc190.

Bar Flôr de Rosa ITALIAN $$

(☑ 82 745 7380; Avenida dos Heróis; mains Mtc400-550; ⊗ 5pm-midnight Mon-Sat) This small, chic, Italian-run place has espresso, a selection of pasta, pizza, soups and sandwiches, and a rooftop terrace for sundowners, plus live music on Friday and Saturday in season. It's near the hospital.

❶ Information

BIM (Avenida Amilcar Cabral; ⊗ 8am-3pm Mon-Fri) Has an ATM (Visa and MasterCard), and changes cash (US dollars, euros and rand).

❶ Getting There & Away

BOAT

There's at least one dhow daily connecting Mozambique Island with Cabaceira Grande and Mossuril, departing the island between about noon and 1pm from the beach down from BIM bank next to Villa Sands hotel, and departing Mossuril about 6am (Mtc25). For Sunset Boulevard, ask to be dropped off at 'São João', from where the *pensão* is just a five- to 10-minute walk up from the beach. From Mossuril village, it's about 1½ hours on foot to Cabaceira Grande.

However, most travellers charter a motorised dhow (about Mtc1500 if you haggle) to the Cabaceiras so they can come back the same day. Hotels on Mozambique Island can also organise Chocas/Cabaceira excursions. For all travel to/from the Cabaceiras, be prepared for lots of wading and walking.

BUS & CHAPA

Mozambique Island is joined by a one-lane, 3.5km bridge (built in 1967) to the mainland (there are half-a-dozen passing places). Most *chapas* (minibuses) stop about 1km before the bridge in Lumbo, where you'll need to get into a smaller pickup to cross over Mossuril Bay, due to vehicle weight restrictions on the bridge. (Thanks to lack of traffic, it's perfectly pleasant to walk the 3.5km across the bridge.)

Leaving Mozambique Island, all transport departs from the bridge.

Lumbo

Chapas to Lumbo cost Mtc10.

Nampula

The only direct cars to Nampula (Mtc200, three hours) are the *tanzaniano* minibuses, with one or two departing daily between 3am and 5am. The best thing to do is to ask at your hotel for help to get a message to the driver to collect you at your hotel pre-dawn. For all later departures, you will need to change vehicles at Monapo and sometimes also at Namialo. Chartering a vehicle from Nampula to Mozambique Island costs from about Mtc3000 one way.

Pemba

For travel direct to Pemba, take the 4am *tanzaniano* from the island to the main junction in Namialo (Mtc100, one hour). Large buses from Nampula start passing the Namialo junction from about 6am and usually have space (about Mtc300, six hours from Namialo to Pemba). If you miss these, there are always smaller vehicles going north.

CAR

Maximum weight is 1.5 tonnes. There's a Mtc10 toll per vehicle, payable on the mainland side.

Around Mozambique Island

Chocas, Cabaceira Pequena & Cabaceira Grande

North of Mozambique Island and across Mossuril Bay is the old Portuguese holiday town of Chocas. The town itself is of minimal interest, but just south along a sandy track roughly paralleling the beach is the traditional fishing village of **Cabaceira Pequena**, with a long, beautiful white-sand beach and views across the bay to Mozambique Island. Minutes inland are the ruins of an old Swahili-style **mosque** and the remains of a **cistern** used as a watering spot by Portuguese sailors.

Further along (northwest) from Cabaceira Pequena is semi-abandoned **Cabaceira Grande**, with a small treasure trove of ruins.

Flocks of pink flamingos stalk the mangroves and tidal pools on the adjacent beach.

Igreja de Nossa Senhora dos Remedios CHURCH

(Cabaceira Grande) This isolated church, tucked behind the mangroves close to the shore, retains a rare beauty enhanced by both its age and its setting. Built on the orders of Portuguese governor Pedro de Castro in 1579 for the Dominicans who maintained a convent on nearby Mozambique Island, it was later taken over by the Jesuits. Surviving details include the huge wooden doors, a gold-leaf altarpiece carved in India and an alfresco cistern once used by mariners.

🛏 Sleeping

Carrusca Mar & Sol   BUNGALOW $

(☑82 516 0173, 26-213302; 4-/7-person bungalows Mtc1750/3500) At Carrusca Mar & Sol it's all about the beach, which has a wild, windswept, desert-island feel, at least during the week (weekends can be unpleasantly crowded). Accommodation wise you're talking fairly rustic. The handful of spacious bungalows have hammocks and terraces, and are set on a rise between the mangroves and one of the best stretches of sand.

★ Coral Lodge 15.41   LODGE $$$

(☑82 902 3612; www.corallodge1541.com; Cabaceira Pequena; s/d all-inclusive US$400/800; ✱@🛜🏊) 🐾 If they gave out six stars for hotels, Coral Lodge might just qualify. Everything gets top marks, from the setting (an idyllic beach with its own natural diving lagoon) and the rooms (the beds have built-in air-con) to the service (akin to having your own butler) and the business ethics (most staff hail from the local village of Cabaceira Pequena).

❶ Getting There & Away

It's easy to charter a boat from Mozambique Island to the beaches at Cabaceira Grande and Pequena. Start haggling at around Mtc2000 for the return trip with a wait.

There's one daily direct *chapa* (minibus) between Nampula and Chocas, departing Nampula between 10am and noon, and departing Chocas about 4am (Mtc200, five hours). Otherwise take any transport between Nampula or Monapo and Mozambique Island to the signposted Mossuril turnoff, 25km southeast of Monapo (Mtc150 from Nampula to the Mossuril turnoff). Sporadic *chapas* go from here to Mossuril (20km), and on to Chocas (12km further), with no vehicles after about 3pm. From Chocas, it's a 30-minute walk at low tide to Cabaceira Pequena, and one to 1½ hours to Cabaceira Grande.

Cuamba

This lively if unexciting rail and road junction was formerly known as Novo Freixo. With its dusty streets, flowering trees and large student population, it's the economic centre of Niassa province and a convenient stop-off if you're travelling to/from Malawi, especially if you're catching the train. The area is known for its garnet gemstones and for its scenic panoramas, especially to the east around Mt Mitucué (Serra Mitucué).

Quinta Timbwa   CHALET $

(☑82 300 0752, 82 692 0250; quintatimbwa@yahoo.com.br; Cruze dos Chiapas; rondavels Mtc2500; ✱) This place is set on a large estate about 2.5km from town, and signposted. It's tranquil and good value, with spotless, pleasant rooms – some in attached rows, some in small rondavels – surrounded by expansive grounds featuring a small lake. It's ideal for families or for anyone with their own transport. There's also a restaurant (mains Mtc350 to Mtc600).

Pensão São Miguel   PENSION $

(☑271-62701; Avenida 3 de Fevereiro; incl breakfast r with fan/air-con Mtc1000/1200; ✱) This long-standing, local-style guesthouse has small, clean rooms crowded behind the restaurant-bar area. Each room has one small double bed. While it's not the most luxurious of establishments, it's the best value-for-price option in the town centre, and located an easy 10-minute walk from the train station and bus stand.

❶ Getting There & Away

BUS & CHAPA

Most transport leaves from Maçaniqueira market, at the southern edge of town and just south of the railway tracks. *Chapas* (minibuses) also come to meet arriving trains. The best time to find transport is between 5am and 6am, and at the station on Tuesday and Saturday afternoons, when the train from Nampula arrives.

TRAIN

A passenger train connects Cuamba and Nampula. It traditionally ran daily (except Monday) in either direction. However, since 2015 it has been reduced to a twice-weekly passenger service leaving Cuamba on Sunday and Thursday at 5am. Hopefully it will revert to its full schedule soon. The journey takes 10 to 12 hours. There are theoretically three classes of carriage (executive/1st/2nd Mtc600/400/170), although they

MOZAMBIQUE CUAMBA

might not function on all trips. It's well worth investing in executive if you can.

Tickets can be purchased between 2pm and 5pm on the day before travel (but not earlier).

Boarding starts at 4am. Arrive early and bring plenty of snacks. As with all Mozambican transport, always check ahead at the station for current schedules.

Lichinga

In Mozambique's remote northwestern corner, Lichinga is what passes for the bright lights. With its dusty unpaved roads, vivid purple jacarandas and vaguely soporific air, you could be excused for thinking you've arrived in a small town as opposed to a provincial capital. Things to enjoy in Lichinga include the cool climate and the equally cool ambience. Most visitors use it as a springboard for Lake Niassa, an hour to the west, but there's a smattering of low-key restaurants and hotels for lingerers.

🛏 Sleeping & Eating

Residencial 2+1   HOTEL $
(📱82 381 1070; Avenida Samora Machel; s/d Mtc2000/2500; ❄) Clean, efficient, central and within easy walking distance of the bus stand, this otherwise journeyman hotel is augmented by its excellent **restaurant** (Avenida Samora Machel; mains Mtc500-700; ⊙ noon-10pm).

Ponto Final   HOTEL $
(📱82 304 3632, 271-20912; Rua Filipe Samuel Magaia; d Mtc2000, s with shared bathroom Mtc1300; ❄) At the northeastern edge of town, this above-average resthouse has clean, low-ceilinged rooms with flat-screen TVs and mosquito nets. Staff are friendly and a local artist has recently produced some lovely African murals in the courtyard.

Massenger Villa   HOTEL $$
(📱82 345 4988; www.massengervilla.com; Rua No 3, Bairro de Massenger; s/d Mtc2720/3360; 🅿❄🛜🏊) This new place a couple of kilometres north of the airport has clean, minimalist rooms, a restaurant and the largest and best swimming pool in town.

Lichinga Hotel by Montebelo   HOTEL $$
(📱271-21280; www.montebelohotels.com; Rua Filipe Samuel Magaia; s/d Mtc4850/5460; ❄🛜🏊) The former Girassol hotel (the company recently rebranded as 'Montebelo'), this place remains Lichinga's most upmarket option and one of the few places in the province catering to business travellers. Despite being a bit of an oasis in an otherwise isolated town (laptop users hog the lobby for wi-fi), it lacks the pizzazz of Montebelos elsewhere.

ℹ Getting There & Away

AIR

LAM (📱271-20434, 271-20847; Praça do Liberados; ⊙ 8.30am-4.30pm Mon-Fri), just off the airport road, operates several flights weekly to/from Maputo, going via Tete (weekly) or Nampula (three times weekly) and sometimes Beira. Flights out of Lichinga tend to be heavily booked, so reconfirm your reservation and show up early at the airport.

BUS & TRUCK

Most transport – bar some buses to Tanzania – departs from beside the market, with vehicles to most destinations leaving by around 6am.

Cuamba via Mandimba

To Cuamba (Mtc500 to Mtc600, eight hours), Sckelane runs buses on Tuesday, Thursday and Saturday leaving at 3am. The same route is also covered by Nagi Investimentos. Most buses pass through the border town of Mandimba (Mtc300).

Marrupa

There's a daily bus to Marrupa (Mtc500, five hours), from where you may be able to get onward travel to Montepuez.

Metangula

To Metangula (Mtc200, 2½ hours) *chapas* (minibuses) leave mostly in the early morning.

Segundo Congresso (Matchedje) & Rovuma River

To Segundo Congresso (Matchedje) and the Rovuma River (Mtc650, six hours), at least one pickup truck goes daily, leaving anywhere between 7am and noon from the dusty street just before the transport stand. Trucks also stop on Avenida Julius Nyerere on the road north out of town (before the airport turnoff). Once over the border bridge, you can get transport to Songea for about Tsh12,000. In both directions, you'll need to have your visa in advance if using this crossing.

ℹ Getting Around

Lúrio Empreendimentos (📱87 161 9022; lurioempreendimentos@teledata.mz; Rua No 3, Bairro de Massenger) has a variety of 4WD vehicles for rent, with or without driver, at very fair rates. A taxi usually waits near Lichinga Hotel by Montebelo. Otherwise, Lúrio Empreendimentos can help with booking taxis.

Lake Niassa

Most people think of Lake Malawi as – well – Malawian, but 25% of its waters lie within Mozambique. Guarding the quieter, less developed side of the lake (which is called Lago Niassa in these parts), the Mozambican shoreline sees a small but steady stream of adventure travellers who quickly realise they've stumbled upon a wild and wonderful African paradise that few others know about.

A small sprinkling of ecolodges and budget bamboo cabins nestles among the sandy coves and giant baobabs that punctuate the shore between Meponda and Cóbuè, offering water activities, barefoot beach fun and integration with local communities.

Within Niassa's deep blue waters are over 500 species of fish, including more than 350 that are unique to the lake. The lake is also home to about a third of the planet's known cichlid (freshwater fish) species, including the brightly coloured mbuna.

Metangula

Metangula is the largest Mozambican lakeshore town – which isn't saying much. About 8km north is the tiny village of **Chuwanga**, which is on an attractive beach and is a popular weekend getaway from Lichinga.

N'Tendele Lodge   CABIN **$$**
(☑87 407 4732; www.ntendele.com; dm/d US$20/80; 🐾) 🌿 Continuing the tradition of sustainable, community-involved lakeside lodges, N'Tendele is a tranquil and beautifully simple place set in 4 hectares of miombo (woodland). It offers unadorned dorm or double rooms as well cottage tents, but, with the wilderness on your veranda, you won't be spending much time in them.

Mbuna Bay   CHALET **$$$**
(☑82 536 7781; www.mbunabay.ch; s/d with full board in bush bungalow US$150/240, in beach chalet US$210/340) 🌿 About 15km south of Metangula, ecofriendly Mbuna Bay has four wooden beachfront cottages, four brick cottages set back in the bush, and one wattle-and-daub cottage. All have creatively designed bathrooms (some open-air), and all are comfortable in a rustic way. Snorkelling, dhow sails, kayaking and yoga can be arranged, as can transfers from Lichinga. Food (included) is entirely vegetarian.

🛈 Getting There & Away

BOAT

Brought into service in 2013, the MV *Chambo* links Metangula with various ports around Lake Niassa in both Malawi and Mozambique. There's a twice-weekly northern route from Metangula via Cóbuè to Likoma Island (Malawi) and Nkata Bay (Malawi), and a once-weekly southern route linking Metangula with Meponda (Mozambique) and Chipoka (Malawi).

The northern run leaves Metangula at 2am on Saturday and Wednesday. The southern route leaves at 2am on Monday. The fare from Metangula to Likoma is US$14.

Departures in Metangula are from the small dhow port just down from Bar Triângulo and below the Catholic church.

CHAPA

Daily *chapas* (minibuses) connect Metangula and Lichinga (Mtc200, two to 2½ hours), most departing Lichinga early. There's also at least one *chapa* (usually an open-backed truck) daily between Metangula and Cóbuè (Mtc250, four hours). Departures in Metangula are from the fork in the road just up from the market at Bar Triângulo; look for the yellow Mcel wall. The final 20km or so of the tarmac road from Lichinga to Metangula is very scenic as the road winds down to the lakeshore.

There are occasional *chapas* between Metangula and Chuwanga, and hitching is easy on the weekend. Otherwise get a Cóbuè *chapa* to drop you at the Chuwanga turnoff, though it's probably just as fast to walk from Metangula. To get to Messumba, you'll need your own 4WD.

Cóbuè

Tiny Cóbuè is the gateway to Mozambique if you're travelling from Malawi via Likoma Island, 7km offshore. The island is surrounded by Mozambican waters but belongs to Malawi.

In addition to being one of the only places in Mozambique where you can procure an on-the-spot visa, Cóbuè's attractions include a lakeside setting dotted with mango trees, the remains of a school once used as a wartime base by Frelimo, and an oversized church, formerly a ruin but recently fixed with a new roof.

House of Chambo   CABIN **$**
(www.houseofchambo.com; Mala Village; cabins per person incl breakfast US$25) Newly opened in 2016, the Chambo hosts three simple but beautifully sited bamboo bungalows right on the beach beside Lake Niassa. On offer are meals, a bar and a raft of activities including

guided safari walks. It's 8km southwest of Cóbuè; you can take a boat or walk.

Rest House Mira Lago
PENSION **$**
(Pensão Layla; r with shared bathroom Mtc750; P)
Directly in the village centre, this place has solar-powered lighting and a row of no-frills, clean rooms. Each has a small double bed. Meals can sometimes be organised with notice.

❶ Getting There & Away

BOAT
The MV *Chambo* stops at Cóbuè twice a week on its run between Metangula and Likoma Island and on to Nkata Bay in Malawi. There are departures north to Likoma Island (US$2, one hour) on Saturday and Wednesday at 8am, and departures south to Metangula (US$12, five hours) on Thursday at 2pm and Sunday at 11am.

Meanwhile, fishing boats depart daily (in the morning) between Cóbuè and Likoma Island (about US$7 one way). Mozambique visas are issued in Cóbuè (US$30) but *not* Metangula. If you're travelling to/from Malawi, you'll need to go to Immigration (on the hill near the large antenna) to get your passport stamped.

BUS & CAR
Chapas (minibuses), usually in the form of open-back trucks, run between Metangula and Cóbuè, usually departing Metangula about 7am and Cóbuè about 8am (Mtc250, four hours).

The road between Cóbuè and Metangula (75km) is in reasonable condition, and there's secure parking at Khango Beach and Rest House Mira Lago in Cóbuè. (Walking between Cóbuè and Metangula takes about two days, going along the river via the villages of Ngoo and Chia.)

Niassa Reserve

The **Niassa Reserve** (Reserva do Niassa; ☏21-329807; http://www.facebook.com/NiassaReserve; adult/child/vehicle per day Mtc200/50/200) is a vast tract of miombo (woodland) and grass savannah dotted with inselbergs (steep, abrupt hills) that supports Mozambique's largest wildlife populations.

Hard to get to, and with park management currently focused on tackling poaching rather than promoting tourism, Niassa gets only a handful of annual visitors. For the time being, aspiring adventurers will need to come equipped with their own transport, food and tents.

The reserve covers 42,000 sq km, an area roughly the size of Denmark.

The reserve's one luxury safari camp, **Lugenda Bush Camp**, closed for major refurbishment in early 2016; check with Kaskazini (p223) for updates. At present, the only accommodation is at several scattered hunting camps (used mainly by trophy hunters on organised excursions) or the rudimentary ranger camp near Mbatamila headquarters, where you can pitch a tent (US$10). To visit, you'll need to bring all your own gear, or arrive on an organised trip.

❶ Information

Reserve headquarters are about 40km southwest of Mecula at Mbatamila.

Wildlife in Niassa is spread relatively thinly over a vast area, with dense foliage and only a skeleton network of bush tracks. As a result, most tourism to date has been exclusively for the well heeled (either photography or hunting oriented), with the most feasible way to visit by charter plane from Pemba. With the gradual upgrading of road connections linking Cabo Delgado and Niassa provinces, this is beginning to change, although the reserve's main market is likely to remain top end for the foreseeable future.

For self-drivers it's possible in theory to do drive-in visits. However, given the lack of a developed network of tracks, this is only recommended for the adventure and the wilderness rather than for the safari or 'Big Four' aspects (there are no rhinos in Niassa). Note that the reserve's tsetse flies are very aggressive and very numerous. Any activity in a vehicle will need to be done with windows up.

❶ Getting There & Away

There are two approaches to the Niassa Reserve, both of which converge on the small town of Marrupa. By far the easiest route is from Lichinga in the west on a good paved road (about five hours). From the east, the road is good through Montepuez to Balama. The Balama–Marrupa section is in poorer condition, but it's passable in the dry season (April to November). Allow a full day from Pemba. There's cheap accommodation available in Montepuez.

At Marrupa there's fuel, camping and basic accommodation. From Marrupa, the remaining 100km stretch up to the Lugenda River and on into the reserve is dirt but in reasonable shape.

The unpaved road from Cuamba to Marrupa is another doable option, especially during the dry season. Petrol is generally available on the roadside in Mecula, although this should not be relied upon, and on the whole, driving itineraries in the reserve will be limited by how much extra fuel you can carry.

NKWICHI LODGE

Apart from its convenient location, the main reason to come to Cóbuè is to get to **Nkwichi Lodge** (www.nkwichi.com; s/d with full board in chalet US$450/690, in private house US$495/760), one of the most appealing and genuinely community-integrated lodges in the region and worth all of the many dollars it costs to stay there.

For setting, service, romance, proximity to nature and integration with the local community, Nkwichi Lodge can rival anywhere in Africa. Gracing the shores of Lake Niassa, its seven hand-crafted bungalows seem to spring naturally from the rocks and foliage, and come equipped with private outdoor baths and showers built into the bush. Several look out onto their own white-sand coves.

There are also two private houses, each with lake views, private chef, and lots of space and privacy.

The lodge lays on activities aplenty, including canoeing, multinight wilderness walking safaris, and visits to the lodge's demonstration farm. It is linked with the Manda Wilderness Community Conservation Area, a privately initiated conservation area along the lakeshore that also promotes community development and responsible tourism. The surrounding bush is full of ospreys, palm-nut vultures, Pel's fishing owls, fish eagles and 200-year-old baobab trees.

Nkwichi is only accessible by boat from Cóbuè or Likoma Island (Malawi). Transfers (45 minutes) can be arranged with reservations.

Once across the Lugenda, you'll need to sign in at the reserve before continuing on towards Mecula and Mbatamila park headquarters – about 45km from the gate, and set in the shadow of the 1441m-high Mt Mecula – where you can arrange a guide.

Montepuez

Montepuez, a busy district capital, previously rivalled Pemba as the largest town in Cabo Delgado province. Today it's known for its marble quarries and as the start of the wild 'road' west across Niassa province towards Lichinga. The main road in Montepuez is Avenida Eduardo Mondlane; most places are either on or just off it.

The transport stand is about two blocks south of Avenida Eduardo Mondlane; turn down the street with Millennium BIM. Several *chapas* (minibuses) daily go between Pemba and Montepuez (Mtc250, three hours). Heading west, there's regular transport to Balama (Mtc180), but from there to Marrupa (for Niassa Reserve) there's no option other than hitching a lift with a tractor or a truck. If you're driving, the Balama–Marrupa stretch is only navigable in the dry season.

VS Lanchonete   FAST FOOD $
([☑]272-51051; Avenida Eduardo Mondlane; snacks Mtc250-400; [☺]8am-9pm) This chicken-and-chips place with plastic picnic tables should

sate your appetite if you're heading towards the wilds of Niassa. Also rents a few clean rooms (from around Mtc1800).

Pemba

The gateway to the north, Pemba sprawls across a small peninsula that juts into the enormous and magnificent Pemba Bay, one of the world's largest natural harbours. Established in 1904 as administrative headquarters for the Niassa Company, Pemba was known for much of its early life as Porto Amelia. Today it's the capital of Cabo Delgado province and a city of three distinct parts. The mildewed *baixa* area is home to the low-lying port, the old town and the lively township of **Paquitequete**. Steeply uphill from here, the busier and less atmospheric town centre is the place to get things done, with banks and offices, a few restaurants and the main bus stand. About 5km east of the town centre is **Wimbi** (also spelled Wimbe) **Beach**, the hub of tourist activity and the favoured destination of most visitors.

[🏃] Activities

There's a small swimming pool at Clube Naval (p222).

CI Divers   DIVING
([☑]272-20102; www.cidivers.co.za; Pieter's Place, Avenida Marginal, Wimbi Beach) The only

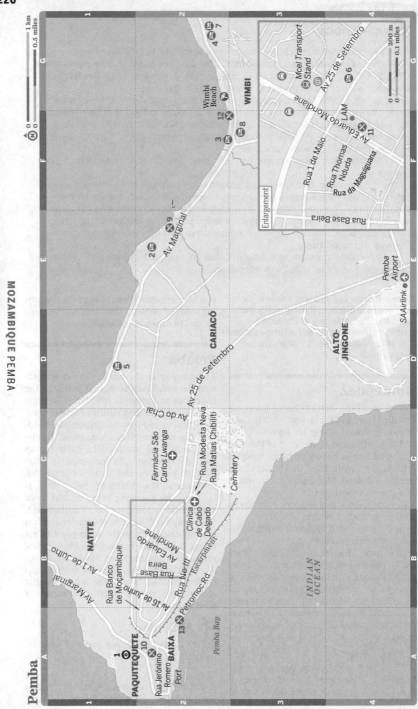

Pemba

MOZAMBIQUE PEMBA

Pemba

⊙ **Sights**
1 Paquitequete..A1

⊙ **Activities, Courses & Tours**
CI Divers...(see 7)

⊙ **Sleeping**
2 Avani Pemba Beach Hotel......................E2
3 Náutilus Hotel.....................................F2
4 Pieter's Place......................................G2
5 Raphael's Hotel...................................D1
6 Residencial Lys...................................G4
7 Residencial Reggio Emilia.....................G2
8 Wimbi Sun Residencial F3

⊗ **Eating**
9 Clube Naval E2
10 Locanda Italiana A2
11 Pastelaria Flor d'Avenida.....................F4
12 Pemba Dolphin F3
Procongel ....(see 13)
13 Wilson's Wharf..................................A2

⊙ **Shopping**
Artes Maconde ....(see 2)

⊙ **Information**
Kaskazini ....(see 2)

independent dive operator in Pemba, CI Divers is based at South African-run Pieter's Place (p221). It offers PADI open-water certification (US$560 for a four-day course) and guided dive immersions (US$70). Boats launch from the Náutilus Hotel and sail out to a 12m to 30m wall replete with coral and marine life roughly 1km out to sea.

🛏 Sleeping

🛏 In & Near Town Centre

Residencial Lys   HOTEL $
(☏272-20951; Rua 1 de Maio; s/d Mtc1500/2000; ☀) Your only overnight option in central Pemba won't win any hotel beauty pageants, though rooms are better than the dark reception area suggests. Bank on air-con and hot and cold water, but not wi-fi.

Raphael's Hotel   HOTEL $$
(☏272-25555; www.raphaelshotel.com; Praça 25 de Setembro; r from US$85; P☀☎❄) A new waterfront, Chinese-owned hotel, Raphael's is handily located halfway between central Pemba and Wimbi Beach. The architecture's hardly photo-worthy, but the rooms are large and well stocked (with coffee, water and shampoo), and there's a downstairs bar featuring a lovely terrace equipped with wicker sofas. Other bonuses include pool, gym, restaurant and strong wi-fi.

🛏 Wimbi Beach

Pemba Magic Lodge   CAMPGROUND, BUNGALOW $
('Russel's Place'; ☏272-21429; www.pembamagiclodge.com; Avenida Marginal; camping per site Mtc700, tent hire Mtc1000, dm/s/d Mtc1000/3500/5200; ☎) In business since 1998, Russel's Place is Pemba's nominal

backpackers, located on the eastern extension of Wimbi Beach (called Nanhimbe) about 3.5km beyond Complexo Náutilus. It offers the full gamut of budget accommodation: campsites, rent-a-tents, a five-bed dorm and private bungalows made out of local materials (one of which sleeps six).

Residencial Reggio Emilia   GUESTHOUSE $$
(☏82 888 0800, 272-21297; www.wix.com/ake elz/Residencial-Reggio-Emilia; 8696 Avenida Marginal; r/apt from Mtc3500/7500; P☀☎) This tranquil spot along the extension of the Wimbi Beach road has 10 clean, spacious rooms - with hot water, air-con, satellite TV, mini fridge and quality mattresses - and a two-bedroom self-catering apartment in quiet grounds. All are appealingly decorated with locally sourced materials such as Palma mats, and all have mosquito screens on the windows. Breakfast (extra) is served on request.

Wimbi Sun Residencial   GUESTHOUSE $$
(☏82 318 1300; bookings@wimbisun.co.mz; 7472 Avenida Marginal; r/d Mtc4000/4500; ☀☎) Clean, modern rooms (the best are the spacious 'suites'), none with nets and all with bathroom and TV, are on offer here. It's at the start of the Wimbi Beach strip, diagonally opposite Complexo Náutilus on the inland side of the road.

Pieter's Place   GUESTHOUSE $$
(☏82 682 2700; www.pietersdiversplace.co.za; Avenida Marginal; r US$60-100; ☀☎) Built around a huge, ancient baobab tree (into which you can climb and have breakfast in an improvised treehouse), Pieter's Place has an amiable African-backpackers feel to it. It's also diving central, thanks to the on-site CI Divers (p219). Building work was being completed on some new rooms in late 2016;

MOZAMBIQUE PEMBA

all will have private bathroom, mosquito nets and coffee-making tray.

Náutilus Hotel

HOTEL $$

(☑86 610 6652; www.thenautiluspemba.com; Avenida Marginal; s/d Mtc5000/7310; ❋ 🛜 ☒) Affiliated with a longstanding restaurant on Wimbi Beach and under new management, these new rondavels built on raised boardwalks on the sand are shaded by palm trees and situated well away from the restaurant bustle. The circular rooms have glass doors opening onto private decks and sitting areas. There's also a beautiful infinity pool to frame the mandarin-orange sunsets.

★ Avani Pemba Beach Hotel

HOTEL $$$

(☑272-21770; www.pembabeachresort.com; 5470 Avenida Marginal; s US$264-366, d US$310-430; P❋@🛜☒) If you're a romantic with a penchant for luxurious beachside hotels that have an Arabian bent, then this five-star establishment is the business. Sitting like a mini-Alhambra in expansive grounds north of Wimbi Beach, it has well-equipped rooms, a dreamy restaurant, gym, spa and infinity pool, a handy travel agent, and staff who touch their heart when they say 'good morning'.

✖ Eating

✖ In & Near Town Centre

Pastelaria Flor d'Avenida

CAFE $

(☑272-20514; Avenida Eduardo Mondlane; mains Mtc300-350; ☺6am-10pm Mon-Sat) It doesn't look much from the outside, but this long-standing, informal eatery with mainly outdoor tables delivers the goods when it comes to coffee and pastries.

Procongel

DELI $

(Petromoc Rd; ☺9am-1pm & 2-5pm Mon-Fri, 9am-1pm Sat) The pricey but well-stocked Procongel is attached to **Wilson's Wharf** (☑84 742 2909; Petromoc Rd; mains Mtc450-850; ☺8am-late Mon-Sat; ❋🛜) in the *baixa*, with produce, imported cheeses and gourmet items.

★ Locanda Italiana

ITALIAN $$

(☑82 688 9050, 272-20672; 487 Rua Jerónimo Romero; pizza & pasta Mtc300-400, mains Mtc500-600; ☺10am-10pm) Something of a vision in the quiet, well-worn streets of the *baixa*, this Italian-run restaurant serves up al dente pasta (the *ragú* is excellent) and wood-fired-oven pizzas in the flower-embellished courtyard of a restored building. If you're

looking for a day off root vegetables and chicken piri-piri, this is the place to go.

✖ Wimbi Beach

Pemba Dolphin

SEAFOOD $$

(☑272-20937; Avenida Marginal; mains Mtc500; ☺7am-late) Directly on Wimbi Beach, the very relaxed Dolphin has a beach-bar ambience, seafood grills and pizzas, and live music from 6.30pm to 9.30pm.

Kauri

INTERNATIONAL $$

(Avenida Marginal; mains Mtc400-800; ☺11am-10pm Tue-Sun) The restaurant at Kauri Resort overlooks the Indian Ocean in more ways than one. Parts of the menu also look to India for inspiration and there are Chinese dishes too. It's the local seafood, however, that tops the bill, particularly the lobster.

Clube Naval

SEAFOOD, CONTINENTAL $$$

(☑82 304 4887, 272-21770; Avenida Marginal; mains Mtc450-1600; ☺11am-10pm; 🚸) The default expat hang-out, the good ole naval club enjoys a prime waterside setting just off the western curve of Wimbi Beach. Sundowners are practically obligatory here, but the restaurant also has a large menu featuring salads, seafood, chicken, ribs, pizzas and desserts. There's a volleyball area on the sand, a swimming pool and a small children's playground.

🛍 Shopping

Artes Maconde

ARTS & CRAFTS

(Avenida Marginal; ☺8am-3pm Mon-Fri, 9am-noon Sat) Even if you don't think you want to buy crafts, it's worth stopping in at the excellent Artes Maconde at Avani Pemba Beach Hotel (p222). It sells a wide range of quality carvings, crafts and textiles sourced from throughout Mozambique as well as elsewhere in the region.

As far as quality of the artistry and uniqueness of the art are concerned, it's one of the best craft shops in the country, and craftspeople come from outlying villages throughout Cabo Delgado province and as far away as the Democratic Republic of Congo (Zaïre) to deliver their wares. It does international air and sea shipping and also takes orders.

ℹ Information

INTERNET

Sycamore Services (☑272-21999; 1282 Avenida 25 de Setembro; per hr Mtc200;

⊙7.30am-8pm Mon-Sat, 8am-noon Sun) Internet connection; it's just after Mcel.

MEDICAL

Clínica de Cabo Delgado (☎272-21462; Rua Modesta Neva 10) For basic medical treatment, although quality is erratic.

Farmácia São Carlos Lwanga (⊙7am-6.30pm Mon-Fri, 8am-5pm Sat) One block back from Avenida 25 de Setembro opposite the church.

TOURIST INFORMATION

Kaskazini (☎272-20371, 82 309 6990; www. kaskazini.com; Pemba Beach Hotel, Avenida Marginal; ⊙8am-3pm Mon-Fri, 9am-noon Sat) Efficient, knowledgeable and a good first stop. It gives free information on Pemba and elsewhere in northern Mozambique, helps with accommodation and flight bookings, and can organise everything from dhow safaris to sunset cruises.

❶ Getting There & Away

AIR

Pemba Airport is 4km southwest of the city centre. **LAM** (☎272-21251; Avenida Eduardo Mondlane; ⊙7am-4.30pm Mon-Fri, 9.30-11.30am Sat) flies daily to/from Maputo (via Nampula and/or Beira) and twice weekly to/from Dar es Salaam (Tanzania) and Nairobi (Kenya). **SAAirlink** (☎272-21700; www. flyairlink.com; Airport) flies twice weekly to Johannesburg.

For charter flights to the Quirimbas Archipelago, book direct with **CR Aviation** (☎84 490 9734; www.craviation.co.mz) or go through travel agency Kaskazini.

Expect to pay from Mtc400 to Mtc500 for a taxi from the airport to town.

BUS & CHAPA

Nearly all transport passes along Avenida 25 de Setembro, Pemba's main drag.

Ibo & Quirimbas Islands

For the Quirimbas get a *chapa* (minibus) from the Mcel Transport Stand to the boat dock at Tandanhangue (Mtc300 to Mtc400, four to eight hours) via Quissanga. *Chapas* leave daily between 4am and 5am.

Moçimboa & Mueda

Maning Nice buses go to Moçimboa da Praia (Mtc300, five to six hours) and on to Mueda (Mtc400, eight hours).

Mozambique Island

For Mozambique Island the best bet is to go to Nampula and then get onward transport from there the next day. You can also try your luck getting out at Namialo junction and looking for onward transport from there, but the timing often doesn't work out, and Namialo is unappealing as an overnight spot.

Nampula & Maputo

The Etrago bus to Maputo (Mtc3500, two days) stops in Nampula (Mtc500, six to seven hours) on its way south. It leaves from the Mcel Transport Stand at 3am Tuesday, Thursday and Saturday. Other companies covering the route include Nagi Investimentos and Esta Na Moda.

❶ Getting Around

BUS & TAXI

There are taxi ranks on Avenida Eduardo Mondlane just down from Mcel and at the same junction along Avenida 25 de Setembro. Town to Wimbi Beach costs Mtc150 to Mtc200. There's also a public bus that runs between 6am and 7pm from town to Wimbi Beach and beyond (Mtc10), and the occasional *chapa* from the Mcel Transport Stand to the Complexo Náutilus roundabout (Mtc10).

CAR

Safi Rentals (☎82 380 8630; www.pemba rentacar.com) comes highly recommended, offering reliable car rentals at very reasonable prices (with a trusted driver if required). Rates include unlimited kilometres, opening the door to many attractions in the north that would otherwise be inaccessible for budget and mid-range travellers. It's also possible to arrange car rentals through Kaskazini.

Murrébuè

Murrébuè is a lovely long stretch of white sand fringed by turquoise Indian Ocean waters that has recently started to gain attention for its optimal kitesurfing conditions. Although it's slowly being developed (two new resorts have opened in the last couple of years), it remains a pleasantly quiet alternative to Pemba's Wimbi Beach. The strip lies 12km south of Pemba.

Most of the Murrébuè lodges can organise airport pick-ups (check when booking). Otherwise regular *chapas* (minibuses) run between Pemba and the beach.

⌘ Sleeping

Ulala Lodge   BUNGALOW **$$**

(☎82 741 5104; www.ulala-lodge.com; s/d in bungalow US$81/92, in stilt bungalow US$150/162; ☎) ⊘ Small is beautiful at Ulala, right on Murrébuè Beach, with six wind- and solar-powered bamboo bungalows and a separate large dining/relaxing area. A couple of the bungalows are raised on stilts just back from the beach; two others cater for families. All have hot water, nets and covered decks and are visited by the sea breeze.

nZuwa Lodge
BUNGALOW, CAMPGROUND $$

(☑82 730 6365; www.nzuwa.com; camping per site US$15, tent rental US$20, bungalows US$100-120; ☏) At the far northern end of the beach, nZuwa offers a rustic, undone Mozambique beach paradise where comfort doesn't have to be compromised. It's all palm-frond-roofed bungalows, hammocks on the beach, epic breakfasts and raspberry-ripple sunsets. Kayaks and snorkelling gear can be borrowed.

Chuiba Bay Lodge
B&B $$$

(☑82 305 0836; www.chuibabaylodge.com; s/d US$200/300; ✳☏✉) You'll feel like a Swahili sultan as you recline in the tropical luxury of the Chuiba Bay. Six stone bungalows with individual, ethnic-chic decor are arranged around a romantically lit pool. The bathrooms are particularly notable, with deep tubs and statuettes holding up the sinks, not to mention the lobby-lounge with its piano and mini library. And...ah...the beach.

Il Pirata
BUNGALOW $$$

(☑82 380 5790; www.murrebue.com; s/d with full board US$110/175) At the northern end of the beach, this Italian-run place is a hub of activity, particularly with regard to kitesurfing. Lessons can be arranged at the on-site Pirate Kites. Accommodation comes in three lovely reed-bamboo bungalows, and there's a lauded Italian restaurant too (open to nonguests at weekends). Airport transfers can be arranged.

Quirimbas Archipelago

Hidden like pirate treasure off Mozambique's north coast, the islands of the Quirimbas archipelago conceal a multitude of secrets, from the brilliant coral reefs of Medjumbe to the ancient baobab trees of Quilaluia. But none of the 31 islands can equal mysterious Ibo, the archipelago's de facto capital. Haunted by a tumultuous history, and now a bubbling blend of Portuguese, Swahili, Indian and African cultures, Ibo feels as though it fell into a stupor in the 1850s and has yet to awaken.

Elsewhere the Quirimbas are as much about natural beauty as history. Their soft white beaches, dotted with low-key, high-end resorts, are rightly legendary, while the bird and marine life, which can be seen on tranquil diving or walking excursions, is immense.

Today many of the southern islands, including Ibo and Matemo, are part of **Quirimbas National Park** (Quirimbas National Park; entry fee US$12), which also includes large inland areas on the fringing coastline.

Ibo Island

Ibo, the best known of the Quirimbas islands, is a one-of-a-kind place that rivals Mozambique Island as one of the nation's historical highlights. Its quiet streets are lined with dilapidated villas and crumbling, moss-covered buildings, and they echo with the footsteps of bygone centuries. Architecturally Ibo is relatively open, with wide streets rather than narrow medieval lanes, although its ambience is strangely insulated; the population of around 3000 is concentrated on the island's northern tip. The best time to visit is during a clear, moonlit night, when the old colonial houses take on a haunting, almost surreal aspect.

Ibo doesn't have many beaches, but as compensation there are magical sunset views over the mudflats just north of the tiny port. With some time, you can also take day excursions to a nearby sandbank or to a lovely patch of beach on the other side of the island.

◉ Sights & Activities

Fort of São João Baptista
FORT

(Mtc50; ⊙7am-noon & 2-5pm) At the island's northern end is the star-shaped Fort of São João Baptista, built in 1791 and designed to accommodate up to 300 people. When Ibo was linked to the slave trade, the fort's dark, cramped lower chambers were used as slave holding points. Today the fort is known for the silver artisans who have set up shop near the entrance. Much of the silver they use comes from melted-down coins and is often of inferior quality, but the distinctive, refined Swahili artisanship is among the best in the region.

Inside the fort is the small, slightly unkempt **Museu Marítimo** (Maritime Museum), focusing on local Mwani culture. Explanations are in Portuguese, but an English translation is available.

You can climb on to to the ramparts to enjoy perfect ocean views.

Raúl Pereira
WALKING
(📞86 208 6046; per person Mtc1200) Raúl is Ibo's history guide, and his relaxed but engaging walking tour of Ibo's wonderful, semi-abandoned Stone Town is practically compulsory if you want to absorb the island's flavour. Raúl can be contacted independently or through Cinco Portas.

🛏 Sleeping

Pensão Café do Ibo
PENSION $
(Ibo Coffee Guesthouse; 📞82 551 7501; Airfield Rd; r Mtc2000-2500) Clean, quiet, slightly cramped rooms are available in this small private home opposite a coffee plantation. It's about a 10-minute walk from the dhow port, following the road towards the airfield with the water to your right.

Karibuni
CABIN, CAMPGROUND $
(📞82 703 2200; camping Mtc120, r Mtc400-700) Karibuni is Ibo on a budget, with very basic rooms in local-style thatched huts and space in a small garden to pitch your tent. Meals can be prepared, but you'll need to bring your own food.

★ Cinco Portas
GUESTHOUSE $$
(📞86 926 2399; www.cincoportas.com; Avenida República; s US$50-80, d US$85-140, apt US$160-195; 🖳) Ibo is an idyll wherever you stay, but Cinco Portas could well offer the best deal when you factor in price, friendly ambience and flawless, nothing-is-too-much-trouble service. Housed in a spruced-up old warehouse with a brilliant waterside setting, its small but comfortable rooms are complemented by lovely communal areas embellished with mahogany carvings and the best restaurant on the island.

Miti Miwiri
BOUTIQUE HOTEL $$
(📞82 543 8564, 26-960530; www.mitimiwiri.com; d/tr/f US$65/80/90; @🖳) One of Ibo's stalwarts, Miwiri reflects the island's magical atmosphere. Its lush walled garden is a popular place for people to hang for drinks, food, sheesha pipes and general info under the mango trees. The hotel occupies one of Ibo's finest old houses, and its large rooms have high ceilings and grand, if not opulent, decor.

Baobibo – Casa de Hospedes
GUESTHOUSE $$
(📞82 815 2892; www.baobibo.com; d US$60-75, ste US$90-110) 🍃 Just up from the dhow port, Baobibo offers several light-filled bungalows made from traditional materials. The clean, well-made bucket showers use recycled rainwater. One bungalow is designed for families. There's a garden, a lovely sitting area and activities – including bike and kayak rental – on tap. Baobibo also runs a campsite on Matemo Island.

★ Ibo Island Lodge
LODGE $$$
(www.iboisland.com; s/d with full board US$460/720; 🖳🖳🖳) This nine-room luxury boutique hotel – the most upmarket accommodation on Ibo – is housed in three restored 19th-century mansions in a prime setting overlooking the water near the dhow port. Furnishings throughout reflect the nuances of Ibo's past (Swahili, Indian, Portuguese and African), with mahogany chests, four-poster beds, and indoor and open-to-the-stars showers.

Ulani Lodge
LODGE $$$
(📞87 595 8114; www.ulanilodge.com; Rua António de Almeida; s/d US$80/100; 🖳🖳) This new Portuguese-owned place in one of Ibo's finest and most lovingly restored mansions opened in late 2016. It offers large, high-ceilinged rooms, a shady garden and pool, and plenty of colonial atmosphere.

✖ Eating

Kumawe
SEAFOOD $
(📞82 741 4616; Rituto; mains Mtc300) 🍃 A couple of homes in the *bairro* known as Rituto offer meals if organised in advance (enquire at Cinco Portas (p225)). A local will pick you up and take you to their small house, where you'll likely dine on the catch of the day, along with *matapa* (cassava leaves sauteed with cashews and coconut milk) and rice.

Medjumbe & Matemo

Idyllic Medjumbe is a narrow sliver of island draped with white coral sand. There are no permanent residents. Instead Medjumbe hosts an airstrip, an old lighthouse and the paradisaical **Anantara Medjumbe Island Resort** (www.medjumbe.anantara.com; per person with full board from US$595; 🖳🖳). It's located approximately 70km due north of Ibo.

The much larger island of Matemo lies 20km north of Ibo and has been inhabited for generations – it was an important cloth-manufacturing centre into the 17th century. Today villages dot much of the north and interior of the island. There's no resort, but camping is available through Baobibo on Ibo, and Ibo's Miti Miwiri can help arrange day trips.

MOZAMBIQUE QUIRIMBAS ARCHIPELAGO

Quilaluia

Until recently, tiny Quilaluia, just south of Quirimba Island, was inhabited only by seasonal fishing communities. Now it's a protected marine sanctuary and home to **Azura Quilálea Private Island** (www.azura-retreats.com/azura-quilalea; r per person with full board US$675-945; ✪) ✎, a low-key, high-quality small resort with nine sea-facing villas. The surrounding waters offer prime diving and snorkelling immediately offshore, while the island itself protects some ancient baobab trees.

Quirimba Island

Just south of Ibo, Quirimba is the most economically active island of the archipelago, with large coconut plantations, a sizeable sisal factory and an airstrip. It's not particularly scenic, though it does have some lovely stretches of sand. You can walk (with a guide) between Quirimba and Ibo at low tide, a beautiful excursion incorporating dense mangroves, expansive beaches and warm tidal pools.

Quirimba was an important Muslim trading centre well before the arrival of the Portuguese. In 1522 it was raided by the Portuguese and the town was destroyed, but it was later rebuilt. In the 16th century Quirimba served as a centre for missionary work.

Quirimba Guesthouse   GUESTHOUSE **$$**
(☑82 308 3930, 86 144 3964; quirimba.island@gmail.com; r US$60) On the grounds of an old coconut estate, this German-run place has six clean rooms and offers food (US$30 for two meals). Bookings are essential.

Vamizi, Rongui & Macalóè

These three islands are part of a privately funded, community-based conservation project. For now, only Vamizi has **accommodation** (www.andbeyond.com/vamizi-island; d all-inclusive from US$1970; ✪) ✎, with lodges on Rongui and Macalóè a possibility in the future.

Historically, the most important of the three islands was Vamizi, a narrow, paradisiacal crescent about midway between Moçimboa da Praia and Palma at the northernmost end of the archipelago. It was long a Portuguese and Arabic trading post – there are the ruins of an old Portuguese fort at its western end. A large village and several marvellous beaches lie to the north and east. All three islands are important seasonal fishing bases.

Moçimboa da Praia

This coastal outpost is the last major town before the Rovuma River and the Tanzanian border. Like Palma, further north, it has become a focus for the lucrative natural-gas industry. Most local residents are Mwani ('People of the Sea') – a Swahili, and hence Muslim, people known for their textiles and silver craftsmanship, as well as for their rich song and dance traditions. Moçimboa da Praia does a brisk trade with Tanzania, both legal and illegal, and from here northwards a few words of Swahili will often get you further than Portuguese.

The town itself is long, stretching over several kilometres between the main road and the sea. In the upper section are a small market, several *pensões* (cheap pensions), a petrol station and the transport stand.

IBO ISLAND COFFEE

One of Ibo's many peculiarities is a rare coffee plant known as *coffea racemose loureiro* that grows wild on the island and is cultivated by the locals for domestic consumption. Unlike Arabica coffee, which requires shade, altitude and sufficient moisture for successful cultivation, Ibo's coffee thrives at sea level and is highly resistant to drought. The plant yields a green fruit that, when harvested, dried and roasted, produces a light, pleasant herbal coffee that is low in caffeine. For a taster cup, head to the **Casa das Conchas** (☉6am-5pm) in the old town.

Thought to have been brought to Ibo by Arabic traders, *racemosa loureiro* coffee was feted by the Portuguese during the colonial period, but it never saw large-scale commercial success. Today a nascent project sponsored by the World Wildlife Fund in tandem with the Slow Food Foundation is aiming to revive production and promote Ibo's coffee as a commercially viable alternative to the island's struggling fishing industry.

About 2km east, near the water, are a few more places to stay, plus police and immigration, a lively fish market and the dhow port.

Hotel Chez Natalie   CHALET, CAMPGROUND $

(☑ 82 439 6080, 272-81092; natalie.bockel@gmail.com; camping Mtc500, d with shared bathroom Mtc1000, 4-person chalets Mtc2800; P ⬙) By far the best bet in town if you have your own transport, Natalie's has large grounds overlooking the estuary, camping and a handful of rustic but elegant family-style four-person chalets with mosquito nets, coffee maker and grill. It's very tranquil. Breakfast and other meals are available by advance arrangement only.

Complexo Vumba   BUNGALOW $$

(☑ 87 609 7554; Avenida Marginal; r from Mtc4600; ❄ ⬙) This place has clean, air-conditioned rooms and is currently favoured by Moçimboa's growing contingent of natural-gas workers. It also has Moçimboa's best **restaurant** (mains from Mtc250; ⌚ 8am-9pm). It's along the road paralleling the beach.

ℹ Getting There & Away

The transport stand is near the market at the entrance to town, and close to the large tree. Several pickups go daily to/from the Rovuma River ('Namoto') via Palma (Mtc250, two hours). The road to Palma is paved and in good shape. To Pemba (Mtc300, five to six hours), Maning Nice buses depart daily by 3am. Several pickups also do the journey, departing by 7am from the main road in front of the market. Maning Nice goes daily to/from Nampula (Mtc500, 13 hours), and several vehicles go daily to/from Mueda (Mtc150, two hours).

Mueda

Mueda is the first (or last) major town on the Mozambique side if you're crossing to/from Tanzania on the Unity Bridge. In 1960 it was the site of the infamous massacre of Mueda (p229). There's a statue commemorating Mueda's role in Mozambican independence and a small museum at the western end of town.

Several bus companies, including Maning Nice, have daily buses to Pemba (Mtc300, nine hours) and Moçimboa da Praia (Mtc150, two hours). They depart at 5am. There's also at least one vehicle (usually a pickup) daily to the Negomano border (Mtc500), including a 7am departure. All transport leaves from the main road opposite the market. After about 10am, it's difficult to find vehicles to any destination.

If you're driving, there are two roads connecting Mueda with the main north–south road. Most traffic uses the good road via Diaca (50km). The alternative route via Muidumbe (about 30km south of Diaca) is scenic, winding through hills and forests, but rougher. (Near Muidumbe is **Nangololo**, a mission station and an important base during the independence struggle, with an old airstrip large enough to take jets.)

Pensão Mtima   PENSION $

(☑ 86 314 5303; Rua 1 de Maio; r Mtc1250, with shared bathroom Mtc350) Just off the main road through town, the Mtima has two classes of room: the basic variety with shared bucket bathroom, and some newer pews with air-con and private bathroom. Don't be put off by the scruffy restaurant (mains Mtc250 to Mtc450): lashings of chicken and chips emerge from the slightly iffy-looking kitchen.

Palma

Traditionally a fishing community known for its basketry and mat weaving, Palma now rivals Tete as Mozambique's fastest-changing city. The reason: natural gas. Huge offshore gas fields were discovered in 2010 and foreign investors have been piling in with their chequebooks ever since. Several plush new hotels aimed at the gas industry have already opened, with more on the way.

Palma sits on the coast nestled among coconut groves 45km south of the Tanzanian border. A melting pot of languages, with Makwe, Makonde, Mwani, Swahili and Portuguese all spoken, it doesn't hold many sights per se, and is usually used as a staging post on the way to Tanzania.

All transport leaves from the Boa Viagem roundabout at the town entrance. Some drivers continue down to the main market.

Chapas (minibuses) from Moçimboa da Praia en route to the Rovuma River pass Palma from about 6am (Mtc300 from Palma to the border). Transport from the Rovuma south to Moçimboa da Praia passes through Palma from about 10am, and there's at least one vehicle from Palma to Moçimboa

ISLAND TO ISLAND WALKS

A unique and interesting day trip is to hike from Ibo (p224) to neighbouring Quirimba Island (p226) immediately to the south – and you don't need to walk on water to do it. At low tide the two islands are effectively joined by a series of sandbars.

Because the timing of the walk depends on the tides and involves navigating along narrow channels through dense mangrove swamps, it's wise to hire a guide – ask at any of Ibo's hotels. With stops, it should take a person of average fitness two to three hours to complete. Once you're on Quirimba Island, your guide can organise a seafood lunch with one of the families who live in the village overlooking the beach. Subsequently you can explore Quirimba's long, untarnished beaches or just watch Mozambican village life as you wait for the tide to come in. A small boat, weaving a curvaceous path through the overhanging mangroves, will ferry you back to Ibo when the water's high enough.

da Praia each morning (Mtc250, one hour) along a good, graded road.

Karibu Palma Hotel HOTEL $$$
(☑87 274 5982; www.karibupalmahotel.com; d incl breakfast from US$107; ❄🛜) Built on the back of Palma's gas boom, this well-appointed new hotel is aimed mainly at business people. Twelve spick-and-span rooms are arranged in smart two-storey blocks overlooking well-manicured gardens. There's also a decent on-site restaurant nestled under a thatched shelter and good buffet breakfasts.

UNDERSTAND MOZAMBIQUE

Mozambique Today

In Mozambique's hotly contested 2014 national elections, Frelimo insider Filipe Nyusi won at the national level. However Renamo, which won at the parliamentary level in five central and northern provinces, alleged widespread irregularities and rejected the results.

Since then, ongoing low-level conflict between Frelimo and Renamo – fuelled also by the discovery of major coal and natural-gas deposits in the country's north – has marred Mozambique's once glowing image as a post-war success story. While economic forecasts remain positive overall, other challenges include corruption and lack of free political debate in the public arena.

History

In the Beginning

The first Mozambicans were small, scattered clans of nomads, possibly distant cousins of the San, who were likely trekking through the bush as early as 10,000 years ago. They left few traces and little is known about this era.

About 3000 years ago, Bantu-speaking peoples from the Niger Delta in West Africa began moving through the Congo basin. Over a period of centuries they journeyed into East and southern Africa, reaching present-day Mozambique sometime around the 1st century AD, where they made their living farming, fishing and raising livestock.

Early Kingdoms

Most of these early Mozambicans set themselves up in small chiefdoms, some of which gradually coalesced into larger states and kingdoms. These included the Karanga (Shona) in central Mozambique and the renowned kingdom of Monomotapa, south and west of present-day Tete.

Southern Mozambique, which was settled by the Nguni and various other groups, remained decentralised until the 19th century, when consolidation under the powerful kingdom of Gaza gave it at least nominal political cohesion.

Arrival of the Arabs

From around the 8th century AD, sailors from Arabia began to arrive along the East African coast. Trade flourished and intermarriage with the indigenous Bantu speakers gave birth to the Swahili language and culture. By the 9th century several settlements had been established, including Kilwa island, in present-day Tanzania, which soon became the hub of Arab trade networks throughout southeastern Africa. Another was Sofala, near present-day Beira, which by the 15th century was the main link connecting Kilwa with the old Shona kingdoms and the inland goldfields. Other early coastal ports and settlements included those at Mozambique Island, Angoche, Quelimane and Ibo Island, all ruled by local sultans.

Portuguese Adventurers

In 1498 Vasco da Gama landed at Mozambique Island en route to India. Within a decade of da Gama's arrival, the Portuguese had established themselves on the island and gained control of numerous other Swahili–Arab trading posts – lured in part by their need for supply points on the sea route to the east and in part by their desire to control the gold trade with the interior.

Over the next 200 years the Portuguese set up trading enclaves and forts along the coast, making Mozambique Island the capital of what they called Portuguese East Africa. By the mid-16th century, ivory had replaced gold as the main trading commodity and by the late 18th century, slaves had been added to the list, with close to one million Africans sold into slavery through Mozambique's ports.

Portugal's Power Struggle

In the 17th century the Portuguese attempted to strengthen their control by setting up *prazos* (vast agricultural estates) on land granted by the Portuguese crown or by wresting control of it from local chiefs.

The next major effort by the Portuguese to consolidate their control came in the late 19th century with the establishment of charter companies, operated by private firms who were supposed to develop the land and natural resources within their boundaries. In reality these charter companies operated as independent fiefdoms and did little to consolidate Portuguese control. With the onset of the 'Scramble for Africa' in the 1880s, Portugal was forced to strengthen its claims in the region. In 1891 a British–Portuguese treaty was signed formalising Portuguese control in the area.

Early 20th Century

One of the most significant events in early-20th-century Mozambique was the large-scale migration of labour from the southern provinces to South Africa and Rhodesia (present-day Zimbabwe). This exodus was spurred by expansion of the Witwatersrand gold mines and by the passage of a new labour law in 1899. The new law divided the Mozambican population into non-indigenous *(não indígenas or assimilados)*, who had full Portuguese citizenship rights, and indigenous *(indígenas)*, who were subject to the provisions of colonial laws and forced to work, to pay a poll tax and to adhere to a form of pass laws.

Another major development was the growing economic importance of the southern part of the country. As ties with South Africa strengthened, Lourenço Marques (now Maputo) took on increasing importance as a major port and export channel and in the late 19th century the Portuguese transferred the capital here from Mozambique Island.

In the late 1920s António Salazar came to power in Portugal. He sealed off the colonies from non-Portuguese investment, abolished the remaining *prazos* and consolidated Portuguese control over Mozambique. Overall, conditions for Mozambicans worsened considerably.

Mueda Massacre

Discontent with the situation grew and a nationalist consciousness gradually developed. In June 1960, at Mueda in northern Mozambique, an official meeting was held by villagers protesting peacefully about taxes. Portuguese troops opened fire on the crowd, killing many demonstrators. Resentment at the 'massacre of Mueda' helped politicise the local Makonde people and became one of the sparks kindling the independence struggle. External support came from several sources, including Julius Nyerere's government in neighbouring Tanganyika (now Tanzania). In 1962, following a meeting of various political organisations working in exile for Mozambican independence, the Frente pela Libertação de Moçambique (Mozambique Liberation Front; Frelimo) was formed in Dar es Salaam (Tanzania), led by Eduardo Chivambo Mondlane.

MOZAMBIQUE HISTORY

Independence Struggle

Frelimo was plagued by internal divisions from the outset. However, under the leadership of the charismatic Mondlane and operating from bases in Tanzania, it succeeded in giving the liberation movement a structure and in defining a program of political and military action to support its aim of complete independence for Mozambique. On 25 September 1964 Mondlane proclaimed the beginning of the armed struggle for national independence.

In 1969 Mondlane was assassinated by a letter bomb at his office in Dar es Salaam. He was succeeded as president by Frelimo's military commander, Samora Moises Machel. Under Machel, Frelimo sought to extend its area of operations to the south. The Portuguese, meanwhile, attempted to eliminate rural support for Frelimo by implementing a scorched-earth campaign and by resettling people in a series of *aldeamentos* (fortified village complexes).

However, struggles within Portugal's colonial empire and increasing international criticism sapped the government's resources. In 1974, at a ceremony in Lusaka (Zambia), Portugal agreed to hand over power to Frelimo and a transitional government was established. On 25 June 1975 the independent People's Republic of Mozambique was proclaimed with Samora Machel as president and Joaquim Chissano, a founding member of Frelimo's intellectual elite, as prime minister.

Early Years of Independence

The Portuguese pulled out virtually overnight, leaving the country in a state of chaos with few skilled professionals and virtually no infrastructure. Frelimo, which found itself suddenly faced with the task of running the country, threw itself headlong into a policy of radical social change.

Frelimo's socialist program proved unrealistic, however, and by 1983 the country was almost bankrupt. Onto this scene came the Resistência Nacional de Moçambique (Mozambique National Resistance; Renamo), a ragtag group that had been established in the mid-1970s by Rhodesia (now Zimbabwe) as part of its destabilisation policy, and later kept alive with backing from the South African military and certain sectors in the West.

Ravages of War

Renamo had no ideology of its own beyond the wholesale destruction of social and communications infrastructure within Mozambique and the destabilisation of the government. Many commentators have pointed out that the war that went on to ravage the country for the next 17 years was thus not a 'civil' war but one between Mozambique's Frelimo government and Renamo's external backers. Recruitment was sometimes voluntary but frequently by force. Roads, bridges, railways, schools and clinics were destroyed. Atrocities were committed on a massive and horrific scale.

The drought and famine of 1983 crippled the country. Faced with this dire situation, Frelimo opened Mozambique to the West in return for Western aid.

In 1984 South Africa and Mozambique signed the Nkomati Accord, under which South Africa undertook to withdraw its support of Renamo, and Mozambique agreed to expel the African National Congress (ANC) and open the country to South African investment. While Mozambique abided by the agreement, South Africa exploited the situation to the full and Renamo's activity did not diminish.

Samora Machel died in a plane crash in 1986 under questionable circumstances and was succeeded by the more moderate Joaquim Chissano. The war between the Frelimo government and the Renamo rebels continued, but by the late 1980s political change was sweeping through the region. The collapse of the USSR altered the political balance, and the new president of South Africa, FW de Klerk, made it more difficult for right-wing factions to supply Renamo.

Peace

By the early 1990s, Frelimo had disavowed its Marxist ideology. A ceasefire was arranged, followed by a formal peace agreement in October 1992 and a UN-monitored disarmament and demobilisation campaign. Since then, Mozambique has been remarkably successful – at least on the surface – in moving beyond its history of war and transforming military conflict into political competition. Most notable was the relatively smooth leadership transition in 2004, when Armando Guebuza of the ruling Frelimo political party was elected to succeed long-serving former president Joaquim Chissano (also of Frelimo). Any easy re-election for Guebuza followed in 2009.

Cuisine

Mozambique's cuisine blends African, Indian and Portuguese influences, and is especially noted for its seafood as well as its use of coconut milk and piri-piri (chilli pepper).

Where to Eat

Roadside or market *barracas* (food stalls) serve plates of local food such as *xima* (a maize- or cassava-based staple) and sauce for about Mtc400 or less.

Most towns have a cafe, *pastelaria* or *salão de chá* serving coffee, pastries and inexpensive snacks and light meals such as omelettes, *pregos* (thin steak sandwiches) and burgers.

Restaurant prices and menu offerings are remarkably uniform throughout the country, ranging from about Mtc300 to Mtc500 for meals such as grilled fish or chicken served with rice or potatoes. Most restaurants also offer hearty Portuguese-style soups.

Markets in all larger towns sell an abundance of fresh tropical fruit along with a reasonably good selection of vegetables. High-quality meats from nearby South Africa are sold in delis and supermarkets.

The Arts

Dance

On Mozambique Island and along the northern coast, watch for *tufo* (a dance of Arabic origin). It is generally performed by women, wearing matching *capulanas* (sarongs) and scarves, and accompanied by special drums (some more like tambourines) known as *taware*.

In the south, one of the best-known dances, particularly in Maputo, is *marrabenta,* which combines Mozambican rhythms with Portuguese folk-music influences. Its energetic swaying and infectious rhythms embody Mozambique's history of struggle and optimistic determination.

The *casas de cultura* (cultural centres), found in every provincial capital, are good places to get information on traditional dance performances. Another excellent contact is Maputo's Centro Cultural Franco-Moçambicano (p179).

Literature

During the colonial era, local literature generally focused on nationalist themes. Two of the most famous poets of this period were Rui de Noronha and Noémia de Sousa.

In the late 1940s José Craveirinha (1922–2003) began to write poetry focusing on the social reality of the Mozambican people and calling for resistance and rebellion, which eventually led to his arrest. Today he is honoured as Mozambique's greatest poet, and his work, including 'Poem of the Future Citizen', is recognised worldwide.

As the armed independence struggle gained strength, Frelimo freedom fighters began to write poems reflecting their life in the forest, their marches and the ambushes. One of the finest of these guerrilla poets was Marcelino dos Santos.

With Mozambican independence in 1975, writers and poets felt able to produce literature without interference. This newfound freedom was soon shattered by Frelimo's war against the Renamo rebels, but new writers emerged, including the internationally acclaimed Mia Couto, whose works include *Voices Made Night* and *The Last Flight of the Flamingo*. Contemporary female writers include Lilia Momple *(The Eyes of the Green Cobra)* and Paulina Chiziane *(Niketche – A Story of Polygamy)*.

Music

The *timbila* orchestras of the Chopi people in southern Mozambique are one of the country's best-known musical traditions.

Modern music flourishes in the cities and the live-music scene in Maputo is excellent. *Marrabenta* is considered Mozambique's national music. It developed in the 1950s in the suburbs of Maputo (then Lourenço Marques) and has a light, upbeat style and distinctive beat inspired by the traditional rural *majika* rhythms of Gaza and Maputo provinces. It is often accompanied by a dance of the same name.

MOZAMBIQUE CUISINE

Sculpture & Painting

Mozambique is known for its woodcarvings, particularly for the sandalwood carvings found in the south and the ebony carvings of the Makonde.

The country's most famous painter is Malangatana Valente Ngwenya – universally known as Malangatana – whose style is characterised by dramatic figures and flamboyant yet restrained use of colour, and by its highly symbolic social and political commentary. Other internationally acclaimed artists include Bertina Lopes and Roberto Chichorro.

Natural Environment

Mozambique has extensive coastal lowlands forming a broad plain 100km to 200km wide in the south and leaving it vulnerable to seasonal flooding. In the north, this plain narrows and the terrain rises to mountains and plateaus on the borders with Zimbabwe, Zambia and Malawi. In central Mozambique, the predominant geographical feature is the Zambezi River valley and its wide delta plains. In many areas of the north, particularly in Nampula and Niassa provinces, towering granite outcrops (inselbergs; literally 'island mountains') dominate the landscape.

Wildlife

ANIMALS

While more than 200 types of mammal wander the interior, challenging access, dense vegetation and skittishness on the part of the animals can make spotting them difficult, and Mozambique shouldn't be viewed as a 'Big Five' destination. Work is proceeding in reviving several parks and reserves, especially Gorongosa National Park, which offers Mozambique's most accessible wildlife watching. However, poaching is taking a heavy toll, especially on the country's elephant population.

BIRDS

Of the approximately 900 bird species that have been identified in the Southern Africa region, close to 600 have been recorded in Mozambique. Among these are numerous aquatic species found primarily in the southern wetlands. On Inhaca Island alone, 300 bird species have been recorded. Rare

and unique species (most of which are found in isolated montane habitats such as the Chimanimani Mountains, Mt Gorongosa and Mt Namúli) include the dappled mountain robin, the chirinda apalis, Swynnerton's forest robin, the olive-headed weaver and the green-headed oriole.

MARINE LIFE

Coastal waters host populations of dolphins, including spinner, bottlenose, humpback and striped dolphins, plus loggerhead, leatherback, green, hawksbill and olive ridley marine turtles. The coast also serves as a winter breeding ground for the humpback whale, which is found primarily between Ponta d'Ouro and Inhambane. Between July and October it's also common to see whales in the north, offshore from Pemba.

Dugongs have been sighted around Inhambane Bay, Angoche, Mozambique Island, Nacala and the Quirimbas and Bazaruto Archipelagos.

Plants

Almost 6000 plant species have been recorded, including an estimated 250 that are thought to be found nowhere else in the world. The Maputaland Centre of Plant Diversity, straddling the border with South Africa south of Maputo, is one of the most important areas of the country in terms of plant diversity and has been classified as a site of global botanical significance. The Chimanimani Mountains are also notable for their plant diversity, with at least 45 endemic species. Other important highland areas include the Gorongosa Massif (Sofala province) and Mt Chiperone, Mt Mabu and Mt Namúli (all in Zambézia province).

National Parks & Reserves

Mozambique has seven national parks: Gorongosa, Zinave, Banhine, Limpopo and Mágoè in the interior; Bazaruto National Park offshore; and Quirimbas National Park, encompassing both coastal and inland areas in Cabo Delgado province. Mágoè, Zinave and Banhine have no tourist infrastructure, although restocking of Zinave with elephants and other wildlife from South Africa's Kruger National Park is currently under way.

Wildlife reserves include Niassa, Marromeu, Pomene, Maputo and Gilé. The Chimanimani National Reserve has a network of rustic camps for hikers.

SURVIVAL GUIDE

ⓘ Directory A–Z

ACCOMMODATION

Accommodation in coastal areas fills during Christmas and New Year's, Easter and other South African school holidays; advance bookings are recommended. Ask about rainy-season and children's discounts.

When quoting prices, many establishments distinguish between a *duplo* (room with two twin beds) and a *casal* (room with double bed). Rates are often quoted in US dollars or South African rand. Payment can almost always be made in meticals, dollars or rand.

ACTIVITIES
Birdwatching

Prime birding areas include:
➡ Bazaruto Archipelago
➡ Gorongosa National Park
➡ Lake Niassa
➡ Maputo Special Reserve

Useful websites with bird lists and announcements of regional birding activities:

African Bird Club (www.africanbirdclub.org)
Fatbirder (www.fatbirder.com)
Indicator Birding (www.birding.co.za)
Southern African Birding (www.sabirding.co.za)

Diving & Snorkelling

Attractions include the chance to sight dolphins, whale sharks, manta rays and dugongs; opportunities to discover new sites; the natural beauty of the Mozambican coast; seasonal humpback-whale sightings; excellent fish diversity; and a generally untouched array of hard and soft corals, especially in the north. You'll also have most spots almost to yourself.

Equipment, instruction and certification are widely available along the coast, including in Ponta d'Ouro, Tofo, Vilankulo, the Bazaruto Archipelago, Pemba and the Quirimbas Archipelago. Prices are comparable to those elsewhere in East Africa but somewhat higher than in South Africa.

Hiking

The best hiking area is the Chimanimani Mountains, which includes Mt Binga, Mozambique's highest peak. The hills around Gurúè offer good walking.

Surfing & Kitesurfing

The best waves are at Ponta d'Ouro in the far south of the country and at Tofinho. Boards can be rented at both places.

Kitesurfing has a small but growing following, especially in the north near Pemba, and around Vilankulo. A good initial contact is Kite Surfing Centre (p193).

Wildlife Watching

The main wildlife-watching destination is Gorongosa National Park. Other possibilities include Niassa Reserve, Maputo Special Reserve and Limpopo National Park. Apart from in Gorongosa, the chances of spotting significant wildlife are small, and Mozambique shouldn't be considered a 'Big Five' destination.

BUSINESS HOURS

Banks 8am to 3pm Monday to Friday
Bars 5pm to late
Cafes 7.30am to 9pm
Exchange bureaus (casas de câmbio) 8.30am to 5pm Monday to Friday, to noon Saturday
Government offices 7.30am to 3.30pm Monday to Friday
Restaurants Breakfast 7am to 11am, lunch noon to 3pm, dinner 6.30pm to 10.30pm
Shops 8am to noon and 2pm to 6pm Monday to Friday, 8am to 1pm Saturday

CHILDREN

Cots & spare beds Easily arranged; average cost Mtc500.
Child seats for hired cars Occasionally available; confirm in advance.
Restaurant high chairs Occasionally available.
Formula, disposable nappies and wet wipes Available in pharmacies, large supermarkets and markets in larger towns.
Child care Easy to arrange informally through your hotel.
Prams Impractical; use a Mozambican-style sling carrier instead.

ELECTRICITY

Electricity is 220V to 240V AC, 50Hz, usually accessed with South African-style three-round-pin plugs or two-round-pin plugs.

ⓘ EATING PRICE RANGES

The following price ranges refer to a standard main course.

$ less than Mtc325 (US$5)

$$ Mtc325–650 (US$5–10)

$$$ more than Mtc650 (US$10)

EMBASSIES & CONSULATES

All of the following embassies are located in Maputo. The closest Australian representation is in South Africa.

British High Commission (☑ 82 313 8580; www.gov.uk/government/world/mozambique; 310 Avenida Vladimir Lenine)

Canadian High Commission (☑ 21-492623; www.canadainternational.gc.ca/mozambique; 1138 Avenida Kenneth Kaunda)

Dutch Embassy (☑ 21-484200; http://mozam bique.nlembassy.org; 324 Avenida Kwame Nkrumah)

French Embassy (☑ 21-484600; www.amba france-mz.org; 2361 Avenida Julius Nyerere)

German Embassy (☑ 21-482700; www.mapu to.diplo.de; 506 Rua Damião de Gois)

Irish Embassy (☑ 21-491440; www.dfa.ie/ mozambique; 3630 Avenida Julius Nyerere)

Malawian High Commission (☑ 21-492676; 75 Avenida Kenneth Kaunda)

Portuguese Embassy (☑ 21-490316; www. maputo.embaixadaportugal.mne.pt/en/; 720 Avenida Julius Nyerere)

South African High Commission (☑ 21-243000; www.dfa.gov.za/foreign/sa_abroad/ sam.htm; 41 Avenida Eduardo Mondlane)

Swazi High Commission (☑ 21-491601, 21-492117; 1271 Rua Luís Pasteur)

Tanzanian High Commission (☑ 21-490112, 21-490110; ujamaa@zebra.uem.mz; 115 Rua 301)

US Embassy (☑ 21-492797; http://maputo. usembassy.gov; 193 Avenida Kenneth Kaunda)

Zambian High Commission (☑ 21-492452; 1286 Avenida Kenneth Kaunda)

Zimbabwean High Commission (☑ 21-490404, 21-488877; zimmaputo@zimfa.gov. zw; 1657 Avenida Mártires de Machava)

INTERNET ACCESS

Internet access is easy and fast in Maputo and other major centres, where there are numerous wi-fi spots and internet cafes. Most mid-range and top-end hotels also offer wi-fi.

MONEY

Mozambique's currency is the metical (plural meticais, pronounced 'meticaish') nova família, abbreviated as Mtc. Visa-card withdrawal from ATMs is the best way of accessing money. For exchange rates see p721.

ATMs

➔ All larger and many smaller towns have ATMs for accessing cash meticals. Most accept Visa cards; Millennium BIM and Standard Bank machines also, and less reliably, accept MasterCard.

➔ Many machines have a limit of Mtc3000 (US$120) per transaction. BCI's limit is Mtc5000 (US$200) and some Standard Bank machines dispense up to Mtc10,000 (US$400) per transaction.

Changing Money

➔ US dollars are easily exchanged everywhere; together with South African rand, they are the best currency to carry.

➔ Only new-design US dollar bills will be accepted. Euros are easy to change in major cities, but elsewhere you're likely to get a poor exchange rate.

➔ *Casas de câmbio* (exchange bureaus) are the most efficient places to change money. They usually give a rate equivalent to or slightly higher than that of the banks and are open longer hours.

➔ It is also possible to change money at some banks; BCI branches are generally good. Most banks don't charge commission for changing cash. Millennium BIM branches will let you change cash only if you have an account.

➔ Changing money on the street isn't safe anywhere and is illegal; asking shopkeepers is a better bet.

Cash

➔ Note denominations include Mtc20, Mtc50, Mtc100, Mtc200, Mtc500 and Mtc1000, and coins include Mtc1, Mtc2, Mtc5 and Mtc10. One metical is equivalent to 100 centavos (Ct); there are Ct1, Ct5, Ct10, Ct20 and Ct50 coins.

➔ Carry a standby mixture of US dollars (or South African rand, especially in the south) and meticals (including a good supply of small-denomination notes, as nobody ever has change) for times when an ATM is nonexistent or not working.

Credit Cards

➔ Credit cards are accepted at most (but not all) top-end hotels, at many midrange places, especially in the south, and at some car-hire agencies; otherwise they're of limited use in Mozambique.

➔ Visa is by far the most useful, and is also the main (often only) card for accessing money from ATMs.

Tipping

In low-budget bars and restaurants, tipping is generally not expected, other than perhaps by rounding up the bill. At upmarket and tourist establishments, tipping is customary (from 10% to 20%, assuming service has been good). Tips are also warranted, and always appreciated, if someone has gone out of their way to do something for you.

Travellers Cheques

Travellers cheques are not accepted for exchange or direct payment in Mozambique.

PUBLIC HOLIDAYS

New Year's Day 1 January
Mozambican Heroes' Day 3 February
Women's Day 7 April
International Workers' Day 1 May
Independence Day 25 June
Lusaka Agreement/Victory Day 7 September
Revolution Day 25 September
Peace & Reconciliation Day 4 October
Christmas/Family Day 25 December

For South African school-holiday dates, see the calendar link at www.saschools.co.za.

SAFE TRAVEL

Mozambique is a relatively safe place and most travellers shouldn't have any difficulties. That said, there are a few areas where caution is warranted. Government travel advisories are a good source of updated information.

Petty theft and robbery are the main risks; watch your pockets or bag in markets; don't leave personal belongings unguarded on the beach or elsewhere; and minimise trappings such as jewellery, watches and external money pouches.

If you leave your vehicle unguarded, don't be surprised if windscreen wipers and other accessories are gone when you return. Don't leave anything inside a parked vehicle.

When at stoplights or slowed in traffic, keep your windows up and doors locked, and don't leave anything on the seat next to you where it could be snatched.

In Maputo and southern Mozambique carjackings and more violent robberies do occur, although most incidents can be avoided by taking the usual precautions: avoid driving at night; keep the passenger windows up and the doors locked if you are in a vehicle (including a taxi) at any time during the day or night; avoid walking alone or in a group at dusk or at night, particularly in isolated areas; and avoid isolating situations in general. Don't walk alone along the beach away from hotel areas. If you're driving and your car is hijacked, hand over the keys immediately.

ⓘ GOVERNMENT TRAVEL ADVISORIES

Australia www.smartraveller.gov.au

Canada www.travel.gc.ca

UK www.gov.uk/government/organisations/foreign-commonwealth-office

New Zealand www.safetravel.govt.nz

USA www.travel.state.gov

All this said, don't let these warnings deter you; simply be a savvy traveller. The vast majority of visitors enjoy this beautiful country without incident.

Hassles & Bribes

More likely than violent crime are simple hassles with underpaid authorities in search of a bribe. The worst offenders here are regular (ie grey-uniformed, non-traffic) police. If you get stopped you shouldn't have any problems as long as your papers are in order. Being friendly, respectful and patient helps (you won't get anywhere otherwise), as does trying to give the impression that you know what you're doing and aren't new in the country. Sometimes the opposite tack is also helpful: feigning complete ignorance if you're told that you've violated some regulation, and apologising profusely. It's also worth remembering that only traffic police are authorised to stop you for traffic infractions. If you're stopped by non-traffic police, you can ask to wait until a traffic-police officer arrives – often this will defuse the bribe attempt.

If you are asked to pay a *multa* (fine) for a trumped-up charge, playing the game a bit (asking to speak to the *chefe* (supervisor) and requesting a receipt) helps to counteract some of the more blatant attempts, as does insisting on going to the nearest *esquadrão* (police station); you should always do these things anyway.

Road Convoys

As of late 2016, timed army convoys were escorting all road traffic on the EN1 between the Save River and Muxungue, as well as on the EN1 between Nhamapadza (Gorongosa area) and Caia, and on the EN7 between Nova Vanduzi and Luenha (en route between Chimoio and Tete). Before you set off, it's highly recommended that you check your country's government travel advisory for updates on the security situation.

TELEPHONE

Land-line area codes must be dialled whenever you're making long-distance calls. As with mobile numbers, there is no initial zero.

Mozambique's country code is +258.

Mobile Phones

Mobile phone numbers are seven digits long, preceded by 82 for Mcel, 84 for Vodafone and 86 for Movitel.

Do not use an initial zero; seven-digit mobile numbers listed with zero at the outset are in South Africa and must be preceded by the South Africa country code (27) when dialling.

All companies have outlets in major towns at which you can buy Sim-card starter packs (from Mtc50), fill out the necessary registration form, and buy top-up cards.

TIME

Mozambique time is GMT/UTC plus two hours. There is no daylight-saving time.

VISAS

Visas are required by all visitors except citizens of South Africa, Swaziland, Zambia, Tanzania, Botswana, Malawi, Mauritius and Zimbabwe.

Travellers residing in a country with Mozambique diplomatic representation are required to obtain visas in advance of arrival in Mozambique or they must pay an additional 25% for visas obtained at the border. However, in an effort to encourage tourism, the government announced in early 2017 that one-month single-entry tourist visas could now be obtained on arrival at 44 land borders (including all major aiports and many major borders, but not the border with Tanzania) for Mtc2000. It is too early to tell how this new announcement will be implemented. Our advice is to try to get your visa in advance, especially if you will be arriving in Maputo via bus from Johannesburg. But failing that, it is well worth trying your luck at the border.

For visas purchased in advance, fees vary according to where you buy your visa and how quickly you need it. The maximum initial length of stay is three months. Express (24-hour to 48-hour) visa service is available at several Mozambican embassies and high commissions, and same-day visa service (within 24 hours) is available at several places, including Johannesburg and Nelspruit (South Africa) and Dar es Salaam (Tanzania), but at a price.

No matter where you get your visa, your passport must be valid for at least six months from the dates of intended travel, and have at least three blank pages.

For citizens of countries not requiring visas, visits are limited to 30 days from the date of entry, after which you'll need to exit Mozambique and re-enter.

The length of each stay for multiple-entry visas is determined when the visa is issued, and varies from embassy to embassy.

Visa Extensions

Visas can be extended at the *migração* (immigration office) in most provincial capitals, provided you haven't exceeded the three-month maximum stay, at a cost of Mtc2000 for one month.

Processing takes two days (with payment of an approximately Mtc200 supplemental express fee) to two weeks.

Don't wait until the visa has expired, as extensions are not granted automatically; hefty fines are levied for overstays.

🛈 Getting There & Away

AIR
Airports & Airlines

Airports in Mozambique:

Maputo International Airport (p180) Mozambique's main airport.

Vilankulo Regional flights.

Beira (p198) Regional flights.

Nampula Airport (p209) Regional flights.

Moçimboa da Praia Regional charter flights.

Pemba Airport (p223) Regional flights.

Airlines servicing Mozambique:

Coastal Aviation (safari@coastal.co.tz) Charter flights between Dar es Salaam (Tanzania) and Moçimboa da Praia, with connections to Pemba and the Quirimbas Archipelago.

Kenya Airways (www.kenya-airways.com) Nairobi (Kenya) to Pemba and Maputo.

Linhas Aéreas de Moçambique (LAM; ☑82 147, 84 147, 21-326001, 21-468800; www.lam.co.mz) The national airline. Offers flights connecting Johannesburg (South Africa) with Maputo, Vilankulo and Beira; and Dar es Salaam (Tanzania) with Pemba, Nampula and Maputo.

SAAirlink (p194) Johannesburg (South Africa) to Vilankulo, Beira, Nampula, Tete and Pemba; and Durban (South Africa) to Maputo.

South African Airways (www.flysaa.com) Johannesburg (South Africa) to Maputo and Vilankulo.

TAP Air Portugal (www.flytap.com) Lisbon (Portugal) to Maputo.

LAKE
Malawi

The MV *Chambo* ferry (Mtc300, 6½ hours between Metangula and Likoma Island; Mtc40, 1½ hours between Cóbuè and Likoma Island; and Mtc500, 12 to 13 hours between Metangula and Nkhata Bay) connects Metangula and Cóbuè twice weekly with Likoma Island (Malawi) and weekly with Nkhata Bay (Malawi). A southern route connecting Metangula with Chipoka (Malawi, Mtc550, 11 to 12 hours) via Meponda is also running. Contact the **Malawi Shipping**

Company (☎ 01-587411; www.malawitourism.com/pages/content/index.asp?PageID=164) for confirmation of prices and schedules.

The journey between Cóbuè and Likoma Island (Malawi) can also be done by local fishing boats (about US$7 one way), which wait each morning at both destinations for passengers.

There are immigration posts in Metangula and Cóbuè (and on Likoma Island and in Nkhata Bay, for Malawi). At the time of research, it was possible to get a Mozambique visa at Cóbuè (although this may soon change) but not at Metangula.

LAND
Malawi

Border Crossings

➡ **Cóbuè** On Lake Niassa.

➡ **Dedza** 85km southwest of Lilongwe.

➡ **Entre Lagos** Southwest of Cuamba.

➡ **Mandimba** Northwest of Cuamba.

➡ **Metangula** On Lake Niassa.

➡ **Milange** 120km southeast of Blantyre.

➡ **Vila Nova da Fronteira** At Malawi's southern tip.

➡ **Zóbuè** On the Tete Corridor route linking Blantyre (Malawi) and Harare (Zimbabwe); this is the busiest crossing.

To & From Blantyre

➡ Via Zóbuè: vehicles go daily from Blantyre to the border via Mwanza. Once in Mozambique (the border posts are separated by about 5km of no-man's land), chapas (converted passenger trucks or minivans) go daily to Tete (Mtc190, 1½ hours Zóbuè to Tete).

➡ Via Vila Nova da Fronteira: daily minibuses go from Blantyre to Nsanje and on to the border. Once across, there are chapas to Mutarara, and from there to Sena and on to Caia on the main north–south road.

➡ Via Melosa (about 2km from Milange town, and convenient for Quelimane and Gurúè): buses go from Blantyre via Mulanje to the border. Once across, several vehicles go daily to Mocuba (Mtc300), from where there is frequent transport south to Quelimane and north to Nampevo junction (for Gurúè) and Nampula.

➡ Entre Lagos (for Cuamba and northern Mozambique): possible with your own 4WD (allow about 1½ hours to cover the 80km from Entre Lagos to Cuamba), or by chapa (about 2½ hours between the border and Cuamba). On the Malawi side, minibuses go from the border to Liwonde. Another option is the weekly Malawi train between the border and Liwonde (currently Thursday morning from Liwonde to Nayuchi on the border, and from Nayuchi back to Liwonde that same afternoon). There is basic accommodation at Entre Lagos if you get stuck.

The closest bank is in Mecanhelas (Mozambique), about 25km away.

➡ Via Mandimba: Malawian transport goes frequently to Mangochi, where you can get minibuses to Namwera, and on to the border at Chiponde. Once in Mozambique (moto-taxis bridge the approximately 1.5km of no-man's land for Mtc50, and then vehicles take you to Mandimba town), several vehicles daily go from Mandimba to both Cuamba (three hours) and Lichinga (Mtc300).

To & From Lilongwe

The Dedza border is linked with the EN103 to/from Tete by a scenic tarmac road. From Tete, there's at least one chapa daily to Ulongwé and on to Dedza. Otherwise, go in stages from Tete via Moatize and the junction about 15km southwest of Zóbuè. Once across, it's easy to find transport for the final 85km to Lilongwe.

South Africa

Border Crossings

Giriyondo (8am to 4pm October to March, to 3pm April to September) 75km west of Massingir town, 95km from Kruger National Park's Phalaborwa Gate.

Kosi Bay (8am to 5pm) 11km south of Ponta d'Ouro.

Pafuri (8am to 4pm) 11km east of Pafuri Camp in Kruger National Park.

Ressano Garcia–Lebombo (6am to midnight) Northwest of Maputo; very busy.

To & From Durban

Luciano Luxury Coach (p180) goes between Maputo and Durban via Namaacha and Big Bend in Swaziland (US$28, nine to 10 hours) departing Maputo at 6.30am Tuesday and Friday and Durban (Pavillion Hotel, North Beach) at 6.30am Wednesday and Sunday.

To & From Kruger National Park

Neither the Pafuri nor the Giriyondo crossing is accessible via public transport. Visas should be arranged in advance. Officially you're required to have a 4WD to cross both borders, and a 4WD is essential for the Pafuri border, which crosses the Limpopo River near Mapai (for which there is a makeshift ferry during the rains). Allow two days between Pafuri and Vilankulo. The basic **Nhampfule Campsite** (☎ 84 301 1719; www.limpopopn.gov.mz; camping Mtc210) at Limpopo National Park's Mapai entry gate has hot-water showers.

Note that if you are entering/leaving South Africa via Giriyondo or Pafuri, you will be required to show proof of payment of one night's lodging within the Great Limpopo Transfrontier Park (ie either in Limpopo National Park or South Africa's Kruger National Park) to fulfil SANParks' requirement for one compulsory overnight within the transfrontier park for all visitors.

To & From Nelspruit & Johannesburg

Large 'luxury' buses do the route daily (US$25 to US$40 one way, nine to 10 hours between Maputo and Johannesburg's Park Station; US$13 to US$15 one way, four hours between Maputo and Nelspruit's Promenade Hotel). All lines also service Pretoria, with a change of buses at Park Station. It's essential to organise your Mozambique visa in advance. Tickets should also be purchased one day in advance of travel.

Cheetah Express (p180) Daily between Maputo and Nelspruit (Mtc1300 return, no one-way tickets), departing Maputo at 6am from Avenida Eduardo Mondlane next to Mundo's (p179), and departing Nelspruit at 4pm from Mediclinic, Crossings and Riverside Mall.

Greyhound (p180) Daily from Johannesburg's Park Station complex at 7.45am, and from Maputo at 7am and 7pm.

Luciano Luxury Coach (p180) Daily Monday to Saturday from Johannesburg (Hotel Oribi, 24 Bezuidenhout Ave, Troyville) at 5pm, and Sunday at 9.30am; and from Maputo daily except Saturday at 8.30pm.

Translux (p180) Operates jointly with City to City; the Translux service is generally the better of the two. Daily from Johannesburg's Park Station at 8.45am (at 7.50am for City to City); and from Maputo at 7.45am (at 7.20am for City to City).

To & From Ponta d'Ouro

The Kosi Bay border crossing is 11km south of Ponta d'Ouro along a sandy track (now 4WD but soon to be paved), and most chapas from Catembe (opposite Maputo, on Maputo Bay) pass here, before stopping at Ponta d'Ouro (Mtc50 from the border to Ponta d'Ouro). Coming from South Africa, there's a guarded car park just over the border where you can leave your vehicle in the shade for R40 per day. Most Ponta d'Ouro hotels do pick-ups from the border from about US$10 to US$15 per person (minimum two people). Allow about five hours for the drive to/from Durban.

Swaziland

Border Crossings

Goba–Mhlumeni (open 24 hours) Southwest of Maputo.

Lomahasha–Namaacha (7am-8pm) In Swaziland's extreme northeastern corner.

To & From Manzini

There are at least one or two direct chapas daily between Maputo and Manzini (Mtc370). It's about the same price and sometimes faster to take a chapa between Maputo and Lomahasha–Namaacha (Mtc70, 1½ hours), walk across the border, and then get Swaziland transport on the other side (about US$5 and three hours from the border to Manzini).

For self-drivers, the Namaacha border is notoriously slow on holiday weekends; the quieter border at Goba (Goba Fronteira), reached via a scenic, winding road from Maputo, is a good alternative. The road from Swaziland's Mananga border (open 7am to 6pm), connecting north to Ressano Garcia–Lebombo, is another option.

Tanzania

Border Crossings

For all Mozambique–Tanzania crossings it is essential to arrange your Mozambique (or Tanzania) visa in advance.

Kilambo 130km north of Moçimboa da Praia, and called Namiranga or Namoto on the Mozambique side.

Moçimboa da Praia (Mozambique) Immigration and customs for those arriving by plane or dhow.

Mtomoni Unity Bridge 2; 120km south of Songea (Tanzania).

Negomano Unity Bridge.

Palma (Mozambique) Immigration and customs for those arriving by dhow or charter flight.

To & From Masasi

The main vehicle crossing over the Rovuma is via the Unity Bridge at Negomano (7.30am to 4pm in Mozambique, 8.30am to 5pm in Tanzania), near the confluence of the Lugenda River. From Masasi, go 35km southwest along the Tunduru road to Nangomba village, from where a good 68km track leads down to Masuguru village. The bridge is 10km further at Mtambaswala. Once over, there is 160km on a bush track with fine, deep, red dust (mud during the rains, and often blocked by trucks). This track continues through low land bordering the Rovuma before climbing up to Ngapa (shown as Moçimboa do Rovuma on some maps), where there is a customs and immigration checkpoint, as well as stunning views down over the Rovuma River basin. From Ngapa to Mueda is 40km further on a reasonable dirt road (four to six hours from the bridge to Mueda, longer during the rains).

Via public transport, there's a daily chapa from Masasi to Mtambaswala (Tsh6000) each morning. On the other side, a chapa leaves Negomano by about 1pm for Mueda (Mtc500). Going in the other direction, if you arrive at Mtambaswala after the chapa for Masasi has left (it doesn't always coordinate with the vehicle arriving from Mueda), there are some basic guesthouses for sleeping.

To & From Mtwara

Vehicles go daily from 6am from Mtwara (Tanzania) to Kilambo (Tsh6000, one hour) and on to the Rovuma River, which is in theory crossed daily by the MV *Kilambo* ferry. The ferry, again in theory, takes half a dozen cars plus passengers (Tsh30,000/500 per vehicle/person). However, its passage depends on tides, rains and mechanical issues. If it is not operating, you'll need to negotiate a ride in a smaller boat or a dugout canoe (about Tsh5000, 10 minutes to over an hour, depending on water levels; dangerous during heavy rains). The border is a rough one, and it's common for touts to demand up to 10 times the 'real' price for the boat crossing. Watch your belongings, especially when getting into and out of the boats, and keep up with the crowd.

Once you're in Mozambique, several pickups go daily to the Mozambique border crossing at Namiranga, 4km further on, and from there to Palma and Moçimboa da Praia (US$13, three hours). The road on the Mozambican side is poor at the border but improves closer to Palma.

To & From Songea

One or two vehicles daily depart from Majengo C area in Songea (Tsh12,000, three to four hours) to Mtomoni village and the Unity 2 bridge. Once across, take Mozambique transport to Lichinga (Tsh30,000, five hours). Pay in stages, rather than paying the entire Tsh40,000 Songea–Lichinga fare in Songea, as is sometimes requested.

Zambia

Border Crossings

Cassacatiza (7am to 5pm) 290km northwest of Tete; main crossing.
Zumbo (7am to 5pm) At the western end of Lake Cahora Bassa.

To & From Zambia

The Cassacatiza border is a seldom used but intriguing route between Mozambique and Zambia's South Luangwa National Park for those with their own vehicles. To cross the border via public transport: chapas go daily from Tete to Matema, from where there's sporadic transport to the border (allow about three hours from Tete to the border). On the other side, there are several vehicles daily to Katete (Zambia), and then on to Lusaka or Chipata.

The border post at Zumbo is accessed with difficulty from Mozambique via Fíngoè and is of interest primarily to anglers and birdwatchers heading to the western reaches of Lake Cahora Bassa. Once at Zumbo, the only possibility for onward transport to Luangwa (Zambia) or Kanyemba (Zimbabwe) is via private charter boat. The government pontoon is not running as of this writing.

Zimbabwe

Border Crossings

Espungabera In the Chimanimani Mountains.
Machipanda On the Beira Corridor linking Harare with the sea.
Mukumbura (7am to 5pm) West of Tete.
Nyamapanda On the Tete Corridor, linking Harare with Tete and Lilongwe (Malawi).

To & From Harare

From Tete there are frequent vehicles to Changara and on to the border at Nyamapanda, where you can get transport to Harare. Through buses between Blantyre and Harare are another option.

From Chimoio you can catch a direct chapa to the border at Machipanda (Mtc80, one hour), from where you'll need to take a taxi 12km to Mutare, and then get Zimbabwean transport to Harare.

The seldom-used route via the orderly little border town of Espungabera is slow and scenic, and an interesting dry-season alternative for those with a 4WD.

Mukumbura (4WD only) is of interest mainly to anglers heading to Cahora Bassa Dam. There is no public transport on the Mozambique side.

ℹ️ Getting Around

AIR
Airlines in Mozambique

Linhas Aéreas de Moçambique (p236) The national airline, with flights linking Maputo with Inhambane, Vilankulo, Beira, Chimoio, Quelimane, Tete, Nampula, Lichinga and Pemba. Always reconfirm your ticket, and check in early. Visa cards are accepted in most offices. Advance-purchase tickets are often significantly cheaper than last-minute fares, and there are many advertised specials. Sample one-way fares and flight frequencies: Maputo to Pemba (US$200, daily), and Maputo to Vilankulo (US$150, daily), Maputo to Lichinga (US$200, five weekly).

CR Aviation (www.craviation.co.mz) Scheduled and charter flights to the Bazaruto Archipelago, Quirimbas Archipelago, Inhaca and Gorongosa National Park.

BOAT

On Lake Niassa there is twice-weekly passenger service on the MV *Chambo* between Metangula, Cóbuè, Mbueca and several other villages along the Mozambican lakeshore.

BUS

➡ Direct services connect major towns at least daily, although vehicle maintenance and driving standards leave much to be desired.

➡ A large bus is called a *machibombo,* and sometimes also an *autocarro.* While there are several larger companies, most routes are served by small, private operators.

➡ Many towns don't have central bus stations. Instead, transport usually leaves from the bus-company garage, or from the start of the road towards the destination. Long-distance transport in general, and all transport in the north, leaves early – between 3am and 7am. Mozambican transport usually leaves quickly and close to the stated departure time.

➡ There is no luggage fee for large buses. For smaller buses and *chapas* (converted passenger trucks or minivans), if your bag is large enough that it needs to be stowed on the roof, you will be charged, with the amount varying depending on distance travelled and size of the bag, and always negotiable.

➡ Where there's a choice, always take buses rather than *chapas.*

➡ The more luggage on the roof, the slower the service.

Reservations

Etrago and Nagi Trans buses should be booked a day in advance. Otherwise, showing up on the morning of travel (about an hour prior to departure) is usually enough to ensure a place.

If you are choosy about your seat (best is in front, on the shady side), get to the departure point earlier.

Routes

Sample journey fares, times and frequencies:

ROUTE	FARE (MTC)	DURATION (HR)	FREQUENCY
Maputo– Vilanculos	950	10	daily
Nampula– Pemba	500	7	daily
Maputo– Beira	1700	17-18	daily
Lichinga– Maputo	4200	2-3 days	weekly

CAR & MOTORCYCLE

➡ A South African or international driving licence is required to drive in Mozambique. Those staying longer than six months will need a Mozambican driving licence.

➡ *Gasolina* (petrol) is scarce off main roads, especially in the north. *Gasóleo* (diesel) supplies are more reliable. On bush journeys, always carry an extra jerry can and top up whenever possible, as filling stations sometimes run out.

➡ Temporary import permits (US$2) and third-party insurance (US$10 to US$15 for 30 days)

are available at most land borders, or in the nearest large town.

➡ In late 2016 Mozambique introduced *livre-trânsito* (free pass) cards. The cards – given to drivers following inspection at the border to minimise traffic-police stops – should be displayed in the front windscreen to show that the car has already been inspected.

Car Hire

➡ There are rental agencies in Maputo, Vilankulo, Beira, Nampula, Tete and Pemba, most of which take credit cards. Elsewhere, you can usually arrange something with upmarket hotels.

➡ Rates start at about US$100 per day for 4WD (US$80 for 2WD), excluding fuel.

➡ None of the major agencies offers unlimited kilometres.

➡ With the appropriate paperwork, rental cars from Mozambique can be taken into South Africa and Swaziland but not into other neighbouring countries. Most South African rental agencies don't permit their vehicles to enter Mozambique.

Insurance

➡ Private vehicles entering Mozambique must purchase third-party insurance at the border (from US$10 to US$15 for 30 days).

➡ It's also advisable to take out insurance coverage at home or (for rental vehicles) with the rental agency to cover damage to the vehicle, yourself and your possessions.

➡ Car-rental agencies in Mozambique have wildly differing policies (some offer no insurance at all, some that do may have high deductibles and most won't cover off-road driving); enquire before signing any agreements.

Road Rules

➡ Traffic in Mozambique drives on the left.

➡ Traffic already in a roundabout has the right of way.

➡ The driver and all passengers are required to wear a seat belt.

➡ It's prohibited to drive while using a mobile phone and required to drive with the vehicle's insurance certificate, and to carry a reflector vest and two hazard triangles.

➡ Speed limits (100km/h on main roads, 80km/h on approaches to towns and 60km/h or less when passing through towns) are radar enforced.

➡ Fines for speeding and other traffic infringements vary, and should always be negotiated (in a polite, friendly way), keeping in mind that official speeding fines range from Mtc1000 up to Mtc5000.

➡ Driving on the beach is illegal.

LOCAL TRANSPORT

Chapa

➺ The main form of local transport is the *chapa*, the name given to any public transport that runs within a town or between towns and isn't a bus or truck. On longer routes, your only option may be a *camião* (truck). Many have open backs, and the sun and dust can be brutal; try for a seat in the cab.

➺ *Chapas* can be hailed anywhere, and prices are fixed. Intra-city fares average Mtc5 to Mtc7. The most comfortable and coveted seat (though you'll likely pay a bit more) is in the front, next to the window.

➺ *Chapa* drivers are notorious for their unsafe driving and there are many accidents. Bus is always a better option. Long-haul *chapas* usually depart early and relatively promptly, although drivers will cruise for passengers before leaving town.

Taxi

Apart from airport arrivals, taxis don't cruise for business, so you'll need to seek them out. While a few have functioning meters, you'll usually need to negotiate a price. Town trips start at Mtc150.

TRAIN

The only passenger train regularly used by tourists is the twice-weekly slow line between Nampula and Cuamba. Vendors are at all stations, but bring extra food and drink. Second class is reasonably comfortable, and most cabins have windows that open. Third class is hot and crowded. Book the afternoon before travel.

MOZAMBIQUE GETTING AROUND

Namibia

POP 2.4 MILLION / ☎ 264

Includes ➡

Windhoek 243

Etosha National
Park 260

The Skeleton Coast ... 275

Swakopmund 277

Walvis Bay 283

Namib-Naukluft
Park 286

Best Places to Eat

➡ Leo's (p250)

➡ Purple Fig Bistro (p258)

➡ Raft (p285)

➡ Anchor @ The Jetty (p285)

➡ Sam's Giardino Hotel (p281)

Best Places to Sleep

➡ Serra Cafema Camp (p275)

➡ Sossusvlei Desert Lodge (p292)

➡ Little Kulala (p291)

➡ Hoanib Skeleton Coast Camp (p277)

➡ Erongo Wilderness Lodge (p254)

Why Go?

Namibia possesses some of the most stunning landscapes in Africa, and a trip through the country is one of the great road adventures. Natural wonders such as that mighty gash in the earth at Fish River Canyon and the wildlife utopia of Etosha National Park enthral, but it's the lonely desert roads, where mighty slabs of granite rise out of swirling sands, that will sear themselves in your mind. It's like a coffee-table book come to life as sand dunes in the world's oldest desert meet the crashing rollers along the wild Atlantic coast.

Among all this is a German legacy, evident in the cuisine and art nouveau architecture and in festivals such as Windhoek's legendary Oktoberfest. Namibia is also the headquarters of adventure activities in the region, so whether you're a dreamer or love hearing the crunch of earth under your boots, travel in Namibia will stay with you long after the desert vistas fade.

When to Go
Windhoek

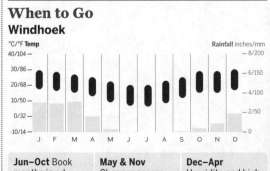

Jun–Oct Book months in advance. Temperatures soar by September.

May & Nov Cheaper accommodation. Heavy rains sometimes in November, May is mild.

Dec–Apr Humidity and high temperatures can make days unpleasant. Prices are low.

WINDHOEK

POP 325,860

If Namibia is Africa for beginners, then Windhoek is very much its capital in more than name only. It's the sort of place that divides travellers, with those who love it for the respite it offers from the rigours of life on the African road facing off against those who find it a little too 'Western' for their African tastes. And they're both right: Windhoek is a modern, well-groomed city where office workers lounge around Zoo Park at lunchtime, tourists funnel through Post St Mall admiring African curios and taxis whizz around honking at potential customers. Neobaroque cathedral spires, as well as a few seemingly misplaced German castles, punctuate the skyline, and complement the steel-and-glass high-rises.

Such apparent incongruities aside, Windhoek makes a great place to begin or break a journey through Namibia or rest at journey's end. The accommodation choices, food variety, cultural sights, shopping and African urban buzz give it an edge not found anywhere else in Namibia.

◉ Sights

Zoo Park
PARK

(Map p248; ◷ dawn-dusk) FREE Although this leafy park served as a public zoo until 1962, today it functions primarily as a picnic spot and shady retreat for lunching office workers. Five thousand years ago the park was the site of a Stone Age elephant hunt, as evidenced by the remains of two elephants and several quartz tools found here in the early 1960s. This prehistoric event is honoured by the park's prominent **elephant column**, designed by Namibian sculptor Dörthe Berner. A rather anachronous mate to the elephant column is the **Kriegerdenkmal**, topped by a rather frightening golden imperial eagle, which was dedicated in 1987 to the memory of German Schutztruppe soldiers who died in the Nama wars of 1893–94.

★ Christuskirche
CHURCH

(Map p248; Fidel Castro St) FREE Windhoek's best-recognised landmark, and something of an unofficial symbol of the city, this German Lutheran church stands on a traffic island and lords it over the city centre. An unusual building, it was constructed from local sandstone in 1907 and designed by architect Gottlieb Redecker in conflicting neo-Gothic and art nouveau styles. The resulting design looks strangely edible, and is somewhat reminiscent of a whimsical gingerbread house. The altarpiece, the *Resurrection of Lazarus*, is a copy of the renowned work by Rubens.

Daan Viljoen Game Park
WILDLIFE RESERVE

(✆061-232393; per person/vehicle N$40/10; ◷sunrise-sunset) This beautiful wildlife park sits in the Khomas Hochland about 18km west of Windhoek. You can walk to your heart's content through lovely wildlife-rich desert hills, and spot gemsboks, kudus, mountain zebras, springboks, hartebeests, warthogs and elands. Daan Viljoen is also known for its birdlife and over 200 species have been recorded, including the rare green-backed heron and pin-tailed whydah. Daan Viljoen's hills are covered with open thorn-scrub vegetation that allows excellent wildlife viewing, and three walking tracks have been laid out. There's also an on-site luxury **lodge** (✆061-232393; www.sunkarros.com; camping N$260, s/d chalets from N$1774/2818; @).

Heinitzburg Castle
CASTLE

(Map p248; 22 Heinitzburg St) FREE Uphill from Robert Mugabe Ave are the three Windhoek 'castles', including the 1914 Heinitzburg, which today houses a hotel (p249) and fine restaurant (p250). The other castles, Schwerinsburg and Sanderburg, are nearby.

Independence Memorial Museum
MUSEUM

(Map p248; ✆061-302236; www.museums.com. na; Robert Mugabe Ave; ◷9am-5pm Mon-Fri, 10am-5pm Sat & Sun) FREE Opened in 2014, this museum is dedicated to the country's anticolonial and independence struggle. The first floor tells the story of Namibia under colonial rule, with the next floor up shifting gears to the resistance movement, while the top floor is dominated by the road to independence. Don't miss taking the glass elevator up the outside of the building for great views out over Windhoek. There's a statue of founding president Sam Nujoma outside.

National Museum of Namibia
MUSEUM

(Map p248; ✆061-302230; www.museums.com. na; Robert Mugabe Ave; ◷9am-6pm Mon-Fri, 3-6pm Sat & Sun) FREE The excellent display on Namibia's independence at the country's historical museum provides some enlightening context to the struggles of this young country. But probably the most interesting part of the museum is the rock-art display, with some great reproductions; it would definitely be worth a nose around before heading to see rock art at the Brandberg or Twyfelfontein. It's housed in Windhoek's

Namibia Highlights

1 Skeleton Coast (p275) and **Kaokoveld** (p272) Getting off the beaten track (and the tarred road) in the true African wilderness.

2 Fish River Canyon (p297) Hiking through one of Africa's greatest natural wonders.

3 Etosha National Park (p260) Crouching by a water hole in one of the world's premier wildlife venues.

4 Waterberg Plateau (p257) Hiking to the top of the plateau for breathtaking views, keeping an eye out for rare sable and roan antelopes.

5 Sossusvlei (p289) Watching the sunrise from the fiery-coloured dunes.

6 Swakopmund (p277) Getting your adrenaline fix at the extreme-sports capital of Namibia.

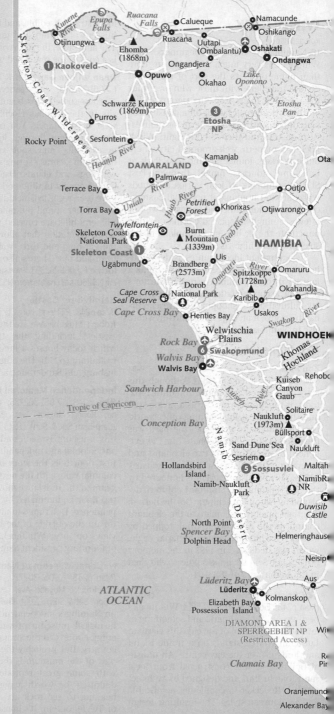

oldest surviving building, dating from the early 1890s; it originally served as the headquarters of the German Schutztruppe.

Owela Museum
MUSEUM

(State Museum; Map p248; www.museums.com.na; 4 Robert Mugabe Ave; ⊙9am-6pm Mon-Fri, 3-6pm Sat & Sun) FREE Part of the National Museum of Namibia. About 600m from the main building, exhibits at the Owela Museum focus on Namibia's natural and cultural history; note it may sometimes close early.

🎎 Festivals & Events

Bank Windhoek Arts Festival
ART

(www.bankwindhoek.com.na; ⊙Feb-Sep) This is the largest arts festival in the country, with events running from February to September.

Mbapira/Enjando Street Festival
CARNIVAL

(⊙Mar) Held around the city centre, featuring colourful gatherings of dancers, musicians and people in ethnic dress.

Windhoek Karneval (WIKA)
CARNIVAL

(windhoek-karneval.org/en; ⊙Apr) Held in late April, this German-style carnival features music performances, a masked ball and a parade down Independence Ave.

Oktoberfest
BEER

(www.windhoekoktoberfest.com; ⊙Oct) True to its partially Teutonic background, Windhoek stages this festival towards the end of October – beer-lovers should not miss it.

👉 Tours

★Cardboard Box Travel Shop
TOURS

(Map p248; ✍061-256580; www.namibian.org; 15 Bismark St) Associated with the backpacker hostel of the same name, this recommended travel agency can arrange both budget and upmarket bookings all over the country. Great website, too.

★Chameleon Safaris
SAFARI

(Map p248; ✍061-247668; www.chameleonsafaris.com; Voight St) This travel agency, attached to the backpacker hostel of the same name, is recommended for all types of safaris around the country.

NAMIBIA WINDHOEK

KATUTURA – A PERMANENT PLACE?

In 1912, during the days of the South African mandate – and apartheid – the Windhoek town council set aside two 'locations', which were open to settlement by black Africans working in the city: the Main Location, which was west of the city centre, and Klein Windhoek, to the east. The following year, people were forcibly relocated to these areas, which effectively became haphazard settlements. In the early 1930s, streets were laid out in the Main Location and the area was divided into regions. Each subdivision within these regions was assigned to an ethnic group and referred to by that name (eg Herero, Nama, Owambo, Damara), followed by a soulless numerical reference.

In the 1950s the Windhoek municipal council, with encouragement from the South African government (which regarded Namibia as a province of South Africa), decided to 'take back' Klein Windhoek and consolidate all 'location' residents into a single settlement northwest of the main city. There was strong opposition to the move, and in early December 1959 a group of Herero women launched a protest march and boycott against the city government. On 10 December unrest escalated into a confrontation with the police, resulting in 11 deaths and 44 serious injuries. Frightened, the roughly 4000 residents of the Main Location submitted and moved to the new settlement, which was ultimately named 'Katutura'. In Herero the name means 'we have no permanent place', though it can also be translated as 'the place we do not want to settle'.

Today in independent Namibia, Katutura is a vibrant Windhoek suburb – Namibia's Soweto – where poverty and affluence brush elbows. The town council has extended municipal water, power and telephone services to most areas of Katutura, and has also established the colourful and perpetually busy Soweto Market, where traders sell just about anything imaginable. Unlike its South African counterparts, Katutura is relatively safe by day, assuming you can find a trustworthy local who can act as a guide.

The tourist office can book township tours but even better is **Katu Tours** (✍081 303 2856; www.katutours.com; tours per person N$450), which offers guided tours by bike. You get a good taste of township life and the chance to meet plenty of locals; it also includes dropping into Penduka, where local women produce a range of handicrafts and textiles. Tours depart at 8am from Katutura and take 3½ hours.

Windhoek

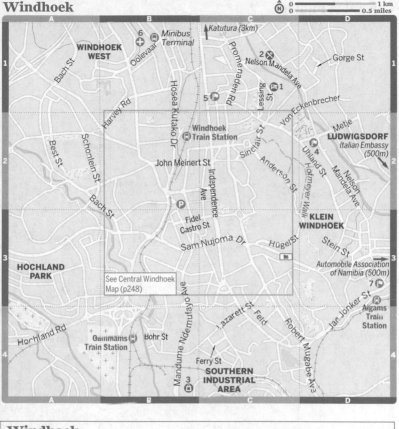

0 ___ 1 km
0 ___ 0.5 miles

Windhoek

🛏 Sleeping
1 Olive Grove C1

🍴 Eating
2 Joe's Beerhouse C1

🍷 Drinking & Nightlife
Joe's Beer House .... (see 2)

🛍 Shopping
3 Safari Den B4

ℹ Information
4 Botswanan Embassy D2
5 French Embassy C1
6 Rhino Park Private Hospital B1
7 South African High Commission D3

🛏 Sleeping

★ **Cardboard Box Backpackers**   HOSTEL $
(Map p248; ☎ 061-228994; www.cardboardbox. com.na; 15 Johann Albrecht St; camping/dm N$90/150, r/tr/q N$450/550/660; @ 🛜 🏊) Hostels are hard to come by in this country but 'The Box' has been doing it for years, with a rep as one of Windhoek's better backpackers. It has a fully stocked bar and swimming pool to cool off in, and travellers have a tough time leaving. Rates include free

coffee and pancakes in the morning, and there are free pick-ups from the Intercape bus stop.

★ **Guesthouse Tamboti**   GUESTHOUSE $
(Map p248; ☎ 061-235515; www.guesthouse-tam boti.com; 9 Kerby St; s/d from N$560/820; ❄ @ 🛜 🏊) Hands-down our favourite place in Windhoek to stay, Tamboti is very well priced, has a great vibe and terrific hosts who will go out of their way to ensure you

Central Windhoek

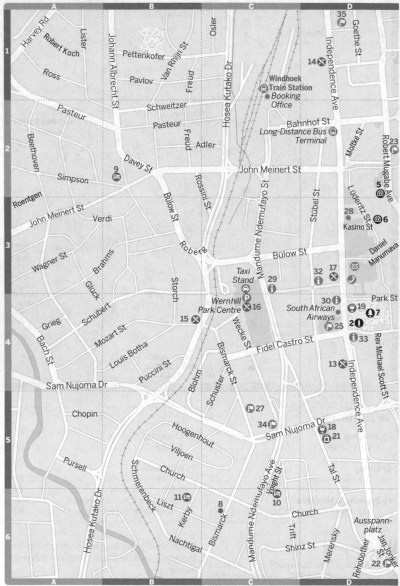

are comfortable (such as driving you to the airport if you have a flight to catch). The rooms here are spacious and well set up – it's situated on a small hill just above the city centre. Book ahead as it's popular.

Belvedere Boutique Hotel BOUTIQUE HOTEL **$$**
(☏ 061-258867; www.belvedere-boutiqueho tel.com; 76 Dr Kwame Nkrumah St; r/ste from N$1650/1875; ❋☏⎙) Highly recommended by travellers, the Belvedere has classically

Christuskirche

styled rooms, quiet grounds and professional service. It's the sort of place that will appeal equally to business travellers and those seeking calm in the big city before heading out into the Namibian wilds.

★ **Hotel Heinitzburg** HOTEL **$$$**
(Map p248; ☎061-249597; www.heinitzburg.com; 22 Heinitzburg St; s/d from N$2137/3154; ❋ @ ⦿) Inside Heinitzburg Castle, which was commissioned in 1914 by Count von Schwerin for his fiancée, Margarethe von Heinitz, Hotel Heinitzburg is a member of the prestigious Relais & Chateaux hotel group, and far and above the most personable upmarket accommodation in Windhoek. Rooms have been updated for the 21st century with satellite TV and air-con.

★ **Olive Grove** BOUTIQUE HOTEL **$$$**
(Map p247; ☎061-302640; www.olivegrove-namibia. com; 20 Promenaden St; s/d standard N$995/1610, luxury N$1319/2370; ❋ @ ⦿) Refined elegance is the order of the day at this boutique hotel in Klein Windhoek, which features 10 individually decorated rooms and two suites awash in fine linens, handcrafted furniture and all-around good taste. Guests in need of some pampering can indulge in a massage, or warm their toes on a cold Windhoek night in front of the crackling fire.

🍴 Eating

Namibia's multicultural capital provides a range of restaurants. It's worth stretching your budget and indulging in the gourmand lifestyle while you're in town. Be advised that reservations are a very good idea on Friday and Saturday nights.

Windhoek is a grocery paradise for self-caterers. The big names are **Pick & Pay** (Map p248; Wernhill Park Centre; ☻9am-6pm Mon-Fri, to 2pm Sat, to 1pm Sun) and **Checkers** (Map p248; Gustav Voigts Centre; ☻8am-7pm Mon-Fri, to 6pm Sat, to 3pm Sun).

Namibia Crafts Cafe CAFE **$**
(Map p248; Old Breweries Complex, cnr Garten & Tal Sts; mains N$35-90; ☻9am-6pm Mon-Fri, to 3.30pm Sat & Sun) This cafe-restaurant-bar is a great spot to perch yourself above Tal St, checking out the local action and taking in the breeze from the outside deck. The extensive drinks menu includes health shakes and freshly squeezed juices. Meals in the way of salads, large pitas, cold-meat platters, open sandwiches and healthy (or just filling) breakfasts hit the spot.

★ **Stellenbosch Wine Bar & Bistro** BISTRO **$$**
(☎061-309141; www.thestellenboschwinebar.com; 320 Sam Nujoma Dr; mains N$81-169; ☻noon-10pm) When well-to-do locals want an enjoyable night out with the guarantee of good

NAMIBIA WINDHOEK

Central Windhoek

◎ Top Sights
1 Christuskirche...................................E4

◎ Sights
2 Elephant Column D4
3 Heinitzburg Castle F6
4 Independence Memorial Museum........E4
5 National Museum of Namibia D2
6 Owela Museum D3
7 Zoo Park...D4

◎ Activities, Courses & Tours
8 Cardboard Box Travel Shop.................C6
Chameleon Safaris ....(see 10)

◎ Sleeping
9 Cardboard Box Backpackers B2
10 Chameleon Backpackers Lodge &
Guesthouse C6
11 Guesthouse Tamboti............................B6
12 Hotel Heinitzburg.................................F6

◎ Eating
13 Checkers...D4
14 La Marmite..D1
Leo's ....(see 12)
Namibia Crafts Cafe ....(see 21)
15 Nice...B4
16 Pick & Pay...C4

17 Restaurant Gathemann........................D3

◎ Drinking & Nightlife
18 Boiler Room @ The Warehouse
Theatre..D5
19 Café Balalaika D4
20 Wine Bar E5

◎ Shopping
Namibia Crafts Centre..................(see 21)
21 Old Breweries Craft Market D5

◎ Information
22 Angolan Embassy..................................D6
23 British High Commission D2
24 Finnish Embassy E2
25 German Embassy..................................D4
26 Kenyan High Commission.....................E1
27 Malawian Embassy C5
28 Ministry of Home Affairs D3
29 Namibia Tourism Board C3
30 Namibia Wildlife Resorts D4
31 US Embassy...E6
32 Windhoek Information & Publicity
Office (Branch Office).........................D3
33 Windhoek Information & Publicity
Office (Main Office)............................D4
34 Zambian High Commission C5
35 Zimbabwean Embassy D1

food, this is their number one pick. With a classy outdoor-indoor setting and thoughtfully conceived international food – beef burger with camembert, Bangladeshi lamb curry, crispy pork belly, baked vanilla cheesecake – and excellent service, we can't think of a single good reason not to join them.

La Marmite   AFRICAN $$
(Map p248; ☑061-240306; 383 Independence Ave; mains N$100; ◎noon-2pm & 6-10pm) Commanding a veritable legion of devoted followers, this humble West African eatery deserves its long-garnered popularity. Here you can sample wonderful North and West African cuisine, including Algerian, Senegalese, Ivorian, Cameroonian (try the curry) and Nigerian dishes, all of which are prepared with the finesse of the finest French haute cuisine. The jolof rice is particularly good.

Nice   INTERNATIONAL $$
(Map p248; ☑061-300710; cnr Mozart St & Hosea Kutako Dr; mains N$65-130; ◎noon-2.30pm Mon-Fri, 6-9pm daily) The Namibian Institute of Culinary Education – or 'Nice' for short – operates this wonderfully conceived 'living classroom' where apprentice chefs can field test their cooking skills. Spanning sev-

eral indoor rooms and a beautiful outdoor courtyard, the restaurant itself is more akin to a stylish gallery (think white tablecloths and clinking wine glasses too). The menu is short and targeted (seafood and game meats feature regularly), and service is very good.

★Leo's   INTERNATIONAL $$$
(Map p248; ☑061-249597; www.heinitzburg.com; 22 Heinitzburg St; mains N$250; ◎noon-3pm & 6.30-9pm) Leo's takes its regal setting in Heinitzburg Castle to heart by welcoming diners into a banquet hall that previously served the likes of royalty. The formal settings of bone china and polished crystal glassware are almost as extravagant as the food itself, which spans cuisines and continents, land and sea.

★Restaurant Gathemann   NAMIBIAN $$$
(Map p248; ☑061-223853; 179 Independence Ave; mains N$90-250; ◎noon-10pm) Located in a prominent colonial building overlooking Independence Ave, this splash-out spot serves gourmet Namibian cuisine that fully utilises the country's unique list of ingredients. From Kalahari truffles and Owamboland legumes to tender cuts of game meat and Walvis Bay oysters, Restaurant Gathemann satisfies the pickiest of appetites.

🍷 Drinking & Nightlife

★ Boiler Room @ The Warehouse Theatre   BAR
(Map p248; ☑061-402253; www.warehousetheatre. com.na; 48 Tal St; ⊗9pm-late) From after-work drinks to live music and a crowd that likes to dance, the Boiler Room at the Warehouse is one of the coolest and most versatile places in town – the latter quality makes us think it might just last the distance.

★ Joe's Beer House   PUB
(Map p247; ☑061-232457; www.joesbeerhouse. com; 160 Nelson Mandela Ave; ⊗noon-11pm) True to its moniker, Joe's stocks a wide assortment of Namibian and German beers, and you can count on prolonged drinking here until early in the morning. It's the favoured drinking hole of Afrikaners and something of a Windhoek institution.

Wine Bar   WINE BAR
(Map p248; ☑061-226514; www.thewinebar shop.com; 3 Garten St; ⊗4-10.30pm Mon-Thu, 4-11.30pm Fri, 5-10.30pm Sat) This bar is in a lovely historic mansion that actually used to store the town's water supply, but now houses the city's premium wine selection. Staff here have an excellent knowledge of their products, pairing an admirable South African wine selection with Mediterranean-style tapas and small snacks. It's a beautiful spot for a glass of wine and a fiery African sunset. There's a wine shop here too.

Café Balalaika   BAR
(Map p248; ☑061-223479; Zoo Park, Independence Ave; ⊗9am-late) This spot, cafe by day, bar by night, features a terrace with the capital's largest rubber tree. There's live music and karaoke, and a cool bar scene with some great beer on tap.

🛍 Shopping

The handicrafts sold in Post St Mall are largely imported from neighbouring countries, though there is still an excellent selection of woodcarvings, baskets and other African curios on offer. You're going to have to bargain hard if you want to secure a good price, though maintain your cool and always flash a smile – you'll win out with politeness in the end! Another spot with a good range of curios is along Fidel Castro St, near the corner of Independence Ave, snaking up the hill towards Christuskirche.

Mall culture is alive and well in Windhoek, and you'll find them scattered throughout the city centre and out in the 'burbs. Most of the stores are South African standards, which generally offer high-quality goods at a fraction of the price back home. Katutura's **Soweto Market** is more reminiscent of a traditional African market, though it's best to visit either with a local or as part of an organised tour.

You can find gear for 4WD expeditions at **Safari Den** (Map p247; ☑061-2909294; www. agra.com.na/safari-den/; 20 Bessemer St; ⊗9am-5pm Mon-Fri, to 2pm Sat, to noon Sun).

★ Namibia Crafts Centre   ARTS & CRAFTS
(Map p248; ☑061-242222; Old Breweries Craft Market, 40 Tal St; ⊗9am-5.30pm Mon-Fri, to 3.30pm Sat & Sun) This place is an outlet for heaps of wonderful Namibian inspiration – leatherwork, basketry, pottery, jewellery, needlework, hand-painted textiles and other material arts – and the artist and origin of each piece is documented.

★ Penduka   ARTS & CRAFTS
(☑061-257210; www.penduka.com; Goreangab Dam; ⊗8am-5pm) Penduka, which means 'wake up', operates a nonprofit women's needlework project at Goreangab Dam, 8km northwest of the city centre. You can purchase needlework, baskets, carvings and fabric creations for fair prices and be assured that all proceeds go to the producers. Ask about their places to stay as an alternative to the city's hotels.

Old Breweries Craft Market   ARTS & CRAFTS
(Map p248; cnr Garten & Tal Sts; ⊗9am-5pm Mon-Fri, to 2pm Sat) This hive of tourist shopping euphoria contains a heap of small and large shops with a range of African arts and crafts on offer. A couple of our favourite shops are **Woven Arts of Africa**, with some wonderfully fine weavings in the form of wall hangings and rugs; and **ArtiSan**, a small, poky shop with genuine Bushmen crafts.

ℹ Information

DANGERS & ANNOYANCES

Central Windhoek is quite relaxed and hassle free. As long as you stay alert, walk with confidence, keep a hand on your wallet and avoid wearing anything too flashy, you should encounter nothing worse than a few persistent touts and the odd con artist.

However, you do need to be especially wary when walking with any kind of bag, particularly on backstreets. Most importantly, don't use bumbags or carry swanky camera or video totes – they're all prime targets.

NAMIBIA WINDHOEK

One popular con is for would-be-thieves to play on the conscience of white tourists and get their attention by posing the question, 'Why won't you talk to a black man?' Ignore this and keep walking. As an extra precaution, always travel by taxi at night, even in the wealthy suburbs. The streets in Windhoek are ominously quiet once the sun goes down, which sadly means that foreign tourists quickly become easy targets.

The most likely annoyance for travellers is petty theft, which more often than not occurs at budget hotels and hostels around the city. As a general rule, you should take advantage of the hotel safe, and never leave your valuables out in the open.

If you're driving, avoid parking on the street, and never leave anything of value visible in your vehicle. Also, never leave your car doors un-locked, even if you're still in the car: a common ploy is for someone to distract you while some-one else opens one of the other doors, grabs a bag and does a runner.

During the day, the safest and most conven-ient parking is the underground lot beneath the Wernhill Park Centre. At night, you should stay at accommodation that provides off-street secure parking.

The township of Katutura and the northwest-ern industrial suburbs of Goreangab, Wanaheda and Hakahana are not as dangerous as their counterparts in South Africa, and are reasonably safe during the daytime. However, if you do visit these neighbourhoods, it's best to either go with a local contact or as part of an organised tour.

MEDICAL SERVICES

Mediclinic Windhoek (☑ 061-4331000; Helio-door St, Eros; ☺ 24hr) Emergency centre and a range of medical services.

Rhino Park Private Hospital (Map p247; ☑ 061-225434, 061-375000; www.hospital.com.na; Sauer St) Provides excellent care and service, but patients must pay up front.

POST

The modern **main post office** (Map p248; Independence Ave; ☺ 8am-4.30pm Mon-Fri, to 11.30am Sat) can readily handle overseas post. It also has telephone boxes in the lobby, and next door is the **Telecommunications Office** (Map p248; Independence Ave; ☺ 8am-4.30pm Mon-Fri, to 11.30am Sat), where you can make international calls and send or receive faxes.

TOURIST INFORMATION

Namibia Tourism Board (Map p248; ☑ 061-2906000; www.namibiatourism.com.na; 1st fl, Channel Life Towers, 39 Post St Mall; ☺ 8am-1pm & 2-5pm Mon-Fri, to 1pm Sat & Sun) The national tourist office can provide information from all over the country.

Namibia Wildlife Resorts (NWR; Map p248; ☑ 061-2857200; www.nwr.com.na; Independ-ence Ave) Books national park accommodation and hikes.

Windhoek Information & Publicity Office (Main Office) (Map p248; ☑ 061-2902596, 061-2902092; www.cityofwindhoek.org.na; Independence Ave; ☺ 7.30am-4.30pm) The friendly staff at this office answer questions and distribute local publications and leaflets, includ-ing *What's On in Windhoek* and useful city maps. There's another **branch** (Map p248; Post St Mall; ☺ 7.30am-noon & 1-4.30pm) that is open the same hours but closes from noon to 1pm.

❶ Getting There & Away

AIR

Chief Hosea Kutako International Airport (WDH; ☑ 061-2996602; www.airports.com.na), which is about 40km east of the city centre, serves most international flights into and out of Windhoek. **Air Namibia** (☑ 061-2996600, 061-2996333; www.airnamibia.com.na; Chief Hosea Kutako International Airport) operates flights daily between Windhoek and Cape Town and Johannesburg, as well as daily flights to and from Frankfurt. Direct services to Amsterdam are also due to begin. Several airlines including Air Namibia also offer international services to and from Maun, Botswana, and Victoria Falls, Zimbabwe.

Eros Airport (ERS; ☑ 061-2955500; www.airports.com.na), immediately south of the city centre, serves most domestic flights into and out of Windhoek. Air Namibia offers around three weekly flights to and from Katima Mulilo, Ondan-gwa, Rundu and Swakopmund/Walvis Bay.

Coming from Windhoek, make sure the taxi driver knows which airport you are going to.

BUS

From the main long-distance **bus terminal** (Map p248; cnr Independence Ave & Bahnhof Sts), the **Intercape Mainliner** (☑ 061-227847; www.intercape.co.za) runs to and from Cape Town, Johannesburg, Victoria Falls and Swakopmund, serving a variety of local destinations along the way. Tickets can be purchased either though your accommodation, from the Intercape Main-liner office at the bus terminal or online – given the popularity of these routes, advance reserva-tions are recommended.

There are some useful shuttle services out to Swakopmund and Walvis Bay such as the **Town Hoppers** (☑ 081 210 3062, 064-407223; www.namibiashuttle.com), departing daily at 2pm (N\$270, 4½ hours) and returning in the morning to Windhoek.

Local combis (minibuses) leave when full from the Rhino Park petrol station (Map p247) in Ka-tutura (get there very early in the morning), and can get you to most urban centres in central and southern Namibia. For northern destinations such as Tsumeb, Grootfontein and Rundu, you need to go to the local minibus station opposite the hospital on Independence Ave, Katutura.

Generally, combi routes do not serve the vast majority of Namibia's tourist destinations, which are located well beyond major population centres. Still, they're a fine way to travel if you want to visit some of the country's smaller towns and cities, and it's great fun to roll up your sleeves and jump into the bus with the locals.

TRAIN

Windhoek train station has a **booking office** (Map p248; ☑ 061-2982175; ⊙7.30am-4pm Mon-Fri), where you are able to reserve seats on any of the country's public rail lines. Routes are varied, and include overnight trains to Keetmanshoop, Tsumeb and Swakopmund, though irregular schedules, lengthy travel times and far better bus connections make train travel of little interest for the majority of overseas travellers.

ⓘ Getting Around

Collective taxis from the main ranks at Wernhill Park Centre follow set routes to Khomasdal and Katutura, and if your destination is along the way, you'll pay around N$10 to N$25. With taxis from the main bus terminals or by radio dispatch, fares are either metered or are calculated on a per-kilometre basis, but you may be able to negotiate a set fare per journey. Plan on N$70 anywhere around the city.

If you're arriving at Chief Hosea Kutako International Airport, taxis typically wait outside the arrivals area. It's a long drive into the city, so you can expect to pay anywhere from N$350 to N$400 depending on your destination. For Eros Airport, fares are much more modest at around N$70. In the city there are always reliable taxis that hang around the tourist office on Independence Ave. If you flag one down off the streets, just be aware there are plenty of cowboys around and often not much English is spoken.

NORTH-CENTRAL NAMIBIA

The crown jewel in Namibia's rich treasure trove of protected areas, Etosha dominates the tourism circuit in North-Central Namibia. However, there are plenty of worthwhile opportunities here for hiking and exploring, and there's a good chance that the tourist crowds will be elsewhere. If you have the time to spare, don't overlook the region's other highlights, which run the gamut from lofty plateaus and art-laden caves to hulking meteorites and dino footprints.

North to Etosha

The immaculate B1 heads north from Windhoek, and provides access to Outjo as well as Tsumeb and Grootfontein. Prominent towns in their own right, together they serve as the launching point for excursions into nearby Etosha National Park. While it's very tempting to strike north with safari fever, it's definitely worth slowing down and taking a bit of time to explore the quirky sights of this comparatively untouristed section of North-Central Namibia.

Erongo Mountains (Erongoberg)

The volcanic Erongo Mountains, often referred to as the Erongoberg, rise as a 2216m massif north of Karibib and Usakos. Among the most beautiful and accessible of Namibia's mountain areas, the Erongo range is best known for its caves and rock art, particularly the 50m-deep Phillips Cave.

Black rhinos and the rare black-nosed impala have been released into the Erongo Conservancy, a 30-farm area in the heart of the range, although both can be difficult to spot. For more information on the rhino, contact the **Erongo Mountain Rhino Sanctuary Trust** (EMRST; www.foerderverein-emrst.de).

North of Ameib, the D1935 skirts the Erongo Mountains before heading north into Damaraland. Alternatively, you can head east towards Omaruru on the D1937. This route virtually encircles the Erongo massif and provides access to minor 4WD roads into the heart of the mountains.

WORTH A TRIP

HARNAS

Harnas Wildlife Foundation & Guest Farm (☑ 081 140 3322, 061-228545; www.harnas.org; camping N$270, s/d igloos N$1520/2500, s/d cottages N$1900/3100, self-catering units from N$1800; ⊙6am-6pm) is a rural development project that likens itself to Noah's Ark. Here you can see wildlife close up, including rescued cheetahs, leopards and lions. A wide range of accommodation is available, including options for full board, and there are plenty of activities here to keep you amused for a couple of days – kids will love it. It's 300km northeast of Windhoek via Gobabis

Phillips Cave CAVE

(day permit N$50) This cave, 3km off the road, contains the famous humpbacked white elephant painting. Superimposed on the elephant is a large humpbacked antelope (perhaps an eland), and around it frolic ostriches and giraffes. The Ameib paintings were brought to attention in the book *Phillips Cave* by prehistorian Abbè Breuil, but his speculations about their Mediterranean origins have now been discounted. The site is open to day hikers via **Ameib Gästehaus** (☑ 081 857 4639; www.ameib.com; camping N$150, s/d from N$750/1400; ✇).

Erongo Plateau Camp CAMPGROUND $

(☑064-570837; www.erongo.iway.na/camp/camp. html; camping N$120) This appealing campsite has four sites with fine views over the plains and mountains. Sites have hot and cold showers, toilets, fireplaces (firewood costs N$25 a bundle) and a tap. Hiking trails and excursions to nearby rock-art sites are highlights.

★**Erongo Wilderness Lodge** LODGE $$$

(☑ 061-239199, 064-570537; www.erongowilderness-namibia.com; tented bungalows with full board s/d from N$2975/5000; ✦@✇) This highly acclaimed wilderness retreat combines spectacular mountain scenery, wildlife viewing, birdwatching and environmentally sensitive architecture to create one of Namibia's most memorable lodges. Accommodation is in one of 10 tented bungalows, which are built on wooden stilts among towering granite pillars crawling with rock hyrax. The restaurant overlooks a water hole where you might see kudus or genets.

Camp Mara CAMPGROUND, GUESTHOUSE $$

(☑064-571190; www.campmara.com; camping N$150, s/d with half board N$1025/1750) This lovely spot by a (usually dry) riverbed has shady, well-tended campsites, as well as eclectic but extremely comfortable rooms with whitewashed walls and creative use of wood in the decor. Activities include day tours into the mountains and Bushman activities.

Omaruru

POP 6300 / ☑064

Omaruru's dry and dusty setting beside the shady Omaruru riverbed lends it a real outback feel and it sits in the heart of some interesting country between Erongo and Okonjima. The town has a growing reputation as an arts-and-crafts centre and in recent years has become home to the **Artist Trail** (www.facebook.com/omaruruartisttrail; ☺Sep), an annual arts event; you can pick up a free copy of the program of events around town.

The town itself is a welcoming little oasis with some great accommodation options, good food and one of the very few wineries in the country – there are few experiences as surreal as enjoying a platter of meats and cheeses under trees while wine tasting in the Namibian outback.

With your own vehicle, the paved C33 passes through Omaruru, and provides the quickest route between Swakopmund and Etosha.

Kristall Kellerei Winery WINERY

(☑064-570083; www.kristallkellerei.com; ☺8am-4.30pm Mon-Fri, to 12.30pm Sat) One of the very few wineries in Namibia, this is a lovely spot to come for lunch. In the afternoon you can enjoy light meals – cheese and cold-meat platters – while tasting their wines and other products, and take a tour of the gardens. Apart from schnapps, the winery produces Colombard, a white wine, and Paradise Flycatcher, a red blend of ruby cabernet, cabernet sauvignon and Tinta Barocca. The winery is 4km east of Omaruru on the D2328.

Central Hotel Omaruru HOTEL $

(☑064-570030; www.centralhotelomaruru.com; Wilhelm Zeraua St; s/d from N$600/900; ✦✇) This place is the town's focal point for eating and drinking, and has rondavels in the huge garden – they are simple concrete setups with small beds, clean linen and good bathrooms. The dining room may well be the only show in town in the evening for dinner. Fortunately, the standard of food is pretty good for a remote pub – there are German favourites plus local game dishes (mains N$80).

River Guesthouse GUESTHOUSE $$

(☑064-570274; www.river-guesthouse.com; 134 Dr I Scheepers St; campsites N$120, s/d/f N$530/830/1050; ☏✇) The camping here is the best in town, with some great shady trees to pitch a tent under and excellent facilities including fireplaces and power outlets. You may just have the family dogs keeping you company as well. The rooms are tidy and comfortable, and surround a shady courtyard well set up for relaxing.

Omaruru Souvenirs & Kaffestube CAFE, SOUVENIRS $

(☑064-570230; Wilhelm Zeraua St; meals N$20-55) The building housing this intimate cafe dates from 1907. This place is a good choice for a strong cup of coffee and traditional German baked goods, as well as for a cold pint of Hansa and some pub grub in the outdoor beer garden. The pies are especially good.

★ **Main Street Cafe** CAFE $$
(📞064-570303; Wilhelm Zeraua St; mains from N$35; ⏰8am-3pm; 🐾) Quiche, hazelnut cheesecake, white-wood furniture...what's not to like about this fine little lunch and breakfast spot that makes a priority of fresh ingredients and friendly service? Oh, and there's great coffee, art on the walls, free wi-fi and so much more.

Erindi Private Game Reserve

📄 064

It may lack the scale of Etosha National Park, but many travellers rank **Erindi** (📞081 145 0000, 064-570800; www.erindi.com) as their most memorable wildlife-watching experience in Namibia. With over 700 sq km of savannah grasslands and rocky mountains, Erindi lacks the zoolike feel of many smaller private reserves in the country and lacks for nothing when it comes to wildlife – you can reliably expect to see elephants and giraffes, with lions, leopards, cheetahs, African wild dogs and black rhinos all reasonable possibilities. Night drives, too, open up a whole new world of nocturnal species. Throw in guided bush walks, visits to a San village and rock-art excursions, and it's not difficult to see why Erindi is fast attracting a growing army of devotees and return visitors.

Erindi lies west of Omaruru, northwest of Okahandja and southwest of Otjiwarongo. There are four entrance gates. To reach the main gate, travel 48km north of Okahandja or 124km south of Otjiwarongo along the B1, then turn west onto the D2414, a decent gravel road, for 40km.

★ **Camp Elephant** CAMPGROUND, CHALET $$$
(📞083 333 1111; www.erindi.com; camping per site N$712, s/d chalets N$1095/2190) In the heart of Erindi, Camp Elephant has 15 excellent self-catering chalets that overlook a water hole that's floodlit at night. The 30 campsites have some lovely greenery and plenty of shade, not to mention good facilities.

★ **Old Traders Lodge** LODGE $$$
(📞083 330 1111; www.erindi.com; s with half board N$3090-4090, d with half board N$5380-7180; 🐾🏊) Erindi's main lodge has 48 luxury rooms that combine the safari feel (thatched roofs and earth tones) with classic wood-and-four-poster-bed interiors. It's never pretentious, and although it can get a little frenetic when the lodge is full, it's a terrific place to stay on a terrific reserve.

Okonjima Nature Reserve

📄 067

The 200 sq km Okonjima Nature Reserve is the epicentre of one of Namibia's most impressive conservation programs. Home of the AfriCat Foundation, it protects cheetahs and other carnivores rescued from human–wildlife conflict situations across the country, and gives them room to move. Aside from excellent accommodation and fascinating education programs, Okonjima offers the opportunity to track wild leopards, as well as cheetahs, African wild dogs and (coming soon) lions within the reserve. There are also self-guided walks, first-rate guides and the chance to be a part of something that makes a genuine difference.

Day visitors are welcome, but we recommend staying here for a minimum of two nights to take full advantage of the activities on offer.

Activities are not included in the room rates, and cost N$670/340 per adult/child for leopard or cheetah tracking, or N$450/225 per adult/child for guided Bushman nature trails.

Unless you visit Okonjima as part of an organised tour, you'll need your own vehicle to visit. The signpost is impossible to miss, 49km south of Otjiwarongo and 130km north of Okahandja along the B1. After taking the turn-off, you pass through a series of gates and the main lodge is 10km off the main road, along a well-graded gravel track.

AfriCat Foundation WILDLIFE
(📞067-687032; www.africat.org; ⏰10am-4pm) This foundation runs education programs and activities within Okonjima Nature Reserve. Day visitors can join the tours that leave from the AfriCat Day Centre at 10.30am and 12.30pm from April to August, and 11am and 1pm from September to March.

The tours take you to the AfriCat Care Centre – where you'll learn about the AfriCat story and the foundation's programmes, as well as visit a large enclosure where cheetahs are held awaiting their return to the wild. You'll also receive a light lunch as part of the tours, which cost N$385/285 per adult/child; children under seven are free.

★ **Omboroko Campsite** CAMPGROUND $
(www.okonjima.com; per adult/child N$330/165; 🏊) These are some of the best campsites in Namibia. There's plenty of shade, firewood is provided, there's a (freezing!) swimming pool,

hot showers and flush toilets, and the five sites are beautifully maintained in the shadow of one of the rocky outcrops that dominate the reserve's core. You're also within the 20 sq km fenced zone and, hence, unlikely to be surprised by wandering predators.

★ **Okonjima Plains Camp**   LODGE $$$
(☑ 067-687032; www.okonjima.com; s/d standard rooms with half board N$2830/4050, view rooms with half board N$3955/6300; ❋ 🤙 🍽) With 10 'view' and 14 'standard' rooms, these newly built lodgings open out onto the Okonjima grasslands, with the ample terraces and abundant glass taking full advantage of the wildlife-rich views. The view rooms in particular are supremely comfortable, spacious and stylish, decorated with a pleasing mix of soothing earth tones and bold colours, as well as plenty of stunning photographs of Okonjima's wildlife.

Okonjima Bush Camp & Suites   LODGE $$$
(☑ 067-687032; www.okonjima.com; s/d with half board N$5700/9900, ste N$8800-14,400; 🤙 🍽) Removed from the main lodge area and hence quieter and more discreet, the Bush Camp and nearby Bush Suites are beautifully turned out. The camp rooms are nicely spaced to ensure maximum privacy and actually have two small adobe bungalows, one for sleeping, the other with a lovely sitting area. The split-level suites are even more beautiful.

AfriCat Day Centre   CAFE $
(light meals from N$40; ⊙ 11.30am-2.30pm) The day centre serves a few simple meal choices at lunchtimes from a menu that changes regularly. There are fine views from the back terrace.

Otjiwarongo

POP 28,250 / ☑ 067

Handy as a jumping-off point for Etosha, and particularly the Waterberg Plateau, Otjiwarongo is especially pleasant in September and October when the town explodes with the vivid colours of blooming jacaranda and bougainvillea. It's a good place to refuel, stock up on supplies and break up the journey.

There's a **Spar Supermarket** (9 Hage Geingob St; ⊙ 8am-8pm Mon-Fri, to noon Sat, to 7pm Sun) in the centre.

There are buses at least daily between Otjiwarongo and Windhoek (from N$288, 3½ hours) with **Intercape Mainliner** (☑ 061-227847; www.intercape.co.za). Minibuses travelling between Windhoek and the north stop at the Engen petrol station. All train services between Tsumeb and Windhoek or Walvis Bay (via Swakopmund) also pass through.

Crocodile Farm   FARM
(cnr Zingel & Hospital Sts; N$50; ⊙ 8am-5pm Mon-Fri, 8am-3pm Sat, 9am-3pm Sun) Otjiwarongo is home to Namibia's first crocodile ranch, which produces skins for export. You can do a worthwhile tour, and there's a shop which has mainly wooden carvings with some jewellery and metalwork, though not much in the way of croc-skin products. The restaurant has a full-blown menu for breakfast and lunch – try any number of croc delicacies, such as a croc wrap or kebabs.

★ **Hadassa Guest House**   GUESTHOUSE $
(☑ 067-307505; www.hadassaguesthouse.com; Lang St; s/d N$640/800; 🤙 🍽) Overseen by the welcoming French owners Orlane and Emmanuel, this fine little guesthouse has the intimate feel of a B&B and the quality of a small, personalised boutique hotel. Rooms are immaculate, the meals are beautifully prepared and service is excellent.

Casa Forno Country Hotel   HOTEL $
(☑ 067-304504; www.casaforno.com; Ramblers Rd; s/d from N$820/920; 🅿 ❋ 🤙) Large and semiluxurious, Casa Forno is decorated in classic Cape Dutch style and it's far enough away from the main street to ensure a quiet night's sleep. The excellent restaurant serves pasta, steaks and other international staples in an agreeable setting.

★ **Bush Pillow**   GUESTHOUSE $$
(☑ 067-303885; bushpillow.co.za; 47 Sonn Rd; s/d incl breakfast N$650/850; 🤙 🍽) This great little guesthouse styles itself as 'executive accommodation' by targeting the business market, but with comfortable rooms and wi-fi connectivity throughout, it also makes an ideal pit stop for travellers. A couple of rooms are set up for families – the kids will love the pool. There's a lovely restaurant as well.

Outjo

POP 8450 / ☑ 067

Given the tourist traffic through this small town, it has retained a surprisingly country, low-key feel. Although it has few attractions, it serves as an increasingly appealing place to rest on your way to/from Etosha. If you're coming from the south, Outjo is the last major rest stop before reaching Okaukuejo, the administrative headquarters of and western gateway to Etosha.

Combis run between the OK Supermarket in Outjo to towns and cities around North-Central Namibia, though there is no public transport leading up to Okaukuejo and the Andersson Gate of Etosha National Park. If you're driving, however, the paved route continues north as far as the park gate. Self-drivers can top up at **Puma** (⊙7am-10pm).

Sophienhof Lodge
LODGE $

(☑067-312999; www.sophienhof-lodge.com; off C39; camping/dm N$200/300, r per person N$440-1650; ⏰⊠) This place just off the C39, 12km southwest of Outjo, gets consistently good reviews from travellers. Accommodation is in good, grassy campsites, sturdy bungalows or the appealing farmhouse; there's even a dorm for budget travellers. In addition to guided walking tours, you can also watch the feeding of rescued cheetahs and ostriches.

Etotongwe Lodge
LODGE $

(☑067-313333; www.etotongwelodge.com; camping N$120, s/d N$580/960; ⏰) This refreshing, professionally run place on the way to Etosha, just outside of town, feels like an unlikely oasis of green. Its neat appearance and trim lawns break up the concrete, stone and thatched roofs spun around an attractive area. Rooms are fairly bare inside, but have some nice African touches and are neat as a pin and very roomy.

★ Outjo Bakery
BAKERY, CAFE $$

(☑067-313055, 081 141 3839; Hage Geingob Ave; breakfast N$48-120, mains N$65-160; ⊙7am-4.30pm Mon-Fri, to 1.30pm Sat; ⏰) Opened in 2016, this stylish place wouldn't look out of place in Windhoek or urban South Africa. All of the international staples are here – pasta, steaks, burgers and open sandwiches – but it's the clean lines, tempting array of bakery items and all-round sophistication of everything from the food to the service that make this place a winner.

Farmhouse
INTERNATIONAL $$

(www.farmhouse-outjo.com; Hage Geingob Ave; mains N$45-105; ⊙7am-9pm; ⏰) This all-rounder is the centre of food and drink in town, serving meals all day every day. Its pleasant beer garden is a great spot to reconnect with social media. Burgers, pies, grills (including game such as kudu, eland and oryx), wraps, pizza, salads and ever-changing daily specials are on offer, as are tempting cakes. It also serves the best coffee in town.

Waterberg Plateau Park
♪ 067

The wild **Waterberg** (per person per day N$80, vehicle N$10) is highly recommended – there is nothing quite like it in Namibia. It takes in a 50km-long, 16km-wide sandstone plateau, looming 150m above the desert plains. It doesn't have the traditional big wildlife attractions (such as lions or elephants). What it does have are some rare and threatened species, including sable and roan antelope, and little-known populations of white and black rhinos. Most animals here have been introduced, and after breeding successfully some are moved to other parks. That said, all of these species can prove difficult to see – most are skittish and the bush is very thick.

Waterberg Plateau Park is only accessible by private car – motorcycles are not permitted anywhere within the park boundaries. From Otjiwarongo it's about 90km to the park gate via the B1, C22 and the gravel D512. While this route is passable to 2WD vehicles, go slow in the final stretches as the road can be in bad shape after the rainy season. An alternative route is the D2512, which runs between Waterberg and Groottontein – this route is OK during winter but can be terrible during summer, the rainy season, when it requires a high-clearance 4WD.

With the exception of walking trails around the Waterberg Resort, both unguided and guided hiking routes in Waterberg must be booked well in advance through Namibia Wildlife Resorts in Windhoek.

May to October is the best time to visit, although year-round is possible. Avoid hiking in the heat of the day from December to February in particular.

Waterberg Unguided Hiking Trail
HIKING

A four-day, 42km unguided hike around a figure-eight track begins at 9am every Wednesday from April to November. It costs N$100 per person, and groups are limited to between three and 10 people. Book through Namibia Wildlife Resorts (p252) in Windhoek. Hikers stay in basic shelters and don't need to carry a tent but must otherwise be self-sufficient. Shelters have drinking water, but you'll need to carry enough to last you between times – plan on drinking at least 3L to 4L per day.

Waterberg Wilderness Trail
HIKING

(per person N$220; ⊙2pm Thu) From April to November the four-day, guided Waterberg Wilderness Trail operates every Thursday. The walks, which are led by armed guides,

NAMIBIA NORTH TO ETOSHA

need a minimum of two people. They begin at 2pm on Thursday from the visitor centre and end early on Sunday afternoon. They cost N$220 per person and must be prebooked through NWR (p252) in Windhoek. There's no set route, and the itinerary is left to the whims of the guide. Accommodation is in simple huts, but participants must carry their own food and sleeping bags.

★ Waterberg
Wilderness Lodge
LODGE, CAMPGROUND $$

(☑067-687018; www.waterberg-wilderness.com; off D2512; camping N$170, tented room N$690, r with half board N$1150-1480; ❋ 🛜 ⊠) Waterberg Wilderness occupies a vast private concession within the park and is a wonderful upmarket choice. The Rust family has painstakingly transformed the property (formerly a cattle farm) by repopulating game animals and allowing nature to return to its pregrazed state. The main lodge rests in a sun-drenched, jacaranda-strewn meadow at the end of a valley, where you'll find red-sandstone chalets adorned with rich hardwood furniture.

Wabi Lodge
LODGE $$$

(☑067-306500; www.wabi.ch; s/d from N$1185/2170; 🛜 ⊠) Wabi is a private luxury set-up almost 30km from Waterberg Plateau on the D2512. The Swiss owners have imparted their heritage on the design and furnishings of the eight bungalows and in the well-prepared food. The lodge runs its own wildlife drives, including night drives where you've a chance to see honey badgers, caracals, genets, brown hyenas, and even cheetahs and leopards.

Grootfontein
POP 23.790 / ☑067

With a pronounced colonial feel, Grootfontein (Afrikaans for Big Spring) has an air of uprightness and respectability, with local limestone constructions and honour guards of jacaranda trees that bloom in the autumn. The springboard for excursions out to Khaudum National Park and the San villages in Otjozondjupa or a way station on your way to/from Etosha's east, Grootfontein can be the last town of any real significance that you see before heading out into the deep bush.

⊙ Sights

German Fort & Museum
FORT

(adult/child N$25/15; ⊙8.30am-4.30pm Mon-Fri) Historical settler history is depicted here through some fascinating black-and-white photos. The Himba, Kavango and Mbanderu collections of artefacts and photographs are also interesting, as is the history of research into the area's rock art. It's a huge museum; put a couple of hours aside at least.

The 1896 fort in which the museum is housed was enlarged several times in the early 20th century and in 1922 a large limestone extension was added.

Hoba Meteorite
NATURAL FEATURE

(adult/child N$20/10; ⊙dawn-dusk) Near the Hoba Farm, the world's largest meteorite was discovered in 1920 by hunter Jacobus Brits. This cuboid bit of space debris is composed of 82% iron, 16% nickel and 0.8% cobalt, along with traces of other metals. No one knows when it fell to earth (it's thought to have been around 80,000 years ago), but since it weighs around 54,000kg, it must have made one hell of a thump.

🛏 Sleeping & Eating

Stone House Lodge
GUESTHOUSE $

(☑067-242842; www.stonehouse.iway.na; 10 Toenessen St; s/d N$450/650; ❋🛜⊠) Probably the best of the in-town options, Stone House has six attractive rooms overseen by Boet and Magda. This guesthouse has a welcoming, family feel to it.

Courtyard Guesthouse
GUESTHOUSE $

(☑067-240027; 2 Gauss St; s/d N$430/660; ❋@🛜⊠) The top spot in Grootfontein is modest by any standard, but its truly enormous rooms (not all – ask to see a few) leave you plenty of space to unpack your bag and take stock of your gear. If you're about to embark on a bush outing, spend the afternoon poolside and bask in comfort while you can. The restaurant (mains N$60 to N$100, open 7am to 10pm) serves fish, salads, pastas and grills dabbling in a bit of everything.

★ Purple Fig Bistro
INTERNATIONAL $$

(☑081 124 2802; www.facebook.com/purplefigbistro; 19 Hage Geingob St; mains N$40-120; ⊙7am-9pm) In the heart of town, the Purple Fig gets good reviews from travellers. Eat under the eponymous fig tree or in the cafe. Light meals take the form of salads, wraps and toasted sandwiches, but there are also burgers, steaks and pancakes. Servings are large, staff are friendly and it's easily the most pleasant place to eat in Grootfontein.

❶ Information

Hospital (☑10111)

Grootfontein

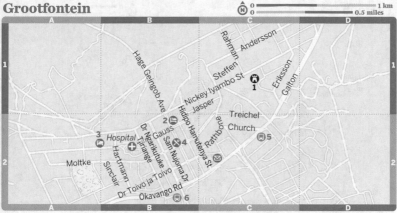

ⓘ Getting There & Away

Minibuses leave for Rundu and Oshakati from one stop along Okavango Rd, with others to Tsumeb and Windhoek from another; all depart when full. The Intercape Mainliner (p252) bus that departs Windhoek for Victoria Falls also passes through Grootfontein (from N$772, six hours) on Monday, Wednesday and Friday; going the other way they pass through on Monday, Thursday and Saturday.

If you're heading out to Tsumkwe, you will need a private vehicle. The gravel road into town is accessible by 2WD if you take it slow, but you will need a high-clearance vehicle to reach the various villages in Oljozondjupa, and a 4WD might be necessary in the rainy season. If you're heading to Khaudum, a sturdy 4WD is a requirement, as is travelling as part of a well-equipped convoy.

Tsumeb

POP 19,280 / ☏ 067

Tsumeb is one Namibian town worth a poke around, especially if you are trying to get a feel for the country's urban side. The streets are very pleasant to wander, made more so by the plentiful shady trees. It's reasonably compact, and there's usually a smile or two drifting your way on the busy streets. There are a few attractions to guide your visit, but it's more about getting a window on the world of an appealing northern Namibian town.

◉ Sights

St Barbara's Church   CHURCH
(cnr Main St & Sam Nujoma Dr) Tsumeb's distinctive Roman Catholic church was consecrated in 1914 and dedicated to St Barbara, the patron saint of mineworkers. It contains some fine colonial murals and an odd tower, which

Grootfontein

◉ Sights
1 German Fort & Museum C1

ⓛ Sleeping
2 Courtyard Guesthouse B2
3 Stone House Lodge A2

✖ Eating
4 Purple Fig Bistro B2

ⓘ Transport
5 Minibuses to Rundu & Oshakati C2
6 Minibuses to Tsumeb &
    Windhoek B2

makes it look less like a church than a municipal building in some small German town.

Tsumeb Mining Museum   MUSEUM
(☏ 067-220447; cnr Main St & 8th Rd; adult/child N$40/10; ⊙ 9am-5pm Mon-Fri, to noon Sat) If you normally skip museums, make an exception here. Tsumeb's story is told in this museum, which is housed in a 1915 colonial building that once served as both a school and a hospital for German troops. In addition to outstanding mineral displays (you've never seen anything like psittacinite!), the museum also houses mining machinery, stuffed birds, Himba and Herero artefacts, and weapons recovered from Lake Otjikoto.

⎙ Sleeping & Eating

Spar (☏ 067-222840; Hage Geingob Dr; ⊙ 8am-6pm Mon-Sat) is Tsumeb's best supermarket.

Mousebird Backpackers & Safaris HOSTEL $
(☏ 067-221777; cnr 533 Pendukeni Iivula-Ithana & 4th Sts; camping N$120, dm/tw N$160/460; ⓐ)

NAMIBIA NORTH TO ETOSHA

Tsumeb

Tsumeb's long-standing backpacker spot continues to stay true to its roots, offering economical accommodation without sacrificing personality or character – there's a really good feel to this place. It's a small house-style set-up with decent communal areas, including a kitchen. The best twin rooms share a bathroom inside the house, although the twin outside does have its own bathroom. The four-bed dorm is also very good.

Kupferquelle Resort RESORT $$
(☏ 067-220139; www.kupferquelle.com; Kupfer St; camping N$115, s/d N$1110/1530; ☀) This modern, resort-style place has lovely, contemporary rooms with high ceilings, quiet terraces and a real sense of space, style and light. Some have kitchens, and all have modern art on the walls. There's an on-site swimming pool and ample grounds. An excellent choice.

❶ Information

Travel North Namibia Tourist Office (☏ 067-220728; 1551 Sam Nujoma Dr; ☎) Inside the guesthouse of the same name. Provides nationwide information; arranges accommodation, transport, car hire and Etosha bookings; and has internet access. No maps available.

❶ Getting There & Away

BUS

Intercape Mainliner (p252) buses make the trip between Windhoek and Tsumeb (from N$340, 5½ hours, twice weekly). Book your tickets in advance online, as this service continues on to Victoria Falls and fills up quickly.

Combis also run up and down the B1 with fairly regular frequency, and a ride between Windhoek

and Tsumeb shouldn't cost more than N$280. If you're continuing on to Etosha National Park, be advised that there is no public transport serving this route.

CAR

Tsumeb is an easy day's drive from Windhoek along paved roads, and serves as the jumping-off point for Namutoni and the Von Lindequist Gate of Etosha National Park. The paved route continues north as far as the park gate, though keep your speed under control as wildlife is frequently seen along the sides of the highway.

Etosha National Park

☐ 067

Etosha National Park (per person per day N$80, per vehicle N$10; ☉ sunrise-sunset), covering more than 20,000 sq km, is one of the world's great wildlife-viewing venues. Unlike other parks in Africa, where you can spend days looking for animals, Etosha's charm lies in its ability to bring the animals to you. Just park your car next to one of the many water holes, then wait and watch while a host of animals – lions, elephants, springboks, gemsboks etc – come not two by two but by the hundreds.

Etosha's essence is the vast **Etosha Pan**, an immense, flat, saline desert that, for a few days each year, is converted by rain into a shallow lagoon teeming with flamingos and pelicans. In contrast, late in the dry season, everything, from the elephants to the once-golden grasslands, seems cast, spectre-like, in Etosha's white chalky dust. And what wildlife there is! Even if you've had a taste of African wildlife watching previously, you are likely to be mesmerised by it here.

🏃 Activities

Etosha's most widespread vegetation type is mopane woodland, which fringes the pan and constitutes about 80% of the vegetation. The park also has umbrella-thorn acacias and other trees favoured by browsing animals, and from December to March this sparse bush country has a pleasant green hue.

Depending on the season, you may observe elephants, giraffes, Burchell's zebras, springboks, red hartebeests, blue wildebeest, gemsboks, elands, kudus, roans, ostriches, jackals, hyenas, lions and even cheetahs and leopards. Among the endangered animal species are the black-faced impala and the black rhinoceros.

Etosha is Namibia's most important stronghold for lions, with more than half of the country's wild lions – 450 to 500 according to the last estimate by peak conservation NGO Panthera (www.panthera.org).

The park's wildlife density varies with the local ecology. As its Afrikaans name would suggest, Oliphantsbad (near Okaukuejo) is attractive to elephants, but for rhinos you couldn't do better than the floodlit water hole at Okaukuejo. We've also seen them by night at the water hole at Olifantsrus and Halali. In general, the further east you go in the park, the more wildebeest, kudus and impalas join the springboks and gemsboks. The area around Namutoni, which averages 443mm of rain annually (compared with 412mm at Okaukuejo), is the best place to see the black-faced impala and the Damara dik-dik, Africa's smallest antelope. Etosha is also home to numerous smaller species, including both yellow and slender mongoose, honey badgers and *leguaans* (water-monitor lizards).

In the dry winter season, wildlife clusters around water holes, while in the hot, wet summer months, animals disperse and spend the days sheltering in the bush. In the afternoon, even in the dry season, look carefully for animals resting beneath the trees, especially prides of lions lazing about. Summer temperatures can reach 44°C, which isn't fun when you're confined to a vehicle, but this is the calving season, and you may catch a glimpse of tiny zebra foals and fragile newborn springboks.

Birdlife is also profuse. Yellow-billed hornbills are common, and on the ground you should look for the huge kori bustard, which weighs 15kg and seldom flies – it's the world's heaviest flying bird. You may also observe ostriches, korhaans, marabous, white-backed vultures and many smaller species.

The best time for wildlife drives is at first light and late in the evening, though visitors aren't permitted outside the camps after dark. While self-drivers should definitely

---

ETOSHA NATIONAL PARK AT A GLANCE

Why Go?

Let's talk numbers: Etosha is home to 114 mammal species as well as 340 bird species, 16 reptile and amphibian species, one fish species and countless insects. Or landscapes: the desolate nature of the pan, the low-cut landscapes and (of course) the water holes mean that wildlife viewing is some of the easiest and most productive on the continent. It's also one of the best places to spot the highly endangered black rhino in Southern Africa.

Gateway Towns

Most people call in at Outjo, if approaching from the south – it's about 100km to Etosha from here on a smooth sealed road. Outjo is a fine place to stock up on supplies at the supermarket, use the internet and indulge in some good food. If you're heading straight to the eastern side of the park (if you're coming from the Caprivi Strip or Rundu, for example), you'll go via Tsumeb, another handy launching point for the park; it's about 110km from the Von Lindequist Gate.

Practicalities

➡ You'll find maps of Etosha National Park across the country and at the shops at most of the park gates. NWR (p252)'s reliable English-German *Map of Etosha* (from N\$40) is the best and also the most widely available. It has the added bonus of park information and quite extensive mammal- and bird-identification sheets.

➡ Etosha's four main entry gates are Von Lindequist (Namutoni), west of Tsumeb; King Nehale, southeast of Ondangwa; Andersson (Okaukuejo), north of Outjo; and Galton, northwest of Kamanjab.

Etosha National Park

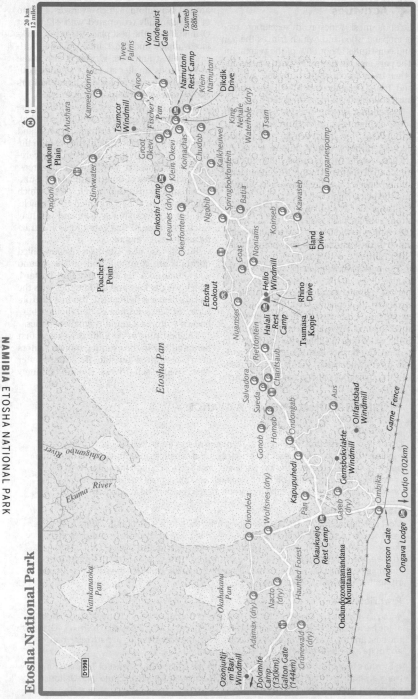

20 km
12 miles

Tsumeb (88km)

Von Lindequist Gate

Twee Palms

Aroe

Namutoni Rest Camp

Klein Namutoni

Dikdik Drive

Tsumcor Windmill

Fischer's Pan

Kameeldoring

Mushara

Groot Okevi

Klein Okevi

Koinachas

King Nehale Waterhole (dry)

Chudob

Tsam

Andoni Plain

Andoni

Stinkwater

Onkoshi Camp

Leeunes (dry)

Okerfontein

Kalkheuwel

Springbokfontein

Ngobib

Batia

Kawaseb

Dungariespomp

Koinseb

Eland Drive

Poacher's Point

Noniams

Goas

Helio Windmill

Rhino Drive

Etosha Lookout

Nuamses

Halali Rest Camp

Tsumasa Kopje

Rietfontein

Etosha Pan

Salvadora

Charitsaub

Sueda

Aus

Gonob

Homob

Ondongab

Olifantsbad Windmill

Oshigambo River

Okondeka

Wolfsnes (dry)

Kapupuhedi Pan

Gemsbokvlakte Windmill

Gaseb (dry)

Ombika

Game Fence

Ekuma River

Natukanaoka Pan

Haunted Forest

Okaukuejo Rest Camp

Ondundozonanandana Mountains

Andersson Gate

Ongava Lodge

Outjo (102km)

Okohakama Pan

Nacto (dry)

Adamax (dry)

Ozonjuitji m'Bari Windmill

Dolomite Camp (130km);

Galton Gate (144km)

Grünewald (dry)

D1998

wake up at dawn, when animals are most active, guided night drives (N$600 per person) can be booked through any of the main camps and are your best chance to see lions hunting, as well as the various nocturnal species. Each of the camps also has a visitor register, which describes any recent sightings in the vicinity.

🛏 Sleeping

In the Park

Olifantsrus Rest Camp   CAMPGROUND $
(📞 061-2857200; www.nwr.com.na; camping N$280) The newest of Etosha's rest camps, out in the recently opened-to-the-public western reaches of the park, fenced Olifantsrus occupies an old elephant-culling site with some of the gruesome paraphernalia still on show. There's a small kiosk, decent sites and a marvellous elevated hide overlooking a water hole.

Halali Rest Camp   LODGE, CAMPGROUND $
(📞 067-229400, 061-2857200; www.nwr.com.na; campsites N$250, plus per person N$150, s/d from N$1150/2040, s/d chalets from N$1530/2800; ❄❄) Etosha's middle camp, Halali, nestles between several dolomite outcrops. The best feature at Halali is its floodlit water hole, which is a 10-minute walk from the rest camp and is sheltered by a glen of trees with huge boulders strewn about. There is a very well serviced campsite here, in addition to a fine collection of semiluxurious chalets.

★Onkoshi Camp   LODGE $$$
(📞 067-687362, 061-2857200; www.nwr.com.na; per person with half board incl transfers from Namutoni N$2750; ❄❄) Upon arrival at Onkoshi (from Namutoni), you'll be chauffeured to a secluded peninsula on the pan's rim and given the keys to one of 15 thatch-and-canvas chalets resting on elevated wooden decks and occupying exclusive locations well beyond the standard tourist route. The opulent interiors blend rich hardwoods, delicate bamboo, elaborate metal flourishes, finely crafted furniture, hand-painted artwork and fine porcelain fixtures.

Okaukuejo Rest Camp   LODGE, CAMPGROUND $$$
(📞 067-229800, 061-2857200; www.nwr.com.na; campsites N$250, plus per person N$150, s/d N$1400/2540, s/d chalets from N$1470/2680; Ⓟ❄❄) Pronounced 'o-ka-kui-yo', this is the site of the Etosha Research Station and it also functions as the official park headquarters and main visitor centre. The Okau-

kuejo water hole is probably Etosha's best rhino-viewing venue, particularly between 8pm and 10pm. Okaukuejo's campsite can get very crowded, but the shared facilities (washing stations, braai pits and bathrooms with hot water) are excellent.

Dolomite Camp   LODGE $$$
(📞061-2857200, 065-685119; www.nwr.com.na; s/d with half board from N$2040/3580; ❄❄) Recently opened in a previously restricted area in western Etosha, Dolomite Camp is beautifully carved into its rocky surrounds. Accommodation is in thatched chalets (actually luxury tents), including a couple with their own plunge pool. The views of surrounding plains are wonderful and there's even a water hole at the camp, so spotting wildlife doesn't mean moving far from your bed.

Outside the Park

★Ongava Lodge   LODGE $$$
(📞061-225178; www.wilderness-safaris.com; s/d with half board N$4771/7632; ❄@❄) One of the more exclusive luxury lodges in the Etosha area, Ongava Lodge is not far south of Andersson Gate. Ongava is actually divided into two properties: the main Ongava Lodge is a collection of safari-chic chalets surrounding a small water hole, while the Ongava Tented Camp has eight East African–style canvas tents situated a bit deeper in the bush.

Onguma Etosha Aoba Lodge   LODGE $$$
(📞067-229100; www.etosha-aoba-lodge.com; s/d with half board from N$2020/3340; ❄@❄) Part of the 70 sq km private Onguma Game Reserve, 10km east of the Von Lindequist Gate, this tranquil lodge is located in tamboti forest next to a dry riverbed. The property comprises 10 cottages that blend effortlessly into their riverine environment. The atmosphere is peaceful and relaxing, and the main lodge is conducive to unwinding with other guests after a long day on safari.

Taleni Etosha Village   TENTED CAMP $$$
(📞067-333413, in South Africa 27-21-930 4564; www.taleni-africa.com; camping N$150, s/d with full board high season N$1951/2928; ❄📶) This little hideaway, just a couple of kilometres outside Etosha, has self-catering safari tents (half- and full-board options available) with outdoor seating area, braai (barbecue), wooden floors, power points and other little luxuries. The tents are nestled into bushland among mopane trees, and the friendly staff can also organise food if you're self-catering. Etosha Village is 2km before the Andersson Gate.

NAMIBIA ETOSHA NATIONAL PARK

Epacha Game Lodge & Spa LODGE $$$
(☑ 061-375300; www.epacha.com; s/d with full board N$3500/5800) Superb rooms are a hallmark of this beautiful lodge on the private 21 sq km Epacha Game Reserve. Night drives, great views from its elevated hillside position and a pervasive sense of quiet sophistication are all well and good, but where else in Etosha can you practise your clay-pigeon shooting? There's also a tented lodge and exclusive private villa on the reserve.

❶ Getting There & Away

There's no public transport into and around the park, which means that you must visit either in a private vehicle or as part of an organised tour.

The vast majority of roads in Etosha are passable to 2WD vehicles. The park speed limit is set at 60km/h, both to protect wildlife and keep down the dust.

The park road between Namutoni and Okaukuejo skirts Etosha Pan, providing great views of its vast spaces. Driving isn't permitted on the pan, but a network of gravel roads threads through the surrounding savannah and mopane woodland and even extends out to a viewing site, the Etosha Lookout, in the middle of the salt desert.

NORTHERN NAMIBIA

The country's most densely populated region, and undeniably its cultural heartland, northern Namibia is a place for some serious African adventure. It is where endless skies meet distant horizons in an expanse that will make you truly wonder if this could be your greatest road trip of all time. There is space out here to think, and you may just find yourself belting down a dirt road hunched over the steering wheel, pondering in detail whatever's on your mind…for many hours.

.Northern Namibia takes its form and identity from the Caprivi Strip, where, alongside traditional villages, a collection of national parks are being repopulated with wildlife after many decades of war and conflict. At the time of independence, these parks had been virtually depleted by poachers, though years of progressive wildlife management have firmly placed the region back on the safari circuit.

Rundu

POP 63,430 / ☑ 066
Rundu, a sultry tropical outpost on the bluffs above the Okavango River, is a major centre of activity for Namibia's growing Angolan community. Although the town has little of specific interest for tourists, the area is home to a number of wonderful lodges where you can laze along the riverside, and spot crocs and hippos doing pretty much the same. As such, it's a fine place to break up the journey between the Caprivi Strip and Grootfontein or Etosha.

★ **N'Kwazi Lodge** LODGE $
(☑ 081 242 4897; www.nkwazilodge.com; camping per adult/child N$100/50, s/d N$600/1000) On the banks of the Okavango, about 20km from Rundu's town centre, this is a tranquil and good-value riverside retreat where relaxation is a by-product of the owners' laidback approach. The entire property blends naturally into the surrounding riverine forest, while the rooms are beautifully laid out, with personal touches; there's a great campsite, although it's sometimes overrun by safari trucks. The lodge represents incredibly good value, with no surcharge for singles and a justifiably famous buffet dinner for N$260 at night.

Hakusembe Lodge LODGE $$
(☑ 061-427200, 066-257010; www.gondwana-collection.com; camping N$140, chalets per person with half board from N$1450; ❄ ❄) Now part of the well-regarded Gondwana Collection chain, this secluded hideaway sits amid lush riverside gardens, and comprises luxury chalets (one of which is floating) decked out in safari prints, wood floors and locally crafted furniture. Activities centre on the river with birdwatching, croc spotting and rather lovely sundowner cruises. It lies 17km down the Nkurenkuru Rd, then 2km north to the riverbank.

Covered Market MARKET
Take a stroll around this large market, which is one of Namibia's most sophisticated informal sales outlets. From July to September, don't miss the fresh papayas sold straight from the trees.

❶ Getting There & Away

BUS
Several weekly Intercape Mainliner (p252) buses make the seven-hour trip between Windhoek and Rundu (fares from N$780). Book your tickets in advance online, as this service continues on to Victoria Falls and fills up quickly.

Combis connect Windhoek and Rundu with fairly regular frequency, and a ride shouldn't cost more than N$600. From Rundu, routes fan out to various towns and cities in the north, with

Rundu

fares costing less than N$60 a ride. Both buses and combis depart and drop off at the Engen petrol station.

CAR & MOTORCYCLE
Drivers will need to be patient on the road (D8) to Rundu from Grootfontein. It's in good condition but passes by many schools where the speed limit drops suddenly – fertile ground for speed cameras.

Khaudum National Park

🎵 066

Exploring the largely undeveloped 3840 sq km **Khaudum National Park** (adult/child/vehicle N$80/free/10; ☺ sunrise-sunset) is an intense wilderness challenge. Meandering sand tracks lure you through pristine bush and across *omiramba* (fossilised river valleys), which run parallel to the east–west-oriented Kalahari dunes. As there is virtually no signage, and navigation is largely based on GPS coordinates and topographic maps, visitors are few, which is precisely why Khaudum is worth exploring – Khaudum is home to one of Namibia's most important populations of lions and African wild dogs, although both can be difficult to see.

In addition to African wild dogs and lions, the park protects large populations of elephants, zebras, giraffes, wildebeest, kudus, oryxes and tsessebes, and there's a good chance you'll be able to spot large herds of roan antelope here. If you're an avid birder, Khaudum supports 320 different species, including summer migratory birds such as storks, crakes, bitterns, orioles, eagles and falcons.

Wildlife viewing is best from June to October, when herds congregate around the water holes and along the *omiramba*. November to April is the richest time to visit for birdwatchers, though you will have to be prepared for a difficult slog through muddy tracks.

From the north, take the sandy track from Katere on the B8 (signposted 'Khaudum'), 120km east of Rundu. After 45km you'll reach the Cwibadom Omuramba, where you should turn east into the park.

From the south, you can reach Sikereti Camp via Tsumkwe. From Tsumkwe, it's 20km to Groote Döbe and another 15km from there to the Dorslandboom turning. It's then 25km north to Sikereti Camp.

Khaudum Camp CAMPGROUND
(GPS: S 18°30.234', E 20°45.180') **FREE** Khaudum Camp is somewhat akin to the Kalahari in miniature, but this is true wilderness camping – shade can be meagre and facilities are nonexistent. The sunsets here are the stuff of legend.

Sikereti Camp CAMPGROUND
(GPS: S 19°06.267', E 20°42.300') **FREE** 'Cigarette' camp, in the south of the park, inhabits a shady grove of terminalia trees, though full appreciation of this place requires sensitivity to its subtle charms, namely isolation and silence. This is true wilderness camping with no facilities whatsoever.

KHAUDUM NATIONAL PARK PRACTICALITIES

Take a satellite phone with you. The park authorities usually require a minimum of two vehicles for exploring the park. Pick up the *Kavango-Zambezi National Parks* map, which is available at some lodges or online via www.thinkafricadesign.com. There's little detail but the GPS coordinates for the major track intersections could save your life. The nearest fuel is at Rundu, Divundu and (sometimes) Tsumkwe.

The Caprivi Strip

Namibia's spindly northeastern appendage, the Caprivi Strip (now officially known as Namibia's Zambezi region, although the name is taking time to catch on...) is typified by expanses of mopane and terminalia broadleaf forest, and punctuated by *shonas* or fossilised parallel dunes that are the remnants of a drier climate. For most travellers, the Caprivi serves as the easiest access route connecting the main body of Namibia with Victoria Falls and Botswana's Chobe National Park.

But Caprivi is also one of Southern Africa's wildlife destinations to watch. After decades of poaching, the region's wildlife is returning and visitors with time and patience can get off the beaten path here, exploring such emerging wildlife gems as Nkasa Rupara and Bwabwata National Parks.

Bwabwata National Park

📞 066

Only recently recognised as a national park, **Bwabwata** (per person per day N$10, per vehicle N$10; ☉ sunrise-sunset) was established to rehabilitate local wildlife populations. Prior to the 2002 Angolan ceasefire, this area saw almost no visitors, and wildlife populations had been virtually wiped out by rampant poaching instigated by ongoing conflict. But the guns have been silent now for well over a decade and the wildlife is making a slow but spectacular comeback. If you come here expecting Etosha, you'll be disappointed. But you might very well see lions, elephants, African wild dogs, perhaps even sable antelope and some fabulous birdlife – and you might just have them all to yourself.

The paved Trans-Caprivi Highway between Rundu and Katima Mulilo is perfectly suited to 2WD vehicles, as is the gravel road between Divundu and Mohembo (on the Botswana border). Drivers may transit the park without charge, but you will incur national park entry fees if you use the loop drive through the park.

Our favourite time to visit is May to August. September and October are also good, but the build-up to the rains brings oppressive heat. The rains usually fall from November to March – getting around can be difficult, but this is the best time for birdwatching.

The nearest airport is at Katima Mulilo, while access to the park by road is via Divundu, Kongola and Katima Mulilo. The park's distinct areas, with the best wildlife at the far eastern and western extremities, mean that it's necessary to plan ahead. The Mahango Game Reserve and Kwando Core Area are, for the moment at least, the most rewarding choices.

East Caprivi Strip

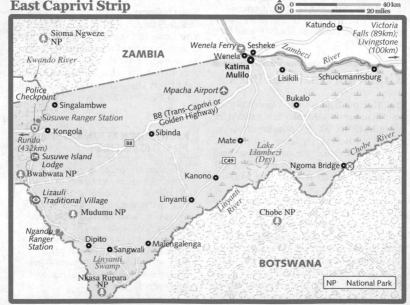

Mahango Game Reserve WILDLIFE RESERVE
(per person/vehicle N$40/10; ☉ sunrise-sunset)
This small but diverse 25 sq km reserve
occupies a broad flood plain north of the
Botswana border and west of the Okavango River. It attracts large concentrations of
thirsty elephants and herd animals, particularly in the dry season. It's particularly nice
to stop beside the river in the afternoon and
watch the elephants swimming and drinking among hippos and crocodiles.

Ngepi Camp LODGE $
(☏066-259903; www.ngepicamp.com; camping
N$140, bush or tree huts per person from N$770)
One of Namibia's top backpacker lodges that
appeals beyond the budget market, Ngepi
makes a great base for the area. Crash for the
night in a bush hut or tree hut, or pitch a tent
on grass by the river's edge and let the sounds
of hippos splashing about ease you into a
restful sleep; we love the outdoor bathtubs.

★**Nambwa**
Tented Lodge LODGE, CAMPGROUND $$$
(www.africanmonarchlodges.com/nambwa-luxury
-tented-lodge; camping N$195, s/d Jul-Oct
N$6415/9930, Apr-Jun & Nov N$5045/7790, Dec-
Mar N$3195/6390; ☎) Nambwa, 14km south
of Kongola, is one of the very few places to
stay in the park itself. It combines an excel-
lent campsite with a luxury lodge, replete
with elevated walkways, stunning interiors
(tree trunks and antique chandeliers, any-
one?) and glorious views out over the flood
plains. Some of Bwabwata's best wildlife
areas are close by, and the lodge overlooks
a water hole that's especially popular with
animals late in the dry season.

Camp Kwando LODGE $$$
(☏081 206 1514; www.campkwando.cc.na; camping
N$150, s with half board N$1130-1840, d with half
board N$2020-2520; ☎) This gorgeous proper-
ty has luxury thatch-and-canvas chalets that
overlook the Kwando River in all its glory.
Elephants and abundant birdlife are frequent
visitors, while the soaring ceilings, prolific
use of wood and four-poster beds are all stunning. There's a grassy and shady campsite.

Katima Mulilo

POP 28,360 / ☏066

Out on a limb at the eastern end of the Caprivi Strip, remote Katima Mulilo is as far
from Windhoek (1200km) as you can get
and still be in Namibia. Once known for
the elephants that marched through the
village streets, Katima is a sprawling town

these days, one that thrives as a border town
– Zambia's border is just 4km away, while
Botswana is less than 100km away to the
southeast – and minor commercial centre.

Air Namibia (www.airnamibia.com.na)
has several weekly departures between
Windhoek's Eros Airport and Katima's Mpa-
cha Airport, located 18km southwest of town.

Three weekly Intercape Mainliner (p252)
buses make the 16-hour run between Windhoek and Katima Mulilo. Book your tickets
(fares from N$530) in advance online, as
this service continues on to Victoria Falls
and fills up quickly.

Combis connect Windhoek and Katima
with fairly regular frequency, and a ride
shouldn't cost more than N$280. From Ka-
tima, routes fan out to various towns and
cities in the north.

Caprivi Houseboat
Safari Lodge HOUSEBOAT, LODGE $$
(☏066-252287; www.zambezisafaris.com; off Ngo-
ma Rd; s/d from N$750/1100) Rustic en-suite
chalet accommodation with mosquito nets,
ceiling fans provide a lovely sense of being
close to nature, but it's the houseboats that
are the real novelty here. These aren't luxury
houseboats, but the fun value is extremely
high and it's certainly a wonderful experi-
ence to spend a night actually *on* the Zambe-
zi. As you'd expect in this part of the world,
the birdwatching is a highlight.

★**Protea Hotel Zambezi Lodge** LODGE $$$
(☏066-251500; www.marriott.com/hotels/travel/
mpapr-protea-hotel-zambezi-river-lodge/; Ngoma Rd; camping N$100, r from N$1058; ❊ @ ☎)
This stunning riverside lodge is perched
on the banks of the Zambezi and features a
floating bar where you can watch the crocs
and hippos below. The campsite is amid a
flowery garden, while accommodation is in
well-equipped modern rooms that open up
to small verandas and ample views.

Nkasa Rupara National Park

☏066

Watch this space – this is one of Namibia's,
perhaps Southern Africa's, most exciting
national parks (per person/vehicle N$40/10).
In years of good rains, this wild and
seldom-visited national park (formerly
called Mamili National Park) becomes Namibia's equivalent of Botswana's Okavango
Delta. Forested islands fringed by reed and
papyrus marshes foster some of the country's richest birdwatching, with more than

430 recorded species to count. Poaching has taken a toll on Nkasa Rupara's wildlife, though – as recently as 2013, the park's largest lion pride was wiped out in retaliation for livestock lost to predators. Since then, things are on the up, thanks to human–wildlife conflict mitigation programmes by Panthera (www.panthera.org). Lions are returning to the area; sightings of wild dogs across the water on the Botswana side are also possible while semiaquatic species such as hippos, crocodiles, pukus, red lechwes, sitatungas and otters will impress.

Wildlife viewing is best from June to August, and is especially good on Nkasa and Lupala islands. It can be oppressively hot from October through to March or April.

Nkasa Lupala Lodge is about 75km from Kongola and 130km from Katima Mulilo. Take the C49 (a maintained gravel road from Kongola and tarred from Katima Mulilo) to Sangwali. From Sangwali, head to the Nkasa Rupara National Park – you'll need a high-clearance 4WD.

Jackalberry Tented Camp TENTED CAMP $$$
(☑081 147 7798; www.jbcamp.com; r N$8600)
Run by the same people who operate Nkasa Lupala Lodge (p268), Jackalberry has just four luxury tents close to the water's edge near the entrance to Nkasa Rupara National Park. With such a small number of tents, the feel is much more intimate and exclusive than most in the area.

★**Livingstone's Camp** CAMPGROUND $
(☑081 033 2853, 066-686208; www.livingstones camp.com; camping Nov-Mar/Apr-Oct N$200/250)
Overlooking the wetlands and marketing itself as an exclusive campsite, Livingstone's has five sites, each with its own shower and toilets and all with front-row seats to the wa-

ter. It can organise wildlife drives into Nkasa Rupara National Park and *mokoro* (dugout canoe) trips on the Kwando River network.

★**Nkasa Lupala Lodge** TENTED CAMP, LODGE $$
(☑081 147 7798; www.nkasalupalalodge.com; r per person N$1930) Located 30km from Mudumu, and just outside the entrance to Nkasa Rupara National Park, this remote luxury, Italian-run lodge sits on the banks of the Kwando–Linyanti River system. The lodge gets rave reviews from travellers and offers activities such as game drives, including night drives. Accommodation is in tents on stilts, from where you may just spot elephants trooping past your deck. The lodge is around 12km beyond Sangwali village, with plenty of signposts along the way.

Nyae Nyae Conservancy

Out in Namibia's northeast, where the horizon shimmers in the haze of the Kalahari, is the land of the Ju/'Hoansi–San. The **Nyae Nyae Conservancy** (☑061-244011; ⊙8am-5pm Mon-Fri) stands at the heart of this remote land where San villages offer a fraught, if fascinating insight into the lives of Southern Africa's longest-standing inhabitants.

With interest in Kalahari cultures growing worldwide, tourist traffic has increased throughout the region, though any expectations you might have of witnessing an entirely self-sufficient hunter-gatherer society will, sadly, not be met here. Hunting is forbidden, and most communities have abandoned foraging in favour of cheap, high-calorie foods such as pap (corn meal) and rice, which are purchased in bulk from shops. Try instead to look beyond the dire realities of the San's economic situation, and attempt to use the experience as a rare opportunity to interact with the modern-day descendants of perhaps all of our ancestors.

Tsumkwe
☑067
Tsumkwe is the only real permanent settlement in the whole of Otjozondjupa, though it's merely a wide spot in the sand that consists of a few rust-covered buildings. Originally constructed as the regional headquarters of the South African Defence Force (SADF), Tsumkwe was then given a mandate as the administrative centre of the *Ju/'Hoansi–San* community, and is home to the Nyae Nyae Conservancy office. While organised tourism in the region is still something of

---

NKASA RUPARA NATIONAL PARK PRACTICALITIES

You must bring everything with you, including your own water, and be prepared for extremely rough road conditions. Although there is generally a ranger to collect park fees at the entrance gate, you're all alone once inside. The simple but handy *Kavango-Zambezi National Parks* map includes a high-level overview of Nkasa Rupara National Park. It's available at Nkasa Lupala Lodge or online via www.think africadesign.com.

a work in progress, Tsumkwe is where you can arrange everything from bush walks to hunting safaris, and inject some much-needed cash into the local community.

Note that you will need your own transport; a 4WD with good clearance is recommended. There are no sealed roads in the region, and only the C44 is passable to 2WD vehicles. Petrol is sometimes available at the Tsumkwe Country Lodge, though it's best to carry a few jerrycans with you. If you're planning to explore the bush around Tsumkwe, it is recommended that you hire a local guide and travel as part of a convoy.

The Dobe border crossing to Botswana requires a 4WD and extra fuel to reach the petrol stations at Maun or Etsha 6, which are accessed by a difficult sand track through northwestern Botswana.

Living Hunter's Museum
of the Ju/'Hoansi   MUSEUM

(D3315; ☉ sunrise-sunset) About 25km out of Tsumkwe, heading towards Khaudum National Park, is the Living Hunter's Museum of the *Ju/'Hoansi,* which is run and managed independently by the San. A lot of effort has gone into representing the old San hunter-gatherer culture as authentically as possible. Cultural interactions on offer include hunting trips (N$250 per person) with San hunters using traditional methods and equipment. There are also bush walks (N$150) and singing/dancing shows.

Tsumkwe Country Lodge   LODGE $

(☏061-374750; camping N$120, s/d from N$680/1000; ❄@❀) The only tourist lodge in Tsumkwe proper is an upmarket affair with a bar, restaurant, small shop and pool. Guests can base themselves here and visit surrounding villages as part of an organised tour.

Nhoma Safari Camp   TENTED CAMP $$$

(☏081 273 4606; www.tsumkwel.iway.na; camping per adult/child N$200/100, s/d luxury tents with full board from N$3625/6000; ❀) The former owners of the Tsumkwe Country Lodge, Arno and Estelle, have lived in the area for much of their lives and are well respected by the local San communities. Their luxury tented camp is perched between a fossilised river valley and a verdant teak grove, though the main attraction continues to be their wonderful excursions into local San villages. The camp is 280km east of Grootfontein and 80km west of Tsumkwe along the C44. You must book in advance to stay here – as mobile phone reception at the camp is unreliable (there's no landline), it's best to email them.

NORTHWESTERN NAMIBIA

For those who like to take a walk (or even a drive) on the wild side, northwestern Namibia is a stark, desolate environment where some of the most incredible landscapes imaginable lie astride 4WD tracks. Along the Skeleton Coast, seemingly endless expanses of foggy beach are punctuated by rusting shipwrecks and flanked by wandering dunes. Here, travellers are left entirely alone to bask in this riveting isolation, bothered only by the concern of whether their vehicles can survive the journey unscathed.

Not to be outdone by the barren coastline, the Kaokoveld is a photographer's dreamscape of wide-open vistas, lonely desert roads and hardly another person around to ruin your shot. A vast repository of desert mountains, this is one of the least developed regions of the country, and arguably Namibia at its most primeval. The Kaokoveld is also the ancestral home of the Himba people, a culturally rich tribal group that has retained its striking appearance and dress. And then there's Damaraland, home to the Brandberg Massif, Namibia's highest peak, and Twyfelfontein, which together contain some of Southern Africa's finest prehistoric rock paintings and engravings. A veritable window into the past, these two sites help to illuminate the hidden inner workings of our collective forebears, who roamed the African savannah so many eons ago.

Damaraland

From the glorious rock formations of Spitzkoppe, Erongo and the Brandberg in the south to the equally glorious red-rock, wild-desert mountains around Palmwag in the north, Damaraland is one of Namibia's most dramatic collections of landscapes. Hidden in the rocky clefts is Twyfelfontein, which along with the Brandberg contains some of Southern Africa's finest prehistoric rock art and engravings, and there's even a petrified forest nearby, as well as palm-fringed, oasislike valleys. Damaraland is also one of Southern Africa's most underrated wildlife-watching areas. One of Namibia's last 'unofficial' wildlife regions, it's home to critically endangered black rhinos, desert-adapted lions and elephants, as well as the full range of Namibia specialities such as gemsbok, zebra, giraffe and spotted hyena.

This combination of wild landscapes and wild creatures is Damaraland at its best. Plan to stay here as long as you can.

The Spitzkoppe

🗹064

One of Namibia's most recognisable landmarks, the 1728m-high **Spitzkoppe** (Groot Spitzkoppe village; per person/car N$50/20; ☉sunrise-sunset) rises miragelike above the dusty Pro-Namib plains of southern Damaraland. Its dramatic shape has inspired its nickname, the Matterhorn of Africa, but similarities between this ancient volcanic remnant and the glaciated Swiss alp begin and end with its sharp peak. First summited in 1946, the Spitzkoppe continues to attract hard-core rock climbers bent on tackling Namibia's most challenging peak.

Under normal dry conditions, a 2WD is sufficient to reach the mountain. Turn northwest off the B2 onto the D1918 towards Henties Bay. After 18km, turn north onto the D3716.

Sptitzkoppe Campsites CAMPGROUND $
(🗹064-464144; www.spitzkoppe.com; camping N$135) These wonderful campsites in the nooks and crannies that surround the Spitzkoppe massif perfectly capture the area's otherworldly landscapes. Operated by the same people as those at Spitzkoppen Lodge, this is a professionally run place with carefully chosen sites and good facilities.

Spitzkoppe Rest Camp CAMPGROUND $
(🗹064-530879; Groot Spitzkoppe village; camping N$110) The sites at this camp are dotted around the base of the Spitzkoppe and surrounding outcrops. Most are set in magical rock hollows and provide a sense of real isolation and oneness with the bouldered surrounds. Facilities at the entrance include a reception office, ecofriendly ablutions blocks and braai stands, plus a bar and restaurant.

★ **Spitzkoppen Lodge** LODGE $$$
(www.spitzkoppenlodge.com; s/d N$2900/5000; 🛜🕸) Due to open not long after our visit, this place promises to be the pick of the Spitzkoppe choices. Run by the same people behind **Kalahari Bush Breaks** (🗹062-568936; www.kalaharibushbreaks.com; s/d N$900/1630; ❄🛜🕸), the lodge consists of 15 wonderfully secluded chalets with gorgeous views all connected by an elevated walkway. The design in places evokes the Spitzkoppe

mountain and there is an enduring sense of isolation and luxury.

The Brandberg

🗹064

Driving around this massive pink granite bulge and marvelling at the ethereal light at sunset is a highlight of the region. But inside lies the real treasure – one of the finest remnants of prehistoric art on the African continent.

The Brandberg (Fire Mountain) is named for the effect created by the setting sun on its western face, which causes this granite massif to resemble a burning slag heap. Its summit, Königstein, is Namibia's highest peak at 2573m.

The Brandberg is a conservancy and the entry fee for admission is N$50 per person and N$20 per car. Note that this includes being allocated a compulsory guide – you cannot just walk around these fragile treasures by yourself. It's good to tip the guide afterwards if you're happy with their service.

To reach Tsisab Ravine from Uis, head 15km north and turn west on the D2359, which leads 26km to the Tsisab car park. To reach Numas Ravine, head 14km south of Uis and follow the D2342 for 55km, where you'll see a rough track turning eastwards. After about 10km, you'll reach a fork; the 4WD track on the right leads to the Numas Ravine car park.

Numas Ravine ROCK ART
Numas Ravine, slicing through the western face of the Brandberg, is a little-known treasure house of ancient paintings. Most people ask their guide to take them to the rock facing the southern bank of the riverbed, which bears paintings of a snake, a giraffe and an antelope. It lies about 30 minutes' walk up the ravine. After another half-hour you'll reach an oasislike freshwater spring and several more paintings in the immediate surroundings.

Tsisab Ravine ROCK ART
Tsisab Ravine is the epicentre of the Brandberg's rock-art magic. The most famous figure in the ravine is the White Lady of the Brandberg, in Maack's Shelter. The figure, which isn't necessarily a lady (it's still open to interpretation), stands about 40cm high and is part of a larger painting that depicts a bizarre hunting procession. In one hand the figure is carrying what appears to be a

flower or possibly a feather. In the other, the figure is carrying a bow and arrows.

Brandberg White Lady Lodge LODGE $$
(☑ 064-684004, 081 791 3117; www.brandbergwl lodge.com; D2359; camping N$110, s/d luxury tents N$550/770, s/tw with half board N$1075/1846) The Brandberg White Lady has something for just about every kind of traveller. Campers can pitch a tent along the riverine valley, all the while taking advantage of the lodge's upmarket facilities, while lovers of their creature comforts can choose from rustic bungalows and chalets that are highlighted by their stone interiors and wraparound patios. There are also luxury tents.

Twyfelfontein Area
☑ 067
Unesco World Heritage–listed Twyfelfontein (Doubtful Spring), at the head of the grassy Aba Huab Valley, is one of the most extensive rock-art galleries on the continent. To date over 2500 engravings have been discovered. Guides are compulsory; note that tips are their only source of income.

There's no public transport in the area and little traffic, Turn off the C39, 73km west of Khorixas, turn south on the D3254 and continue 15km to a right turning signposted Twyfelfontein. It's 5km to the petroglyph site.

Burnt Mountain MOUNTAIN
Southeast of Twyfelfontein rises a barren 12km-long volcanic ridge, at the foot of which lies the hill known as Burnt Mountain, an expanse of volcanic clinker that ap-

pears to have been literally exposed to fire. Virtually nothing grows in this eerie panorama of desolation. Burnt Mountain lies beside the D3254, 3km south of the Twyfelfontein turn-off.

Petrified Forest LANDMARK
(Versteende Woud; adult/child/car N$80/free/10; ☉ sunrise-sunset) The petrified forest is an area of open veld scattered with petrified tree trunks up to 34m long and 6m in circumference, which are estimated to be around 260 million years old. The original trees belonged to an ancient group of cone-bearing plants that are known as *Gymnospermae*, which includes such modern plants as conifers, cycads and welwitschias. Because of the lack of root or branch remnants, it's thought that the trunks were transported to the site in a flood.

Abu Huab Rest Camp CAMPGROUND $
(camping N$120) Well-shaded, close to the Twyfelfontein rock art and often visited by desert elephants, Abu Huab is an appealing choice for self-drivers, at least at first glance. There's also a small bar, but service at the whole place definitely needs a rethink and facilities (such as the nonexistent electricity) need an overhaul.

★ Camp Kipwe LODGE $$$
(☑ 061-232009; www.kipwe.com; s/d with half board low season N$2800/4100, high season N$2490/5280; ❄ ✆ ☒) Brilliantly located amongst the boulders and rocks littered throughout its premises, Kipwe is languidly

NAMIBIA DAMARALAND

TWYFELFONTEIN'S ROCK ENGRAVINGS

Mostly dating back at least 6000 years to the early Stone Age, Twyfelfontein's **rock engravings** (adult/child/car N$80/free/10; ☉ sunrise-sunset) were probably the work of ancient San hunters, and were made by cutting through the hard patina covering the local sandstone. In time, this skin reformed over the engravings, protecting them from erosion. From colour differentiation and weathering, researchers have identified at least six distinct phases, but some are clearly the work of copycat artists and are thought to date from the 19th century.

In the ancient past, this perennial spring most likely attracted wildlife, creating a paradise for the hunters who eventually left their marks on the surrounding rocks. Animals, animal tracks and geometric designs are well represented here, though there are surprisingly few human figures. Many of the engravings depict animals that are no longer found in the area – elephants, rhinos, giraffes and lions – and an engraving of a sea lion indicates contact with the coast more than 100km away.

Twyfelfontein became a national monument in 1952. Unfortunately, the site did not receive formal protection until 1986, when it was designated a natural reserve. In the interim, many petroglyphs were damaged by vandals, and some were even removed altogether. Restoration work continues.

draped over the stunning landscape in very unobtrusive large rondavels with thatched roofs that blend in beautifully with their surrounds and have lovely views. There are nine standard rooms and one honeymoon suite (rooms 3 and 4 are family rooms with kids' tents); all come with outdoor bathrooms so you can stargaze while you wash.

★ Doro Nawas Camp   LODGE $$$

(☑ 061-225178; www.wilderness-safaris.com; s/d Jun-Oct N$6510/11,270, rates vary rest of year; 🛜 ☒) Part of the elite Wilderness Safaris portfolio, Doro Nawas is a magnificent place. The thatched rooms are massive and luxurious, the terraces open onto vast views and there's a great mix of excursions, from Twyfelfontein rock art to wildlife drives in search of desert-adapted elephants and lions. Prices are high by Namibian standards, but the quality and service are unimpeachable.

Palmwag

☑ 061

The 5000 sq km Palmwag Concession and the surrounding areas together make up a rich wildlife area amid stark red hills and plains, surrounded by a bizarre landscape of uniformly sized red stones. It serves as something of a buffer zone between Etosha in the north and the Skeleton Coast, with a reasonable chance that you'll see black rhinos (most of the camps offer rhino tracking), desert elephants and lions, as well as spotted hyenas, giraffes, gemsboks and other antelope. The area is home to a handful of luxury lodges, and also serves as a study centre for the Save the Rhino Trust (SRT), making it a good mix of great wildlife watching and serious conservation, quite apart from being stunningly beautiful country.

Palmwag is on the D3706, 157km from Khorixas and 105km from Sesfontein. Coming from the south, you'll cross the Red Line, 1km south of Palmwag Lodge – you can carry meat heading north, but not south.

Hoada Campsite   CAMPGROUND $

(☑ 081 289 0982, 061-228104; www.grootberg.com/hoada-campsite; camping N$185; ☒) Run by Grootberg Lodge, this superb campsite sits among towering boulders with excellent facilities including a fine swimming pool, flush toilets and outdoor showers.

★ Desert Rhino Camp   TENTED CAMP $$$

(☑ 061-225178; www.wilderness-safaris.com; s/d with full board high season N$11,600/17,010; ☒) The safari-style tents in a remote corner of Damaraland are certainly luxurious and a worthy member of the elite Wilderness Safaris' Classic collection. But even more than the rooms, it's the ethos of this place – the camp has been at the centre of efforts to save Namibia's black rhino population – that impresses. Rhino tracking, and the chance to see desert lions and elephants, are other highlights.

Damaraland Camp   LODGE $$$

(☑ 061-225178; www.wilderness-safaris.com; s/d with full board high season N$9030/13,120; ☒) This solar-powered desert outpost 60km south of Palmwag has all-encompassing views of stark, truncated hills and is an oasis of luxury amid a truly feral and outlandish setting. When you're not living out your end-of-world fantasies in your luxury tent with wood floors, adobe walls and outdoor showers, you can do a few laps in the novel pool that occupies a rocky gorge formed by past lava flows.

Grootberg Lodge   LODGE $$$

(☑ 067-333212, 061-228104; www.grootberg.com; s/d with half board N$1950/2930) This place has the best views we witnessed on our most recent research trip in Namibia, and the valley of this stunning setting is where you can track black rhino – yes, you get to drive down into that valley! An extraordinary location brought home by the very steep approach track, this is a genuinely wild, open space – there are no fences. Rooms are large and luxurious, but it's the views that you'll remember most.

The Kaokoveld

The Kaokoveld is largely devoid of roads and is crossed only by sandy tracks laid down by the South African Defence Force (SADF) decades ago. In this harsh wilderness of dry and arid conditions, wildlife has been forced to adapt in miraculous ways – consider the critically endangered desert elephant, which has especially spindly legs suited for long walks in search of precious water.

It's that sort of place, where a sense of mystery and scenes of singular beauty are your companions while travelling out here.

Opuwo

POP 7660 / ☑ 065

In the Herero language, Opuwo means 'the end', which is certainly a fitting name for this dusty collection of concrete commercial buildings ringed by traditional rondavels and huts. While first impressions are unlikely to be very positive, a visit to Opuwo is one of the cultural highlights of Namibia, particularly for anyone interested in interacting with the Himba people. As the unofficial capital of Himbaland, Opuwo serves as a convenient jumping-off point for excursions into the nearby villages, and there is a good assortment of lodges and campsites to choose from.

The paved C41 runs from Outjo to Opuwo, which makes Himbaland accessible even to 2WD vehicles. Although there is a temptation to speed along this long and lonely highway, keep your lead foot off the pedal north of the veterinary control fence, as herds of cattle commonly stray across the road. If you're heading deeper into the Kaokoveld, be advised that Opuwo is the last opportunity to buy petrol before Kamanjab, Ruacana or Sesfontein.

Ohakane Lodge　　　　　LODGE $

(☑ 065-273031, 081 295 9024; ohakane@iway.na; s/d N$620/1030; ❊❊) This well-established

and centrally located lodge sits along the main drag in Opuwo and does good business with tour groups. Fairly standard but fully modern rooms are comfortable enough, but if it's in your budget, it's worth shelling out a bit more for a bungalow at the Opuwo Country Lodge.

★Opuwo Country Lodge　　　HOTEL $$$

(☑ 065-273461, 064-418661; www.opuwolodge. com; camping N$160, s/d standard rooms incl breakfast N$1260/1800, s/d luxury rooms incl breakfast N$1820/2560; ❊@❊) Far and away the area's swankiest accommodation option with lovely rooms, the hilltop Opuwo Country Lodge is an enormous thatched building (reportedly the largest in Namibia) that elegantly lords it over the town below. The hotel faces across a valley towards the Angolan foothills, and most of your time here will be spent soaking your cares away in the infinity-edge pool.

Kaoko Information Centre　　　TOURIST INFORMATION

(☑ 065-273420, 081 284 3681; ⊙8am-6pm) KK and Kemuu, the friendly guys at this information centre (look for the tiny, tiny yellow shack), can arrange visits to local Himba villages in addition to providing useful information for your trip through the Kaokoveld region.

NAMIBIA THE KAOKOVELD

THE HIMBA, ETIQUETTE & TAKING PICS

In the past, rural Himba people were willing models for photography. These days, however, you are likely to encounter traditionally dressed Himba people who will wave you down and ask for tips in exchange for having their photograph taken. Naturally, whether you accept is up to you, but bear in mind that encouraging this trade works to draw people away from their traditional lifestyle, and propels them towards a cash economy that undermines long-standing values and community cooperation.

It's recommended that instead you trade basic commodities for photographs. In times of plenty, Himba grow maize to supplement their largely meat- and milk-based diet, though rain is highly unpredictable in Namibia. Pap (corn meal) is a very desirable gift for the Himba, as is rice, bread, potatoes and other starches. Try to resist giving sugar, soft drinks and other sweets, as the majority of Himba may never meet a dentist in their lifetime.

If you would like to have free rein with the camera, visiting a traditional village – if done in the proper fashion – can yield some truly amazing shots. Needless to say, a guide who speaks both English and the Himba language is essential to the experience. You can either join an organised tour through your accommodation, or stop by the Kaoko Information Centre in Opuwo.

Before arriving in the village, please do spend some time shopping for gifts – entering a village with food items will garner a warm welcome from the villagers, who will subsequently be more willing to tolerate photography. At the end of your time in the village, buying small bracelets and trinkets directly from the artisan is also a greatly appreciated gesture.

Epupa Falls

📍 061

At Epupa, which means 'falling waters' in Herero, the Kunene River fans out into a vast flood plain and is ushered through a 500m-wide series of parallel channels, dropping a total of 60m over 1.5km. The greatest single drop, an estimated 37m, is commonly identified as the Epupa Falls. Here the river tumbles into a dark, narrow, rainbow-wrapped cleft, a stunning sight to behold, particularly when the Kunene is in peak flow from April to May.

Although you'd think this remote corner of the Kaokoveld would be off the tourist trail, Epupa Falls is a popular detour for overland trucks and organised safaris, and can get swamped with tourists. But if you're passing through the area, the falls are certainly worth the detour – the sight of so much water in the middle of the dry Kaokoveld is miraculous to say the least, and if the pools are free from crocs, a dip is a possibility.

The road from Okongwati is accessible to high-clearance 2WD vehicles, but it's still quite rough. As the rugged 93km 4WD river route from Swartbooi's Drift may take several days, it's far quicker to make the trip via Otjiveze/Epembe.

Epupa Camp LODGE, CAMGROUND $$$

(📞 061-237294; www.epupa.com.na; camping N$120, s/d with full board N$1800/2800; 🏊) Located 800m upstream from the falls and with a lovely riverside setting, Epupa Camp offers beautifully situated accommodation among a grove of towering baobab and palm trees. There are nine luxury tents filled to the brim with curios, and a slew of activities on offer, including Himba visits, boat trips, sundowner hikes, birdwatching walks and trips to rock-art sites. Five campsites are also available.

Omarunga Lodge LODGE, CAMPGROUND $$$

(📞 064-403096; www.natron.net/omarunga-camp/main.html; camping N$100, s/d chalets with full board N$2458/3916; 🏊) This German-run camp operates through a concession granted by a local chief, and has a well-groomed campsite beneath the palm trees with modern facilities as well as a dozen luxury chalets. It's a very attractive spot, but it can't hold a candle to the slightly more upmarket Epupa Camp. Don't be tempted to swim in the river – crocodiles lurk!

The Northwest Corner

📍 064

West of Epupa Falls is the Kaokoveld of travellers' dreams: stark, rugged desert peaks, vast landscapes, sparse, scrubby vegetation, drought-resistant wildlife, and nomadic bands of Himba people and their tiny settlements of beehive huts. This region, which is contiguous with the Skeleton Coast Wilderness, has been designated the Kaokoveld Conservation Area and it's one of Namibia's true gems. It's also a pretty rough ride on bad tracks – getting here and around is part of the adventure.

From Okongwati, the westward route through Etengwa leads to either Van Zyl's Pass or Otjihaa Pass. From Okauwa (with a landmark broken windmill) to the road fork at Otjitanda, which is a Himba chief's *kraal* (hut), the journey is extremely rough and slow going. Along the way, stop off for a swim at beautiful Ovivero Dam. From Otjitanda, you must decide whether you're heading west over Van Zyl's Pass (which may only be traversed from east to west!) into Otjinjange (Marienflüss) and Hartmann's Valleys, or south over the equally beautiful, but much easier, Otjihaa Pass towards Orupembe.

You can also access Otjinjange (Marienflüss) and Hartmann's Valleys without crossing Van Zyl's Pass by turning north at the three-way junction in the middle of the Onjuva Plains, 12km north of Orupembe. At the T-junction in Rooidrum (Red Drum), you can decide which valley you want. Turn right for Otjinjange (Marienflüss) and left for Hartmann's. West of this junction, 17km from Rooidrum, you can also turn south along the fairly good route to Orupembe, Purros (provided that the Hoarusib River isn't flowing) and on to Sesfontein.

Alternatively, you can head west from Opuwo on the D3703, which leads 105km to Etanga; 19km beyond Etanga, you'll reach a road junction marked by a stone sign painted with white birds. At this point, you can turn north towards Otjitanda (27km away) or south towards Otjihaa Pass and Orupembe.

Otjinjange & Hartmann's Valleys NATURAL SITE

Allow plenty of time to explore the wild and magical Otjinjange (better known as Marienflüss) and Hartmann's Valleys – broad sandy and grassy expanses descending gently to the Kunene River. Note that camping outside campsites is prohibited at both valleys.

Van Zyl's Pass   NATURAL SITE

The beautiful, but frightfully steep and challenging, Van Zyl's Pass forms a dramatic transition between the Kaokoveld plateaus and the vast, grassy expanses of Otjinjange Valley (Marienflüss). This winding 13km stretch isn't suitable for trailers and may only be passed from east to west, which means you'll have to return via Otjihaa Pass or through Purros.

Ngatutunge Pamwe
Camp Site   CAMPGROUND $

(Purros Campsite; camping N$60; ✿) The community-run Ngatutunge campsite is perched along the Hoarusib River 2km from Purros village, and surprisingly has hot showers, flush toilets, well-appointed bungalows, a communal kitchen and (believe it or not!) a swimming pool. It's also a good spot for hiring guides to visit nearby Himba villages or observing desert-adapted wildlife.

★ Serra Cafema Camp   TENTED CAMP $$$

(www.wilderness-safaris.com; s/d high season N$16,320/25,140; ✿) One of Namibia's most opulent and remote safari experiences, Serra Cafema is a breathtaking place. Stunning desert scenery, combined with a special riverside location and excellent cultural immersion opportunities with the local Himba are big selling points here. The public areas open onto some gorgeous views, while the rooms, each with a private terrace overlooking the river, are large and lovely.

The Skeleton Coast

This treacherous coast – a foggy region with rocky and sandy coastal shallows, rusting shipwrecks and soaring dunes – has long been a graveyard for unwary ships and their crews, hence its forbidding name. Early Portuguese sailors called it *As Areias do Inferno* (The Sands of Hell), as once a ship washed ashore, the fate of the crew was sealed. This protected area stretches from Sandwich Harbour, south of Swakopmund, to the Kunene River, taking in around 20,000 sq km of dunes and gravel plains to form one of the world's most inhospitable waterless areas in the world's oldest desert.

Dorob National Park

Declared a national park in December 2010, Dorob extends beyond the Swakop River and down to Sandwich Harbour in the south, while its northern border is the Ugab River. Its undoubted highlight is the Cape Cross Seal Reserve. It's also extremely popular among fisherfolk. The most interesting area for visitors is a 200km-long and 25km-wide strip that extends from Swakopmund to the Ugab River.

At the time of writing, there were no entrance fees for Dorob.

There's no public transport along this coast – you'll need your own wheels. The coastal C34 road is in part built from salt but is in generally excellent condition. If you're coming from the north, take the C43 road south from Palmwag, then west along the C39.

★ Sandwich Harbour   HARBOUR

Sandwich Harbour, 56km south of Walvis Bay in Dorob National Park, is one of the most dramatic sights in Namibia – dunes up to 100m-high plunge into the Atlantic, which washes into the picturesque lagoon. The harbour is now deserted and a stirring wilderness devoid of any human settlement. Birdwatchers will have a field day and Sandwich Harbour 4x4 (p284) facilitate half- and full-day trips down here.

Cape Cross Seal Reserve

The best-known breeding colony of Cape fur seals along the Namib coast is at this **reserve** (per person/car N$80/10; ☉10am-5pm), where the population has grown large and fat by taking advantage of the rich concentrations of fish in the cold Benguela Current. The sight of more than 100,000 seals basking on the beach and frolicking in the surf is impressive to behold, though you're going to have to contend with the overwhelming odoriferousness of piles and piles of stinky seal poo. Bring a handkerchief or bandana to cover your nose – seriously, you'll thank us for the recommendation.

No pets or motorcycles are permitted, and visitors may not cross the low barrier between the seal-viewing area and the rocks where the colony lounges.

Cape Cross lies 46km north of Henties Bay along the coastal salt road. There's no public transport here, but a 2WD is all you'll need to get here from the south.

Campsites

CAMPGROUND $

(camping N$100) There are campsites on the water's edge 1.7km back along the coast from the seal colony. They're far enough away from the stink and have uninterrupted sea views, but facilities are basic and they only open from November to July. They operate on a first-come, first-served basis – ask at the entry to the reserve.

★ **Cape Cross Lodge** LODGE, CAMPGROUND $$$
(✆064-461677, 064-694012; www.capecross. org; camping per adult/child N$100/50, s/d N$1600/2450; ❀🛜) Cape Cross Lodge has an odd but strangely appealing architecture, which is self-described as a cross between Cape Dutch and fishing village style. The nicer rooms have spacious outdoor patios that overlook the coastline, though you really can't choose a bad room at this all-around

stunner of a lodge, conveniently located just before the official reserve entrance.

Skeleton Coast Park

📌064
At Ugabmund, 110km north of Cape Cross, the salt road passes through the entry gate to the Skeleton Coast Park, where rolling fogs and dusty sandstorms encapsulate its eerie, remote and wild feel. Despite the enduring fame of this coastline, surprisingly few travellers ever reach points north of Cape Cross. In order to preserve this incredibly fragile environment, Namibian Wildlife Resorts (NWR) imposes strict regulations on individual travellers seeking to do more than transit through the park. If you plan to linger, visit the NWR offices in Windhoek (p252) or Swakopmund (p283).

NAMIBIA THE SKELETON COAST

SKELETONS ON THE COAST

Despite prominent images of rusting ships embedded in the hostile sands of the Skeleton Coast, the most famous shipwrecks have long since disappeared. The harsh winds and dense fog that roll off the South Atlantic are strong forces of erosion, and today there are little more than traces of the countless ships that were swept ashore during the height of the mercantile era. In addition, the few remaining vessels are often in remote and inaccessible locations.

One such example is the *Dunedin Star,* which was deliberately run aground in 1942 just south of the Angolan border after hitting some offshore rocks. The ship was en route from Britain around the Cape of Good Hope to the Middle East war zone, and was carrying more than 100 passengers, a military crew and cargo.

When a rescue ship arrived two days later, getting the castaways off the beach proved an impossible task. At first, the rescuers attempted to haul the castaways onto their vessel by using a line through the surf. However, as the surge grew stronger, the rescue vessel was swept onto the rocks and wrecked alongside the *Dunedin Star*. Meanwhile, a rescue aircraft, which managed to land on the beach alongside the castaways, became bogged in the sand. Eventually all the passengers were rescued, though they were evacuated with the help of an overland truck convoy. The journey back to civilisation was two weeks of hard slog across 1000km of desert.

Further south on the Skeleton Coast – and nearly as difficult to reach – are several more intact wrecks. The *Eduard Bohlen* ran aground south of Walvis Bay in 1909 while carrying equipment to the diamond fields in the far south. Over the past century, the shoreline has changed so much that the ship now lies beached in a dune nearly 1km from the shore.

On picturesque Spencer Bay, 200km further south and just north of the abandoned mining town of Saddle Hill, is the dramatic wreck of the *Otavi*. This cargo ship beached in 1945 following a strong storm, and is now dramatically perched on Dolphin's Head, the highest point on the coast between Cape Town's Table Mountain and the Angolan border. In 1972 Spencer Bay also claimed the Korean cargo ship *Tong Taw*, which is currently one of the most intact vessels along the entirety of the Skeleton Coast.

More accessible wrecks include *South West Seal* (1976), just south of Toscanini and north of Henties Bay, and the *Zeila* (2008), 14km south of Henties Bay; the latter is close enough to the towns to attract touts and hangers-on.

You can get a free transit permit to pass between Ugabmund and Springbokwater, which can be obtained at the gates. To transit the park, you must pass the entry gate before 1pm and exit through the other gate before 3pm the same day. Note that transit permits aren't valid for Torra Bay or Terrace Bay.

The Skeleton Coast Park is accessed via the salt road from Swakopmund, which ends 70km north of Terrace Bay. The park is also accessible via the C39 gravel road which runs between Khorixas and Torra Bay. Note that motorcycles are not permitted in the Skeleton Coast Park.

Ugab River Rhino Camp CAMPGROUND $
(www.rhino-trust.org.na; GPS: S 20°57.44', E 14°08.01'; camping N$60) Outside the Skeleton Coast Park, this campsite is administered by the Save the Rhino Trust. This remote landscape is truly enigmatic, and those who've visited have only glowing comments. To get there, turn east onto the D2303, 40km north of Cape Cross; it's then 70km to the camp. Watch out for black rhinos!

Terrace Bay Resort CHALET $$$
(camping N$145, s/d N$990/1600, 4- to 10-person beach chalets per person N$610) Open year-round, this resort is a luxurious alternative to camping at Torra Bay. Around the camp you may spot black-backed jackals or brown hyenas, and the scenery of sparse coastal vegetation and lonely dunes is the Skeleton Coast at its finest. The site has a restaurant, a shop and a petrol station. Terrace Bay is 49km north of Torra Bay.

Skeleton Coast Wilderness Area

The Skeleton Coast Wilderness Area, stretching between the Hoanib and Kunene Rivers, makes up the northern third of the Skeleton Coast and is a part of the Skeleton Coast Park. This section of coastline is among the most remote and inaccessible areas in Namibia, though it's here in the wilderness that you can truly live out your Skeleton Coast fantasies. Since the entire area is a private concession and your only option for visiting is staying in the luxury lodge, you're going to have to part with some serious cash to visit.

The Skeleton Coast Wilderness Area is closed to private vehicles. Access is restricted to fly-in trips.

★**Hoanib Skeleton Coast Camp** LODGE $$$
(061-225178; www.wilderness-safaris.com; s/d all-inclusive high season N$16,350/26,100, rates vary rest of year;) Now here's something special. So far from the nearest publicly accessible road, and built in a splendid amalgam of canopied canvas and light woods, this uberluxurious tented camp is one of the most beautiful places to stay in Namibia. With a more contemporary look than many safari camps in the region, and all the better for it, Hoanib exudes light and space and end-of-the-earth romance.

CENTRAL NAMBIA

Central Nambia zeroes in on the tourist trade but it does so Namibian-style, offering epic road journeys, big skies and mesmerising landscapes. In that sense its not unlike other parts of the country – except here it is home to two large cities and a spectacular desert.

Walvis Bay and Swakopmund were originally established as port towns during the colonial era. The drive into them defines their surreal nature as desert wildernesses, which is magically replaced by (in the case of Swakopmund) a Germanic urban landscape that would be a colonial relic if it weren't for the life and energy brought to bear by a thriving tourist industry.

Adventure sports and Swakopmund go hand in hand. From quad biking up the crest of a soaring seaside dune to jumping out of a plane at 3000m, Swakop is where you can test your limits and go wild amid a stunningly beautiful natural setting unlike any other on the planet.

The region is defined by the Namib Desert though, a barren and desolate landscape of undulating apricot-coloured dunes interspersed with dry pans that culminates in the monumental peaks of Sossusvlei.

Swakopmund

POP 44,730 / 064
Sandwiched between Atlantic rollers and the Namib Desert, Swakopmund is one of those great traveller way stations along the African road. At once Namibia's adventure capital and a surreal colonial remnant, part destination in its own right and part launch pad for an exploration of the Skeleton Coast and Namib Desert, this is a city with as much personality as it has sea frontage. Like Lüderitz on the south coast,

NAMIBIA SWAKOPMUND

with its half-timbered German architecture, seaside promenades and pervasive *Gemütlichkeit* (a distinctively German appreciation of comfort and hospitality), Swakopmund, especially out of season, can feel like a holiday town along Germany's North Sea and Baltic coasts transplanted onto African soil. But the city is also thoroughly African and its multidimensional appeal means that most people end up staying longer than they planned.

Swakopmund

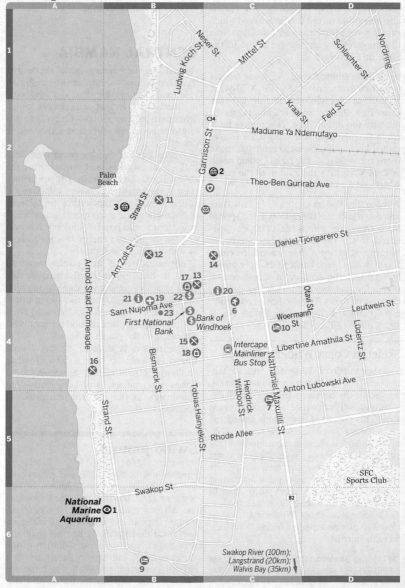

◉ Sights

Goanikontes   FARM

If you're on a quest to see welwitschias, continue east along the Welwitschia Drive to the **Moon Landscape**, a vista across eroded hills and valleys carved by the Swakop River. Here you may want to take a quick 12km return side trip north to the farm and oasis of Goanikontes, which dates from 1848. It lies beside the Swakop River amid fabulous desert mountains, and serves as an excellent picnic site.

Kristall Galerie   GALLERY

(☑064-406080; cnr Garnison St & Theo-Ben Gurirab Ave; N$30; ⊙9am-5pm Mon-Sat) This architecturally astute gallery features some of the planet's most incredible crystal formations, including the largest quartz crystal that has ever been found. The adjacent shop sells lovely mineral samples, crystal jewellery, and intriguing plates, cups and wine glasses that are carved from local stone.

★National Marine Aquarium   AQUARIUM

(☑064-4101214; Strand St; adult/child N$40/20; ⊙10am-4pm Tue-Sun) This recently overhauled waterfront aquarium provides an excellent introduction to the cold offshore world in the South Atlantic Ocean. Most impressive is the tunnel through the largest aquarium, which allows close-up views of graceful rays, toothy sharks (you can literally count the teeth!) and other little marine beasties.

Swakopmund Museum   MUSEUM

(☑064-402046; Strand St; adult/student N$30/15; ⊙8am-1pm & 3-5pm Mon-Fri, 10am-noon Sat) When ill winds blow, head for this museum at the foot of the lighthouse, where you can hole up and learn about the town's history. The museum occupies the site of the old harbour warehouse, which was destroyed in 1914 by a 'lucky' shot from a British warship. Displays include exhibits on Namibia's history and ethnology, including information on local flora and fauna. Especially good is the display on the !nara melon, a fruit which was vital to the early Khoikhoi people of the Namib region.

🏃 Activities

Adventure sports and Swakopmund go hand in hand. From quad biking up the crest of a soaring seaside dune to jumping out of a plane at 3000m, Swakop is one of the top destinations in Southern Africa for extreme-sports enthusiasts. Although filling your days with adrenaline-soaked activities is certainly not cheap, there are few places in the world where you can climb up, sandboard down and soar over towering sand dunes.

NAMIBIA SWAKOPMUND

Most activity operators don't have offices in town, which means that you need to arrange all of your activities through either your accommodation or the Namib-i (p283) tourist information centre.

★ **Alter Action** ADVENTURE SPORTS
(☑064-402737; www.alter-action.info; lie down/stand up US$40/55) Sandboarding with Alter Action is certain to increase your heart rate. If you have any experience snowboarding or surfing, it's highly recommended that you have a go at the stand-up option. You will be given a snowboard, gloves, goggles and enough polish to ensure a smooth ride.

★ **Ground Rush Adventures** ADVENTURE SPORTS, SCENIC FLIGHTS
(☑064-402841; www.skydiveswakop.com.na; tandem jumps N$2500, handycam/professional video N$500/900) Ground Rush Adventures provides the ultimate rush, and skydiving in Swakopmund is sweetened by the outstanding dune and ocean backdrop. The crew at Ground Rush have an impeccable safety record to date, and they make even the most nervous participant feel comfortable about jumping out of a plane at 3000m and freefalling for 30 seconds at 220km/h.

Living Desert Tours WILDLIFE
(☑081 127 5070, 064-405070; www.livingdesert namibia.com; half-day tours N$650) Get up close and personal with the Namib's fascinating wildlife on this excellent 4WD excursion. You'll go in search of the transparent Namib dune gecko, legless lizards, sidewinder snakes and other desert-adapted species.

Okakambe Horse Stables HORSE RIDING
(☑064-405258, 081 124 6626; www.okakambe. iway.na; 1/2hr ride N$650/820) Meaning 'horse' in the local Herero and Oshivambo languages, Okakambe specialises in horse riding and trekking through the desert. The German owner cares immensely for her horses, so you can be assured that they're well fed and looked after. Discounts are available for larger groups and longer outings, while more experienced riders can organise multi-day treks. You'll find it 12km east of Swakopmund on the D1901.

★ **Pleasure Flights** SCENIC FLIGHTS
(☑064-404500; www.pleasureflights.com.na) One of the most reputable light-plane operators in Namibia, Pleasure Flights has been offering scenic aerial cruises for almost 20 years. Given so much of Namibia's South Atlantic coastline is inaccessible on the ground, this is a fabulous way to get a glimpse. Destinations include the Salt Works, Sandwich Harbour, Welwitschia Drive, the Brandberg Mountains, Sossusvlei, the Skeleton Coast and beyond.

Swakop Cycle Tours CYCLING
(☑081 251 5916; www.swakopcycletours.com; bicycle/walking tours from N$380/285, bicycle rental per half-/full day N$195/255; ☉9am & 2pm) Visit the local Mondesa township to see how locals live as part of this 3½-hour cycle tour. Prices include a guide, bike and helmet

Swakopmund

◉ Top Sights
1 National Marine Aquarium B6

◉ Sights
2 Kristall Galerie C2
3 Swakopmund Museum B3

➌ Activities, Courses & Tours
4 Alter Action E4
5 Ground Rush Adventures E4
6 Pleasure Flights C4

🛏 Sleeping
7 Desert Sky Backpackers C5
8 Sam's Giardino Hotel F4
9 Stiltz B6
10 Swakop Lodge C4

🍴 Eating
11 22° South B3

12 Cafe Anton B3
13 Die Muschel Art Cafe B3
14 Hansa Hotel Restaurant C3
15 Kücki's Pub B4
16 Tug A4

🛍 Shopping
17 Die Muschel Book & Art Shop B3
18 Peter's Antiques B4

ℹ Information
19 Bismarck Medical Centre B4
20 Namib-i C3
21 Namibia Wildlife Resorts B4
22 Swakopmunder Buchhandlung
Commercial Bank B4

ℹ Transport
23 Air Namibia B4

rental, and local food tasting. It also arranges 2½-hour city walking tours and bicycle rental.

🕝 Tours

⭐ Hata Angu Cultural Tours   CULTURAL
(📞 081 124 6111; www.culturalactivities.in.na; tours from N$400; ⏰ 10am & 3pm) These four-hour tours are a refreshing change from your typical Swakop adventure. Here you'll meet an African herbalist, try homemade local dishes, drink at a local shebeen in a Swakop township and even shake hands with a chief. They can also organise sandboarding.

Hafeni Cultural Tours   CULTURAL TOUR
(📞 064-400731, 081 146 6222; hafenictours@gmail.com; 4hr tour N$450) If you're interested in arranging a visit to the Mondesa township, Hafeni Cultural Tours runs a variety of different excursions that provide insight into how the other half of Swakopmunders live. It also offers Himba cultural tours, and day excursions to Cape Cross, Spitzkoppe and the flamingos of Walvis Bay.

🛏 Sleeping

Desert Sky Backpackers   HOSTEL $
(📞 064-402339; www.desertskylodging.com; Anton Lubowski Ave; camping/dm N$160/200, d N$650, with shared bathroom N$600; 📶) This centrally located backpackers' haunt is an excellent place to drop anchor in Swakopmund. The indoor lounge is simple and homey, while the outdoor picnic tables are a nice spot for a cold beer and warm conversation. Free coffee is available all day, and you're within stumbling distance of the pubs if you want something stronger.

Swakop Lodge   HOSTEL $
(📞 064-402030; 42 Nathaniel Maxuilili St; dm/s/d N$150/450/650; ❋📶📶) This backpacker-orientated hotel is the epicentre of the action in Swakopmund, especially since this is where many of the adrenaline activities depart from and return to, and where many of the videos are screened each night. The hotel is extremely popular with overland trucks, so it's a safe bet that the attached bar is probably bumping and grinding most nights of the week.

⭐ Sea Breeze Guesthouse   GUESTHOUSE $$
(📞 064-463348; www.seabreeze.com.na; Turmalin St; s/d incl breakfast N$900/1285; 📶) This upmarket guesthouse is right on the beach about 4.5km north of town, and is an excellent option if you're looking for a secluded retreat. Ask to see a few of the rooms, as several of them have spectacular sea views; there's also a great family room. There's plenty of advice available on what to see and do around town. Follow the Strand north and keep an eye out for signs.

Stiltz   LODGE $$
(📞 064-400771; www.thestiltz.com; Am Zoll; s/d from N$1260/1680) Balanced atop 3.5m-high stilts with a bird's-eye view over the coast and town, the Stiltz is unlike anywhere else in Swakopmund. The rooms vary in size and design – some are slightly cavernous, others are warm and perfectly proportioned – but it's the views that will live longest in the memory.

⭐ Atlantic Villa   BOUTIQUE HOTEL $$
(📞 064-463511; www.atlantic-villa.com; Plover St; s/d N$980/1380, with sea view N$1200/1720, ste N$2100/2940) Styling itself as a boutique guesthouse, Atlantic Villa is a stylish place. Expect clean-lined rooms decked all in white with Nespresso coffee machines; many rooms have ocean views. In the northern part of town, it's also blissfully quiet.

⭐ Sam's Giardino Hotel   HOTEL $$
(📞 064-403210; www.giardinonamibia.com; 89 Anton Lubowski Ave; s/d from N$1000/1500; 📶📶) Sam's Giardino Hotel is a wonderfully personal place in the backstreets emphasising superb wines, fine cigars and relaxing in the rose garden with a friendly dog named Beethoven. There's a lovely front garden and a lot of common areas with books, and a grotto with stacks of wine bottles. The rooms are simple but very comfortable. Book ahead for the five-course dinner (N$280) and some wine tasting (N$190).

⭐ Desert Breeze Lodge   LODGE $$$
(📞 064-406236, 064-400771; www.desertbreeze swakopmund.com; off B2; s/d from N$1570/2140) Set on Swakopmund's southern outskirts but still close to the centre, Desert Breeze has sweeping views of the sand dunes from its perch above the Swakop riverbed. The 12 luxury bungalows here are lovely, modern and comfortable but it's the views you come here for – they are, quite simply, sublime.

🍴 Eating

Die Muschel Art Cafe   CAFE $
(📞 081 849 5984; off Tobias Hainyeko St, Brauhaus Arcade; snacks & light meals N$26-50; ⏰ 9am-6pm

Mon-Fri, 8.30am-5pm Sat, 10am-5pm Sun) The size of a postage stamp and cute as a button, this fine little cafe next to the bookshop of the same name does great coffee to go with its oven-baked rolls and cupcakes. Enjoy it all at one of the tables on the pedestrianised street outside.

Cafe Anton CAFE $

(☑064-400331; 1 Bismarck St; light meals N$40-70; ⏲7am-7pm) This much-loved local institution, located in the Schweizerhaus Hotel, serves superb coffee, *Apfelstrudel*, *Kugelhopf* (cake with nuts and raisins), *Mohnkuchen* (poppyseed cake), *Linzertorte* (cake flavoured with almond meal, lemon and spices, and spread with jam) and other European delights. The outdoor seating is inviting for afternoon snacks in the sun.

★22° South ITALIAN $$

(☑064-400380; Strand St; mains N$80-190; ⏲noon-2.30pm & 6-9.30pm Tue-Sun) Inside the ground floor of the lighthouse, this atmospheric place is run by an Italian-Namibian couple who prepare Swakopmund's best (and homemade) Italian food. It's a slightly more formal option than the many pizzerias around town, and the quality of the food is similarly elevated.

★Kücki's Pub PUB FOOD $$

(☑064-402407; www.kuckispub.com; Tobias Hainyeko St; mains N$95-160) A Swakopmund institution, Kücki's has been in the bar and restaurant biz for a couple of decades. The menu is full of seafood and meat dishes alongside comfort food, and everything is well prepared. The warm and congenial atmosphere is a welcome complement to the food.

Hansa Hotel Restaurant INTERNATIONAL $$$

(☑064-400311; www.hansahotel.com.na; 3 Hendrick Witbooi St; mains N$100-245; ⏲8am-9pm) It's hard to top history, and the Hansa Hotel is steeped in it. In the main dining hall at this classic colonial spot, you can indulge in culinary excesses and wash them down with a bottle from the extensive wine list. Lunch is served on the outside terrace while seafood and game meats are the specialities.

Tug SEAFOOD $$$

(☑064-402356; www.the-tug.com; off Strand St; mains N$75-315; ⏲5-10pm Mon-Thu, 6-10pm Fri, noon-3pm & 6-10pm Sat & Sun) Housed in the beached tugboat *Danie Hugo* near the jetty, the Tug is something of an obligatory destination for any restaurant-goer in Swakopmund. Regarded by many as the best restaurant in town, the Tug is an atmospheric, upmarket choice for meat and seafood, though a sundowner cocktail with the angelfish burger in North African spices will do just fine.

🛍 Shopping

Cosdef Arts & Crafts Centre ARTS & CRAFTS

(☑064-406122; www.cosdef.org.na; ⏲9am-5pm) This worthy project supports local artisans and unemployed people by providing a shopfront for their work. The quality is high and the overall message, one of building sustainability in local communities, is one that deserves support. For an idea of what's available, check out https://namibiacraft-collections.wordpress.com or its Facebook page. Opening hours were in a state of flux at the time of writing, at least on weekends.

Die Muschel Book & Art Shop BOOKS

(☑064-402874; Hendrick Witbooi St; ⏲8.30am-6pm Mon-Fri, 8.30am-1pm & 4-6pm Sat, 10am-6pm Sun) Swakopmund's best bookshop, with German- and English-language books. It's great for guides and maps, and esoteric works on art and local history are also available here.

Peter's Antiques ANTIQUES

(☑064-405624; www.peters-antiques.com; 24 Tobias Hainyeko St; ⏲9am-1pm & 3-6pm Mon-Fri, 9am-1pm & 4-6pm Sat, 4-6pm Sun) This place is an Ali Baba's cave of treasures, specialising in colonial relics, historic literature, West African art, politically incorrect German paraphernalia, and genuine West African fetishes and other artefacts from around the continent.

ℹ Information

DANGERS & ANNOYANCES

Although the palm-fringed streets and cool sea breezes in Swakopmund are unlikely to make you tense, you should always keep your guard up in town. Regardless of how relaxed the ambience might be, petty crime unfortunately occurs.

If you have a private vehicle, be sure that you leave it all locked up with no possessions inside visible during the day. At night, you need to make sure you're parked in a gated parking lot and not on the street. Also, when you're choosing a hotel or hostel, be sure that the security precautions (ie an electric fence and/or a guard) are up to your standards. Finally, although Swakopmund is generally safe at night, it's best to stay in a group, and when possible, take a taxi to and from your accommodation.

MEDICAL SERVICES

Bismarck Medical Centre (☏ 064-405000; cnr Bismarck St & Sam Nujoma Ave) To visit a doctor, go to this recommended centre.

MONEY

There are plenty of banks in the centre of town with ATMs; try around the corner of Tobias Hainyeko St and Sam Nujoma Ave.

POLICE

Police (☏ 402431, 10111)

POST

Main post office (Garnison St) Also sells telephone cards and offers fax services.

TOURIST INFORMATION

Namib-i (☏ 064-404827; Sam Nujoma Ave; ☺ 8am-1pm & 2-5pm Mon-Fri, 9am-1pm & 3-5pm Sat, 9am-1pm Sun) This tourist information centre is a very helpful resource. In addition to helping you get your bearings, it can also act as a booking agent for any activities and tours that happen to take your fancy.

Namibia Wildlife Resorts (NWR; ☏ 064-402172; www.nwr.com.na; Woermannhaus, Bismarck St; ☺ 8am-1pm & 2-5pm Mon-Fri, park permits only 8am-1pm Sat & Sun) Like its big brother in Windhoek, this office sells Namib-Naukluft Park and Skeleton Coast permits, and can also make reservations for other NWR-administered properties around the country.

❶ Getting There & Away

AIR

Air Namibia (☏ 064-405123; www.airnamibia. com.na) has several flights a week between Windhoek's Eros Airport and Walvis Bay, from where you can easily catch a bus or taxi to Swakopmund.

BUS

There are twice-weekly buses between Windhoek and Swakopmund (from N$200, five hours) on the Intercape Mainliner (p252) from the company's bus stop. You can easily book your tickets in advance online.

Also consider **Town Hopper** (☏ 064-407223; www.namibiashuttle.com), which runs private shuttle buses between Windhoek and Swakopmund (N$270), and also offers door-to-door pick-up and drop-off service.

Finally, combis run this route fairly regularly, and a ride between Windhoek and Swakopmund shouldn't cost more than N$120. Swakopmund is also a minor public-transport hub, serving various regional destinations, including Walvis

Bay by combi, with fares averaging between N$25 and N$50.

Walvis Bay

POP 100,000 / ☏ 064

Walvis Bay (vahl-fis bay), 30km south of Swakopmund, is pleasant enough, particularly around the new waterfront development and along the esplanade. The town proper is not so compact and your own wheels make life a lot easier. It's a good alternative to staying in Swakopmund if that city is too much of a scene for you – Walvis Bay has a far more relaxed feel to it. And the accommodation options and food choices are excellent.

Unlike Swakopmund, Walvis Bay was snatched by the British years before the German colonists could get their hands on it. As a result, Walvis Bay is architecturally uninspiring, and lacks the Old World ambience of its northerly neighbour. In marked contrast, the area around Walvis Bay is home to a number of unique natural attractions, including one of the largest flocks of flamingos in the whole of Southern Africa.

The only real port between Lüderitz and Luanda (Angola), the natural harbour at Walvis Bay is the result of the sand spit Pelican Point, which forms a natural breakwater and shelters the city from the strong ocean surge.

◉ Sights

Salt Works   BIRD SANCTUARY

Southwest of the lagoon (p286) is this 3500-hectare salt-pan complex, which currently supplies over 90% of South Africa's salt. As with the one in Swakopmund, these pans concentrate salt from seawater with the aid of evaporation. They are also a rich feeding ground for shrimp and larval fish. It's one of the three wetlands around Walvis Bay (along with the lagoon and Bird Island), which together form Southern Africa's single most important coastal wetland for migratory birds.

Dune 7   LANDMARK

In the bleak expanse just off the C14, 6km by road from town, Dune 7 is popular with locals as a slope for sandboarding and skiing. The picnic site, which is now engulfed by sand, has several shady palm trees tucked away in the lee of the dune.

Walvis Bay

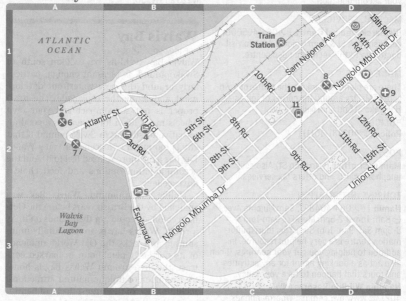

🏃 Activities

Sea-kayaking, boat trips, birdwatching and excursions to Sandwich Harbour (56km south) are all highlights of a visit to Walvis Bay. If that's not enough action for you, try Swakopmund to the north.

Mola Mola Safaris   BOATING
(☑ 081 127 2522, 064-205511; www.mola-namibia. com; Waterfront) This professional marine-safari company offers fully customisable boating trips around the Walvis Bay and Swakopmund coastal areas, where you can expect to see dolphins, seals and countless birds. Prices are dependent on your group size and length of voyage, but the standard three-hour Marine Dolphin Cruise starts at N$620/420 per adult/child.

Sandwich Harbour 4x4   TOUR
(☑ 064-207663; www.sandwich-harbour.com; Waterfront; adult/child half-day N$1100/850, full day N$1300/1050) Sandwich Harbour 4x4 runs half- and full-day trips down to spectacular Sandwich Harbour, 56km south of Walvis Bay. It also runs an excellent full-day Sandwich Harbour and sea-kayaking combo for N$1850/1350 per adult/child.

Eco Marine Kayak Tours   KAYAKING
(☑ 064-203144; www.emkayak.iway.na) Sea-kayaking trips around the beautiful Walvis Bay wetlands and beyond are conducted by this outfit. Note that there is no central office, though bookings can be made over the phone or through your accommodation.

🛏 Sleeping

Courtyard Hotel Garni   HOTEL $
(☑ 064-213600, 064-206252; 16 3rd Rd; s/d from N$450/550; @ 🎧 🛜 🛝) This low-rise place in a quiet neighbourhood near the water has generous rooms that are a bit beaten around the edges – it's comfortable enough and there are nice common areas, but it's probably a tad overpriced in peak season (when rates are known to double) and the beds are quite small. Kitchenettes are useful for self-caterers. Guests can access the indoor heated pool and sauna.

★ Langholm Hotel   HOTEL $$
(☑ 064-209230; www.langholmhotel.com; 2nd St W; s/d from N$1070/1228) Getting consistently good reviews from travellers, the excellent Langholm sits on a quiet street a couple of blocks back from the water. It satisfies both business and leisure travellers with profes-

Walvis Bay

◎ Sights
1 Bird Paradise..F2

✆ Activities, Courses & Tours
Mola Mola Safaris ....(see 6)
2 Sandwich Harbour 4x4 ....A2

⊨ Sleeping
3 Courtyard Hotel Garni........................B2
4 Langholm Hotel..................................B2
5 Oyster Box Guesthouse B2

⊗ Eating
6 Anchor @ The Jetty A2
7 Raft A2
8 Willi Probst Bakery & Cafe...................D1

ⓘ Information
9 Welwitschia Medical Centre D1

ⓘ Transport
10 Air Namibia C1
11 Intercape Mainliner Bus Stop C2

sional service and stylish rooms with strong colours and a contemporary aesthetic.

★**Oyster Box Guesthouse**　　GUESTHOUSE **$$**
(☑ 061-249597, 064-202247; www.oysterbox guesthouse.com; cnr Esplanade & 2nd West, s N$865-1109, d N$1374-1730; ❋ ⛶) More like a classy boutique hotel, this guesthouse is a stylish affair right on the waterfront, a short walk from Raft restaurant. Rooms are very contemporary and bedding includes crisp sheets and fluffy pillows. Helpful staff can book activities for you around town and arrange transport. A lovely choice.

✗ Eating

Willi Probst Bakery & Cafe　　CAFE **$**
(☑ 064-202744; http://williprobstbakery.webs. com; cnr 12th Rd & 9th St; light meals N$25-60; ❂ 6.30am-3pm Mon-Sat) If you're feeling nostalgic for Swakopmund (or Deutschland, for that matter), take comfort in knowing that Probst specialises in stodgy German fare: pork, meatballs, schnitzel and the like, while pies and breakfast pizzas mix things up a little. A range of sweet treats ensures that it is everyone's friend.

★**Anchor @ The Jetty**　　INTERNATIONAL **$$**
(☑ 064-205762; Esplanade, Waterfront; breakfast/ mains from N$45/75; ❂ 7.30am-10pm Tue-Sat, to 3pm Sun & Mon) The food is good at the Anchor but the real attraction is the location overlooking the water. It makes a particularly lovely spot for breakfast, and if you're tired of eating stodgy food, it does a pretty mean fruit salad. Later on, seafood dominates things. Sit at a table right on the water and watch the morning cruise boats slink out of the bay.

★**Raft**　　SEAFOOD **$$**
(☑ 064-204877; theraftrestaurant.com; Esplanade; mains N$77-227; ❂ 11am-11pm Mon-Sat, to 2pm Sun) This Walvis Bay landmark sits on stilts offshore, and has a great front-row view of the ducks, pelicans and flamingos. Here you can expect high-quality meats and seafood in addition to spectacular sunsets and ocean views. The seafood extravaganza is well worth the extravagant N$367 price tag.

ⓘ Information

MEDICAL SERVICES
Welwitschia Medical Centre (13th Rd; ❂ 24hr) For medical services.

POLICE
Police (☑ 10111; cnr 11th St & 13th Rd)

NAMIBIA WALVIS BAY

FLAMINGOS AT WALVIS BAY

Lesser and greater flamingos flock in large numbers to pools along the Namib Desert coast, particularly around Walvis Bay and Lüderitz. They're excellent fliers, and have been known to migrate up to 500km overnight in search of proliferations of algae and crustaceans.

The lesser flamingo filters algae and diatoms (microscopic organisms) from the water by sucking in and vigorously expelling water from its bill. The minute particles are caught on fine hairlike protrusions, which line the inside of the mandibles. The suction is created by the thick fleshy tongue, which rests in a groove in the lower mandible and pumps back and forth like a piston. It has been estimated that a million lesser flamingos can consume over 180 tonnes of algae and diatoms daily.

While lesser flamingos obtain food by filtration, the greater flamingo supplements its algae diet with small molluscs, crustaceans and other organic particles from the mud. When feeding, it will rotate in a circle while stamping its feet in an effort to scare up a tasty potential meal.

The greater and lesser flamingos are best distinguished by their colouration. Greater flamingos are white to light pink, and their beaks are whitish with a black tip. Lesser flamingos are a deeper pink – often reddish – colour, with dark-red beaks.

Located near Walvis Bay are three diverse wetland areas:

Lagoon This shallow and sheltered 45,000-hectare lagoon, southwest of Walvis Bay and west of the Kuiseb River mouth, attracts a range of coastal water birds in addition to enormous flocks of lesser and greater flamingos. It also supports chestnut banded plovers and curlew sandpipers, as well as the rare Damara tern.

Salt Works (p283) Southwest of the lagoon is this 3500-hectare saltpan complex, which currently supplies over 90% of South Africa's salt. As with the one in Swakopmund, these pans concentrate salt from seawater with the aid of evaporation. They also act as a rich feeding ground for prawns and larval fish.

Bird Paradise Immediately east of town along the C14 at the municipal sewage purification works is this nature sanctuary, which consists of a series of shallow artificial pools, fringed by reeds. An observation tower and a short nature walk afford excellent birdwatching.

Together they form Southern Africa's single most important coastal wetland for migratory birds, with up to 150,000 transient avian visitors stopping by annually, including massive flocks of both lesser and greater flamingos.

POST

Post office (Sam Nujoma Ave) Provides public telephones and fax services.

ℹ️ Getting There & Away

Air Namibia (📞 064-203102; www.airnamibia.com.na) has around seven flights a week between Windhoek's Eros Airport and Walvis Bay's Rooikop Airport, located 10km southeast of town on the C14.

All buses and combis to Walvis Bay run via Swakopmund. The Intercape Mainliner stop is at the Spur Restaurant on Ben Gurirab St. There are also other private bus services running between Windhoek and Walvis Bay.

Hitching isn't difficult between Walvis Bay and Swakopmund, but weather conditions can be rough if heading for Namib-Naukluft Park or the Skeleton Coast.

Namib-Naukluft Park

Welcome to the Namib, the oldest desert on earth and certainly one of the most beautiful and accessible desert regions on the planet. This is sand-dune country par excellence, silent, constantly shifting and ageless, and an undoubted highlight of any visit to Namibia. The epicentre of its appeal is at Sossusvlei, Namibia's most famous strip of sand, where gargantuan dunes tower more than 300m above the underlying strata. Elsewhere, the land lives up to its name: the Nama word 'Namib' inspired the name of the entire country and rather prosaically means 'vast dry plain'. And then there are the Naukluft Mountains – barren and beautiful, and filled with an appeal all of their own.

The **Namib-Naukluft National Park** (per person per day N$80, per vehicle N$10; ☉sunrise-sunset) takes in around 23,000 sq km of arid and semi-arid land, and protects various areas of vast ecological importance in the Namib and the Naukluft. The park also abuts the NamibRand Nature Reserve, the largest privately owned property in Southern Africa, forming a massive wildlife corridor that promotes migratory movement.

Naukluft Mountains

♪ 063 / ELEVATION 1973M

The Naukluft Mountains, which rise steeply from the gravel plains of the central Namib, are characterised by a high plateau bounded by gorges, caves and springs cut deeply from dolomite formations. The Tsondab, Tsams and Tsauchab Rivers all rise in the massif, and the relative abundance of water creates an ideal habitat for mountain zebras, kudus, leopards, springboks and klipspringers. In addition to wildlife watching, the Naukluft

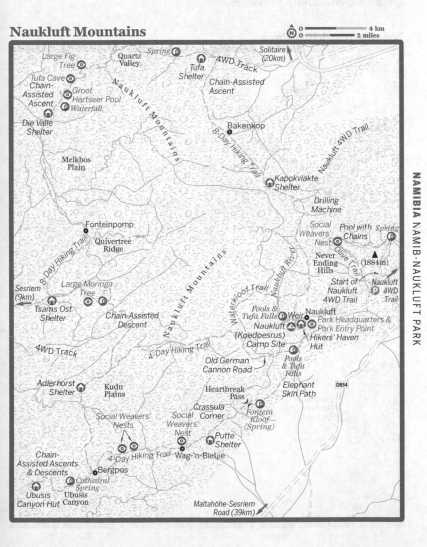

Naukluft Mountains

N 0 ——— 4 km
   0 ——— 2 miles

NAMIBIA NAMIB-NAUKLUFT PARK

is home to a couple of challenging treks that open up this largely inaccessible terrain.

The Naukluft is best reached via the C24 from Rehoboth and the D1206 from Rietoog; petrol is available at Büllsport and Rietoog. From Sesriem, 103km away, the nearest access is via the dip-ridden D854.

Naukluft 4WD Trail Off-Road SCENIC DRIVE

Off-road enthusiasts will love the 73km, two-day Naukluft 4WD Trail. It begins near the start of the Olive Trail and follows a loop near the northeastern corner of the Naukluft area. Accommodation is provided in one of the stone-walled A-frames at the 28km point. Facilities include shared toilets, showers and braai pits. Up to four vehicles/16 people are permitted here at a time.

Olive Trail HIKING

The 11km Olive Trail, named for the wild olives that grow alongside it, is one of Namibia's most popular hikes and deservedly so. It begins at the car park 4km northeast of the park headquarters. The walk runs clockwise around the triangular loop and takes four to five hours.

Namib-Naukluft Park

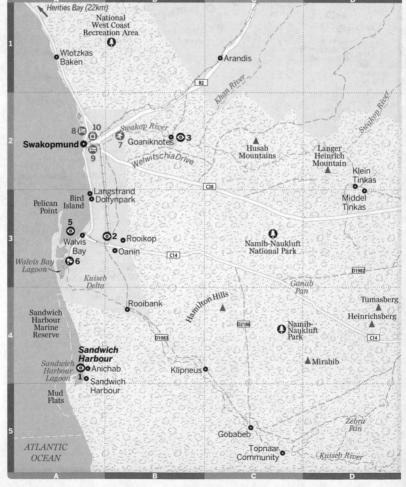

Waterkloof Trail
HIKING

This lovely 17km anticlockwise loop takes about seven hours to complete, and begins at the Naukluft (Koedoesrus) campsite, located 2km west of the park headquarters. The trail traverses a lovely range of landscapes and habitats, from riverbank to canyon, plateau to rocky ridge.

★ Tsauchab River Camp
CAMPGROUND $

(☑ 063-293416; www.tsauchab.com; campsites N$150, plus per adult/child N$110/65, s/d chalets N$760/1400; 🛜 ⚟) If you're an avid hiker (or just love excellent settings!), you're in for a treat. The scattered campsites here sit beside the Tsauchab riverbed – one occupies a huge hollow tree – and each has a private shower block, a sink and braai area. The stone-built chalets grow in number with each passing year; also down in the riverbed, they're lovely and quiet.

★ Zebra River Lodge
LODGE $$

(☑ 061-301934; www.zebra-river-lodge.com; s/d with full board from N$1275/1610; 🛜 ⚟) Occupying a magical setting in the Tsaris Mountains, this is Rob and Marianne Field's private Grand Canyon. Go for one of the more expansive rock chalets – you'll feel like you're sleeping inside the mountain and they're some of Namibia's more original rooms.

Sesriem & Sossusvlei
☑ 063

Appropriate for this vast country with its epic landscapes – its number one tourist attraction – Sossusvlei still manages to feel isolated. The dunes, appearing other-worldly at times, especially when the light hits them just so near sunrise, are part of the 32,000 sq km sand sea that covers much of the region. The dunes reach as high as 325m, and are part of one of the oldest and driest ecosystems on earth. However, the landscape here is constantly changing – wind forever alters the shape of the dunes, while colours shift with the changing light, reaching the peak of their brilliance just after sunrise.

The gateway to Sossusvlei is Sesriem (Six Thongs), which was the number of joined

Namib-Naukluft Park

◎ **Top Sights**
1 Sandwich Harbour A4

◎ **Sights**
2 Dune 7 ....B3
3 Goanikontes B2
4 Kuiseb Canyon E4
5 Lagoon..A3
    Moon Landscape ....(see 3)
6 Salt Works..A3

◉ **Activities, Courses & Tours**
7 Okakambe Horse Stables...................B2

◉ **Sleeping**
8 Atlantic Villa......................................A2
9 Desert Breeze Lodge.........................A2
    Sea Breeze Guesthouse ....(see 8)

◎ **Shopping**
10 Cosdef Arts & Crafts Centre A2

NAMIBIA NAMIB-NAUKLUFT PARK

leather ox-wagon thongs necessary to draw water from the bottom of the nearby gorge. Sesriem remains a lonely and far-flung outpost, home to little more than a petrol station and a handful of tourist hotels and lodges.

⊙ Sights

★**Sossusvlei**   PAN
(round trip N$100) Sossusvlei, a large ephemeral pan, is set amid red sand dunes that tower up to 325m above the valley floor. It rarely contains any water, but when the Tsauchab River has gathered enough volume and momentum to push beyond the thirsty plains to the sand sea, it's completely transformed. The normally cracked dry mud gives way to an ethereal blue-green lake, surrounded by greenery and attended by aquatic birdlife, as well as the usual sand-loving gemsbok, and ostriches.

This sand probably originated in the Kalahari between three and five million years ago. It was washed down the Orange River and out to sea, where it was swept northward with the Benguela Current to be deposited along the coast. The best way to get the measure of this sandy sprawl is to climb a dune, as most people do. And of course, if you experience a sense of déjà vu here, don't be surprised – Sossusvlei has appeared in many films and advertisements worldwide, and every story ever written about Namibia features a photo of it.

At the end of the 65km 2WD road from Sesriem is the 2WD car park; only 4WDs can drive the last 4km into the Sossusvlei Pan itself. Visitors with lesser vehicles park at the 2WD car park and walk, hitch or catch the shuttle to cover the remaining distance. If you choose to walk, allot about 90 minutes, and carry enough water for a hot, sandy slog in the sun.

★**Deadvlei**   NATURAL FEATURE
Although it's much less famous than its neighbour Sossusvlei, Deadvlei is actually the most alluring pan in the Namib-Naukluft National Park – it's arguably one of Southern Africa's greatest sights. Sprouting from the pan are seemingly petrified trees, with their parched limbs casting stark shadows across the baked, bleached white canvas. The juxtaposition of this scene with the cobalt-blue skies and the towering orange sands of Big Daddy, the area's tallest dune (325m), is simply spellbinding.

It's an easy 3km return walk from the Deadvlei/Big Daddy Dune 4WD parking area – follow the waymarker posts.

Sesriem & Sossusvlei

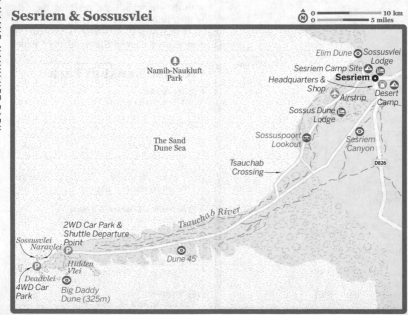

★ Hidden Vlei   NATURAL FEATURE

This unearthly dry vlei (low, open landscape) amid lonely dunes makes a rewarding excursion. It's a 4km return hike from the 2WD car park. The route is marked by white-painted posts. It's most intriguing in the afternoon, when you're unlikely to see another person.

★ Sesriem Canyon   CANYON

The 3km-long, 30m-deep Sesriem Canyon, 4km south of the Sesriem headquarters, was carved by the Tsauchab River through the 15-million-year-old deposits of sand and gravel conglomerate. There are two pleasant walks: you can hike upstream to the brackish pool at its head or 2.5km downstream to its lower end. Check out the natural sphinx-like formation on the northern flank near the canyon mouth.

Dune 45   VIEWPOINT

The most accessible of the large red dunes along the Sossusvlei road is Dune 45, so-called because it's 45km from Sesriem. It rises over 150m above the surrounding plains, and is flanked by several scraggly and often photographed trees.

🛏 Sleeping

Advanced reservations are essential, especially during the high season, school holidays and busy weekends. For an overview of accommodation options in the area, visit **Sossusvlei Accommodation** (www.sossusvlei.org/accommodation).

Sossus Oasis Campsite   CAMPGROUND $

(☑ 063-293632; www.sossus-oasis.com; camping N$180) Nicer than the main Sesriem Camp Site but outside the main gate, Sossus Oasis has an on-site petrol station, kiosk, restaurant and decent if dusty sites with good shade and a private ablutions block for each site.

★ Little Kulala   LODGE $$$

(☑ 061-225178; www.wilderness-safaris.com; s/d all-inclusive Jun-Oct N$13,480/20,750, rates vary rest of year) Part of Wilderness Safaris' Classic portfolio, Little Kulala is simply stunning. Expansive rooms, each with their own plunge pools, watch over rippling sands and silhouetted desert trees with the sand sea dominating the view not far away. Meals are outstanding, there's a well-stocked wine cellar, the public areas are gorgeous and the whole effect is of a near-perfect sophisticated oasis.

Kulala Desert Lodge   LODGE $$$

(☑ 061-225178; www.wilderness-safaris.com; s/d all-inclusive Jun-Oct N$6510/11,270, rates vary rest of year) If you've stayed in a Wilderness Safaris lodge before, you know the deal. If you haven't, you're in for a treat. Semiluxurious canvas tents and great food are just the start, as the whole property faces off towards the sand dunes in the middle distance. It's close enough to the park entrance for a quick arrival but far enough away to feel like you're kilometres from anywhere.

ℹ️ Information

Sesriem Canyon and Sossusvlei are part of the Namib-Naukluft National Park and are open year-round. If you want to see the sunrise over Sossusvlei, you must stay inside the park, either at the **Sesriem Camp Site** (☑ 061-2857200; www.nwr.com.na/resorts/sesriem-camp; camping N$200) or the **Sossus Dune Lodge** (☑ 061-2857200; www.nwr.com.na/resorts/sossus-dune-lodge; s/d chalets with half board N$3190/5940; ☀) . From both places, you are allowed to start driving to Sossusvlei before the general public are allowed through the main gates. If you're content with simply enjoying the morning light, however, you can stay in Sesriem or Solitaire and simply pass through the park gate once the sun rises above the horizon – be prepared for queues at the park gate, however.

All visitors headed for Sossusvlei must check in at the park office and secure a park entry permit.

Namib-Naukluft park entry at Sossusvlei is N$80 per adult, N$10 per car.

ℹ️ Getting There & Away

Sesriem is reached via a signposted turn-off from the C14, and petrol is available in town. There is no public transport leading into the park, though hotels can arrange tours if you don't have your own vehicle.

The road leading from the park gate to the 2WD car park is paved, though the speed limit remains 60km/h. Although the road is conducive to higher speeds, there are oryxes and springboks dashing about, so drive with extreme care.

Solitaire Area

☑ 062, 063 & 064

Solitaire is a lonely and aptly named settlement of just a few buildings about 80km north of Sesriem along the A46. Although the town is nothing more than an open spot in the desert, the surrounding area is home to several guest farms and lodges, which can serve as an alternative base for exploring Sossusvlei. Otherwise, the town is little more than a place to refuel.

Solitaire is connected to Sesriem by the unpaved C19, and petrol is available in town.

Check to see if the shuttle service is still running from Solitaire petrol station to Sosusvlei for N$150 return; also check with the station for the times the service runs. We reckon you're better off getting there under your own steam, but it does provide another option.

★ **Agama River Camp**   LODGE, CAMPGROUND $$$
(☑ 063-683245; www.agamarivercamp.com; camping N$150, s/d chalets N$1700/2680) This relatively new lodge is in a handy spot between Solitaire and Sesriem (34km from Sesriem). The chalets are supremely comfortable and have rooftop decks so you can sleep under the stars. There's also an excellent campsite, while in the main lodge there's a sundowner deck and lounge; meals are only available if booked well in advance.

★ **Moon Mountain**   TENTED CAMP $$$
(☑ 061-305176; www.moonmountain.biz; s/d from N$2210/4000; ☒) Off the C19 between Sesriem and Solitaire, this extraordinary tented camp clings to a steep hillside and the result is vertigo-inducing, sunset-facing views. The wood-floored tents open up to maximise the sense of flying above the desert but even so you'll just want to sit on your balcony (or in your private splash pool) all evening. Stunning bathrooms round out a wonderful package. The suites are even more decadent.

NamibRand Nature Reserve

☑ 061

Bordering Namib-Naukluft Park, **NamibRand Nature Reserve** (www.namibrand. org) is essentially a collection of private farms that together protect over 200,000 hectares of dunes, desert grasslands and wild, isolated mountain ranges. Currently, several concessionaires operate on the reserve, offering a range of experiences amid one of Namibia's most stunning and colourful landscapes. A surprising amount of wildlife can be seen here, including large herds of gemsboks, springboks and zebras, as well as kudus, klipspringers, spotted hyenas, jackals, and Cape and bat-eared foxes.

Access by private vehicle is restricted in order to maintain the delicate balance of the reserve. Accommodation prices are also extremely high, which seeks to limit the tourist footprint. As a result, you must book in advance through a lodge, and then arrange either a 4WD transfer or a chartered fly-in.

NamibRand Family Hideout   FARMSTAY $
(☑ 061-226803; www.nrfhideout.com; camping N$150) Run on solar energy and making a virtue of its remoteness, NamibRand Family Hideout is run by Andreas and Mandy, who offer a warm welcome, two wonderfully isolated campsites and accommodation in the farmhouse (sleeps 10). Much of the old farm infrastructure, now defunct, has been left in situ to evoke the property's sheep-farming days. Farm rates vary with the number of people staying.

★ **Sossusvlei Desert Lodge**   LODGE $$$
(☑ in South Africa 27-11-809 4300; www.andbe yond.com; per person all-inclusive high/low season N$10,185/6345; ☒☜☒) This stunning place frequently appears in *Condé Nast* as one of the top lodges in the world, and we're inclined to agree. The property contains 10 chalets, which are constructed from locally quarried stone and appear to blend effortlessly into the surrounding landscape. The interiors showcase contemporary flair with lovely earth tones, and feature personal fireplaces, marble baths and linen-covered patios.

Wolwedans Dune Lodge   LODGE $$$
(☑ 061-230616; www.wolwedans.com; s/d all-inclusive from N$6930/9900; ☒☒) One of the more affordable lodges in the NamibRand, Wolwedans Dune Lodge features an architecturally arresting collection of raised wooden chalets that are scattered amid towering red sand dunes. Service is impeccable, and the atmosphere is overwhelmingly elegant, yet you can indulge your wild side at any time with chauffeured 4WD dune drives and guided safaris.

SOUTHERN NAMIBIA

If you're beginning a regional odyssey in South Africa, one of the best ways to approach Namibia is from South Africa's vast Northern Cape, crossing the border into the infinite, desert-rich south of the country. Once in Namibia, the landscape, noticeably starker than its southern neighbour, is tinged with a lunar feel from the scattered rocky debris, and is marked from the irrepressible movement of the oldest sand dunes on the planet.

Although the tourist trail in Namibia firmly swings north towards Etosha National Park, the deserts of southern Namibia sparkle beneath the sun – quite literally – as they're filled with millions of carats of diamonds.

The port of Lüderitz has long been a traveller's favourite. A surreal colonial relic that has largely disregarded the 21st century, Lüderitz clings fiercely to its European roots, with traditional German architecture set against a backdrop of fiery sand dunes and deep blue seas.

Your first sight of Fish River Canyon will, more than any place in Namibia, leave you with feelings of awe and grandeur – it is Mother Earth at her very finest. One of the largest canyons in the world, it's also one of the most spectacular.

The Central Plateau

The central plateau is probably not where you'll spend most of your time in Namibia. Most travellers encounter the region on their way elsewhere – the plateau is bisected by the B1, which is the country's main north–south route, stretching from the South African border to Otjiwarongo. What this means is that, for most drivers, this excellent road is little more than a mesmerising broken white line stretching towards a receding horizon – a paradise for lead-foot drivers and cruise-control potatoes.

Even so, with most of the central plateau's towns on or just off the main B1 route, there are numerous places to break up the journey, whether as a base for exploring the region's natural attractions, for fuel stops, or even as detour destinations in their own right. Of the latter, Bethanie, Gondwana Cañon Park, Keetmanshoop and Seeheim are probably the pick.

Keetmanshoop

POP 20,980 / ☑ 063

Keetmanshoop (*kayt*-mahns-*hoo*-up) sits at the main crossroads of southern Namibia, and this is why you may end up here. More of a place to overnight than spend any time, it's nonetheless a friendly enough little town.

There are a few examples of German colonial architecture, including the 1910 **Kaiserliches Postampt** (Imperial Post Office; cnr 5th Ave & Fenschel St), and the **town museum** (cnr Kaiser St & 7th Ave; ⊘ 7.30am-4.30pm Mon-Fri) **FREE**, housed in the 1895 Rhenish Mission Church, which itself is arguably more interesting than the contents of the museum inside. The ramshackle bits and pieces on display are good for killing an hour or so.

Intercape Mainliner (p252) runs buses between Windhoek and Keetmanshoop (from N$522, 5½ hours, four weekly). Book your tickets in advance online, as this service continues on to Cape Town, South Africa, and fills up quickly.

Combis also run up and down the B1 with fairly regular frequency, and a ride between Windhoek and Keetmanshoop shouldn't cost more than N$180. Less regular combis connect Keetmanshoop to Lüderitz, with fares averaging around N$250.

Trans-Namib (p321) operates a night train between Windhoek and Keetmanshoop (from N$160, 12 hours, daily except Saturday).

Bernice B&B GUESTHOUSE $
(☑ 063-224851; bernicebeds@iway.na; 129 10th St; s/d N$240/360) Although down a side road, Bernice B&B is extremely well signed from any direction that you approach town – just follow the signs! Book ahead, as it does get busy. There are family options, digital satellite TV and good-size rooms, which are a little dated but otherwise well kept and nice enough.

Quivertree Forest
Rest Camp CAMPGROUND, BUNGALOWS $
(☑ 063-683421; www.quivertreeforest.com; camping N$120, s/d/tr/q bungalows from N$620/965/1260/1950; 🖾) About 14km east of town, the Quivertree Forest Rest Camp proudly boasts Namibia's largest stand of *kokerboom* (quiver trees). Day rates (per person N$60) include use of picnic facilities and entry to the Giant's Playground, a bizarre natural rock garden 5km away. Accommodation is simple but adequate.

Duwisib Castle
☑ 063

A curious neobaroque structure located about 70km south of Maltahöhe, smack-dab in the middle of the barren desert, this European **castle** (N$70; ⊘ 8am-1pm & 2-5pm) is smaller than some grandiose descriptions suggest and really worth a stop only if you're passing by. The portraits and scant furniture certainly give it a European feel though and the pleasant courtyard is a good place to relax in the shade of some majestic trees.

There isn't any public transport to Duwisib Castle. If you're coming from Helmeringhausen, head north on the C14 for 62km and turn northwest onto the D831. Continue for 27km, then turn west onto the D826 and travel a further 15km to the castle.

Duwisib Castle Rest Camp　　　CAMPGROUND $
(camping N$110) This very amenable rest camp (with a sparkling amenities block) occupies one corner of the castle grounds and is well set up with campsites containing bin, braai and bench seating. The adjoining kiosk sells snacks, coffee and cool drinks. Book through the NWR office (p252) in Windhoek.

Duwisib Guest Farm　　　GUESTHOUSE $$
(☑ 063-293344; www.farmduwisib.com; camping N$110, s/d with half board N$980/1720) Located 300m from the castle, this pleasant guest farm has rooms with views of the main attraction, and self-catering family units that sleep up to eight people. While you're there, be sure to check out the historic blacksmith shop up the hill.

Aus

POP 300 / ☑ 063

A stop on the long drive west to Lüderitz, Aus is home to a former prison camp and also boasts two highly recommended guest farms where you can slow down and spend some time soaking up the desolate beauty of the shifting sands.

Aus is 125km east of Lüderitz on the B4. Travel in this region typically requires a private vehicle.

Aus Information Centre (☑ 063-258151; ☺ 8am-5pm Mon-Fri, to 2pm Sat & Sun) has a cafe, internet and lots of information on the area's natural environment, history and wild horses. Ask here about the Aus Walking Trail, which begins at the info centre.

Desert Horse Inn　　　LODGE $$
(☑ 063-258021; www.klein-aus-vista.com; N$120, r per person from N$990; 🕸🛜🐾) This 10,000-hectare ranch, 3km west of Aus, is a hiker's paradise with six different trails you can do, from 4km to 20km in length. Accommodation is provided in the main lodge, which is cast in soothing earth tones and

with lovely large rooms. Meals are available at the main lodge. Apart from the wonderful hiking, activities include horse riding and 4WD tours of the ranch's vast desert concession.

Eagle's Nest Chalets　　　CHALET $$$
(www.klein-aus-vista.com; chalets per person N$1325) These two- to four-person self-catering chalets mix the deliciously remote with proximity to the affiliated Desert Horse Inn (p294) facilities 7km away; if you don't feel like cooking, you can eat at the lodge restaurant. Built in stone and glass, and with their backs to the barren mountains, this fine place offers sweeping views and a glorious sense of space and light.

Lüderitz

POP 12,540 / ☑ 063

Before travelling to Lüderitz, pause for a moment to study the country map and how the town is sandwiched between the barren Namib Desert and the windswept South Atlantic coast. As if Lüderitz' unique geographical setting wasn't impressive enough, its surreal German art nouveau architecture will seal the deal. A colonial relic scarcely touched by the 21st century, Lüderitz recalls a Bavarian *dorfchen* (small village), with churches, bakeries and cafes. Unlike its more well-heeled Teutonic rival Swakopmund, Lüderitz feels stuck in a time warp, a perception that delivers both gloom and a certain charm (at least for visitors). In short, it's one of the most incongruous places in Africa.

But it's the natural environment surrounding the town where southern Namibia really comes alive. The rocky coastline of the Lüderitz peninsula harbours flamingo flocks and penguin colonies, while the adjacent Sperrgebiet National Park is arguably the country's wildest and most pristine landscape.

☉ Sights

The Lüderitz Peninsula, much of which lies outside the Sperrgebiet, makes an interesting half-day excursion from town.

Agate Bay, just north of Lüderitz, is made of tailings from the diamond workings. There aren't many agates these days, but you'll find fine sand partially consisting of tiny grey mica chips.

A picturesque and relatively calm bay, **Sturmvogelbucht** is a pleasant place for a braai, though the water temperature would be amenable only to a penguin or polar bear. The rusty ruin in the bay is the remains of a 1914 Norwegian whaling station; the salty pan just inland attracts flamingos and merits a quick stop.

At **Diaz Point**, 22km by road from Lüderitz, is a classic lighthouse and a replica of the cross erected in July 1488 by Portuguese navigator Bartolomeu Dias on his return from the Cape of Good Hope. Portions of the original have been dispersed as far as Lisbon, Berlin and Cape Town. From the point, there's a view of a nearby seal colony and you can also see cormorants, flamingos, wading birds and even the occasional pod of dolphins.

Also at the point is a **coffee shop** serving hot/cold drinks, toasties, oysters, beer and great chocolate cake. It's possible to **camp** (campsite N$95, per person N$55) out here as well as on rocky, flat ground roped off between the lighthouse and water. There are decent amenities although the site is more exposed to the wind than Shark Island.

Halifax Island, a short distance offshore south of Diaz Point, is home to Namibia's best-known jackass-penguin colony. Jackass or Cape penguins live in colonies on rocky offshore islets off the Atlantic Coast. With binoculars, you can often see them gathering on the sandy beach opposite the car park.

Grosse Bucht (Big Bay), at the southern end of Lüderitz Peninsula, is a wild and scenic beach favoured by flocks of flamingos, which feed in the tidal pools. It's also the site of a small but picturesque shipwreck on the beach.

Just a few kilometres up the coast is **Klein Bogenfels**, a small rock arch beside the sea. When the wind isn't blowing a gale, it makes a pleasant picnic spot.

Felsenkirche
CHURCH

(Kirche St; ⊙ 4-5pm Mon-Sat) FREE The prominent Evangelical Lutheran church dominates Lüderitz from high on Diamond Hill. It was designed by Albert Bause, who implemented the Victorian influences he'd seen in the Cape. With assistance from private donors in Germany, construction of the church began in late 1911 and was completed the following year. The brilliant stained-glass panel situated over the altar was donated by Kaiser Wilhelm II, while the Bible was a gift from his wife. Come for the views over the water and the town.

☞ Tours

Lüderitz Safaris & Tours
ADVENTURE

(☑ 063-202719; ludsaf@africaonline.com.na; Bismarck St) Provides useful tourist information, organises visitor permits for the Kolmanskop ghost town and books seats on the schooner *Sedina* (N$375 per person), which sails past the Cape fur seal sanctuary at Diaz Point and the penguin colony on Halifax Island. It also conducts guided oyster tours with time for tastings, and is generally a great information service with very knowledgeable staff.

⊨ Sleeping

★ Hansa Haus Guesthouse
GUESTHOUSE $

(☑ 063-203699; www.hansahausluderitz.co.za; 85 Mabel St; s/d from N$552/650; ☎) This family-run guesthouse in an early-20th-century German-style house is one of the better places in town. The wood floors, white-linen look and the sea breezes (especially on the upstairs terrace) round out a lovely package.

★ Haus Sandrose
APARTMENT $

(☑ 063-202630; www.haussandrose.com; 15 Bismarck St; s/d from N$530/760) Haus Sandrose is comprised of uniquely decorated self-catering rooms surrounding a sheltered garden. The bright rooms are good value and exude a cheerful and roomy feel; note some rooms are bigger than others It's a great location and very friendly.

★ Kairos B&B
B&B $

(☑ 063-203080, 081 650 5598; http://kairoscottage.com/; Shark Island; s/d N$480/680) This brand-spanking-new, cheerful, whitewashed building houses a promising new guesthouse and overlooks the water just before Shark Island. It's in a lovely location and is just a few minutes' drive from the town centre. Also here is a coffee shop serving breakfast and lunch.

Lüderitz Backpackers Lodge
HOSTEL $

(☑ 063-202000; www.namibweb.com/backpackers.htm; 2 Ring St; camping N$90, dm/d/f N$120/300/450) Housed in a historic colonial mansion, this is the only true backpackers spot in town, with rudimentary accommodation. The vibe is congenial and low-key, and the friendly management is helpful in sorting out your onward travels. And of course, the usual backpacker amenities are on offer here, including a communal kitchen, braai pit, TV lounge and laundry facilities. Prices may increase when it's busy.

Lüderitz

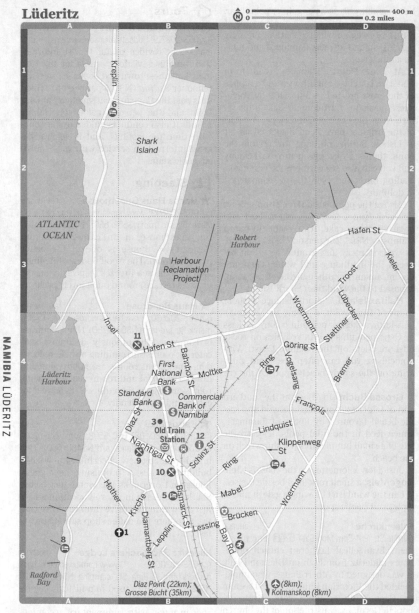

N
0   400 m
0   0.2 miles

Lüderitz Nest Hotel   HOTEL **$$$**
(☏063-204000; www.nesthotel.com; 820 Diaz St;
s/d from N$1320/2100; ❄❄) Lüderitz' oldest
upmarket hotel occupies a jutting peninsula
in the southwest corner of town, complete
with its own private beach. Each room is styl-
ishly appointed with modern furnishings and
faces out towards the sea. Amenities include
a pool, sauna, kids playground, car hire, ter-
raced bar and a collection of gourmet restau-
rants. This hotel is what you would expect:
decent service, clean and good facilities. It's

Lüderitz

⊙ **Sights**
1 Felsenkirche B6

🔵 **Activities, Courses & Tours**
2 Coastways Tours Lüderitz.................... C6
3 Lüderitz Safaris & Tours B5

🛏 **Sleeping**
4 Hansa Haus Guesthouse C5
5 Haus Sandrose.......................................B5
6 Kairos B&B A1

7 Lüderitz Backpackers Lodge C4
8 Lüderitz Nest Hotel A6

🍴 **Eating**
9 Barrels B5
10 Diaz Coffee Shop B5
11 Garden Cafe B4

ℹ **Information**
12 Namibia Wildlife Resorts B5

overpriced but its drawcard is the magnificent water views from the rooms.

🍴 Eating

★Diaz Coffee Shop   CAFE $
(🖉 081-700 0475; cnr Bismarck & Nachtigal Sts; mains from N$45; ⊗8am-9pm) The cappuccinos are strong, the pastries are sweet, and the ambience wouldn't at all seem out of place in Munich. Patrons sit in a large room with some comfy seating and receive quick service; the food, such as hot wraps or chicken shwarma, is delicious. The coffee shop has recently broadened its horizons to become an evening oyster and wine bar – very cool. Try the speciality coffee...if you dare.

★Garden Cafe   CAFE $
(🖉 081-124 8317; 17 Hafen St; light meals from N$25) The garden setting, white-wood furnishings, great coffee and filled rolls add up to one of our favourite little haunts in town. The baked treats, Black Forest gateau among them, are also highlights. Travellers tend to agree with our positive experience – we're yet to hear a bad word said about this place.

Barrels   GERMAN $$
(🖉063-202458; 5 Nachtigal St; mains N$50-120; ⊗6-10pm Mon-Fri) A wonderfully festive bar-restaurant accented by occasional live music, Barrels offers rotating daily specials highlighting fresh seafood and German staples. Portions are hefty and the buffet (N$150) is great value.

ℹ Information
Stay well clear of the Sperrgebiet, unless you're part of an organised tour, as much of the area remains strictly off limits despite its national-park status. The northern boundary is formed by the B4 and extends almost as far east as Aus. The boundary is patrolled by some fairly ruthless characters, and trespassers will be prosecuted (or worse).

Several banks on Bismarck St change cash and travellers cheques.
NWR (NWR; 🖉063-202752; www.nwr.com.na; Schinz St; ⊗7.30am-1pm & 2-4pm Mon-Fri) This local office can help with national-park information.

ℹ Getting There & Away
Air Namibia (p252) travels about three times a week between Windhoek and Lüderitz. The airport is 8km southeast of town.

Somewhat irregular combis connect Lüderitz to Keetmanshoop, with fares averaging around N$250. Buses depart from the southern edge of town at informal bus stops along Bismarck St.

Lüderitz and the scenery en route are worth the 334km trip from Keetmanshoop via the tarred B4. When the wind blows – which is most of the time – the final 10km into Lüderitz may be blocked by a barchan dune field that seems bent upon crossing the road. Conditions do get hazardous, especially if it's foggy, and the drifts pile quite high before road crews clean them off. Obey local speed limits, and avoid driving at night if possible.

Fish River Canyon
🖉 063
Nowhere else in Africa will you find anything quite like **Fish River Canyon** (per person per day N$80, per vehicle N$10). Whether you're getting a taste of the sheer scale and beauty of the place from one of the lookouts, or hiking for five days to immerse yourself in its multifaceted charm, Fish River Canyon is a special place.

At one level, the numbers don't lie: the canyon measures 160km in length, up to 27km in width, and the dramatic inner canyon reaches a depth of 550m. But as impressive as these numbers are, it's difficult to get a sense of perspective without actually

SPERRGEBIET NATIONAL PARK

Although it was off limits to the public for most of the last century, in 2008 the Namibian government inaugurated the Sperrgebiet (Forbidden Area) as a national park. Geographically speaking, the park encompasses the northern tip of the Succulent Karoo Biorne, an area of 26,000 sq km of dunes and mountains that appear dramatically stark, but represent one of 25 outstanding global 'hotspots' of unique biodiversity.

The Sperrgebiet originally consisted of two private concessions: Diamond Area 1 and Diamond Area 2. The latter, home to the Kolmanskop ghost town and Elizabeth Bay, has been open to the public for some time now. Since 2004 parts of the former have also been opened up to specialist conservation groups, though given the diamond industry's security concerns, access has been carefully controlled.

Kolmanskop (N$75; ⊘ 9.30am & 11am Mon-Sat, 10am Sun) Named after early Afrikaner trekker Jani Kolman, whose ox wagon became bogged in the sand here, Kolmanskop was originally constructed as the Consolidated Diamond Mines (CDM) headquarters. Although Kolmanskop once boasted a casino, bowling alley and a theatre with fine acoustics, the slump in diamond sales after WWI and the discovery of richer pickings at Oranjemund ended its heyday. By 1956, the town was totally deserted, and left to the mercy of the shifting desert sands.

Coastways Tours Lüderitz (☑ 063-202002; www.coastways.com.na) This highly reputable company runs multiday self-catering 4WD trips deep into the Sperrgebiet (from Lüderitz to Walvis Bay, for example). Note that the cost of the permit is included in the price of the relevant tour.

NAMIBIA FISH RIVER CANYON

experiencing the enormous scope of the canyon, something best done on the monumental five-day hike that traverses half its length. The reward is nothing less than an unforgettable relationship with one of Africa's greatest natural wonders.

⊙ Sights

Main Viewpoint VIEWPOINT
This viewpoint has probably the best – and most photographed – overall canyon outlook, with views that take in the sharp river bend known as Hell's Corner. Better still, it's accessible to everyone, not just those hiking the full five-day canyon trail.

🏃 Activities

Hiking is obviously the main event here, but following the death of an ill-prepared hiker in 2001, the NWR decided to strictly prohibit day hikes and leisure walks into Fish River Canyon.

Fish River Hiking Trail HIKING
(per person N$250; ⊘ 15 Apr-15 Sep) The five-day hike from Hobas to Ai-Ais is Namibia's most popular long-distance walk – and with good reason. The magical 85km route, which follows the sandy riverbed past a series of ephemeral pools, begins at Hikers'

point, and ends at the hot-spring resort of Ai-Ais.

Due to flash flooding and heat in summer months, the route is open only from 15 April to 15 September. Groups of three to 30 people may begin the hike every day of the season, though you will have to book in advance as the trail is extremely popular. Reservations can be made at the NWR office (p252) in Windhoek.

Officials may ask to see a doctor's certificate of fitness, issued less than 40 days before your hike, though if you look young and fit, they're unlikely to ask. Hikers must arrange their own transport to and from the start and finish, as well as accommodation in Hobas and Ai-Ais.

Thanks to the typically warm, clear weather, you probably won't need a tent, but you must carry a sleeping bag and food. In Hobas, check on water availability in the canyon. In August and September, the last 15km of the walk can be completely dry and hikers will need several 2L water bottles to manage this hot, sandy stretch. Large plastic soft-drink bottles normally work just fine.

➜ **Hiking Route**

From Hobas, it's 10km to **Hikers' Viewpoint**, which is the start of the trail – hikers must find their own transport to this point.

The steep and scenic section at the beginning takes you from the canyon rim to the river, where you'll have a choice of fabulous sandy campsites beside cool green river pools.

Although some maps show the trail following the river quite closely, it's important to note that the best route changes from year to year. This is largely due to sand and vegetation deposited by the previous year's floods. In general, the easiest hiking will be along the inside of the river bends, where you're likely to find wildlife trails and dry, nonsandy terrain that's free of vegetation tangles, slippery stones and large boulders.

After an exhausting 13km hike through the rough sand and boulders along the east bank, the **Sulphur Springs Viewpoint** track joins the main route. If you're completely exhausted at this stage and can't handle the conditions, this trail can be used as an emergency exit from the canyon. If it's any encouragement, however, the going gets easier as you move downstream, so why not head a further 2km to **Sulphur Springs**, set up camp and see how you feel in the morning?

Sulphur Springs (more commonly called Palm Springs) is an excellent campsite with thermal sulphur pools (a touch of paradise) to soothe your aching muscles. The springs, which have a stable temperature of 57°C, gush up from the underworld at an amazing 30L per second and contain not only sulphur but also chloride and fluoride.

Legend has it that during WWI, two German prisoners of war hid out at Sulphur Springs to escape internment. One was apparently suffering from asthma, and the other from skin cancer, but thanks to the spring's healing powers, both were cured. It's also said that the palm trees growing here sprang up from date pips discarded by these two Germans.

The next section of the hike consists mostly of deep sand, pebbles and gravel. The most direct route through the inside river bends requires hikers to cross the river several times. The **Table Mountain** formation lies 15km beyond Sulphur Springs, and a further 15km on is the first short cut, which avoids an area of dense thorn scrub known as Bushy Corner. Around the next river bend, just upstream from the **Three Sisters** rock formation, is a longer short cut past **Kanebis Bend** up to **Kooigoedhoogte Pass**. At the top, you'll have a superb view of **Four Finger Rock**, an impressive rock tower consisting of four thick pinnacles (though they more closely resemble a cow's udder than fingers).

After descending to the river, you'll cross to the west bank and start climbing over yet another short cut (although you can also follow the river bend). At the southern end of this pass, on the west bank of the river, lies the **grave of Lieutenant Thilo von Trotha**, who was killed here in a 1905 confrontation between the Germans and the Nama.

The final 25km into Ai-Ais, which can be completed in one long day, follows an easy but sandy and rocky route. South of von Trotha's grave, the canyon widens out and becomes drier. Be advised that towards the end of winter, the final 15km are normally completely dry, so you will need to carry sufficient water.

🛏 Sleeping

Accommodation inside the park must be prebooked through the NWR office (p252) in Windhoek. In addition to the accommodation inside and close to the park, other excellent possibilities can be found at Gondwana Cañon Park.

Hobas Camp Site   CAMPGROUND $
(camping N$170, s/d N$1080/1760; ☀) Administered by NWR, this pleasant and well-shaded campground near the park's northern end is about 10km from the main viewpoints. Facilities are clean and there's a kiosk and swimming pool, but no restaurant or petrol station. Rooms in bush chalets were under construction when we last passed through.

Ai-Ais Hot Springs Spa   RESORT $$
(www.nwrnamibia.com/ai-ais.htm; camping N$190, mountain-river-view d N$1330/1620; ☀) Administered by NWR, amenities here include washing blocks, braai pits and use of the resort facilities, including the hot springs. The rooms are tidy, if a touch overpriced, and there are also slightly more expensive river-view rooms. There are family chalets available and an on-site restaurant and small grocery store.

★ Fish River Lodge   LODGE $$$
(✉061-228104, 063-683005; www.fishriverlodge-namibia.com; s/d N$1995/3056) With 20 chalets located on the western rim of the canyon, Fish River Lodge is a magical spot to enjoy the landscape. Rooms are gorgeous, modern and come with superlative views. Activities include the five-night canyon hike

(85km, April to September), or a day hike for the less ambitious.

Access to the lodge is from the D463, which links the B4 in the north and the C13 to the west.

ℹ️ Information

The main access points for Fish River Canyon are at Hobas, near the northern end of the park, and Ai-Ais, near the southern end. Both are administered by the NWR. Accommodation must be booked in advance through the Windhoek office (p252). Daily park permits (N$80 per person and N$10 per vehicle) are valid for both Hobas and Ai-Ais.

The **Hobas Information Centre** (⊙7.30am-noon & 2-5pm), at the northern end of the park, is also the check-in point for the five-day canyon hike. Packaged snacks and cool drinks are available here, but little else. If you're on your way to view the canyon, use the toilets here – there are none further on.

The Fish River typically flows between March and April. Early in the tourist season, from April to June, it may diminish to a trickle, and by mid-winter, to just a chain of remnant pools along the canyon floor.

ℹ️ Getting There & Away

There's no public transport to Hobas or Ai-Ais, and you'll really need a private vehicle to get around. The drive in from Grünau to Hobas is on a decent gravel road, accessible most of the year in a 2WD, although it can be problematic immediately after heavy rain.

Gondwana Cañon Park

📞 061

Founded in 1996, the 100,000-hectare Gondwana Cañon Park was created by amalgamating several former sheep farms and removing the fences to restore the wilderness country immediately northeast of |Ai- |Ais Richtersveld Transfrontier Park. Water holes have been established and wildlife is returning to this wonderful, remote corner of Namibia. In the process, the park absorbed the former Augurabies-Steenbok Nature Reserve, which had been created earlier to protect not only steenboks but also Hartmann's mountain zebras, gemsboks and klipspringers. Predators are still yet to arrive in numbers, but expect that to change as word gets out...

Gondwana Cañon Park can be accessed via private vehicle along the C37, south of Seeheim.

Cañon Mountain Camp LODGE $$

(📞061-244558; r N$1080; ❄️) One of the more budget-orientated properties in the area, this remote mountain camp occupies a high-altitude setting amid dolerite hills. Self-caterers can take advantage of the fully equipped kitchen, braai pits and communal lounges. The whitewashed walls evoke a cross between New Mexico and the south of Spain.

★ Canyon Lodge LODGE $$$

(📞061-427200, 063-693014; www.gondwana-collection.com; camping from N$120, s/d from N$2035/3256; ❄️📶❄️) This mountain retreat is one of Namibia's most stunning accommodation options and it comes at a price that is surprisingly reasonable. The whole place, but especially the luxury stone bungalows, is sympathetically integrated into its boulder-strewn backdrop. The outlook is dramatic and the bungalows, with flagstone floors, have great privacy. The restaurant, housed in a 1908 farmhouse, is tastefully decorated with historic farming implements and has rambling gardens.

Canyon Roadhouse GUESTHOUSE $$$

(📞061-230066; www.gondwana-collection.com; camping N$175, s/d from N$1511/2422; 📶❄️) This wonderful (and terribly kitsch) place attempts to recreate a roadhouse out on the wildest stretches of Route 66 – at least as it exists in the collective imagination. Buffets are served on an antique motorcycle, and the stunning window shades and bar stools are made from used air filters from heavy-duty vehicles. Rooms (which are all the same) are brightly coloured with low-slung roofs and modern touches.

Noordoewer

📞 063

Noordoewer sits astride the Orange River, which has its headwaters in the Drakensberg Mountains of Natal (South Africa) and forms much of the boundary between Namibia and South Africa. Although the town primarily serves as a border crossing and a centre for viticulture, it is a good base for organising a canoeing or rafting adventure on the Orange River.

Noordoewer is located just off the B1 near the South African border, and is only accessible by private transport.

Canoe and rafting trips are normally done in stages and last three to six days. The popular trips from Noordoewer north to Aussenkehr aren't treacherous by any stretch – the white water never exceeds Class II – but they do provide access to some wonderfully wild canyon country. Other possible stages include Aussenkehr to the Fish River mouth; Fish River mouth to Nama Canyon (which has a few more serious rapids); and Nama Canyon to Selingsdrif.

Amanzi Trails CANOEING
(☑ in South Africa 27 21-559 1573; www.amanzi trails.co.za) This well-established South African company is based in Amanzi River Camp, and specialises in four- and five-night guided canoe trips down the Orange River costing N$2990/3380 per person. It also arranges shorter self-guided trips and longer excursions up Fish River for more experienced clients.

Felix Unite CANOEING
(☑ in South Africa 27 87 354 0578; www.felixunite. com) Another highly reputable South African operator, Felix Unite, based in Camp Provenance, specialises in five-day guided canoe and rafting trips down the Orange River costing N$3295 per person. It can also combine these excursions with lengthier trips around the Western Cape of South Africa.

Amanzi River Camp CAMPGROUND $
(☑ in South Africa 27 21-559 1573; http:// amanzitrails.co.za/amanzi-river-camp/; camping per adult/child N$130/80, s/d/tr/q chalets N$430/550/670/790) This well-situated camp, 15km down Orange River Rd, sits on the riverbank. It's the launch point for Amanzi Trails, so you can stock up on supplies, indulge in a hot meal and get a good night's rest before embarking on your canoe trip.

Camp Provenance CAMPGROUND $$
(☑ in South Africa 27-21-702-9400; www.felixunite. com; camping N$120, r N$965-1725) Approximately 10km west of Noordoewer is this safari-chic river camp and launch point for Felix Unite. Purists can pitch their own tent on the grassy field, while lovers of creature comforts can bed down in a permanent tent or chalet, and stockpile their reserves for the paddling ahead.

UNDERSTAND NAMIBIA

Namibia Today

As a relative newcomer to the world of nations, Namibia has mastered political stability and economic prosperity better than most African veterans. This is a country that works. Yes, many of its people live in grinding poverty and wealth disparity is a major issue, but the country's overall economic performance and social harmony continue to impress and there's nothing to suggest that these are likely to change any time soon.

Namibia's economy continues to roll along nicely. Although it was affected by the global recession in 2008–09, its mineral deposits ensured its economy rebounded as uranium and diamond prices recovered. By 2015 the country was again reporting a growth rate in excess of 5%.

There is much to be excited about when it comes to the country's economic future. Offshore oil and natural-gas exploration has thrown up some promising signals; the country is one of the world's largest producers of diamonds and uranium, with large deposits of gold, copper and zinc; while its tourism industry goes from strength to strength. In 2014, for example, the tourism sector was responsible for nearly one out of every five jobs in the country, according to the World Travel and Tourism Council. Nearly one million visitors come to Namibia every year – a lot when you remember that the country's total population is only 2.44 million people.

But like so many other countries, Namibia faces a massive challenge in ensuring that the country's prosperity benefits all Namibians. Crippling droughts have caused widespread hardship in a country that grows around half of its cereal requirements and where, according to the UN, nearly one-third of the population lives below the poverty line and roughly the same number is unemployed.

History

Namibia's history is a familiar African story, beginning with ancient peoples and the stories they told on remote rock walls, and entering the modern world with colonial repression and a brutal war of independence. But that's not where the story ends. Instead,

NAMIBIA NAMIBIA TODAY

Namibia has emerged from such turbulence as a confident, independent country where the future looks far brighter than its past.

European Exploration & Incursion

In 1486 the Portuguese captain Diego Cão sailed as far south as Cape Cross, where he erected a stone cross in tribute to his royal patron, João II. The following year, another cross was erected by Bartolomeu Dias at Lüderitz, but it wasn't really until the early 17th century that Dutch sailors from the Cape colonies began to explore the desert coastline, although they refrained from setting up any permanent stations.

Soon after, however, growing European commercial and territorial interests were to send ambitious men deeper into Namibia's interior, and in 1750 the Dutch elephant hunter Jacobus Coetsee became the first European to cross the Orange River. In his wake came a series of traders, hunters and missionaries, and by the early 19th century there were mission stations at Bethanie, Windhoek, Rehoboth, Keetmanshoop and various other sites. In 1844 the German Rhenish Missionary Society, under Dr Hugo Hahn, began working among the Herero. More successful were the Finnish Lutherans, who arrived in the north in 1870 and established missions among the Owambo.

By 1843 the rich coastal guano deposits of the southern Namib Desert were attracting commercial attention. In 1867 the guano islands were annexed by the British, who then proceeded to take over Walvis Bay in 1878. The British also mediated the largely inconclusive Khoisan–Herero wars during this period.

The Scramble for Africa

The Germans, under Chancellor Otto von Bismarck, were late entering the European scramble for Africa. Bismarck had always been against colonies; he considered them an expensive illusion, famously stating, 'My map of Africa is here in Europe.' But he was to be pushed into an ill-starred colonial venture by the actions of a Bremen merchant called Adolf Lüderitz.

Having already set up a trading station in Lagos, Nigeria, in 1881, Lüderitz convinced the Nama chief, Joseph Fredericks, to sell Angra Pequena, where he established his second station trading in guano (excrement of seabirds; used to make manure and a gunpowder ingredient). He then petitioned the German chancellor for protection. Bismarck, still trying to stay out of Africa, politely requested the British at Walvis Bay to say whether they had any interest in the matter, but they never bothered to reply. Subsequently, in 1884, Lüderitz was officially declared part of the German Empire.

Initially, German interests were minimal, and between 1885 and 1890 the colonial administration amounted to three public administrators. Their interests were served largely through a colonial company (along the lines of the British East India Company in India prior to the raj), but the organisation couldn't maintain law and order.

In the 1880s, due to renewed fighting between the Nama and Herero, the German government dispatched Curt von François and 23 soldiers to restrict the supply of arms from British-administered Walvis Bay. This seemingly innocuous peacekeeping regiment slowly evolved into the more powerful Schutztruppe (German Imperial Army), which constructed forts around the country to combat growing opposition.

At this stage, Namibia became a fully fledged protectorate known as German South West Africa. The first German farmers arrived in 1892 to take up expropriated land on the central plateau, and were soon followed by merchants and other settlers. In the late 1890s the Germans, the Portuguese in Angola and the British in Bechuanaland (present-day Botswana) agreed on Namibia's boundaries.

Reaping the Whirlwind

Meanwhile, in the south, diamonds had been discovered at Grasplatz, east of Lüderitz, by South African labourer Zacharias Lewala. Despite the assessment of diamond-mining giant De Beers that the find probably wouldn't amount to much, prospectors flooded in to stake their claims. By 1910 the German authorities had granted exclusive rights to Deutsche Diamanten Gesellschaft (German Diamond Company).

For all the devastation visited upon the local populace, Germany was never to benefit from the diamond riches it found. The outbreak of WWI in 1914 was to mark the end of German colonial rule in South West Africa. By this time, however, the Germans had all but succeeded in devastating the Herero tribal structures, and had taken over all Khoikhoi and Herero lands. The more fortunate Owambo, in the north, managed to avoid German conquest, and they were only subsequently overrun during WWI by Portuguese forces fighting on the side of the Allies.

In 1914, at the beginning of WWI, Britain pressured South Africa into invading Namibia. The South Africans, under the command of Prime Minister Louis Botha and General Jan Smuts, pushed northward, forcing the outnumbered Schutztruppe to retreat. In May 1915 the Germans faced their final defeat at Khorab near Tsumeb and, a week later, a South African administration was set up in Windhoek.

By 1920 many German farms had been sold to Afrikaans-speaking settlers, and the German diamond-mining interests in the south were handed over to the South Africa–based Consolidated Diamond Mines (CDM), which later gave way to the Namdeb Diamond Corporation Limited (Namdeb).

South African Occupation

Under the Treaty of Versailles in 1919, Germany was required to renounce all of its colonial claims, and in 1920 the League of Nations granted South Africa a formal mandate to administer Namibia as part of the Union of South Africa.

While the mandate was renewed by the UN following WWII, South Africa was more interested in annexing South West Africa as a full province in the Union, and decided to scrap the terms of the mandate and rewrite the constitution. In response, the International Court of Justice determined that South Africa had overstepped its boundaries, and the UN established the Committee on South West Africa to enforce the original terms of the mandate. In 1956 the UN further decided that South African control should be terminated.

Undeterred, the South African government tightened its grip on the territory, and in 1949 granted the white population parliamentary representation in Pretoria. The bulk of Namibia's viable farmland was parcelled into some 6000 farms for white settlers, while other ethnic groups were relegated to newly demarcated 'tribal homelands'. The official intent was ostensibly to 'channel economic development into predominantly poor rural areas', but it was all too obvious that it was simply a convenient way of retaining the majority of the country for white settlement and ranching.

As a result, a prominent line of demarcation appeared between the predominantly white ranching lands in the central and southern parts of the country, and the poorer but better-watered tribal areas to the north. This arrangement was retained until Namibian independence in 1990, and to some extent continues to the present day.

Swapo

Throughout the 1950s, despite mounting pressure from the UN, South Africa refused to release its grip on Namibia. This intransigence was based on its fears of having yet another antagonistic government on its doorstep, and of losing the income that it derived from the mining operations there.

Forced labour had been the lot of most Namibians since the German annexation, and was one of the main factors that led to mass demonstrations and the increasingly nationalist sentiments in the late 1950s. Among the parties was the Owamboland People's Congress, founded in Cape Town under the leadership of Samuel Daniel Shafiishuna Nujoma and Herman Andimba Toivo ya Toivo.

In 1959 the party's name was changed to the Owamboland People's Organisation, and Nujoma took the issue of South African occupation to the UN in New York. By 1960 his party had gathered increased support, and it eventually coalesced into the South-West African People's Organisation (Swapo), with its headquarters in Dar es Salaam, Tanzania.

In 1966 Swapo took the issue of South African occupation to the International Court of Justice. The court upheld South Africa's right to govern South West Africa, but the UN General Assembly voted to terminate South Africa's mandate and replace it with a Council for South West Africa (renamed the Commission for Namibia in 1973) to administer the territory.

In response, on 26 August 1966 (now called Heroes' Day), Swapo launched its campaign of guerrilla warfare at Ongulumbashe in northern Namibia. The next year, one of Swapo's founders, Toivo ya Toivo, was convicted of terrorism and imprisoned in South Africa, where he would remain until 1984. Nujoma, however, stayed in Tanzania and avoided criminal prosecution. In 1972 the UN finally declared the South African occupation of South West Africa officially illegal and called for a withdrawal, proclaiming Swapo the legitimate representative of the Namibian people.

In 1975 Angola gained independence under the Cuban-backed Popular Movement for the Liberation of Angola (MPLA). Sympathetic to Swapo's struggle for independence in neighbouring Namibia, the fledgling government allowed it a safe base in the south of the country, from where it could step up its guerrilla campaign against South Africa.

South Africa responded by invading Angola in support of the opposition party, National Union for the Total Independence of Angola (Unita), an act that prompted the Cuban government to send hundreds of troops to the country to bolster up the MPLA. Although the South African invasion failed, and troops had to be withdrawn in March 1976, furious and bloody incursions into Angola continued well into the 1980s.

In the end, it was neither solely the activities of Swapo nor international sanctions that forced the South Africans to the negotiating table. On the contrary, all players were growing tired of the war, and the South African economy was suffering badly. By 1985 the war was costing R480 million (around US$250 million) per year, and conscription was widespread. Mineral exports, which once provided around 88% of the country's gross domestic product, had plummeted to just 27% by 1984.

Independence

In December 1988 a deal was finally struck between Cuba, Angola, South Africa and Swapo that provided for the withdrawal of Cuban troops from Angola and South African troops from Namibia. It also stipulated that the transition to Namibian independence would formally begin on 1 April 1989 and would be followed by UN-monitored elections held in November 1989 on the basis of universal suffrage. Although minor score settling and unrest among some Swapo troops threatened to derail the whole process, the plan went ahead, and in September 1989 Sam Nujoma returned from his 30-year exile. In the elections, Swapo garnered two-thirds of the votes, but the numbers were insufficient to give the party the sole mandate to write the new constitution, an outcome that went some way to allaying

fears that Namibia's minority groups would be excluded from the democratic process.

Following negotiations between the Constituent Assembly (soon to become the National Assembly) and international advisers, including the USA, France, Germany and the former USSR, a constitution was drafted. The new constitution established a multiparty system alongside an impressive Bill of Rights. It also limited the presidential executive to two five-year terms. The new constitution was adopted in February 1990, and independence was granted a month later, with Nujoma being sworn in as Namibia's first president.

Post-Independence

In those first optimistic years of his presidency, Sam Nujoma and his Swapo party based their policies on a national reconciliation program aimed at healing the wounds left by 25 years of armed struggle. They also embarked on a reconstruction program based on the retention of a mixed economy and partnership with the private sector.

These moderate policies and the stability they afforded were well received, and in 1994 President Nujoma and his party were re-elected with a 68% landslide victory over the main opposition party, the Democratic Turnhalle Alliance (DTA). Similarly in 1999, Swapo won 76.8% of the vote, although concerns arose when President Nujoma amended the constitution to allow himself a rather unconstitutional third term.

Other political problems included growing unrest in the Caprivi Strip, starting in 1999 with a failed attempt by rebels to seize Katima Mulilo. Continued fighting drove Caprivians out (and kept tourists away) until the conflict ended in 2002.

In 2004 the world watched warily to see if Nujoma would cling to power for a fourth term, and an almost audible sigh of relief could be heard in Namibia when he announced that he would finally be stepping down in favour of his chosen successor, Hifikepunye Pohamba.

Like Nujoma, Pohamba is a Swapo veteran, and he swept to power with nearly 77% of the vote. In 2009 he was re-elected for a second term. He left behind the land ministry, where he presided over one of Namibia's most controversial schemes – the expropriation of land from white farmers. This policy formed part of the 'poverty agenda', which, along with Namibia's HIV/AIDS crisis, the unequal distribution of income, managing the country's resource wealth fairly and the challenge of raising living standards for Namibia's poor, would become the defining domestic issues of his presidency.

In 2011 it was announced that Namibia had found offshore oil reserves amounting to 11 billion barrels, although it remains unclear whether the deposits will prove to be commercially viable. In the same year, the government's ongoing efforts to seek redress for colonial wrongs continued to bear fruit when the skulls of 20 Herero and Nama people were returned to Namibia from a museum in Germany.

In line with the constitution, and in keeping with Namibia's impressive postindependence record of largely peaceful transitions, President Pohamba honoured his pledge to stand aside in 2014. His successor, Hage Geingob, easily won elections in November of that year. Unusually for Namibia, political unrest marred the lead-up to the election and one protester was shot by police. Even so, international observers praised Namibia for its free and fair elections (and for its use of electronic voting, an African first). This, and the size of Swapo's electoral victory (Swapo won 87% of the vote in presidential polls and 80% of parliamentary seats), suggest that its dominance of Namibian politics is unlikely to change any time soon.

The Namibian People

Namibia's population in 2016 was estimated at 2,436,469 people, with an annual population growth rate of 1.98%. At approximately two people per square kilometre, Namibia has one of Africa's lowest population densities, while nearly 60% of the population is aged under 25.

The population of Namibia comprises 12 major ethnic groups. Half the people come from the Owambo tribe (50%), with other ethnic groups making up a relatively small percentage of the population: Kavango (9%), Herero/Himba (7%), Damara (7%), Afrikaner and German (6%), Nama (5%), Caprivian (4%), San (3%), Baster (2%) and Tswana (0.5%).

Like nearly all other sub-Saharan nations, Namibia is struggling to contain its HIV/AIDS epidemic, which is impacting heavily on average life expectancy and population growth rates. HIV/AIDS became the leading cause of death in Namibia in 1996, and in 2015 just under 9% of the population was HIV positive. Life expectancy in Namibia has dropped to 63.6, although that figure is again climbing. By 2021 it is estimated that up to a third of Namibia's children under the age of 15 could be orphaned.

Owambo

As a sort of loose confederation, the Owambo have always been strong enough to deter outsiders, including the slavers of yore and the German invaders of the last century. They were historically an aggressive culture, which made them the obvious candidates to fight the war of independence. They also make up Namibia's largest ethnic group (about 50% of the population) and, not surprisingly, most of the ruling Swapo party.

The Owambo traditionally inhabited the north of the country, and are subdivided into 12 distinct groups. Four of these occupy the Kunene region of southern Angola, while the other eight comprise the Owambo groups in Namibia. The most numerous group is the Kwanyama, which makes up 35% of Namibia's Owambo population and dominates the government.

Recently, large numbers of Owambo have migrated southward to Windhoek, or to the larger towns in the north, to work as professionals, craftspeople and labourers. They have enjoyed considerable favour from the government over the years and, with the exception of white Namibians of European descent, are among the most successful of the tribal groups.

Herero/Himba

Namibia's 120,000 Herero occupy a few regions of the country, and are divided into several subgroups. The largest groups include the Tjimba and Ndamuranda in Kaokoveld, the Maherero around Okahandja, and the Zeraua, who are centred on Omaruru. The Himba of the Kaokoveld are also a Herero subgroup, as are the Mbandero, who occupy the colonially demarcated territory formerly known as Hereroland, around Gobabis in eastern Namibia.

The Herero were originally part of the early Bantu migrations south from central Africa. They arrived in present-day Namibia in the mid-16th century and, after a 200-year sojourn in the Kaokoveld, they moved southward to occupy the Swakop Valley and the central plateau. Until the colonial period, they remained as seminomadic pastoralists in this relatively rich grassland, herding and grazing cattle and sheep.

However, bloody clashes with the northward-migrating Nama, as well as with German colonial troops and settlers, led to a violent uprising in the late 19th century, which culminated in the devastating Battle of Waterberg in August 1904. In the aftermath, 80% of the country's Herero population was wiped out, and the remainder were dispersed around the country, terrified and demoralised. Large numbers fled into neighbouring Botswana, where they settled down to a life of subsistence agriculture (although they have since prospered to become the country's richest herders).

The characteristic Herero women's dress is derived from Victorian-era German missionaries. It consists of an enormous crinoline worn over a series of petticoats, with a horn-shaped hat or headdress. If you happen to be in Okahandja on the nearest weekend to 23 August, you can witness the gathering of thousands of Hereros immaculately turned out in their traditional dress, come to honour their fallen chiefs on Maherero Day.

The Himba, a tribal group numbering not more than 50,000 people, are a seminomadic pastoral people who are closely related to the Herero, yet continue to live much as they have for generations. The women in particular are famous for smearing themselves with a fragrant mixture of ochre, butter and bush herbs, which dyes their skin a burnt-orange hue and serves as a natural sunblock and insect repellent. As if this wasn't striking enough, they also use the mixture to cover their braided hair, which has an effect similar to dreadlocking. Instead of wearing Western clothes, they prefer to dress traditionally, bare-breasted, with little more than a pleated animal-skin skirt in the way of clothing.

Similar to the Masai of Kenya and Tanzania, the Himba breed and care for herds of cattle in addition to goats and sheep. Unlike the East African savannah, Himba homelands are among the most extreme environments in the world, and their survival is ultimately dependent on maintaining strong community alliances. It was this very climatic harshness and resulting seclusion from outside influences that enabled the Himba to maintain their cultural heritage over the centuries.

During the 1980s and early 1990s, the Himba were severely threatened by war and drought, though they have experienced a tremendous resurgence in recent years. At present, the population as a whole has succeeded in gaining control of their homelands, and in exerting real political power on the national stage.

Women in Namibia

In a culture where male power is mythologised, it's unsurprising that women's rights lag behind. Even today, it's not uncommon for men to have multiple sexual partners and, until recently, in cases where husbands abandoned their wives and their children, there was very little course for redress. Since independence, the Namibian government has been committed to improving women's rights with bills such as the Married Persons Equality Act (1996), which equalised property rights and gave women rights of custody over their children.

Even the government acknowledges that achieving gender equality is more about changing grass-roots attitudes than passing laws. According to a US Department of State Human Rights Report in 2015, domestic violence was widespread, and endemic social problems such as poverty, alcoholism and the feeling of powerlessness engendered by long-term unemployment only served to increase women's vulnerability to violence. According to the US Department of State, the Namibian government has passed one of the most comprehensive legislative acts against rape in the world. However, women's groups and NGOs point out that many sexual crimes against women are never reported and never reach the authorities.

Namibian women do feature prominently in local and civic life, and many a Namibian woman took a heroic stance in the struggle for independence.

In 2016 women held 43 out of 104 seats in the National Assembly, an impressive 41.35% of all MPs, while women have been increasingly appointed to ministerial roles under the ruling party's much-touted 'zebra policy', whereby every ministry must have a male and a female in the top two positions. In the private sector, however, women remain underrepresented in senior leadership positions.

Women are also undoubtedly the linchpin of the Namibian home. They shoulder a double responsibility in raising children and caring for family members as well as contributing to the family income. This load has only increased with the horrendous effects of HIV/AIDS on the family structure – in 2015 just over 13% of the adult Namibian population was living with HIV/AIDS, down from 18% in 2009.

Female literacy (84.5% in 2015) is actually higher than for men (79.2%), but maternal mortality remains high (265 per 100,000 live births, compared to 129 in Botswana and 138 in South Africa).

Economy

The country's economy is dominated by the extraction and processing of minerals for export. Although mining only accounts for 11.5% of the GDP, it provides more than half of foreign-exchange earnings. Most famously, Namibia's large alluvial diamond deposits have earned it the enviable reputation as one of the world's primary sources for gem-quality stones. However, the country is also regarded as a prominent producer of uranium, lead, zinc, tin, silver and tungsten.

The Namibian economy continues to perform strongly, with growth rates falling slightly in recent years, but still an extremely healthy 4.5% in 2015. Unemployment, however, remains high, with an official rate of 28.1% in 2014 – unofficially, the figure stands closer to 50%, with close to three-quarters of 15- to 19-year-olds unemployed.

The mining sector employs only about 2% of the population, while about half the population depends on subsistence agriculture for its livelihood. Namibia normally imports about 50% of its cereal requirements, and in drought years, food shortages are a major problem in rural areas. Although the fishing industry is also a large economic force, catches are typically canned and marked for export.

In recent years, tourism has grown considerably throughout the country, though white Namibians still largely control the industry.

The Namibian economy is closely linked to the regional powerhouse of South Africa, and the Namibian dollar is pegged one-to-one to the South African rand.

Architecture

While most visitors to Namibia have already set their sights on the country's natural wonders, there are a surprising number of architectural attractions to discover as well. Striking German colonial structures continue to stand as testament to the former European occupation of Namibia.

While most of Windhoek has modernised with the chock-a-block concrete structures that typify most African cities, there are a few remaining colonial gems. Towering over the city is the German Lutheran Christuskirche (p243), which masterfully uses local sandstone in its European-leaning neo-Gothic construction. Another notable structure is the Alte Fest (Old Fort), which was constructed in 1890 by Curt von François and his men to serve as the barracks for the German army. It remains the oldest surviving building in the city, and now serves a much more peaceful function as the National Museum (p243).

If you truly want to experience the shining jewels in Namibia's architectural crown, you're going to need to head out to the coast. Here, improbably squeezed between the icy waters of the South Atlantic and the overbearing heat of the Namib Desert, are the surreal colonial relics of Swakopmund (p277) and Lüderitz (p294). Walking the streets of either town, you'd be easily forgiven for thinking that you were in a Bavarian *dorfchen* (small village) transplanted onto the shores of southwestern Africa. Somewhat forgotten by time and history, both towns are characterised by a handsome blend of German imperial and art nouveau styles, which become all the more bizarre when viewed against the backdrop of soaring dunes and raging seas.

Environment

Namibia's natural world is a grand epic of extraordinary landforms (from sand-dune deserts that reach the coast to the haunting, barren mountain ranges of the interior) and these shelter a wonderful array of wildlife, especially in the country's north. But this is also one of the driest countries on earth and issues of desertification and water scarcity loom large over the country's future. And unlike neighbouring Botswana, Namibia allows commercial or trophy hunting.

The Land

The Namib, the desert of southwestern Africa that so appropriately gives its name to

NAMIBIA ARCHITECTURE

the driest country south of the Sahara, is the oldest desert on the planet. It is a scorched earth of burned and blackened-red basalt that spilled from beneath the earth 130 million years ago, hardening to form what we now know as Namibia. Precious little can grow or thrive in this merciless environment. That anything survives out here owes everything to the sheer ingenuity of the natural world and the resilience of its human population.

Northwestern Namibia is synonymous with the Skeleton Coast, a formidable desert coastline engulfed by icy breakers. As you move inland, the sinister fogs give way to the wondrous desert wilderness of Damaraland and the Kaokoveld. The former is known for its unique geological features, including volcanic mounds, petrified forests, red-rock mesas and petroglyph-engraved sandstone slabs. The latter is known as one of the last great wildernesses in Southern Africa. Despite their unimaginably harsh conditions, both regions are also rich in wildlife, which has adapted to the arid environment and subsequently thrived.

The Namib Desert extends along the country's entire Atlantic coast, and is scored by a number of rivers, which rise in the central plateau, but often run dry. Some, like the ephemeral Tsauchab, once reached the sea, but now end in calcrete pans. Others flow only during the summer rainy season, but at some former stage carried huge volumes of water and carved out dramatic canyons such as Fish River (p297) and Kuiseb. Much of the surface between Walvis Bay and Lüderitz is covered by enormous linear dunes, which roll back from the sea towards the inland gravel plains that are occasionally interrupted by isolated mountain ranges.

Wildlife

If you're here to see wildlife, you'll want to spend most of your time in the north, in the country's three main wildlife areas: Kaokoveld, where elusive desert elephants and black rhinos follow the river courses running to the Skeleton Coast; the Caprivi Strip and Khaudum National Park, where Namibia's last African wild dogs find refuge and lions are making a comeback; and, best of all, Etosha National Park, one of the world's finest wildlife reserves.

Further south is one of the largest wildlife reserves in Africa, the Namib-Naukluft Park, which covers an astonishing 6% of Namibian territory. Much of it is true desert, and large mammals occur in extremely low densities, though local species include Hartmann's mountain zebras as well as more widespread Southern African endemics such as springboks and gemsboks. For aficionados of smaller life, the Namib is an endemism hotspot – on the dunes, desert-adapted birdlife flickers into view, alongside reptiles and desert-specialist insects.

The severe Namibian coast is no place to expect abundant big wildlife, although it's the only spot in the world where massive fur-seal colonies are patrolled by hunting brown hyenas and black-backed jackals. The coast also hosts flamingos and massive flocks of summer waders, including sanderlings, turnstones and grey plovers, while Heaviside's and dusky dolphins can often be seen in the shallow offshore waters.

HUNTING

Unlike in neighbouring Botswana, hunting is legal in Namibia, although it is strictly regulated and licensed. The Ministry of the Environment and Tourism along with the Namibia Professional Hunting Association (www.napha-namibia.com) regulate hunting, which accounts for 5% of the country's revenue from wildlife.

The Namibian government views its hunting laws as a practical form of wildlife management and conservation. Many foreign hunters are willing to pay handsomely for big wildlife trophies, and farmers and ranchers frequently complain about the ravages of wildlife on their stock. The idea is to provide farmers with financial incentives to protect free-ranging wildlife. Management strategies include encouraging hunting of older animals, evaluating the condition of trophies and setting bag limits in accordance with population fluctuations.

In addition, quite a few private farms are set aside for hunting. The owners stock these farms with wildlife bred by suppliers – mainly in South Africa – and turn them loose into the farm environment. Although community-based hunting concessions have appeared in the Otjozondjupa area, these still aren't widespread.

WHERE TO WATCH WILDLIFE

Undoubtedly Namibia's most prolific wildlife populations are in Etosha National Park (p260), one of Africa's premier wildlife reserves. Its name means 'Place of Mirages', for the dusty salt pan that sits at its centre. During the dry season, huge herds of elephants, zebras, antelope and giraffes, as well as rare black rhinos, congregate here against an eerie, bleached-white backdrop. Predators, too, are commonly sighted here.

Namibia's other major parks for good wildlife viewing are Bwabwata National Park (p266) and Nkasa Rupara National Park (p267) in the Caprivi Strip.

Along the coast, penguins and seals thrive in the chilly Atlantic currents; the colony of Cape fur seals at Cape Cross Seal Reserve (p275) is one of the country's premier wildlife-watching attractions.

Not all of Namibia's wildlife is confined to national parks. Unprotected Damaraland (p269), in the northwest, is home to numerous antelope species and other ungulates, and is also a haven for desert rhinos, elephants, lions, spotted hyenas and other specially adapted subspecies.

In 2009 the Namibian government opened Sperrgebiet National Park, a vast 16,000 sq km expanse of land home to the threatened desert rain frog, dramatic rock formations and disused diamond mines. The area's haunting beauty, which is highlighted by shimmering salt pans and saffron-coloured sand dunes, provides one of the world's most dramatic backdrops for adventurous wildlife watchers. The Sperrgebiet fringe is also home to one of Africa's only populations of wild horses.

MAMMALS

Northern Namibia is one of Southern Africa's most rewarding wildlife-watching destinations. The greatest prizes here are desert elephants, black rhinos, lions, leopards, cheetahs and, if you're really lucky, African wild dogs. Other unusual sightings include the elusive Hartmann's mountain zebra.

More commonly sighted species include ostriches, zebras, warthogs, greater kudus, giraffes, gemsboks, springboks, steenboks, mongoose, ground squirrels and small numbers of other animals, such as black-backed jackals and bat-eared foxes. If you're *really* lucky, you might encounter caracals, aardwolfs, pangolins (go on, dream a little...) and brown hyenas.

Along the country's desert coasts you can see jackass penguins, flamingos and Cape fur seals.

BIRDS

Despite Namibia's harsh and inhospitable desert landscape, more than 700 bird species have been recorded in the country. The richest pickings for birders are in the lush green Caprivi Strip, which borders the Okavango Delta. Here, particularly in the Mahango Game Reserve, you'll find the same exotic range of species as in Botswana's Okavango Panhandle, Okavango Delta and Linyanti regions. Wetland species include the African jacana, snakebird, ibis, stork, egret, shrike, kingfisher, great white heron and purple and green-backed heron. Birds of prey include Pel's fishing owl (which is much prized among birders), goshawk, several species of vulture, and both the bateleur and African fish eagle.

The coastal wildfowl reserves support an especially wide range of birdlife: white pelicans, flamingos, cormorants and hundreds of other wetland birds. Further south, around Walvis Bay and Lüderitz, flamingos (p286) and jackass penguins share the same desert shoreline.

Situated on a key migration route, Namibia also hosts a range of migratory birds, especially raptors, which arrive around September and October and remain until April. The canyons and riverbeds slicing across the central Namib Desert are home to nine species of raptor. Throughout the desert regions, you'll also see the intriguing social weaver, which builds an enormous nest that's the avian equivalent of a 10-storey block of flats. Central Namibia also boasts bird species found nowhere else, such as the Namaqua sand-grouse and Grey's lark.

Other iconic species that birders may want to build their trips around include Hartlaub's francolin (in the rocky uplands of central and northern Namibia), Rüppell's bustard (on the Namib Desert fringe), Barlow's lark (the far south, around Sperrgebiet), Rüppell's parrot (acacia woodlands and dry riverbeds), Monteiro's hornbill (arid woodlands in the interior), dune lark (dry riverbeds of the Namib), Herero chat (arid interior in the centre and north), rockrunner (arid interior in the centre and north) and Carp's tit (northern woodlands).

ENDANGERED SPECIES

Namibia has a number of endangered species, among them the black rhino, desert elephant, lion and African wild dog. It is also considered a key battleground in the fight to save the cheetah. Poaching continues to take its toll on a number of flagship species, especially the rhino.

In the eastern reaches of the Caprivi Strip, and across the border in Botswana's Chobe National Park, a small population of puku antelope survives, the last of its kind in Southern Africa (although healthy, if declining, populations survive in Tanzania and northern Zambia).

Overfishing and the 1993–94 outbreak of 'red tide' along the Skeleton Coast have decimated the sea-lion population, both through starvation and commercially inspired culling.

The stability of some bird and plant species, such as the lichen fields, the welwitschia plant, the Damara tern, the Cape vulture and numerous lesser-known species, has been undoubtedly compromised by human activities (including tourism and recreation) in formerly remote areas. However, awareness of the perils faced by these species is increasing among operators and tourists alike, which adds a glimmer of hope to the prospects of their future survival.

NATIONAL PARKS & RESERVES

PARK	FEATURES	ACTIVITIES	BEST TIME
Dorob National Park	Stretches from the Ugab River in the north down to Sandwich Harbour in the south (it consumes the old National West Coast Tourist Recreation Area); coastal dune belt; desert plants; sand dunes; vast gravel plains; prolific birdlife; major river systems	Fishing; birdwatching	Jun-Nov
Etosha National Park	22,275 sq km; semi-arid savannah surrounding a salt pan; 114 mammal species	Wildlife viewing; birdwatching; night drives	May-Sep
Fish River Canyon (part of |Ai- |Ais Richtersveld Transfrontier Park)	Africa's longest canyon (161km); hot springs; rock strata of multiple colours	Hiking; bathing	May-Nov
Khaudum National Park	3840 sq km; bushveld landscape crossed by fossilised river valleys	Wildlife viewing; hiking; 4WD exploration	Jun-Oct
Namib-Naukluft Park	50,000 sq km; Namibia's largest protected area; rare Hartmann's zebras	Wildlife watching; walking	year-round
Nkasa Rupara National Park	320 sq km; mini-Okavango; 430 bird species; canoe trails through park	Wildlife viewing; birdwatching; canoe trips	Sep-Apr
Mudumu National Park	850 sq km; lush riverine environment; 400 bird species	Wildlife watching; birdwatching; guided trails	May-Sep
Skeleton Coast Park	20,000 sq km; wild, foggy wilderness; desert-adapted animals	Wildlife viewing; walking; fly-in safaris	year-round
Waterberg Plateau Park	400 sq km; table mountain; refuge for black and white rhinos and rare antelope	Wildlife viewing; rhino tracking; hiking	May-Sep

National Parks & Reserves

VISITING THE NATIONAL PARKS IN NAMIBIA

Access to most wildlife parks is limited to closed vehicles only. A 2WD is sufficient for most parks, but for Nkasa Rupara National Park, Khaudum National Park and parts of Bwabwata National Park, you need a sturdy 4WD with high clearance.

Entry permits are available on arrival at park entrances. Campsites and resorts should be booked in advance, although it is possible to make a booking on arrival, subject to availability.

FOREIGNERS	COST PER DAY
adult	N$80 (Etosha, Cape Cross, |Ai- |Ais/Fish River, Skeleton Coast, Naukluft Park, Waterberg); N$40 all other parks
child (under 16)	free
camping	cost varies
vehicles	N$10

NAMIBIA WILDLIFE RESORTS (NWR)

The semiprivate Namibia Wildlife Resorts (p252) in Windhoek manages a large number of rest camps, campsites and resorts within the national parks. If you haven't prebooked (ie if you're pulling into a national park area on a whim), there's a good chance you'll find something available on the spot, but have a contingency plan in case things don't work out. This is not advised for Etosha or Sossusvlei, which are perennially busy.

SURVIVAL GUIDE

ⓘ Directory A–Z

ACCOMMODATION

B&Bs

B&Bs are mushrooming all around the country. As they are private homes, the standard, atmosphere and welcome tend to vary a great deal. Generally speaking, B&Bs are a pleasure to frequent and can be one of the highlights of any trip to Namibia. Some places don't actually provide breakfast (!), so it pays to ask when booking.

For listings, pick up the *Namibia B&B Guide* or contact the Accommodation Association of Namibia (www.accommodation-association. com), which also lists a number of self-catering flats and guest farms.

Camping

Namibia is campers' heaven, and wherever you go in the country you'll find a campsite nearby. These can vary from a patch of scrubland with basic facilities to well-kitted-out sites with concrete ablution blocks with hot and cold running water and a kiosk.

In many of the national parks, campsites are administered by Namibia Wildlife Resorts (p252) and need to be booked beforehand online or through its offices in Windhoek, Swakopmund and Cape Town. These sites are all well maintained, and many of them also offer accommodation in bungalows. Unlike in Botswana, most campsites, at least in national parks, are fenced.

To camp on private land, you'll need to secure permission from the landowner. On communal land – unless you're well away from human habitation – it's a courtesy to make your presence known to the leaders in the nearest community.

Most towns also have caravan parks with bungalows or rondavels, as well as a pool, restaurant and shop. Prices are normally per site, with a maximum of eight people and two vehicles per site; there's normally an additional charge per vehicle. In addition, a growing number of private rest camps, with rooms and campsites and well-appointed facilities, are springing up in rural areas and along major tourist routes.

Guest Farms

Farmstays are a peculiarly Namibian phenomenon, whereby tourists can spend the night on one of the country's huge private farms. They give an intriguing insight into the rural white lifestyle, although, as with B&Bs, the level of hospitality and the standard of rooms and facilities can vary enormously. The emphasis is on personal service and quaint rural luxury, and bedding down on a huge rural estate in the middle of the bush can be a uniquely Namibian experience.

As an added bonus, many of these farms have designated blocks of land as wildlife reserves, and offer excellent wildlife viewing and photographic opportunities. With that said, many also serve as hunting reserves, so bear this in mind when booking if you don't relish the thought of trading trophy stories over dinner.

For all farmstays, advance bookings are essential.

Hostels

In Windhoek, Swakopmund, Lüderitz and other places, you'll find private backpacker hostels, which provide inexpensive dorm accommodation, shared ablutions and cooking facilities. Most offer a very agreeable atmosphere, and they are extremely popular with budget travellers. On average, you can expect to pay around

ⓘ PRACTICALITIES

Electricity
Electrical plugs are three round pins (like South Africa).

Media
There are a decent number of commercial newspapers, of which the *Namibian* and the *Windhoek Advertiser* are probably the best. The *Windhoek Observer*, published on Saturday, is also good.

Weights & Measures
Namibia uses the metric system.

N$100 per person per night. Some also offer private doubles, which cost around N$250 to N$400.

Hotels

Hotels in Namibia are much like hotels anywhere else, ranging from tired old has-beens to palaces of luxury and indulgence. Rarely, though, will you find a dirty or unsafe hotel in Namibia given the relatively strict classification system, which rates everything from small guesthouses to four-star hotels.

One-star hotels must have a specific ratio of rooms with private and shared facilities. They tend to be quite simple, but most are locally owned and managed and provide clean, comfortable accommodation with adequate beds and towels. Rates range from around N$350 to N$500 for a double room, including breakfast. They always have a small dining room and bar, but few offer frills such as air-conditioning.

Hotels with two- and three-star ratings are generally more comfortable, and are often used by local business people. Rates start at around N$450 for a double, and climb to N$650 for the more elegant places.

There aren't really many four-star hotels in the usual sense, though most high-end lodges could qualify for a four-star rating. To qualify, a hotel needs to be an air-conditioned palace with a salon, valet service and a range of ancillary services for business and diplomatic travellers.

Safari Lodges

Over the last decade the Namibian luxury safari lodge has come along in leaps and bounds, offering the kind of colonial luxury that has been associated with Botswana.

Most of the lodges are set on large private ranches or in concession areas. Some are quite affordable family-run places with standard meals or self-catering options. In general they are still more affordable than comparable places

in Botswana or the Victoria Falls area, yet more expensive than those in South Africa.

ACTIVITIES

Given its stunning landscapes, Namibia provides a photogenic arena for the multitude of outdoor activities that are on offer. These range from the more conventional hiking and 4WD trails to sandboarding down mountainous dunes, quad biking, paragliding, ballooning and camel riding. Most of these activities can be arranged very easily locally, and are relatively well priced.

4WD Trails

Traditionally, 4WD trips were limited to rugged wilderness tracks through the Kaokoveld, Damaraland and Otjozondjupa, but recent years have seen the rise of fixed-route 4WD trails established for 4WD enthusiasts. Participants must pay a daily fee, and are obligated to travel a certain distance each day and stay at prespecified campsites. You'll need to book at least a few weeks in advance through Namibian Wildlife Resorts (p252). Contact it to see which trails are currently available. You could also try www.namibian.org/travel/adventure/4x4_action.htm, which includes a booking service; and www.drivesouthafrica.co.za/blog/best-4x4-trails-in-namibia for more information.

Canoeing & Rafting

Along the Orange River, in the south of the country, canoeing and rafting trips are growing in popularity. Several operators in Noordoewer (p301) offer good-value descents through the spectacular canyons of the Orange River, along the South African border. White-water rafting on the Kunene River is available through the inexpensive **Kunene River Lodge** (☑ 065-274300; www.kuneneriverlodge.com; camping N$160, s/d chalets N$720/1440, r N$950/1900; ▧) at Swartbooi's Drift, and also through several more upmarket operators.

Hiking

Hiking is a highlight in Namibia, and a growing number of private ranches have established wonderful hiking routes for their guests.

You'll also find superb routes in several national parks. Multiday walks are available at Waterberg Plateau, the Naukluft Mountains, the Ugab River, Daan Viljoen Game Park and Fish River Canyon, but departures are limited, so book as far in advance as possible.

Hiking groups on most national-park routes must consist of at least three but no more than 10 people, and it's advised that each hiker obtain a doctor's certificate of fitness (forms are available from the Windhoek NWR office) issued no more than 40 days before the start of the hike. If you're young and you look fit, this requirement might be waived on most trails, with the exception of the demanding 85km hike in Fish River Canyon. The NWR can recommend doctors, but again, in most cases this requirement is waived.

While this might seem restrictive to folks who are accustomed to strapping on a pack and taking off, it does protect the environment from unrestrained tourism, and it ensures that you'll have the trail to yourself – you'll certainly never see another group.

If you prefer guided hiking, get in touch with **Trail Hopper** (☏ 061-264521; www.namibweb. com/trailhopper.htm), which offers hikes all over the country, including Fish River Canyon, a five-day Brandberg Ascent and a Naukluft Mountain Trek. Prices depend on the size of the group.

Rock Climbing

Rock climbing is popular on the red rocks of Damaraland, particularly the Spitzkoppe and the Brandberg, but participants need their own gear and transport. For less experienced climbers it's a dangerous endeavour in the desert heat, so seek local advice beforehand, and never attempt a climb on your own.

Sandboarding

A popular activity is sandboarding, which is commercially available in Swakopmund and Walvis Bay. You can choose between sled-style sandboarding, in which you lie on a Masonite board and slide down the dunes at very high speeds, or the stand-up version, in which you schuss down on a snowboard.

CHILDREN

Many parents regard Africa as just too dangerous for travel with children, but in reality Namibia presents few problems to families travelling with children. We travelled with our own children in the country and not only survived unscathed but had a wonderful time.

As a destination Namibia is relatively safe healthwise, largely due to its dry climate and good medical services. There's a good network of affordable accommodation and an excellent infrastructure of well-maintained roads. In addition, foreigners who visit Namibia with children are usually treated with great kindness, and a widespread local affection for the younger set opens up all sorts of social interaction.

The greatest difficulty is likely to be the temperature (it can get *very* hot) and distances can be vast.

For invaluable general advice on taking the family abroad, see Lonely Planet's *Travel with Children*.

Practicalities

While there are few attractions or facilities designed specifically for children, Namibian food and lodgings are mostly quite familiar and manageable. Family rooms and chalets are normally available for only slightly more than double rooms. These normally consist of one double bed and two single beds. Otherwise, it's usually easy to arrange more beds in a standard double room for a minimal extra charge.

Camping can be exciting, but you'll need to be extra vigilant so your kids don't just wander off unsupervised, and you'll also need to be alert to potential hazards such as mosquitoes and campfires. Most mosquito repellents with high levels of DEET may be unsuitable for young children. They should also wear sturdy enclosed shoes to protect them from thorns, bees and scorpion stings.

If you're travelling with kids, you should always invest in a hire car, unless you want to be stuck for hours on public transport. Functional seatbelts are rare even in taxis, and accidents are common – a child seat brought from home is a good idea if you're hiring a car or going on safari. Even with your own car, distances between towns and parks can be long, so parents will need to provide essential supplemental entertainment (toys, books, games, a Nintendo DS etc).

Canned baby foods, powdered milk, disposable nappies (diapers) and the like are available in most large supermarkets.

CUSTOMS REGULATIONS

Most items from elsewhere in the Southern African Customs Union – Botswana, South Africa, Lesotho and Swaziland – may be imported duty-free. From elsewhere, visitors can import duty-free 400 cigarettes or 250g of tobacco, 2L of wine, 1L of spirits and 250mL of eau de cologne. Those aged under 18 do not qualify for the tobacco or alcohol allowances. There are no limits on currency import, but entry and departure forms ask how much you intend to spend or have spent in the country – we have left this blank every time we've entered the country and have never been questioned on it.

Vehicles may not be sold in Namibia without payment of duty. For pets, you need a health certificate and full veterinary documentation (note that pets aren't permitted in national parks or reserves).

DANGERS & ANNOYANCES

Namibia is one of the safest countries in Africa. It's also a huge country with a very sparse population, and even the capital, Windhoek, is more like a provincial town than an urban jungle. Unfortunately, however, crime is on the rise in the larger cities, in particular Windhoek, but a little street sense will go a long way here.

Scams

A common scam you might encounter in Namibia is the pretty innocuous palm-ivory nut scam practised at various petrol stations. It starts with a friendly approach from a couple of young men, who ask your name. Without you seeing it they then carve your name onto a palm-ivory nut and then offer it to you for sale for anything up to N\$70, hoping that you'll feel obligated to buy the personalised item. You can obtain the same sort of thing at any curio shop for around N\$20. It's hardly the crime of the century, but it pays to be aware.

A more serious trick is for one guy to distract a parked motorist while their accomplice opens a door and grabs the bags from the back seat or from the front passenger seat. Always keep the doors of your vehicle locked, and be aware of distractions. It's rare but it does happen – Walvis Bay has been something of a hotspot for this scam in the past.

The Sperrgebiet

En route to Lüderitz from the east, keep well clear of the Sperrgebiet (Forbidden Zone), the prohibited diamond area. Well-armed patrols can be overly zealous. The area begins immediately south of the A4 Lüderitz–Keetmanshoop road and continues to just west of Aus, where the off-limits boundary turns south towards the Orange River. It's best to have a healthy respect for boundaries.

Theft

Theft isn't rife in Namibia, but Windhoek, Swakopmund, Walvis Bay, Tsumeb and Grootfontein have problems with petty theft and muggings, so it's sensible to conceal your valuables, not leave anything in your car and avoid walking alone at night. It's also prudent to avoid walking around cities and towns bedecked in expensive jewellery, watches and cameras. Most hotels provide a safe or secure place for valuables, although you should be cautious of the security at some budget places.

Never leave a safari-packed vehicle anywhere in Windhoek or Swakopmund, other than in a guarded car park or private parking lot.

Theft from campsites can also be a problem, particularly near urban areas. Locking up your tent may help, but anything left unattended is still at risk.

Vegetation

An unusual natural hazard is the euphorbia plant. Its dried branches should never be used in fires as they release a deadly toxin when burnt. It can be fatal to inhale the smoke or eat food cooked on a fire containing it. If you're in doubt about any wood you've collected, leave it out of the fire. Caretakers at campsites do a good job of removing these plants from around pitches and fire pits, so you needn't worry excessively. As a precaution, try to only use bundles of wood that you've purchased in a store to start fires. If you're bush camping, it's best to familiarise

yourself with the plant's appearance. There are several members of the family, and you can check out their pictures either online or at the tourist information centres in Windhoek.

DISCOUNT CARDS

Travellers with student cards score a 15% discount on Intercape Mainliner buses, and occasionally receive discounts on museum admissions. Seniors over 60, with proof of age, also receive a 15% discount on Intercape Mainliner buses, and good discounts on domestic Air Namibia fares.

EMBASSIES & CONSULATES

It's important to realise what your own embassy – the embassy of the country of which you are a citizen – can and can't do to help you if you get into trouble. Generally speaking, it won't be much help in emergencies if the trouble you're in is remotely your own fault. Remember that you are bound by the laws of the country you are in. Your embassy will not be sympathetic if you end up in jail after committing a crime locally, even if such actions are legal in your own country. The embassies listed here are all in Windhoek.

Angola (Map p248; ☑ 061-227535; 3 Dr Agostino Neto St; ☺9am-4pm)

Botswana (Map p247; ☑ 061-221941; 101 Nelson Mandela Ave; ☺8am-1pm & 2-5pm)

Finland (Map p248; ☑ 061-221355; www.finland.org.na; 2 Crohn St, cnr Bahnhof St; ☺9am-noon Mon, Wed & Thu)

France (Map p247; ☑ 061-276700; www.ambafrance-na.org; 1 Goethe St; ☺8am-12.30pm & 2-5.45pm Mon-Thu, to 1pm Fri)

Germany (Map p248; ☑ 061-273100; www.windhuk.diplo.de; 6th fl, Sanlam Centre, 154 Independence Ave; ☺9am-noon Mon-Fri, plus 2-4pm Wed)

Kenya (Map p248; ☑ 061-226836; www.khcwindhoek.com; 5th fl, Kenya House, 134 Robert Mugabe Ave; ☺8.30am-1pm & 2-4.30pm Mon-Thu, to 3pm Fri)

Malawi (Map p248; ☑ 061-221391; 56 Bismarck St, Windhoek West; ☺8am-noon & 2-5pm Mon-Fri)

South Africa (Map p247; ☑ 061-2057111; www.dirco.gov.za/windhoek; cnr Jan Jonker St & Nelson Mandela Dr, Klein Windhoek; ☺8.15am-12.15pm)

UK (Map p248; ☑ 061-274800; www.gov.uk/government/world/organisations/british-high-commission-windhoek; 116 Robert Mugabe Ave; ☺8am-noon Mon-Thu)

USA (Map p248; ☑ 061-2958500; https://na.usembassy.gov; 14 Lossen St; ☺8.30am-noon Mon-Thu)

Zambia (Map p248; ☑ 061-237610; www.zahico.iway.na; 22 Sam Nujoma Dr, cnr Mandume Ndemufeyo Ave; ☺9am-1pm & 2-4pm)

Zimbabwe (Map p248; ☑ 061-228134; www.
zimwhk.com; Gamsberg Bldg, cnr Independence Ave & Grimm St; ⊘ 8.30am-1pm &
2-4.45pm Mon-Thu, to 2pm Fri)

GAY & LESBIAN TRAVELLERS

As in many African countries, homosexuality is
illegal in Namibia, based on the common-law offence of sodomy or committing 'an unnatural sex
crime'. Namibia is also very conservative in its
attitudes, given the strongly held Christian beliefs of the majority. In view of this, discretion is
certainly the better part of valour, as treatment
of gay men and lesbians can range from simple
social ostracism to physical attack. In 1996
Namibia's president, Sam Nujoma, continued
his very public campaign against homosexuals,
recommending that all foreign gays and lesbians
be deported or excluded from the country. One
minister called homosexuality a 'behavioural
disorder which is alien to African culture', while
in 2005 the Deputy Minister of Home Affairs and
Immigration, Teopolina Mushelenga, claimed
that lesbians and gays had caused the HIV/AIDS
pandemic and were 'an insult to African culture'.

The climate for gays and lesbians in Namibia
has, however, eased somewhat in recent years.
With no prosecutions recorded under the sodomy law since independence, the United Nations
Human Rights Committee called in 2016 for
the law against sodomy to be abolished and for
laws to be introduced prohibiting discrimination on the grounds of sexual orientation. The
call received the public support of Namibia's
ombudsman and stirred little public debate. In
the same year, an Afrobarometer opinion poll
found that 55% of Namibians would welcome, or
would not be bothered by, having a homosexual
neighbour. Namibia was one of only four African
countries polled to have a majority in favour of
the proposition.

INTERNET ACCESS

Internet access is firmly established and widespread in Namibia, and connection speeds are
fairly stable. Most larger or tourist-oriented
towns have at least one internet cafe. Plan on
spending around N$50 per hour online. An in-
creasing number of backpacker hostels, hotels
in larger towns and some lodges and guesthouses also offer wi-fi internet access, although this
rarely extends beyond the hotel reception area.

MAPS
Country Maps

The best paper map of Namibia is the *Namibia*
(1:1,000,000) map published by Tracks4Africa
(www.tracks4africa.co.za). Updated every couple of years using detailed traveller feedback,
the map is printed on tear-free, waterproof paper
and includes distances and estimated travel
times. Used in conjunction with Tracks4Africa's

unrivalled GPS maps, it's far and away the best
mapping product on the market.

If for some reason you are unable to get hold of
the Tracks4Africa map, other options include the
Namibia map produced by Reise-Know-How-Ver-
lag (1:250,000) or the Freytag & Berndt map
(1:200,000). *Shell Roadmap – Namibia* or *InfoMap Namibia* are good references for remote
routes. InfoMap contains GPS coordinates and
both companies produce maps of remote areas
such as Namibia's far northwest and the Caprivi
Strip.

Good for an overview rather than serious
navigation is the *Namibia Map* endorsed by the
Roads Authority, which shows major routes
and lists accommodation. Even the Globe-
trotter *Namibia* map is easy to read and quite
detailed. Also consider Nelles Vertag's *Namibia*
(1:1,500,000) and Map Studio, which also publishes a *Namibia* map (1:1,550,000) and a road
atlas (1:500,000).

National Park Maps

You'll find maps of Etosha National Park across
the country. NWR's reliable English-German *Map
of Etosha* (from N$40) is the pick and also most
widely available. It has the added bonus of park
information and quite extensive mammal- and
bird-identification sheets.

A welcome recent addition to Namibia's mapping portfolio is the simple but handy *Kavango-Zambezi National Parks* map, which includes
high-level overviews of Namibia's far northeastern parks: Khaudum, Mahango, Bwabwata,
Mudumu and Nkasa Rupara. It's available at
some lodges or online at www.thinkafrica
design.com.

MONEY

Money can be exchanged in banks and exchange
offices. Banks generally offer the best rates.

ATMs

Credit cards can be used in ATMs displaying the
appropriate sign or to obtain cash advances
over the counter in many banks; Visa and MasterCard are among the most widely recognised.
You'll find ATMs at all the main bank branches
throughout Namibia, and this is undoubtedly the
simplest (and safest) way to handle your money
while travelling.

Cash

While most major currencies are accepted in
Windhoek and Swakopmund, once away from
these two centres you'll run into problems with
currencies other than US dollars, euros, UK
pounds and South African rand (you may even
struggle with pounds). Play it safe and carry US
dollars – it makes life much simpler.

When changing money, you may be given
either South African rand or Namibian dollars;

if you'll need to change any leftover currency outside Namibia, the rand is a better choice.

There is no currency black market, so beware of street changers offering unrealistic rates.

Credit/Debit Cards

Credit cards and debit cards are accepted in most shops, restaurants and hotels, and credit- and debit-card cash advances are available from ATMs. Check charges with your bank.

Credit-card (but not debit-card) cash advances are available at foreign-exchange desks in most major banks, but set aside at least an hour or two to complete the rather tedious transaction.

Keep the card supplier's emergency number handy in case your card is lost or stolen.

Tipping

Tipping is welcomed everywhere, but is expected only in upmarket tourist restaurants, where it's normal to leave a tip of 10% to 15% of the bill. Some restaurants add a service charge as a matter of course. As a rule, taxi drivers aren't tipped, but it is customary to give N$2 to N$5 to petrol-station attendants who clean your windows and/or check the oil and water. Note that tipping is officially prohibited in national parks and reserves.

At safari lodges, guides and drivers of safari vehicles will also expect a tip, especially if you've spent a number of days in their care.

Most safari companies suggest the following as a rule of thumb:
➝ guides/drivers – US$10 per person per day
➝ camp or lodge staff – US$10 per guest per day (usually placed in a communal box)
➝ transfer drivers and porters – US$3

OPENING HOURS

Banks 8am or 9am-3pm Monday to Friday, 8am-12.30pm Saturday

Drinking and entertainment 5pm to close (midnight-3am) Monday to Saturday

Eating breakfast 8 to 10am, lunch 11am to 3pm, dinner 6 to 10pm; some places open 8am to 10pm Monday to Saturday

Information 8am or 9am-5pm or 6pm Monday to Friday

Petrol stations Only a few open 24 hours; in outlying areas fuel is hard to find after hours or on Sunday.

Post offices 8am to 4.30pm Monday to Friday, 8.30-11am Saturday

Shopping 8am or 9am-5pm or 6pm Monday to Friday, 9am-1pm or 5pm Saturday; late-night shopping to 9pm Thursday or Friday

POST

Domestic post generally moves slowly; it can take weeks for a letter to travel from Lüderitz to Katima Mulilo, for example. Overseas airmail post is normally more efficient.

PUBLIC HOLIDAYS

Banks, government offices and most shops are closed on public holidays; when a public holiday falls on a Sunday, the following day also becomes a holiday.

New Year's Day 1 January

Good Friday March/April

Easter Sunday March/April

Easter Monday March/April

Independence Day 21 March

Ascension Day April/May

Workers' Day 1 May

Cassinga Day 4 May

Africa Day 25 May

Heroes' Day 26 August

Human Rights Day 10 December

Christmas Day 25 December

Family/Boxing Day 26 December

TELEPHONE

The Namibian fixed-line phone system, run by Telecom Namibia (www.telecom.na), is very efficient, and getting through to fixed-line numbers is extremely easy. However, as in the rest of Africa, the fixed-line system is rapidly being overtaken by the massive popularity of mobile phones.

Fixed-line calls to the UK/US and Europe cost around N$3.60 to N$5 per minute at peak times; to neighbouring countries it's around N$2.40 to N$4.14 per minute. Click on 'Tariffs' and then 'International Services' on the website for exact charges.

Given the increasing number of wi-fi hotspots in the country, using Skype is also becoming a more common (and much cheaper) alternative. MTC (www.mtc.com.na) is the largest mobile service provider in Namibia, operating on the GSM 900/1800 frequency, which is compatible with Europe and Australia but not with North America (GSM 1900) or Japan. The other provider is Telecom Namibia (www.telecom.na).

There is supposedly comprehensive coverage across the country, although in reality it's hard to get a signal outside the major towns and along the major highways. The more remote you are, the less likely you'll get coverage, which is why a satellite phone is an attractive backup proposition if you're travelling extensively away from population areas.

Both providers offer prepaid services. For visitors to the country, you're better off paying a one-off SIM-card fee then buying prepaid vouchers at the ubiquitous stores across Namibia.

You can easily buy a handset in any major town in Namibia, which will set you back from N$600.

Most Namibian mobile-phone numbers begin with ☑ 081, which is followed by a seven-digit number.

TOURIST INFORMATION

The level of service in Namibia's tourist offices is generally high, and everyone speaks impeccable English, German and Afrikaans.

Namibia's national tourist office, Namibia Tourism (p252), is in Windhoek, where you'll also find the local Windhoek Information & Publicity Office (p252). There's also a branch of the latter in the Post Street Mall that is open the same hours, but closed from noon to 1pm.

Also in Windhoek is the office of Namibia Wildlife Resorts (p252), where you can pick up information on national parks and make reservations at any NWR campsite.

Other useful tourist offices include Lüderitz Safaris & Tours (p295) in Lüderitz and Namib-i (p283) in Swakopmund.

TRAVELLERS WITH DISABILITIES

There are very few special facilities, and people with limited mobility will not have an easy time in Namibia. All is not lost, however – with an able-bodied travelling companion, wheelchair travellers will manage here. This is mainly because Namibia has some advantages over other parts of the developing world: footpaths and public areas are often surfaced with tar or concrete; many buildings (including safari lodges and national-park cabins) are single-storey; car hire is easy and hire cars can be taken into neighbouring countries; and assistance is usually available on internal and regional flights. In addition, most safari companies in Namibia, including budget operators, are happy to 'make a plan' to accommodate travellers with special needs.

VISAS

Nationals of many countries, including Australia, the EU, USA and most Commonwealth countries, do not need a visa to visit Namibia. Citizens of most Eastern European countries do require visas.

Tourists are granted an initial 90 days, although most immigration officials will ask how long you plan to stay in the country and tailor your visa duration accordingly.

Visas may be extended at the **Ministry of Home Affairs** (Map p248; ☑ 061-2922111; www.mha.gov.na; cnr Kasino St & Independence Ave; ⊙ 8am-1pm Mon-Fri) in Windhoek. For the best results, be there when the office opens at 8am and submit your application at the 3rd-floor offices (as opposed to the desk on the ground floor).

WOMEN TRAVELLERS

On the whole Namibia is a safe destination for women travellers, and we receive few complaints from women about any sort of harassment. Having said that, Namibia is still a conservative society. Many bars are men only (by either policy or convention), but even in places that welcome women, you may be more comfortable in a group or with a male companion. Note that accepting a drink from a local man is usually construed as a come-on.

The threat of sexual assault isn't any greater in Namibia than in Europe, but it's best to avoid walking alone in parks and backstreets, especially at night. Hitching alone is not recommended. Never hitch at night and, if possible, find a companion for trips through sparsely populated areas.

In Windhoek and other urban areas, wearing shorts and sleeveless dresses or shirts is fine. However, if you're visiting rural areas, wear knee-length skirts or loose trousers and shirts with sleeves. If you're poolside in a resort or lodge where the clientele is largely foreign, then revealing swimwear is acceptable; otherwise err on the side of caution and see what other women are wearing.

ℹ Getting There & Away

Unless you are travelling overland, most likely from Botswana or South Africa, flying is by far the most convenient way to get to Namibia. The country isn't exactly a hub of international travel, nor is it an obvious transit point along major international routes, but it does have an increasing number of routes, including to Frankfurt and Amsterdam. Otherwise, you're most likely to fly via South Africa.

ENTERING THE COUNTRY

Entering Namibia is straightforward and hassle-free: upon arrival and departure, you must fill out an immigration card. If arriving by air, queues can be long, particularly when a couple of planes arrive at the same time (fill out the arrival cards while in the queue to save time), but once you finally reach the counter it's usually straightforward. If you are entering Namibia across one of its land borders, the process is similarly painless: you will need to have all the necessary documentation and insurance for your vehicle. Most nationalities (including nationals from the UK, USA, Australia, Japan and all the Western European countries) don't even require a visa.

If travelling with children, parents should be aware of the need to carry birth certificates and may require other documents (see p719).

All visitors entering Namibia must hold a passport that is valid for at least six months after their intended departure date from Namibia. Also, allow a few empty pages for stamp-happy immigration officials, especially if you'll be crossing over to see Victoria Falls in Zambia and Zimbabwe. In theory, you should also hold proof of departure, either in the form of a return or onward ticket. In practice, this is rarely asked for.

AIR

Most international airlines stop at Johannesburg or Cape Town in South Africa, where you'll typically switch to a **South African Airways** (Map p248; ☑ 061-273340; www.flysaa.com; Independence Ave, Windhoek) flight for your final leg to Windhoek. South African Airways has daily flights connecting Cape Town and Johannesburg to Windhoek. Johannesburg is also the main hub for connecting flights to other African cities.

For North American travellers, it's worth checking the price of a flight via Frankfurt, as this may be cheaper than a direct flight to South Africa.

Book well in advance for flights from the following neighbouring countries.

Botswana Air Namibia runs several flights a week between Windhoek and Maun.

Zambia You will need to transit through Jo'burg for flights to Lusaka or Livingstone.

Zimbabwe Air Namibia flies to Victoria Falls a few times a week.

Most international flights into Namibia arrive at Windhoek's Chief Hosea Kutako International Airport (p252), 42km east of the capital.

Windhoek's in-town Eros Airport (p252) is mainly for small charter flights, although Air Namibia (p252) also runs flights to Katima Mulilo, Ondangwa and Walvis Bay from here.

The main domestic carrier is Air Namibia (www.airnamibia.com.na), which flies routes to other parts of Southern Africa as well as long-haul flights to Frankfurt.

LAND

Thanks to the Southern African Customs Union, you can drive through Namibia, Botswana, South Africa and Swaziland with a minimum of ado. To travel further north requires a *carnet de passage,* which can amount to heavy expenditure.

If you're driving a hire car to/from Namibia, you will need to present a letter of permission from the rental company saying the car is allowed to cross the border.

Border Crossings

Namibia has a well-developed road network with easy access from neighbouring countries. The main border crossings into Namibia:

Angola Oshikango, Ruacana, Rundu
Botswana Buitepos, Mahango, Ngoma
South Africa Noordoewer, Ariamsvlei
Zambia Katima Mulilo

All borders are open daily, and the main crossings from South Africa (Noordoewer and Ariamsvlei) are open 24 hours. Otherwise, border crossings are generally open at least between 8am and 5pm, although most open from 6am to 6pm. Immigration posts at some smaller border crossings close for lunch between 12.30pm and 1.45pm. It is always advisable to reach the crossings as early in the day as possible to allow time for any potential delays. For more information on opening hours, check out the website www.namibweb.com/border.htm.

Angola

To enter Namibia overland, you'll need an Angolan visa permitting overland entry. At Ruacana Falls, you can enter the border area temporarily without a visa to visit the falls by signing the immigration register.

Botswana

The most commonly used crossing is at Buitepos/Mamuno, between Windhoek and Ghanzi, although the Caprivi border posts at Mohembo/Mahango and Ngoma (the latter is a short drive from Kasane in Botswana) are also popular. The Mpalila Island/Kasane border is only available to guests who have prebooked accommodation at upmarket lodges on the island.

The Mohembo/Mahango crossing connects northeastern Namibia with Shakawe, Maun and the Okavango Panhandle. Drivers crossing here pass through Mahango Game Reserve at Popa Falls. Entry is free if you're transiting, or US$5 per person per day plus US$5 per vehicle per day if you want to drive around the reserve (which is possible in a 2WD). No motorbikes are permitted in the reserve.

There is also a little-used border crossing at Gcangwa–Tsumkwe along a 4WD-only track close to Botswana's Tsodilo Hills.

South Africa

Namibia's border crossings with South Africa are among the country's busiest, but they're generally hassle-free. The crossings at Noordoewer and Ariamsvlei are open 24 hours (although we advise against driving at night on either side of the border). There is an additional border post along the coast, between Alexander Bay and Oranjemund (6am to 10pm), but it's closed to tourists and anyone without permission from the diamond company Namdeb.

Zambia

The border crossing between Zambia and Namibia is at Katima Mulilo in Namibia's Caprivi Strip. The Namibian side of things is generally quick and easy, but Zambian formalities can take a little longer.

Visas into Zambia cost US$50 per person for most nationalities, while you'll also have to pay the Zambian road toll (US$48), carbon tax (ZM150) and third party vehicle insurance (ZM487, valid for one month and payable even if you already have insurance) if you're bringing in a vehicle. There is a bank next to the border crossing. Changing money at the bank is preferable to the young men who will approach your vehicle with wads of kwatcha. If you arrive outside banking hours and are left with no choice, make sure you know the current exchange rates, count your money carefully and don't let them hurry you into a quick exchange that will rarely be to your benefit.

If you're heading to Liuwa National Park and other places in Zambia's far west, an excellent sealed road (so new it wasn't even on Tracks4Africa's GPS system when we drove it) runs from the border all the way to Mongu and Kalabo, at the entrance to Liuwa National Park.

If you're on your way to Livingstone, the road is sealed but not in great condition. It is, however, accessible in a 2WD.

Zimbabwe

There's no direct border crossing between Namibia and Zimbabwe. To get there you must take the Chobe National Park transit route from Ngoma Bridge through northern Botswana to Kasane/Kazungula, and from there to Victoria Falls.

Bus

There's only really one main inter-regional bus service connecting cities in Namibia with Botswana and South Africa. Intercape Mainliner (p252) has services between Windhoek and Johannesburg and Cape Town (South Africa). It also travels northeast to Victoria Falls, and between larger towns within Namibia. There are also long-distance Intercape Mainliner services running between Windhoek and Livingstone.

Tok Tokkie Shuttle (☑ 061-300743; www. shuttlesnamibia.com) makes the 12-hour Windhoek–Gaborone run, departing Windhoek at 6pm on Wednesday and Friday, and from Gaborone at 1pm on Thursday and Saturday. One-way fares are N$500 and there's free wi-fi and air-con on board.

Otherwise, you may need to hitch from Gobabis to the border, cross the border on foot (bearing in mind that this crossing is about 1km long) then probably hitch from the border to Ghanzi, unless you happen to coincide with the daily minibus between the Mamuno border crossing and Ghanzi.

Car & Motorcycle

Crossing borders with your own vehicle or a hire car is generally straightforward, as long as you have the necessary paperwork: the vehicle registration documents if you own the car, or a letter from the hire company stating that you have permission to take the car over the border, and proof of insurance. The hire company should provide you with a letter that includes the engine and chassis numbers, as you may be asked for these.

Note that Namibia implements a road tax, known as the Cross-Border Charge (CBC) for foreign-registered vehicles entering the country. Passenger vehicles carrying fewer than 25 passengers are charged N$140 per entry, and N$90 for motorbikes. It is very important that you keep this receipt as you may be asked to produce it at police roadblocks, and fines will ensue if you can't.

ℹ Getting Around

Namibia is a sparsely populated country, and distances between towns can be vast. However, there is an excellent infrastructure of sealed roads, and to more remote locations there are well-maintained gravel and even salt roads. With such a low population density, it's hardly surprising that the public-transport network is limited. Public buses do serve the main towns, but they won't take you to the country's major sights. By far the best way to experience Namibia is in the comfort of your own hire car.

AIR

Air Namibia (www.airnamibia.com.na) has an extensive network of local flights operating out of Windhoek's Eros Airport (p252). There are six flights per week to Rundu, Katima Mulilo and Ondangwa.

From Windhoek's Hosea Kutako International Airport (p252), domestic destinations include Lüderitz and Oranjemund (three times per week) and Walvis Bay (daily).

BUS

Namibia's bus services aren't extensive. Luxury services are limited to the Intercape Mainliner (p252), which has scheduled services from Windhoek to Swakopmund, Walvis Bay, Grootfontein, Rundu, Katima Mulilo, Keetmanshoop and Oshikango. Fares include meals on the bus.

There are also local combis, which depart when full and follow main routes around the country. From Windhoek's Rhino Park petrol station they depart for dozens of destinations.

CAR

The easiest way to get around Namibia is in your own car, and an excellent system of sealed roads runs the length of the country, from the South African border at Noordoewer to Ngoma Bridge on the Botswana border and Ruacana in the northwest. Similarly, sealed spur roads connect the main north–south routes to Buitepos, Lüderitz, Swakopmund and Walvis Bay. Elsewhere, towns and most sights of interest are accessible on good gravel roads. Most C-numbered highways are well maintained and passable to all vehicles, and D-numbered roads, although a bit rougher, are mostly (but not always) passable to 2WD vehicles. In the Kaokoveld, however, most D-numbered roads can only be negotiated with a 4WD.

Nearly all the main car-rental agencies have offices at Hosea Kutako International Airport.

Motorcycle holidays in Namibia are also popular due to the exciting off-road riding on offer. Unfortunately, however, it's difficult to rent a bike in Namibia, though the bigger car companies generally have a couple in their fleet. Note that motorcycles aren't permitted in the national parks, with the exception of the main highway routes through Namib-Naukluft Park.

Driving Licence

Foreigners can drive in Namibia on their home driving licence for up to 90 days, and most (if not all) car-rental companies will accept foreign driving licences for car hire. If your home licence isn't written in English, you'd be better off getting an International Driving Permit (IDP) before you arrive in Namibia.

Fuel & Spare Parts

The network of petrol stations in Namibia is good, and most small towns have a station. Mostly diesel, unleaded and super (leaded) are available, and prices vary according to the remoteness of the petrol station. Although the odd petrol station is open 24 hours, most are open 7am to 7pm.

All stations are fully serviced (there is no self-service), and a small tip of a couple of Namibian dollars is appropriate, especially if the attendant has washed your windscreen.

As a general road-safety rule, you should never pass a service station without filling up, and it is advisable to carry an additional 100L of fuel (either in long-range tanks or jerrycans) if you're planning on driving in more remote areas. Petrol stations do run out of fuel in Namibia, so you can't always drain the tank and expect a fill-up at the next station. In more remote areas, payment may only be possible in cash.

Spare parts are readily available in most major towns, but not elsewhere. If you're planning on some 4WD touring, it is advisable to carry the following: two spare tyres, jump leads, fan belt, tow rope and cable, a few litres of oil, wheel spanner and a complete tool kit. A sturdy roll of duct tape will also do in a pinch.

If you're hiring a car, make sure you check you have a working jack (and know how to use it!) and a spare tyre. As an extra precaution, double-check that your spare tyre is fully pressurised as you don't want to get stuck out in the desert with only three good wheels.

Hire

Whatever kind of vehicle you decide to rent, you should always check the paperwork carefully, and thoroughly examine the vehicle before accepting it. Car-rental agencies in Namibia have some very high excesses due to the general risks involved in driving on the country's gravel roads. You should also carefully check the condition of your car and never ever compromise if you don't feel totally happy with its state of repair.

Always give yourself plenty of time when dropping off your hire car to ensure that the vehicle can be checked over properly for damage etc. The car-rental firm should then issue you with your final invoice before you leave the office.

Insurance

No matter who you hire your car from, make sure you understand what is included in the price (unlimited kilometres, tax, insurance, collision waiver and so on) and what your liabilities are. Most local insurance policies do not cover damage to windscreens and tyres.

Third-party motor insurance is a minimum requirement in Namibia. However, it is also advisable to take damage (collision) waiver, which costs around US$25 extra per day for a 2WD, and about US$50 per day for a 4WD. Loss (theft) waiver is also an extra worth having.

For both types of insurance, the excess liability is about US$1500 for a 2WD and US$3000 for a 4WD. If you're only going for a short period of time, it may be worth taking out the super collision waiver, which covers absolutely everything, albeit at a price.

Road Hazards

Namibia has one of the highest rates of road accidents in the world – always drive within speed limits, take account of road conditions and be prepared for other vehicles travelling at high speed. Avoid driving at night when speeding vehicles and faulty headlights can make things perilous. Both domestic and wild animals can also be a hazard, even along the main highways. And remember that the chances of hitting a wild or domestic animal is far, far greater after dark.

In addition to its good system of sealed roads, Namibia has everything from high-speed gravel roads to badly maintained secondary routes, farm roads, bush tracks, sand tracks, salt roads and challenging 4WD routes. Driving under these conditions requires special techniques, appropriate vehicle preparation, a bit of practice and a heavy dose of caution.

Around Swakopmund and Lüderitz, watch out for sand on the road. It's very slippery and can easily cause a car to flip over if you're driving too fast. Early-morning fog along Skeleton Coast roads is also a hazard, so keep within the prescribed speed limits.

Road Rules

To drive a car in Namibia, you must be at least 21 years old. Like most other Southern African countries, traffic keeps to the left side of the road. The national speed limit is 120km/h on sealed roads out of settlements, 80km/h on gravel roads and 40km/h to 60km/h in all national parks and reserves. When passing through towns and villages, assume a speed limit of 60km/h, even in the absence of any signs.

Highway police use radar, and love to fine motorists for speeding (officially about N$70 for every 10km you exceed the limit, but often far more – much seems to be at the discretion of the police officer in question...). Sitting on the roof of a moving vehicle is illegal, and wearing seatbelts (where installed) is compulsory in the front (but not back) seats. Drunk-driving is also against the law, and your insurance policy will be invalid if you have an accident while drunk. The legal blood-alcohol limit in Namibia is 0.05%. Driving without a licence is also a serious offence.

If you have an accident causing injury, it must be reported to the authorities within 48 hours. If vehicles have sustained only minor damage, and there are no injuries – and all parties agree – you can exchange names and addresses and sort it out later through your insurance companies.

In theory, owners are responsible for keeping their livestock off the road, but in practice animals wander wherever they want. If you hit a domestic animal, your distress (and possible vehicle damage) will be compounded by the effort involved in finding the owner and the red tape involved when filing a claim.

HITCHING

Although hitching is possible in Namibia (and is quite common among locals), it's illegal in national parks, and even main highways receive relatively little traffic. On a positive note, it isn't unusual to get a lift of 1000km in the same car. Truck drivers generally expect to be paid, so agree on a price beforehand; the standard charge is N$15 per 100km.

Lifts wanted and offered are advertised daily at Cardboard Box Backpackers (p247) and **Chameleon Backpackers Lodge** (Map p248; 5-7 Voight St) in Windhoek. At the Namibia Wildlife Resorts (p252) office, also in Windhoek, there's a noticeboard with shared car hire and lifts offered and wanted.

Hitching is never entirely safe in any country. If you decide to hitch, understand that you are taking a small but potentially serious risk. Travel in pairs and let someone know where you're planning to go if possible.

LOCAL TRANSPORT

Public transport in Namibia is geared towards the needs of the local populace, and is confined to main roads between major population centres. Although cheap and reliable, it is of little use to the traveller, as most of Namibia's tourist attractions lie off the beaten track.

TRAIN

Trans-Namib Railways (☎ 061-2982032; www.transnamib.com.na) connects some major towns, but trains are extremely slow – as one reader remarked, they move 'at the pace of an energetic donkey cart'. In addition, passenger and freight cars are mixed on the same train, and trains tend to stop at every post, which means that rail travel isn't popular and services are rarely fully booked.

Windhoek is Namibia's rail hub, with services south to Keetmanshoop, west to Swakopmund and east to Gobabis. Trains carry economy and business-class seats, but although most services operate overnight, sleepers are not available. Book at train stations or through the Windhoek booking office at the train station; tickets must be collected before 4pm on the day of departure.

South Africa

POP 53 MILLION / 🗗 27

Includes ➜

Cape Town	323
Garden Route	371
Durban	406
Zululand	419
Bloemfontein	441
Johannesburg	449
Soweto	464
Pretoria	465

Best Places to Eat

➜ Test Kitchen (p349)

➜ Great Eastern Food Bar (p459)

➜ Foliage (p361)

➜ Mali's Indian Restaurant (p414)

➜ La Sosta (p366)

➜ Hog House Brewing Co (p349)

Best Places to Sleep

➜ Tintswalo Atlantic (p346)

➜ Thonga Beach Lodge (p425)

➜ Motel Mipichi (p458)

➜ Hog Hollow (p378)

Why Go?

When Archbishop Desmond Tutu called South Africa the 'Rainbow Nation', his words described the very essence of what makes this country extraordinary. The blend of peoples and cultures that he referred to is instantly evident, but the country's diversity stretches far beyond its people.

Without straying beyond South Africa's borders you can sleep under the stars in a desert or hike to snow-capped peaks. The hills of Zululand and the Wild Coast provide a bucolic antidote to the bustle of large cities like Johannesburg and Durban. Wildlife watching ranges from remote safari walks to up-close encounters with waddling penguins.

Variety continues in the cuisine, with the delicate (West Coast seafood), the hearty (Karoo meat feasts), the fragrant (Cape Malay stews) and the spicy (Durban curries) all represented. And southwest of it all sits Cape Town, where gourmands, art lovers, thrill seekers and beach babes come together to sip, surf and sunbathe in beautiful surrounds.

When to Go
Cape Town

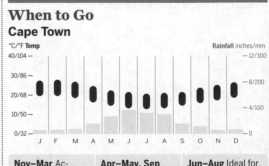

Nov–Mar Accommodation in national parks and the coast books up months in advance.	Apr–May, Sep & Oct Sunny weather. Best wildlife-watching conditions from autumn onwards.	Jun–Aug Ideal for wildlife watching. Rainy season in Cape Town and the Western Cape.

CAPE TOWN

POP 3.74 MILLION / ✐ 021

Prepare to fall in love, as South Africa's 'Mother City' is an old pro at capturing people's hearts. And who wouldn't swoon at the sight of magnificent Table Mountain, its summit draped with cascading clouds, its flanks coated with unique flora and vineyards, its base fringed by golden beaches?

Few cities can boast such a wonderful national park at their heart or provide the range of activities that take full advantage of it. From the brightly painted facades of the Bo-Kaap and the bathing chalets of Muizenberg, to striking street art and the Afro-chic decor of guesthouses, this is one good-looking metropolis. Above all it's a multicultural city where nearly everyone has a fascinating, sometimes heartbreaking, story to tell.

Long before the Dutch East India Company (Vereenigde Oost-Indische Compagnie; VOC) established a base here in 1652, the Cape Town area was settled by the San and Khoekhoen peoples, collectively known as the Khoe-San. The indigenous people shunned the Dutch, so the VOC imported slaves from Madagascar, India, Ceylon, Malaya and Indonesia. In time the slaves intermixed with the Khoe-San; their offspring formed the basis of sections of today's coloured population.

In the 150-odd years of Dutch rule, Kaapstad, as the Cape settlement became known, thrived and gained a wider reputation as the 'Tavern of the Seven Seas', a riotous port used by sailors travelling between Europe and the East. Following the British defeat of the Dutch in 1806 at Bloubergstrand, 25km north of Cape Town, the colony was ceded to the British Crown. The slave trade was abolished in 1808, and all slaves emancipated in 1833.

An outbreak of bubonic plague in 1901 was blamed on black African workers (it actually came on boats from Argentina) and gave the government an excuse to introduce racial segregation. Blacks were moved to two locations; one near the docks and the other at Ndabeni on the eastern flank of Table Mountain. This was the start of what would later develop into the townships of the Cape Flats.

◉ Sights

◉ City Bowl, Foreshore, Bo-Kaap & De Waterkant

The City Bowl, where the Dutch first set up shop, includes many historic sights and businesses. Landfill created the Foreshore district in the 1940s and 1950s, now dominated by Duncan Dock and the convention centre. Tumbling down Signal Hill are the colourfully painted houses of the Bo-Kaap and, to the northeast, Cape Town's pink precinct De Waterkant, a retail and party hub.

★ Bo-Kaap   AREA

(Map p332; ☐Dorp/Leeuwen) Meaning 'Upper Cape', the Bo-Kaap with its vividly painted low-roofed houses, many of them historic monuments, strung along narrow cobbled streets, is one of the most photographed sections of the city. Initially a garrison for soldiers in the mid-18th century, this area was where freed slaves started to settle after emancipation in the 1830s. The most picturesque streets are Chiappini, Rose and Wale.

★ Company's Gardens   GARDENS

(Map p332; City Bowl; ◷7am-7pm; ☐Dorp/Leeuwen) These shady green gardens, which started as the vegetable patch for the Dutch East India Company, are a lovely place to relax. They are planted with a fine collection of botanical specimens from South Africa and the rest of the world, including frangipanis, African flame trees, aloes and roses. Cecil Rhodes' statue stands in the centre of the gardens, and there's a newly recreated VOC Vegetable Garden.

Open House   PUBLIC ART

(Map p332; cnr Dorp & Long Sts, City Bowl; ☐Dorp/Leeuwen) This creation by Kimberley-born artist Jacques Coetzer was the winning design in a World Design Capital competition for a piece of public art. Rising up three stories to 10.5m, the bright-red house facade with stairs and balconies is envisioned as a place where people can go to speak, sing, cry or simply wave to passers by. Coetzer drew inspiration from corrugated metal structures, RDP homes (Reconstruction and Development Programme – government subsidised houses) and Long Street itself.

Greenmarket Square   ARCHITECTURE, MARKET

(Map p332; Greenmarket Sq, City Bowl; ☐Church/Longmarket) This cobbled square is Cape Town's second-oldest public space after the Grand Parade. It hosts a lively and colourful crafts and souvenir market daily. Apart from the Old Town House, the square is also surrounded by some choice examples of art deco architecture, including Market House, an elaborately decorated building with balconies and stone-carved eagles and flowers on its facade.

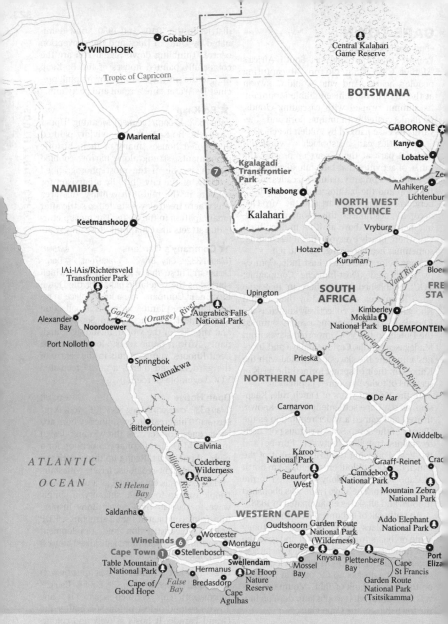

South Africa Highlights

❶ Cape Town (p323)
Tackling Table Mountain, paddling with penguins or just lazing on Atlantic beaches.

❷ Kruger National Park (p476) Joining rangers at on a safari of the most involving kind – on foot.

❸ Drakensberg (p427) Hiking towards the peaks of

the Drakensberg range for a view of the Amphitheatre, an 8km mountain curtain.

❹ Soweto (p464) Brushing up on recent history and

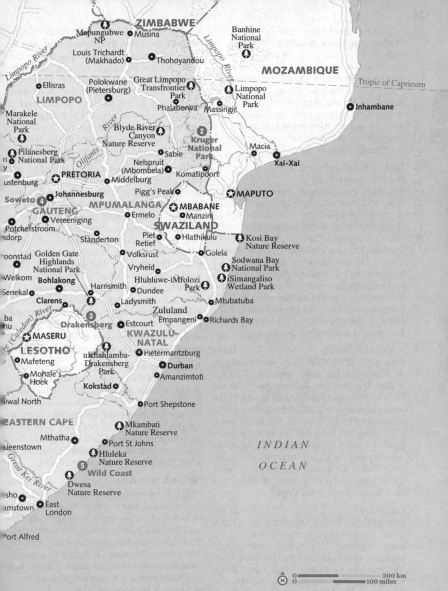

ZIMBABWE

Mapungubwe NP
Musina
Louis Trichardt (Makhado)
Thohoyandou

MOZAMBIQUE

Banhine National Park

Tropic of Capricorn

Ellisras
Polokwane (Pietersburg)

LIMPOPO

Great Limpopo Transfrontier Park
Phalaborwa
Massingir
Limpopo National Park

Inhambane

Marakele National Park

Blyde River Canyon Nature Reserve
Sable

❷ **Kruger National Park**

Macia

Pilanesberg National Park
Olifants
Nelspruit (Mbombela)
Komatipoort

Xai-Xai

Rustenburg
PRETORIA
Middelburg

Pigg's Peak

Soweto ❹
Johannesburg
GAUTENG
Vereeniging

✪ **MAPUTO**

Potchefstroom
sdorp

Ermelo
MPUMALANGA
✪ **MBABANE**
Manzini
SWAZILAND
Hlathikulu

oonstad
Golden Gate Highlands National Park
Standerton
Piet Retief
Volksrust
Golela

Kosi Bay Nature Reserve

Welkom
Bohlakong
Vryheid
Sodwana Bay National Park
iSimangaliso Wetland Park

Senekal
Harrismith
Hluhluwe-iMfolozi Park
Dundee

Clarens
Ladysmith
Zululand
Mtubatuba

ba
Drakensberg
❸
Estcourt
Empangeni
Richards Bay

MASERU
KWAZULU-NATAL

LESOTHO
ukhahlamba-Drakensberg Park
Pietermaritzburg

Mafeteng
Durban

Mohale's Hoek
Amanzimtoti

Kokstad

iwal North
Port Shepstone

EASTERN CAPE
Mkambati Nature Reserve

Mthatha
Port St Johns

ueenstown
Hluleka Nature Reserve

❺ **Wild Coast**

Dwesa Nature Reserve

isho
East London

amstown

ort Alfred

INDIAN

OCEAN

N 0   200 km
   0   100 miles

learning about township life in bustling Soweto.

❺ **Wild Coast** (p401) Choosing between a hammock and the beach at one of the laid-back hostels.

❻ **Winelands** (p355) Sipping on world-class wines and enjoying posh nosh in the magnificent Cape Dutch surrounds.

❼ **Kgalagadi Transfrontier Park** (p501) Watching a black-maned lion nap under a thorn tree in the crimson Kalahari wonderland.

Next to Market House, the dazzling-white **Protea Insurance Building** was built in 1928 and renovated in 1990. Opposite is **Shell House**, once the South African headquarters of Shell, now a hotel and restaurant.

On the corner of Shortmarket St is **Namaqua House**; Baran's cafe here has a wraparound balcony providing a great view over the square. **Kimberley House** is built of sandstone and decorated with an attractive diamond-theme design.

Michaelis Collection at the Old Town House
MUSEUM

(Map p332; www.iziko.org.za; Greenmarket Sq, City Bowl; adult/child R20/10; ⊙10am-5pm Mon-Sat; 🚇Church/Longmarket) On the south side of Greenmarket Sq is the beautifully restored Old Town House, a Cape rococo building dating from 1755 that was once City Hall. It now houses the impressive art collection of Sir Max Michaelis. Dutch and Flemish paintings and etchings from the 16th and 17th centuries (including works by Rembrandt, Frans Hals and Anthony van Dyck) hang side by side with contemporary works – the contrasts between old and new are fascinating.

Iziko Slave Lodge
MUSEUM

(Map p332; ☑021-467 7229; www.iziko.org.za; 49 Adderley St, City Bowl; adult/child R30/R15; ⊙10am-5pm Mon-Sat; 🚇Groote Kerk) Dating back to 1660, the Slave Lodge is one of the oldest buildings in South Africa. Once home to as many as 1000 slaves, the lodge has a fascinating history; it has also been used as a brothel, a jail, a mental asylum, a post office, a library and the Cape Supreme Court in its time. Today, it's a museum mainly devoted to the history and experience of slaves and their descendants in the Cape.

Long Street
ARCHITECTURE

(Map p332; City Bowl; 🚇Dorp/Leeuwen) A stroll along Long St is an essential element of a Cape Town visit. This busy commercial and nightlife thoroughfare, partly lined with Victorian-era buildings featuring lovely wrought-iron balconies, once formed the border of the Muslim Bo-Kaap. Along it you'll find the **Palm Tree Mosque** (185 Long St; ⊙closed to public), dating from 1780, the **SA Mission Museum** (40 Long St; ⊙9am-6pm Mon-Fri) FREE, the oldest Mission church in South Africa, and the city's newest public art installation Open House (p323).

Castle of Good Hope
MUSEUM

(Map p332; www.castleofgoodhope.co.za; cnr Castle & Darling Sts, City Bowl, entrance on Buitenkant St; adult/child R30/15; ⊙9am-4pm; 🅿; 🚇Castle)

Built by the Dutch between 1666 and 1679 to defend Cape Town, this stone-walled pentagonal castle remains the headquarters for the Western Cape military command. There are free guided tours of the site (11am, noon and 2pm Monday to Saturday), and don't miss climbing up to the castle's bastions for an elevated view of the castle's layout. The **Military Museum** is interesting, as are the displays of antiques and decorative arts in the **William Fehr Collection** (⊙9am-4pm; 🚇Castle).

Houses of Parliament
NOTABLE BUILDING

(Map p332; ☑021-403 2266; www.parliament.gov.za; Parliament St, City Bowl; ⊙tours 9am-2pm Mon-Fri; 🚇Roeland) FREE A tour around parliament is fascinating, especially if you're interested in the country's modern history. Opened in 1885, the hallowed halls have seen some pretty momentous events; this is where British Prime Minister Harold Macmillan made his 'Wind of Change' speech in 1960, and where President Hendrik Verwoerd, known as the architect of apartheid, was stabbed to death in 1966. Call ahead and present your passport to gain entry.

⊙ Gardens & Surrounds

Ranging from the cluster of museums at the south end of the Company's Gardens, up the slopes of Table Mountain, is the wider area known as Gardens. Neighbourhoods here include Tamboerskloof, Oranjezicht, Higgovale and Vredehoek – all desirable residential suburbs with views of Table Bay and immediate access to Table Mountain. Kloof St and Kloof Nek Rd are the main retail strips.

★ Table Mountain
MOUNTAIN

(Map p342; www.tmnp.co.za) Around 600 million years old, and a canvas painted with the rich diversity of the Cape floral kingdom, Table Mountain is truly iconic. You can admire Table Mountain National Park and one of the 'New Seven Wonders of Nature' (www.new-7wonders.com) from multiple angles, but you really can't say you've visited Cape Town until you've stood on top of it.

Signal Hill
VIEWPOINT

(Map p342; 🚇Kloof Nek) The early settlement's lookout point is so named because it was from here that flags were hoisted when a ship was spotted, giving the people below time to prepare goods for sale and dust off their tankards. Walk, cycle or drive to the summit, which is part of Table Mountain National Park, by taking the first turn-off to the right off Kloof Nek Rd onto Military Rd.

South African Museum MUSEUM
(Map p336; ☎021-481 3800; www.iziko.org.za/
museums/south-african-museum; 25 Queen Victoria St, Gardens; adult/child R30/15; ☺10am-5pm;
☒Michaelis) South Africa's oldest museum contains a wide and often intriguing series of exhibitions, many of the country's natural history. The best galleries are the newest, showcasing the art and culture of the area's first peoples, the Khoekhoen and San, and including the famous Linton Panel, an amazing example of San rock art. There's an extraordinary delicacy to the paintings, particularly the ones of graceful elands.

South African Jewish Museum MUSEUM
(Map p336; www.sajewishmuseum.co.za; 88 Hatfield St, Gardens; adult/child R60/free; ☺10am-5pm Sun-Thu, to 2pm Fri; P; ☒Annandale) You need a photo ID to enter the secure compound that's home not only to this imaginatively designed museum but also to the functioning and beautifully decorated **Great Synagogue**, a 1905 building in neo-Egyptian style. The museum partly occupies the beautifully restored **Old Synagogue** (1863). The excellent permanent exhibition Hidden Treasures of Japanese Art showcases a collection of exquisite *netsuke* (carved pieces of ivory and wood). There are also temporary exhibitions that are usually worth seeing.

South African National Gallery GALLERY
(Map p336; ☎021-481 3970; www.iziko.org.za/museums/south-african-national-gallery; Government Ave, Gardens; adult/child R30/15; ☺10am-5pm; ☒Annandale) The impressive permanent collection of the nation's premier art space harks back to Dutch times and includes some extraordinary pieces. But it's often contemporary works, such as the *Butcher Boys* sculpture by Jane Alexander – looking rather like a trio

---

CAPE TOWN'S TOP TOURS

If you're short on time, have a specific interest, or want some expert help in seeing Cape Town, there's a small army of tour guides and companies waiting to assist you. The best will provide invaluable insight into Capetonian food and wine, flora and fauna, and history and culture.

Laura's Township Tours (☎082 979 5831; www.laurastownshiptours.co.za; from R400) Gugulethu-based Laura Ndukwana gets rave reviews for her tours of her 'hood. She also runs a breakfast club, where she feeds 40 kids daily before they go to school. Itineraries include a Sunday-morning visit to a charismatic evangelist church, and cooking tours (R700).

Venture Forth (☎021-555 3864, 086 617 3449; www.ventureforth.co.za; per person from R570) Excellent guided hikes and rock climbs with enthusiastic, savvy guides.

Vamos (☎072 499 7866; www.vamos.co.za; walking/cycling tours R320/400) Personable guide Siviwe Mbinda (www.townshiptourscapetown.co.za) is one of the cofounders of this company, offering two- to three-hour walking and cycling tours around Langa. Itineraries often include a performance by the Happy Feet gumboot dance troupe that Siviwe established. Vamos can also arrange homestays in Langa.

Table Mountain Walks (☎021-715 6136; www.tablemountainwalks.co.za; from R550 per person) Offers a range of guided day hikes in different parts of the park, from ascents of Table Mountain to rambles through Silvermine.

Uthando (Map p328; ☎021-683 8523; www.uthandosa.org; 48 2nd Ave, Harfield Village; tour R912) These township tours cost more because half of the money goes towards the social upliftment projects that the tours visit and are specifically designed to support. Usually three or so projects are visited: they could be anything from an organic farm to an old folks' centre.

Walk in Africa (Map p332; ☎021-823 8790; www.walkinafrica.com; 32 Loop St) Steve Bolnick, an experienced and passionate safari and mountain guide, runs this company. Their five-day, four-night Mountain in the Sea walk runs from Platteklip Gorge to Cape Point, partly following the Hoerikwaggo Trail.

City Sightseeing Cape Town (☎086 173 3287; www.citysightseeing.co.za; adult/child 1 day R170/90, 2 days R270/180) These hop-on, hop-off buses, running two main routes, are perfect for a quick orientation, with commentary available in 16 languages. The open-top double-deckers also provide an elevated platform for photos. Buses run at roughly half-hourly intervals between 9am and 4.30pm, with extra services in peak season.

Cape Town & the Peninsula

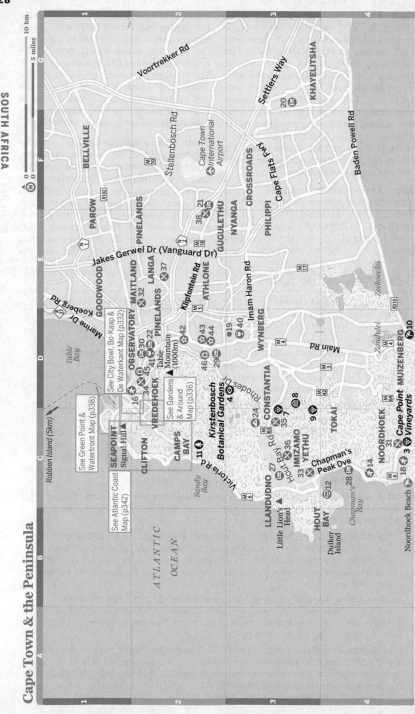

ATLANTIC OCEAN

False Bay

Seal Island

Silvermine Nature Reserve 5

39

KALK BAY

CLOVELLY

FISH HOEK

Kommetjie Rd

Simon's Town Rd

Boulders Visitor Centre

SIMON'S TOWN

Boulders Penguin Colony

BOULDERS

SCARBOROUGH

Red Hill

Long Beach

Kommetjie Beach 25

M65

M6

M66

M65

M65

M4

M65

23

26 13

Paulsberg

Smitswinkel Bay

Cape of Good Hope

Buffelsfontein Visitor Centre

Buffels Bay

6

2

Platboom Beach

Cape Point

15

Maclear Beach

Diaz Beach

Cape Town & the Peninsula

◉ Top Sights
1 Boulders Penguin Colony D6
2 Cape of Good Hope D8
3 Cape Point Vineyards........................... C4
4 Kirstenbosch Botanical Gardens......... D3
5 Silvermine Nature Reserve.................. D5

◉ Sights
6 Buffels Bay.. D8
7 Eagle's Nest... C3
8 Groot Constantia................................. D3
9 Klein Constantia.................................. C3
10 Muizenberg Beach................................ D4
11 Table Mountain National Park C2

◉ Activities, Courses & Tours
12 Animal Ocean C4
13 Cape of Good Hope Trail...................... D7
14 Chapman's Peak Drive C4
Gary's Surf School...................... (see 10)
15 Hoerikwaggo Trail................................ D8
16 Que Pasa... D2
Sea Kayak Trips .... (see 17)
17 Simon's Town Boat Company D6
18 Sleepy Hollow Horse Riding C4
19 Uthando D3
Water Slide ....(see 10)

◉ Sleeping
Bella Ev.. (see 10)
Boulders Beach Lodge .... (see 1)
20 Kopanong.. G3
21 Liziwe Guest House F2
22 Observatory Backpackers.................... D2
23 Olifantsbos Guest House C7
24 Orange Kloof Camp C3
Simon's Town Boutique
Backpackers............................... (see 17)
25 Slangkop Camp................................... B5
26 Smitswinkel Camp................................ D7
27 Thulani River Lodge............................. C3
28 Tintswalo Atlantic C4
29 Vineyard Hotel & Spa D2

30 Wish U Were Here D2

◉ Eating
31 Foodbarn C4
32 Hog House Brewing Co......................... E2
33 Hout Bay Coffee C3
Jonkershuis .... (see 8)
34 Kitchen.. D2
35 La Colombe C3
Lighthouse Cafe ....(see 17)
36 Massimo's C3
37 Mzansi... E2
38 Mzoli's... E2
39 Olympia Café & Deli.............................D5
Pot Luck Club................................(see 30)
Test Kitchen.................................(see 30)

◉ Drinking & Nightlife
40 Banana Jam D3
Brass Bell.....................................(see 39)
Espressolab Microroasters..........(see 30)
41 Taproom D2
Tiger's Milk ....(see 10)

◉ Entertainment
Artscape......................................(see 16)
42 Baxter Theatre.................................... D2
43 Newlands Rugby Stadium..................... D2
44 Sahara Park Newlands D2

◉ Shopping
45 Chapel...D2
Clementina Ceramics ....(see 30)
Cocofair ....(see 30)
Grandt Mason Originals................(see 45)
Imiso Ceramics.............................(see 30)
Kalk Bay Modern ....(see 39)
46 Montebello D2
Mü & Me..(see 30)
Neighbourgoods Market ....(see 30)
The Old Biscuit Mill......................(see 30)
Woodstock Exchange ....(see 45)

of Tolkienesque orcs who have stumbled into the gallery – that stand out the most.

◉ Green Point & Waterfront

Green Point's common includes a landscaped park and the Cape Town Stadium, built for the 2010 World Cup. Fronting Table Bay is the V&A Waterfront shopping, entertainment and residential development (commonly known simply as the Waterfront), as well as the residential Mouille Point.

★**V&A Waterfront**   AREA
(Map p338; www.waterfront.co.za; P; ◻Nobel Sq)
This historic working harbour has a spec-

tacular setting and many tourist-oriented attractions, including masses of shops, restaurants, bars, cinemas and cruises. The Alfred and Victoria Basins date from 1860 and are named after Queen Victoria and her son Alfred. Too small for modern container vessels and tankers, the Victoria Basin is still used by tugs, fishing boats and other vessels. In the Alfred Basin you'll see ships under repair.

★**Robben Island**   LANDMARK
(☎021-413 4200; www.robben-island.org.za; adult/child R320/180; ⊙ferries depart at 9am, 11am, 1pm & 3pm, weather permitting; ◻Nobel Sq) Used as a prison from the early days of the VOC right up until 1996, this Unesco World Heritage

Site is preserved as a memorial to those (such as Nelson Mandela) who spent many years incarcerated here. You can only go here on a tour, which lasts around four hours including ferry rides, departing from the **Nelson Mandela Gateway** (Map p338; Clock Tower Precinct, V&A Waterfront; ⊙9am-8.30pm; 🚇Nobel Sq) FREE, beside the Clock Tower at the Waterfront. Booking online well in advance is highly recommended as tours can sell out.

The standard tours, which have set departure and return times, include a walk through the old prison (with the obligatory peek into Mandela's cell), as well as a 45-minute bus ride around the island with commentary on the various places of note, such as the lime quarry in which Mandela and many others slaved, and the church used during the island's stint as a leper colony. If you're lucky, you'll have about 10 minutes to wander around on your own. Even if you don't plan a visit to the island, it's worth dropping by the free museum at the Nelson Mandela Gateway, with its focus on the struggle for equality. Also preserved as a small museum is the Waterfront's **Jetty 1** FREE, the departure point for Robben Island when it was a prison.

Two Oceans Aquarium
AQUARIUM

(Map p338; www.aquarium.co.za; Dock Rd, V&A Waterfront; adult/child R150/70; ⊙9.30am-6pm; 🚼; 🚇Aquarium) This excellent aquarium features denizens of the deep from the cold and the warm oceans that border the Cape Peninsula. The ragged-tooth sharks were released into the wild in 2016, but there are still penguins, turtles, an astounding kelp forest open to the sky, and pools in which kids can touch sea creatures. Qualified divers can get into the water for a closer look (R790, including dive gear).

Zeitz MOCAA Museum
MUSEUM

(Map p338; www.zeitzmocaa.museum; Fish Quay, V&A Waterfront; 🅿; 🚇Waterfront Silo) The Waterfront's giant old grain silos are in the process of being transformed into a state-of-the-art museum with some 80 proposed gallery spaces for the contemporary Southern African art collection of entrepreneur Jochen Zeitz. The new building, designed by Thomas Heatherwick, is set to open in September 2017. Entrepreneur Jochen Zeitz's impressive art collection will provide the finished museum's permanent exhibition within.

The Springbok Experience
MUSEUM

(Map p338; ☎021-418 4741; www.sarugby.co.za; Portswood House, V&A Waterfront; adult/child R75/50; ⊙9am-5pm; 🚼; 🚇Nobel Sq) You don't have to be rugby crazy to enjoy this new attraction which celebrates the history of rugby in South Africa and, in particular, the trials and triumphs of the national team, the Springboks. There are several interactive displays (one purports to show whether you'd make the grade as a Springbok player), and the historical aspects – including the international boycotts of the team during apartheid – are covered in detail.

Zeitz MOCAA Pavilion
MUSEUM

(Map p338; www.waterfront.co.za/activities/land-operators/zeitz-mocca-pavilion; North Wharf, V&A Waterfront; ⊙noon-8pm Wed-Sun; 🚇Nobel Sq) FREE Until its Thomas Heatherwick–designed home in the Waterfront's old grain silo opens in 2017, a taster of the Zeitz MOCAA's collection of contemporary African art is displayed in this small pavilion next to the Bascule Bridge. Exhibits here change regularly, and several are put on in conjunction with the Chavonnes Battery Museum.

Green Point Urban Park
PARK

(Map p338; www.gprra.co.za/green-point-urban-park.html; Bay Rd, Green Point; ⊙7am-7pm; 🅿; 🚇Stadium) One of the best things to come out of the redevelopment of Green Point Common for the 2010 World Cup is this park and biodiversity garden. Streams fed by Table Mountain's springs and rivers water the park, which has three imaginatively designed areas – People & Plants, Wetlands, and Discovering Biodiversity – that, along with educational information boards, act as the best kind of outdoor museum. Guided tours of the park (adult/child R35/11) can be arranged through the Cape Town Stadium (p331).

Cape Town Stadium
STADIUM

(Map p338; ☎021-417 0120; Granger Bay Blvd, Green Point; tours adult/child R45/17; ⊙tours 10am, noon & 2pm Tue-Sat; 🅿; 🚇Stadium) Shaped like a giant, traditional African hat and wrapped with a Teflon-mesh membrane designed to catch and reflect natural light, this R4.5 billion stadium, built for the 2010 World Cup, is Cape Town's most striking piece of contemporary architecture. The hour-long tours will take you behind the scenes into the VIP and press boxes as well as the teams' dressing rooms.

◉ Southern Suburbs

The lush eastern slopes of Table Mountain are covered by the areas known collectively as the Southern Suburbs. Here you'll find Kirstenbosch Botanical Gardens, the rugby

City Bowl, Bo-Kaap & De Waterkant

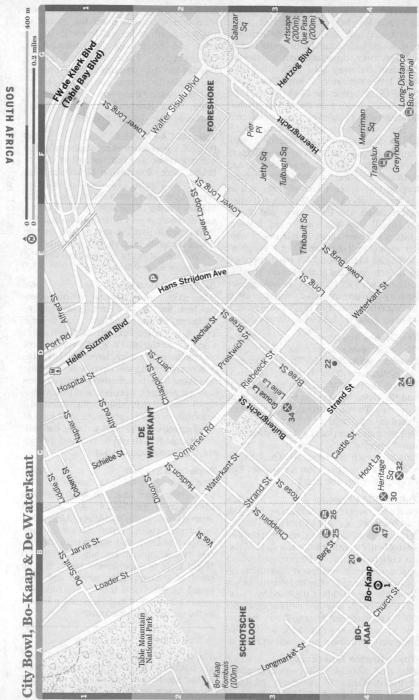

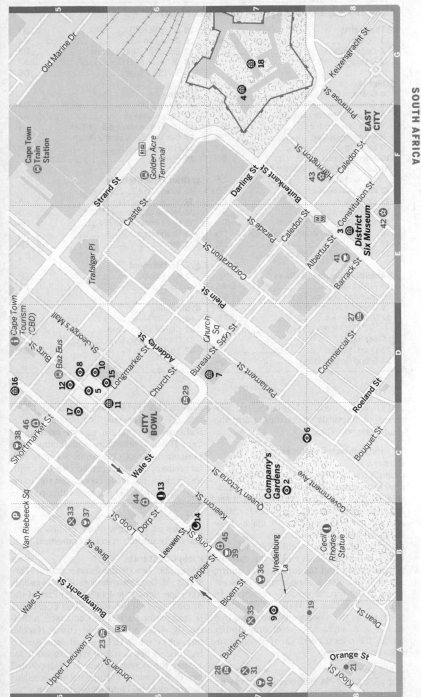

SOUTH AFRICA

City Bowl, Bo-Kaap & De Waterkant

Top Sights
1 Bo-Kaap B4
2 Company's Gardens C7
3 District Six Museum E8

Sights
4 Castle of Good Hope G7
5 Greenmarket Square D5
6 Houses of Parliament C8
7 Iziko Slave Lodge D7
8 Kimberley House D5
9 Long Street A7
10 Market House D5
11 Michaelis Collection at the Old
    Town House C6
12 Namaqua House D5
13 Open House C6
14 Palm Tree Mosque B6
15 Protea Insurance Building D5
16 SA Mission Museum D5
17 Shell House C5
18 William Fehr Collection G7

Activities, Courses & Tours
19 Abseil Africa A8
20 Bo-Kaap Cooking Tour B4
21 Downhill Adventures A8
22 Walk in Africa D4

Sleeping
23 Dutch Manor A5
24 Grand Daddy Hotel D4

25 La Rose B&B B4
26 Rouge on Rose B4
27 Scalabrini Guest House D8
28 St Paul's B&B Guesthouse A7
29 Taj Cape Town D6

Eating
30 Africa Café C4
31 Bacon on Bree A7
32 Chef's Warehouse & Canteen C4
33 Clarke's Bar & Dining Room B5
34 Hemelhuijs C3
35 Plant A7

Drinking & Nightlife
36 Beerhouse B7
37 Honest Chocolate Cafe B5
38 House of Machines C5
39 Lady Bonin's Tea Bar B7
40 Orphanage A7
41 Truth E8

Entertainment
42 Assembly E8
43 Fugard Theatre F8

Shopping
44 African Music Store C6
45 Clarke's Bookshop B7
46 South African Market C5
47 Streetwires B4

and cricket grounds of Newlands, the centuries-old vineyards of Constantia and the shady forests of Tokai.

★ **Kirstenbosch Botanical Gardens**   GARDENS
(Map p328; ☎ 021-799 8782; www.sanbi.org/gardens/kirstenbosch; Rhodes Dr, Newlands; adult/child R60/15; ⊙ 8am-7pm Sep-Mar, to 6pm Apr-Aug, conservatory 9am-5pm year-round) Location and unique flora combine to make these 52,800-sq-km botanical gardens among the most beautiful in the world. The main entrance at the Newlands end of the gardens is where you'll find the information centre, an excellent souvenir shop and the conservatory. Added for the garden's centenary in 2013, the Tree Canopy Walkway (informally known as the 'Boomslang', meaning tree snake) is a curvaceous steel and timber bridge that rises through the trees and provides amazing views.

Groot Constantia   MUSEUM, WINERY
(Map p328; ☎ 021-794 5128; www.grootconstantia. co.za; Groot Constantia Rd, Constantia; tastings R75,

museum adult/child R20/free, cellar tours R100 incl tasting; ⊙ 9am-6pm daily; ℗) Simon van der Stel's manor house, a superb example of Cape Dutch architecture, is maintained as a museum at Groot Constantia. Set in beautiful grounds, the estate can become busy with tour groups, but is big enough for you to escape the crowds. The large tasting room is first on your right as you enter the estate. Further on is the free orientation centre, which provides an overview of the estate's history, and the beautifully restored homestead.

Klein Constantia   WINERY
(Map p328; www.kleinconstantia.com; Klein Constantia Rd, Constantia; tastings R50; ⊙ tastings 10am-5pm Mon-Sat, to 4pm Sun; ℗) Part of the original Constantia estate, Klein Constantia is famous for its Vin de Constance, a deliciously sweet muscat wine. It was Napoleon's solace on St Helena, and Jane Austen had one of her heroines recommend it for having the power to heal 'a disappointed heart'. It's worth visiting for its excellent tasting room and informative displays.

Eagle's Nest WINERY
(Map p328; ☑021-794 4095; www.eaglesnest-wines.com; Constantia Main Rd, Constantia; tasting R50; ☺10am-4.30pm; P) Book ahead for pic-nics (R395 for two), which you can enjoy in the shady grounds beside a stream; other-wise there are various food platters and light snacks available.

⊙ Simon's Town & Southern Peninsula

On the False Bay side of the peninsula are the charming communities of Muizenberg, Kalk Bay and Simon's Town. More wildlife and landscapes are protected within the nation-al park at Cape Point. On the Atlantic coast side, Kommetjie is beloved by surfers, and the broad beach at Noordhoek by horse riders.

★ **Cape of Good Hope** OUTDOORS
(Map p328; www.tmnp.co.za; adult/child R135/70; ☺6am-6pm Oct-Mar, 7am-5pm Apr-Sep; P) Commonly called Cape Point, this 77.50-sq-km section of Table Mountain National Park includes awesome scenery, fantastic walks, great birdwatching and often desert-ed beaches. Bookings are required for the two-day Cape of Good Hope Trail (p340), a spectacular 33.8km circular route with one night spent at the basic Protea and Restio huts. Contact the **Buffelsfontein Visitor Centre** (Map p328; ☑021-780 9204; ☺9.30am-5.30pm) for further details. Some 250 species of birds have been spotted here, including cormorants and a family of ostriches that hang out near the Cape of Good Hope, the southwestern-most point of the continent.

There are many bus tours to the reserve but, if you have the time, hiking or cycling through it is much more rewarding. Bear in mind, though, that there is minimal shade and that the weather can change quickly.

It's not a hard walk uphill, but if you're feeling lazy take the **Flying Dutchman Fu-nicular** (www.capepoint.co.za; one way/return adult R48/58, child R18/24; ☺9am-5.30pm), which runs up from beside the restaurant to the souvenir kiosk next to the old lighthouse (which dates from 1860). A 1km trail runs from here to its successor. Ignore the signs: it takes less than 30 minutes to walk along a spectacular ridgeway path to look down on the new lighthouse and the sheer cliffs plunging into the pounding ocean.

★ **Boulders Penguin Colony** BIRD SANCTUARY
(Map p328; www.tmnp.co.za; Simon's Town; adult/child R70/35; ☺8am-5pm Apr-Sep, to 6.30pm Feb, Mar, Oct & Nov, 7am-7.30pm Dec & Jan; P; ☒Si-mon's Town) Some 3km southeast of Simon's Town, this picturesque area, with enormous boulders dividing small, sandy coves, is home to a colony of 2100 delightful Afri-can penguins. A boardwalk runs from the **Boulders Visitor Centre** (☑021-786 2329; 1 Kleintuin Rd, Seaforth, Simon's Town; ☺8am-4pm) at the Foxy Beach end of the protected area (part of Table Mountain National Park; p339) to Boulders Beach, where you can get down on the sand and mingle with the wad-dling penguins. Don't, however, be tempted to pet them: they have sharp beaks that can cause serious injuries.

The bulk of the colony, which has grown from just two breeding pairs in 1982, seems to prefer hanging out at Foxy Beach, where, like nonchalant, stunted supermodels, they ignore the armies of camera-touting tourists snapping away from the viewing platform.

The aquatic birds, which are an endan-gered species, were formerly called jackass penguins on account of their donkey-like braying – you'll have a chance to hear it if you turn up during the main breeding season, which peaks from March to May. Parking is available at either end of the reservation, on Seaforth Rd and on Bellevue Rd, where you'll also find accommodation and places to eat.

★ **Silvermine Nature Reserve** NATURE RESERVE
(Map p328; ☑021-780 9002; www.tmnp.co.za; Ou Kaapse Weg; adult/child R50/25; ☺6am-6pm) This section of Table Mountain National Park is named after the fruitless attempts by the Dutch to prospect for silver in this area from 1675 to 1685. Today its focal point is the Sil-vermine Reservoir (built in 1898), which is a beautiful spot for a picnic or leisurely walk on a wheelchair-accessible boardwalk. The reservoir waters are tannin-stained and al-though there are signs forbidding swimming, you'll often find locals taking a dip here.

★ **Cape Point Vineyards** WINERY
(Map p328; ☑021-789 0900; www.cpv.co.za; 1 Chapmans Peak Dr, Noordhoek; tastings R10 per wine; ☺tastings 11am-6pm, restaurant noon-3pm & 6.30pm-8.30pm Mon-Wed, Fri & Sat; P) Known for its fine sauvignon blanc, this small vine-yard has a spectacular setting overlooking Noordhoek Beach. Enjoy the wines with a picnic (noon to 5pm, R395 for two, bookings essential) in the grounds, or at their restau-rant. Their Thursday evening community market (4.30pm to 8.30pm), selling mainly food, is a weekly highlight for locals and great for kids, who can play on the lawns.

Gardens & Around

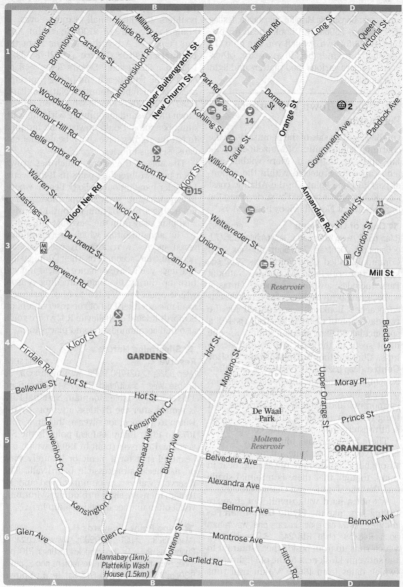

Muizenberg Beach   BEACH
(Map p328; Beach Rd, Muizenberg; P; R Muizenberg) Popular with families, this surf beach is famous for its row of colourfully painted Victorian bathing chalets. Surfboards can be hired and lessons booked at several shops along Beach Rd; lockers are available in the pavilions on the promenade. The beach shelves gently and the sea is generally safer here than elsewhere along the peninsula. At the eastern end of the promenade is a fun **water slide** (1hr/day pass R40/80; ⏰1.30-5.30pm Mon-Fri, 9.30am-5.30pm Sat & Sun).

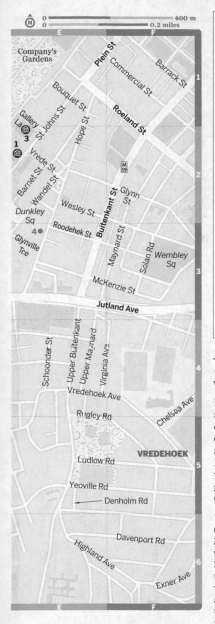

Gardens & Around

◎ Sights
1 South African Jewish Museum E2
2 South African Museum D2
3 South African National Gallery E2

☺ Activities, Courses & Tours
4 Coffeebeans Routes............................E3

⊟ Sleeping
5 Ashanti Gardens C3
6 Backpack C1
7 Belmond Mount Nelson Hotel.............C3
8 Hippo Boutique Hotel..........................C2
9 La Grenadine C2
10 Once in Cape Town.............................C2

✕ Eating
11 Aubergine D3
   Chef's Table...................................(see 7)
12 Kyoto Garden Sushi.............................B2
13 Manna Epicure B4

☺ Drinking & Nightlife
14 Chalk & Cork..C2
   Yours Truly ....(see 10)

⊟ Shopping
15 KIN B2

☉ East City, District Six, Woodstock & Observatory

Immediately east of the City Bowl is a creative industries enclave that occupies part of what was once the mixed residential area of District Six – now a series of empty plots awaiting development. Woodstock and Salt River continue to attract the attention of developers and the art set, but are yet to fully gentrify. Bohemia rules at Observatory near Cape Town University.

★ **District Six Museum**　　　　MUSEUM
(Map p332; ☎ 021-466 7200; www.districtsix.co.za; 25A Buitenkant St, East City; adult/child R30/15, walking tours per person R150; ⊙ 9am-4pm Mon-Sat; ◙ Lower Buitenkant) It's impossible not to be emotionally touched by this museum which celebrates the once lively multiracial area that was destroyed during apartheid in the 1960s and 1970s, its 60,000 inhabitants forcibly removed. Inside the former Methodist Mission Church, home interiors have been recreated, alongside photographs, recordings and testimonials, all of which build an evocative picture of a shattered but not entirely broken community. Many township tours stop here first to explain the history of the pass laws.

Buffels Bay　　　　BEACH
(Map p328; Cape of Good Hope, Table Mountain National Park) Within the Cape Point section of Table Mountain National Park (p339), this sheltered bay offers sweeping views across False Bay and a sea pool for safe swimming.

Green Point & Waterfront

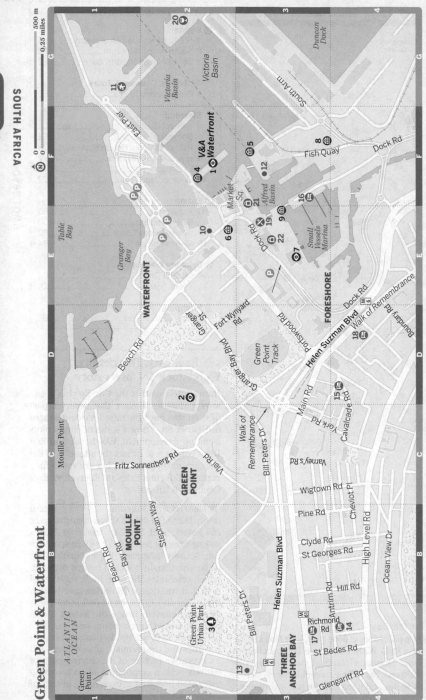

500 m
0.25 miles

Green Point

ATLANTIC OCEAN

Table Bay

Mouille Point

Granger Bay

WATERFRONT

East Pier

Victoria Basin

Victoria Basin

V&A Waterfront

Market Sq

Alfred Basin

Fish Quay

Duncan Dock

South Arm

Dock Rd

Dock Rd

Small Vessels Marina

FORESHORE

Walk of Remembrance

Dock Rd

Boundary Rd

Portswood Rd

Fort Wynyard Rd

Granger St

Green Point Track

Helen Suzman Blvd

GREEN POINT

Beach Rd

Fritz Sonnenberg Rd

Viel Rd

Granger Bay Blvd

Bill Peters Dr

Walk of Remembrance

Main Rd

York Rd

Cavalcade Rd

Varney's Rd

Wigtown Rd

Cheviot Pl

MOUILLE POINT

Bay Rd

Beach Rd

Stephan Way

Pine Rd

Clyde Rd

St Georges Rd

High Level Rd

Ocean View Dr

Green Point Urban Park

Bill Peters Dr

Helen Suzman Blvd

Hill Rd

Antrim Rd

Richmond Rd

St Bedes Rd

THREE ANCHOR BAY

Glengariff Rd

⊙ Sea Point to Hout Bay

Sea Point blends into ritzier Bantry Bay and Clifton before culminating in the prime real estate of Camps Bay. Beyond here, urban development is largely curtailed by the national park until you reach delightful Hout Bay, which has good access to both the city and the vineyards of Constantia.

★ Sea Point Promenade   OUTDOORS
(Map p342; Beach Rd, Sea Point; 🚌 Promenade) Ambulating along Sea Point's wide, paved and grassy promenade is a pleasure shared by Capetonians from all walks of life – it's a great place to observe the city's multiculturalism. There are kids' playgrounds, a well-maintained outdoor gym, and several public art works that are worth taking the time to see.

The coast here is rocky and swimming is dangerous, although you can get in the water at **Rocklands Beach**. If you're too thin-skinned for the frigid sea, try the **Sea Point Pavilion** (Map p342; Beach Rd, Sea Point; adult/child R22/11; ⊙7am-7pm Oct-Apr, 9am-5pm May-Sep; 🚌 Sea Point Pool), towards the promenade's southern end.

★ Clifton Beaches   BEACH
(Map p342; Victoria Rd, Clifton; 🚌 Clifton, Clifton 2nd, Clifton 3rd, Clifton 4th) Giant granite boulders break up the four beaches at Clifton, all accessible by steps from Victoria Rd. As they're almost always sheltered from the wind, they offer top sunbathing spots. Vendors hawk drinks and ice creams along the beach and sun loungers and shades are available. However, there are no public toilets.

The most northern and longest of the beaches are **Clifton 1st** and **2nd**. **Clifton 3rd** is the gay beach, though plenty of straight folk frequent it, too, while **Clifton 4th** is popular with families. Before hopping in the sea, remember that the water comes straight from the Antarctic, so swimming here is exhilarating (ie freezing).

Table Mountain National Park   PARK
(Map p328; 🗗 021-712 2337; www.sanparks.org/parks/table_mountain) Stretching from Signal Hill to Cape Point, this 220-sq km park is a natural wonder, its range of environments including granite and sandstone mountains, giant boulder strewn beaches and shady forests. For the vast majority of visitors the main attraction is the 1086m-high mountain itself, the top of which can easily be accessed by the **cableway** (🗗 021-424 8181; www.tablemountain.net; Tafelberg Rd; adult one-way/return from R135/255, child R65/125; ⊙8.30am-6pm Feb-Nov, 8am-9.30pm Dec & Jan; 🚌 Lower Cable Car), which runs every 10 to 20 minutes. The park provides the venue for a host of adventure activities including hiking, abseiling, mountain biking, rock climbing, paragliding, bird and wildlife watching, snorkelling and diving.

Camps Bay Beach   BEACH
(Map p342; Victoria Rd, Camps Bay; 🚌 Camps Bay) With soft white sand and a backdrop of the spectacular Twelve Apostles of Table Mountain, Camps Bay is one of the city's most popular beaches. However, it has drawbacks: it's one of the windiest beaches here; it gets crowded, particularly on weekends; there are no lifeguards on duty; and the surf is strong. So please take care if you do decide to swim.

Green Point & Waterfront

◉ Top Sights
1 V&A Waterfront F2

◉ Sights
2 Cape Town Stadium D2
3 Green Point Urban Park A2
4 Jetty 1 .... F2
5 Nelson Mandela Gateway F3
6 The Springbok Experience E2
7 Two Oceans Aquarium E3
8 Zeitz MOCAA Museum F3
9 Zeitz MOCAA Pavilion E3

◐ Activities, Courses & Tours
10 Awol Tours E2
11 Cape Town Helicopters G1
12 Historical Walking Tour F3
13 Kaskazi Kayaks A3

◔ Sleeping
14 Ashanti Green Point A4
15 Atlantic Point Backpackers D4
16 Cape Grace F3
17 Head South Lodge A3
18 Villa Zest D4

◉ Eating
19 V&A Food Market E3

◔ Drinking & Nightlife
Bascule .... (see 16)
20 Shimmy Beach Club G2

◔ Shopping
21 KIN F3
22 Watershed E3

CAPE TOWN FESTIVALS

Cape Town International Jazz Festival (www.capetownjazzfest.com; ☉ late Mar/early Apr) Cape Town's biggest jazz event, attracting big names from both South Africa and overseas, is usually held at the Cape Town International Convention Centre at the end of March. It includes a free concert in Greenmarket Sq.

Cape Town Minstrel Carnival (www.capetown-minstrels.co.za; ☉ Jan & Feb) *Tweede Nuwe Jaar* (2 January) is when the satin- and sequin-clad minstrel troupes traditionally march through the city for the Kaapse Klopse (Cape Minstrel Festival) from Keizergracht St, along Adderley and Wale Sts to the Bo-Kaap. Throughout January into early February there are Saturday competitions between troupes at Athlone Stadium.

Cape Argus Pick 'n' Pay Cycle Tour (www.cycletour.co.za; ☉ mid-Mar) Held on a Saturday, this is the world's largest timed cycling event, attracting more than 30,000 contestants. The route circles Table Mountain, heading down the Atlantic Coast and along Chapman's Peak Dr. Forget driving around town on the day.

🏃 Activities

Que Pasa
DANCING
(Map p328; www.quepasa.co.za; Jazzart Studios, Artscape, 1-10 DF Malan St, Foreshore; classes per hour from R80; 🚇 Civic Centre) A variety of dance classes, including swing and salsa, are held here on different nights of the week. Que Pasa also runs classes and events at the Slug & Lettuce pub at the River Club in Observatory.

Cape Town Tandem Paragliding
PARAGLIDING
(☎076 892 2283; www.paraglide.co.za; flight R1150) Feel like James Bond as you paraglide off Lion's Head, land near the Glen Country Club, and then sink a cocktail at Camps Bay. Novices can arrange a tandem paraglide, where you're strapped to an experienced flyer who takes care of the technicalities. Make enquiries on your first day in Cape Town as the weather conditions have to be right.

Cape Town Helicopters
SCENIC FLIGHTS
(Map p338; ☎021-418 9462; www.helicopterscapetown.co.za; 220 East Pier, Breakwater Edge, V&A Waterfront; from R1650 per person; 🚇 Waterfront) Unforgettable views of the Cape Peninsula are guaranteed with these scenic flights. A variety of packages are available from a 30 minute journey out to Robben Island and back to the hour-long journey down to Cape Point (R4400).

★ Constantia Valley Wine Route
WINERIES
(www.constantiawineroute.com) South Africa's wine industry began here back in 1685 when Governor Simon van der Stel chose the area for its wine-growing potential and named his farm Constantia. After Van der Stel's death in 1712 his 7.63-sq-km estate was split up and the area is now the location for this wine route, comprising eight vineyards.

★ Sea Kayak Trips
KAYAKING
(Map p328; ☎082 501 8930; www.kayakcapetown.co.za; Simon's Town Jetty, Simon's Town; 🚇 Simon's Town) Paddle out to the penguin colony (p335) at Boulders (R300) with this Simon's Town–based operation.

Cape of Good Hope Trail
HIKING
(Map p328; R280, excl reserve entry fee) You'll need to book to walk the two-day/one-night Cape of Good Hope Trail, which traces a spectacular 33.8km circular route through the reserve. Accommodation is included at the basic Erica, Protea and Restio huts (each sleep six) at the southern end of the reserve. You'll need to bring your own food and a sleeping bag. Contact the reserve's Buffelsfontein Visitor Centre (p335) for further information.

Gary's Surf School
SURFING
(Map p328; ☎021-788 9839; www.garysurf.co.za; 34 Balmoral Bldg, Beach Rd, Muizenberg; 2hr lesson R450; ☉8.30am-5pm; 🚇 Muizenberg) If genial surfing coach Gary Kleynhans and his team can't get you standing on a board within a day, you don't pay for the lesson. You can also hire boards and wetsuits (per hour/day R100/500) or join a sandboarding trip to the dunes at Kommetjie (R300).

Hoerikwaggo Trail
HIKING
(Table Mountain National Park; Map p328; ☎021-712 7471; www.sanparks.org) Envisioned as an epic six-day, 80km trail stretching from Cape Point to the upper cable-car station on Table Mountain, the Hoerikwaggo Trail is still to fully get off the ground. Certain stretches of the trail are open, though some cut through private land and advance permission is required. It's best to contact the park to confirm which sections are open and to get the relevant trail fees.

Sleepy Hollow Horse Riding HORSE RIDING
(Map p328; ☑021-789 2341, 083 261 0104; www.
sleepyhollowhorseriding.com; Sleepy Hollow Ln,
Noordhoek; per person R530) This reliable operation can arrange horse riding along the
wide, sandy beach at Noordhoek, as well as
in the mountainous hinterland. Two-hour
rides leave at 9am, 1pm and 4.30pm.

Skydive Cape Town ADVENTURE SPORTS
(☑082 800 6290; www.skydivecapetown.co.za;
R2300) Based about 20km north of the city
centre in Melkbosstrand, this experienced
outfit offers tandem skydives. Needless to
say, the views – once you stop screaming
– are spectacular. Flights take off from the
Delta 200 Airfield at Melkbosstrand; they
don't offer Cape Town pick ups, but can recommend transport operators if you don't
have your own vehicle.

★**Animal Ocean** SNORKELLING, DIVING
(Map p328; ☑072 296 9132; www.animalocean.
co.za; Hout Bay Harbour, Hout Bay; snorkelling/
diving per person R800/1600; ▣; ▢Fishmarket)
Although it's weather-dependent (and not
for those who suffer seasickness), don't miss
the chance to go snorkelling or diving with
some of the thousands of playful, curious
Cape fur seals that live on Duiker Island,
and swim in the shark-free waters around it.
All necessary gear, including thick neoprene
wetsuits, is provided. Trips run only from
September to April.

★**Chapman's Peak Drive** DRIVING, CYCLING
(Map p328; www.chapmanspeakdrive.co.za; Chapman's Peak Drive; cars/motorcycles R42/27; ▢Hout
Bay) Take your time driving, cycling or walking along 'Chappies', a 5km toll road linking
Hout Bay with Noordhoek – it's one of the
most spectacular stretches of coastal highway
in the world. There are picnic spots and viewpoints, and it's certainly worth taking the
road at least one way en route to Cape Point.

☞ Tours

Abseil Africa ADVENTURE SPORTS
(Map p332; ☑021-424 4760; www.abseilafrica.
co.za; 297 Long St; abseiling R995) The 112m
drop off the top of Table Mountain with
this long-established outfit is a guaranteed
adrenaline rush. Don't even think of tackling it unless you've got a head (and a stom-
ach) for heights. You can tag on a guided
hike up Platteklip Gorge for R455. They also
offer guided hikes without the abseil (R495).

Abseil Africa also offers kloofing (canyoning) trips around Cape Town. The sport of
clambering into and out of kloofs (cliffs or

gorges) also entails abseiling, climbing, hiking, swimming and jumping.

Coffeebeans Routes CULTURAL
(Map p336; ☑021-461 3572; www.coffeebeans-
routes.com; 22 Hope St, Gardens; tours from R800;
▢Roodehek) The concept – hooking up visitors with interesting local personalities,
including musicians, artists, brewers and
designers – is fantastic. Among innovative
routes are ones focusing on South Africa's
recent revolutionary history, creative enterprises, and organic and natural wines.

Downhill Adventures CYCLING
(Map p332; ☑021-422 0388; www.downhillad-
ventures.com; cnr Orange & Kloof Sts, Gardens;
▢Upper Loop/Upper Long) Get the adrenaline
pumping with Downhill's cycling trips, including a thrilling ride down from the lower
cable station on Table Mountain (R995), as
well as more leisurely pedals in the Tokai
Forest, or through the Constantia Winelands
and the Cape of Good Hope. You can also
hire bikes here (R400 per day) and arrange
surf or sandboarding lessons.

Kaskazi Kayaks KAYAKING, TOUR
(Map p338; ☑083 230 2726, 083 346 1146; www.
kayak.co.za; Shell service station, 179 Beach Rd,
Three Anchor Bay; per person R350; ⊙1-5.30pm
Tue-Fri, 9am-1pm Sat; ▢Three Anchor Bay) This
outfit runs two-hour guided kayak trips
(weather dependent) from Three Anchor
Bay to either Granger Bay or Clifton. There
are astounding views of the mountains and
coastline, as well as possible close encounters with dolphins, seals and penguins.
Whale sightings in season are also on the
cards. Kaskazi can also arrange cycle tours
and rental, and tandem paraglides.

Historical Walking Tour HISTORY
(Map p338; ☑ bookings 021-408 4600; Chavonnes
Battery Museum, V&A Waterfront; adult/child
R150/20; ⊙11am & 2pm; ▢Nobel Sq) One of the
best ways to get an insight into the history
of the Waterfront and its development, as
well as make sense of this sprawling site, is
to sign up for a 45-minute historical walking
tour starting from the Chavonnes Battery
Museum.

Awol Tours CYCLING
(Map p338; ☑021-418 3803; www.awoltours.
co.za; Information Centre, Dock Rd, V&A Waterfront;
▢Nobel Sq) Discover Cape Town's cycle lanes
on this superb city bike tour (daily, three
hours, R600) from Awol's Waterfront base.
Other pedalling itineraries including the
Winelands, Cape Point and the township of

Atlantic Coast

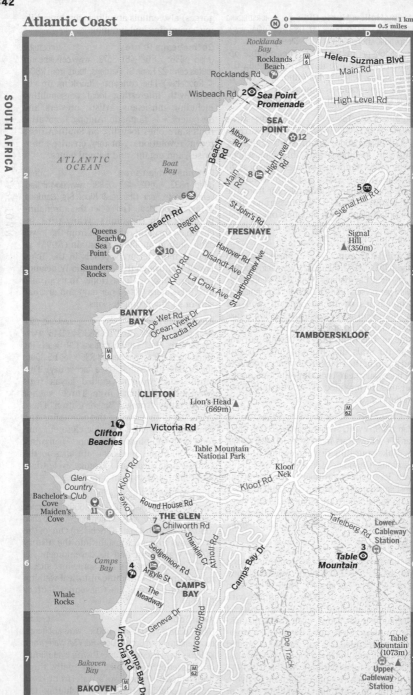

Masiphumelele – a great alternative to traditional township tours. They also offer guided hikes on Table Mountain (from R1250).

Simon's Town Boat Company BOATING
(Map p328; ☑ 083 257 7760; www.boatcompany.co.za; Town Pier, Simon's Town; harbour cruise adult/child R50/30; ☒ Simon's Town) Hop aboard the popular *Spirit of Just Nuisance* cruise around the harbour, as well as longer boat trips to Cape Point (adult/child R550/400) and Seal Island (adult/child R400/300). During the whale-watching season they also offer cruises that allow you to get up close to these magnificent animals.

🛏 Sleeping

🛏 City Bowl, Foreshore, Bo-Kaap & De Waterkant

Scalabrini Guest House HOSTEL $
(Map p332; ☑ 021-465 6433; www.scalabrini.org.za; 47 Commercial St, City Bowl; dm/s/d or tw R260/500/660; ◉🛜; ☒ Roeland) The Italian monastic order Scalabrini Fathers have provided welfare service to Cape Town's poor and to refugees since 1994. Housed in a former textile factory, they run several social programs, and a pleasant guesthouse with 11 immaculately clean en suite rooms – plus a great kitchen for self-catering where you can watch satellite TV.

St Paul's B&B Guesthouse B&R $
(Map p332; ☑ 021-423 4420; www.stpaulsguesthouse.com; 182 Bree St, City Bowl; s/d R600/900, with shared bathroom R500/800; P🛜; ☒ Upper Long/Upper Loop) This spotless B&B in a very handy location is a quiet alternative to the noise-plagued Long St backpackers. The simply furnished and spacious rooms have high ceilings, and there's a vine-shaded courtyard where you can relax or eat breakfast.

★ **Dutch Manor** HISTORIC HOTEL $$
(Map p332; ☑ 087 095 1375; www.dutchmanor.co.za; 158 Buitengracht St, Bo-Kaap; s/d incl breakfast R1800/2900, parking per day R70; P❄🛜; ☒ Dorp/Leeuwen) Four-poster beds, giant armoires and creaking floorboards lend terrific atmosphere to this six-room property crafted from a 1812 building. Although it overlooks busy Buitengracht, the noise is largely kept at bay thanks to modern renovations. Dinners can be prepared on request by the staff, who can also arrange Bo-Kaap walking tours for R70 (nonguests R100) with a local guide.

Rouge on Rose BOUTIQUE HOTEL $$
(Map p332; ☑ 021-426 0298; www.rougeonrose.co.za; 25 Rose St, Bo-Kaap; s/d incl breakfast R1300/1800; ❄🛜; ☒ Old Fire Station) This great Bo-Kaap option offers nine rustic-chic suites with kitchenettes, lounges and lots of workspace. The fun wall paintings are by a resident artist and all rooms have luxurious, open bath spaces with standalone tubs.

La Rose B&B B&B $$
(Map p332; ☑ 021-422 5883; www.larosecapetown.com; 32 Rose St, Bo-Kaap; s/d incl breakfast from R800/1000; P❄🛜; ☒ Old Fire Station) Adheena and Yoann are the very welcoming South African–French couple running this charming B&B, which has been so successful it's expanded into nearby properties. It's beautifully decorated and has a rooftop garden with the best views of the area. Yoann's speciality is making authentic crêpes for the guests.

Taj Cape Town LUXURY HOTEL $$$
(Map p332; ☑ 021-819 2000; www.tajhotels.com; Wale St, City Bowl; r/ste incl breakfast R9750/16,000; P❄◉🛜🏊; ☒ Groote Kerk) India's luxury hotel group has breathed new life into the old Board of Executors building, set at the corner of Wale and Adderley. There's plenty of heritage here but a

Atlantic Coast

◉ Top Sights
1 Clifton Beaches.....................................A5
2 Sea Point Promenade C1
3 Table Mountain D6

◉ Sights
4 Camps Bay Beach B6
5 Signal Hill D2

◉ Activities, Courses & Tours
6 Sea Point Pavilion B2

🛏 Sleeping
7 Camps Bay Retreat................................B6
8 Glen Boutique Hotel...............................C2
9 POD B6

◉ Eating
10 Kleinsky's Delicatessen B3

◉ Drinking & Nightlife
11 Bungalow..A5

◉ Entertainment
12 Studio 7..C2

new tower also houses the chic contemporary-styled rooms, many offering spectacular views of Table Mountain. Service and facilities, including the excellent restaurant Bombay Brasserie, are top grade.

Grand Daddy Hotel
BOUTIQUE HOTEL $$$

(Map p332; ☑021-424 7247; www.granddaddy. co.za; 38 Long St, City Bowl; r or trailer from R2245, parking per day R60; P✿@☎; ☐Mid-Long/ Church) The Grand Daddy's star attraction is its rooftop 'trailer park' of penthouse suites, made from seven vintage, artistically renovated Airstream trailers. The hotel's regular rooms are also stylish and incorporate playful references to South African culture. Its Daddy Cool bar has been blinged to the max with gold paint and trinkets.

🛏 Gardens & Surrounds

As long as you don't mind hiking up hills to get to bed, you'll find some fabulous guesthouses in Gardens.

Ashanti Gardens
HOSTEL $

(Map p336; ☑021-423 8721; www.ashanti.co.za; 11 Hof St, Gardens; dm R260, d R1200, s/d with shared bathroom R550/780; P✿@☎; ☐Government Ave) This is one of Cape Town's slickest backpackers, with much of the action focused on the lively bar and deck that overlook Table Mountain. The beautiful old house, decorated with a tasteful collection of contemporary art, holds the dorms; there's also a lawn where you can camp (R140 per person).

Platteklip Wash House
CHALET $

(☑012-428 9111, 021-712 7471; www.tmnp.co.za; Deer Park, Vredehoek; d R920, extra person R480; P; ☐Herzlia) The old wash houses on the park's edge have been converted into some very stylish accommodation. The decoration in the living room includes pieces by top Capetonian craftspeople, while outside are a sunken campfire circle and hammocks to settle into.

Backpack
HOSTEL $

(Map p336; ☑021-423 4530; www.backpackers. co.za; 74 New Church St, Tamboerskloof; dm R320, s/d R1260/1800, s/d with shared bathroom from R920/1260; P✿@☎; ☐Upper Long/Upper Loop) This Fair Trade in Tourism–accredited operation offers affordable style, a buzzing vibe and fantastic staff. Its dorms may not be Cape Town's cheapest but they're among its best, while the private rooms and self-catering apartments are charmingly decorated. There's a lovely mosaic-decorated pool and relaxing gardens with Table Mountain views to chill out in. Rates do not include breakfast.

⭐ La Grenadine
GUESTHOUSE $$$

(Map p336; ☑021-424 1358; www.lagrenadine. co.za; 15 Park Rd, Gardens; r/2-bed cottage incl breakfast from R2180/3980; ✿@☎; ☐Ludwig's Garden) Expat couple Maxime and Mélodie ladle on the Gallic charm at this imaginatively renovated former stables, where the ancient stone walls are a feature of the rooms. The garden planted with fruit trees is a magical oasis, the lounge is stacked with books and vinyl LPs, and breakfast is served on actress Mélodie's prized collection of china.

⭐ Mannabay
BOUTIQUE HOTEL $$$

(☑021-461 1094; www.mannabay.com; 8 Bridle Rd, Oranjezicht; r/ste incl breakfast from R5500/6600; P✿@☎⊠; ☐Upper Orange) Nothing is too much bother for the staff at this knockout property decorated with stunning contemporary art by local artists. The seven guest rooms are decorated in different themes: Versailles, world explorer, Japan etc. Its high hillside location on the edge of the national park provides amazing views. Rates include high tea, which is served in the library lounge.

Belmond Mount Nelson Hotel
HOTEL $$$

(Map p336; ☑021-483 1000; www.mountnelson. co.za; 76 Orange St, Gardens; r/ste incl breakfast from R8735/10,985; P✿@☎⊠; ☐Government Ave) The sugar-pink-painted 'Nellie' is a colonial charmer with its chintz decor and doormen in pith helmets. It's great for families since it pushes the boat out for the little ones, with kid-sized robes and bedtime cookies and milk – not to mention the large pool and three hectares of gardens, including tennis courts.

Hippo Boutique Hotel
BOUTIQUE HOTEL $$$

(Map p336; ☑021-423 2500; www.hippotique. co.za; 5-9 Park Rd, Gardens; d/ste incl breakfast R2420/2950; P✿@☎⊠; ☐Lower Kloof) A brilliantly located and appealing boutique property that offers spacious, stylish rooms, each with a small kitchen for self-catering. Larger, arty suites, with mezzanine-level bedrooms and themes such as Red Bull and Mini Cooper, are worth the extra spend.

🛏 Green Point & Waterfront

Staying at the Waterfront is extremely convenient for shopping and restaurants, but the hotels here can be pricey. Head to Green Point if you seek something more affordable.

Atlantic Point Backpackers
HOSTEL $

(Map p338; ☑021-433 1663; www.atlanticpoint. co.za; 2 Cavalcade Rd, Green Point; dm R270, d R1080, with shared bathroom from R980; P@☎; ☐Upper Portswood) This playfully designed and well-run place is steps away from Green Point's main drag. Features include a big balcony and bar, loft lounge covered in Astroturf, a tiny pool to cool off in and bicycle rental (R70 per day).

Ashanti Green Point HOSTEL $
(Map p338; ☑ 021-433 1619; www.ashanti.co.za; 23 Antrim Rd, Three Anchor Bay; dm R250, d R1200, s/d with shared bathroom R570/820; P@�

 St Bedes) More chilled than the branch in Gardens (p344), this Ashanti has a breezy hillside position with sea views and is nicely decorated with old Cape Town photos. Pancakes are served for breakfast.

Villa Zest BOUTIQUE HOTEL $$
(Map p338; ☑ 021-433 1246; www.villazest.co.za; 2 Braemar Rd, Green Point; s/d incl breakfast from R1590/1790; P✳@

; Upper Portswood) This Bauhaus-style villa has been converted into a quirkily decorated boutique hotel. The lobby is lined with an impressive collection of '60s and '70s groovy electronic goods, including radios, phones, Polaroid cameras and eight-track cassette players. The seven guest rooms have bold, retro-design papered walls and furniture accented with furry pillows and shag rugs.

Head South Lodge BOUTIQUE HOTEL $$
(Map p338; ☑ 021-434 8777; www.headsouth.co.za; 215 Main Rd, Three Anchor Bay; s/d incl breakfast from R995/1250; P✳@

; Ellerslie) A homage to the 1950s, with retro furnishings and collection of Tretchikoff prints hung en masse in the bar. Its big rooms, decorated in cool white and grey, are hung with equally striking modern art by Philip Briel.

Cape Grace LUXURY HOTEL $$$
(Map p338; ☑ 021-410 7100; www.capegrace. com; West Quay Rd, V&A Waterfront; r/ste from R8100/15,000; P✳@

; Nobel Sq) One of the Waterfront's most appealing hotels, the Cape Grace sports an arty combination of antiques and crafts decoration – including hand-painted bed covers and curtains – providing a unique sense of place and Cape Town's history.

Southern Suburbs

Orange Kloof Camp TENTED CAMP $
(Map p328; ☑ 021-712 7471; www.tmbp.co.cz; off Hout Bay Rd, Cecelia Forest; tent for 2 people R590) Perhaps the best of the Table Mountain National Park (p339) tented camps. It's tucked away in a beautiful area near Constantia Nek and provides direct access to the last strand of Afro-montane forest in the park. Perma-

nently erected tents sit beneath reed roofs, each with two single beds and a small deck.

Vineyard Hotel & Spa LUXURY HOTEL $$$
(Map p328; ☑ 021-657 4500; www.vineyard.co.za; Colinton Rd, Newlands; r/ste incl breakfast from R3320/5420; P✳@

; Claremont) Built around the 1799 home of Lady Anne Barnard, the rooms at this delightful hotel have a contemporary look and are decorated in soothing natural tones. It's surrounded by lush gardens with views onto Table Mountain. Friendly staff, the fabulous Angsana Spa, a great gym and pool, and top gourmet restaurant, Myoga, complete the picture.

Simon's Town & Southern Peninsula

Smitswinkel Camp TENTED CAMP $
(Map p328; ☑ 021-712 7471; www.tmnp.co.za; Cape Point; tent for 2 people R725) The bright and spacious permanent tents here are the only ones within the Table Mountain National Park to offer en suite bathrooms. There are also shared kitchen and braai (barbecue) facilities. The camp is steps from the entrance to the Cape of Good Hope section of the park. Note that it does get windy here.

Slangkop Camp TENTED CAMP $
(Map p328; ☑ 021-712 7471; www.tmnp.co.za; off Lighthouse Rd, Kommetjie; tent for 2 people R590) Near the lighthouse at Kommetjie, beneath a forest of rare, indigenous milkwood trees, this camp has simple tents permanently pitched on wooden decks. Each tent has two single beds; ablutions and braai facilities are shared.

Simon's Town Boutique Backpackers HOSTEL $
(Map p328; ☑ 021-786 1964; www.capepax.co.za; 66 St George's St, Simon's Town; dm R220, s/d 650/760, s/d with shared bathroom R500/640;

; Simon's Town) Best-value place to stay in Simon's Town, with spacious, ship-shape rooms – several overlooking the harbour. Friendly staff can help you arrange a host of activities in the area, and there's bike hire for R200 per day. Rates do not include breakfast.

★ Bella Ev GUESTHOUSE $$
(Map p328; ☑ 021-788 1293; www.bellaevguesthouse.co.za; 8 Camp Rd, Muizenberg; r incl breakfast from R900; P@

; Muizenberg) This charming guesthouse, with a delightful courtyard garden, could be the setting for an Agatha Christie mystery, one in which the home's owner has a penchant for all things Turkish – hence the Ottoman slippers for guests' use.

Boulders Beach Lodge   B&B $$

(Map p328; ☎021-786 1758; www.bouldersbeach.co.za; 4 Boulders Pl, Simon's Town; s/d/apt incl breakfast from R750/1300/2200; P@🖘; 🚇Simon's Town) Penguins waddle right up to the doors of this smart guesthouse, with rooms decorated in wicker and wood and a range of self-catering units, where the rates also include breakfast. Its excellent restaurant has an outdoor deck. Note: penguins are not the quietest of creatures, so you may want to bring earplugs.

Olifantsbos Guest House   COTTAGE $$$

(Map p328; ☎021-780 9204; www.tmnp.co.za; Cape of Good Hope; up to 4 people R3620, extra adult/child R480/240; P) Escape from it all at this pretty whitewashed cottage, with an isolated position just steps from the beach and the pounding waves of the Atlantic. Together with its annexe, it sleeps a maximum of 12 people.

🛏 Cape Flats & Northern Suburbs

★Liziwe Guest House   B&B $

(Map p328; ☎021-633 7406; www.sa-venues.com/visit/liziwesguesthouse; 121 NY 112, Gugulethu; r from R600; P@; 🚇Nyanga) Liziwe has made her mansion into a palace, with four delightful en suite rooms all sporting TVs and African-themed decor. She was featured on a BBC cooking show, so you can be sure her food is delicious; breakfast is R70 extra, dinner R80. Plus her place is walking distance to Mzoli's (p348).

Kopanong   B&B $

(Map p328; ☎021-361 2084, 082 476 1278; www.kopanong-township.co.za; 329 Velani Cres, Section C, Khayelitsha; s/d R430/800; P; 🚇Khayelitsha) Thope Lekau, called 'Mama Africa' for obvious reasons, runs this excellent B&B with her equally ebullient daughter, Mpho. Her substantial brick home offers two stylishly decorated guest rooms, each with their own bathroom. Dinner (R120) is delicious. If they're already booked out, Thope can assist with finding homestays in the area.

🛏 East City, District Six, Woodstock & Observatory

★Wish U Were Here   HOSTEL $

(Map p328; ☎021-447 0522; www.wishuwerehere-capetown.com; 445 Albert Rd, Salt River; dm/d R255/960, s/d with shared bathroom R530/830; 🖘; 🚇Kent) The designers clearly had a lot of fun with this place just a short stroll from the Old Biscuit Mill. One dorm is Barbie-doll pink; a romantic double has a bed made from a suspended fishing boat; another is styled after an intensive care unit! The building's wraparound balcony overlooks the Salt River roundabout (which is noisy during the day).

Observatory Backpackers   HOSTEL $

(Map p328; ☎021-447 0861; www.observatory-backpackers.com; 235 Lower Main Rd, Observatory; dm from R180, r R550, s/d with shared bathroom from R400/490; 🖘; 🚇Observatory) There's a funky African theme to this very appealing backpackers, just a short walk away from the heart of the Obs action further down Lower Main Rd. The spacious, shady backyard and lounges are a plus. Breakfast is not included, but there is a bakery right next door.

🛏 Sea Point to Hout Bay

Thulani River Lodge   B&B $$

(Map p328; ☎021-790 7662; www.thulani.eu; 14 Riverside Tce, Hout Bay; r/ste incl breakfast from R1550/2100; P@🖘☀; 🚇Imizamo Yethu) *Thulani* is Zulu for 'peace and tranquillity' – the perfect description for this treasure, a thatched mansion in a lush valley through which the Disa River flows towards Hout Bay. From the four-poster bed in the honeymoon suite and you'll be treated to a sweeping panorama of the back of Table Mountain.

★Tintswalo Atlantic   LUXURY HOTEL $$$

(Map p328; ☎021-201 0025; www.tintswalo.com; Chapman's Peak Dr, Hout Bay; s/d with half board from R7020/9370; P☀@🖘☀; 🚇Hout Bay) Destroyed in a disastrous fire in March 2015, this heralded hotel is happily up and running again. Luxurious Tintswalo hugs the edge of a beautiful rocky bay within the Table Mountain National Park (p339), a favourite resting ground for whales. Expect sublime views and rooms rich with natural materials.

★Glen Boutique Hotel   BOUTIQUE HOTEL $$$

(Map p342; ☎021-439 0086; www.glenhotel.co.za; 3 The Glen, Sea Point; d/ste incl breakfast from R2135/6490; P☀@🖘☀; 🚇The Glen) This gorgeous 'straight-friendly' boutique hotel occupies an elegant old house and a newer block behind. Spacious rooms are decorated in natural tones of stone and wood. In the middle is a fabulous pool and spa, and outdoor dining for their restaurant.

POD   BOUTIQUE HOTEL $$$

(Map p342; ☎021-438 8550; www.pod.co.za; 3 Argyle Rd, Camps Bay; r/ste incl breakfast from R4200/14,300; P☀@🖘☀; 🚇Camps Bay) Offering clean, contemporary design, POD is perfectly angled to catch the Camps Bay action from its bar and spacious pool and deck area. The cheapest rooms have mountain rather than sea views; luxury rooms have their own private plunge pools.

Camps Bay Retreat LUXURY HOTEL $$$
(Map p342; ☑021-437 8300; www.campsbayretreat.com; 7 Chilworth Rd, The Glen; d/ste incl breakfast from R5550/8200; P☀@🅟🅢; 🚌Glen Beach) Based in the grand Earl's Dyke Manor (dating from 1929), this splendid place is set in a secluded nature reserve a short walk from the Camps Bay strip. Choose between rooms in either the main house or the contemporary Deck House, reached by a rope bridge over a ravine. There are also four pools, including some fed by a stream from Table Mountain.

✖ Eating

✖ City Bowl, Foreshore, Bo-Kaap & De Waterkant

★Plant VEGAN $
(Map p332; ☑021-422 2737; www.plantcafe.co.za; 8 Buiten St, City Bowl; mains R40-70; ◎9am-10pm Mon-Sat; 🅟; 🚌Upper Loop/Upper Long) As their name suggests, Plant serves only vegan food, and it's so tasty that you may become converted to the cause. Mock cheese and egg substitutes are incorporated in sandwiches and salads, and giant portobello mushrooms or a mix of flaked potato and seaweed do service as alternative burgers. Their vegan cupcakes and brownies are delicious.

Bacon on Bree SANDWICHES $
(Map p332; ☑021-422 2798; http://baconbonbree.com; 217 Bree St; sandwiches R55-90; ◎7.30am-5pm Mon-Fri, 8.30am-3pm Sat & Sun) The 'number one baconporium in the Cape' serves superb sandwiches and decadent salads named for movies and TV shows, though the stars of this performance are the cured meats of owner Richard Bosman, a renowned local charcuterie master. The breakfasts are also excellent.

Clarke's Bar & Dining Room AMERICAN $
(Map p332; ☑021-422 7648; www.clarkesdining.co.za; 133 Bree St, City Bowl; mains R55-85; ◎7am-5pm Mon, 7am-10.30pm Tue-Fri, 8am-3pm Sat & Sun; 🚌Dorp/Leeuwen) A focus of the Bree St hipster scene is this convivial spot with counter seating that pays homage to the US diner tradition. All-day breakfast dishes include grilled cheese sandwiches and huevos rancheros. There are reubens and pork-bel-

ly sandwiches from lunchtime, as well as burgers and mac and cheese.

★Hemelhuijs INTERNATIONAL $$
(Map p332; ☑021-418 2042; www.hemelhuijs.co.za; 71 Waterkant St, Foreshore; mains R100; ◎9am-4pm Mon-Fri, to 3pm Sat; 🅢; 🚌Strand) A quirky yet elegantly decorated space – think deer heads with broken crockery and contemporary art – showcases the art and culinary creations of Jacques Erasmus. The inventive food is delicious and includes lovely fresh juices, daily bakes, and signature dishes such as sandveld potato and saffron gnocchi with blackened quail breast and smoked aubergine.

★Chef's Warehouse & Canteen TAPAS $$$
(Map p332; ☑021-422 0128; www.chefswarehouse.co.za; Heritage Sq, 92 Bree St, City Bowl; tapas set for 2 R620; ◎noon-2.30pm & 4.30-8pm Mon-Fri, noon-2.30pm Sat; 🚌Church/Longmarket) Hurry here for a delicious and very generous spread of small plates from chef Liam Tomlin and his talented crew. Flavours zip around the world, from a squid with a tangy Vietnamese salad to comforting Coq au Vin. If you can't get a seat (there are no bookings) try their take-away hatch **Street Food** in the space under the stoop.

Africa Café AFRICAN $$$
(Map p332; ☑021-422 0221; www.africacafe.co.za; 108 Shortmarket St, City Bowl; set banquets R280; ◎6-11pm Mon-Sat; 🚌Church/Longmarket) Touristy, yes, but still one of the best places to sample African food. Come with a hearty appetite as the set feast comprises some 15 dishes from across the continent, of which you can eat as much as you like. The talented staff go on song-and-dance walkabout around the tables midmeal.

✖ Gardens & Surrounds

Kyoto Garden Sushi JAPANESE $$
(Map p336; ☑021-422 2001; www.kyotogardensushi.com; 11 Lower Kloofnek Rd, Tamboerskloof; mains R100-200; ◎5.30-11pm Mon-Sat; 🚌Ludwig's Garden) Beechwood furnishings and subtle lighting lend a calm, Zen-like air to this superior Japanese restaurant, owned by an LA expat, but with an expert chef turning out sushi and sashimi. Splurge on the sea urchin.

Manna Epicure BAKERY $$
(Map p336; ☑021-426 2413; www.mannaepicure.com; 151 Kloof St, Gardens; mains R90-130; ◎8am-9pm; 🚌Welgemeend) Come for a deliciously simple breakfast or lunch, or for late-afternoon cocktails and tapas on the veranda

of this white-box cafe. The freshly baked breads alone – coconut or pecan and raisin – are worth dragging yourself up the hill for.

★ **Chef's Table** INTERNATIONAL **$$$**
(Map p336; 021-483 1864; www.belmond.com/mountnelsonhotel; Belmond Mount Nelson Hotel, 76 Orange St, Gardens; lunch R500, dinner without/with wine R745/1285; ☉noon-3pm Fri, 6.30-9pm Mon-Sat; P ✐; ☐Government Ave) There are several dining options at the Mount Nelson Hotel, but for a real treat book one of the four tables with a front-row view onto the drama and culinary magic unfolding inside the kitchen. The food is superb (vegetarians are catered for) and presented by the chefs who will take you on a behind-the-scenes tour.

★ **Aubergine** INTERNATIONAL **$$$**
(Map p336; 021-465 0000; www.aubergine.co.za; 39 Barnet St, Gardens; 3-course lunch R445, 3-/4-/5-course dinner R580/720/875; ☉noon-2pm Wed-Fri, 5-10pm Mon-Sat; ✐; ☐Annandale) German-born Harald Bresselschmidt is one of Cape Town's most consistent chefs, producing creative, hearty dishes that are served with some of the Cape's best wines. Don't over-order, as portions are large. Vegetarian menus are available and the service and ambiance are impeccable.

✗ Green Point & Waterfront

V&A Food Market AFRICAN **$**
(Map p338; www.waterfrontfoodmarket.com; Pump House, Dock Rd, V&A Waterfront; mains from R75; ☉10am-6pm May-Oct, to 8pm Nov-April; P 🛜 📶; ☐Nobel Sq) There's no need to spend big to eat well (and healthily) at the Waterfront, thanks to this colourful, market-style food court in the old Pump House. Grab a coffee or freshly squeezed juice to go with a wrap or muffin, or opt for a larger meal such as Thai, Indian or Cape Malay curry.

✗ Southern Suburbs

Jonkershuis CAPE MALAY **$$**
(Map p328; 021-794 6255; www.jonkershuis-constantia.co.za; Groot Constantia Rd, Constantia; mains R90-140; ☉9am-10pm Mon-Sat, to 5pm Sun; P) This casual brasserie-style restaurant in the grounds of Groot Constantia (p334) has a pleasant, vine-shaded courtyard and tables looking onto the manor house. Sample Cape Malay dishes (including a tasting plate for R188) or cured meats with a glass or two of the local wines, or satisfy your sweet tooth with the desserts.

★ **La Colombe** FRENCH **$$$**
(Map p328; 021-794 2390; www.lacolombe.co.za; Silvermist, Main Rd, Constantia; lunch/dinner tasting menu R890/990; ☉12.30-2.30pm & 7.30-9.30pm; P) There's a new location on the Silvermist estate for this storied Constantia restaurant, but little else has changed. British chef Scot Kirton rustles up skilful dishes combining French and Asian techniques and flavours, such as smoked-tomato risotto and miso-seared scallops. The coolly elegant setting and personable service couldn't be better.

✗ Simon's Town & Southern Peninsula

★ **Foodbarn** INTERNATIONAL **$$**
(Map p328; 021-789 1390; www.thefoodbarn.co.za; cnr Noordhoek Main Rd & Village Ln, Noordhoek Village; mains R80-130; ☉noon-2.30pm daily, 6.30-9.30pm Tue-Sat noon-2.30pm daily, 6.30-9.30pm Tue-Sat; P 🛜) ✐ Masterchef Franck Dangereux might have opted for the less stressful life in Noordhoek, but that doesn't mean this operation skimps on quality. Expect rustic, delicious bistro dishes.

★ **Olympia Café & Deli** BAKERY **$$**
(Map p328; 021-788 6396; www.facebook.com/OlympiaCafeKalkBay; 134 Main Rd, Kalk Bay; mains R80-120; ☉7am-9.30pm; ☐Kalk Bay) Setting a high standard for relaxed rustic cafes by the sea, Olympia bakes its own breads and pastries. It's great for breakfast, and its Mediterranean-influenced lunch dishes are delicious, too – particularly the heaped bowls of mussels.

★ **Lighthouse Cafe** INTERNATIONAL **$$**
(Map p328; 021-786 9000; www.thelighthousecafe.co.za; 90 St Georges St, Simon's Town; mains R65-100; ☉8.30am-4pm Sun-Tue, to 10pm Wed-Sat; ☐Simon's Town) Relaxed, beachcomber-chic cafe, with a menu big on seafood – there's a delicious and filling Mauritian bouillabaisse and fish and chips made to Jamie Oliver's recipe. They also do burgers, pizza and mezze platters.

✗ Cape Flats & Northern Suburbs

Mzoli's BRAAI **$**
(Map p328; 021-638 1355; 150 NY111, Gugulethu; meals R50-100; ☉11am-6pm; ☐Nyanga) Tourists, TV stars and locals gather at this busy butchery serving some of Cape Town's tastiest grilled meat. First buy your meat and make sure you get them to add their special sauce. Take it to the kitchen to be braaied

(barbecued) and then find a table outside. It gets super-hectic here at weekends, so arrive early.

★**Hog House Brewing Co.**   BARBECUE **$$**
(Map p328; ☑021-810 4545; http://hhbc.co.za; Unit 4 Technosquare, 42 Morningside Rd, Ndabeni; meals R100-150; ☺5pm-9pm Mon-Sat; ☑) It couldn't be in a more obscure spot – within a business park in an industrial part of town – but this barbecue restaurant is perpetually busy. The creations of chef PJ Vadas include smoked meats so tender you could cut them with a spoon. The veggie side dishes are just as impressive – you've never eaten cauliflower and broccoli this good.

★**Mzansi**   AFRICAN **$$**
(Map p328; ☑073 754 8502; www.mzansi45.co.za; 45 Harlem Ave, Langa; buffet R180; ☺noon-10pm; ☐Langa) As much a cultural experience as a gastronomic one, Mzansi rates highly among travellers. Food is served buffet-style and features some traditional dishes, including *pap* (maize porridge). Host Mama Nomonde brings a personal touch with tales of her life in the Cape Flats, and there's live music in the form of a marimba band. Book ahead.

✕ East City, District Six, Woodstock & Observatory

★**Kitchen**   SANDWICHES, SALADS **$**
(Map p328; www.lovethekitchen.co.za; 111 Sir Lowry Rd, Woodstock; sandwiches & salads R60-70; ☺8am-3.30pm Mon-Fri; ☑; ☐District Six) Of all the swanky restaurants in town, it was this little charmer that Michelle Obama chose for lunch, proving the First Lady has excellent taste. Tuck into plates of divine salads, rustic sandwiches made with love, and sweet treats via tea served from china teapots.

★**Pot Luck Club**   INTERNATIONAL **$$**
(Map p328; ☑021-447 0804; www.thepotluckclub. co.za; Silo top fl, Old Biscuit Mill, 373-375 Albert Rd, Woodstock; dishes R90-120; ☺12.30-2.30pm & 6-10.30pm Mon-Sat, 11am-3pm Sun; ☐Kent) The sister restaurant to The Test Kitchen is a more affordable Luke Dale-Roberts' option. Sitting at the top of an old silo, it offers panoramic views of the surrounding area, but it's what's on the plate that tends to take the breath away. The dishes are designed to be shared; we defy you not to order a second plate of the Chalmar beef with truffle-café-au-lait sauce.

★**Test Kitchen**   INTERNATIONAL **$$$**
(Map p328; ☑021-447 2622; www.thetestkitchen. co.za; Shop 104A, Old Biscuit Mill, 375 Albert Rd,

Woodstock; gourmand menu without/with wine R1600/2250; ☺6.30-9pm Tue-Sat; ℗; ☐Kent) Luke Dale-Roberts' creates inspirational dishes with top-quality local ingredients at his flagship restaurant – generally agreed to be the best in Africa. However, the award-winning UK-born chef is so famous now that bookings several months in advance are essential. Pescatarian and vegetarian menus are available on request.

✕ Sea Point to Hout Bay

★**Kleinsky's Delicatessen**   DELI **$**
(Map p342; www.kleinskys.co.za; 95 Regent Rd, Sea Point; mains R40-70; ☺8am-5pm Mon-Fri, 8am-3pm Sat & Sun; ☎; ☐Tramway) An homage to classic, Jewish-style delis, Kleinsky's is a great addition to Sea Point's casual dining scene, serving dishes such as toasted bagels with smoked salmon or house-made chopped liver, chicken soup with matzo balls, and *latkes* (potato pancakes). They serve good coffee, too. The walls act as a gallery for local artists.

★**Massimo's**   ITALIAN **$$**
(Map p328; ☑021-790 5648; www.pizzaclub. co.za, Oakhurst Farm Park, Main Rd, Hout Bay; mains R50-135; ☺noon-9.30pm; ℗☎☑☀; ☐Imizamo Yethu) They do pasta and *spuntini* (tapas-style small plates), but it's the wood-fired thin-crust pizzas that are Massimo's speciality – and very good they are, too. It's all served up with warmth and humour by the Italian Massimo and his Liverpudlian wife Tracy. There are plenty of vegetarian options, too, plus one of the best kids' play areas in Cape Town.

★**Hout Bay Coffee**   CAFE
(Map p328; www.facebook.com/HoutbayCoffee; Mainstream Shopping Centre, Main Rd, Hout Bay; ☺9am-5pm Mon-Fri, to 3pm Sat & Sun; ☐Military) Sip excellent coffee at this rustic cafe, set in an 18th-century extension to the original 17th-century woodcutters' cottage at Hout Bay. The outdoor area is shaded by a 150-year-old Norfolk Pine, with tables and chairs made from an old fishing boat. They also bake filo-pastry chicken pies, luscious chocolate cakes and wheat-free quiche with free-range eggs.

● Drinking & Nightlife

★**Lady Bonin's Tea Bar**   TEAHOUSE
(Map p332; ☑021-447 1741; www.ladyboninstea.com; 213 Long St; ☺8am-4.30pm Mon-Fri, 9.30am-2.30pm Sat; ☐Upper Loop/Upper Long)

A charmingly decorated, relaxing place in which to sample organic and sustainable artisan teas, fruity and herbal brews, and vegan baked treats.

★ Orphanage
COCKTAIL BAR

(Map p332; ☑021-424 2004; www.theorphanage. co.za; cnr Orphange & Bree Sts, City Bowl; ☺5pm-2am Mon-Thu & Sat, to 3am Fri; ▣Upper Loop/Upper Long) Named after the nearby lane, the mixologists here prepare some tempting artisan libations with curious names including Knicker-Dropper Glory, Dollymop and Daylight Daisy, using ingredients as varied as peanut butter, kumquat compote and 'goldfish'! It's dark, sophisticated and stylish, with outdoor seating beneath the trees on Bree.

★ Beerhouse
BAR

(Map p332; www.beerhouse.co.za; 223 Long St, City Bowl; ☺11am-2am; ▣Upper Loop/Upper Long) With 99 brands of bottled beer, both local and international, and several more brews on tap, this brightly designed and spacious joint in the heart of Long St beer will have beer lovers thinking they've died and gone to heaven. The balcony is a great spot from which to watch the world go by.

★ Honest Chocolate Cafe
BAR

(Map p332; www.honestchocolate.co.za; 64A Wale St, City Bowl; ☺9am-6pm Mon-Fri, to 9pm Sat, to 4pm Sun; ▣Dorp/Leeuwen) Following a successful crowdfunding campaign, Honest Chocolate, who make their artisan sweet treats at the Woodstock Exchange (p353), have launched this homage to fine dark chocolate in liquid, solid, ice-cream and cake form. It's a chocoholic's dream come true, with even vegan and gluten-free options.

House of Machines
BAR

(Map p332; ☑021-426 1400; www.thehouseof-machines.com; 84 Shortmarket St, City Bowl; ☺7am-12.30am Mon-Fri, from 9am Sat; ▣Church/Mid-Long) Combining a motorbike workshop with barbers, a boutique and a live music/DJ space, this is a homage to Americana, with tasty, inventive bourbon cocktails, US craft beers and Evil Twin Coffee from NYC.

★ Chalk & Cork
WINE BAR

(Map p336; ☑021-422 5822; www.chalkandcork. co.za; 51 Kloof St, Gardens; ☺11am-10pm Mon-Sat, to 6pm Sun; ▣Lower Kloof) This wine bar and restaurant has a pleasant courtyard fronting Kloof St. The menu runs from breakfast dishes to tapas and sharing platters, but you're welcome to drop in for just the wines, plenty of which is served by the glass and sourced from some of the region's best estates.

★ Yours Truly
BAR

(Map p336; www.yourstrulycafe.co.za; 73 Kloof St, Gardens; ☺6am-11pm; ▣Ludwig's Garden) Fronting the **Once in Cape Town backpackers** (Map p336; ☑021-424 6169; www.onceincapetown. co.za; 73 Kloof St, Gardens; dm/d incl breakfast R275/1065; ▣@☎; ▣Ludwig's Garden), this place is hopping from early morning to late nights. Travellers mingle with hipster locals, who come for the excellent coffee, craft beer, gourmet sandwiches, thin-crust pizzas and the occasional DJ event.

★ Shimmy Beach Club
CLUB

(Map p338; ☑021-200 7778; www.shimmybeach-club.com; South Arm Rd, V&A Waterfront; cover after 3pm R150; ☺11am-2am Mon-Fri, 9am-2am Sat, 11am-6pm Sun; ▣Waterfront Silo) Drive past the fish processing factories to discover this glitzy mega-club and restaurant, arranged around a small fake beach with a glass-sided pool. Perhaps unsurprisingly, they have pool parties with scantily clad dancers shimmying to grooves by top DJs, including the electro-jazz group Goldfish, who have a summer Sunday residency here (bookings advised).

★ Bascule
BAR

(Map p338; ☑021-410 7082; www.basculebar.com; Cape Grace Hotel, West Quay Rd, V&A Waterfront; ☺9am-1am; ▣Nobel Sq) Over 450 varieties of whisky are served at the Grace's sophisticated bar, with a few slugs of the 50-year-old Glenfiddich still available (at just R10,000 a tot). Outdoor tables facing the marina are a superb spot for drinks and tasty tapas. Make a booking for one their whisky tastings (from R350), in which you can sample various drams paired with food.

★ Banana Jam
CRAFT BEER

(Map p328; www.bananajamcafe.co.za; 157 2nd Ave, Harfield Village, Kenilworth; ☺11am-11pm Mon-Sat, 5-10pm Sun; ☎; ▣Kenilworth) Real beer lovers rejoice – this convivial Caribbean restaurant and bar has over 30 beers on tap (including their own brews) and bottled ales from all the top local microbrewers, including Jack Black, Darling Brew and CBC.

★ Tiger's Milk
BAR

(Map p328; ☑021-788 1869; www.tigersmilk.co.za; cnr Beach & Sidmouth Rds, Muizenberg; ☺11am-2am Mon-Fri, from 8am Sat & Sun; ☎; ▣Muizenberg) There's a panoramic view of Muizenberg beach through the floor-to-ceiling window of this hangar-like bar and restaurant. Although it's open all day for food (good pizza and steaks), the vibe – with its long bar counter, comfy sofas and quirky decor (a BMW bike and a giant golden cow's head hanging on exposed brick walls) – is more nightclub.

★Brass Bell
BAR

(Map p328; www.brassbell.co.za; Kalk Bay station, Main Rd, Kalk Bay; ⊘8.30am-11pm; ⊒Kalk Bay) Follow the tunnel beneath the train tracks to reach this institution, lapped by the waves of False Bay. On a sunny day there are few better places to drink and eat (mains R60 to R130) by the sea. You can also take a dip in the adjacent tidal pools before or after.

★Taproom
MICROBREWERY

(Map p328; ⊘021-200 5818; www.devilspeakbrewing.co.za; 95 Durham Ave, Salt River; ⊘11am-2am Mon-Sat, noon-6pm Sun; ⊒Upper Salt River) Devil's Peak Brewing Company make some of South Africa's best craft beers. Their taproom and restaurant provide a panoramic view up to Devil's Peak itself. The food is hearty fare (think burgers and fried chicken), designed to balance their stellar selection of on-tap beers. There are also barrel-aged brews and one-off experiments available on tap.

★Truth
COFFEE

(Map p332; www.truthcoffee.com; 36 Buitenkant St, East City; ⊘7am-6pm Mon-Thu, 8am-midnight Fri & Sat, 8am-2pm Sun; ⊛; ⊒Lower Buitenkant) This self-described 'steampunk roastery and coffee bar', with pressed-tin ceilings, naked hanging bulbs and mad-inventor style metalwork, is an awe-inspiring space in which to mingle with city slickers. Apart from coffee, craft beers, baked goods and various sandwiches, burgers and hot dogs are on the menu.

★Espressolab Microroasters
COFFEE

(Map p328; www.espressolabmicroroasters.com; Old Biscuit Mill, 375 Albert Rd, Woodstock; ⊘8am-4pm Mon-Fri, to 2pm Sat; ⊒Kent) Geek out about coffee at this lab staffed with passionate roasters and baristas. Their beans, which come from single farms, estates and co-ops from around the world, are packaged with tasting notes such as those for fine wines.

★Bungalow
BAR

(Map p342; ⊘021-438 2018; www.thebungalow.co.za; Glen Country Club, 3 Victoria Rd, Clifton; ⊘noon-2am; ⊒Maiden's Cove) This restaurant and lounge bar with a Euro-chic vibe is a great place for beers, cocktails or a boozy meal, after which you can crash on a daybed under a billowing white awning, or dangle your feet in the tiny bar-side splash pool. A DJ creates a more clubby atmosphere by night. Bookings are advised.

☆ Entertainment

Artscape
THEATRE

(Map p328; ⊘021-410 9800; www.artscape.co.za; 1-10 DF Malan St, Foreshore; ⊒Civic Centre) Consisting of three different-sized auditoriums, this behemoth is the city's main arts complex. Theatre, classical music, ballet, opera and cabaret shows – Artscape offers it all. If you're into swing and salsa, Que Pasa (p340) also run regular classes at the Jazzart Studio here. The desolate area means it's not recommended to walk around here at night; there's plenty of secure parking.

★Baxter Theatre
THEATRE

(Map p328; ⊘021-685 7880; www.baxter.co.za; Main Rd, Rondebosch; tickets R75-150; ⊒Rosebank) Since the 1970s the Baxter has been the focus of Capetonian theatre. There are three venues – the main theatre, the concert hall and the studio – and between them they cover everything from kids' shows to African dance spectaculars. They have an ongoing relationship with the Royal Shakespeare Company thanks to Capetonian Sir Anthony Sher, who has performed here.

Sahara Park Newlands
CRICKET

(Map p328; ⊘021-657 2043; www.wpca.org.za; 146 Campground Rd, Newlands; tickets R20-550; ⊒Newlands) If it weren't for a nearby megabrewery messing up the view towards Table Mountain, Newlands would be a shoo-in for the title of world's prettiest cricket ground. With room for 25,000, it's used for all international matches. Local team the Nashua Mobile Cape Cobras play here during the season, which runs from September to March.

Newlands Rugby Stadium
RUGBY

(Map p328; ⊘021-659 4600; www.wprugby.com; 8 Boundary Rd, Newlands; ⊒Newlands) This hallowed ground of South African rugby is home to the Stormers (www.thestormers.com). Super-12 games and international matches are played here.

Fugard Theatre
THEATRE

(Map p332; ⊘021-461 4554; www.thefugard.com; Caledon St, East City; ⊒Lower Buitenkant) Named for Athol Fugard, South Africa's best-known living playwright, this impressive arts centre was created from the former Congregational Church Hall. The largest theatre doubling up as a 'bioscope' – a fancy word for a digital cinema where top international dance and opera performances are screened.

Assembly
LIVE MUSIC

(Map p332; www.theassembly.co.za; 61 Harrington St, East City; cover R30-50; ⊒Lower Buitenkant)

In an old furniture assembly factory, this live-music and DJ-performance space has made its mark with an exciting, eclectic line-up of both local and international artists. They also hold the audio-visual event Pecha Kucha (www.pechakucha-capetown.co.za), generally once a month.

★ **Studio 7** LIVE MUSIC
(Map p342; www.studio7sessions.com; 213 High Level Rd, Sea Point; Rhine) A few years ago, musician Patrick Craig set up a members-only music club in his living room. Top local and international musicians play acoustic gigs here in very relaxed, intimate surroundings. Usually no more than 40 tickets are sold (online) – check the website for details, as it's a fantastic venue for true music lovers.

🛍 Shopping

★ **South African Market** FASHION, CRAFTS
(SAM; Map p332; ☑ 089 690 6476; www.ilovesam.co.za; 67 Shortmarket St, City Bowl; ⊙10am-6pm Mon-Fri, 10am-3pm Sat; Church/Longmarket) A showcase for local design talent across fashion, jewellery, homewares, stationery and art works with a great selection of men's, women's and kids' wear here, including the cute graphic T-shirts of Mingo Lamberti.

★ **Streetwires** ARTS & CRAFTS
(Map p332; www.streetwires.co.za; 77 Shortmarket St, Bo-Kaap; ⊙9am-5pm Mon-Fri, 9am-1pm Sat; Church/Longmarket) The motto is 'anything you can dream up in wire we will build'. And if you visit this social project, designed to create sustainable employment, and see the wire sculptors at work, you'll see what that means! The amazing range, includes working radios and chandeliers, life-sized animals and artier products such as the Nguni Cow range.

Clarke's Bookshop BOOKS
(Map p332; ☑ 021-423 5739; www.clarkesbooks.co.za; 199 Long St, City Bowl; ⊙9am-5pm Mon-Fri, 9.30am-1pm Sat; Dorp/Leeuwen) Take your time leafing through the best range of books on South Africa and the continent, with a great second-hand section upstairs. If you can't find what you're looking for here, it's unlikely to be in any of the many other bookshops along Long St (although there's no harm in browsing).

African Music Store MUSIC
(Map p332; ☑ 021-426 0857; 134 Long St, City Bowl; ⊙9am-6pm Mon-Fri, to 2pm Sat; Dorp/Leeuwen) The range of local music here, including jazz, *kwaito* (a form of township music), dance and trance recordings, can't

be surpassed; and the staff are knowledgeable about the music scene. You'll also find DVDs and other souvenirs.

★ **KIN** ARTS & CRAFTS
(Map p336; www.kinshop.co.za; 99B Kloof St, Gardens; ⊙9.30am-5pm Mon-Sat; Ludwig's Garden) You're sure to find a unique gift or item for yourself at this creative boutique representing over a hundred South African artists and designers, ranging from ceramics and jewellery to prints and bags. They also have a branch at the Waterfront (p352), which stocks more African-themed designs.

★ **Watershed** SHOPPING CENTRE
(Map p338; www.waterfront.co.za/shop/watershed; Dock Rd, V&A Waterfront; ⊙10am-6pm; Nobel Sq) The best place to shop for souvenirs in Cape Town, this exciting revamped retail market gathers together over hundreds of top Capetonian and South African brands in fashion, arts, crafts and design – there's something here for every pocket. On the upper level is an exhibition space, and a wellness centre offering holistic products and massages.

KIN ARTS & CRAFTS
(Map p338; ☑ 076 822 5786; www.kinshop.co.za; Shop 11B, Alfred Mall, V&A Waterfront; ⊙9am-9pm; V&A Waterfront) Second branch of a creative boutique representing over a hundred South African artists and designers; their main shop is in Gardens (p352).

★ **Montebello** ARTS & CRAFTS
(Map p328; www.montebello.co.za; 31 Newlands Ave, Newlands; ⊙9am-5pm Mon-Sat, to 3pm Sun; Newlands) This development project has helped several great craftspeople and designers along the way. In the leafy compound, artists studios are scattered around the central craft shop, where you can buy a great range of gifts, including some made from recycled materials. There's also a plant nursery, the excellent cafe **Gardener's Cottage** and car-washers.

★ **Kalk Bay Modern** ARTS & CRAFTS
(Map p328; ☑ 021-788 6571; www.kalkbaymodern.co.za; 136 Main Rd, Kalk Bay; ⊙9.30am-5pm; Kalk Bay) This wonderful gallery is stocked with an eclectic and appealing range of arts and crafts, and there are often exhibitions by local artists showing here. Check out the Art-i-San collection of printed cloth, a fair-trade product made by the !Kung Bushmen in Namibia.

★ **Neighbourgoods Market** MARKET
(Map p328; www.neighbourgoodsmarket.co.za; Old Biscuit Mill, 373-375 Albert Rd, Woodstock; ⊙9am-2pm Sat; Kent) The first, and still the best,

of the artisan goods markets that are now common across the Cape. Food and drinks are gathered in the main area where you can pick up groceries and gourmet goodies or just graze, while the separate Designergoods area hosts a must-buy selection of local fashions and accessories. Come early unless you enjoy jostling with crowds.

★ **Woodstock Exchange** SHOPPING CENTRE
(Map p328; www.woodstockexchange.co.za; 66 Albert Rd, Woodstock; ⊗8am-5pm Mon-Fri, to 2pm Sat; ᖆWoodstock) There's a fair amount of original retail at the Exchange, including the atelier and showroom of **Grandt Mason Originals**, (www.g-mo.co.za) which uses luxurious fabrics from ends of rolls and swatch books to make one-off footwear; **Chapel** (www.store.chapelgoods.co.za) leather goods; **Charlie. H**, who crafts kimonos, halter dresses, and skirts from printed fabrics; and boutique **Kingdom**, which mixes fashion and accessories with interior design.

★ **The Old Biscuit Mill** SHOPPING CENTRE
(Map p328; www.theoldbiscuitmill.co.za; 373-375 Albert Rd, Woodstock; ⊗10am-4pm Mon-Fri, 9am-2pm Sat; ᖆKent) This former biscuit factory houses an ace collection of arts, craft, fashion and design shops, as well as places to eat and drink. Favourites include **Clementina Ceramics** (www.clementina.co.za) and **Imiso Ceramics** (☑021-447 2627; www.imisoceramics.co.zat) for ceramics; the organic bean-to-shop chocolate factory **Cocofair** (www.cocoafair.com); and **Mü & Me** (www.muandme.nett) for supercute graphic art for cards, wrapping paper, stationery and kids' T-shirts.

ⓘ Information
MEDICAL SERVICES
Medical services in Cape Town are of a high standard; make sure you have health insurance and be prepared to pay for services immediately. In an emergency call ☑107 (landlines only), or ☑112 if using a mobile phone, for directions to the nearest hospital.

Many doctors make house calls; look under 'Medical' in the phone book or ask at your hotel.
Netcare Christiaan Barnard Memorial Hospital (☑021-480 6111; https://www.netcare.co.za/139/netcare-christiaan-barnard-memorial-hospital; 181 Longmarket St, City Bowl; ᖆChurch/Longmarket) Excellent private hospital. Reception is on the 8th floor.
Netcare Travel Clinic (☑021-419 3172; www.travelclinic.co.za; 11th fl, Picbal Arcade, 58 Strand St, City Bowl; ⊗8am-4pm Mon-Fri; ᖆAdderley) For vaccinations and travel health advice.

DON'T MISS

CAPE TOWN COOKING COURSES
Bo-Kaap Cooking Tour (Map p332; ☑074 130 8124; www.bokaapcookingtour.co.za; Rose St; per person R700) After a short walking tour of the Bo-Kaap and a bit of spice shopping, join Zainie in her home for a hands-on Cape Malay cooking class.

Groote Schuur Hospital (☑021-404 9111; www.westerncape.gov.za/your_gov/163; Main Rd, Observatory; ᖆObservatory) Has a casualty (emergency) department.

POST
There are post office branches across Cape Town; see www.sapo.co.za to find the nearest. The post is reliable but can be slow. If you're mailing anything of value, consider using private mail services, such as **Postnet** (www.postnet.co.za), which uses DHL for international deliveries.

TOURIST INFORMATION
The head office of **Cape Town Tourism** (Map p332; ☑021-487 6800; www.capetown.travel; Pinnacle Bldg, cnr Castle & Burg Sts, City Bowl; ⊗8am-5.30pm Mon-Fri, 8.30am-2pm Sat, 9am-1pm Sun; ᖆChurch/Mid-Long) is centrally located and there are plenty of satellite offices around the city, including one at the airport.

ⓘ Getting There & Away
Most likely you'll arrive at Cape Town International Airport. If coming from within South Africa, it's possible that your arrival point will be Cape Town's combined rail and bus station. The city is also on the international cruise circuit, with liners docking either at the Waterfront or in the docks. Flights, tours and rail tickets can all be booked online at www.lonelyplanet.com/travelservices.

AIR
Cape Town International Airport (CPT; Map p328; ☑021-937 1200; www.airports.co.za), 22km east of the city centre, has a tourist information office located in the arrivals hall.

There are many direct international flights into Cape Town. Generally it's cheaper to book and pay for domestic flights within South Africa on the internet (rather than via a local travel agent).

BUS
Interstate buses arrive at the bus terminus (Map p332) at **Cape Town Railway Station**, where you'll find the booking offices for the following bus companies, all open from 6am to 6.30pm daily.

ⓘ TO/FROM THE AIRPORT

MyCiTi buses Run every 30 minutes between 4.45am and 10.15pm to the city centre and the Watefront. A single trip fare is R90; if you use a 'myconnect' card (which costs a non-refundable R30), the fare varies between R57.80 and R69.50 – depending on whether you travel in peak or off-peak hours, and use a standard fare or the MyCiTi Mover fares package.

Backpacker Bus (☑ 082 809 9185; www.backpackerbus.co.za) Book in advance for airport transfers (from R220 per person) and pick-ups from hostels and hotels.

Taxi Expect to pay around R250 for a nonshared taxi.

Greyhound (Map p332; ☑ 021-418 4326; www.greyhound.co.za; Cape Town Railway Station; ⊗ 6am-6.30pm)

Intercape (☑ 021-380 4400, 0861 287 287; www.intercape.co.za; Cape Town Railway Station; ⊗ 6am-6.30pm)

Translux (Map p332; ☑ 0861 589 282, 021-449 6209; www.translux.co.za; Cape Town Railway Station; ⊗ 6am-6.30pm)

Baz Bus (Map p332; ☑ 0861 229 287; www.bazbus.com; 32 Burg St; ⊗ 6am-6.30pm) Offers hop-on, hop-off fares and door-to-door service between Cape Town and Jo'burg/Pretoria via Northern Drakensberg, Durban and the Garden Route.

TRAIN

Long distance trains arrive at Cape Town Railway Station on Heerengracht in the City Bowl. There are services Wednesday, Friday and Sunday to and from Jo'burg via Kimberley on the **Shosholoza Meyl** (☑ 0860 008 888; www.shosholozameyl.co.za): these sleeper trains offer comfortable accommodation and dining cars. Other services include the luxurious **Blue Train** (☑ 021-449 2672; www.bluetrain.co.za) and **Rovos Rail** (☑ 021-421 4020; www.rovos.com).

ⓘ Getting Around

BUS
Golden Arrow

Golden Arrow (☑ 0800 656 463; www.gabs.co.za) buses run from the **Golden Acre Bus Terminal** (Map p332; Grand Pde), with most services stopping early in the evening. You might find them handy for journeys into the Cape Flats, Northern Suburbs and even as far south as Simon's Town. Fares start from R5.50.

MyCiTi Buses

The **MyCiTi** (☑ 0800 656 463; www.myciti.org.za) network of commuter buses runs daily between 5am and 10pm, with the the most frequent services being between 8am and 5pm. Routes cover the city centre up to Gardens and out to the Waterfront; along the Atlantic seaboard to Camps Bay and Hout Bay; up to Tamboerskloof along Kloof Nek Rd, with a shuttle service to the cableway; to Woodstock and Salt River; to Blouberg and Table View; to Khayelitsha; and to the airport.

Fares have to be paid with a stored-value 'myconnect' card (a non-refundable R30), which can be purchased from MyCiTi station kiosks and participating retailers. It's also possible to buy single-trip tickets (R35 or R90 to or from the airport). A bank fee of 2.5% of the loaded value (with a minimum of R1.50) will be charged, eg if you load the card with R200 you will have R195 in credit. The card, issued by ABSA (a national bank), can also be used to pay for low-value transactions at shops and businesses displaying the MasterCard sign.

Fares charged depend on the time of day (peak-hour fares are charged from 6.30am to 8.30am and 4pm to 6pm, Monday to Friday) and whether you have pre-loaded the card with MyCiTi Mover package (amount of between R50 and R1000), which can cut the standard fares by 30%.

For journeys of under 5km (ie from Civic Centre to Gardens or the Waterfront), standard fares are R8.90 at peak times (as above) and R5.90 at all other times; city centre to Table View is peak/off-peak R12.50/9.40; city centre to airport peak/off-peak R69.50/57.80; city centre to Hout Bay peak/off-peak R12.50/9.40.

TAXI

Consider taking a nonshared taxi at night or if you're in a group. Rates are about R10 per kilometre. **Uber** (www.uber.com) is very popular and works well.

Excite Taxis (☑ 021-448 4444; www.excitetaxis.co.za)

Marine Taxi (☑ 0861 434 0434, 021-447 0384; www.marinetaxis.co.za)

Rikkis (☑ 086 174 5547; www.rikkis.co.za)

Telecab (☑ 021-788 2717, 082 222 0282) For transfers from Simon's Town to Boulders and Cape Point.

Touch Down Taxis (☑ 083 652 0786)

TRAIN

Cape Metro Rail (☑ 0800 656 463; www.capetownrails.freeblog.site) trains are a handy way to get around, although there are few (or no) trains after 6pm on weekdays and after noon on Saturday.

The difference between MetroPlus (first class) and Metro (economy class) carriages in price and comfort is negligible. The most important line for visitors is the Simon's Town line, which runs through Observatory and around the back of Table Mountain, through upper-income suburbs such as Newlands, and on to Muizenberg and the False Bay coast. These trains run at least every hour from 6am to 9pm and during peak times (6am to 9am and 3pm to 6pm) as often as every 15 minutes.

Metro trains also run out to Strand on the eastern side of False Bay, and into the Winelands to Stellenbosch and Paarl. They are the cheapest and easiest means of transport to these areas. For all routes security is best at peak times when the carriages are busy.

Some MetroPlus/Metro fares are: Observatory (R9.50/7), Muizenberg (R12.50/8.50), Simon's Town (R15.50/9.50), Paarl (R18.50/12) and Stellenbosch (R18.50/12).

WESTERN CAPE

The splendours of the Western Cape lie not only in its world-class vineyards, stunning beaches and mountains, but also in lesser-known regions, such as the wide-open spaces of the Karoo, the nature reserves and the wilderness areas. Make sure you get out into these wild, less-visited areas for bird-watching and wildlife adventure, as well as pure relaxation under vast skies.

The Western Cape offers a huge range of activities, from sedate endeavours such as wine tasting and scenic drives to more hair-raising encounters such as skydiving and rock climbing.

The melting pot of cultures in the region also begs to be explored. Khoe-San rock art is at its best in the Cederberg mountains and there are some fine opportunities to visit black townships and be entranced by the fascinating culture of the Xhosa people.

Winelands

Venturing inland and upwards from Cape Town you'll find the Boland, meaning 'upland'. It's a superb wine-producing area, and indeed the best known in South Africa. The magnificent mountain ranges around Stellenbosch and Franschhoek provide ideal microclimates for the vines.

There's been colonial settlement here since the latter half of the 17th century, when the Dutch first founded Stellenbosch and the French Huguenots settled in Franschhoek. Both towns pride themselves on their innovative young chefs, many based at wine estates, and the region has become the mainspring of South African cuisine. Along with Paarl,

these towns make up the core of the Winelands, but there are many more wine-producing places to explore. Pretty Tulbagh, with its many historical buildings, is known for MCC (Méthode Cap Classique – the local version of Champagne), and Robertson's scattered wineries often offer free tastings.

Stellenbosch

POP 155,000 / ☑ 021

Stellenbosch is an elegant, historical town with stately Cape Dutch, Georgian and Victorian architecture along its oak-lined streets – and it is so much more than that. Full of interesting museums, quality hotels and a selection of bars, clubs and restaurants, it is constantly abuzz with locals, students, Capetonians and tourists.

Established by the governor of the Cape (Simon van der Stel) in 1679 on the banks of the Eerste River, Stellenbosch was – and still is – famed for its rich soil, just what was needed to produce vegetables and wine for ships stopping off at the Cape.

◉ Sights

Stellenbosch University Botanical Garden   PARK

(☑021-808 3054; cnr Neethling & Van Riebeeck Sts; ⊗8am-5pm) FREE This glorious inner-city garden is an unsung Stellenbosch sight and well worth a wander. Themed gardens include a bonsai area and tropical glasshouse, and there's a host of indigenous plants. For those not mad about botany, it's a peaceful place to walk and there's a pleasant tea garden for coffee, cake or a light lunch (mains R55 to R130).

WINERIES

There are too many good wineries in the Stellenbosch area to list; it's sometimes best to drive around and stop on a whim. You'll find supurb tours at brandy distillery **Van Ryn Brandy Cellar** (☑021-881 3875; www.vanryn.co.za; off Rte 310; tour with tastings R75-100, tour only R40; ⊗9am-6pm Mon-Fri, 9am-4pm Sat & 11am-4pm Sun Oct-Apr, closed Sun May-Sep), amongst stunning contemporary architecture at **Waterkloof** (☑021-858 1292; www.waterkloofwines.co.za; Sir Lowry's Pass Village Rd, Somerset West; tastings from R30; ⊗10am-5pm Mon-Sat, 11am-5pm Sun; ⓟ) 🍷, and at **Vergelegen** (☑021-847 2100; www.vergelegen.co.za; Lourensford Rd, Somerset West; entrance adult/child R10/5, tastings from R30; ⊗9.30am-4.30pm, garden tour 10am, cellar tour 11.30 am & 3pm; ⓟ♿), where vines were first planted in 1700.

Western Cape

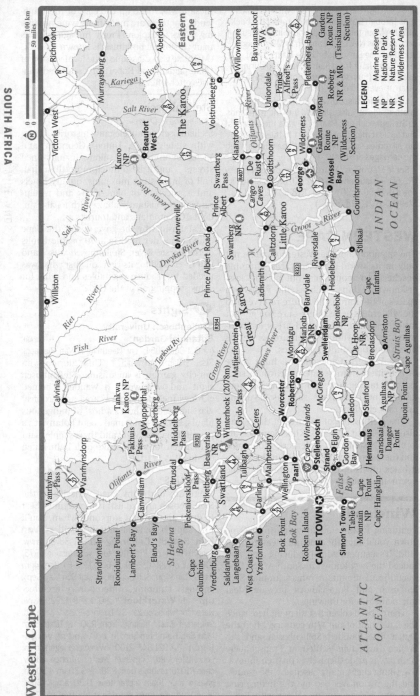

LEGEND

MR   Marine Reserve
NP   National Park
NR   Nature Reserve
NR & MR
WA   Wilderness Area

Fantastic reds are produced at **Hartenberg Estate** (☎021-865 2541; www.hartenbergestate. com; Bottelary Rd; tastings R25; ⊙9am-5pm Mon-Fri, 9am-4pm Sat & 10am-4pm Sun Oct-Apr, closed Sun May-Sep; ⊕) and **Warwick Estate** (☎021-884 4410; www.warwickwine.com; tastings R50, wine safari R80; ⊙9am-5pm; P⊕). For wine lovers without wheels, **Bergkelder** (☎021-809 8025; www.bergkelder.co.za; George Blake St; tour & tasting R60; ⊙9am-5pm Mon-Fri, 9am-2pm Sat; P) is a short walk from town.

★**Villiera**   WINERY
(☎021-865 2002; www.villiera.com; ⊙9am-5pm Mon-Fri, 9am-3pm Sat) FREE Villiera produces several excellent Méthode Cap Classique wines and a highly rated and very well-priced shiraz. Excellent two-hour wildlife drives (adult/child R150/75) with knowledgeable guides take in the various antelopes, zebras, giraffes and bird species on the farm.

Spier   WINERY
(☎021-809 1100; www.spier.co.za; Rte 310; tastings from R40; ⊙9am-5pm Mon-Wed, to 6pm Thu-Sat, 11am-6pm Sun; P⊕) Spier has some excellent shiraz, cabernet and red blends, though a visit to this vast winery is less about wine and more about the other activities available. There are superb bird-of-prey displays, Segway tours through the vines, three restaurants, and picnics to enjoy in the grounds. Look out for special events, particularly the Spier Winelands Express, a train trip running from Cape Town in the summer months.

Vergenoegd   WINERY
(☎021-843 3248; http://vergenoegd.co.za; Baden Powell Dr; tastings from R35; ⊙9am-5pm Mon-Sat, 10am-4pm Sun; ⊕) Vergenoegd has become a real destination winery. Other than tastings, there's lots of kid-friendly fun, a chance to meet the workforce of ducks that help keep the vineyards pest-free and all kind of hands-on activities (you can blend your own tea, coffee, wine and olive oil). Picnics (adult/child R450/125) can be nibbled on the lawns or in the old barn.

Delaire Graff Estate   WINERY
(☎021-885 8160; www.delaire.co.za; Helshoogte Pass; tastings 3/5 wines R50/70; ⊙tastings 10am-5pm; P) The views are stunning from this 'vineyard in the sky', which has a gorgeous hotel and spa and two gourmet restaurants. Its wines also gets top marks from the critics.

👉 **Tours**

Joining a tour is probably the best way to see the wineries, not least because it means you don't have to worry about driving back to your digs. There are various options, from basic hop-on, hop-off transport to bespoke trips including a gourmet lunch.

★**Bikes 'n Wines**   TOURS
(☎021-823 8790; www.bikesnwines.com; tours from R595) 🌿 This carbon-negative company comes highly recommended. Cycling routes range from 9km to 21km and take in three or four Stellenbosch wineries. There are also Cape Town city tours and trips to lesser-visited wine regions such as Elgin, Wellington and Hermanus.

Vine Hopper   TOURS
(☎021-882 8112; www.vinehopper.co.za; cnr Dorp & Market Sts; 1-/2-day pass R300/540) A hop-on/hop-off bus with three routes each covering five or six estates. There are seven departures per day, departing from Stellenbosch Tourism (p359), where you can buy tickets.

Guided Walk   WALKING
(☎081 813 5533; ⊙10am & 1pm) FREE If you've had all the wine you can take, Stellenbosch's many historical buildings are worth a visit. Free guided walks leave from St Mary's Church on the Braak. Tips are greatly welcomed. Private tours are also available (R100 per person).

Easy Rider Wine Tours   TOURS
(☎021-886 4651; www.winetour.co.za; 12 Market St) This long-established company operates from the Stumble Inn and offers good value for a full-day trip at R600 including lunch and all tastings.

🛏 **Sleeping**

Contact Stellenbosch Tourism (p359) for sleeping options if your initial choices are booked up.

★**Banghoek Place**   HOSTEL $
(☎021-887 0048; www.banghoek.co.za; 193 Banghoek Rd; dm/r R180/600; P🐾🛜🏊) This stylish suburban hostel provides a quiet budget alternative, away from the centre. The recreation area has satellite TV and a pool table and there's a nice swimming pool in the garden.

Ikhaya Backpackers   HOSTEL $
(☎021-883 8550; www.stellenboschbackpackers. co.za; 56 Bird St; dm R150, d with shared bathroom R420; 🛜) The superb, central location means you're within easy stumbling distance of the bars. Rooms are in converted apartments, so each dorm comes with its own kitchen and bathroom, shared with the adjoining double rooms.

Stellenbosch

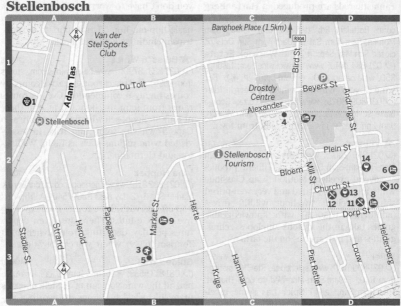

Stumble Inn
HOSTEL $

(☎021-887 4049; www.stumbleinnbackpackers.
co.za; 12 Market St; camping R65, dm R145, d with
shared bathroom R420; P🛜🛜🏊) Stellenbosch's
party hostel is split over two houses – the
second building is quieter, away from the bar.
Travellers have expressed concerns about security so take extra care with your belongings.

Stellenbosch Hotel
HISTORIC HOTEL $$$

(☎021-887 3644; www.stellenboschhotel.co.za;
162 Dorp St, cnr Andringa St; s/d incl breakfast from
R1190/1490; ❄🛜) A comfortable country-style
hotel with a variety of rooms, including some
with self-catering facilities and others with
four-poster beds. A section dating from 1743
houses the Stellenbosch Kitchen, a good spot
for a drink and a spot of people-watching.

D'Ouwe Werf
HISTORIC HOTEL $$$

(☎021-887 4608; www.oudewerfhotel.co.za; 30
Church St; s/d incl breakfast from R2400/2500;
❄🛜🏊) This appealing, old-style hotel dates
back to 1802, though it recently had a dramatic facelift. Deluxe rooms are furnished with
antiques and brass beds, while the superior
and luxury rooms are bright and modern.

🍴 Eating

⭐Schoon de Companje
DELI $

(www.decompanje.co.za; 7 Church St; mains R55-
100; ⊙7am-6pm Tue-Fri, 8am-6pm Sat, 8am-

1.30pm Sun; 🛜) A vibrant bakery and deli
priding itself on locally sourced ingredients.
The menu features salads, sandwiches and
mezze-style platters, as well as fresh cakes
and pastries and local craft beer. There are
tables on the pavement, while inside has a
market-hall feel, with plenty of seating and
some shops to browse.

Root 44 Market
MARKET $

(www.root44.co.za; Rte 44, Audacia Winery; dishes
R40-80; ⊙10am-4pm Sat & Sun; 🚸) A large indoor–outdoor market with plenty of crafts
and clothing as well as wine by the glass,
draught craft beer and a host of food stalls
serving everything from pad Thai to burgers
to giant slabs of cake.

⭐Rust en Vrede
FUSION $$$

(☎021-881 3757; www.rustenvrede.com; Annandale
Rd; 4-course menu R720, 6-course menu with/with-
out wines R1450/850; ⊙noon-3pm Mon-Sat, 6.30-
11pm Tue-Sat) Chef John Shuttleworth presides
over this stylish winery restaurant. Expect
innovative dishes like rabbit-leg wontons or
artichoke-and-vanilla mousse. Book ahead.

Jardine
FUSION $$$

(☎021-886-5020; http://restaurantjardine.co.za;
1 Andringa St; lunch R165, 3-/6-course dinner
R320/420; ⊙noon-2pm & 6.30-8pm Wed-Sat) Celebrated chef George Jardine of the long-established Jordan Restaurant opened this small

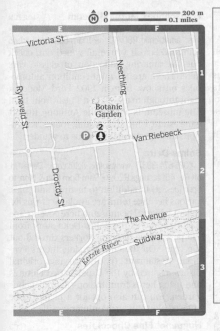

Stellenbosch

⊙ Sights
1 Bergkelder A1
2 Stellenbosch University Botanical
   Garden E2

⊙ Activities, Courses & Tours
3 Adventure Shop B3
   Easy Rider Wine Tours .... (see 9)
4 Guided Walk C2
5 Vine Hopper B3

⊙ Sleeping
6 D'Ouwe Werf D2
7 Ikhaya Backpackers D2
8 Stellenbosch Hotel D2
9 Stumble Inn B3

⊗ Eating
10 Helena's D2
11 Jardine D2
12 Schoon de Companje D2

⊙ Drinking & Nightlife
13 Brampton Wine Studio D2
14 Craft Wheat & Hops D2

and very special spot in 2016 The emphasis is on local produce showcased in simple but extraordinarily good dishes. Book ahead.

Helena's SOUTH AFRICAN $$$
(☏ 021-883 3132; www.helenasrestaurant.co.za; 33 Church St, Coopmanhuijs Boutique Hotel; lunch R80 220, dinner R135-265; ⊙ 12.30pm-2.30pm & 7pm-10pm Mon-Sat, lunch only Sun) A cosy, charming restaurant within a boutique hotel. The menu is small but features some traditional dishes and lots of locally sourced goodies – the mushroom risotto is superb. Bookings essential.

🍷 Drinking & Nightlife

★ Brampton Wine Studio WINE BAR
(☏ 021-883 9097; www.brampton.co.za; 11 Church St; ⊙ 10am-9pm) Play games and scribble on tables while sipping shiraz at this trendy pavement cafe that also serves as Brampton winery's tasting room. Sandwiches and wraps (R50 to R130) are served throughout the day.

Craft Wheat & Hops CRAFT BEER
(☏ 021-882 8069; http://craftstellenbosch.co.za; Andringa St; ⊙ 11am-9.30pm Mon-Sat) This place has 15 local microbrewery beers on tap and another dozen in bottles. There's a decent wine list and a great selection of spirits. Open sandwiches (R50 to R70) are served and there's a nice tapas menu available after 4pm.

ⓘ Information

Stellenbosch Tourism (☏ 021-883 3584; www.stellenbosch.travel; 36 Market St; ⊙ 8am-5pm Mon-Fri, 9am-2pm Sat & Sun; ☏) The staff are extremely helpful. Pick up the excellent brochure Historical Stellenbosch on Foot (R5), with a walking-tour map and information on many of the historic buildings (also available in French and German).

ⓘ Getting There & Away

Long-distance bus services charge high prices for the short sector to Cape Town and do not take bookings.

Shared taxis to Paarl leave from the stand on Bird St (about R50, 45 minutes).

Metro trains run the 46km between Cape Town and Stellenbosch (1st/economy class R22.50/12, about one hour). For inquiries, call Metro Rail (p354). To be safe, travel in the middle of the day. If coming from Jo'burg, change to a metro train at Wellington.

ⓘ Getting Around

Stellenbosch is navigable on foot and, being largely flat, is good cycling territory. Bikes can be hired from the **Adventure Shop** (☏ 021-882 8112; www.adventureshop.co.za; cnr Dorp & Mark Sts; per hour/day R80/250), next to Stellenbosch Tourism.

Franschhoek

POP 17,500 / ☎ 021

French Huguenots settled in this spectacular valley over 300 years ago, bringing their vines with them. Ever since, the town has clung to its French roots, and July visitors will find that Bastille Day is celebrated here. Franschhoek bills itself as the country's gastronomic capital, and you'll certainly have a tough time deciding where to eat. Plus, with a clutch of art galleries, wine farms and stylish guesthouses thrown in, it really is one of the loveliest towns in the Cape.

◉ Sights

★La Motte
WINERY

(☎ 021-876 8000; www.la-motte.com; Main Rd; tastings R50; ◷ 9am-5pm Mon-Sat) There's enough to keep you occupied for a full day at this vast estate just west of Franschhoek. As well as tastings on offer of the superb shiraz range, wine-pairing lunches and dinners are served at the **Pierneef à la Motte** (☎ 021-876 8800; www.la-motte.com; Main Rd; mains R160-210; ◷ Tue & Wed noon-3pm, Thu-Sun noon-3pm & 7-10pm) restaurant. The restaurant is named for South African artist Jacob Hendrik Pierneef and a collection of his work is on show at the on-site museum.

★Boschendal
WINERY

(☎ 021-870 4210; www.boschendal.com; Rte 310, Groot Drakenstein; tastings R75, cellar tours R50, vineyard tours R80; ◷ 9am-5.30pm, cellar tours 10.30am, noon, 1.30pm & 3pm, vineyard tours 11.30am) This is a quintessential Winelands estate, with lovely architecture, food and wine. There are excellent vineyard and cellar tours; booking is essential. Boschendal has three eating options: the huge buffet lunch (adult/child R295/145) in the 1795 homestead, bistro lunches featuring produce grown on the farm at The Werf (mains R200) or a picnic hamper (basket for two R440; bookings essential), served under parasols on the lawn from September to May.

Grande Provence
WINERY

(www.grandeprovence.co.za; Main Rd; tastings from R40, cellar tours R30; ◷ 10am-7pm, cellar tours 11am & 3pm Mon-Fri) A beautifully revamped, 18th-century manor house that is home to a stylish restaurant and a splendid gallery showcasing contemporary South African art. There is a range of tasting options, including grape-juice tasting for the kids (R20) plus the chance to blend your own wine. It's within walking distance of the town centre.

Franschhoek Motor Museum
MUSEUM

(☎ 021-874 9002; www.fmm.co.za; Rte 45, L'Ormarins; adult/child R80/40; ◷ 10am-5pm Mon-Fri, to 4pm Sat & Sun) If you're all wined out, check out the amazing collection of classic cars here. There are 80 mint-condition automobiles on show, from a 1902 Ford Model A right through to a McLaren F1 car from 1991. The museum is part of the Anthonij Rupert wine estate, which has tasting rooms, restaurants and spectacular grounds to wander.

Solms-Delta
WINERY

(☎ 021-874 3937; www.solms-delta.com; Delta Rd, off Rte 45; tastings R20; ◷ 9am-5pm Sun & Mon, to 6pm Tue-Sat) In addition to tastings and sales, various heritage tours are available at this excellent winery. The museum here covers Cape history and tells the Solms-Delta story from the perspective of farm workers throughout the years. On the culinary side, there's Fyndraai Restaurant (p361), serving original dishes inspired by the Cape's varied cultures and using herbs from the on-site indigenous garden. You can also opt for a picnic, to be enjoyed along an enchanting riverside trail.

Huguenot Fine Chocolates
FOOD

(☎ 021-876 4096; www.huguenotchocolates.com; 62 Huguenot St; ◷ 8am-5.30pm Mon-Fri, from 9am Sat & Sun) An empowerment program gave the two local guys who run this chocolatier a leg up and now people are raving about their confections. There are daily chocolate-making demonstrations including a tasting (R50) at 11am and 3pm – advance bookings recommended.

Huguenot Memorial Museum
MUSEUM

(☎ 021-876 2532; www.museum.co.za; Lambrecht St; adult/child R10/2; ◷ 9am-5pm Mon-Sat, 2-5pm Sun) This museum celebrates South Africa's Huguenots and houses the genealogical records of their descendants. Behind the main complex is a pleasant cafe, in front is the **Huguenot Monument** (◷ 9am-5pm) FREE, opened in 1948, and across the road is the **annexe** (www.museum.co.za; adult/child R10/2; ◷ 9am-5pm Mon-Sat, 2-5pm Sun) (admission included), which offers displays on the Anglo-Boer War and natural history.

☞ Tours

Franschhoek Wine Tram
TOURS

(☎ 021-300 0338; www.winetram.co.za; 32 Huguenot Rd; adult/child R220/90) This is a fun alternative to the usual Winelands tour. The tram line is short and only two wineries have a stop. The rest of the hop-on, hop-off service makes use of an open-sided bus.

There are four routes, each visiting up to nine wineries. Bookings are advisable and dress warmly – the bus in particular can get pretty chilly.

Paradise Stables   HORSE RIDING
(☑ 021-876 2160; www.paradisestables.co.za; per hr R250; ⊙ Mon-Sat) As well as hour-long rides through Franschhoek's surrounds, there are four-hour trips taking in two vineyards (R850 including tastings).

📖 Sleeping

Otter's Bend Lodge   HOSTEL $
(☑021-876 3200; www.ottersbendlodge.co.za; Dassenberg Rd; camping per site R200, drn/d R175/550; 🐾) A delightful budget option in a town not known for affordable accommodation. Basic doubles lead to a shared deck shaded by poplar trees, and there's space for a couple of tents on the lawn. There are also two four-sleeper cabins (R850) with kitchenette, one of which is wheelchair-friendly. It's a 15-minute walk from town and close to a winery.

⭐ Reeden Lodge   CHALET $$
(☑021-876 3174; www.reedenlodge.co.za; Anne Marie St; cottage from R1200; 🕹🐾) A good-value, terrific option for families, with well-equipped, self-catering cottages sleeping from two to 10 people, situated on a farm about 10 minutes' walk from town. Parents will love the peace and quiet and their kids will love the sheep, tree house and open space.

Le Ballon Rouge   GUESTHOUSE $$
(☑ 021-876 2651; www.ballonrouge.co.za; 7 Reservoir East St; s/d incl breakfast from R1000/1200; 🟦🕹🐾) A small guesthouse with good-quality rooms and stylish suites with stunning bathrooms.

Le Quartier Français   BOUTIQUE HOTEL $$$
(☑ 021-876 2151; www.lqf.co.za; Wilhelmina St, cnr Berg St; r incl breakfast from R5300; 🟦🕹🐾) Set around a leafy courtyard and pool, the guest rooms at this fabulous hotel are very large with fireplaces, huge beds and stylish decor. If you're feeling flush, try the Four Quarters suites (from R9800) which come with private pools and a butler service.

Akademie Street   BOUTIQUE HOTEL
(☑ 082 517 0405; www.aka.co.za; 5 Akademie St; r incl breakfast from R6000; 🅿🕹🐾) If there's anywhere in South Africa that you're going to blow the budget, Franschhoek might as well be it. The opulent rooms at this quiet hotel are a fine place to splurge. Part of the guesthouse dates back to 1860 and rooms honour

the building's history with heavy four-poster beds and occasional antiques, though there is a distinctly modern flair.

🍴 Eating

Franschhoek Market   MARKET $
(☑ 082 786 7927; 29 Huguenot Rd; mains R30-70; ⊙ 9am-2pm Sat) Based in the grounds of the church, this market has a real country fete vibe. Shop for crafts and lunch on a range of light dishes, or buy a bag of goodies to take on a picnic.

Lust Bistro & Bakery   BISTRO $$
(☑ 021-874 1456; www.lustbistro.com; Rte 45, cnr Simondium Rd; mains R80-150; ⊙ 7.30am-5pm Mon-Sat, 8am-4pm Sun) At Vrede en Lust winery, this is a refreshingly unfussy place to eat in a region known for haute cuisine. The focus is on sandwiches and pizzas, with all bread freshly baked. Try the sourdough pizza base. Daily blackboard specials include some Asian-inspired eats and on Sunday there's a buffet lunch where you pay by the weight of your plate – bookings essential.

Fyndraai Restaurant   SOUTH AFRICAN $$
(☑021-874 3937; www.solms-delta.com; Delta Rd, off R45; mains R85-165; ⊙9am-5pm; 🕹) Original dishes inspired by the Cape's varied cultures and using herbs from the on-site indigenous garden. A handy glossary on the menu helps you to learn some traditional foodstuffs.

⭐ Le Quartier Français:
Tasting Room   FUSION $$$
(☑ 021-876 2151; www.lqf.co.za; 16 Huguenot St; 8-course menu with/without wine R1495/975; ⊙ 7-11pm Tue-Sat) Tasting Room is consistently rated as one of South Africa's top restaurants, and with good reason. Chef Margot Janse whips up a surprise eight-course menu. Bookings essential.

Foliage   FUSION $$$
(☑ 021-876 2328; http://foliage.co.za; 11 Huguenot St; mains R130-240; ⊙noon-3pm & 7-9pm Mon-Sat) Chef and owner Chris Erasmus has brought the foraging culture to the Cape at this hugely popular restaurant. Forest-floor ingredients such as river cress, dandelion and forest mushrooms compliment decadent dishes such as crayfish-butter curry and braised kudu shank. The restaurant is decked out with creations from Chris' artist wife, Alisha. Book ahead.

Ryan's Kitchen   FUSION $$$
(☑ 021-876 4598; www.ryanskitchen.co.za; Huguenot Rd, Place Vendome; mains R165-240, 4-course

menu with/without wine R720/520; ⊙12.30-2.30pm & 6.30-9.30pm Mon-Sat) Loved by locals and recommended by travellers, this long-running restaurant marries South African ingredients with fine-dining techniques. Watch chefs prepare intricate dishes such as Madagascan sea bass with seaweed-soya broth in the open kitchen. The menu changes every two weeks.

ℹ Information

Franschhoek Wine Valley Tourism (☏ 021-876 2861; www.franschhoek.org.za; 62 Huguenot St; ⊙ 8am-5pm Mon-Fri, 9am-5pm Sat, 9am-4pm Sun) Staff can provide you with a map of the area's scenic walks (R15) and issue permits (R40) for hikes in the Mont Rochelle Nature Reserve, as well as book accommodation.

ℹ Getting There & Away

Franschhoek is 32km east of Stellenbosch and 32km south of Paarl. The best way to reach Franschhoek is in your own vehicle. Some visitors choose to cycle from Stellenbosch, but roads are winding and can be treacherous. Alternatively, take a shared taxi from Stellenbosch (R25) or Paarl station (R28).

Paarl

POP 112,000 / ☏ 021

Surrounded by mountains and vineyards, and set on the banks of the Berg River, Paarl is the Winelands' largest town. It's often overlooked by people heading for Stellenbosch and Franschhoek, but it does have its own charm, including interesting Cape Dutch architecture and gracious homesteads, a good range of places to stay and some decent restaurants. The main road is over 11km long, so not exactly walkable, but there are a couple of wineries within an easy stroll of the train station.

⊙ Sights

Drakenstein Prison   HISTORIC SITE
On 11 February 1990, when Nelson Mandela walked free from incarceration for the first time in over 27 years, the jail he left was not on Robben Island, but here. Then called the Victor Verster, this was where Mandela spent his last two years of captivity in the warders' cottage, negotiating the end of apartheid. It's still a working prison, so there are no tours, but there's a superb statue of Mandela, fist raised in *viva* position.

Afrikaans Language Museum   MUSEUM
(☏ 021-863 4809; www.taalmuseum.co.za; 11 Pastorie Ave; adult/child R20/5; ⊙ 8.30am-4.30pm Mon-Fri) Paarl is considered the wellspring of the Afrikaans language, a fact covered by this interesting museum. It also shows, thanks to a multimedia exhibition, how three continents contributed to the formation of the language.

There's a discount if you buy a combo ticket for the **Taal Monument** (☏ 021-863 0543; www.taalmuseum.co.za; adult/child R25/5; ⊙ 8am-5pm Apr-Nov, 8am-8pm Dec-Mar) as well.

🏃 Activities

Bainskloof Pass   SCENIC DRIVE
Bainskloof is one of the country's great mountain passes, with a superb caravan park halfway along. It's a magical drive, which, if you have the lungs for it, would be even better experienced on a bicycle. Rte 303 runs from Wellington across Bainskloof to meet Rte 43, which runs south to Worcester and north to Ceres.

🛏 Sleeping

Berg River Resort   CAMPGROUND $
(☏ 021-001 8805; www.bergriverresort.co.za; camping per site from R430, chalets from R860; 🏊) An attractive camping ground with simple chalets (sleeping two) beside the Berg River, 5km from Paarl on Rte 45 towards Franschhoek. Facilities include canoes, trampolines and a cafe. It gets very crowded during school holidays and prices rise dramatically.

Cape Valley Manor   GUESTHOUSE $$
(☏ 021-872 4545; www.capevalleymanor.co.za; Plein St; s/d incl breakfast from R850/990; P 🛜 🏊) In a peaceful side street not far from Main St, Cape Valley has four individually decorated rooms and a delightful garden – a great spot to open that bottle of wine you bought while touring the vineyards.

Under Oaks   GUESTHOUSE $$
(☏ 021-869 8535; http://underoaks.co.za; Noord Agter Paarl Rd, Northern Paarl; s/d R960/1350; P @ 🛜) On a peaceful wine farm just 3km north of central Paarl, Under Oaks has spacious rooms decked out in muted shades. There's wine tasting on the premises as well as a rustic pizzeria and some magnificent mountain vistas.

Grande Roche Hotel   LUXURY HOTEL $$$
(☏ 021-863 5100; www.granderoche.com; Plantasie St; ste from R3850; P ❄ 🛜 🏊) A superluxurious hotel set in a Cape Dutch manor house, offering wonderful mountain views, a heated swimming pool and the award-winning Bosman's Restaurant (p363). It's a short walk to Paarl's main road.

✕ Eating

★ Tea Under the Trees
BISTRO $

(☑ 072 871 9103; www.teaunderthetrees.co.za; Main Rd, Northern Paarl; mains R40-55; ☺ 9am-4pm Mon-Fri Oct-Apr) The only downside to this fabulous tea garden is that it's only open for half the year. Based on an organic fruit farm, it's a wonderful place to sit under century-old oak trees and enjoy an al fresco cuppa, a light lunch or a large slice of home-baked cake. There's no indoor seating. Saturdays tend to get booked well in advance.

Glen Carlou
INTERNATIONAL $$

(☑ 021-875 5528; www.glencarlou.co.za; mains R95-170; ☺ 11am-3pm) The food at this stylish winery is on a par with the views: magnificent. Dishes, such as spiced duck-leg confit, parmesan mousse and lamb shoulder with sweetbreads, come with a recommended wine pairing. There are also some adventurous dishes like pork-head terrine with crispy pig's ears. Book ahead on weekends.

★ Bosman's Restaurant
INTERNATIONAL $$$

(☑ 021-863 5100; www.granderoche.com; Plantasie St; 3-courses R525; ☺ lunch & dinner) This elegant spot within the Grande Roche Hotel is one of the country's top restaurants, serving multicourse gourmet dinners and more casual bistro-style lunches (mains from R190). Bookings highly recommended.

Noop
FUSION $$$

(☑ 021-863 3925; www.noop.co.za; 127 Main St; mains R120-225; ☺ 11am-11pm Mon-Sat) Recommended by locals all over the Winelands, this restaurant and wine bar has a comprehensive menu of upmarket dishes like herb-crusted lamb rump, roast duck and wild-mushroom risotto. Check out the South African dessert platter, featuring Malva pudding, Amarula Anglaise and milk-tart ice cream.

❶ Information

Paarl Tourism (☑ 021-872 4842; www.paarlonline.com; 216 Main St; ☺ 8.30am-5pm Mon-Fri, 10am-1pm Sat & Sun) This office has an excellent supply of information on the whole region.

❶ Getting There & Away

BUS
All the major long-distance bus companies offer services going through Paarl. The bus segment between Paarl and Cape Town is disproportionately expensive, so consider taking the cheaper train to Paarl and then linking with the buses. The long-distance bus stop is opposite the Shell petrol station on Main St as you enter town from the N1.

TRAIN
Metro trains run roughly every hour between Cape Town and Paarl (1st/economy class R22.50/17, 1¼ hours). Services are less frequent on weekends. Take care to travel on trains during the busy part of the day for safety reasons.

You can travel by train from Paarl to Stellenbosch; take a Cape Town–bound train and change at Muldersvlei. If coming from Jo'burg, change to a metro train at Worcester.

❶ Getting Around
If you don't have your own transport, your only option for getting around Paarl, apart from walking and cycling, is to call a taxi; try **Paarl Taxis** (☑ 021-872 5671; www.paarltaxisandtours.co.za).

WINE TASTING IN PAARL

Paarl has dozens of wineries worth a visit. Here are a few of our favourites.

Spice Route (☑ 021-863 5200; www.spiceroute.co.za; Suid-Agter-Paarl Rd; tastings from R40; ☺ 9am-5pm; 🍴) Known for its complex red wines, particularly the flagship syrah.

Babylonstoren (☑ 021-863 3852; www.babylonstoren.com; Simondium Rd, Klapmuts; R10; ☺ 10am-5pm) The highlight is the formally designed garden; reserve a place on a 10am tour.

Fairview (☑ 021-863 2450; www.fairview.co.za; Suid-Agter-Paarl Rd; wine & cheese tastings R40; ☺ 9am-5pm) Great-value tastings and a good restaurant.

Backsberg (☑ 021-875 5141; www.backsberg.co.za; tastings from R20; ☺ 8.30am-5pm Mon-Fri, 9.30am-4.30pm Sat, 10.30am-4.30pm Sun; 🍴) 🍷 Famous for its lavish outdoor lunches; book ahead for the Sunday lamb spit braai.

Nederburg Wines (☑ 021-862 3104; www.nederburg.co.za; tastings from R40, cellar tours R50; ☺ 9am-5pm Mon-Fri, 10am-4pm Sat & Sun, tours 10.30am & 3pm Mon-Fri, 11am Sat & Sun) A big, professional label with a vast range.

KWV Emporium (☑ 021-863 3803; www.kwvwineemporium.co.za; Kohler St; tastings R60, cellar tours R50; ☺ 9am-4.30pm Mon-Sat, 11am-4pm Sun, cellar tours 10am, 10.30am & 2.15pm) Award-winning wines and cellar tours just a short walk from the train station.

The Overberg

Literally meaning 'over the mountain', Over-berg refers to the region east of the Hotten-tots Holland range, where rolling wheat fields are bordered by the Breede River, the coast and the peaks of three mountain ranges.

There are no unattractive routes leading to the Overberg; the N2 snakes up Sir Low-ry's Pass, which has magnificent views from the top, while Rte 44 stays at sea level and winds its way round Cape Hangklip, skirt-ing the Kogelberg Biosphere Reserve. It's a breathtaking coastal drive, on a par with Chapman's Peak Dr in Cape Town, but with-out the toll.

Hermanus is a major draw for whales in the calving season (June to December) and for people wanting to watch them from eas-ily accessed points throughout the town. If you're keen to escape the throngs that gather here, head for less crowded whale-watching spots in Gansbaai, Arniston and the magical De Hoop Nature Reserve.

Hermanus

POP 10,500 / ☑ 028

What might have once been a small fishing village is today a large, bustling town with an excellent range of accommodation, res-taurants and shops. Only 122km from Cape Town, Hermanus is perfect for a day trip as well as being extremely popular with South African holidaymakers. The growth surge in recent years is mainly due to the presence in Walker Bay, from June to December, of large numbers of southern right whales. Hermanus is generally considered the best land-based destination in the world from which to watch whales.

The town stretches over a long main road but the centre is easily navigable on foot. There's a superb cliff-path walk and plenty of other hikes in the hills around the town, as well as good wine tasting, and the Her-manus Whale Festival (p364) in September. The town gets very crowded at this time and during the December and January school holidays.

◉ Sights

Fernkloof Nature Reserve NATURE RESERVE
(☑028-313 0819; www.fernkloof.com; Fir Ave; ◎9am-5pm) FREE This 15-sq-km reserve is wonderful if you're interested in *fyn-bos* (fine bush). There's a 60km network of hiking trails for all fitness levels, and views over the sea are spectacular. A hiking map is available from the tourist information office. Guided tours are available – book ahead.

Old Harbour HISTORIC SITE
This harbour clings to the cliffs in front of the town centre. The **Old Harbour Museum** (adult/child R20/5; ◎9am-1pm & 2-5pm Mon-Sat, noon-4pm Sun) doesn't really have a lot going for it, but outside there's a display of old fishing boats and the admission fee includes entrance to the more interesting Whale House Museum (p364) and **Photographic Museum** (Market Sq; adult/child R20/5; ◎9am-4.30pm Mon-Sat, noon-4pm Sun). There's a per-manent craft market in the square as well.

Whale House Museum MUSEUM
(Market Sq; adults/child R20/5; ◎9am-4.30pm Mon-Sat, 12pm-4pm Sun) There's lots of info on whales, including daily audio-visual shows. Admission fee included in ticket for Old Har-bour Museum and Photographic Museum.

🏃 Activities

★**Cliff Path Walking Trail** HIKING
FREE This scenic path meanders for 10km from New Harbour, 2km west of town, along the sea to the mouth of the Klein River; you can join it anywhere along the cliffs. It's simply the finest thing to do in Hermanus, whales or not.

🎊 Festivals & Events

Hermanus Whale Festival CULTURAL
(www.whalefestival.co.za; ◎Sep) Held in the middle of whale season, this festival features everything from live music and kids' enter-tainment to car rallies and food markets.

🛏 Sleeping

Hermanus Backpackers HOSTEL $
(☑028-312 4293; www.hermanusbackpackers. co.za; 26 Flower St; dm R160, d R470, with shared bathroom R420; ◎❄☀) This is a great place with upbeat decor, good facilities and clued-up staff who can help with activities. The simple, help-yourself breakfast is free, and evening braais are R120. It's a pretty chilled spot and the annexe around the corner is even quieter.

★**Potting Shed** GUESTHOUSE $$
(☑028-312 1712; www.thepottingshedaccom-modation.co.za; 28 Albertyn St; s/d incl breakfast R920/1150; P❄☀) This friendly guesthouse offers delightful personal touches, including homemade whale-shaped biscuits on arriv-al. The neat rooms are comfortable and have bright, imaginative decor. There's a spacious loft studio and the owners also operate styl-

ish self-catering apartments (four people R1150) closer to the sea.

Marine
LUXURY HOTEL $$$

(☑028-313 1000; www.themarine.co.za; Marine Dr; r incl breakfast from R5300; P❋✿⊠) The town's poshest option is right on the sea with immaculate grounds and amenities, including two sea-facing restaurants. The Pavilion (R170; ☺7-10.30am) is only open for breakfast, while Origins (mains R120-475; ☺noon-2.30pm & 7-9.30pm) boasts gourmet fare with a focus on seafood.

Harbour House Hotel
HOTEL $$$

(☑028-312 1799; www.harbourhousehotel.co.za; 22 Harbour Rd; r incl breakfast from R2600; P❋✿⊠) Some of the bright, modern rooms have kitchenettes and all have a balcony or terrace. It's a delightful seaside hotel and the ocean views from the infinity pool are phenomenal.

✖ Eating

Bistro at Just Pure
CAFE $$

(☑028-313 0060; www.justpurebistro.co.za; Park Ln, cnr Marine Dr; mains R65-115; ☺8.30am-4.30pm Mon-Fri, to 3pm Sat & Sun; ☎) ❁ Adjoining a shop selling natural cosmetics, this seafront bistro is all about fresh, local, organic ingredients. Try the 'famous' cheesecake and watch whales from the patio as you eat.

Burgundy Restaurant
SEAFOOD $$

(☑028-312 2800; www.burgundyrestaurant. co.za; Marine Dr; mains R90-220; ☺8am-9pm) This long-standing restaurant is still going strong, popular with both locals and tourists as much for its superb sea view as for its menu. Seafood is the star, though vegetarians and carnivores are also well served.

★ Pear Tree
FUSION $$$

(☑028 313 1224; http://peartree-hermanus.co.za; 2 Godfrey Cottages, Village Sq; mains R110-180; ☺11am-11pm) One of the town's top restaurants is an intimate venue decorated in bodega style – all bare brick and wine bottles. The small menu features delights like pulled lamb pasta with truffle oil, braised pork belly and naartjie Malva pudding (a traditional sticky sponge pudding with citrus fruit) with pink peppercorns. Book ahead.

ⓘ Information

Although it is not the main tourism office, Hermanus Tourism (☑028-313 1602; www. hermanustourism.info; Market Sq; ☺9am-5pm Mon-Fri, 9am-4pm Sat, 10am-2pm Sun) is in a much more convenient location. Staff are exceptionally helpful.

The larger tourism office (☑028-312 2629; www.hermanustourism.info; Mitchell St, Old Station Bldg; ☺8am-5pm Mon-Fri, 9am-4pm Sat, 10am-2pm Sun) is just north of the town and can help with accommodation bookings.

ⓘ Getting There & Away

Bernardus Tours (☑028-316 1093; www. bernardustransfershermanus.co.za) offers shuttles to Gansbaai (R450, 30 minutes) and Cape Town (R900, 1½ hours).

The hostels run a shuttle service (R75 one-way, 30 minutes) to the Baz Bus (p354) drop-off point in Botrivier, 50km west of town. There are no regular bus services to Hermanus from Cape Town.

De Hoop Nature Reserve

Covering 340 sq km and extending 5km out to sea, this reserve has a magnificent coastline, with long stretches of pristine beach and huge dunes. It's an important breeding and calving area for the southern right whale. You'll find exceptional coastal *fynbos* and animals such as endangered Cape mountain zebras and bonteboks. There is also prolific birdlife, including the Western Cape's only remaining breeding colony of the rare Cape vultures.

🏃 Activities

Whale Trail
HIKING

(☑021-483 0190; www.capenature.co.za; per person R1695) Although there are numerous day walks, an overnight mountain-bike trail and good snorkelling along the coast, the De Hoop Nature Reserve's most interesting feature is the five-day Whale Trail. The 55km hike offers excellent opportunities to see whales between June and December. Accommodation is in modern, fully equipped self-catering cottages.

Birdwatching
BIRDWATCHING

Some 260 bird species have been recorded in the reserve. Head to Potberg to catch a glimpse of the only remaining breeding colony of Cape vultures in the Western Cape.

ⓘ Getting There & Away

The reserve is about 260km from Cape Town, and the final 57km from either Bredasdorp or Swellendam is unsealed. The only access to the reserve is via Wydgeleë on the Bredasdorp-to-Malgas road. Note that if you approach via Malgas, you'll have to take the manually operated pont (river ferry) over the Breede River (between dawn and dusk).

The village of Ouplaas, 15km from the entrance, is the nearest place to buy fuel and supplies.

Swellendam

POP 17,500 / ✏ 028

Surrounded by the undulating wheat lands of the Overberg and protected by the Langeberge mountain range, Swellendam is perfectly positioned for exploring the Little Karoo and makes a good stopover on the way further east to the Garden Route. One of the oldest towns in South Africa (it dates back to 1745), it has beautiful Cape Dutch architecture and a worthwhile museum.

◎ Sights

Marloth Nature Reserve NATURE RESERVE
(✏ 028-514 1410; www.capenature.co.za; adult/child R40/20) Perched in the Langeberge, 1.5km north of town, this reserve is particularly pretty in October and November when the ericas are in flower. If the day hikes don't hit the spot, try the demanding Swellendam Hiking Trail, generally regarded as one of South Africa's top hikes. You can choose to walk any distance from two to six days. There are two basic overnight huts, and you'll need to be self-sufficient. Entrance to the reserve is via Andrew Whyte St.

Drostdy Museum MUSEUM
(✏ 028-514 1138; www.drostdymuseum.com; 18 Swellengrebel St; adult/child R25/5; ◎ 9am-5pm Mon-Fri, 10am-3pm Sat & Sun) The centrepiece of this excellent museum is the beautiful *drostdy* (residence of an official) itself, which dates from 1747. The museum ticket also covers entrance to the nearby **Old Gaol** (◎ 9am-5pm Mon-Fri, 10am-3pm Sat & Sun), where you'll find part of the original administrative buildings and a watermill; and **Mayville** (Hermanus Steyn St; ◎ 9am-5pm Mon-Fri, 10am-3pm Sat & Sun), another residence dating back to 1853, with a formal Victorian garden.

🏃 Activities

Two Feathers Horse Trails HORSE RIDING
(✏ 082-494 8279; 5 Lichtenstein St, Swellendam Backpackers Adventure Lodge; 1½ hour beginner ride R300) There are horse rides in the mountains lasting from an hour to a couple of days. Both inexperienced and experienced riders catered for. Advance booking essential.

🛏 Sleeping

Swellendam Backpackers Adventure Lodge HOSTEL $
(✏ 028-514 2648; www.swellendambackpackers. co.za; 5 Lichtenstein St; s/d R350/550; 🌐) This excellent hostel is set on a huge plot of land bordering the Marloth Nature Reserve.

Horse riding, permits to the reserve and day trips to Cape Agulhas (R750) can all be arranged. The Baz Bus (p354) stops right outside.

★**Cypress Cottage** GUESTHOUSE $$
(✏ 028-514 3296; www.cypress-cottage.co.za; 3 Voortrek St; s/d R500/900; 🅿 ❄ 🌐 🍽) There are six individually decorated rooms in this 200-year-old house with a gorgeous garden and a refreshing pool. It's within walking distance of the church, museum and a handful of restaurants.

Braeside B&B B&B $$
(✏ 028-514 3325; www.braeside.co.za; 13 Van Oudtshoorn Rd; s/d incl breakfast from R800/1200; 🅿 ❄ 🌐 🍽) This quiet, gracious Cape Edwardian home boasts a lovely garden, fantastic views and knowledgeable, gay-friendly hosts.

Bloomestate GUESTHOUSE $$$
(✏ 028-514 2984; www.bloomestate.com; 276 Voortrek St; s/d incl breakfast from R1725/2300; 🅿 ❄ 🌐 🍽) A modern, friendly guesthouse set on a beautiful property, which offers Zen-like privacy to go with the luxurious, colourful rooms. Health and beauty treatments are available and, if relaxing around the pool isn't enough, you can hop in the spa bath that's sitting on a deck under the trees.

🍴 Eating

Old Gaol on Church Square SOUTH AFRICAN $$
(www.oldgaolrestaurant.co.za; 8A Voortrek St; light meals R50-120; ◎ 7.30am-10pm Wed-Fri, 8am-5pm Sat-Tue; 🚗) It might not be in the Old Gaol any more, but the food at this empowerment venture is still just as good. There's lots of seating outside under the trees where you can enjoy delicious cakes, traditional breads and Cape Malay dishes. Service is slow.

★**La Sosta** ITALIAN $$$
(✏ 028-514 1470; www.lasostaswellendam.com; 45 Voortrek St; mains R135-190) Once voted the top Italian restaurant in the country, La Sosta is something special. The beautifully presented food includes treats like butternut-and-truffle ravioli, lamb carpaccio and coconut panna cotta. To taste it all, opt for the set 6-course menu (R420). Bookings advisable.

Field & Fork FUSION $$$
(✏ 028-514 3430; 26 Swellengrebel St; mains R160-195; ◎ 6pm-10pm Mon-Sat) Locals rave about this stylish place based in the Old Gaol building. The small menu features intricate dishes that use local ingredients such as springbok, Karoo lamb and Franschhoek trout. There's also a three-course set menu (R325).

WORTH A TRIP

CAPE AGULHAS

Cape Agulhas is the southernmost tip of Africa, where the Atlantic and Indian Oceans collide. It's a rugged, windswept coastline and the graveyard for many a ship. Most people head straight for a photo with the sign marking where the oceans meet.

If you don't have your own wheels, contact the backpacker hostels in Hermanus or Swellendam to arrange a tour.

Sights

Agulhas National Park (☏ 028-435 6078; www.sanparks.org; adult/child R148/74) Other than the photo opportunities of being at Africa's southernmost point, where the Atlantic and Indian oceans meet, there is a range of hikes from 3km to 10km in length. Recommended is the 5.5km Rasperpunt Trail, which takes in the *Meisho Maru* shipwreck. An information booklet for each hike is available at the park office for R10.

Cape Agulhas Lighthouse (☏ 028-435 6078; adult/child R26/13; ⏲ 9am-5pm) It's worth climbing the 71 steps to the top. There's an interesting museum inside.

Sleeping

Cape Agulhas Backpackers (☏ 082 372 3354; www.capeagulhasbackpackers.com; Duiker St, cnr Main St, Struisbaai; camping R100, dm R150, d R400; P �📶) Along the coast in Struisbaai, this is a good base for exploring the area. It's in a prime kite-surfing spot, and offers lessons as well as surfboard rentals.

National Park Accommodation (☏ central reservations 012-428 9111; www.sanparks.org; cottage/chalet R900/1245) There is charming self-catering accommodation dotted about the national park, some of which has sea views.

Information

Tourism Bureau (☏ 028-435 7185, www.discovercapeagulhas.co.za; Agulhas Lighthouse; ⏲ 9am-5pm) In the Cape Agulhas lighthouse.

ⓘ Information

Swellendam Tourism Bureau (☏ 028-514 2770; www.swellendamtourism.co.za; 22 Swellengrebel St; ⏲ 9am-5pm Mon-Fri, 9am-2pm Sat & Sun) A helpful office based in the Old Gaoler's Cottage. It rents mountain bikes (R150 per day) and staff can advise on biking routes.

ⓘ Getting There & Away

All three major bus companies (Voortrek St) pass through Swellendam on their runs between Cape Town (R300, three hours) and Port Elizabeth (R420, eight hours), stopping opposite the Swellengrebel Hotel on Voortrek St. The Baz Bus (p354) stops at Swellendam Backpackers.

Bontebok National Park

Some 6km south of Swellendam is this **national park** (☏ 028-514 2735; adult/child R100/50; ⏲ 7am-7pm Oct-Apr, 7am-6pm May-Sep), proclaimed in 1931 to save the remaining 30 bontebok. The project was successful, and bontebok as well as other antelope and mountain zebras can be found in this smallest of South Africa's national parks. The *fynbos* that flowers in late winter and spring and an abundance of birdlife are features of the park. You can swim in in the Breede River, but the finest way to experience the park is by walking one of its three-day trails, with no fear of bumping into a predator.

Take the N2 west of Swellendam. The entrance is signposted and is 5km along a gravel road to the south.

🛏 Sleeping

Campsites   CAMPGROUND $
(www.sanparks.org; from R245; P) There are pleasant campsites alongside the Breede River, some with electricity.

Lang Elsie's Kraal   CHALET $$
(www.sanparks.org; chalet from R1285; P) These 10 chalets have decks overlooking the river. Two of the chalets are adapted for people with special needs.

Route 62

Following Rte 62 will take you through some spectacular scenery changes, from the rugged mountain passes between Montagu and

Calitzdorp, to the arid semidesert of the Little Karoo region around Oudtshoorn. It's touted as the longest wine route in the world and is a great alternative to the N2 if you're travelling from Cape Town towards the Garden Route.

Montagu

POP 15,000

Coming into Montagu along Rte 62 from Robertson, the road passes through a narrow arch in the Langeberg mountains, and suddenly the town appears before you. Its wide streets are bordered by 24 restored national monuments, including some fine art deco architecture. There's a wide range of activities, including hot springs, a number of walks and superlative rock climbing, as well as excellent accommodation and some good restaurants.

◎ Sights

Montagu Museum   MUSEUM
(☑023-614 1774; 41 Long St; adult/child R5/2; ◎9am-1pm & 1.30-5pm Mon-Fri, 10.30am-12.30pm Sat & Sun) Interesting displays and some good examples of antique furniture can be found at this museum in the old mission church.

🏃 Activities

Montagu is one of the Western Cape's top spots for rock climbing.

★Montagu Rock Climbing   CLIMBING
(☑082 696 4067; www.montaguclimbing.com; 45 Mount St; 2hr climbing trip R550) Justin Lawson offers gear rental as well as guided climbing and abseiling for beginners.

Avalon Springs   HOT SPRINGS
(☑023-614 1150; www.avalonsprings.co.za; Uitvlucht St; R55; ◎8am-10pm; ⛟) Water from underground mineral springs finds its way into the swimming pools of the Avalon Springs Hotel, just north of town. The water gushes from a rock face underground at 43°C, and is renowned for its healing properties. The pools are commercialised (including waterslides) and can get unpleasantly busy on weekends and in school holidays. Try to visit during off-peak times.

Bloupunt Trail   HIKING
(R43) The Bloupunt Trail is 15.6km long and can be walked in six to eight hours; it traverses ravines and mountain streams, and climbs to 1000m. Starts from the car park at the northern end of Tanner St. You can book the overnight huts (per person R150) near the start of the trail through the tourism bu-

reau; they are basic (wood stoves, showers and toilet facilities) but cheap.

Cogmanskloof Trail   HIKING
(R43) The Cogmanskloof Trail is 12.1km and takes four to six hours; it's fairly strenuous. Starts from the car park at the northern end of Tanner St.

ᐊ Tours

★Protea Farm   ECOTOUR
(☑023-614 3012; www.proteafarm.co.za; adult/child R120/50; ◎tours 10am Wed & Sat) Wonderful three-hour tractor rides explore Protea Farm, 29km from Montagu. There are sweeping views of the Breede River Valley and the trip includes snacks and drinks. There's an option to extend the day with a traditional lunch of *potjiekos* (pot stew) with homemade bread for R120/50 per adult/child. Farm accommodation is available (two-person cottage from R650).

🛏 Sleeping

You can book overnight huts (per person R150) near the start of the Cogmanskloof Trail through the tourism bureau; they are basic (wood stoves, showers and toilet facilities) but cheap.

De Bos   CAMPGROUND $
(☑023-614 2532; www.debos.co.za; Bath St; camping R80, dm/d R125/420; ⛟⛟) A genuine farmstay for backpackers – there's a river, chickens and pecan trees on this 500-sq-m property with basic self-catering cottages (from R480). It's an easy walk into town. Refurbishments to smarten up the cottages were beginning when we visited.

★7 Church Street   GUESTHOUSE $$
(☑023-614 1186; www.7churchstreet.co.za; 7 Church St; s/d incl breakfast from R1300/1500; ⛟⛟⛟⛟) A friendly, upmarket guesthouse in a charming Karoo building. Affable owners Mike and May offer large, well-appointed rooms, manicured gardens in which to relax and a particularly memorable breakfast. They also supply honest tourist info on the region.

Avalon Springs Hotel   HOTEL $$
(☑023-614 1150; www.avalonsprings.co.za; Warmbronne Hot Springs; d from R1100, apt from R1500; ⛟⛟⛟) This colossal place has smart rooms in the main building and enormous apartments (sleeping two) on stilts. Features include the outdoor hot-spring pools, massages, a gym and plenty of kid-friendly activities. There's a shuttle bus into Montagu. Rates are considerably cheaper Sunday to Thursday.

Mimosa Lodge HOTEL $$
(☑023-614 2351; www.mimosa.co.za; Church St; s/d incl breakfast from R860/1260; �☒) A delightful, upmarket lodge in a restored Edwardian landmark building with lovely gardens and a pool with a thatched-roof gazebo for shade. The attached restaurant serves four-course dinners (R380) and is open to nonguests. Wines from the owner's vineyard are served.

✗ Eating

★ **Barn on 62** CAFE $
(☑082 824 2995; 60 Long St; mains R50-80; ☺Tue-Sun 8.30am-4pm; ℗☶) Grab a spot under the trees and enjoy a lunch of home-baked pie and salad or a slice of cake with Montagu's best cup of coffee. There's a kids' play area in the garden. It's at the start of Long St as you arrive from Barrydale and ideal for a lunch stop if you're just passing through.

Rambling Rose FARM STALL $$
(☑083 401 4503; 36 Long St; mains R65-120; ☺8am-5pm Wed-Mon; ℗�) Great for brunch, lunch or cake, this shop-cum-restaurant serves local fodder on its shady patio. The shop sells all manner of local produce. It's an ideal stop if you're just passing through.

Simply Delicious@Four Oaks FUSION $$
(☑023-614 3483; www.four-oaks.co.za; 46 Long St; mains R85-145; ☺6.30-9.30pm Mon-Sun) Set in a lovely old house, the style is minimalist rather than the usual country decor and the food is tasty and unfussy.

ℹ Information

Tourism Bureau (☑023-614 2471; www.montagu-ashton.info; 24 Bath St; ☺8.30am-5.30pm Mon-Fri, 9am-5pm Sat, 9.30am-4pm Sun) An extremely efficient and helpful office. Opening hours are slightly shorter between May and October.

ℹ Getting There & Away

Buses stop at Ashton, 9km from Montagu. Translux (p527) buses stop here on the run between Cape Town (R270, three hours) and Port Elizabeth (R450, eight hours).

Most accommodation establishments in town offer (prebooked) shuttles from Ashton to Montagu, but you can also jump in a shared taxi (R20), which stops at **Foodzone** (Bath St).

Oudtshoorn

POP 29,000 / ☑044

In the late 1860s, no self-respecting society lady in the Western world would be seen dead without an ostrich plume adorning her headgear. The fashion lasted until the slump of 1914 and during this time the 'feather barons' of Oudtshoorn made their fortunes.

You can still see their gracious homes, along with other architectural pointers to Oudtshoorn's former wealth such as the CP Nel Museum (formerly a school). The town remains the 'ostrich capital of the world' and is now the prosperous tourist centre of the Little Karoo. Ostrich leather is much sought after (and expensive), feathers, eggs and biltong are available everywhere, and the meat is always on the menu (a healthy option, flavour-wise akin to beef but low in cholesterol).

Oudtshoorn has much more to offer than ostriches, though. It makes a great base for exploring the Little Karoo, the Garden Route (it's 55km to George along the N12) and the Great Karoo to the north.

◉ Sights

Cango Caves CAVE
(☑044-272 7410; www.cango-caves.co.za; adult/child R100/60; ☺9am-4pm) Named after the Khoe-San word for 'a wet place', the Cango Caves are heavily commercialised but impressive. The one-hour tour gives you just a glimpse, while the 90-minute Adventure Tour (adult/child R150/90) lets you explore deeper into the caves. It does involve crawling through tight and damp places, so is not recommended for the claustrophobic or unfit. Advance booking for both tours is essential. The caves are 30km north of Oudtshoorn.

CP Nel Museum MUSEUM
(www.cpnelmuseum.co.za; 3 Baron van Rheede St; adult/child R25/5; ☺8am-5pm Mon-Fri, 9am-1pm Sat) Extensive displays about ostriches and Karoo history make up this large and interesting museum, housed in a striking sandstone building completed in 1906 at the height of ostrich fever. Included in the ticket price is admission to **Le Roux Townhouse** (High St, cnr Loop St; ☺9am-5pm Mon-Fri), decorated in authentic period furniture and as good an example of a 'feather palace' as you're likely to see.

⭑ Activities

There are four show farms that offer guided tours of 45 minutes to 1½ hours. There's little to choose between them; we found the staff at **Highgate Ostrich Show Farm** (www.highgate.co.za; adult/child R140/90; ☺8am-5pm; ℗) very knowledgeable – it's 10km from Oudtshoorn en route to Mossel Bay. Nearby is **Safari Ostrich Show Farm** (www.

safariostrich.co.za; adult/child R118/59; ☺8am-4pm; ℗). **Cango Ostrich Show Farm** (www.cangoostrich.co.za; Cango Caves Rd; adult/child R90/55; ☺8am-4.30pm) is on the way to the Cango Caves, while **Chandelier Ostrich Show Farm** (www.chandelier.co.za; N12; adult/child R80/50; ☺9am-4pm) is south of Oudtshoorn on the road to George.

★ **Meerkat Adventures**   WILDLIFE WATCHING
(☑084 772 9678; www.meerkatadventures.co.za; per person R550) This unique wildlife encounter sees you sitting around at sunrise, coffee in hand, as meerkats emerge from their burrows to warm up in the morning sun. It's considered a trip highlight by many. Passionate conservationist Devey Glinister operates the experience on De Zeekoe Farm, 9km west of Oudtshoorn. No children under 10 years.

Two Passes Route   SCENIC DRIVE
A wonderful day's excursion is the round-trip from Oudtshoorn to Prince Albert taking in two magnificent passes. Head up the unsealed **Swartberg Pass** and all the way down to Prince Albert, then return via the **Meiringspoort Pass**. Halfway down the latter is a waterfall and small visitor centre. Both passes are engineering masterpieces. Ask at your accommodation or the tourism bureau for a route map.

Backpackers Paradise   MOUNTAIN BIKING
(☑044-272 3436; 148 Baron van Rheede St; tours R450) The backpackers will arrange a ride for you and your bike (bikes provided as part of the package) so you can cycle back down the Swartberg Pass.

🛏 Sleeping

Backpackers Paradise   HOSTEL $
(☑044-272 3436; www.backpackersparadise.net; 148 Baron van Rheede St; camping R100, dm R160, d R500, with shared bathroom R460; ℗ 🛜 🏊) In a large old house, this lively hostel has a bar, ostrich braais and free ostrich-egg breakfasts (in season, you'll be given an egg – cook it any way you please). It also offers discounts to attractions in the area and can set you up with a host of activities.

Karoo Soul Travel Lodge   HOSTEL $
(☑044-272 0330; www.karoosoul.com; 1 Adderley St; dm R150, d with shared bathroom R420; ℗ 🛜 🏊) The gracious old house is more about doubles than dorms, though there is one small dorm. Try to get one of the west-facing doubles for a romantic sundowner from your bed, or ask about the garden cottages with en suite (R550).

★ **La Pension**   GUESTHOUSE $$
(☑044-279 2445; www.lapension.co.za; 169 Church St; s/d incl breakfast R750/1180; ℗ ❄ 🛜 🏊) A reliable choice with spacious, stylish rooms and superb bathrooms, La Pension also has one self-catering cottage, plus a good-size pool and a large, immaculate garden.

Oakdene Guesthouse   GUESTHOUSE $$
(☑044-272 3018; www.oakdene.co.za; 99 Baron van Rheede St; s/d R995/1360; ❄ 🛜 🏊) The new owners have totally refurbished the rooms, which are fitted out with modern decor largely made of recycled wine crates. The rooms perfectly marry the modern with the classic – in keeping with the house's status as one of Oudtshoorn's oldest buildings.

Queen's Hotel   HOTEL $$$
(☑044-272 2101; www.queenshotel.co.za; 5 Baron van Rheede St; s/d R1020/1650; ❄ 🛜 🏊) Bang in the middle of town, this attractive old-style country hotel with spacious, understated rooms is refreshingly cool inside and has an inviting appeal. The attached **Colony Restaurant** (mains R85-160; ☺6-11pm) serves a range of local and international dishes.

🍴 Eating

Café Brulé   CAFE $
(☑044-279 2412; 5 Baron van Rheede St, Queen's Hotel; mains R40-70; ☺7am-5pm; 🛜) A popular cafe, recommended for its freshly baked bread and cakes. There's a 'dish up and weigh' buffet on Wednesday, Thursday and Friday.

Nostalgie   BISTRO $$
(☑044-272 4085; www.nostalgiebnb.co.za; 74 Baron van Rheede St; mains R60-110; ☺7am-10pm) This quaint tea garden, complete with lace tablecloths, is best as a place for breakfast, or coffee with a slice of home-baked cake. That said, there are more than a dozen ostrich dishes on the lunch and dinner menu, including carpaccio, burger, kebabs and pie.

Black Swan   INTERNATIONAL $$
(☑044-272 0982; http://blackswanoudtshoorn.co.za; 109 Baron van Rheede St; mains R90-125; ☺5pm-10pm; 🛜) There are tables outside and in the atmospheric dining room at this large restaurant at the northern end of town. The menu is small but fairly varied and of course includes the requisite ostrich steaks.

★ **Jemima's**   SOUTH AFRICAN $$$
(☑044-272 0808; www.jemimas.com; 94 Baron van Rheede St; mains R120-180; ☺11am-11pm) With a small menu specialising in traditional South African fare, this long-running restaurant is set in an attractive old house and

garden. After your meal try a *swepie,* a mix of brandy and *jerepigo* (a dessert wine).

❶ Information

Oudtshoorn Tourism Bureau (☑044-279 2532; www.oudtshoorn.com; Voortrekker St, cnr Baron van Rheede St; ☺8.30am-5pm Mon-Fri, 9.30am-12.30pm Sat) Behind the CP Nel Museum.

PostNet (Queen's Mall, Voortrekker Rd; R40 per hour; ☺8.30am-5pm Mon-Fri, to 12.30pm Sat) Internet access.

❶ Getting There & Away

Buses stop in the Riverside Centre off Voortrekker St. Intercape (p354) has services to Johannesburg (R750, 14½ hours), Cape Town (R520, eight hours) and Mossel Bay (R390, two hours).

The Baz Bus (p354) stops at George, from where you can arrange a transfer to Oudtshoorn with Backpackers Paradise (R150 one-way).

Shared taxis leave from behind the Spar supermarket on Adderley St en route to George (R60, 30 minutes) or Cape Town (R300, three hours). Bookings are required for the latter – contact the tourism bureau.

Garden Route

High on the must-see lists of most visitors to South Africa is the Garden Route, and with good reason: you can't help but be seduced by the glorious natural beauty. The distance from Mossel Bay in the west to Storms River in the east is just over 200km, yet the range of topography, vegetation, wildlife and outdoor activities is remarkable.

The coast is dotted with excellent beaches, while inland you'll find picturesque lagoons and lakes, rolling hills and eventually the mountains of the Outeniqua and Tsitsikamma ranges that divide the verdant Garden Route from the arid Little Karoo.

Mossel Bay

POP 30,000 / ☑044

At first glance Mossel Bay is the ugly sister of the Garden Route. It was a hugely popular destination until the 1980s, when the building of the world's largest gas-to-oil refinery and concomitant industrial sprawl uglified it, and it fell into a slump. But if you can see beyond the unimpressive approach road, you'll find some fine beaches, gnarly surf spots, a wealth of activities and good places to stay. It has a way to go to catch up with its more glamorous neighbours, but it's trying hard to grab back some of its former glory.

◉ Sights

★Dias Museum Complex   MUSEUM
(☑044-691 1067; www.diasmuseum.co.za; Market St; adult/child R20/5; ☺9am-4.45pm Mon-Fri, 9am-3.45pm Sat & Sun; P⛟) This excellent museum offers insight into Mossel Bay's role as an early stomping ground for European sailors. Named for 15th-century Portuguese explorer Bartholomeu Dias, the museum contains the 'post office tree' where sailors left messages for one another, the 1786 Dutch East India Company (Vereenigde Oost-Indische Compagnie; VOC) granary, a small aquarium and a local history museum. The highlight is the replica of the caravel that Dias used on his 1488 voyage of discovery.

Cape St Blaize Lighthouse   LIGHTHOUSE
(adult/child R20/10; ☺10am-3pm) There are wonderful views from the lighthouse. The St Blaize Cave, dating back to the Stone Age, is rather neglected and frequented by vandals.

☆ Activities

Oystercatcher Trail   HIKING
(☑044-699 1204; www.oystercatchertrail.co.za; per person incl accommodation/with full board R5600/6850) Hikers can tackle this fabulous coastal trail over five days. It follows the coastline from Mossel Bay to Gourits River via Cape St Blaize, where you're likely to see the endangered black oystercatcher bird. You can self-cater or choose the fully catered option.

Waves School of Surfing   SURFING
(☑078 297 3999; www.wavesschoolofsurfing.com; 47 Marsh St; 1½ hour lesson R300) Mossel Bay is one of the Garden Route's top surfing spots; beginners can get started here.

Skydive Mossel Bay   ADVENTURE SPORTS
(☑082 824 8599; www.skydivemosselbay.com; Mossel Bay Airfield; from R2550) Tandem skydives start from 3000m and when the weather and tides cooperate you get to land on Diaz Beach.

White Shark Africa   DIVING
(☑044-691 3796; www.whitesharkafrica.com; 7 Church St; adult/child R1550/850) Full-day cage-diving trips to view great white sharks, including lunch, drinks and snacks.

☞ Tours

Point of Human Origins   CULTURAL
(☑071 690 8889; www.humanorigin.co.za; tours R450) Led by an archaeology professor, this fascinating four-hour tour includes a hike to

Garden Route

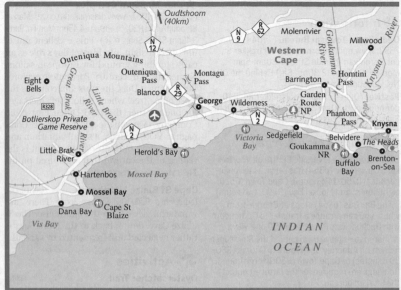

the Pinnacle Point Caves, where discoveries have shed light on human life from 162,000 years ago.

Romonza
BOATING

(☎ 044-690 3101; Mossel Bay Harbour; 1hr boat trips R150) Regular boat trips head out to Seal Island to see the seals, birds and dolphins that frequent these waters. In late winter and spring this outfit also runs whale-watching trips (R680, 2½ hours).

🛏 Sleeping

Bakke Santos Caravan Park
CAMPGROUND, CHALET $

(☎ 044-690 3760; www.debakkesantos.co.za; Santos Beach; camping per site from R225, chalet from R550) One of three caravan parks in Mossel Bay, all of which have ocean views. It also has basic chalets.

Mossel Bay Backpackers
HOSTEL $

(☎ 044-691 3182; www.mosselbaybackpackers. co.za; 1 Marsh St; dm R150, d R500, with shared bathroom R350; 🛜🏊) This well-run and long-established backpackers has swallowed the adjoining guesthouse, meaning there are some excellent en suite rooms on offer alongside dorms and basic doubles. There's even a honeymoon suite, complete with spa bath (R600). Staff can arrange activities.

Park House Lodge & Travel Centre
HOSTEL $

(☎ 044-691 1937; www.park-house.co.za; 121 High St; camping R110, dm R170, s/d R450/600, with shared bathroom R350/460; 🛜) This place, in a gracious old sandstone house next to the park, is friendly, smartly decorated and has beautiful gardens. Breakfast is R60, and staff can organise activities.

★ Point Village Hotel
HOTEL $$

(☎ 044-690 3156; www.pointvillagehotel.co.za; 5 Point Rd; s/d R500/900; 🛜) The quirky, fake lighthouse on this exceptionally well-priced hotel's exterior is a sign of what's inside: a range of fun, funky, bright rooms and friendly service. Rooms have a kitchenette and some have balconies. There are also two- and three-bedroom apartments with good sea views (from R1500).

Eight Bells Mountain Inn
LODGE $$

(☎ 044-631 0000; www.eightbells.co.za; s/d from R660/1155; 🅿🛜🏊) This country inn is 35km north of Mossel Bay on Rte 328 to Oudtshoorn (50km). It's in a lovely mountain setting at the foot of the Robinson Pass and its large grounds have something for everyone from children to squash players. You'll find a variety of rooms; the rondavels (round huts with conical roofs) are fun. Prices rise sharply during school holidays.

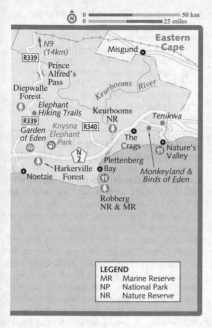

LEGEND

MR	Marine Reserve
NP	National Park
NR	Nature Reserve

Protea Hotel Mossel Bay HOTEL $$$
(044-691 3738; www.oldposttree.co.za; Market St; r from R1700; P❄🛜🏊) Part of the Protea chain, this is a classy hotel set in the old post office building. Its restaurant, **Café Gannet** (www.proteahotels.com/mosselbay; Market St; mains R50-230; 7am-10pm), has a large seafood, meat and pizza menu.

✕ Eating

Carola Ann's CAFE $
(044-690 3477; www.carolaann.com; 12 Church St; mains R50-85; 8am-5pm Mon-Fri, to 2pm Sat) Close to the museum, Carola Ann's serves inventive breakfasts, delicious, healthy lunches and not-so-healthy slabs of cake. Grab a packet of the chocolate-chip cookies for the road. Delicious.

★ Blue Shed Coffee Roastery CAFE
(044-691 0037; www.blueshedroasters.co.za; 33 Bland St; 6.30am-7pm; 🛜) Enjoy great coffee and homemade cakes at this funky cafe with eclectic decor and ocean views from the deck. It's an awesome spot to spend a couple of hours chilling or playing vinyl on the old-school jukebox.

★ Kaai 4 BRAAI $$
(044-691 0056; www.kaai4.co.za; Mossel Bay Harbour; mains R40-100; 10am-10pm) Boasting one of Mossel Bay's best locations, this low-

key restaurant has picnic tables on the sand overlooking the ocean. Most of the dishes – including stews, burgers, boerewors (farmer's sausages) and some seafood – are cooked on massive fire pits and there's local beer on tap.

ⓘ Information

Tourism Bureau (044-691 2202; www. visitmosselbay.co.za; Market St; 8am-6pm Mon-Fri, 9am-4pm Sat & Sun) Staff are very friendly and can help with accommodation bookings. Pick up a brochure detailing a self-guided walking tour of historic Mossel Bay.

ⓘ Getting There & Around

Mossel Bay is off the highway, so the long-distance buses don't come into town; they drop passengers at the Voorbaai Shell petrol station, 8km away. The hostels can usually collect you if you give notice, but private taxis (R80) are often waiting for bus passengers who need onward travel. If none are there call 082 932 5809, or during the day take a shared taxi (R10). The Baz Bus (p354) will drop you in town.

Translux (p527), Greyhound (p524) and Intercape (p354) buses stop here on their Cape Town–Port Elizabeth runs. Intercape fares from Mossel Bay include Knysna (R350, two hours), Plettenberg Bay (R350, 2½ hours), Cape Town (R480, six hours) and Port Elizabeth (R510, 6½ hours).

Pleasure trips run out of the Boat Terminal.

George

POP 114,000

George, founded in 1811, is the largest town on the Garden Route yet remains little more than a commercial centre and transport hub with not much to keep visitors for long. It has some attractive old buildings, including the tiny St Mark's Cathedral and the more imposing Dutch Reformed Mother Church, but it's 8km from the coast and for most of its visitors its chief draw is the range of championship golf courses.

◉ Sights

Outeniqua Transport Museum MUSEUM
(www.outeniquachootjoe.co.za/museum.htm; 2 Mission St; adult/child R20/10; 8am-4.30pm Mon-Fri, 8am-2pm Sat; P) The starting point and terminus for journeys on the Outeniqua Power Van (p374), this museum is worth a visit if you're even remotely interested in trains. A dozen locomotives and 15 carriages, as well as many detailed models, have found a retirement home here, including a carriage used by the British royal family in the 1940s. There's also an impressive collection of classic cars.

☞ Tours

Outeniqua Power Van
TOURS

(☏082 490 5627; adult/child R130/110; ☺Mon-Sat) A trip on this motorised trolley van is one of the best things to do in George. It takes you from the Outeniqua Transport Museum on a 2½-hour trip into the Outeniqua mountains. You can even take a bike and cycle back down the Montagu Pass

🛏 Sleeping & Eating

Outeniqua Travel Lodge
HOSTEL $

(☏082 316 7720; www.outeniqualodge.com; 19 Montagu St; dm/s/d R140/390/530; P🐾😻) It's a way from the centre, but this is a great budget option with en suite rooms in a quiet, residential area. Staff are friendly and can arrange activities.

★French Lodge International
GUESTHOUSE $$

(☏044-874 0345; www.frenchlodge.co.za; 29 York St; s/d incl breakfast from R700/900; P🐾@😻) Rooms are in luxurious thatched-roof rondavels set around the pool, with satellite TV and bathrooms with spa baths.

Fancourt Hotel
LUXURY HOTEL $$$

(☏044-804 0000; www.fancourt.co.za; Montagu St, Blanco; d incl breakfast from R3960; P🐾😻) This is the area's most luxurious option, about 10km from the centre, and has three 18-hole golf courses designed by Gary Player. There's a health spa and four restaurants.

Old Townhouse
STEAK $$

(☏044-874 3663; Market St; mains R75-200; ☺11.30am-5pm & 6-10pm Mon-Fri, 6-10pm Sat) In the one-time town administration building, this long-standing restaurant is known for its excellent steaks and ever-changing game-meat options. The homemade ice cream is a great way to finish off a meal.

ℹ Information

George Tourism (☏044-801 9295; www.georgetourism.org.za; 124 York St; ☺7.45am-4.30pm Mon-Fri, 9am-1pm Sat) Information for George and the surrounding area.

ℹ Getting There & Away

Kulula (p526), Airlink (p526) and SA Express (p526) fly to **George airport** (☏044-876 9310), which is 7km west of town.

Buses stop in George on their route between Cape Town and Port Elizabeth and between Jo'burg and the Garden Route. Greyhound (p524) services stop at the Caltex petrol station on York St, while Translux (p527) and Intercape (p354) stop at the main station at the end of Hibernia St.

Intercape fares include Knysna (R320, 1½ hours, twice daily), Plettenberg Bay (R320, two hours), Port Elizabeth (R410, 5½ hours, twice daily), Cape Town (R410, seven hours, twice daily), Bloemfontein (R540, 10 hours, daily) and Jo'burg (R700, 16 hours, daily).

The Baz Bus (p354) drops off passengers in town.

Garden Route National Park

Formerly the Wilderness National Park, this section has been incorporated into the vast and scattered **Garden Route National Park** (☏044-877 0046; www.sanparks.org; adult/child R120/60; ☺7am-6pm) along with the Knysna Forests and Tsitsikamma. The park covers a unique system of lakes, rivers, wetlands and estuaries that are vital for the survival of many species. There are several nature trails for all levels of fitness, taking in the lakes, the beach and the indigenous forest. The Kingfisher Trail is a day walk that traverses the region and includes a boardwalk across the intertidal zone of the Touws River. The lakes offer anglers, canoeists, windsurfers and sailors an ideal venue. Canoes can be hired at Eden Adventures in Wilderness.

🛏 Sleeping

There are two similar camping grounds in the park with basic but comfortable accommodation, including in rondavels: **Ebb & Flow North** (camping per site from R190, d rondavel R450, without bathroom R400), which is the smaller of the two, and **Ebb & Flow South** (camping per site from R190, cabins from R725), which also has four-person log cabins (R1370). Prices for all accommodation rise considerably in December and January.

ℹ Getting There & Away

The park is tricky to access by public transport – if you don't have your own car, hiking in or joining a tour are your only options. By car, access is via the N2, 2km east of Wilderness village. Gates are open 7am to 6pm.

Knysna

POP 51,000 / ☏044

Embracing an exquisitely beautiful lagoon and surrounded by ancient forests, Knysna (pronounced ny-znah) is probably the most famous town on the Garden Route. Formerly the centre of the timber industry, supplying yellowwood and stinkwood for railway lines, shipping and house-building, it still

Knysna

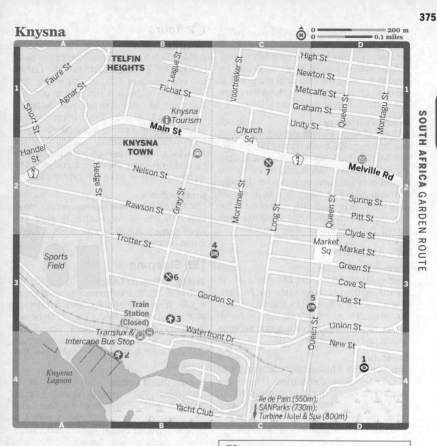

has several shops specialising in woodwork and traditional furniture. The lagoon has always been popular with sailing enthusiasts, and there are plenty of boat trips on offer.

With its serene setting, arty and gay-friendly vibe, excellent places to stay, eat and drink, and wide range of activities, Knysna has plenty going for it. But if you're after something quiet and undeveloped, you might like to look elsewhere – particularly in high season, when the numbers of visitors threaten to overwhelm the town.

◉ Sights

Featherbed Nature Reserve NATURE RESERVE
(www.knysnafeatherbed.com; guided day tour adult/child R450/105) You can visit this reserve, which occupies the western head, on a boat trip from the Knysna Waterfront.

Knysna Lagoon PARK
FREE The Knysna Lagoon opens between two sandstone cliffs known as the Heads –

Knysna

◉ Sights
1 Mitchell's Brewery D4

◉ Activities, Courses & Tours
2 Featherbed Company B4
3 Knysna Cycle Works........................... B3

◉ Sleeping
4 Inyathi Guest Lodge C3
5 Jembjo's Knysna Lodge..................... D3

◉ Eating
6 Chatters Bistro.................................... B3
7 Olive Tree C2

once proclaimed by the British Royal Navy to be the most dangerous harbour entrance in the world. There are good views from the eastern head, and from the Featherbed Nature Reserve on the western head.

Although regulated by SANParks (p377), Knysna Lagoon is not a national park or wilderness area. Much is still privately owned, and the lagoon is used by industry and for recreation. The protected area starts just to the east of Buffalo Bay and follows the coastline to the mouth of the Noetzie River.

Mitchell's Brewery BREWERY
(☏ 044-382 4685; www.mitchellsbrewing.com; 10 New St; tastings R75, tour & tasting R150; ☺ 10am-6pm Mon-Sat, tours Mon-Fri 12.30pm & 2.30pm; P) South Africa's oldest microbrewery has moved to bright, new premises on the edge of the lagoon. You can join a tour, or just taste their range of English-style beers in the beer garden. Pub meals (R55 to R90) are also served. Bookings essential for tours.

🏃 Activities

Elephant Day Walks HIKING
(adult/child R68/34) A series of forest walks in the Diepwalle area. Keep an eye out for signs of the legendary Knysna elephants living in the forest. There are still thought to be up to five elephants here, with a rare sighting caught on camera in early 2016.

Scootours ADVENTURE SPORTS
(☏ 079 148 3751; http://scootours.co.za; adult/child R450/195) Explore the Knysna Forest on a monster scooter – that is, a (non-motorised) scooter with chunky tyres capable of navigating the terrain. The guided tours last two hours and include transfers to the forest.

Knysna Kayak Hire KAYAKING
(www.knysnacharters.com; per hour R100) A peaceful way to explore the lagoon – just steer clear of the Heads!

Trip Out WATER SPORTS
(☏ 083 306 3587; www.tripout.co.za; 2hr surfing class R400) Offers surfing classes for beginners in nearby Buffalo Bay, snorkelling around the Heads (R350) and boat cruises, as well as a full-on kloofing day trip (R900).

Knysna Cycle Works CYCLING
(☏ 044-382 5153; www.knysnacycles.co.za; Waterfront Park, Queen St; per day R200; ☺ 8.30am-5pm Mon-Fri, 9am-1pm Sat) Long-running agency that rents out mountain bikes and supplies maps of the region's trails.

Featherbed Company BOATING
(☏ 044-382 1693; www.knysnafeatherbed.com; Remembrance Dr, off Waterfront Dr; boat trips adult/child from R130/70) Operates various vessels and runs a trip that allows you to explore the nature reserve on foot (adult/child R450/105).

👉 Tours

⭐ Emzini Tours CULTURAL
(☏ 044-382 1087; www.emzinitours.co.za; adult/child R400/150; ☺ 10am & 2pm Mon-Sat) Led by township resident Ella, the three-hour trip visits some of Emzini's community projects. Tours can be tailored to suit your interests, but generally end at Ella's home for tea, drumming and a group giggle as you try to wrap your tongue around the clicks of the Xhosa language. Other options include a music and drumming experience and a hands-on lunch where you help prepare the food.

Brother Zeb CULTURAL
(☏ 076 649 1034; www.judahsquare.co.za; tours from R90) The unforgettable Brother Zeb leads tours of Judah Square, Kysna's Rastafarian community.

🛏 Sleeping

Jembjo's Knysna Lodge HOSTEL $
(☏ 044-382 2658; www.jembjosknysnalodge.co.za; 4 Queen St; dm R140, d R500, with shared bathroom R400; ☎) A small, friendly hostel run by two former overland truck drivers. There's lots of info on activities in the area, mountain bikes to rent (R90 per day) and a free DIY breakfast.

Inyathi Guest Lodge CHALET $
(☏ 044-382 7768; www.inyathiguestlodge.co.za; 38 Trotter St; chalet from R450; ☎) This lodge has changed address and had a complete overhaul, but the cheery owners and tasteful African decor remain. Accommodation is in self-catering chalets each with its own private garden. It's an excellent budget option for those who don't fancy a backpackers.

Brenton Cottages CHALET $$
(☏ 044-381 0082; www.brentononsea.net; 242 CR Swart Drive, Brenton-on-Sea; 2-person cabin R740, 6-person chalet R1480; P ❄ ☎ ⛱) On the seaward side of the lagoon, the hills drop to Brenton-on-Sea, overlooking a magnificent 8km beach. The cottages have a full kitchen while cabins have a kitchenette; many have ocean views. There are plenty of braai areas dotted around the manicured lawns.

⭐ Under Milk Wood CHALET $$$
(☏ 044-384 0745; www.milkwood.co.za; George Rex Dr; s/d cabin from R815/1250) Perched on the shores of Knysna Lagoon are these highly impressive self-catering log cabins, each with its own deck and braai area. There's no pool but there is a small beach. The water-facing chalets are more expensive and prices skyrocket in December.

Turbine Hotel & Spa
BOUTIQUE HOTEL $$$

(☎044-302 5746; www.turbinehotel.co.za; Sawtooth Lane, Thesen's Island; s/d incl breakfast R2350/3140; P☎☎☎) The clever design of this power station-turned-boutique hotel makes it one of Knysna's coolest places to stay. Elements of the original building have been cleverly incorporated into the rooms and public areas. It's a great location a short walk from cafes and restaurants and some rooms have magnificent views of the lagoon.

✖ Eating

★ Ile de Pain
CAFE, BAKERY $

(☎044-302 5707; www.iledepain.co.za; Thesen's Island; mains R55-95; ⊙8am-3pm Tue-Sat, 9am-1.30pm Sun; ☎☎) A wildly popular bakery and cafe that's as much a hit with locals as it is with tourists. There's an excellent breakfast menu, lots of fresh salads, some inventive lunch specials and quite a bit for vegetarians.

Chatters Bistro
PIZZA $$

(☎044-382 0203; www.chattersbistro.co.za; 9A Gray St; mains R60-130; ⊙noon-10pm Tue-Sun) Restaurants seem to come and go in Knysna, but this pizza joint has been around a while. You'll also find burgers, pasta and some salads, plus a pleasant garden to enjoy them in.

Olive Tree
BISTRO $$

(☎044-382 5867; 21 Main St; mains R100-170; ⊙6-9pm Mon-Sat) One of Knysna's more upmarket restaurants is a romantic spot with a blackboard menu that changes regularly. Bookings advisable.

East Head Café
INTERNATIONAL $$

(☎044-384 0933; www.eastheadcafe.co.za; 25 George Rex Dr, Eastern Head; mains R75-145; ⊙8am-3.30pm; ☎☎) There's an outdoor deck overlooking the lagoon and ocean, lots of fish and seafood, plus a few vegetarian dishes. It's a very popular spot so expect to wait for a table in high season. They don't accept reservations.

❶ Information

You'll find a couple of internet cafes on Main Rd. Access is around R40 per hour, or most cafes provide free, if not altogether reliable, wi-fi.

Knysna Tourism (☎044-382 5510; www.visitknysna.co.za; 40 Main St; ⊙8am-5pm Mon-Fri, 8.30am-1pm Sat year-round, plus 9am-1pm Sun Dec, Jan & Jul) An excellent office, with very knowledgeable staff.

SANParks (☎044-302 5600; www.sanparks.org; Long St, Thesen's Island; ⊙7.30am-4pm Mon-Fri)

❶ Getting There & Away

BUS

Translux (p527) and Intercape (p354) stop at the Waterfront; Greyhound (p524) stops at the Engen petrol station (Main St); Baz Bus (p354) drops at all the hostels. For travel between nearby towns on the Garden Route, you're better off looking for a shared taxi than travelling with the major bus lines, which are very expensive for short sectors.

Intercape destinations include George (R310, 1½ hours), Mossel Bay (R310, two hours), Port Elizabeth (R350, 4½ hours), Cape Town (R450, eight hours) and Jo'burg (R720, 17½ hours).

SHARED TAXI

The main shared taxi stop is at the corner of Main and Gray Sts. Routes include Plettenberg Bay (R20, 30 minutes, daily) and Cape Town (R170, 7½ hours, daily). If you want a private taxi, try **Eagle Cabs** (☎076 797 3110).

Plettenberg Bay

POP 6500 / ☎044

Plettenberg Bay, or 'Plett' as it's more commonly known, is a resort town through and through, with mountains, white sand and crystal-blue water making it one of the country's top tourist spots. As a result, things can get very busy and somewhat overpriced, but the town retains a relaxed, friendly atmosphere and does have very good-value hostels. The scenery to the east in particular is superb, with some of the best coast and indigenous forest in South Africa.

⊙ Sights

Monkeyland
WILDLIFE RESERVE

(☎044-534 8906; www.monkeyland.co.za; The Crags; 1hr tour adult/child R230/115; ⊙8am-5pm) This very popular attraction helps rehabilitate wild monkeys that have been in zoos or private homes. The walking safari through a dense forest and across a 128m-long rope bridge is superb. A combo ticket with Birds of Edencosts R280/140 per adult/child.

Birds of Eden
BIRD SANCTUARY

(☎044-534 8906; www.birdsofeden.co.za; The Crags; adult/child R230/115; ⊙8am-5pm) This is one of the world's largest free-flight aviaries with a 200-sq-m dome over the forest. A combo ticket with Monkeyland costs R360/180 per adult/child.

⚡ Activities

Apart from lounging on the beaches or hiking on the Robberg Peninsula there's a lot to do in Plett; check with Albergo for Back-packers, which can organise most things, often at a discount. At the Crags you'll find several animal parks in close proximity.

Learn to Surf Plett   SURFING
(☎082 436 6410; www.learntosurfplett.co.za; 2hr group lesson incl equipment R400) A long-running surfing outfit that also offers stand-up paddle-boarding lessons (R200 per hour).

Ocean Safaris   BOATING
(☎082 784 5729; www.oceansafaris.co.za; Hopwood St, Milkwood Centre; dolphin/whale watching R450/700) Boat trips to view dolphins and whales in season. The trips are permitted on 30-person boats.

Sky Dive Plettenberg Bay   ADVENTURE SPORTS
(☎082 905 7440; www.skydiveplett.com; Plettenberg Airport; tandem jump from R2300) This recommended operator offers dives with outstanding views on the way down.

⌖ Tours

Ocean Blue Adventures   BOATING
(☎044-533 5083; www.oceanadventures.co.za; Hopwood St, Milkwood Centre; dolphin/whale watching R440/700) Trips on 30-person boats to view dolphins and whales in season. Children go for half price.

🛏 Sleeping

Abalone Beach House   HOSTEL $
(☎044-535 9602; www.abalonebeachhouse.co.za; 13 Milkwood Glen, Keurboomstrand; d R700, d with shared bathroom R600; P🤶) This upmarket and extremely friendly backpackers is two minutes' walk from a magnificent beach; surf and body boards are provided free. To reach the house follow the Keurboomstrand signs from the N2 (about 6km east of Plett), then turn into Milkwood Glen.

Nothando Backpackers Hostel   HOSTEL $
(☎044-533 0220; www.nothando.com; 5 Wilder St; dm R160, d R550, with shared bathroom R480; P🤶) This excellent, five-star budget option is owner-run and it shows. There's a great bar area with satellite TV, yet you can still find peace and quiet in the large grounds. Rooms are worthy of a budget guesthouse.

Albergo for Backpackers   HOSTEL $
(☎044-533 4434; www.albergo.co.za; 8 Church St; camping R130, dm R210, d with shared bathroom R600; P🤶) Well-run and friendly, Albergo can organise just about any activity in the area and there are free body boards to use. The upstairs dorm has huge windows and a spacious balcony.

★**Hog Hollow**   LODGE $$$
(☎044-534 8879; www.hog-hollow.com; Askop Rd, The Crags; s/d incl breakfast R2495/3680; P❄🤶🏊) Hog Hollow, 18km east of Plett along the N2, provides delightful accommodation in African-art-decorated units overlooking the forest. Each luxurious unit comes with a private wooden deck and hammock. You can walk to Monkeyland (p377) from here; staff will collect you if you don't fancy the walk back.

🍴 Eating

Le Fournil de Plett   CAFE $
(☎044-533 1390; Church St, cnr Main St; mains R70-85; ⊙8am-5pm Mon-Fri, to 4pm Sat, to 1pm Sun; 🤶) Enjoy a good cup of coffee and a freshly baked pastry in the courtyard or on the balcony overlooking Plett's main road. There's also a small lunch menu, largely focusing on salads and sandwiches.

Table   ITALIAN $$
(☎044-533 3024; www.thetable.co.za; 9 Main St; mains R70-130; ⊙noon-11pm Mon-Sat, to 5pm Sun; 🥗) A funky, minimalist venue with pizzas featuring an array of inventive toppings.

★**Nguni**   STEAK $$$
(☎044-533 6710; www.nguni-restaurant.co.za; 6 Crescent St; mains R135-200; ⊙11am-10pm Mon-Fri, from 6pm Sat) Tucked away in a quiet courtyard, this is one of Plett's most upscale eateries. The speciality is Chalmar beef, though you'll also find lots of South African favourites including ostrich, Karoo lamb and traditional dishes such as bobotie (curry topped with beaten egg baked to a crust). Reservations recommended.

ℹ Information

There are internet cafes on Main St.

Plett Tourism (☎044-533 4065; www.plett -tourism.co.za; Melville's Corner Shopping Centre, Main St; ⊙9am-5pm Mon-Fri, 9am-1pm Sat) Plenty of useful information on accommodation plus walks in the surrounding hills and reserves.

ℹ Getting There & Away

All the major buses stop at the Shell Ultra City on the N2; the **Baz Bus** (p354) comes into town. **Intercape** (p354) destinations from Plett include George (R330, two hours), Port Elizabeth (R330, 3½ hours), Cape Town (R450, nine hours), Jo'burg (R720, 18 hours) and Graaff-Reinet (R460, 6½ hours).

If you're heading to Knysna you're better off taking a shared taxi (Kloof St, near cnr High St; R20) (30 minutes). Long-distance shared taxis stop at the Shell Ultra City on the N2.

Central Karoo

The seemingly endless Karoo has a truly magical feel. It's a vast, semi-arid plateau (its name is a Khoe-San word meaning 'land of thirst') that features stunning sunsets and starscapes. Inhabited by humans and their ancestors for over half a million years, the region is rich in archaeological sites, fossils, San paintings, wildlife and some 9000 plant species.

The Karoo covers almost one-third of South Africa's total area and is demarcated in the south and west by the coastal mountain ranges, and to the east and north by the mighty Gariep (Orange) River. It's often split into the Great Karoo (north) and the Little Karoo (south), but the Karoo doesn't respect provincial boundaries and sprawls into three provinces.

Prince Albert

POP 7050

To many urban-dwelling South African people, Prince Albert – a charming village dating back to 1762 – represents an idyllic life in the Karoo. If you have your own transport, you can easily visit on a day trip from Oudtshoorn or even from the coast. Alternatively, stay in Prince Albert and make a day trip to Oudtshoorn via the spectacular Swartberg and Meiringspoort Passes, or – if the weather isn't too hot – consider going on a hike.

Despite being surrounded by very harsh country, the town is green and fertile (producing peaches, apricots, grapes and olives), thanks to the run-off from the mountain springs. It's something of a foodie town and there's an **Olive Festival** each April.

☞ Tours

Dennehof Tours　　　　　　　　　TOURS
(☑ 023-541 1227; www.dennehof.co.za; 20 Christina de Wit St, Dennehof Guesthouse, Prince Albert; day tour R1050) Guide Lindsay Steyn is a mine of information on the region and offers superb full-day tours taking in the top of the Swartberg Pass before descending the vertiginous road to 'Hell' for lunch. There are also cycling tours of the Swartberg Pass and surrounding region.

☞ Sleeping

Bushman Valley　　　　　　　　　CHALET $
(☑ 082 452 8134; www.bushmanvalley.com; Rte 407 (Klaarstroom Rd); s/d cottage R500/700; P ☀) Prince Albert's only real budget option is 3km south of town and a fantastic base

for hiking in the Swartberg mountains. Hiking permits are available, and a guide (not essential) is R40 per person. The thatched cottages have decent kitchen facilities or you can camp in the grounds (from R120).

Karoo Lodge　　　　　　　GUESTHOUSE $$
(☑ 023-541 1467; www.karoolodge.com; 66 Church St; r from R1050; P ✳ ☎ ☀) This owner-run guesthouse has an enormous garden with plenty of shady spots. The restaurant (mains R85 to R140) largely showcases Karoo fare. It's open to nonguests (dinner Wednesday to Sunday) but bookings are essential.

✗ Eating

Lazy Lizard　　　　　　　　　　CAFE $
(☑ 023-541 1379; 9 Church St; mains R60-100; ⏱ 7.30am-5pm; ☎) This bright, cosy house offers the best coffee in town and stocks home-baked goodies and crafts. The menu offers a little of everything. Try its legendary apple pie.

★ Gallery　　　　　　　　　　FUSION $$
(☑ 023-541 1057; www.princealbertgallery.co.za; 57 Church St; mains R90-170; ⏱ 6-9.30pm) Prince Albert's smartest dining option has an ever-changing menu featuring modern takes on local classics such as Karoo lamb and game steaks. There's also a couple of imaginative vegetarian choices.

ⓘ Information

Prince Albert Tourism (☑ 023-541 1366; www. princealbert.org.za; 42 Church St; ⏱ 9am-5pm Mon-Fri)

ⓘ Getting There & Away

Most people visit by driving over one of the area's passes from Oudtshoorn, or from the N1 between Cape Town and Jo'burg. There is no direct bus or train service to Prince Albert; the closest drop-off point is at Prince Albert Rd, 45km northwest of town. The **train** (p354) is cheaper than the bus, and private taxis from the station cost upwards of R200, or you could arrange a pickup with your accommodation.

West Coast & Swartland

The windswept coastline and desolate mountains on the western side of Western Cape are a peaceful, largely undeveloped paradise. You'll find whitewashed fishing villages, fascinating country towns, unspoilt beaches, a lagoon and wetlands teeming with birds, plus one of the best hiking regions in the country.

The West Coast National Park is a must for birdwatchers and lovers of seascapes, while inland lies the richly fertile Olifants River Valley, where citrus orchards and vineyards sit at the foot of the Cederberg mountains – a hiker's heaven. This remote area has spectacular rock formations and a wealth of San rock paintings. Between the coast and the mountains lies the Swartland, undulating hills of wheat and vineyards. Swartland (black land) received its name from *renosterveld*, a threatened indigenous vegetation that turns dark grey in summer.

West Coast National Park

Encompassing the clear, blue waters of the Langebaan Lagoon and home to an enormous number of birds is the **West Coast National Park** (☑022-772 2144; www.sanparks.org; adult/child R75/37, Aug & Sep R150/75; ☺7am-7pm). The park covers around 310 sq km and protects wetlands of international significance and important seabird breeding colonies. Wading birds flock here by the thousands in summer. The most numerically dominant species is the curlew sandpiper, which migrates north from the sub-Antarctic in huge flocks. The offshore islands are home to colonies of African penguins.

The park is famous for its wildflower display, usually between August and September – it can get fairly crowded during this time. Aside from the white-sand beaches and turquoise waters of the ocean and lagoon, the park's greatest allure is that it is under-visited. If you visit midweek (outside school holidays) you might find that you're sharing the roads only with zebras, ostriches and the occasional leopard tortoise.

🛏 Sleeping & Eating

★**Duinepos**　　　　　　　CHALET **$$**
(☑022-707 9900; www.duinepos.co.za; s/d chalet from R650/950; 🅿🐾) Bright, modern and well-equipped chalets in the heart of the park. It's an excellent birdwatching spot.

SANPark Cottages　　　　　CABIN **$$**
(www.sanparks.org; cottage from R1450; 🅿) Abrahamskraal Cottage is the plusher of the two, but Jo Anne's Beach Cottage has the better location, an easy walk from the lagoon. Both come with a decent kitchen and a large dose of tranquillity.

Geelbek Visitor's Centre & Restaurant　　　SOUTH AFRICAN **$$**
(☑022-772 2134; mains R85-135; ☺9am-5pm) There's a wide menu, focusing on traditional

fare. It's also an information centre for the park and can help with accommodation.

ℹ Getting There & Away

Drive from Cape Town (120km) or Langebaan (7km).

Cederberg Wilderness Area

Some of the Western Cape's finest scenery is found in the desolate **Cederberg Wilderness Area** (☑027-482 2403; www.capenature.co.za; adult/child R60/35). As you drive, bike or hike or rock climb through the bizarre-shaped, weathered-sandstone formations, glowing ochre in the fabulous Cederberg light, you'd be forgiven for whistling the soundtrack to an old Western movie. The 830-sq-km wilderness area boasts San rock art, craggy mountains, clear streams and bumpy dirt roads you can imagine a horse and cart racing along. The peaks and valleys extend roughly north–south for 100km, between Vanrhynsdorp and Citrusdal. The highest peaks are Sneeuberg (2027m) and Tafelberg (1969m).

The region is famous for its plant life – mountain *fynbos* abounds, and wildflowers erupt in spring. Vegetation varies with altitude, with the eponymous cedar stands living between 1000m and 1500m. There are small populations of baboons, rheboks, klipspringers and grysboks; and predators such as caracals, Cape foxes, honey badgers and elusive leopards.

◎ Sights

Stadsaal Caves　　　　　HISTORIC SITE
(adult/child R40/20) Once occupied by the San, these sandstone caves are glorious at sunset. First visit the rock-art site, on the right as you drive through the gate, then explore the network of caves with their marvellous views. Permits are available from Sanddrif (Dwarsrivier Farm).

Astronomical Observatory　　OBSERVATORY
(www.cederbergobs.org.za; entry by donation; ☺8pm Sat) A group of hobbyists run this superb mini observatory. Bring a bottle of wine with you.

🛏 Sleeping

Sanddrif　　　CHALETS, CAMPGROUND **$$**
(☑044-004 0060, 027-482 2825; www.sanddrif.com; Dwarsrivier Farm; camping per site R200, 4-person chalet R850) A great base in the Cederberg, with a winery, brewery, astronomical observatory and a range of top-notch hikes nearby.

Accommodation is in simple chalets or campsites, all with wonderful mountain views. Hiking maps and permits are available.

Algeria CAMPGROUND $$
(☑ 027-482 2403; www.capenature.co.za; camping per site R300, chalet from R580, cottage from R800) The main camping spot in the area has exceptional grounds in a shaded site alongside the Rondegat River. There is a swimming hole and lovely picnic spots. There are a number of two-person chalets here and six new cottages sleeping four people each. It gets busy at weekends and school holidays. Entrance to the camping ground closes at 4.30pm (9pm on Friday).

Clanwilliam
POP 7700

The adjacent dam and some adventurous dirt roads into the Cederberg make the compact town of Clanwilliam a popular weekend resort. The dam is a favourite with water-skiers, though once the current project to raise the dam are fulfilled, this and the landscape of the region will change somewhat.

Clanwilliam is the centre of the **rooibos** (red bush) tea industry. It's made from the leaves of the *Aspalathus linearis* plant, which only grows in the Cederberg region. Rooibos contains no caffeine and much less tannin than normal tea and is said to have health benefits. Tours of the Elandsberg Rooibos Estate, 22km west of Clanwilliam, are an excellent way to follow the process from planting to packaging. The owners of Rooibos Teahouse in town have also set up the Rooibos Route (www.rooibos-route.co.za), which takes in restaurants, tea producers and accommodation highlighting the region's most famous export.

◉ Sights

Sevilla Rock Art Trail HISTORIC SITE
(www.travellersrest.co.za; permits R40) There are nine rock-art sites along a relatively easy 3km hike here. A pamphlet helping to explain the sites is available. It's based at the Traveller's Rest, 36km from Clanwilliam on the way to Bushmans Kloof.

⚲ Tours

Elandsberg Rooibos Estate TOURS
(☑ 027-482 2022; www.elandsberg.co.za; tour per person R140) This rooibos estate 22km west of Clanwilliam offers informative tours following the process from planting to packaging. Accommodation is available here.

⌶ Sleeping

Daisy Cottage COTTAGE $
(☑ 027-482 1603; Foster St; per person R350) In a quiet street close to the town centre, this adorable thatched cottage has a beautiful garden. There are two bedrooms plus a sleeper couch.

Bushmans Kloof LUXURY HOTEL $$$
(☑ 027-482 8200; www.bushmanskloof.co.za; s/d with full board from R5650/8000; ✴🕲🖳) This upmarket private reserve, 46km east of Clanwilliam along the Pakhuis Pass, is known for excellent San rock-art sites and extensive animal- and birdlife. Guests are assigned a guide and can partake in all manner of retreat-type activities or just gorge on excellent food.

✕ Eating

Nancy's Tearoom CAFE $
(☑ 027-482 2661; 33 Main St; mains R65-100; ⊙8.30am-4.30pm Mon-Fri, to 2pm Sat) Enjoy light meals on the shady patio at this friendly spot. Locals rave about the scones – try one with a rooibos cappuccino. Nancy's is a stop on the Rooibos Route (www.rooibos-route.co.za) and you'll find the tea in a number of dishes including bobotie, cheesecake and even rooibos lemon meringue.

Reinhold's SOUTH AFRICAN $$
(☑ 083 389 3040; Main St; mains R100-170; ⊙7-9pm Tue-Sat) The music and the menu at this à la carte restaurant will take you back 50 years, but it's a long-standing favourite and there are few other places to eat in town. It specialises in fish and grills.

⚕ Drinking & Nightlife

★**Rooibos Teahouse** TEAHOUSE
(☑ 027-482 1007; www.rooibosteahouse.co.za; 4 Voortrekker St; ⊙8am-5.30pm Mon-Fri, to 2pm Sat) An absolute must for tea enthusiasts. There are more than 100 blends and flavours of rooibos available. The tea tasting (R70) is highly recommended – choose seven teas to taste, perhaps with a slice of cake. Tutored tastings can be arranged for groups of four or more (bookings essential). There's also a shop selling all the teas on the menu.

ⓘ Information

Information Centre (☑ 027-482 2024; Main St; ⊙8.30am-4.30pm Mon-Fri, to 12.30pm Sat) Opposite the old jail, dating from 1808, which doubles as the town's museum. Ask about the historical walkabout (R50), a one-hour guided tour of South Africa's seventh-oldest town.

ⓘ Getting There & Away

Buses that go through Citrusdal also pass Clanwilliam, stopping at the Cedar Inn petrol station out of town – you'll need to arrange for your accommodation to collect you. Shared taxis running between Springbok (R320, five hours) and Cape Town (R160, three hours) go through Clanwilliam – the tourism office can help with bookings.

EASTERN CAPE

From lush tropical forests to uninhabited desert expanses, from easygoing hammock time to adrenaline-pumping adventures, the Eastern Cape offers a wide range of topography and experiences. Compared with the wealthier and more developed Western Cape, it can feel like a different country and provides opportunities to learn about Xhosa culture. Some of South Africa's finest hiking (and slackpacking) trails wind along the province's largely undeveloped coastline and through its mountainous, waterfall-filled landscapes.

Private wildlife reserves and national and regional parks abound; see the Big Five (lion, leopard, buffalo, elephant and rhino) or migrating whales and dolphins. You'll find tranquillity and culture in the towns of the semi-arid Karoo; the imposing Drakensberg peaks and little-known valleys in the Highlands; good surfing in the Indian Ocean, coupled with amazing cultural experiences on the Wild Coast; and history throughout, including the legacy of some famous local sons – Nelson Mandela, Oliver Tambo and Steve Biko.

Garden Route East

This region includes the western edge of the Eastern Cape coast, an extension of the well-travelled Garden Route and, for that reason, is probably the most visited part of the province. Tsitsikamma National Park is deservedly well known but other lesser-known destinations such as Baviaanskloof Wilderness Area are also worthy of attention.

Nature's Valley

POP 460

Nature's Valley is nestled in yellowwood forest next to a magnificent beach and lagoon in the Tsitsikamma section of the Garden Route National Park. This is where the 46km Otter Trail (p384) ends and the 60km Tsitsikamma Mountain Trail (p384) begins. There are also plenty of shorter hikes in this part of the park, which is referred to as the De Vasselot Section. A range of accommodation options and eateries are found above the village, signposted from Rte 102 as it runs 9km down to Nature's Valley from the N2 near Kurland Village. After passing Nature's Valley, Rte 102 loops back to the N2, crossing it at the Tsitsikamma toll plaza, 14km east of Kurland Village.

🏃 Activities

Bloukrans Bridge Bungee ADVENTURE SPORTS
(☏ 042-281 1458; www.faceadrenalin.com; bungee jumps R950; ⊗9am-5pm) At 216m, this is one of the highest bungee jumps in the world. If you're not sure whether you have the guts to take the plunge, walk out to the jumping-off point under the bridge for R120. Jumps take place 21km west of Storms River directly under the N2. Unexpectedly scary is the post-jump upside-down hang while you wait to be reeled back up. Photos and video of your glorious lapse of judgement are available.

If jumping is not for you, you can instead take in the spectacle of people leaping off the bridge from the safety of the cliff-top terrace or bar-restaurant

🛏 Sleeping

Rocky Road HOSTEL $
(☏ 044-534 8148; www.rockyroadbackpackers. com; Loredo South; dm R150, safari tent s/d R240/380; 🅿🛜) 🍴 Rocky Road is like an enchanted clearing in the wood. Swing chairs, a donkey-boiler Jacuzzi (fired up on Fridays) and magical bathrooms are scattered on the fringes of indigenous forest. Walking trails lead through the trees, and accommodation options include comfortable safari tents and cabins with adjoining bathrooms. It is signposted from Rte 102 about 1km from the N2.

Nature's Valley Rest Camp CAMPGROUND $$
(☏ 044-531 6700; www.sanparks.org; camping per site R205, chalets R970) The national park campsite is a lovely spot at the edge of the river east of town, and it's a 2km walk from the beach. There are clean bathrooms and shared kitchens and laundry. Keep food well stored; there are pesky primates everywhere. In addition to accommodation charges, guests must pay the park's daily conservation fee (adult/child R80/40).

🍴 Eating

Nature's Valley Trading Store PUB FOOD $
(☏ 044-531 6835; 135 St Michael's Ave; mains R70-100; ⊗9.30am-8pm) A spade's throw from the

Eastern Cape

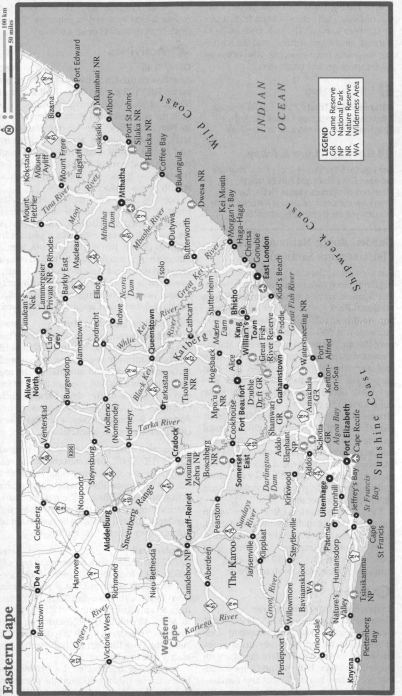

LEGEND
GR   Game Reserve
NP   National Park
NR   Nature Reserve
WA   Wilderness Area

beach. Hiking boots and champagne empties of Otter Trail veterans hang from a tree in the beer garden. The pub grub includes burgers, steaks and seafood, and the adjoining shop sells basic groceries. Also offers local information and brochures.

ℹ️ Information

Nature's Valley Trust (📞044-531 6820; www. naturesvalleytrust.co.za; Lagoon Dr; ⏰8am-4pm Mon-Fri) At the entrance to the village.

ℹ️ Getting There & Away

Baz Bus (p354) stops at Rocky Road en route between Cape Town and Port Elizabeth. The other bus companies stop in Plettenberg Bay, from where accommodation in Nature's Valley will pick you up, if given advance notice.

Garden Route National Park (Tsitsikamma Section)

Cut through by dark, coffee-coloured churning rivers, deep ravines and dense forests, the Tsitsikamma section of the **Garden Route National Park** (📞042-281 1607; www.sanparks. org; adult/child R180/90; ⏰gate 6am-9.30pm) encompasses 650 sq km between Plettenberg Bay and Humansdorp, as well a Marine Protected Area covering 80km of coastline and stretching 5km out to sea. A 77m-long suspension bridge spans the Storms River Mouth near the rest camp of the same name (not to be confused with the village of Storms River), where several walking trails pass thickets of ferns, lilies, orchids, coastal and mountain *fynbos*, and yellowwood and milkwood trees, some hundreds of years old. Millennia-old sandstone and quartz rock formations line the gorges and rocky shoreline, and southern right whale and dolphins are visible out in the ocean.

Elusive Cape clawless otters, after which the Otter Trail (a multiday hike) is named, inhabit this park; there are also baboons, monkeys, small antelope and furry little dassies. Birdlife is plentiful, including endangered African black oystercatchers.

👁 Sights

Baviaanskloof Wilderness Area   PARK
(Baviaanskloof Mega Reserve; 📞044-272 9908; www.baviaans.co.za; R40; ⏰sunrise-4pm) One of South Africa's largest conservation areas, Baviaanskloof is a World Heritage Site with leopards, antelope, buffaloes and Cape mountain zebras between the Kouga and Baviaanskloof Mountains. Stretching between the

towns of Patensie and Willowmore, the region is best explored in your own vehicle (with high clearance) or on a tour.

🏃 Activities

Otter Trail   HIKING
(📞in Pretoria 012-426 5111; www.sanparks.org; per person R1075) The 45km Otter Trail is one of South Africa's most acclaimed hikes, hugging the coastline from Storms River Mouth to Nature's Valley. The five-day, four-night walk, involves fording a number of rivers and gives access to some superb stretches of coast. A good level of fitness is required for the walk, as it goes up- and downhill quite steeply in many places.

Book at least nine months ahead (six months if you are flexible about dates). There are often cancellations, however, so it's always worth trying, especially if you are in a group of only two or three people. Single hikers are permitted; you'll be tagged onto a group so you do not walk by yourself. Accommodation is in six-bed rest huts with mattresses (without bedding), rainwater tanks, braais and firewood. Camping is not allowed.

Tsitsikamma Mountain Trail   HIKING
(www.mtoecotourism.co.za; per night R155) This 62km trail begins at Nature's Valley and ends at Storms River, taking you inland through the forests and mountains. The full trail takes six days, but you can also opt for two, three, four or five days, because each overnight hut has its own access route. Porterage is also available, as are day hikes (R50) and mountain-bike trails.

Untouched Adventures   KAYAKING
(📞073 130 0689; www.untouchedadventures. com) Offers a popular three-hour kayak and lilo trip up Storms River (R450), plus scuba diving and snorkelling in the national park Marine Protected Area (trips are weather dependent). Located beneath the restaurant at Storms River Mouth Rest Camp (p385).

Dolphin Trail   HIKING
(📞042-280 3588; www.dolphintrail.co.za; s/d R5900/7080) Ideal for well-heeled slackpackers who don't want to hoist a rucksack or sleep in huts, this two-day, 17km hike runs from Storms River Mouth Rest Camp (p385) to Misty Mountain (p386), and then onto the Fernery Lodge & Chalets (p386) for the last night. Book through the trail's website at least a year in advance.

Luggage is transported by vehicle between the overnight stops, and the price also includes three nights of accommodation, all meals, guides and a 4WD trip back to Storms River Mouth.

Sleeping

Storms River Mouth

Rest Camp CAMPGROUND, CHALET **$$**
(☎042-281 1607; www.sanparks.org; camping per site from R300) This camp offers accommodation ranging from rustic forest huts (from R610) to chalets (from R1155), family cottages with four single beds (R1760), and waterfront 'oceanette' cottages (from R995). Most have single beds with bedding and, apart from the forest huts, kitchens (including utensils) and bathrooms. Rates do not include the park's conservation fee (adult/child R180/90).

ⓘ Getting There & Away

There is no public transport to either Nature's Valley Rest Camp or Storms River Mouth. Greyhound (p524), Intercape (p354), Translux (p527) and City to City (p527) stop in Plettenberg Bay and Storms River Bridge. Baz Bus (p354) gets you closer to the rest camps, stopping in the Crags (near Nature's Valley), at Bloukrans Bridge and at Storms River en route between Cape Town and Port Elizabeth.

Hiking Trail Transfers (☎082 696 5335; www.ottertrailtransfers.co.za) offers transfers to walkers on the Otter and Tsitsikamma Mountain Trails.

Storms River

POP 1670

Tree-lined Storms River is a little hamlet with an excellent selection of accommodation options and a well-developed tourist industry, in large part because of its location in the Tsitsikamma section of Garden Route National Park near Bloukrans Bridge. Don't confuse Storms River with the turn-off 4km to the west for Storms River Mouth (Stormsriviermond in Afrikaans), located in the park.

◉ Sights

Big Tree FOREST
(adult/child R16/9; ☺8am-5pm, to 6pm Sep-Apr; ℗) Just east of Storms River on the other side of the N2 is a 36m-high yellowwood that's over 800 years old, and a forest with many fine examples of candlewood, stinkwood and assegai. The 4.2km Ratel Trail begins here, with signs describing the trees in this forest; it's one of the best preserved in South Africa.

🏃 Activities

Segway Tours OUTDOORS
(☎042-281 1868; www.tsitsikammabackpackers. co.za; from R350; ☺8am-5pm) After a short

training session, knowledgeable guides lead one-hour Segway tours through the village and surrounding forest. The longer tour (two hours; R500) includes a stop at the Big Tree (p385). Operates out of **Tsitsikamma Backpackers** (☎042-281 1868; www.tsitsikammabackpackers.co.za; 54 Formosa St; dm R180, d R600, with shared bathroom R500; ℗@🐾) .

Blackwater Tubing ADVENTURE SPORTS
(☎079 636 8008; tubenaxe.co.za; cnr Darnell & Saffron Sts; half/full day from R545/900) Tubing trips on the Storms River run out of **Tube 'n Axe backpackers** (☎042-281 1757; www. tubenaxe.co.za; cnr Darnell & Saffron Sts; camping/dm R105/190, r R630, with shared bathroom R600; ℗🐾⌨). Because the river is susceptible to flooding, there may be no departures for several days after rains of any significance. It's worth asking how the river is flowing; with lower water levels you'll be doing almost as much walking as floating.

Tsitsikamma Canopy Tours ECOTOUR
(☎042-281 1836; www.stormsriver.com; Darnell St; incl lunch and park entrance R595) This massive operation is the oldest branch in a nationwide network of canopy tours. Ten zip lines up to 100m long cut through the forest covering high in the trees; it's more relaxing than thrilling. The three-hour guided tour departs every half-hour from 8.30am to 3.30pm. Guided forest drives and hikes also offered.

Tsitsikamma Falls Adventure ADVENTURE SPORTS
(☎042-280 3770; www.tsitsikammaadventure. co.za; Witelsbos; abseil R100, zip-line R375) Abseil 36m down a beautiful waterfall or explore the Kruis River gorge on eight zip-lines up to 211m long. Around 12km east of the Storms River just off the N2.

Sleeping

★Dijembe Backpackers HOSTEL **$**
(☎042-281 1842; www.dijembebackpackers. com; cnr Formosa & Assegai Sts; camping/dm/d R80/150/450; ℗🐾) 🐾 Reflecting the spirit of its nature-loving owner – who might arrive with a rescued horse, hang from the rafters and lead a drum circle, all in the space of a typical evening – much of this intimate backpackers is made from recycled wood. There's a Jacuzzi on the upper deck, free pancake breakfasts and township tavern visits, plus nightly bonfires and dinners (R70). Accommodation includes safari tents and a cottage in the back garden.

At the Woods
GUESTHOUSE $$

(☑ 042-281 1446; www.atthewoods.co.za; 43 Formosa St; s/d incl breakfast R890/1190; P🖥🎆) This stylish guesthouse has an arty feel, with ceramics on the walls, colourful cushions on the beds and turquoise garden furniture. Rooms upstairs have wooden balconies; number six is particularly spacious.

★ Fernery Lodge & Chalets
RESORT $$$

(☑ 042-280 3588, 081 422 9617; www.forestferns. co.za/Fernery; s/d incl breakfast from R1800/2400; P🖥🎆) Hugging the edge of a cliff overlooking the Sandrift River gorge with falls and pools, the Fernery takes full advantage of its dramatic setting. Luxurious chalets and suites are scattered throughout; a Jacuzzi hovers over the void; and the restaurant is a cosy nook with floor-to-ceiling windows.

Misty Mountain Reserve
CHALET $$$

(☑ 042-280 3699; www.mistymountainreserve. co.za; s/d/f from R1395/1860/2200) A string of large, individual A-frame cottages set back from a bluff over the ocean, each with a large Jacuzzi bath and some with a separate lounge. Meals are available, and on-site activities include walking and mountain-biking on trails through the indigenous forest.

✗ Eating

Marilyn's 60's Diner
DINER $

(☑ ext. 267 042-281 1711; www.facebook.com/marilyns60sdiner; Darnell St; mains R50-75; ⊗ 10am-9pm) This wonderfully incongruous Americana-inspired diner dominates the village centre. The menu mixes South African and American classics; dishes of varying quality range from hot dogs, curry and calamari to the 'A Little Less Conversation' sandwich. The burgers are decent but it's really all about the decor.

① Information

Just off the N2 is **Storms River Information Centre** (☑ 042-281 1098; Gamassi St; ⊗ 9am-5.30pm), which has a wall of brochures and can help with accommodation, including self-catering options. Across from Marilyn's 60's Diner is a small supermarket and liquor store with an ATM.

① Getting There & Away

Baz Bus (p354) stops at the backpackers in Storms River en route between Cape Town and Port Elizabeth, and your accommodation can organise shuttles to the Tsitsikamma section of Garden Route National Park and local activities. The main bus companies stop at Storms River Bridge, 5km east of town on the N2; arrange a pickup with your accommodation from there.

Sunshine Coast

The Sunshine Coast covers a significant chunk of the Eastern Cape coastline, including Port Elizabeth, the seaside towns of Jeffreys Bay and Port Alfred, and numerous sandy beaches. In the hinterland are the best wildlife-watching areas within easy reach of the coastline between Cape Town and Durban: Addo Elephant National Park and the nearby private reserves.

The region has an English heritage and flavour, thanks to the influence of the 1820 Settlers. These hardy Brits landed at Algoa Bay and, having tried to farm in the midst of internecine clashes between the Boers and the Xhosa, they ultimately ended up in Grahamstown, Port Elizabeth and beyond.

Jeffreys Bay
POP 27,107 / ☑ 042

Once just a sleepy seaside town, 'J-Bay' is now one of the world's top surfing destinations. It's certainly South Africa's foremost centre of surfing and surf culture. Boardies from all over the planet flock here to ride waves such as the famous Supertubes, generally rated as one of the world's most perfect waves. June to September are the best months for experienced surfers, but novices can learn at any time of year.

◉ Sights & Activities

For nonsurfers, there's windsurfing, kite-surfing, stand-up paddle-boarding, sandboarding, horse riding, dolphin- and whale-watching from the beaches, and birdwatching at Kabeljous Estuary, which makes a pleasant 6km coastal walk from town (for security reasons, don't go by yourself). Alternatively, wander down the boardwalk to **Supertubes** to watch impressive displays of surf skill.

Dolphin Beach
BEACH

A beautiful and largely untouched expanse of sand, perfect for a prebreakfast stroll.

Son Surf School
SURFING

(☑ 076 501 6191; www.surfschools.co.za; 1½hr lesson R300) Good for intermediate surfers who want a refresher or to improve their technique. Beginner and advanced classes are also on offer.

Wavecrest Surf School
SURFING

(☑ 073 509 0400; www.wavecrestsurfschool.co.za; 6 Drommedaris St; 2hr lesson incl board & wetsuit R300) Long-running operation offering daily lessons. Good for children and beginners.

Jeffreys Bay Adventures
OUTDOORS

(☑042-293 4214; http://jeffreysbayadventures.co.za; 10 Dageraad St) As well as surf lessons (2hrs R250), this outfit offers sandboarding (R200), trips to a nearby waterfall (R200) and horse rides along the beach (R450). It's based at Island Vibe (p387).

AfricaSUP
WATER SPORTS

(☑042-293 0155; www.africasup.com; 19 Da Gama Road; 1½hr lesson R300) If you fancy a different way to get wet, try stand-up paddle-boarding. As well as beginner lessons, they also rent out equipment (1½hr R250).

🛌 Sleeping

Beach Music
GUESTHOUSE $

(☑042-293 2291; www.beachmusic.co.za; 33 Flame Cres; s R230-430, d R350-700; P🖥) This airy house with a garden leading straight to the beach is great value. The first-floor lounge and kitchen have superb ocean views – including a glimpse of Supertubes – and the tastefully decorated rooms have small private patios.

Island Vibe
HOSTEL $

(☑042-293 1625; www.jbay.islandvibe.co.za; 10 Dageraad St; dm R160-170, d R550-650; P🖥) Party central in J-Bay, Island Vibe is 500m south of the city centre, and the attendant raft of surfers attests to its prime beachfront location. Accommodation ranges from four- to 12-bed dorms and wooden cabins (numbers one and two have private balconies overlooking the beach), to a beach house and a flashpackers, both with en suite rooms.

African Ubuntu
HOSTEL $

(☑042-296 0376; www.jaybay.co.za; 8 Cherry St; camping/dm R100/140, d R450, with shared bathroom R340; @🖥) A suburban home transformed into an intimate and friendly backpackers by its passionate surfer owner. The garden, braai area and bar are good places to chill. You can see Magnatubes and Boneyards – two choice surf spots – from the balcony, and surfboard rental and activities can be organised. Rates include breakfast.

Funky Town
GUESTHOUSE $$

(☑042-293 3860; www.accommodationjbay.co.za; 12a Oosterland St; r R700-800; P🖥🏊) The eight rooms here are all brightly decorated with original art hanging on the walls. There's also a penthouse apartment (R1700) with kitchen and sitting area. For the rest there's a shared kitchen and TV lounge inside and a braai area, pizza oven, hot tub and pool in the garden. Bikes and boards are available to hire.

African Perfection
B&B $$

(☑042-293 1401; www.africanperfection.co.za; 20 Pepper St; s/d incl breakfast from R600/R900; P🖥) Occupying prime real estate in front of Supertubes, this luxury option is perfect for surfing voyeurs. Every room comes with a private balcony offering stunning sea views; the fabulous four-sleeper penthouse suite (R3250) has a fully equipped kitchen.

🍴 Eating

★InFood Deli
INTERNATIONAL $

(☑042-2931880; www.infood.co.za; cnr Schelde & Jeffrey Sts; mains R50-80; ⏰7am-5pm Mon-Sat; 🖥) The sandwiches, burgers and other fare at this cafe, bakery and deli are far from ordinary. This is not surprising, considering the owner-chef's impressive CV – including once having cooked for Prince William. The mix of organic, locally sourced ingredients (such as Karoo *fynbos* honey) and wide-ranging culinary tastes (quesadillas, handmade pasta and Thai chicken curry) makes this a worthy foodie destination.

★Nina's
INTERNATIONAL $$

(☑042-296 0281; 126 Da Gama Rd, Wavecrest Centre; mains R65-155; ⏰7am-10pm) Most locals recommend Nina's, with its stylish decor of surfboards and coastal scenes around a paper-disc chandelier. Service can be slow, but the food is worth the wait. Seafood abounds on the wide-ranging menu, which also features burgers, curries, pizza, pasta, Thai food and nachos; the specials menu is a winner, offering dishes such as ostrich fillet and grilled tuna.

Die Walskipper
SEAFOOD $$

(☑042-292 0005; www.walskipper.co.za; Marina Martinique; mains R95-195; ⏰noon-8pm Tue-Sat, noon-3pm Sun) A finer location you couldn't hope to find. Die Walskipper clings to quiet Clapton Beach within the Marina Martinique, a 5km drive south of town. The seafood-focused menu features platters loaded with crayfish, mussels, prawns and calamari alongside some traditional meaty fare such as lamb shank, springbok and oxtail.

❶ Information

Most ATMs are on Da Gama Rd, the main thoroughfare.

Jeffreys Bay Tourism (☑042-293 2923; www.jeffreysbaytourism.org; Da Gama Rd; ⏰9am-5pm Mon-Fri, to noon Sat) Friendly and helpful, and can make bookings for accommodation and activities.

Post Office (cnr De Reyger St & Verbena Cres)

ⓘ Getting There & Away

Baz Bus (p354) stops at several J-Bay backpackers en route between Cape Town and Port Elizabeth.

AdventureNow (📱 076 781 3912; www.adventurenow.co.za; Da Gama Rd) runs shuttles to/from destinations including Storms River (up to three people R640), Bloukrans Bridge (R860) and Port Elizabeth Airport (R550).

Long-distance buses (St Francis St, Mentors Plaza) plying the Cape Town–Port Elizabeth–Durban route stop at the Mentors Plaza Caltex garage, at the junction of St Francis St and the N2.

Shared taxis depart when full, generally on the hour, from the corner of Goedehoop and St Francis Sts; it's R35 to Humansdorp (25 minutes) and R80 to Port Elizabeth (1¼ hours).

Local taxis, including **J-Bay Cabs** (📱 083 611 1003), charge about R10 per kilometre.

Port Elizabeth

POP 1.15 MILLION / 📞 041

Port Elizabeth (PE for short) fringes Algoa Bay at the western end of the Sunshine Coast, and offers many good bathing beaches and surf spots. It's also a convenient gateway to worthy destinations in either direction along the coast, as well as to the eastern Karoo. Sadly, with the notable exception of vibrant Richmond Hill and a few other urban-regeneration projects, the city centre remains rather rundown. Many of the more upmarket shops, restaurants and bars are found in the suburban shopping centres.

PE, its industrial satellite towns of Uitenhage and Despatch, and the massive surrounding townships, are collectively referred to as Nelson Mandela Bay.

⊙ Sights

Port Elizabeth's major attractions as a holiday destination are its wide sandy beaches and the warm waters of the Indian Ocean. Sardinia Bay, 20km south of the centre past the airport, is easily the nicest in the area, though beware of strong currents. There are broad beaches south of Central; Kings Beach stretches from the harbour to Humewood, and there are more beaches at Summerstrand, which are all fairly sheltered.

South End Museum MUSEUM
(📱 041-582 3325; cnr Walmer Blvd & Humewood Rd, South End; admission by donation; ⊙ 9am-4pm Mon-Fri, 10am-3pm Sat & Sun; 🅿) Multimedia exhibits relate the history of South End, a vibrant multicultural district destroyed by apartheid bulldozers during forced removals between 1965 and 1975 (under the infamous Group Areas Act). The inhabitants were relocated to other parts of the city, designated by race. Book ahead for a one-hour guided walking tour of the area (R60).

Marine Rehabilitation & Education Centre BIRD SANCTUARY
(SAMREC; www.samrec.org.za; Cape Recife Nature Reserve; adult/child R30/20; ⊙ 9.30am-4pm; 🅿) Most of the world's remaining 25,000 breeding pairs of endangered African penguins are found around Algoa Bay; they are threatened by currents pushing their food far out to sea, causing them to digest much of it before they get back to their chicks. At this centre, learn more from volunteers and watch the penguins chilling by the pool, or having a feed at 2.30pm. There is a cafe here and coastal walking trails in the area.

Bayworld AQUARIUM
(📱 041-584 0650; www.bayworld.co.za; Beach Rd, Brookes Hill; adult/child R40/30; ⊙ 9am-4.30pm; 🅿) This ageing complex includes a museum, an oceanarium and a snake park. Alongside the many stuffed and pickled marine mammals in the museum is some beautiful Xhosa beadwork incorporating modern materials, and a replica of the Algoasaurus dinosaur, once native to the area. There's a snake interaction at noon, and seal and penguin presentations at 11am and 3pm.

Nelson Mandela Metropolitan Art Museum GALLERY
(📱 041-506 2000; www.artmuseum.co.za; 1 Park Dr, St George's Park; ⊙ 9am-5pm Mon & Wed-Fri, 1-5pm Tue) **FREE** The museum housed in two handsome buildings at the entrance to St George's Park has a small gallery of paintings and sculpture by contemporary South African artists, some older British and Eastern Cape works, plus temporary exhibitions and graduate shows.

🏃 Activities

PE is not known as the 'windy city' for nothing; windsurfers and sailors will find what they need at Hobie Beach (p389), 5km south of Central. There are some excellent dive sites around Port Elizabeth, with shipwrecks and reefs all over Algoa Bay. Both Marine Training & Consulting and Pro Dive offer PADI Open Water courses starting at around R3300, with dives from R300 per dive.

Surf Centre SURFING
(📱 041-585 6027; www.surf.co.za; Main Rd, Walmer Park Shopping Centre, Walmer) PE's best surf breaks are found between the harbour wall and Summerstrand, and at Pollok beach. The

Surf Centre sells and hires out surfboards and bodyboards. Its surf school will teach you how to use them (1½ hour lesson R250).

Pro Dive
DIVING

(☎041-581 1144; www.prodive.co.za; 189 Main Rd, Walmer) Pro Dive offers PADI Open Water courses starting at around R3950, with dives from R295 plus equipment rental.

Hobie Beach
WINDSURFING

The beach of choice for windsurfers, sailors and kite-surfers.

Marine Training & Consulting
DIVING

(☎041-581 5121; www.watersportmtc.com; 10 Albert Rd, Walmer) Formerly known as Ocean Divers International, this long-running set-up offers PADI Open Water courses starting at R3350, with dives from R300 per dive (excluding gear rental).

☞ Tours

Raggy Charters
BOATING

(☎073 152 2277; www.raggycharters.co.za; Algoa Bay Yacht Club) This respected outfit offers a range of oceanic boat trips, including half-day tours (R1400) with a qualified marine biologist to St Croix, Jahleel and Benton Islands, variously focused on penguins, whale and dolphins. Shorter sunset cruises (R500) to Cape Recife Lighthouse offer opportunities to spot birds and marine life. Bookings essential.

Calabash Tours
CULTURAL

(☎084 552 4414; www.calabashtours.co.za; Summerstrand Hotel, Marine Drive) Runs real local trips, ranging from Addo Elephant National Park safaris (R1100) to several township tours (R550 to R695), including visits to *shebeens* (taverns) and story-telling in residents' homes. The guides are locals who are proud of the Port Elizabeth townships' part in the anti-apartheid struggle, and they highlight places of historical and political interest along the way.

🛏 Sleeping

★Tree Tops Guest House
GUESTHOUSE $

(☎041-581 0147; www.treetopsguesthouse.co.za; 44 Albert Rd, Walmer; s/d from R450/570; P☀❄🖥) In a suburban area close to the airport, this friendly guesthouse has simple, great-value rooms each with a fridge, microwave, TV and en suite bathroom. The cheapest rooms are without air conditioning. Owners offer a free airport shuttle.

Island Vibe
HOSTEL $

(☎041-583 1256; www.islandvibe.co.za; 4 Jenvey Rd, Summerstrand; dm/d R170/600; P@❄🖥)

This 'flashpackers' in a nondescript suburban house is less characterful than its sister in Jeffreys Bay (p387), but makes a comfortable base with numerous facilities. The bar, pool table, Foosball table and outdoor Jacuzzi liven up the 'burbs, while the well-equipped kitchen, secure parking and en suite rooms are welcome. Pollok Beach and the Pipe surf break are within walking distance.

Forest Hall Guest House
GUESTHOUSE $$

(☎041-581 3356; www.foresthall.co.za; 84 River Rd, btwn 9th & 10th Aves, Walmer; s/d incl breakfast from R700/1000; P❄🖥) At this gracious suburban property, huge rooms with lots of natural light and private patios open onto a beautiful garden with an Italianate swimming pool.

Windermere
BOUTIQUE HOTEL $$$

(☎041-582 2245; www.thewindermere.co.za; 35 Humewood Rd; s/d incl breakfast R2100/2300; P☀❄🖥) Located on a quiet street, only a block from the beach, is this oasis of design-savvy luxury. There are plush and contemporary furnishings throughout the nine palatial rooms, which offer sea glimpses from their balconies. Additional attractions include a bar, a garden plunge pool overlooked by creeper-covered walls, and African art books scattered throughout.

🍴 Eating

The Boardwalk
INTERNATIONAL $

(☎041-507 7777; www.suninternational.com/boardwalk; Marine Dr, Summerstrand; ⊙7am-11pm) The Boardwalk has numerous chain restaurants.

★Two Olives
MEDITERRANEAN $$

(☎081 744 2496; www.twoolives.co.za; 3 Stanley St, Richmond Hill; mains R75-170, tapas R50-70; ⊙noon-3pm & 5.30-10.30pm Tue-Sat, 5.30-10.30pm Mon, noon-3pm Sun) One of the most upmarket restaurants in Richmond Hill, Two Olives serves a range of Spanish- and Greek-inspired dishes in its busy dining room and on the wraparound balcony (warning: it can get pretty breezy out there). The lamb shank is as delicious as it is enormous. For the not so hungry, try the tapas menu. Reservations recommended.

Something Good
CAFE $$

(☎041-583 6986; off Marine Dr, Pollok Beach; mains R60-90; ⊙8am-10.30pm; ❄🍴) This roadhouse-cum-beach bar is an excellent spot for a sundowner, with a breezy interior, beachfront decks and a children's playground. Dishes include gourmet pizzas, burgers, seafood (try the Cajun calamari)

Port Elizabeth

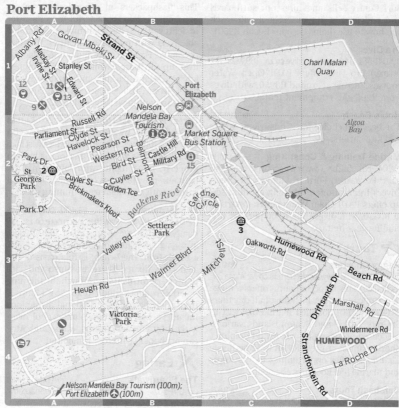

and for the health conscious, bunless burgers and healthy breakfasts.

Fushin
ASIAN **$$**

(☎041-811 7874; www.fushin.co.za; 15 Stanley St, Richmond Hill; mains R70-110; ☺noon-10pm) This restaurant's experienced owner and chef creates high-quality sushi and handmade Singapore-inspired noodle dishes, as well as creative fare like stuffed giant squid.

🍷 Drinking & Nightlife

★ For the Love of Wine
WINE BAR

(☎072 566 2692; www.ftlow.co.za; 1st fl, 20 Stanley St, Richmond Hill; ☺noon-10pm Mon-Sat) At this excellent wine bar and boutique, you can sample the output of Stellenbosch and beyond (tastings and wine by the glass start at R25), with craft beer and cheese platters also offered. If the wraparound porch feels too inviting to leave, you can order from a few local restaurants to eat here.

Beer Yard
BAR

(☎041-582 2444; 1 Cooper St, Richmond Hill; ☺noon-10pm Mon-Sat) With a Bedouin tent and small pool in the backyard, this craft-beer and cider bar encapsulates Richmond Hill's urban buzz. Burgers (R60 to R75) and thin-crust pizzas (R50 to R85) are on the menu, plus beer from the adjoining microbrewery.

☆ Entertainment

Port Elizabeth Opera House
OPERA, THEATRE

(☎041-586 2256; www.peoperahouse.co.za; Whites Rd, Central) The oldest theatre in both Africa and the southern hemisphere, the PE Opera House hosts a wide range of performances, including plays, poetry, concerts and comedy.

🔒 Shopping

Wezandla Gallery & Craft Centre
ARTS & CRAFTS

(☎041-585 1185; www.wezandla.co.za; 27 Baakens St, Central; ☺9am-5pm Mon-Fri, 9am-1pm Sat)

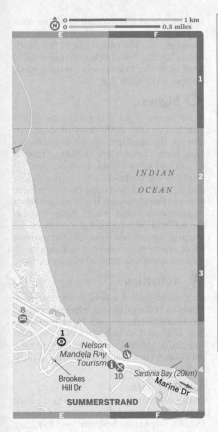

Port Elizabeth

◎ Sights
1 Bayworld E4
2 Nelson Mandela Metropolitan Art
    Museum A2
3 South End Museum C3

✦ Activities, Courses & Tours
4 Hobie Beach F4
5 Marine Training & Consulting A4
6 Raggy Charters C2

🛏 Sleeping
7 Tree Tops Guest House A4
8 Windermere E3

✖ Eating
9 Fushin...A1
10 The Boardwalk F4
11 Two Olives A1

🍷 Drinking & Nightlife
12 Beer Yard A1
13 For the Love of Wine...........................A1

✪ Entertainment
14 Port Elizabeth Opera House................B2

🛍 Shopping
15 Wezandla Gallery & Craft Centre........B2

This brightly coloured arts and crafts centre has a huge array of items made by local groups, plus a small coffee shop.

ⓘ Information

Nelson Mandela Bay Tourism (☏041-585 8884; www.nmbt.co.za; Donkin Reserve; ⊙8am-4.30pm Mon-Fri, 9.30am-3.30pm Sat) has an excellent supply of information and maps, and a cafe with city views. There are also branches at the **Boardwalk** (☏041-583 2030; Marine Dr, Summerstrand; ⊙8am-7pm) (a good stop for information about the whole province) and the **airport** (☏041-581 0456; Port Elizabeth Airport; ⊙7am-9.30pm). Wezandla craft shop also dispenses info.

ⓘ Getting There & Away

AIR
Port Elizabeth Airport (☏041-507 7319; www. airports.co.za; Allister Miller Rd, Walmer) is about 5km from the city centre.

South African Airways (☏041-507 7220; www flysaa.com) and its subsidiaries Airlink, SA Express and Mango, and **FlySafair** (p526) and **Kulula** (p526) all fly daily to/from cities including Cape Town (from R900, 1¼ hours), Durban (from R1500, 1¼ hours) and Jo'burg (from R800, 1¾ hours). A taxi to the centre costs about R120.

BUS
Greyhound (p524), **Translux** (☏041-392 1303; www.translux.co.za; Ring Rd, Ernst & Young Bldg, Greenacres Shopping Centre) and City to City (p527) depart from the Greenacres Shopping Centre, about 4km inland from the city centre. Intercape (p354) departs from its office behind the old post office.

To Cape Town
Greyhound (p524), Translux (p391), Intercape (p354) and City to City (p527) have daily buses to/from Cape Town (R450, 12 hours) via the Garden Route. Baz Bus (p354) runs a hop-on, hop-off service five days a week in both directions between Port Elizabeth and Cape Town (R2300 one way; 15 hours).

To Johannesburg
Greyhound (p524), Translux (p391), Intercape (p354) and City to City (p527) have daily buses

to/from Jo'burg (R500, 16 hours) via Bloemfontein (R480, 9½ hours).

To Durban

Greyhound (p524), Translux (p391), Intercape (p354) and City to City (p527) have daily buses to/from Durban (R520, 14½ hours) via Grahamstown (R290, two hours) and East London (R450, 4½ hours). Baz Bus (p354) runs a hop-on, hop-off service four days a week in both directions between Port Elizabeth and Durban (R2180 one way; 15¼ hours).

CAR

All the big car-rental operators have offices in Port Elizabeth or at the airport.

Avis (☑ 041-501 7200; www.avis.co.za; Port Elizabeth Airport)

Hertz (☑ 041-508 6600; www.hertz.co.za; Port Elizabeth Airport)

SHARED TAXI

Vehicles run to local destinations from the shared taxi rank (Strand St, Central) beneath the flyover.

TRAIN

Shosholoza Meyl (p354) runs to/from Jo'burg (20 hours, Wed, Fri & Sun) via Cradock and Bloemfontein. Choose between tourist class (sleeper, R500) or less-recommended economy class (seat only, R320).

ⓘ Getting Around

Algoa Bus Company (☑ 080 142 1444; www.algoabus.co.za) runs most routes (R8.70 one way) around the city and to the surrounding suburbs every 25 minutes, leaving from the Market Square bus station (Strand St).

Addo Elephant National Park

Located 70km north of Port Elizabeth, and encompassing both the Zuurberg mountains and the Sundays River Valley, South Africa's third-largest **national park** (☑ 042-233 8600; www.sanparks.org; adult/child R232/116; ⊙ 7am-7pm) protects the remnants of the huge elephant herds that once roamed the Eastern Cape. When Addo was proclaimed a national park in 1931, there were only 11 elephants left; today there are more than 600 in the park, and you'd be unlucky not to see some. Addo, which was once farmland, now encompasses five biomes and about 1800 sq km, and extends to the coastline between the mouths of the Sundays and Bushman's Rivers. The coastal section includes Alexandria Dunefield, the southern hemisphere's largest and least degraded coastal dunefield,

and islands with significant breeding colonies of African penguins, Cape gannets and Cape fur seals. The park is one of few which boasts the 'Big Seven', thanks to sightings of great white sharks and southern right whale (in season) in Algoa Bay.

⊙ Sights

A day or two at Addo is a highlight of any visit to this part of the Eastern Cape, not only for the elephants but for the lions, zebras, black rhinos, Cape buffaloes, spotted hyenas and myriad birds. Look out, too, for southern right whales, great white sharks and the rare flightless dung beetle, endemic to Addo. Female beetles bury elephant dung underground to eat, which both fertilises the soil and encourages the growth of the bright-green spekboom plants – the leaves of which are the main source of moisture for elephants and are nicknamed 'elephant's food'.

🏃 Activities

Book in advance for wildlife drives, horse riding and other activities, especially during the high season (October to March). Also bear in mind that for most SANParks activities and accommodation, you must pay the park's daily conservation fee on top of SANParks' quoted price.

Self-Drive Safaris

During summer it's best to arrive at the park by mid-morning and stake out one of the waterholes, where the elephants tend to gather during the heat of the day. In winter, early mornings are the best time to see animals.

The elephants of Addo were once addicted to – and even fought violently over – the oranges and grapefruits fed to them by the park's first rangers to encourage them to stay within the park's boundaries. A fruit ban has been in place since the late 1970s; however, as the old adage goes, 'elephants have good memories' and the smell alone could provoke an old-timer. And, of course, do not get out of your car except at designated climb-out points.

As at most parks in Southern Africa, it's not compulsory to hire a guide to explore Addo in your own vehicle. You can just turn up, pay the entrance fee and try your luck spotting elephants between the trees. For novice wildlife watchers, hiring a hop-on SANParks guide (R180 plus park entry fee; available 8am to 5pm) to ride along can be a helpful way of picking up a few tips for spotting animals.

💤 Sleeping

★Chrislin African Lodge   LODGE $$
(📞042-233 0022; www.chrislin.co.za; off Rte 335; s/d incl breakfast from R995/1200; 🅿❄🛜🏊) 🍃 Chrislin is set among lawns, trees and aloes on a former citrus farm. The lodge offers thatched huts with stylish African decor and heat-banishing walls of cow dung and mud, and luxurious units. Activities including open-vehicle Addo safaris (half/full day R950/1500) are offered, as are three-course dinners (R195) featuring home-grown fruit, veg and herbs. It's a refreshingly cool and rustic spot after a day spotting elephants.

Addo Rest Camp   CAMPGROUND, LODGE $$
(📞in Pretoria 012-428 9111; www.sanparks.org; camping per site 1-2 people R285, cabins R870; ❄🏊) Addo's main rest camp, at the park headquarters, has myriad cottages, chalets, safari tents and rondavels, some overlooking the floodlit waterhole where elephants slake their thirst. Options range from camping, to two-person safari tents with shared bathroom (from R755), to luxurious houses (from R4000) with two en suite bedrooms, air-conditioning and DSTV.

★Camp Figtree   RESORT $$$
(📞082 611 3603; www.campfigtree.co.za; s/d incl breakfast from R2175/2900; @🏊) 🍃 Offering colonial-chic luxury, this property takes full advantage of breathtaking panoramic views from its perch in the Zuurberg mountains above Addo. Tastefully appointed cottages with elephantine bathrooms and private porches share the grounds with a pool, library, and restaurant which serves afternoon tea. Pampering aside, there's emphasis on the environmental – electricity is limited and ingenious solar-powered jar lamps are used at night. Figtree is around 11km from the R335 turn-off towards the Zuurberg Pass.

🍴 Eating

Cattle Baron   STEAK $$
(📞042-233 8674; Addo Rest Camp; mains R65-180; ⏲7am-9pm; 🅿) This surprisingly stylish restaurant in the park offers fine dining inside and a covered deck outside. Breakfast and lunch buffets are offered, while the meat-oriented à la carte menu is brimming with choice, especially if you're keen on steaks.

Lenmore   PIZZA
(📞087 700 0614; www.lenmore-addo.com; Main Rd, Addo; mains R85-125; ⏲noon-9pm Mon-Sat, to 3pm Sun) A wide selection of salads, steaks, chicken dishes and pasta make up the menu

here, but the best bet is to opt for a pizza. The deli and bakery make for a good place to stock up on picnic fodder.

ℹ️ Information

The 'town' of Addo is nothing more than a few shops, a petrol station and a bank with ATMs sharing a dusty car park on Rte 335. Addo Rest Camp also has a shop and petrol station.

ℹ️ Getting There & Away

Private shuttles operate between Port Elizabeth and Addo – ask at PE's tourist information office for recommended operators. Countless companies offer Addo day trips and overnight tours, but the best way to explore is in a hire car.

The park's sealed and gravel roads are mostly passable in a 2WD vehicle, though some may be out of action after been heavy rain – if in doubt, call the park headquarters.

Grahamstown

POP 50,217 / 📞 046

Grahamstown is referred to as GOG (Good Old Grahamstown) or, more commonly, the City of Saints because of its 40 or so religious buildings (mostly churches). The historic capital of Settler Country, it is also one of South Africa's liveliest university towns, and hosts several annual festivals, including one of the world's largest arts festivals. With its dreaming spires, weathered edifices and pastel shopfronts, the town centre has some fine examples of Georgian, Victorian and early Edwardian architecture.

Yet its genteel conservatism and English prettiness belie a bloody history; the Cape Frontier Wars, fought locally between European settlers and the Xhosa, continued for most of the 19th century. Once rulers of the region, the Xhosa were defeated by British and Boer forces after a fierce struggle.

Socially, while the university students dominate the town, packing out pubs and bars, artists and alternative spirits are settling here and, as the population ages, a more sophisticated side is developing.

◎ Sights

★Observatory Museum   MUSEUM
(www.ru.ac.za/albanymuseum; Bathurst St; adult/child R10/5; ⏲8am-4.30pm Mon-Fri) As well as several rooms of Victorian furniture and memorabilia, this 1850 house contains the wonderful camera obscura. Built in 1882, and the only one of its kind in the world outside the UK, the camera obscura is a series of lenses that reflects a perfect panoramic

image of Grahamstown onto a flat, white disc in a tower in the roof. Think of it as Victorian CCTV. Staff give fascinating demonstrations with a virtual tour of the town.

National English Literary Museum
LIBRARY, MUSEUM

(☑046-622 7042; www.nelm.org.za; 25 Worcester St; ☺8.30am-1pm & 2-4.30pm Mon-Fri) FREE Housed in a snazzy new building on the outskirts of town, the museum was about to reopen when we visited. The collection here contains South African manuscripts, first editions and works going back to 1797, with all the famous writers represented. The collection is in storage; phone ahead if there is something specific you would like to see. The new building also houses a cultural centre with two theatres and exhibitions on South African literature.

Birch's Gentlemen's Outfitters
HISTORIC BUILDING

(High St) Birch's is one of a number of historic shopfronts overlooking Church Sq. It has a marvellously old-fashioned 'slider' (a pulley system that sends money and change across the ceiling to and from the central till) and a vacuum pipe system used to send notes between floors. Staff will demonstrate the slider if you ask nicely.

International Library of African Music
MUSEUM

(ILAM; ☑046-603 8557; www.ru.ac.za/ilam; Prince Alfred St, Rhodes University; ☺8am-12.45pm & 2-5pm Mon-Fri) FREE There are 200 or so instruments to examine here – listen to field recordings and try to emulate what you've heard on *nyanga* (pan) pipes from Mozambique, a *kora* (stringed instrument) from Southern Africa or a Ugandan *kalimba* (thumb piano). Call ahead for an appointment.

🕝 Tours

Otto Ntshebe
CULTURAL

(☑082 214 4242; ottours@webmail.co.za; half-day tour R450) Local guide Otto Ntshebe runs tours of the township, known as Fingo Village, by foot or donkey cart, including visits to a local home.

✨ Festivals & Events

National Arts Festival
ART

(☑046-603 1103; www.nationalartsfestival.co.za; ☺Jul) Africa's largest arts festival runs for 10 days at the beginning of July. Remember two things: book ahead, as accommodation at this time can be booked out a year in advance; and bring something warm, as nights

can be freezing. The associated Fringe and Fingo Festivals, the latter showcasing art, music and theatre from the townships, offer hundreds more performances.

🛏 Sleeping

Bon Tempo
FARMSTAY $

(☑083 281 0257; www.bontempo.co.za; off Rte 67, Manley Flats; cottage R400-450; ℗) On a farm 20km from town en route to Bathurst, whimsical Bon Tempo offers rustic cottages and a gallery of penis sculptures. Meals available.

Kwam eMakana
HOMESTAY $

(☑072 448 0520; kwamemakana@gmail.com; s/d incl breakfast R375/550) Over 30 homestays offered by Xhosa mamas in Grahamstown's townships. Meals are available.

High Corner
GUESTHOUSE $$

(☑046-622 8284; www.highcorner.co.za; 122 High St; s/d incl breakfast R790/1080, s/d cottage R620/960; ℗❄🅿📶🏊) An account of this gracious house's 200-year history is the first thing you see you see upon entering. Rooms are split between the main building, with its antique furniture and elegant, high-ceilinged lounge and breakfast room, and modern self-catering cottages at the back.

Graham Hotel
HOTEL $$

(☑046-622 2324; www.grahamhotel.com; 123 High St; s/d incl breakfast R1185/1550; ℗❄🅿🏊) This modern hotel is recommended less for its standard rooms than for its many facilities, including African restaurant Calabash and **Champs Action Bar** (☺11am-11pm).

🍴 Eating

Festival Gallery Coffee Shop
CAFE $

(☑046-603 1103; 38 Somerset St; sandwiches R50; 🛜) While you're waiting for your cappuccino and slice of cake, browse the latest exhibition featuring paintings and sculpture from local artists.

★ Haricot's Deli & Bistro
DELI $$

(☑046-622 2150; www.haricots.co.za; 32 New St; mains R60-130; ☺bistro noon-3pm & 6-9.30pm, deli 9am-5pm Mon-Fri, to 2pm Sat; 🛜) Eavesdrop on faculty gossip at Grahamstown's best eatery, which is simultaneously a relaxed courtyard cafe and refined restaurant. The menu has a strong Mediterranean influence with Asian and Moroccan twists, resulting in gourmet dishes such as pork loin in milk and braised lamb with white wine.

Its deli heaves with wholesome goodies including quiches, pastries, gluten-free muffins and flourless chocolate cake.

Calabash
SOUTH AFRICAN $$

(✆046-622 2324; 123 High St; mains R95-130; ☺11am-11pm; ✐) Traditional South African food, including specialties like Xhosa hot-pots and *samp* (maize and beans), are served up in a warm, reed-ceilinged dining room. Vegetarian options and standard burger and pasta fare are on the menu as well.

❶ Information

The **tourist office** (✆046-622 3241; www.grahamstown.co.za; 63 High St; ☺8.30am-5pm Mon-Fri, 8am-noon Sat; ☎) has booklets and information on self-guided walking tours and various themed historical routes.

❶ Getting There & Away

Greyhound (p524), Translux (p527), Intercape (p354) and City to City (p527) buses depart from the Frontier Hotel (cnr High & Bathurst Sts) and the Conference Centre (Grey St) on their daily runs to Cape Town (R490, 14 hours), Port Elizabeth (R290, two hours), Durban (R500, 12 hours) and Jo'burg (R480, 13 hours).

Shared taxis depart from Jacob Zuma Dr, the eastern continuation of Beaufort St.

Port Alfred

POP 9747

Known as 'the Kowie' for the picturesque canal-like river that flows through its centre, Port Alfred is blessed with beautiful beaches, with some to the north backed by massive sand dunes. Upscale vacation homes line the marina and the hills surrounding town. It's generally a quiet place, except for visiting Grahamstown students. Things get busier during the rowing regatta in late September, and from mid-December to January, when the town bustles with holidaymakers.

🏃 Activities

Apart from the pristine beaches, there are good right- and left-hand surf breaks at the river mouth. Drifting up the Kowie River also makes for a relaxing few hours; riverine euphorbia and private wildlife reserves meet the shore, African fish eagles circle overhead, and fishers dig for mud prawns to use as bait.

Kowie River Cruises
BOATING

(✆073 162 1611; www.kowierivercruises.co.za; Ski Boat Club Jetty; adult/child R75/50) Cruises in the *Lady Biscay*, an enclosed 13m-long barge.

Kowie Canoe Trail
CANOEING

(✆046-624 2230; www.kowiecanoetrail.co.za; 64 Albany Rd; per person R250) This is a fairly easy 21km canoe trip upriver from Port Alfred, with an overnight stay in a hut at Horseshoe Bend in the Watersmeeting Nature Reserve. Mattresses, water and wood are provided, but you'll need your own food and bedding. Your bags can be transported for an extra fee.

Outdoor Focus
OUTDOORS

(✆046-624 4432; www.outdoorfocus.co.za; Beach Rd) A one-stop shop for activities, Outdoor Focus rents out canoes (one hour/day R70/250), and organises river cruises (adult/child R80/50) and sea trips (from R250). It can book the two-day Kowie Canoe Trail (p395), which is a fairly easy 21km canoe trip upriver from Port Alfred, with a night in a hut at Horseshoe Bend in the Watersmeeting Nature Reserve and an optional 12km hike. Other activities include diving, sand-boarding, horse riding and skydiving.

Kowie Hiking Trail
HIKING

(✆076 557 1324) An 8km trail through Kowie Nature Reserve – maps are available from the tourist office (p396).

Three Sisters Horse Trails
HORSE RIDING

(✆082 645 6345; www.threesistershorsetrails.co.za; per hour/half-day R350/750) Offers rides taking in beach and forest, and overnight trips along a river valley. Located 15km from town on Rte 72 towards East London.

🛏 Sleeping

★ Lookout
GUESTHOUSE $$

(✆046-624 4564; www.thelookout.co.za; 24 Park Rd; s/d/tr from R500/840/1180; ▣☎☎☎) Perched on a hill, this contemporary white-washed home has three units with kitchenettes and wonderful views.

Panorama
B&B $$

(✆046-624 5853; www.portalfredpanorama.co.za; 15 Wesley Hill; s/d incl breakfast R450/720; ▣☎) Dutch–South African couple Rob and Marianne are gracious hosts at this well-priced hilltop guesthouse with winning views. Rob, a pilot and speedboat owner, is full of suggestions for local activities.

My Pond Hotel
HOTEL $$

(✆046-624 4626; www.mypondhotel.com; Van der Riet St; d incl breakfast from R1050; ▣☎) This sleek boutique-style hotel on the Kowie River is operated and staffed by a hotel management school, so service is especially conscientious. The restaurant, Lily (p396), serves contemporary South African cuisine.

Richmond House
CHALET $$$

(✆046-624 8543; www.richmondhousecottages.com; Wesley Hill; cottage 2/4 people R1780/3300;

P 🌐) Three luxury self-catering cottages among lawns and coral trees on the site of a historic homestead atop Wesley Hill. Offers seclusion and tranquillity in the town centre.

✗ Eating

★ Zest Café
MEDITERRANEAN $

(Van der Riet St; mains R70-90; ⊗8am-5pm Mon-Fri, to 3pm Sat; 🌐) This friendly little Mediterranean-style refuge occupies a flowery courtyard scattered with pastel furniture. Besides good ol' pizzas, try one of the more inventive dishes such as spicy seafood, red pepper and almond tagine or vegetable rösti stack.

Lily
SOUTH AFRICAN $$

(✎ 046-624 4626; http://mypondhotel.com; 33 Van der Riet St, My Pond Hotel; mains R90-145; ⊗ noon-9pm) Lily serves contemporary South African cuisine, including recommended lamb and mint spring rolls, butternut-and-biltong chicken and traditional oxtail.

Graze by the River
HEALTH FOOD $$

(✎ 046-624 8095; 38 Van der Riet St; mains R85; ⊗ 9am-4pm Mon, Tue & Thu-Sun, dinner by appointment) 🍴 This eccentric spot at the back of a curio shop serves slow food, organic veg and ethically produced meat, fish and dairy products. They also roast coffee beans and smoke meat and fish. Daily dinner specials include line-caught cob, fresh tuna steaks and 30-day matured rump steaks.

ℹ Information

Sunshine Coast Tourism Port Alfred
(✎ 046-624 1235; www.sunshinecoasttourism. co.za; Causeway Rd; ⊗ 9am-4.30pm Mon-Fri, 9-12.30pm Sat) Has brochures and maps, plus information about accommodation and activities including boat cruises and fishing charters.

ℹ Transport

Baz Bus (p354) passes through four days a week between Port Elizabeth (R295, two hours) and Durban (R1970, 13 hours).

From the **shared taxi rank** (Biscay Rd) outside the Heritage Mall, there are daily services to Port Elizabeth (R95), Grahamstown (R40) via Bathurst (R25), and East London (R115).

Avis and Budget car hire have offices here.

Amathole

Running inland from East London, the Amathole region (pronounced 'ama-*tawl*-eh', from the Xhosa for 'calves') includes the eponymous mountain range, home to the enchanting village of Hogsback, and some wild and little-visited nature reserves. A good part of this area was the apartheid-era Xhosa homeland of Ciskei. If meeting Xhosa people against a mountain backdrop sounds appealing, a few backpacker hostels offer cultural experiences on a par with the Wild Coast.

East London

POP 267,007 / ☎ 043

In terms of population, geography and economy, this industrial and manufacturing centre (and the country's only river port) is an important Eastern Cape city. However, despite East London's bay-front location, which curves round to huge sand hills, stopping in this grey and rundown city is not recommended, especially when more appealing destinations lie nearby. You may pass through, though; with its airport and location at the meeting of the Sunshine and Wild Coasts, East London is a transport hub. Much of the centre is dilapidated, dotted with falling-to-pieces Victorian buildings and 1960s and '70s monstrosities. Wealthy neighbourhoods with sizeable homes and neatly clipped lawns and gardens extend north of Eastern Beach.

⊙ Sights

East London Museum
MUSEUM

(✎ 043-743 0686; www.elmuseum.za.org; 319 Oxford St; adult/child R15/5; ⊗ 9am-4.30pm Mon-Thu, to 4pm Fri) One of the first coelacanths, a type of fish thought to have become extinct over 50 million years ago, was discovered nearby in 1938; the stuffed original is on display here. Given the Eastern Cape's rich past the museum is worth a visit, with an excellent natural-history collection, and exhibits on subjects from trace-fossil human footprints to maritime history.

Ann Bryant Art Gallery
MUSEUM

(✎ 043-722 4044; 9 St Marks Rd; ⊗ 9am-5pm Mon-Fri, to noon Sat) FREE This mixed late Victorian and early Edwardian mansion has a good collection of South African paintings from landscapes to city scenes, featuring the likes of Pierneef and Cecil Skotnes plus contemporary local work. Pick up a catalogue on the way in. There's a small coffee shop in the coach house.

🛏 Sleeping

Sugarshack Backpackers
HOSTEL $

(✎ 043-722 8240; www.sugarshack.co.za; Eastern Esplanade; camping/dm from R80/100) Just steps from Eastern Beach, this faux log-cabin complex has three- to 12-bed dorms and mini-cabins (d R320) – all have seen better days. The upstairs deck and self-catering kitchen have great ocean views, and guests get free beer with meals at the equally raucous neighbouring Buccaneers Pub & Grill.

The Hampton HOTEL $$
(☏ 043-722 7924; www.thehampton.co.za; 2 Marine Tce; s/d incl breakfast from R950/1150; [P][✷][☎]) This renovated 1920s landmark building with a waterfront location and contemporary furnishings is a good choice for the centre. Sea-facing rooms, while more expensive, have panoramic views.

Quarry Lake Inn HOTEL $$$
(www.quarrylakeinn.co.za; Quartzite Drive, off Pearce St; s/d incl breakfast R1215/1700; [P][✷][☎][≋]) One of East London's best sleeping options, this small hotel offers bright, spotless rooms, a good breakfast, a small pool and friendly staff. Weekend rates are cheaper. It's in the northern suburbs, not far from Rte 72.

✖ Eating

★ **Grazia Fine Food & Wine** MEDITERRANEAN $$
(☏ 043-722 2009; www.graziafinefood.co.za; Upper Esplanade; mains R75-170; ⊙noon 10pm) This stylish, centrally located restaurant has large windows with sea views as well as an outdoor deck for dining. The Italian-born owner has helped create a sophisticated menu with a variety of European influences; the menu includes pasta, pizza, meat and seafood. Reservations recommended.

Sanook Cafe BURGERS $$
(☏ 043-721 3215; www.sanook.co.za; 11 Chamberlain Rd; mains R70-130; ⊙9am-10pm Mon-Sat; ☎) It's official – the gourmet-burger and craft-beer craze has reached East London, and Sanook does it particularly well. Burgers are juicy, tasty and come with a range of inventive toppings. Try the trio of sliders with a taster tray of Eastern Cape–brewed beer. Pizza, steak and salads also grace the menu at this vibrant, cheery spot.

ℹ Information

Buffalo City Tourism (☏ 043-705 1167; www.bctourism.co.za; Airport; ⊙9am-5pm)

ℹ Transport

AIR
East London Airport (☏ 043-706 0306; www.airports.co.za; Rte 72) is 10km southeast of the centre. **South African Airways** (☏ 043-706 0220; www.flysaa.com), SA Express (p526) and

Kulula (p526) fly daily to Jo'burg (from R680, 1½ hours). SA Express and FlySafair (p526) serve Cape Town (from R1000, two hours). SA Express also flies to Durban (from R1650, one hour) daily.

BUS
Baz Bus (p354) stops at Sugarshack en route between Port Elizabeth and Durban.

All the major bus lines serve the central **bus station** (Moore St, Windmill Park), near Eastern Beach. Greyhound (p524), Translux (p527), Intercape (p354) and City to City (p527) offer daily services to Mthatha (R290, three hours), Port Elizabeth (R450, 4½ hours), Durban (R420, 9½ hours), Cape Town (R550, 16 hours) and Jo'burg (R450, 16 hours).

SHARED TAXI
Shared taxis leave from Oxford St and the surrounding streets. On the corner of Buffalo and College Sts (near East London Zoo) are long-distance taxis to destinations north of East London, including Mthatha (R115, four hours). A few blocks south, on the corner of Caxton and Gillwell Sts, are taxis for local destinations including King William's Town (R25, one hour).

TRAIN
On Wednesdays, Fridays and Sundays, Shosholoza Meyl (p354) runs a tourist-class (with sleepers) train both to and from Jo'burg (R490, 20 hours) via Queenstown (R160, 4½ hours) and Bloemfontein (R310, 13 hours). Less recommended economy class (seat only) is also available on this route (to Queenstown/Bloemfontein/Jo'burg R110/200/300).

Hogsback
POP 1029

There's something about Hogsback that inspires people. An Edenic little village 1300m up in the beautiful Amathole Mountains above Alice, the village's name is derived from the 'bristles' (known geologically as a 'hogsback') that cover peaks of the surrounding hills.

Artists, poets, alternative therapists and other like-minded folk have helped create an environmentally inclined community here – an easy sensibility to adopt with fabulous views of mountains and forested valleys. The town's climate and history of green-fingered English settlers mean it's blessed with gorgeous (though seasonal) market-garden estates. Expect occasional snowfall and freezing temperatures in winter. Locals will tell you that JRR Tolkien, who lived in Bloemfontein until he was three, visited Hogsback, sowing the seed of his fantastical novels. That is extremely unlikely, but the area may well have inspired him via his son Christopher, who came here while stationed in South Africa with the British Royal Air Force.

⊙ Sights

Mirrors Gallery & Crystal Corner   GALLERY
(Bramble Close; admission by donation; ⊙10am-5pm) Mirrors has a magical 180-sq-m garden with a stone circle and labyrinth, a gallery of owner Ken's landscape photography, and a crystal shop.

Ecoshrine   SCULPTURE
(www.ecoshrine.co.za; 22 Summerton Dr; adult/child R20/free; ⊙9am-5pm Wed, Sat & Sun) Well-known mixed-media artist Diana Graham, a passionate environmental advocate, has created a cement sculpture garden dedicated to the forces of nature. The images, which Graham will explain, cover the origins of the earth, and ecological and scientific themes. The property has beautiful views (when the haze in the valley has cleared off) and can be reached from the village centre by road or a forest walking trail.

🏃 Activities

There are some great walks, bike rides and drives through the area's indigenous forests and pine plantations. A recommended hike (three to five hours) leaves from behind Away with the Fairies backpackers and passes various waterfalls. Purchase a R10 hiking permit at the backpackers.

True to Hogsback's alternative leanings, various invigorating and energy-balancing massages and treatments are available.

🛏 Sleeping

Away with the Fairies   HOSTEL $
(☑045-962 1031; www.awaywiththefairies.co.za; Ambleside Close; camping/dm/r from R90/160/475; P🛜🏊) 🍃 Terrific views abound at this magical, mystical clifftop backpackers: take an al fresco bath in the cliff-side tub, or climb 15m to the tree-house perched in the forest among parrots and monkeys. Activities on offer include Xhosa lessons, picnics in the forest, pancakes at sunrise, fishing, hiking, tree hugging and creative writing workshops.

★Edge Mountain Retreat   LODGE $$
(☑045-962 1159; www.theedge-hogsback.co.za; Perry Bar Lane; s/d incl breakfast R495/900, self-catering cottages R650-1800; P🛜) The tastefully decorated cottages and garden rooms are strung out along a dramatic plateau edge, which once marked the border

between the apartheid-era Ciskei homeland and South Africa proper. The cottages vary in size but all have log fires and a small kitchen. The vibe here is peace and relaxation. It's an unbeatable place for a healthy rest or a romantic weekend.

🍴 Eating

★The Edge Restaurant   INTERNATIONAL $$
(Perry Bar Lane; mains R75-130; ⊙7.30am-8.30pm) 🍃 The Edge's charming garden restaurant serves French toast with local berries and Hogsback's best coffee for breakfast, recommended tapas boards and wood-fired pizzas for lunch, and hearty but refined meat dishes for dinner. Throw in homemade bread, fresh, organic local produce, a cosy dining room, and paths leading to the nearby labyrinth and viewpoint. Dinner bookings essential.

ℹ Information

There's an ATM in the small supermarket, just off the main road, and a petrol station.

The helpful **information centre** (☑045-962 1245; www.hogsbackinfo.co.za; Main Rd; ⊙9am-3pm Mon-Sat, to 1pm Sun) can provide accommodation advice and maps for walks.

ℹ Getting There & Away

The way up to Hogsback on Rte 345 (the turnoff is 4km east of Alice) is sealed, but try to arrive in daylight due to mountain bends and occasional itinerant livestock. Coming from Queenstown and the north, take Rte 67 towards Fort Beaufort and turn off in Seymour, following the good gravel road to Elundini and the backpackers there; after 22km, this road meets Rte 345 south of Hogsback. Do not attempt the more direct dirt road to/from Cathcart in a 2WD car.

The easiest way to get to Hogsback without a car is in the shuttle run by Away with the Fairies (p398) on Tuesday, Wednesday, Friday and Sunday. It picks up at Sugarshack Backpackers in East London (R150, two hours), Buccaneers Lodge in Chintsa (R180, 2½ hours), East London Airport (R180, two hours) and King William's Town (R120, 1½ hours).

By shared taxi, you can get to Hogsback from Alice (R38), but you must change in Auckland.

City to City (p527) stops in Alice daily en route between East London (R140, two hours) and Pretoria via Queenstown, Bloemfontein and Jo'burg.

Eastern Karoo

The Karoo is the vast and beautiful semidesert stretching across the great South African plateau inland from the Cape coast; its southeastern section covers a chunk of the

Eastern Cape. The dry region, with its variety of grasses, hardy shrubs, *tolbos* (tumbleweed in Afrikaans) and succulents, including the trademark red aloe, is a surprisingly rich cultural and historic destination. Graaff-Reinet, the architectural 'jewel of the Karoo', is complemented by artistic Nieu Bethesda and literary Cradock, while **Camdeboo and Mountain Zebra National Parks** offer stunning scenery and rare Cape mountain zebras. Throughout, the overwhelming sense of space, peace and freedom stand in sharp contrast to the busier coastline – and make the region perfect road-trip territory.

Between December and February temperatures in Karoo towns can reach 45°C, and things barely cool down in March and April. June and July see the thermometer plummet to -5°C, with snow in the mountain passes and frosts.

Graaff-Reinet

POP 26,585

Cradled in a curve of the Sundays River and encircled by the Camdeboo National Park, Graaff-Reinet is often referred to as the 'jewel of the Karoo'. South Africa's fourth-oldest town, the 'far-off colony of Graaff-Reinet', as the Dutch East India Company called the remote spot when they established it in 1786, has a superb architectural heritage. More than 220 buildings designated as national monuments include gabled Cape Dutch houses, flat-roofed Karoo cottages and ornate Victorian villas. Add in small-town charm, some excellent accommodation and restaurants, plus a handful of museums, and you'll begin to understand why Graaff-Reinet acquired its nickname.

◉ Sights

Urquhart House MUSEUM
(Somerset St; adult/child R25/10; ⊙8am-1pm & 1.45-4pm Mon-Fri) Shows how well-to-do 19th-century families lived, complete with wooden floors and period furniture.

Old Library MUSEUM
(cnr Church & Somerset Sts; adult/child R25/10; ⊙8am-1pm & 1.45-4pm Mon-Fri, 9am-1pm Sat & Sun) This former library, built in 1847, houses a wide-ranging collection of historical artefacts. There's fossils from the Karoo, displays on Khoe-San rock paintings and slavery, and an exhibition about local son Robert Sobukwe, founder of the Pan African Congress (PAC).

Reinet House MUSEUM
(Murray St; adult/child R25/10; ⊙8am-4pm Mon-Fri, 9am-1pm Sat & Sun) This Dutch Reformed parsonage, built between 1806 and 1812, is a beautiful example of Cape Dutch architecture. The cobblestone rear courtyard has a grapevine that was planted in 1870 and is one of the largest in the world.

Hester Rupert Art Museum MUSEUM
(☑049-807 5700; www.rupertartmuseum.co.za; Church St; adult/family R10/20; ⊙9am-12.30pm & 2-5pm Mon-Fri, to noon Sat & Sun) Located in one of South Africa's oldest churches, a Dutch Reformed Mission church consecrated in 1821, this collection of South African paintings (and a few sculptures) from the 1950s and '60s includes the likes of Irma Stern.

Old Residency MUSEUM
(Parsonage St; adult/child R25/10; ⊙8am-1pm & 1.45-4pm Mon-Fri, 9am-noon Sat & Sun) A well-preserved, 19th-century house with creaking wooden floors and a large collection of firearms, as well as historical photos.

⛵ Tours

Camdeboo Adventure Tours ADVENTURE
(☑049-892 3410; www.karoopark.co.za; 81 Caledon St; tours per person R400) Buks and Chantelle Marais of Camdeboo Cottages and Karoopark Guest House organise sundowner trips to the Valley of Desolation and wildlife viewing drives in Camdeboo National Park. They also do trips further afield to Mountain Zebra National Park and Baviaanskloof Wilderness Area. Two people minimum per tour.

Karoo Connections TOURS
(☑049-892 3978; www.karooconnections.co.za; 7 Church St) Based at McNaughton's Bookshop, David McNaughton organises a range of tours and transfers, including a sundowner tour of the Valley of Desolation by open Land Rover (R475 per person), a half-day trip to Nieu Bethesda (R700; full day including Bushman rock art and fossils R1100), and wildlife-watching drives to Camdeboo (R400) and Mountain Zebra National Parks.

🛏 Sleeping

Profcon Resort COTTAGES, CAMPGROUND $
(☑049-892 2887; www.profconresort.co.za; 82 Somerset St; camping R200, d R500, cottages from R580; 🅿❄🛜🐾) A well-run complex with modern rooms, garden cottages and numerous facilities including a children's playground.

Aa 'Qtansisi
GUESTHOUSE **$$**

(☑ 049-891 0243; www.aaqtansisi.co.za; 69 Somerset St; s/d incl breakfast R750/1200; ❋ 🛜 ≋) Translating as 'We welcome you' in Khoe-San (to pronounce the name, drop the 'Q'), Aa 'Qtansisi's eight lavish rooms are inspired by the owner's travels, with themes including the Karoo, a French chateau and Morocco. The trellis-covered backyard is a tempting oasis with a plunge pool and hammocks, and the gourmet breakfast includes a fruit platter and shot glass of muesli and nuts. Dinner is also available (R150).

Camdeboo Cottages
GUESTHOUSE **$$**

(☑049-892 3180; www.camdeboocottages.co.za; 16 Parliament St; r from R750, cottage from R950; P ❋ 🛜 ≋) Behind their whitewashed facades and green shutters, these eight mid-19th-century cottages mix colonial furniture and modern amenities. Yellowwood floors, insulating reed-and-clay roofs, claw-footed baths and vintage cake tins on the dresser meet electric blankets, radiators and DSTV.

Buiten Verwagten
GUESTHOUSE **$$**

(☑ 049-892 4504; www.buitenverwagten.co.za; 58 Bourke St; s/d incl breakfast R875/1300; ❋ 🛜 ≋) Every aspect of this Victorian-era home is tastefully curated by its friendly and professional owners. Inside are high ceilings, cedar and pine floors, and elegant antiques; outside are a trellis-covered veranda, a perfectly manicured lawn and a courtyard pool. There are two self-catering rooms at the back.

★ Drostdy Hotel
HISTORIC HOTEL **$$$**

(☑049-892 2161; www.newmarkhotels.com; 30 Church St; s/d from R1400/1600; P ❋ 🛜 ≋) Even more magnificent following a multi-million-rand renovation, the town's flagship hotel offers a fine mix of historic charm and modern luxury. Accommodation is in mid-19th-century cottages, originally built for freed slaves. A long list of facilities make it a world-class hotel, including a spa, an art gallery, three pools in a manicured garden, and restaurants with top South African chefs.

✖ Eating

Our Yard
CAFE **$**

(50 Somerset St; mains R50-70; ☺8am-5pm Mon-Fri, to 2pm Sat; 🍴) This 'roastery and culture stop' serves coffees from all over the world, light meals, scones and cakes in a shady courtyard. Also here are a gallery and T-shirt shop.

★ Polka Cafe
SOUTH AFRICAN **$$**

(☑ 087 550 1363; www.polkacafe.co.za; 52 Somerset St; lunch/dinner mains R75/130; ☺7.30am-10pm Mon-Sat) Polka's nouvelle cuisine improves upon conventional fare and South African classics with subtle twists, beautiful presentation and taste upgrades. Karoo lamb, matured steaks and bobotie are on the dinner menu; lighter lunches include savoury pancakes and thin-crust pizzas.

ⓘ Information

Graaff-Reinet Tourism (☑049-892 4248; www.graaffreinet.co.za; 13A Church St; ☺8am-5pm Mon-Fri, 9am-noon Sat) This helpful office has accommodation information and an abundance of maps.

ⓘ Getting There & Away

Intercape (p354) and Translux (p527) serve Cape Town (R430, 12 hours) and Jo'burg (R470, 11 hours) daily; the latter also runs to East London (R260, six hours) and Port Elizabeth (R250, four hours). Tickets and information are available at the tourist office.

Long-distance buses stop at **Kudu Motors** (Church St). Shared taxis leave from Market Sq. Major destinations are Port Elizabeth (R260) and Cape Town (R520).

Avis has an office opposite Karoopark Guest House on Caledon St.

Camdeboo National Park

Covering an area of 194 sq km, **Camdeboo National Park** (☑049-892 3453; www.sanparks. org; adult/child R84/42; ☺Lakeview Gate 6am-7pm Oct-Mar, 7am-6pm May-Aug, 6.30am-6.30pm Apr & Sep; P) has plenty of animals, but the real attractions are the spectacular geological formations, and great views of Graaff-Reinet and the sun-baked Karoo plains. The park's name comes from the Khoekhoen for 'green valleys' – probably a reference to the spekboom growing here, which remain verdant throughout the winter.

⊙ Sights

Valley of Desolation
VIEWPOINT

(off Rte 63; ☺6am-7.30pm Oct-Mar, 7am-6pm May-Aug, 6.30am-7pm Apr & Sep) The Valley of Desolation is the park's most popular sight. It's a hauntingly beautiful valley with an outstanding view – the rugged, piled dolerite columns here are set against the backdrop of the endless Karoo plains. Graaff-Reinet is also visible, nestled in a bend of the Sundays River. The valley viewpoint, 14km from town, can be reached by car on a steep but sealed road, and there's a 1.5km circuit walk. The best times to visit are sunrise and sunset.

🏃 Activities

Eerstefontein Day Trail
HIKING

FREE The Eerstefontein Day Trail runs through the park's western section past the Valley of Desolation; there are three route options with distances of 5km, 11km and 14km. The park reception has a map.

🛏 Sleeping

Lakeview Tented Camp
TENTED CAMP $

(tent for 2 people R650; **P**) Near Nqweba Dam, this campsite has pre-erected safari tents furnished with twin beds and a table and chairs on the deck. There's a shared kitchen and ablutions.

Nqweba Campsite
CAMPGROUND $

(camping R225; **P**) This campsite near the dam of the same name has 15 gravel sites beneath thorn trees, each with a braai, and a self-catering kitchen.

❶ Getting There & Away

You'll need your own vehicle to visit the wildlife-watching area; otherwise, book a tour in Graaff-Reinet.

The Wild Coast

This shipwreck-strewn coastline rivals any in the country in terms of beauty, stretching over 350km from just east of East London to Port Edward. Often referred to as the 'Transkei' (the name of the apartheid-era homeland that once covered most of this area), the region also stretches inland, covering pastoral landscapes where clusters of rondavels scatter the rolling hills covered in short grass.

The local Xhosa people are some of the friendliest you'll meet anywhere in South Africa, and you might be invited inside a home or, at the very least, a *shebeen* (tavern). South of the Mbashe River lives the Gcaleka tribe; the Mpondomise live to the north. In this land of far-flung river estuaries and backpackers resembling Xhosa settlements, numerous outdoor activities and cultural tours are on offer. Birdlife is abundant, especially in the parks.

Chintsa

POP 1803 / 📞 043

Less than an hour's drive north of East London, Chintsa is worlds away from the big city. It comprises two small villages – Chintsa East and Chintsa West, on either side of the Chintsa River Mouth – fronted by a spectacular white-sand beach with good, swimmable surf. It's a great place to hang out for a few days (or weeks) on this part of the coast.

◎ Sights

Inkwenkwezi Game Reserve
WILDLIFE RESERVE

(📞043-734 3234; www.inkwenkwezi.com; tented bush camp incl meals & activities per person from R1900) Between the Chintsa East and West turnoffs, the private, upmarket Inkwenkwezi features the Big Five (although the elephants and lions are kept separately) and five biomes. In addition to wildlife drives (per person from R795), the reserve offers guided mountain biking, hiking and canoeing. Bookings essential for all activities.

🛏 Sleeping

★ Buccaneers Lodge
HOSTEL $

(📞043-734 3012; www.cintsa.com; Chintsa West; camping/dm/r/cottage/suite from R100/160/410/900/995; **P**@🛜🏊) Offering an accessible taste of the Wild Coast, fabulous 'Buccs' is a sort of all-inclusive holiday resort for backpackers, beach bums and travellers interested in Xhosa culture. Sleeping options cover the spectrum from comfortable four- to 12-bed dorms and safari tents, to self-catering cottages and gorgeous suites for two with sea-facing decks.

A mind-boggling range of activities, tours and cultural experiences is offered, while on-site entertainments include free use of canoes and boogie boards, complimentary wine and Sunday breakfast, beach volleyball, yoga and spa treatments. Meals are served, family-style, in the charming candle-lit dining room and outdoor deck.

Areena Riverside Resort
RESORT $

(📞043-734 3055; www.areenaresort.com; Glengariff; camping/r/cottage from R165/470/850; **P**🏊) Hugging the tree-shaded shore of the Kwelera River, Areena has self-catering rondavels, thatched cottages, timber chalets, riverside tents and caravan sites – and a 3.5-sq-km wildlife reserve. There's a tennis court, a bar-restaurant open Wednesday to Saturday (mains R70 to R120), plus abseiling, zip-lining, sea kayaking and river cruises. Prices rise steeply in December and over Easter.

🍴 Eating

Barefoot Café
PUB FOOD $

(Chintsa East; mains R65; ⊗4pm-late Mon & Wed-Fri, from 9am Sat & Sun) What nightlife there is in Chintsa centres on this casual bar-restaurant where foreign volunteers, backpackers

Wild Coast

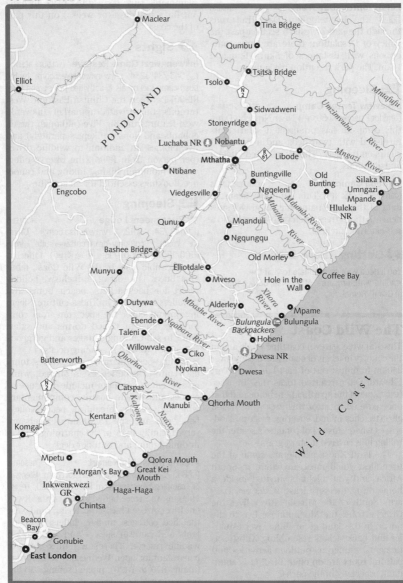

and locals mix. Burgers, peri peri chicken, pizzas and beer-battered fish are on the menu. Kitchen closes at 8.30pm.

Emerald Vale BREWERY **$$**
(☏043-738 5397; www.emeraldvalebrewery.co.za; Chintsa East; tour & tasting R70, mains R70-100; ⊙11am-7pm Wed-Sun, tours by appt noon & 4pm; P 🛜 🐾) Half-hour tours of this brewery in a converted barn on a working farm include tasters of the four ales. The bar-restaurant serves food to complement the beer, including burgers and a few veggie options. There's a playground and milkshake bar for the kids.

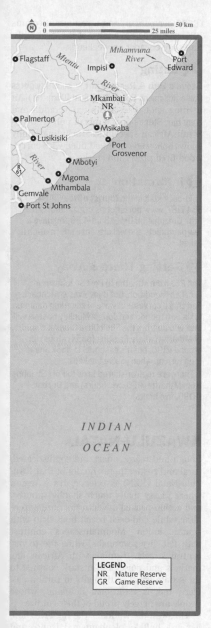

LEGEND
NR Nature Reserve
GR Game Reserve

ℹ Getting There & Away

Baz Bus (p354) stops at Buccaneers en route between Port Elizabeth and Durban. Many accommodation options at this end of the Wild Coast will arrange a transfer from East London with prior notice.

With your own transport, follow the brown signpost to Chintsa from the N2, about 30km north of East London. Chintsa East and West are both about 15km further on.

Coffee Bay

POP 258 / 📞 047

Because of its beautiful kilometre-long beach and easy access to dramatic surrounding scenery, this once-remote village has become something of an essential Wild Coast stop for backpackers and South African hippies. No-one is sure how tiny Coffee Bay got its name, but there is a theory that a ship, wrecked here in 1863, deposited its cargo of coffee beans on the beach. The village today is a scruffy nondescript place, where locals hover around the backpackers enclave, trying to sell *dagga* (marijuana), curios and day trips.

Popular activities such as guided hikes, horse riding, cultural visits and surfing trips can be organised through town's various accommodation options.

🛏 Sleeping

Coffee Shack　　　　　　　　　　HOSTEL $
(📞 047-575 2048; www.coffeeshack.co.za; camping/dm/r R90/150/500, r with shared bathroom R400; 🅿 🛜) An enduringly popular beachfront option for travellers looking to surf and party, Coffee Shack doesn't let standards slip among the merrymaking. The complex is rather labyrinthine, with bright paint masking its sometimes-institutional feel, but there are rondavels across the river with more privacy. Camping is out back with ocean views.

Ocean View Hotel　　　　　　　　HOTEL $$
(📞 047-575 2005; www.oceanview.co.za; s/d with half board from R850/1500; 🅿 🛜 🏊) This 45-year-old hotel offers a great mix of old-fashioned charm and modern elements, with generous buffet meals, a lovely thatched beach bar and chalet-style rooms with private patio overlooking the sea or garden. Located at the far end of the main beach from the Coffee Bay melee, it offers activities including guided hikes, horse riding and cultural tours.

🍴 Eating

Papazela's　　　　　　　　　　　PIZZA $$
(pizzas R90; ⊙ 3-11pm) This popular shack serves wood-fired pizzas with predictably wacky names, eaten with fingers and accompanied by sweeping beach views and cold quarts of beer.

ⓘ Getting There & Away

A sealed road runs to Coffee Bay from the N2 at Viedgesville – beware of children, potholes and stray farm animals. Backpacker shuttles (R80) meet the Baz Bus (p354) at the Shell Ultra City garage, 4km south of Mthatha. Shared taxis also run from from Mthatha (R35, one hour).

Port St Johns

POP 6441 / ☎ 047

Dramatically located at the mouth of the Mzimvubu (or Umzimvubu) River and framed by towering cliffs covered with tropical vegetation, the laid-back town of Port St Johns is the original Wild Coast journey's end. There's a vibrant, if somewhat run-down, quality to the town, which is the largest between East London and Port Edward.

Bull Zambezi sharks calve upriver and there have been several fatal attacks in recent years, all at Second Beach. Until shark nets are installed, it's recommended that you do nothing more than wade off the town's beaches, and even then with caution.

🛏 Sleeping

Amapondo Backpackers   HOSTEL $
(☎ 083 315 3103; www.amapondo.co.za; Second Beach Rd; camping R90, dm from R150, s/d with shared bathroom from R300/390; P 🛜) A mellow place where several low-slung buildings line a hillside with excellent views of Second Beach. A rambling network of verandas, leafy walkways and chill spaces leads to the simple rooms, while smarter cottages stand on the hill above. An excellent range of activities is offered, include horse riding, cultural tours, canoeing, hiking to Silaka and sundowners at the airstrip.

Jungle Monkey   HOSTEL $
(☎ 047-564 1517; www.junglemonkey.co.za; 3 Berea Rd; camping/dm/r R90/120/450, r with shared bathroom R390; P @ 🛜 ☀) Music booms through the trees as you approach this casual hang-out, with its desert-island bar-restaurant overlooking the pool. Rooms are reasonably comfortable and distant from any party noise, while dorms are more basic. Hiking, activities and day trips are on offer. It's located between town and Second Beach.

Port St Johns River Lodge   LODGE $$
(☎ 047-564 0005; www.portstjohnsriverlodge. co.za; Mzimvubu Dr; s/d incl breakfast R640/1000; P ✳ 🛜 ☀) One of a few riverside lodges north of town, this well-run complex has comfortable rooms, self catering chalets

(R500 per person) and a restaurant (mains R85) gazing across a lawn at the river cliffs. Rates are cheaper on weekends.

✖ Eating

Steve's Pub & Restaurant   SOUTH AFRICAN $$
(Main Rd; mains R65-120; ⊗ 8am-10pm; 🛜) An inviting spot with a covered veranda and cosy bar, Steve's does a mix of pub grub and South African specialities, including bunny chow (hollowed-out bread filled with curry), wood-fired pizzas and steaks.

ⓘ Information

Laid-back staff in the **tourist office** (☎ 047-564 1187; www.portstjohns.org.za/tourism. htm; Umzimvubu Dr; ⊗ 8am-4.30pm) have a few pamphlets and will dispense information if asked.

ⓘ Getting There & Away

The R61 from Mthatha to Port St Johns is in excellent condition, but it involves switchbacks and sharp curves – beware of speeding minibus taxis. Amapondo and Jungle Monkey hostels will pick you up from the Shell Ultra City, 4km south of Mthatha (where Baz Bus (p354) stops) for around R100, but it's essential to book ahead (and turn up when you've booked).

There are regular shared taxis to Port St Johns from Mthatha (R50, two hours) and Durban (R190, five hours).

KWAZULU-NATAL

Rough and ready, smart and sophisticated, rural and rustic: there's no doubt that Kwa-Zulu-Natal (KZN) is eclectic. It's a region where glassy malls touch shabby suburbs, and action-packed adventurers ooze adrenaline while laid-back beach bods drip with suntan lotion. Mountainscapes contrast with flat, dry savannahs, while the towns' central streets, teeming with African life, markets and noise, are in stark contrast to the sedate tribal settlements in rural areas. Here, too, is traditional Zululand, whose people are fiercely proud of their culture.

Throw in the wildlife – the Big Five (lion, leopard, buffalo, elephant and rhino) and rare marine species – the historic intrigue of the Battlefields, fabulous hiking opportunities, and the sand, sea and surf of coastal resort towns, and you get a tantalising taste of local heritage and authentic African highlights that should be on every 'must-do' list.

KwaZulu-Natal

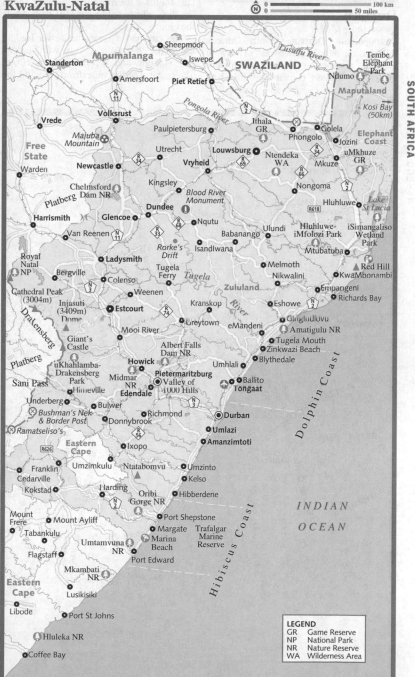

0   100 km
0   50 miles

Sheepmoor

Standerton

Iswepe

SWAZILAND

Lusutfu River

Tembe
Elephant
Park

Ndumo

Amersfoort

Piet Retief

Mpumalanga

Pongola River

Maputaland

*Kosi Bay
(50km)*

Vrede

Volksrust

Paulpietersburg

Ithala
GR

Phongolo

Golela

Jozini

**Elephant
Coast**

*Majuba
Mountain*

Utrecht

Louwsburg

Ntendeka
WA

uMkhuze
GR

**Free
State**

Warden

Newcastle

Vryheid

Mkuze

Chelmsford
Dam NR

Kingsley

Nongoma

Hluhluwe

*Lake
St Lucia*

Harrismith

Glencoe

Dundee

*Blood River
Monument*

Nqutu

Ulundi

Hluhluwe-
iMfolozi Park

iSimangaliso
Wetland
Park

Van Reenen

Babanango

Mtubatuba

Royal
Natal
NP

Bergville

Ladysmith

*Rorke's
Drift*

Isandlwana

Melmoth

Red Hill

Cathedral Peak
(3004m)

Colenso

Tugela
Ferry

Tugela

Nikwalini

KwaMbonambi

Injasuti
(3409m)
Dome

Weenen

Zululand

Eshowe

Empangeni

Richards Bay

Drakensberg

Giant's
Castle

Estcourt

Kranskop

River

Gingindlovu

Mooi River

Greytown

eMandeni

Amatigulu NR

Albert Falls
Dam NR

Tugela Mouth

Platberg

uKhahlamba-
Drakensberg
Park

Howick

Umhlali

Zinkwazi Beach
Blythedale

Sani Pass

Hilton

Midmar
NR

Pietermaritzburg

Edendale

*Valley of
1000 Hills*

Ballito

Tongaat

Underberg

Bulwer

Richmond

*Bushman's Nek
& Border Post*

Donnybrook

Durban

Ramatseliso's

Ixopo

Umlazi

**Eastern
Cape**

Amanzimtoti

Franklin

Umzimkulu

Ntatabomvu

Umzinto

Cedarville

Kelso

Kokstad

Harding

Oribi
Gorge NR

Hibberdene

Mount
Frere

Mount Ayliff

Port Shepstone

*INDIAN
OCEAN*

Tabankulu

Margate

Trafalgar
Marine
Reserve

Umtamvuna
NR

Marina
Beach

Flagstaff

Port Edward

Mkambati
NR

**Eastern
Cape**

Lusikisiki

Hibiscus Coast

Libode

Port St Johns

Dolphin Coast

Hluleka NR

Coffee Bay

LEGEND
GR   Game Reserve
NP   National Park
NR   Nature Reserve
WA   Wilderness Area

Durban

POP 600,000 / ☏ 031

Cosmopolitan Durban, South Africa's third-largest city (known as eThekweni in Zulu), is sometimes passed over for her 'cooler' Capetonian cousin. But this isn't fair; there's a lot more to fun-loving Durbs (as she's affectionately known) than meets the eye.

The city had a major makeover leading up to the 2010 World Cup, with a sleek new stadium and a revamped waterfront. The renewal of the waterfront area and the

Durban

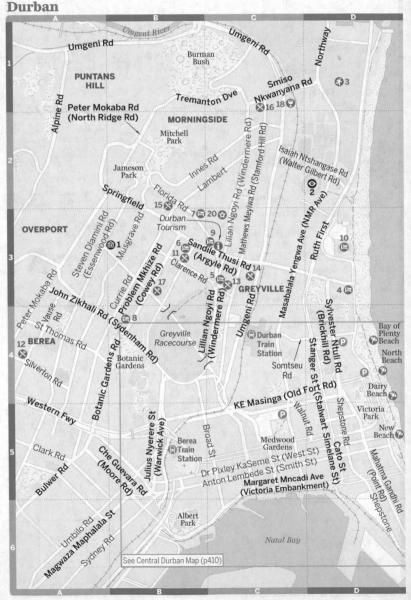

See Central Durban Map (p410)

sweeping away of the old sleaze has given municipal authorities new confidence and ambition – there are plans to extend the waterfront promenade right down the south coast.

Home to the largest concentration of people of Indian descent outside of India, Durban also boasts an unmistakeably Asian feel, with the marketplaces and streets of the Indian area replete with the sights, sounds and scents of the subcontinent.

History

It took some time for Durban to be established. Natal Bay, around which the city is based, provided refuge for seafarers at least as early as 1685, and it's thought that Vasco da Gama anchored here in 1497. Though the Dutch bought a large area of land around the bay from a local chief in 1690, their ships didn't make it across the sand bar at the entrance to the bay until 1705, by which time the chief had died, and his son refused to acknowledge the deal.

Natal Bay attracted little attention from Europeans until 1824, when Englishmen Henry Fynn and Francis Farewell set up a

INDIAN OCEAN

South Beach

Erskine Ter

Addington Beach

uShaka Beach

KwaZulu-Natal Tourism Authority

19 THE POINT

Durban

◎ Sights
1 Campbell Collections B3
2 Moses Mabhida Stadium D2

✪ Activities, Courses & Tours
3 Durban Country Club D1
   STS Sport .... (see 2)

◔ Sleeping
4 Blue Waters D3
5 Concierge C3
6 Gibela Backpackers Lodge B3
7 Madeline Grove B3
8 Napier House B4
9 Quarters C3
10 Southern Sun Suncoast Hotel D3

✖ Eating
11 9th Avenue Bistro B3
12 Cafe 1999 .... A4
13 Freedom Cafe C3
14 Hollywood Bets C3
15 House of Curries B2
16 Mali's Indian Restaurant C1
17 Market B3

◕ Drinking & Nightlife
18 S43 .... C1
   Unity Brasserie & Bar .... (see 12)

✪ Entertainment
19 Chairman E6
   Sun Coast Casino .... (see 10)
20 Zack's C3

◧ Shopping
   African Art Centre .... (see 9)
   Station Drive Precinct .... (see 18)

base here to trade for ivory with the Zulu. Shaka, a powerful Zulu chief, granted land around the bay to the trading company and it was accepted in the name of King George IV.

The settlement was slow to prosper, partly because of the chaos Shaka was causing in the area. By 1835 it had become a small town with a mission station, and that year it took the name D'Urban, after the Cape Colony governor.

In 1837 the Voortrekkers crossed the Drakensberg and founded Pietermaritzburg, 80km northwest of Durban. The next year, after Durban was evacuated during a raid by the Zulu, the Boers claimed control. It was reoccupied by a British force later that year, but the Boers stuck by their claim. The British sent troops to Durban to secure the settlement but were defeated by the Boers at the Battle of Congella in 1842.

The Boers retained control for a month until a British frigate arrived (fetched by Dick King, who rode the 1000km of wild country between Durban and Grahamstown in Eastern Cape in 10 days) and dislodged them. The next year Natal was annexed by the British, and Durban began its growth as an important colonial port city. In 1860 the first indentured Indian labourers arrived to work the cane fields. Despite the unjust system – slave labour by another name – many free Indian settlers arrived in 1893, including Mohandas Gandhi.

⊙ Sights

⊙ Beachfront

Durban's beachfront has experienced a resurgence thanks to the massive revamp that was completed prior to the World Cup. The new promenade – a pedestrian superhighway – runs behind the beaches but offers little shade. Both the beaches and promenade extend from the Blue Lagoon (at the mouth of the Umgeni River) to uShaka Marine World on the Point, an area known as the 'Golden Mile', although it's much longer. The road behind this is OR Tambo Pde (Marine Pde), and it's lined with high-rise hotels and a sprinkling of cafes.

Excellent signage at the beaches provides maps and names of the different beaches, although it's really one stretch of sand with different names. At Suncoast Beach, in front of the casino, umbrellas and chairs are available on a first come, first served basis. Due to its location at the strip's southern end, uShaka Beach is often slightly more

sheltered and is close to cafes and a small car park. Keep an eye out for the incredible sand sculptures done by locals, depicting anything from mermaids to lions. The uShaka Beach has activities including surfing lessons and kayaking. Warning: the surf and currents at Durban's beaches can be dangerous. Always swim in patrolled areas; these are indicated by flags.

uShaka Marine World   AMUSEMENT PARK
(Map p410; ☑031-328 8000; www.ushakamarineworld.co.za; uShaka Beach, the Point; Wet'n'Wild or Sea World adult/child R175/130, combo ticket for both parks R200/160; ⊙9am-5pm) Divided into areas including Sea World and Wet'n'Wild, uShaka Marine World boasts one of the largest aquariums in the world, the biggest collection of sharks in the southern hemisphere, marine animals and exhibits, a mock-up 1940s steamer wreck featuring two classy restaurants, a shopping centre, and enough freshwater rides to make you seasick. There are various options to 'meet' dolphins, seals and rays, but animal welfare groups suggest such interactions create stress for these creatures.

Moses Mabhida Stadium   STADIUM
(Map p406; ☑031-582 8242; www.mmstadium. com; 44 Isaiah Ntshangase Rd (Walter Gilbert Rd), Stamford Hill; SkyCar adult/child R60/30, Adventure Walk per person R90, Big Swing per person R695; ⊙SkyCar 9am-5pm, Adventure Walk 10am, 1pm & 3pm Sat & Sun, Big Swing 9.30am-4.30pm Mon-Fri, 8am-5pm Sat & Sun) Durbanites are proud of their state-of-the-art stadium, constructed for the 2010 World Cup. Resembling a giant basket, it seats 56,000 people, and its arch was inspired by the 'Y' in the country's flag. Visitors can head up to the arch in a SkyCar, puff up on foot (550 steps) on an Adventure Walk or plunge off the 106m arch on the giant Big Swing. All options offer great views of Durban.

⊙ City Centre

City Hall   NOTABLE BUILDING
(Map p410; Anton Lembede St (Smith St), City Centre) Dominating the city centre is the opulent 1910 Edwardian neo-baroque City Hall. In front of the hall is Francis Farewell Sq.

Natural Science Museum   MUSEUM
(Map p410; ☑031-311 2256; Anton Lembede St (Smith St), City Centre; ⊙8.30am-4pm Mon-Sat, 11am-4pm Sun) FREE This museum at City Hall boasts an impressive, if pleasantly retro, display of stuffed birds and insects, plus

African animals. Check out the cockroach and dung-beetle displays, the reconstructed dodo and the life-size dinosaur model.

Art Gallery GALLERY
(Map p410; 031-311 2262; Anton Lembede St (Smith St), City Centre; 8.30am-4pm Mon-Sat, 11am-4pm Sun) FREE Under City Hall's impressive dome is this gallery with a small but interesting collection of South African artworks, including paintings, mixed media and ceramics. It also has temporary and rotating exhibitions.

KwaMuhle Museum MUSEUM
(Map p410; 031-311 2233; www.durbanhistorymuseums.org.za; 130 Bram Fischer Rd (Ordnance Rd), City Centre; 8.30am-4pm Mon-Sat) FREE This was formerly the Native Administration headquarters, where Durban's colonial authorities formulated the structures of urban racial segregation (the 'Durban System'), which were the blueprints of South Africa's apartheid policy. Exhibitions on apartheid are housed in various rooms leading off a central courtyard.

Old Courthouse Museum MUSEUM
(Map p410; 031 311 2229; www.durbanhistorymuseums.org.za; 77 Samora Machel St (Aliwal St), City Centre; 8.30am-4pm Mon-Fri, to 12.30pm Sat) FREE Found in the beautiful 1866 courthouse behind City Hall, this museum offers a worthwhile insight into the highs and lows of colonial living. There's also a moving exhibit on the sadly brief life of journalist Nathaniel (Nat) Wakasa, as well as a collection of model ships that kids (and more than a few adults) will enjoy.

Victoria Embankment

Sugar Terminal NOTABLE BUILDING
(Map p410; 031-365 8100; 25 Leuchars Rd; adult/concession R16/8; tours 8.30am, 10am, 11.30am & 2pm Mon-Thu, 8.30am, 10am & 11.30m Fri) Maydon Wharf, which runs along the southwestern side of the harbour and south of Margaret Mncadi Ave, is home to the Sugar Terminal, which offers an insight into the sugar trade. The trade was the backbone of Durban's early economy.

Port Natal Maritime Museum MUSEUM
(Map p410; 031-322 9598; www.durbanhistorymuseums.org.za; Maritime Dr; adult/child R5/3; 8.30am-4pm Mon-Sat, 11am-4pm Sun) On a service road running parallel to Margaret Mncadi Ave you can explore two former steam tugs and see the huge wicker basket once used for hoisting passengers onto ocean liners.

Indian Area

Juma Mosque MOSQUE
(Map p410; 031-304 1518; cnr Denis Hurley St (Queen St) & Dr Yusuf Dadoo St (Grey St); 9am-4pm Mon-Thu, to 11am Sat) The largest mosque in the southern hemisphere; call ahead for a guided tour. Next to the mosque between Dr AB Xuma St and Cathedral Rd, and near the Catholic Emmanuel Cathedral, is the 1927 Madrassa Arcade, a bazaar-like shopping space with a distinctly Indian flavour.

Berea & Around

Durban Botanic Gardens GARDENS
(Map p410; 031-309 9240; www.durbanbotanicgardens.org.za; John Zikhali Rd (Sydenham Rd); 7.30am-5.15pm) FREE A 2000-sq-metre garden featuring one of the rarest cycads *(Encephalartos woodii)*, as well as many species of bromeliad, this is a lovely place to wander. On weekends bridal parties galore pose with their petals for photographers. The gardens play host to an annual concert series featuring the KwaZulu-Natal Philharmonic Orchestra and other concerts.

Campbell Collections GALLERY
(Map p406; 031-207 3432; www.campbell.ukzn.ac.za; 220 Gladys Mazibuko Rd (Marriott Rd); R20; by appointment only) These collections are well worth seeing. Muckleneuk, a superb house designed by Sir Herbert Baker, holds the documents and artefacts collected by Dr Killie Campbell and her father Sir Marshall Campbell (KwaMashu township is named after him), and these are extremely important records of early Natal and Zulu culture.

Killie Campbell began collecting works by black artists 60 years before the Durban Gallery did so, and she was the first patron of Barbara Tyrrell, who recorded the traditional costumes of the indigenous peoples. Tyrrell's paintings beautifully convey clothing and decoration, and the grace of the people wearing them.

North & West Durban

Umgeni River Bird Park WILDLIFE RESERVE
(031-579 4601; www.umgeniriverbirdpark.co.za; Riverside Rd; adult/child R52/33; 9am-5pm) Found on the Umgeni River, north of the centre, this bird park makes for a relaxing escape from the throng. You can see many African bird species in lush vegetation and aviaries. Don't miss the free-flight bird show at 11am and 2pm Tuesday to Sunday, featuring birds from around the world.

Central Durban

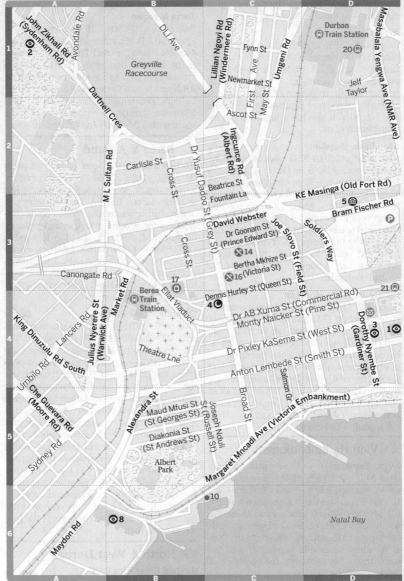

Temple of Understanding TEMPLE
(☑031-403 3328; www.iskcondurban.net; Bhaktieedanta Sami Circle; ☺10am-1pm & 4-9pm) Situated in Durban's west, this is the biggest Hare Krishna temple in the southern hemisphere. The unusual building, designed in the shape of a lotus flower, also houses a well-respected vegetarian restaurant (open 11am to 7pm). Follow the N3 towards Pietermaritzburg and then branch off to the N2 south. Take the Chatsworth turn-off and turn right towards the centre of Chatsworth.

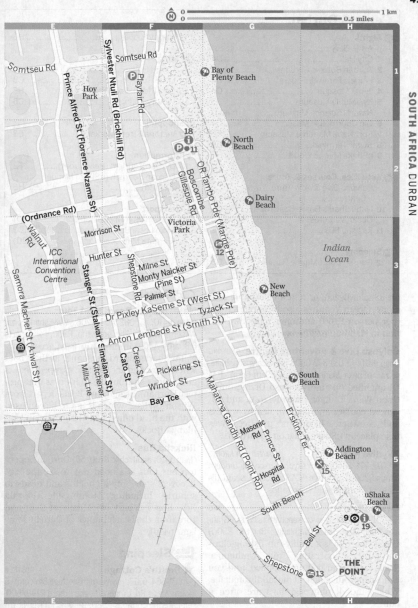

🏃 Activities

Durban Country Club GOLF

(Map p406; ☎031-3131777; www.dcclub.co.za; Isaiah Ntshangase Rd; green fee R385) Close to the coast and with views of the Moses Mabhida Stadium, the Durban Country Club is a fine place to swing a club.

Ocean Ventures SURFING, KAYAKING

(Map p410; ☎086 100 1138; www.oceanventures.co.za; uShaka Marine World; lessons R200, board hire per hr from R120; ⊙8am-4pm) Learn to surf

Central Durban

◉ Sights
Art Gallery .... (see 1)
1 City Hall D4
2 Durban Botanic Gardens A1
3 Francis Farewell Square D4
4 Juma Mosque C4
5 KwaMuhle Museum D3
Natural Science Museum .... (see 1)
6 Old Courthouse Museum E4
7 Port Natal Maritime Museum E5
8 Sugar Terminal B6
9 uShaka Marine World H6

❸ Activities, Courses & Tours
Calypso Dive & Adventure
Centre ....(see 9)
10 Natal Sharks Board Boat Tour C6
Ocean Ventures ....(see 9)
11 Ricksha Bus F2

ⓔ Sleeping
12 Garden Court Marine Parade G3

13 Happy Hippo H6

❽ Eating
Cargo Hold .... (see 9)
14 Little Gujarat C3
15 Surf Riders Food Shack H5
16 Victory Lounge C3

ⓐ Shopping
17 Victoria Street Market B3

❶ Information
18 Durban Tourism (Beachfront) F2
19 Durban Tourism (uShaka Marine
World) H6

❶ Transport
20 Durban Intercity Bus Station D1
21 Main Local Bus Terminal D3
Margate Mini Coach ....(see 20)

on uShaka Beach, or rent a board and go it alone. Ocean Ventures also hires out kayaks (per person R100) and offer tours and tuition in stand-up paddle-boarding.

Calypso Dive & Adventure Centre   DIVING
(Map p410; ☑031-332 0905; www.calypsoushaka. co.za; uShaka Marine World; ◉9am-6pm) PADI-qualified operator Calypso Diving offers Open Water courses (from R4450), and advanced courses and dives in nearby wrecks and elsewhere. Beginners' practice dives take place in uShaka's lagoon aquarium.

Skydive KZN   ADVENTURE SPORTS
(☑072 214 6040; www.skydivekzn.co.za; tandem jumps R2000) Skydive KZN offers a seagull's view of Durban and surrounds.

Casea Charters   FISHING
(☑031-561 7381; www.caseacharters.co.za; Grannies Pool, Main Beach, Umhlanga; 3hr trip R500) Casea Charters is a family-run fishing-charter business operating from Umhlanga. Rods, tackle and bait are supplied, and you can keep your catch at no additional fee. Whale and dolphin sightings are often a bonus.

STS Sport   CYCLING
(Map p406; ☑031-312 9479; www.stssport.co.za; Shop 6, Moses Mabhida Stadium; per hr R50; ◉8am-6pm) Bicycles for hire, including tandems. You'll need to leave identification and R100 as a deposit; unfortunately, you can't lock up the bikes along the way.

🖝 Tours

Natal Sharks Board Boat Tour   BOATING
(Map p410; ☑082 403 9206; www.shark.co.za; Wilson's Wharf; 2hr boat trip R300; ◉departs 6.30am) A fascinating trip is to accompany Natal Sharks Board personnel in their boat when they tag and release trapped sharks and other fish from the shark nets that protect Durban's beachfront. Boats depart from Wilson's Wharf, which is not to be confused with the head office, which is located in Umhlanga Rocks.

Ricksha Bus   BUS
(Map p410; adult/child R100/50) Durban's open-top bus tour is a good way to see the city. It covers some city highlights and heads to suburbs including Morningside (Florida Rd). Buses depart twice daily at 9am and 1pm from the beach branch of Durban Tourism (p416).

🛏 Sleeping

⭐**Smith's Cottage**   HOSTEL $
(☑031-564 6313; www.smithscottage.8m.com; 5 Mount Argus Rd, Umgeni Heights; dm/d R190/500, self-catering cottages R980; ⓟ🛜🞱) This is an excellent budget option within chirping distance of the Umgeni River Bird Park. It's set around a suburban garden and has a couple of free-standing (smallish) cabins, a large 12-bed dorm with attached kitchen and a smaller four-bed dorm inside the house. The whole place has a great feel and the hosts couldn't be friendlier.

Happy Hippo HOSTEL $
(Map p410; ☏ 031-368 7181; www.happyhippo
durban.co.za; 222 Mahatma Gandhi Rd (Point Rd);
dm R165, s/d R470/600, with shared bathroom
R380/460; ☏) Close to the beach is this spacious, well-run, warehouse-style accommodation choice. There are bright colours, vast
spaces and an awesome rooftop bar, which
make for a laid-back stay, though some travellers report it's noisy; rooms are off communal areas.

★ **Concierge** BOUTIQUE HOTEL $$
(Map p406; ☏ 031-309 4434; www.the-concierge.
co.za; 36-42 St Mary's Ave, Greyville; s/d incl break-
fast R965/1200; ☏☀☏) One of Durbs' most
cutting-edge sleeping options, this cleverly
conceived spot – 12 cosy rooms in four pods
– is more about the design (urban, funky,
shape-oriented) than the spaces (smallish but
adequate). For breakfast, roll out of bed and
head to Freedom Cafe, also on the premises.

Madeline Grove B&B $$
(Map p406; www.madeline.co.za; s/d incl break-
fast from R700/990; ☏☏☀) Close to Florida Rd's bars and restaurants, this largish
guest house has a range of rooms, including
some with balconies and a couple of smaller
budget friendly options (s/d R425/750).

Napier House B&B $$
(Map p406; ☏ 031-207 6779; www.napierhouse.
co.za; 31 Napier Rd, Berea; s/d incl breakfast
R700/950; ☏☀☏☀) On a poky little street
near the Botanic Gardens, this is an excel-
lent, homey B&B that is terrific value. The
former colonial residence has five en suite
rooms that are spacious, light and tastefully
organised and have large bathrooms. Break-
fast is a highlight, as are the friendly hosts.

Mackaya Bella GUESTHOUSE $$
(☏ 031-205 8790; www.mackayabella.co.za;
137 Penzance Rd; s/d incl breakfast R660/900;
☏☀☏☀) ✿ Located near the universi-
ty, this pretty spot has a lovely indigenous
garden (featuring the Mackaya Bella plant)
and stylish rooms in a relaxed home-style
environment. There are also budget single
rooms available (R400) with a minimum
three-night stay. Best to reserve ahead as it's
popular with university-associated guests.

Gibela Backpackers Lodge HOSTEL $$
(Map p406; ☏ 031-303 6291; www.gibelaback
packers.co.za; 119 Ninth Ave, Morningside; dm/s/d
R280/535/750; ☏@☏☀) This hostel (a taste-
fully converted 1950s Tuscan-style home)
gets lots of good reports from travellers,
including those travelling by themselves. It

even provides a continental breakfast – to
be enjoyed in an attractive indoor-outdoor
dining area. It definitely suits those look-
ing to get away from the hostel party scene.
Friendly owner Elmar knows everything
there is to know about life in Durban.

Blue Waters HOTEL $$
(Map p406; ☏ 031-327 7000; www.bluewaters
hotel.co.za; 175 Snell Pde; s/d incl breakfast from
R800/900; ☏☀☏) At the northern end of
the beachfront, away from the promenade
crowd, Blue Waters is a classic hotel that
has recently undergone an extensive renovation. Rooms have brilliant ocean views, soft
bedding and stylish furnishings. It also has
a complicated pricing structure depending
on the day of the week you stay – the rate
displayed here is an average only.

Garden Court Marine Parade HOTEL $$$
(Map p410; www.tsogosun.com; r incl breakfast
from R1400; ☏☀☏☀) A superb beachfront
option, Garden Court has recently had a
snazzy overhaul and now boasts sleek, mod-
ern rooms all with ocean views.

Southern Sun Suncoast Hotel HOTEL $$$
(Map p406; ☏ 031-314 7878; www.tsogosunhotels.
com; 20 Battery Beach Rd; s/d incl breakfast from
R1500/1700; ☏☀☏☀) This hotel, adjacent to
the casino, is a safe if businesslike bet. It has
over 100 sleek and contemporary rooms with
flash trimmings. Be aware that the 'Philadel-
phia suite' design means that the bathrooms
are incorporated into the bedrooms themselves (read: little privacy among friends).
Awesome vista from the top floor.

Quarters BOUTIQUE HOTEL $$$
(Map p406; ☏ 031-303 5246; www.quarters.co.za;
101 Florida Rd, Morningside; s/d from R1200/1700;
☏☀☏) Right in the throbbing heart of Dur-
ban's busiest eating and drinking quarter,
this attractive boutique hotel – at two neigh-
bouring locations – balances colonial glam-
our with small-scale home comforts. There's
an on-site restaurant at both.

✖ Eating

Freedom Cafe CAFE $
(Map p406; ☏ 031-309 4453; www.tastefreedom.
co.za; 37-43 St Mary's Ave; mains R65-95; ☉7am-
4pm, to 9pm Fri; ☏) An upmarket, colourful,
funky place in an imaginatively convert-
ed space with a pebble-strewn courtyard.
Asian-influenced food includes Vietnam-
ese pulled pork; there are also vegetari-
an options and a kids' menu. It's behind
Concierge.

★ Mali's Indian Restaurant INDIAN $$

(Map p406; ☑ 031-312 8535; 77 Smiso Nkwanya Rd (Goble Rd), Morningside; mains R90-120; ⊘12.30pm-3pm & 6-10pm Tue-Thu, to 10.30pm Fri-Sun) In a city that boasts a huge Indian population, this place is about as good as Indian food gets in Durban's restaurant scene. North and South Indian dishes are available at this friendly, family-run spot.

Surf Riders Food Shack BURGERS $$

(Map p410; ☑ 031-825 8528; 17 Erskine Tce, Addington Beach; mains R65-115; ⊘7am-6pm; 🛜) Marking a resurgence of beachfront dining, Surf Riders has tables alongside the promenade where surfers, travellers and hip locals meet to chomp on gourmet burgers, woodfired pizzas, tacos and a few seafood dishes. There's craft beer on tap, or for something healthier try a protein shake with your morning oats.

Market INTERNATIONAL $$

(Map p406; ☑ 031-309 8581; www.marketrestaurant.co.za; 40 Gladys Mazibuko Rd (Marriott Rd), Greyville; mains R80-160; ⊘Mon 7.30am-4pm, Tue-Sat 7.30am-9.30pm, Sun 8.30am-3.30pm; 🛜) 🍴 The breakfasts, casual lunches and more formal dinners here are delectable. Imaginative dishes include the likes of calamari, quinoa, feta, red pesto and macadamia salad; produce is locally sourced, free range and organic, where possible. The cafe's tree-lined courtyard and fountain are the perfect antidote to the hot weather and the craft beer is reasonably priced.

Cafe 1999 INTERNATIONAL $$

(Map p406; ☑ 031-202 3406; www.cafe1999.co.za; Silverton Rd, Silvervause Centre, Berea; tapas R60, mains R95-180; ⊘12.30-2.30pm Mon-Fri, 6.30-10.30pm Mon-Sat) This classy restaurant looks unassuming inside, but assume that you will get seriously good modern Mediterranean fusion food here. Tapas including stuffed and deep-fried olives, kudu carpaccio and chilli prawns all hit the spot. There are always lots of daily specials, and friendly wait staff to run you through them.

9th Avenue Bistro INTERNATIONAL $$$

(Map p406; ☑ 031-312 9134; www.9thavenuebistro.co.za; Ninth Ave, Avonmore Centre, Morningside; mains R150-190; ⊘noon-2.30pm Tue-Fri, 6-9.30pm Mon-Sat) The setting, in the car park of the Avonmore Centre, isn't anything to rave about, but the fine-dining experience is. This smart, modern spot serves up fabulously reliable international fare. The tasting menu changes (often with venison, and the likes of smoked ostrich fillet), while the bistro standards include braised lamb shoulder and line-caught fish of the day.

Cargo Hold SEAFOOD $$$

(Map p410; ☑ 031-328 8065; www.ushakamarineworld.co.za; uShaka Marine World, the Point; mains R120-190; ⊘noon-3pm & 6-9.30pm Mon-Sat, noon-5pm Sun) A seafood encounter of the most novel kind. On the *Phantom Ship* in uShaka Marine World (p408), your dining companions are fish with very large teeth – the restaurant shares a glass wall with

BUNNY CHOW

You can't leave Durban without sampling bunny chow. It's the ultimate takeaway food, where the container (a loaf of bread) is part of the meal and the only utensils are your hands and a chunk of bread. The hollowed-out loaf is filled with curry – usually beans, chicken or lamb – which you scoop out with pieces of the loaf. You can order a quarter or half loaf – a quarter is usually plenty for one person. Bunny chow is available in restaurants and backstreet dives throughout Durban. Here are a few choice spots.

Hollywood Bets (Map p406; ☑ 031-309 4920; cnr Linze & De Mazenod Rds, Greyville; mains R50-85; ⊘9am-8pm) This cafe tacked onto a betting shop is an unlikely lunch spot, but the bunnies here are legendary and indeed, award-winning.

House of Curries (Map p406; ☑ 031-303 6076; 275 Florida Rd, Morningside; mains R50-120; ⊘9am-10.30pm) On Florida Rd, this is a more salubrious spot than many to sample bunny chow.

Little Gujarat (Map p410; 43 Dr Goonam St; mains R30-70; ⊘7am-5pm Mon-Sat; 🍴) A long-running city-centre takeout, specialising in vegetarian dishes.

Victory Lounge (Map p410; 187 Dr Yusuf Dadoo St; bunny chow R30-70; ⊘9am-4pm Mon-Fri) This hole-in-the-wall is a stalwart of the bunny chow scene. Locals swear by the mutton version.

the aquarium's shark tank. Well known for casting some high-quality fish dishes with Spanish flavours.

🍸 Drinking & Nightlife

⭐ S43   BREWERY
(Map p406; ☑031-303 2747; 43 Station Dr, Berea; ⊙noon-midnight Tue-Sat) This warehouse-like space alongside the train tracks is in a complex of arty enterprises that is set to gentrify this formerly downtrodden district. Beers from That Brewing Company are brewed and served here – the APA and Weiss are particularly good. The menu is inspired by global street food and features burgers, pulled-pork tacos and of course, bunny chow.

Unity Brasserie & Bar   BREWERY
(Map p406; ☑ 031-201 3470; www.unitybar.co.za; 117 Silverton Rd; ⊙ noon-10.30pm Mon-Thu, to midnight Fri & Sat) This cosy bar has quality craft beer on tap from a range of breweries from Durban, Johannesburg and the Cape. It's a very friendly place, with families welcome during the day and early evening.

☆ Entertainment

Chairman   LIVE MUSIC
(Map p406; ☑031-332 0087; www.thechairman-live.com; 146 Mahatma Gandhi Rd (Point Rd); cover R150; ⊙7pm-2am Thu-Sat) This classy lounge-bar is in an up-and-coming part of Durban, but for now it's best to grab a cab to get here. A very classy joint that's both old-style and new-age, it challenges convention. It's essentially a jazz lounge, but it's well worth going just to taste one of the excellent cocktails.

Zack's   LIVE MUSIC
(Map p406; ☑031-312 0755; www.zacks.co.za; Lilian Ngoyi Rd (Windermere Rd), Windermere Centre; ⊙8am-late) Weekends see this unassuming restaurant liven up with performances from local rock, jazz and blues bands. There's another venue at Wilson's Wharf.

Rainbow Restaurant & Jazz Club   JAZZ
(☑031-702 9161; www.therainbow.co.za; 23 Stanfield Lane, Pinetown) In Pinetown, 15km west of the centre, this was the first place in Natal to cater to blacks in a so-called 'white area' in the 1980s. With a reputation as the centre of the jazz scene and still the preferred local haunt, it stages gigs on the first or last Sunday of the month. See the website for info.

Sun Coast Casino   CASINO
(Map p406; ☑031-328 3000; www.suncoastcasino.co.za; Suncoast Blvd, OR Tambo Pde (Marine Pde)) The glitzy, art deco–style casino is popular with locals and features slot machines, cinemas and some well-attended restaurants. The beach in front of the casino – Suncoast Beach – is a safe and pleasant spot to lie and bake. It has lawn, deckchairs and umbrellas.

🛍 Shopping

Station Drive Precinct   SHOPPING CENTRE
(Map p406) Following trends set in Cape Town and Johannesburg, Station Drive is an artsy complex that's helping to regenerate a run-down part of town. Shops within include designer-clothing boutiques, photography studio, distillery and a brewpub. There is a market here on Sunday mornings and a host of events on the first Thursday of each month.

Victoria Street Market   MARKET
(Map p410; ☑031-306 4021; www.thevsm.co.za; 151-155 Bertha Mkhize St (Victoria St), City Centre; ⊙8am-5pm Mon-Fri, 8am-3pm Sat & Sun) At the western end of Bertha Mkhize St, this is the hub of the Indian community. It offers a typically rip-roaring subcontinental shopping experience, with more than 160 stalls selling wares from across Asia. Watch your wallet and don't take valuables. Note: most shops run by Muslims close between noon and 2pm on Friday.

African Art Centre   ARTS & CRAFTS
(Map p406; ☑031-312 3084; www.afriart.org.za; Florida Rd; ⊙8.30am-5pm Mon-Fri, 9am-3pm Sat) This not-for-profit gallery has an excellent selection of high-quality work by rural craftspeople and artists.

ℹ Information

DANGERS & ANNOYANCES

As with elsewhere in South Africa, crime against tourists and locals can and does occur in Durban. Be aware and careful, but not paranoid. Muggings and pickpocketing, once a problem around the beach esplanade, have declined since that area's upgrade, but be careful here at night. Extra care should also be taken around the Umgeni Rd side of the train station and the Warwick Triangle markets.

At night, with the exception of the casino and around the Playhouse theatre (if something is on), central Durban becomes a ghost town as people head to the suburbs for entertainment. Always catch a cab to and from nightspots, as well as uShaka Marine World (and ride with others, if possible).

Parking is generally OK outside suburban restaurants, but don't leave your car in the street all night: use off-street parking (most accommodation options offer this). Never leave valuables exposed on your car seats, even while driving.

The best advice is from locals, so ask around when you get here.

GAY & LESBIAN TRAVELLERS

Durban has a fairly good gay scene. One of the best places to find gay-friendly events, bars and accommodation is Durban Pride (www.durbanpride.org.za). Another good resource is the KwaZulu-Natal Gay & Lesbian Tourism Association (www.kzngalta.org.za). Also check out the Gay Durban blog (http://gaydurban.blogspot.ca), which is written by the owners of a gay-friendly guesthouse in Morningside. Each August, the Durban Gay & Lesbian Film Festival (www.dglff.org.za) is hosted – check the website for venue details.

INTERNET ACCESS

Wi-fi access is available at most cafes, hostels, guesthouses and hotels, and in some restaurants. Internet cafes are less common than they used to be, but still exist. Access is around R40 per hour.

MEDICAL SERVICES

Entabeni Hospital (☑ 031-204 1300, 24hr trauma centre 031-204 1377; 148 Mazisi Kunene Rd (South Ridge Rd), Berea) The trauma centre charges around R700 per consultation, the balance of which is refunded if the full amount is not utilised.

St Augustines (☑ 031-268 5000; 107 JB Marks Rd, Berea) KwaZulu-Natal's largest private hospital has a good emergency department.

Travel Doctor (☑ 031-360 1122; www.durbantraveldoctor.co.za; 45 Bram Fischer Rd (Old Ordanance Rd), International Convention Centre; ⊙ 8.30am-4pm Mon-Fri, 8.30-11am Sat) For travel-related advice.

Umhlanga Hospital (☑ 031-560 5500; 323 Umhlanga Rocks Dr, Umhlanga) Handy for the North Coast and north Durban.

MONEY

There are banks with ATMs and change facilities across the city. These include Standard Bank, FNB, Nedbank and ABSA.

American Express Musgrave Centre (☑ 031-202 8733; FNB House, 151 Musgrave Rd, Musgrave)

Bidvest Bank (☑ 031-202 7833; Shop 311, Level 3, Musgrave Centre, Musgrave Rd, Berea; ⊙ 9am-5pm Mon-Fri, to 1pm Sat)

POST

There are post offices in the major shopping centres, including the Musgrave and Windermere Centres. The **main post office** (Map p410; cnr Dr Pixley KaSeme St (West St) & Dorothy Nyembe St (Gardiner St); ⊙ 8am-5pm Mon-Fri, to 1pm Sat) is near City Hall.

TOURIST INFORMATION

Durban Tourism (Map p406; ☑ 031-322 4164; www.durbanexperience.co.za; 90 Florida Road, Morningside; ⊙ 8am-4.30pm Mon-Fri) A useful information service on Durban and surrounds. It can help with general accommodation and arranges tours of Durban and beyond. There are also branches at the **beachfront** (Map p410; ☑ 031-322 4205; www.durbanexperience.co.za; Old Pavilion Site, OR Tambo Pde (Marine Pde); ⊙ 8am-5pm) and another at **uShaka Marine World** (Map p410; ☑ 031-337 8099; www.durbanexperience.co.za; 1 Bell St; ⊙ 8am-4.30pm Mon-Fri).

King Shaka Airport Tourist Information Office (☑ 031-322 6046; international arrivals hall; ⊙ 7am-9pm) Durban Tourism, KwaZulu-Natal Tourism Authority and Ezemvelo KZN Wildlife all share a desk (the last is open 8am to 4.30pm Monday to Friday only) at the airport.

KwaZulu-Natal Tourism Authority (KZN Tourism; Map p406; ☑ 031-366 7500; www.zulu.org.za; 29 Canal Quay Rd, Ithala Trade Centre, the Point; ⊙ 8.30am-4.30pm Mon-Fri) Has lots of glossy brochures, but assistance stops there.

❶ Getting There & Away

AIR

King Shaka International Airport (DUR; ☑ 032-436 6585; kingshakainternational.co.za) is at La Mercy, 40km north of the city.

Several airlines link Durban with South Africa's other main centres. Internet fares vary greatly depending on the day of the week, the month and even the time of day.

Kulula (p526) A budget airline linking Durban with Jo'burg, Cape Town and Port Elizabeth.

Mango (☑ 0861 001 234; www.flymango.com) A no-frills airline that is a subsidiary of SAA, with flights to Jo'burg and Cape Town.

South African Airlink (SAAirlink; ☑ 032-436 2602; www.flyairlink.co.za) Flies daily to Nelspruit, Bloemfontein and George.

South African Airways (SAA; ☑ 032-815 2009; www.flysaa.com) Flies at least once daily to most major regional airports in South Africa.

BUS

Long-distance buses leave from the bus station (Map p410) near the Durban train station. Enter the station from Masabalala Yengwa Ave (NMR Ave), not Umgeni Rd. Long-distance bus companies have their offices here.

Note: tickets for all long-distance buses can be bought from Shoprite/Checkers shops and online at www.computickettravel.com.

Baz Bus (p354) is based in Cape Town. You can hop on and off as often as you like along the route for a given price, and can be picked up and dropped off at selected hostels. The seven-/14-/21-day pass (R2600/4100/5100) allows you to travel in any direction and as often as you like within the period. See the website for routes.

Greyhound (p524) Has daily buses to Jo'burg (R350, eight hours), Cape Town (R750, 22 to

27 hours), Port Elizabeth (R600, 15 hours) and Port Shepstone (R350, 1¾ hours). Within KZN, Greyhound buses run daily to Pietermaritzburg (R250, one hour) and Ladysmith (R360, four hours), among other destinations.

Intercape (p354) Has several daily buses to Jo'burg (R400, eight hours). For connections to Mozambique, buses head to Maputo (via Jo'burg; R800, 22 hours).

Margate Mini Coach (Map p410; ☑ 039-312 1406; www.margatecoach.co.za) Head to Durban station or King Shaka International Airport to hop on this bus, which links Durban and Margate three times a day (R210, 2½ hours), and also Port Edward (R240, three hours).

Translux (p527) Runs daily buses to nationwide destinations, including Jo'burg (R300, eight hours) and Cape Town (R720, 27 hours).

CAR

Hiring a car is one of the best options in KZN; car travel is by far the easiest way of getting around. Most major car-rental companies have offices at the airport and in the city.

Aroundabout Cars (☑ 086 0422 4022; www.aroundaboutcars.com)

Avis (☑ 086 102 1111; www.avis.co.za)

Budget (☑ 032-436 5500; www.budget.co.za)

TRAIN

Durban train station (Masabalala Yengwa Ave/NMR Ave) is huge. The local inner-city or suburban trains are not recommended for travellers; these are not commonly used and even hardy travellers report feeling unsafe.

However, mainline passenger long-distance services are another matter – they are efficient and arranged into separate male and female sleeper compartments. These are run by Shosholoza Meyl (p354) and include the *Trans Natal*, which leaves Durban on Friday and Sunday evening for Jo'burg (sleeper R360, 14 hours) via Pietermaritzburg and Ladysmith.

Premier Classe (☑ 086 000 8888, 031-361 7167; www.premierclasse.co.za) The fully serviced luxury Premier Classe has trains between Jo'burg and Durban on Wednesday, Friday and Sunday. Tickets should be booked in advance (R1230, about 14 hours).

Rovos Rail (☑ 012-315 8242; www.rovosrail.co.za) The *Rovos* is a luxury steam train on which, from a mere R18,950, you can enjoy old-world luxury on a three-day choof from Durban to Pretoria via the Battlefields and nature reserves.

ⓘ Getting Around

TO/FROM THE AIRPORT

Some hostels run their own taxi shuttle services for clients at competitive prices. By taxi, the same trip costs around R500.

The **King Shaka Airport Shuttle Bus** (☑ 031-465 5573; www.shuttle.airportbustransport.co.za; per person R80; ☺ to airport 4.30am-8pm, from airport 7.30am-10.30pm) runs hourly between hotels and key locations in Durban and the beachfront via Umhlanga Rocks.

BUS

The useful **Durban People Mover** (☑ 031-309 2731; www.durban.gov.za/City_Services/ethekwini_transport_authority/Pages/People_Mover.aspx; ☺ 5am-10pm) shuttle bus operates along several routes. Tickets (R16) can be purchased on board and allow you to get on and off as many times as you like within a day. Single-leg tickets cost R5.50. The service runs daily between 5am and 10pm. The bus links the beachfront to the city centre and runs the length of the beachfront from uShaka Marine World to Suncoast Casino, with designated stops (including the Victoria Street Market and City Hall) along the way.

Durban Transport (☑ 031-309 3250) runs the bus services Mynah and Aqualine. Mynah covers most of the city and local residential areas. Trips cost around R5 and you get a slight discount if you pre-purchase 10 tickets. Stops include North Beach, South Beach, Musgrave Rd/Mitchell Park Circle, Peter Mokaba Ridge/Vause, Botanic Gardens and Kensington Rd. The larger Aqualine buses run through the greater metropolitan area.

TAXI

Always use metered cabs. A taxi between the beach and Florida Rd, Morningside, usually costs about R50. Companies running a reliable 24-hour service include **Mozzie Cabs** (☑ 031-303 5787; www.mozziecabs.mobi), **Zippy Cabs** (☑ 031-202 7067; www.zippycabs.co.za) and **Eagle** (☑ 0800 330 336; www.eagletaxicabs.co.za). Uber also operates in Durban and is usually cheaper than metered cabs.

South Coast

South of Durban is a 160km-long string of seaside resorts and suburbs running from Amanzimtoti to Port Edward, near the Eastern Cape border. There's a bit of a *Groundhog Day* feel about this mass of shoulder-to-shoulder getaways that are spread out along two routes – the N2 and the R102. However, the coastal region's sandy beaches are interspersed with some pretty gardens and grassy areas, especially in the southern section. The region is a surfers' and divers' delight (the latter because of Aliwal Shoal dive site), and in summer it's packed. Inland, the sugar cane, bananas and palms provide a pleasant, lush, green contrast to the beach culture. The attractive Oribi Gorge Nature

Reserve, near Port Shepstone, provides beautiful forest walks, eating and accommodation options.

Oribi Gorge Nature Reserve

The **Oribi Gorge Nature Reserve** (☎072 042 9390; www.kznwildlife.com; adult/child R30/15; ⊙6am-6pm summer, 7.30am-4.30pm winter) is inland from Port Shepstone, off the N2. The spectacular gorge, on the Umzimkulwana River, is one of the highlights of the South Coast with beautiful scenery, animals and birds, plus walking trails and pretty picnic spots. The reception office is accessed via the N2 on the southern side of the gorge. Accommodation is in simple huts with private bathrooms, a shared kitchen and a marvellous location atop the gorge.

🏃 Activities

Wild 5 Adventures   ADVENTURE SPORTS
(☎082 566 7424; www.wild5adventures.co.za; Oribi Gorge Hotel) Organises activities within the Oribi Gorge Nature Reserve, including a 100m Wild Swing (free-fall jump and swing) off Lehr's Falls (R550), abseiling (R400), white-water rafting (R550) and a zip-line across the gorge (R250). It's located 11km off the N2 along the Oribi Flats Rd.

🛏 Sleeping

Leopard Rock Lookout Chalets   CHALET **$$**
(☎074 124 0902; www.leopardrockc.co.za; Main Oribi Gorge Rd; chalet incl breakfast R1600) Accommodation here is in four pleasant chalets, although it's the vista that's the winner. The dining deck boasts a superb view of the uMzumkulu Gorge. Thoughtful touches include a welcome pack of South African goodies like braai spice, rusks and rooibos. The coffee shop's open 9am to 4pm Wednesday to Sunday.

Margate, Ramsgate & Southbroom

The tourist hub of Margate is a claustrophobic concrete jungle with a string of loud and lively bars. You're better off heading to nearby Ramsgate, with a nice little beach, or to the lush green confines of Southbroom, the posh neck of the woods but delightful for the fact that it's within a bushbuck (large antelope) conservancy.

🏃 Activities

2nd Breath   DIVING
(☎039-317 2326; www.2ndbreath.co.za; cnr Bank St & Berea Rd, Margate; 5-day Open Water course

R4100) Highly qualified PADI professional who takes classes and safety issues seriously.

🛏 Sleeping

Vuna Valley Lodge   HOSTEL **$**
(☎039-311 3602; www.vunavalleyventureskzn. co.za; 9 Mitchell Rd, Banners Rest; s/d R375/600; ❄) By the entrance to the Umtamvuna Nature Reserve – inland from Port Edward – Vuna Valley has stylish double cabins and more budget (but very pleasant) rooms in the main house with separate entrances and spectacular gorge views. Walking, cycling and canoeing opportunities are nearby.

Treetops Lodge   B&B **$$**
(☎039-317 2060; www.treetopslodge.co.za; 3 Poplar Rd, Margate; s/d incl breakfast R450/800; ❄) This pleasant, leafy place has neat, if dated, double rooms, plus a self-catering unit. The rooms overlook a charming garden, and there's a massive shared balcony with your own table and chairs.

🍴 Eating

Waffle House   WAFFLES **$**
(☎039-314 9424; www.wafflehouse.co.za; Marine Dr, Ramsgate; mains R60-80; ⊙8am-5pm; 🅿) People flock to this pleasant spot on the edge of a lagoon for fresh Belgian-style waffles with every sweet and savoury topping under the sun. There are queues in the holiday season.

Trattoria La Terrazza   ITALIAN **$$**
(☎039-316 6162; www.trattoria.co.za; Outlook Rd, Southbroom; mains R90-160; ⊙12.30pm-10pm) Ask for a food recommendation in the area and the answer is overwhelmingly this Italian option. It has a popular meaty menu, including the likes of tender, grain-fed beef fillet and seafood such as West Coast mussels and seared baby squid. The setting, on an estuary, is gorgeous. Reservations recommended.

ℹ Information

South Coast Tourism (☎039-312 2322; Panorama Pde, Main Beach, Margate; ⊙8am-5pm Mon-Fri, to 1pm Sat & Sun) Information is available from here.

ℹ Getting There & Away

Margate Mini Coach (☎031-312 1406; www. margate.co.za) links Durban and Margate three times daily (one-way R240).

Intercity Express (☎031-305 9090; www. intercity.co.za) runs regular buses between Margate and Jo'burg (R430, 10 hours).

North Coast

This coastal strip from Umhlanga Rocks north to Tugela River is a profusion of up-market time-share apartments and retirement villages with some pleasant beaches. The section from Zimbali, slightly north of Umhlanga, to the Tugela is known as the Dolphin Coast. It gets its name from the bottlenose dolphins that favour the area, attracted by the continental shelf and warm water.

The area is home to a fascinating mix of peoples: descendants of former colonialists, Indians, French-Mauritian sugar-cane growers and indentured labourers from the Indian subcontinent, plus, of course, the Zulu people.

King Shaka is said to have established a military camp on the coast; royal handmaidens gathered salt from tidal pools, a practice since immortalised in the name Salt Rock. A memorial to King Shaka can be found at KwaDukuza (Stanger), slightly inland.

Umhlanga Rocks & uMdloti Beach

The buckle of Durban's chichi commuter belt, Umhlanga is a cosmopolitan mix of upmarket beach resort, moneyed suburbia and myriad malls. Umhlanga means 'Place of Reeds' (the 'h' is pronounced something like 'sh'). Further north, uMdloti Beach has some good restaurants. Both locations are convenient to the airport.

Sights

Natal Sharks Board   MUSEUM
(☑031-566 0400; www.shark.co.za; 1A Herrwood Dr, Umhlanga Rocks; ☺8am-4pm Mon-Fri, presentations & dissections 9am & 2pm Tue-Thu) FREE This research institute is dedicated to studying sharks, specifically in relation to their danger to humans. There are audiovisual presentations and shark dissections (adult/child R45/25). The museum has replicas of sharks and a wealth of information on the animals and their tumultuous relationship with mankind. The Natal Sharks Board is signposted; it's about 2km out of town, up steep Umhlanga Rocks Dr (the M12 leading to the N3).

Umhlanga Lagoon
Nature Reserve   NATURE RESERVE
(☺6am-6pm) FREE Found on a river mouth just north of town, the reserve is home to many bird species (despite its small size: 2600 sq m). Trails lead through stunning dune forest, across the lagoon and onto the beach.

Sleeping

On the Beach Backpackers   HOSTEL $$
(☑031-562 1591; www.durbanbackpackers.com; 17 The Promenade, Glenashley; dm/s/d R200/650/950; P🛜🏊) There are million-rand views from the double rooms here that overlook the water. Or you can slum it in a dorm for a much more reasonable price. A great spot for lazing on the coast, this light and airy house-turned-backpackers is 4km south of Umhlanga in Glenashley. It's on the Baz Bus (p354) route.

Oyster Box   HOTEL $$$
(☑031-514 5000; www.oysterboxhotel.com; 2 Lighthouse Rd, Umhlanga; r incl breakfast R6800) For chic, ocean-facing luxury you can't do much better than this popular hotel next to the lighthouse. Rooms have all the usual trimmings and if you've forgotten anything you can grab a bag packed with umbrella, bats, balls and sunscreen before heading to the beach. The daily curry buffet is legendary.

Eating

Ile Maurice   FRENCH $$$
(☑031-561 7609; www.ilemauricerestaurant.co.za; 9 McCausland Cres, Umhlanga Rocks; mains R175-250; ☺noon-2.30pm & 6.30-10pm Tue-Sun; 🅿) For a special seaside splurge with a Gallic touch, try this chic eatery serving a variety of French and Mauritian dishes, including a range of fish and seafood, juicy steaks and a good selection for vegetarians.

Information

Umhlanga Tourism Information Centre
(☑031-561 4257; www.umhlangatourism.co.za; Shop 1A, Chartwell Centre, Chartwell Dr, Umhlanga Rocks; ☺8.30am-5pm Mon-Fri, 9am-1pm Sat) An excellent resource with knowledgeable staff.

Getting There & Away

Metro buses 716 and 706 run between Umhlanga and Durban.

Zululand

Evoking images of wild landscapes and tribal rhythms, this beautiful swath of KwaZulu-Natal offers a different face of South Africa, where fine coastline, mist-clad hills and traditional settlements are in contrast to the ordered suburban developments around Durban. Dominated by the Zulu tribal group, the region offers fascinating historical and contemporary insights into one of the country's most enigmatic cultures. However, while the name Zulu (which means Heaven) aptly describes the rolling expanses that dominate the landscape here, it doesn't tell the whole story. Intense poverty and all the social problems that come with that are still commonplace, and much of the population struggles in a hand-to-mouth existence. If you head off the main roads this becomes glaringly obvious.

The region is most visited for the Hluhluwe-iMfolozi Park and its many traditional Zulu villages, where you can learn about Zulu history and the legendary King Shaka.

Eshowe

POP 14,800

Situated amid a beautiful indigenous forest and surrounded by green rolling hills, Eshowe has its own particular character. The centre has a rural, rough-and-tumble atmosphere, but the suburbs are leafy and quiet. It is well placed for exploring the wider region and there are decent attractions and accommodation options.

Eshowe has been home to four Zulu Kings (Shaka, Mpande, Cetshwayo and Dinuzulu). It was Cetshwayo's stronghold before he moved to Ondini and, like Ondini, it was destroyed during the Anglo-Zulu War. The British occupied the site and built Fort Nongqayi in 1883, establishing Eshowe as the administrative centre of their newly captured territory.

◉ Sights

Dlinza Forest Reserve FOREST
(www.kznwildlife.com/dlinza-forest; adult/child R40/10; ⊙6am-5pm Sep-Apr, 8am-5pm May-Aug) When war approached, King Shaka is said to have hidden his wives in the thick swath of forest that now makes up this 2-sq-km reserve. There is prolific birdlife – look out for crowned eagles (*Stephanoaetus coronatus*), as well as a few walking trails, some of which are believed to have been made by British soldiers stationed here after the Anglo-Zulu War. The 125m-long Dlinza Forest Aerial Boardwalk offers some great views.

Fort Nongqayi Museum Village MUSEUM
(www.eshowemuseums.org.za; Nongqayi Rd; adult/child R40/10; ⊙7.30am-4pm Mon-Fri, 9am-4pm Sat & Sun) Based around three-turreted Fort Nongqayi, the museum village also includes the **Zululand Historical Museum**, with artefacts and Victoriana; the excellent **Vukani Museum** with its Zulu basketry collection;

and a **missionary chapel**. Well worth a look is the small but delightful butterfly house: a walk-in greenhouse where visitors can enjoy indigenous vegetation and hundreds of (mostly local) African butterfly species.

You can walk from here to Mpushini Falls (40 minutes return), but note that bilharzia (snail fever) has been reported here.

🏃 Activities

Dlinza Forest Aerial Boardwalk WALKING
(www.kznwildlife.com/dlinza-broadwalk; adult/child R40/10; ⊙6am-5pm Sep-Apr, 8am-5pm May-Aug) Within the Dlinza Forest Reserve (p420), the 125m-long boardwalk offers some great views of the canopy and birdlife. This is the start of the Prince Dabulamanzi Trail, a three-day circuit through nature reserves and rivers. The boardwalk is included in the entrance fee to the reserve.

⛵ Tours

Zululand Eco-Adventures CULTURAL
(☏035-474 2298; www.zululandeco-adventures.com; 36 Main St) Offers a large range of genuine Zulu adventure activities, from weddings and coming-of-age ceremonies to visits to witch doctors.

🛏 Sleeping

Dlinza Forest Accommodation CABIN $$
(☏035-474 2377; www.dlinzaforestaccommodation.co.za; 2 Oftebro St; s/d R500/650; 🕸) These four self-catering log cabins are neat, modern, clean and spacious. Follow the signs to the Dlinza Forest Reserve; the guesthouse is just beyond the entrance.

George Hotel HOTEL $$
(☏035-474 4919; www.thegeorge.co.za; 38 Main St; s/d R695/795; P🕸🏊) Dripping with character, this grand old hotel (1902) is a good midrange option. Rooms are a bit old and rickety (and water pressure can be hit-and-miss), but the huge beds are very comfy. The budget wing has been completely renovated and offers good value (s/d R400/600). The restaurant menu is limited, but the food is well prepared. Two of the hotel's best features are its veranda, perfect for a sunset drink, and its lounge, with ancient reading material and a cosy vibe.

🍴 Eating

Adam's Outpost INTERNATIONAL $
(☏035-4741787; 5 Nongqayi St, Fort Nongqayi Museum; mains R50-70; ⊙Mon-Fri & Sun 9am-4pm) Find refuge in the garden cafe and cosy, cor-

rugated-iron restaurant, complete with real fireplaces and candles – easily the standout in Eshowe's culinary roll call. Try a chicken mango salad or beef curry for lunch.

ℹ️ Information

ABSA (Osborne Rd, Miku Bldg) Changes money and has an ATM.

ℹ️ Getting There & Away

Minibus shared taxis leave from the bus and taxi rank (downhill from KFC near the Osborne and Main Sts roundabout – go across the bridge and to the right) to Empangeni (R60, one hour), which is the best place from which to catch taxis deeper into Zululand, and Durban (R110, 1½ hours).

Ulundi

POP 20,000

Once the hub of the powerful Zulu empire and until 2004 a joint capital of KZN (with Pietermaritzburg, which gained pre-eminence), Ulundi today is an unattractive, merely functional place that resembles a temporary settlement rather than an important Zulu centre. Brightly coloured boxlike houses have replaced traditional huts, and its small centre shopping mall has a transitory feel. However, there are historic Zulu sites, including the interesting Ondini, to explore in the immediate area. Ulundi also offers alternative access to Hluhluwe-iMfolozi Park.

◉ Sights

Mgungundlovu   HISTORIC SITE
(www.heritagekzn.co.za) The military settlement of Mgungundlovu (Ungungundhlovu), Dingaan's capital from 1829 to 1838, is southwest of Ulundi on Rte 34 (the road linking Vryheid and Melmoth). It was here that Pieter Retief and the other Voortrekkers were killed by their host in 1838, the event that precipitated the Boer-Zulu War. Signs point to the Piet Retief memorial marking the spot. In 1990 excavations revealed the site of Dingaan's *indlu* (great hut) nearby. A **multimedia information centre** (☎035-450 0916; adult/child R30/15; ⊙8am-4pm Mon-Fri, 9am-4pm Sat & Sun) has high-tech displays and info. From Ulundi head southwest along Rte 66 to Rte 34, turn right and continue on Rte 34 for several kilometres. Mgungundlovu is signed off Rte 34 to the west; it's another 5km to the site.

Ondini   HISTORIC SITE
(High Place; ☎035-870 2050; www.heritagekzn.co.za; adult/child R40/15; ⊙8am-4pm Mon-Fri, 9am-4pm Sat & Sun) Established as Cetshwayo's

capital in 1873, Ondini was razed by British troops after the Battle of Ulundi (July 1879), the final engagement of the 1879 Anglo-Zulu War. The royal kraal section of the Ondini site has been rebuilt and you can see where archaeological digs have uncovered the floors of identifiable buildings. The floors, made of mud and cow dung, were preserved by the heat of the fires, which destroyed the huts above. The huge area is enclosed in a defensive perimeter of gnarled branches.

Spirit of eMakhosini Monument   MONUMENT
(⊙8am-4pm Mon-Fri, 9am-4pm Sat & Sun) On Rte 34 and 2km north of Mgungundlovu, signs point west to Spirit of eMakhosini monument, which is perched on a hill. It comprises a massive bronze Zulu beer pot, surrounded by 18 bronze reliefs depicting Zulu life, and seven large horns symbolising the seven kings buried in the valley. Guides will explain the site's significance.

KwaZulu Cultural-Historical Museum   MUSEUM
(⊙8am-4pm Mon-Fri, 9am-4pm Sat & Sun) This museum, located within Ondini (p421), has excellent exhibits on Zulu history and culture. It also has one of the country's best collections of beadwork on display. There's a good selection of books for sale.

☞ Tours

Tinta Safaris   HISTORY
(☎035-870 2500; www.tintasafaris.co.za) Family-run enterprise offering guided tours of the eMakhosini Valley and Battlefields.

🛏️ Sleeping

Garden Court   BUSINESS HOTEL $$$
(☎035-870 1012; www.tsogosun.com/garden-court-ulundi; Princess Magogo St; r incl breakfast R1500; P❄🛜🏊) Rooms here are spacious, with attention to detail and no-nonsense comforts. The hotel's restaurant serves meals throughout the day.

ℹ️ Getting There & Away

The minibus shared taxi park is opposite the Garden Court hotel, with services to destinations including Vryheid (R80, 1½ hours) and Eshowe (R75, 1½ hours).

The Elephant Coast

Up there on the podium with the world's great ecotourism destinations, and near the top of the scribbled list marked 'Places I Must See in South Africa', the Elephant Coast (formerly 'Maputaland') is a phenomenal stretch of natural beauty, with a fabulously diverse mix of environments and wildlife.

This large stretch of coastline includes some of the country's true highlights, including the perennially photogenic iSimangaliso Wetland Park that runs from Lake St Lucia in the south to Kosi Bay in the north. Uncompromisingly untamed, this region, away from the scattered resort towns, offers a glimpse of precolonial Africa. Slightly further inland, the incredible Hluhluwe-iMfolozi Park is KZN's answer to Kruger National Park.

The climate becomes hotter as you go north and, thanks to the warm Indian Ocean, summers are steamy and tropical. The humid coastal air causes dense mists on the inland hills, reducing visibility to a few metres.

Hluhluwe-iMfolozi Park

Rivalling Kruger National Park in its beauty and variety of landscapes, **Hluhluwe-iMfolozi Park** (☑035-550 8476, central reservations 033-845 1000; www.kznwildlife.com; adult/child R175/90; ☉5am-7pm Nov-Feb, 6am-6pm Mar-Oct) is one of South Africa's best-known, most evocative parks. Indeed, some say it's better than Kruger for its accessibility – it covers 960 sq km (around a 20th of the size of Kruger) and there's plenty of wildlife including lions, elephants, rhinos (black and white), leopards, giraffes, buffaloes and African wild dogs.

Stunning Hluhluwe-iMfolozi has a mountainous landscape providing jaw-dropping views in all directions. The lack of thick vegetation in parts of the park, such as the drive from Memorial gate to Hilltop Camp, makes for excellent wildlife spotting. You are almost certain to see white rhino here.

◉ Sights

Centenary Centre   MUSEUM
(☉8am-4pm) **FREE** The Centenary Centre, a wildlife-holding centre with an attached museum, information centre and excellent craft market, is in the eastern section of iMfolozi. It incorporates rhino enclosures and antelope pens, and was established to allow visitors to view animals in transit to their new homes. To see the animals, ask at the Centenary Centre kiosk; you must be accompanied by a guide (around R20 per person).

Bhejane Waterhole & Hide   VIEWPOINT
Great place to see wildlife congregating, especially in winter.

🏃 Activities

Wildlife Drives
Wildlife drives here are very popular. Hilltop Camp offers morning and evening drives, while Mpila Camp does evening drives only. The camp-run drives are open to resort residents only and cost R325 per person. Most visitors to the area self-drive.

Hiking
One of iMfolozi's main attractions is its extraordinary trail system, in a special 240-sq-km wilderness area (note: these trails are seasonal and there's a four-person minimum) where there are no roads, only walking tracks. The trail walks are guided and last from two to five days. They are run by KZN Wildlife (p437) and all food, water, cooking equipment etc is provided. Accommodation is in tented camps and you can certainly expect to see wildlife. These walks are truly once-in-a-lifetime experiences and thus extremely popular, so book ahead.

The **Base Camp Trail** (R3900, three nights) is, as the name suggests, at a base camp. Trailists carry day packs on the daily outings. The **Short Wilderness Trail** (R2350, two nights) is at satellite camps with no amenities (bucket shower) but are fully catered. Similar is the **Extended Wilderness Trail** (R3450, three nights), but guests must carry their gear for 7km into camp. On the **Primitive Trail** (R2900, four nights) you carry equipment, help prepare the food (provided) and sleep under the stars. Some consider this trail to be more fun than the others because you are able to participate more (for example, hikers must sit up in 1½-hour watches during the night).

🛏 Sleeping

Hilltop Camp   CABIN $$
(☑035-562 0848; s/d rondavel R610/850, 2-person chalets R1600; ✺) The signature resort on the Hluhluwe side: a cold drink followed by dinner on the patio with mountains silhouetted into the distance is a memorable experience.

Mpila Camp   TENTED CAMP, CHALET $$
(tent for 2 people & chalet R870) The main accommodation centre on the iMfolozi side, spectacular and peaceful Mpila Camp is perched on top of a hill in the centre of the reserve. The safari tents are the most fun, but self-contained chalets are available, too. Note: there's an electric fence, but wildlife (lions, hyenas, wild dogs) can still wander through.

Muntulu Bush Lodge
LODGE $$

(www.kznwildlife.com; 6 people R4320, extra adult/child R720/360) Muntulu Bush Lodge is perched high above the Hluhluwe River and has four en suite bedrooms with verandas. There's a cook on hand to rustle up some grub and guided walks are available.

❶ Getting There & Away

You can access the park via three gates. The main entrance, Memorial gate, is about 15km west of the N2, about 50km north of Mtubatuba. The second entrance, Nyalazi gate, is accessed by turning left off the N2 onto R618 just after Mtubatuba on the way to Nongoma. The third, Cengeni gate, on iMfolozi's western side, is accessible by road (tarred for 30km) from Ulundi.

iSimangaliso Wetland Park

The **iSimangaliso Wetland Park** (http://isimangaliso.com), a Unesco World Heritage Site, stretches for 220 glorious kilometres from the Mozambique border to Maphelane, at the southern end of Lake St Lucia. With the Indian Ocean on one side and a series of lakes (including Lake St Lucia) on the other, the 3280-sq-km park protects five distinct ecosystems, offering everything from offshore reefs and beaches to lakes, wetlands, woodlands and coastal forests. Loggerhead and leatherback turtles nest along the park's shores; whales and dolphins appear offshore and the park is occupied by numerous animals, including antelopes, hippos and zebras. The ocean beaches pull big crowds during the holiday season for everything from diving to fishing. iSimangaliso means 'Miracle' or 'Wonder' and, given its extraordinary beauty, it's an appropriate title.

◉ Sights

Cape Vidal
BEACH

(http://isimangaliso.com; ⊙ 5am-7pm Nov-Mar, 6am-6pm Apr-Oct) Twenty kilometres north of Mission Rocks (p423) (30km from St Lucia Estuary), taking in the land between Lake Bhangazi and the ocean, is Cape Vidal. Some of the forested sand dunes are 150m high and the beaches are excellent for swimming. There's also decent wildlife-viewing en route to the beach and you'll likely have the sightings of hippos, antelopes, buffaloes and crocs to yourself. You have to pay the Eastern Shores entry fee to access the beach.

Mission Rocks
WATERFRONT

About 14km north of the entrance, Mission Rocks is a rugged and rock-covered shoreline. At low tide you can view a fabulous array of sea life in the rock pools. (Note: you cannot swim here.)

Eastern Shores
PARK

(☏ 035-590 1633; www.isimangaliso.com; adult/child/vehicle R45/25/55; ⊙ 5am-7pm Nov-Mar, 6am-6pm Apr-Oct) The Eastern Shores has four scenic routes – pan, *vlei* (marshland), coastal dune and grassland – that reflect their different features and ecosystems. The Eastern Shores has an excellent accommodation option: Ezemvelo KZN Wildlife (p437) manages the pretty Cape Vidal Camp, near the shores of Lake Bhangazi. Minimum charges apply.

Mt Tabor Lookout
VIEWPOINT

About 4km before Mission Rocks is the Mt Tabor lookout (signed), which provides a wonderful view of Lake St Lucia and the Indian Ocean.

🏃 Activities

As part of the iSimangaliso Wetland Park Authority's responsible-tourism practices, every few years an ecotour operator must officially reapply for a permit – known as a concession – to operate activity tours. Go to www.isimangaliso.com for a list of current companies and organisations.

Birdwatching is a delight in St Lucia and beyond. Check out the Zululand Birding Route website (www.zululandbirdingroute.co.za) for heaps of info plus guide services.

Whatever you do, keep aside some money in the kitty for a whale-watching experience. In season, there's a high chance of spotting whales here, as well as dolphins and other sea creatures. Trips cost around R1000 per person. You can also head upriver on boat tours to view hippos and crocodiles. Most trips operate from St Lucia, though Sodwana Bay Lodge (p425) offers whale-watching out of Sodwana Bay. Sodwana Bay is a hotbed for scuba diving and deep-sea fishing.

Horse Riding

Hluhluwe Horse Safaris
HORSE RIDING

(☏ 035-562 1039; www.hluhluwehorsesafaris.co.za; 1½hr ride R495, 2½hr ride R795) Horse riding is a wonderful way to see wildlife; these rides are in the False Bay region. You may spot antelope species, as well as other animals. A second option heads to Falaza Game reserve, where you can see rhinos, buffaloes and giraffes. It operates out of Wildebeest Ecolodge.

Wildlife Watching

Fascinating night turtle tours operate from Cape Vidal. Sodwana Bay Lodge (p425) runs trips at Sodwana Bay, as does Kosi Bay Lodge at Kosi Bay.

uMkhuze Game Reserve has some of the best wildlife viewing in the country, and there are a number of operators offering excellent day and night trips on the Eastern and Western Shores. Operators are listed on www.isimangaliso.com. Self-guided drives are also rewarding ways to seek out wildlife.

The Eastern Shores (p423), in the southern part of iSimangaliso Wetland Park, is among the most accessible from St Lucia Estuary. It affords opportunities for self-guided drives through the wonderful network of wildlife-viewing roads (there's everything from hippos to antelope, and prolific birdlife). Part of a rehabilitation scheme with Western Shores, this area is where hundreds of thousands of square metres of plantation land has been returned to its former state (yes, that's why there are all those tree stumps).

Sleeping

Cape Vidal Camp CAMPGROUND, CABIN $$
(☏033-845 1000; www.kznwildlife.com; camping per site 1-4 people R520, 5-bed log cabins from R1040) The Eastern Shores' excellent accommodation option, pretty Cape Vidal Camp is set near the shores of Lake Bhangazi. It's managed by Ezemvelo KZN Wildlife (p437); minimum charges apply.

KOSI BAY

The jewel of iSimangaliso Wetland Park, **Kosi Bay** (http://isimangaliso.com; adult/child/vehicle R43/21/43; ☉6am-6pm) features a string of four lakes, starting from an estuary lined with some of the most beautiful and quiet beaches in South Africa. Fig, mangrove and raffia-palm forests provide the greenery (it's the only place in South Africa with five mangrove species in one place). Within the estuary mouth is excellent snorkelling. Note: stonefish are present here, so protect your feet if walking in the estuary.

Hippos, Zambezi sharks and some crocs live within the lake system. More than 250 bird species have been identified here, including rare palmnut vultures.

You'll need a 4WD and permit to visit. KwaNgwanase is the nearest service centre, some 10km west of the reserve, and you will find shops and an ATM here.

Note that Kosi Bay is in a high-risk malaria zone and precautions should be taken.

◉ Sights

Kosi Mouth OUTDOORS
(adult/child/vehicle R40/20/40) You need a 4WD to reach Kosi Mouth, where traditional Thonga fishing kraals still provide an income to local families. The sandy mouth offers great swimming, though stonefish are present so be sure to wear shoes.

Sleeping

Ezemvelo KZN Wildlife CAMPGROUND, CABIN $$
(☏central reservations 033-845 1000; www.kznwildlife.com; camping per site 1-4 people R440, 2-/6-bed cabins R740/1480) Offers camping and fully equipped, pleasant cabin accommodation within lush forest surrounds on the western shore of Lake Nhlange – minimum charges apply. Popular with fishers.

Utshwayelo Lodge CAMPGROUND, CHALET $$
(☏082 909 3113; www.kosimouth.co.za; camping R400, sahara tents R595, chalets R840; ☢) This lovely community-run camp offers basic but neat bamboo-lined two-sleeper chalets with a communal kitchen. It also has permanent tents with wooden decks and communal ablutions. It's right by the entrance to the park at the Kosi Mouth access road. Issues car-entry permits to Kosi Mouth.

Kosi Bay Lodge LODGE $$
(☏083 262 4865; www.kosibaylodge.co.za; r per person from R360; ☢) The rooms are a little worn, but good value and the resort has decent facilities including a pool, restaurant and bar. The comprehensive activities menu includes turtle-watching trips (R680 per person).

Kosi Forest Lodge LODGE $$$
(☏035-474 1473; www.isibindi.co.za; s/d with full board R3055/4700; ☢) The only private lodge in iSimangaliso's Kosi Bay region, and surrounded by the sand forest's Umdoni trees, this intimate 16-bed lodge offers a dreamy, luxurious – given the remote circumstances and lack of electricity – experience. Accommodation is in romantic safari tents. They're a blend of *Out of Africa* (wooden decor and muted furnishings) and natural (the ultimate in ingenious outdoor bathrooms). There are activities (some included in the nightly rate) on tap, and guest transfers are available.

LAKE SIBAYA & COASTAL FOREST

Remote grassland plains, lush forests and pristine beaches are the main features of the magical Coastal Forest. Its beauty can, in part, be explained by its location – this area is one of the most remote sections of iSimangaliso. Highlights include Black Rock (a rugged rocky peninsula easily reached by climbing over sand dunes) and Lala Nek, a beautiful and seemingly never-ending stretch of sand.

Further south sits Lake Sibaya, the largest freshwater lake in South Africa. It covers between 60 and 70 sq km, depending on the water level. Hippos, crocs and a large range of birdlife (more than 280 species) occupy the lake. Canoeing trips can be arranged through Thonga Beach Lodge.

Entrance to this area of iSimangaliso is free. Gates are open 6am to 6pm.

Sleeping

Mabibi Camp CAMPGROUND $
(☑035-474-1504; www.mabibicampsite.co.za; camping R124, chalet R680) If you can get here, you'll have heaven to yourself – almost. This rustic community-owned camp is right next to upmarket Thonga Beach Lodge (p425), but this is luxury of a different kind – nestled in a swath of forest and only a hop, skip and 137 steps (via a stairway) from the beach. Bring your own tent, food and gear.

Thonga Beach Lodge LODGE $$$
(☑035 474 1473; www.thongabeachlodge.co.za; s/d with full board R6435/9900; ❋☀) Popular with European visitors, this isolated and luxurious beach resort offers spacious huts scattered through coastal forest. Spectacular ocean views – whales sometimes pass by – and activities provide the entertainment, while the wide, white beach and spa treatments (at extra cost) are a welcome relief after the rigours of a safari. The cuisine is excellent, especially the buffet lunches.

SODWANA BAY

Get past the approach to the park – a mishmash of lodges, signs and temporary-looking constructions – and you're in for a pleasant surprise. **Sodwana Bay** (☑035-571 0051; http://isimangaliso.com; adult/child/vehicle R35/30/50; ☉24hr) is bordered by lush forest on one side and glittering sands on another. The area is best known for its scuba diving – the diversity of underwater seascapes and marine flora and fauna makes it one of South Africa's diving capitals. Serious deepsea fishing occurs here, too; you can be inundated with huntin', shootin', fishin' types who head out in their water machines. On that note: avoid the silly season (summer holidays) when thousands throng here to take the plunge – literally. At all other times it's a beautifully peaceful place. That said, most people come here for the diving or fishing; outside of that, there's not much to do here but walk along the beach and admire the gorgeous surrounds

Activities

Sodwana Bay Lodge Scuba Centre DIVING
(☑035-571 0117; www.sodwanadiving.co.za; Sodwana Bay Lodge; PADI Open Water course R3750) This place has a fine reputation for diving and safety and also working with the local community. Half-day try-dives (R1100) are available for beginners while the already qualified can rent equipment (full set R240 per day).

Sleeping

Sodwana Bay Lodge LODGE $$
(☑035-571 9101; www.sodwanabaylodge.co.za; s/d with half board R925/1700) This resort has neat boardwalks, banana palms and pine-filled, slightly dated rooms. The chalets here are very comfortable, with huge decks. It caters to divers and offers various dive and accommodation packages, which can be great value. It's on the main road on the approach to the park. Sodwana Bay Lodge Scuba Centre (p425) is on the premises.

Ezemvelo KZN Wildlife CAMPGROUND $$
(☑central reservations 033-845 1000; www.kznwildlife.com; camping per site 1-4 people from R480, 4-bed cabins R1410; @) Has hundreds of well-organised campsites plus cabins set within the park's coastal forest. Minimum charges apply. There's a shop selling basic supplies here.

ST LUCIA

Although not officially within the iSimangaliso Wetland Park, the pleasant village of St Lucia is a useful base from which to explore the park's southern sections. In high season St Lucia is a hotbed of activity as the population swells with visitor numbers. The main drag, McKenzie St (a former hippo pathway), is packed with restaurants, lively hostels and bars, but the quieter avenues behind it offer a touch more hush and a good selection of B&Bs. Hippos sometimes amble down the town's quieter streets (beware: these are not cute, just dangerous).

Activities

Advantage Tours CRUISE
(St Lucia Tours; ☑035-590 1259; www.advantage-tours.co.za; 1 McKenzie St, Dolphin Centre) Runs daily whale-watching boat tours (R995 per person) between June and September, weather permitting. You can also head up-

river on boat tours to view hippos and crocodiles (R190 per person).

Euro Zulu Safaris ECOTOUR
(035-590 1635; www.eurozulu.com; per person incl dinner & drinks R995) Fascinating night turtle-watching tours operate (from November to March) from Cape Vidal and Kosi Bay. Other tours include the usual selection of game drives and boat trips.

Shakabarker Tours TOUR
(035-590 1162; www.shakabarker.co.za; 43 Hornbill St) Shakabarker Tours operates out of St Lucia and conducts a range of excellent wildlife trips, including tours of local wildlife parks and a guided bike ride (R250 per person) around St Lucia with a Zulu guide.

St Lucia Kayak Safaris KAYAKING
(035-590 1233; www.kayaksafaris.co.za) St Lucia Kayak Safaris offers novel ways to enjoy the wetland, including a 2½-hour trip (R295) starting from Honeymoon Bend in the estuary with a wildlife guide. This outfit also offers snorkelling at Cape Vidal.

Sleeping

Monzi Safaris GUESTHOUSE $
(035-590 1697; www.monzisafaris.com; 81 McKenzie St; tent/r R380/420;) St Lucia's best budget option is part upmarket guesthouse, part well-maintained backpacker hostel. The backpacker section has clean, simple rooms with shared bathroom, or pre-erected tents with fans and plug points on a covered balcony. There's an excellent entertainment area with pool table, bar and sparkling pool. The luxury wing offers large tents with en suite bathroom (d R880).

Lodge Afrique LODGE $$
(071 592 0366; www.lodgeafrique.com; 71 Hornbill St; s/d incl breakfast R950/1700;) Smart 'African chic'–style chalets crammed into a suburban block but with lush surrounds. It's a safe bet, if not booked out by groups; reservations required.

Sunset Lodge CABIN $$
(035-590 1197; www.sunsetstlucia.co.za; 154 McKenzie St; cabins R695-1500;) Seven well-maintained, self-catering log cabins, lined in dark wood and with a safari theme. Affords a lovely view overlooking the estuary from your private patio – you can watch the hippos, mongooses and monkeys wander onto the lawn. Rates significantly lower outside high season.

Eating

Braza PORTUGUESE $$
(73 McKenzie St; mains R65-200; 11am-10pm) Cuisine with a touch of Portugal, Brazil, Mozambique and Angola – at least that's what this lively place promotes. It translates as good meaty dishes and grills, although a decent vegetarian platter is on offer (but not on the menu). Anything featuring the chorizo is superb.

Ski Boat Club PUB FOOD $$
(035-590 1376; St Lucia Estuary; mains R50-160; noon-10pm;) The food is far from spectacular but the setting more than compensates. Take a dip in the pool or keep an eye out for crocs and hippos in the estuary from your table in the garden. It's the ideal spot for a sundowner and a local favourite.

Information

Internet Cafe (035-590 1056; 310 McKenzie St; per 30min R25; 8am-6pm) By far the best service; at BiB's International Backpackers.

UMKHUZE GAME RESERVE

The **uMkhuze Game Reserve** (035-573 9004, 031-845 1000; www.kznwildlife.com; adult/child/vehicle R40/30/50; 5am-7pm Nov-Mar, 6am-6pm Apr-Oct) is, in a phrase, a trip highlight. Established in 1912 to protect the nyala antelope, and now part of iSimangaliso Wetland Park, this reserve of dense scrub and open acacia plains covers some spectacular 360 sq km. It successfully re-introduced lions in 2014, and just about every other sought-after animal is represented, as well as more than 400 bird species, including the rare Pel's fishing owl (Scotopelia peli). The reserve has fabulous hides, some at waterholes; the pans, surrounded by fever trees, offer some of the best wildlife viewing in the country. It's 15km from Mkuze town (18km from Bayla if heading north).

Activities

Fig Forest Walk WALKING
(www.kznwildlife.com; per person R230) Don't miss the wonderful Fig Forest Walk, an escorted walk across multilevel walkways. It's offered by Mantuma.

Sleeping

Mantuma CHALET, TENTED CAMP $$
(033-845 1000; www.kznwildlife.com; hut per person R220, d chalets R870) Mantuma is in a lovely setting and is unfenced, so there's often wandering wildlife, especially nyala. It's

an old camp – the accommodation has seen better days – but it's clean, well positioned and good value. You're better off self-catering than relying on the restaurant.

Tembe Elephant Park

Heading west along a dirt road to the N2 from Kosi Bay, South Africa's last free-ranging elephants are protected in the sandveld (dry, sandy coastal belt) forests of **Tembe Elephant Park** (☏031-267 0144; www.tembe. co.za; adult/child/vehicle R30/15/35; ☉6am-6pm). This transfrontier park on the Mozambique border is owned by the Tembe tribe and managed by Ezemvelo KZN Wildlife (p437). Around 230 elephants live in its 300 sq km; these are the only indigenous elephants in KZN, and the largest elephants in the world, weighing up to 7000kg. The park boasts the Big Five (lion, leopard, buffalo, elephant and rhino), plus more than 300 bird species.

🛏 Sleeping

Tembe Lodge   LODGE $$$
(☏082 651 2868; www.tembe.co.za; s/d with full board & activities from R2200/3400; ✖) Tembe Lodge offers accommodation in delightful, secluded, upmarket safari tents built on wooden platforms (the tents have bathrooms).

ℹ Getting There & Away

If driving from Durban along the N2, fill up with petrol at Mkuze. The turnoff to Tembe is at Jozini. There's a sealed road all the way to the park entrance, but only 4WD vehicles are allowed to drive through the park itself. If you don't have a 4WD, secure parking is available and visitors are collected in open safari vehicles.

Ndumo Game Reserve

Just west of Tembe Elephant Park, **Ndumo Game Reserve** (☏035-591 0004, central reservations 035-845 1000; www.kznwildlife.com; adult/child/vehicle R45/25/45; ☉5am-7pm Oct-Mar, 6am-6pm Apr-Sep) is beside the Mozambique border and close to the Swaziland border, about 100km north of uMkhuze. On some 100 sq km, there are black and white rhinos, hippos, crocodiles and antelope species, but it's the birdlife on the Phongolo and Usutu Rivers, and their flood plains and pans, that attracts visitors. The reserve is known locally as a 'mini Okavango'.

Wildlife-viewing and birdwatching guided walks (R130) and vehicle tours (R240) are available. This is the southernmost limit of the range of many bird species and the reserve is a favourite with birdwatchers, with more than 400 species recorded.

Fuel and limited supplies are usually available 2km outside the park gate. Camping and rest huts are offered by Ezemvelo KZN Wildlife ; minimum charges apply.

🛏 Sleeping

Ndumo Rest Camp   CAMPGROUND $$
(☏central reservations 033-845 1000; www.kznwildlife.com; camping R130, 2-bed huts R750) The simple rest camp has campsites and rest huts with shared ablutions and a communal kitchen. Guided walks (R130) and game drives (R240) are available.

ℹ Getting There & Away

The road to Ndumo is paved all the way. You need your own vehicle to reach the park.

Drakensberg & uKhahlamba-Drakensberg Park

If any landscape lives up to its airbrushed, publicity-shot alter ego, it is the jagged, green sweep of the Drakensberg's tabletop peaks. This forms the boundary between South Africa and the mountain kingdom of Lesotho, and offers some of the country's most awe-inspiring landscapes.

Within the area is a vast 2430-sq-km sweep of basalt summits and buttresses; this section was formally granted World Heritage status in 2000, and was renamed uKhahlamba-Drakensberg Park. Today, some of the vistas are recognisably South African, particularly the unforgettable curve of the Amphitheatre in Royal Natal National Park.

Drakensberg means 'Dragon Mountains'; the Zulu named it Quathlamba, meaning 'Battlement of Spears'. The Zulu word is a more accurate description of the sheer escarpment, but the Afrikaans name captures something of the Drakensberg's otherworldly atmosphere.

🏃 Activities

The Drakensberg range is one of the best hiking destinations in Africa. Valleys, waterfalls, rivers, caves and the escarpment, which rises to an impressive 3000m, provide spectacular wilderness experiences for walkers of all levels. Climbing is popular throughout the Drakensberg; only experienced climbers should attempt peaks in this region.

Drakensberg

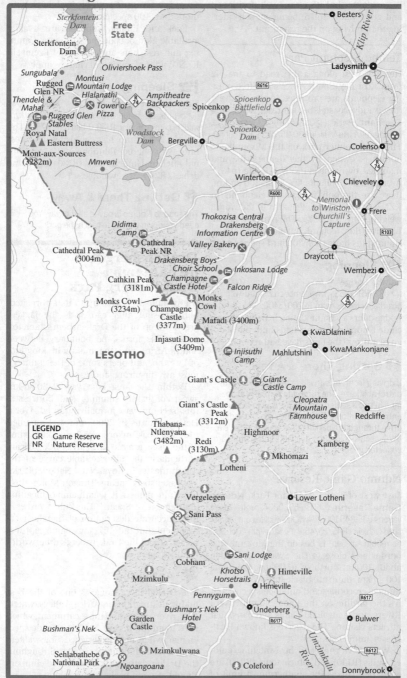

Besters

Sterkfontein Dam

Free State

Klip River

Ladysmith

Sterkfontein Dam

Sungubala

Oliviershoek Pass

R616

Rugged Glen NR

Montusi Mountain Lodge

Hlalanathi

Ampitheatre Backpackers

Spioenkop

Spioenkop Battlefield

Thendele & Mahai

Tower of Pizza

Spioenkop Dam

Rugged Glen Stables

Royal Natal

Woodstock Dam

Bergville

Eastern Buttress

Colenso

Mont-aux-Sources (3282m)

Mnweni

Winterton

N3

Chieveley

R600

R74

Memorial to Winston Churchill's Capture

Frere

Didima Camp

Cathedral Peak NR

Thokozisa Central Drakensberg Information Centre

R103

Cathedral Peak (3004m)

Valley Bakery

Draycott

Cathkin Peak (3181m)

Drakensberg Boys' Choir School

Champagne Castle Hotel

Inkosana Lodge

Wembezi

Falcon Ridge

Monks Cowl (3234m)

Monks Cowl

Champagne Castle (3377m)

Mafadi (3400m)

R29

LESOTHO

Injasuti Dome (3409m)

Injisuthi Camp

KwaDlamini

Mahlutshini

KwaMankonjane

Giant's Castle

Giant's Castle Camp

Cleopatra Mountain Farmhouse

Redcliffe

Giant's Castle Peak (3312m)

Thabana-Ntlenyana (3482m)

Highmoor

Kamberg

LEGEND
GR   Game Reserve
NR   Nature Reserve

Redi (3130m)

Mkhomazi

Lotheni

Vergelegen

Lower Lotheni

Sani Pass

Sani Lodge

Cobham

Khotso Horsetrails

Himeville

Mzimkulu

Pennygum

Himeville

R617

Bushman's Nek Hotel

Underberg

R617

Bulwer

Bushman's Nek

Garden Castle

Umzimkulu River

R612

Sehlabathebe National Park

Ngoangoana

Mzimkulwana

Coleford

Donnybrook

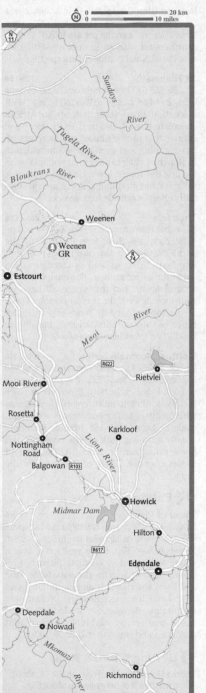

Broadly speaking, there are three main degrees of difficulty: gentle day walks, moderate half-day hikes and strenuous 10- to 12-hour hikes. Overnight treks and multiday hikes are for more serious and experienced hikers.

The trails are accessed through any of the park's entrances – Royal Natal National Park (renowned for its excellent day walks), Cathedral Peak, Monk's Cowl, Injisuthi and Giant's Castle, and the remote wilderness areas in the Southern Drakensberg.

To plan any walk, hike or trek, make sure you obtain the relevant 1:50,000-scale maps that show trails and have essential information for hikers. You should always seek advice on the current status of any trail – consult with experienced hikers, accommodation owners and Ezemvelo KZN Wildlife officers. You must always fill in a register, and permits are needed on all hikes within the park – organise them with Ezemvelo KZN Wildlife offices at the various trailheads. The only trail accommodation is at Giant's Castle; in some areas hikers can use caves, but always carry a tent.

If you prefer to hike with a guide, most accommodation options can arrange an experienced guide, or enquire at park offices. Guides for overnight hikes can be booked through Ezemvelo KZN Wildlife – rates per guide vary and there is also a R60 permit fee (per person per night). Hikers are not allowed to light fires, so you'll need to bring a stove.

April to July are good months for hiking. Summer hiking can be made frustrating, and even dangerous, by rain and flooding rivers; in winter, frost is the main hazard, and snow occurs occasionally. Snakes inhabit the area.

Northern Berg

An ideal stopover on the journey between Durban and Jo'burg, the Northern Berg is crowned with the beautiful Royal Natal National Park, with some excellent day walks and wonderfully empty spaces.

ROYAL NATAL NATIONAL PARK

Fanning out from some of the range's loftiest summits, the 80-sq-km **Royal Natal National Park** (☏ 036-438 6310; www.kznwildlife. com; adult/child/vehicle R40/20/45; ☉ 5am-7pm summer, 6am-6pm winter) has a presence that far outstrips its relatively meagre size: many of the surrounding peaks rise as high into the air as the park stretches across. With some of the Drakensberg's most dramatic and accessible scenery, the park is crowned by the sublime Amphitheatre, an 8km wall of cliff and canyon that's spectacular from below and even more so from up on high. Here, the Tugela Falls drop 850m in five stages (the top one often freezes in winter). Looming up behind is Mont-aux-Sources (3282m), so called because the Tugela, Elands and Western Khubedu Rivers rise here; the last eventually becomes the Senqu (Orange) River and flows all the way to the Atlantic. The park is renowned for its excellent day walks and hiking opportunities.

Other notable peaks in the area are the Devil's Tooth, the Eastern Buttress and the Sentinel. Rugged Glen Nature Reserve adjoins the park on the northeastern side.

◉ Sights

San Rock Art
HISTORIC SITE

(guided walk R40; ⊙9am-4pm) Of several San rock-art sites within the park, this is the only one open to tourists. You can organise a guided walk with community guides. The return trip takes about an hour, including time to rest and chat. Look for the 'San Rock Art' sign near the first bridge after entry.

☃ Activities

Elijah Mbonane
HIKING

(☑073 137 4690; elijahmbonane@yahoo.com) Offers guided hikes ranging from hour-long strolls to overnight treks. Prices vary greatly depending on number of hikers and length of the walk – minimum charge R800.

Rugged Glen Stables
HORSE RIDING

(☑036-438 6422; 2hr rides R240) Just outside the Royal Natal National Park gates, Rugged Glen Stables organises a wide range of horse-riding activities, including two-day trails.

🛏 Sleeping

Amphitheatre Backpackers
HOSTEL $

(☑082 855 9767; www.amphibackpackers.co.za; R74, 21km north of Bergville; camping R95, dm R180, d R360-720; 🅿🛜) This place gets mixed reviews from travellers – some report feeling pressured to do the organised trips (when there are other options around); others enjoy the rolled-out convenience. Amenities, though, are superb, including a bar, Jacuzzi, sauna and restaurant. Facing out over the Amphitheatre, it has a selection of sleeping options from dorms to comfortable four-person en suite rooms and a great campsite.

Rugged Glen Campsite
CAMPGROUND $

(☑central reservations 033-845 1000; www.kznwildlife.com; camping per site R220) A basic campground with an impressive setting inside Royal Natal National Park (p429).

★Hlalanathi
RESORT $$

(☑036-438 6308; www.hlalanathi.co.za; camping R195, 2-/4-bed chalets R1100/1800; ▣) With a location lifted straight from an African chocolate-box lid and next to the local golf course, this pretty, unpretentious resort offers camping and excellent accommodation in thatched chalets on a finger of land overlooking the Tugela River. Go for a site facing the river and mountains. Prices are substantially cheaper outside high season.

Thendele
CHALET $$

(☑central reservations 033-845 1000; www.kznwildlife.com; s/d chalet from R750/1000) The park's fabulous main camp has two- and four-bed chalets as well as cottages and a lodge for larger groups. The chalets are set around lawns and driveways; all have in-your-face views of the peaks opposite. Those at the top are slightly more expensive because of their wondrous views, but all are good. It's a great base for walkers.

Montusi Mountain Lodge
LODGE $$$

(☑036-438 6243; www.montusi.co.za; s/d with half board from R2360/3750; 🛜▣) With oodles of bush-lodge exclusivity, this opulent place blends a thatch-and-fireplace homeliness with plenty of luxury comforts in very swish chalets. There's guided hiking, including a daily morning walk on the property, and horse riding can be arranged. The turn-off is just after the Tower of Pizza; follow the signs.

🍴 Eating

Tower of Pizza
ITALIAN $

(☑036-438 6480; www.towerofpizza.co.za; pizza R75-100; ⊙noon-8.30pm Tue-Thu, to 9pm Fri & Sat, 10am-9pm Sun) Yep, there really is a tower, where very good wood-fired pizza is prepared. Grab a table on the outside decking and enjoy the clean air and mountain views at this excellent place near the Drakensberg mountains. Be warned: it doesn't accept cash – credit cards only! It also offers quaint rondavels and cottages (s/d R590/1000).

ⓘ Getting There & Away

The road into Royal Natal runs off Rte 74, about 30km northwest of Bergville and about 5km from Oliviershoek Pass.

Central Berg

Crowned with some of the Drakensberg's most formidable peaks, including Giant's Castle peak (3312m), Monk's Cowl (3234m) and Champagne Castle (3377m), the Central Berg is a big hit with hikers and climbers. But with dramatic scenery aplenty, this beautiful region is just as popular with those who prefer to admire their mountains from a safe distance. Champagne Valley, leading into Monk's Cowl, is full of cafes and accommodation options for all budgets. The sedate little town of Winterton is the gateway to the Central Drakensberg. The tiny, parochial Winterton Museum offers an insight into San rock art (there are some excellent photos with notes) and the history of local peoples, and there are photos relating to the Spioenkop battle.

CATHEDRAL PEAK NATURE RESERVE

In the shadow of the ramparts of Cathedral Peak, **Cathedral Peak Nature Reserve** (☑036-488 8000; www.kznwildlife.com; adult/child R35/20; ☺6am-6pm) backs up against a colossal escarpment of peaks between Royal Natal National Park and Giant's Castle, west of Winterton. With the Bell (2930m), the Horns (3005m) and Cleft Peak (3281m) on the horizon, this is a beautifully photogenic park.

The **Didima San Rock Art Centre** (☑036-488 1332; adult/child R20/5; ☺8am-4pm), at Didima Camp 1km into the park, offers an insight into San rock art, though the multimedia exhibit has been out of action for some time. If you plan to visit the centre, tell staff at the gate – an extra fee (adult/child R20/5) will be tacked onto your ticket price.

🛌 Sleeping

Didima Camp CAMPGROUND, CHALET **$$**
(☑central reservations 033-845 1000; www.kznwildlife.com; camping R200, chalets from R1020; P@☲) One of Ezemvelo KZN Wildlife's swankiest offerings, this upmarket thatched lodge, constructed to resemble San rock shelters, boasts huge views, a restaurant, tennis courts and a range of two- and four-bed self-catering chalets (full-board options are also available, on request). The nearby campsites have braai facilities, shared ablutions and kitchen and lovely views. Minimum charges apply.

ℹ Information

Head to the **Park Office** (☑ 036-488 8000; www.kznwildlife.com) for information on hikes in the area.

ℹ Getting There & Away

Cathedral Peak is 45km southwest of Winterton on a sealed road. There is no public transport unless you hitch a ride on a staff shuttle heading to the hotel.

MONK'S COWL & CHAMPAGNE VALLEY

Within uKhahlamba-Drakensberg Park, **Monk's Cowl** (☑036-468 1103; www.kznwildlife.com; adult/child R40/20; ☺6am-6pm), another stunning slice of the Drakensberg range, offers superb hiking and rock climbing. Within the reserve are the three peaks Monk's Cowl, Champagne Castle and Cathkin Peak.

The area en route to the park is known as **Champagne Valley**. This is full of cafes, pleasant accommodation options, bakeries, and enough (nonhiking) tourist activities to keep you busy for days.

The **Thokozisa** complex, 13km out of Winterton on Rte 600 and at the crossroads to Cathedral Peak, Monk's Cowl and Giant's Castle (via Estcourt), is a useful spot to orient yourself. It has a clutch of craft shops.

◎ Sights

Falcon Ridge WILDLIFE RESERVE
(☑082 774 6398; adult/child R85/40; ☺displays 10.30am Tue-Sun) Seven kilometres from the Drakensberg Sun turn-off is Falcon Ridge, with awesome raptor-flying demonstrations and talks.

🏃 Activities

Drakensberg Canopy Tour ADVENTURE SPORTS
(☑036-468 1981; www.drakensbergcanopytour.co.za; per person R595; ☺8am-1pm) Drakensberg Canopy Tour boasts superlatives – 12 slides, of which seven are over 100m; the highest point is 65m and the longest is 179m. You 'fly' above a beautiful canopy of an ancient indigenous forest, with a stream and waterfalls. It's an extreme sport – don't attempt it if you have vertigo. Book ahead.

Ushaka Horse Trails HORSE RIDING
(☑072 664 2993; www.monkscowl.com; 4 Bell Park Dam Rd; 2hr/day R250/850) One-hour to full-day horse trails are available through Ushaka Horse Trails. Ring for directions.

🛌 Sleeping

Inkosana Lodge HOSTEL **$**
(☑036-468 1202; www.inkosana.co.za; camping R125, dm R225, d 850, with shared bathroom R650; P☎☲) Travellers rave about this lodge. Its indigenous garden, rustic swimming dam, clean rooms and lovely rondavels make it

one of the best spots around. Although promoted as a 'backpacker lodge', it's range of rooms would suit any discerning traveller. Centrally located for activities in and around the area, it's on Rte 600, en route to Champagne Castle.

Wits End Mountain Resort CHALET $$
(☎036-468 1133; www.witsend.co.za; Rte 600; chalets per person R410; 🗺🏊) The excellent four-, six-, and eight-sleeper chalets here have a braai area, a large kitchen and wonderful views. Cheaper rates on weekdays.

Ardmore Guest Farm LODGE $$
(☎087 997 1194; www.ardmore.co.za; rondavels per person with half board from R615; P🗺🏊) A refreshing change from the area's resorts, this pleasant place, situated on a working farm, has a range of comfortable options. There are cottages and thatched rondavels – some with log fires – and meals are served in the original farmhouse.

✗ Eating

★Valley Bakery BAKERY, CAFE $
(☎036-468 1257; Rte 600; mains R35-60; ☺8am-5pm Mon-Fri, to 2pm Sat; 🗺🍴) Baguettes, croissants and a range of sticky treats are baked on the premises (the owners even grow and grind their wheat). A quaint wrought-iron veranda is the place for a wonderful selection of breakfasts, including eggs Benedict or muesli with fresh fruit. Wraps, sandwiches and homemade pies feature later in the day.

Dragon's Rest Pub & Restaurant PUB FOOD $$
(☎036-468 1218; mains R70-100; ☺10.30am-2.30pm & 6-8.30pm) Sit outside at this delightful place and drink in the dam-side and mountain views while enjoying some fine Berg cooking and a cold drink. Inside is a log fire and a cosy bar. Service is painfully slow but the food is tasty and the setting sublime. It's near the auditorium of the boys' choir.

☆ Entertainment

Drakensberg Boys' Choir School LIVE PERFORMANCE
(☎036-468 1012; www.dbchoir.com; R600; from R110) Just off Dragon Peaks Rd are South Africa's singing ambassadors, the Drakensberg Boys' Choir School. There are public performances at 3.30pm on Wednesday during school terms.

ⓘ Information

The **park office** (☎036-468 1103; camping R190-210; ☺8am-12.30pm & 2-4.30pm) is 3km

beyond Champagne Castle Hotel, which is at the end of the Rte 600 running southwest from Winterton. The **Central Drakensberg Information Centre** (☎036-488 1207; www.cdic.co.za; Rte 600, Info Centre Building; ☺9am-5pm), based in the Thokozisa complex, 13km outside Winterton, is also helpful.

ⓘ Getting There & Away

From the south, take the Estcourt North/Giant's Castle turnoff from the N3 and head towards Loskop. Turn left onto the R600 at Thokozisa. If you're coming from the north, look out for Rte 600 as you enter Winterton. The road is paved all the way to Monk's Cowl. The last section is steep and winding.

GIANT'S CASTLE

Established in 1904, mainly to protect the eland, **Giant's Castle** (☎036-353 3718; www.kznwildlife.com; adult/child R40/20; ☺5am-10pm Oct-Mar, 6am-10pm Apr-Sep, reception 8am-4.30pm) is a rugged, remote and popular destination, with varying dramatic landscapes. The Giant's Castle ridge itself is one of the most prominent features of the Berg. (If coming from the south on the N3, use the off-ramp exit 175, not marked on all maps.)

As is the case elsewhere, there are many excellent day walks and longer trails here. The office at Giant's Castle Camp (p433) gives out a basic map of the trails (distances not stated). Here, too, is a shop selling basic provisions, and fuel is available.

⊙ Sights

Lammergeier Hide VIEWPOINT
(☎036-353 3718; www.kznwildlife.com; per person R260, minimum R780) The rare lammergeier, also known as the bearded vulture (*Gypaetus barbatus*), which is found only in the Drakensberg, nests in the reserve. Reserve staff sometimes give guests bones to put out to encourage the birds to feed here. The Lammergeier Hide is the best place to see these raptors. The hide is extremely popular, so it's essential to book in advance. You need a 4WD or a sturdy pair of hiking boots to reach the hide and there are no facilities whatsoever.

Main Cave HISTORIC SITE
(per person R40; ☺9am-3pm) The Giant's Castle area is rich in San rock art. It's thought that the last San lived here at the beginning of the 20th century. To see some of these paintings, you can visit Main Cave, 2.3km south of Giant's Camp. A guide waits at the cave's entrance where, every hour, he conducts an explanatory tour.

🛌 Sleeping

Giant's Castle Camp
CHALET $$

(☎ 036-353 3718, central reservations 033-845 1000; www.kznwildlife.com; trail huts per person R60, chalets from R870) The main camp here is an impressive and remote set-up 8km from the main gate. Two-, four- and six-bed chalets have fireplace, kitchenette, floor-to-ceiling windows, TV and thatched verandah. The restaurant has a lovely deck with superb mountain views (but when the summer mists descend visibility gets down to a few metres). Hiker accommodation is available in caves and in an eight-bed hut.

🛈 Getting There & Away

If coming from the north or south along the N3, take Rte 29 to Giant's Castle (it links with Estcourt, to the east). From Winterton or Champagne Valley you can get here on Rte 10 and then south via Draycott (from Draycott there's 25km of good gravel road meandering through pine plantation, which joins the tar at White Mountain Lodge – from here it's 23km on tarred roads to Giant's Castle, hooking up with Rte 29).

Infrequent minibus shared taxis do the run from Estcourt to villages near the main entrance (KwaDlamini, Mahlutshini and KwaMankonjane), but these are still several kilometres from Giant's Camp.

Southern Berg

Best accessed from the pleasant towns of Himeville and Underberg, the Southern Berg boasts one of the region's highlights: the journey up to Lesotho over Sani Pass.

It is also renowned as a serious hiking area. As well as some great walks (including the fabulous Giant's Cup Trail), the region also offers a smorgasbord of wilderness areas.

SANI PASS

The drive up Sani Pass is a trip to the roof of South Africa: a spectacular ride around hairpin bends up into the clouds to the kingdom of Lesotho. At 2865m, this is the highest pass in the country and the vistas (on a clear day) are magical, offering stunning views out across the Umkhomazana River to the north and looming cliffs to the south. There are hikes in almost every direction, and inexpensive horse rides are available. Amazingly, this is also the only road link between Lesotho and KwaZulu-Natal.

At the top of the pass, just beyond the Lesotho border crossing, is Sani Top Chalet – various operators run 4WD trips up to the chalet. Although that has been talk of sealing the pass for years, it remains a gravel road and a 4WD is required.

🛌 Sleeping

Sani Lodge
HOSTEL $

(☎ 033-702 0330; www.sanilodge.co.za; camping R85, dm/d with shared bathroom R150/430, s/d rondavel R270/540) At the bottom of the pass and on a sealed road, Sani Lodge tops the pops in the local-knowledge stakes, offering a range of fabulous tours and activities and insider tips about the region through its company, Drakensberg Adventures. Some of the rooms are basic (the rondavels are

GIANT'S CUP TRAIL

If you are planning to stretch your legs anywhere in South Africa, this is the place to do it. Without doubt, the Giant's Cup Trail (60km, five days and five nights), running from Sani Pass to Bushman's Nek, is one of the nation's great walks. Any reasonably fit person can walk it, so it's very popular. Early booking, through Ezemvelo KZN Wildlife (p437), is advisable in local holiday seasons. Weather-wise, the usual precautions for the Drakensberg apply – expect severe cold snaps at any time of the year. Fees are based on the composition of the hiking party.

The stages are: day one, 14km; day two, 9km; day three, 12km; day four, 13km; and day five, 12km (note that it's not a circuit walk). An unofficial sixth day can take you from Bushman's Nek up into Lesotho to Sehlabathebe National Park (passports required). Highlights include the Bathplug Cave, with San rock art, and the breathtaking mountain scenery on day four. You can make the trail more challenging by doing two days in one, and you can do side trips from the huts if the weather is fine. Maps are sold at Sani Lodge for R45.

Camping is not permitted on this trail, so accommodation is in limited shared huts (www.kznwildlife.com; per person R100), hence the need to book ahead. No firewood is available, so you'll need a stove and fuel. Sani Lodge (p433) is almost at the head of the trail; arrange for the lodge to pick you up from Himeville or Underberg.

nicer), but it makes up for this with its communal, ski lodge–style atmosphere.

❶ Getting There & Away

Daily minibus shared taxis bring people from Mokhotlong (Lesotho) to South Africa for shopping; if there's a spare seat going back, this is the cheapest way to head over the pass to Lesotho, and you are taken to a town, not just the isolated lodge at the top of the pass. Ask at the tourist office. You need a passport to cross into Lesotho. The border is open from 6am to 6pm daily, but check beforehand; times alter. Make sure you allow sufficient time to arrive at either end. Also be aware that coming back into South Africa will require another visa.

SOUTHERN DRAKENSBERG WILDERNESS AREAS

The areas of Highmoor, Kamberg, Lotheni and Cobham are south of Giant's Castle and are administered by Ezemvelo KZN Wildlife (p437). These areas are more isolated, although they're accessible for those with time. The region is good for hiking (the rates for overnight-hiking permits are dependent on what you do.)

◉ Sights

Kamberg Nature Reserve NATURE RESERVE
(☑ 033-267 7251; www.kznwildlife.com; adult/child R40/20; ⊙ 5am-7pm Oct-Mar, 6am-6pm Apr-Sep) Southeast of Giant's Castle, Kamberg Nature Reserve has a number of antelope species and a mustn't-miss rock-art experience. It begins with a multimedia presentation, then you join a three-hour guided walk to the famous Game Pass Shelter, known as the 'Rosetta Stone' of Southern African rock art, for it was here that archaeologists first interpreted the symbolism of the San paintings. You can get to Kamberg from Nottingham Road or Rosetta, off the N3 south of Mooi River. Chalets available from R660.

Highmoor Nature Reserve NATURE RESERVE
(☑ central reservations 033-845 1000; www.kznwildlife.com; adult/child R40/20; ⊙ 5am-7pm Oct-Mar, 6am-6pm Apr-Sep) Although more exposed and less dramatic than some of the Drakensberg region, the undulating hills of the reserve make for pleasant walks. It's also one of the few places where you're driving 'on top of' the foothills. There are two caves – Aasvoel Cave and Caracal Cave – both 2.5km from the main office, and Fultons Rock, which has rock art (a 4km easy walk), plus caves for overnight hikers. Trout fishing is also popular.

🛌 Sleeping

Ezemvelo KZN Wildlife CHALET $
(☑ 033-267 7251; www.kznwildlife.com; chalet from R660) Ezemvelo KZN Wildlife has well-equipped two-bed chalets in the Kamberg section, tastefully decorated with small kitchens and floor-to-ceiling glass overlooking lawns and mountains. Accommodation in the Highmoor section is limited to camping. Bring your own supplies if you're staying in either reserve.

Cleopatra Mountain Farmhouse RESORT $$$
(☑ 033-267 7243; www.cleomountain.com; Balgowan; per person with half board from R2295) If God were to top off the beauty of the Drakensberg with a gourmet treat, Cleopatra Mountain Farmhouse would be it. Guests enjoy a nightly six-course menu of quality produce prepared innovatively and accompanied by rich, creamy sauces. Each of the 11 rooms is decked out in a theme and features quirky touches, such as a picket-fence bedhead and Boer memorabilia.

UNDERBERG & HIMEVILLE

Clustered in the foothills of the southern Drakensberg, the small farming town of Underberg fills up in summer, when Durbanites head to the peaks for a breath of the fresh stuff. It has good infrastructure, and is the place to go for money and shopping and to organise activities in the region. Only a few kilometres from Underberg, Himeville is a pretty, if sedate, jumping-off point for the southern Drakensberg. Except for an excellent museum, a characteristic old pub and a cluster of reasonable B&Bs, there's not much else here. Minibus shared taxis run between Himeville and Underberg (R12, 10 minutes).

◉ Sights

Himeville Museum MUSEUM
(☑ 033-702 1184; Arbuckle St; admission by donation; ⊙ 9am-3pm Tue-Sat) One of the best rural museums in the country. Housed in the last *laager* (tavern) built in South Africa (c 1896), the museum now contains an incredible array of bric-a-brac, from the Union Jack flown at the siege of Ladysmith to a map of El Alamein signed by Montgomery.

🏃 Activities

Khotso Horsetrails HORSE RIDING
(☑ 033-701 1502; www.khotsotrails.co.za; horse rides per hour/day R190/650) Offers rides and treks (plus tubing and fishing) in the area

and into Lesotho – owner Steve is described by readers as 'South Africa's Crocodile Dundee'. It's about 7km northwest of Underberg on Drakensberg Gardens Rd.

☞ Tours

Sani Pass Tours TOURS
(🖉 033-701 1064; www.sanipasstours.com; Shop 22, Trout Walk Centre, Underberg) Highly regarded tours up the Sani Pass (per person R830) as well as multiday tours into Lesotho.

🛏 Sleeping

Khotso Backpackers HOSTEL $
(🖉 033-701 1502; www.khotso.co.za; Treetower Farm, Underberg; camping R100, dm R160, d from R550, without bathroom R430; 🛜) A good budget choice, located in a rural environment. The owners lead horse rides (p434) into Lesotho and surrounds, and you can get your adrenaline fix by rafting and tubing. It's about 7km northwest of Underberg on Drakensberg Gardens Rd.

Himeville Arms HISTORIC HOTEL $$
(🖉 033-702 1305; www.himevillehotel.co.za; Arbuckle St, Himeville; r from R830) Now operated by the Premier Hotels group, this old-fashioned inn dates back to the start of the 20th century. Rooms blend antique furniture with modern decor and there's an atmospheric old bar.

✗ Eating

Pucketty Farm DELI $
(🖉 033-701 1035; www.puckettyfarm.co.za; Main Rd, Underberg; mains R50-90; ⊙9am-4.30pm) Beatrix Potter meets Jamie Oliver: there's more to this extraordinarily cute place than meets the eye. There's a huge selection of great-value gourmet products, plus an art gallery and a small tea garden. Perfect for self-caterers. The farm is 1.5km southeast of the Himeville turn-off.

ℹ Information

First National Bank (Old Main Rd, Underberg) and **Standard Chartered Bank** (Underberg Village Mall, Underberg) have ATMs.

ℹ Getting There & Away

One daily minibus shared taxi runs between central Kokstad and Underberg, departing Underberg (Spar car park) at 9am and Kokstad at 2pm. (Baz Bus and bus arrivals in Kokstad are at Mount Currie Inn, 2.5km from the centre; you will have to ask the minibus to take you there, for an extra cost.) Minibus taxis run between Himeville and Underberg (R12, 10 minutes) and from Underberg to Pietermaritzburg (R80, 1½ hours).

The Midlands

The Midlands run northwest from Pietermaritzburg (KwaZulu-Natal's capital) to Estcourt, skirting the Battlefields to the northeast. West of Pietermaritzburg is picturesque, hilly country, with horse studs and plenty of European trees. It was originally settled by English farmers.

Today, the region appeals more to art and craft lovers; it promotes itself heavily as the Midlands Meander, a slightly contrived concoction of craft shops, artistic endeavours, tea shops and B&Bs, winding along and around the R103 west of the N3, northwest of Pietermaritzburg.

Pietermaritzburg

POP 223,500 / 🖉 033
Billed as the heritage city, and KZN's administrative and legislative capital, Pietermaritzburg and its grand historic buildings hark back to an age of pith helmets and midday martinis. While many buildings have been converted into museums, much of the CBD has, sadly, lost its gloss, especially in the past few years. This is partly due to the dire state of the local-government coffers. Elsewhere, the inner suburbs – plus Hilton, a suburb 9km northwest of the city centre – are green, leafy and pretty.

Pietermaritzburg comprises a very contemporary mix: the city is home to students attending the numerous private schools in the area, a large Zulu community and a sizable Indian population. Pietermaritzburg is a reasonable base from which to tackle the Midlands Meander.

◉ Sights

Tatham Art Gallery GALLERY
(🖉 033-392 2800; www.tatham.org.za; Chief Albert Luthuli St (Commercial Rd); ⊙10am-5pm Tue-Sun) FREE In keeping with Pietermaritzburg's self-styled role as the 'heritage city', one of its finest sights, the art gallery, was started in 1903 by Mrs Ada Tatham. Housed in the beautiful Old Supreme Court, it contains a fine collection of French and English 19th- and early-20th-century works.

KwaZulu-Natal National Botanical Garden GARDENS
(🖉 033-344 3585; www.sanbi.org; 2 Swartkops Rd, Prestbury; adult/child R22/15; ⊙8am-6pm Oct-Apr,

Pietermaritzburg

Pietermaritzburg

◉ Sights
1 Msunduzi Museum C1
2 Tatham Art Gallery C1

✖ Eating
3 Tatham Art Gallery Cafe C1
4 Traffords D2

❶ Transport
5 Long-Distance Bus Company
    Offices C2
6 Long-Distance Bus Company
    Offices C2

to 5.30pm May-Sep) Located 2km west of the train station on the continuation of Hoosen Haffejee St and spread over 4200 sq m, these gardens have exotic species and indigenous mist-belt flora. Guided tours are offered on weekdays and there's a weekly farmers market here on Saturday mornings from 6am.

Msunduzi Museum MUSEUM
(📞 033-394 6834; www.voortrekkermuseum.co.za; 351 Langalibalele St (Longmarket St); adult/student R10/5; ⏰ 9am-4pm Mon-Fri, to 1pm Sat; 🅿) Formerly known as Voortrekker Museum, Msunduzi Museum comprises a complex that incorporates the **Church of the Vow**, the home of Andries Pretorius, a Voortrek-

ker house and a former school now housing exhibits on the history of the region and its varied inhabitants. The Church of the Vow was built in 1841 to fulfil the Voortrekkers' promise to God at the Battle of Blood River. The words of the vow are in the **Modern Memorial Church**.

🛏 Sleeping

Tancredi B&B B&B $$
(📞 082 818 1555; www.tancredi.co.za; 41 Woodhouse Rd, Scottsville; s/d incl breakfast R640/890; 🅿🛜) Just south of the city centre in a quiet suburb, Tancredi has seven rooms in a beautifully restored Victorian house. The topnotch breakfast and personal service from owner Ann make this a popular spot.

**Pietermaritzburg
B&B Network** ACCOMMODATION SERVICES $$
(📞 073 154 4444; www.pmbnetwork.co.za; d R600-1500) A group of local B&Bs that help promote each other.

Smith Grove B&B B&B $$
(📞 033-345 3963; www.smithgrove.co.za; 37 Howick Rd; s/d incl breakfast R595/850; ❄🛜) This beautiful renovated Victorian home offers English-style B&B comforts with spacious, individually styled rooms, each in a different colour. There are freestanding bathtubs,

and the pick of the rooms is No 5 on the 2nd floor, facing away from the main road with two good-size windows to enjoy the views.

Redlands Hotel & Lodge HOTEL $$$
(☑ 033-394 3333; www.redlandshotel.co.za; cnr Howick Rd & George MacFarlane Lane; s/d incl breakfast from R1370/1780; P❉🛜⚟) Swish and stately, this elegant place offers contrived but tasteful colonial-style surrounds. It's a favourite among government dignitaries. The spacious grounds add to the escape-from-it-all ambience. It's north of the centre off Howick Rd, past the Royal Agricultural Showgrounds.

🍴 Eating

Tatham Art Gallery Cafe CAFE $
(Chief Albert Luthuli St (Commercial Rd); mains R60-90; ☺10am-4pm Mon Sat) Dip into quiche, beef curry or lasagne at the upstairs cafe at Tatham Gallery, or grab a table on the outside balcony. Also on offer are sweet treats like muffins and brownies.

Traffords INTERNATIONAL $$$
(☑ 033-394 4364; http://traffords.co.za; 43 Miller St; mains lunch R65-120, dinner R95-160; ☺noon-3pm Tue-Fri, 6.30-10.30pm Tue-Sat; ✎) This place serves up quality international cuisine in appealingly quaint surrounds: the rooms of a converted heritage home. Choose from the likes of cherry-tobacco duck or smoked, black-pepper-rubbed entrecôte. Lunches include more salad-based offerings. Vegetarians are also catered for. Decor is of the preloved linen tablecloth variety – it's like having an elegant meal in the home you'd love to have.

ℹ Information

There are several banks located across town and in major shopping malls.

ABSA (cnr Langalibalele St (Longmarket St) & Buchanan St) Has an ATM and change facilities.

First National Bank (Church St) In a handy location in the city centre.

Ezemvelo KZN Wildlife Headquarters
(☑ 033-845 1000; www.kznwildlife.com; Peter Brown Dr, Queen Elizabeth Park; ☺reception 8am-4.30pm Mon-Fri, reservations 8am-5.30pm Mon-Thu, to 4.30pm Fri, to 12.30pm Sat) Provides information and accommodation bookings for all Ezemvelo KZN Wildlife parks and reserves. To get to the office, head out to Howick Rd (an extension of Chief Albert Luthuli St) and after several kilometres you'll come to a roundabout. Veer right and head over the N3. This road has a very small sign directing you to 'Country Club', which is 2km further. It's hard to get to without your own transport, although

some minibus shared taxis pass the roundabout on their way to Hilton. Note that at least 48 hours' notice is required for bookings.

Main Post Office (Langalibalele St)

Medi-Clinic (☑ 033-845 3911, 033-845 3700; www.mediclinic.co.za; 90 Payn St; ☺24hr emergency) Well-equipped hospital with emergency department on the banks of the Umsinduzi River.

Msunduzi Pietermaritzburg Tourism (☑ 033-345 1348; www.pmbtourism.co.za; Publicity House, 117 Chief Albert Luthuli St; ☺8am-5pm Mon-Fri, to 1pm Sat) The tourist office has brand spanking new premises just behind the current office – although when it officially moves is anybody's guess.

Police Station (☑10111, 033-845 2400; Jabu Ndlovu St)

ℹ Getting There & Away

AIR

The **airport** (☑ 033-386 9577) is 7km south of the city. A taxi costs around R90. **Airlink** (☑ 033-386 9286; www.flyairlink.com) operates flights Johannesburg (R800, one hour).

BUS

The offices of most bus companies, including Greyhound (p524) and Intercape (p354), are in Berger St, or directly opposite in McDonalds Plaza. Translux (p527) and its no-frills affiliate, City to City (p527), are based at the train station.

Destinations offered from Pietermaritzburg include Jo'burg (R330, seven hours), Pretoria (R330, seven hours) and Durban (R220, 1½ hours). Offices are generally open 7am or 8am until 11pm. Tickets for all major services can be purchased at Checkers/Shoprite or online at www.computickettravel.com.

NUD Express (☑ 079 696 7108; www.under bergexpress.co.za) offers a daily service to Durban's King Shaka International Airport (R300) and Durban Central (R300). You must book these services; note that the buses are not known for their reliability in sticking to times.

Baz Bus (p354) travels between Durban and Pietermaritzburg three times a week.

SHARED TAXI

Minibus taxis to Durban leave from behind City Hall (R70, 1½ hours), while those to Underberg depart from the corner of West and Pietermaritz Sts. Destinations from this stop also include Ladysmith (R90, 2½ hours), Underberg (R80, 2½ hours), and Jo'burg (R200, eight hours).

TRAIN

Shosholoza Meyl (p354) offers a service to Johannesburg (R320, 12 hours) on Friday and Sunday.

❶ Getting Around

To order a taxi, phone **Metro Taxis** (☑ 033-397 1912; www.metrotaxis.co.za).

Battlefields

Big wildlife, big mountains and big waves may top the agenda for many visitors to the province, but the history of KwaZulu-Natal is intrinsically linked to its battlefields, the stage on which many of South Africa's bloodiest chapters were played out. The province's northwestern region is where fewer than 600 Voortrekkers avenged the murder of their leader, Piet Retief, by defeating a force of 12,000 Zulu at Blood River, and where the British Empire was crushed by a Zulu army at Isandlwana. Here they subsequently staged the heroic defence of Rorke's Drift, where the Boers and the Brits slogged it out at Ladysmith and Spioenkop. These days, the region offers some luxurious accommodation options, and for history buffs it can be most rewarding.

See www.battlefields.kzn.org.za or pick up KZN Tourism's *Battlefields Route* brochure.

Ladysmith

POP 65,000 / ☑ 036

Ladysmith was named after the wife of Cape governor Sir Harry Smith. The town achieved fame during the 1899–1902 Anglo-Boer War, when it was besieged by Boer forces for 118 days. Musical group Ladysmith Black Mambazo has its roots here, but the town's pretty colonial vestiges are looking a little tired these days. Apart from its historical aspect, it's a reasonable, bustling base for the area's battlefield tours.

◉ Sights

Siege Museum   MUSEUM

(☑ 036-637 2992; Murchison St; adult/child R12/5; ☺ 8am-4pm Mon-Fri, 9am-noon Sat) The excellent museum, next to the town hall in the old Market House (built 1884), was used to store rations during the Anglo-Boer War siege. It has displays about the war, stocks information about the town and surrounds, and can provide a list of battlefield tour guides.

Castor & Pollux   MONUMENT

Outside the town hall are two guns, Castor and Pollux, used by the British in defence of Ladysmith.

Fort   NOTABLE BUILDING

(King St) Opposite Settlers Dr is a wall with loopholes from the original fort, built as a refuge from Zulu attack and now part of the police station.

🛏 Sleeping

Memra Guest House   GUESTHOUSE $$

(☑ 036-631 7072; www.memra.co.za; 14 St Augustine Ave; r R800; ❄) Travellers rave about the personal attention at this small guesthouse with six simple rooms.

Buller's Rest Lodge   B&B $$

(☑ 036-637 6154; www.bullersrestlodge.co.za; 59 Cove Cres; s/d incl breakfast from R740/1010; 🛜❄) It's worth digging in at this smart thatched abode. There's the snug 'Boer War' pub, scrumptious home cooking (R160 for three courses), and views from the attractive sun-deck–bar area. Turn right at Francis Rd off Harrismith (Poort) Rd, and follow the signs.

✖ Eating

Guinea Fowl   INTERNATIONAL $$

(☑ 036-637 8163; San Marco Centre, cnr Harrismith & Francis Rds; mains R90-140; ☺ noon-3pm & 6-9.30pm Mon-Sat) One of the only reasonable restaurants in Ladysmith, this eatery does curries along with steak, chicken and seafood dishes at a shopping centre. Burgers available too.

❶ Information

The museum doubles as a tourism office.

ABSA (cnr Queen & Murchison Sts) Two branches on the same crossroads, one with ATM.

Police Station (☑ 036-638 3309; King St) By the NG Church.

❶ Getting There & Away

BUS

Bus tickets can be purchased from Shoprite/Checkers in the Oval Shopping Centre. **Greyhound** (p524) buses depart from the Guinea Fowl petrol station (not to be confused with the restaurant) on Murchison Rd, and they connect Ladysmith with Durban (R360, four hours), Jo'Burg/Pretoria (R380, seven hours) and Cape Town (R660, 19 hours).

SHARED TAXI

The main minibus taxi rank is east of the town centre near the corner of Queen and Lyell Sts. Taxis bound for Jo'burg are nearby on Alexandra St. Destinations include Pietermaritzburg (1½ hours), Durban (2½ hours) and Jo'burg (five hours).

Isandlwana & Rorke's Drift

If you've seen *Zulu* (1964), the film that made Michael Caine a star, you will doubtless have heard of Rorke's Drift, a victory of the misty-eyed variety, where on 22 and 23 January 1879, 139 British soldiers successfully defended a small mission station from around 4000 Zulu warriors. Queen Victoria lavished 11 Victoria Crosses on the survivors and the battle was assured its dramatic place in British military history.

However, for the full picture you must travel 15km across the plain to Isandlwana, the precursor to Rorke's Drift. It's here that, only hours earlier, the Zulus dealt the Empire one of its great Battlefields disasters by annihilating the main body of the British force in devastating style. Tellingly, *Zulu Dawn* (1979), the film made about Isandlwana, never became the cult classic *Zulu* is now. Victories sell better than defeats.

◉ Sights

Rorke's Drift Battlefield HISTORIC SITE
(☑034-642 1687; adult/child R30/15; ☺9am-4pm) Rorke's Drift Orientation Centre, on the site of the original mission station, is excellent. The Zulu know this site as Shiyane, their name for the hill at the back of the village. The *Rorke's Drift–Shiyane Self-Guided Trail* brochure (R5) is a helpful reference. *Zulu* was actually filmed in the Drakensberg, so the scenery around Rorke's Drift may come as a bit of a disappointment to those familiar with the film. The landscape is still beautifully rugged, however.

Isandlwana Battlefield HISTORIC SITE
(☑034-271 0634; adult/child R30/15; ☺9am-4pm) The Isandlwana Visitors Centre has a small museum; the entrance fee includes the battlefield. The battlefield itself is extremely evocative. White cairns and memorials mark the spots where British soldiers fell. It's best seen with a local guide.

⌸ Sleeping

Isandalwana Lodge LODGE $$$
(☑034-271 8301; www.isandlwana.co.za; s/d with full board R4320/7200; P✿❖) Top marks for location: the lodge's stunning rooms have expansive views over Mt Isandlwana, the Anglo-Zulu battle site. For such a modern construction, the lodge ingeniously blends into the landscape. Specials are offered throughout the year.

Rorke's Drift Hotel LODGE $$$
(☑034-642 1760; www.rorkesdrifthotel.com; s/d with half board R1440/2140) The common areas and restaurant of this giant rotunda – a wide expanse with massive sofas and an enormous central fireplace – promise big things. The rooms are less appealing, with not-quite-there but pleasant enough decor. The nearest place to Rorke's Drift, the restaurant is a popular snack spot for day-trippers.

❶ Getting There & Away

The battle sites are southeast of Dundee. Isandlwana is about 70km from Dundee, off R68; Rorke's Drift is 42km from Dundee, accessible from R68 or R33 (the R33 turn-off is 13km south of Dundee). The roads to both battlefields can be dusty and rough. A dirt road connects Isandlwana and Rorke's Drift.

Blood River

On 16 December 1838 a small force of Voortrekkers avenged the massacre of Piet Retief by crushing an army of 12,000 Zulu. More than 3000 Zulu died – the river ran red with their blood – while the Voortrekkers sustained a few casualties. The battle became a seminal event in Afrikaner history, seen as proof that the Boers had a divine mandate to 'civilise' Southern Africa, and that they were, in fact, a chosen people.

It has been argued that the importance of Blood River was deliberately heightened and manipulated for political ends. The standard interpretation of the victory meshed with the former apartheid regime's world view: untrustworthy black savages beaten by Boers on an Old Testament–style mission from God.

The story of this historic battle is told at two rewarding sites, the Blood River Heritage Site and Ncome Museum, which speak from the perspective of the Voortrekkers and Zulus respectively.

◉ Sights

Blood River Heritage Site MUSEUM
(☑034-632 1695; www.bloedrivier.org.za; adult/child R35/20, car R15; ☺8am-4.30pm) The Blood River battle site is marked by a full-scale bronze recreation of the Boers' 64-wagon *laager* (an encampment fortified by a circle of wagons). The cairn here tells the story of the legendary battle. It's located 20km southeast of Rte 33; the turn-off is 27km from Dundee and 45km from Vryheid.

Ncome Museum   MUSEUM
(☏ 034-271 8121; www.ncomemuseum.co.za; admission by donation; ⊗ 8am-4.30pm) The interesting Ncome Museum offers the Zulu perspective of the Battle of Blood River. The museum takes the shape of buffalo horns, the traditional method of attack. A symbolic display of Zulu shields (in metal) represents the Zulu regiments that fought in the battle.

FREE STATE

A place of big skies and open pastureland, the Free State is ideal for a road trip. Broad horizons are interrupted only briefly by a smattering of towns and villages and, apart from Bloemfontein, the urban centres are small and manageable. The Eastern Highlands, around the Drakensberg and the Lesotho border, is a vast area of rocky mountains, steep valleys and summer electrical storms. It's spectacular country, well known for its fruit farms, especially cherries. There are some excellent accommodation options in this part of the country, along with the stunning and walkable Golden Gate Highlands National Park. The Free State tends to be a place travellers pass through rather than a destination in its own right. However

Free State

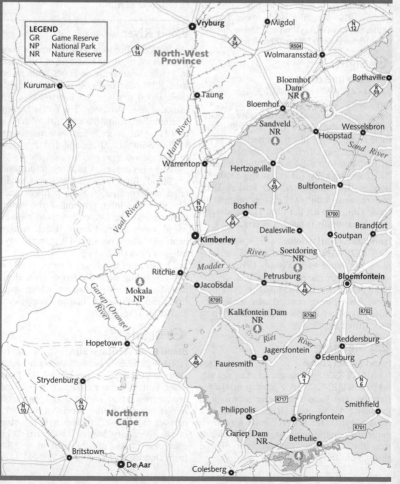

it's well worth exploring for its natural beauty, adventure sports and history – especially Bloemfontein, which, although historically an Afrikaner city, is also the birthplace of the African National Congress (ANC).

Bloemfontein

POP 256,500 / ☎ 051

With the feel of a small country village, despite its double-capital status – it's the Free State's capital and the judicial capital of the country – Bloemfontein is one of South Africa's most pleasant cities. Although it doesn't possess the type of big-name attractions that make it worth a visit in its own right, you'll likely pass through 'Bloem' at some point on your way across South Africa's heartland and there are some small-scale sights to keep you occupied for a day or two.

Note that some areas of downtown are not considered safe, especially at night, so seek local advice before going for a wander around the central business district. Apart from this the city has a relaxed, welcoming feel and some excellent eating and accommodation options.

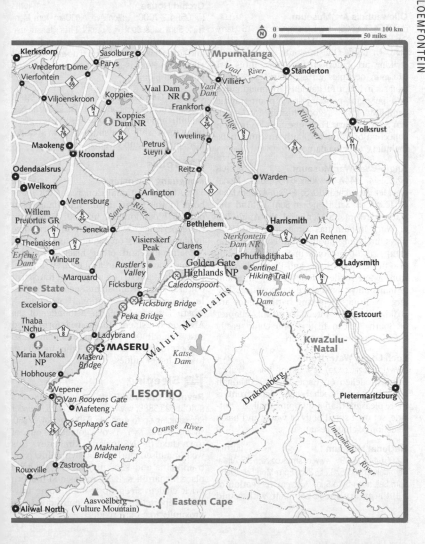

◉ Sights

★ Naval Hill
PARK

(☏051-412 7016; ⊙8am-6pm) FREE This was the site of the British naval-gun emplacements during the Anglo-Boer War. There are good views from the top of the hill, which is also home to the **Franklin Game Reserve**. Walking is permitted, and you may see ostriches, zebras and giraffes wandering about. Also on top is a **planetarium**, operated by the University of the Free State, and a gigantic **statue of Nelson Mandela** overlooking the city. There are plans to open a restaurant next to the statue. Entry is from Union Ave.

Oliewenhuis Art Museum
GALLERY

(☏051-447 9609; www.nasmus.co.za; 16 Harry Smith St; ⊙8am-5pm Mon-Fri, 9am-4pm Sat & Sun; 🖈) FREE One of South Africa's most striking art galleries, the Oliewenhuis Art Museum occupies an exquisite 1935 mansion set in beautiful gardens. An imaginative and poignant contemporary photographic exhibition gives a good insight into modern South Africa. The museum also holds a collection of works by South African artists, including Thomas Baines.

Anglo-Boer War Museum
MUSEUM

(☏051-447 3447; www.anglo-boer.co.za; Monument Rd; adult/child R10/5; ⊙8am-4.30pm Mon-Fri, 10am-5pm Sat, 11am-5pm Sun) Behind the National Women's Memorial, the Anglo-Boer War Museum has some interesting displays, including photos from concentration camps set up not only in South Africa but also in Bermuda, India and Portugal. Apart from a few modern touches, this museum remains unchanged since its inception. The large paintings depicting battle scenes are striking. If you're interested in this chapter of South African history you could easily spend a couple of hours here.

Loch Logan Waterfront
MALL

(www.lochlogan.co.za) Yes, Bloem has a Waterfront, modelled on Cape Town's. Although it's a bit tacky, Loch Logan Waterfront is more pleasant than a shopping mall. It's outside, set on a small body of water and has a selection of chain restaurants.

National Museum
MUSEUM

(☏051-447 9609; www.nasmus.co.za; 36 Aliwal St; adult/child R5/3; ⊙8am-5pm Mon-Fri, 10am-5pm Sat, noon-5pm Sun) A great recreation of a 19th-century street, complete with sound effects, is the most interesting display at this museum. It also has a shop and a cafe.

National Women's Memorial
MEMORIAL

(Monument Rd) Commemorating the 26,000 women and children who died in British concentration camps during the 1899–1902 Anglo-Boer War, the National Women's Memorial depicts a bearded Afrikaner setting off on his horse to fight the British, bidding a last farewell to his wife and baby, who are to perish in one of the camps. It's a powerful image and one still buried in the psyche of many Afrikaners.

Orchid House
GARDENS

(☏051-412 7000; Union Ave; ⊙10am-4pm Mon-Fri, to 5pm Sat & Sun; 🖈) FREE This glasshouse has a beautiful, if small, collection of flowers and some dazzling orchids. The surrounding **Hamilton Park** is an ideal place to take the kids for a picnic.

Franklin Game Reserve
WILDLIFE RESERVE

(☏051-405 8124; ⊙8am-6pm) FREE Atop Naval hill, the Franklin Game Reserve is a great place for a walk or a short drive to spot zebras, antelope and giraffes.

☞ Tours

Manguang Township
CULTURAL

The African National Congress (ANC) was born in the township of Manguang, 5km outside Bloemfontein, in 1912. Today, you can experience township life and learn some important history on a guided tour.

Manguang and other black townships around the Bloem area played an integral role in the fight to end apartheid. Tours visit culturally important sights such as **Mapikela House** (now a national monument), where Thomas Mapikela, a founder of the ANC, once resided. Tours are informal and cost about R500. The operators change, so it's best to ask at the tourist office for an up-to-date list of guides.

🛏 Sleeping

Reyneke Caravan Park
CARAVAN PARK $

(☏051-523 3888; www.reynekepark.co.za; Brendar Rd; camping up to 4 people R300, s/d R470/560, chalets R980; ⊠) Two kilometres out of town (take the N8 towards Kimberley), this well-organised park has a swimming pool, trampoline and kids' play area. It's a good place for families. Basic rooms and modern brick chalets sleep up to four. Some travellers report that it can be noisy due to its proximity to a busy road.

★**Matanja** GUESTHOUSE $$
(☑079 494 9740; www.matanja.co.za; 74A Albrecht St, Dan Pienaar; s/d incl breakfast R585/780; ❀) Small luxuries, such as goose-down duvets and a stylish, rustic ambience, set this little B&B apart. There are honesty fridges in the bedrooms, and with only four rooms there's attention to detail. Your comfort seems a priority to the owners, who will even arrange breakfast in bed. Prebooking recommended.

Franklin View GUESTHOUSE $$
(☑083 262 1245; www.franklinview.co.za; 9E Innes Avenue, Waverley; s/d incl breakfast R795/1100; P❀❀❀) Located on the slopes of Naval Hill, Franklin View has awesome views over the city and a huge balcony where breakfast is served. Rooms are stylish, with lots of bare brick and heavy wooden furniture.

Urban Hotel HOTEL $$
(☑051-444 3142; www.urbanhotel.co.za; cnr Parfitt Ave & Henry St; r incl breakfast R750; ❀❀) This hotel fills an important niche in Bloem's accommodation market; it's at the cheaper end of midrange, and service reflects this. Very modern rooms, however, are quite decadent, with lovely bathrooms and great beds. Try to get an upstairs room near the back. It's in an excellent location, too, close to all the Westdene and Waterfront action.

Hobbit Boutique Hotel BOUTIQUE HOTEL $$
(☑051-447 0663; www.hobhit.co.za; 19 President Steyn Ave, Westdene; r incl breakfast from R1000; ❀@❀) This charming Victorian guesthouse, comprising two 1921 houses, is popular with visiting dignitaries and perfect for literati and romantic types. The cottage-style bedrooms have painted bathtubs, plus a couple of teddy bears apiece. The reading room has a chess table, and the local Tolkien society meets here to discuss all things JRR. Check out the pub and lovely outdoor patio. At night there's a turn-down service with sherry and chocolate.

Protea Hotel Willow Lake HOTEL $$$
(☑051-412 5400; www.protea.marriott.com; 101 Henry St; r from R1400; ❀@❀❀) Part of a popular national chain, the Protea offers very stylish rooms. Plump bedding and a shower cubicle that looks like it belongs at NASA complete the experience. It's a genuine touch of luxury. Close to the Waterfront, and overlooking the zoo.

✖ **Eating**

Picnic CAFE $
(☑051-430 4590; Loch Logan Waterfront; mains R60-90; ❀Mon-Sat 8am-5pm, to 2pm Sun) A cool place with a great outlook over the water, perfect for a long, lazy chill-out. The food is excellent – especially the salads and sandwiches. Enjoy the fresh bread, quality ingredients and homemade touches such as tomato chutney (recommended on rye with ham and camembert).

★**Seven on Kellner** INTERNATIONAL $$
(☑051-447 7928; www.sevenonkellner.co.za; 7 Kellner St, Westdene; mains R80-165; ❀noon-2pm Mon-Fri, from 6.30pm Mon-Sat) Set in an old house with inside and outside dining options, Seven on Kellner offers an informal, intimate atmosphere. Poultry, meat and seafood dishes are delicately prepared with expert hands along a Middle Eastern– and Indian-inspired theme. Excellent wine list.

Avanti ITALIAN $$
(☑051-447 4198; www.avantirestaurant.co.za; 53 2nd Ave; mains R70-220; ❀11.30am-10pm Mon-Sat, to 3pm Sun) With a covered terrace and heavy leather chairs, this stylish place serves more than just pizza and pasta (although it does those too, and does them well). The lamb loin chops are delicious, and there's a good range of wines to pair them with.

New York STEAK $$
(☑051-447 7279; www.newyorkrestaurant.co.za; cnr 2nd Ave & Reid St; mains R80-180; ❀11.30am-3pm & 6-10pm Sun-Thu, 6-10pm Sat) Locals love this upmarket steakhouse, with its decor invoking 1920s New York, for special occasions. The menu features seafood, chicken and burgers, but it's the saucy steaks that steal the show. There are a couple of vegetarian options alongside all the meat.

Braza PORTUGUESE $$
(☑051-447 2821; Loch Logan Waterfront; mains R80-160; ❀11am-10pm Mon-Sat, to 9pm Sun) The Portuguese-inspired cuisine here will appeal to both meat lovers and seafood aficionados. Outside tables are right on the water's edge.

● **Drinking & Nightlife**

No. 16 Stoep & Beer Garden BEER GARDEN
(☑051-430 2542; 16 2nd Ave; ❀11am-4am Tue-Sat) A hip addition to the 2nd Avenue scene, No. 16 combines gourmet burgers (R70 to R90) and craft beer in a city beer garden setting. There's live music most nights and

more than 30 beers to choose from. The kitchen closes at 11pm.

Stereo Cafe
COFFEE, CAFE

(☏051-430 1135; 60 2nd Ave; ☺7am-4pm Mon-Fri, 8am-1pm Sat; ☎) This small, hip roastery is Bloem's best place for a cup of Joe.

Mystic Boer
PUB

(☏051-430 2206; www.diemysticboer.co.za; 84 Kellner St; ☺2pm-4am Mon-Fri, noon-4am Sat, 5pm-2am Sun; ☎) Bloem's most popular long-standing pub and live-music venue provides an eccentric twist on Afrikaner

Bloemfontein

culture – check out the psychedelic pictures of long-bearded Boers on the walls. There are regular gigs by unsigned rock and hip-hop groups. The bar specialises in tequila; pizza and burgers provide the fuel.

ℹ Information

There are banks with ATMs all over the city centre and at Loch Logan Waterfront. the American Express Foreign Exchange office is at Mimosa Mall.

Main Post Office (Groenendal St) Near Hoffman Sq.

Tourist Information Centre (☏ 051-405 8489; www.bloemfonteintourism.co.za; 60 Park Rd; ⏱ 8am-4.15pm Mon-Fri, to noon Sat) A mildly useful tourist office.

ℹ Getting There & Away

AIR

Bloemfontein airport is 10km from the city centre. A number of international airlines fly into Bloem via Cape Town or Jo'burg.

Mango (☏ 086 100 1234; www.flymango.com) connects Bloem with Cape Town (R950, 1½ hours). **Fly Blue Crane** (☏ 087 330 2424; www.flybluecrane.com) has flights to Jo'burg (R900, one hour) and Cape Town (R1200, 1½ hours). **CemAir** (☏ in Johannesburg 011-395 4473; www.flycemair.co.za) has flghts to Jo'burg (R1200, one hour), Port Elizabeth (R1600, 1½ hours) and George (R1800,1½ hours)

A taxi from the airport (there's often only one available) to the city centre is around R220.

BUS & SHARED TAXI

Long-distance buses (Park Rd) leave from the tourist centre on Park Rd. **Translux** (☏ 0861

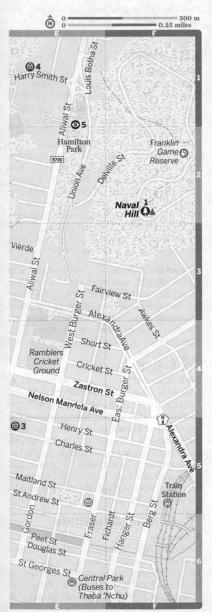

Bloemfontein

◉ **Top Sights**
1 Naval Hill F2

◉ **Sights**
2 Loch Logan Waterfront C4
3 National Museum E5
4 Oliewenhuis Art Museum E1
5 Orchid House E1

🛏 **Sleeping**
6 Hobbit Boutique Hotel C2
7 Protea Hotel Willow Lake A4
8 Urban Hotel A4

🍴 **Eating**
9 Avanti C2
10 Braza C5
11 New York C3
12 Picnic C4
13 Seven on Kellner D4

🍷 **Drinking & Nightlife**
14 Mystic Boer B3
15 No. 16 Stoep & Beer Garden B3
16 Stereo Cafe C2

589 282; www.translux.co.za) runs daily buses to Cape Town (R520, 13 hours), Durban (R370, nine hours), East London (R360, nine hours), Jo'burg/Pretoria (R300, five hours) and Port Elizabeth (R500, nine hours)

Greyhound (☏ 083 915 9000; www.greyhound.co.za; Park Rd) and **Intercape** (☏ in Cape Town 021-380 4400; www.intercape.co.za; Park Rd) also have similar services.

Most minibus shared taxis (cnr Power & Fort Sts) leave from near the train station and head to Maseru, Lesotho (R90, three hours), Kimberley (R120, four hours) and Jo'burg (R190, six hours). There's usually at least one bus daily, but times vary.

TRAIN

Shosholoza Meyl (p354) operates services three times weekly via Bloemfontein between Jo'burg (tourist/economy R230/130, about seven hours) and Port Elizabeth (R330/210). There's also a service that passes by Bloem on the run between Jo'burg and East London (13 hours, R310/200).

Northern Free State

With a pretty countryside of rolling hills, the northern Free State offers a growing number of hiking, mountain-biking and fishing opportunities. Near Parys in the far north, at Vredefort Dome, is one of the world's largest visible meteor craters, now one of South Africa's eight Unesco World Heritage Sites. (The crater is too wide to get a good photo of from the ground; to get a real impression of it, you'll need to take a flight.)

Further south is a golden region of maize farms and sunflowers. The small towns around here are rural enclaves where people live and work, and they see few tourists.

Parys & Vredefort Dome Area

POP 8100

Parys is a small, vibrant town that sits beside the Vaal River just 120km south of Jo'burg. It is home to a few impressive buildings, including the 1915 **Anglican Church**, built from blue-granite blocks. The immediate area is quite beautiful, with its valleys, ravines and cliffs, a covering of lush flora, and many resident plants, animals and birds. But it's the adventure-sport options and the art-and-craft outlets lining the main street that draw most of the town's visitors – particularly Jo'burgers on the weekend. Parys is also handy for visiting **Vredefort Dome**, an enigmatic area of hills created by the impact of a gigantic meteorite two billion years ago.

🏃 Activities

Stone Adventures OUTDOORS

(☏ 056-811 4664; www.stoneadventures.co.za; Kopjeskraal Rd) Stone Adventures, based at the Stonehenge in Africa lodge, can arrange tandem skydives (from R2400), an 8km rafting trip to Rocky Ridge (R220), abseiling with 13m (R170) and 44m drops (R200), and other activities, including a geological tour of Vredefort Dome.

🛏 Sleeping

Otters' Haunt GUESTHOUSE $

(☏ 084 245 2490, 056-818 1814; www.otters.co.za; Kopjeskraal Rd; r/cottage from R350; @ �︁🛆) Some of the accommodation at this cheerfully overgrown place is getting a bit tatty, but the secluded location right on the Vaal River is unbeatable. Options include bungalows, thatched-roof cabins set around a swimming pool, and a three-bedroom cottage with its own pool. Turn left after you cross the bridge out of town and continue for 2km along the river. All sleeping options come with kitchenettes and/or access to braais. Grab a canoe and go for a paddle downstream, or tackle something else from the long list of activities on offer.

Mirabel Guesthouse GUESTHOUSE $$

(☏ 079 120 1199; www.mirabel.co.za; 5 De Villiers St; s/d incl breakfast from R500/850; 🅿) There are five rooms to choose from at this riverfront guesthouse, each with its own unique decor. It's a very short walk to some good restaurants.

🍴 Eating

O's Restaurant INTERNATIONAL $$

(☏ 056-811 3683; www.osrestaurant.co.za; 1 de Villiers St; mains R95-200; ⊙ 11am-10pm Wed-Sat, to 3pm Sun) In this stylish, thoroughly satisfying restaurant down by the river, have some garlic mussels followed by peri peri–topped steak, or fillet flambé prepared at your table. The pizza menu is also worth a browse, and there are some kids' meals, too. Dine in the elegant interior, out on the deck or amidst the foliage in the gorgeous garden.

🍺 Drinking & Nightlife

Pickled Pig PUB

(☏ 056-817 7814; 71 Bree St) This dark, cosy pub, more like an alcove than a full-blown bar, is accessed via a small courtyard off Bree St. A local favourite, it's good for a refreshing ale after an afternoon's browsing in the local shops or a dusty drive around Vredefort. There's an excellent selection of local and international beers.

The owners also run the **Plum Tree** restaurant across the road, whose menu is made available for breakfast and lunch; at night, the pub serves delicious homemade pies, including oxtail and pepper steak.

ⓘ Information

Parys Info Centre (☑ 056-811 4000; www. parys.info; 30 Water St; ☺ 8am-5pm Mon-Fri, 9am-1pm Sat & Sun) can provide a map of the town and detailed information on accommodation options and activity providers.

ⓘ Getting There & Away

The R59 leads into Parys, which is just west of the N1 heading north from Jo'burg. Translux (p445) buses connect Parys with Bloemfontein (R240, 3½ hours) and Jo'burg (R190, 1½ hours).

Eastern Highlands & Southern Free State

With the Kingdom of Lesotho tucked into its crook, the mighty Eastern Highlands are the Free State's star attraction. The wild, rugged border winds its way past snow-shrouded mountains in winter and amber foliage in autumn – the views are spectacular, particularly in the northwest around Clarens.

Encompassing an area roughly from Rte 26 and Rte 49 east of Bethlehem to Harrismith, the region boasts sandstone monoliths towering above undulating golden fields, the fantastic Golden Gate Highlands National Park and trendy Clarens, South Africa's cutest country-village art destination.

Golden Gate Highlands National Park

Right before the darkness erases the remaining flecks of colour from the sky, something magical happens in **Golden Gate Highlands National Park** (☑ 058-255 1000; www.sanparks.org/parks/golden_gate; adult/child R176/88). The jagged sandstone outcrops fronting the foothills of the wild, maroon-hued Maluti Mountains glow golden in the dying light; lemon-yellow rays silhouette a lone kudu standing still in a sea of mint-green grasses before the sky explodes in a fiery collision of purple and red. The park might not boast any of the Big Five, but it does feature fantastic nightly sunsets.

There are quite a few animals in the park, though, including grey rheboks, blesboks, elands, oribi antelope, Burchell's zebras, jackals, baboons and numerous bird species, including the rare bearded and Cape vultures as well as the endangered bald ibis. The park is popular with hikers on long treks, but there are also shorter **walking trails**. Buy your entry permit at the park reception.

⊙ Sights

Basotho Cultural Village   VILLAGE
(tours R50; ☺ 8am-4.30pm Mon-Fri, 8am-5pm Sat & Sun) Within the park you'll find the small Basotho Cultural Village, essentially an open-air museum peopled by actors depicting various aspects of traditional Sotho life. A two-hour guided **hiking trail** explores medicinal and other plants, and a rock-art site. You can stay in two-person, self-catering rondavels (R810); check in at Glen Reenen, about 15km away.

🏃 Activities

Rhebok Hiking Trail   HIKING
(per person R175) This well-maintained, circular 33km trail is a two-day trek and offers a great way to see the park. On the second day the track climbs up to a viewpoint on the side of **Generaalskop** (2732m), the highest point in the park, from where Mont-aux-Sources and the Maluti Mountains can be seen. The return trail to Glen Reenen passes **Langtoon Dam**. The trail starts at the Glen Reenen Rest Camp, located next to the park reception. It has some steep sections, so hikers need to be reasonably fit. The trail is limited to 18 people and must be booked through the park board in advance – check the park's website.

🚗 Tours

Oribi Loop   DRIVING
The 4.2km Oribi Loop offers magnificent scenery. You may spot its namesake antelope wandering about, but its highlight is the view of the Drakensberg.

Blesbok Loop   DRIVING
This 6.7km scenic route traverses low-cut, stony grasslands. The mountain views and sense of isolation make it well worth the drive.

🛌 Sleeping

Glen Reenen Rest Camp   CAMPGROUND $
(☑ 058-255 1000; www.sanparks.org; camping R235, 2-person rondavels from R810) This place

is conveniently located on the main road, buried among the craggy limestone, and has well-maintained chalets and campsites by the river. A shop sells basic supplies.

Golden Gate Hotel HOTEL **$$**
(☑ 058-255 0000; www.goldengatehotel.co.za; r incl breakfast from R1200, 2-person chalet from R1250) In the heart of the park, this stately old lodge with great mountain views offers self-catering chalets and upmarket rooms. It recently underwent an extensive renovation adding more rooms (decorated as African seasons) and modern interiors. There's also a restaurant, bar and coffee shop.

❶ Getting There & Away

The R712 cuts through Golden Gates Highlands National Park. You don't have to pay the entrance fee in order to drive through, but be careful to adhere to strict speed limits.

Clarens

POP 800 / ☑ 058

The jewel of the Free State, Clarens is one of those places you stumble upon and find yourself talking about long after you depart. With a backdrop of craggy limestone rocks, verdant green hills, fields of spun gold and the magnificent Maluti Mountains, Clarens is a picture-perfect village of whitewashed buildings and quiet, shady streets. It makes a bucolic country retreat.

It's also an art destination, with many galleries focusing on quality works by well-known South African artists. Charming guesthouses (ranging from very simple to extraordinarily posh), gourmet restaurants, eclectic cafes and myriad adventure activities round out the appeal.

The town fills up with beer enthusiasts on the last weekend in February for the annual **Clarens Craft Beer Festival** – one of the country's largest. Tickets sell out and accommodation gets booked months in advance, so plan ahead.

🏃 Activities

Clarens Xtreme ADVENTURE SPORTS
(☑ 058-256 1260; www.clarensxtreme.co.za; Sias Oosthuizen St) Head over to this one-stop shop for all things outdoors. Popular activities include quad biking (from R250), white-water rafting (R450) on the dam-fed Ash River (some rapids rate as high as Class IV), mountain biking (half-/full day R250/350) in the mountains behind Clarens

with views over the town and valley, and zip lining (R160) through an adventure park.

🛏 Sleeping

Clarens Inn & Backpackers HOSTEL **$**
(☑ 076 369 9283; www.clarensinn.com; 93 Van Reenen St; dm R180, s/d from R180/360, self-catering cottages from R400; 🛜) The town's best budget option offers single-sex dorms and basic doubles, built around a central courtyard with a big open fire pit and outdoor bar. The locale is rustic and tranquil, pushed up against the mountain at the bottom of Van Reenen St (look for it after the Le Roux turn-off).

★ Patcham Place B&B **$$**
(☑ 058-256 1017; www.patchamplace.co.za; 30 Church St; s/d incl breakfast from R830/1112; P 🛜) A good central option often offering better value in this range than competitors around town – a recent makeover included the addition of satellite TV in its five airy rooms, which have fab views from the balconies. The bathrooms are spotless and the beds firm, and there's even a small kitchen for guest use.

Lake Clarens Guesthouse GUESTHOUSE **$$**
(☑ 058-256 1436; www.lakeclarensgh.co.za; Lake Clarens Dr; s/d incl breakfast R630/1160) This well maintained, four-star guesthouse offers buckets of intimate country charm. Fresh flowers, giant bathtubs, heated floors and silky-soft linens are all highlights of the slightly old-fashioned bedrooms.

🍴 Eating

Gosto PORTUGUESE **$$**
(☑ 076 792 8189; cnr Main & Van Zyl Sts; mains R80-160; ⏰ noon-9pm) This stylish place on the square serves Portuguese and Mozambican dishes like *trinchado* (braised beef); peri peri chicken; juicy, spicy prawns and egg tarts.

Clementines Restaurant INTERNATIONAL **$$**
(☑ 058-256 1616; www.clementines.co.za; cnr Van Zyl & Church Sts; mains R80-160; ⏰ noon-3pm & 6pm-late Tue-Sun; ☑) The food at this souped-up country kitchen tastes just as good as it looks on the gourmet international menu, featuring everything from rainbow trout with almond butter to tender ostrich fillets. Professional service, intimate ambience, a lengthy wine list and vegie options are more perks. Make sure to check out the daily specials on the wall.

🍷 Drinking & Nightlife

Clarens Brewery   BREWERY
(☑058-256 1193; www.clarensbrewery.co.za; 326 Main St; ☺10am-7pm Mon-Sat, to 6pm Sun) Finely crafted local brews such as English ale, stout and IPA go down very well at this exposed-brick bar across from Clarens Sq. You can sample the range – which also includes a number of ciders – for free before choosing your preferred pint.

🔒 Shopping

Art & Wine Gallery on Main   ART
(☑058-256 1298; www.artandwine.co.za; 279 Main St; ☺9am-5pm) Offers a fantastic selection of regional wines and paintings.

ℹ Getting There & Away

Clarens is best reached by private transport.

Ficksburg

POP 5400

Ficksburg is a lovely little mountain village on the banks of the Mohokare (Caledon) River that's home to some fine **sandstone buildings**; keep an eye out for the town hall and the post office. Nestled into the purple-hued Maluti range, Ficksburg is particularly fetching in winter, when dollops of snow cover the craggy peaks.

Mild summers and cold winters make this area perfect for growing stone fruits, and Ficksburg is the centre of the Free State's cherry industry. There's a Cherry Festival in November, but September and October are the best times to see the trees in full bloom.

🎆 Festivals & Events

Cherry Festival   FOOD & DRINK
(☑051-933 6486; www.cherryfestival.co.za) Although September and October are the best times to see the trees in full bloom, the annual Cherry Festival is held in November. The festival features live music, kiddie fun and events such as cherry-pip spitting contests and the finals of 'Ficksberg's Got Talent'.

🛏 Sleeping

Imperani Guest House
& Coffee Shop   GUESTHOUSE $$
(☑051-933 3606; www.imperaniguesthouse.co.za; 53 McCabe Rd; s/d incl breakfast from R550/780; ☏⊠) In a quiet spot, the Imperani has an African-flavoured, country-cottage vibe. The spotless, modern rooms have wooden floors and big windows and are in thatched-roof buildings. In a big, airy *boma* (an open-air, thatched-roof hut) nearby, the on-site **restaurant** is a good lunch stop if you're passing through Ficksburg.

Along with strong coffee, the restaurant does excellent wraps for lunch. It also offers salads and other light meals at breakfast and lunch. There's a very good kids menu, too.

GAUTENG

If you're in search of urban vibes, Gauteng will enthrall you. This small province is the throbbing heart of the South African nation and the economic engine of Africa. Its epicentre is Johannesburg (Jo'burg), the country's largest city. And what a city! Jo'burg's centre is undergoing an astonishing rebirth and its cultural life has never been so dynamic. Once considered a place to avoid, Jo'burg is now one of the most inspiring and happening metropolises in the world.

For a change of scene, head to Pretoria, a short drive north. The country's administrative capital is decidedly less urbane but somewhat grander with stately buildings, attractive museums and jacaranda-lined streets.

Gauteng also has a unique geological history that's evident at the World Heritage–listed Cradle of Humankind. This vast valley full of caves and fossils is one of the African continent's most important archaeological sites.

Johannesburg

POP 4.4 MILLION / ☑011

Johannesburg, more commonly known as Jo'burg or Jozi, is a rapidly changing city and the vibrant heart of South Africa. After almost 20 years of decline and decay, the city is now looking optimistically towards the future. Its centre is smartening up and new loft apartments and office developments are being constructed at a rapid pace. The hipster-friendly urban neighbourhood of Maboneng is considered one of the most successful urban-renewal projects in the world. However, the wealth divide remains stark, and crime and poverty haven't been eliminated. The affluence of Rosebank and Sandton breeds discontent in desperately poor neighbouring townships such as Alexandra.

Still, Jo'burg is an incredibly friendly, unstuffy city and there's a lot to see here, from sobering reminders of the country's recent past at the Apartheid Museum to the progressive streets of Melville. So delve in and

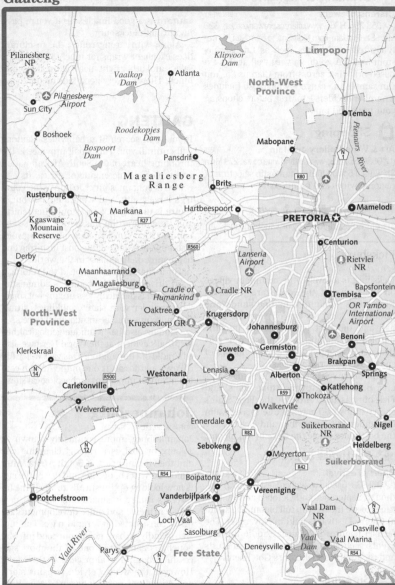

experience the buzz of a city undergoing an incredible rebirth.

◉ Sights

Since the mass exodus of white-owned businesses in the 1990s, a steady recovery has been led by both the creative sector and far-sighted property developers. Public art is prettying up the streets and old warehouses, and art deco buildings have been snapped up by those who consider themselves to have good taste.

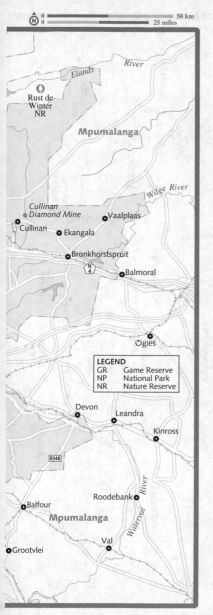

central Jozi. Large areas of the Inner City are being revitalised, upgraded and modernised. Sure, there remain a number of dodgy enclaves, but what was before a no-go zone is regaining attractiveness.

One of the most appealing (and safest) areas is Marshalltown, Jo'burg's old financial and corporate district, where you'll find many mining-company and bank head offices. Amid the imposing skyscrapers you'll find some excellent cafes, plenty of small-scale sights and even a few inspiring parks where you can hone your people-watching skills.

Newtown's revival has slowed in recent years as other areas have risen in the hip stakes, but it's still home to some decent museums and a few restaurants.

During the day, you can walk pretty safely around the area west of the Carlton Centre and south of Jeppe St (recently renamed Rahima Moosa St), but it pays to keep your wits about you, especially around Park Station. Don't flash around valuables such as cameras and watches, and avoid carrying bags.

Johannesburg Art Gallery GALLERY
(JAG; Map p456; ☎ 011-725 3130; Joubert Park, Inner City; ⊗10am-5pm Tue-Sun) **FREE** The JAG has the largest art collection in Africa and regularly rotates its incredible collection of 17th- and 18th-century European landscape and figurative paintings with works by leading South African painters and traditional African objects and retrospectives by black artists. It's on the Sophie de Bruyn St (Noord St) side of Joubert Park (the park itself is best avoided).

Top of Africa VIEWPOINT
(Map p456; ☎ 011-308 1331; www.gauteng.net/attractions/carlton_centre; 50th fl, Carlton Centre, 150 Commissioner St, Inner City; adult/child R15/10; ⊗9am-6pm Mon-Fri, to 5pm Sat, to 2pm Sun) The iconic **Carlton Centre** (223m) has been Africa's tallest building for more than 40 years now. The basement shelters a buzzing **shopping mall**. For awesome city vistas, head to the **observation deck** at the top (entrance is via a special lift one floor below street level).

👁 Inner City & Newtown

Ask South Africans what they think about downtown Johannesburg and the chances are they'll say 'unsafe' and 'run down'. Savvy locals though, will speak differently about

Mary Fitzgerald Square SQUARE
(Map p456; Rahima Moosa St (Jeppe St), Inner City) Named after South Africa's first female trade unionist, this square is the best place to start a visit to central Jo'burg. Lined with an array of heads, carved from old railway sleepers by Newtown artists, it's bordered by the

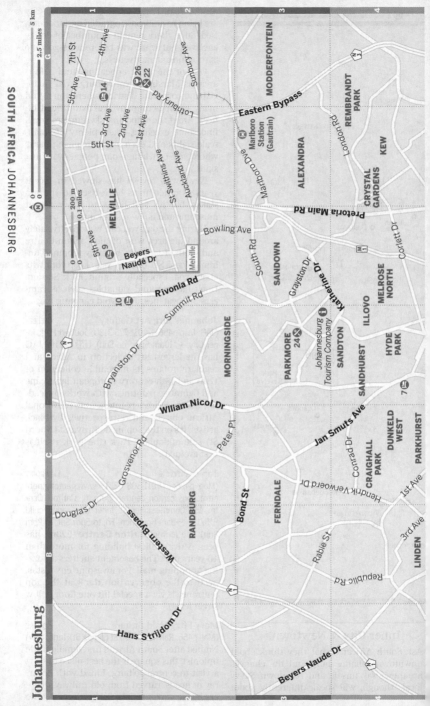

Johannesburg

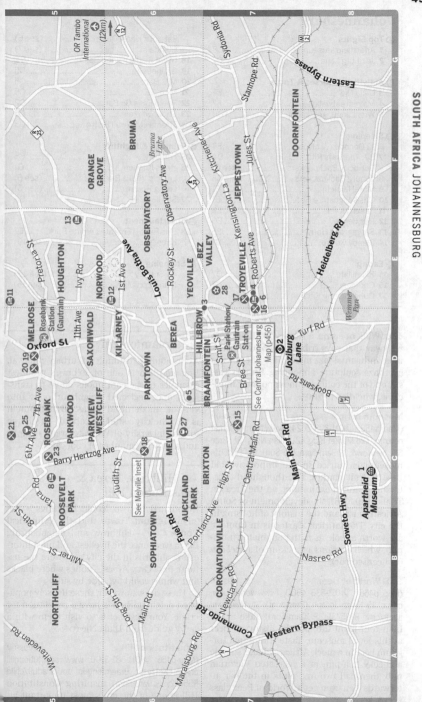

Johannesburg

◎ Top Sights
1 Apartheid Museum C8
2 Joziburg Lane D7

◎ Activities, Courses & Tours
3 Dlala Nje E7
4 Mainstreetwalks.....................................E7
5 Wits Language School...........................D6

◎ Sleeping
6 12 Decades Art Hotel.............................E7
7 Backpackers Ritz D4
  Curiocity Backpackers ....(see 4)
8 Joburg Backpackers C5
9 Motel Mipichi E1
10 Oasis Signature Hotel E1
11 Peech Hotel E5
12 Residence E6
13 Satyagraha House E5
14 Sleepy Gecko...G1

◎ Eating
15 Bismillah... C7
16 Canteen.. D7
17 Cube Tasting Kitchen E7

Eat Your Heart Out .... (see 6)
Glenda's .... (see 7)
18 Great Eastern Food Bar C6
19 Grillhouse D5
20 Milk Bar D5
21 Nice C5
22 Pablo Eggs Go Bar.................................G2
23 Shadowboxer...C5
24 Thomas Maxwell Bistro D3

◎ Drinking & Nightlife
25 Foundry... C5
26 Hell's Kitchen G1
  Lenin's Vodka Bar .... (see 6)
  Living Room .... (see 6)
27 Stanley Beer Yard C6

◎ Entertainment
28 Ellis Park – Emirates Airline Park.......... E7
  Katzy's ....(see 19)

◎ Shopping
44 Stanley .... (see 27)
Market on Main.............................(see 16)

Jazz Walk of Fame, a Hollywood Blvd–style walkway that pays tribute to South Africa's most influential jazz musicians. There's also a bronze sculpture honouring Brenda Fassie, one of the country's most popular musicians, who died in 2004.

Museum Africa　MUSEUM
(Map p456; ☎011-833 5624; www.themuseumafrica.org; Old Market Bldg, 121 Lilian Ngoyi St (Bree St), Newtown; ◎9am-5pm Tue-Sun) FREE This museum is housed in the impressive old Bree St fruit market. The thoughtful curatorship features exhibitions on the Treason Trials of 1956–61, the development of South African music and the history of housing in the city. The satirical 'Cartoons in Context' are worth a look, as is the Sophiatown display, which contains a mock-up of a *shebeen* (unlicensed bar).

SAB World of Beer　MUSEUM
(Map p456; ☎011-836 4900; www.worldofbeer.co.za; 15 Helen Joseph (President) St, Newtown; adult/child R105/35; ◎10am-6pm) Take a 1½-hour tour jaunt through the history of beer at this jovial museum. Taste traditional sorghum beer in a mock African village, sample a cheeky half-pint at a recreated Victorian pub, then nail two free pints in the bar afterwards. You even get a World of Beer glass keepsake.

◎ Braamfontein

A resounding triumph of urban renewal, Braamfontein is one of Jo'burg's proudest examples of the continuous effort to transform once-neglected neighbourhoods into vibrant, modernised areas. Braamfontein is also the city's student capital – it's home to the University of Witwatersrand campus and a growing number of cool cafes.

◎ Hillbrow, Berea & Constitution Hill

Dominated by two iconic buildings – the 269m **Telkom Tower** and the cylindrical **Ponte City** – Hillbrow and neighbouring Berea were once the liveliest and most interesting suburbs in the city and were the nation's first 'Grey Areas' – zones where blacks and whites could live side by side.

These days, however, these densely populated neighbourhoods have a reputation for crime. Your best bet is to visit them with a savvy guide from Dlala Nje (p455).

Constitution Hill　MUSEUM
(Map p456; ☎011-381 3100; www.constitutionhill.org.za; Kotze St, Braamfontein; tours adult/child R55/22; ◎9am-5pm) Inspiring Constitution Hill is one of the city's most important at-

tractions. It offers travellers interested in the modern South African story an integral understanding of the legal and historical ramifications of the struggle. The development focuses on South Africa's new Constitutional Court, built within the ramparts of the Old Fort, which dates from 1892 and was once a notorious prison – many of the country's high-profile political activists, including Nelson Mandela and Mohandas (Mahatma) Gandhi, were once held there.

The modern structure incorporates sections of the old prison walls, plus large windows that allow visitors to watch the proceedings.

◉ Maboneng

On a stretch of the eastern fringe of downtown Jo'burg, this once-gritty enclave is the darling of the many architectural and creative hubs springing up across the city. A breeding ground of creativity and innovation packed full of galleries, artist and cultural spaces, cool bars, coffee shops, restaurants, fashion shops and startups, Maboneng is an exemplar of Jo'burg's vision for the future and is a hipster paradise. Be sure to explore its dynamic streets and soak up its unique atmosphere.

◉ Southern Jo'burg

★ Apartheid Museum   MUSEUM
(Map p452; ☑011-309 4700; www.apartheidmuseum.org; cnr Gold Reef Rd & Northern Parkway, Ormonde; adult/child R80/65; ◎9am-5pm; P) The Apartheid Museum illustrates the rise and fall of South Africa's era of segregation and oppression, and is an absolute must-see. It uses film, text, audio and live accounts to provide a chilling insight into the architecture and implementation of the apartheid system, as well as inspiring stories of the struggle towards democracy. It's invaluable in understanding the inequalities and tensions that still exist today. Located 8km south of the city centre, just off the M1 freeway. Visiting the museum is an overwhelming experience; particularly distressing is a small chamber in which hang 131 nooses, representative of the 131 government opponents who were executed under antiterrorism laws.

★ Joziburg Lane   MARKET
(Map p452; www.joziburglane.co.za; 1 Eloff St, Marshalltown; ◎10am-5pm Tue-Sat) Yet another gentrified quarter of the city, Joziburg Lane occupies the ground floor of One Eloff, a magnificent art deco building that once stood derelict and is now filled with loft-style apartments. Browse artists' studios, graze on cheese platters, curries and traditional African eats in the hip eateries and sip on good coffee and craft beer. The shops and cafes stay open until 10pm on Fridays. City walks with JoburgPlaces start from here.

☞ Tours

Dlala Nje   WALKING
(Map p452; ☑011-402 2373; www.dlalanje.org; Shop 1, Ponte City, Hillbrow) Run by Nickolaus Bauer and Mike Luptak, this pioneering company offers unique tours to three of Jo'burg's most impoverished and misunderstood areas: Hillbrow, Berea and the West African immigrant community of Yeoville. This is a great opportunity to change negative perceptions about these districts and learn more about the diverse communities that live there.

Mulaudzi Alexandra Tours   CYCLING
(☑071 279 3654, 061 365 7695; www.alexandra-tours.co.za; ◎2hr/4hr tour R450/550) Explore Alexandra, one of South Africa's oldest townships, in the company of friendly Jeff Mulaudzi. Born and raised in Alexandra, this young entrepreneur offers a two- to four-hour bicycle tour where you'll venture into the heart of this lesser-known township. It's a truly enlightening experience. Jeff meets visitors at the Marlboro Gautrain station, where secure parking is available.

JoburgPlaces   CULTURAL, WALKING
(☑082 894 5216; www.joburgplaces.com) Gerald Garner's inner-city tours are sure to change your perceptions about downtown Jo'burg. A hot favourite is the five-hour Regenerated Inner City Walk, which explores the way central Johannesburg has changed over recent years. Other walking tours include Western Edge to Gandhi Sq (three hours), Inner City Swimming Pools (six hours) and Fashion District and Little Addis (five hours).

Mainstreetwalks   CULTURAL, WALKING
(Map p452; ☑011-614 0163; www.mainstreetwalks.co.za; tours per person from R200) Led by young entrepreneur Bheki Dube, who also manages Curiocity Backpackers (p457), Mainstreetwalks specialises in tours of Maboneng, where it is based, but it also offers excellent tours of the Inner City, Troyeville and the utterly fascinating Little Addis Ethiopian district. And if you want to get a taste

Central Johannesburg

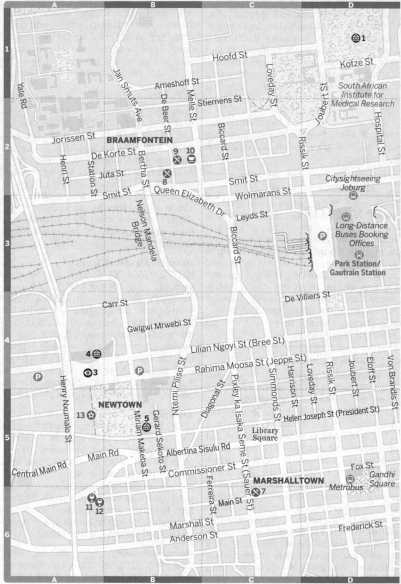

SOUTH AFRICA JOHANNESBURG

of Jo'burg nightlife, the Underground Pub Crawl is a must.

Past Experiences   CULTURAL, WALKING
(☎083 701 3046, 011-678 3905; www.pastexperiences.co.za) Run by Jo Buitendach and her team of hip guides, Past Experiences offers a range of fascinating tours that have a special focus on graffiti, street art and shopping. Participants have the opportunity to learn about artists' histories and the local graffiti culture. Tours take in Braamfontein, Newtown and the Fashion District.

Ⓝ 0 _____ 500 m
0 _____ 0.25 miles

Central Johannesburg

◉ Sights
1	Constitution Hill	D1
2	Johannesburg Art Gallery	E3
3	Mary Fitzgerald Square	A4
4	Museum Africa	A4
5	SAB World of Beer	B5
6	Top of Africa	E5

⊗ Eating
7	City Perk Café	C6
8	Post	B2
9	Smokehouse & Grill	B2

◐ Drinking & Nightlife
10	Doubleshot Coffee & Tea	B2
11	Good Luck Bar	A6
12	Mad Giant	A6

✪ Entertainment
13	Bassline	A5

ⓐ Shopping
	Neighbourgoods Market	(see 9)
	Sheds@1Fox	(see 11)

na, Afrikaans, English and sign language. Part of the University of Witwatersrand.

🛏 Sleeping

Curiocity Backpackers HOSTEL $
(Map p452; ☎ 011-614 0163; www.curiocityback-packers.com; 302 Fox St, Maboneng; dm R200, s/d with shared bathroom R330/530; ⓟ 🛜) This is a superlative place to stay thanks to the dedication of young proprietor Bheki Dube. Occupying a converted printing house in the desirable Maboneng precinct, this quirky, offbeat backpackers features clean dorms, unadorned yet neat rooms and a rooftop suite. It also has a buzzing bar, kitchen facilities and a small restaurant. The congenial atmosphere is hard to beat.

Joburg Backpackers HOSTEL $
(Map p452; ☎ 011-888 4742; www.joburgback-packers.com; 14 Umgwezi Rd, Emmarentia; dm R180, d R530, s/d with shared bathroom R340/440; ⓟ 🛜 ⊛) This discreet hostel in the leafy streets of Emmarentia is clean, safe and well run, with a range of well-appointed rooms and a relaxed country feel. The en suite rooms are terrific value and open onto big grassy lawns; the eight- and 10-bed dorms are spacious and spotless. No meals are served, but Greenside's eateries are a 10-minute stroll away.

🎓 Courses

Wits Language School LANGUAGE
(Map p452; www.witslanguageschool.com; Professional Development Hub, Gate 6, 92 Empire Rd, Braamfontein) Courses in Zulu, Sesotho, Tswa-

Map streets (left)

Pretoria St

HILLBROW
Esselen St
Kapteijn St

Edith Cavell St
Klein St
Twist St
Quartz St
Claim St
Catherine St

Pietersen St

Smit St

Wolmarans St

Leyds St

Joubert Park

Bok St

King George St
Klein St

🏛 2

Sophie de Bruyn St (Noord St)

De Villiers St

Plein St

Lilian Ngoyi St (Bree St)

Rahima Moosa St (Jeppe St)

Kerk St

INNER CITY

Pritchard St

Von Wellingh St
Kruis St
Smal St Mall

Helen Joseph St (President St)

Albertina Sisulu Rd

Commissioner St

Troye St
Polly St
Mooi St
Gold St
Nugget St

🏛 6

Delvers St

Main St

Marshall St

Anderson St

Wanderers St

Nugget St

Sleepy Gecko
GUESTHOUSE $

(Map p452; ☑082 745 0434, 011-482 5224; www.
sleepygecko.co.za; 84 3rd Ave, Melville; s/d incl breakfast from R500/700; P❋@≋) The laid-back
Gecko is an attractive and very popular guesthouse right at the heart of the 7th St mischief.
The rooms outside the house, in a semide-
tached annexe, are preferable, with less noise
and more natural light – our favourites are
Fossil and Amarula. The communal areas
include a spacious, homey dining area and a
small front-yard swimming pool.

Backpackers Ritz
HOSTEL $

(Map p452; ☑011-325 7125; www.backpackers-ritz.
co.za; 1A North Rd, Dunkeld West; dm/s/d with shared
bathroom R180/360/540; P♠≋) A longstanding institution, the Ritz scores high on its
excellent shared facilities, prime location and
beautiful views. It's owned by three brothers, who ensure that a family atmosphere is
maintained on its sprawling, leafy grounds.
The 12- to 14-bed dorms are spacious, though
the rooms could do with a lick of paint.

★12 Decades Art Hotel
BOUTIQUE HOTEL $$

(Map p452; ☑011-026 5601; www.12decadeshotel.
co.za; 7th fl, Main Street Life Bldg, 286 Fox St, Ma-
boneng; s/d R950/1260; P❋♠) This terrific
concept hotel in the heart of the Maboneng
precinct has 12 7th-floor rooms (the rest are
residential), each one designed by different
international artists and inspired by a par-
ticular era in the city's history. The Sir Abe
Bailey Suite takes on a late-19th-century
Chinese gold rush aesthetic, while Perpetual
Liberty is decidedly more contemporary. A
special experience. No breakfast is served,
but there's no shortage of eateries nearby.

★Motel Mipichi
BOUTIQUE HOTEL $$

(Map p452; ☑011-726 8844; www.motelmipichi.
co.za; 35 4th Ave, Melville; s/d incl breakfast from
R645/895; P♠) A gem of a place. The design
duo behind Motel Mipichi turned two semi-
detached 1930s abodes into a genuine alternative to the traditional Melville guesthouse
experience. Mipichi is a minimalist delight,
with six calming rooms speckled with pastel splotches and walk-through showers.
The open-plan kitchen and living area, with
original Portuguese tiles, is an ideal place to
decompress. Book ahead.

★Oasis Signature Hotel
HOTEL $$

(Map p452; ☑011-807 4351; www.oasisguesthouse.
co.za; 29 Homestead Rd, Rivonia; s/d incl breakfast
from R1190/1490; P❋♠≋) This is a delightful
suburban hideaway, presided over by an as-
tute couple who cater for businesspeople and
holidaymakers with equal aplomb. The lush
garden surrounds feature a kidney-shaped
pool and a spacious *lapa* (South African
thatched gazebo). The 14 rooms vary in size
and price, but all are stylish and thoughtfully
furnished. The breakfast smorgasbord is wor-
thy of special mention.

★Residence
BOUTIQUE HOTEL $$$

(Map p452; ☑011-853 2480; www.theresidence.
co.za; 17 4th Ave, Houghton; d incl breakfast R3165-
4975; P❋@♠≋) If you could smell charm,
this super-smooth boutique hotel set in a former embassy would reek of it to high heaven.
This quiet little paradise is the epitome of a
refined cocoon, with 17 opulent, individually
designed suites and swish communal areas.
After a day of turf pounding, take a dip in the
stress-melting pool or relax in the spa.

★Satyagraha House
GUESTHOUSE $$$

(Map p452; ☑011-485 5928; www.satyagraha-
house.com; 15 Pine Rd, Orchards; d incl breakfast
from R2520; P♠) A wonderful urban sanc-
tuary, Satyagraha is the former home of
Mohandas (Mahatma) Gandhi, who lived
here between 1907 and 1908. This heritage
building has been restored into an innova-
tive guesthouse and museum, with seven
rooms built to resemble a traditional Afri-
can village. The intimate history of Gandhi's
time here is on display to reward guests in
unexpected ways. Meals are vegetarian.

Peech Hotel
BOUTIQUE HOTEL $$$

(Map p452; ☑011-537 9797; www.thepeech.co.za;
61 North St, Melrose; d incl breakfast R2420-2800;
P❋♠≋) Your money goes far with these
four converted duplex apartment blocks
amid a beautifully landscaped garden. The
16 rooms are amply sized and feature subtle,
trendy design details, but it's the setting that's
the pull here. Another plus is the pool.

✗ Eating

★Eat Your Heart Out
DELI $

(Map p452; ☑072 586 0600; www.eatyourheartout.
co.za; cnr Kruger & Fox Sts, Maboneng; mains R50-
80; ⊙7.30am-4pm Tue-Sun; ♠) The best spot in
Maboneng to start the day. The Israeli breakfast – omelette, toasted pita, diced salad, pickled cabbage and cottage cheese – is the highlight, while the bagels and cheesecakes will
leave your taste buds reeling. Healthy fruit
juices, great coffee and sweet treats are also
on offer, and there's outdoor seating.

Pablo Eggs Go Bar
BREAKFAST $

(Map p452; ☑063 335 9348; 27th St, Melville;
dishes R40-100; ⊙6.30am-4pm) You have to

love this place for the name alone, but the Middle Eastern–inspired all-day breakfast menu also keeps the hipsters and foodies coming back. Try the upmarket Egg 'n' Soldiers, where fingers of toast are replaced by asparagus wrapped in bacon.

Post
CAFE $

(Map p456; ☑ 072 248 2078; 70 Juta St, Braamfontein; mains R45-75; ☺ 6.30am-4pm Mon-Fri, 8.30am-2pm Sat; ☎) Fill up at this great little cafe before (or after) delving into Braamfontein. Come for delicious breakfasts, gourmet sandwiches, fresh salads and changing lunch specials. The chalkboard menu adds to the casual atmosphere. Oh, and it serves delectable coffee.

★ Great Eastern Food Bar
ASIAN $$

(Map p452; ☑ 011-482 2910; Bamboo Centre, cnr 9th St & Rustenburg Rd, Melville; mains R60-140; ☺ noon-11pm Tue-Fri, 1-11pm Sat, 1-8pm Sun) If you think Jozi is a dud at creative Asian food, prepare to eat your words – and everything in sight – at this exciting, well-priced, obscenely delicious eatery located on the roof of the trendy Bamboo Centre. Owner-chef Nick Scott turns out succulent concoctions prepared with top-of the-line ingredients. Musts include kimchi dumplings, sashimi tacos and smoked trout.

★ Smokehouse & Grill
STEAK $$

(Map p456; ☑ 011-403 1395; cnr Juta & De Beer Sts, Braamfontein; mains R75-215; ☺ noon-10pm Mon-Sat) Students, hipsters, moms and pops: everyone dives into this busy steakhouse for a rockin' feed. Get messy with slow-pit-smoked ribs, slabs of juicy steak and succulent burgers, or watch the waist with the lightly seasoned grilled-chicken options or classic salads. Good wines and beers, too.

City Perk Café
CAFE $$

(Map p456; ☑ 011-838 9755; www.cityperkcafe.co.za; 70 Fox St, Marshalltown, Inner City; mains R60-150; ☺ 7.30am-4.30pm Mon-Fri; ☎) Good luck at securing a seat at this superpopular cafe that makes splendid breakfasts, sandwiches, wraps, grills and salads, as well as serving decent coffee at affordable prices. Lunch for under R80? Count us in! There's ample outdoor seating on warm days.

Shadowboxer
PUB FOOD $$

(Map p452; 131 Green Way; mains R100-300; ☺ 7am-midnight Mon-Sat, to 10pm Sun) How do you decide with so many choices? Starting by picking your table in either the cool warehouse-style interior or on the leafy streetside balcony. Easy enough. But the choices are endless on the extensive food menu ranging from pizza to pub grub to gourmet meals.

Glenda's
BISTRO $$

(Map p452; ☑ 011-268 6369; http://glendas.co; Hyde Sq, cnr Jan Smuts Ave & North Rd; R90-180; ☺ 7am-5pm Mon & Tue, to 10pm Wed-Sat, 8am-3pm Sun) Glenda's is a romantic tropical kingdom where the floral detailing extends from the decor and table settings to the impeccable presentation of the meals. Brunch is likely to turn into a three-course affair with sweet treats like Madagascan vanilla flapjacks served with maple-roasted pears, a temptation that shouldn't be resisted.

Milk Bar
CAFE $$

(Map p452; ☑ 083-649 3339; www.facebook.com/milkbarSA; 21 Keyes Ave; mains R80-150; ☺ 6.30am-6.30pm Mon & Tue, to 11pm Wed & Thu, to 8pm Fri, 8:30am-3pm Sat & Sun) To experience African design and the African aesthetic at its best, pop into the Rosebank branch of Milk Bar. Bright colours and traditional African fabrics make this cute little cafe a feast for the eyes. The interesting takes on traditional meals, like mini bunny chows, are a feast for the tastebuds.

Nice
CAFE $$

(Map p452; ☑ 011-788 6286; www.niceon4th.co.za; 37 4th Ave, Parkhurst, cnr 14th St; mains R80-200; ☺ 7.30am-4pm Tue-Sun) Mismatched crockery and bunches of fresh wildflowers adorn all surfaces of this quirky cafe-cum-bookshop, but the main reason to visit Nice is for the imaginative breakfasts and light meals. The signature bread baskets with perfectly poached eggs and crispy bacon washed down with a creamy cappuccino are a brunch-lover's dream.

Canteen
INTERNATIONAL $$

(Map p452; ☑ 011-334 5947; Arts on Main, 264 Fox St, Maboneng; mains R70-180; ☺ noon-2.30pm & 6-9pm Tue & Wed, 9am-9pm Thu-Sun) One of the best spots to chill in the 'hood, this lively eatery inside hip Arts on Main boasts a lovely setting, with a large, festive 'garden party' courtyard shaded by olive trees and a rooftop bar. Foodwise, the emphasis is on burgers, salads, pasta and meat dishes.

Bismillah
INDIAN $$

(Map p452; ☑ 011-838 8050; www.bismillahrestaurant.co.za; 78 Mint Rd, Fordsburg; mains R40-135; ☺ 8am-10.30pm) Over in Fordsburg you'll find the best Indian food in Jo'burg, and Bismillah is, we reckon, the pick of the lot. The menu is classic North Indian – tandooris, tikkas, biryanis and masalas are all here, plus a few surprises – while the service is refreshingly earnest. Best of all, it's super cheap.

★ **Grillhouse**   STEAK $$$
(Map p452; ☑011-880 3945; www.thegrillhouse. co.za; The Firs Shopping Centre, cnr Oxford Rd & Bierman Ave, Rosebank; mains R75-300; ☺noon-2.30pm & 6.30-9.30pm Sun-Fri, 6.30-9.30pm Sat) Get an honest-to-goodness Jozi steakhouse experience at this New York–style institution inside The Firs. Rub elbows with other red-meat lovers and choose your cut: prime sirloin, T-bone, spare ribs or fillet. Thick chops of veal, ostrich medallions and various seafood options are also on tap, as are heaping portions of character thanks to the skilled waiters and cosy decor.

There's also an incredible selection of single malts and fabulous local wines.

★ **Thomas Maxwell Bistro**   BISTRO $$$
(Map p452; ☑011-784 1575; www.thomasmaxwell.co.za; 140 11th St, Parkmore; mains R110-210; ☺12.30-2.30pm & 6.30-9.30pm Mon-Fri, 6.30-9.30pm Sat) The king of bistros in Parkmore, bustling Thomas Maxwell is never short of a discriminating mob. That's all thanks to three winning details: its rustic-chic decor; the uplifting Jozi-meets-NYC mood; and of course the stellar, crowd-pleasing menu. Highlights include the outstanding rabbit risotto, steak tartare and sirloin wasabi.

Cube Tasting Kitchen   FUSION $$$
(Map p452; ☑082 422 8158; www.cubekitchen. co.za; 24 Albrecht St, Maboneng; tasting menu R800; ☺6.15-11pm Tue-Sat) The multicourse banquet served at this minimalist inner city spot features innovative dishes such as Sunday roast served as a salad (featuring deep-fried gnocchi and green-pea puree) and modern take on Durban curry. Reservations highly recommended.

🍷 Drinking & Nightlife

Jo'burg has an ever-revolving bar scene and you'll find everything from crusty bohemian haunts to chic cocktail lounges to conservative wine bars here. Maboneng and Braamfontein have some great lively places, but much of the nightlife is in the northern suburbs, particularly around Melville, Greenside and Rosebank.

★ **Mad Giant**   BREWERY
(Map p456; www.madgiant.co.za; 1 Fox St, Newtown; ☺noon-10pm Mon-Sat, to 6pm Sun) A superlative addition to Jozi's inner city, Mad Giant combines excellent craft beers (brewed on site) with delectable tapas dishes inspired by Asian street food. The warehouse-like space is filled with furniture seemingly fashioned from a giant Meccano set. Outside there's a bustling beer garden serving burgers and the like.

Doubleshot Coffee & Tea   COFFEE
(Map p456; www.doubleshot.co.za; cnr Juta & Melle Sts, Braamfontein; ☺8am-6pm Mon-Sat) Coffee, tea and a few baked treats is all you'll get at this roaster but, man, are they good. The espresso is dark and intense, brewed by competent baristas and swilled by a bevy of cool kids and clued-in corporate people.

Good Luck Bar   BAR
(Map p456; ☑084-683 4413; http://goodluckbar. co.za; 1 Fox St; ☺10am-2am Wed-Sat, 10am-11pm Sun) With exposed bricks and iron beams, visible piping and a long bar, the Good Luck Bar has obvious remnants of its previous life as a warehouse for buses and trams. In its latest incarnation as a grungy live music-venue and bar, you are just as likely to bump into an Afrikaans death-metal band member as you are to stumble into a '90s rave.

Foundry   CRAFT BEER
(Map p452; ☑011-447 5828; www.foundrycafe. co.za; Parktown Quarter, cnr 3rd & 7th Aves, Parktown North; ☺11.30am-10.30pm Mon-Sat, to 5pm Sun) Sitting on a street filled with cool bars, this place stands out for the bistro-style fare (try the maple-bacon and blue-cheese pizza) and the impressive selection of craft beer from around the country. Book ahead if you hope to get table on a weekend evening.

Hell's Kitchen   BAR
(Map p452; ☑079 980 9591; www.hellskitchen. co.za; 4 7th St, Melville; ☺12.30pm-1.30am Mon-Sat, noon-10pm Sun) Forget which year it is as you enter this speakeasy-style bar that has rooms hidden behind bookshelves. An extensive cocktail menu, cold craft beer and food prepared on an open flame will snap you back to the present. Drop by for a lazy Sunday lunch when awesome specials include a meal and a drink.

Living Room   BAR
(Map p452; ☑011-029 0556; www.livingroomjozi. co.za; 20 Kruger St, Maboneng; ☺10am-5pm Mon-Wed, 11am-9pm Thu-Sat, 11am-7pm Sun) Four storeys above the bustling city, Living Room is a plant-filled oasis that offers great views of Jo'burg. Enjoy cold beers, cocktails and bar snacks as you watch the city go by at this rooftop jungle decorated with fairy lights. Keep an eye on their website for the regular live-music and comedy events.

Stanley Beer Yard   CRAFT BEER
(Map p452; ☑ 011-481 5791; www.44stanley.co.za; 44 Stanley Ave, Milpark; ⊙ noon-11pm Tue-Sun) The cognoscenti of Jo'burg's beer world pack this attractive haven inside the 44 Stanley precinct. It serves brews from around the country as well as delectable pub grub and hosts live bands on Saturday (from 2pm). Inside is an eye-catching interior complete with armchairs and a huge log fire; outside are long wooden tables under olive trees.

Lenin's Vodka Bar   COCKTAIL BAR
(Map p452; www.lenins.co.za; 300 Commissioner St, Maboneng; ⊙ 4pm-midnight Wed-Sat, from noon Sun) This Maboneng gem is famous for one thing and one thing only: vodka. With more than 50 varieties, you're sure to find something to tickle your fancy. Non-vodka drinkers have a good choice of other drinks on the menu. Bag a table in the moodily lit interior or on the shady terrace. In between drinks, snack on salads and sandwiches.

☆ Entertainment

Katzy's   JAZZ
(Map p452; ☑ 011-880 3945; www.katzys.co.za; The Firs Shopping Centre, cnr Oxford Rd & Bierman Ave, Rosebank; ⊙ noon-midnight Mon-Wed, to 2am Thu-Fri, 6.30pm-2am Sat) One of the loveliest hangouts in the neighbourhood, this swanky den recalls the atmosphere of an old NYC jazz club. You'll find mellow, live jazz five nights a week, as well as the tasty carnivore menu of the restaurant next door, The Grillhouse. A cover charge (R150) applies on Thursday, Friday and Saturday nights. It also boasts an exceptional menu of whiskies, cognacs and bourbons.

Ellis Park – Emirates Airline Park   RUGBY
(Map p452; ☑ 011-402 2960; www.lionsrugby.co.za; cnr Currey & Staib Sts, Doornfontein) The spiritual home of Jo'burg rugby, just east of the city centre, was the scene of one of the new nation's proudest moments – victory in the 1995 World Cup. Local supporters are fanatical: a Saturday afternoon at the rugby can be an almost religious experience. Renamed Emirates Airline Park in January 2015, it's still widely known as Ellis Park.

Bassline   LIVE MUSIC
(Map p456; ☑ 011-838 9145; www.bassline.co.za; 10 Henry Nxumalo St, Newtown) This is still the most respected live-music venue in Jo'burg, gaining prominence as a Melville jazz haunt in the late '90s before getting on the world-music tip and relocating to Newtown in 2004. Today it covers the full range of international musicianship and more-popular reggae, rock and hip hop styles.

🛍 Shopping

★ Neighbourgoods Market   FOOD
(Map p456; www.neighbourgoodsmarket.co.za; cnr Juta & de Beer Sts, Braamfontein; ⊙ 9am-3pm Sat) Cape Town's wondrous community market has come to Braamfontein to continually 're-invent the public market as civic institution'. The two-storey brick warehouse fills with artisan purveyors and their foodie fans, who hoover up healthy brunches, 'slow' beer and stiff coffee. Upstairs you can grab a bench and watch the sun shine off city buildings.

Sheds@1Fox   ARTS & CRAFTS, FOOD
(Map p456; www.1fox.co.za; 1 Fox St, Ferreirasdorp; ⊙ noon-5pm Fri, 10am-7pm Sat, 10am-4pm Sun) This venue occupying a former industrial warehouse on the western edge of downtown Jo'burg is a shining example of redevelopment and preservation. It's now a thriving marketplace with gourmet outlets as well as a collection of food stands, bars and craft stalls.

Market on Main   FASHION, FOOD
(Map p452; www.marketonmain.co.za; Arts on Main, 264 Fox St, Maboneng; ⊙ 10am-3pm Sun) This beloved market is housed in a refurbished industrial building packed with food stands selling freshly baked goods, gourmet edibles and other temptations. You'll also find local fashion designers, artists' studios and a microbrewery.

44 Stanley   FASHION & ACCESSORIES
(Map p452; www.44stanley.co.za; 44 Stanley Ave, Milpark) The antithesis of consumer tack, 44 Stanley is a blueprint for future mall development. It's in a previously disused building with shady courtyards and features an eclectic collection of local designers, speciality boutiques and interesting restaurants.

ℹ Information

DANGERS & ANNOYANCES
Johannesburg has a larger-than-life reputation when it comes to crime, but most visits are trouble-free.

The city centre, once a no-go area, is fine during the day but best avoided after dark. The surrounding neighbourhoods of Braamfontein, Ferreirasdorp, Newtown and Maboneng are generally busy at night and safe to visit – just be vigilant when walking back to your car. Avoid Hillbrow and Yeoville unless you're with a guide.

Car-jackings do happen in the city, so keep your wits about you when stopped at traffic lights after dark.

INTERNET ACCESS

You'll find internet cafes dotted around the city centre and in malls; access is around R30 per hour. Free wi-fi is widespread in cafes and restaurants.

MEDICAL SERVICES

Jo'burg's medical services are good, but they can be pricey, so make sure you get insurance before you leave home.

Charlotte Maxeke Johannesburg Hospital (☑ 011-488 4911; M1/Jubilee Rd, Parktown) Jo'burg's main public hospital.

Netcare Rosebank Hospital (☑ 011-328 0500; www.netcare.co.za; 14 Sturdee Ave, Rosebank; ☺7am-10pm) A private hospital in the northern suburbs, with casualty (emergency), GP and specialist services.

MONEY

There are banks with ATMs and exchange facilities at every commercial centre.

POLICE

Police (☑10111; Main Rd)

POST

Main Post Office (Map p456; ☑ 011-336 1361; www.postoffice.co.za; Rahima Moosa St (Jeppe St); ☺8.30am-4.30pm Mon-Fri, to noon Sat) Has a poste restante service.

TOURIST INFORMATION

Guesthouses or hostels as well as tour guides are your best sources of tourist information.

Johannesburg Tourism Company (Map p452; ☑ 087 151 2950; www.joburgtourism.com; 4th fl, Nelson Mandela Square, Sandton; ☺8am-5pm Mon-Fri) A private endeavour; covers the city of Jo'burg.

❶ Getting There & Away

AIR

OR Tambo International Airport

South Africa's major international and domestic airport is **OR Tambo International Airport** (Ortia; ☑ 011-921 6262; www.airports.co.za). It's about 25km east of central Johannesburg in Kempton Park.

If you're in a hurry, some domestic flights are definitely worth considering. Smaller budget airlines Kulula (p526), Safair (p526) and Mango (p416) link Jo'burg with major destinations.

For regular flights to national and regional destinations try **South African Airways** (SAA; ☑ 0861 359 722; www.flysaa.com), **Airlink** (☑ 0861 606 606; www.flyairlink.com) and

SA Express (p526). All flights can be booked through SAA, which also has offices in the domestic and international terminals of OR Tambo.

Lanseria Airport

Jo'burg has a second airport, **Lanseria** (☑ 011-367 0300; www.lanseria.co.za), located north-west of the city in Randburg. It's often cheaper to fly in and out of Lanseria as it's a smaller airport. It's a joy to rent a car here and drive onto near-empty roads. There is no public transport from the airport.

BUS

There are a number of international buses that leave Jo'burg from the Park Station (Map p456) complex and head for Mozambique, Lesotho, Botswana, Namibia, Swaziland and Zimbabwe.

The main long-distance bus lines (national and international) also depart from and arrive at the Park Station transit centre, in the northwestern corner of the site, where you'll also find their booking offices.

The nearest large town to Kruger National Park is Nelspruit. Phalaborwa is a good option if you're staying at a more northerly Kruger National Park camp such as Olifants.

Baz Bus (p354) Connects Jo'burg with the most popular parts of the region (including Durban, the Garden Route and Cape Town) and picks up at hostels in Jo'burg and Pretoria, saving you the hassle of going into the city to arrange transport. (Note that Baz Bus no longer services Swaziland.) All hostels have current timetables and prices. A seven-day travel pass costs R2600.

Citybug (☑ 0861 334 433; www.citybug.co.za) Runs a shuttle service between Jo'burg and Nelspruit (R440, 3½ hours), stopping in Pretoria and a few smaller towns along the way.

City to City (p527) National and international bus services.

Greyhound (☑ 083 915 9000; www.greyhound.co.za) National and international bus services.

Intercape (p354) National and international bus services.

Lowveld Link (☑ mobile 083 918 8075; www.lowveldlink.com) Runs a shuttle between the airport and Nelspruit (R410, four hours), via Pretoria.

Translux (p527) National and international bus services.

CAR

All the major car-rental operators have counters at OR Tambo and at various locations around the city, and many offer deals with unlimited mileage.

TRAIN

Long-distance train services link Jo'burg with a number of destinations including Pretoria, Cape Town, Bloemfontein, Kimberley, Port Elizabeth,

Durban, Komatipoort and Nelspruit. A number of these services have sleeper compartments. Tickets can be booked through Shosholoza Meyl (p529) or at Jo'burg's Park Station.

ℹ️ Getting Around

BUS

Rea Vaya (☑ 0860 562 874; www.reavaya. org.za) These buses were introduced in the build-up to the 2010 World Cup as a way of addressing the lack of safe, reliable public transport between Soweto (and other townships) and downtown Johannesburg. The network has rapidly expanded since then and includes the Inner City, Newtown, Braamfontein and Auckland Park. The fleet is colourful and comfortable, and timetables are more strictly adhered to than metro lines. An inner-city circular route costs R6.20, while a full trip from the feeder routes to the Inner City costs R12.90.

Citysightseeing Johannesburg (Map p456; ☑ 0861 733 287; www.citysightseeing.co.za; Park Station) Starting from Park Station, these hop-on, hop-off red buses run to 11 major tourist sites around central Johannesburg, including Gandhi Sq, Constitutional Hill and Carlton Centre, as well as the Apartheid Museum, Gold Reef City, Newtown and Braamfontein. They run from roughly 9am to 6pm. A ticket valid for one day costs R190. There's a discount for online bookings.

Metrobus (Map p456; ☑ 0860 562 874; www. mbus.co.za; Gandhi Sq) A reasonable network of buses across the city.

SHARED TAXI

Most Jo'burgers get around in shared minibus taxis. The standard fare in the inner suburbs and the city centre is R8, while longer journeys are R12. There's a complex system of hand/finger signals to tell a passing taxi where you want to go, so it's best to look as though you know where you're going and raise a confident index finger (drivers will stop if they're going the same way).

If you take a minibus shared taxi into central Jo'burg, be sure to get off before it reaches the end of the route, and avoid the taxi rank – it's a mugging zone. Getting a minibus taxi home from the city is a more difficult proposition.

TAXI

There are taxis in Jo'burg, but they are relatively expensive. They all operate meters, but it's wise to ask a local the likely price and agree on a fare from the outset.

Rose Taxis (☑ 011-403 9625; www.rosetaxis. com) is a reputable firm. These days, most Jo'burgers prefer to use **Uber** (www.uber.com/ cities/johannesburg).

TRAIN

Jo'burg's pride and joy, the rapid-transit **Gautrain** (☑ 0800 428 87246; www.gautrain.co.za) offers a direct service between the airport, Sandton, Rosebank, Park Station, Pretoria and Hatfield. Trains depart every 12 minutes at peak times (5.30am to 8.30am and 3pm to 6pm Monday to Friday), and every 20 to 30 minutes outside peak times. A one-way ticket between Pretoria and Park Station costs R72.

If you're travelling in peak periods, or staying near a station, it's a fast, state-of-the-art and

---

WORTH A TRIP

CRADLE OF HUMANKIND

The area to the west of Jo'burg is one of the world's most important palaeontological zones, focused on the Sterkfontein hominid fossil fields. The area is part of the 470-sq-km **Cradle of Humankind** (www.maropeng.co.za), a Unesco World Heritage Site. Most Jo'burg-based tour operators offer full- and half-day tours of the area, but it's also an easy drive if you have your own wheels.

Sterkfontein Caves (☑ 014-577 9000; www.maropeng.co.za; Sterkfontein Caves Rd; adult/ child R165/97, with Maropeng R190/125; ⊘9am-5pm) About 10km away from Maropeng (it's signposted), this place includes a permanent hominid exhibit and a walkway past the excavation site. Tours down into the caves, one of the most significant archaeological sites in the world, leave every 30 minutes (the last tour is at 4pm). A discount ticket that covers the caves and Maropeng must be purchased by 1pm.

Maropeng (☑ 014-577 9000; www.maropeng.co.za; Rte 400, off Rte 563, Hekpoort Rd; adult/ child R120/65, with Sterkfontein Caves R190/125; ⊘9am-5pm; 🖈) Maropeng is well worth a visit. Housed in a building that looks like a giant grassy mound on one side and shiny modern steel on the other, it's an all-in-one information centre, visitor attraction and entertainment complex. The exhibits here show how the human race has progressed since its very beginnings. There are active fossil sites, restaurants, a curio shop and a 5000-seat amphitheatre for outdoor events.

cost-effective way to enter/exit the city. You must purchase a Gold Card (R15) first, then load it with credit for your desired journey.

Soweto

POP 1.3 MILLION / ☎ 011

The 'South West Townships' have evolved from an area of forced habitation to an address of pride and social prestige and a destination in their own right. Travellers come to be part of the welcoming township life and to visit places of historical significance. And while it was considered foolhardy to get there on your own a decade ago, it's now safe to visit the main sights independently.

Mirroring much of South Africa, the rising middle class lives here alongside shack dwellers and the mass unemployed, yet all are equally buoyed by the history of Soweto as an icon of the struggle. Many who break the cycle decide to stay and reinvest, and most laud their Sowetan upbringing. The townships are the heart of the nation and none beats louder than Soweto.

⊙ Sights

★Hector Pieterson Museum   MUSEUM
(☑ 011-536 0611; cnr Pela & Kumalo Sts, Orlando West; adult/child R30/10; ⊙10am-5pm Mon-Sat, to 4pm Sun) This powerful museum illuminates the role of Sowetan life in the history of the independence struggle. On 16 June 1976, a peaceful student protest against the introduction of Afrikaans as a language of instruction in black secondary schools was violently quelled by police. In the resulting chaos police opened fire and a 13-year-old boy, Hector Pieterson, was shot dead.

Walter Sisulu Square of Dedication   SQUARE
(www.waltersisulusquare.co.za; cnr Union Ave & Main Rd) Located in Kliptown, the oldest settlement in Jo'burg to accommodate all races, the Walter Sisulu Square of Dedication is the site where the Freedom Charter was adopted on 26 June 1955. Once a football field, its facilities now include an information centre, a hotel, banks, curio shops and the conical brick Freedom Charter Monument.

Mandela House Museum   MUSEUM
(☑ 011-936 7754; www.mandelahouse.com; cnr Vilakazi & Ngakane Sts, Orlando West; adult/child R60/20; ⊙9am-5pm) Nelson Mandela lived with his first wife, Evelyn, and later with his second wife, Winnie, in this four-room house, just off Vilakazi St. The museum includes interactive exhibits on the history

of the house and some interesting family photos. Just down Vilakazi St, by Sakhumzi Restaurant, is the home of Archbishop Desmond Tutu.

Freedom Charter Monument   MONUMENT
(Walter Sisulu Sq of Dedication, Kliptown) This brick tower right on Walter Sisulu Sq symbolises freedom and democracy. It's built where the Freedom Charter was adopted by the Congress of the People in 1955.

Home of Archbishop
Desmond Tutu   NOTABLE BUILDING
(Vilakazi St) Close to the Mandela House Museum on busy Vilakazi St is the home of Archbishop Desmond Tutu. (A plaque marks the location but the house is not open to visitors.)

Hector Pieterson Memorial   MEMORIAL
(Kumalo St, Orlando West) North of Vilakazi St is Hector Pieterson Sq, named after the 13-year-old shot dead in the run-up to the Soweto uprising in 1976. The poignant memorial features the iconic photo of the limp-bodied boy being carried from the protest.

🏃 Activities

★Orlando Towers   ADVENTURE SPORTS
(☑ 071-674 4343; www.orlandotowers.co.za; cnr Chris Hani Rd & Dynamo St; viewing platform/ bungee jumping R80/550; ⊙ noon-5pm Thu, 10am-6pm Fri-Sun) Built originally for Orlando's Power Station, the towers host one of the world's more incongruous bungee jumps. Once painted a drab white, one tower is now decorated with a colourful mural depicting, among others, Nelson Mandela, singer Yvonne Chaka Chaka and a football stadium. The other tower displays the FNB logo (the bank commissioned the murals in 2002). Abseiling and rap jumping (forward abseiling) are also available (R450). There's a braai restaurant at the towers' base.

☞ Tours

Lebo's Soweto Bicycle Tours   CYCLING
(☑ 011-936 3444; www.sowetobicycletours.com; 2hr/1-day tour R430/680) Soweto's clay paths and grassy nooks make for fabulous cycling terrain. Walking tours are also offered, and there are tuk-tuk (auto rickshaw) tours for the less energetic. The tours are organised by Lebo's Soweto Backpackers, with discounts available for guests.

Taste of Africa   TOURS
(www.tasteofafrica.co.za) Offers an excellent 24-hour tour (per person R950) where you

can explore Soweto with locals, far off the beaten track.

🛏 Sleeping

There are many B&Bs in Soweto, most in the immediate vicinity of Vilakazi St.

Lebo's Soweto Backpackers · HOSTEL $

(☏011-936 3444; www.sowetobackpackers.com; 10823A Pooe St, Orlando West; camping R100, dm/s/d with shared bathroom R170/270/420; 🅿🛜) For a real township experience, this well-established hostel set by lovely parklands is your answer. It's a healthy walk from the Vilakazi St action, but guests love the shaded beer garden, restaurant (meals from R60) and pool table. Dorms are neat and clean; the double rooms are excellent value. Friendly staff encourage interactivity, and all kinds of tours are available. Free Baz Bus (p354) shuttles to Johannesburg can be arranged.

Nthateng's B&B · GUESTHOUSE $$

(☏011-051 9362, 082 335 7956; nthatengmd@gmail.com; 6991 Inhlwathi St, Orlando West; s/d incl breakfast R500/695; 🅿🛜) Dark woods, tan linens, sandy-coloured walls and a few kitschy touches give this spacious guesthouse an air of early-'80s post-disco chill. However, Nthateng is an animated host who insists on top-shelf personal tours, delicious breakfasts and a *mi casa es su casa* state of mind. It's in an ideal location near the museum and restaurants.

Soweto Hotel · HOTEL $$$

(☏011-527 7300; www.sowetohotel.co.za; Walter Sisulu Sq of Dedication, Kliptown; s/d incl breakfast from R1900/2200; 🅿@🛜) You wouldn't guess from the outside, but this muscular concrete building overlooking a square shelters stylish, tranquil rooms, all in beiges and maroons; the jazz design continues in the restaurant and bar. The restaurant tends to be eerily empty and staff aren't always on the ball, but it's in a historically important part of Soweto that most travellers don't see.

🍴 Eating

The most tourist-friendly and atmospheric eateries are on Vilakazi St.

Chaf Pozi · BARBECUE $$

(☏081 797 5756; www.chafpozi.co.za; cnr Chris Han & Nicholas Sts; set menus R110-275; ⊙11am-6pm Mon-Thu, 11am-2am Fri & Sat, noon-10pm Sun) At the base of the Orlando Towers, this large *shisa nyama* (barbeque) restaurant is popular with locals and those needing a beer after leaping from the towers (attached to a bungee rope, that is). The well-seasoned meat is served in a range of set menus that also include mealie pap (maize porridge), vegetables and sauces.

Vuyo's · AFRICAN $$

(☏011-536 1838; www.thrivecafe.co.za; 8038 Vilakazi St, Orlando West; mains R50-130; ⊙10am-10pm; 🛜) A surprisingly hip restaurant with a sleek, design-led interior, this cool culinary outpost demonstrates Soweto's changing sensibilities. Serving up inventive dishes showcasing South African ingredients like *mogodo* (tripe), boerewors (farmer's sausage) and *morogo* (wild spinach), it's frequented more by locals than tourists. A good place to hang out and soak up the atmosphere while nursing a beer on the upstairs terrace.

🍷 Drinking & Nightlife

Kofi · CAFE

(www.kofiafrika.co.za; 7166 Vilakazi St, Orlando West; 8am-7.30pm Mon-Thu, to 8.30pm Fri & Sat) Part of the Box Shop, an initiative to assist new small businesses, Kofi is Soweto's coolest cafe. Excellent coffee is served alongside a few sandwiches, salads and breakfasts. There are plans to open a roastery here in the future.

ℹ Information

There are banks with ATMs in Walter Sisulu Square of Dedication. Foreign exchange is available at the Soweto Hotel, also in the square.

Soweto Tourism and Information Centre (☏011-342 4316; www.joburgtourism.com; Walter Sisulu Sq of Dedication, Kliptown; ⊙8am-5pm Mon-Fri) has a few brochures and can help with tours.

ℹ Getting There & Away

Many tourists take a half- or full-day guided tour of Soweto, but you can choose to travel independently using the safe Rea Vaya (p463) bus system. It's also pretty straightforward (and safe) to drive to Soweto with your own wheels.

Pretoria

POP 741,000 / ☏012

South Africa's administrative centre is a handsome city, with a number of gracious old houses in the city centre; large, leafy suburbs; and wide streets that are lined with a purple haze of jacarandas in October and November. It's more of an Afrikaner city than Jo'burg, and its bars and restaurants

Central Pretoria

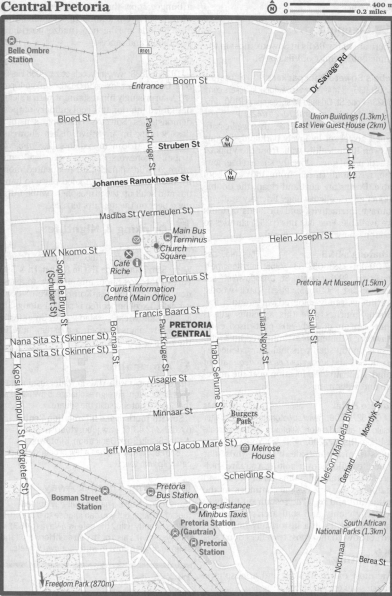

0 — 400 m
0 — 0.2 miles

Belle Ombre Station

R101

Boom St

Entrance

Dr Savage Rd

Bloed St

Union Buildings (1.3km);
East View Guest House (2km)

Paul Kruger St

Struben St

N4

Du Toit St

Johannes Ramokhoase St

N4

Madiba St (Vermeulen St)

Main Bus Terminus

Helen Joseph St

WK Nkomo St

Church Square

Café Riche

Pretorius St

Sophie De Bruyn St (Schubart St)

Tourist Information Centre (Main Office)

Pretoria Art Museum (1.5km)

Francis Baard St

PRETORIA CENTRAL

Nana Sita St (Skinner St)

Nana Sita St (Skinner St)

Bosman St

Paul Kruger St

Lilian Ngoyi St

Sisulu St

Kgosi Mampuru St (Potgieter St)

Thabo Sehume St

Visagie St

Minnaar St

Burgers Park

Jeff Masemola St (Jacob Maré St)

Melrose House

Nelson Mandela Blvd

Moerdyk St

Gerhard

Scheiding St

Pretoria Bus Station

Bosman Street Station

Long-distance Minibus Taxis

Pretoria Station (Gautrain)

Pretoria Station

South African National Parks (1.3km)

Normaal

Berea St

Freedom Park (870m)

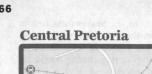

are less cosmopolitan – sedate Pretoria was once at the heart of the apartheid regime and its very name a symbol of oppression. Today it's home to a growing number of black civil servants and foreign embassy workers, who are infusing the city with a new sense of multiculturalism. Officially, the greater Pretoria region, which also includes Centurion and a number of smaller towns and townships, is called Tshwane.

⊙ Sights

Freedom Park MEMORIAL
(📋012-336 4000; www.freedompark.co.za; cnr Koch
St & 7th Ave; entry incl guided tour R100; ☺8am-
4.30pm, tours 9am, noon & 3pm) This stunning
memorial adopts an integrated approach to
South Africa's war history and is a place of
architectural imagination and collective healing. Located across the kopje (rocky hill) from
the austere Voortrekker Monument (p467),
Freedom Park honours fallen South Africans
in all major conflicts. Highlights include the
**Isivivane Garden of Remembrance; Sikh-
imbuto**, the wall of inscribed names of fallen
heroes; **//hapo**, a museum and interpretative centre covering Southern African history; and **Mveledzo**, a spiral path that cuts into
the natural landscape.

Voortrekker Monument MONUMENT, VIEWPOINT
(📋012-326 6770; www.vtm.org.za; Eeufees Rd;
adult/child R70/35; ☺8am-6pm Sep-Apr, to 5pm
May-Aug) The imposing Voortrekker Monument was constructed between 1938 and
1949 to honour the journey of the Voortrekkers, who journeyed north over the coastal
mountains of the Cape into the heart of the
African veld. The monument is 3km south
of the city and is clearly signposted from the
N1 freeway. It is surrounded by a 3.4-sq-km
nature reserve.

Church Square SQUARE
At Pretoria's heart, **Church Square** is surrounded by imposing public buildings, including the **Palace of Justice**, where the
Rivonia Trial that sentenced Nelson Mandela
to life imprisonment was held, on the northern side; the **OuRaadsaal (Old Government) building** on the southern side; the **Old
Capitol Theatre** in the northwestern corner;
First National Bank in the northeast; the
Old Nederlandsche Bank building, which
adjoins Café Riche and houses the tourist information centre; and the **main post office**
on the western side.

Union Buildings NOTABLE BUILDING
(Government Ave) FREE These sweeping sandstone buildings are the headquarters of government and home to the presidential offices. The **gardens** are often used for public
celebrations, and Nelson Mandela's inaugu-
ration took place here back in 1994. Statues
of a few former heads of state inhabit the
grounds, including a magnificent statue of
an open-armed, grinning Mandela. There's
also a WWI memorial here, and a memorial
to the South African police. The buildings

themselves aren't open to the public, but the
grounds are open seven days a week.

Pretoria Art Museum GALLERY
(📋021-358 6750; www.pretoriaartmuseum.co.za;
cnr Francis Baard & Wessels Sts, Arcadia Park; adult/
child R22/5; ☺10am-5pm Tue-Sun) This art museum specialises in South African art from
throughout the country's history. It also features regularly changing exhibitions.

Melrose House HISTORIC BUILDING
(📋012-322 2805; 275 Jeff Masemola St; adult/
child R22/5; ☺10am-5pm Tue-Sun) This stately
mansion built in 1886 is of strong historical
significance – on 31 May 1902, the Treaty of
Vereeniging, which marked the end of the
Anglo-Boer War (1899–1902), was signed in
the dining room. Highlights of the house include a grand billiard room with a vibrant
stained-glass smoking nook and a conservatory containing a collection of political cartoons from the Anglo-Boer War.

🛏 Sleeping

Pumbas Backpackers HOSTEL $
(📋012-362 5343; www.pumbas.co.za; 1232 Arcadia St, Hatfield; camping R100, dm R170, s/d with
shared bathroom R300/400; ℗☺🛜❄) Although
this budget-friendly hostel won't knock your
socks off, it features an assortment of tidy and
serviceable private rooms and dorms and is
optimally placed in Hatfield, a short stroll
from the Gauteng station. There's a kitchen
for guest use and a pocket-sized pool.

1322 Backpackers International HOSTEL $
(📋012-362 3905; www.1322backpackers.com;
1322 Arcadia St, Hatfield; dm R170-190, r R550, s/d
with shared bathroom from R250/450; ℗@🛜❄)
This hostel is a welcoming retreat, where
travellers congregate around a backyard
pool and a buzzing little bar. You can stay
in neat three- to eight-bed dorms, or smallish, converted wood-and-brick sheds at the
bottom of the garden (chilly in winter, a bit
stifling in summer). Shared bathrooms are
clean and all guests have kitchen access.
Continental breakfast is included.

★**Foreigners Friend
Guesthouse** GUESTHOUSE $$
(📋082 458 4951; www.foreignersfriends.co.za;
409A Om die Berg St, Lynnwood; s/d incl breakfast
from R850/1150; ℗❄🛜❄) Character and
charm – somewhere between a boutique
hotel and a B&B, this enchanting abode is
an oasis of tranquillity in a wonderfully qui-
et neighbourhood. It has 10 well-organised,

spacious rooms; a well-furnished ground-floor living area; a lush garden and a spiffing swimming pool. A beautifully presented breakfast is served on a breezy terrace.

East View Guest House
GUESTHOUSE **$$**

(☑082 451 6516; eastview1@mweb.co.za; 175 East Ave, Arcadia; s/d incl breakfast R700/850; P🖥🛜⛱) At this calm haven in a little-known backstreet, Lynette Blignaut offers the perfect small B&B experience, with six fresh rooms done out in taupe and grey shades, and modern bathrooms. It occupies an imposing villa in the embassy district, close to the Union Buildings. Breakfasts are copious – mmm, the homemade muffins! – and evening meals can be arranged.

Ambiance Guesthouse
GUESTHOUSE **$$**

(☑083 280 0981; www.ambianceguesthouse.com; 28 3rd St, Menlo Park; s/d R660/930; P🛜⛱) This elegant villa in the leafy suburb of Menlo Park is just the ticket for those seeking a stylish home-away-from-home experience in Pretoria. The four rooms are different in design and colour scheme and open onto a delightful garden complete with a nifty pool; our choice is 'Petit Paris', replete with claw-footed bath. Breakfast costs R60.

Alpine Attitude
BOUTIQUE HOTEL **$$$**

(☑012-348 6504; http://alpineattiude.co.za; 522 Atterbury Rd, Menlo Park; s R1300-1600, d R1600-2000; P❋🛜⛱) Looking for a night somewhere extra special? Make a beeline for this unique boutique hotel. The seven rooms have been creatively designed – each one has its own theme and decor. The Transparent room, where pretty much everything (except the bedding and walls) is see-through, has to be seen to be believed. Amenities include restaurant, bar and pool. Breakfast included.

Courtyard Arcadia Hotel
HOTEL **$$$**

(☑012-342 4940; www.clhg.com; cnr Park & Hill Sts, Arcadia; d R1900; P❋🛜⛱) At the upper end of the City Lodge chain spectrum is this Cape Dutch manor house in the heart of the embassy district. The 69 rooms, which occupy several residences, are a little pedestrian for the grandeur of the setting, but service is assured and the evening happy hours are a nice touch. Booking online gets you the best deal.

🍴 Eating

Café Riche
BISTRO **$**

(☑012-328 3173; 2 WF Nkomo St (Church St); mains R45-90; ⏱6am-6pm; 🛜) This historic, early-20th-century European bistro in the heart of Church Sq is the ideal place to sip

beer and watch the South African capital roll through its day. The street tables are quickly nabbed by local office workers and politicians, while inside the atmospheric bar, unhurried staff serve sandwiches, pastries, salads and very simple bistro meals.

★ Carbon Bistro
STEAK **$$**

(☑012-340 0029; www.carbonbistro.co.za; mains R80-170; ⏱11am-11pm Mon-Sat, to 3pm Sun) This places oozes hipster chic, with its minimalist decor, craft-beer taps, gin bar and cuts of steak you've never heard of. Knowledgeable, friendly staff will explain the meaty menu and pour bespoke cocktails featuring a range of South African gins. And if all that seems too much, grab a draught G&T and watch the world go by from the patio.

Crawdaddy's
BRASSERIE **$$**

(☑012-460 0889; www.crawdaddys.co.za; cnr Middle & Dey Sts, Brooklyn Plaza, Brooklyn; mains R90-180; ⏱11am-10pm Mon-Sat, to 9pm Sun) An old favourite with hungry locals, this brasserie never fails to satisfy the requirements of its loyal punters. The key to its success is an eclectic menu that ranges from curries and stir-fries to grilled meats and seafood. It has several dining rooms and an open-air terrace that overlooks a busy intersection.

Geet
INDIAN **$$**

(☑012-460 3199; www.geetindianrestaurant.com; 541 Fehrsen St, Brooklyn; mains R90-175; ⏱11am-3pm & 5-10pm Mon-Sat, 11am-6pm Sun; 🍽) You wouldn't guess it from the humble surrounds here, but chef Gita Jivan concocts first-class Indian dishes, fusing Indian flavours with European presentation. The huge menu emphasises North Indian delights, and vegetarians can feast well. The whisky lounge, where you can dine sitting on cushions, is a treat.

Blue Crane
SOUTH AFRICAN **$$**

(☑012-460 7615; www.bluecranerestaurant.co.za; 156 Melk St, New Muckleneuk; mains R60-170; ⏱7.30am-3pm Mon, to 10pm Tue-Fri, 9am-10pm Sat, 9am-3pm Sun; 🛜🍴) As part of the Austin Roberts Bird Sanctuary, Blue Crane is famous to ornithologists worldwide (and anyone else who enjoys a cold Castle lager at sunset), with a menu that begins with breakfast and moves on to steaks, salads, burgers and sandwiches. There are various dining rooms, including an atmospheric *boma* and a splendid deck overlooking a pond.

Pacha's
SOUTH AFRICAN **$$$**

(☑012-460 3220; www.pachas.co.za; 27 Maroelana St, Hazelwood; mains R95-220; ⏱noon-2.30pm & 6-9.30pm Mon-Fri, 6-9.30pm Sat, noon-2.30pm

Sun) The address of choice for those looking for both style and substance. It's a pleasant modern restaurant with large picture windows, an aquarium and quality furniture, but high-quality meat dishes, including some traditional fare, are the main attraction here. Feeling more surf than turf? There's also a good selection of seafood dishes.

Kream INTERNATIONAL $$$
(012-346 4642; www.kream.co.za; 570 Fehrsen St, Brooklyn Bridge; mains R120-220; noon-10pm Mon-Sat, to 2.30pm Sun) A bold concept in a conservative city, Kream, in many ways, *is* the cream of the crop. The uber-trendy menu features exotic starters and the usual grilled suspects for main course. The white-chocolate and passion-fruit cheesecake with a dram from the long whisky list is a fine way to finish a night.

Drinking & Nightlife

★ Capital Craft CRAFT BEER
(012-424 8601; www.capitalcraft.co.za; Greenlyn Village Centre, cnr Thomas Edison St & 12th St East, Menlo Park; noon-midnight Tue, 10.30am-midnight Wed-Sat, 10.30am-8pm Sun) Pretoria's premier beer hangout is a huge place whose long tables, both inside the cool bar and out in the garden, are perpetually packed. The focus here is craft beer from around the country. The selection is impressive – try a few tasters before ordering a pint. Want something to soak up all that ale? The pulled-pork sandwich is superb.

Eastwoods PUB
(012-344 0243; www.eastwoods.co.za; 391 Eastwood St, Arcadia; 8am-2am Mon-Sat, to 10pm Sun) This hugely popular pub is often packed, especially at lunchtime and after work hours. There's a large outdoor deck, and banquette seating and a big bar inside. It has won the 'Best Pub in Pretoria' award several times and serves up good meals throughout the day, as well as local beers and a large selection of cocktails and spirits.

ⓘ Information

There are banks with ATMs and change facilities across town.

American Express (012-346 2599; Fehrson St, Brooklyn Mall, Brooklyn; 9am-5pm)
Hatfield Clinic (012-362 7180; www.hatmed. co.za; 454 Hilda St; 8am-7pm Mon-Thu, to 6pm Fri, to 1pm Sat, to noon Sun) A well-known suburban clinic.

Hatfield Post Office (Hatfield Sq; 8am-4.30pm Mon-Fri, to noon Sat) The most commonly used post office.
Main Post Office (Church Sq; 8.30am-4.30pm Mon-Fri, 8am-noon Sat) In a historic building on the main square.
South African National Parks (SANParks; 012-428 9111; www.sanparks.org; 643 Leyds St, Muckleneuk; office 7.30am-3.45pm Mon-Fri, call centre 7.30am-5pm Mon-Fri, 8am-1pm Sat) Your best bet for all wildlife-reserve bookings and enquiries.
Tourist Information Centre (012-358 1430; www.tshwanetourism.com; Old Nederlandsche Bank Bldg, Church Sq; 7.30am-4pm Mon-Fri) Parking here can be tricky. There's another branch in **Hatfield** (012-358 1675; www. tshwanetourism.com; Kingston House, 311 Eastwood St, Hatfield; 7.30am-4pm Mon-Fri).
Tshwane District Hospital (012-354 5958; Dr Savage Rd) For medical emergencies.

ⓘ Getting There & Away

BUS
The **Pretoria Bus Station** (Railway St) is next to Pretoria's train station. You will also find the major companies' booking and information offices here, as well as a good cafe and an ATM.

Most Translux (p527), City to City (p527), Intercape (p354) and Greyhound (p462) services running from Jo'burg to Durban, the South Coast and Cape Town originate in Pretoria. Services running north up the N1 also stop here. (Translux, Greyhound and Intercape fares from Pretoria are identical to those from Jo'burg, regardless of the one-hour difference in time.) If you only want to go between the two cities, it will cost about R200.

Baz Bus (p354) will pick up and drop off at Pretoria hostels.

Long-distance minibus taxis leave from the rank close to the train station.

TRAIN
The historic Pretoria train station is an attractive location to commence or complete a journey.

The Gautrain (p463) service offers regular high-speed connections with Hatfield, Johannesburg (Park Station, Rosebank and Sandton) and onward to the airport. The fare from Pretoria to Sandton is R57.

For long distances, Shosholoza Meyl (p529) trains running through Pretoria are the *Trans Karoo* (daily from Pretoria to Cape Town) and the *Komati* (daily from Jo'burg to Komatipoort via Nelspruit). The luxury **Blue Train** (www. bluetrain.co.za), which links Pretoria, Jo'burg and Cape Town, originates here.

Because of a high incidence of crime, we don't recommend travelling between Pretoria and Jo'burg by Metro.

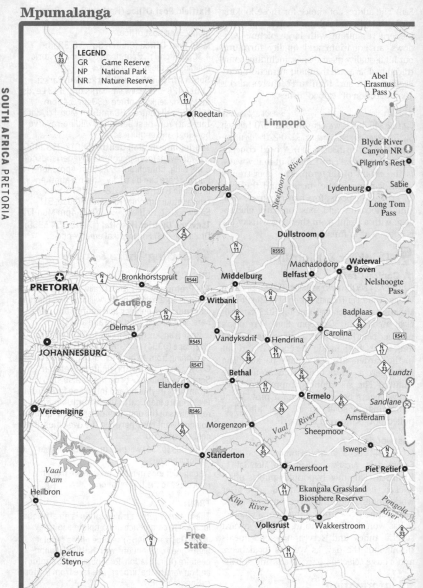

SOUTH AFRICA PRETORIA

ℹ️ **Getting Around**

There's an extensive network of local buses. A booklet of timetables and route maps is available from the enquiry office in the **main bus terminus** (☎ 012-308 0839; Church Sq) or from pharmacies. Fares range from R6 to R14, depending on the distance. Handy services include buses 5 and 8, which run between Church Sq and Brooklyn via Burnett St in Hatfield.

Minibus taxis run pretty much everywhere and the standard fare is about R6. They're not very convenient for travellers, however – most visitors prefer to use taxis.

You can get a metered taxi from **Rixi Taxis** (☎ 086 100 7494; www.rixitaxi.co.za; per km around R10). Locals tend to opt for Uber, which is operational in Pretoria.

MPUMALANGA

Mpumalanga is one of South Africa's smallest provinces and one of its most exciting. Visually it is a simply beautiful region, with vistas of mountains, lush, green valleys and a collection of cool-climate towns. Its natural assets make it a prime target for outdoor enthusiasts, who head here to abseil down waterfalls, throw themselves off cliffs, negotiate rivers by raft, inner tube or canoe, and hike or bike numerous wilderness trails.

Mpumalanga's major draw, though, is the massive Blyde River Canyon, which carves its way spectacularly through the Drakensberg Escarpment. It is one of South Africa's iconic sights and on a clear day one of the many vantage points can leave you breathless.

And, of course, the province provides access to the southern half of Kruger National Park (p476), with an excellent selection of lodges and wilderness activities right on the mighty park's doorstep.

Nelspruit (Mbombela)

POP 58,700 / ☎ 013

Nelspruit (now officially called Mbombela) is Mpumalanga's largest town and the provincial capital. While not unpleasant, it's more a place to get things done than a worthwhile destination for tourists. There are, however, good accommodation options and a couple of excellent restaurants, so it makes a good-enough stopover on the way elsewhere. It's also a good place to organise a trip to Kruger National Park.

⊙ Sights

**Lowveld National
Botanical Garden**   GARDENS
(☎ 013-752 5531; www.sanbi.org; adult/child R30/14; ⊗8am-6pm) Outside of town, this 15,000-sq-m botanical garden (established 1969) is home to tropical African rainforest and is a nice place for a stroll among the flowers and trees. Over 240 bird species have been recorded here. It's on Rte 40 about 2km north of the junction with the N4.

Chimpanzee Eden   ZOO
(☎ 079 777 1514; www.chimpeden.com; Rte 40; adult/child R190/85) This chimp centre, 12km south of Nelspruit on Rte 40, acts as a sanctuary for rescued chimpanzees. Here you can see chimps in a semi-wild environment and learn about the primates' behaviour and plight. The entry fee includes a guided tour (at 10am, noon and 2pm).

🛏 Sleeping

Nelspruit Backpackers HOSTEL $

(☎ 013-741 2237; www.nelback.co.za; Andries Pretorius St; camping R100, dm R160, s/d with shared bathroom R280/450) With a large pool and deck overlooking the adjoining nature reserve, this family home in suburbia is a relaxing budget option. There are rooms in the main house, which has a communal lounge and kitchen, and a couple more in the garden. Tours to Blyde River Canyon and Kruger National Park are available.

Old Vic Travellers Inn HOSTEL $

(☎ 013-744 0993; www.krugerandmore.co.za; 12 Impala St; dm R160, d R560, d with shared bathroom R460, 4-person self-catering houses R900; @🛜🖨) A friendly, somewhat upscale backpackers, with self-catering facilities and lots of information on the area. Double rooms are a bit dark but clean and well kept, and shared bathrooms are in good order. A big, rambling garden leads down to the river. It's about 3km south of the centre and is a Baz Bus stop.

★ Utopia in Africa GUESTHOUSE $$$

(☎ 013-745 7714; www.utopiainafrica.co.za; 6 Daleen St; s/d incl breakfast from R910/1480; ❄🛜🖨) Simplicity, elegance and a masterly design that keeps the premises cool using the afternoon breeze mark this exceptional accommodation. Rooms are beautifully furnished and have balconies overlooking a nature reserve. Head south on Madiba Dr, turn left onto Dr Enos Mabuza Dr, then left onto Halssnoer St (which becomes Augusta) and keep following it – Utopia is well signposted from here.

Francolin Lodge GUESTHOUSE $$$

(☎ 013-744 1251; www.francolinlodge.co.za; 4 Du Preez St; s/d incl breakfast R1295/2030; @🛜🖨) This is a top Nelspruit guesthouse. The rooms have double-height ceilings, private patios and corner bathrooms with views. There's also a small spa and an excellent restaurant on-site. The easiest way to approach it is off the N4 coming into town from the east – it's well signposted.

🍴 Eating

Food Fundi SANDWICHES $

(☎ 013-755 1091; www.thefoodfundi.co.za; Shop 16, Pick n Pay Centre, Sitrus Cres; mains R40-70; ⏱7am-6pm Mon-Fri, 8am-5pm Sat, 8am-2pm Sun) Using fresh lowveld ingredients, this outstanding cafe is an excellent choice for breakfast or lunch. Wraps, sandwiches (try the rooibos-smoked chicken, toasted cashew nuts, pineapple chutney and feta), salads and burgers all decorate the menu. Craft beer, wine and sweet treats are also available.

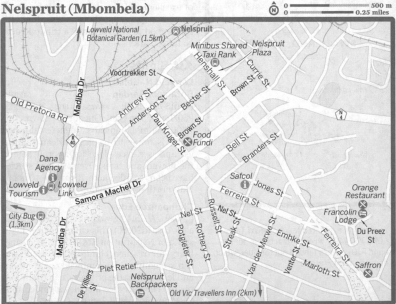

Nelspruit (Mbombela)

Saffron TAPAS $$

(☑ 013-744 1146; www.saffronnelspruit.co.za; 56 Ferreira St; tapas R30-60; ☺ 6-9pm Tue-Sat) Serving quality tapas dishes, such as house-smoked pork loin with honey-mustard cream, and onion-marmalade tartlets topped with goat cheese, Saffron is a fine addition to Nelspruit's growing culinary scene. Dine in the intimate interior or outside on the lovely deck. Book ahead, as it's popular with locals and visitors alike.

★ Orange Restaurant FUSION $$$

(☑ 013-744 9507; www.eatatorange.co.za; 4 Du Preez St; mains lunch R60-120, dinner R90-180; ☺ noon 10pm Mon Sat, 6 9pm Sun) Put on your finest and treat yourself to some beautifully prepared cuisine – such as artful servings of ostrich carpaccio – at this classy restaurant at the Francolin Lodge. The terrific views are the icing on the cake.

❶ Information

Dana Agency (☑ 013-753 3571; www.dana agency.co.za; Shop 13, Nelspruit Crossing Mall; ☺ 8am-4.30pm Mon-Fri, 9am-noon Sat) This long-standing agent can help with air tickets and other travel arrangements.

Lowveld Tourism (☑ 013-755 1988; www. krugerlowveld.com; cnr Madiba & Samora Machel Drs; ☺ 7am-6pm Mon-Fri, 8am-1.30pm Sat) This helpful office at Nelspruit Crossing Mall (behind News Cafe) takes bookings for all national parks, including Kruger, and can help arrange accommodation and tours.

Safcol (South African Forestry Co Ltd; ☑ 013-754 2724; www.safcol.co.za; 10 Streak St) Provides information and takes bookings for hikes in the area.

❶ Getting There & Away

AIR

Kruger Mpumalanga International Airport (KMIA; ☑ 013-753 7500; www.kmiairport.co.za) The closest commercial airport to Nelspruit.

Airlink (☑ 013-750 2531, 0861 606 606; www. flyairlink.com) There are daily flights with Airlink to Jo'burg (R1600 to R2200, one hour), Cape Town (R3600 to R4400, 2½ hours) and Durban (R2500 to R3200, 1 hour).

BUS

The major bus companies all stop in Nelspruit as they travel between Jo'burg/Pretoria (R315, five hours) and Maputo (Mozambique; R320, three hours) via Nelspruit. Tickets are sold at the **offices** (Promenade Mall, Samora Machel Dr) in Promenade Mall.

Greyhound (☑ 083 915 9000; www.grey hound.co.za)

CAR

Avis (☑ 013-750 1015; www.avis.co.za), **Europcar** (☑ 013-750 2871; www.europcar. co.za) and **First** (☑ 013-750 2538; www.first-carrental.co.za) all have offices at the airport. There is also a branch of **Avis** (☑ 011-387 8560; Meander Cr, Riverside Park) north of the city, near the Botanical Gardens.

SHARED TAXI

The local bus and minibus-taxi rank is behind Nelspruit Plaza near the corner of Bester and Henshall Sts. Minibus-taxi destinations and fares include White River (R15, 20 minutes), Barberton (R30, 40 minutes), Hazyview (R40, one hour), Graskop (R50, 1½ hours) and Jo'burg (R200, five hours).

City Bug (☑ 086-133 4433; www.citybug. co.za) Operates a twice-weekly shuttle to Durban (one-way R660, nine hours) and several per day to Pretoria (R440, 3½ hours) and OR Tambo International Airport (R440, 3½ to 4½ hours). All services depart from Graniet St, off Rte 104 near the Ilanga Mall.

Lowveld Link (☑ 013-750 1174; www.lowveld link.com) Operates a convenient daily shuttle from Nelspruit to Pretoria, OR Tambo International Airport and Sandton (one way R410, four-five hours). It leaves from the Lowveld Tourism office.

TRAIN

Shosholoza Meyl (p354) operates a seat-only service which travels twice weekly between Jo'burg (R170, ten hours) and Komatipoort (R100, 2½ hours) via Nelspruit.

Blyde River Canyon

Increasingly popular with international visitors, Blyde River Canyon is the third-largest canyon in the world and one of South Africa's most outstanding natural sights. The canyon's scale and beauty make a trip here a memorable experience – especially if you're lucky enough to visit on a fine day.

Landscape lovers will be in heaven driving the R532, which largely follows the edge of the canyon north from Graskop. En route, there are numerous scenic stops, taking in waterfalls and lookout points. Each stop has its own nominal entry fee. Most people stick to driving – but if you can spare a day, hiking here is a magical experience.

◉ Sights

Echo Caves CAVE

(☑ 013-238 0015; www.echocaves.co.za; admission & guided tour adult/child R60/25; ☺ 8.30am-4.30pm Mon-Sat, to 4pm Sun) Echo Caves are off Rte 36, where Stone Age relics have been found. The caves get their name from dripstone formations that echo when tapped.

Blyde River Canyon Nature Reserve
NATURE RESERVE

(☏021-424 1037; www.mtpa.co.za) Bordering much of the 30km-long Blyde River Canyon, the 260 sq km Blyde River Canyon NR winds its way north from Graskop, following the Drakensberg Escarpment and meeting the Blyde River as it snakes down to the lowveld. The majority of visitors drive along the canyon's edge, and there are plenty of viewpoints along the way where you can stop and gaze in awe. If you have enough time, however, the canyon is even better explored on foot. There are separate entrance fees for each attraction within the reserve.

🏃 Activities

Blyde River Canyon Hiking Trail
HIKING

(Rte 60) This popular and very scenic 30km trail (R80; 2½ days) begins at Paradise Camp and finishes at Bourke's Luck Potholes, overnighting in simple hiker huts. Bookings should be made through the **Mpumalanga Tourism and Parks Agency** (www.mtpa. co.za; ☏013-759 5300), or at the Bourke's Luck Potholes visitors centre. As it's a one-way route, you'll need to sort out onward transport from the end of the trail.

Belvedere Day Walk
WALKING

This reasonably strenuous 10km walk takes you in a circular route to the Belvedere hydroelectric power station at Bourke's Luck Potholes. Bookings should be made at Potholes; the walk takes approximately five hours. When walking here, don't go to the river; instead turn left at the guesthouse and down a path to some beautiful waterfalls and rock pools. The power station was built in 1911 and was once the largest of its kind in the southern hemisphere.

🛏 Sleeping

Forever Blyde Canyon
RESORT $$

(☏0861 226 966; www.foreverblydecanyon.co.za; camping R210, chalets from R925; 🅿️🛜🏊) This rambling resort has a wide choice of accommodation. The solid brick chalets are very well set up, and the pricier ones are worth it for the views and extra space. (For jaw-dropping views of the rock formation, the Three Rondavels, ask for Nos 89 to 96.)

Watch out for the cheeky baboons – they've been known to jump through windows and help themselves to your breakfast!

Thaba Tsweni Lodge
LODGE $$

(☏013-767 1380; www.blyderivercanyonaccommodation.com; d from R850; 🅿️) Beautifully located just a short walk from Berlin Falls in the heart of the panorama route are several self-catering chalets with stone walls, African-print bedspreads, kitchens, private garden areas with braai facilities, wood-burning fireplaces and beautiful views. It's just off Rte 352 in the direction of Berlin Falls.

Graskop
POP 4000 / ☏013

While it's a popular stop with the tour buses, little Graskop somehow seems to swallow them quite well, leaving plenty of room around town for everyone else. The compact town is one of the most appealing in the area, with a sunny disposition, sleepy backstreets and gently sloping hills in every direction. There are good guesthouses, restaurants and craft shops to keep visitors happy. On summer afternoons, restaurant terraces are full and there's a friendly buzz.

It's also a useful base for exploring the Blyde River Canyon, and the nearby views over the edge of the Drakensberg Escarpment are magnificent.

🏃 Activities

There's good hiking and mountain biking in the area. Panorama Info (p475) can point you in the right direction, or you can hire bikes (per day R200) from Graskop Valley View Backpackers.

Big Swing
ADVENTURE SPORTS

(☏079 779 8713; www.bigswing.co.za; s/tandem jump R350/R600, zip line only R100; ⏰Tue-Sun 9am-4pm) One of the highest cable gorge swings in the world, Big Swing has a free-fall of 68m (that's like falling 19 storeys in less than three seconds) into Graskop Gorge. You then swing like a pendulum across the width of the gorge – which gives you an outstanding view. It's 1km out of town on the Hazyview road. Once you've taken the plunge, celebrate with a nerve-steadying drink at the lodge next door. There's also a 135m highwire 'foefie slide' (zip line).

🛏 Sleeping

★Graskop Valley View Backpackers
HOSTEL $

(☏013-767 1112; www.valley-view.co.za; 47 De Lange St; camping R100, dm R150, d R390, s/d wth shared bathroom RR260/320; 🖰🛜🏊) This friendly backpackers has a variety of rooms in excellent condition, plus rondavels and a self-catering flat. The owners can organise adventure tours and rent out mountain bikes for private use (per day R200). Highly recommended. Take the road to Sabie, turn left at the first four-way stop and take another left on De Lange St.

★ **Graskop Hotel** HOTEL $$
(☎013-767 1244; www.graskophotel.co.za; cnr Hoof & Louis Trichardt Sts; s/d incl breakfast R770/1100; ❄☎🛋) This classy hotel is one of our favourites in the province. Rooms here are slick, stylish and individual; several feature art and design by contemporary South African artists. Rooms out the back are little country cottages with dollhouse-like furniture (but are extremely comfortable), an impression exemplified by the glass doors opening onto the lush garden at the rear. Book ahead.

✕ Eating

Harrie's Pancakes CRÊPES $
(cnr Louis Trichardt & Kerk Sts; pancakes R50-80; ⊙8am-7pm) The chic white minimalist interior, full of modern art and quirky touches, is somewhat at odds with the cuisine. You won't find breakfast style pancakes here but mostly savoury and exotic fillings, as well as some sweet offerings. Its reputation perhaps outdoes what it delivers, but Harrie's is a nice spot for a breakfast croissant and fresh-brewed coffee.

❶ Information

There is no official tourist office and the private enterprises seems to open and close frequently. **Panorama Info** (☎ 013-767 1377; www.panoramainfo.co.za; cnr Louis Trichardt & Kerk Sts; ⊙9am-4.30pm Mon-Fri, to 4pm Sat & Sun) has some pamphlets and maps.

First National Bank (Kerk St) has an ATM just north of Louis Trichardt St.

❶ Getting There & Away

The minibus shared taxi stand (Hoof St) is at the south end of town, with daily morning departures to Pilgrim's Rest (R12, 30 minutes), Sabie (R30, 40 minutes) and Hazyview (R40, one hour).

Sabie

POP 9200 / ☎013
Sabie is a lovely little town, and one of Mpumalanga's best places to base yourself. There are some excellent eating options and a good range of accommodation, and

the lush, mountainous countryside makes a delightful backdrop. Once you venture out of town you'll quickly discover hidden waterfalls, streams and walking trails. It's a favourite with outdoorsy types who can enjoy the heart-pumping opportunities – including rafting, canyoning (known as kloofing around these parts) and hiking – that abound in the area.

◉ Sights

Waterfall fanatics will be in their element here – the area around Sabie positively gushes with **falls** (admission to each R5 to R10). They include **Sabie Falls**, just north of town on Rte 532 to Graskop; the 70m **Bridal Veil Falls**, northwest of Sabie, off Old Lydenburg Rd; the 68m **Lone Creek Falls**, also off Old Lydenburg Rd, and with wheelchair access on the right-hand path; and the nearby **Horseshoe Falls**, about 5km southwest of Lone Creek Falls. The popular **Mac-Mac Falls**, about 12km north of Sabie, off Rte 532 to Graskop, take their name from the many Scots on the local mining register. About 3km southeast of the falls are the **Mac-Mac Pools**, where you can swim.

🏃 Activities

Sabie Xtreme Adventures ADVENTURE SPORTS
(☎013-764 2118; www.sabiextreme.co.za; Main St) This outfit, based in Sabie Backpackers Lodge, can organise kloofing, candlelight caving, rafting, tours of Blyde River Canyon (p474) and more.

🛏 Sleeping

Sabie River Camp CAMPGROUND $
(☎013-764 3282; www.sabierivercamp.co.za; camping R110) Every level of camping is offered here, from sites where you pitch your own, to ready-pitched tents with beds and bedding (s/d R250/350) and en suite safari tents with their own private kitchen (s/d R350/500). It's in a lovely location on the banks of the Sabie River just out of town, off the road to Graskop.

★ **Woodsman** INN $$
(☎013-764 2015; www.thewoodsman.co.za; 94 Main St; s/d incl breakfast R560/795) A landmark pub, the Woodsman offers accommodation next door in an uninspiring brick building. They're not all that flash, but rooms are spacious with powerful showers, and there are small balconies upstairs. Best of all, it's stumbling distance to Sabie's best two eating options: the Woodsman itself and Wild Fig Tree.

Sabie Townhouse
B&B $$

(☑ 013-764 2292; www.sabietownhouse.co.za; Power St; s/d incl breakfast R650/1150; @ 🛜 🏊) This pretty river-stone house has a pool and terrace, and fabulous views over the hills. Travellers rave about the warm hospitality from Greg and family. The Zebra suite (s/d including breakfast R1250/1550) is the pinnacle of luxury here, with king-size bed, private patio and hot tub – best of all is the breakfast-in-bed service when you book this room.

✖ Eating

★ Wild Fig Tree
SOUTH AFRICAN $$

(☑ 013-764 2239; cnr Main & Louis Trichardt Sts; light meals R50-70, mains R90-130; ⊙ 8.30am-9pm Mon-Sat, to 8pm Sun) There's a meat-driven menu and a warm atmosphere here, with candles and African-print wall hangings. Try some of the more unusual game-meat options, including crocodile curry or ostrich kebabs. The ploughman's or trout platter makes a terrific lunch. With seating on a breezy balcony, it's a very pleasant place to while away a Sabie afternoon.

Woodsman
GREEK $$

(☑ 013-764 2015; 94 Main St; mains R80-155; ⊙ 7am-late) Half pub, half restaurant, the Woodsman offers great food with a Greek twist. Souvlaki, grilled calamari, *mezedhes* (starter plate) and other offerings are mixed with more local dishes: pan-fried trout and ostrich in red wine and oregano also feature. Most folk will find their spot, be it raucous beer drinking at the bar or fine dining by candelit table on the balcony.

🍷 Drinking & Nightlife

Sabie Brewery
BREWERY

(☑ 013-764 1005; www.sabiebrewery.com; 45 Main Rd; ⊙ 11am-6pm Sun-Wed, to 9pm Thu-Sat) Based in a 1921 trading post, this microbrewery is a new addition to Sabie's drinking and dining scene. Grab a taster platter of the full range to enjoy on the wooden deck overlooking Main St. It's a nice spot for a sundowner. Pub grub on offer includes burgers, cheese platters, curry and pies (mains R60 to R120).

ℹ Information

First National Bank (Market Sq) Has an ATM.

Sabie Internet Cafe (☑ 013-764 2875; Main St; per 30min R25; ⊙ 8am-5pm Mon-Fri, 9am-2pm Sat) Reliable internet access.

Komatiland Ecotourism (p473) Organises hikes in the region.

Tourist Information Office (Market Sq, Main St; ⊙ 9am-4pm Mon-Fri, to noon Sat, to 2pm Sun) Helpful office with accommodation recommendations and plenty of information on the local area.

Trips SA (☑ 013-764 1177; www.sabie.co.za; Main St) Information centre and booking agent for tours and accommodation.

ℹ Getting There & Away

There are daily buses from Jo'burg to Nelspruit (Mbombela), from where you can get minibus shared taxis to Sabie (R40, one hour between Nelspruit and Sabie). Minibus shared taxis also run frequently to and from Hazyview (R40, one hour). Minibus taxis stop next to the Engen petrol station.

KRUGER NATIONAL PARK

In terms of wildlife, **Kruger** (SAN Parks; ☑ 012-428 9111; www.sanparks.org) is one of the world's greatest national parks. The diversity, density and sheer numbers of animals is almost unparalleled, and all of Africa's iconic safari species – elephant, lion, leopard, cheetah, rhino, buffalo, giraffe, hippo and zebra – live out their dramatic days here, along with a supporting cast of 137 other mammals and over 500 varieties of bird.

Beautiful granite kopjes (hills) pepper the bushveld in the south, the Lebombo Mountains rise from the savannah in the east, and tropical forests cut across the far north of the 19,485-sq-km park.

A vast network of roads allows you to (incredibly) explore on your own, guided wildlife activities are abundant and accommodation is both plentiful and great value. The only downside is that it can sometimes become overly busy, meaning you essentially have to wait in line for your turn to view the latest sighting.

◉ Sights

Kruger encompasses a variety of landscapes and ecosystems, with each favouring particular species. That said, elephants, impalas, buffaloes, Burchell's zebras, wildebeest, kudus, waterbucks, baboons, vervet monkeys, leopards and smaller predators are widespread, and birdlife is incredible, especially along waterways. Rivers are hubs of activity; the major ones flow from west to east, including the Limpopo, Luvuvhu, Shingwedzi, Letaba, Olifants, Timbavati, Sand and Sabie. All of them are lined with riverine forest (often with enormous fig trees), which supports a wealth of wildlife.

While your drives along the extensive road network will throw up the majority of your animal sightings, there are numerous lookouts that offer great opportunities to see wildlife, or simply enjoy a stunning view.

👁 Southern Kruger

Southern Kruger is perhaps the most physically beautiful section of the park, with numerous granite kopjes climbing above the undulating grasslands and the thick stands of acacias, bushwillows, sycamore figs and flowering species such as the red-and-orange coral tree. The changes in elevation in the west offer you some staggering views over the wilderness that at times can look like a never-ending sea of green.

Its flora is fed by the park's highest amount of rainfall, some 50% more than in the north. This has in turn led to Kruger's highest proportion of wildlife calling the area home. The terrain is particularly favoured by white rhinos, buffaloes and zebras, but the thickness of the bush in some areas can make it harder to spot predators. Lions, hyenas and leopards are still spotted regularly, however, and wild dogs and cheetahs make occasional appearances.

This is the most visited section of Kruger.

👁 Central Kruger

With the exception of the Lebombo Mountains that flank the Mozambique border to the east, the landscape between the Sabie and Olifants Rivers is less varied than in the south, with large swaths of open savannah, particularly west and southeast of Satara. The buffalo grass and red grass in these areas is interspersed with knobthorn, leadwood and marula trees, and hosts large populations of impalas, zebras, wildebeest, kudus, giraffes and elephants. Joining them are predators, especially lions. Leopards are commonly sighted, and the road between Satara and Orpen is one of the most likely places in Kruger to spot cheetahs.

👁 Northern Kruger

North of the Olifants River the rolling landscape becomes more and more dominated by the elephant's favourite dish: the mopane tree. So it's no surprise that huge herds roam this region. Towards the Lebombo Mountains in the east the trees are so stunted by the clay soils on the basalt plains that the elephants' backs rise above the canopy. The

> ### ℹ KRUGER NP ENTRY
>
> Park entry for international visitors costs R304/152 per adult/child per day or for an overnight stay (SANParks' Wild Card (p520) applies). During school holidays park stays are limited to 10 days, and five days at any one rest camp (10 days if you're camping).
>
> Throughout the year authorities restrict the total number of visitors, so in the high season arrive early if you don't have a booking. Bicycles and motorcycles are not permitted.

mopaneveld also attracts large herds of buffalo and numerous tsessebes, elands, roans and sables. Leopards, lions and rhinos are less numerous.

Kruger's far north, around Punda Maria and Pafuri, lies completely in the tropics and supports a wider variety of plants (baobabs are particularly noticeable), high wildlife concentrations and an exceptional array of birds not found further south. Between the Luvuvhu and Limpopo Rivers is a gorgeous tropical riverine forest with figs, fever trees and jackalberries. The far north is a winter grazing ground for elephants, and lions and leopards are also regularly encountered.

🏃 Activities

Despite its mammoth size, Kruger is exceptionally well organised and there are numerous opportunities to enrich your wildlife watching throughout.

Wildlife Walks

The bush becomes so much more alive when you step out on foot and leave the security blanket of your vehicle behind. And it's often not the large wildlife that captures your imagination – the smallest of creatures, whether insects, reptiles or birds, take on a new light of importance and you truly start to understand how the environment works.

Most SANParks rest camps offer three-hour **morning bush walks** (R500) with knowledgeable armed guides, as do all of the lodges in the private concessions. Bergen-dal, Letaba and Skukuza currently also offer **afternoon walks** (R400), and Olifants offers **river walks** (R275), too. SANParks options can be booked in advance or arranged at the relevant camp upon arrival.

If you truly want to embrace the wilderness, book one of the park's **wilderness trails** or **backpack trails** well in advance

Kruger National Park

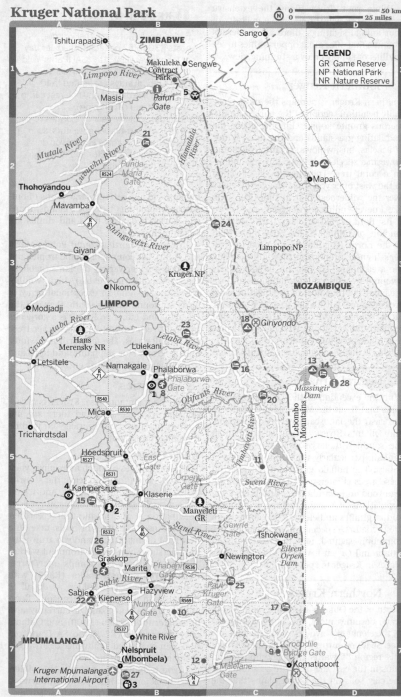

of your trip. Lasting four days (departing Wednesday and Sunday), these guided walks provide some of the park's most memorable experiences. The catered wilderness trails are based out of a remote camp with basic huts or safari tents, and are not overly strenuous, covering around 20km per day. Backpack trails are more rugged, with the group camping wild each evening (minimum of four people required). All walking groups limit numbers to eight participants, and no children under 12 are permitted.

Wildlife Drives

Self-driving is fantastic for so many reasons, but do strongly consider joining some guided drives – they are a great way to maximise your safari experience. For starters, all the SANParks options roam the park when you can't (i.e. before camps open and after they've closed), and guides will often shed light on species and behaviours that you weren't aware of. Guides at lodges in private concessions can also take you closer to the wildlife, as off-road driving is permitted in most.

SANParks operates three-hour **sunrise drives** and **sunset drives** at almost all rest camps, bushveld camps and many park gates. Costs (R280 to R390) depend on whether a 10- or 20-seat vehicle is used. Two-hour **night drives** (R230 to R320), which are great for nocturnal animals such as bush babies, hippos and big cats, are common, too. Book in advance or upon arrival. Children under the age of six are not permitted.

☞ Tours

Lonely Bull Back-Pack Trail   WILDLIFE
(☏ 012-428 9111; www.sanparks.org; 4 days R2700)
Following along the Letaba River and crossing various dry riverbeds, this trail throws up some great sightings of buffaloes, elephants and even leopards. You must be self-sufficient, with your own tent, cooking equipment and food. Water is available. Based from **Shimuwini Bushveld Camp** (☏ 013-735 6683, reservations 012-428 9111; www.sanparks.org; 4-/5-/6-person cottages from R1230/2040/2200).

Olifants River Back-Pack Trail   WILDLIFE
(☏ 012-428 9111; www.sanparks.org; 4 days R2700)
The trail's superb riverine setting offers the chance to get close to elephants, hippos, crocs and more. It's also known for birds, including the African fish eagle and the rare Pel's fishing owl. You must provide your own camping and cooking kit, as well as food and drink.

Kruger National Park

◉ Sights
1 Amarula Lapa B4
2 Blyde River Canyon Nature Reserve B6
3 Chimpanzee Eden.. .... B7
4 Echo Caves A5
5 Pafuri Picnic Area B1

✪ Activities, Courses & Tours
6 Big Swing A6
7 EcoTraining B1
8 Hans Merensky Estate B4
9 Lebombo Motorised Eco Trail C7
Lonely Bull Back-Pack Trail .... (see 23)
10 Napi Wilderness Trail B7
Olifants River Back-Pack Trail .... (see 20)
11 Sweni Wilderness Trail C5
12 Wolhuter Wilderness Trail B7

🛏 Sleeping
Berg-en-dal Rest Camp .... (see 12)
13 Campismo Aguia Pesqueira D4
14 Covane Community Lodge D4
Daan & Zena's .... (see 8)
15 Forever Blyde Canyon A5
Graskop Valley View
   Backpackers .... (see 6)
Kaia Tani .... (see 8)
16 Letaba Rest Camp C4
17 Lower Sabie Rest Camp C7

18 Machampane Wilderness Camp C4
19 Nhampfule Campsite D2
20 Olifants Rest Camp C4
Pretoriuskop Rest Camp .... (see 10)
21 Punda Maria Rest Camp B2
22 Sabie River Camp A6
Satara Rest Camp .... (see 11)
Sefapane .... (see 8)
23 Shimuwini Bushveld Camp B4
24 Shingwedzi Rest Camp C3
25 Skukuza Rest Camp C6
26 Thaba Tsweni Lodge A6
27 Utopia in Africa B7

✗ Eating
Buffalo Pub & Grill .... (see 8)

✪ Drinking & Nightlife
Sabie Brewery .... (see 22)

ⓘ Information
Bollanoto Tourism Centre .... (see 8)
28 Massingir Gate D4
Panorama Info .... (see 6)

ⓘ Transport
Minibus Shared Taxi Stand .... (see 6)
Minibus Taxis .... (see 22)

Water can be collected en route. Walks commence from Olifants Rest Camp.

Lebombo Motorised Eco Trail DRIVING
(☑012-426 5117, 012-428 9111; www.sanparks.org; per vehicle (max 4 people) R9000; ☺Apr-Oct) Covering a rugged 500km over five days (Sunday to Thursday), the Lebombo Motorised Eco Trail is Kruger's premier 4WD trail. Departing from Crocodile Bridge, the route skirts the park's entire eastern boundary before finishing at Pafuri picnic spot near Crooks Corner. Besides providing your own 4WD and camping kit, you must bring all your food, drink and cooking equipment.

Wolhuter Wilderness Trail WILDLIFE
(☑012-428 9111; www.sanparks.org; 4 days incl meals R4500) Wolhuter is the original wilderness trail, and is based in southern Kruger in an area inhabited by lions and white rhinos. The trail has great history, as does the ground it covers – Stone and Iron Age relics abound. Take it all in from high atop a granite kopje. Meet prior at **Berg-en-dal Rest Camp** (☑013-735 6106, reservations 012-428 9111; www.sanparks.org; camping per site R305, d bungalows with kitchen R1350; ❋🌊).

Napi Wilderness Trail WILDLIFE
(☑012-428 9111; www.sanparks.org; 4 days incl meals from R4500) Following the Mbyamithi and Napi Rivers between Pretoriuskop and Skukuza, Napi is known for its black and white rhino sightings at seasonal pans (waterholes). Camp consists of four safari tents. Trips commence at Pretoriuskop Rest Camp.

Sweni Wilderness Trail WILDLIFE
(☑012-428 9111; www.sanparks.org; 4 days incl meals R4500) A highly rewarding trail, Sweni is known for herds of wildebeest, zebras and buffaloes (and the lions that stalk them). It's an evocative environment with vast grassy plains. Sweni starts and finishes at Satara Rest Camp.

🎓 Courses

EcoTraining OUTDOORS
(☑013-752 2532; www.ecotraining.co.za) Various one-week to one-month field-guide training courses for budding professionals and enthusiastic amateurs. Go Bear Grylls wild in the bush for a week on the Wilderness Trails Skills option.

🛏 Sleeping

★**Letaba Rest Camp** BUNGALOW, CAMPGROUND **$$**
(☑013-735 6636, reservations 012-428 9111; www.sanparks.org; camping per site R305, d huts/safari

tents with shared bathroom R735/685, bungalows with/without kitchen from R1305/1215; ❋🌊) One of Kruger's best rest camps, this leafy haven has shady lawns, resident bushbucks, SAN-Parks' most attractive pools and a wide variety of accommodation, with great views from bungalows (No 32, of BD3U class is best) and six-person cottages (ask for newly refurbished No 101, class FQ6). There's a **Mugg & Bean** (www.themugg.com; mains R55-140), too.

★**Satara Rest Camp** BUNGALOW, CAMPGROUND **$$**
(☑013-735 6306, reservations 012-428 9111; www.sanparks.org; camping per site from R265, d bungalows with/without kitchen R1355/1220; ❋🌊) Satara – the second-largest option after Skukuza (p480) – may lack the riverside views of other camps, but it's optimally situated in the heart of 'big cat' territory, with open plains making viewing easier. An incongruous **Debonairs Pizza** (www.debonairspizza.co.za; pizzas R35-80) outlet joins **Mugg & Bean** (www.themugg.com; mains R55-140) here.

★**Olifants Rest Camp** BUNGALOW, COTTAGE **$$**
(☑013-735 6606, reservations 012-428 9111; www.sanparks.org; d bungalows with/without kitchenette R1460/1120; 🌊) High atop a bluff, this camp offers fantastic views down to the Olifants River, where elephants, hippos and numerous other animals roam. Bungalow Nos 1 and 9 (of BBD2V class) have the best views, as do the eight-person Nshawu and Lebombo self-catering guest houses (from R4300). There's also a new camp pool.

★**Skukuza Rest Camp** BUNGALOW, CAMPGROUND **$$**
(☑013-735 4152, reservations 012-428 9111; www.sanparks.org; camping per site R305, d safari tents without bathroom R595, d bungalows with/without kitchen R1310/1200; ❋🛜🌊) Although more town than camp, Kruger's largest camp is unobtrusive and has a great location on the Sabie River. There's an extensive range of accommodation, including four-/six-person cottages (from R2320). The attractive pool areas will lead you to linger. Additional services include bank, ATM, post office, doctor, library, museum and information centre.

★**Lower Sabie Rest Camp** BUNGALOW, CAMPGROUND **$$**
(☑013-735 6056, reservations 012-428 9111; www.sanparks.org; camping per site R305, huts without bathroom R595, d safari tents/bungalows with kitchen R955/1310; ❋🌊) Kruger's most popular rest camp is set on a gorgeous bend of the Sabie River that attracts elephants, hippos, buffaloes and other animals. LST2U-class safari tents and BD2U/BD3U bungalows

have river views. The riverside dining area of the **Mugg & Bean** (www.themugg.com; mains R55-140) is one of Kruger's most scenic, though the pool area is less so.

Pretoriuskop

Rest Camp   BUNGALOW, CAMPGROUND **$$**
([☑]013-735 5128, reservations 012-428 9111; www.sanparks.org; camping per site R305, d huts without bathroom R595, d bungalows with/without kitchen R1320/1160; [✿][✱]) Kruger's oldest and highest (thus coolest) camp is next to Numbi Gate. Located within an attractive region dotted with granite outcrops and frequented by rhinos, it's pretty too, with bougainvillea, flowering trees and a natural rock swimming pool. A wide choice of accommodation, ranging up to nine-person guest houses (from R4000). Food is limited to a Wimpy fast-food outlet (free wi-fi).

Shingwedzi

Rest Camp   BUNGALOW, CAMPGROUND **$$**
([☑]013-735 6806, reservations 012-428 9111; www.sanparks.org; camping per site from R265, d huts without bathroom R570, d bungalows with/without kitchen R1150/950; [✱][✱]) Tall mopane trees and palms shade this relaxed camp, with a mix of old-style bungalows in circle A and some large, new modern options in circle B (Nos 32–95 and 69–79 of BD2 class, and Nos 38–41 of the BG2 class). Although it's on the Shingwedzi River, only the **Tindlovu restaurant** (mains R55-150) offers views.

Punda Maria

Rest Camp   BUNGALOW, CAMPGROUND **$$**
([☑]013-735 6873, reservations 012-428 9111; www.sanparks.org; camping per site from R265, d bungalows with/without kitchen R1185/950, safari tents with kitchen R1125; [✱][✱]) Quaintly residing up a forested slope in far northern Kruger, this petite camp has plenty of old-world charm, with picturesque thatched-roof bungalows dating back to the 1930s. While those options are a little cramped, seven new 'luxury' safari tents provide more comfort and space (Nos 2 and 3 of ST2 class are the most private).

🛈 Getting There & Away

There are nine South African entry gates with unified hours of operation, which vary slightly by season (opening times range from 5.30am to 6am; closing times from 5.30pm to 6.30pm). Camp gate times are almost in complete unison with the park gates, and fines are issued for late arrival. It's also possible to enter Kruger from Mozambique at the Giriyondo and Pafuri border crossings (p524).

LIMPOPO

Limpopo is a huge and diverse province characterised by culture, history, vast open spaces and wildlife. In a single visit to Mapungubwe National Park visitors can walk through the country's most significant Iron Age site, gaze from a rocky bluff over the riverine landscape where South Africa, Botswana and Zimbabwe meet, and observe iconic animals such as meerkats and rhinos. Culture and traditional art shine in the enigmatic region of Venda, an area dotted with hilltops, lakes and forests of great spiritual significance. Nature takes centre stage in the Waterberg, where the eponymous Unesco biosphere reserve has endless skies, a landscape of distinctly South African beauty and great safari opportunities, particularly in Marakele National Park.

It's easy to rush through Limpopo, either en route to Kruger National Park on its eastern edge, or to Zimbabwe via Musina, but investing in a detour or two will pay rather lovely dividends.

Polokwane

POP 130,000

Once called 'the bastion of the north' by Paul Kruger, but now a little rough around the edges, Polokwane (formerly Pietersburg) is Limpopo's provincial capital. Although not unpleasant, it's a mish-mash of lively, semi-organised chaos (roughly between Civic Sq and the Indian Centre) and security fences sheltering vast gardens and clipped lawns (in the prim and proper eastern suburbs). Geographically, it's handy for visitors to use as a stopover, with plenty of decent guesthouses, two good information centres and a few interesting attractions in and around town.

◉ Sights

Polokwane Game Reserve   WILDLIFE RESERVE
([☑]015-290 2331; adult/child/vehicle R23/18/35; [◷]7am-5.30pm, last entry 3.30pm May-Sep, 7am-6.30pm, last entry 4.30pm Oct-Apr) Go on safari at this 32.5-sq-km reserve less than 5km south of Polokwane. It's one of the country's largest municipal nature reserves, with 21 wildlife species, including zebras, giraffes and white rhinos, plus a good network of roads and **hiking trails**.

Polokwane Art Museum   MUSEUM
([☑]015-290 2177; cnr Grobler & Hans van Ransburgh Sts, Library Gardens; [◷]9am-4pm Mon-Fri, 10am-noon Sat) [FREE] This museum is worth

Limpopo

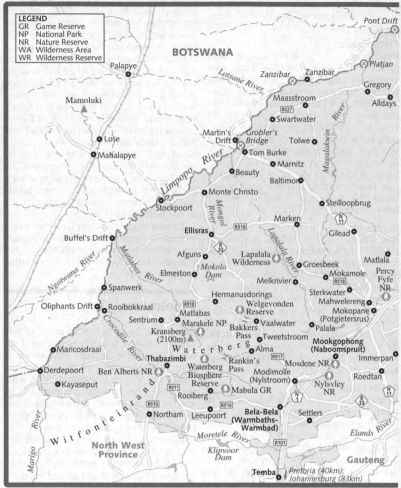

LEGEND
GR Game Reserve
NP National Park
NR Nature Reserve
WA Wilderness Area
WR Wilderness Reserve

ducking into for its modern take on colonialism, many depictions of Nelson Mandela and interesting displays on women and art in South Africa. It features artists from Limpopo and across the country.

Bakone Malapa Open-Air Museum MUSEUM
(☑ 073 216 9912; adult/child R12/7; ⊙ 8am-4pm Mon-Fri) Located 9km south of Polokwane on Rte 37 to Chuniespoort, this museum evokes the customs of the Northern Sotho people who lived here 300 years ago. The tour of the recreated village shows pots being made and demonstrations of tools, such as the antelope-horn trumpet and palm-root matches.

Hugh Exton Photographic Museum MUSEUM
(☑ 015-290 2186; Civic Sq; ⊙ 9am-3.30pm Mon-Fri) **FREE** Set in a restored 19th-century church, this museum covers Polokwane's first half-century and the second Anglo-Boer War through the work of the prolific photographer Hugh Exton (1864–1955), who left behind 23,000 glass negatives.

🛏 Sleeping

★**Plumtree Lodge** GUESTHOUSE $$
(☑ 015-295 6153; www.plumtree.co.za; 138 Marshall St; s/d incl breakfast R790/1030; ❀ 🐾 🖥) This German-run guesthouse's bungalow

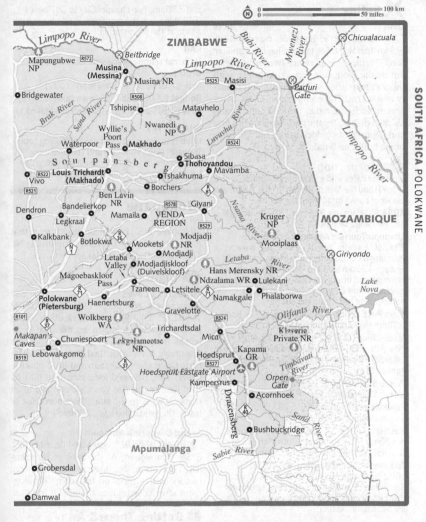

rooms are some of the most spacious and appealing in town. Standard features are high ceilings, lounge areas, minibars, DSTV and desks where you can tap into the free wi-fi. A poolside *lapa* (circular building with low walls and a thatched roof) bar and generous breakfast complete the package.

African Roots   GUESTHOUSE **$$**
(☏015-297 0113; www.africanroots.info; 58a Devenish St; s/d incl breakfast R750/950; ✲ 🛜 🛋) Based in a revamped 1920s farmhouse, the rooms here have original steel pressed ceilings and pine floors that blend comfortably with the modern facilities. Each one has its own entrance

into either the garden or pool area. Popular with businesspeople and tourists.

Protea Hotel – Ranch Resort   HOTEL **$$$**
(☏015-290 5000; www.theranch.co.za; Farm Hollandrift; r R1100-2900; ✲ 🛜 🛋) If it's a touch of luxury you're after and you don't mind being out of town, this ranch offers four-star rooms that feature varnished wooden furniture and large bathrooms with marble sinks. It's based on a private game reserve, where hyenas, giraffes, buffaloes and various antelope wander. You'll find it 25km southwest of Polokwane (on the N1).

✖ Eating

Dish INTERNATIONAL **$$**
(☑ 079 553 3790; 96 Burger St; mains R70-115; ☺ 9am-4pm Mon & Sat, to 10pm Tue-Fri, 11am-2pm Sun) The dining experience here is as pleasant as the food; in a renovated house with indoor and outdoor tables, the Dish is homely and warm. The menu covers most bases and includes lasagne, seafood, steak and chicken dishes. Try the garlic snails with feta and pepperdews to kick things off. There's a lunch buffet on Sundays.

❶ Information

There are cafes with wi-fi in the Savannah Centre (Rte 71) and the Mall of the North (N1). There are plenty of banks throughout the centre.

ABSA (70 Hans van Rensburg St) Has an ATM and exchange facilities.

Limpopo Tourism Agency (☑ office 015-293 3600, visitor info 015-290 2010; www.golimpopo.com; Southern Gateway, ext 4, N1; ☺ 8am-4.30pm Mon-Fri) Covers the whole province and offers the useful *Limpopo Explorer* map and *Know Limpopo* guide. On the N1, approaching town from the south.

Main Post Office (Landdros Mare St; ☺ 8am-5.30pm Mon-Fri, to 1pm Sat)

Medi-Clinic (☑ 015-290 3600, 24hr emergency 015-290 3747; www.mediclinic.co.za; 53 Plein St) Private hospital with 24-hour emergency centre.

Police Station (☑ 015-290 6000; Bodenstein St, cnr Schoeman St)

Polokwane Hospital (☑ 015-287 5000; Dorp St, cnr Hospital St) Public hospital.

PostNet (☑ 015-265 1341; Mall of the North; per 30min R25; ☺ 8am-4.30pm Mon-Fri, to 1pm Sat) Has reliable internet connections.

Tourism Information Centre (☑ 015-290 2010; cnr Thabo Mbeki & Church Sts, Civic Sq; ☺ 8am-5pm Mon-Fri) The best source for Polokwane information; has brochures and a list of accommodation.

❶ Getting There & Away

AIR

Polokwane Airport (☑ 015-288 1622; www.polokwaneinternationalairport.co.za) is 5km north of town.

Airlink (☑ 015-781 5823; www.flyairlink.com) Subsidiary of South African Airways with offices at the airport, flies daily to/from Jo'burg (one way from R1500).

BUS

Translux (☑ 0861 589 282; www.translux.co.za; Thabo Mbeki St, cnr Joubert St) Runs services to Jo'burg (R230, four hours) via Pretoria (R230, 3½ hours) at 10.30am, 11.15am

and 2.30pm. Two cheaper City to City buses (R190) leave in the mornings. Buses leave from a stop at the train station.

CAR

Major car rental agencies are located at the airport.

Avis (☑ 015-288 0171; www.avis.co.za)
Budget (☑ 015-288 0169; www.budget.co.za)
First (☑ 015-291 1579; www.firstcarrental.co.za)

SHARED TAXI

Minibus taxis run to destinations including Louis Trichardt (R60, 1½ hours) and Thohoyandou (R70, 2½ hours) from the rank at the Indian Centre, on the corner of Church and Excelsior Sts.

Mokopane

POP 30,000

Mokopane is a sizeable Bushveld town that makes a good place to break a trip up the N1. The main attraction is Makapan's Caves.

⊙ Sights

Makapan's Caves CAVE
(Makapansgat; ☑ 079 515 6491, 014-736 4328; adult/student R25/15) This National Heritage Site is of great palaeontological significance – artefacts from throughout the Stone and Iron Ages have been unearthed here. In the **Historic Cave**, chief Makapan and 1000-plus followers were besieged for a month in 1854 by Paul Kruger and the Voortrekkers. You must prebook visits to the site, 23km northeast of town; the guide also speaks French.

Arend Dieperink Museum MUSEUM
(☑ 015-491 9735; 97 Thabo Mbeki Dr; adult R22; ☺ 8am-4pm Mon-Fri) At the back of the tourism association, this museum recounts local history, with a focus on the town's development after Voortrekkers founded it in 1852.

❶ Getting There & Away

Translux and City to City have daily buses to Jo'burg (R210, 3¾ hours) via Pretoria; to Phalaborwa (R220, 3¾ hours) via Tzaneen; and to Sibasa (R190, four hours) via Polokwane and Louis Trichardt.

Minibus shared taxis leave from outside Shoprite on Nelson Mandela Dr; from Mokopane to Polokwane it's about R40.

Bela-Bela

POP 45,000

Bela-Bela is a hot, chaotic, seemingly perpetually busy place, but works as a spot to break a journey, especially if you like to indulge in 'warm baths'. Bela-Bela (aka Warmbaths) takes its name from the town's hot springs, which bubble out of the earth at a rate of 22,000L per hour and were discovered by the Tswana in the early 19th century. Bathing in the soporific pools is a popular treatment for rheumatic ailments.

⊙ Sights

Bambelela WILDLIFE RESERVE
(☑ 014-736 4090; www.bambelela.org.za; adult/child R100/50; ⊘ by appointment) This private rehabilitation centre focusses on vervet monkeys, with more than 300 being cared for here. Join a 1½ hour tour to learn more about the monkeys, from newborns through to those about to be released into the wild. Advance booking is essential. It's 20km northeast of town.

🏃 Activities

Hydro SPA
(☑ 014-736 8500; www.foreverwarmbaths.co.za; Chris Hani Dr; per person R130; ⊘ 7am-4pm &

5-10pm) At Warmbaths (a Forever Resort), the Hydro spa has a series of interlinked indoor and outdoor pools. Children head to the cold pools with twisty slides, while those who prefer a relaxing experience can wallow in warm baths (at 38°C to 42°C) or peruse the many other enhancers and therapies involving the cleansing waters.

🛏 Sleeping

Flamboyant Guesthouse B&B $
(☑ 076 259 7111; www.flamboyantguesthouse.com; 5 Flamboyant St; s/d incl breakfast R350/500; ❋) Among the jacaranda trees on the northern edge of town, the Flamboyant has flowery patios aplenty, decor that may take you back a few years and a personable owner. It's a no-frills place, but excellent value.

🍴 Eating

Toeka se Dae INTERNATIONAL $
(☑ 082 570 7923; www.toekasedae.co.za; Rte 516, Roodekuil Padstal; mains R40-70; ⊘ 9am-6pm) Pull up a chair fashioned from old tyres,

---

WORTH A TRIP

THE WATERBERG

Paul Kruger used to damn troublesome politicos with the phrase 'Give him a farm in the Waterberg', but that fate may not strike you as such a hardship. The 150km-long range, which stretches northeast from Thabazimbi past Vaalwater, is protected by the 15,000-sq-km Waterberg Biosphere Reserve, one of Africa's two savannah biospheres. Rising to 2100m, it has a mild climate and some wild terrain for spotting the Big Five (lion, leopard, buffalo, elephant and rhino), with rivers and distinctive mountains scything through bushveld and *sourveld* (a type of grassland).

Marakele National Park

This mountainous **national park** (☑ 014-777 6928; www.sanparks.org/parks/marakele/; adult/child R176/88; ⊘ 6am-5.30pm) is at the southwest end of the Waterberg Biosphere Reserve. The animals grazing beneath the red cliffs include elephants, black and white rhinos, giraffes, zebras, leopards and cheetahs. A great place to eyeball the landscape from is the vulture-viewing point (be warned: the road up is precipitous), where you can also see one of the world's largest colonies of the endangered Cape vulture (800-plus breeding pairs).

The park is divided into two sections, with the second section (you press a buzzer to open the gate) wilder and richer in wildlife (the Big Five are present). However, the gravel roads are in much better shape in the first section, so if it's been raining that may be as far as you want to go.

Bontle Camp (☑ in Pretoria 012-428 9111; www.sanparks.org; camping per 2-person site R305, d safari tents R1315) The park has tent sites at Bontle and safari tents with private bathroom and well-equipped kitchens.

Tlopi Tent Camp (☑ in Pretoria 012-428 9111; www.sanparks.org; tents R1360) This two-bed tented accommodation is 15km from reception. The furnished tents, overlooking a dam where antelope and wildebeest come to drink, have a bathroom and open-air kitchen, with refrigerator and braai (barbecue). Note: you'll have to bring your own food, as there is no shop in the park.

WORTH A TRIP

MAPUNGUBWE NATIONAL PARK

Stunningly stark, arid, rocky landscapes reverberate with cultural intrigue and wandering wildlife at **Mapungubwe National Park** (☏ 015-534 7923; www.sanparks.org/parks/mapungubwe; adult/child R176/88; ⊗ 6am-6.30pm Sep-Mar, 6.30am-6pm Apr-Aug). A Unesco World Heritage Site, Mapungubwe contains South Africa's most significant Iron Age site, plus animals ranging from black and white rhinos to the rare Pel's fishing owl and meerkats.

The park will realise its full potential when plans to incorporate it into an 8000-sq-km transfrontier conservation area stretching into Botswana and Zimbabwe are implemented by the respective governments. (In 2016, not much progress had been made on this.)

The park is as much about history as wildlife. In 1933 archaeologists unearthed a 13th-century grave site on Mapungubwe Hill, containing ornaments, jewellery, bowls and amulets, much of it covered in gold foil. The most spectacular of these pieces was a small, gold-covered rhinoceros. Apartheid kept this discovery under wraps, as the regime attempted to suppress any historical information that proved black cultural sophistication.

Interpretative Centre (guided tour R50; ⊗ 8am-4pm) The impressive centre, one of the country's finest modern buildings, was designed in sympathetic resemblance to the landscape. Inside it is contemporary, air-conditioned and has tastefully curated exhibits. There's plenty of information on the Mapungubwe cultural landscape, including finds from archaeological digs. Keep an eye out for the exquisite beadwork and the **replica of the famous gold rhino**.

Leokwe Camp (☏ in Pretoria 012-428 9111; www.sanparks.org; chalets from R1345; ❄ ☀) These chalets are the best we've seen in any South African national park. They include a huge living space, fully equipped kitchen, outside braai (barbecue) area and a traditional rondavel-thatch-roof design. There are also outdoor showers.

Limpopo Forest Camp (☏ in Pretoria 012-428 9111; www.sanparks.org; luxury tents R1250) This lovely forest location has well-equipped safari tents, with kitchen area containing fridge/freezer and a separate bedroom area with twin beds and a fan.

The park is a 60km drive from Musina on Rte 572 to Pont Drift. A 2WD will get you around but the tracks are pretty rough and you'll see more with a 4WD. The western side of the park is rougher again and you'll need a 4WD to really see it

number plates or tin baths and admire the inimitably quirky decor at this farm stall 15km out of town. Lunches are nothing spectacular – a familiar menu of burgers, toasted sandwiches and a few South African specialities – but it's a fun pit stop. You'll find it on the R516, southeast of Bela-Bela.

ℹ Getting There & Away

Minibus shared taxis run from Ritchie St, between the Forever Resort and Elephant Springs Hotel, to destinations including Polokwane (R80, 2½ hours) and Jo'burg (R90, two hours).

Musina

POP 43,000

Some 18km south of the Beitbridge border crossing into Zimbabwe, Musina (aka Messina) hums with typical border-town tension. It's busy, there are traffic snarls, and you should keep your wits about you when walking the streets. You will probably pass

through the town en route to the spectacular Mapungubwe National Park; the drive passes through a starkly beautiful landscape on empty, baobab-lined roads.

◉ Sights

Musina Nature Reserve   NATURE RESERVE
(☏ 015-534 3235; ⊗ 9am-6pm) **FREE** With South Africa's highest concentration of baobabs, the reserve is 5km south of the town off the N1, and has animals such as zebras, giraffes and the rare sable antelope.

🛏 Sleeping

Ilala Country Lodge   LODGE **$**
(☏ 076 138 0699; www.ilalacountrylodge.co.za; Rte 572; s/d incl breakfast R550/700; ☀) The sweeping views of the Limpopo River Valley into Zimbabwe at this old country lodge are something special. And there are few better places in Limpopo for a cold drink in the evening. The accommodation is superb value, with rooms sleeping four in the main homestead,

and huge chalets with lounge area, braai facilities and separate kitchen. It's 8km northwest of town, on the way to Mapungubwe.

Old Mine Guest House GUESTHOUSE $$
(☑ 082 568 3215; www.oldmineguesthouse.com; 1 Woodburn Ave; s/d R700/800; ✿ 🛜 ⚞) In a residence built in 1919 by the first manager of Musina's copper mine, this guesthouse reeks of class and olde-worlde charm (it is seemingly out of place in Musina!). A veranda overlooks the leafy grounds, and there are stylish rooms and self-catering units with private outdoor patio areas.

ℹ Information

ABSA (6 National Rd) Has change facilities and an ATM. Located on the N1 as it passes through the centre of town.

Musina Tourism (☑ 015-534 3500; www.golimpopo.com; National Rd; ⊗ 8am-4pm Mon-Fri) In a thatched hut on the way into town on the N1 from Polokwane. Very helpful office.

PostNet (National Rd; per hr R60; ⊗ 8.30am-4.30pm Mon-Fri, 8-11am Sat) Internet access.

ℹ Getting There & Away

The Zimbabwe border at Beitbridge, 15km north of Musina, is open 24 hours. There is a large taxi rank on the South African side of the border; taxis between the border and Musina cost R40 (20 minutes). If you want to take a minibus shared taxi further south than Musina, catch one here – there are many more than in Musina.

Greyhound (☑ 083 915 9000; www.greyhound.co.za) buses between Johannesburg (R440, seven hours) and Harare (R440, nine hours) stop in Musina and across the border in Beitbridge at the Ultra City.

Car rental is available at **Avis** (☑ 015-534 0124; www.avis.co.za; 3 National Rd, Musina Hotel; ⊗ 8am-5pm Mon-Fri, to noon Sat) for about R300 a day.

Venda

With perhaps the most enigmatic ambience of the Soutpansberg region, this is the traditional homeland of the Venda people, who moved to the area in the early 18th century. Even a short diversion from the freeway takes you through an Africa of mist-clad hilltops, dusty streets and mud huts. A land where myth and legend continue to play a major role in everyday life, Venda is peppered with lakes and forests that are of great spiritual significance, and its distinctive artwork is famous nationwide.

Elim

POP 16,500

The backwater town of Elim, some 25km southeast of Louis Trichardt, can be used as a base for touring the Venda and Tsonga-Shangaan art-and-craft studios, where you might come across a zebra-dung notebook or a ceremony taking place at a studio. There are also some worthwhile cooperatives, including the **Twananani weavers**.

🛏 Sleeping

Shiluvari Lakeside Lodge LODGE $$$
(☑ 015-556 3406; www.shiluvari.com; Albasini Dam; s/d incl breakfast R1115/1590; ⚞) Set amongst the greenery on the shores of Albasini Dam, this lodge is immersed in the local culture and countryside. Thatched chalets, standard rooms and a family suite, reached on walkways lined with sculptures, are adorned with local craftwork (which can be purchased in the on-site shop). There's also a **country restaurant** and **pub**.

🛍 Shopping

Mukondeni Pottery Village ARTS & CRAFTS
(☑ 076 873 5771; Mukondeni) This group of 15 women produce traditional- and contemporary-design pottery, including, pots, bowls and beads.

ℹ Information

Ribolla Tourism Association (☑ 015-556 4262; www.openafrica.org; Old Khoja Bldg) produces a useful brochure.

ℹ Getting There & Away

Translux buses serve Jo'burg (R280, seven hours).

Valley of the Olifants

These days the Valley of the Olifants may be largely devoid of pachyderms, but the subtropical area feels exotic in places. The region is culturally rich, being the traditional home of the Tsonga-Shangaan and Lobedu peoples.

Phalaborwa, a popular entry point to the Kruger National Park, is the start of the 'Kruger to Beach' trail to the Mozambican coast. The main town of Tzaneen and the pretty village of Haenertsburg make pleasant bases for trips to the scenic Modjadji and Magoebaskloof areas.

Letaba Valley

The Letaba Valley, east of Polokwane, is subtropical and lush, with tea plantations and fruit farms overlooked by forested hills. At Haenertsburg, known locally as 'The Mountain', Rte 71 climbs northeast over the steep Magoebaskloof Pass. There are plenty of places where you can stop for short hikes that are signposted from the road. A less scenic route to Tzaneen is via Rte 528, which runs along the gentler George's Valley.

Tzaneen

POP 14,600

An affluent town with a chaotic street layout, Tzaneen makes a very pleasant place to base yourself for a few days on your way to Kruger, down to the Blyde River Canyon or deeper into Limpopo's arts-and-crafts territory further north. The town has personality, although when we passed through, the town centre was looking worse for wear, with especially terrible litter. However, there are a few attractions and the cool mountainous retreat of Haenerstsburg is well worth a visit if not an overnight stop. It's often hot around here, but sudden downpours cool things off.

◉ Sights

Kings Walden   GARDENS

(www.kingswalden.co.za; Old Coach Rd, Agatha) **FREE** If steamy Tzaneen is making you droop, climb to this spectacular 300-sq-m English garden at 1050m in the African bush. The views of the Drakensberg Mountains from the sweeping lawn are interrupted only by a lightning-struck tree, and leafy walkways wind away from the swimming pool. From town, take Joubert St south then turn right onto Claude Wheatley St. There's no charge for the gardens but it's good form to get a drink or some cake from the restaurant.

Tzaneen Museum   MUSEUM

(Agatha St; by donation; ◷9am-4pm Mon-Fri, to noon Sat) The town museum has an impressive collection of artefacts, ranging from a 'house guard' totem used by the Rain Queens to some pretty spine-chilling Congolese masks. It's particularly interesting if you're visiting Modjadji or the Venda region.

🛏 Sleeping

Satvik Backpackers   HOSTEL $

(☑084 556 2414; www.satvik.co.za; George's Valley Rd; camping per person R85, dm/d/cottage R140/350/710) These cottages, on a slope above a dam, have a kitchen and a braai, along with views of wooded hills. Activities such as fishing are offered, but watch out for the crocs and hippos. Head out of town south on Agatha St – it's about 4km away.

★**Kings Walden**   HOTEL $$$

(☑015-307 3262; www.kingswalden.co.za; Old Coach Rd, Agatha; s/d incl breakfast R1150/2060; 🛜🐾) The sizeable rooms here are as dreamy as the gardens and mountains they overlook, with fireplaces, antiquated prints everywhere, and bathrooms you could get lost in. Picnic hampers can be provided; four-course dinners are R320 per person.

✕ Eating

Highgrove Restaurant   INTERNATIONAL $$

(☑015-307 7242; Agatha St; mains R60-120; ◷7am-8.30pm) Based at Highgrove Lodge, this is one of Tzaneen's most reliable restaurants. Dishes include steaks, pasta, burgers and hearty breakfasts. With a lovely poolside setting, it's a lovely spot for dinner.

❶ Information

ABSA (Danie Joubert St) Has an ATM and exchange facilities.

Limpopo Parks & Tourism Board (☑015-307 3582; www.tzaneeninfo.co.za; Old Gravelotte Road; ◷8am-4.30pm Mon-Fri) On Rte 71 towards Phalaborwa.

Post Office (Lannie Lane) Behind Danie Joubert St.

❶ Getting There & Away

There is a daily Translux bus to Phalaborwa (R190, one hour), and to Jo'burg (R300, 7 hours) and Polokwane (R220, two hours). **Checkers** (Letaba Blvd shopping centre) sells tickets.

Most minibus shared taxis depart from the rank behind the Tzaneng Mall; destinations include Polokwane (R70, two hours).

Phalaborwa

POP 13,000

Phalaborwa makes an ideal starting point if you're intending to explore central and northern Kruger. For people with limited time in South Africa, it is possible to visit Kruger NP by flying from Jo'burg to Phalaborwa and hiring a car at the airport (with its thatched terminal building). Phalaborwa rocks between suburban tidiness and the bush, with a green belt in the centre and the occasional warthog grazing on a lawn.

The town is also a gateway to Mozambique – it's possible to drive across Kruger and into Mozambique via the Giriyondo Gate in a vehicle with good clearance.

◉ Sights

Amarula Lapa DISTILLERY
(☑015-781 7766; www.amarula.com; Rte 40; ⊗9am-6pm Mon-Fri, to 4pm Sat) FREE The best way to enjoy a glass of creamy Amarula liqueur is to visit the Amarula Lapa, located next to the production plant, 10km west of Phalaborwa. Groups of at least five can visit the plant during harvest season; at other times, exhibits and a seven-minute DVD explain all.

🏃 Activities

Hans Merensky Estate GOLF
(☑015-781 3931; www.hansmerensky.com; 3 Copper Rd; 9-/18-hole round R280/495) Just south of Phalaborwa is an 18-hole championship golf course with a difference: here you might have to hold your shot while wildlife (elephants included) crosses the fairways. Be careful – the wildlife is indeed 'wild'.

Africa Unlimited WILDLIFE WATCHING
(☑015-781 7466; www.africaunltd.co.za) Offers activities including culture tours, river cruises, bush walks, visits to animal rehabilitation centres and trips through Kruger to Mozambique.

🛌 Sleeping

Daan & Zena's GUESTHOUSE $
(☑015-559 8732; www.daanzena.co.za; 15 Birkenhead St; r R500, apt R900; ❉ 🛜 🏊) Though looking a bit worn around the edges these days, Daan & Zena's is brought to life by lashings of colour and a friendly atmosphere, and it still presents great value. The two-room flats across the road from the main establishment are spacious and well equipped; No 1 has a door leading onto a lovely grassed area.

★Kaia Tani GUESTHOUSE $$
(☑015-781 1358; www.kaiatani.com; 29 Boekenhout St; r per person incl breakfast R690; ❉ 🛜 🏊) This 'exclusive guesthouse' delivers a lot of style for your money. The six rooms with traditional African furniture have flourishes such as rope-lined wooden walls, and a thatch restaurant-bar overlooks the rock swimming pool. It's off Essenhout St.

Sefapane LODGE $$$
(☑015-780 6700; www.sefapane.co.za; Copper Rd; standard rondavels per person from R1700; ❉ 🛜 🏊) With a whiff of exclusivity, this 1000-sq-m resort has a restaurant and sunken bar, a long list of safaris for guests and mushroom-shaped rondavels. There are spacious self-catering 'safari houses' overlooking a dam, and donations are made to projects for local children. Lots of packages available, from two to seven nights.

🍴 Eating

★Buffalo Pub & Grill PUB FOOD $$
(☑015-781 0829; 1 Lekkerbreek St; mains R80-150; ⊗11am-11pm; ❉) If you've emerged from Kruger feeling like a hungry lion, stop here for some pub grub. It's a very meat-driven menu – for a lean steak alternative try the ostrich or impala fillet. Excellent service, and there's a terrace for alfresco dining.

ℹ Information

Bollanoto Tourism Centre (☑087 151 1164; www.phalaborwa.co.za; Hendrick van Eck St; ⊗8am-6pm Mon-Fri) Helpful info office.
Cyber World (Tambotie St, Tambotie Park; wi-fi per hr R40, internet per hr R50; ⊗8am-5.30pm Mon-Fri, 9am-1pm Sat; 🛜) Good, reliable internet connections.

ℹ Getting There & Away

AIR
Airlink (☑015-781 5823; www.flyairlink.com), which has an office at the airport, flies daily to Jo'burg (from R1750). The airport is 2km north of town.
SA Express (p526)

BUS
Translux connects Phalaborwa with Jo'burg (R320, eight hours) via Tzaneen (R190, one hour), Polokwane (R250, 3½ hours) and Pretoria (R320, seven hours); City to City buses travel to Jo'burg (R250, 9½ hours) via Middelburg.

CAR
Hiring a car is often the cheapest way of seeing Kruger National Park, starting at about R280 per day. Major car rental companies have offices at the airport; they're generally open 8am to 5pm Monday to Friday, and also to meet flights or by appointment at weekends.
Avis (☑015-781 3169; www.avis.co.za)
Hertz (☑015-781 3565)

NORTH WEST PROVINCE

This stretch of bushveld between Pretoria and the Kalahari is famous for Sun City, the southern hemisphere's answer to Las Vegas. Though its slot machines and kitsch edifices are grotesquely fascinating, you may prefer a different kind of gambling in nearby Pilanesberg National Park. Wager that lions and rhinos will wander to the waterhole you have staked out – sightings on self-drive safaris come with a serendipitous thrill.

Alternatively, improve your odds of spotting elusive predators in Pilanesberg and Madikwe Game Reserve by joining a guided drive or walk. And for that once-in-a-lifetime, romantic *Out of Africa*–style experience, a night in the bush at Madikwe's exclusive lodges can't be beat.

Conveniently, these opportunities to encounter both big cats and one-armed bandits are all within four hours' drive of Jo'burg. En route, the Magaliesberg area offers detours from the N4, ranging from zip lining to rural accommodation near Rustenburg.

Rustenburg

POP 105,000

Sitting on the edge of the Magaliesberg range, Rustenburg is a big country town with an urban grittiness to its crowded central business district. Pedestrians weave between honking cars on Nelson Mandela Dr (the main drag through the long downtown area), and sidewalks heave with vendors selling mobile-phone cases and the like in front of takeaway chicken shops and undertakers. It's Rustenburg's location, however, just 40km southeast of Sun City and Pilanesberg National Park, that is its main selling point – it's an option for travellers wishing to visit these major attractions without paying high accommodation rates.

🛏 Sleeping

Bushwillows B&B   B&B $

(📱082 680 5890; wjmcgill@lantic.net; r per person incl breakfast R250; 🖥) This country retreat is owned by local wildlife artist Bill McGill, whose paintings decorate the breakfast room. Birdwatching tours to areas such as Pilanesberg are offered. Coming from the Waterfall Mall, look for the white sign on the right af-

North West Province

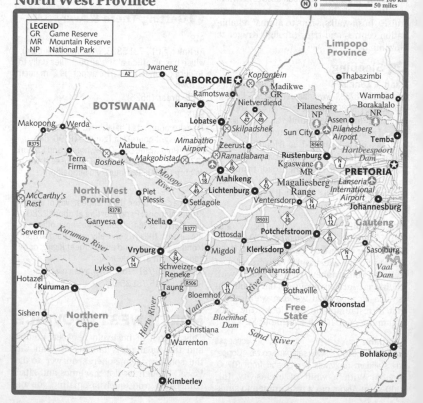

ter 5km. From there, it's 2km up the hill. The rooms are basic and the decor frozen in time, but this matters little in light of the warm welcome you'll get, and the wonderful view of the Magaliesberg from the terrace.

★ Boubou
B&B $$

(☑ 083 457 9954; www.boubou.co.za; Doornlaagte, Kommissiesdrift; s/d incl breakfast from R770/1160; P ☎ ⊡ ⊛) This tranquil option in a small nature reserve will likely have you extending your stay in Rustenburg. There's excellent birdwatching and you might spot a range of antelope from your pool lounger. Rooms come with great big comfy beds and French doors opening out onto the garden. Guests can use the kitchen; traditional meals are available if you book ahead. It's 28km out of town, off the R52 to Koster.

✖ Eating

Brauhaus am Damm
GERMAN $$

(☑ 014-004 0382; www.brauhaus.co.za; Rte 24, Olifants Nek Dam; mains R70-130; ⊙ Tue-Sat 11am-10pm, Sun to 4pm) On a sunny afternoon join Rustenburg locals and Gauteng weekenders at this cavernous restaurant with a large deck overlooking the Olifants Nek Dam. German food like sausage platters and *eisbein* (pork knuckle) come accompanied by award-winning beers from the on-site microbrewery, one of few in the country with a female brewer at the helm. The *weissbier* (wheat beer) is excellent. It's 20km south of Rustenburg on the R24.

ℹ Information

Tourist Information Centre
(☑ 014-597 0904; www.tourismnorthwest.co.za; cnr Nelson Mandela St & Kloof Rd; ⊙ 8am-4.30pm Mon-Fri, to noon Sat) Rustenburg's helpful, well-stocked tourist information centre is located in the municipal offices that sprawl between Nelson Mandela Dr and Fatima Bhayat St just west of the Rte 24 turn-off. It provides sundry brochures and a local map.

ℹ Getting There & Away

Rustenburg is just off the N4, about 120km northwest of Jo'burg and 110km west of Pretoria. Intercape has buses from Johannesburg (R200, 1½ hours) but if you want to explore the surrounding region, you'll need to hire a car.

Sun City

At **Sun City** (☑ 014-557 1580; www.suninternational.com/sun-city; day visitors R60, hotel guests free; ⊙ 24hr; ⚑), the legendary creation of entrepreneur Sol Kerzer, Disneyland collides with ancient Egypt in Africa's version of Vegas. Filled with gilded statues of lions and monkeys, acres of artificial beaches, 1200 hotel rooms and line upon line of clinking slot machines, it serves no other purpose than to entertain. Yet while there's no question this gambling-centric resort is almost grotesquely gaudy, a visit can be pretty damn fun.

The complex is dominated by the Lost City, an extraordinary piece of kitsch claiming to symbolise African heritage. It has even less to do with African culture than Disneyland Paris has to do with French, but it's entertaining.

Should the gambling weigh on your conscience, you can rest easy in regards to at least one area – the resort is green. Yes, despite the show of lavishness, Sun City has received awards for practising sustainable, environmentally friendly tourism.

◉ Sights

Entertainment Centre
CASINO

(⊙ 24hr; ⚑) As well as housing smoking and nonsmoking casinos, this two-storey centre has food courts, shops, cinemas and the Superbowl performance venue. Its style might best be described as 'nouveau Flintstone', embellished by a jungle theme.

🏃 Activities

Visit the Welcome Centre (p492) for the lowdown on the mind-boggling range of activities available. These include golfing (on two different courses), jet skiing, parasailing, a crocodile park and zip lining, plus wildlife drives at the neighbouring Pilanesberg National Park.

Maze
OUTDOORS

(www.suninternational.com/sun-city/activities/maze; adult/child R120/60; ⊙ 9am-9pm) An enormous labyrinth in the form of an archaeological site.

Valley of the Waves
WATER PARK

(www.suninternational.com/sun-city; adult/child R120/70, hotel guests free; ⊙ 9am-6pm Sep-Apr, 10am-5pm May-Aug) This water park is gaudy and outlandish even by Sun City's standards – and children love it. Its centrepiece is the **Roaring Lagoon**, a 6500-sq-metre wave pool with palm-fringed beach. Slides, flumes and chutes such as the 70m-long **Temple of Courage** get the adrenaline flowing; tubing on the **Lazy River** and swimming in the **Royal Bath** pool offer slower-paced fun.

☞ Tours

Mankwe Gametrackers   SAFARI, OUTDOORS
(☎014-552 5020; www.mankwegametrackers.
co.za; Welcome Centre; ⏰5am-7pm) From Sun
City, this tour and outdoor activity company
runs two three-hour **wildlife drives** (adult/
child R510/255) to Pilanesberg National
Park each day, usually departing at 5.30am
and 5pm (times vary depending on the time
of year). It also runs four-hour, early-morning **wildlife walks** (per person R550) in the
park (ages 16 and over only).

🛏 Sleeping

Palace of the Lost City   RESORT $$$
(☎bookings 011-780 7855; www.suninternational.
com/palace; r incl breakfast from R4600; ❉🛜🏊)
Ranked one of the top hotels in the world by
travel magazines and websites, this hotel does
a good job at redefining the fantasy of luxury.
The rooms are done up with bold-coloured
carpets and duvets and hand-painted ceil-
ings, but seem a bit unimaginative when
compared with the awesome public spaces.

Cascades   RESORT $$$
(☎bookings 011-780 7855; www.suninternation-
al.com/sun-city/cascades; r incl breakfast from
R4500; ❉🛜🏊) In this azure, Mediterrane-
an-inspired environment, waterfalls cascade
into a lake and cocktails go down nicely in
the beach bar. There are multiple pools, alfresco island dining at Santorini restaurant,
and luxuries such as dressing rooms in the
palatial bedrooms.

Soho   CASINO HOTEL $$$
(☎bookings 011-780 7855; www.suninternational.
com/sun-city/soho; r incl breakfast from R2990;
❉🛜🏊) Sun City's liveliest hotel (and its first)
packs in casinos, slot machines and an enter-
tainment centre, as well as multiple restau-
rants and bars. With foliage hanging in the
jungle-themed foyer and oversize roulette
chips stacked outside the Raj Indian restau-
rant, it's a good choice for anyone looking for
a little hedonism with their gambling.

Cabanas   RESORT $$$
(☎bookings 011-780 7855; www.suninternational.
com/sun-city/cabanas; r incl breakfast from R1900;
❉🛜🏊) Sun City's most informal and affordable option is the best one for families,
with facilities and activities for children. The
modern rooms have retro styling and upmarket conveniences, and the atmosphere
is laid-back, from the balconied foyer and
onward. Family rooms with a fold-out sofa
and up to eight beds are available.

ℹ Information

The **Welcome Centre** (☎014-557 1543; ⏰8am-
7pm Mon-Fri, to 10pm Sat & Sun) at the entrance
to the Entertainment Centre has maps and any
information you could possibly need. Also here
are lockers and a branch of Hertz car rental.

ℹ Getting There & Away

Sun City is less than three hours' drive northwest
of Jo'burg, signposted from the N4. Coming from
Gauteng on the N4, the most straightforward
route is to stay on the freeway past Rustenburg
and take Rte 565 via Phokeng and Boshoek.

The car park for nonguests is at the entrance,
about 2km from the Entertainment Centre.
Buses and an elevated monorail Sky Train (the
latter offering good views of the complex and
Pilanesberg) shuttle people from the car park to
the Entertainment Centre and Cascades, passing Sun City Cabanas and Sun City Hotel.

Tours from Gauteng combine Sun City and
Pilanesberg.

Ingelosi Shuttles (☎014-552 3260; www.
ingelositours.co.za; Welcome Centre; per 2
people R1150) offers a shuttle service from set
pickup points in Johannesburg.

Pilanesberg National Park

Occupying an eroded alkaline crater north
of Sun City, in a transition zone between
the Kalahari and wet lowveld vegetation,
the 550-sq-km **Pilanesberg National Park**
(☎014-555 1600; www.pilanesbergnationalpark.
org; adult/child R65/20, vehicle R20, map R20;
⏰5.30am-7pm Nov-Feb, 6am-6.30pm Mar, Apr, Sep
& Oct, 6.30am-6pm May-Aug) is a wonderfully
scenic place to see a variety of South African
wildlife.

Conceived in the late 1970s as a back-
to-nature weekend escape for nearby city
dwellers, Pilanesberg remains a haven
where lions, buffaloes and day-trippers still
roam. But although the park may appear
developed in comparison with some South
African wildernesses, don't mistake it for a
zoo: the animals roaming the extinct vol-
cano crater are 100% wild. All the Big Five
are here, as are cheetahs, caracals, African
wild dogs, jackals, hyenas, giraffes, hippos,
zebras, a wide variety of antelope (including
sables, elands and kudus) and 300-plus bird
species.

🏃 Activities

Most lodges in the park offer sunrise and
sunset wildlife drives, but with nearly 200km
of excellent gravel roads, Pilanesberg was

designed with self-drive safaris in mind. Although you have a better chance of spotting cats on one of the ranger-led wildlife drives, steering yourself is cheaper, and more rewarding when you do see an animal. You'll never forget the first time you brake to let a lumbering elephant cross your path – from the size of these animals to how tough and wrinkly a pachyderm's rump looks up close.

Driving yourself around the park also means you can move at your own pace. And in Pilanesberg, this means slowly. Devote at least a few hours to sitting with a cooler full of beverages and a pair of binoculars in a public hidesand wait for the action to come to you. Basically big, raised, covered decks with chairs that have been camouflaged so the wildlife doesn't notice you, these hides have been purposefully constructed next to water sources that attract thirsty animals.

Keep in mind that no matter which way you choose to explore the park, Pilanesberg is still an urban reserve. It's very popular, and the number of folks driving around, combined with the guided-tour vehicles, means there's usually a lot of traffic. Pilanesberg has strict regulations about driving off-road – you can't do it. If your vision of the perfect safari includes a remote bush location, few roads and even fewer cars, drive three hours further northwest and shell out the extra cash to stay in Madikwe Game Reserve instead.

Mankwe Gametrackers SAFARI
(☏014-555 5469; www.mankwegametrackers.co.za; Manyane) Provides outdoor adventure activities in Pilanesberg.

🖝 Tours

Mankwe Gametrackers SAFARI
(☏014-556 2710; www.mankwegametrackers.co.za; Bakgatla; ⊙5am-7pm) This outdoor adventure company runs a variety of organised activities within the park. The three-hour **wildlife drives** (adult/child R510/255; 5.30am, 9.30am and 5pm) provide a good introduction to wildlife watching, and you have a better chance of spotting animals when driven around by a knowledgeable ranger. Another option is a four-hour **wildlife walk** (per person R550); you must be aged 16 or older to take part.

🛏 Sleeping

Kwa Maritane LODGE $$$
(☏014-552 5100; www.legacyhotels.co.za/en/hotels/kwamaritane; s/d with half board R3500/4900;

❄️📶🏊) Kwa Maritane's smart thatched rooms encircle its pool, and the restaurant veranda has a bird's-eye view of bush-covered hills and rocky cliffs. The **Kwa Lefakeng restaurant** puts on various buffets and carveries, or else you can order à la carte out on the terrace.

Manyane RESORT, CAMPGROUND $$$
(☏014-555 1000; www.goldenleopardresorts.co.za; camping R180, chalet s/d incl breakfast R2110/2220; ❄️🏊) Manyane's thatched African chalets are comfortable and well-equipped. The restaurant borders an enticing pool, with a number of its tables sitting on a patio under thatched awnings. Baboons regularly scamper through the dry and dusty camping area.

Bakgatla RESORT, CAMPGROUND $$$
(☏014-555 1000; www.goldenleopardresorts.co.za; camping R160, chalet incl breakfast from R1900; ❄️🏊) This resort is nestled among some hills and has as its centrepiece a massive U-shaped pool. The restaurant was being extensively renovated when we visited; there's also a superette with basic supplies at the conference centre. The colonial-style chalets have private patios.

❶ Getting There & Away

Tours from Gauteng combine Pilanesberg and Sun City. Bakubung and Kwa Maritane gates are convenient if you're driving from Sun City. If you're driving down from Limpopo on the Rte 510 (between Rustenburg and Thabazimbi), Manyane and Bakgatla gates are your closest entry point.

❶ Getting Around

Kubu/Kgabo Dr, crossing the park between Bakubung and Bakgatla Gates, is tarred, as are Tau Link and Tshwene Dr, which link Kubu/Kgabo Dr and Manyane Gate. The gravel roads are in good condition and passable in 2WD cars.

There is a 40km/h speed limit in the park and you can't go much faster on the roads skirting Pilanesberg. Be aware of cattle and donkeys wandering onto the road; locals may wave to warn you of a herd ahead.

Madikwe Game Reserve

Madikwe (☏018-350 9938; www.experience-madikwe.com; adult/child R180/90; ⊙6am-6pm) is the country's fourth-largest reserve, covering 760 sq km of bushveld, savannah grassland and riverine forest on the edge of the Kalahari. It offers Big Five wildlife watching and dreamy lodging among striking (and malaria-free) red sand and clay-thorn bushveld.

Experiencing Madikwe isn't cheap, but you get what you pay for at these exclusive bush hideaways. The animals have become used to the sturdy, open-sided jeeps and don't view them as a threat. So when your guide pulls up to a herd of buffalo and cuts the engine, you usually have time to snap some good shots without your subjects tearing off.

🏃 Activities

Madikwe does not allow self-drive safaris or day visitors, which means you must stay at one of its 16 lodges to explore the reserve. Rangers communicate via radio with the other drivers in the reserve, so if a family of lions napping in the shade of a thorn tree is spotted nearby, your driver will hear about it. Restrictions on driving off road are minimal and the jeeps are tough enough to tackle most terrain, getting you close to the animals.

🛏 Sleeping

★ **Mosetlha Bush Camp**
& Eco Lodge   LODGE $$$
(☏ 011-444 9345; www.thebushcamp.com; Abjaterskop Gate; s/d per person incl full board R2795/4590) 🌿 Madikwe's second-oldest lodge is also the reserve's only non-five-star option, but Mosetlha's relatively low rates are not its only attraction. With nine open-fronted cabins around the camp fire, Mosetlha is truly off the grid – it has no electricity or running water. But staying in the unfenced camp, which animals wander into at night, is romantic rather than rough.

Buffalo Ridge Safari Lodge   LODGE $$$
(☏ 011-234 6500; www.buffaloridgesafari.com; Wonderboom Gate; s/d chalet incl full board R5900/9100; ❄☀) This swish lodge exemplifies the sustainable, community-based tourism envisioned by Madikwe's founders – owned by the Balete people from the local village of Lekgophung, it was the first of its kind in South Africa. Designed by a well-known local architect, Buffalo Ridge has eight ultraprivate thatched chalet suites that blend seamlessly into the bushveld.

ℹ️ Getting There & Away

Madikwe is next to the Kopfontein Gate/Tlokweng Gate border crossing with Botswana, about 400km northwest of Johannesburg and Pretoria via the N4 and Rte 47/49 (the road is referred to by both numbers).

Madikwe's main gates are Abjaterskop and Wonderboom, adjoining Rte 47/49 on the reserve's western side; Tau and Deerdepoort on the northern side; and Molatedi on the eastern side. All the lodges can be reached from Rte 47/49; when you make a reservation, your lodge will give you directions.

There is one charter flight per day between OR Tambo International Airport in Jo'burg and the landing strip in Madikwe. Tickets cost around R4000 return, and are arranged through your lodge at the time of booking.

If driving yourself from Madikwe to Sun City and Pilanesberg, ask your lodge for directions and take the back roads. This route is quicker and bypasses the R75 charge at the Swartruggens toll gate on the N4. This shortcut is not recommended en route to Madikwe as it's trickier in that direction and getting lost is more likely.

Without your own transport, the best option is to organise a transfer through your lodge. Alternatively, take a Gaborone (Botswana) bus and arrange for your lodge to pick you up from the Kopfontein border crossing, where the bus will stop.

Mahikeng

POP 15,200

The capital of North West Province is a friendly place with a sizeable middle-class black population. It's quite rundown and not worth a special visit, but if you're passing through, Mahikeng Museum makes an interesting pit stop.

Many locals still refer to the town as 'Mafikeng', which it was called until the name change was approved in 2010.

👁 Sights

Mafikeng Museum   MUSEUM
(☏ 018-381 0773; Martin St, cnr Carrington St; by donation; ⊙ 8am-4pm Mon-Fri, 10am-12.30pm Sat) Among the many displays in this excellent regional museum are exhibits charting the rise of the Boy Scout Movement and a presentation on the famous 217-day siege (from the Second Anglo-Boer War), with original photographs and documents, and information about the role played by the town's black population. It occupies the former **town hall**, which was built in 1902.

🛏 Sleeping & Eating

Protea Hotel Mafikeng   HOTEL $$
(☏ 018-381 0400; www.proteahotels.com/mahikeng; 80 Nelson Mandela Dr; r from R900; P❄@☎☀) The Protea is a stylish accommo-

dation option, and one of the more pleasant places in town to loiter, with its pillars and the vintage photos of old Mahikeng decorating reception. Rooms feature white fluffy duvets with lots of pillows, heavy curtains, mood lighting and international TV channels. Facilities include a bar and restaurant.

Crossing Mall   FAST FOOD
(Sekame St, cnr Nelson Mandela Dr) The main shopping mall in town has a handful of decent chain restaurants – Nando's or Ocean Basket are the best options. There's a supermarket and liquor store here, too.

❶ Information

North West Parks & Tourism Board (☑018-381 7341; www.tourismnorthwest.co.za; 14 Tillard Street; ☺8am-4.30pm Mon-Fri) It doesn't have much printed material, but the staff are helpful and can provide a map of town.

❶ Getting There & Away

Mahikeng is 25km southeast of the Ramatlabama border crossing with Botswana. The best way to get there is by car. From Pretoria or Rustenburg take the N4 to Zeerust and then veer off on Rte 27 to Mahikeng. The town is also on the N18, which heads south towards Northern Cape and Free State.

City to City (p527) has a daily service between Mahkeng and Jo'burg (R160, five hours).

NORTHERN CAPE

With only a million people inhabiting its 373,000 sq km, the Northern Cape is South Africa's last great frontier. Its scattered towns are hundreds of kilometres apart, connected by empty roads across the sublime, surreal wilderness expanses of Namakwa, the Kalahari and Upper Karoo. Under the remorseless sun, vehicles share park roads with lions, dune boards swish down roaring sands, and Kimberley's pubs serve cold beer as they have since the 19th-century diamond rush.

It's a raw, elemental land, where gnarly camel thorn, quiver and Halfmens trees break the boundless horizons. Yet some of nature's greatest tricks here are instances of rejuvenating beauty. The Gariep (Orange) River waters the dry region, creating the Green Kalahari with its vineyards and epic Augrabies Falls. Following the rains, red Kalahari sands shimmer with grasses, and Namakwa's spring blooming carpets rocky hills and plains with wildflowers.

Kimberley

POP 97,000

Kimberley, the provincial capital, is the centre of the region known as the Diamond Fields. The city that gave birth to De Beers and 'A Diamond is Forever' remains a captivating place, with a Wild West vibe.

The last earth was shovelled at the landmark Big Hole back in 1914, but the Northern Cape's capital remains synonymous with diamonds. Step inside an atmospheric old pub, with dark interiors, scarred wooden tables and last century's liquor ads, and you'll feel you've been transported back to Kimberley's rough-and-ready mining heyday. Wander the period-perfect Victorian mining settlement at the Big Hole Complex, and you'll leave imagining Cecil Rhodes is alive and well and pointing his horse towards Rhodesia.

The Northern Cape's only real city is also home to fantastic museums, some wonderful accommodation and Galeshewe, a township with plenty of its own history.

◉ Sights

★ Big Hole   MUSEUM
(☑053-839 4600; www.thebighole.co.za; West Circular Rd; adult/child R100/60; ☺8am-5pm, tours on the hour) Although the R50 million that turned the Big Hole into a world-class tourist destination came from De Beers, touring the world's largest hand-dug hole gives an honest impression of the mining industry's chequered past in Kimberley. Visits start with an entertaining 20-minute film about mining conditions and characters in late-19th-century Kimberley, and a walk along the Big Hole viewing platform. The open-air steel contraption, jutting over the 1.6km-round, 215m-deep chasm, enhances the vertigo-inducing view of the 40m-deep turquoise water.

Wildebeest Kuil
Rock Art Centre   ARCHAEOLOGICAL SITE
(☑053-833 7069; www.wildebeestkuil.itgo.com; Rte 31; adult/child R25/12; ☺9am-4pm Mon-Fri, by appt Sat & Sun) On a site owned by the !Xun and Khwe San people, who were relocated from Angola and Namibia in 1990, this small sacred hill has 400-plus rock engravings dating back millennia. Visits start with a video detailing the troubled history of the !Xun and Khwe, followed by an excellent interpretative **guided tour**. The centre is 16km northwest of town, en route to Barkly West. A minibus

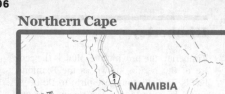

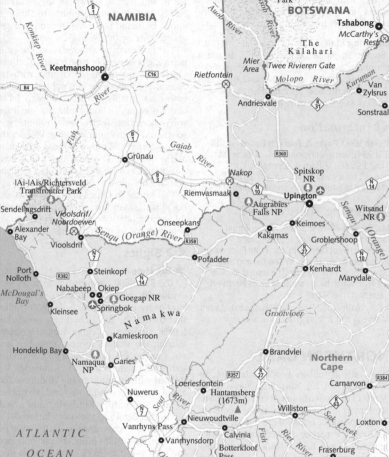

shared taxi costs R35; a private taxi costs R360 return, including waiting time.

Magersfontein
HISTORIC SITE

(☎ 053-833 7115; adult/child R15/8; ⊙ 8am-5pm) This was the site of an important battle in the Second Anglo-Boer War. There's a small museum, as well as a decent audio-visual exhibit that shows what life in the trenches was like in 1899. It's 30km southwest of the city on the Modder River road. Local tour guide Steve Lunderstedt offers a ghost-themed evening tour here.

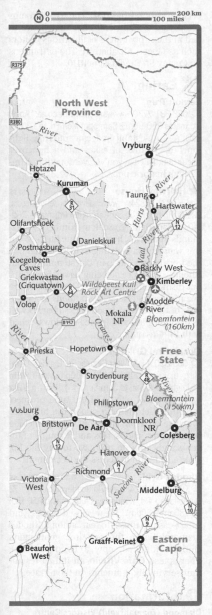

timeline offering a one-stop lesson in South African history, alongside landmark events in Kimberley's past. There's also an exhibit on the history of the building – built by De Beers in 1897 as a sanatorium – and a mockup of the room where Rhodes sat out the Siege of Kimberley.

Duggan-Cronin Gallery GALLERY
(Edgerton Rd; by donation; ⊘ 9am-5pm Mon-Fri; P) This ethnographic gallery holds a wonderful collection of photographs of southern African tribes taken in the 1920s and 1930s, before many aspects of traditional life were lost. Photographer Alfred Duggan-Cronin lived in this 19th-century house before his death in 1954. There's a section dedicated to Hugh Tracey, who travelled southern Africa in the mid-20th century, capturing traditional African music. You can listen to many of his recordings and see some candid caught-in-a-moment-of-happiness photos.

William Humphreys Art Gallery GALLERY
(☑ 053-831 1724; www.whag.co.za; 1 Cullinan Cres, Civic Centre; adult/child R5/2; ⊘ 8am-4.45pm Mon-Fri, 10am-4.45pm Sat, 9am-noon Sun) One of the country's best public galleries, with changing exhibitions of contemporary South African work, as well as a surprisingly good collection of European masters. The **cafe** sits in a lovely garden and is one of Kimberley's nicest spots for tea and cake.

⚲ Tours

Local guides Steve Lunderstedt and Jaco Powell (p498) offer historical and ghost-themed walks around the Kimberley area.

The **Kimberley Meander** (www.kimberleymeander.co.za) website has information on other local guided tours.

★**Steve Lunderstedt Tours** WALKING, HISTORY
(☑ 083 732 3189; from R200; ⊘ 6.30pm) Given its history of diamond-digging and Anglo-Boer conflict, Kimberley is fertile ground for ghosts. Local historian and raconteur Steve Lunderstedt has been exploring the city for 20 years. As much historical tour as paranormal hunt, his four-hour jaunt has six stops, starting at the **Honoured Dead Memorial**. Bookings are essential; 10 people are required for a tour to go ahead.

Second Anglo-Boer War Battlefields DRIVING
Several battles were fought in the area, including Magersfontein, Modder River and Graspan, all southwest of Kimberley off the N12. The most important was Magersfontein

McGregor Museum MUSEUM
(☑ 053-839 2700; www.museumsnc.co.za; Atlas St; adult/child R25/15; ⊘ 9am-5pm Mon-Sat, 2-5pm Sun) This comprehensive museum warrants a visit of a couple of hours. It covers the Second Anglo-Boer War and South Africa's role in WWI, and has an incredibly detailed

(p496), where entrenched Boers decimated the famous Highland Brigade. There's an infomation centre and an audiovisual display depicting life in the trenches. Better still, take a tour with Steve Lunderstedt (p497), who also offers a ghost-themed evening at Magersfontein.

Jaco Powell Tours WALKING, HISTORY
(⌨ 082 572 0065; per person R200) Jaco offers three-hour walking tours (book in advance, minimum 10 people) departing from the **Honoured Dead Memorial** at 6pm – just in time for the skies to darken and your guide to inform you that the vault is supposedly haunted with the souls of 27 British soldiers who perished during the siege of Kimberley.

🛌 Sleeping

Heerengracht Guest House GUESTHOUSE $
(⌨ 053-831 1531; www.heerengracht.co.za; 42 Heerengracht Ave, Royldene; s without bathroom R400, d from R550; 🅿🛜🏊) This bare-brick setup on a leafy suburban street has rooms and spacious self-catering units (R850). It's walking distance from two malls with fast-food eateries. The clientele is largely made up of business travellers, so rates are cheaper on weekends. Breakfast is R75.

★ 75 on Milner GUESTHOUSE $$
(⌨ 082 686 5994; www.milnerlodge.co.za; 75 Milner St; s/d from R720/890; 🅿🛜🏊) Highly recommended by travellers, this very friendly guesthouse has spacious, well-equipped rooms with fridge, microwave and cable TV. Rooms are set around a small patio and there's a good-size pool. Little touches set it apart, including a welcome drink, snacks in the room and superb information on local attractions.

Australian Arms Guesthouse GUESTHOUSE $$
(⌨ 053-832 1526; www.australianarms.co.za; Tucker St, Big Hole Complex; s/d incl breakfast from R800/880; 🅿) It's based in the reconstructed mining settlement, and the highlight of a stay is walking around the largely deserted mining village at night, imagining diamond dealers of yore drinking in the taverns after a long day's digging. The comfortable but unspectacular rooms have B&W photos of Kimberley, free-standing baths, DSTV and a fridge.

★ Kimberley Club BOUTIQUE HOTEL $$$
(⌨ 053-832 4224; www.kimberleyclub.co.za; 72 Du Toitspan Rd; s/d from R1010/1450; 🅿🛜) Founded by Rhodes and his diamond cronies as a private club in 1881, and rebuilt following a fire in 1896, this reputedly haunted building

became a hotel in 2004. The 21 bedrooms are period-elegant, and offer the chance to pad in the slipper-steps of illustrious visitors such as Queen Elizabeth II. The entrance is on Currey St. Breakfast is R110.

🍴 Eating

Lemon Tree CAFE $
(⌨ 053-831 7730; www.nclemontree.co.za; Angel St; mains R50-90; ⊙ 8am-5pm Mon-Fri, to 1.30pm Sat) A long-established cafe offering light lunches, a range of cakes and a hangover breakfast, in case you've overdone it in Kimberley's historic pubs.

★ Halfway House PUB FOOD $$
(⌨ 053-831 6324; www.halfwayhousehotel.co.za; 229 Du Toitspan Rd, cnr Carrington Rd; mains R60-140; ⊙ 11am-11pm; 🛜) Soak up Kimberley's diamonds-and-drink history – quite literally – in this watering hole dating to 1872. It might be the world's only 'drive-in' bar, stemming from Rhodes' insistence on being served beer without dismounting his horse. The interiors are beautifully historic, with spittoons along the base of the scarred, wood-backed bar, as well as old liquor ads and frosted windows etched with Rhodes quotes.

Occidental Grill Bar PUB FOOD $$
(⌨ 053-830 4418; West Circular Rd, Big Hole Complex; mains R70-150; ⊙ 10am-10pm Mon-Thu, to midnight Fri & Sat, to 3pm Sun; 🛜) With a long bar and B&W photos of old-time prospectors, this Victorian-era saloon is a fun place to pause on a Big Hole tour. Dishes include bunny chow, chops, ribs and a couple of token salads. You do not have to pay the Big Hole admission to access the Occidental.

Rhodes Grill INTERNATIONAL $$
(⌨ 053-832 4224; www.kimberleyclub.co.za; 72 Du Toitspan Rd, Kimberley Club; mains R50-130; ⊙ 6.30am-9.30pm) Wear closed shoes and smart-casual dress to eat among Rhodes memorabilia in the one-time gentlemen's club he founded, now a boutique hotel. There's also **Café Vitello**, an Italian restaurant serving light lunches on the terrace.

ℹ Information

Diamond (Diamantveld) Visitors Centre
(⌨ 053-830 6779; www.kimberley.co.za; 121 Bultfontein Rd; ⊙ 8am-5pm Mon-Fri) Pick up the *Kimberley Meander* brochure, with suggested self-guided walking and driving tours.
Small World Net Café (⌨ 053-831 3484; 42 Sidney St; per hr R30; ⊙ 8am-5pm Mon-Fri) Offers (slow) internet access.

❶ Getting There & Away

AIR

Taxis connect the city centre with the airport, 6km south.

SA Express (☑ 053-838 3337; www.flyexpress.aero) Flies to/from Jo'burg (R1000, one hour) and Cape Town (R1000, 1½ hours).

Hamba Nathi (☑ 053-831 3982; www.hambanathi.co.za; 121 Bultfontein Rd, Diamond Visitors Centre) Sells airline tickets.

BUS

Tickets 4 Africa (☑ 053-832 6040; tickets4africa@hotmail.com; 121 Bultfontein Rd, Diamond Visitors Centre) sells tickets for **Greyhound** (☑ 083 915 9000; www.greyhound.co.za), **Intercape** (☑ in Cape Town 021-380 4400; www.intercape.co.za) and **City to City** (☑ 0861 589 282; www.citytocity.co.za). There are direct services to Cape Town (R550, 12 hours) and Jo'burg (R400, seven hours). Intercape runs services to Upington (R340, seven hours) on Friday and Sunday via Bloemfontein (R300, two hours).

Translux (☑ 0861 589 282; www.translux.co.za) also services Kimberley.

CAR

Avis, Budget, Europcar, First, Hertz, Sixt and Tempest have desks at Kimberley airport. Hire rates start at around R300 per day.

TAXI

Rikki's Taxis (☑ 053-842 1764; www.rikkistaxis.co.za) is a reliable option.

TRAIN

Shosholoza Meyl (p354) Trans-Karoo trains stop in Kimberley en route between Jo'burg (economy/sleeper R160/240, eight hours) and Cape Town (R300/470, 17½ hours).

Blue Train (☑ in Cape Town 021-449 2672; www.bluetrain.co.za) Stops for a tour of the Big Hole Complex en route from Pretoria to Cape Town.

Mokala National Park

Named after the Tswana for 'camel thorn', the dominant tree found in South Africa's newest national park, **Mokala** (☑ 053-204 8000; www.sanparks.org/parks/mokala/; adult/child R148/74; ⊘ 6.30am-6pm mid-Mar–Apr, Aug & Sep, 7am-5.30pm May-Jul, 6am-7pm Oct–mid-Mar) encompasses grassy plains studded with rocky hills and these trademark trees. Indigenous to Southern Africa, camel thorns can range from small, spiny shrubs standing barely 2m to 16m-tall trees with wide, spreading crowns. The species is an important resource for both the people and wildlife living in this harsh region – the local tribes use the gum and bark to treat coughs, colds and nosebleeds. (Some people even roast the seeds as a coffee substitute.) Mammals in the 200-sq-km park include black and white rhinos, roan antelope, Cape buffaloes, giraffes and zebras.

Organised activities include sunset wildlife drives, fly-fishing and bush braais. All activities should be booked ahead.

🛏 Sleeping

Motswedi Campsite   CAMPGROUND $
(www.sanparks.org/parks/mokala/; camping R400) A superb campground with just six sites, all overlooking a waterhole. Each site has its own washing facilities and kitchen.

Stofdam Bird Hide   HUT $
(☑ 053-204 8000; www.sanparks.org/parks/mokala/; per night R555) A much sought after and very rustic sleeping option that sleeps up to four people. It cannot be booked online and only one-night stays are possible. Bring all your own bedding and cooking utensils. Book directly through the park.

★ Kameeldoorn Tree House   CABIN $$
(☑ 053-204 8000; www.sanparks.org/parks/mokala/; d R1380) A simply delightful self-catering cabin accommodating one or two people, nestled in a tree in the centre of the park. Bookings should be made directly through the park, rather than central reservations. Book well in advance.

Mosu Lodge   LODGE $$
(www.sanparks.org/parks/mokala/; bungalows from R770; ❋ ☲) Mokala's most upmarket accommodation, with amenities such as electric blankets, fireplaces and DSTV in the self-catering luxury executive suites. The smart poolside bar-restaurant is open all day, serving dishes from vegetable stir-fry to venison pie (mains R60 to R120).

Lilydale Rest Camp   CHALET $$
(www.sanparks.org/parks/mokala/; chalets R870; ❋ ☲) Lilydale is on the banks of the Riet River, which has good fly-fishing. Its self-catering units, especially the thatched chalets, are perfect for getting back to nature.

❶ Getting There & Away

To enter the park, head about 60km southwest of Kimberley on the N12, then turn right at the 'Mokala Mosu' sign and follow the dirt road for 21km. It's possible to cross the park and exit by the Lilydale Gate, then follow a dirt road for 16km and meet the N12 about 40km southwest of Kimberley. In the rainy season, the roads might not be passable with a 2WD – always call in advance to check.

Upington

POP 57,000

Home to lush gardens and hundreds of date palm trees, Upington is a prosperous, orderly town on the banks of the Gariep (Orange) River. The central hub for the Green Kalahari, it's a good place to recoup after a long desert slog – although it gets blazing hot in summer. Wide boulevards, slightly cluttered with supermarkets and chain stores, fill the town centre. Step onto a side street near the river, however, and you'll enter a peaceful world where refreshing, watery views and rows of palms hold quiet court.

If you yearn to see the Northern Cape's most remote parts but don't have the means to do so on your own, this is also a good place to organise a guided tour.

◉ Sights

Die Mas Van Kakamas WINERY
(☑054-431 0245; www.diemasvankakamas.co.za; ☺8am-5pm Mon-Fri, 9am-2pm Sat) These winemakers experiment with a wider range of grape varieties than most other area vineyards, though the *jerepigo* and *hanepoot* wines that the Gariep (Orange) River region is known for are still the best. Activities include farm tours, hiking trails, donkey-cart trips and quad biking; there's self-catering accommodation and campsites. It's well sign-posted from the N14 as you enter Kakamas.

Bezalel WINERY
(☑054-491 1325; www.bezalel.co.za; N14; tastings R60; ☺9am-5pm Mon-Fri, to 1pm Sat) Possibly the most varied tasting of any estate in the country, with samples of wine, port, brandy, various cream-based liqueurs and the challenge of swigging *mampoer* (moonshine) without grimacing. There's a **restaurant** (mains R60 to R95) and a leafy courtyard where you can enjoy your chosen tipple. It's 25km southwest of Upington on the N14.

Kalahari-Orange Museum MUSEUM
(4 Schröder St; adult/child R10/2; ☺9am-12.30pm & 2-5pm Mon-Fri) Occupying the mission station established by Reverend Schröder in 1875, this museum focuses on local social history, with domestic and agricultural artefacts. Displays cover the story of the Upington 26, who were wrongly jailed under apartheid.

Orange River Cellars WINERY
(☑054-495 0040; www.orangeriverwines.com; 158 Schröder St; tastings from R10; ☺10am-6pm Mon-Fri, to 3pm Sat) At this swanky new tasting centre there's a vast range of well-priced wines to taste, including dessert and sparkling wines, as well as a juice tasting for kids and nondrinkers. Platters are available if you fancy pairing your wine with cheese, olives or biltong.

🏃 Activities

★ Sakkie se Arkie CRUISE
(☑082 564 5447; www.arkie.co.za; Park St; adult/child R100/60; ☺5.30pm Fri-Sun, daily during holidays) Soak up the last rays of the Kalahari sun over the Gariep (Orange) River on the top deck of Sakkie's barge. Dire Straits, Afrikaans pop and other classics keep everyone entertained on the two-hour sunset cruise as the water turns silvery and the bartender lines up cold beers. A river-taxi service lets you arrive at your guesthouse in style.

⌖ Tours

Upington is the best place to organise a Kalahari adventure.

Kalahari Safaris ADVENTURE
(☑054-332 5653; www.kalaharisafaris.co.za) Runs small-group (two to five people) trips to locations including the Kgalagadi and Augrabies Falls parks, Witsand Nature Reserve and Namakwa. Tours last from one to seven days and cater to all budgets.

🛏 Sleeping

Island View House B&B $$
(☑054-331 1328; www.islandviewhouse.co.za; 10 Murray Ave; s/d incl breakfast R700/900; ❄️ 🛜 🏊) The Mocké family offers a friendly welcome and modern rooms with showers and a shared lounge, kitchen and balcony.

Die Eiland Holiday Resort CHALET $$
(☑054-334 0287; resort@kharahais.gov.za; camping from R125, huts without bathroom from R300, chalets from R770; 🏊) A palm-lined avenue leads to 'the Island', in a wonderful natural setting on the river's southeastern bank. The basic self-catering chalets have kitchenettes with stove and microwave, and tiny bathrooms with shower.

Aqua Viva GUESTHOUSE $$
(☑054-331 2524; www.aquaviva.co.za; 26A Schröder St; s/d R660/840; ❄️) Tucked behind the Protea Hotel, this is a peaceful place whose spacious

rooms are sparsely but stylishly decorated. They come with large bathrooms, comically small TVs and a shared veranda leading on to a lawn overlooking the river.

★**Le Must River Residence** GUESTHOUSE **$$$**
(☑054-332 3971; www.lemustupington.com; 14 Budler St; s/d incl breakfast from 1190/1700; ❋❀⊠) This elegant riverside getaway has 11 African-themed rooms with antique furnishings and crisp linen. Sitting rooms and terraces open onto the artful garden with its Italianate pool.

Protea Hotel Oasis HOTEL **$$$**
(☑054-337 8500; www.proteahotels.com; 26 Schröder St; r from R1450; ❋❀⊠) The Oasis offers some of Upington's most stylish accommodation. The swimming pool and restaurant are at the Protea Upington, across the road. Breakfast is R175.

✖ Eating

Bi-Lo Bistro INTERNATIONAL, SUSHI **$$**
(☑054-338 0616; 9 Green Point Rd; mains R60-120; ☺7am-10pm; ❀⊛) Birds hop between palm trees and kids play on the swings at this popular spot in the suburbs. The vast menu features everything from steak to sushi – the latter is surprisingly decent.

Irish Pub & Grill PUB FOOD **$$**
(☑054-331 2005; 20 Schröder St; mains R70-150; ☺9am-11pm) For sundowners or an early evening meal, you can't beat this Irish bar's patio overlooking the river. The menu features pizza, a few salads and plenty of meat.

❶ Information

Post Office (Schröder St)
Upington Tourist Office (☑054-338 7152; www.northerncape.org.za; Mutual St; ☺7.30am-4.30pm Mon-Fri) This office's location in the municipal building is temporary; there are plans to move it back to the library.

❶ Getting There & Away

AIR
South African Airways (☑0861 606 606; www.flysaa.com) flies to/from Jo'burg (R2200, 1½ hours) and Cape Town (R2500, 1½ hours). The airport is 6km north of town, off the N10.

BUS
Intercape (☑021-380 4400; www.intercape. co.za; Lutz St) buses go to Bloemfontein (R390, nine hours, Thursday and Saturday), Cape Town (R600, 14 hours, Thursday, Friday

and Sunday), Jo'burg (R750, 11 hours, daily) and Windhoek, Namibia (R660, 12 hours, Tuesday, Thursday, Friday and Sunday). Buses leave from the Intercape office on Lutz St.

CAR
Rental agencies, including Avis and Europcar, have offices at Upington airport.

SHARED TAXI
Destinations of minibus taxis include Springbok (R240, four hours) and Windhoek, Namibia (R650, 13 hours).

Kgalagadi Transfrontier Park

A long, hot road leads between crimson dunes from Upington to Africa's first transfrontier **park** (☑054-561 2000; www.sanparks. org/parks/kgalagadi/; adult/child R304/152), one of the world's last great, unspoilt ecosystems. Once you enter the magical park, tucked away alongside Namibia in the Northern Cape and southwest Botswana, you'll soon see why the journey was well worth the effort.

The Kgalagadi is a wild land of harsh extremes and frequent droughts, where shifting red and white sands meet thorn trees and dry riverbeds. Yet despite the desolate landscape, it's teeming with wildlife. From prides of black-maned lions to packs of howling spotted hyenas, there are some 1775 predators here. It's one of the best places in the world to spot big cats, especially cheetahs. Add in giant, orange-ball sunsets and black-velvet night skies studded with twinkling stars, and you'll feel like you've entered the Africa of storybooks.

---

❶ KGALAGADI SELF-DRIVE WATCHING WILDLIFE

We found the section between Urikaruus and Mata-Mata to be particularly good for predator sightings, while the east–west routes linking the two rivers are rich in scenery and birdlife. The semi-arid countryside also supports large populations of reptiles, rodents, small mammals and antelopes. Most of the animals are remarkably tolerant of vehicles, allowing you to get extraordinarily close.

Kgalagadi Transfrontier Park

0 ——— 40 km
0 ——— 20 miles

Kgalagadi Transfrontier Park

⊙ Sights
1 Kgalagadi Transfrontier Park B4

⊜ Sleeping
2 !Xaus.......................................A4
3 !Xaus Lodge............................A4
4 Kalahari Tented Camp A3
5 Twee Rivieren Rest Camp.........B4
6 Twee Rivieren B4

facilities. The cottages have between two and four single beds; the chalet has six. The cheaper campsites don't have power.

★**Kalahari Tented Camp**　　CAMPGROUND $$$
(d safari tents from R1500; ☒) Kgalagadi's most luxurious wilderness camp has 14 stilted desert tents with rustic furnishings and views of a waterhole in the Auob riverbed – a popular hangout for herds of wildebeest. It provides a remote, rustic feel while being only 3km from the conveniences of Mata-Mata (and over three hours from Twee Rivieren Gate).

!Xaus Lodge　　LODGE $$$
(☑ in Cape Town 021-701 7860; www.xauslodge. co.za; s/d incl full board R5700/8800; ☒) ✍ Kgalagadi's most upmarket option is owned and operated by the local San community. The lodge is a dreamy fantasy in ochre, overlooking a circular pan so perfect it almost looks artificially constructed. Cultural activities and excellent wildlife drives round out a wonderful package.

🚶 Activities

The park operates sunrise, sunset, night and full-morning **wildlife drives** (adult/ child from R220/110) and three-hour **walking safaris** (adult from R330, no one under 12 years). Both depart from Twee Rivieren, Nossob, Mata-Mata and Kalahari Tented Camp. We recommend trying at least one guided activity; you have a better chance of spotting predators when accompanied by a trained ranger. At least two people are needed for safaris to depart.

For an extra fee, there are 4WD trails to tackle (per vehicle R2950).

ⓘ Information

Botswana Wildlife (☑ 267 318 0774; dwnp@ gov.bw; Gaborone)
South African National Parks (SANParks; ☑ 012-428 9111; www.sanparks.org/parks/ kgalagadi)

ⓘ Getting There & Away

Twee Rivieren Gate is 270km northwest of Upington on the tarred Rte 360.

A 4WD vehicle is useful but not essential – the park's four main routes are gravel/sand roads but they're in decent condition and can be driven in a 2WD if you take care. Beware of patches of deep sand and loose gravel on the park's roads, which can make corners treacherous. The speed limit is 50km/h. Allow plenty of time to get to the camps as no driving is permitted after dark.

🛌 Sleeping

Twee Rivieren　　CHALET $$
(camping from R265, cottages/chalets from R1275/1635; ❄ ☒) The largest camp in the park is also the most convenient, located next to the park entrance and with the most

Augrabies Falls National Park

The Khoe-San people called it 'Aukoerbis', meaning 'place of great noise', and when the waterfall for which this **park** (☏ 054-452 9200; www.sanparks.org/parks/augrabies/; adult/child R176/88; ⊙ 7am-6.30pm) is named is fat with rainy-season run-off, its thunderous roar is nothing short of spectacular. This is the world's sixth-tallest falls, formed where the Gariep (Orange) River crashes into an 18km-long ravine with 200m-high cliffs. The main falls drop 56m, while the adjoining Bridal Veil Falls plunge 75m. It's a short walk from the visitor centre to the viewing platforms. The park has a harsh climate, with an average rainfall of just 107mm and summer temperatures that reach 46°C.

The falls are of course the main draw, but the 500-sq-km park also offers little-known wildlife-watching opportunities. The park's 52 mammal species include giraffes, various antelope, African clawless otters and endangered Hartmann's mountain zebras. You're less likely to spot predators, but caracals, black-backed jackals and African wild cats all roam here.

✦ Activities

The road to the rest camp and the main lookout over the falls is tarred and you can easily reach the viewpoints at Ararat and Oranjekom in a 2WD. If you take it slowly, you can explore further without a 4WD, though you'll need one to complete the 94km-long **Wilderness Road**. Call in advance to check the state of the roads as heavy rains can cause havoc. There are also two-hour **guided night drives** available – book ahead directly with the park.

Dassie Trail   HIKING

This three-hour, 9km trail is well worth doing, particularly if your time is fairly short. The hike involves clambering over rocks through some magical landscapes.

Klipspringer Trail   HIKING

(per person R265; ⊙ Apr–mid-Oct) The three-day, 36km Klipspringer Trail leads along the southern banks of the Gariep (Orange) River. You'll spend two nights in rustic huts with bunk beds, toilets, firewood and rudimentary cooking utensils, but no electricity or showers, and you need to bring drinking water. There's a minimum requirement of two hikers; advance booking is essential.

Kalahari Outventures   RAFTING, CANOEING

(☏ 082 476 8213; www.kalahari-adventures.co.za; Augrabies; half-day rafting trip R450) The flagship rafting trip, Augrabies Rush, is a half-day tour taking in Grade II and Grade III rapids on a 9km section of the Gariep (Orange) River, finishing 300m above the main falls. Overnight and multiday river expeditions are also offered, as are **hot-air balloon rides** and **wildlife-watching** trips.

🛏 Sleeping

Augrabies Falls Lodge & Camp   HOTEL $$

(☏ 054-451 7203; www.augfallslodge.co.za; Rte 359; camping per site R275, s/d R535/790; ❄) One of a number of sleeping options on the road to the park (8.5km from the park gate), this 1950s building has a modernised interior that is adorned with African art. The spacious rooms have pleasant furnishings and balconies with views across the countryside. There's a restaurant (mains R80, breakfast R35), bar and a four-person self-catering room (R895).

Augrabies Rest Camp   CHALET, CAMPGROUND $$

(www.sanparks.org/parks/augrabies/; camping R235, chalets/cottages from R1200/1900; ❄ ❄) Within the park and close enough to the falls to hear them after rains, the rest camp has self-catering chalets, two-bedroom cottages and a campsite with washing facilities. The restaurant offers a decent selection of dishes; it's open 7am to 8pm.

ℹ Getting There & Away

The park is 39km northwest of Kakamas; head west on the N14 for 8km, then northwest on Rte 359. Minibus taxis do pass by the approach road – but you'll then have to walk the remaining 3km to the gate.

Namakwa

A land of immense skies and stark countryside, rugged Namakwa is truly South Africa's Wild West. The roads seemingly stretch forever through vast, empty spaces, and scorching days lead to dramatically quiet and still nights, when the stars appear bigger and brighter than anywhere else. From exploring the misty shipwrecked diamond coastline on the country's far western edge to four-wheel driving through the Mars-like landscape of remote |Ai-|Ais/Richtersveld Transfrontier Park, its pleasures are simple yet flabbergasting.

Namakwa is also a proficient magician, who performs its favourite trick each spring, shaking off winter's bite with an explosion of colour and covering the sunbaked desert in a spectacular, multihued wildflower blanket.

The region takes its name from the Nama (also known as Namkwa or Namaqua, which means 'Nama people'), a Khoekhoen tribe from northwest Namakwa (previously known as Namaqualand).

|Ai-|Ais/Richtersveld Transfrontier Park

Sculpted by millions of years of harsh elemental exposure, South Africa's most remote **national park** (☑ 027-831 1506; www.sanparks. org/parks/richtersveld/; adult/child R210/105; ⊙ 7am-7pm Oct-Apr, to 6pm May-Sep) is a seemingly barren wilderness of lava rocks, human-like trees and sandy moonscapes studded with semiprecious stones. The 6000 sq km of surreal mountain desert joins South Africa's Richtersveld National Park with Namibia's |Ai-|Ais Hot Springs Game Park.

Accessible only by 4WD, the Richtersveld is South Africa's final wild frontier. The South African section of the park covers 1850 sq km, and is most beautiful during the spring wildflower season, when, like elsewhere in Namakwa, it turns into a technicolour wonderland. Hiking here is demanding but spectacular – trails traverse jagged peaks, grotesque rock formations, deep ravines and gorges. This is a place for those who seek to wander way off the beaten track and even those who crave a little survivalist action. There are almost no facilities so you need to be completely self-sufficient.

⫷ Tours

Richtersveld Tours   TOURS
(☑ 082 335 1399; www.richtersveldtours.com; per day from R1950) Offers 4WD tours, including all meals and equipment.

⊨ Sleeping

★ **Tatasberg**   CABIN $$
(d cabins R895) The delightful cabins at this camp each have a covered deck with magnificent views over the Gariep (Orange) River. Made from corrugated tin, reed and canvas, they have a striking, rustic feel that blends perfectly with the park's scenery. Each has two single beds, a fridge, gas stove and shower.

Gannakouriep   CABIN $$
(d cabins R895) Staying in these stone-and-canvas cabins is like upmarket camping. Great efforts have been made to showcase the camp's magnificent setting in a rocky valley. Each cabin comes with two beds, a gas stove and solar-powered fridge.

Sendelingsdrift   CAMPGROUND, CHALET $$
(camping R245, d chalets R895; ❋ ❋❋) The two- to four-bed self-catering chalets at the park entrance are surprisingly comfortable, with porches overlooking the river. You'll be glad of the air-con if you dare to visit in summer.

❶ Getting There & Away

A tar road leads 82km from Port Nolloth to Alexander Bay, from where a 90km gravel road leads to Sendelingsdrift Gate. This section is passable in a car but you need a 4WD vehicle in the park – sedans are not permitted. You can hire a 4WD vehicle and buy a decent map in Springbok – ask at the tourist office.

You can cross the Gariep (Orange) River into Namibia on a pontoon at Sendelingsdrift; it operates from 8am to 4.15pm, weather permitting.

It's highly recommended that you travel in convoy as the harsh terrain is challenging even for experienced 4WD drivers. Day visits are impractical considering the park's remoteness – you need at least three days, and preferably closer to a week.

Springbok

POP 12,800

Springbok sits in a valley surrounded by harsh rocky hills that turn into a rainbow tapestry during the spring wildflower season. When the flowers aren't blooming there's little to see or do here, although the town's remoteness, desolate landscape and 300-plus days of sunshine make it a pleasant enough stopover. Springbok is 120km south of the Vioolsdrif crossing to Namibia, from where it is about 800km to Windhoek (Namibia).

From an edgy frontier town, Springbok has grown into a busy service centre for Namakwa's copper and diamond mines. Farmers from remote outlying areas also point their bakkies (pick-up trucks) to the main drag, Voortrekker St, for their weekly shopping trips; Springbok is a good place to rest up and do jobs before continuing into the wilderness.

⊙ Sights

Goegap Nature Reserve   NATURE RESERVE
(☑027-718 9906; R30; ⊙7.30am-4pm) This 150-sq-km semidesert reserve, 15km east of Springbok past the airport, supports some 600 indigenous plant species, 45 mammal species and 94 types of bird. It is one of the best places in the region to take a walk during flower season, with circular 4km and 7km **hiking trails**. There is a 13km circuit for cars and trails for 4WD vehicles, and accommodation is available in basic four-bed huts (R160) and campsites (R90).

Namakwaland Museum   MUSEUM
(☑027-718 8100; Monument St; ⊙8am-1pm & 2-4pm Mon-Fri) **FREE** Springbok's former synagogue, built in 1929, has been converted into the town's small museum. It's mostly a ramshackle collection of bric-a-brac, though the matchstick model of the immense church in the dusty *dorp* (village) of Pella is impressive. Next door, the town's first **Dutch Reformed church** sits empty, though there are vague plans to convert it into a gallery showcasing local artists' work.

🛏 Sleeping

Cat Nap Accommodation   HOSTEL $
(☑027-718 1905; richtersveld.challen@kingsley. co.za; 99 Voortrekker St; dm R180, s/d R450/650; ❄) The walls of this spacious old house are adorned with nature photos, and rooms are cosy, African-themed affairs. There's a self-catering kitchen and dorm beds in the barn, although they're incredibly close together and it gets hot in summer.

★Kliprand Guesthouse   GUESTHOUSE $$
(☑027-712 2604; 2 King St; s/d R660/1200; 🛜❄) A friendly place in a quiet side street close to Springbok's top restaurant. Rooms are bright and cosy and there's a large swimming pool in the garden. Breakfast is R85.

Mountain View   GUESTHOUSE $$
(☑027-712 1438; www.mountview.co.za; 2 Overberg Ave; s/d incl breakfast from R800/950; ❄🛜❄) Perched in a tranquil location up against the hills, this guesthouse has four-star rooms – some of which open onto a garden leading to the pool, which has wonderful views.

Annie's Cottage   GUESTHOUSE $$
(☑027-712 1451; www.anniescottage.co.za; 4 King St; s/d incl breakfast R950/1200; ❄🛜❄) The ornate bedrooms are cutesy in places, but the Afro-themed rooms are fun; you can also request the honeymoon suite at no extra cost. Afternoon tea and cake are served and there is a self-catering room in the garden.

✗ Eating

★Tauren Steak Ranch   STEAK $$
(☑027-712 2717; 2 Hospital St; mains R65-150; ⊙11.30am-late Mon-Fri, from 6pm Sat) Meat lovers rejoice: Tauren serves steaks weighing up to a kilogram, with a host of delectable sauces. The menu also features burgers, a few vegetarian choices and pizzas with toppings including biltong and *boerewors* (farmer's sausage). The ambience is country-relaxed, with *boeremusiek* on the stereo.

Pot & Barrell   PUB FOOD
(☑027-718 1475; 30 Voortrekker Rd; ⊙9am-11pm) Serves basic pub grub like burgers and snack baskets and has a decent beer selection.

ℹ Information

Tourist Office (☑027-712 8035; www.experiencenortherncape.com; Voortrekker St; ⊙8am-4.15pm Mon-Thu, to 3pm Fri) Has some maps and info on southern Namibia as well as Namakwa.

ℹ Transport

Buses, including **Intercape** (☑021-380 4400; www.intercape.co.za), serve Cape Town (R500, nine hours) and Windhoek, Namibia (R650, 13 hours). Buses leave from the Engen garage on Voortrekker St.

Minibus shared taxis serve Upington (R270, four hours), Port Nolloth (R120, two hours) and Cape Town (R450, 8½ hours). Contact the **Namakwaland Taxi Association** (☑027-718 2840; Van der Stel St, cnr Namaqua St) for bookings.

UNDERSTAND SOUTH AFRICA

South Africa Today

More than two decades after Nelson Mandela came to power, life in South Africa remains dominated by social inequality. Central Cape Town's mountain and beach communities contrast with the townships sprawling across the Cape Flats, lining the N2 with shacks and portaloos. Seeing First-World wealth alongside African poverty is confronting for first-time visitors. Yet every day, millions of South Africans embrace progress by trying to understand and respect the vastly different outlooks of people from other economic and racial groups.

What makes South Africa an uplifting place to visit is the dissolution of racial divisions. Projects are in place that aim to empower inhabitants of the townships and former homelands, and to provide work in a country with 25% unemployment. Finding common ground can be challenging in this cultural melting pot with 11 official languages, but race relations are informed by the miracle that Mandela et al performed.

Reflecting pan-African issues, South Africa has the world's largest population of people with HIV/AIDS (around seven million people). Educational efforts face numerous taboos, and *sangomas* (traditional healers) preach superstitious lore; every day, funerals commemorate supposed tuberculosis victims.

South Africa's record on gender issues exemplifies the country's contradictions. Its constitution, adopted in 1996, is the world's most progressive, promoting the rights of women and LGBT people (same-sex marriage is legal), among others. Yet the street-level reality is far harsher, with one of the world's highest reported incidences of rape, including 'corrective' rape of lesbians.

When Mandela died in 2013 South Africa came together in a way not seen since the 2010 World Cup. Madiba's death was, though, a reminder that the ANC is losing its apartheid-busting glow, as it presides over a country where crime, corruption and institutional incompetence are rife.

Now serving his second term, President Jacob Zuma will be remembered for the Marikana massacre, in which police killed 34 people after opening fire on striking miners; Nkandlagate, in which Zuma was accused of spending R246 million (US$24.6 million) of public funds to upgrade Nkandla, his sprawling homestead in Zululand; and Guptagate, in which a wealthy Indian family has amassed a large amount of influence in government through Zuma and his family members, who have been given various directorships at Gupta-run companies.

The next elections will be held in 2019, marking the end of Zuma's tenure. Assuming the Democratic Alliance and their coalitions can live up to their promises, it's thought that the ANC's majority in the National Assembly could come to an end.

History

Visit South Africa and you'll see reminders of its past at every turn. The country's human drama is reflected in the faces and body language of its citizens. It's on display in centuries-old rock paintings and modern-day urban graffiti, in isolated battlefields and sober apartheid-era memorials. It permeates every corner with its pain and injustice but also with its hope. Be prepared to immerse yourself in one of the most anguished yet most inspiring stories to be found anywhere.

The Great Trek

From 1836, groups of Boers dissatisfied with British rule in the Cape Colony trekked off into the interior in search of freedom. In a decade of migration known as the Great Trek, increasing numbers of Voortrekkers (pioneers) abandoned their farms and crossed the Senqu (Orange) River. Reports from early missions told of vast, uninhabited– or at least poorly defended – grazing lands.

Tensions between the Boers and the government had been building for some time, but the reason given by many trekkers for leaving was the 1833 act banning slavery.

The Great Trek coincided with the *difaqane* (forced migration) and the Boers mistakenly believed that what they found – deserted pasture lands, disorganised bands of refugees and tales of brutality – was the normal state of affairs. This gave rise to the Afrikaner myths that the Voortrekkers moved into unoccupied territory or arrived at much the same time as black Africans.

The Voortrekkers Meet the Zulu

The Great Trek's first halt was at Thaba 'Nchu, near present-day Bloemfontein, where a republic was established. Following disagreements among their leadership, the various Voortrekker groups split, with most crossing the Drakensberg into Natal to try to establish a republic there. As this was Zulu territory, the Voortrekker leader, Piet Retief, paid a visit to King Dingaan, and was promptly massacred by the suspicious Zulu. This massacre triggered others, as well as a revenge attack by the Boers. The culmination came at the Battle of Blood River (1838) in Natal. While the Boers sustained some injuries, more than 3000 Zulu were killed, reportedly causing the Ncome River to run red.

After this victory (the result of vastly superior weapons), the Boers felt their expansion really did have that long-suspected stamp of divine approval. The 16 December victory at Blood River was celebrated as the Day of the Vow until 1994, when it was renamed the Day of Reconciliation.

The Boer Republics

Several short-lived Boer republics sprang up, but soon the only serious contenders were the Orange Free State and the Transvaal. The republics' financial position was always precarious and their economies depended entirely on cattle. Just when it seemed that the republics, with their thinly spread population of fiercely independent Boers, were beginning to settle into stable states, diamonds were discovered near Kimberley in 1869. Britain stepped in quickly and annexed the area.

The Boers were disturbed by the foreigners, both black and white, who poured in following the discovery and were angry that their impoverished republics were missing out on the money the mines brought in.

Anglo-Boer Wars

Longstanding Boer resentment became a full blown rebellion in the Transvaal and the first Anglo-Boer War, known by Afrikaners as the War of Independence, broke out. It was over almost as soon as it began, with a crushing Boer victory at the Battle of Majuba Hill in 1881, and the republic regained its independence as the Zuid-Afrikaansche Republiek (ZAR; South African Republic).

With the discovery of a huge reef of gold in the Witwatersrand (the area around Johannesburg) in 1886 and the ensuing explosive growth of Jo'burg itself, the ZAR was suddenly host to thousands of *uitlanders* (foreigners), black and white.

This only intensified the Boers' grievances that had begun during the earlier diamond rush. In 1899 the British demanded voting rights for the 60,000 foreign whites on the Witwatersrand. Paul Kruger (ZAR president 1883–1900) refused, and demanded that British troops be withdrawn from the republic's borders, leading to the second Anglo-Boer War.

The conflict was more protracted than its predecessor, as the British were better prepared. By mid-1900, Pretoria, the last of the major Boer towns, had surrendered. Yet resistance by Boer *bittereinders* (bitter enders) continued for two more years with guerrilla-style battles, which in turn were met by scorched-earth tactics by the British. In May 1902, the Treaty of Vereeniging brought a superficial peace. Under its terms, the Boer republics acknowledged British sovereignty.

British Rule

The British response after their victory was a mixture of appeasement and insensitive imperialism. The nonwhites were scarcely considered, other than as potential labour, despite the fact that they constituted more than 75% of the combined population of the provinces.

Political awareness was growing, however. Mohandas (later Mahatma) Gandhi was working with the Indian populations of the Natal and Transvaal, and men such as John Jabavu, Walter Rubusana and Abdullah Abdurahman laid the foundations for new nontribal black political groups.

Afrikaners found themselves in the position of being poor farmers in a country where big mining ventures and foreign capital rendered them irrelevant. Afrikaans came to be seen as the *volkstaal* (people's language) and a symbol of Afrikaner nationhood. The former Boer republics were given representative government in 1906–07, and moves towards union began almost immediately.

Union of South Africa

The Union of South Africa was established in 1910. The British High Commission Territories of Basotholand (now Lesotho), Bechuanaland (now Botswana), Swaziland and Rhodesia (now Zimbabwe) continued to be ruled directly by Britain. English and Dutch became the official languages – Afrikaans was not recognised as an official language until 1925.

The first government of the new union was the South African National Party (later known as the South African Party, or SAP). A diverse coalition of Boer groups under General Louis Botha, with General Jan Smuts as his deputy, the party followed a generally pro-British, white-unity line. General Barry Hertzog raised divisive issues, championing Afrikaner interests, advocating separate development for the two white groups and independence from Britain. He and his supporters formed the National Party (NP).

Soon after the union was established a barrage of repressive legislation was passed. It became illegal for black workers to strike; skilled jobs were reserved for whites; blacks were barred from military service; and pass laws, restricting black freedom of movement, were tightened. In 1912, Pixley ka Isaka Seme formed a national democratic organisation to represent blacks. It was initially called the South African Native Congress, but from 1923 it was known as the African National Congress (ANC).

In 1913 the Natives Land Act set aside 8% of South Africa's land for black occupancy. Blacks were not allowed to buy, rent or even become sharecroppers outside their designated areas. Thousands of squatters were evicted from farms and forced into increasingly overcrowded reserves, or into the cities.

In 1914 South Africa, as a part of the British Empire, was drawn into war with Germany and saddled with the responsibility of dealing with German South West Africa (now Namibia). After the war, South West Africa became part of South Africa under a 'mandate' from the League of Nations.

Rise of Afrikaner Nationalism

In 1924 the NP, under Hertzog, came to power in a coalition government, and Afrikaner nationalism gained a greater hold. Dutch was replaced by Afrikaans (previously only regarded as a low-class dialect of Dutch) as an official language of the Union, and the so-called *swart gevaar* (black threat) was made the dominant issue of the 1929 election. Hertzog joined briefly in a coalition with the more moderate Jan Smuts in the mid-1930s, after which Smuts took the reins. However, any hopes of turning the tide of Afrikaner nationalism were dashed when Daniel François (DF) Malan led a radical breakaway movement, the Purified National Party, to the central position in Afrikaner political life. The Afrikaner Broederbond, a secret Afrikaner brotherhood that had been formed in 1918 to protect Afrikaner culture, soon became an extraordinarily influential force behind both the NP and other organisations designed to promote the *volk* (people; ie the Afrikaners).

Due to the booming wartime economy, black labour became increasingly important to the mining and manufacturing industries, and the black urban population nearly doubled. Enormous squatter camps grew up on the outskirts of Johannesburg and, to a lesser extent, outside the other major cities. Conditions in the townships were appalling, but poverty was not only suffered by blacks: wartime surveys found that 40% of white schoolchildren were malnourished.

Apartheid

In the months leading up to the 1948 elections, the NP campaigned on its policy of segregation, or 'apartheid' (an Afrikaans term for the state of being apart). It was voted in, in coalition with the Afrikaner Party (AP), and under the leadership of DF Malan.

Thus it was that apartheid, long a reality of life, became institutionalised under Malan. Within short order, legislation was passed prohibiting mixed marriages, making interracial sex illegal, classifying every individual by race and establishing a classification board to rule in questionable cases. The noxious Group Areas Act of 1950 set aside desirable city properties for whites and banished nonwhites into the townships. The Separate Amenities Act created, among other things, separate beaches, buses, hospitals, schools and even park benches.

The existing pass laws were further strengthened: blacks and coloureds were compelled to carry identity documents at all times and were prohibited from remaining in towns, or even visiting them, without specific permission.

In 1960 tensions came to a head: on 21 March 1960, Robert Sobukwe, who had founded ANC splinter group the Pan African Congress (PAC), along with many thousands of followers protested against the hated pass laws at police stations in Gauteng and the Western Cape. Police opened fire on the demonstrators surrounding a police station in Sharpeville, a township near Vereeniging. In what became known as the Sharpeville massacre, at least 67 people were killed and 186 wounded; most were shot in the back.

Soon thereafter, Prime Minister Hendrik Verwoerd, credited with the unofficial title of 'architect of apartheid', announced a referendum on whether the country should become a republic. The change was passed by a slim majority of voters. Verwoerd withdrew South Africa from the Commonwealth, and in May 1961 the Republic of South Africa came into existence.

ANC Begins the Long Walk

The further entrenchment of apartheid pushed the hitherto relatively conservative ANC into action. In 1949 it had developed an agenda that for the first time advocated open resistance in the form of strikes, acts of public disobedience and protest marches. Resistance continued throughout the 1950s and resulted in occasional violent clashes. In 1959 a group of disenchanted ANC members, seeking to sever all links with the white government, broke away to form the more militant PAC.

To many domestic and international onlookers, the struggle had crossed a crucial line at Sharpeville, and there could no longer be any lingering doubts about the nature of the white regime. In the wake of the shooting, a massive stay away from work was organised, and demonstrations continued. Prime Minister Verwoerd declared a state of emergency, giving security forces the right to detain people without trial. More than 18,000 demonstrators were arrested, including much of the ANC and PAC leadership, and both organisations were banned.

In response, the ANC and PAC began a campaign of sabotage through the armed wings of their organisations, Umkhonto we Sizwe (Spear of the Nation, MK) and Poqo ('Pure' or 'Alone'), respectively. In July 1963, 17 members of the ANC underground movement were arrested and tried for treason at the widely publicised Rivonia Trial. Among them was Nelson Mandela, an ANC leader and founder of Umkhonto we Sizwe, who had already been arrested on other charges. In June 1964, Mandela and seven others were sentenced to life imprisonment. Oliver Tambo, another member of the ANC leadership, managed to escape South Africa and lead the ANC in exile. On 20 April 1964, during the Rivonia Trial, Nelson Mandela said, 'I have fought against White domination and I have fought against Black domination. I have cherished the ideal of a democratic and free society in which all persons live together in harmony and with equal opportunities. It is an ideal which I hope to live for and to achieve. But if needs be, it is an ideal for which I am prepared to die.'

Decades of Darkness

With the ANC banned, and Mandela and most of its leadership in jail or exile, South Africa moved into some of its darkest times. Apartheid legislation was enforced with increasing gusto, and the walls between the races were built ever higher. Most odious was the creation of separate 'homelands' for blacks. Ten homelands were created within South Africa's borders – black-only 'countries' that were meant to be autonomous from South Africa, though no one outside the country recognised them. Residents were stripped of their South African ciitizenship and left in a puppet state wth no infrastructure and plenty of corruption.

During the 1970s, resistance again gained momentum, first channelled through trade unions and strikes, and then spearheaded by the South African Students' Organisation under the leadership of the charismatic Steve Biko. Biko, a medical student, was the main force behind the growth of South Africa's Black Consciousness Movement, which stressed the need for psychological liberation, black pride and nonviolent opposition to apartheid.

Things culminated in 1976, when the Soweto Students' Representative Council organised protests against the use of Afrikaans (regarded as the language of the oppressor) in black schools. On 16 June, police opened fire on a student march led by Tsietsi Mashinini – a central figure in the book *A Burning Hunger: One Family's Struggle Against Apartheid* and now immortalised by a large monument in Soweto. This began a round of nationwide demonstrations, strikes, mass arrests, riots and violence that, over the next 12 months, took more than 1000 lives.

In September 1977, Steve Biko was killed by security police. South Africa would never be the same. A generation of young blacks committed themselves to a revolutionary struggle against apartheid ('Liberation before Education' was the catch-cry) and black communities were politicised.

Winds of Change

In the early 1980s, a fresh wind began to blow across South Africa. Whites constituted only 16% of the total population, in comparison with 20% 50 years earlier, and the percentage was continuing to fall. Recognising the inevitability of change, President PW

Botha told white South Africans to 'adapt or die'. Numerous reforms were instituted, including the repeal of the pass laws. But Botha stopped well short of full reform, and many blacks (as well as the international community) felt the changes were only cosmetic. Protests and resistance continued at full force as South Africa became increasingly polarised and fragmented, and unrest was widespread. A white backlash gave rise to a number of neo-Nazi paramilitary groups, notably the Afrikaner Weerstandsbeweging (AWB), led by Eugène Terre'Blanche. The opposition United Democratic Front (UDF) was also formed at this time. With a broad coalition of members, led by Archbishop Desmond Tutu and the Reverend Allan Boesak, it called for the government to abolish apartheid and eliminate the homelands.

International pressure also increased, as economic sanctions began to dig in harder, and the value of the rand collapsed. In 1985 the government declared a state of emergency, which was to stay in effect for five years. The media were censored and by 1988, according to ANC estimates (and backed up by those of human-rights groups), 30,000 people had been detained without trial and thousands had been tortured.

Mandela is Freed

In 1986 President Botha announced to parliament that South Africa had 'outgrown' apartheid. The government started making a series of minor reforms in the direction of racial equality while maintaining an iron grip on the media and on all anti-apartheid demonstrations.

In late 1989, a physically ailing Botha was succeeded by FW de Klerk. At his opening address to parliament in February 1990, De Klerk announced that he would repeal discriminatory laws and legalise the ANC, the PAC and the Communist Party. Media restrictions were lifted, and De Klerk released political prisoners not guilty of common-law crimes. On 11 February 1990, 27 years after he had first been incarcerated, Nelson Mandela walked out of the grounds of Victor Verster Prison a free man.

From 1990 to 1991 the legal apparatus of apartheid was abolished. A referendum – the last of the whites-only vote held in South Africa – overwhelmingly gave the government authority to negotiate a new constitution with the ANC and other groups.

Rough Road to Democracy

Despite the fact that the state of emergency had been lifted and the military presence removed, the period between apartheid and democracy was in fact one of the most violent times in South African history. There were groups on both sides who resented their leaders entering into talks with the opposition and made every effort to end the peace talks – usually by violent means. Between 1990 and 1994 there were over 12,000 political killings.

Although Mandela and De Klerk initially enjoyed mutual respect, Mandela soon became suspicious of De Klerk's loyalty to democracy following a record number of deaths, many seemingly carried out by the police. He believed that these murders and disappearances had ultimately been ordered by the government – and that meant by De Klerk. Mandela referred to the authority ordering the deaths as the Third Force. There were also many everyday South Africans opposed to the talks who likewise perpetuated violent attacks. Chaos reigned in the townships, where rival factions fought – when the police stepped in, the violence escalated further. Many ANC members had trained for guerrilla warfare and clung hopelessly to the idea that they could overthrow the government using violence and without having to accommodate white demands. In July 1991 Nelson Mandela was officially elected president of the ANC, despite an increasing distrust for a man in secret negotiations with the oppressive government.

Throughout the negotiation process huge problems were caused by the Zulu Inkatha Freedom Party (IFP), both in their own province and in townships around the country where Zulus lived and clashed with other groups. Throughout apartheid KwaZulu had enjoyed special status, with leader Chief Mangosuthu Buthelezi sitting on a fence somewhere between African rights and white capitalism. As violence reached a new high, ANC followers demanded that the armed struggle recommence and with the country verging on anarchy, all talks collapsed. The world looked on in despair.

Slowly, the government gave in to each of Mandela's demands and in doing so gradually lost control of the negotiations process. Suddenly, Mandela had the upper hand. His former comrade in MK, Joe Slovo, drafted a constitution that appeased the National

Party. Slovo included what he called 'sunset clauses', which allowed current public servants to continue their term, working alongside ANC members in a power-sharing plan that would ensure a smooth government changeover.

Elections

In 1993 an interim constitution was finalised, guaranteeing freedom of speech and religion, access to adequate housing and numerous other benefits, and explicitly prohibiting discrimination on almost any grounds. Finally, at midnight on 26/27 April 1994, the old national anthem 'Die Stem' (The Call) was sung and the old flag was lowered, followed by the raising of the new rainbow flag and the singing of the new anthem 'Nkosi Sikelel i Afrika' (God Bless Africa). The election went off fairly peacefully, amid a palpable feeling of goodwill throughout the country. Due to their efforts in bringing reconciliation to South Africa, Mandela and De Klerk were jointly awarded the Nobel Peace Prize in 1993.

The ANC won 62.7% of the vote, less than the 66.7% that would have enabled it to rewrite the constitution. As well as deciding the national government, the election decided the provincial governments, and the ANC won in all but two provinces. The NP captured most of the white and coloured vote and became the official opposition party.

In 1996, after much negotiation and debate, South Africa's parliament approved a

NELSON MANDELA

Nelson Rolihlahla Mandela, one of the millennium's greatest leaders, was once vilified by South Africa's ruling whites and sentenced to life imprisonment. Twenty-seven years later, he emerged from incarceration calling for reconciliation and forgiveness.

Mandela, son of a Xhosa chief, was born on 18 July 1918 in the village of Mveso on the Mbashe River. After attending the University of Fort Hare, Mandela headed to Johannesburg, where he soon became immersed in politics. He finished his law degree and, together with Oliver Tambo, opened South Africa's first black law firm. Meanwhile, in 1944, along with Tambo and Walter Sisulu, Mandela formed the Youth League of the African National Congress (ANC). During the 1950s, Mandela was at the forefront of the ANC's civil disobedience campaigns, for which he was arrested in 1952, and tried and acquitted. After the ANC was banned in the wake of the Sharpeville massacre, Mandela led the establishment of its underground military wing, Umkhonto we Sizwe. In 1964 Mandela was brought to stand trial for sabotage and fomenting revolution in the widely publicised Rivonia Trial. After brilliantly arguing his own defence, he was sentenced to life imprisonment, and spent the next 18 years in the infamous Robben Island prison before being moved to the mainland.

Throughout his incarceration, Mandela repeatedly refused to compromise his political beliefs in exchange for freedom, saying that only free men can negotiate.

In February 1990, Mandela was finally released, and in 1991 he was elected president of the ANC. In 1993 Mandela shared the Nobel Peace Prize with FW de Klerk and, in the country's first free elections the following year, was elected president of South Africa. In his much-quoted speech 'Free at Last!', made after winning the 1994 elections, he focused the nation's attention firmly on the future, declaring, 'This is the time to heal the old wounds and build a new South Africa.'

In 1997 Mandela – or Madiba, his traditional Xhosa name – stepped down as ANC president, although he continued to be revered as an elder statesman. On 5 December 2013 Nelson Mandela, aged 95 years, died from an ongoing respiratory infection. South Africans grieved openly for the man who had given so much of himself to his country. South African president Jacob Zuma said, 'Our nation has lost its greatest son. Nothing can diminish our sense of a profound and enduring loss.' The world also grieved for the man who had inspired so many with his moral authority. One of the largest gatherings of world leaders came together for the memorial service.

The legacy of Nelson Mandela is what he achieved with unswerving determination, generosity of spirit and lack of vengeance. And his gift to South Africans was the major role he played in bringing peace and reconciliation to a country torn by racial discrimination. It is a legacy that reverberates far beyond his country's borders.

revised version of the 1993 constitution that established the structure of the country's new, democratic government. The national government consists of a 400-member National Assembly, a 90-member National Council of Provinces and a head of state (the president), who is elected by the National Assembly.

A South African president has more in common with a Westminster-style prime minister than a US president, although as head of state the South African president has some executive powers denied to most prime ministers. The constitution is most notable for its expansive Bill of Rights.

In 1999 South Africa held its second democratic elections. Two years previously Mandela had handed over ANC leadership to his deputy, Thabo Mbeki, and the ANC's share of the vote increased to put the party within one seat of the two-thirds majority that would allow it to alter the constitution.

The Democratic Party (DP) – traditionally a stronghold of liberal whites, with new support from conservatives disenchanted with the NP, and from some middle-class blacks – won official opposition status.

By any account, Mbeki had huge shoes to fill as president – although how close he came is the subject of sharply divided debate – and his years in office can only be characterised as a roller-coaster ride. In the early days of his presidency, Mbeki's effective denial of the HIV/AIDS crisis invited global criticism, and his conspicuous failure to condemn the forced reclamation of white-owned farms in neighbouring Zimbabwe and to speak out publicly against his long-time comrade, Zimbabwean president Robert Mugabe, unnerved both South African landowners and foreign investors.

Truth & Reconciliation

Following the first elections, focus turned to the Truth and Reconciliation Commission (1994–99), which worked to expose crimes of the apartheid era. The dictum of its chairman Archbishop Desmond Tutu was: 'Without forgiveness there is no future, but without confession there can be no forgiveness.' Many stories of horrific brutality and injustice were heard by the commission, offering some catharsis to people and communities shattered by their past.

The commission operated by allowing victims to tell their stories and perpetrators to confess their guilt, with amnesty on offer to those who made a clean breast of it. Those who chose not to appear before the commission would face criminal prosecution if their guilt could be proven. Yet, while some soldiers, police and 'ordinary' citizens confessed their crimes, many of the human-rights criminals who gave the orders and dictated the policies failed to present themselves (PW Botha was one famous no-show).

South Africa in Recent Years

In 2005 Mbeki dismissed his deputy president Jacob Zuma in the wake of corruption charges against him, setting off a ruthless internal ANC power struggle, which Zuma won. In September 2008, in an unprecedented move by the party, Mbeki was asked to step down as president.

The charges against Zuma were dropped and, as widely expected, the ANC won the 2009 election, with Jacob Zuma declared president. Zuma managed to balance out considerable domestic and international criticism with his approachable personality and strong grassroots popularity. There is a widely held view, however, that he has demonstrated weak leadership and failed to fulfill promises to create jobs and alleviate poverty. The opposition has also brought new charges of corruption against him.

In the 2014 elections, the country's media excitedly talked up the chances of the Democratic Alliance (DA) – the official opposition that is an amalgamation of the old Democratic Party and numerous smaller parties. Disenchantment with perceived corruption, crime and slow progress on providing critical services to poor communities fed a growing desire for change. In the end, though, the ANC won comfortably with 62.1% of the vote (down from 65.9% in 2009); the Democratic Alliance won 22.2%, highlighting the mammoth task it faces in wresting government from the ANC.

Perhaps the most surprising result was from the Economic Freedom Fighters – a new political party headed by Julius Malema, a former ANC youth leader kicked out of his former party for corruption and bringing the ANC into disrepute. Though he enjoys grassroots popularity for his talk of economic equality and fighting poverty, his radical views against 'white monopoly power' and on the need for faster land redistribution has worried many. Once one of Zuma's greatest supporters, he now rails against his former mentor and the corrupt practices that he accuses the ANC of perpetrating.

The ability of opposition parties to pressure the government to tackle the country's problems continues to be an important test of South Africa's political maturity. Corruption, crime, economic inequality, quality education and AIDS all loom as major challenges.

Given the country's turbulent recent history, ongoing crime problems and issues of corruption – the latter two are always talking points among the populace – it's not surprising that there is a range of views among South Africans about the future of the 'rainbow nation'. Most of them would agree, however, that the country today is an immeasurably more optimistic and relaxed place than it was in 1990, despite the massive problems that it still confronts.

The Culture

Dubbed the 'rainbow nation' by Archbishop Desmond Tutu, South Africa has become more integrated in the two decades since its first democratic elections. There's still a long way to go, perhaps a generation or two, but people tend to live and work more harmoniously these days, and the nation is divided less by colour than by class.

The numerous issues that stir racial tension and shake international confidence in South Africa include government corruption and the disparity between rich and poor; land reform and farm attacks; the controversial Black Economic Empowerment and affirmative action; and inflammatory tirades from the likes of Economic Freedom Fighters (EFF) leader Julius Malema. All have contributed to the weakening rand: between 2011 and 2015 its value dropped from roughly seven to the US dollar to 12 to the dollar. The rand's lowest point came in December 2015, when President Zuma unexpectedly fired finance minister Nhlanhla Nene. The minister had threatened to stand in the way of deals Zuma was trying to make with cronies at the country's national airline, SAA.

The country's reputation for crime continues to dent its considerable appeal as a tourism destination. It is important to keep things in perspective so as not to miss out on three inspiring and hope-filled countries at the tip of Africa. Visiting South Africa provides a rare chance to experience a nation that is rebuilding itself after profound change. A backdrop to all this change is magnificent natural scenery, and the remarkably deep bond – perhaps best expressed in the country's literature – that most South Africans feel for their land.

People & Economy

South Africa's Gauteng province, which includes Johannesburg and Pretoria, is the economic engine of the country, generating over a third of South Africa's GDP – and 10% of Africa's. It's also the most densely populated and urbanised province. At the other end of the scale is the rural and underdeveloped Eastern Cape, where around 25% of adults are illiterate.

Millions of immigrants from across the continent make their way to South Africa to take advantage of the country's powerhouse economy. While some arrive legally, many illegal immigrants live in the townships of Jo'burg and other cities, causing resentment among some locals, who accuse the outsiders of taking jobs, committing crime and increasing pressure on service delivery.

Beyond economics, different racial groups have complicated relationships. While much of the focus in South Africa has been on black–white relations, there is also friction and distrust between black people, coloured people and South Africans of Indian descent. Yet, locals are often surprisingly open when they talk about the stereotypes and prejudices that exist across racial lines. Relations within racial groups are also complex: just ask a Zulu what he or she thinks about Xhosas or quiz English-speaking white people about their views on Afrikaners.

Racial Groups

BLACK

The vast majority of South Africans – about 80% – are black Africans. Although subdivided into dozens of smaller groups, all ultimately trace their ancestry to the Bantu speakers who migrated to Southern Africa in the early part of the 1st millennium AD. Due to the destruction and dispersal caused by the *difaqane* (forced migration) in the 19th century, and to the forced removals and separations of the apartheid era, tribal affiliation tends to be much weaker in South Africa than in other areas of the continent.

Today, discussions generally focus on ethnolinguistic groupings. With the constitution's elevation of 11 languages to the status of 'official' language, the concept of ethnicity is also gaining a second wind. The largest ethnolinguistic group is the Nguni, which includes Zulu, Swazi, Xhosa and Ndebele peoples. Other major groups are the Sotho-Tswana, the Tsonga-Shangaan and the Venda.

The Zulu maintain the highest-profile ethnic identity, and 23% of South Africans speak Zulu as a first language – including President Zuma. The second-largest group is the Xhosa, who have been extremely influential in politics. Nelson Mandela was Xhosa, as were many figures in the apartheid struggle, and Xhosa have traditionally formed the heart of the black professional class. About 16% of South Africa's population uses Xhosa as a first language.

Other major groups include the Basotho (found primarily in and around Lesotho and South Africa's Free State), the Swazi (most of whom are in Swaziland) and the Tswana (who live primarily in the North West Province and Northern Cape, as well as neighbouring Botswana). The Ndebele and Venda peoples, found mostly in Mpumalanga and Limpopo respectively, are fewer in number, but have maintained very distinct cultures.

COLOURED

During apartheid, 'coloured' was generally used as a catch-all term for anyone who didn't fit into one of the other racial categories. Despite this, a distinct coloured cultural identity has developed over the years – forged, at least in part, by white people's refusal to accept coloureds as equals, and coloureds' own refusal to be grouped socially with blacks. Coloured people are renowned for their sharp sense of humour and quick-witted patter, which has helped them through hardships such as the notorious forced population removals from Cape Town's District Six (covered at the District Six Museum).

Among the diverse ancestors of today's coloured population are Afrikaners and others of European descent, West African slaves, political prisoners and exiles from the Dutch East Indies, and some of South Africa's original Khoe-San peoples. One of the largest subgroups of coloureds is the Griqua.

Another major subgroup is the Cape Muslims, also know as the Cape Malays, with roots in places as widely dispersed as India, Indonesia and parts of East Africa. They have preserved their Asian-influenced culture and cuisine, which you can experience on a walking tour of Cape Town's Bo-Kaap neighbourhood.

Today, most coloured people live in the Western and Northern Capes, with a significant population also in the Eastern Cape.

About 20% speak English as their first language, while about 80% are Afrikaans speakers; one of the oldest Afrikaans documents is a Quran transcribed using Arabic script. South Africa's roughly 4.6 million coloured people comprise about 9% of the total population.

WHITE

Most of South Africa's approximately 4.6 million white people (about 9% of South Africans) are either Afrikaans-speaking descendents of the early European settlers or English speakers. The Afrikaners, who constitute about 5% of the country's total population, have had a disproportionate influence on South Africa's history. Rural areas of the country, with the exception of the Eastern Cape, KwaZulu-Natal and the former homelands, continue to be dominated by Afrikaners, who are united by language and often by membership in the Dutch Reformed Church – the focal point of life in country towns.

While a few Afrikaners still dream of a *volkstaat* (an independent, racially pure Boer state), the urbanised middle class has become considerably more moderate. Happily, the further the distance between the apartheid era and the 'new South Africa', the more room there is for all Afrikaners to be proud of their heritage. Two reflections of this are the growing popularity of Oudtshoorn's Klein Karoo National Arts Festival and the blossoming Afrikaans indie music scene.

About two-thirds of South Africa's white English speakers trace their roots to the British immigrants who began arriving in South Africa in the 1820s. Other white South Africans include about 70,000 Jews, a Greek community numbering 50,000-plus people and a similar number of Portuguese.

ASIAN

The majority of South Africa's almost 1.3 million Asians are Indians. Many are descended from the indentured labourers brought to KwaZulu-Natal in the 19th century, while others trace their ancestry to the free 'passenger Indians' who came to South Africa during the same period as merchants and businesspeople. During apartheid, Indians were both discriminated against by whites and seen as white collaborators by some blacks.

Today's South African Indian population is primarily Hindu, with about 20% Muslims and small numbers of Christians. Close to

90% live in Durban and other urban areas of KwaZulu-Natal. Most speak English as a first language; Tamil or Hindi and Afrikaans are also spoken.

There are more than 300,000 Chinese people in South Africa, concentrated primarily in Johannesburg but running shops nationwide, and small numbers of other East Asians.

Women

Women have enjoyed a uniquely high profile during South Africa's turbulent history: they were at the centre of the anti-pass law demonstrations and bus boycotts of the 1950s, protesting under the slogan 'You strike the woman and you strike the rock.' Women are also well represented in South Africa's current parliament, the constitution guarantees women's rights, and the ruling African National Congress (ANC) party has a 50%-women quota system.

However, the daily reality for many South African women is very different, with poverty, sexual violence and HIV infection overshadowing other gains. South Africa has one of the world's highest rape rates, with more than 65,000 offences reported to the police annually. In one study, one in four men admitted to having raped a woman. A woman is raped every five minutes and gang rape is common. The brutal gang rape and mutilation of teenager Anene Booysen in the Overberg town of Bredasdorp in 2013 was a 'Delhi moment' for South Africa, sparking protests about the horrific epidemic and echoing the previous year's outcry in India.

Women are statistically more likely than men to be infected with HIV, and many women become infected at an early age. Worsening the situation is the threat of sexual violence, which often undermines the ability of young women to ensure their partner is wearing a condom.

Religion

Religion plays a central role in the lives of most people in South Africa and church attendance is generally high. Christianity is dominant, with almost 80% of South Africans identifying themselves as Christians. Major South African denominations include the Dutch Reformed Church, which has more than a million members and more than 1000 churches across the country, and the considerably more flamboyant Zion

Christian Church (ZCC), with up to six million followers.

About 15% of South Africans are atheist and agnostic, while Muslims, Hindus and Jews combined make up less than 5% of the population. Up to two-thirds of South Africa's Indians have retained their Hindu faith. Islam has a small but growing following, particularly in the Cape. There is a declining Jewish community of about 70,000 people, mostly in Jo'burg and the Cape.

African traditional believers make up around 1% of South Africa's population, compared with 20% in neighbouring Lesotho. However, their traditions and practices have a significant influence on the cultural fabric and life of the region. Visting the *sangoma* (traditional healer) for some *muti* (traditional medicine) is a widespread practice, even amongst those who practise Christianity.

Arts

LITERATURE

South Africa has an extraordinarily rich literary history, and there's no better way to get a sense of the country than by delving into some local reads.

Many of the first black South African writers were missionary-educated, including Sol Plaatje. In 1930 his epic romance *Mhudi* became one of the first books published in English by a black South African. The first major South African novel published internationally was Olive Schreiner's *Story of an African Farm* (1883), which depicts colonial life in the Karoo.

In 1948 South Africa made an impression on the international literary scene with Alan Paton's global-bestseller *Cry, the Beloved Country*. Today, this beautifully crafted tale is still one of the country's most widely recognised titles.

Nadine Gordimer's acclaimed *A Guest of Honour* was published in 1970. The country's first Nobel laureate in literature (1991), her most famous novel, *July's People* (1981), depicts the collapse of white rule.

In the 1960s and '70s Afrikaner writers gained prominence as powerful voices for the opposition. Poet and novelist Breyten Breytenbach was jailed for becoming involved with the liberation movement, while André Brink's novel *Looking on Darkness* was the first Afrikaans book to be banned by the apartheid government. His autobiography, *A Fork in the Road* (2009), gives a fascinating account of anti-apartheid activities by Afrikaners.

The 1970s also gave rise to several influential black poets, including Mongane Wally Serote, a veteran of the liberation struggle. His work gives insights into the lives of black South Africans during the worst years of oppression.

JM Coetzee, now residing in Australia, gained international acclaim with his novel *Disgrace* (1999), which won him his second Booker Prize. Coetzee was awarded the Nobel Prize for Literature in 2003.

One of the most prominent contemporary authors is Zakes Mda. With the publication of *Ways of Dying* in 1995, Mda became an acclaimed novelist. His memoir, *Sometimes There is a Void* (2011), is a transfixing account of his exile in Lesotho and eventual return to South Africa.

VISUAL ARTS

South African art had its beginnings with the San, who left their distinctive designs on rock faces and cave walls throughout the region. When European painters arrived, many of their early works centred on depictions of Africa for colonial enthusiasts back home, although with time, a more South Africa–centred focus developed.

Black artists were sidelined for many decades. Gerard Sekoto was one of the first to break through the barriers of racism, becoming a major figure in South African modern art. Throughout the apartheid era, racism, oppression and violence were common themes. Many black artists who were unable to afford materials adopted cheaper alternatives, such as lino prints.

A recent lack of public funds for the arts sector has meant that it has become more reliant on corporate collectors and the tourism industry. Contemporary art ranges from the vibrant crafts sold in the Venda region (or on the side of the road in cities and tourist areas) to high-priced paintings hanging in galleries. Innovative township artists are using 'found' materials such as telephone wire, safety pins, beads, plastic bags and tin cans. Local sculpture is also diverse; artists working in various media include the Venda woodcarvers and bronze sculptor Dylan Lewis.

See www.artthrob.co.za for news, features and listings on South Africa's contemporary visual arts scene.

Environment

The Land & Sea

A windswept and beautiful coast is the face that South Africa turns to the rest of the world – tempestuous and tamed, stormy and sublime. It spans two oceans as it winds its way down the Atlantic seaboard in the west and up into the warmer Indian Ocean waters to the east. In all, the country has more than 2500km of coastline. Two major ocean currents shape the country's climate and provide for a rich marine life. The chilly Benguela current surges up from Antarctica along the country's Atlantic Coast and is laden with plankton. The north-to-south Mozambique/Agulhas current gives the east coast its warmer waters.

And this is just the start of the region's topographical wealth. Head further inland, and you'll find yourself climbing from the eastern lowlands (lowveld) to the cool heights of the Drakensberg Escarpment and onto the vast plateau (highveld) that forms the heart of the country. This plateau, which averages about 1500m in height, drops off again in the northwestern part of the country to the low-lying Kalahari basin.

Wildlife

South Africa is home to the world's three largest land mammals (the African elephant, white rhino and hippopotamus), its tallest (giraffe), fastest (cheetah) and smallest (pygmy shrew). The country's 800-plus bird species include the world's largest (ostrich), the heaviest flying bird (Kori bustard) and the smallest raptor (pygmy falcon).

Off its long coastline is a rich diversity of marine life – 11,000 species have been recorded. Eight whale species are found in South African waters, including the largest mammal in the world, the blue whale. Although it's the great white shark that snares most of the headlines, turtles, seabirds and penguins are also popular sightings.

Endangered mammals include black rhinos (sometimes spotted in uMkhuze Game Reserve, and Hluhluwe-iMfolozi Park); riverine rabbits (found only near rivers in the central Karoo); wild dogs (Hluhluwe-iMfolozi Park and Kruger National Park); and roan antelope. Endangered bird species include the African penguin and the Cape vulture.

The wattled crane and the blue swallow are threatened.

National Parks & Protected Areas

South Africa has close to 600 national parks and reserves, many featuring wildlife, while others are primarily wilderness sanctuaries or hiking areas. All national parks charge a daily conservation fee, which is discounted for South African residents and nationals of Southern African Development Community (SADC) countries.

In addition to its national parks, South Africa is party to several transfrontier conservation areas. These include Kgalagadi Transfrontier Park, combining the Northern Cape's former Kalahari Gemsbok National Park with Botswana's Gemsbok National Park; the Maloti-Drakensberg Peace Park, which links Sehlabathebe National Park and other areas of the Lesotho Drakensberg with their South African counterparts in uKhahlamba-Drakensberg; and the Great Limpopo Transfrontier Park, which spans the borders of South Africa, Mozambique and Zimbabwe. Private wildlife reserves also abound.

In total, just over 5% of South African land has national park status, with an estimated 4% to 5% more enjoying other types of protective status. The government has started teaming up with private landowners to bring private conservation land under government protection, with the goal of increasing the total amount of conservation land to over 10%.

In addition to this, South Africa has 19 Marine Protected Areas (MPAs) designed to protect and stabilise fish and other marine-life populations against overfishing, pollution, uncontrolled tourism and mining. The world's seventh largest MPA was declared in 2013 and lies 2000km southeast of the country's coastline around Prince Edward and Marion Islands. Marine life falling under the protection of the new MPA includes albatrosses, penguins, fur seals, killer whales and Patagonian toothfish.

More information is available through online resources:

CapeNature (☏ 021-483 0190; www.cape nature.co.za) Promotes nature conservation in the Western Cape, and is responsible for permits and bookings for Western Cape reserves.

Ezemvelo KZN Wildlife (☏ 033-845 1000; www.kznwildlife.com) Responsible for wildlife parks in KwaZulu-Natal.

South African National Parks (SANParks; ☏ 012-428 9111; www.sanparks.org) The best place to start your safari.

Environmental Issues

South Africa is the world's third most biologically diverse country. It's also one of Africa's most urbanised, with over 50% of the population living in towns and cities. Major challenges for the government include managing increasing urbanisation while protecting the environment.

Land degradation is one of the country's most serious problems, with about one-quarter of South Africa's land considered to be severely degraded. In former homeland areas, years of overgrazing and overcropping have resulted in massive soil depletion. This, plus poor overall conditions, is pushing people to the cities, further increasing urban pressures. The distorted rural–urban settlement pattern is a legacy of the apartheid era, with huge population concentrations in townships that generally lack adequate utilities and infrastructure.

South Africa receives an average of only 500mm of rainfall annually, and droughts are common. To meet demand for water, all major South African rivers have been dammed or modified. While this has improved water supply to many areas, it has also disrupted local ecosystems and caused increased silting in waterways.

South Africa has long been at the forefront among African countries in conservation of its fauna. However, funding is tight and will likely remain so as long as many South Africans still lack access to basic amenities. Rhino poaching across the country, and particularly in Kruger National Park, is exacerbated by underfunding. Potential solutions include public/private-sector conservation partnerships, and increased contributions from private donors and international conservation bodies such as the World Wide Fund for Nature (WWF).

Estimates have put South Africa's potential shale-gas deposits at 485 trillion cubic feet of gas. That's gained a lot of interest from oil companies, and according to Econometrix (in a report commissioned by Shell) the shale-gas industry could be worth R200 billion annually to GDP and lead to the creation of 700,000 jobs. Until 2012, South Africa, like many countries had placed a moratorium on hydraulic fracturing (fracking) to extract the gas. There are serious environmental concerns about the safety of the technology used in fracking, which uses large amounts of clean water mixed with sand and a 'chemical cocktail' to crack underground rocks and release the shale gas. Since the moratorium was lifted, the debate over fracking in South Africa's Northern Cape (in the Karoo) has continued to rage, with these serious environmental concerns – pitted against vested economic interests – in particular large oil companies. In March 2016, the government announced that fracking would commence within 12 months.

SURVIVAL GUIDE

❶ Directory A–Z

ACCOMMODATION

You can often get away with booking a few days in advance, or not at all, but if you're travelling at Christmas or Easter, plan several months ahead. Book national-park accommodation a month in advance.

Lodges Can be uber-luxe or fairly rustic but tend to boast some of the best locations.

Guesthouses Often owner-run, with comfortable rooms, hearty breakfasts and priceless local information.

Self-catering cottages Usually spacious and excellent value for money.

Backpacker hostels Often have a bar, swimming pool and campsites; ideal for budget or solo travellers.

Hotels Everything from stylish boutique hotels to vast and luxurious chains brands.

Seasons Rates rise steeply during the summer school break (mid-December to early January) and the Easter break (late March to mid-April). Room prices sometimes double and minimum stays are imposed; advance bookings are essential. The other school holidays (late June to mid-July and late September to early October) are classified as either high or shoulder season. You can get excellent deals during the winter low season, which is also the best time for wildlife-watching.

Discounts Discounted midweek and multinight rates are common, so always ask. Occasionally, in towns geared towards business travellers rather than tourists, such as mining centres, rates can be more expensive during the week.

ACTIVITIES

Thanks to South Africa's diverse terrain and pleasant climate, almost any outdoor activity is possible to do here, from abseiling to zip lining. Good facilities and instruction mean that most activities are accessible to all visitors, whatever their experience level.

Birdwatching

With its enormous diversity of habitats, South Africa is a paradise for birdwatchers. There are birdwatching clubs nationwide, and most parks and reserves can provide birding lists, with some information from SANParks (www.sanparks. org). Many parks, reserves and accommodation also have field guides, but it's still worth bringing your own.

BirdLife South Africa (www.birdlife.org.za) Useful information and links. Promotes avitourism (birding ecotourism) routes.

Birding Africa (www.birdingafrica.com) Day trips from Cape Town and tours further afield, covering birds and flowers.

Bird-Watch Cape (www.birdwatch.co.za) Small, Cape Town–based outfit for twitchers, with tours including nationwide 17- and 27-day packages.

Cape Birding Route (www.capebirdingroute. org) Information relating to western South Africa, from Cape Point to the Kalahari.

Greater Limpopo Birding Routes (www.limpopobirding.com) Lists guides and four routes, including one taking in the Soutpansberg mountains and Limpopo River Valley.

Indicator Birding (www.birding.co.za) Information, articles and tours. Based in Gauteng.

Southern African Birding (www.sabirding. co.za) Multimedia guides and information.

Zululand Birding Route (www.zululandbirdingroute.co.za) Avitourism project in an area of northern KwaZulu-Natal featuring over 600 bird species.

Canoeing, Kayaking & Rafting

South Africa has few major rivers, but those it has flow year-round and offer rewarding rafting and canoeing. Rafting is highly rain-dependent, with the best months in most areas from December/January to April.

PRICE RANGES

Rates quoted are for high season (November to March), with a private bathroom. Exceptions are noted in listings. Reviews are ordered by budget and, within those categories, by preference. Price ranges are based on the cost of a double room.

$ less than R700

$$ R700–1400

$$$ more than R1400

In Cape Town, Johannesburg and the Garden Route, prices are higher:

$ less than R1050

$$ R1050–2100

$$$ more than R2100

Felix Unite (☑ 087 354 0578; www.felixunite. com) Runs trips on the Breede and Gariep (Orange) Rivers.

Induna Adventures (www.indunaadventures. com) White-water rafting and tubing ('geckoing') on the Sabie River.

Intrapid (www.raftsa.co.za) Rafting trips on rivers including the Gariep (Orange), Doring and Palmiet.

Kaskazi Kayaks (www.kayak.co.za) Sea kayaking trips in Cape Town and Gordon's Bay.

PaddleYak (www.seakayak.co.za) Sea kayak shop, news and tours.

Hiking

South Africa is a wonderful destination for hiking, with an excellent system of well-marked trails varied enough to suit every ability.

Accommodation Some trails offer accommodation, from camping and simple huts with electricity and running water to hotels on slackpacking trails in the Eastern Cape and elsewhere. Book well in advance.

Guided walks Various parks, including Kruger, offer hikes ranging from two- to three-hour bush walks to overnight or multiday wilderness trails. Accompanied by armed rangers, you won't cover much distance, but they offer the chance to experience the wild with nothing between you and nature. Numerous tour operators also offer guided hikes in areas such as the Wild Coast and Drakensberg – excellent ways to get off the beaten track and experience African village life.

Off-trail hiking Some designated wilderness areas offer this. Routes are suggested, but it's basically up to you to survive on your own.

Regulations Many trails have limits as to how many hikers can be on them at any one time, so book ahead. Most longer routes and wilderness areas require hikers to be in a group of at least three or four, although solo hikers may be able to join a group.

Safety This is not a major issue on most trails, but longer trails have seen muggings and burglaries of accommodation, while robberies and attacks can occur on the contour paths on Table Mountain, neighbouring Lion's Head, Signal Hill and especially Devil's Peak. Check with the local hiking club or park office. On longer and quieter trails, hike in a group, and limit the valuables you carry; in Cape Town, do not walk alone, and avoid early mornings, evenings and other quiet times. The Table Mountain plateau is usually safe.

When to Go Hiking is possible year-round, although you'll need to be prepared in summer for extremes of heat and wet. The best time in the northern half of the country is March to October. For Cape Town and the Western Cape, spring (September to November) and autumn (March to May) offer cool, dry weather.

Horse Riding & Pony Trekking

In South Africa it's easy to find horse rides ranging from hours to days, and for all experience levels. Riding trips are offered in several South African national parks.

Fynbos Trails (www.fynbostrails.com) In the Western Cape.

Haven Horse Safaris (www.havenhotel.co.za) One of many operators offering rides on the beaches of the Wild Coast and Eastern Cape.

Horizon Horseback Adventures (www.riding-nafrica.com) In the Waterberg, Limpopo.

Khotso Trails (www.khotsotrails.co.za) In the Southern Drakensberg, including Lesotho.

Savannah Horse Trails (www.savannahhorse-trails.co.za) In the Waterberg, Limpopo.

Mountain Biking

There are trails almost everywhere in South Africa, from the Garden Route to the Kalahari. Cape Town is an unofficial national hub for the activity.

Bike Hub (www.bikehub.co.za) General cycling site, with articles, classifieds and a popular forum.

Linx Africa (www.linx.co.za/trails/lists/bike-list.html) Lists trails by province.

MTB Routes (www.mtbroutes.co.za) Maps the locations of more than 400 bike trails nationwide.

Rock Climbing

Top spots for climbing include Table Mountain, the Cederberg, Montagu, the Drakensberg and Waterval Boven, near Nelspruit in Mpumalanga.

Climb ZA (www.climbing.co.za) News, articles, directory and forum.

Mountain Club of South Africa (www.mcsa.org.za) Information and links to regional clubs.

SA Climbing Info Network (www.saclimb.co.za) Has listings and photos of climbing and bouldering routes.

Surfing

The best time of the year for surfing the southern and eastern coasts is autumn and early winter (from about April to July). Boards and gear can be bought in most of the big coastal cities. New boards typically cost about R4500.

Good spots for beginners – with lessons and gear hire aplenty – are Muizenberg (Cape Town), Jeffreys Bay and Durban.

Wavescape (www.wavescape.co.za) Surf forecasting and coastal lifestyle website.

Zig Zag (www.zigzag.co.za) South Africa's main surf magazine.

Whale Watching

South Africa is considered one of the world's best spots to sight whales from land. Whale-watching spots dot the southern and eastern coastlines, from False Bay to iSimangaliso Wetland Park; Hermanus, where southern right whales come to calve, is the unofficial whale-watching capital.

Southern right and humpback whales are regularly seen offshore between June/July and November, with occasional spottings of Bryde's and killer whales.

Wildlife Watching

South Africa's populations of large animals are one of the country's biggest attractions. In comparison with other countries in the region (Botswana and Zambia, for example), wildlife watching in South Africa tends to be very accessible, with good roads and accommodation for all categories of traveller. It is also comparatively inexpensive, although there are plenty of pricier choices for those seeking a luxury experience in the bush.

CUSTOMS REGULATIONS

➛ You're permitted to bring 2L of wine, 1L of spirits and other alcoholic beverages, 200 cigarettes and up to R5000 worth of goods into South Africa without paying duties.

➛ Imported and exported protected-animal products such as ivory must be declared.

➛ Visit www.southafrica.info/travel/advice/redtape.htm for more information.

DANGERS & ANNOYANCES

Caused by South Africa's poverty and social inequality, crime is the national obsession. Apart from car accidents, it's the major risk that you'll face here. However, try to keep things in perspective: despite the statistics and newspaper headlines, the majority of travellers visit without incident. The risks are highest in Jo'burg, followed by some townships and other urban centres.

You can minimise risks by following basic safety precautions, including the following:

➛ Store your travel documents and valuables in your room (if it's secure), in a safe or at least out of sight.

➛ If your room does not have a safe or is not secure, inquire if there is a safe in reception.

➛ Don't flash around valuables such as cameras, watches and jewellery.

➛ Don't look like you might be carrying valuables; avoid wearing expensive-looking clothes.

➛ Completely avoid external money pouches.

➛ Divide your cash into a few separate stashes, with some 'decoy' money or a 'decoy' wallet ready to hand over if you are mugged.

➛ Keep a small amount of cash handy and separate from your other money, so that you don't need to pull out a large wad of bills for making purchases.

➛ Avoid groups of young men; trust older, mixed-sex groups.

➛ Don't keep money in your back pocket.

➛ Listen to local advice on unsafe areas.

➛ Avoid deserted areas day and night, including isolated beaches and parts of Cape Town's mountains.

➛ Avoid the downtown and CBD areas of larger towns and cities at night and weekends.

➛ If you're visiting a township, join a tour or hire a trusted guide.

➛ Try not to look apprehensive or lost.

➛ If you get a local phone number, bear in mind that 419-style telephone and SMS scams are rife.

DISCOUNT CARDS

➛ A valid student ID will get you discounts on bus tickets, museum admission and so on.

➛ **UR Card** (www.urcard.co.za), sold online and by backpackers and tourist businesses, offers discounts on accommodation, transport, tours and activities. The card costs R199, but there are other fees involved.

➛ If you're planning to spend more than eight days in national parks, seriously consider buying a **Wild Card** (www.sanparks.org/wild). A year pass for individual foreigners is R2210 (R3455 per couple, R4130 per family), which gives free access to more than 80 parks and reserves run by SANParks, Ezemvelo KZN Wildlife, Cape Nature, Msinsi and Swazi organisations.

➛ Some cities also offer discount cards for a number of their attractions.

EMBASSIES & CONSULATES

Most countries have their main embassy in Pretoria, with an office or consulate in Cape Town (which may become the embassy during Cape Town's parliamentary sessions).

Most open for visa services and consular matters on weekday mornings, between about 9am and noon. For more information, see www.dirco.gov.za/foreign/forrep/index.htm.

EMERGENCY & IMPORTANT NUMBERS

South Africa's country code	☏ 27
International access code	☏ 00
Ambulance	☏ 10177
Emergencies (from mobiles)	☏ 112
Police	☏ 10111

GAY & LESBIAN TRAVELLERS

South Africa's constitution is one of the few in the world that explicitly prohibits discrimination on the grounds of sexual orientation. Gay sexual relationships are legal and same-sex marriages are recognised. There are active gay and lesbian communities and scenes in Cape Town and Jo'burg, and to a lesser degree in Pretoria and Durban. Cape Town is the focal point, and is the most openly gay city on the continent.

But despite the liberality of the new constitution, it will be a while before attitudes in the more conservative sections of society begin to change towards acceptance. Particularly in rural areas, and in both black and white communities, homosexuality remains frowned upon, if not taboo.

INTERNET ACCESS

→ Internet access is widely available in South Africa, though connections may be slower than you're used to at home.

→ Accommodation options usually offer wi-fi or, less commonly, a computer with internet access for guest use.

→ We have used the (☏) icon where an establishment has a wi-fi network.

→ The (@) icon is used in sleeping reviews where an accommodation option offers a computer with internet access for guest use.

→ Many malls, cafes, bars and restaurants (including chains) have wi-fi, often for free. Alternatively, it may be through a provider such as **Skyrove** (www.skyrove.com) or **Red Button** (www.redbutton.co.za), for which you will need to buy credit online using a credit card, or from the hot-spot owner.

→ Look out for the **AlwaysOn** (www.alwayson.co.za) network, which generally allows you 30 minutes free connection per hotspot if you sign up. It's available at airports and some cafes, malls and banks.

→ If you are staying for some time, a USB modem or smart-phone data package may be useful, as wi-fi can be temperamental.

→ Local mobile-phone companies such as **MTN** (www.mtn.co.za) sell USB modems and data packages.

→ There are internet cafes in major towns and, sometimes, smaller locations. Charges are about R30 per hour.

MONEY

ATMs are found throughout the country and cards are widely accepted. Inform your bank of your travel plans before leaving home to avoid declined transactions.

Cash

→ South Africa's currency is the rand (R), which is divided into 100 cents. Notes are R10, R20, R50, R100 and R200; the coins are R1, R2 and R5, and five, 10, 20 and 50 cents. Transactions are often rounded up or down by a few cents.

→ The rand is weak against Western currencies, making travelling in South Africa less expensive than in Europe and North America.

→ The best currencies to bring in cash are US dollars, euros or British pounds, but a debit or credit card will be more useful, as many businesses only accept rand.

→ Cash is readily exchanged at banks and foreign-exchange bureaus in the major cities.

Credit Cards

Because South Africa has a reputation for scams, many banks abroad automatically prevent transactions in the country. If you plan to use a credit card in South Africa, contact your bank before leaving home and inform it of your travel plans to avoid having your purchases declined automatically.

Travellers Cheques

→ Thomas Cook and American Express travellers' cheques in major currencies can be cashed at banks, foreign-exchange bureaus and some hotels – with varying commissions.

→ Buying cheques in a stronger currency such as US dollars will work out better than buying them in rand.

→ If you buy rand or rand cheques, watch the market, as the currency can be pretty volatile; failing that, buying them just before departure will minimise the effects of devaluation.

→ There are **American Express** (www.americanexpressforex.co.za) foreign-exchange offices in major cities.

→ Keep at least some of your exchange receipts, as you'll need them to reconvert leftover rand when you leave.

Tipping

Wages are low here, and tipping is expected.
Restaurants & Cafes 10% to 15% of the total in restaurants; 10% in cafes.

Hotels A standard tip of R10 to R20 is welcomed.

Car guards Offer R2, or R5 for longer periods.

Petrol stations Anything from R2 – more if the attendant also washes the windscreen and checks the tyres.

Taxis Tips not expected but rounding up the fare will be appreciated.

OPENING HOURS

Banks 9am–3.30pm Mon–Fri, 9–11am Sat

Post offices 8.30am–4.30pm Mon–Fri, 8.30am–noon Sat

Government offices 8am–3pm Mon-Fri, 8am–noon Sat

Cafes 8am–5pm

Restaurants 11.30am–3pm & 6.30–10pm (last orders); many open 3–7pm

Bars 4pm–2am

Businesses & shopping 8.30am–5pm Mon–Fri, 8.30am–1pm Sat; many supermarkets also 9am–noon Sun; major shopping centres until 9pm daily

POST

➤ Both domestic and international deliveries are generally reliable but can be slow. There are periodic postal strikes, which further delay delivery times.

➤ For mailing anything valuable or important, use a private mail service such as **PostNet** (www.postnet.co.za).

➤ Do not receive anything of value from overseas, as parcels are often impounded by customs.

PUBLIC HOLIDAYS

New Year's Day 1 January

Human Rights Day 21 March

Good Friday March/April

Family Day March/April

Freedom Day 27 April

Workers' Day 1 May

Youth Day 16 June

National Women's Day 9 August

Heritage Day 24 September

Day of Reconciliation 16 December

Christmas Day 25 December

Day of Goodwill 26 December

TELEPHONE

South Africa has good telephone facilities, operated by **Telkom** (www.telkom.co.za). A good way to avoid high charges when calling home, or to make reverse-charge calls, is to dial a 'Home Direct' number, which puts you through to an operator in your country. Call Telkom's 24-hour international call centre to find out the number for your country.

Mobile Phones

➤ South Africa's 10-digit mobile numbers begin with ☑ 06, 07 or 08.

➤ The major mobile networks are **Cell C** (www.cellc.co.za), **MTN** (www.mtn.co.za), **Virgin Mobile** (www.virginmobile.co.za) and the Vodafone-owned **Vodacom** (www.vodacom.co.za).

➤ You can hire a mobile phone through your car-rental provider.

➤ A cheaper alternative is to use a local prepaid SIM card in your own phone, provided it's unlocked and on roaming. SIM cards and credit are available almost everywhere in shops and malls throughout the cities and larger towns. A new SIM should cost under R10; they tend to be more expensive in airport shops.

➤ You need some form of ID and proof of South African address to buy and 'RICA' (register) a SIM card. The proof of address can be a signed statement from your host or accommodation that you are residing with them, or an accommodation receipt.

➤ Various prepaid plans and airtime or data bundles are available. On Vodacom's Anytime Per Second plan, for example, calls cost R1.20 per minute, local SMS texts are R0.50 and international texts R1.74.

Phone Codes

Telephone numbers in South Africa are 10 digits, including the local area code, which must always be dialled. There are several four-digit nationwide prefixes, followed by six-digit numbers. These include:

➤ ☑ 080 (usually 0800; toll free)

➤ ☑ 0860 (charged as a local call)

➤ ☑ 0861 (flat-rate calls)

TOURIST INFORMATION

Almost every town in the country has a tourist office. These are often private entities, which will only recommend member organisations and may add commissions to bookings they make on your behalf. They are worth visiting, but you may have to push to find out about all the possible options.

In state-run offices, staff are often badly informed and lethargic; asking for assistance at your accommodation may prove more useful.

South African Tourism (www.southafrica.net) has a helpful website, with practical information and inspirational features.

VISAS

➤ Travellers from most Commonwealth countries (including Australia, Canada and the UK), most Western European countries, Japan and the USA are issued with a free, 90-day visitor's permit on arrival. From 16 January 2017 New Zealand citizens will require visas.

➡ Your passport should be valid for at least 30 days after the end of your intended visit, and should have at least two blank pages.

➡ Children aged under 18 must show an unabridged birth certificate, with additional paperwork needed in some cases. Your airline will likely alert you to these immigration regulations when you buy your flight.

➡ Immigration officers rarely ask to see it, but you should technically be able to present evidence of a return flight, or onward travel, from South Africa.

➡ If you have an onward flight, print a copy of your e-ticket, or ask your airline's help desk at the departing airport to print a copy of your itinerary.

➡ If you aren't entitled to a visitor's permit, you'll need to obtain a visa at a South African diplomatic mission in your home country, or one nearby.

➡ Visas are not issued at the borders.

➡ If you do need a visa, get a multiple-entry visa if you plan to visit Lesotho, Swaziland or any other neighbouring country. This avoids the hassle of applying for another South African visa.

➡ For any entry – whether you require a visa or not – you need to have at least two completely blank pages in your passport, excluding the last two pages.

➡ For more information, visit the websites of the **Department of Home Affairs** (www.dha. gov.za) and **Brand South Africa** (www.southafrica.info/travel/advice/disabled.htm).

VOLUNTEERING

Volunteering is a growing area, with opportunities nationwide. But there are some rip-off operators, often around animal-related projects. Book through local rather than foreign organisations, get previous volunteers' opinions, and check that most of your payment will go to the schemes involved rather than middlemen.

To work on an unpaid, voluntary basis for a short period, a visitor's permit or visa suffices. If you want to take a lengthy placement (in South Africa, for example, longer than the 90 days afforded by a visitor's permit), the organisation facilitating your placement should help you apply for the correct visa.

Shorter experiences of a few hours, days or weeks are available through accommodation options and tourist businesses, which often give ongoing support to one or two local schemes. But keep in mind that while short visits are interesting for the visitor, they may be of limited use to the project, beyond any fee paid for the trip. Some prominent volunteer organisations have actually suggested that short-term volunteers may do more harm than good.

African Conservation Experience (www.conservationafrica.net) Conservation projects and courses in Southern Africa.

African Impact (www.africanimpact.com) Volunteering and internship opportunities in areas including healthcare and conservation.

Aviva (www.aviva-sa.com) Cape Town-based organisation offering wide-ranging volunteering opportunities, including great white shark and African penguin conservation.

GoAbroad.com (www.goabroad.com/volunteer-abroad) Listings of opportunities in South Africa, Lesotho and Swaziland.

Greater Good SA (www.greatergoodsa.co.za) Has details on many local charities and development projects.

Grow (www.facebook.com/GROWMokhotlong) There are opportunities with this NGO implementing community-development programs in eastern Lesotho.

How 2 Help (www.h2h.info) Publishes a guide focusing on smaller, grassroots development projects.

Kick4Life (www.kick4life.org) Opportunities in Lesotho including the annual football tour, which mixes HIV education and soccer matches.

Life Skills (www.lifeskillsinsa.com) Reforestation and other green projects on the Garden Route.

One World 365 (www.oneworld365.org) Opportunities in areas including human rights, conservation, English teaching and healthcare.

Streetfootballworld (www.streetfootballworld.org) A starting point for football-related volunteering opportunities.

Travel Now Now (www.travelnownow.co.za) Province-by-province listings of opportunities.

Uthando South Africa (www.uthandosa.org) A tour company that supports a range of charitable projects.

Wilderness Foundation (www.wildernessfoundation.org) Conservation NGO running projects throughout Southern Africa.

World Wide Opportunities on Organic Farms (www.wwoofsa.co.za) Opportunities to stay and work on organic farms across South Africa; **Fynbos Estate** (www.fynbosestate.co.za) near Cape Town is recommended.

ℹ Getting There & Away

AIR
South African Airways (SAA; ☎ 0860 606 606; www.flysaa.com) is South Africa's national airline, with an excellent route network and safety record. In addition to its long-haul flights, it operates regional and domestic routes together with its partners Airlink (p526) and SA Express (p526).

OR Tambo International Airport (p462), east of Jo'burg, is the major hub for Southern Africa.

The other principal international airports are Cape Town International Airport (p353) and King Shaka International Airport (Durban; p416).

LAND
Car & Motorcycle

➜ If you rent a car in South Africa and plan to take it across an international border, you'll need a permission letter from the rental company.

➜ South African car-rental companies typically charge around R1500 for cross-border travel to Botswana, Namibia and Zimbabwe; R2000 for Mozambique.

➜ Most companies permit entry to most neighbouring countries; some may be reluctant regarding Mozambique.

➜ You don't usually need a letter to take a car into Lesotho or Swaziland and most companies will not charge for this.

➜ Check that the right information is on the permission letter; companies often get it wrong.

➜ Taking a car across a border also raises the insurance excess.

Botswana

There are 15 official South Africa–Botswana border posts, open between at least 8am and 3pm.

Some of the more remote crossings are impassable to 2WD vehicles and may be closed during periods of high water. Otherwise, the crossings are hassle-free.

Citizens of most Western nations do not require a visa to enter Botswana. People who do require a visa should apply in advance through a Botswanan mission (or a British mission in countries without Botswanan representation).

Grobler's Bridge/Martin's Drift (8am-6pm) Northwest of Polokwane (Pietersburg).

Kopfontein Gate/Tlokweng Gate (6am-midnight) Next to Madikwe Game Reserve; a main border post.

Pont Drift (8am-4pm) Convenient for Mapungubwe National Park (Limpopo) and Tuli Block (Botswana).

Ramatlabama (6am-10pm) North of Mahikeng; a main border post.

Skilpadshek/Pioneer Gate (6am-midnight) Northwest of Zeerust; a main border post.

Swartkopfontein Gate/Ramotswa (6am-10pm) Northwest of Zeerust.

Twee Rivieren (7.30am-4pm) At the South African entrance to Kgalagadi Transfrontier Park.

Bus Intercape (p354) runs daily between Gaborone (Botswana) and Jo'burg (R290 to R390, seven hours) via Pretoria.

Lesotho

All of Lesotho's borders are with South Africa and are straightforward to cross.

The main crossing is at Maseru Bridge, east of Bloemfontein. Queues here are sometimes very long upon exiting and, on some weekend evenings, entering Lesotho; use other posts if possible.

You need a 4WD to cross at Sani Pass, Ramatseliso's Gate and Ongeluksnek.

Bus Shared taxis connect Jo'burg and Maseru. It's quicker and easier to catch a bus to Bloemfontein, then continue by shared taxi to Maseru (three hours).

South African bus lines, including **Intercape** (p354), also link Bloemfontein with Ladybrand (2½ hours), a few kilometres from the Maseru Bridge crossing.

Leaving Maseru, long-distance shared taxis leave from the rank at Maseru Bridge.

Other possible shared-taxi routes:
➜ Butha-Buthe to/from Fouriesburg (Free State).
➜ Leribe (Hlotse) to/from Ficksburg (Free State).
➜ Quthing to/from Sterkspruit (Eastern Cape).
➜ Qacha's Nek to/from Matatiele (Eastern Cape).

Mozambique

Citizens of Western countries should apply in advance for tourist visas at a Mozambican mission. Border visas may be issued to people coming from countries where there is no Mozambican consular representation, but travellers in this situation should check with the Mozambican high commission in Pretoria (or Mbabane).

Giriyondo (⏱ 8am-4pm Oct-Mar, 8am-3pm Apr-Sep) Between Kruger National Park's Phalaborwa Gate and Massingir (Mozambique).

Kosi Bay/Ponta d'Ouro (8am-4pm) On the coast, well north of Durban.

Lebombo/Ressano Garcia (Komatipoort) The main crossing, east of Nelspruit; also known as Komatipoort.

Pafuri (☎ 013-735 6888; ⏱ 6am-6pm with slight seasonal variations) In Kruger National Park's northeastern corner.

Bus Bus companies including **Greyhound** (☎ customer care (24hr) 011-611 8000, reservations 083 915 9000; www.greyhound.co.za), Intercape (p527) and Translux (p527) run daily 'luxury' coaches between Jo'burg/Pretoria and Maputo (Mozambique) via Nelspruit and Ressano Garcia (Komatipoort; R320 to R410, eight hours). Passengers must have a valid Mozambique visa before boarding the bus. (This route can also be tackled in shared taxis.)

Mozambique-based Cheetah Express (p732) runs shuttles between Nelspruit and Maputo.

Taxis run between Maputo and the Namaacha/Lomahasha post on the Swazi border (1¾ hours); some continue to Manzini (3¼ hours).

Namibia

Citizens of most Western nations do not require a visa to enter Namibia for up to three months. People who do require a visa should apply in advance through a Namibian mission. Border posts include the following:

Alexander Bay/Oranjemund (6am-10pm) On the Atlantic coast; access is reliant on the ferry.

Nakop/Ariamsvlei (24 hours) West of Upington.

Rietfontein/Aroab (8am-4.30pm) Just south of Kgalagadi Transfrontier Park.

Vioolsdrif/Noordoewer (24 hours) North of Springbok, en route to/from Cape Town.

Bus Intercape (p527) buses run from Windhoek (Namibia) to Cape Town (R780 to R950, 21½ hours) on Monday, Wednesday, Friday and Sunday, returning Tuesday, Thursday, Friday and Sunday.

Swaziland

There are 11 South Africa–Swaziland border posts, all of which are hassle-free, including the following. Note that small posts close at 4pm.

Golela/Lavumisa (⊙7am-10pm) En route between Durban and Swaziland's Ezulwini Valley.

Josefdal/Bulembu (⊙8am-4pm) Between Piggs Peak and Barberton (Mpumalanga); 4WD or a car with high clearance recommended.

Mahamba (⊙8am-8pm) The best crossing to use from Piet Retief in Mpumalanga. Casinos nearby attract traffic, especially on weekends – good places to look for lifts into and out of the country.

Mananga (⊙8am-6pm) Southwest of Komatipoort.

Matsamo/Jeppe's Reef (⊙8am-8pm) Southwest of Malelane and a possible route to Kruger National Park. Casinos nearby attract traffic, especially on weekends – good places to look for lifts into and out of the country.

Onverwacht/Salitje (⊙8am-6pm) North of Pongola in KwaZulu-Natal.

Oshoek/Ngwenya (⊙7am-10pm) The busiest crossing (and a good place to pick up lifts), about 360km southeast of Pretoria.

Bus Daily shuttles run between Jo'burg and Mbabane.

Shared taxi routes:

➤ Jo'burg to/from Mbabane (four hours); some continue to Manzini.

➤ Durban to/from Manzini (eight hours).

➤ Manzini to/from Maputo (3¼ hours).

Zimbabwe

➤ Citizens of most Western nations need a visa to enter Zimbabwe, and these should be purchased at the border.

➤ Beitbridge (24hr), on the Limpopo River, is the only border post between Zimbabwe and South Africa.

➤ There's lots of smuggling, so searches are thorough and queues often long.

➤ The closest South African town to the border is Musina (15km south), where you can change money.

➤ Ignore touts on the Zimbabwe side trying to 'help' you through Zimbabwe immigration and customs; there's no charge for the government forms needed for immigration.

Bus Greyhound (p524) and Intercape (p527) operate daily buses between Jo'burg and Harare (Zimbabwe; 17 hours, R500), and between Jo'burg and Bulawayo (Zimbabwe; 14 hours, R475) both via Pretoria.

Shared taxis run south from Beitbridge to Musina and beyond.

ⓘ Getting Around

Car A great option, with affordable rental rates, a good road network and the car-based South African lifestyle; the drawback is dangerous drivers.

Baz Bus (www.bazbus.com) The backpacker shuttle is a convenient and social option between Cape Town, Durban and Jo'burg/Pretoria.

Train Tourist class is an underused secret (with sleeper coaches and dining car), linking Jo'burg to Cape Town and the coast.

Bus Lines including Greyhound, Intercape and Translux are useful, covering the country in comfortable vehicles at reasonable rates.

Shared Minibus Taxi These are OK for short journeys but less practical over long distances as there are various safety and security issues.

AIR

Domestic fares are affordable depending on the route. A budget flight from Jo'burg to Cape Town, a popular route served by numerous airlines, costs from R1000, while Cape Town to East London, a less competitive route, costs from R1800.

There are a number of budget airlines connecting all the major South African cities and it rarely works out cheaper to fly with the main carrier, South African Airways (SAA).

Keep costs down by booking online months before travelling.

Airlines in South Africa

Airlink (☑ 0861 606 606; www.flyairlink.com) South African Airways' partner has a good network, including smaller destinations such as Upington, Mthatha and Maseru.

SA Express (☑ 0861 729 227; www.flyexpress. aero) This South African Airways partner has a good network, including direct flights between Cape Town and Hoedspruit (for Kruger National Park).

South African Airways (p523) The national airline, with an extensive domestic and regional network.

Budget Airlines

South Africa's budget airlines also offer hotel bookings, car rentals and holiday packages.

Fly Blue Crane (☑ 087 330 2424; www.fly-bluecrane.com) Connects Jo'burg, Cape Town, Bloemfontein, Kimberley and Mthatha

CemAir (☑ 011-395 4473; www.flycemair. co.za) A small airline connecting Port Elizabeth, Bloemfontein, George, Plettenberg Bay and Margate.

Kulula (☑ 0861 585 852; www.kulula.com) Budget airline connecting Jo'burg, Cape Town, Durban, George and East London. It also offers discounts on domestic flights with sister airline British Airways.

Mango (p416) The South African Airways subsidiary flies between Jo'burg, Cape Town, Durban, Port Elizabeth, George and Bloemfontein.

FlySafair (☑ 0871 351 351; www.flysafair.co.za) A new airline offering cheap fares between Jo'burg, Cape Town, Durban, Port Elizabeth, East London and George.

BICYCLE

As long as you're fit enough to handle the hills, South Africa offers some rewarding cycling. It has scenic and diverse terrain, abundant campsites, and numerous quiet secondary roads. The major drawback is sharing the tarmac with South Africa's often erratic and aggressive drivers.

Good areas The roads around the Cape peninsula and Winelands are popular, although busy; the Wild Coast is beautiful and challenging; the northern lowveld offers wide plains.

Public transport Trains can carry bicycles, but most bus lines don't want bicycles in their luggage holds, and shared taxis don't carry luggage on the roof.

Purchase Larger South African cities, especially Cape Town, have a good selection of mountain bikes for sale. Jo'burg and Cape Town are the best places to look for touring bikes. To resell your bicycle at the end of your trip, try

hostel notice boards, bike shops and clubs, and www.gumtree.co.za.

Rental For day rides, some hostels offers short-term mountain bike rental. Rentals can also sometimes be arranged through bike shops in the cities, though you'll usually be required to leave a credit-card deposit.

Safety Distances between major towns are often long, although, except in isolated areas such as the Karoo, you're rarely far from a village or farmhouse. Many roads don't have a hard shoulder; on those that do, motorists use the shoulder as an unofficial slow lane. It's illegal to cycle on highways, and roads near urban areas are too busy and hazardous. Before heading off anywhere, contact other cyclists, through local cycling clubs or bicycle shops, to get recent information on the routes you're considering. Bring a good lock to counter the ever-present risk of theft, store the bike inside your accommodation (preferably inside your room) and chain it to something solid.

Spare parts Mountain bikes and parts are widely available in the cities. It's often difficult to find specialised parts for touring bikes, especially outside Cape Town and Jo'burg. Establish a relationship with a good bike shop in a city before you head off into the veld, in case you need something couriered to you.

Weather Much of the country (except for the Western Cape and west coast) gets most of its rain in summer (late November to March), often in the form of violent thunderstorms. When it isn't raining, summer days can be unpleasantly hot, especially in the steamy lowveld.

BUS

A good network of buses, of varying reliability and comfort, links the major cities.

Classes There are no class tiers on the bus lines, although major companies generally offer a 'luxury' service, with features such as air-con, a toilet and films.

Discounts The major bus lines offer student, frequent traveller and senior-citizen discounts, as well as specials – check their websites for details.

Fares Roughly calculated by distance, although short runs are disproportionately expensive. Your fare may also be based on the bus's whole journey (so travelling from Jo'burg to Bloemfontein costs the same as travelling from Pretoria). Prices rise during school holidays.

Safety Lines are generally safe. Note, however, that many long-distance services run through the night. On overnight journeys, travellers should take care of their valuables and women might feel more comfortable sitting near the front of the bus.

Ticket purchase For the main lines, purchase tickets at least 24 hours in advance, and as far in advance as possible for travel during peak periods. Tickets can be bought through bus offices, **Computicket** (☑ 0861 915 4000; www.computickettravel.com) and Shoprite/Checkers supermarkets.

Bus Lines

City to City (☑ 0861 589 282; www.citytocity.co.za) In partnership with Translux, it operates the routes that once carried people between the homelands and the cities under apartheid. The no-frills service is less expensive than the other lines, and serves many off-the-beaten-track places, including townships and mining towns. Destinations include Mthatha (for the Wild Coast), Nelspruit (for Kruger National park), Beitbridge (for Zimbabwe), Cape Town and Durban.

Greyhound (p524) An extensive nationwide network of comfortable buses, including Jo'burg to Durban via Richards Bay. Also operates other lines including the cheaper Citiliner buses.

Intercape (☑ 0861 287 287; www.intercape.co.za) An extensive network stretching from Cape Town to Limpopo and beyond. For longer hauls (including Cape Town to Windhoek, Namibia, and Mossel Bay to Jo'burg), it's worth paying extra for a reclining seat on an overnight Sleepliner bus.

Translux (☑ 0861 589 282; www.translux.co.za) The main long-distance operator, serving destinations including Cape Town, Durban, Bloemfontein, Port Elizabeth, East London, Mthatha, Nelspruit and the Garden Route.

Baz Bus

A convenient alternative to standard bus lines, **Baz Bus** (www.bazbus.com) caters almost exclusively to backpackers and travellers. It offers hop-on, hop-off fares and door-to-door services between Cape Town and Jo'burg via the Garden Route, Port Elizabeth, Mthatha, Durban and the Northern Drakensberg.

Baz Bus drops off and picks up at hostels, and has transfer arrangements with those off its route in areas such as the Wild Coast. You can book directly with Baz Bus or at most hostels.

Point-to-point fares are more expensive than on the major bus lines, but it can work out economically if you take advantage of the hop-on/hop-off feature. Sample one-way hop-on, hop-off fares from Cape Town: Jo'burg R5400, Durban R4470, Port Elizabeth R2300.

One-/two-/three-week travel passes cost R2600/R4100/5100.

CAR & MOTORCYCLE

South Africa is a spectacular country for a road trip. Away from the main bus and train routes, having your own wheels is the best way to get around, and if you're in a group, hiring a car is often the most economical option.

Road maps, a worthwhile investment, are readily available in South Africa.

Automobile Associations

Automobile Association of South Africa (AASA; ☑ 0861 000 234, 011-799 1500; www.aa.co.za) offers a vehicle breakdown service, which can be useful if you'll be driving in the areas it covers.

Its fleet of emergency response vehicles operates out of Johannesburg, Pretoria, Durban, Cape Town, Pietermaritzburg, Port Elizabeth, Nelspruit, Polokwane (Pietersburg), Bloemfontein, Rustenburg, Somerset West, Stellenbosch and East London, with AA-approved operatives available elsewhere.

Membership costs from R85 per month.

Members of foreign clubs in the **Fédération Internationale de l'Automobile** (www.fia.com) group have access to AASA – contact your club to find out what is available to you in South Africa.

Driving Licence

➡ You can use your driving licence from your home country, provided it is in English (or you have a certified translation).

➡ For use in South Africa, it should also carry your photo. Otherwise you'll need an international driving permit.

➡ Police generally ask to see foreign drivers' passports, so keep a photocopy in your car.

Hire

➡ Car rental is inexpensive in South Africa compared with Europe and North America, starting at around R200 per day for longer rentals.

➡ Many companies levy a surcharge for drivers aged below 21.

➡ Most companies ask for a credit card, and will not accept a debit card. Most use a chip-and-pin machine, so you'll need to know your credit card's pin number.

➡ For low rates, book online months in advance.

➡ Many companies stipulate a daily mileage limit, with an extra fee payable for any mileage over this limit. This can be a drawback if you're planning a long road trip. Four hundred kilometres a day is generally sufficient. If you plan one- or two-day stopovers along the way, 200km a day might be sufficient.

➡ A few local companies offer unlimited mileage. If you rent through an international company, and book through an overseas branch, you may get unlimited mileage for no extra cost, except at peak times (such as December to January).

➡ Make sure that quoted prices include the 14% value-added tax (VAT).

➡ One-way rental is charged according to the distance of the relocation.

➡ South Africa has rental operations in cities, major towns and airports, but it's generally cheapest to hire in a hub such as Jo'burg or Cape Town.

Insurance

Insurance for third-party damage and damage to or loss of your vehicle is highly recommended, though it's not legally required for private-vehicle owners. Generally it is only available on an annual basis.

If you're renting a vehicle, insurance with an excess should be included, with an excess waiver or reduction available for extra.

Check that hire-car insurance or the rental agreement covers hail damage, a costly possibility during the summer in the highveld and lowveld regions.

Insurance providers include:

Automobile Association of South Africa (p527)
Old Mutual iWyze (www.oldmutual.co.za/personal/insurance/car-insurance)
Outsurance (www.outsurance.co.za)
Sansure (www.sansure.co.za)

Road Conditions

➡ A good network of highways covers the country.

➡ Major roads are generally in good condition.

➡ Outside large towns and cities, you may encounter gravel (dirt) roads, most of which are graded and reasonably smooth.

➡ Check locally on tertiary and gravel roads' condition, which can deteriorate when it rains.

➡ In rural areas, beware of hazards such as dangerous potholes, washed-out roads, unannounced hairpin bends, and livestock, children and dogs in the road.

➡ The N2 highway through the Wild Coast region is in bad condition.

Road Hazards

➡ South Africa's roads can be treacherous, with a horrific accident rate, and well over 10,000 deaths annually.

➡ Notably dangerous stretches of highway: N1 between Cape Town and Beaufort West, and between Polokwane (Pietersburg) and Louis Trichardt (Makhado); N2 between Cape Town and Caledon, along the Garden Route, between East London and Kokstad, and Durban and Tongaat; N12 between Springs and Witbank; N4 between Middelburg and Belfast.

➡ The main hazards are your fellow drivers. Motorists from all sections of society drive sloppily and often aggressively. Be particularly wary of minibus-taxi drivers, who operate under pressure on little sleep in sometimes shoddy vehicles.

➡ Overtaking blind and with insufficient passing room are common.

➡ On major roads, drivers coming up behind you will flash their lights at you and expect you to move into the hard shoulder to let them pass, even if you are approaching a corner and regardless of what is happening in the hard shoulder. Motorists often remain hard on your tail until you move over.

➡ Drivers on little-used rural roads often speed and assume that there is no other traffic.

➡ Watch out especially for oncoming cars at blind corners on secondary roads.

➡ Despite roadblocks and alcohol breath-testing in South Africa, particularly in urban areas, drink driving is widespread.

➡ Do not be seduced by the relaxed local attitude to drink driving; you can end up in a cell, so nominate a designated driver.

➡ Farm animals, wildlife (particularly baboons) and pedestrians stray onto the roads, especially in rural areas. If you hit an animal in an area where you're uncertain of your safety, continue to the nearest police station and report it there.

➡ In roads through townships (such as the N2 from Cape Town International Airport to the city), foreign objects are occasionally placed in the road and motorists robbed when they pull over after driving over the object. Continue to a garage and police station to inspect your car and report the incident.

➡ During the rainy season, thick fog can slow you to a crawl, especially in the higher areas of KwaZulu-Natal.

➡ In the highveld and lowveld, summer hail storms can damage your car.

Road Rules

➡ Driving is on the left-hand side of the road.

➡ Seatbelts are mandatory for the driver and all passengers where they are fitted.

➡ The main local idiosyncrasy is the 'four-way stop' (crossroad), found even on major roads. All vehicles are required to stop, with those arriving first the first to go (even if they're on a minor cross street).

LOCAL TRANSPORT
Bus

➡ Several urban areas, including Cape Town, Durban, Pretoria and Jo'burg, have city bus networks.

➡ Fares are cheap.

➡ Routes, which are often signboarded, are extensive.

➡ Services often stop running early in the evening, and there aren't many on weekends.

➡ In terms of safety and convenience, only Cape Town's MyCiTi buses and Durban People Mover are recommended.

Shared Taxi

Minibus shared taxis run almost everywhere – around cities, to the suburbs and to neighbouring towns. Riding them offers an insight into local life, but be aware that there are safety issues.

➡ They leave when full – though 'full' in South Africa isn't as packed as in many African countries.

➡ Most accommodate 14 to 16 people. Slightly larger 'sprinters' accommodate about 20.

➡ Away from train and bus routes, shared taxis may be the only choice of public transport.

➡ At weekends they generally have reduced services or no departures.

➡ Car taxis are sometimes shared.

➡ In some towns, and on some longer routes, a shared car taxi may be the only transport option.

➡ Shared car taxis are more expensive than minibus taxis, and comparable in safety.

Private Taxi

➡ Larger cities have private taxi services.

➡ There are taxi stands in popular areas.

➡ Phoning for a cab is often safer; you will have to wait for the taxi to arrive, but the vehicle will likely be better quality than those at the stands.

➡ Rates vary between cities; in Cape Town, they average R10 per kilometre, often with a minimum charge of R30 or more.

➡ Uber is popular in larger cities and operates in Cape Town, Johannesburg, Pretoria, Durban and Port Elizabeth.

TRAIN

South Africa's **Shosholoza Meyl** (☎ 011-774 4555, 0860 008 888; www.shosholozameyl. co.za) offers regular services connecting major cities.

For an overview of services, descriptions of trains and valuable advice, visit **The Man in Seat Sixty-One** (www.seat61.com).

Classes

Both of the following are affordable options. Unlike on long-distance buses, fares on short sectors are not inflated.

Tourist class Recommended: scenic, authentic but safe, and more comfortable than taking the bus, albeit often slower. The overnight journey from Jo'burg to Cape Town is a wonderful way to get a sense of the country's vastness:

entering the Karoo as night falls and eating a celebratory lunch as the train swishes through the Winelands. There's a dining car and showers, and the fare includes accommodation in a two-berth coupé or four-berth compartment. Depending on what's available, couples are given coupés and single travellers and groups are put in compartments. If you are travelling alone and you want a coupé to yourself, you'll need to buy two tickets. There's an additional R60 charge for bedding hire. Cars can be transported on the Jo'burg–Cape Town and Jo'burg–Durban routes.

Economy class Does not have sleeping carriages and is not a comfortable or secure option for overnight travel.

Tickets & Fares

➡ At the time of writing, Jo'burg to Cape Town in tourist/economy class cost R690/440.

➡ The easiest way to purchase tickets is through travel agent **African Sun Travel** (www. southafricanrailways.co.za).

➡ African Sun charges a commission (about R100 for Cape Town–Jo'burg tickets and R80 for Jo'burg–Durban tickets).

➡ Tickets can be purchased up to three months in advance, and must be bought at least 48 hours before departure.

➡ Tourist-class sleepers can get fully booked a month or two ahead, especially on popular routes such as Jo'burg–Cape Town.

➡ Bookings can be made at train stations, by phone or through Shosholoza Meyl's website. You must then collect and pay for your tickets at a station within two days.

➡ A more complicated and lengthy option is to deposit the money in Shosholoza Meyl's bank account and send the company proof of payment; it takes four days for funds to clear in Shosholoza Meyl's account.

Routes

Jo'burg–Cape Town Via Kimberley and Beaufort West; 26 hours; tourist (Tuesday to Friday and Sunday) and economy (Wednesday, Friday and Sunday).

Jo'burg–Durban Via Ladysmith and Pietermaritzburg; 14 hours; tourist and economy (Friday and Sunday).

Jo'burg–East London Via Bloemfontein; 20 hours; tourist and economy (Wednesday, Friday and Sunday).

Jo'burg–Port Elizabeth Via Bloemfontein; 20 hours; tourist and economy (Wednesday, Friday and Sunday).

East London–Cape Town Via Queenstown and Beaufort West; 28 hours; economy (Tuesday and Sunday).

Swaziland

POP 1.4 MILLION / 268

Includes ➜
Mbabane 532
Ezulwini Valley 534
Malkerns Valley 537
Malolotja Nature
Reserve 541
Hlane Royal
National Park 541
Mlawula Nature
Reserve 542

Best Places to Eat

➜ eDladleni (p533)
➜ Lihawu Restaurant (p536)
➜ Ramblas Restaurant (p533)

Best Places to Sleep

➜ Stone Camp (p543)
➜ Sondzela Backpackers (p539)
➜ Brackenhill Lodge (p532)
➜ Lidwala Backpacker Lodge (p555)
➜ Phophonyane Falls Ecolodge & Nature Reserve (p543)

Why Go?

The intriguing kingdom of Swaziland is diminutive but boasts a huge checklist for any visitor. Rewarding wildlife watching? Tick. Adrenaline-boosting activities such as rafting and mountain biking? Tick. Lively and colourful local culture, with celebrations and ceremonies still common practice? Tick. Plus there are superb walking trails, stunning mountain and flatland scenery, varied accommodation options and excellent, high-quality handicrafts.

Unlike South Africa, Swaziland has managed to hold on to that slow-down-this-is-Africa feeling and that's why it's gaining in popularity. Everything remains small and personable and the atmosphere is remarkably relaxed. Instead of making a flying visit here on your way to Kruger National Park, KwaZulu-Natal or Mozambique, consider staying at least a week to do the country justice. If you plan a visit during the winter months, try to make it coincide with the Umhlanga festival, one of Africa's biggest cultural events.

When to Go
Mbabane

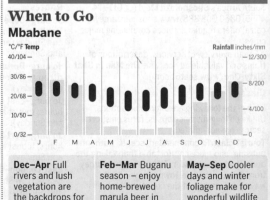

Dec–Apr Full rivers and lush vegetation are the backdrops for photography and adventuring.	**Feb–Mar** Buganu season – enjoy home-brewed marula beer in rural Swaziland.

May–Sep Cooler days and winter foliage make for wonderful wildlife viewing in the lowveld.

Swaziland Highlights

1 Mkhaya Game Reserve
(p543) Watching wildlife, including rare black rhinos, in the wild.

2 Malolotja Nature Reserve (p541) Walking or hiking in this enchanting wilderness area.

3 Great Usutu River
(Lusutfu River; p543)
Shooting over whitewater rapids on a day-long adventure.

4 Malkerns Valley (p537) Browsing the craft shops here and in the nearby Ezulwini Valley (p534).

5 Mlilwane Wildlife Sanctuary (p539) Exploring on foot, horseback or by bike.

6 Sibebe Rock (p532) Climbing this massive granite dome outside the capital and soaking up the lovely views.

7 Hlane Royal National Park (p541) Coming face-to-face with a pride of lions or watching white rhinos congregate at the accessible watering hole.

MBABANE

POP 38,000 / ELEV 1243M

Mbabane's main draw? Its lovely setting in the craggy Dlangeni Hills. Swaziland's capital and second-largest city, Mbabane is a relaxed and functional place perched in the cool highveld. During the colonial era, the British originally had their base in Manzini but moved it in 1902 to Mbabane to take advantage of the cooler climate in the hills.

There's a handful of good restaurants and places to stay, but for the traveller the nearby Ezulwini and Malkerns Valleys have most of the attractions and, on the whole, a better choice of accommodation.

◉ Sights

Sibebe Rock LANDMARK

(Pine Valley; E30; ⊙8am-4pm Mon-Sat) About 8km northeast of Mbabane is Sibebe Rock, a massive granite dome hulking over the surrounding countryside. It's the world's second largest monolith, after Australia's Ul-

uru, but is considerably less visited. Much of the rock is completely sheer, and dangerous if you should fall, but climbing it is a good adrenaline charge if you're reasonably fit and relish looking down steep rock faces. Community guides operate guided hikes (E50 per person) – ask at the visitor centre.

Alternatively, Swazi Trails (p534) in Ezulwini Valley runs half-day nontechnical climbs up the rock (E750 per person, including transport).

🛏 Sleeping

Mbabane is a bit short on decent budget accommodation; the Ezulwini or Malkerns Valleys (only 14km and 18km away) have a better selection.

Bombaso's Guesthouse HOSTEL $

(☏7681 9191, 7804 0603; www.swazilandhappenings.co.za/photos_bombasos.htm; Lukhalo St, off Pine Valley Rd; dm/s/d E200/550/650, s/d with shared bathroom E450/550; P🐾🛜🏊) Bombaso's offers a buzzy vibe and has a variety of accommodation options, including a self-catering cottage (E850). No meals are served, but there are excellent kitchen facilities. Jason and Lwazi, who run the place, are well clued-up about the country. It's about 2km north of the centre, with easy public transport.

★Brackenhill Lodge GUESTHOUSE $$

(☏2404 2887; www.brackenhillswazi.com; Mountain Dr; s/d incl breakfast E675/950; P🛜🏊) With its wonderfully relaxing atmosphere and bucolic setting, this little cracker located 4.5km northeast of Mbabane is sure to win your heart. It offers eight comfortable, well-equipped and airy rooms, and its 162 hectares have several walking trails, great birdlife and splendid panoramas. Facilities include gym, sauna, swimming pool and even tennis courts. Lovely owners; evening meals on request.

The Place GUESTHOUSE $$

(☏7828 5090, 7638 1880; www.theplaceswaziland. com; Mantsholo St; s/d incl breakfast E900/1365; P✳🛜🏊) Opposite the golf course, this modern guesthouse has impeccable, well-equipped rooms with sparkling bathrooms and a small kitchenette. The free-standing units open onto a manicured garden and a pool, and there's a reputable restaurant next door. A great find.

Foresters Arms LODGE $$

(☏2467 4177; www.forestersarms.co.za; MR19, Mhlambanyatsi; s/d incl breakfast E670/1140; P🛜🏊) Hidden 27km southwest of Mba-

Mbabane

N   0 —— 200 m
    0 —— 0.1 miles

Ramblas Restaurant (500m); The Place (500m); Bombaso's Guesthouse (1.8km)

Mbovane St
Mabandla St
Hill St
Gwamile St
Polinjane River
Coronation Park
Mandela
Indingilizi Gallery & Restaurant
Msakato St
Zwide St
Somhlolo St (Gilfillan St)
eDish (550m)
Howe St
Post St
Shield St
Smuts St
Libandla St
Western Distributor
Dzeliwe St
Mbabane Riverside Dr
Dr Sishayi Rd
Mhlonhlo St
Mbabane River
Bus & Minibus Taxi Rank
Msunduza St
Tourism Information Office
Nonshared Taxi Rank
West St
Swazi Market
TransMagnific
Plaza Mall Dr
Sozisa Rd (Mbabane Bypass Rd)
Sky World (1km)
Ministry of Home Affairs Immigration Department (300m)
Mountain Inn (1.2km)

bane in picturesque hills, Foresters Arms has a haunting but beautiful remoteness. The air is clean, the views suggestive, the peace tangible. It's a superb staging post between KwaZulu-Natal and Kruger National Park, with cosy rooms, attractive gardens and a smorgasbord of activities (horse riding, mountain biking and hiking). Another highlight is the on-site restaurant.

Follow the MR19 from Mbabane in the direction of Mhlambanyatsi.

Mountain Inn   INN **$$**
(☑ 2404 2781; www.mountaininn.sz; Sihawu Cres, Highland View; s/d incl breakfast from R1025/1210; ⓟ❄️🛜🏊) This sprawling inn is a bit bland and its decor feels dated, but it's friendly, unpretentious and a safe bet. It comprises three wings linked by a covered walkway; South Wing rooms proffer stupendous views over the valley but are more expensive than the North Wing rooms. There's a pool, a library, lawns and a well-regarded restaurant.

It's about 4km south of the city centre, in a tranquil neighbourhood.

✗ Eating

There are supermarkets, chain restaurants and fast-food outlets at Swazi Plaza, which is the main shopping mall in the city centre.

eDish   CAFE **$**
(☑ 2404 5504; Computronics House, Somhlolo St (Gilfillan St); E45-75; ⊗ 8am-5pm Mon-Sat; ⓟ🛜) With gourmet sandwiches, comfy couches, good coffee, cold beer and a deck offering fine Mbabane views, eDish is a worthy place to spend an hour. Best of all, there is free wifi at decent speeds.

Indingilizi Gallery & Restaurant   CAFE **$**
(☑ 2404 6213; 112 Dzeliwe St; mains E50-80; ⊗ 8am-5pm Mon-Fri, 8.30am-1pm Sat) Indingilizi is that easy-to-miss 'secret spot' that locals like to recommend. This small outdoor cafe is at the back of an art gallery and offers breakfasts, snacks and light lunches. There's no obvious sign marking the place – look out for a grey building with red doors.

★ eDladleni   SWAZI **$$**
(☑ 2404 5743; http://edladleni.100webspace.net/index.html; Manzini/Mbabane Hwy, Mvubu Falls; mains E55-80; ⊗ noon-3pm & 6-10pm Tue-Sun; 🍴) Delicious food, a serene setting and cracking views – if you're after an authentic Swazi experience, eDladleni is hard to beat. Here you can tuck into traditional specialities that are hard to find elsewhere, and it's got excellent vegetarian options. It's about 6km from

INCWALA

Incwala (also known as Ncwala) is the most sacred ceremony of the Swazi people, a 'first fruits' ceremony where the king gives permission for his people to eat the first crops of the new year. It takes place in late December/early January and lasts one week: dates are announced shortly beforehand. It's a fiercely traditional celebration and visitors should take note of strict rules, including restrictions on dress and photography.

Mbabane, off the main highway (follow the sign 'Mvubu Falls'); check the website for directions. The charismatic owner, Dolores Godeffroy, is committed to reviving traditional recipes based on local produce. Service can be rather slow and opening hours are unreliable – it's wise to call ahead.

Ramblas Restaurant   INTERNATIONAL **$$**
(☑ 2404 4147; www.ramblasswaziland.webs.com; Mantsholo St; mains E70-160; ⊗ 8am-10pm Mon-Sat; 🛜) Mbabane's top choice for good cuisine and a buzzing ambience is a stone's throw from the golf course. It's well worth the trip for an eclectic menu including great salads, meat dishes, burgers and appetising desserts. It occupies a small villa with an agreeable terrace; inside, colourful paintings and shades of grey and red create a sophisticated mood.

ⓘ Information

INTERNET ACCESS

Mbabane has internet centres in Swazi Plaza and in the Mall. Access starts from around E30 per hour.

MEDICAL SERVICES

Mbabane Clinic (☑ 2404 2423; www.theclinicgroup.com; Mkhonubovu St; ⊗ 24h) For emergencies try this well-equipped clinic in the southwestern corner of town, just off the bypass road.

MONEY

Mbabane's banks with ATMs include **First National Bank** (⊗ 8.30am-2.30pm Mon-Fri, 9-11am Sat), **Nedbank** (⊗ 8.30am-2.30pm Mon-Fri, 9-11am Sat) and **Standard Bank** (⊗ 8.30am-2.30pm Mon-Fri, 9-11am Sat); these are located in Swazi Plaza.

POLICE

Police (☑ 999, 2404 2221; Mhlonhlo St)

POST

Post Office (Msunduza St; ⊘8am-4pm Mon-Fri, 8.30-11am Sat) You can also make international (though not reverse-charge) calls here.

TOURIST INFORMATION

Tourism Information Office (☑2404 2531; www.thekingdomofswaziland.com; Swazi Mall, Dr Sishayi Rd; ⊘8am-5pm Mon-Fri, 9am-1pm Sat) At Swazi Plaza. Has maps and brochures.

ⓘ Getting There & Away

Mbabane's main **bus and minibus-taxi rank** (Dr Sishayi Rd) is just behind Swazi Plaza. Minibus shared taxis leave for Jo'burg (E220, four hours) throughout the day.

There are several minibus taxis daily to Ngwenya and the Oshoek border post (E30, 50 minutes), and Malkerns Valley (E30, 45 minutes). All vehicles heading towards Manzini (E40, 35 minutes) and points east pass through the Ezulwini Valley, although most take the highways, bypassing the valley itself.

Nonshared taxis (Dr Sishayi Rd) congregate just outside the transport park behind Swazi Plaza. Nonshared taxis to the Ezulwini Valley cost from E150, more to the far end of the valley (from E200). Expect to pay from E160 to get to King Mswati III International Airport (p540).

TransMagnific (☑2404 9977; www.goswaziland.co.sz; Cooper Centre, Sozisa Rd) and **Sky World** (☑2404 9921, mobile 7664 0001; www.skyworld.co.sz; Checkers Business Park, Sozisa Rd) offer a daily luxury shuttle service between Johannesburg (stopping at OR Tambo International Airport and Sandton) and Mbabane for E600. Other destinations include Durban (E780) and Nelspruit (from E450).

If you're driving, you can get petrol at Engen (Sozisa Rd) or Total (Sozisa Rd) on Sozisa Rd.

CENTRAL SWAZILAND

The country's tourist hub, central Swaziland is a heady mix of culture, nature and epicurean indulgences, and has plenty to keep you occupied for a few days. There are wildlife reserves to explore, museums to visit, great restaurants to sample and quality handicrafts to bring home.

Ezulwini Valley

What a difference a few kilometres can make! Swaziland's tourism centre, the Ezulwini Valley, begins just outside Mbabane but feels a world away from the hullabaloo of the capital. With an excellent selection of places to stay and wonderful craft shopping, it's a convenient base for many visitors.

⊙ Sights

Mantenga Cultural Village & Nature Reserve   NATURE RESERVE
(☑2416 1151; www.sntc.org.sz/reserves/mantenga.asp; E100; ⊘8am-6pm) The entrance fee to this tranquil, thickly forested reserve covers a guided tour of the Swazi Cultural Village, a 'living' cultural village with authentic beehive huts and cultural displays, plus a *sibhaca* dance (performed daily at 11.30am and 3.15pm) and a visit to the impressive Mantenga Falls. The reserve is also great for hiking; day hikers pay only E50. Although it's not a big wildlife park, it offers a chance to see vervet monkeys, baboons, warthogs, nyalas and duikers. Birdlife abounds, including the endangered southern bald ibis. It's located 1km from Mantenga Lodge and is well signposted from the MR103.

🏃 Activities

Swazi Trails   ADVENTURE SPORTS
(☑2416 2180, mobile 7602 0261; www.swazitrails.co.sz; Mantenga Craft Centre; ⊘8am-5pm) Based in the Mantenga Craft Centre, this is one of the country's major activity companies and the place to go to for caving, rafting, hikes and general cultural and highlights tours. Also houses the Ezulwini Tourist Office.

Cuddle Puddle   HOT SPRINGS
(☑2416 1164; MR103, Ezulwini Valley; adult/child E30/15; ⊘6am-11pm) For personal pampering, head to the Royal Valley's own mineral hot springs. The magnesium-rich waters are a constant 32°C. There's also a spa, complete with sauna, gym and massage.

👉 Tours

Mandla Masuku/ Ekhaya Cultural Tours   CULTURAL
(☑mobile 7644 3257; www.ekhayatours.com; half/full day R1200/1450, minimum 2 people; ⊘daily by reservation) For a taste of rural Swazi life – including a visit to Lobamba, a school and a family – a good contact is local Mandla Masuku of Ekhaya Cultural Tours. If you have your own vehicle, Mandla will hop in your car for a reduced rate (half/full day E800/1000). Tours are offered in English and French.

All Out Africa   ADVENTURE
(☑2416 2260; www.alloutafrica.com; MR103; ⊘8am-5pm) Runs a range of adventure trips and activities throughout Swaziland, plus to Kruger National Park. Highly recommended is the half-day cultural tour through Lobamba (per person E450; minimum two people). It's housed in Lidwala Backpacker Lodge .

🛏 Sleeping

⭐**Lidwala Backpacker Lodge** HOSTEL **$**
(☏ mobile 7690 5865; www.lidwala.co.sz; MR103, Ezulwini Valley; camping per person R100, dm E180, d E440-590; 🅿 🛜 ⊠) What a magical setting! This comfortable, well-run spot is nestled in a splendid garden with a pool, among big boulders and a chuckling stream. Rooms are a typical dorm-style, backpacker set-up, with

Ezulwini & Malkerns Valleys

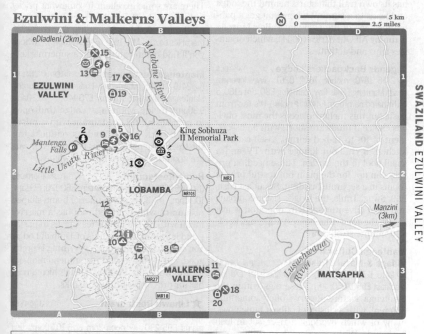

🧭 N   0 —————— 5 km
0 —————— 2.5 miles

Ezulwini & Malkerns Valleys

◎ Sights
1 Eludzidzini Royal Residence.................B2
King Sobhuza II Memorial Park......(see 3)
2 Mantenga Cultural Village & Nature Reserve.....................................A2
3 National Museum.................................B2
Parliament.......................................(see 3)
4 Somhlolo National Stadium.................B2

✚ Activities, Courses & Tours
5 All Out Africa.....................................B2
6 Cuddle Puddle....................................A1
7 Swazi Trails..B2

🛏 Sleeping
Legends Backpackers Lodge.........(see 9)
Lidwala Backpacker Lodge............(see 5)
8 Malandela's B&B.................................B3
Mantenga Cultural Village & Nature Reserve.........................(see 2)
9 Mantenga Lodge & Restaurant............A2
10 Mlilwane Wildlife Sanctuary Main Camp...B3
11 Rainbird Chalets.................................C3
12 Reilly's Rock Hilltop Lodge..................A2
13 Royal Swazi Spa..................................A1

14 Sondzela Backpackers.........................B3

✗ Eating
15 Boma Restaurant................................A1
Calabash..(see 15)
16 Gables Shopping Centre......................B2
17 Lihawu Restaurant..............................B1
Malandela's Restaurant.................(see 8)
Mantenga Restaurant.....................(see 9)
18 Sambane Coffee Shoppe......................C3

✪ Entertainment
House on Fire...................................(see 8)

🛍 Shopping
Baobab Batik...................................(see 20)
19 Ezulwini Craft Market.........................B1
Gone Rural......................................(see 8)
Mantenga Craft Centre...................(see 9)
20 Swazi Candles....................................C3

🛈 Information
21 Big Game Parks...................................B3
Ezulwini Tourist Office...................(see 7)
Malandela's Tourist Information & Internet Cafe........(see 8)

a laid-back, friendly feel. The separate safari tents are popular (E150 per person), while the private rooms are smallish but neat.

There are kitchen and laundry facilities; meals are available. Fancy hiking? Lidwala has its own trail that starts behind the lodge and leads to a summit where you get a panoramic view of the Ezulwini Valley. Lidwala is run by All Out Africa (p534), which organises trips and activities.

Legends Backpackers Lodge HOSTEL **$**
(☎2416 1870, mobile 7602 0261; www.legends.co.sz; Mantenga Falls Rdy; camping E80, dm E160, d with shared bathroom E440; P 📶 🏊) It's far from flash, but this mellow place is the most obvious choice if funds are short, with an assortment of 10- to 12-bed dorms, a self-catering kitchen, a chill-out lounge with TV and a small pool in the garden. Those needing privacy can opt for the plain but restful private rooms in a separate building. Breakfast costs E50. Swazi Trails, the lodge's sister company and local adventure-activity operator, is just across the road. The nearest supermarket is a 10-minute stroll away.

Mantenga Cultural Village & Nature Reserve BUNGALOW **$$**
(☎2416 1178, 2416 1151; www.sntc.org.sz; s/d incl breakfast E550/850; P) These digs within the Mantenga Nature Reserve offer something different, with a cluster of offbeat bungalows, many of which overlook a river, set in lush bushland. With wooden furnishings and modern amenities (but no air-con), they represent a nice balance between comfort, rustic charm and seclusion. Overnight guests don't pay entry to the nature reserve. A pleasant restaurant is nearby, set in a rainforest.

Mantenga Lodge & Restaurant HOTEL **$$**
(☎2416 1049; www.mantengalodge.com; Mantenga Falls Rd; incl breakfast s E605-820, d E810-1035; P ❄ 📶 🏊) We're suckers for the relaxing atmosphere that prevails in this oasis of calm. The 38 rooms of varying standards (and different prices) are nothing too out of the ordinary, but they're set in a lush wooded area where you can mooch around, and the pool is an instant elixir when it's swelteringly hot. Another plus is the attached restaurant.

Royal Swazi Spa HOTEL **$$$**
(☎2416 5000; www.suninternational.com; MR103, Ezulwini Valley; s/d incl breakfast from E1690/1890; P ❄ @ 📶 🏊) With a palatial facade and grounds to match, the Royal Swazi certainly looks the part, though the rooms are in need of a revamp. Still, they have the requisite comforts and the hotel features a host of facilities and amenities, including two restaurants, three bars, a large pool, a spa, a casino and a golf course.

Eating

There are some excellent if somewhat pricey restaurants in the valley. For cheaper eats, head to the **Gables Shopping Centre** (www.thegables.co.sz; MR 103; ⏰8am-10pm), where you'll find chain eateries and a supermarket.

Mantenga Restaurant INTERNATIONAL **$$**
(☎2416 1049; Mantenga Lodge & Restaurant, Mantenga Falls Rd; mains E70-140; ⏰6.30am-9.30pm) Inside Mantenga Lodge (but open to nonguests), this restaurant with a raised wooden deck has a fabulous outlook over the trees. The pasta dishes and grilled meats are good deals, as are the sandwiches.

Boma Restaurant INTERNATIONAL **$$**
(☎2416 2632; Nyonyane Rd; mains E60-120; ⏰11am-10.30pm; 👪) This atmospheric, boma-shaped restaurant with thatched roof has a massive menu with all the favourites – grills to pastas – and is within the grounds of Timbali Lodge. You can't really go wrong, everything is pretty good, but if you want a recommendation, go for the wood-fired pizzas. There's also a cosy bar for pre- or post-dinner drinks.

★ **Lihawu Restaurant** FUSION **$$$**
(☎2416 7035; www.lihawu.co.sz; Royal Villas; mains E95-230; ⏰noon-2pm & 6-10.30pm; 🍷) Within the swish Royal Villas resort nestles Swaziland's most elegant restaurant, with a tastefully decorated dining room and an outdoor eating area that overlooks a swimming pool. The menu is Afro-fusion, with meaty signature dishes such as oxtail stew and pork belly, but there are a couple of vegetarian options. Needless to say the accompanying wine list is top class.

Calabash GERMAN, FRENCH **$$$**
(☎2416 1187; Nyonyane Rd; mains E120-290; ⏰noon-2.30pm & 6-10pm) Grilled *eisbein* (pig knuckle) and *escargots bourguignons* (Burgundy snails) in Swaziland? Yes, it's possible. German and French cuisine are the highlights at this long-standing and dated, but smart, place located at the upper end of the Ezulwini Valley. It has an impressive wine cellar.

Shopping

Ezulwini Craft Market ARTS & CRAFTS
(MR103, Ezulwini Valley; ⏰8am-5pm) Don't miss this well-stocked market that's opposite the Zeemans Filling Station on the corner of

MR103 and Mpumalanga Loop Rd. Look for the blue tin roofs. The stalls sell a vast array of local carvings, weavings and handicrafts.

Mantenga Craft Centre ARTS & CRAFTS
(✆2416 1136; Mantenga Falls Rd, Ezulwini Valley; ⊗8am-5pm) This colourful, compact craft centre has several shops featuring everything from weaving and tapestries to candles, woodcarvings and T-shirts.

ℹ Information

There are ATMs at the Gables Shopping Centre.

Big Game Parks (✆2528 3943; www.biggame-parks.org; Mlilwane Wildlife Sanctuary; ⊗8am-5pm Mon-Fri, 8.30am-12.30pm Sat)

Ezulwini Tourist Office (✆2416 2180, mobile 7602 0261; www.swazitrails.co.sz; Mantenga Craft Centre, Ezulwini Valley; ⊗8am-5pm)

Medi-Sun Clinic (✆2416 2800; Mantenga Dr; ⊗24hr) Behind Gables Shopping Centre.

Post Office (⊗8am-4pm Mon-Fri, 8.30-11am Sat)

ℹ Getting There & Away

Nonshared taxis from Mbabane to the Ezulwini Valley cost E120 to E200, depending on how far down the valley you go.

During the day you could get on a minibus bound for Manzini, but make sure the driver knows that you want to alight in the valley, as many aren't keen on stopping.

Lobamba

POP 11,000

Welcome to Swaziland's spiritual, cultural and political heart. Within the Ezulwini Valley lies Lobamba, an area that has played host to Swaziland's monarchy for over two centuries. It's home to some of the most notable buildings in the country. Despite its importance, Lobamba feels surprisingly quiet – except during the spectacular Incwala (p533) and Umhlanga (p538) ceremonies, when the nation gathers on the surrounding plains for several days of intense revelry.

There are no sleeping options or notable eating places in Lobamba itself, but plenty of places to stay and eat in the Ezulwini and Malkerns Valleys.

Minibus taxis running between Ezulwini and Malkerns stop in Lobamba several times a day. Fares to both destinations are about E10.

National Museum MUSEUM
(✆2416 1179; adult/child E80/30; ⊗8am-4.30pm Mon-Fri, 10am-4pm Sat & Sun) This museum has some interesting displays of Swazi culture, as well as a traditional beehive village and cattle enclosure, and several of King Sobhuza II's 1940s cars. There's a discounted combo ticket if you visit both the museum and the King Sobhuza II Memorial Park (p537; adult/child E120/40).

King Sobhuza II Memorial Park MEMORIAL
(✆2416 2131; adult/child E80/30; ⊗8am-4.30pm Mon-Fri, 10am-4pm Sat & Sun) Adjacent to the parliament, this memorial was established as a tribute to King Sobhuza II, who led Swaziland to independence from British rule in 1968. Its main highlight is a 3m-tall bronze statue of the late, revered king. There's a small museum with pictures and documents about his life. The king's mausoleum is also within the park. There's a discounted combo ticket if you visit both the museum and the National Museum (adult/child E120/40).

Somhlolo National Stadium NOTABLE BUILDING
Built for Swaziland's independence in 1968, the 20,000-capacity national stadium hosts soccer matches, as well as important state occasions such as coronations (like that of Mswati III), and soccer matches. It is named after King Sobhuza I, also known as Somhlolo, founding father of the Swazi nation.

Parliament NOTABLE BUILDING
(✆2416 2407) Opened in 1969 as a post-independence gift from the departing British, this hexagonal building topped with a brass dome is a major landmark in Lobamba. It is sometimes open to visitors; if you want to visit, wear neat clothes and use the side entrance. Call for opening times.

Eludzidzini Royal Residence NOTABLE BUILDING
At the end of a palm-lined avenue south of Lobamba lies Eludzidzini, the queen mother's royal residence. It's not open to the public except during festivities, notably the Incwala (p533) ceremony or the Umhlanga (reed) dance (p538). It's just off the MR103 south of Ezulwini.

Malkerns Valley

About 7km south of Lobamba/Ezulwini Valley on the MR103 is the turn-off to the fertile Malkerns Valley, known for its arts and crafts outlets. Together with the Ezulwini Valley, if offers a scenic and fun drive.

🛏 Sleeping

Malandela's B&B B&B $$
(✆2528 3339, 2528 3448; www.malandelas.com; MR27; s/d incl breakfast E580/800; ℙ@🛜🖾)

DON'T MISS

UMHLANGA REED DANCE FESTIVAL

The *Umhlanga* (reed) dance is Swaziland's best-known cultural event. Though not as sacred as the Incwala, it serves a similar function in drawing the nation together and reminding the people of their relationship to the king. It is something like a week-long debutante ball for marriageable young Swazi women, who journey from all over the kingdom to help repair the queen mother's home at Lobamba. It takes place in late August or early September.

This is a wonderfully relaxing option with six tastefully designed rooms, a pool and a terrific sculpture garden. Each room has a different theme and decoration; our fave is the super-sized Purple. There's an excellent restaurant if you're feeling too lazy to travel elsewhere. Wi-fi costs extra. Malandela's is along the MR27, about 1km from the junction with the MR103. Book ahead.

Rainbird Chalets CHALET $$

(☑7603 7273; www.rainbirdchalets.com; s/d incl breakfast E700/1200; P✱✲) It's the bucolic setting that's the pull here. Eight chalets – three log and five brick A-frames – are set in a manicured private garden near the owners' house and overlook a small dam. All are fully equipped and feature smart bathrooms. Breakfast is served on a verandah blessed with soul-stirring views of surrounding hills.

✖ Eating

There are some lovely cafes in Malkerns, but for dinner you'll find more choice in the Ezulwini Valley (p536).

★Sambane Coffee Shoppe CAFE $

(☑7604 2035; Swazi Candles craft centre; mains E50-100; ☺8.15am-5pm; ✦) If you need to re-energise after a bout of shopping in the adjoining handicrafts outlets, there's no better place than this delightful cafe. It has a fine selection of homemade cakes, sandwiches, burgers and salads. Tip: arrive early, as it's usually packed to the rafters with hungry tourists at lunchtime.

Malandela's Restaurant INTERNATIONAL $$

(☑2528 3115; www.malandelas.com; Malandela's complex, MR27, Malkerns Valley; mains E80-150; ☺9am-11pm; ☎) This restaurant in the Malandela's complex is a reliable option, with an eclectic menu featuring grilled meats, seafood dishes, frondy salads and scrumptious house desserts – don't miss out on the chocolate cake. There's pleasant outdoor seating; indoors there's a fire for when it's chilly, and it's candlelit at night.

☆ Entertainment

★House on Fire LIVE MUSIC

(☑2528 2110; www.house-on-fire.com; Malandela's complex, MR27) People visit this especially for the ever-mutating cultural site–living gallery and experimental-performance space. Part of the Malandela's complex, the well-known venue hosts everything from African theatre, music and films to raves and other forms of entertainment. Since 2007, it has hosted the annual MTN Bushfire Festival.

🔒 Shopping

★Swazi Candles ARTS & CRAFTS

(☑2528 3219; www.swazicandles.com; Swazi Candles craft centre; ☺8am-5pm) A mandatory stop for the souvenir hunter, this is one of the most famous handicrafts outlets in Southern Africa. Here you can wax lyrical about these creative coloured candles – in every African-animal shape and hue; it's fun to watch the workers hand-mould the designs. It's 7km south of the MR103 turn-off for Malkerns.

Gone Rural ARTS & CRAFTS

(☑2550 4936; www.goneruralswazi.com; Malandela's complex, M27; ☺8am-5pm Mon-Sat, 9am-5pm Sun) The place to go for good-quality woven goodies – baskets, mats and bowls – made by groups of local women. The shop is found within the Malandela's complex, but you can also arrange to visit the workshop and meet the creators behind the artworks.

Baobab Batik ARTS & CRAFTS

(☑2528 3242; www.baobab-batik.com; ☺8am-5pm) This fair-trade enterprise employs more than 30 local artisans who produce beautiful printed wall hangings, clothing and cushion covers. It's based at the Swazi Candles craft centre.

ℹ Information

Malandela's Tourist Information & Internet Cafe (Mandalela's complex; per hr E45; ☺8am-5pm) Internet access and basic tourist info.

ℹ Getting There & Away

Minibus shared taxis run between here and the Ezulwini Valley for around E12. As the craft shops and sleeping places are spread out, you'll really need a car to get around.

Mlilwane Wildlife Sanctuary

While it doesn't have the drama or vastness of some of the bigger South African parks, the tranquil Mlilwane Wildlife Sanctuary near Lobamba is well worth a visit: it's beautiful, tranquil and easily accessible. The landscape is another highlight; its terrain is dominated by the Nyonyane Mountain, whose exposed granite peak is known as Execution Rock (1110m). Small wonder that the reserve is an outdoor-lover's paradise, with a wide range of activities available.

The reserve supports a diversity of fauna (mostly large herbivores and birds) and flora, and has no dangerous wildlife to worry about (except hippos). The best wildlife and bird-watching areas are the water hole at the main camp and the main dam to the north. The enclosed area near Reilly's Rock shelters some rare species of antelope and is accessible only on a guided drive. All activities can be booked at Mlilwane Wildlife Sanctuary Main Camp.

Heading to the sanctuary from Mbabane or Ezulwini Valley, take the MR103 to the south. Drive past Lobamba; the turn-off to the reserve is well signposted on the right. After initial check-in at Sangweni main gate, visitors enjoy 24-hour park access.

★ **Sondzela Backpackers**　　HOSTEL $
(☏2528 3943; www.biggameparks.org/sondzela; camping per person E100, dm E115, s/d with shared bathroom E275/390, rondavel s/d with shared outside bathroom E295/430; P🐾) Sondzela is a top choice for budgeteers, located in the southern part of the Mlilwane Wildlife Sanctuary. It boasts fine, breezy dorms, clean private doubles and a clutch of lovely rondavels with wraparound views. And it doesn't end there. The delightful gardens, kitchen, swimming pool and a hilltop perch provide one of the best backpackers' settings in Southern Africa.

Breakfast and hearty traditional dinners (cooked on the outside braai) are available for a song. If you're driving, you'll need to use the main Mlilwane Wildlife Sanctuary entrance, pay the entry fee and drive through the park to reach Sondzela. Alternatively, Sondzela's own shuttle bus departs the lodge at 8am and 5pm, and from Malandela's B&B in Malkerns Valley 30 minutes later.

Mlilwane Wildlife Sanctuary Main Camp　　CAMPGROUND $$
(☏2528 3943/4; www.biggameparks.org/mlilwane; camping E105, hut s/d E555/790, rondavel s/d E625/890; P🐾) This homey camp is set in a scenic wooded location about 3.5km from the entry gate, complete with well-appointed rondavels and simple huts – including traditional beehive huts (s/d E580/830) – and the occasional snuffling warthog. The Hippo Haunt Restaurant serves excellent grilled meat and overlooks a water hole. There are often dance performances in the evening, and the pool is another drawcard.

Reilly's Rock Hilltop Lodge　　LODGE $$$
(☏2528 3943/4; www.biggameparks.org/reilly; s/d with half board from E1410/2170; P) Promoted as 'quaintly colonial', this is a delightfully tranquil, old-world, nonfussy luxury experience at its best. The main house is in an incredible setting – a Royal Botanic Garden with aloes, cycads and an enormous jacaranda – and shelters four rooms with striking views of the valley and Mdzimba Mountains. Entry to the reserve is included. Generous dinners are served in the dining room and full breakfasts are enjoyed on the verandah, in sight of beautiful birds and even small antelope.

Manzini

Swaziland's largest town, Manzini is a chaotic commercial and industrial hub whose small centre is dominated by office blocks and a couple of shopping malls running down two main streets. With the exception of the market, Manzini itself has limited appeal for the tourist. That said, it's a key transport hub, so you're likely to pass through if you're getting around on public transport. Accommodation is limited; you're best to head to the nearby Malkerns or Ezulwini Valleys.

Manzini Market　　MARKET
(cnr Mhlakuvane & Mancishane Sts; ⊙7am-5pm Mon-Sat) Manzini's main drawcard is its colourful market; its upper section is packed with handicrafts from Swaziland and elsewhere in Africa. Thursday morning is a good time to see the rural vendors and Mozambican traders bringing in their handicrafts and textiles to sell to the retailers.

George Hotel　　BUSINESS HOTEL $$
(☏2505 2260; www.tgh.co.sz; cnr Ngwane & Du Toit Sts; s/d incl breakfast from E1070/1520; P❄🐾) Don't be discouraged by this hotel's modest exterior and unspectacular location up the main road. Manzini's fanciest hotel attempts an international atmosphere and features a respectable collection of various-size comfy rooms (tip: ask for a poolside one), two stylish restaurants, a lovely garden with a pool, a small spa and conference facilities.

CULTURAL EXPERIENCES

Headed by proud local Myxo Mdluli, **Woza Nawe Tours** (☑2505 8363; www.swaziculturaltours.com) runs highly recommended village visits (day tour R1210) and overnight stays (adult/child E1450/725) to Kaphunga, 55km southeast of Manzini. The fee includes transport, meals and a guide. Guests join in on whatever activities are going on in the village – including cooking, planting and harvesting.

Gil Vincente Restaurant   PORTUGUESE $$
(☑2505 3874; Ngwane St; mains R80-150; ◷9am-10pm Tue-Sun) Gourmands saunter here for well-prepped Portuguese-inspired dishes with a twist, a respectable wine list, efficient service and smart decor. Sink your teeth into a juicy *bitoque* (beefsteak with fried egg) or a succulent *bacalhau* (cod). Had enough protein? Pastas and salads are also available.

ⓘ Getting There & Away

The main **bus and minibus-taxi park** (Louw St) is at the northern end of Louw St, where you can also find some nonshared taxis. A minibus shared-taxi trip up the Ezulwini Valley to Mbabane costs E40 (35 minutes). Minibus taxis to Mozambique (E120) also depart from here.
King Mswati III International Airport (SHO; ☑2518 4390; www.swacaa.co.sz)

NORTHWESTERN SWAZILAND

Lush hills undulating off towards the horizon, green velvet mountains cloaked in layers of wispy cloud, majestic plantations and woodlands, streams and waterfalls, and plunging ravines: these are the main features of Swaziland's beautiful northwest. As well as boasting the best scenery in Swaziland, this area offers some excellent hiking and accommodation options.

Ngwenya

Tiny Ngwenya, 5km east of the border with Mpumalanga, is the first town you'll reach if you're arriving in Swaziland via Oshoek. If you can't wait until you reach the Ezulwini Valley to go shopping, there are excellent craft outlets here. For history buffs, the Ngwenya iron-ore mine is well worth a detour.

◉ Sights

Ngwenya Iron-Ore Mine   HISTORIC SITE
(E30; ◷8am-4pm) Ngwenya is one of the world's oldest known mines. The **Visitors Centre** has an interesting display of photographs and information, including the original excavation tools. To visit the mine, even if you are travelling by vehicle, you will need to be accompanied by a ranger, who will explain the mine's history (note: tips are appreciated). The entrance is signposted off the MR3. Note that although the mine is part of Malolotja Nature Reserve, you can't continue in to the rest of the reserve from here.

⌂ Sleeping

Hawane Resort   RESORT $$
(☑2444 1744; www.hawane.co.sz/pages/accomm.html; Hawane; dm E120, chalet s/d incl breakfast E630/990; P🗚🛜🏊) Framed by the Malolotja peaks, these quirky chalets are a blend of traditional Swazi materials (wattle and grass) with glass, with ethnic African interiors. Backpackers are stabled in a converted barn. The resort restaurant serves African cuisine (dinner buffet E180). It's a convenient base for visiting Malolotja Nature Reserve (p541), though some visitors say it's overpriced and service is lackadaisical. Horse riding is available on the premises. Use of the wi-fi costs E20 per stay. It's about 5km up the Piggs Peak road from the junction of the MR1 and MR3, and 1.5km off the main road.

🛍 Shopping

★**Ngwenya Glass**   ARTS & CRAFTS
(☑2442 4142; www.ngwenyaglass.co.sz; Ngwenya Glass Complex; ◷8am-4pm; 🖪) One of Swaziland's major tourist attractions, this superb glass-blowing factory and boutique showcases a fantastic selection of animal figurines, vases, decorative art glass and tableware, all made from recycled glass. On weekdays you can watch the glass-blowers at work from an overhead balcony. Magical!

The on-site cafe serves light lunches (mains E45 to E75), freshly squeezed juice and big wedges of chocolate cake.

Quazi Design Process   ARTS & CRAFTS
(☑in Mbabane 2422 0193; www.quazidesign.com; Ngwenya Glass Complex; ◷8am-4pm) 🖉 Run by a group of women, this sustainable outlet sells modern accessories of cutting-edge design, made in Mbabane from recycled paper.

Malolotja Nature Reserve

One of Swaziland's premier natural attractions, the beautiful **Malolotja Nature Reserve** (☑2444 3048, mobile 7660 6755; www.sntc.org.sz/reserves/malolotja.asp; adult/child E30/20; ☺6am-6pm) is a true wilderness area that's rugged and, in the most part, unspoiled. The reserve is laced by streams and cut by three rivers, including the Komati, which flows east through a gorge in a series of falls and rapids until it meets the lowveld. No prizes for guessing that this spectacular area is a fantastic playground for nature-lovers and ornithologists, with more than 280 species of bird.

Fans of flora will also get their kicks here; wildflowers and rare plants are added attractions, with several (including the Woolly, Barberton and Kaapschehoop cycads) found only in this region of Africa. Don't expect to see plenty of large mammals, though. It's the scenery that's the pull here, rather than the wildlife. That said, you'll certainly come across various antelope species as well as small groups of zebras and wildebeest.

Malolotja offers some of the most inspirational **hiking** trails in Swaziland. Walking options range from short walks to multi-day hikes. Well-known and much enjoyed walks include the 11.5km Malolotja Falls Trail, with superb views of the Malolotja Valley, and the 8km Komati River Trail. Printouts of hiking trails are available for free at reception inside the reserve. Also check the SNTC website (www.sntc.org.sz/tourism/malolotjawalks.asp) for descriptions of walks and trails.

The entrance gate for Malolotja is about 35km northwest of Mbabane, along the Piggs Peak road (MR1). It's well signposted.

Malolotja Canopy Tour   OUTDOORS
(☑mobile 7660 6755; www.malolotjacanopytour.com; per person E650; ☺8am-2pm) This tour is a definite must-do for those wanting to experience the Malolotja Nature Reserve from a different perspective. Here you will make your way across Malolotja's stunning, lush tree canopy on 10 slides (11 wooden platforms) and via a 50m-long suspension bridge. It's very safe, and no previous experience is required. From the restaurant inside the park you're driven to a base point, from where it's a 15-minute walk to the canopy starting point. Tours leave every 30 minutes.

Malolotja Cabins   CABIN $
(☑2444 3048; www.sntc.org.sz/tourism/malolotja.asp; s/d E400/600; ℗🐾) These fully equipped, self-catering wooden cabins, each sleeping a

MAGUGA DAM LODGE

Scenically positioned on the southern shore of Maguga Dam, the laid-back **Maguga Dam Lodge** (☑2437 3975; www.magugalodge.com; camping per person E145; s/d incl breakfast E690/1045; ℗🕸🛜🏊) is blessed with commanding views of the dam and surrounding hills. It comprises two well-equipped camping grounds, a clutch of spacious and light-filled rondavels and an excellent restaurant overlooking the dam. Various activities are on offer, including fishing, cultural tours, hiking and boat cruises.

maximum of five, are near Malolotja Nature Reserve reception and afford lovely mountain views. If cooking's not your thing, there's a restaurant (also near reception). Wi-fi is available at reception and costs E25 per hour.

Malolotja Camping   CAMPGROUND $
(camping per person E100) Camping is available at the well-equipped main site near reserve reception, with ablutions (hot shower) and braai area, or along the overnight trails (E70; no facilities).

NORTHEASTERN SWAZILAND

The northeastern Swaziland lowveld nestles in the shadow of the Lubombo Mountains, within an easy drive of the Mozambique border. This remote corner is the country's top wildlife-watching region: you'll find a duo of excellent wildlife parks – Hlane Royal National Park and Mkhaya Game Reserve – as well as a couple of lesser-known nature reserves that also beg exploration. If it's action you're after, the superb rapids of the Great Usutu River (Lusutfu River) provide an incredible playground.

Hlane Royal National Park

Hlane Royal National Park belongs in the elite of Swaziland's wildlife parks, and it's easy to see why. Here you can expect to see most safari A-listers, with the exception of buffaloes. This well-organised reserve is the country's largest protected area, and is home to elephants, lions, leopards, white rhinos and many antelope species, and offers wonderfully low-key wildlife and bird-life watching. And it's so easy to enjoy it: hippos and elephants are found around Ndlovu Camp just metres from your cottage. There's plenty to keep you occupied, including bushwalking, wildlife drives, mountain biking and cultural tours.

There's a good network of roads that can be tackled in a 2WD, but note that you'll need to book a guided wildlife drive to explore the lion enclosure. All activities can be booked at Ndlovu Camp.

🏃 Activities

Mountain Biking
Mountain biking is a fun and ecofriendly way to commune with Hlane's bushveld. Guided mountain-bike outings led by expert rangers cost E255 and last two hours. Tours start from Ndlovu Camp at sunrise.

Bushwalks
Hlane offers guided walking trails and birding trips (per person E205), which afford the opportunity to see elephants and rhinos. Serious walkers or bush fanatics can book the one- or two-night fully catered Ehlatsini Bush Trails (full board from E1340, April to September only), which take in some lesser-known areas of the park. Book ahead for the overnight trails.

Wildlife Drives
Hlane's major attraction are its large mammals and predators, and the easiest way to spot them is on a wildlife drive in an open vehicle. The 2½-hour sunrise and sunset drives (per person E345), only for those overnighting at Ndlovu Camp (p542), are best for wildlife and photography; they include the lion enclosure, where you have good chances to see the big cats. A dedicated white-rhino drive (1½ hours, E245) will allow you to get up close and personal with these endangered giants.

Guided Tours
Growing weary of antelope, rhinos and lions? Bookmark the Ndlovu Camp's 'Umphakatsi Experience' cultural tour (two hours; per person E115, minimum four people), during which you'll visit a chief's village and learn about traditional Swazi culture.

Swazi Travel   WILDLIFE
(🖉 2416 2180; www.swazi.travel; day tour from R1850) This company offers day tours to Hlane Royal National Park, collecting from the Ezulwini Valley.

🛌 Sleeping

Hlane has two good camps – Bhubesi is the smaller and quieter of the two. Both can be booked through Big Game Parks (p537).

Ndlovu Camp   CAMPGROUND, COTTAGE $$
(🖉 2528 3943; www.biggameparks.org/hlane; camping E115, rondavel s/d E610/870, cottage s/d from E650/930; 🅿) Ndlovu Camp is a delightfully mellow spot, with spacious grounds and an atmospheric restaurant that serves outstanding food. Accommodation is in rondavels and self-catering cottages with no electricity (paraffin lanterns are provided). You can also pitch your tent on a grassy plot. Ndlovu is just inside the main gate and near a water hole that draws hippos and rhinos.

In the evening, don't miss the traditional dance performance around the campfire.

Bhubesi Camp   BUNGALOW $$
(🖉 2528 3943; www.biggameparks.org/hlane; s/d E650/930; 🅿) Set in a pristine setting about 14km from Ndlovu Camp, Bhubesi Camp features tasteful four-person, self-catering stone bungalows that overlook a river and green lawns and are surrounded by lush growth. Electricity is available, but there's no restaurant.

🍴 Eating

There is a restaurant at Hlane's Ndlovu Camp, overlooking a water hole frequented by rhinos. Self-caterers should stock up before arriving. There are also braai (barbecue) areas for day visitors – bring all supplies with you.

ℹ Information

All Hlane activities can be booked at Ndlovu Camp, where you'll also find bird and mammal lists, plus info on recent sightings.

ℹ Getting There & Away

The gate to Hlane is signposted about 7km south of Simunye. If you don't have your own transport, you can book a tour through Swazi Travel.

Mlawula Nature Reserve

The low-key Mlawula Nature Reserve, where the lowveld plains meet the Lubombo Mountains, boasts antelope species and a few spotted hyenas, among others, plus rewarding birdwatching. Keep your expectations in check, though; wildlife is more elusive here than anywhere else in the country and visitor infrastructure is fairly limited. The park's

DON'T MISS

PHOPHONYANE FALLS ECOLODGE & NATURE RESERVE

Phophonyane Falls Ecolodge & Nature Reserve (☏2431 3429; www.phophonyane. co.sz; s/d safari tent with shared bathroom E915/1310, s/d beehive hut E1525/2190, d cottage E2050; ⓟ ≋), a little morsel of paradise about 14km north of Piggs Peak, is a dream come true for those seeking to get well and truly off the beaten track. It lies on a river in its own nature reserve of lush indigenous forest. Accommodation is in comfortable cottages, stylish beehives or luxury safari tents overlooking cascades.

There's a network of walking trails around the river and waterfall. Day visitors to the reserve are charged E40/30 per adult/child. Excellent meals are available in the stylish dining area. Turn at signs indicating Phophonyane Falls; then it's 4.5km on dirt road.

real highlight is its network of walking trails amid beautifully scenic landscapes. There are 10 self-guided walks ranging from a one-hour stroll to a full-day hike. Ask for the *Trails and Day Walks* flier at the gate.

The turn-off for the entrance gates to the Mlawula Nature Reserve is about 10km north of Simunye, from where it's another 4km from the main road. You'll need your own transport to explore the reserve.

Siphiso Campground CAMPGROUND $
(www.sntc.org.sz; adult/child E100/30) A basic campsite within the Mlawula Nature Reserve, which offers shared ablutions and shady trees.

Magadzavane Lodge CHALET $$
(☏2383 8885; magadzavane@sntc.org.sz; Mlawula Nature Reserve; s/d incl breakfast E600/900; ⓟ ⓦ ≋) This great option offers 20 enticing chalets in southern Mlawula, on the edge of the Lubombo escarpment, with magnificent views of the valley below. There's a restaurant and a small infinity pool. From the northern gate, it's a 17km drive on a gravel road; the last kilometres are very steep (but manageable in a standard vehicle in dry weather). It's also possible to reach here via the southern gate.

Mkhaya Game Reserve

The crowning glory of Swaziland's parks, the top-notch and stunning **Mkhaya Game Reserve** (☏2528 3943; www.mkhaya.org) is famous for its black and white rhino populations (it boasts that you're more likely to meet rhinos here than anywhere else in Africa and, judging from our experience, this is true). Its other animals include roan and sable antelope, giraffes, tsessebe, buffaloes and elephants, along with a rich diversity of birds. If you're lucky, you might spot the elusive narina trogon and other rare bird

species. Note that children under 10 are not allowed in the park.

The Mkhaya Game Reserve is near the hamlet of Phuzumoya, off the Manzini–Big Bend road (it's signposted off the MR8). Rangers meet you at the gate to transfer you to camp. There is secure parking at the ranger base station.

One of the highlights of Swaziland is rafting the **Great Usutu River** (Lusutfu River). The river varies radically from steep creeks to sluggish flats, but in the vicinity of Mkhaya Game Reserve it passes through a gorge, where a perfect mix of rapids can be encountered all year round.

Swazi Trails (p534) is the best contact to organise a rafting trip – it offers full- and half-day trips (E1300/1100 per person, including lunch and transport, minimum two people). Abseiling and cliff jumps are added for extra adrenaline in the winter months.

For an off-the-scale challenge rating, the company's adventure-caving trips offer a rare window into the elite world of cave exploration. A few kilometres from Mbabane, the vast Gobholo Cave is 98% unexplored. You can choose between the 8.30am departure (E800) and the 4.30pm dinner trip (E950; it includes a hot-spring soak, pizza and beer).

★Stone Camp LODGE $$$
(☏2528 3943; www.mkhaya.org; Mkhaya Game Reserve; s/d with full board & activities from E2620/3940; ⓟ) A dream come true for nature-lovers, Stone Camp consists of a series of rustic and luxurious semi-open stone-and-thatch cottages (a proper loo with a view!), located in secluded bush zones. The price includes wildlife drives, walking safaris and meals, and is excellent value compared to many of the private reserves in Southern Africa. Simply arrive, absorb and wonder. No electricity, but paraffin lanterns are provided.

Mkhaya's signature activity, guided bushwalks are an ideal way to approach wildlife, especially white rhinos. You periodically disembark from the open vehicle and track rhinos on foot, under the guidance of an experienced ranger. You'll learn plenty about rhino behaviour. Unforgettable!

Bush walks take place at 11am. Note that they're offered to Stone Camp overnight guests only.

Wildlife drives through Mkhaya in an open vehicle are included in Stone Camp's accommodation rates. For overnight guests, they take place in the early morning and late afternoon. As day trips (per person E735), they start at 10am and include lunch.

UNDERSTAND SWAZILAND

Swaziland Today

Democratic freedom is an issue in Swaziland, where absolute monarch King Mswati III has been accused of silencing opponents. In 2014, the country was excluded from a trade pact giving duty-free access to the US market, due to human rights concerns. Despite calls for greater democracy, pride in the monarchy lingers, and some propose a constitutional monarchy. The rural, homogeneous country has many challenges, including widespread poverty, a declining economy reliant on South Africa and the world's highest HIV prevalence at 28.8%. Life expectancy hovers around 50 years – among the lowest in the world.

History

Beginnings of a Nation

The area that is now Swaziland has been inhabited for millennia, and human-like remains possibly dating back as far as 100,000 years have been discovered around the Lubombo Mountains in eastern Swaziland. However, today's Swazis trace their ancestors to much more recent arrivals. By around AD 500, various Nguni groups had made their way to the region as part of the great Bantu migrations. One of these groups settled in the area around present-day Maputo (Mozambique), eventually founding the Dlamini dynasty. In the mid-18th century, in response to increasing pressure from other clans in the area, the Dlamini king, Ngwane III, led his people southwest to the Pongola River, in present-day southern Swaziland and northern KwaZulu-Natal. This became the first Swazi heartland.

Ngwane's successor, Sobhuza I, established a base in the Ezulwini Valley, which still remains the centre of Swazi royalty and ritual. Next came King Mswazi (or Mswati), after whom the Swazi take their name. Despite pressure from the neighbouring Zulu, Mswazi succeeded in unifying the whole kingdom.

From the mid-19th century, Swaziland attracted increasing numbers of European farmers in search of land for cattle, as well as hunters, traders and missionaries.

Over the next decades, the Swazis saw their territory whittled away as the British and Boers jostled for power in the area. In 1902, following the second Anglo-Boer War, the Boers withdrew and the British took control of Swaziland as a protectorate.

Struggle for Independence

Swazi history in the early 20th century centred on the ongoing struggle for independence. Under the leadership of King Sobhuza II (guided by the capable hands of his mother, Lomawa Ndwandwewho, who acted as regent while Sobhuza was a child), the Swazis succeeded in regaining much of their original territory. This was done in part by direct purchase and in part by British government decree. This was a major development, as Swazi kings are considered to hold the kingdom in trust for their subjects, and land ownership is thus more than just a political and economic issue.

Independence was finally achieved – the culmination of a long and remarkably nonviolent path – on 6 September 1968, 66 years after the establishment of the British protectorate.

The first Swazi constitution was largely a British creation, and in 1973 the king suspended it on the grounds that it did not accord with Swazi culture. Four years later parliament reconvened under a new constitution vesting all power in the king.

Sobhuza II died in 1982, at that time the world's longest-reigning monarch. In 1986 the young Mswati III ascended the throne, where he continues today to represent and maintain the traditional Swazi way of life and to assert his pre-eminence as absolute monarch. Despite an undercurrent of political dissent, political parties are still unable to participate in elections.

The Culture

People & Economy

Swaziland's economic scene is almost completely wrapped up in that of its larger neighbour. About two-thirds of Swazi exports go to South Africa and more than 90% of goods and services are imported. Overall, some 70% of Swazis live in rural areas and rely on subsistence farming for survival.

Swazi culture is very strong and quite distinct from that of South Africa. The monarchy influences many aspects of life, from cultural ceremonies to politics. While some Swazis are proud of the royal traditions and suspicious of those who call for greater democracy, a growing number of human-rights and opposition activists believe power should be transferred from the king to the people.

Women in Swaziland

Swazi women's rights have recently improved dramatically. The 2005 constitution guarantees women equal political, economic and social rights and reserves one-third of parliamentary seats for women, but this is not always instituted, and discriminatory practices continue. Traditional social systems discriminate against women, and one survey conducted by Unicef found that one-third of Swazi females had experienced sexual violence before they turned 18. But it is estimated that over 70% of small businesses in Swaziland are operated by women, who tend to be more entrepreneurial than their countrymen.

Environment

Swaziland is one of Africa's smallest countries at only 17,364 sq km in area, but with a remarkable diversity of landscapes, climates and ecological zones. These range from low-lying savannah to the east, rolling hills towards the centre, and rainforest and perpetually fog-draped peaks in the northwest.

Wildlife

Swaziland has about 120 mammal species, representing one-third of Southern Africa's

SWAZI LITERATURE

Most of the books available about Swaziland were written by Brits during the colonial era. Noted indigenous writers include James Shadrack Mkhulunyelwa Matsebula, who pioneered the use of Swati as a written language. Stanley Musa N Matsebula's novels, including *Siyisike Yinye Nje* (We Are in the Same Boat; 1989), opened up the debate about gender inequality in Swaziland.

nonmarine mammal species. Many (including elephants, rhinos and lions) have been introduced, and larger animals are restricted to nature reserves and private wildlife farms. Mongoose and large-spotted genets are common, and hyenas and jackals are found in the reserves. Leopards are rarely seen.

Swaziland's varied terrain supports abundant birdlife, including the blue crane, ground woodpecker and lappet-faced vulture. More species have been spotted in Swaziland than in the larger Kruger National Park.

National Parks & Protected Areas

About 4% of Swaziland's area is protected. Its conservation areas tend to be low-key, with fewer visitors than their South African counterparts, and good value for money. They include Mlilwane Wildlife Sanctuary, Mkhaya Game Reserve, Malolotja Nature Reserve, which is mainly for hiking, and Hlane Royal National Park. Mlilwane, Mkhaya and Hlane are included in South Africa's Wild Card program (www.sanparks.org/wild).

Environmental Issues

Three of Swaziland's major waterways (the Komati, Lomati and Usutu Rivers) arise in South Africa, and Swaziland has been closely involved in South Africa's river-control efforts. Drought is a recurring problem in eastern lowveld areas. Other concerns include lack of community participation in conservation efforts, low levels of environmental awareness and lack of government support.

SURVIVAL GUIDE

ℹ Directory A–Z

ACCOMMODATION

Rates are reasonable in Swaziland and much lower than you would find in Europe or North America. There is a handful of backpackers hostels and camping is possible on the grounds of many accommodation options.

Backpackers

Backpacker accommodation is found in areas including the Ezulwini Valley. Prices and facilities are similar to those in South Africa.

Camping

Apart from in Swaziland's national parks, nature reserves and lodges, there are few official campsites. It's usually possible to free-camp, but get permission from elders in the nearest village before setting up, both out of respect for the local community and to minimise security risks. You may be offered a hut for the night; expect to pay a token fee of about E20 for this.

ACTIVITIES

Swaziland's geographical diversity makes for some fabulous hiking experiences and you'll find short and long trails throughout the country, many within the excellent parks and nature reserves. The terrain can also be explored on horseback, by mountain bike and from the soggy seat of a river raft or canoe.

Canoeing

Swazi Trails (www.swazitrails.co.sz) offers trips on Swaziland's Great Usutu River (Lusutfu River) and around the country.

Hiking

➡ Some of the nature reserves are particularly good for hiking, including Malolotja with its 200km of trails.

➡ In most rural areas, you can follow the generations-old tracks that criss-cross the countryside.

➡ If you're hiking during the summer, be prepared for torrential downpours and even occasional hailstorms.

Horse Riding

There are stables offering fully kitted-out horse rides in the Ezulwini Valley, Malkerns, Mlilwane Wildlife Sanctuary and Malolotja Nature Reserve. Rides can last anything from an hour or two to a full week.

Wildlife Watching

From sightings of rare birds in Mlilwane Wildlife Sanctuary and Mlawula Nature Reserve, to up-close encounters with black and white rhino at Mkhaya Game Reserve, Swaziland's top draw is its range of accessible – and very affordable –

BOOK YOUR STAY ONLINE

For more accommodation reviews by Lonely Planet authors, check out hotels. lonelyplanet.com. You'll find independent reviews, as well as recommendations on the best places to stay. Best of all, you can book online.

wildlife experiences. Guided wildlife drives are on offer throughout the country and in most parks you can self-drive, but there are also opportunities to cycle, hike and ride horses in the parks.

CHILDREN

Swaziland is a good family destination, with a child-friendly attitude and a relaxed pace. The main caveat is that malaria is a real risk in lower-lying areas of the country.

Many hotels in Swaziland offer family-friendly accommodation, and there are amusements such as minigolf to keep children occupied.

Informal childcare arrangements can be made; if you are staying in a good lodge or hotel, staff may be able to assist.

Nappies, powdered milk and baby food are available in Mbabane and Manzini, with only a limited selection in smaller towns.

DANGERS & ANNOYANCES

Petty crime such as pickpocketing and phone- and bag-snatching can happen in urban areas. Always take common-sense precautions and be vigilant at all times. Never walk around alone at night or flaunt valuables.

Schistosomiasis (bilharzia) and malaria are both present in Swaziland, although it is taking serious steps to be the first country in sub-Saharan Africa to move to malaria-free status.

EMBASSIES & CONSULATES

Embassies and consulates are found in Mbabane and the Ezulwini Valley. Missions in South Africa generally have responsibility for Swaziland.

German Liaison Office (📞 2404 3174; www. southafrica.diplo.de; 3rd fl, Lilunga House, Samhlolo St; ⊘ 9am-noon Mon-Fri)

Mozambican High Commission (📞 2404 1296; moz.high@swazi.net; Princess Drive Rd, Highlands View)

Netherlands Honorary Consul (📞 2404 3547; southafrica.nlembassy.org)

South African High Commission (📞 2404 4651; www.dfa.gov.za; 2nd fl, the New Mall, Dr Sishayi Rd; ⊘ 9am-3pm Mon-Fri)

US Embassy (📞 2417 9000; http://swaziland. usembassy.gov; nr MR103 & Cultural Center Drive, Lobamba; ⊘ 7.30am-5pm Mon-Thu, to 1.30pm Fri)

EMERGENCY & IMPORTANT NUMBERS

Ambulance	✆ 977
Fire	✆ 933
Police	✆ 2404 2221, 999

GAY & LESBIAN TRAVELLERS

Swaziland is one of the most conservative countries in Southern Africa. Male homosexual activities are illegal, and gay relationships are culturally taboo, with homosexuals subjected to discrimination and harassment.

INTERNET ACCESS

Wi-fi is still rare in Swaziland, even in many accommodation establishments. You will find a few (paid-for) wi-fi spots and internet cafes in Mbabane, Manzini and Malkerns Valley.

MONEY

ATMs are common throughout Swaziland. Cards might not be accepted in rural spots so keep a small stash of cash handy.

Swaziland's currency is the lilangeni (plural emalangeni, E), divided into 100 cents. It is fixed at a value equal to the South African rand. Rand are accepted everywhere, though you will invariably be given emalangeni in change.

Moneychangers

➜ FNB and Nedbank change cash and travellers cheques – their rates are similar, but commissions vary.

➜ Most banks ask to see the purchase receipt when cashing travellers cheques

➜ Nedbank, FNB and Standard Bank have branches in Mbabane, Manzini, Matsapha and around the country.

Tipping

Wages are low in Swaziland, and tipping is expected – 10% to 15% in restaurants.

OPENING HOURS

Banks 8.30am–2.30pm Mon–Fri, 9–11am Sat
Post offices 8am–4pm Mon–Fri, 8.30–11am Sat
Government offices 8am–4pm Mon–Fri
Cafes 8am–5pm
Restaurants 11.30am–3pm & 7–10pm (last orders); many open 3–7pm
Bars noon–2am
Businesses and shopping 8.30am–5pm Mon–Fri, 8.30am–1pm Sat

POST

Domestic and international deliveries are generally reliable in Swaziland but can be slow.

PUBLIC HOLIDAYS

New Year's Day 1 January
Good Friday March/April
Easter Monday March/April
King Mswati III's Birthday 19 April
National Flag Day 25 April
Workers' Day 1 May
King Sobhuza II's Birthday 22 July
Umhlanga Reed Dance Festival August/September
Somhlolo (Independence) Day 6 September
Christmas Day 25 December
Boxing Day 26 December
Incwala Ceremony December/January

TELEPHONE

➜ Swaziland has a reasonably good telephone network, operated by SwaziTelecom (www.sptc.co.sz/swazitelecom).

➜ There are no area codes.

➜ Swaziland's eight-digit landline and mobile-phone numbers respectively begin with 2 and 7.

➜ Dial ✆ 94 to make a reverse-charge call.

➜ International calls are most easily made using MTN phonecards.

➜ Outside the major towns, dial 94 to book international calls.

➜ MTN Swaziland (www.mtn.co.sz) provides the mobile-phone network.

➜ You can buy SIM cards for a nominal fee and South African SIMs work on roaming.

TIME

➜ Swaziland is on SAST (South Africa Standard Time), which is two hours ahead of GMT/UTC.

➜ There is no daylight-saving period.

➜ Most timetables and businesses use the 24-hour clock.

TOURIST INFORMATION

Swaziland has tourist offices in Mbabane and the Ezulwini and Malkerns Valleys; elsewhere they are thin on the ground.

PRACTICALITIES

Media

Times of Swaziland (www.times.co.sz) and **Swazi Observer** (www.observer.org.sz) carry local news.

Electricity

The electricity supply in Swaziland is 220V. Plugs have three large round pins as used in South Africa.

Weights & Measures

Swaziland uses the metric system.

Swaziland National Trust Commission (www.sntc.org.sz)

Swaziland Tourism (www.thekingdomof swaziland.com)

Swazi.travel (www.swazi.travel)

VISAS

➡ Visitors from most Western countries don't need a visa to enter Swaziland for up to 30 days.

➡ To stay for longer than 30 days, apply at the **Ministry of Home Affairs immigration department** (☑ 2404 2941; www.gov.sz; Home Affairs & Justice Bldg, Mhlambanyatsi Rd, Mbabane; ☺ 8am-4pm Mon-Fri).

➡ Visas cannot be obtained on arrival in Swaziland.

➡ Visa applications must be accompanied by documents including a letter of invitation.

ⓘ Getting There & Away

AIR

There are Airlink subsidiary **Swaziland Airlink** (☑ in South Africa 0861 606 606, in Swaziland 2335 0107; www.flyswaziland.com) flights into Swaziland (King Mswati III International Airport) from Johannesburg (Jo'burg).

Departure tax is E100.

LAND

Most travellers enter Swaziland overland. Car rental is available from **Avis** (☑ 2333 5299; www.avis.co.za; King Mswati III International Airport; ☺ 7am-6pm) and **Europcar** (☑ 2518 4393; www.europcar.com; Matshapa Airport; ☺ 8am-5pm Mon-Fri, 11am-5pm Sat & Sun), but it's usually cheaper to rent a car in South Africa.

There are no restrictions on bringing your own bicycle into Swaziland. Repair shops and bicycle supplies are in short supply so come well prepared.

Border Crossings

There are 12 Swaziland–South Africa border posts, all of which are hassle-free, including the following. Note that small posts close at 4pm.

Mhlumeni/Goba (☺ 24hr) To/from Mozambique.

Lavumisa/Golela (☺ 7am-10pm) En route between Durban and Swaziland's Ezulwini Valley.

Bulembu/Josefdal (☺ 8am-4pm) Between Piggs Peak and Barberton (Mpumalanga); the road is in a terrible state and barely passable in a 2WD.

Namaacha/Lomahasha (☺ 7am-10pm) The busy post in extreme northeast Swaziland is the main crossing to/from Mozambique.

Mahamba (☺ 7am-10pm) The best crossing to use from Piet Retief in Mpumalanga. Casinos nearby attract traffic, especially on weekends – good places to look for lifts into and out of the country.

Mananga (8am-6pm) Southwest of Komatipoort.

Jeppe's Reef/Matsamo (8am-8pm) Southwest of Malelane and a possible route to Kruger National Park. Casinos nearby attract traffic, especially on weekends – good places to look for lifts into and out of the country.

Salitje/Onverwacht (8am-6pm) North of Pongola in KwaZulu-Natal.

Ngwenya/Oshoek (7am-midnight) The busiest crossing (and a good place to pick up lifts), about 360km southeast of Pretoria.

ⓘ Getting Around

There is a good network of minibus shared taxis covering Swaziland.

BICYCLE

Swaziland is an excellent cycling destination, for which you need a mountain bike. Stock up on spare parts in South Africa. Summer thunderstorms and flooding are an issue. Transporting bicycles on public transport is uncommon, as buses and taxis are generally crowded.

Avoid the main towns and the heavily travelled Ezulwini Valley. Short pedals are available on the mountain-bike trails of Hlane Royal National Park and Mlilwane Wildlife Sanctuary, which respectively offer guided rides and bike rental.

BUS

Minibus shared taxis are the main form of public transport in Swaziland. They run almost everywhere, with frequent stops en route. They leave when full; no reservations are necessary.

Local buses connect towns and villages throughout the country. Most start and terminate at the main stop in central Mbabane; they are lightly cheaper than minibuses but are slow and often overcrowded.

CAR & MOTORCYCLE

It usually works out cheaper to rent a vehicle in South Africa and drive it over the Swazi border (you'll need a permission letter from the rental company to cross the border; this costs about R300). You'll find rentals in Swaziland in Mbabane and King Mswati III International Airport (p540).

LOCAL TRANSPORT
Private Taxi

Larger cities have private taxi services. It's best to phone for a taxi rather than hailing one on the street – the vehicle will likely be better quality and you can ask your accommodation for a reputable company.

Shared Taxi

Minibus shared taxis don't have stellar road-safety records, but fares are cheap and the network is comprehensive. The downside is that journeys can be slow, with constant stops and long waits to fill the seats.

Victoria Falls

Includes ➡

Zambia 553
Livingstone 554
Zimbabwe 559
Victoria Falls 559

Best Places to Eat

➡ Cafe Zambezi (p557)

➡ Lola's Tapas & Carnivore Restaurant (p562)

➡ Olga's Italian Corner (p557)

➡ Lookout Cafe (p561)

➡ Boma (p562)

Best Places to Sleep

➡ Victoria Falls Hotel (p561)

➡ Jollyboys Backpackers (p555)

➡ Stanley Safari Lodge (p557)

➡ Victoria Falls Backpackers (p561)

Why Go?

Taking its place alongside the Pyramids and the Serengeti, Victoria Falls (*Mosi-oa-Tunya* – the 'smoke that thunders') is one of Africa's original blockbusters. And although Zimbabwe and Zambia share it, Victoria Falls is a place all of its own.

As a magnet for tourists of all descriptions – backpackers, tour groups, thrill seekers, families, honeymooners – Victoria Falls is one of Earth's great spectacles. View it directly as a raging mile-long curtain of water, in all its glory, from a helicopter ride or peek precariously over its edge from Devil's Pools; the sheer power and force of the falls is something that simply does not disappoint.

Whether you're here purely to take in the sight of a natural wonder of the world, or for a serious hit of adrenalin via rafting or bungee jumping into the Zambezi, Victoria Falls is a place where you're sure to tick off numerous items from that bucket list.

When to Go

There are two main reasons to go to Victoria Falls – to view the falls, and to experience the outdoor activities – and each has its season.

July to December is the season for white-water rafting, especially August for hard-core rapids.

From February to June you'll experience the falls at their full force, so don't forget your raincoat.

From July to September you'll get the best views of the falls, combined with lovely weather and all activities to keep you busy.

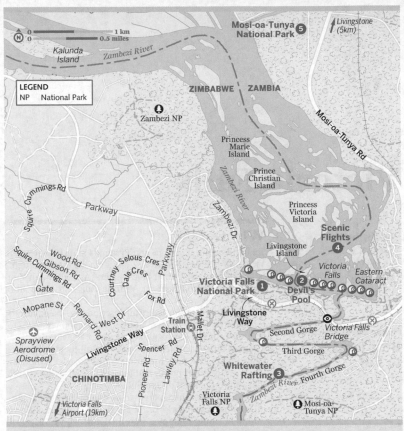

Victoria Falls Highlights

❶ Victoria Falls National Park (p559) Taking in the full force of the falls with unobstructed views.

❷ Devil's Pool (p554) Experiencing the world's most extreme infinity pool.

❸ Whitewater rafting (p551) Taming Grade-5 rapids along the Zambezi.

❹ Scenic flights (p552) Taking the 'flight of the angels' helicopter ride over Victoria Falls.

❺ Mosi-oa-Tunya National Park (p554) Tracking white rhino on foot on a walking safari.

SEVENTH NATURAL WONDER OF THE WORLD

Victoria Falls is the largest, most beautiful and most majestic waterfall on the planet, and is the Seventh Natural Wonder of the World as well as a Unesco World Heritage Site. A trip to Southern Africa would not be complete without visiting this unforgettable place.

Up to one million litres of water fall – per second – down a 108m drop along a 1.7km wide strip in the Zambezi Gorge; it's an awe-some sight. Victoria Falls can be seen, heard, tasted and touched; it is a treat that few other places in the world can offer, a 'must see before you die' spot.

Victoria Falls is spectacular at any time of year, yet varies in the experiences it offers.

🏃 Activities

While it's the falls that lures travellers to the region, its awesome outdoor adventure scene is what makes them hang around. From world-class whitewater rafting, bungee jumping and high-adrenalin activities, to scenic flights and walking with rhinos, Victoria Falls is undoubtedly one of the world's premier adventure destinations.

Abseiling

Strap on a helmet, grab a rope and spend the day rappelling down the 54m sheer drop cliff face of Batoka Gorge from US$55.

Birdwatching

Twitchers will want to bring binoculars to check out 470 species of bird that inhabit the region, including Schalow's turaco, Taita falcon, African finfoot and half-collared kingfisher. Spot them on foot in the parks or on a canoe trip along the Zambezi.

Bridge Walk

For those not interested in bungee jumping off the bridge, walking along it is a good alternative. Strapped in with a harness, the guided tours take the walkways running just beneath the Victoria Falls Bridge, and offer a good way to learn about this engineering marvel, as well as fantastic photo ops. It's US$65 per person. Don't forget your passport.

Bungee Jumping & Bridge Swinging

One of the most famous bungee jumps in the world, the leap here is from atop of the iconic Victoria Falls bridge, plunging 111m into the Zambezi River. It's a long way down, but man it's a lot of fun. It costs US$160 per person.

Otherwise there's the bridge swing where you jump feet first, and free fall for four seconds; you'll end up swinging, but not upside down. There are two main spots: one right off the Victoria Falls Bridge, and the other a bit further along the Batoka Gorge. Costs for single/tandem are US$160/240.

Combine bungee with a bridge swing and bridge slide, and it'll cost US$210.

Canoeing & Kayaking

If whitewater rafting isn't for you, there's more relaxed guided canoe trips along the Upper Zambezi River on two-person inflatable canoes. Options include half (US$110) or whole day (US$125 to US$155) trips, and overnight jaunts (US$250 to US$285) and longer trips are available.

There's even more relaxed three-hour guided sunset river float trips where you can kick back and let someone else do the paddling for US$100, including refreshments.

On the Zambian side, take on the Zambezi's raging rapids in an inflatable kayak on a full-day trip (US$155).

Crocodile Cage Diving

On the Zimbabwe side of the falls, bring along your bathers for a close encounter with a Nile croc, where you plunge within the safety of a cage into a croc-filled enclosure wearing a mask and breathing apparatus. It costs US$70

Cultural Activities

Spend an hour in the evening by a campfire drumming under the African sky, which includes a traditional meal, for US$25. On the Zimbabwe side you can visit a local's home for lunch (US$23) or dinner (US$25)

Hiking

There's a good choice of guided walks in the area. One of the most popular treks is the trek down Batoka Gorge to the Boiling Pot (US$48) where you can get up close and personal with Victoria Falls. You can only do this from late August to December.

Horse Riding

Indulge in a bit of wildlife spotting from horseback along the Zambezi. Rides for 2½ hours cost US$100, and full-day trips for experienced riders are US$155.

Jet Boating

This hair-raising trip costs US$120, and is combined with a cable-car ride down into the Batoka Gorge.

Quadbiking

Discover the spectacular landscape surrounding Livingstone, Zambia, and the Batoka Gorge, spotting wildlife as you go on all-terrain quad bikes. Trips vary from ecotrail riding at Batoka Land to longer-range cultural trips in the African bush. Trips are one hour (US$95) or 2½ hours (US$165).

Rafting

This is one of the best white-water rafting destinations in the world, both for experienced rafters and newbies. Rafting can be done on either side of the Zambezi River, so it doesn't matter what side of the border you're on – you'll find Grade 5 rapids. Expect very long rides with huge drops and big kicks; it's not for the faint-hearted.

The best time for rafting is between July and mid-February (low water season); peak season is around August to October. Day trips run between rapids 1 and 21 (to rapid 25 on the Zambian side), covering a distance of around 25km.

VICTORIA FALLS ACTIVITIES

The river fills up between mid-February and July (high water season), when day trips move downstream from rapids 11 to 25, covering a distance of around 18km. Only half-day trips are offered during this time. The river will usually close for its 'off season' around April or May, depending on the rain pattern for the year.

Trips are cheaper on the Zimbabwe side, costing about US$120 (versus US$160 in Zambia), but Zambia has the benefit of the cable car (and a few additional rapids) as opposed to the steep climb out on the Zimbabwe side.

Overnight and multiday jaunts can also be arranged.

An add-on activity to rafting is **riverboarding**, which is basically lying on a boogie board and careering down the rapids. A package including rafting for a half/full day is US$170/190. Otherwise get in touch with **Bundu Adventures** (013-324406, 0978-203988; www.bunduadventures.com; 1364 Kabompo Rd, Gemstone Restaurant) about its **hydrospeed surfing** trips, where you can ride rapid number 2 on an Anvil board for US$70 for three hours.

River Cruises

River cruises along the Zambezi range from breakfast cruises to civilised jaunts on the grand *African Queen* and all-you-can-drink sunset booze cruises. Prices range from US$48 to US$85, excluding park fees. They're great for spotting wildlife, though some tourists get just as much enjoyment out of the bottomless drinks. Highly recommended.

Scenic Flights

Just when you thought the falls couldn't get any more spectacular, discover the 'flight of angels' helicopter ride that flies you right by the drama for the undisputed best views available. Rides aren't cheap, but they're worth it. **Zambezi Helicopter Company** (013-43569; www.zambezihelicopters.com; flights 13-/25-min US$150/284, plus US$12 govt fee) and **Bonisair** (0776 497888; www.bonisair.com; 15-/22-/25-mins US$150/235/277) in Zimbabwe, and **United Air Charter** (0955 204282, 0213-323095; www.uaczam.com; Baobab Ridge, Livingstone; 15/20/30min US$165/235/330) and **Batoka Sky** (0213-323589; www.seasonsinafrica.com; 15-min flights from US$155) in Zambia all offer flights. Flights cost from US$150 for 15 minutes over the falls, with longer trips available to take in the surrounding area.

On the Zambian side you can take a microlight flight with Batoka Sky, which offers another way to get fabulous aerial views.

Steam Train Journeys

To take in the romance of yesteryear, book yourself a ride on a historical steam train on the **Bushtracks Express** (013-45176; www.gotothevictoriafalls.com; 205 Courtney Selous Cr),

---

THE FALLS VIEWING SEASONS

Though spectacular at any time of year, the falls has a wet and dry season and each brings a distinct experience.

When the river is higher and the falls fuller it's the Wet, and when the river is lower and the falls aren't smothered in spray it's the Dry. Broadly speaking, you can expect the following conditions during the year:

January to April The beginning of the rainy season sees the falls begin their transitional period from low to high water, which should give you decent views, combined with experiencing its famous spray.

May to June Don't forget your raincoat, as you're gonna get drenched! While the falls will be hard to see through the mist, it'll give you a true sense of its power as 500 million litres of water plummets over the edge. The mist during this time can be seen from 50km away. If you want views, don't despair, this is the best time for aerial views with a chopper flight taking you up and over this incredible sight.

July to October The most popular time to visit, as the mist dissipates to unveil the best views and photography options from directly across the falls, while the volume maintains its rage to give you an idea of its sheer force – but only from the Zimbabwe side. However, those on the Zambian side will be able to experience Devil's Pool, which is accessible from August.

November to January The least popular time to visit, as temperatures rise and the falls are at their lowest flow. But they're impressive nevertheless, as the curtain of water divides into sections. The advantage of this time of year is you're able to swim right up to the edge of Devil's Pool on the Zambian side.

a 1953 class 14A Garratt steam train that will take you over the iconic Victoria Falls bridge at sunset with gourmet canapés and unlimited drinks. It's US$125 (including transfers, alcohol and snacks), with departures on Tuesday and Friday either at 5pm or 5.30pm; check the website for the latest schedule. Even if you're not booked on a trip it's worth getting along to the station to watch the drama of its departure.

In Zambia the **Royal Livingstone Express** (📞 0213-4699300; www.royal-livingstone-express.com; Mosi-oa-Tunya Rd; US$180 incl dinner, drinks & transfers; ⏰ 4.30pm Wed & Sat) takes you on a 3½-hour ride including five-course dinner and drinks on a 1924 10th-class or 12th-class steam engine. The journey takes you to through Mosi-oa-Tunya National Park on plush leather couches, en route to the Victoria Falls Bridge for a sundowner. It's priced at $180 per person, including return transfers within Livingstone.

Wildlife Safaris

There are plenty of options for wildlife watching in the area, both in the national park in the immediate area and further afield, as well as private game reserves.

In Zambia the game reserve section of Mosi-oa-Tunya National Park is home to white rhino, and hence a popular spot to tick off that last member from the big five in the wild. You're able to track them on foot for US$80 per person (including park fees), but you can only do this as part of a walking tour. Get in touch with Livingstone Rhino Walks (p555) or Savannah Southern Safaris (p554) for bookings; note that you need to be over 12 years of age.

The Zambezi National Park in Zimbabwe is much bigger in scale and has a greater diversity of wildlife (including a few cats) and some wonderful lodges and campsites along the Zambezi.

On both sides of the border river cruises (from US$48) along the Zambezi River are another popular way to see various wildlife including elephants, hippos and plenty of birdlife.

Another convenient option, only 15km from Victoria Falls town, is the Stanley and Livingstone Private Game Reserve. Set on a 4000-hectare private reserve here you can track the Big Five, including black rhino that have been translocated from Hwange National Park. A standard three-hour game drive costs US$100, or you can do a night drive and a bush dinner (US$137).

Hwange National Park (www.zimparks.org; national parks accommodation per day guests/nonguests US$10/20; ⏰ main gate 6am-6pm) in Zimbabwe is the other option, with one of the largest number of elephants in the world, as well as good sightings of predators. A day trip will cost around US$220 (minimum four people), or otherwise it's a two-hour bus ride away.

You can travel further afield, with operators arranging day trips to Chobe National Park in Botswana for US$160 (excluding visas). It's only a one-hour drive from Victoria Falls, and includes a breakfast boat cruise, a game drive in Chobe National Park, lunch and transfer back to Victoria Falls by 5pm. Wildlife viewing is excellent: lions, elephants, wild dogs, cheetahs, buffaloes and plenty of antelopes.

Zipline, Flying Fox & Gorge Swings

Glide at 106km/h along a zipline (single/tandem US$69/111), or soar like a superhero from one country to another (from Zim to Zam) on the 'bridge slide' as you whiz over Batoka Gorge (single/tandem US$45/70). Other similar options are flying-fox rides (US$42).

A *slightly* less terrifying variation of the bungee jump is the gorge swing (US$95), where you take the plunge foot first before swinging across the gorge like a human pendulum.

❶ Information

Hands down the best independent advice is from **Backpackers Bazaar** (📞 013-45828, 013-44511, 013-42208; www.backpackersbazaarvicfalls.com; off Parkway, Shop 5, Bata Bldg; ⏰ 8am-5pm Mon-Fri, 9am-4pm Sat & Sun) in the town of Victoria Falls, run by the passionate owner, Joy, who has a wealth of all info and advice for Victoria Falls and beyond. In Livingstone, the folks at Jollyboys Backpackers (p555) are also extremely knowledgeable on all the latest happenings. Both are good places to book activities and onward travel.

ZAMBIA

📞 260

As Zambia continues to ride the wave of tourism generated by the falls, it manages to keep itself grounded, offering a wonderfully low-key destination. The waterfront straddling the falls continues its rapid development and is fast becoming one of the most exclusive destinations in Southern Africa.

Livingstone

POP 136,897 / ☑ 0213

The relaxed and friendly town of Livingstone, set just 11km from Victoria Falls, is a fantastic base for visiting the Zambian side of the natural world wonder. It attracts travellers not only to experience the falls but also to tackle the thrilling adventure scene, and has taken on the role of a backpacking mecca. Its main thoroughfare, Mosi-oa-Tunya Rd, leads south to a wonderful stretch of the Zambezi River around 7km from town.

◉ Sights

★ Victoria Falls World Heritage National Monument Site
WATERFALL

(Mosi-au-Tunya National Park; adult/child/guide US$20/10/10; ☺6am-6pm) This is what you're here for. The mighty Victoria Falls is part of the Mosi-oa-Tunya National Park, located 11km outside town before the Zambia border. From the centre, a network of paths leads through thick vegetation to various viewpoints.

For close-up views of the **Eastern Cataract**, nothing beats the hair-raising (and hair-wetting) walk across the footbridge, through swirling clouds of mist, to a sheer buttress called the **Knife Edge**.

★ Devil's Pool
VIEWPOINT

(www.devilspool.net; Livingstone Island; from US$90) One of the most thrilling experiences – not only at the falls but in all of Africa – is the hair-raising journey to **Livingstone Island**. Here you will bathe in Devil's Pool – nature's ultimate infinity pool, set directly on the edge of Victoria Falls. You can leap into the pool and then poke your head over the edge to get an extraordinary view of the 100m drop. Here also you'll see the plaque marking the spot where David Livingstone first sighted the falls.

Mosi-oa-Tunya National Park
NATIONAL PARK

(adult/child US$15/7.50; ☺6am-6pm) This park is divided into two sections: the Victoria Falls area and the wildlife sector. The latter is only 3km southwest of Livingstone, and most famous for its population of white rhino, which you can track on foot. For their protection, the rhino are accompanied by anti-poaching rangers round-the-clock. You can only see them as part of a pre-booked tour (US$80 per person, inclusive of park fees and hotel transfer), booked through Livingstone Rhino Walks or Savannah Southern Safaris.

Livingstone Museum
MUSEUM

(☑0213-324429; www.museumszambia.org; Mosi-oa-Tunya Rd; adult/child US$ 5/3; ☺9am-4.30pm) The excellent Livingstone Museum is the oldest, largest and best museum in the country. It's divided into sections covering archaeology, history, ethnography and natural history. Highlights include its collection of original David Livingstone memorabilia (including signed letters), tribal artefacts (from bark cloth to witchcraft exhibits), a life-sized model of an African village, taxidermy displays and coverage of modern-day Zambian history.

☞ Tours

Savannah Southern Safaris
WILDLIFE, WALKING

(☑0973 471486; www.savannah-southern-safaris.com) Offers a range of nature tours, but it's best known for its walks to see white rhino in Mosi-au-Tunya National Park. For two or more people it's US$70, or US$80 for individuals, inclusive of transport and park fees. Note you need to be over 12 years of age.

ⓘ VISAS

You will need a visa to cross between Zimbabwe and Zambia. These are available at the border, open from around 6am to 10pm.

You can't get multi-entry visas at the Victoria Falls crossings; you'll usually need to apply at your home country embassy before travelling.

➡ **Crossing into Zambia** A day visit costs US$20 for 24 hours (but you'll need a Zimbabwean double-entry to return), a single-entry visa costs US$50 and double entry is US$80.

➡ **Crossing into Zimbabwe** A single-entry visa costs US$30 for most nationalities (US$55 for British/Irish and US$75 for Canadian). Double entry is US$45 for most nationalities (US$75 for British/Irish and unavailable for Canadians).

Note that the KAZA Uni-Visa (which formerly allowed travel between the two countries) was suspended in 2016. It's worth checking, though, before you leave to see if it's back in effect.

There are also tours to visit local communities, as well as Livingstone walking tours.

Livingstone Rhino Walks
SAFARI

(☑ 0213-322267; www.livingstonerhinosafaris.com; per person US$80) This Livingstone-based tour operator specialises in walking safaris to see white rhino in Mosi-au-Tunya National Park. Visitors must be over 12 years of age. The price is inclusive of park entry fees and transfers in the Livingstone area.

🛏 Sleeping

★ Jollyboys
Backpackers
HOSTEL, CAMPGROUND $

(☑ 0213-324229; www.backpackzambia.com; 34 Kanyanta Rd; campsite per person US$9, dm US$12-15, d from US$65, d/tr/q with shared bathroom US$45/50/80; ❄@🤖≋) 🏊 The clued-in owner knows exactly what backpackers want, making Jollyboys popular for good reason. From its friendly staff, social bar and restaurant to the sunken reading lounge and sparkling pool, it's a great place to hang out. Dorms and bathrooms are spotless (with a flashpacker option, too), while the private rooms comprise A-frame garden cottages or very comfortable rooms with air-con and attached bathroom.

Rose Rabbit
Zambezi River Bushcamp
TENTED CAMP $

(☑ in Zimbabwe 0784 007283, 0773 368608; www.facebook.com/theroserabbit; Rapid 21, Lower Zambezi River; per person campsite/dm/tented camping/treehouse US$10/15/20/40) This riverside beach camp is one for independent travellers looking for a different scene. Right on rapid 21 of the Lower Zambezi, it will suit not only rafting enthusiasts but also a more free-spirited crowd who are into bonfire jamborees, swimming and hanging out by the beach. As well as campsites, there are dorms, tented camps and A-frame treehouse digs.

Livingstone
Backpackers
HOSTEL, CAMPGROUND $

(☑ 0213-324730; www.livingstonebackpackers.com; 559 Mokambo Rd; campsite US$7, dm from US$12, d US$45, with shared bathroom US$65; 🤖≋) Resembling the *Big Brother* household, this place can be a bit 'party central', particularly when the Gen Y volunteer brigade is on holiday. You'll find them lounging by the pool, in the hot tub, at the bar, or in the sandy outdoor cabana, swinging in hammocks, cooking barbecues or tackling the rock-climbing wall. There is also an open-air kitchen and living room. Very friendly staff.

Fawlty Towers
BACKPACKERS, LODGE $

(☑ 0213-323432; www.adventure-africa.com; 216 Mosi-oa-Tunya Rd; dm US$12, r from US$50, with shared bathroom US$45; ❄@🤖≋) As well as some of the nicest and most spacious dorms we've seen, things have been spruced up here into a guesthouse full of upmarket touches – no longer catering exclusively to backpackers. There's free wi-fi, large well-maintained lawns, a great pool, a bar, a homely lounge, free pancakes for afternoon tea, a self-catering kitchen, and no Basil or Manuel in sight.

Olga's Guesthouse
GUESTHOUSE $$

(☑ 0213-324160; www.olgasproject.com; cnr Mosi-oa-Tunya & Nakatindi Rds; s/d/f incl breakfast US$40/60/80; ❄🤖) 🏊 With a good location

---

ZIM OR ZAM?

Victoria Falls straddles the border between Zimbabwe and Zambia, and is easily accessible from both countries. However, the big question for most travellers is: do I visit the falls from the town of Victoria Falls, Zimbabwe, or from Livingstone, Zambia? The answer is simple: visit the falls from both sides and, if possible, stay in both towns. You'll need to pay for extra visas, but you've come this far so it's worth it.

From the Zimbabwean side, you're further from the falls, though the overall views are much, much better. From the Zambian side, for daring souls you can literally stand on top of the falls from Devil's Pool, though from here your perspective is narrowed.

The town of Victoria Falls was built for tourists, so it's easily walkable and located right next to the entrance to the Falls. It has a natural African bush beauty. As for whether it's safe given Zimbabwe's ongoing political issues, the answer is a resolute 'yes'.

Livingstone is an attractive town with a relaxed ambience and a proud, historic air. Since the town of Victoria Falls was the main tourist centre for so many years, Livingstone feels more authentic, perhaps because locals earn their livelihood through means other than tourism. Livingstone is bustling with travellers year-round, though the town is fairly spread out, and is located 11km from the falls.

Livingstone

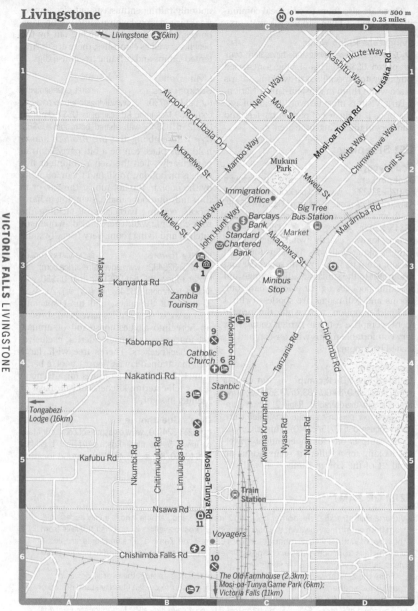

in the centre of town, Olga's offers clean, spacious rooms with cool tiled floors, teak furniture and slick bathrooms just a few feet away. Profits go towards helping an organisation supporting local youth. Another bonus is its on-site Italian restaurant, Olga's Italian Corner.

ZigZag
GUESTHOUSE $$

(☎0213-322814; www.zigzagzambia.com; 693 Linda Rd, off Mosi-oa-Tunya Rd; s/d/tr incl breakfast

Livingstone

◉ Sights
1 Livingstone Museum.............................B3

◉ Activities, Courses & Tours
2 Royal Livingstone Express...................B6

◉ Sleeping
3 Fawlty Towers B4
4 Jollyboys Backpackers B3
5 Livingstone Backpackers C4
6 Olga's Guesthouse...............................C4
7 ZigZag...B6

◉ Eating
8 Cafe Zambezi.......................................B5
9 Da Canton...B4
10 Golden Leaf...B6
Olga's Italian Corner ....(see 6)
ZigZag...(see 7)

◉ Shopping
11 Wayawaya B6

US$50/70/90; (P ✻ @ 🛜 ⊠) Don't be deceived by the motel-meets-caravan-park exterior: the rooms here are more boutique B&B with loving touches throughout. Rooms are spotless, and set on a sprawling garden property with an assortment of fruit trees, picnic tables, a plush pool and a playground for kids. Its great restaurant is another drawcard, too.

Victoria Falls Waterfront   LODGE, CAMPGROUND $$
(📋0213-320606; www.thevictoriafallswaterfront. com; Sichango Dr; campsite per person US$13, s/d tented camping US$36/48, s/d incl breakfast chalet from US$165/215; ✻ 🛜 ⊠) Sharing space with the luxury resorts along the banks of the Zambezi, this is the only waterfront lodge that caters to budget travellers. For this reason it's a popular place, with a wilderness charm (crocs inhabit a small creek on the property), and a choice of camping, domed tents or alluring riverside chalets. Its pool with decking and bar overlooking the river is unsurprisingly popular at sunset.

★ Stanley Safari Lodge   LODGE $$$
(📋in Malawi 0265-1794491; www.stanleysafaris. com; Stanley Rd; per person with full board & activities from US$510; @ 🛜 ⊠) Intimate and indulgent, Stanley is a 10km drive from the falls in a peaceful spot surrounded by mopane (woodland). Rooms scattered among the landscaped bush garden are as plush as can be expected at these prices; the standouts are the rustic open-air suites where you can soak up nature from your own private plunge pool. When you tire of that, curl up by the fire in the open-air lounge. Rates are all-inclusive.

Tongabezi Lodge   LODGE $$$
(📋0979 312766, 0213-327468; www.tongabezi.com; cottage/house per person incl full board & activities from US$775/875; ✻ 🛜 ⊠) Has sumptuous, spacious cottages, open-faced 'treehouses'

and private dining decks. The houses are good for families and have private plunge pools. Guests are invited to spend an evening on nearby Sindabezi Island (from US$595 per person), a luxurious, rustic getaway.

✕ Eating

★ Da Canton   GELATERIA $
(Mosi-Oa-Tunya Rd; gelato small/large cup ZMW8/24, pizza from ZMW19; ◷9am-11pm) While all the Italian food here is tasty and authentic, it's the homemade gelato that has locals raving. The Italian owner makes all 18 flavours, including all the classics and some original concoctions.

★ Cafe Zambezi   AFRICAN $$
(📋0978 978578; www.facebook.com/cafezambezi; 217 Mosi-oa-Tunya Rd; mains US$6-10; ◷7.15am-midnight; 🛜⊠) Head straight through to the courtyard, sunny by day and candlelit by night. Bursting with local flavour, the broad menu covers local favourites of goat meat, smoky crocodile tail and mopane (woodland) caterpillars. Authentic wood-fired pizzas are a winner or sink your teeth into impala or eggplant-and-haloumi burgers.

★ Olga's Italian Corner   ITALIAN $$
(www.olgasproject.con; cnr Mosi-oa-Tunya & Nakatindi Rds; pizza & pasta ZMW35-88; ◷7am-10pm; 🛜⊠) Olga's does authentic wood-fired thin-crust pizzas, as well as delicious homemade pasta classics all served under a large thatched roof. Great options for vegetarians include the lasagne with its crispy blackened edge served in the dish. All profits go to a community centre to help disadvantaged youth.

Golden Leaf   INDIAN $$
(📋0213-321266; 1174 Mosi-Oa-Tunya Rd; mains ZMW54-95; ◷12.30-10pm) As soon as those aromas hit you upon arrival you'll realise Golden Leaf is the real deal when it comes to authentic

Indian food. It's a good option for vegetarians with a lot of choices including house-made paneer dishes, creamy North Indian curries and tandoori dishes in the evenings.

ZigZag   CAFE $$
(Mango Tree Cafe; www.zigzagzambia.com/the-mango-tree-cafe; 693 Linda Rd, off Mosi-oa-Tunya Rd; mains from ZMW25-62; ⊘7am-9pm; 🛜) ZigZag does drool-inducing homemade muffins, excellent Zambian coffee and smoothies using fresh fruit from the garden. Its changing menu of comfort food is all made from scratch, and you can expect anything from drop scones (pikelets) with bacon and maple syrup to thin-crust pizzas and burgers.

🍷 Drinking & Nightlife

The Sundeck   BAR
(http://royal-livingstone.anantara.com/the-sun decks; Mosi-au-Tunya Rd; cocktail from ZMW40; ⊘10.30am-7pm; 🛜) Just the spot for a sundowner, this open-air bar within the Royal Livingstone Hotel overlooks a dramatic stretch of the Zambezi. As well as the usual bar drinks there's a choice of old-fashioned cocktails such as the Manhattan, Americano and champagne cocktail. There's also decent burgers, mezze platters and salads. From here it's a 15-minute walk to the falls.

🛍 Shopping

Wayawaya   FASHION & ACCESSORIES
(www.wayawaya.no; Mosi-oa-Tunya Rd; ⊘9am-5pm) 🖊 A social enterprise founded by two Norwegian girls, Wayawaya sells quality, contemporary handmade bags put together by local women. Its principles are based on the slow fashion movement, and you can meet all the ladies when visiting. Get in touch if you want to volunteer.

ℹ️ Information

DANGERS & ANNOYANCES
Don't walk from town to the falls as there have been a number of muggings along this stretch of road – even tourists on bicycles have been targeted. It's a long and not terribly interesting walk anyway, and simply not worth the risk (especially given there are elephants around). Take a taxi or free shuttle from your guesthouse. While Livingstone is generally a very safe town, avoid walking around town once it becomes dark.

IMMIGRATION
Immigration Office (☏0213-3320648; www.zambiaimmigration.gov.zm; Mosi-oa-Tunya Rd; ⊘8am-1pm & 2-5pm Mon-Fri)

MEDICAL SERVICES
SES-Zambia (www.ses-zambia.com; Mosi-au-Tunya Rd, AVANI Victoria Falls Resort; ⊘8am-5pm) The best medical facility in the area, both for emergency services and general medicine. It's within the **AVANI resort** (☏0978 777044; www.minorhotels.com/en/avani; Mosi-oa-Tunya Rd).

MONEY
The following banks accept MasterCard and Visa, but can occasionally go offline during power outages.
Barclays in town (cnr Mosi-oa-Tunya Rd & Akapelwa St) and at the AVANI resort.
Standard Chartered Bank (Mosi-oa-Tunya Rd) In town.
Stanbic (Mosi-oa-Tunya Rd) In town.

POLICE
Police (☏0213-320116, 0213-323575; Maramba Rd)

POST
Post Office (Mosi-oa-Tunya Rd) Has a poste restante service.

TOURIST INFORMATION
Tourist Centre (☏0213-321404; www.zambia tourism.com; Mosi-oa-Tunya Rd; ⊘8am-5pm Mon-Fri, 8am-noon Sat) Mildly useful and can help with booking tours and accommodation, but Jollyboys and Fawlty Towers have all the information you need.

ℹ️ Getting There & Away

AIR
Livingstone's newly renovated airport – officially known as Harry Mwanga Nkumbula International Airport – is located 6km northwest of town. It has an ATM and free wi-fi. It's around a US$5 taxi ride into town, or US$8 to the waterfront hotels.
South African Airways (☏0213-323031; www.flysaa.com) and **British Airways** (Comair; ☏in South Africa +27 10-3440130; www.british airways.com) have daily flights to and from Johannesburg (1¾ hours); the cheapest economy fare starts at around US$270 return.
Proflight Zambia (☏0977 335563, in Lusaka 0211-252452; www.proflight-zambia.com) flies daily from Livingstone to Lusaka for around US$210 one way (1¼ hours).

BUS & MINIBUS
Plenty of minibuses and shared taxis ply the route from the Big Tree Bus Station at Livingstone's town market along Senanga Rd in Livingstone. Note that plans are in place to relocate the bus terminal to Nakatindi Rd. As muggings have been reported, it is best to take a taxi if you arrive at night.

CAR & MOTORCYCLE

If you're driving a rented car or motorcycle, be sure to carefully check all info regarding insurance, and that you have all the necessary papers for checks and border crossings such as 'owners' and 'permission to drive' documents, insurance papers and a copy of the carbon tax receipt. Expect to pay around US$100 in various fees when crossing the border into Zimbabwe.

TRAIN

While the bus is a much quicker way to get around, the train to Lusaka is for lovers of slow travel or trains. The operative word here is *slow*, taking anywhere from 15 to 20 hours for the trip to Lusaka (economy/business/1st-class sleeper ZMW 70/90/135), via Choma, departing 8pm on Monday and Friday. Bring your own food. Reservations are available at the **train station** (☑ 0961 195353), which is signed off Mosi-oa-Tunya Rd.

❶ Getting Around

CAR & MOTORCYCLE

Hemingways (☑ 0213-323097; www.heming wayszambia.com) in Livingstone has new 4WD Toyota Hiluxes for around US$225 per day. Vehicles are fully kitted out with everything you need, including cooking and camping equipment. Drivers must be over 25.

Voyagers (☑ 0213-320517, 0213-323259; www. voyagerszambia.com; 163 Mosi-oa-Tunya Rd) Zambian operator affiliated with Europcar has reasonably priced 4WDs for around US$100 per day.

TAXIS

Minibuses run regularly along Mosi-oa-Tunya Rd to Victoria Falls and the Zambian border (ZMW5,15 minutes). Blue taxis cost ZMW60 to ZMW80 from the border to Livingstone. Coming from the border, shared taxis are parked just over from the waiting taxis, and depart when full. The going rate for one day's taxi hire around Livingstone and the falls is about US$25.

ZIMBABWE
☑ 263

There may still be a long way to go, but finally things seem to be looking up for Zimbabwe. All the bad news that has kept it in the glare of the spotlight – rampant land reform, hyperinflation and food shortages – fortunately now seem to be a thing of the past. In reality, safety has never been a concern for travellers here and, even during the worst of it, tourists were never targets for political violence. Word of this seems to have spread, as tourists stream back to the Zim side of the falls.

Victoria Falls

POP 33,360 / ☑ 013

A genuine bucket-list destination, Victoria Falls remains one of Africa's most famous tourist towns. Not only does it offer the best views of the iconic falls, but it also has a world-class adventure-tourism scene and wildlife safaris.

It's home to the country's tourism industry, and despite Zimbabwe's political issues, it's always been a safe spot for tourists; locals are exceptionally friendly. While for a few years it felt like a resort in off-season, there's no mistake about it now – it's officially reopened for business.

Though built specifically for tourism, it retains a relaxed local feel, and has neat, walkable streets (though not at dark, because of the wild animals) lined with hotels, bars and some of the best crafts you'll find anywhere in Southern Africa.

❂ Sights

★**Victoria Falls National Park**　WATERFALL
(US$30; ☉6am-6pm) Here on the Zimbabwe side of the falls you're in for a real treat. Some two-thirds of Victoria Falls are located here, including the main falls themselves, which flow spectacularly year-round. The walk is along the top of the gorge, following a path with various viewing points that open up to extraordinary front-on panoramas of these world-famous waterfalls.

★**Jafuta Heritage Centre**　CULTURAL CENTRE
(www.elephantswalk.com/heritage.htm;　Adam Stander Dr, Elephant's Walk; admission by donation; ☉8am-5pm) **FREE** This impressive little museum details the cultural heritage of Zimbabwe's indigenous ethnic groups. There's good background information on the Shona, Ndebele, Tonga and Lozi people, as well as fascinating artefacts, jewellery and costumes.

Zambezi National Park　NATIONAL PARK
(☑013-42294; www.zimparks.org; day/overnight US$15/23; ☉6am-6pm) Just 5km from the town centre is this vastly underrated national park, comprising 40km of Zambezi River frontage and a spread of wildlife-rich mopane (woodland) and savannah. It's best known for its herds of sable, elephant, giraffe, zebra and buffalo, plus the occasional (rarely spotted) lion, leopard and cheetah. It's easily accessible by 2WD vehicle.

Victoria Falls

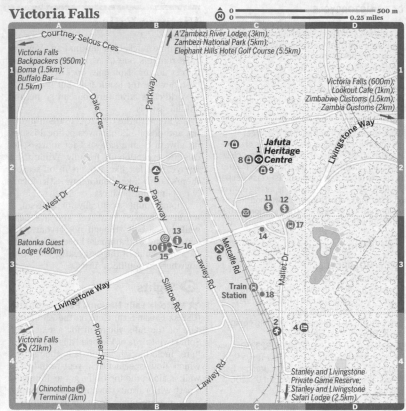

Victoria Falls

◉ Top Sights
1 Jafuta Heritage Centre...........................C2

✪ Activities, Courses & Tours
2 Bushtracks Express C4
3 Wild Horizons B2

🛏 Sleeping
4 Victoria Falls Hotel................................C4
5 Victoria Falls Restcamp & Lodges........B2

✖ Eating
Africa Café ....(see 8)
In Da Belly Restaurant.....................(see 5)
6 Lola's Tapas & Carnivore
Restaurant..C3

🍷 Drinking & Nightlife
Stanley's Terrace..............................(see 4)

🛍 Shopping
7 Big Curio Open Market C2
8 Elephant's Walk Shopping & Artist
Village...C2
Matsimela...(see 8)
Ndau Collection ....(see 8)
Prime Art Gallery ....(see 8)
9 Tshaka's Den Complex............................C2

ℹ Information
10 Backpackers Bazaar................................B3
11 Barclays Bank...C2
12 Standard Chartered Bank.......................C2
13 Zimbabwe Tourism Authority................B3

ℹ Transport
14 Avis..C3
15 FastJet B3
16 Hertz..B3
17 Intercape Pathfinder...............................C3
18 Train Ticket Office..................................C3

Stanley and Livingstone Private Game Reserve
WILDLIFE RESERVE

(Victoria Falls Private Game Reserve; ☑ 013-44571; www.stanleyandlivingstone.com/activities) This private 4000-hectare game reserve 12km from town has the Big Five, including the critically endangered black rhino, which you're almost guaranteed to see. Game drives are US$100, US$135 for a night drive with a bush dinner.

🛏 Sleeping

★ Victoria Falls Backpackers
HOSTEL, CAMPGROUND $

(☑ 013-42209; www.victoriafallsbackpackers.com; 357 Gibson Rd; camping/dm per person US$10/18, d US$60, with shared bathroom US$50; @ 🛜 🏊) One of the best budget choices in town, this long-standing backpackers received a much-needed revamp when the original owners returned. The eclectic mix of rooms are scattered among the well-tended garden property full of quirky touches. Other notable features are its bar, small inviting pool, games room and TV lounge, plus self-catering kitchen, massage and fish spa.

Victoria Falls Restcamp & Lodges
CAMPGROUND, LODGE $

(☑ 013-40509; www.vicfallsrestcamp.com; cnr Parkway & West Dr; camping/dm US$16/20, s/d dome tents from US$29/40, s/d chalets without bathroom US$35/46, cottages from US$127; ❄ 🛜 🏊) A great alternative for independent travellers, it has a relaxed holiday-camp feel, within secure grassy grounds, with a choice of no-frills dorms, lodge-style rooms (or pricier air-con rooms with bathroom) and safari tents. There's a lovely pool and fantastic open-air restaurant, In Da Belly. Wi-fi available (for a fee).

Zambezi National Park Lodge
CHALETS, CAMPGROUND $$

(☑ 013-42294; www.zimparks.org; camping $17, cottage $138; ❄) These wonderful two-bedroom cottages are right on the Zambezi river. You'll need to bring your own food, but all come with fridges, full kitchen, couches, TV, bathtubs and even air-con. There's an outdoor barbecue area too. Further into the park are basic bush campsites (firewood US$5), but with no water or ablutions.

★ Victoria Falls Hotel
LUXURY HOTEL $$$

(☑ 0772 132175, 013-44751; www.victoriafallshotel.com; 1 Mallet Dr; s/d incl breakfast from US$423/455; ❄ 🛜 🏊) Built in 1904, this historic hotel (the oldest in Zimbabwe) oozes elegance and sophistication. It occupies an impossibly scenic location, looking across manicured lawns (with roaming warthogs) to the gorge and bridge. You can't see the falls as such, but you do see the spray from some rooms. Taking high tea here at Stanley's Terrace is an institution.

Stanley and Livingstone Safari Lodge
LODGE $$$

(☑ 013-44571; www.stanleyandlivingstone.com; Stanley & Livingstone Private Game Reserve; r per person incl full board & activities US$436; ❄ 🛜 🏊) Set on a private game reserve 15km from Victoria Falls, this luxury lodge will suit visitors without the time to visit a national park but who want to be surrounded by wildlife. Rooms on the luxurious grounds feature all the modern comforts combined with Victorian-style bathrooms featuring clawfoot tubs, lounge suite and patio.

Batonka Guest Lodge
GUESTHOUSE $$$

(☑ 013-47189/90; www.batonkaguestlodge.com; Reynard Rd; s/d incl breakfast US$195/300; ❄ 🛜 🏊) 🍃 Mixing modern comforts with colonial charm, Batonka is an excellent choice for those not wanting a large-scale resort. It has a relaxed ambience, with rooms overlooking a landscaped lawn and inviting pool. Rooms have stylish bathrooms, cable TV and filter coffee. The reception/bar/restaurant is in a homestead-style building with wraparound veranda and a boutique interior design with original artwork throughout.

Elephant Camp
LODGE $$$

(☑ 013-44571; www.theelephantcamp.com; s/d incl full board US$838/1118; @ 🛜 🏊) One of the best spots to splash out; the luxurious 'tents' have a classic lodge feel and are set on a private concession within the Victoria Falls National Park. Each room has its own outdoor private plunge pool and balcony decking to spot grazing animals or the spray of the falls. You might get to meet Sylvester, the resident cheetah.

🍴 Eating

★ Lookout Cafe
CAFE $$

(☑ 0782 745112; www.wildhorizons.co.za/the-lookout-cafe; Batoka Gorge; mains US$12-15; ⊙ 8am-7pm; 🛜) A stunning location overlooking Batoka Gorge. Enjoy views of the bridge and the Zambezi river while tucking into a burger or crocodile kebab, or a cold drink on its open-air deck or grassy lawn

Victoria Falls & Mosi-oa-Tunya National Parks

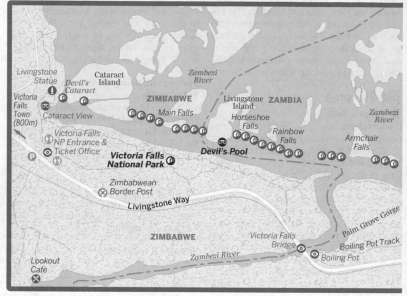

terrace. It's operated by **Wild Horizons** ([☑] 013-44571, 0712 213721; www.wildhorizons. co.za; 310 Parkway Dr), so you'll get the added entertainment of watching daredevils take the plunge or soar across the gorge.

Africa Café CAFE **$$**
(www.elephantswalk.com/africa_cafe.htm; Adam Stander Dr, Elephant's Walk; breakfast/burgers US$7/11; ⊙8am-5pm; [☎][✎]) This appealing outdoor cafe does the best coffee in Victoria Falls, made by expert baristas using beans sourced from Zimbabwe's eastern highlands. There's plenty of seating scattered about to enjoy big breakfasts, burgers, vegetarian dishes and desserts such as its signature baobab-powder cheese cake. There's a bar, too.

★**Lola's Tapas &
Carnivore Restaurant** SPANISH, AFRICAN **$$**
([☑] 013-42994; 8B Landela Complex; dishes US$8-20; ⊙8am-10pm; [☎]) Run by welcoming host Lola from Barcelona, this popular eatery combines a menu of Mediterranean cuisine with local game meats, with anything from crocodile ravioli to paella with kudu. Other items include zebra burgers, impala meatballs, and more traditional tapas dishes.

There's also a full spread of all-you-can-eat game meat for US$30.

★**Boma** AFRICAN **$$**
([☑] 013-43211; www.victoria-falls-safari-lodge.com; Squire Cummings Rd, Victoria Falls Safari Lodge; buffet US$40; ⊙dinner 7pm, cafe from 7am) Enjoy a taste of Africa at this buffet restaurant set under a massive thatched roof. Here you can dine on smoked crocodile tail, BBQ warthog, guinea fowl stew and wood-fired spit roasts; and the more adventurous can try a mopane worm (you'll get a certificate from the chef for your efforts). There's also traditional dancing (8pm), interactive drumming (8.45pm) and fortune telling by a witch doctor. Bookings essential.

**In Da Belly
Restaurant** AFRICAN, INTERNATIONAL **$$**
([☑] 013-332077; Parkway, Victoria Falls Restcamp & Lodges; meals US$5-15; ⊙7am-9.30pm) Under a large thatched hut, looking out to a sparkling pool, this relaxed open-air eatery has a menu of warthog schnitzel, crocodile curry and impala burgers, as well as one of the best breakfast menus in town. The name is a play on Ndebele, one of the two major population tribes in Zimbabwe.

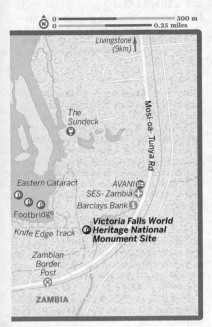

🍷 Drinking & Nightlife

★ Stanley's Terrace
HIGH TEA

(☎013-44751; www.victoriafallshotel.com/stanleys-terrace; Mallet Dr, Victoria Falls Hotel; high tea for 1-/2-people US$15/30; ☺high tea 3-6pm; 🛜) The Terrace at the stately Victoria Falls Hotel just brims with English colonial ambience. High tea is served to a postcard-perfect backdrop of the gardens and Victoria Falls Bridge, with polished silverware, decadent cakes and three-tiered trays of finger sandwiches. (Cucumber? Why yes, of course.) A jug of Pimms makes perfect sense on summer day at US$24. The only thing missing is croquet.

Buffalo Bar
BAR

(www.victoria-falls-safari-lodge.com; Squire Cummings Rd, Victoria Falls Safari Lodge; ☺7am-10pm) Unquestionably the best sundowner spot in town; enjoy a gin-and-tonic on its outdoor terrace overlooking distant animals on the plains of Zambezi National Park. Part of the Victoria Falls Safari Lodge, it's a good pre-dinner spot if you've got a booking at the hotel's Boma restaurant. Otherwise come during the day for the 1pm vulture feeding.

🛍 Shopping

★ Elephant's Walk Shopping & Artist Village
SHOPPING CENTRE

(☎0772 254552; www.elephantswalk.com; Adam Stander Dr; ☺9am-5pm) A must for those in the market for quality Zimbabwean and African craft, this shopping village is home to boutique stores and galleries owned by a collective that aims to promote and set up local artists.

At the back of Elephant's Walk Village you'll find local vendors at **Big Curio Open Market** (Adam Stander Dr), and the **Tshaka's Den Complex** (☺7.30am-6pm), both of which sell locally made handicraft and Shona sculpture.

Matsimela
COSMETICS

(www.matsimela.co.za; Adam Stander Dr, Elephant's Walk; ☺8am-5pm) South African body-care brand Matsimela has set up shop here with an enticing aroma of natural scented soaps, body scrubs and bath bombs (anything from rose and lychee to baobab-seed oil). They also offer massage treatments (from US$30), manicures and pedicures.

Prime Art Gallery
ART

(☎0772 239805; www.primeart-gallery.com; Adam Stander Dr, Elephant's Walk; ☺8am-5pm) This quality gallery, run by two friendly brothers, represents more than 40 local artists, most notably it has original pieces by Dominic Benhura, Zimbabwe's pre-eminent current-day Shona sculptor whose worked has been exhibited around the world.

Ndau Collection
JEWELLERY

(☎013-386221; www.ndaucollectionstore.com; Adam Stander Dr, Elephant's Walk; ☺8am-6pm) This upmarket showroom stocks handmade individual pieces, including silver bracelets, rings and necklaces, made at its on-site studio. They also sell exquisite antique African trade beads to be incorporated into custom-made jewellery. Its range of organic fragrances made using local ingredients is also popular, as are its croc-skin purses and briefcases.

ℹ Information

DANGERS & ANNOYANCES

Mugging is not such a problem any more, but at dawn and dusk wild animals such as elephants and warthogs do roam the streets away from the town centre, so take taxis at these times. Although it's perfectly safe to walk to and from the falls, it's advisable to stick to the more touristed areas.

INTERNET ACCESS

Most lodges and restaurants offer wi-fi; otherwise there are a few internet cafes about town, including **Econet** (Park Way; per 30min/1hr US$1/2; ⊙8am-5pm Mon-Fri, to 1pm Sat & Sun).

MONEY

Barclays Bank (off Livingstone Way)
Standard Chartered Bank (off Livingstone Way)

POST

Post Office (off Livingstone Way)

TOURIST INFORMATION

Backpackers Bazaar (p553) Definitive place for all tourist info and bookings.
Zimbabwe Tourism Authority (☑0772 225427, 013-44202; zta@vicfalls.ztazim.co.zw; Park Way; ⊙8am-6pm) A few brochures, but not very useful.

❶ Getting There & Away

AIR

Victoria Falls Airport is located 18km southeast of town. Its new international terminal opened in late 2015.

While nothing compared to the heydays of the 1980s and '90s, there's still no shortage of flights arriving at Victoria Falls. Most come from Johannesburg (US$150 to US$500 return). There are also regular flights from Harare with FastJet and Air Zimbabwe for as little as US$20.

Check out www.flightsite.co.za or www.travelstart.co.za, where you can search all the airlines including low-cost carriers (and car-hire companies) for the cheapest flights and then book yourself.

Air Namibia (☑0774 011320, 0771 401918; www.airnamibia.com)
Air Zimbabwe (☑0712 212121, 013-443168, 013-44665; www.airzimbabwe.aero)
British Airways (☑013-2053; www.britishairways.com)
FastJet (☑86 7700 6060; www.fastjet.com/zw; cnr Livingstone Way and Parkway Dr; ⊙9am-4pm Mon-Fri, to 1pm Sat)
South African Airways (☑04-702702; www.flysaa.com)

BUS & SHARED TAXI

Though its standards have dropped in recent years, **Intercape Pathfinder** (☑0778 888880; www.intercapepathfinder.com) easily remains the safest and most comfortable bus company in Zimbabwe.

To Bulawayo & Harare

Intercape Pathfinder has departures for Hwange National Park (US$10, two hours), Bulawayo (US$15, six hours) and Harare (US$35, 12 hours) on Wednesday, Friday and Sunday at 7.30am from outside the Kingdom Hotel. You can book tickets online. If you're heading to Hwange National Park, you'll need to tell the driver beforehand as it only stops there on request. There's no direct bus to Harare, so you'll have to transfer to an awaiting bus at Bulawayo.

From Chinotimba Bus Terminal, Bravo Tours and Extra City have departures throughout the day to Bulawayo (US$13) and Harare (US$25). Buy tickets at the bus station. They can also drop you on the main road outside Hwange National Park, but you'll need to pre-arrange transport from there.

Note that, due to the prevalence of elephants and donkeys on the road, it's best to avoid this journey at night.

To Johannesburg

These days it's almost quicker to fly, but you can take the Intercape Pathfinder from Vic Falls to Bulawayo, then connect with Intercaper Greyhound to Johannesburg.

CAR & MOTORCYCLE

If you're driving a rented car into Zambia, you need to make sure you have insurance and carbon tax papers, as well original owner documents. When you enter Zambia you are issued with a Temporary Import Permit, valid for while you are in the country. This must be returned to immigration for them to acquit the vehicle.

TRAIN

A popular way of getting to/from Victoria Falls is by the overnight *Mosi-oa-Tunya* train that leaves Victoria Falls daily at 7pm for Bulawayo (economy/2nd/1st class US$8/10/12, 12 hours). First class (comprising two-berth compartments) is the only way to go. Be aware that delays of several hours aren't uncommon, and you'll need to bring your own food. Make reservations at the **ticket office** (⊙7am-noon & 2-7pm) inside the train station.

The luxurious **Rovos Rail** (📞 in South Africa 012-315 8242; www.rovos.com; from US$1650) to Pretoria also departs from here.

ℹ Getting Around

CAR & MOTORCYCLE

Zimbabwe Car Hire (📞 0783 496253, 09-230306; www.zimbabwecarhire.com; Victoria Falls Airport) gets positive reviews for its good rates, and is a good place for 4WDs. All the big name companies, such as **Hertz** (📞 013-47012; www.hertz.co.za; 1 Bata Bldg, Parkway; ⊙ 8am-5pm Mon-Fri), **Avis** (📞 091 2511128; www.avis.com; 251 Livingstone Way) and **Europcar** (📞 013-43466; Victoria Falls Airport), have offices in town and at the airport.

TAXI

A taxi around town costs about US$10, or slightly more after dark.

Zambia

POP 15.5 MILLION

Includes ➜
Lusaka........................ 567

South Luangwa
National Park 578

North Luangwa
National Park 584

Lower Zambezi
National Park 585

Liuwa Plain
National Park 594

Lake Tanganyika 601

Best Places to Sleep

➜ Chizombo (p580)

➜ Chiawa Camp (p587)

➜ Kapishya Hot Springs Lodge (p599)

➜ Ndole Bay Lodge (p602)

➜ Mukambi Plains Camp (p591)

Best Places to Eat

➜ Sugarbush Cafe (p571)

➜ Courtyard Café (p604)

➜ Luangwa Bridge Camp (p578)

➜ Thorn Tree Guesthouse (p600)

Why Go?

The rewards of travelling in Zambia are those of exploring remote, mesmerising wilderness as full of an astonishing diversity of wildlife as any part of Southern Africa. Adventures undertaken here will lead you deep into the bush where animals, both predators and prey, wander through unfenced camps, where night-time means swapping stories around the fire and where the human footprint is nowhere to be seen. Where one day you can canoe down a wide, placid river and the next raft through the raging rapids near world-famous Victoria Falls.

Though landlocked, three great rivers – the Kafue, the Luangwa and the Zambezi – flow through Zambia, defining both its geography and the rhythms of life for many of its people. For the independent traveller, however, Zambia is a logistical challenge, because of its sheer size, dilapidated road network and upmarket facilities. For those who do venture here, the relative lack of crowds means an even more satisfying journey.

When to Go
Lusaka

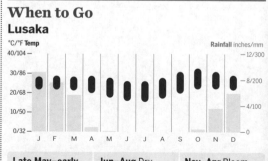

Late May–early Oct Dry season, with prime wildlife viewing; tourist high season.

Jun–Aug Dry, cooler temperatures and sometimes frosty nights.

Nov–Apr Blooming landscapes during the rainy ('emerald') season. Wildebeest and bat migration.

LUSAKA

All roads lead to Lusaka, the geographic, commercial and metaphorical heart of Zambia. However, the nation's capital and largest urban zone, with its mishmash of dusty tree-lined streets, bustling African markets, Soviet-looking high-rise blocks and modern commerce, doesn't easily justify exploration by the casual visitor. There are no real attractions, grand museums to drool over or historical treasures to unearth. Nonetheless, for some, the city's genuine African feel, cosmopolitan populace and quality restaurants and accommodation are reason enough to spend a night or two. If you feel like letting loose, expat bars and the home-grown nightclub scene will see you through to the wee hours.

◉ Sights

Lusaka National Park   NATIONAL PARK
(☑ 0955 472433; adult/child US$30/15) The idea of seeing a rhino in the wild just 15km from the capital seems absurd, but this new national park (opened in 2015) allows you to do just that. Set over 46 sq km, it's home to eland, zebra, giraffe and wildebeest, among others. But it's the white rhino that brings people here. While you'll be able to tick it off from the list of Big Five, most likely you'll see them in their holding pen, so it can feel more like a zoo than national park.

Lilayi Elephant Nursery   WILDLIFE RESERVE
(☑ 0211-840435; www.lilayi.com; adult/child/under 12yr ZMW50/20/free; ☉ 11.30am-1pm) On the southern outskirts of town is this elephant nursery set up by Game Rangers International (a Zambian conservationist NGO), which works with rescuing and rehabilitating orphaned elephants in Kafue National Park. You can see them being fed from 11am to 1.30pm daily; Monday is free entry. You can also do wildlife drives on its 650-hectare property. There's a lovely restaurant and lodge where, if you're staying, you can get a behind-the-scenes look at the elephants.

Presidential Burial Site
National Monument   MAUSOLEUM
(Embassy Park; adult/child US$15/7; ☉ 8.30am-4.30pm) This mausoleum is where the late Zambian presidents Levy Patrick Mwanawasa (1948–2008), Frederick Chiluba (1943–2011) and Michael Sata (1937–2014) are buried. Remarkably both Mwanawasa and

Sata died while in office; the latter's tomb will be completed in 2018. It's an interesting enough sight, but the US$15 entry is a bit steep, though does include a guided tour.

Henry Tayali Visual Arts Centre   GALLERY
(www.henrytayaliartgallery.wordpress.com; Showgrounds, Lion Lane; ☉ 9am-5pm Mon-Fri, to 4pm Sat & Sun) A lovely space exhibiting quality contemporary works by local artists, and all are for sale.

Namwandwe Gallery   GALLERY
(☑ 0976 608538, 0977 549802; www.namwandwe.com; Leopards Hill Rd; by donation; ☉ 8am-6pm) Featuring the impressive private collection of businessman and patron of the arts John Kapotwe, Namwandwe is hands-down the best in the country for contemporary Zambian art. The gallery space is within his private home (an attraction in itself) and features paintings, sculptures, masks and fabrics by both established and up-and-coming artists. It's located 15km southeast of the city centre.

Lusaka National Museum   MUSEUM
(Nasser Rd; adult/child US$5/3; ☉ 9am-4.30pm) This big square box of a building resembling a Soviet-era Moscow ministry has upstairs galleries displaying exhibits on urban culture and Zambian history as well cultural, ethnographic and archaeological displays. Contemporary Zambian paintings and sculpture are shown downstairs.

Lusaka City Market   MARKET
(Lumumba Rd; ☉ 7am-5pm) Fronted by the chaotic and congested eponymously named bus station, as well as a veritable Maginot Line of sidewalk vendors, reaching the entrance to the Lusaka City Market is an achievement in and of itself. Unfortunately, while large, lively and packed to the rafters, the clothing and housewares sold in the warren of stalls aren't of much interest to the average traveller.

⌁ Sleeping

★ Natwange Backpackers   HOSTEL $
(☑ 0966 303816, 0977 886240; www.natwange backpackers.com; 6808 Kapuka Rd; dm/s/d incl breakfast with shared bathroom US$12/30/40; ☎ ✸) In quiet residential street, this lovely and secure home offers a relaxed atmosphere for independent travellers. Rooms are clean, though can be a little cramped, and all share bathrooms. It has plenty of lawn with fruit trees and a nice little pool and gym. There are several lounge areas to

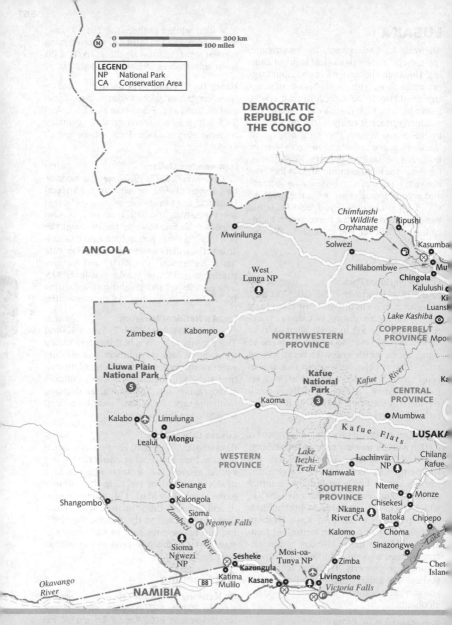

Zambia Highlights

1 **South Luangwa National Park** (p578) Bushwalking like a detective following the tracks of wild animals.

2 **Zambezi River** (p585) Paddling a canoe down this mighty river past pods of hippos, menacing-looking crocs and thirsty elephants.

3 **Kafue National Park** (p590) Spotting leopards in this behemoth wilderness area where wildlife dreams unfold amid stunning landscapes.

4 Lake Tanganyika (p601)
Lazing on white sandy beaches and snorkelling with tropical fish on this beautiful lake in the country's far north.

5 Liuwa Plain National Park (p594) Witnessing the wildebeest migration unfold at Zambia's 'mini Serengeti'.

6 Shiwa Ng'andu (p599)
Taking a step back in time and a leap to another continent at a remarkably well-preserved English manor estate.

hang out, and a fully equipped kitchen for self-caterers.

Tanuger Travels HOSTEL $
(☑ 0972 662588; www.tanuger.com; cnr Sibweni & Chigwilizano Rds; dm US$15, r US$60, with shared bathroom US$40; 🛜🖾) Set up by a bunch of local female friends, this funky and vibrant hostel offers a homely, social and relaxed atmosphere. There's plenty of artwork about, including graffiti-splashed walls, plus a swimming pool, firepit, giant chess board and free pool table. Its members-only bar is one of the liveliest in town, and a great place to meet travellers and locals alike.

Lusaka Backpackers HOSTEL $
(☑ 0977 805483; www.lusakabackpackers.com; 161 Mulombwa Cl; 4-/8-bed dm US$12/15, r US$55, with shared bathroom US$40; @🛜🖾) One of the more established and respected backpackers in Lusaka, this place is deservedly popular with those on a budget. The centrepiece of activity is the patio area out front with a small pool and a tiki bar, which can get lively and loud, especially on weekends. Nearby is also its Wanderers Lodge, which offers cheaper rooms and camping.

Wanderers Lodge HOSTEL $
(☑ 0971 763508; www.wandererslusaka.com; 848 Lagos Rd, Rhodes Park; camping US$5, dm/s/d US$10/25/30; 🛜) The sister lodge to the popular Lusaka Backpackers, this centrally located lodge offers some of cheapest rooms in town, along with camping facilities.

Eureka Camping Park CAMPGROUND, CHALET $
(☑ 0977 803051, 0966 822448; www.eurekacamp. com; Kafue Rd; camping US$14, dm US$20, r from US$60, with shared bathroom from US$40; 🛜🖾) The grassy campsite here, shaded by big trees, is popular with overlanding groups. The security is good, while the swimming pool and bar (which sells burgers and breakfasts) are nice touches. There are braai facilities for cooking and charcoal for sale. Chalets are cool and comfortable and modelled on the traditional thatch hut. It's about 12km south of the city centre.

Kilimanjaro Country Lodge LODGE $$
(☑ 0955 611779, 0975 838461; www.kilimanjaro zambia.com; Leopards Hill Rd; s/d incl breakfast US$85/100, mains ZMW50-100; ⊗cafe 7am-8pm; 🛜🖾) A good out-of-town option – especially for groups and families – around 7.5km east of the city centre, Kilimanjaro consists of several well-kept, low-slung buildings on

a manicured lawn. The 11 rooms are spacious and simply furnished and management is responsive to any requests. A perk is free laundry for guests staying more than a night.

Bongwe Barn GUESTHOUSE $$
(☑ 0973 589419; www.bongwesafaris.com/guest house.html; 609 Zambezi Rd, Roma; r US$55-75; 🛜🖾) If you've outgrown the whole backpacker scene, but still want something informal and homely – and social, if inclined – then Bongwe's your place. Run by UK expat Stacey, the staff here are exceptionally friendly and helpful, and rooms (some of which share bathrooms) are spotless and spacious. There's a stocked kitchen, couches in the living room and a sparkling pool to relax by.

Pioneer Camp CAMPGROUND, CHALET $$
(☑ 0966 432700; www.pioneercampzambia.com; Palabana Rd, off Great East Rd; camping US$10, chalet with shared/private bathroom from US$88/132; 🛜🖾) An isolated 25-acre camp, surrounded by bird-rich woodland, Pioneer is the accommodation of choice for many expats living outside Lusaka, especially those with an early flight out of the country. Most of the widely dispersed and simply furnished thatch-roofed chalets have flagstone floors, small verandas and large bathrooms. The well-kept facilities for campers are up the front next to the small plunge pool.

★ Latitude 15 Degrees BOUTIQUE HOTEL $$$
(☑ 0211-268802; http://15.latitudehotels.com; Leopards Lane, Kabulonga; s/d incl breakfast US$244/297; ❄🛜🖾) Lusaka's best accommodation is this fashionable hotel with an architecturally designed building that resembles a chic contemporary gallery. Its rooms are plush with king-sized beds, standalone tubs, coffee makers, fast wi-fi, cable TV and plenty of art decorating its walls. Guests also have access to the 'Other Side' executive members-only lounge. Its restaurant (mains ZMW140-180; ⊗7-10am, noon-3pm & 6-9.30pm) is also very popular. It's just off Leopards Hill Rd.

Wayside Bed & Breakfast GUESTHOUSE $$$
(☑ 0211-273439; www.wayside-guesthouse. com; 39 Makeni Rd, Makeni; s/d incl breakfast US$80/120; 🛜🖾) This upmarket and peaceful guesthouse is one of the best in Lusaka, with only a handful of snug en-suite rooms. It used to be a farm and today the sizeable grounds are devoted to the owners' love

of gardening, and really are magnificent. Three rooms in a separate cottage have air-conditioning and there's a lounge with TV and comfortable couches.

Southern Sun Ridgeway
HOTEL $$$

(☑ 0211-251666; www.southernsun.com; cnr Church Rd & Independence Ave; s/d incl breakfast US$169/204; ✳ 🛜 ☒) Deservedly popular with in-the-know expats and a coterie of international business and government types, the Southern Sun is a no-brainer for those seeking an affordable low-key, comfortable city-centre option. Rooms are tastefully done in muted tones. A quality restaurant, pub, small gym, large outdoor pool area and free wi-fi round out the offerings.

✕ Eating

★ Deli
CAFE, BAKERY $

(Lunzua Rd, Rhodes Park; mains from ZMW25, coffee ZMW14; ⊙ 7am-4pm Mon-Fri, 8.30am-12.30pm Sat; 🛜) Boasting the best barista in Lusaka (the winner of an international competition) as well as an enviable garden setting, the Deli is a good place to plant yourself for a few hours. The sophisticated kitchen turns out all-day breakfasts like eggs and French toast, speciality sandwiches like Asian pork meatball and classics like pastrami, wood-fired pizzas and homemade ice cream.

Gigibontà
GELATERIA $

(Foxdale Court, Zambezi Rd; from ZMW16) Around the back of Foxdale Court shopping centre, this small outlet makes delicious homemade gelato using fresh ingredients, with 26 flavours to choose from. Proceeds go towards funding local community projects.

Zambean Coffee
CAFE $

(6 Nyati Close, Rhodes Park; coffee/sandwiches from ZMW17/70; ⊙ 8.30am-4pm Mon-Fri, to 1pm Sat; 🛜) Run by a couple of friendly Zimbabwean expats, this lovely little garden cafe is a great spot to grab a well-made Zambian coffee, a quality breakfast and gourmet sandwiches on home-baked breads. They also have a good list of South African wines.

Lusaka Garden Club
CAFE $

(off Nangwenya Rd, Showgrounds; coffee ZMW12, mains ZMW50; ⊙ 8am-5pm Mon-Sat) A lovely little garden oasis within the Showgrounds that's a nice to spot to relax with a filter coffee, an Aussie lamington, sandwich, or heartier meat and *nshima* dishes.

★ Sugarbush Cafe
INTERNATIONAL, ORGANIC $$

(☑ 0967 648761; www.facebook.com/sugarbushcafezam; Leopards Hill Rd, Sugarbush Farm; breakfast ZMW40-75, mains ZMW75-120; ⊙ 8am-5pm Tue-Sat, 8.30am-4.30pm Sun; 🛜) This picture-postcard idyllic cafe is worth every kwacha of the journey it takes to get here. Chill out for an afternoon at one of the picnic tables munching on homemade bread and pastries, salads made with organic homegrown vegetables, and expertly prepared sandwiches, pasta and meat dishes, as well as a glass of wine, or Pimms by the jug.

Casa Portico
ITALIAN $$

(☑ 0211-250111; 27 Ngumbo Rd, Longacres; mains from ZMW85; ⊙ 7am-10pm Mon-Thu, to midnight Fri & Sat, to 8pm Sun) Italian owned and operated, this garden restaurant offers as authentic cuisine as you'll get outside Italy. There's homemade pastas (go the tagliatelle ragu), home-baked panini, and imported Italian cheeses and meats. It's a good spot, too, for a glass of Prosecco or well-made Negroni cocktails.

Marlin
STEAK $$

(☑ 0211-252206; Los Angeles Blvd, Longacres Roundabout; mains ZMW85-110; ⊙ noon-2.30pm & 7-10pm Mon & Wed-Sat, noon-2.30pm Tue) Housed in the colonial-era Lusaka Club with decor that probably hasn't been touched since the '60s, this wood-panelled favourite serves some of the best steaks in Lusaka. While it does serve gargantuan portions of every cut of meat under the sun, most guests come for the aged fillet with mushroom or pepper sauce. Reservations are strongly recommended.

🍷 Drinking & Nightlife

★ Bongwe Pub & Grill
PUB

(www.facebook.com/bongwebarn; 609 Zambezi Rd, Roma; ⊙ 2pm-late) A favourite watering hole for many locals, expats and tourists (and basically anyone who likes a drink) is this tropical dive bar, set in an open-air shack centred around a palm tree. There's a pool table, sports on the TV and always someone around for a chat. On Fridays it's usually pumping and regularly has local bands and DJs.

Sky Bar
BAR

(www.facebook.com/roma.sky.bar.lusaka; Foxdale Court, Zambezi Rd; ⊙ 2pm-midnight) A decent rooftop bar atop of Foxdale Court shopping centre, Sky Bar attracts a young crowd

Lusaka

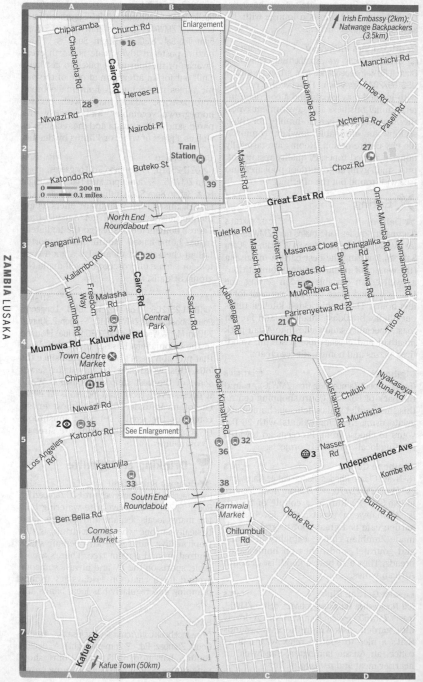

ZAMBIA LUSAKA

Irish Embassy (2km); Natwange Backpackers (3.5km)

Enlargement

Chiparamba
Church Rd
● 16
Cairo Rd
Chachacha Rd
Heroes Pl
Nkwazi Rd
28 ●
Nairobi Pl
Katondo Rd
Buteko St
Train Station
0   200 m
0   0.1 miles
39

Manchichi Rd
Lubambe Rd
Limbe Rd
Nchenja Rd
Paseli Rd
27
Chozi Rd
Omelo Mumba Rd
Makishi Rd
Great East Rd

North End Roundabout
Tuletka Rd
Provitent Rd
Masansa Close
Chingalika Rd
Namambozi Rd
Panganini Rd
Makishi Rd
Broads Rd
Mwilwa Rd
Kalambo Rd
✚ 20
5
Freedom Way
Malasha Rd
Cairo Rd
Mulombwa Cl
Bwinjimfumu Rd
Lumumba Rd
37
Sadzu Rd
Kabelenga Rd
Parirenyetwa Rd
Tito Rd
Central Park
21
Mumbwa Rd   **Kalundwe Rd**
Church Rd
Town Centre Market
Chiparamba
15
Dedan Kimathi Rd
Dushambe Rd
Nyakaseya Ituna Rd
Chilubi
Nkwazi Rd
Muchisha
2 ◉   ▣ 35
See Enlargement
Katondo Rd
36
▣ 32
3
Nasser Rd
Los Angeles Rd
Katunjila
38
Independence Ave
Kombe Rd
33
South End Roundabout
Kamwaia Market
Burma Rd
Ben Bella Rd
Obote Rd
Comesa Market
Chilumbuli Rd

Kafue Rd
Kafue Town (50km)

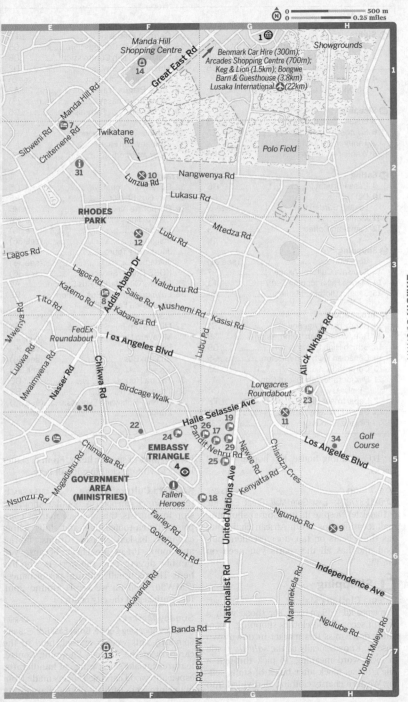

ZAMBIA LUSAKA

Manda Hill Shopping Centre

Great East Rd

14

Benmark Car Hire (300m);
Arcades Shopping Centre (700m);
Keg & Lion (1.5km); Bongwe
Barn & Guesthouse (3.8km)
Lusaka International (22km)

1

Showgrounds

Sibweni Rd

Manda Hill Rd

Chitemene Rd

7

Twikatane Rd

31

Lunzua Rd

10

Nangwenya Rd

Polo Field

RHODES PARK

Lukasu Rd

Lagos Rd

12

Lubu Rd

Mtedza Rd

Lagos Rd

Katemo Rd

Addis Ababa Dr

Nalubutu Rd

Tito Rd

Saise Rd

Mushemi Rd

Kasisi Rd

8

Kabanga Rd

Mwenya Rd

Lubwa Rd

FedEx Roundabout

Los Angeles Blvd

Lubu Rd

Alick Nkhata Rd

Mwaimwena Rd

Nasser Rd

Chikwa Rd

Birdcage Walk

Longacres Roundabout

23

30

22

Haile Selassie Ave

19

11

6

Chimanga Rd

24

26

17

34

Golf Course

EMBASSY TRIANGLE

4

29

25

Los Angeles Blvd

Pandit Nehru Rd

Ngwee Rd

Chisidza Cres

GOVERNMENT AREA (MINISTRIES)

Fallen Heroes

18

United Nations Ave

Kenyatta Rd

Nsunzu Rd

Mogadishu Rd

Ngumbo Rd

9

Fairley Rd

Government Rd

Nationalist Rd

Manenekela Rd

Independence Ave

Jacaranda Rd

Banda Rd

Mutunda Rd

Ngulube Rd

Yotam Muleya Rd

13

Lusaka

◎ **Sights**
1 Henry Tayali Visual Arts Centre............G1
2 Lusaka City Market...............................A5
3 Lusaka National Museum.....................C5
4 Presidential Burial Site National
   Monument...F5

🛏 **Sleeping**
5 Lusaka Backpackers............................C3
6 Southern Sun Ridgeway.......................E5
7 Tanuger Travels...................................E2
8 Wanderers Lodge.................................F3

🍴 **Eating**
9 Casa Portico.......................................H6
10 Deli...F2
   Lusaka Garden Club......................(see 1)
11 Marlin..G5
12 Zambean Coffee..................................F3

🛍 **Shopping**
   Bookworld.....................................(see 14)
13 Kabwata Cultural Village.....................F7
14 Manda Hill Shopping Centre................F1
15 Salaula Clothing Market......................A4

ℹ **Information**
16 Bimm Travel Agency............................B1
17 Botswanan High Commission..............G5
18 British High Commission.....................G5
19 Canadian High Commission................G5
20 Corpmed..B3
21 Democratic Republic of Congo
   Embassy...C4
22 Department of Immigration..................F5
23 Dutch Embassy....................................H4
   Finland Embassy..........................(see 23)

24 German Embassy..................................F5
25 Kenyan High Commission....................G5
26 Malawian High Commission.................G5
27 Mozambican Embassy..........................D2
   River Safari Company......................(see 5)
28 Steve Blagus Travel.............................A2
   Swedish Embassy.........................(see 23)
29 Tanzanian High Commission...............G5
30 Voyagers...E4
31 Zambia Tourism Agency.......................E2
   Zimbabwean High
   Commission.................................(see 23)

ℹ **Transport**
32 Buses for Zimbabwe.............................C5
33 City Bus Station...................................B5
34 Corporate Air.......................................H5
   CR Holdings..................................(see 36)
   Falcon..(see 36)
   Insight...(see 36)
   Jonda Bus Tours............................(see 36)
   Juldan...(see 36)
   KOBS Coach Service.....................(see 36)
35 Lusaka City Market Bus Station...........A5
36 Lusaka Inter-City Bus Station.............C5
   Mazhandu Family Bus
   Services...(see 36)
37 Millennium Bus Station........................A4
   Mwayera Buses..............................(see 32)
   Power Tools...................................(see 36)
   Shalom Bus...................................(see 36)
   Taqwa..(see 36)
38 Tazara House.......................................C6
39 Train Station..B2
   Zambia-Botswana Express..........(see 36)
   Zupco..(see 32)

for DJs spinning house, hip hop and R&B tracks.

Keg & Lion SPORTS BAR
(📞 0211-377824; East Gate Mall, Great East Rd; ⏰ 11am-late) Despite its uninspired shopping mall location, this South African chain pub has three beers on tap, does excellent pub food and has all the sports you need on the TV.

🛍 Shopping

Salaula Clothing Market CLOTHING
(Lumumba Rd; ⏰ 9am-6pm) For those with a love of secondhand clothes shopping, absolutely don't miss this market in downtown Lusaka. Known locally as the *salaula* trade (a local word meaning 'to pick through a pile'), it has block after block of stalls selling Western charity clothing all divided into heaped piles of specific items. From designer labels to vintage clothing, it's all here.

Kabwata Cultural Village ARTS & CRAFTS
(Burma Rd; ⏰ 7am-6pm) A popular shopping stop for tourists, this open-air market comprises thatch-roofed huts and stalls selling carvings, baskets, masks, drums, fabrics and more. Prices are cheap because you can buy directly from the workers who live here. There's usually cultural performances (ZMW30) held on weekends around 2pm. It's southeast of the city centre.

Sunday Market MARKET
(Arcades Shopping Centre, Great East Rd; ⏰ 9am-6pm Sun) This weekly market, held in the car park at the Arcades Shopping Centre, features Lusaka's best range of handicrafts, especially wood carvings, curios made from malachite and African prints. Bargaining

is expected, though it's a relaxed, low-pressure affair.

Bookworld
BOOKS

(www.bookworldzambia.com; Manda Hill Shopping Centre, Great East Rd; ⊙9am-6pm) Stocks a good selection of Zambia-specific nonfiction and cultural books, as well as fiction, international magazines and newspapers.

Manda Hill Shopping Centre
SHOPPING CENTRE

(Great East Rd) The swish Manda Hill Shopping Centre has all the usual retail, restaurants and banks you get in shopping malls.

ℹ Information

IMMIGRATION

Department of Immigration (✆0211-252622; www.zambiaimmigration.gov.zm; Kent Building, Haile Selassie Rd)

INTERNET ACCESS

I-Zone Internet (Arcades Shopping Centre, Great East Rd; ⊙9am-9pm) Reliable, fast internet access, plus printing facilities.

MEDICAL SERVICES

Corpmed (✆0211-222612; Cairo Rd; ⊙24hr) Located behind Barclays Bank. Has a doctor on duty 24 hours and is probably the city's best-equipped facility. Also runs its own ambulance service.

Specialty Emergency Services (✆737; www.ses-zambia.com) For evacuations. Has bases in Lusaka, Livingstone and Kitwe but operates throughout the country. Also has ambulances and in-patient care.

MONEY

Banks (Barclays and others) and bureaux de change are located in Arcades, Levy Junction and Mana Hill shopping centres, along Cairo Rd and elsewhere in Lusaka, such as on Haile Selassie Ave.

SAFE TRAVEL

Like most African cities, pickpockets take advantage of crowds, so be alert in the markets and bus stations and along the busy streets immediately west of Cairo Rd. Take care of your mobile phone and bring along only the cash you need in your pockets. Soweto Market, only a few blocks from the city markets on Lumumba Rd, in particular is notorious for robbery and pickpockets (if in a car, wind windows up and lock doors); there is a township nearby with a bad reputation. At night, most streets are dark and often empty, so even if you're on a tight budget, take a taxi.

The suburb of Rhodes Park, between Cairo Rd and Embassy Triangle, which is quite upmarket during the week, takes on a sleazy twist at weekends when prostitutes display their wares at night, especially along Mwilwa Rd.

TOURIST INFORMATION & TRAVEL AGENCIES

Bimm Travel Agency (✆0211-220641; www.bimmzambia.com; Shop 3, Luangwa House, Cairo Rd) Located just south of the post office, this agency is reliable and locally run. It can also arrange car hire. There's another branch at Levy Junction.

Bush Buzz (✆0978 773930, 0977 801374; www.bush-buzz.com) Organises trips to Kafue, Lower Zambezi and South Luangwa National Parks.

Steve Blagus Travel (✆0211-227739; www.sbltravel.com; 24 Nkwazi Rd; ⊙8am-4pm Mon-Fri, to 11.30am Sat) The agency for Amex and a dozen upmarket lodges/camps; also organises regional and domestic tours.

Voyagers (✆0211-253064; www.voyagerszambia.com; Suez Rd; ⊙8am-5pm Mon-Fri, to 11am Sat) Perhaps the most popular agency in Zambia (with other offices in Ndola, Chingola and Kitwe), Voyagers arranges flights and hotel reservations, and partners with Europcar for car hire.

Zambia Tourism Agency (✆0211-229087; www.zambiatourism.com; 1st fl, Petroda House, Great East Rd, ⊙8am-1pm & 2-5pm Mon-Fri) Information and maps of Lusaka are limited, but has an excellent website.

ℹ Getting There & Away

AIR

Lusaka International Airport is about 20km northeast of the city centre. Taxis between the airport and central Lusaka cost anywhere from ZMW200 to ZMW250. There's no airport bus but the upmarket hotels send minibuses (usually for a fee) to meet international flights, so you may be able to arrange a ride into town with the minibus driver (for a negotiable fee).

Arriving at the airport there are ATMs, foreign-exchange booths, car-rental offices and mobile-phone companies selling SIM cards. For departures, once through security for international flights, there's a restaurant and basic bar, and a couple of shops selling curios.

BUS & MINIBUS

Domestic

From a tourist point of view, the only real bus station you'll need to worry about is the **Lusaka Inter-City Bus Station** (Dedan Kimathi Rd). Here you can find a bus to all long-distance destinations in Zambia and across the border.

A range of buses from different companies cover most tourist destinations (all leaving from this bus station unless otherwise stated) – we've quoted the highest prices because they represent the best companies, with the most comfortable buses (two-storey with reclining seats). It's certainly worth double-checking the schedules and booking your tickets one or two days before you leave.

Much less safe are the buses and minibuses from in front of the massive and chaotic **Lusaka City Market Bus Station** (Lumumba Rd), which leave for nearby towns such as Kafue (not to be confused with the national park; ZMW30, one hour, 10 to 15 daily), Chirundu (ZMW55, 2½ hours, five to seven daily), Siavonga (ZMW70, three hours, three to five daily) and Luangwa Bridge (ZMW95, four hours, one or two daily); destinations are more or less signposted. To add to the confusion, minibuses to places not far south of Lusaka also leave from the **City Bus Station** (Kulima Towers Bus Station; off Chachacha Rd), also called the Kulima Towers Station. So it's possible to get to Kafue, Chirundu and Siavonga from here too.

Minibuses heading to the north (eg the Manda Hill Shopping Centre) depart from the **Millennium Bus Station** (Malasha Rd).

Copperbelt

Juldan (Lusaka Inter-City Bus Station), **Power Tools** (📞 0960 812019; Lusaka Inter-City Bus Station) and **Mazhandu Family** (📞 0977 805064; Lusaka Inter-City Bus Station) buses, among others, go to Copperbelt destinations such as Ndola (ZMW85, four hours, five daily) and Kitwe (ZMW90, five hours, five daily); Kapiri Mposhi (ZMW60, 2½ hours, five daily) is also reached along this route.

East Zambia

Travelling east, many companies operate services to Chipata (ZMW160), the road link for South Luangwa or Malawi; **Jonda Bus Tours** (📞 0977 412616; Lusaka Inter-City Bus Station) has departures from 5am.

Northeast

Tracking northeast, Juldan and Power Tools are two of the better companies, making a beeline for Serenje (ZMW145, five to six hours), Mpika (ZMW160, 10 hours), Kasama (ZMW130, 14 hours, four daily) and Mpulungu (ZMW180, 18 hours, four daily).

Southwest

Heading southwest, as you'd expect, there are plenty of buses to Livingstone (ZMW120, six to seven hours, at least seven daily) with either Mazhandu Family or **Shalom** (📞 0977 414932; Lusaka Inter-City Bus Station) being the recommended bus services. It's best to purchase the ticket the day before or phone ahead of time to get seat details.

West Zambia

Heading west, catch an 8am Juldan or Shalom bus through Kafue National Park and onto Mongu (ZMW130, eight hours); for Kafue camps just off the highway, it's ZMW120 and three hours.

International

All buses mentioned here (unless stated otherwise) leave from the Lusaka Inter-City Bus Station.

Botswana

Zambia-Botswana Express (📞 0977 800042, 0966 800042; Lusaka Inter-City Bus Station) has buses to Gaborone (ZMW300, 22 hours, Sunday and Wednesday at 9pm) via Kasane and Francistown; Mazhandu Family has a 5am departure for the border at Kazungula.

East Africa

Falcon (📞 0977 212516, 0977 945874; Lusaka Inter-City Bus Station) and **Taqwa** (📞 0977 157763; Lusaka Inter-City Bus Station) both make the run to Dar es Salaam (ZMW500, 27 hours, six weekly), Tanzania, but services can be haphazard (and the train is a more interesting and adventurous experience). For the pathologically masochistic, you can even board Nairobi- (ZMW900) and Kampala- (Uganda)-bound buses, which take two to three days.

Malawi

For Malawi, there's no direct service to Blantyre, but **KOBS Coach Service** (📞 0955 714545; Lusaka Inter-City Bus Terminal) has five services a week to Lilongwe (ZMW220, 10 hours, 4.30am), where you can change buses.

Namibia

Insight (📞 0976 599441; Lusaka Inter-City Bus Station) has buses to Windhoek (ZMW550, 24 hours) departing at 5.30am.

South Africa

For South Africa, buses cost around ZMW450 for the journey that heads to Johannesburg (18 to 24 hours) via Livingstone, Harare, Masvingo and Pretoria.

Shalom departs daily at 9am, while Mazhandu Family, **CR Holdings** (Lusaka Inter-City Bus Station) and Juldan also have services through the week.

Zimbabwe

Buses heading to Zimbabwe leave just across from the Lusaka Inter-City bus station. **Mwayera Buses** (www.facebook.com/mwayerabuses; Dedan Kimathi Rd, opp Lusaka Inter-City Bus Station) head via Chirundu, while **Zupco** (opp Lusaka Inter-City Bus Station, Dedan Kimathi Rd) goes via Siavonga border crossings. It's US$20 to Harare (eight hours via Chirundu) and US$10 to Siavonga (three hours). There are usually around three buses per day.

TRAIN

The train travelling to Livingstone (economy/business/sleeper class ZMW70/90/135, 14 hours), via Choma, leaves Lusaka at 7am on Saturday and Tuesday, and arrives in Livingstone at the ungodly hour of 2am. Quite simply, it's not worth it. But if you insist, tickets are available from the reservations office inside the **train station** (☑ 0961 195353; btwn Cairo & Dedan Kimathi Rds). Get there early and be prepared for hustle and bustle. Slow, 'ordinary' trains to Ndola (standard class ZMW40, 12 hours), via Kapiri Mposhi (ZMW25, eight hours), depart Friday and Monday at 7pm.

The Tazara train runs between Kapiri Mposhi and Dar es Salaam (Tanzania) on Tuesday (ZMW334) at 4pm and Friday (ZMW278) at 2pm, taking 38 to 48 hours. Get tickets from **Tazara House** (☑ 0979 484980; 2nd Fl, Tazara House, off Independence Ave; ☺ 8am-5pm Mon-Fri).

ⓘ Getting Around

CAR & MOTORCYCLE

The roads can get extremely clogged around Lusaka at peak traffic times. Speed limits are enforced in and around the city. Do not park your vehicle on the streets unless you have someone to keep an eye on it for you; hotels, restaurants and shopping centres all have guarded car parks. If you drive around at night, you increase the risk of an accident or carjacking; after dark, leave the car at your hotel and take a taxi.

Several international car-rental companies have counters at the airport, including **Avis** (☑ airport 0211-271020; www.avis.com) and **Europcar/Voyagers** (☑ 0212-620314; www.europcarzambia.com). **Benmark Transways & Car Hire** (☑ 0211-292192; ben@benmarkcarhire.com; cnr Parliament & Great East Rds) rents out cars for travel within Lusaka for around US$35 per day.

If you want a car and driver to help get you around Lusaka, you're better off hiring a taxi for the day; your lodge will be able to recommend a trusted driver for around US$40 to US$50 a day, depending on how much distance you will cover.

LOCAL TRANSPORT

Local minibuses run along Lusaka's main roads, but there are no route numbers or destination signs, so the system is difficult to work out. There is also a confusing array of bus and minibus stations.

Otherwise it is possible to flag down a minibus along a route. For instance, from the South End Roundabout, the 'Kabulonga' minibus goes along Independence Ave to Longacres Roundabout and then heads back towards the city along Los Angeles Blvd and Church Rd; the 'Chakunkula' or 'Chelston' minibus shuttles down Kafue Rd to Kafue town; and the 'Chilanga' minibus heads to Chilanga, via Kafue Rd. The standard fare is ZMW2 to ZMW3.

TAXI

Official taxis can be identified by the numbers painted on the doors and their colour – light blue – but hundreds of unofficial taxis also cruise the streets (you'll hear them honk their horn as they go past you on the street, looking for business).

Official taxis can be hailed along the street or found at numerous places near the main hotels and markets. Fares are negotiable, but if you're unsure, ask at your accommodation first for an approximate price; always agree on the fare before setting out.

EASTERN ZAMBIA

Eastern Zambia contains a couple of the country's wilderness gems. It's a sparsely populated region with one long highway, the Great East Rd, meandering out to the border with Malawi and onto Lilongwe. The two key national parks of the Luangwa Valley complement each other beautifully: stunning South Luangwa is the most set-up park for tourism in Zambia, as well as being one of the best in the region for wildlife watching and the most accessible park for budget tourists in Zambia; North Luangwa is wild and difficult to reach – access is usually by private charter flights – and spectacular for exploring on foot. Splitting the two parks is the lesser visited Luambe National Park, under new private management and one to look out for with animal numbers on the rise.

Chipata

The primary commercial and urban centre in this eastern district, Chipata is a fast-growing, traffic-clogged town in a valley surrounded by a fertile agricultural region. For travellers, it's simply a stop on the way to South Luangwa National Park or Malawi, which is only 30km away. There are a few decent accommodation options, petrol stations, ATMs and several large shopping malls with restaurant chains and supermarkets to stock up on food and other supplies.

Deans Hill View Lodge CAMPGROUND, LODGE $
(☑ 0216-223698; www.deanshillviewlodge.com; Plot 3278, Kanjala Hill, Fort Jameson; camping/

WORTH A TRIP

GREAT EAST ROAD: FROM LUSAKA TO CHIPATA

The Great East Rd crosses the Luangwa River on a large suspension bridge about halfway between Lusaka and Chipata. There are several places en route to break your trip.

Tikondane Community Centre (☑0979 176960; www.tikondane.org; Katete; camping/dm/r US$5/6/25, s/d with shared bathroom from US$10/15; 🖘) This grassroots initiative does wonderful work in assisting to empower local communities. It's a great place to hang around and help out as a volunteer. Otherwise you can spend the night at its Tiko Lodge, which offers camping, dorms and basic rooms in various configurations. The food here is another reason to stop by, with intriguing local dishes on offer.

Luangwa Bridge Camp (☑0977 395037; www.bridgecampzambia.com; Feira Rd; camping/r US$10/85, meals ZMW95-175; ⊘8am-9pm) A great place to break up the drive between Lusaka and Chipata, Luangwa Bridge Camp offers a good menu and drinks list, and scenic spot overlooking the river. It does filtered Zambian coffee, cold drinks, burgers, pizzas and steaks, as well as gourmet items such as deep-fried crumbed camembert or a tempura prawn burger with onion rings.

dm/d ZMW60/100/300, s/d with shared bathroom ZMW150/250; 🖘) This laid-back lodge is perched at the top of a hill with great views of the valley and Chipata below. Simple rooms are set in a two-storey stone-and-thatch chapel-like building. The shared ablutions are kept clean, and camping is out on a nice big sloping garden. Meals are served in a cosy dining area with bar, or there's a kitchen for self-caterers.

Mama Rula's   CAMPGROUND, LODGE **$$**
(☑0965 790225, 0977 790226; www.mamarulas.com; camping US$10, s/d incl breakfast US$32/60, s/d with shared bathroom US$15/30; @) Owned and operated by a South African/Zimbabwean family, this long-running operation is in a leafy compound around 4km out of Chipata along the road to Mfuwe. Simply furnished rooms with mosquito nets are in a low-slung building; nearby are small but clean cheaper rooms with shared bathroom facilities and a campsite popular with overland groups. Its social bar is Chipata's best spot for a beer.

Meals (T-bone steaks or schnitzel with chips and salad around ZM60 to ZMW120) are served in the bar festooned with South African rugby flags. Transport to and from town is ZMW50, or ZMW100 to the border.

❶ Getting There & Away

The main **bus station** is located in the tangle of streets about 1.5km north of the town centre.

Of the handful of bus companies offering services to Lusaka, Johabie (ZMW160, seven hours, 4am and 7am) is easily the most recommended. Touts from competing companies can be very aggressive in trying to steer you, or rather manhandle you, towards their waiting vehicle.

Buses also leave here to Mfuwe (around ZMW50, 2½ hours, 1.30pm) for South Luangwa National Park. A taxi to Mfuwe (ZMW450, three-plus hours) is another option.

It's best to arrive an hour early to guarantee a seat; always choose the bus closest to being filled, otherwise you might have a long, uncomfortable wait.

KOBS Coach Service has departures to Lilongwe, Malawi (ZMW80, four hours) at 5.30am pretty much daily (except Thursday and Sunday).

Minibuses (ZMW25) for the Malawi border depart from 7am to 5pm from the **Puma petrol station** (Great East Rd) on the main drag in town; otherwise, a taxi should run at around ZMW100 (30 minutes). Once you've passed through Zambian customs (open 24 hours), it's a few minutes' walk to the Malawian entry post. From the border crossing you can catch a shared taxi to nearby Mchinji (MK300) before getting a minibus all the way to Lilongwe.

South Luangwa National Park

For scenery, variety and density of animals, **South Luangwa National Park** (per person/self-drive vehicle US$25/30; ⊘6am-6pm) is one of the best parks in Zambia, if not Africa. Impalas, pukus, waterbucks, giraffes and buffaloes wander on the wide-open plains; leopards, of which there are many in the park, hunt in the dense woodlands; herds of elephants wade through the marshes; and hippos munch serenely on Nile cabbage in the Luangwa River. The bird life is a highlight: about 400 species have been recorded – large birds like snake eagles, bateleurs and ground hornbills are normally easy to spot.

South Luangwa National Park

South Luangwa National Park

◎ **Top Sights**
1 South Luangwa National Park A2

🛏 **Sleeping**
2 Chamilandu Bushcamp A3
3 Chizombo...A1
4 Croc Valley...A1
5 Flatdogs Camp A1
6 Kawaza Village B2
7 Luwi Bush Camp A1
8 Marula Lodge..A1
9 Mfuwe Lodge..A1
10 Nkonzi Camp...A1
11 Nkwali...A2
12 Nsefu Camp...B2
Track & Trail River Camp............(see 8)
13 Wildlife Camp A2
14 Zungulila..A3

✖ **Eating**
Dorphil Restaurant ....(see 8)

🛍 **Shopping**
15 Tribal Textiles.......................................B2

The focal point is Mfuwe, an uninspiring though more prosperous than average village with shops as well as a petrol station and market. Around 1.8km further along

is **Mfuwe Gate**, the main entrance to the park, where a bridge crosses the Luangwa River.

Much of the park is inaccessible because of rains between November and April.

🏃 Activities

All lodges/camps run excellent day or night wildlife drives and some have walking safaris (June to November). These activities are included in the rates charged by the upmarket places, while the cheaper lodges/camps can organise things with little notice. A three-hour morning or evening wildlife drive normally costs around US$40, while a wildlife walk is about US$50.

Budget Safaris

While South Luangwa is one of the easier parks to navigate for those without their own vehicle, an all-inclusive safari is still an excellent way to see the park. The following offer some more affordable safaris:

Jackalberry Safari (www.jackalberry safaris.net; 3-/4-/5-day safari per person US$645/995/1195) Popular all-inclusive multiday safaris that offer top value for money with stays at its lovely, remote Nkonzi Camp.

Edward Selfe Photography Safaris (☏ 0976 750967; www.edwardselfephotography. com; 6 days from US$2870) One for budding wildlife photographers, these tours are run by an experienced nature photographer.

River Safari Company (☏ in South Africa 021-426 2838; www.riversafaricompany.com; 161 Mulombwa Cl; 3-/4-day safari per person US$545/695) Budget safaris run out of Lusaka Backpackers.

Kiboko Safaris (☏ 0975 713820; www.kiboko-safaris.com; 4-day safari per person US$515) Operating out of Lilongwe, Malawi; offers multiday trips in its tented camp along the Luangwa River.

🛏 Sleeping

Most lodges and camps in South Luangwa are along the banks of the river; those deep in the park are all-inclusive and at the very top end price-wise.

Budget travellers will be treated to some of the best-value accommodation in Africa, where you don't need to spend a cashload for waterfront views or wildlife encounters.

Many lodges close during the rainy season (November to April), but those around Mfuwe open year-round.

🛏 Around Mfuwe Gate

★ Marula Lodge   LODGE $

(📞 0216-246073; www.marulalodgezambia.com; Mfuwe; dm US$10, dome tents per person US$15, r from US$40; 📶💺) Occupying a stretch of riverfront with plenty of lawn, Marula offers one of the best choices in the park for budget travellers. Options include waterfront domed tents, upstairs dorm rooms with a view and some charming, comfortable chalets with private bathroom. The shared bathroom for those in the tents and dorms offers a unique experience in a wonderful circular open-air structure built around a lovely mahogany tree.

There's also a self-catering kitchen, an atmospheric thatched restaurant/bar serving up Western mains, and an inviting swimming pool that makes it worth hanging around another day.

Croc Valley   LODGE $

(📞 0216-246074; www.crocvalley.com; camping/safari tent US$12/15, r from US$40, with shared bathroom from US$25; @📶💺) One of several places catering to independent travellers along this stretch of the river, Croc Valley offers great options. In a sprawling compound set under a tangle of trees lining the riverbank, there's both camping and good-value 'backpacker rooms' with shared amenities. Otherwise it has air-conditioned safari tents of varying levels of luxury and more standard tents with open-air, thatch-walled bathrooms.

Wildlife Camp   LODGE, CAMPGROUND $

(📞 0216-246026; www.wildlifecamp-zambia.com; camping US$12, safari tent s/d US$55/90, chalet s/d US$85/136; 📶💺) This spacious, secluded spot about 5km southwest of Mfuwe village is popular with both overland groups and independent travellers. There are nine simple stone-and-thatch chalets (two with basic kitchenettes), five airy tented ones and a big, open area for campers with its own bar and pool area. Its tented camps have some of the best views in the park.

Track & Trail
River Camp   CHALET, CAMPGROUND $$

(📞 0977 600556, 0974 244850, in Lusaka 0211-246020; www.trackandtrailrivercamp.com; camping US$12.50, s/d all-inclusive US$495/850; 📶💺) Set on a riverfront property about 400m east of Mfuwe Gate, Track & Trail offers varying levels of luxurious chalets and lovely camping grounds shaded by a giant African fig. Its pool with elevated deck and lounge chairs overlooking the river is one of the park's finest.

Flatdogs Camp   TENTED CAMP $$

(📞 0216-246038; www.flatdogscamp.com; safari tents U$52-97, all-inclusive chalets per person US$395; @💺) On a large, leafy property along a kilometre of riverfront, Flatdogs has 11 safari tents of varying features. All are well kept and have outdoor showers. Groups of four can consider the 'tree house' (US$405), which has two open-air bedrooms overlooking a flood plain frequented by all manner of wildlife (a telescope is on hand for stargazing).

Kawaza Village   HUT $$

(www.kawazavillage.co.uk; per person day visit incl lunch US$20, overnight per person with full board US$70) This enterprise run by the local Kunda people gives tourists the opportunity to visit a real rural Zambian village while helping the local community. Four rondavels (each sleeps two) with open-air reed showers and long-drop toilets are reserved for visitors who are encouraged to partake in village life, learning how to cook *nshima* (maize porridge), attending church services and visiting schools.

Mfuwe Lodge   LODGE $$$

(📞 0216-245041; www.bushcampcompany.com; per person all-inclusive US$545; 📶💺) 🌿 Laid out along an enviable stretch of a well-trafficked oxbow lagoon only 2km from the Mfuwe Gate, this resort-like lodge, one of the largest, is also certainly one of the nicest and most well run. The 18 separate cottages (12 face the lagoon and six the hippo pool) are imaginatively designed with private verandas (and hanging wicker 'basket chairs') and colourful bathrooms with big windows.

★ Chizombo   LODGE $$$

(📞 0216-246025; www.normancarrsafaris.com/camps/chizombo; per person all-inclusive US$1300; ❋📶💺) One of the park's most exquisite lodges, Chizombo offers luxury villas done out in designer soft white tones, with spacious, breezy and immaculate areas furnished with a classy vintage decor. Each of the six villas has its own massive decking area with a sofa and private plunge pool overlooking the wildlife-viewing areas.

SOUTH LUANGWA'S FLORA & FAUNA

The lifeblood of South Luangwa park is the wide Luangwa River, which rises in far north-eastern Zambia, near the Malawi border, and flows southward for 800km through the broad Luangwa Valley. Although it flows all year, it gets very shallow in the dry season (May to October) when vast midstream sandbanks are exposed – usually covered in groups of hippos or crocodiles basking in the sun. Steep exposed banks mean animals prefer to drink at the park's numerous oxbow lagoons, formed as the river continually changes its course, and this is where wildlife viewing is often best, especially as the smaller waterholes run dry.

Vegetation ranges from open grassy plains to the strips of woodland along the riverbank, dominated by large trees including ebony, mahogany, leadwood and winterthorn, sometimes growing in beautiful groves. As you move away from the river onto higher ground, the woodland gets denser and finding animals takes more patience.

Not that you'll ever be disappointed by Luangwa's wildlife. The park is famous for its buffalo herds, which are particularly large and dramatic when they congregate in the dry season and march en masse to the river to drink. Elephant numbers are also very healthy, even though ivory poaching in the 1980s had a dramatic effect on the population. This park is also a great place to see lions and leopards (especially on night drives), and local specialities include Cookson's wildebeest (an unusual light-coloured subspecies) and the endemic Thornicroft's giraffe, distinguished from other giraffes by a dark neck pattern.

Even the zebras here are unusual; called Crawshay's zebras, their stripes are thin, numerous and extend down to the hooves, under the belly, with no shadow stripe – they are an intermediate form between the 'standard' East African form and the extra-stripy subspecies in Mozambique.

There's a stunning variety wildlife on the plains: the numerous antelope species include bushbuck, waterbuck, kudu, impala and puku. Roan antelopes, hartebeests and reedbucks are also here, but encountered less often.

Luangwa's population of wild dogs, one of the rarest animals in Zambia (and Africa), seems to be on the increase, especially around the Mfuwe area from November to January; there has been a resurgence in numbers around the Nsefu sector as well. An organisation that works to protect and rehabilitate wild dog populations is the Zambia Carnivore Programme (www.zambiacarnivores.org) – healthy packs require huge areas to roam for their nomadic lifestyles, and it is trying to open up a viable corridor for the dogs between South Luangwa and the Lower Zambezi National Parks.

The birdlife in South Luangwa is also tremendous. As small lagoons dry out, fish writhe in the shallows and birds mass together as 'fishing parties'. Pelicans and yellow-billed storks stuff themselves silly, and become so heavy they can't fly. Herons, spoonbills and marabou storks join the fun, while grasses and seeds around the lagoons attract a moving coloured carpet of queleas and Lilian's lovebirds. Other ornithological highlights are the stately crowned cranes and the unfeasibly colourful Carmine bee-eaters, whose migration here every August is one of the world's great wildlife spectacles – some visitors come just to see these flocks of beautiful birds busy nesting in the sandy riverbanks.

The **South Luangwa Conservation Society** (CLS; ☑ in South Africa 096 2492386; www.slcszambia.org) helps to protect this wonderful natural heritage through its anti-poaching efforts, with regular patrols throughout the park.

Southern Camps

Zungulila
LODGE $$$

(☑ 0216-245041; www.bushcampcompany.com; per person all-inclusive US$720; ☺ Jun-Dec) Imagine a *Vogue* shoot with an *Out of Africa* theme and you'll have the sophisticated design aesthetic of this camp. Spacious safari tents evoke colonial-era fantasies with copper-plated taps and Middle Eastern rugs; each has its own sun deck with tiny circular plunge pool and outdoor shower. Zungulila's decadent signature treats are the sundowners enjoyed barefoot in folding chairs in the shallow river.

ZAMBIA SOUTH LUANGWA NATIONAL PARK

BUSHCAMP COMPANIES

Only a handful of companies offer lodging within the park proper, primarily in what are generally referred to as 'bush camps'. Despite the misleading name, these are very comfortable, ranging from simple thatch-roofed chalets to stylishly furnished tents with gold-plated taps and plunge pools. Most have only three to five rooms and offer customised itineraries that take guests to multiple camps by vehicle or on foot.

Bushcamp Company (www.bushcampcompany.com) Sophisticated and expertly managed Bushcamp operates six uniquely designed camps (Bilimungwe, Chamilandu, Chindeni, Kapamba, Kuyenda and Zungulila), which are all in the southern section of the park, as well as its base **Mfuwe Lodge** (p580).

Norman Carr Safaris (www.normancarrsafaris.com) Operates five somewhat more rustic camps (Chizombo, Kakuli, Luwi, Mchenja and Nsolo) mainly in the remote sections of the park; its base is at Kapani Lodge.

Robin Pope Safaris (www.robinpopesafaris.net) With its base at **Nkwali** (p582) not far south of Mfuwe Gate, Robin Pope Safaris operates three camps (Luangwa River Camp, Nsefu and Tena Tena), several remote mobile walking camps in the north sector of the park and two houses for rent (Robin's House and Luangwa Safari House).

The other companies in the park that are the highly recommended: **Remote Africa** (www.remoteafrica.com; Chikoko, Mwaleshi and Tafika) in the northern section run by John and Carol Coppinger; **Sanctuary Retreats** (www.sanctuaryretreats.com; Chichele and Puku Ridge) and **Shenton Safaris** (www.kaingo.com; Mwamba and Kaingo).

Chamilandu Bushcamp LODGE **$$$**
(☑ 0216-245041; www.bushcampcompany.com; per person all-inclusive US$720; ☉ mid-Jun–Nov) Built along the banks of the Luangwa River, Chamilandu Bushcamp's stilted thatch-and-reed chalets are utterly exposed to the elements; they have no fourth wall, only three sides of expert carpentry work. You'll never want to spend more time in a bathroom! Sunrise offers another revelation when the true brilliance of the camp's design comes to light. It's a two-hour drive south of Mfuwe.

🛏 Northern Camps

Nkwali LODGE **$$$**
(☑ 0216-245090; www.robinpopesafaris.net; per person all-inclusive US$665; 🅰) A long-standing, classic Luangwa lodge, Nkwali has just six small cottages with delightful open-air bathrooms. They're all very comfortable but with no unnecessary frills, which gives a feel of the bush – rustic but also quite classy. If you're after privacy, the two-bedroom Safari House has traditional African decor and a private guide, hostess and chef!

Nsefu Camp LODGE **$$$**
(www.robinpopesafaris.net; per person all-inclusive US$835) Luangwa's first tourist camp (now protected as a historic monument) has an excellent location smack bang in the middle of the Nsefu sector on an open plain awash with wildlife and with hot springs nearby. The stylishly furnished rondavels retain a 1950s atmosphere (along with the rest of the camp), complete with brass taps in the bathrooms and good-sized windows with river views.

★ Luwi Bush Camp LODGE **$$$**
(☑ 0216-246015, 0216-246025; www.normancarr safaris.com/camps/luwi; per person all-inclusive US$840) One of Norman Carr Safari's original remote luxury wilderness camps in South Luangwa, Luwi nails the rustic:luxury ratio with each of its open-plan thatch-and-reed chalets overlooking the plains. It's dismantled at the end of each season to minimise environmental impact.

★ Nkonzi Camp TENTED CAMP **$$$**
(☑ 0966 411320; www.jackalberrysafaris.net; 3 days per person all-inclusive US$610; ☉ June 1–Oct 31) Run by Jackalberry Safaris, Nkonzi is a bush camp within the national park that offers a wonderful (and relatively more affordable) wilderness experience; it's excellent value for those looking to spend a few days on safari. The seasonal site offers tented accommodation with double bed and attached open-air bathrooms constructed from reed material. Rates include activities led by experienced owner/guide Gavin Opie.

Eating

Dorphil Restaurant INTERNATIONAL $
(☑ 0216-246196; mains ZMW25; ☺ 6am-9pm)
Highly recommended by area expats and
one of the few places to eat in the village of
Mfuwe is friendly Dorphil Restaurant. The
owner/chef Dorika prepares samosas, spring
rolls, T-bones with *nshima* and pizza, served
at a few outdoor tables under a thatch roof.

Shopping

Tribal Textiles ARTS & CRAFTS
(☑ 0216-245137; www.tribaltextiles.co.zm; ☺ 7am-
4.30pm) This enterprise employs a team of
local artists to produce, among other things,
bags, wall hangings, bed linens and sarongs,
much of which are sold abroad. Tribal Textiles has some striking original designs and
it's quite a refined place to shop or take a
short (free) tour around the factory.

Getting There & Away

AIR

Many people reach South Luangwa by air. Mfuwe
Airport is about 20km southeast of Mfuwe Gate
and served by Proflight (www.proflight-zambia.
com), with several daily flights from Lusaka
(from US$150 one way). A flight to Lower Zam-
bezi was introduced in late 2016. **Ulendo Airlink**
(☑ in Malawi 01-794638; www.flyulendo.com)
flies from Lilongwe (Malawi) to Mfuwe.

At Mfuwe Airport's little terminal there's a
bureau de change, Barclays Bank and Zanaco
ATMs, and a cafe by the car park where you can
grab a coffee and meal while waiting for your
flight. Almost every lodge meets clients at the
airport (the charge is often included in the room
rates). Otherwise a taxi to locations near the
Mfuwe gate should cost around ZMW80.

BUS

There are several buses from Mfuwe village
for Chipata (around ZMW50) and Lusaka
(ZMW220); Jonada Bus is probably the most
reliable. Note that when you arrive there's a
facility for you to call your lodge to pick you up
as it's not safe to walk due to the prevalence of
wildlife.

Shared taxi and minibuses are other options
and depart from the **BP petrol station** early in
the morning, typically before 7am.

CAR

While the vast majority of visitors come and
go using the main park entrance at Mfuwe,
the Chifungwe Gate is an option if arriving/
departing from the north of the country via
Mpika. The route is open during the dry season
only, and passes over the Muchinga Escarpment
along a steep rocky track, which you'll need
to pass along at a snail's pace – hence it's one
for experienced 4WD drivers only. The turnoff
to Chifungwe is signed about 40km south of
Mpika along the Great North Rd, from where it's
a further 50km or so to the gate. All up expect
the journey from Mpika to Mfuwe to take six to
seven hours.

If you're heading to or arriving to Luambe or
North Luangwa national parks, you'll take the
Chikwinda Gate and follow a track along the east
side of the Luangwa River. There are several river
crossings, so it's only passable during the dry season and again for experienced 4WD drivers only.

For alternative routes to Mfuwe Gate, be sure to
call ahead to enquire about the state of the roads.

Getting Around

For independent drivers, South Luangwa is
probably the easiest park to access (with the
exception of Kafue) and to drive around. A limited section of all-weather gravel roads are in
excellent condition near Mfuwe Gate and there's

ZAMBIA SOUTH LUANGWA NATIONAL PARK

WORTH A TRIP

LUAMBE NATIONAL PARK

Despite the relative proximity of North and South Luangwa National Parks, driving between them is long and hard, and it would take over 11 hours if you were to try the trip
in one go. However, most who venture this route stop after around six hours in small
Luambe National Park (entry US$35, per vehicle US$20).

A destination in its own right, Luambe is a great option for those wanting to see the
same animals as South Luangwa, minus the crowds. Though tiny in size, it's one of the
country's oldest parks, gazetted in 1938.

Luambe Camp (☑ in South Africa 072 298 0777; www.luambe.com; Luambe National Park;
per person all-inclusive US$395; ☺ Apr-Nov) is the place to stay in the northwest pocket of
the park, only 3km off the roadway on the Luangwa River. It's run by a team of passionate conservationists aiming to put the park back on to the tourist map.

It's another five hours or so from here to Buffalo camp in North Luangwa.

lots of smaller tracks. You should be able to pick up a very basic map at the gate. The bush opens up off the side of the roads (even early after the rainy season in May), making wildlife spotting fairly easy, especially along the river.

If you're not staying at an all-inclusive place and you want to arrange a 4WD (up to nine people; around US$125 per 24 hours) for wildlife viewing or to explore villages in the area contact Ben Koobs, the owner of **Personal Touch** (📱0978 459965, 0966 602796; www.tptouch.com).

Be aware that it's never entirely safe to walk anywhere in the park (even within your lodge you'll need to be highly vigilant) as there are no fenced boundaries, so wildlife roams freely inside and out of the park.

North Luangwa National Park

This **park** (admission US$20, self drive US$25; ◷6am-6pm) is large, wild and spectacular, but nowhere near as developed or set up for tourism as its southern counterpart. The big draw of North Luangwa is its walking safaris, where you can get up close to the wildlife in a truly remote wilderness.

The range of wildlife in North Luangwa is similar to South Luangwa's (except there are no giraffes), and the park is particularly famous for its small population of black rhino and huge buffalo herds (sometimes up to 1000-strong), which in turn attract large numbers of lions and hyenas. The bush here is dense in places, so the animals are slightly harder to see than at South Luangwa, and there are very few tracks for vehicles, so the emphasis is firmly on walking.

North Luangwa's eastern boundary is the Luangwa River, but the heart of the park is the Mwaleshi River – a permanent watercourse and vital supply for wildlife.

There is no public transport to North Luangwa. Most guests fly in and out on charter flights arranged by their lodge (typical price per person from Mfuwe to one of the airstrips is ZMW1000 one way); the result is that only several hundred people visit the park each year.

If you are coming to the park independently remember that you need to be well set-up with a fully equipped, high-clearance 4WD, and your accommodation prebooked. Also, get advice regarding the state of the roads into the park and make sure you've got maps that cover the area (and GPS); they should be supplemented by a map of the park, usually available at Mano Gate and detailing where you're allowed to drive.

Mwaleshi Camp CAMPGROUND $$$
(📱0216-246185; www.remoteafrica.com; per person all-inclusive from US$710; ◷Jun 15–Oct 31) A top-notch operation – at once luxurious, in terms of care from the staff, and relaxed. It's a bush camp with accommodation in four charmingly simple chalets made from reeds and thatch with open-roofed bathrooms. Walking is the main activity and that's a fortunate thing once you've tasted the excellent food. Spotted hyenas are commonly seen in this area, as are buffaloes and, of course, lions.

Buffalo Camp LODGE $$$
(📱0976 970444; www.shiwasafaris.com; per person self-catering/all-inclusive US$100/280) Located in the south of the park, Buffalo Camp is a quiet, secluded place. It's good value (and unusually welcomes children) and the six traditional-style thatch-roofed chalets overlook the river. Book ahead for the 'self-catering rates', normally only available when there's a paucity of guests on the all-inclusive package. Transfers for those without vehicles are usually possible from Kapishya Lodge or Mpika (maximum four people).

SOUTHERN ZAMBIA

This region is a real highlight of Zambia with some wonderful natural attractions. There are great national parks, the Lower Zambezi in particular highly regarded for both its wildlife (especially elephants) and its scenic landscape. The area is also home to the remote Lochinvar National Park, renowned for its pristine wetlands. Then there's the massive Lake Kariba, with Siavonga's sandy beaches and Chikanka Island (smack in the middle of the lake) providing fascinating views of the night sky and a glimpse of the 60 elephants that make their way between the islands. If you're lucky enough to see a storm roll in over the steely waters from Zimbabwe, it'll be an experience you'll long remember. Siavonga offers the chance to experience the more rural side of the country.

Chirundu

This dusty and bedraggled border town is on the main road between Lusaka and Harare. The only reason to stay here is if you're going on to Zimbabwe or planning to explore the

Lower Zambezi National Park. Other than a few shops and bars, as well as a Barclays Bank with ATM and a number of money-changers, there's little else to note.

That said, west of town, near the Siavonga turnoff, is the **Fossil Forest**. From a sign on the main road, paths lead through the bush. At first, things are pretty uninspiring, but further in huge trunks of petrified trees are visible, complete with age rings and grains of bark now preserved as stone.

Minibuses leave regularly for Chirundu from Lusaka (ZMW40, three hours, five to seven daily). To reach Siavonga (on Lake Kariba) from Chirundu, catch a minibus towards Lusaka, get off at the obvious turnoff to Siavonga and wait for something else to come along.

There is no petrol station in town. Gwabi Lodge and Kiambi Safaris have a couple of fuel pumps, but there is a limited supply, so it's safer to stock up in Lusaka or Kafue.

Wagtail River Club LODGE $
(📞0965 623067, 0979 279468; www.wagtailriver camp.com; camping US$10, r per person US$45, with shared bathroom US$20; 🛜🐾) The former Zambezi Breezers has been rebadged as Wagtail River Club, but it's the exact same place. It still boasts a wonderful grassy spot overlooking the Zambezi River and is still run by the same Dutch owner. It's only 6km from Chirundu, and has a variety of accommodation including a wide lawn for riverbank camping, and simple, clean tented chalets with small decks.

Gwabi Lodge CAMPGROUND, CHALET $$
(📞0966 345962; www.gwabiriverlodge.com; camping/stone tents US$9/14, s/d chalets from US$54/88; 🅿🛜🐾) This long-running lodge owned by a Zimbabwean family is set on large, leafy grounds 12km northeast of Chirundu. There's a well-equipped camping ground (popular with overland backpackers) and solid stone-floor chalets with TVs. The highlight is the lovely elevated outlook over the Kafue River, with the decking area in front of the restaurant providing a great spot to observe birds and hippos.

Lower Zambezi National Park

One of the country's premier wildlife-viewing areas, the **Lower Zambezi National Park** (adult/self-drive vehicle US$25/30; ⊙6am-6pm) covers a large stretch of wilderness area along the northeastern bank of the Zambezi River. Several smaller rivers flow through the park, which is centred on a beautiful flood plain alongside the Zambezi, dotted with acacias and other large trees, and flanked by a steep escarpment on the northern side, covered with thick miombo woodland. On the opposite bank, in Zimbabwe, is Mana Pools National Park, and together the parks constitute one of Africa's finest wildlife areas.

The best wildlife viewing is on the flood plain and along the river itself. Mammal species include elephant, puku, impala, zebra, buffalo, bushbuck, leopard, lion, cheetah and wild dog, and more than 400 bird species have been recorded.

The best time to visit is May to October; however, temperatures average around 40°C in the latter half of October.

🏃 Activities

Canoe Safari
One of the best ways to see the Lower Zambezi is by canoe safari.

Drifting silently in a canoe past the riverbank allows you to get surprisingly close to birds and animals without disturbing them. Nothing beats getting eye-to-eye with a drinking buffalo, or watching dainty bushbuck tiptoe towards the river's edge. Excitement comes as you negotiate a herd of grunting hippos or hear a sudden 'plop' as a croc you hadn't even noticed slips into the water nearby.

Most of the camps and lodges have canoes, so you can go out with a river guide for a few hours. Longer safaris are even more enjoyable; ask your lodge what is available.

Wildlife Watching
Most lodges offer wildlife-viewing activities by boat or by safari vehicle and are not fenced. Keep in mind, however, that while theoretically on offer, most of the lodges in the Game Management Area (GMA), especially those closer to Chirundu than to Chongwe Gate, don't take their wildlife drives in the park proper.

The main entrance is at **Chongwe Gate** along the southwestern boundary. The southwestern sector of the park is the easiest to reach and the most scenic, and has excellent wildlife viewing, so as you might expect, it's a popular area. As you go further into the central part of the park, the surroundings become wilder and more open

Lower Zambezi National Park

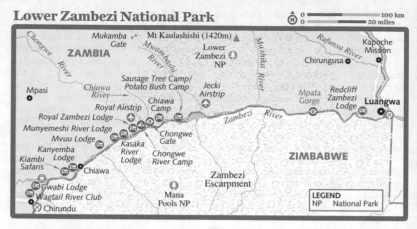

and there's more chance of having the place to yourself. Although the park is technically open all year, access is impossible in the rainy season and most lodges close down from at least mid-December to the end of February.

The elephant population was ravaged by poaching until the early 1990s, but thanks to the efforts of Conservation Lower Zambezi (www.conservationlowerzambezi.org), an organisation funded by the area's lodges and private grants, they are making a strong comeback now, with the surrounding Chiwa Game Management Area particularly dense with elephants. However, despite regular anti-poaching flights and regular ZAWA patrols, illegal hunting remains a big concern. Hence here you'll likely find elephants more on the aggressive side, so take absolute care if you're driving, especially given the road is tight.

The eastern part of the park is different in character as here the hills are close to the Zambezi and there's virtually no flood plain. The park's eastern boundary is the dramatic **Mpata Gorge** where the steep hillsides plunge straight into the river, and the only access is by boat.

🛏 Sleeping

All lodges here are found stretched out along the banks of the Zambezi river. Here you'll find some of the most stunning luxury safari lodges in Zambia; however, budget travellers also have some lovely camping options in the GMA leading into the park, which likewise has plenty of wildlife.

Munyemeshi River Lodge LODGE $
(☑ 0979 565646, 0211-231466; www.munyemeshi. co.zm; r ZMW450; ☒) An affordable waterfront lodge close to the park, Munyemeshi's stone-and-thatch chalets are rough around the edges, but at these prices you can't be too choosy. It was undergoing renovations at the time of research, so call ahead to see if it's going to remain as a budget lodge. There's no restaurant, so it's one for selfcaterers, with a fully equipped kitchen on hand.

Kiambi Safaris CAMPGROUND, CHALETS $$
(☑ 0977 876003, 0977 186106; www.kiambi.com; camping US$12, tent rental US$28, chalets s/d with full board from US$208/306; ❄ ☎ ☒) This wellrun and atmospheric operation at the confluence of the Zambezi and Kafue Rivers has a smattering of different, relatively affordable accommodation options. Set in attractive, verdant surrounds, chalets and cottages are comfortable and characterful. Campsites come with a powerpoint and firepit, and a tent if you don't have one. The social restaurant and bar is another highlight.

Mvuu Lodge CAMPGROUND, TENTED CAMP $$
(☑ 0966 363762, in South Africa 012-660 5369; www.mvuulodge.com; camping US$28, tented camping US$38, luxury tent per person all-inclusive US$175) A large, leafy property with an informal vibe, Mvuu is built on the edge of the tree-lined riverbank. Comfortable elevated safari tents with balconies are on either side of a casual lounge and dining area. The communal campfire encourages guests to share their tales of leopard and lion sightings.

★**Chiawa Camp**   CHALET $$$
(✆0211-261588; www.chiawa.com; per person all-inclusive US$1120; ☾mid-Apr–mid-Nov; @🛜⊠) In a spectacular position at the confluence of the Chiawa and Zambezi Rivers, this luxurious lodge inside the park was the first in the Lower Zambezi. As a pioneer in this area, the owner Grant Cummings knows the park intimately and his guiding expertise is highly regarded. The large walkin canvas-thatch tents feature pine-clad private bathrooms.

The bar-lounge has an upstairs deck with majestic views over the river and there's a viewing platform high up in the trees.

The food is top notch and for the romantics among you (and honeymooners), candlelit private tables can be set up in the bush, on a boat or, at full moon, on a sand bar in the middle of the river.

Chiawa's sister camp, **Old Mindoro**, is a classic old-school safari bush camp unlike anything else in the park and receives rave reviews.

★**Royal Zambezi Lodge**   TENTED CAMP $$$
(✆0979 486618; www.royalzambezilodge.com; per person all-inclusive from US$990; ☾year-round; 🛜⊠) The epitome of luxury bush mixed with a colonial-era vibe, Royal is only a short drive to the eponymous airstrip as well as Chongwe Gate. Despite its understated opulence – think brass fixtures, claw-footed tubs and private day beds on decks overlooking the river – it's unpretentious and exceptionally friendly. Its bar built around the trunk of a sausage tree is a well-received feature.

In addition, there's a full-service spa (the only one on the Zambezi) and a small pool, essentially in the river; rest your elbows on the edge and you might see a hippo glide by only a few feet away. Kids and families are welcome and there are discounts in the 'green' season when rains tend to be heavy and quick; although wildlife drives might be impossible, canoe trips are still on and there are few other visitors around.

Chongwe River Camp   TENTED CAMP $$$
(✆0968 351098, 0973 965851; www.chongwe.com; per person all-inclusive US$725; ☾Apr–mid-Nov; 🛜⊠) Right on the Chongwe River that marks the boundary between the GMA and the national park, this camp has an enviable position with plenty of wildlife around the camp but without the park fees. The confluence of the Zambezi is within view and a menagerie of wildlife grazes on a spit of grassland with the park's escarpment in the background – an absolutely Edenic view.

❶ Getting There & Away

AIR
Proflight (✆0211-271032; www.proflight-zambia.com) has daily flights between Lusaka and Royal Airstrip (30 minutes; in the GMA just a few kilometres west of Chongwe Gate) and Jeki Airstrip (40 minutes; in the heart of the park). Almost every guest staying at one of the top-end lodges in the park flies into and out of Jeki, while Royal is very convenient for the lodges near Chongwe Gate. All include transfers from the airstrip.

From 2017 Proflight will also offer flights between Lower Zambezi and Mfuwe in South Luangwa National Park, which will make life considerably easier for those heading between the two parks.

Charter flights are also available with Nkwazi Air (www.ngwaziaircharters.com).

CAR
Uncomfortable minibuses run from Lusaka to Chirundu; departures run throughout the morning, but you have to sort out transport from town to your accommodation.

There's no public transport to Chongwe Gate, nor anything to the eastern and northern boundaries, and hitching is very difficult. Most people visit the park on an organised tour, and/or stay at a lodge that offers wildlife drives and boat rides as part of the deal. The lodges also arrange transfers from Lusaka – generally a minivan to Chirundu and then boat to the lodge (rates and travel times vary depending on the distance from Chirundu).

There are also tracks via the north for those heading to the eastern side of the park but these are far less used: there's an approach road accessed from the Great East Rd, 100km east of Lusaka, that will take you to Mukanga Gate; and there's a track from Leopards Hill in Lusaka, which is earmarked for improvement, though this could be many years in the future. Seek local advice before attempting either of these routes.

For budget travellers, ask at Bongwe Barn (p570) and Lusaka Backpackers (p570) in Lusaka or Jollyboys (p555) in Livingstone for deals on budget safaris into the Lower Zambezi.

❶ Getting Around

Remember that you'll need a well-equipped 4WD to access and get around the park. You must drive slowly in the GMA area and the park itself – watch especially for elephants along the roadside at all times. There are several loops inside the park for wildlife viewing, but these change

KARIBA DAM

Lake Kariba was formed in the 1960s, its waters held back by the massive Kariba Dam, built to provide electricity for Northern and Southern Rhodesia (later Zambia and Zimbabwe) and as a symbol of the Central African Federation in the days before independence. Today Kariba measures 280km long by 12km to 32km wide, with an area of over 5500 sq km, making it one of the largest artificial lakes in the world. Underground power stations on both sides of the dam produce over 1200 megawatts between them.

As well as being a source of power, Lake Kariba is an important commercial fishing centre. Small sardine-like fish called *kapenta* were introduced from Lake Tanganyika, and they thrived in the new mineral-rich waters. In recent years overfishing has led to a decline in catches, but some rigs still operate, and you'll often see their lights twinkling on the horizon.

A visit to the dam with your own wheels is quite straightforward. Head down to the Zimbabwean border crossing at Siavonga/Kariba; it's a few kilometres from the wall. Enter the immigration building (on the right-hand side down some stairs as you face the border gate). Tell them that you just want to visit the wall and that you are coming back to Zambia and not going onto Zimbabwe. They will give you a stamped pass to the dam wall and ask you to leave some ID behind (driving licence or passport are OK). At the gate, show them your pass and you'll be let through. From here it's a short drive or walk to the wall. Once there, park your car and walk out over the wall: the views are spectacular and it's well worth the trip – particularly if you admire gargantuan engineering projects. You should be allowed to take pictures of the wall but not the power station. Remember that the authorities don't like cameras around here and have a fear of terrorism or sabotage to the dam. So do what they tell you. On the way back, surrender your pass at the border gate, and don't forget to pick up your ID from immigration.

from year to year, especially after the rainy season, so pick up a guide at any of the gates.

One adventurous way to visit the park is by canoe along the Zambezi. Most lodges offer two- or three-day canoe trips, with stops at seasonal camps along the river or makeshift camps on midstream islands.

For fuel in the park, Kiambi Safaris generally has petrol and diesel; otherwise Gwabi Lodge is the closest option.

Lake Kariba

Beyond Victoria Falls, the Zambezi River flows through the Batoka Gorge then enters the waters of Lake Kariba. Formed behind the massive Kariba Dam, this is one of the largest artificial lakes in the world. It's enormous, and a spectacular sight with the silhouettes of jagged Zimbabwean peaks far across its shimmering waters. For those who make it here, this remoteness is the very attraction.

The main base for activities on and around the lakeshore is Siavonga, which is a small town with accommodation. Sinazongwe, almost halfway between Livingstone and Siavonga, is even less set up for tourism. Only 17km away across the water,

closer to Zimbabwe (150m away) than Zambia, is Chete (27 sq km), the largest island on the lake. It has lions, leopards, elands, waterbucks, bushbucks, impalas and kudus, and of course hippos and crocs, as well as an astonishing variety of birds – but no roads or accommodation.

Siavonga

Siavonga, the main town and resort along the Zambian side of Lake Kariba, has a location to be envied. Set among hills and verdant greenery, just a few kilometres from the massive Kariba Dam, views of the lake pop up from many vantage points, especially from the lodges. Yet, as it is set up primarily for the conference/business market and wealthy urban Zambians (especially from Lusaka) who tear down here towing their sleek boats and stay in their holiday bungalows, independent travellers without their own wheels might not find enough upside to offset the challenges of a visit. The lodges can organise activities in and around the lake, including boat trips to the dam wall, sunset cruises, fishing trips, longer-distance boat trips and one-day to four-night canoe safaris on the Zambezi.

Minibuses from Lusaka (ZMW70, three hours, three to five daily) leave when bursting to capacity for Siavonga and the nearby border. Alternatively get a bus towards Chirundu and get dropped off at the Siavonga turnoff; from here take a local pickup (ZMW15) the rest of the way.

Leaving Siavonga, minibuses depart from near the market. There are no official taxis in Siavonga, but your hotel can arrange a car to the border; otherwise, minibuses head here as well.

Eagles Rest   CAMPGROUND, CHALET $$
(☑0967 688617, 0978 869126; www.eaglesrest resort.com; camping/tent hire US$1025, s/d/tr incl breakfast US$50/75/90; ✳ 🞱) While it's all a little bit tired and in need of a refurb, this laidback beachfront resort is still the best spot for independent travellers. It has its own little sandy area (no swimming, however), pool and beach bar. It's the only campsite around town, and its chalets are spacious with stone floors and great decking outside with patio furniture overlooking the lake.

Lake Kariba Inns   HOTEL $$
(☑0977 770480, 0211-511290; www.karibainns. com; s/d from ZMW825/945; ✳ @ 🛜 🞱) With a commanding hilltop location with lush gardens (home to some roaming zebra) and lake views, this hotel has relatively luxurious rooms (some with verandas) and is a good choice if you don't mind sharing space with conference attendees. The restaurant (buffet ZMW150) and sports bar overlook the pool area, which is itself perched high above the lake.

Sinazongwe

Near the southwestern end of Lake Kariba and far from its cousin Siavonga at the other end of the lake, Sinazongwe is a small Zambian town used by *kapenta* fishers as an outpost. The centre of town is actually up on a hill away from the lake's edge and the whole area has little tourism footprint. It's a lovely place to come to get away from it all.

Ask in Choma for minibuses that can take you to Sinazongwe. By car, head to Batoka, just north of Choma. From here take the turnoff to Maamba. After about 50km look for the turn-off to Sinazongwe; the town is a short distance down this dirt road. All up it's around a 5½-hour drive from Lusaka. Note: if visiting during the rainy season, you'll need a 4WD.

WORTH A TRIP

CHIKANKA ISLAND CAMP

Chikanka Island Camp (☑0976 667752; www.lakeview-zambia.com; camping ZMW100, s/d incl breakfast ZMW750/1350; 🞱) is located on a beautiful private island 18km from Sinazongwe – it's mostly wooded, with impala, kudu, zebra, bushbuck and the occasional elephant dropping in. Crocs and hippos patrol the shores, so don't even think about taking a dip.

The camp features a mix of stone-and-thatch chalets with views overlooking the lake. Fishing for tiger fish and bream is a big draw, as are boat trips and wildlife safaris to Chete Island. Campers are welcome to pitch a tent. Meals are available to order or there's braai facilities for self-caterers.

To get here you'll need to transfer from its sister accommodation Lakeview Lodge at Sinazongwe on the mainland, a 40-minute boat trip (ZMW950).

Lakeview Lodge   LODGE $$
(☑0976 667752; www.lakeview-zambia.com; camping ZMW100, s/d incl breakfast ZMW420/714; 🞱) A kilometre from the town of Sinazongwe, Lakeview Lodge has comfortable chalets with ceiling fans and a secluded terrace overlooking the lake and verdant grounds. There's also a campsite to pitch a tent, as well as a pool, small beach area and a braai, making it a good spot to chill out for a few days.

Choma

This busy market town, the capital of the Southern Province, is strung out along the highway 188km northeast of Livingstone. Most visitors zip through on their way to Lusaka or Livingstone, but Choma is a convenient stopover or staging post for trips to the southern section of Kafue National Park or to Lake Kariba. Other than the **museum** (adult/child US$5/3; ⊙9am-4pm) there's not much to distinguish the town, but it has all of the facilities and services travellers need, including a Spar supermarket, international banks with ATMs, internet, a couple of petrol stations and decent accommodation.

All daily buses and trains between Livingstone and Lusaka stop at Choma. The bus to either Lusaka or Livingstone is ZMW60 or ZMW75 and there are many departures throughout the day.

Leon's Lodge

LODGE $

(☑ 0978 666008; off Livingstone Rd; r ZMW250-450; ✸) Marked by two enormous stone carved lions out front, and rather luxurious-looking thatched chalets, Leon's has clean and large rooms that come with satellite TV and fridge. There's a small bar and restaurant on site, both of which are rarely attended to, consistent with what is fairly patchy service across the board. It's along a backstreet running parallel with the main road.

New Choma Hotel

HOTEL $

(☑ 0213-220836; Livingstone-Lusaka Rd; r incl breakfast ZMW175-250; ✸) Far from flash, this gritty hotel nonetheless has a convenient central location along the main strip. Rooms are spacious and have TV, fridge and air-con. At its rear is a great Indian restaurant and bar, which can get noisy at night, however.

Lochinvar National Park

This small, 410 sq km park (adult US$10; ☉ 6am-6pm), northwest of Monze, consists of grassland, low wooded hills and the seasonally flooded Chunga Lagoon – all part of a huge, impressive wetland site called the Kafue Flats. You may see buffalo, wildebeest, zebra, kudu and some of the 30,000 Kafue lechwe residing in the park. Bushbuck, oribi, hippo, jackal, reedbuck and common waterbuck are also here. Lochinvar is a haven for birdlife too, with more than 400 species recorded.

While all safaris in the park are self-drive, you're likely to be able to arrange for a ranger to accompany you for around US$20. The network of tracks around the park is still mostly overgrown, with only the track from the gate to Chunga Lagoon reliably open.

Moorings Campsite

CAMPGROUND $

(☑ 0977 521352; www.mooringscampsite.com; camping/tent rental US$8/15, chalet s/d US$30/50) This is perhaps the most beautifully landscaped campsite in Zambia. It's a lovely secluded spot on an old farm with plenty of grass and there are open-walled thatch rondavels scattered around the campsite and a braai next to them

for cooking. It's perhaps the best place to break a journey between Lusaka and Livingstone, or to access Lochinvar National Park.

WESTERN ZAMBIA

When it comes to tourism, west Zambia doesn't do things by half measures: it's either wildly popular or just plain wild.

At one end of the spectrum is Victoria Falls. Being one of Africa's most famous attractions – combined with a world-class outdoor adventure scene – it's home to the country's tourism industry. The other big hitter is Kafue National Park, one of the continent's largest parks and a truly magnificent spot with all the big animals, and a thousand different landscapes.

Conversely, in the bulk of this vast west region you'll be hard pressed to see a single traveller. It's by far Zambia's least-visited area, which for many is its very appeal. It has huge tourism potential, however, with thundering waterfalls and remote wilderness areas such as Liuwa Plain National Park. Barotseland is also here, home to the Lozi people and the site of the colourful Kuomboka, Zambia's best-known traditional ceremony.

Kafue National Park

Covering more than 22,500 sq km, **Kafue National Park** (adult/vehicle US$20/15; ☉ 6am-6pm) is the largest in Zambia and one of the biggest in the world. With terrain ranging from the lush riverine forest of the Kafue River to the vast grassland of the Busanga Plains, the park rewards wildlife enthusiasts with glimpses of various carnivores and their nimble prey. There's a good chance of sighting lions and leopards, and, if you're lucky, cheetahs in the north of the park, plus elephants, zebras and numerous species of antelope. There are some 500 species of birds too.

The main route into the park is via the sealed highway running between Lusaka and Mongu, which loosely divides the park into its northern and southern sectors. Kafue is one of the few parks in Zambia that's easily accessible by public transport, with a handful of camps just off the highway.

For a budget safari into the park, check with Lusaka Backpackers (p570) and Bongwe Barn (p570) in Lusaka, or the **Mobile Safari Company** (☑ 0963 005937; www.wild-kaf ue.com; 2 nights/3 days from US$425) based in Livingstone.

🛏 Sleeping

🛏 Northern Sector

★ **Mayukuyuku**   CAMPGROUND, TENTED CAMP **$$$**
(☑ 0972 179266, 0977 721284; www.kafue camps.com; Northern Sector; camping US$25, all-inclusive chalet per person US$495; ☎) This rustic bush camp, small and personal, is in a gorgeous spot on the river with a well-landscaped camping area and four tastefully furnished thatch-roofed safari tents. Each of the latter has hammocks, chairs and table out the front and great outdoor bathrooms (even campers get open-air toilets and showers). If you don't have your own gear, you can rent tents (US$15/30 small/large tent).

★ **Mukambi Plains Camp**   TENTED CAMP **$$$**
(☑ 0974 424013; www.mukambisafaris.com; Northern Sector; per person all-inclusive US$775, minimum 5-night stay; ☺ 15 Jul-Oct) The approach to this bucolic oasis, basically an island just 7km from the park's northern border, is made all the more dramatic by the wooden walkway over a prairie of 'floating grass'. The four simply but comfortably outfitted safari tents succeed in the exact balance between luxury and offering a safari experience, and feature outdoor bathrooms with bucket showers.

🛏 Southern Sector

Chibila Camp   LODGE **$**
(☑ 0211-251630; www.conservationzambia.org/camps-and-lodges; Southern Sector; r member/non-member ZMW100/150) Just outside the park in the GMA, Chibila offers three basic, bargain-priced rooms that overlook Lake Itezhi-tezhi. Rooms come with attached bathroom, and while you need to bring along your own food, the team here are happy to cook it up for you. It's a peaceful spot among woodland and boulders, where plenty of hyrax dart about.

There are no wildlife drives on offer here, so you'll either need your own wheels or you can arrange safaris with one of the neighbouring lodges, including Hippo Bay Bush Camp or New Kalala Camp.

Hippo Bay Bush Camp   CAMPGROUND, CHALET **$$**
(☑ 0962 841364; www.hippobaycamp.com; Southern Sector; camping US$20, chalets US$60-100) Hippo Bay is easily one of the best budget options in south Kafue. It has six rustic, well-priced thatched reed chalets with attached bathroom, or a campsite with flush toilets and hot water. There's a braai and firewood to cook meals, but otherwise you can drive to its nearby sister Konkamoya Lodge for meals (breakfast/lunch US$15, dinner US$30) and drinks. Wildlife drives cost US$35.

New Kalala Camp   CAMPGROUND, CHALET **$$**
(☑ 0211-290914, 0979 418324; www.newkalala.com; camping/tent hire ZMW100/200, s/d from ZMW500/700; ✴☀) Just outside the park boundary in the GMA is this locally run place with large, bland chalets in a rocky setting overlooking beautiful Lake Itezhi-Tezhi. There's a choice of thatched chalets or new concrete rondavels; the latter have lake views. All come with TV, fridge and air-con. The campsite is separate from the lodge in a patch of shady trees.

★ **KaingU Safari Lodge**   CAMPGROUND, TENTED CAMP **$$$**
(☑ in Lusaka 0211-256992; www.kaingu-lodge.com; Southern Sector; camping US$20-25, tented camping with full board & 2 activities US$450; ☺ Apr-Dec; ☎) Set on a magical stretch of the Kafue River, this lodge overlooks a primordial stretch of lush islands among the rapids, with delightful birdwatching. The four tastefully furnished Meru-style tents are raised on rosewood platforms with stone bathrooms and large decks to enjoy the view. There are also three campsites, each with its own well-kept thatch ablution and braai facilities.

Mukambi Safari Lodge   CHALET **$$$**
(☑ 0974 424013; www.mukambi.com; Southern Sector; per person with full board US$350; ☎☀) Easily the most accessible of the Kafue lodges and easy to reach from Lusaka, Mukambi makes a great base to explore the park. Tastefully designed rondavels with Adirondack-style chairs on each front porch are set back from the riverfront on a lawn with a manicuring assisted by visiting hippos in the evenings. Activities such as wildlife drives and boat cruises are additional (US$45).

Konkamoya Lodge   CHALET **$$$**
(☑ 0962 841364; www.konkamoya.com; Southern Sector; per person all-inclusive US$500; ☺ mid-

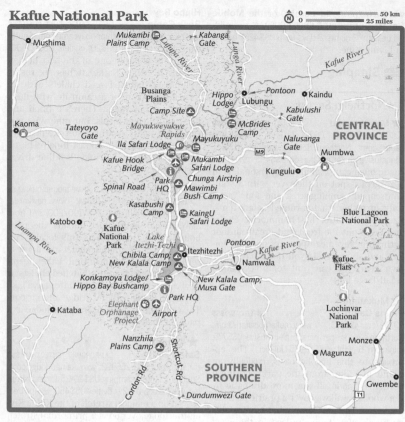

Jun–mid-Nov; ☎) One of the best lodges in the southern sector, Konkamoya has a wonderful location on the southern shores of Lake Itezhi-Tezhi. Enjoy dramatic views of skeletal tree trunks rising from the water and grassy plains that attract plenty of wildlife. Its enormous and luxurious stilted safari tents come with wicker furniture and panoramic outlooks.

Kasabushi Camp CAMPGROUND, CHALET **$$$**
(☏0971 807226; www.kasabushi.wordpress. com; Southern Sector; camping US$20, tent hire US$15-20, chalet per person all-inclusive US$350; ⊙chalets May-Dec, campsite year-round) Run by husband-and-wife team Andy and Libby, Kasabushi gets great reviews for both its tranquil riverside campsite and luxury chalets. Separated from the campsite, its two rosewood chalets are thoughtfully and lovingly designed and open directly to the river. The camping area has wonderful views and atmospheric outdoor showers. There's also a

natural rock swimming pool built into the riverbank.

❶ Getting There & Away

Most guests of the top-end lodges/camps fly in on chartered planes.

Given there's a sealed road passing through the centre of the park, you can easily catch a Mongu-bound bus here from Lusaka (ZMW120, 3½ hours). On the highway ask to be let off either near Mukambi Safari Lodge (contact Mukambi for pick-up; only a couple hundred metres away wildlife roams free) or Mayukuyuku (arrange pick-up from the highway for US$35). For a ride back to Lusaka, wait out by Hook Bridge or the stop by Mukambi between 11am and 11.30am. Juldan or Shalom are two of the more recommendable bus companies.

Alternatively, take the slow daily bus, or one of the more regular minibuses from Lusaka to Itezhitezhi village (ZMW75, four hours). From the village bus stop wait around for a lift (because of the number of wild animals, it's not safe to hike).

If you're driving, be aware that the tsetse flies in the park are horrendous. It pays to have air-conditioning so you can close the windows.

There are several gates, but the main ones are: Nalusanga Gate (200km from Lusaka), along the eastern boundary; Dundumwezi Gate for the southern sector, accessed from the town of Kalomo if coming from Livingstone or Choma; Kabanga Gate if entering or exiting from the north; and Tateyoyo Gate for either sector if you're coming from the west. Rangers are also stationed at the two park headquarters: one at Chunga Camp and another 8km south of Musa Gate, at the southern end of Lake Itezhi-Tezhi.

For those heading south from the main road, the newly upgraded Spinal Rd is by far the best option. If coming from Lusaka it's accessed off the Lusaka–Mongu highway about 10km after the Kafue Hook Bridge (or 82km from Nalusanga Gate); look for the sign to Chunga. To get to the lodges along the eastern side of the Kafue River, you'll have to take a boat trip across (inclusive in the rates); otherwise from June to November there's a very rough, though scenic, dirt track that mostly hugs the eastern bank of the river.

Mongu

The largest town in Barotseland, and the capital of the Western Province, is on high ground overlooking the flat and seemingly endless Liuwa Plain. This is a low-key town with plenty of activity on the streets but little to draw travellers outside of the annual Kuomboka ceremony, when thousands flock here and room prices skyrocket.

The town is quite spread out with no real centre and the highlight is the spectacular panoramic view over the flood plains. From a harbour on the southwestern outskirts of town, an 8km canal runs westwards to meet a tributary of the Zambezi. The river port is a settlement of reed-and-thatch buildings, where local fishers sell their catch, and it's a good spot for people-watching as longboats glide down the river transporting people and goods to nearby villages.

◉ Sights

While in Mongu itself there isn't much to see, you can head to Limulunga, 15km north of town, for an interesting little museum and the palace of the litunga (the king of the Lozi). Otherwise head to the main palace of the litunga in the village of Lealui, 15km northwest of Mongu.

Nayuma Museum   MUSEUM
(Limulunga; adult/child US$5/2.50; ⊙8am-4.30pm) This small, dusty museum has some good info on the Lozi people, the litunga (Lozi king) and Kuomboka ceremony. It has various artefacts and cultural exhibits, as well as a large model of the *nalikwanda* boat used in the Kuomboka. There are some fascinating shots of royal pageantry in a black-and-white photo exhibition titled, 'A Retrospective in the Forties' by Max Gluckman. It also has interesting pictures of the historical line of the litungas.

Lealui Palace   PALACE
(Lealui; ⊙by appointment Mon-Fri) FREE Lealui village is the site of the main palace of the litunga (king of the Lozi). The palace is a large single-storey Lozi house, built with traditional materials (wood, reeds, mud and thatch); it was being renovated at the time of research and was scheduled to reopen 2017. Avoid visiting on weekends when the *litunga's* kotu (court) is closed, because you need permission from his *indunas* (advisors) to get a close look at the palace and even to take photos.

🛏 Sleeping

Country Lodge   LODGE $
(☎0977 222216; countrylodge@iconnect.zm; 3066 Independence Ave; r incl breakfast ZMW250-600; 🅿🖥) Close to the centre of town, this modern and well-run place sees its fair share of conferences, weddings and the like. The rooms are plainly decorated but come with amenities like satellite TV and nice modern bathrooms. There's a bar and restaurant onsite.

Greenview Guesthouse   CAMPGROUND, GUESTHOUSE $
(☎0217-221029; www.limagarden.com; Limulunga Rd; camping per person ZMW80, s/d from ZMW70/200; 🖥) Located next to the church, chalets here sleep two people and are fantastic value; newer ones come with air-conditioning, shiny tiled floors and DSTV. Spacious inside and set in nice, grassy grounds with views of the flood plains, they may well be the best deal in Mongu. It's on the road to Limulunga; keep an eye out for the sign on the left.

🛍 Shopping

Mumwa Craft Association   ARTS & CRAFTS
(☎0964 015014; Lusaka Rd; ⊙7.30am-6pm Mon-Sat) A visit here is well worth your time.

Proceeds from sales of expertly made basketry and woodcarvings – at low prices – are ploughed back into the local communities that produce them. Located next to the Total petrol station on the road to Lusaka.

Liuwa Plain National Park

About 100km northwest of Mongu, near the Angolan border, **Liuwa Plain National Park** (☎ 0964 168394; liuwa@africanparks.co.zm; adult/child US$30/10) is 3600 sq km of true wilderness. The remote park is characterised by expanses of flat, grassy flood plains, and is most famous for the second-largest wildebeest migration in Africa; in the wet season you'll find a wall-to-wall gathering of herds.

The park is also notable for having one of the highest population densities of hyena in the world, as well as a stunning variety of birdlife. Other wildlife include lion, cheetah, wild dog, zebra, buffalo, lechwe, wildebeest, tsessebe and Roan antelope.

Since 2004 the park has been managed by African Parks (www.african-parks.org), an international organisation that assists governments in funding conservation projects and reviving animal numbers across Africa.

A sizeable community of Lozi people live both within and around the park, and you'll pass several of their villages en route, characterised by their thatched rondavels.

Most visitors are here to see the November migration of wildebeest, which congregate here in vast numbers that turn the park into a 'mini Serengeti'. Although it's often called a migration, in reality the wildebeest are here year-round, so it's more a meander from one sector of the park to another. While November is undoubtedly the best time to visit, you can see them at other times in the northern part of the park in large numbers.

Liuwa Plain is accessible from May/June to December. However the best time to go is November, just after the rains start (the later the better). Leave before the flood waters rise, however, or you'll be stuck for months.

🛏 Sleeping

For completely self-sufficient travellers, there are five well-maintained campsites in the park.

Sikhale Camp Site   CAMPGROUND $
(www.african-parks.org/the-parks/liuwa-plain; per person US$ adult/child US$15/7) In the far northern part of the park, Sikale is the place to camp for those wanting to see wildebeest during the drier months. Lions also often head up this way. There's no running water or flush toilets, so you'll need to be totally self-sufficient. It's about a 4½-hour drive from Kalabo.

Katoyana   CAMPGROUND $
(www.african-parks.org/the-parks/liuwa-plain; camping adult/child US$15/7) One of Liuwa's best campsites is this lovely shaded spot that's well placed for the wildebeest gatherings, as well as for spotting birdlife, hyenas and lions. It's a 2½-hour drive from the main gate at Kalabo.

ℹ Getting There & Away

The new pristine tarmac road from Mongu to the park's headquarters in Kalabo (70km, 45 minutes) has drastically improved accessibility to the park. At Kalabo you need to cross the river via the rope-pulled pontoon (per vehicle ZMW40); from that point it's 12km to the park boundary. There is no petrol in Kalabo, so be sure to fill up in Mongu and carry a full jerry can.

Access to Liuwa Plain National Park is restricted from around May to December. Despite a network of tracks, Liuwa is serious 4WD territory; a lot of the tracks are very sandy, wet or both. Although the trackless, featureless, endless plains appear benign, it's also very easy to get lost. Taking a scout with you is highly recommended and also financially assists the national park; this can be organised at the park headquarters. A GPS is advisable.

Senanga

Senanga has a real 'end of the line' feel, particularly if you've come from Lusaka. That said, the main street can be surprisingly lively, especially in the evening, and the views of the Zambezi are beautiful. It is the best place to break up a journey between Mongu and Ngonye Falls or Sesheke.

Minibuses and pickups run between Senanga and Mongu (ZMW50, two hours) several times a day. For Livingstone it's an 8½-hour bus journey (ZMW140), departing daily at 3pm apart from Sundays.

Senanga Safaris   CHALET $
(☎ 0976 020143; r incl breakfast ZMW200-350; ▣) The best accommodation in Senanga are these comfortable rondavels with splendid views over the Zambezi plains. It's spoiled only by the giant satellite TV dish in the garden. The bar sells cold beer and the res-

taurant serves stock-standard meals, where staff are for the most part disinterested.

Ngonye Falls

Located about 130km north of Sesheke are the **Ngonye Falls** (Sioma Falls; entry US$5, vehicle US$15; ⊙ 6am-6pm), a 1km-wide chain of waterfalls, rapids and rocky islands cutting across the Zambezi River. It's beautiful and very impressive and would be a major attraction if it wasn't so difficult to reach. Imagine something almost as majestic as Victoria Falls, but with almost no other person (local or foreign) in sight. It's worth visiting anytime of the year, but it peaks around June to July.

Wildlife is being introduced to the area of the park surrounding the falls, including zebra and sitatunga among others.

While it's easy to get a view of the falls, getting a really good view is much harder as you need to get out onto an island in front of the falls – ask at the National Parks office if there are any boats that might take you

there. Otherwise Ngonye River Camp (p595) can arrange boat trips.

🛏 Sleeping

Ngonye River Camp LODGE $

(📞 0975 144820; www.ngonyerivercamp.com; per person camping US$10, tented camping from US$15, chalet US$35) This scenic camp on the sandy banks of the Zambezi, about 5km from Ngonye Falls, is a laid-back spot where you can pitch a tent (or hire one of theirs) or stay in a chalet. They offer boat trips to the falls as well as canoeing trips, fishing and village tours. Meals are available and there's complimentary filter coffee.

Campsite CAMPGROUND $

(camping US$10) A lovely campsite, just a five-minute walk from the falls, with hot-water showers, toilets and a shelter for food preparation. There's a camp attendant to provide firewood and light campfires.

ⓘ Getting There & Away

The falls are reached along a nice stretch of tarmac running from Sesheke to Sioma, which

---

KUOMBOKA CEREMONY

The Kuomboka (literally, 'to move to dry ground') is probably one of the last great Southern African ceremonies. It is celebrated by the Lozi people of western Zambia, and marks the ceremonial journey of the *litunga* (the Lozi king) from his dry-season palace at Lealui, near Mongu, to his wet-season palace on higher ground at Limulunga. It usually takes place in late March or early April, and sometimes ties in with Easter. The dates are not fixed, however; they're dependent on the rains. In fact, the Kuomboka does not happen every year and is not infrequently cancelled because of insufficient flood waters; the 2012 ceremony was called off because it's against Lozi tradition to hold the Kuomboka under a full moon. While the new road here means the journey by boat is no longer necessary, tradition dictates the ceremony continues as is – though since there's a road a lot more people come to watch!

In 1933 a palace was built by Litunga Yeta III on permanently dry ground at the edge of the plain at a place called Limulunga. Although the Kuomboka was already a long-standing tradition, it was Yeta III who first made the move from Lealui to Limulunga a major ceremony.

Central to the ceremony is the royal barge, the *nalikwanda*, a huge wooden canoe, painted with black-and-white stripes, that carries the *litunga*. It is considered a great honour to be one of the hundred or so paddlers on the *nalikwanda*, and each paddler wears a headdress of a scarlet beret with a piece of a lion's mane and a knee-length skirt of animal skins. Drums also play a leading role in the ceremony. The most important are the three royal war drums, *kanaona, munanga* and *mundili*, each more than one-metre wide and said to be at least 170 years old.

The journey from Lealui to Limulunga takes about six hours. The *litunga* begins the day in traditional dress, but during the journey changes into the full uniform of a British admiral, complete with regalia and ostrich-plumed hat. The uniform was presented to the *litunga* in 1902 by the British King, Edward VII, in recognition of the treaties signed between the Lozi and Queen Victoria.

links up to Senanga. Plenty of buses ply the route – but you'll need to make sure they're Sioma-bound, as the road splits just before the new Sioma bridge.

The falls themselves are also easily accessible, less than 1km east of the main road. If driving, for the falls follow the signs to Sioma when you reach the split in the road, from where it's a further 5km over the new bridge.

Sesheke

The sleepy border town of Sesheke is a handy base for those crossing the border to Namibia (via the bridge to Katima Mulilo), or onward travel to northwest Zambia.

Buses link Sesheke with Natakindi Rd in Livingstone (ZMW70, three hours, two daily), usually at 7am and 5pm. Occasional minibuses also link Sesheke with Katima Mulilo, otherwise it's a ZMW15 taxi ride to the Nambian border which is open 6.30am to 6pm.

★ **Brenda's Best & Baobab Bar**   CAMPGROUND, CHALET **$**
(☎0963 786882; brendasbaobab@gmail.com; Mulambwe St; camping ZMW50, s/d incl breakfast ZMW200/300) Run by the friendly Brenda and her Dutch husband, this relaxed guesthouse is easily the best place to stay in Sesheke. The thatch-roofed double-storey chalets are built around a lovely lawn and a massive baobab overlooking fantastic views of the Zambezi.

NORTHERN ZAMBIA

Those with a spirit of adventure and who love wild, open spaces will be at home in Zambia's untamed north. The region starts after the 'Pedicle', the slice of DRC territory that juts sharply into Zambia, almost splitting it in two. From here onwards the old Great North Rd shoots its way straight up to Tanzania, passing national parks, vast wilderness areas and waterfalls along the way.

Attractions in the north include Lake Tanganyika where you can relax on white sandy beaches; Kasanka National Park, to watch the spectacular bat migration; Mutinondo Wilderness, a vast area of whaleback hills, rivers and valleys so untouched you feel almost like you have been transported to a prehistoric era; and the eerie Shiwa Ng'andu, a grand English mansion buried deep in the Zambian bush with a relaxing hot springs on tap.

Serenje

Serenje is a relatively uninspiring rural town spread out around the Great North Rd. The only reason for travellers to pass through is for a convenient refuelling stop or to spend the night on the way to more exciting destinations.

There are two main hubs in the town: the turnoff at the junction, with a petrol station, a couple of shops and a few basic restaurants; and the town centre, 3km north of the Great North Rd, with a bank, the bus station and some lodges.

All buses between Lusaka (ZMW90, five hours) and Kasama (ZMW90, five hours) pass through Serenje. Most of the big buses stop beside the petrol station at the junction with the Great North Rd, while minibuses stop in town.

Mapontela Inn   GUESTHOUSE **$**
(☎0979 587262; r ZMW180-235; ⊙restaurant 7am-9pm) Located along the main road in the centre of town is this charming guesthouse that's the best in Serenje. Opening out onto the leafy courtyard are a number of homely brick cottage rooms with fans and spotless bathrooms. The attached restaurant (meals ZMW35 to ZMW70), with a patio overlooking the street, serves tasty staples and is a good place to sample Zambian food.

Kasanka National Park

One of Zambia's least-known wilderness areas and a real highlight of a visit to this part of the country is the privately man-

> ### ⓘ FIBWE HIDE
>
> A trip to Kasanka isn't complete without viewing the park from the heights of the **Fibwe Hide**, a 15-minute drive from Wasa Lodge. Ascend 20m up an old mahogany tree via a rickety wooden ladder to a platform where you can sit and watch the swamps below. Come at dawn and dusk for the best chance of spotting sitatungas.
>
> **Pontoon Campsite** (www.kasankanationalpark.com; camping US$20) and **Kasanka Conservation Centre** (camping ZMW59, dm/r ZMW99/190) are good budget bets.

aged **Kasanka National Park** (⟡ in South Africa 072-298 0777; www.kasankanationalpark. com; adult US$8; ◷ 6am-6pm). At just 390 sq km, it's pretty small compared to most African parks, it doesn't have a huge range of facilities and it sees very few visitors – and this is what makes it special. There are no queues of jeeps to get a look at a leopard here; instead, you'll discover great tracts of miombo woodland, evergreen thicket, open grassland and rivers fringed with emerald forest, all by yourself.

Kasanka is most famous for its fruit bat migration in November and December, which sees up to 10 million of the nocturnal creatures arrive. The park is also known for its swampland, and this is the terrain to see the park's shy and retiring star, the sitatunga.

For sleeping, Pontoon Campsite and Kasanka Conservation Centre are good budget bets.

★**Wasa Lodge**　　　　　　LODGE $$
(⟡ in South Africa 072-298 0777; www.kasankana tionalpark.com; per person self-catering chalets US$70, all-inclusive US$420) Doubling as the park headquarters, accommodation here consists of thatched bungalows overlooking Lake Wasa. Larger chalets are airy and cool with wide balconies and lovely stone showers. There are multiple vantage points – including the deck of the large bar and dining area – to look out over the swamp to spot hippos, puku and sometimes even sitatungas.

ℹ Getting There & Away

From Lusaka, take a bus (ZMW130) in the direction of Mansa, or take any bus from Lusaka to Serenje and change onto a minibus (ZMW45) for Mansa. After turning off the Great North Rd, ask the driver to drop you at Kasanka National Park (near Mulembo village), not at Kasanka village, which is much further away. From the gate to Wasa Lodge is 12km; you can radio Wasa Lodge for a lift. It is also possible to charter a taxi from Serenje directly to Wasa Lodge; ZMW200 is about what you can expect to pay.

If you have your own vehicle, continue north along the Great North Rd from Serenje for 36km, then turn left onto the road towards Mansa. It's then 55km on a good road to the Kasanka entrance gate, clearly signposted on the left. There is no fuel available in the park, so stock up at Serenje.

There's an airstrip used for charter flights arranged through **Skytrails Charters** (⟡ 0979

KASANKA TO THE GREAT NORTH ROAD DRIVE

Drivers with a taste of adventure (and time on their side) may like to take the 'back route' from Kasanka direct to the Great North Rd, which winds past several attractions, including a memorial to explorer David Livingstone and lovely Lake Waka-Waka. The roads are generally in poor condition, so you'll need a 4WD or high-clearance vehicle.

In between Kasanka National Park and the Bangweulu Wetlands is the **Nakapalayo Tourism Project** (⟡ 0977 561714; r incl full-board & activities per person US$60, r only & activities per person US$40), a community initiative that allows tourists to experience life in a real Zambian village. Visitors can camp or stay in huts with double beds and mosquito nets. Activities revolve around village life and include learning how to pound cassava, meeting local healers and bush walks to learn about traditional uses for plants and trees.

337206; www.skytrailszambia.com), which is based there. For further information and prices, contact the Kasanka Trust (www.kasanka.com).

Bangweulu Wetlands

The **Bangweulu Wetlands** (www.african-parks.org/the-parks/bangweulu; adult ZMW50) is a watery wilderness of lakes, seasonally flooded grasslands, swamp and unspoiled miombo woodland that lies 50km to the north of Kasanka. This rarely visited part of Zambia is the only place in Africa to see major numbers of black lechwes (antelopes with long, curved antlers). Bangweulu is also known for its birds. Some 400 species have been noted, and a particular highlight for twitchers is the strange and rare shoebill stork.

It's one of several national parks run by African Parks. During the rainy season, be sure to call ahead to enquire about accessibility into the area.

June to July is the best time to see the lechwe herds as the waters have begun receding, leaving vast plains of fresh green grass.

Nsobe Camp
CAMPGROUND $

(www.african-parks.org; camping ZMW50; ☺ May-Jan) This is a basic campsite with braai area, hot showers, flush toilets and a couple of thatched cooking shelters. Note it's closed February to April.

Nkondo Safari Camp
TENTED CAMP $

(www.african-parks.org; per person ZMW250) Open year-round, Nkondo offers a comfortable self-catering option with safari tents with attached bathroom. There's a common kitchen to cook up meals. It's set among miombo woodlands with plenty of wildlife about.

Shoebill Island Camp
CAMPGROUND $$$

(www.african-parks.org) This camp rests in the heart of the wetlands and is splendidly positioned on a tiny permanent island with only birds, hippos, lechwes and the occasional passing fisher for company. It was closed from 2016 for a refurb with plans of reopening mid-2017.

❶ Getting There & Away

The only way into the wetlands is by 4WD or chartered plane. Dirt roads lead here from Kasanka via Lake Waka-Waka and the Nakapalayo Tourism Project. The Chikuni ranger post and Nsobe Camp are 65km on from Nakapalayo, and from here it's another 10km to Shoebill Island Camp if it's dry. (In the wet, you'll have to travel this last stretch by boat.) You will definitely need a fully equipped 4WD to attempt this trip as the going is tough. Set off from Kasanka in the early morning in order to reach Bangweulu before it gets dark. You can also get here along the Great North Rd via Lavushi Manda National Park; the African Parks team can provide a detailed information sheet about getting to the wetlands.

Samfya

Perched on the western shore of Lake Bangweulu, about 10km east of the main road between Mansa and Serenje, is Samfya, a small and dusty trading centre with little going for it except for its excellent white sandy beaches on the western shores of this beautiful lake. In the local language *bangweulu* means 'where the water meets the sky' and if you watch the lake at sunset, when the lake and hazy clouds both turn the same shade of blue, it's not hard to see why. Though locals are insistent it's safe to swim, the occasional crocodile is known to pass by.

Samfya is regularly served by minibuses from Serenje (ZMW95, five hours). Buses from Lusaka (ZMW120, 12 hours) may drop you in town or at the junction 10km away, from where local pickups shuttle passengers to and fro.

Samfya Beach Hotel
HOTEL $

(☎ 0969 121916; camping ZMW100, r ZMW200-500) Sitting on Cabana Beach, this place has a pretty good location but the rooms are small and have very basic bathrooms. Camping is an affordable option for those with a tent. As of late 2016 it was undergoing a much-needed renovation. Take the first turning on the left in town and it's about 2km north of the centre.

Mutinondo Wilderness

This is one of the most stunning places in northern Zambia. Mutinondo is a beautiful 100-sq-km wilderness littered with whaleback hills or inselbergs: huge, sweeping hulks of stone in varying shades of black, purple, green and brown. The landscape here feels unspoiled and ancient.

It's beautiful walking country and there are more than 60km of wilderness trails. Scramble to the top of one of those great granite beasts and it is easy to imagine a time when Stone Age hunters wandered the endless valleys, woodland and rivers below.

The network of rivers and waterfalls at Mutinondo are incredibly clear and calm, and safe to swim in (and to drink). Canoes are also available.

Mammal sightings are rare here, although Mutinondo is an important birding destination. There are about 345 species here including plenty of rare specimens that are difficult to find outside the country. Notable are the Ross's turaco, Anchieta's sunbird and the bar-winged weaver.

The turnoff to Mutinondo is 164km past Serenje heading north on the Great North Rd. It's signposted to the right; Mutinondo is 25km down a 2WD-friendly track. Travelling by bus from Lusaka, ask for a ticket to Kalonje Railway Station (ZMW150, six hours). Road transfers for a maximum of five people can be arranged from the Great North Rd turnoff (ZMW290). There's also an airstrip at nearby Mpika for charter flights, from where the team at Mutinondo can pick up guests for US$125.

Mayense Campsite
CAMPGROUND $

(www.mutinondozambia.com; camping US$8-15, rondavel US$35-45, tented camping US$100) This fantastic campsite offers a user-friendly spot to pitch a tent. Each pitch has cooking areas and bird-proof cupboards to protect supplies. The large, open-air showers (constructed out of sustainable materials) have hot water, sinks have framed pieces of information to read while teeth-brushing, and the eco-toilets have magazines to browse and strategically placed slots for views over the bush.

★**Mayense Camp**　　　　　LODGE $$$
(☑0978 198198; www.mutinondozambia.com; s/d all-inclusive from US$145/260; ☞) Built into the hillside are Mayense's individually designed chalets, each with outstanding views. All are beautiful in their simplicity and blend in seamlessly with their natural environment. Some are built into the granite rocks, with a huge handmade bath with a view, while others are open to the elements so it feels as if you're sleeping in the wild.

Mpika

Mpika is a busy crossroads town on the Great North Rd. The old road (M1) runs north to Kasama and Mpulungu, while the newer road (T2) runs northeast to the Tanzanian border at Nakonde. It is a good supply stop, and can also serve as a base to tackle South or North Luangwa national parks if you have a 4WD.

Buses and minibuses stop at the junction where the Kasama road and the Great North Rd divide. Destinations include Lusaka (ZMW140 to ZMW160, 9½ hours), Kasama (ZMW80), Serenje (ZMW85) and Mpulungu (ZMW110). There are also daily services to Nakonde on the Tanzanian border, but the buses usually pass through around midnight on their way from Lusaka.

Mpika's huge and impressive Tazara train station is about 7km southwest of the town centre, and is reachable by minibus when trains are due.

From here you can access South Luangwa via the rarely used Chifungwe Gate. The turn off is 40km south of Mpika along the Great North Rd. As it passes over the escarpment road it's a challenging route only to be attempted by experienced drivers in a 4WD.

★**Bayama's Lodge, Pub & Grill**　　LODGE $
(☑0977 316143, 0977 410839; www.bayama.de; r US$20-35, meals from US$5; ✳☞) Bayama's Lodge is a real gem for a backwater like Mpika. Under German-Zambian ownership,

it is just off the Great North Rd and offers budget rooms or larger chalets. The best feature is a lively restaurant-bar serving mains such as T-bone steaks and homemade pizzas. The bar has cold beer, tunes and a popular pool table.

Shiwa Ng'andu

Deep in the northern Zambian wilderness sits Shiwa Ng'andu, a grand country estate and labour of love of eccentric British aristocrat Sir Stewart Gore-Brown. The estate's crowning glory is Shiwa Ng'andu manor house, which is a magnificent English-style mansion. Driving up to the house through farm buildings, settlements and workers' houses it almost feels like an old feudal domain: there's a whole community built around it, including a school and a hospital, and many of the people now working at Shiwa Ng'andu are the children and grandchildren of Sir Stewart's original staff. Today Gore-Brown's grandchildren live on and manage the estate, which is a working farm.

Shiwa House　　　　　　　HISTORIC SITE
(www.shiwangandu.com; tours US$20; ☺tour 9-11am Mon-Sat, closed to nonguests Sun) The main draw to the area is the surreal sight of Shiwa House, a massive English-style manor materialising seemingly out of nowhere in the middle of rural Zambia. Built in the 1920s, the decaying grand mansion built on a stately lawn is full of old family heirlooms, photographs and stories. There are guided tours of the estate (or there's a self-guided option with booklet), which include a wildlife drive to spot the property's 24 mammal species including puku, kudu, zebra and wildebeest.

Kapishya Hot Springs　　　HOT SPRINGS
(nonguests/guests of Kapishya Lodge US$8/free; ☺6am-6pm) Located on the premises of Kapishya Hot Springs Lodge, the setting here makes it a marvellous place to take a soak in its blue-green steaming lagoon of bathhot water surrounded by thick palms. If staying at Kapishya Lodge, then you can use the springs for free. It's about 20km west of Shiwa House.

🛏 Sleeping & Eating

★**Kapishya Hot Springs Lodge**　　LODGE $$
(☑0211-229261, 0976 970444; www.shiwasafaris.com; camping US$15, d from US$75, per person all-inclusive US$165; ☞✳) Featuring a scenic river location, with nearby hot springs and

lush rainforest, this lodge is popular for good reason. The chalets are light and spacious, with wooden decks complete with fireplaces and views and there's a lovely campsite with hot showers and barbecue areas. The pool and hot springs are wonderful spots to unwind. Excellent meals are also available.

Shiwa House HISTORIC HOTEL **$$$**
(☑ 0211-229261; www.shiwasafaris.com; per person with full board from US$470) This old place is suitably attired for a grand old English manor, with fireplaces, four-poster beds, oil paintings and big old roll-top baths. There's a glorious guest sitting-room looking out onto the front lawn, which is even more atmospheric at night when lit by candles and a crackling fire. Tasty dinners are taken in the rather splendid dining room.

❶ Getting There & Away

To reach Shiwa House, head north along the Great North Rd by bus (or car) from Mpika for about 90km towards Chisoso. Look for the signpost to the west, from where a 20km dirt road leads to the house. Kapishya Hot Springs and the lodge are a further 20km along this track.

You can also get to Shiwa from the Mpika to Kasama road – this time look for the signpost pointing east and it's then 42km down the dirt track to Kapishya. There is no public transport along this last section, but vehicle transfers are available from the Great North Rd turnoff for US$35 per vehicle.

Kasama

Kasama is the capital of the Northern Province and the cultural centre of the Bemba people. With its wide, leafy streets and handsome, old, tin-roofed colonial houses, it is the most appealing of the northern towns. Kasama's environs are home to ancient rock art and a beautiful waterfall, as well as to the **Kusefya Pangwena festival** (www.zambiatourism.com).

Buses and minibuses leave for Lusaka (ZMW130, 12 hours) daily. Buses go via Mpika (ZMW80, two hours) and Serenje (ZMW95, four hours). Northbound buses go to Mbala (ZMW35, two hours) and Mpulungu (ZMW50, three hours). Cheaper local minibuses run to Mpulungu, Mbala and Mpika.

The Tazara train station is 6km south of the town centre. The express train to Nakonde (for the Tanzanian and Malawian border) and Dar Es Salaam (1st class ZMW205)

leaves in the small hours of Friday night/Saturday morning. Trains to Mpika (ZMW35) and Kapiri Mposhi (ZMW87) pass through on Tuesday night.

Kasama Rock Art HISTORIC SITE
(adult/child US$15/7, camping US$10; ⊙ 6am-6pm) Archaeologists rate the Kasama rock art as one of the largest and most significant collections of ancient art in Southern Africa, though their quality is outdone in Zimbabwe and Namibia. The works are attributed to Stone Age hunter-gatherers (sometimes known as Twa) and are up to 2000 years old. Many are abstract designs, but some of the finest pictographs show human figures and animals, often capturing a remarkable sense of fluidity and movement, despite being stylised with huge bodies and minute limbs.

★ **Thorn Tree Guesthouse** GUESTHOUSE **$**
(☑ 0214-221615; kansato@iconnect.zm; 612 Zambia Rd; s/d from ZMW210/270, f from ZMW350; 🞱 🞵) The Thorn Tree is family-run, homey and very popular, so book ahead to avoid disappointment. Rooms are either in the main house sharing spick-and-span facilities or in larger family rooms, including a three-room cottage. There's a bar and a restaurant serving fresh farm produce; they also roast their own coffee beans on site, so you'll get a decent brew here.

Mbala

Once the colonial centre of Abercorn, this sleepy town sits on the periphery of the Great Rift Valley. From here the road drops about 1000m from the highest settlement in Zambia down to Lake Tanganyika and Mpulungu, the lowest town in the country. Today the only reason to visit is its museum, or as a stop-off point for Kalambo Falls. In practical terms, there's some decent spots for lunch, an ATM, fuel station and some general stores.

Buses run daily to Mpulungu (ZMW15, 50 minutes), Kasama (ZMW45, two hours), Mpika (ZMW110, four to five hours), Serenje (ZMW135, seven hours) and Lusaka (ZMW180, 13 to 15 hours).

Moto Moto Museum MUSEUM
(adult/child ZMW30/15; ⊙ 9am-4.45pm) This museum in a 1970s modernist building is well worth a visit if you're in the area. It has a large and diverse collection, much of which details the cultural life and history of

the Bemba people. Items on display include old drums, traditional musical instruments and an array of smoking paraphernalia. Particularly noteworthy is an exhibition detailing how young Bemba women were traditionally initiated into adulthood. It includes a life-size, walk-in example of an initiation hut, with background info.

Lake Chila Lodge
LODGE $

(📞0977 795241; lakechilalodge@yahoo.com; Lake Chila; camping ZMW150, r incl breakfast ZMW250-500) The most atmospheric place to stay in Mbala is this welcoming lodge located on the shores of Lake Chila, about 2km from town. Rooms are set in spacious chalets with satellite TV and hot showers; the cheaper rondavels offer the best value. The lodge includes a lively little bar-restaurant (mains ZMW20 to ZMW40), which makes for a good road-trip pit stop.

Lake Tanganyika

Spreading over a massive 34,000 sq km, and reaching almost 1500m deep, cavernous Lake Tanganyika is the second-deepest lake in the world and contains about 15% of the earth's fresh water. Believed to be up to 15 million years old and lying in the Great Rift Valley, the shores of the lake reach Tanzania, Burundi, the Democratic Republic of the Congo and Zambia. The climate here is always very hot, especially at the end of the dry season.

Of most interest to visitors are its white sandy beaches that, along with palm trees and snorkelling in crystal clear waters with multicoloured tropical fish, can make it feel more like Thailand than Zambia.

All of the lodges can arrange boat transfers. Most boat transfers are included in the rates with the exception of Mishembe Bay and campers at Isanga Bay Lodge, in which case return transfers are US$100 to US$150. Otherwise you can try the water taxi service (ZMW25), which departs Monday, Wednesday and Friday – leaving Mpulungu at 3pm, and making the return journey about 5am or 6am. However, be warned: it gets very full.

Travel by road is possible, but only with a 4WD as the road is in very poor condition, with plenty of deep sandy stretches. Some taxis may be willing to tackle the road and will charge about ZMW400.

★ Mishembe Bay (Luke's Beach)
BUNGALOW, CAMPGROUND $

(📞0976 664999; www.facebook.com/mishembebayzambia; camping per person US$10, lodge US$25) With its stunning white sands, palm trees and thatched bungalows, Luke's Beach resembles some secluded Southeast Asian beach paradise. The stilted thatched bungalows are luxurious on the outside, yet remain bare bones within to suit the budget traveller, and feature magnificent views of the water. You'll need to bring along all your own food, but there's a kitchen where you can cook.

Staying here gives you the advantage of being a 1½-hour walk to Kalambo Falls. To get here the boat transfer is around ZMW500 return. The owner Luke is the son of the owners from Thorn Tree in Kasama.

Kalambo Falls Lodge
LODGE $$

(📞0973 248476, 0977 430894; www.kalambolodge.com; all-inclusive per person US$70) While it doesn't have a white sandy beach, Kalambo Falls Lodge's waterfront location remains equally spectacular – whether enjoyed from the rooms or lazing on a sunbed. Run by a friendly Zambian-Danish couple, Victoria and Peter, rates include accommodation, activities, food and transfers, making it excellent value. The honeymoon suite in a stone chalet with clawfoot bath is a great option for couples.

Isanga Bay Lodge
RESORT, CAMPGROUND $$

(📞0973 472317; www.isangabay.com; camping US$15, r incl breakfast US$80-100) Lake Tanganyika's most popular all-round choice is this South African–managed resort fronted by a pure white sandy beach. Undoubtedly the best pick here are the beach-facing bungalows in magnificent thatched structures; however, it's also a popular spot to pitch a tent; campers can access the same facilities including its lovely restaurant.

Mpulungu

Resting at the foot of mighty Lake Tanganyika, Mpulungu is a crossroads between Eastern, Central and Southern Africa. As Zambia's only international port, it's the terminal for the ferry across the lake to Tanzania. It's also a busy commercial fishing port and several fisheries are based here, some of them exporting tropical fish to aquariums around the world. The streets are fairly lively and busy, especially at night, but there is no real reason to come here unless travelling to Nsumbu National Park, Ndole Bay, the lodges along Lake Tanganyika or northeast to Tanzania. Although it's always very hot, don't be tempted to swim in the lake in this area because there are a few crocs.

Long-distance buses link Mpulungu with Lusaka (ZMW180, 16 hours) via Kasama (ZMW50, three hours) and Mpika (ZMW110, six hours). Minibuses also depart from near the BP petrol station in Mpulungu for Mbala (ZMW15, 40 minutes).

The MV *Liemba*, a hulking ex-German warship, leaves from Mpulungu harbour every second Friday, arriving in Kigoma (Tanzania) on Sunday. Fares for foreigners travelling in 1st, 2nd and economy class are US$100, US$90 and US$70, respectively. Visas can be issued on the ferry and cost US$50 single-entry.

Nkupi Lodge LODGE $
(☑0977 455166; camping/dm ZMW60/75, rondavels with shared/private bathroom from ZMW150/300) The best place for independent travellers is this shady campsite and lodge, a short walk out of town near the lake. It has plenty of space for tents as well as a number of spacious rondavels. There's also a self-catering kitchen and a bar, or otherwise meals are available with plenty of notice. The friendly owners Charity and Dinesh can assist with onward transport to Tanzania.

Nsumbu National Park

Hugging the southern shores of Lake Tanganyika, little-visited **Nsumbu National Park** (Sumbu National Park; adult US$10; ⏱6am-6pm) is a beautiful 2020 sq km of hilly grassland and escarpment, interrupted by rivers and wetlands. Back in the 1970s, this was one of the leading national parks in Africa with the largest density of rhino on the continent, and Kasaba Bay was like the St Tropez of Zambia, with the jet set flying in from South Africa and beyond. Like other remote parks in Zambia, Nsumbu was virtually abandoned in the 1980s and 1990s and poaching seriously depleted wildlife stocks here; however, conditions have improved over the past decade. Poaching has come under control, and animal numbers have increased, in part thanks to a buffer zone created by two Game Management Areas that adjoin the park.

A government ferry chugs up and down the lake ($US5, seven hours), heading north to Nsumbu at 7.30am Monday to Friday. For more comfort, boat charters to Ndole Bay Lodge are US$350 to US$750 (two hours).

Driving here is also an option with a 4WD. The most direct route is along the paved Great North Rd passing Mpika and Kasama before reaching Mporokoso, from where it's rough dirt road for the remaining 135km to the beginning of the park at Mutundu Gate.

★**Ndole Bay Lodge** LODGE, CAMPGROUND $$
(☑088-2165 2077; www.ndolebaylodge.com; camping US$15, chalets with full board from US$100; 🛜🏊) Set on a pretty beach just outside Nsumbu National Park, this family-owned lodge has several spacious chalets dotted around the grounds, all made from natural local materials. The newest rooms are stunning and include beautiful furnishings and a huge attached bathroom with Balinese-style outdoor showers. There is also a campsite right under the trees on the sandy beach.

Kalambo Falls

At 221m in height **Kalambo Falls** (adult/child/car US$15/7/15, camping US$15) is twice as high as Victoria Falls, and the second-highest single-drop waterfall in Africa (the highest being Tugela Falls in South Africa). From spectacular viewpoints near the top of the falls, you can see the Kalambo River plummeting off a steep V-shaped cliff cut into the Rift Valley escarpment down into a deep valley, which then winds towards Lake Tanganyika.

Most people visit as a day trip from one of the lodges along Lake Tanganyika or Mbala, though there's a campsite (US$15 per person; bring food and drinking water) for those who want to stay overnight.

The best way for travellers without a car to get here is from Mpulungu. A thrice-weekly taxi boat service (ZMW25) stops at villages east of Mpulungu. It moves quite slowly and makes plenty of stops so just getting to the base of the falls can take all day. Avoid arriving in the dark as it's two to three hours' walk uphill to the viewpoint near the top of Kalambo Falls (and the campsite). It's also possible to hire a private boat from Mpulungu harbour, which will cost around US$150 for a return trip. Ask around at the market near the lake in Mpulungu.

Another alternative is to stay in one of the lakeshore lodges near the falls, from where you could hike to the falls or get them to arrange a boat trip.

THE COPPERBELT

While the Copperbelt Province is the industrial heartland of Zambia, there are a few interesting spots for tourists too. The most important is the Chimfunshi Wildlife Orphanage, one of the largest chimpanzee sanctuaries in the world. The Copperbelt's major towns – Kitwe, Ndola and Chingola – are nice spots for a break, with museums, comfortable hotels and some good restaurants.

The region is home to the country's lucrative copper-mining industry, which is once again prospering following a slump during the 1970s.

Kapiri Mposhi

This uninspiring transit town, about 200km north of Lusaka, is at the southern end of the Tazara railway from Dar es Salaam (Tanzania) and at the fork in the roads to Lusaka, the Copperbelt and northern Zambia.

There's only basic lodging available here, none of which is really recommendable, so it's not really a great town to hang around for the night.

Buses and minibuses from Lusaka (ZMW60, 2½ hours) leave regularly and are a quicker and more convenient option than the irregular local trains.

If disembarking the international train service (p614) from Dar es Salaam run by Tazara railway company, there's a passport check before exiting the station, then from outside the station there's a mad rush for buses to Lusaka and elsewhere. Thieves and pickpockets thrive in the crowds and confusion, so stay alert.

Ndola

Ndola, the capital of the Copperbelt Province (and third largest in Zambia), is a prosperous, sprawling city that makes a good spot to break up the journey or spend the night en route to the Chimfunshi Wildlife Orphanage (p604). Once you get off its main thoroughfare, and hit its genteel, well-tended residential streets, there is no real evidence of its industrial base. Interestingly it's only 10km from the border with the Democratic Republic of Congo.

Copperbelt Museum MUSEUM
(☑ 0212-617450; Buteko Ave; adult/child US$5/3; ☉ 8am-4.30pm) Definitely worth a visit, this museum starts upstairs with its cultural and ethnography galleries exhibiting artefacts used in witchcraft, personal ornaments, smoking and snuffing paraphernalia, and musical instruments such as talking drums. Downstairs it showcases the local mining industry with displays on its history, gemstones and the processing of copper.

🛏 Sleeping & Eating

★**Katuba Guesthouse** GUESTHOUSE $
(☑ 0212-671341, 0978 450245; www.katubaguesthouse.com; 4 Mwabombeni Rd; d incl breakfast ZMW350-450; ❈ ☜) Comfortable, clean and relaxed, this friendly guesthouse is within a secure residential compound in a well-heeled neighbourhood with jacaranda-lined streets. Rooms are spacious and come with fast wi-fi, cable TV and reliable hot water. Meals are available in the evening (ZMW50), along with cold beers, and there's a complimentary continental breakfast in the morning.

Savoy Hotel HOTEL $
(☑ 0212-611097; www.savoyhotel.co.zm; Buteko Ave; s/d incl breakfast ZMW350/400; ❈ @ ☒) It's a bit of a hulking concrete block from the outside and the 154 rooms add up to the largest hotel in the Copperbelt; however, inside the Savoy is upholding standards well – old-fashioned, true, but not without a certain charm.

Michelangelo ITALIAN $$
(☑ 0212-620325; 126 Broadway; pizzas from ZMW50, mains ZMW90-150; ☉ 7.30am-9.40pm Mon-Fri, 8am-2pm & 7-10pm Sat; ❈ ☜) Long regarded as one of Ndola's best restaurants, this Italian cafe-terrace under a designer awning does thin-crust pizzas, pastas and Western mains. Coffee, gelato or a homemade pastry round the meal off nicely. There is also a small boutique hotel (room from US$130) attached. On Sundays it is only open to hotel guests and local residents.

ℹ Getting There & Away

Ndola is located about 320km north of Lusaka, about a 4½-hour drive along a well-maintained but busy stretch of highway.

One of only three cities in Zambia to have an international airport, Ndola's airport has flights daily between Lusaka, South Africa, Ethiopia and Kenya. The airport is 3.5km south of the public bus station.

Ethiopian Airlines (☑ 0950 585343, 0211-236401; www.ethiopianairlines.com) Direct flights to Addis Ababa.

Kenya Airways (☑ 0212-620709; www.kenya-airways.com) Daily flights to Nairobi.

Proflight Zambia (☑ 0211-271032; www.proflight-zambia.com) Daily flights to Lusaka.

South African Airlink (☑ 0977 777224; www.saairlink.co.za) Offers daily flights to Johannesburg.

Long-distance buses depart from the stand next to the Broadway–Maina Soko roundabout and run to Lusaka (ZMW85, five hours), Kitwe (ZMW20, two hours) and Chingola (ZMW60, 2½ hours). Joldan is a recommended company. The gritty **public bus station** (Chimwemwe Rd) has frequent local chicken buses and minibuses to Kitwe (ZMW17, 45 minutes).

The **train station** (☑ 0212-617641; off President Ave Nth) is 700m north of the Copperbelt Museum, but trains to Lusaka (ZMW40, 12 hours, Monday and Friday) are infrequent and slow.

There are several international car-hire companies such as **Avis** (☑ 0212-620741) at the airport, as well as **Voyagers** (☑ 0212-621333; www.voyagerszambia.com/ndola.php; Arusha St; ⊙ 8am-1pm & 2-5pm Mon-Fri, 9am-noon Sat) travel agency, which can also help with car rental.

Kitwe

Zambia's second-largest city and the centre of the country's mining industry, Kitwe seems far larger than quiet Ndola. Business travellers (read mining consultants) stop here for the good selection of accommodation and eating places.

Kitwe is about 60km northwest of Ndola. The **public bus station** is situated 500m west of Independence Ave, and the **train station** (☑ 0212-223078) is at the southern end of Independence Ave. Frequent minibuses and buses run to Lusaka (ZMW90, five hours), Ndola (ZMW17, 45 minutes) and Chingola (ZMW17, 30 minutes).

Voyagers (☑ 0212-225056; www.voyagerszambia.com/kitwe.php; Enos Chomba Ave) is very helpful and can organise car hire and other travel arrangements.

Dazi Lodge　　　　　　　　　　LODGE $$
(☑ 0977 404132; dazilodge2002@yahoo.com; 17 Pamo Ave; r incl breakfast ZMW500-750; ⊙ restaurant 6am-midnight; ☒) It's a bit overpriced, especially as there's no air-con, but Dazi's en-suite rooms are sparkling clean. There's an appealingly kitsch bamboo bar on the lawn near the swimming pool, and a good restaurant, making it a decent place to hang out.

★ **Mukwa Lodge**　　　　　　　LODGE $$$
(☑ 0212-224266; www.mukwalodge.co.zm; 26 Mpezeni Ave; s/d incl breakfast ZMW895/1195; ❋ @ ⊛ ☒) This lodge has gorgeous stone-floor rooms that are beautifully furnished, and the bathrooms are as good as any in Zambia. It's a delightful place to stay that's well worth the indulgence. There are also suites across the road at its excellent restaurant, the Courtyard Cafe.

★ **Courtyard Cafe**　　　　INTERNATIONAL $$
(☑ 0212-224266; www.mukwalodge.co.zm; Mukwa Lodge, 26 Mpezeni Ave; mains ZMW55-70; ⊙ noon-2pm & 6-9pm; ⊛) A part of the boutique Mukwa Lodge, this attached restaurant is hands down Kitwe's best place to eat. Its menu is split between Portuguese and Indian, and both are authentic and exquisite. Its classy decor comprises flagstone floor, heavy wood furniture, French doors onto the garden, plenty of windows and exposed red brick.

Chingola

As the closest town to the Chimfunshi Wildlife Orphanage, Chingola sees its fair share of travellers stopping over for the night. And given it's essentially a huge mine with a settlement wrapped around it, all up it's a surprisingly pleasant and relaxed town. For sleeping, try **Hibiscus Guest House** (☑ 0967 513448, 0977 513448; www.hibiscusguesthouse.com; 33 Katutwa Rd; s/d incl breakfast ZMW350/400; ❋ @ ⊛ ☒) or **Emerald Lodge** (☑ 0963 893542; emeraldlodge.manager@emeraldlodgeconsort.com; cnr Consort Ave & Kabundi Rd; r incl full breakfast ZMW450-900; ❋ ⊛).

Chingola's bus station is in the centre of town. Frequent buses and minibuses (ZMW16, 30 minutes) run to the station from Kitwe, 50km to the southeast.

Chimfunshi Wildlife Orphanage

On a farm deep in the African bush, about 65km northwest of Chingola, is this impressive **chimpanzee sanctuary** (www.chimfunshi.de/en; day visit adult/child US$6/3; ⊙ 8am-4pm) that's undoubtedly the standout highlight in the Copperbelt region. Home to around 120 adult and young chimps, most have been rescued from poachers and traders in the neighbouring Democratic Republic of Congo or other parts of Africa. It's one of the largest sanctuaries of its kind in the world. This is not a natural wildlife experience, but it's still a unique and fascinating opportunity to observe the chimps as they feed, play and socialise.

You can overnight at self-catering cottages (www.chimfunshi.de/en; adult/child with shared bathroom US$30/15) or camp (☏0968 568830, 0212-311293; www.chimfunshi.de/en; camping US$15).

From Chingola, you'll need to make the slow, bumpy and incredibly dusty journey across the unsealed Chingola–Solwezi road (hopefully construction will be completed by 2017) for 50km or so until you see the Chimfunshi Wildlife Orphanage sign. From here it's a further 15km. All up count on a two-hour drive from Chingola.

Although most arrive using a private vehicle, you can catch public transport for most of the way here. Take any Solwezi-bound bus and ask to be dropped off at Muchinshi, near to the turnoff to the chimp orphanage, from where you'll need to have pre-arranged a pick up for the remainder of the 25km journey (ZMW100 per person); it's important to prearrange this as mobile phone coverage at the orphanage is poor.

UNDERSTAND ZAMBIA

Zambia Today

Politically speaking it's been a tumultuous few years for Zambia: since late 2014, it's had three presidents (including one who's died), two elections and an overall tense atmosphere characterised by disputed results, riots and violence.

After ruling for three years, President Sata passed away in late 2014 following a long, undisclosed illness, aged 77. He became the second president to die in office within six years, after Levy Mwanawasa passed away in 2008. His temporary replacement was vice president Guy Scott, a white Zambian, who took over the leadership for three months until scheduled elections in 2015; due to the Constitution, Scott wasn't able to run for presidency on the basis of his British parents not being born in Zambia.

In 2015 the defence minister Edgar Lungu was inaugurated as Zambia's sixth president. He won in a narrow victory with 48.4% of the vote, taking over leadership for the remaining one year of Sata's five-year term.

He defeated opposition leader Hakainde Hichilema (better known as HH), who denounced the election as fraudulent.

It was a process to repeat itself all over again a year later in the 2016 elections. This time round was marred by political violence, opposition arrests and alleged voting fraud. Lungu again emerged victorious with 50.35% of the vote to Hichilema's 47.67%. Once again there were widespread claims that the results were rigged, and the matter was taken to Zambia's Constitutional Court. The case was duly thrown out, and Lungu was sworn in for his five-year term on 13 September 2016.

The 59-year-old President Lungu faces challenges rising from a number of ongoing issues, namely tackling corruption, nationwide power cuts that continue to cripple the economy, wildlife poaching and the influence of Chinese investment in the mining, agriculture and manufacturing sectors.

History

The first of the 'modern' (still present today) ethnic groups of Zambia to arrive were the Tonga and Ila peoples (sometimes combined as the Tonga-Ila), who migrated from the Congo area in the late 15th century. By 1550 they had occupied the Zambezi Valley and plateau areas north of where Lake Kariba is now – and which is still their homeland today. Next to arrive were the Chewa. Between the 14th and 16th centuries they followed a long and circuitous route via Lakes Mweru, Tanganyika and Malawi before founding a powerful kingdom covering much of present-day eastern Zambia, as well as parts of Malawi and Mozambique. Today the Chewa are still the largest group in eastern Zambia.

The Bemba (most notably the ruling Ngandu clan) had migrated from Congo by crossing the Luapula River into northern Zambia by around 1700. Meanwhile, the Lamba people migrated to the area of the Copperbelt in about 1650. At around the same time, the related Lala settled in the region around Serenje.

In western Zambia, the Lozi people established a dynasty and the basis of a solid political entity that still exists. The Lozi's ancestors may have migrated from what is now Angola as early as AD 450.

Early 19th Century

In the early 19th century, the fearsome reputation of the newly powerful and highly disciplined warrior army under the command of Shaka Zulu in KawZulu Natal (South Africa) led to a domino effect as groups who lived in his path fled elsewhere and in turn displaced other groups. This included the Ngoni, who fled to Malawi and Zambia, as well as the Makololo who moved into southern Zambia, around the towns of Kalomo and Monze, and who were eventually forced further west into southwest Zambia, where they displaced more Tonga people.

Also around this time, the slave trade, which had existed for many centuries, increased considerably. Swahili-Arabs, who dominated the trade on the east coast of Africa, pushed into the interior; many people from Zambia were captured and taken across Lake Malawi and through Mozambique or Tanzania to be sold in the slave markets of Zanzibar.

The Colonial Era

David Livingstone, the Scottish explorer, journeyed through large swaths of Zambia, including the lower Zambezi, where he came upon a magnificent waterfall never before seen by a European, naming it Victoria Falls in homage to royalty back home. On a subsequent trip, Livingstone died while searching for the source of the Nile in northern Zambia. His heart was buried under a tree near the spot where he died, in Chief Chitambo's village, southeast of Lake Bangweulu.

In 1885 claims over African territory by European powers were settled at the Berlin Conference and the continent was split into colonies and spheres of influence – Britain claimed Rhodesia (Zambia and Zimbabwe) and Malawi.

This 'new' territory did not escape the notice of entrepreneur Cecil John Rhodes, who was already establishing mines and a vast business empire in South Africa. Rhodes' British South Africa Company (BSAC) laid claim to the area in the early 1890s and was backed by the British government in 1895 to help combat slavery and prevent further Portuguese expansion in the region.

Two separate territories were initially created – North-Western Rhodesia and North-Eastern Rhodesia – but these were combined in 1911 to become Northern Rhodesia. In 1907 Livingstone became the capital. At around the same time, vast deposits of copper were discovered in the area now called the Copperbelt.

In 1924 the colony was put under direct British control and in 1935 the capital was moved to Lusaka. To make them less dependent on colonial rule, settlers soon pushed for closer ties with Southern Rhodesia and Nyasaland (Malawi), but various interruptions (such as WWII) meant that the Federation of Rhodesia and Nyasaland did not come about until 1953.

Independence & Kaunda

In Zambia the United National Independence Party (UNIP) was founded in the late 1950s by Dr Kenneth Kaunda, who spoke out against the federation on the grounds that it promoted the rights of white settlers to the detriment of the indigenous African population. As other African countries gained independence, Zambian nationalists opposed colonial forces through civil disobedience and a small but decisive conflict called the Chachacha Rebellion.

Northern Rhodesia became independent a year after the federation was dissolved and changed its name to Zambia. While the British government had profited enormously from Northern Rhodesia, the colonialists chose to spend a large portion of this wealth on the development of Southern Rhodesia (now Zimbabwe).

After gaining independence, Zambia inherited a British-style multiparty political system. Kaunda, as leader of the majority UNIP, became the new republic's first president. The other main party was the African National Congress (ANC), led by Harry Nkumbula. But Kaunda disliked opposition. In one swift move during 1972, he disbanded the Zambian ANC, created the 'second republic', declared UNIP the sole legal party and made himself the only presidential candidate.

Consequently Kaunda remained in power for the next 27 years. His rule was based upon 'humanism' – his own mix of Marxism and traditional African values. The civil service was increased, and nearly all private businesses (including the copper mines) were nationalised. But corruption and mismanagement, exacerbated by a fall in world copper prices, doomed Zambia to become one of the poorest countries in the world by the end of the 1970s. The economy continued to flounder, and Zambia's trade routes to the coast through neighbouring countries (such as Zimbabwe and Mozambique) were closed in retaliation for Kaunda's support for several liberation movements in the region.

By the early 1980s Rhodesia gained independence (to become Zimbabwe), which allowed Kaunda to take his country off a war footing, and the Tazara railway to Dar es Salaam (Tanzania) was completed, giving Zambia unencumbered access to the coast. Yet the economy remained on the brink of collapse: foreign-exchange reserves were almost exhausted, serious shortages of food, fuel and other basic commodities were common, and unemployment and crime rates rose sharply.

In 1986 an attempt was made to diversify the economy and improve the country's balance of payments. Zambia received economic aid from the International Monetary Fund (IMF), but the IMF conditions were severe and included cutting basic food subsidies. Subsequent price rises led to country-wide riots in which many people lost their lives. Kaunda was forced to restore subsidies.

The winds of change blowing through Africa during the late 1980s, coupled with Zambia's disastrous domestic situation, meant that something had to give. Following another round of violent street protests against increased food prices in 1990, which quickly transformed into a general demand for the return of multiparty politics, Kaunda was forced to accede to public opinion.

He announced a snap referendum in late 1990 but, as protests grew more vocal, he was forced to legalise opposition parties and announce full presidential and parliamentary elections for October 1991. Not surprisingly, UNIP (and Kaunda) were resoundingly defeated by the Movement for Multiparty Democracy (MMD), led by Frederick Chiluba, a former trade-union leader. Kaunda stepped down without complaint, which may have saved Zambia from descending into anarchy.

The 1990s

President Chiluba moved quickly to encourage loans and investment from the IMF and World Bank. Exchange controls were liberalised to attract investors, particularly from South Africa, but tough austerity measures were also introduced. Once again food prices soared. The civil service was rationalised, state industries privatised or simply closed, and thousands of people lost their jobs.

By the mid-1990s the government's failure to bring about any perceptible improvements to the economy and the standard of living in Zambia allowed Kaunda to confidently re-enter the political arena. He attracted strong support and soon became the UNIP leader. Leading up to the 1996 elections, the MMD panicked and passed a law forbidding anyone with foreign parents to enter politics (Kaunda's parents were from Malawi). Despite intercessions from Western aid donors and world leaders like Nelson Mandela – not to mention accusations that Chiluba's parents were from the Democratic Republic of the Congo (Zaïre) – the law was not repealed. The UNIP withdrew all its candidates in protest and many voters boycotted the election. Consequently Chiluba and the MMD easily won, and the result was grudgingly accepted by most Zambians.

In the 21st Century

The political shenanigans continued unabated at the start of the new millennium: in mid-2001 vice-president Christon Tembo was expelled from parliament by Chiluba, so he formed an opposition party the Forum for Democratic Development (FDD). Later, Paul Tembo, a former MMD national secretary, joined the FDD but was assassinated the day before he was due to front a tribunal about alleged MMD corruption.

Chiluba was unable to run for a third presidential term in December 2001 (though he badly wanted to change the Constitution so he could). He anointed his former vice-president, Levy Mwanawasa, as his successor, but Mwanawasa only just beat a coalition of opposition parties known as the United Party for National Development (UPND). Again, allegations from international observers about the MMD rigging the results and buying votes fell on deaf ears. To Chiluba's horror, Mwanawasa stripped his predecessor of immunity from prosecution and proceeded to launch an anti-corruption drive, which targeted the former president. In August 2009, after a long-running trial, Chiluba was cleared of embezzling US$500,000 by Zambia's High Court. His wife, however, was not so lucky, having been given a jail term earlier in the year for receiving stolen funds while her husband was in office. In a separate case in 2007, the High Court in Britain ruled Chiluba and four of his aides conspired to rob Zambia of about US$46 million, but in Zambia he was acquitted of such charges in 2009. Only two years later he passed away from a heart attack, aged 68.

Although Zambia remains a poor country, its economy experienced strong growth in the early part of the 21st century with GDP growing at around 6%. However, the country is still very dependent on the world prices of its principal minerals (copper and cobalt).

As well as combating global markets, natural disasters have played a significant role in the country's fortunes. Although a bumper harvest was recorded in 2007, floods in 2008–09 were declared a national disaster and killed dozens of people – the Zambezi River, which flooded much of western Zambia, was said to be at its highest level in 60 years, and crops were severely affected.

In September 2011, Michael Sata, nicknamed 'King Cobra', and his party the Patriotic Front (PF) won national elections. The populist strain in Sata's policy was apparent by his decision to revalue the country's currency. Motivated more by symbolism than economics, it was a move that indicated a sincere focus on redirecting the country's wealth to the majority of Zambians who remained impoverished. He also announced a significant increase in the minimum wage in September 2012, and his administration encouraged Zambian participation and ownership in the tourism industry. However, his presidency was tainted by heavy-handed tactics to clamp down on political opposition. Sata passed away while still in power on 28 October 2014 after battling a long illness, plunging Zambia into a period of political uncertainty and leaving his successor with numerous political, economic and environmental challenges.

Way of Life

Zambia's population is made up of between 70 and 80 different ethnic groups (the final count varies according to your definition of ethnicity, but the Zambian government officially recognises 73 groups). Despite these numbers there is considerable homogeneity among the tribes of Zambia. This is partly due to a long history of people moving around the country, settling new areas or looking for work, and also because after independence President Kaunda fostered national unity, while still recognising the disparate languages and cultures. Intermar-

riage among the officially recognised groups is also common. Hence Zambia is justifiably proud of its relative lack of ethnic problems, and its official motto on the coat of arms reads: 'One Zambia, One Nation'.

The vast majority (99%) of Zambians are indigenous Africans. The final 1% are Zambian citizens of Indian or European origin (mostly involved in business, commerce, farming and the tourist industry). Many white and Asian families have lived here for generations – although race relations are still sometimes a little strained.

Environment

Landlocked Zambia is one of Africa's most eccentric legacies of colonialism. Shaped like a mangled butterfly, its borders don't correspond to any tribal or linguistic area. And Zambia is huge. At some 752,000 sq km, it's about the size of France, England and the Republic of Ireland combined.

Zambia is chock full of rivers. The Luangwa, the Kafue and the mighty Zambezi dominate western, southern and eastern Zambia, flowing through a beautiful mix of flood plains, forests and farmland. In the north, the main rivers are the Chambeshi and the Luapula, both sources of the Congo River. Northern Zambia has many smaller rivers, too, and the broken landscape helps create a stunning scenery of lakes, rapids and waterfalls.

Of course, Zambia's most famous waterfall is Victoria Falls, where the Zambezi River plunges over a mile-wide cliff before thundering down the long, zigzagging Batoka Gorge. The Zambezi flows into Lake Kariba, created by a dam but still one of the largest lakes in Africa. In northern Zambia is the even larger Lake Tanganyika – it's 675km long, the second deepest in the world, and holds roughly one-sixth of the earth's fresh water.

In the south and east, Zambia is cut by deep valleys, some of of which are branches of the Great Rift Valley. The Zambezi Valley is the largest, and defines the county's southern border, while the 700km-long Luangwa Valley is lined by the steep and spectacular Muchinga Escarpment.

Even the flats of Zambia can be stunning: the endless grassy Busanga Plains in Kafue National Park attract fantastic wildlife, while the Liuwa Plain – part of the even larger Upper Zambezi flood plain that makes up much of western Zambia – is home to Africa's second-largest wildebeest migration.

Some of Zambia's other geographical highlights include the breathtaking high, rolling grasslands of the Nyika Plateau, the seasonally flooded wetlands of the Kafue Flats, the teak forests of the Upper Zambezi, and the Kariba and Mpata Gorges on the Lower Zambezi.

Wildlife

Because of Zambia's diverse landscape, plentiful water supplies, and position between Eastern, Southern and Central Africa, the diversity of animal species is huge. The rivers, of course, support large populations of hippos (at around 40,000, the Zambezi River has Africa's highest population) and crocs, and the associated grasslands provide plenty of fodder for herds of zebras, impalas and pukus (an antelope common in Zambia, but not elsewhere). Although the tiger fish of the Zambezi are related to the South American piranha, there's no record of a human being attacked (however, they are attracted to blood in the water).

Huge herds of rare black lechwe live near Lake Bangweulu, and endemic Kafue lechwe settle in the area around the Kafue River. Kasanka National Park is one of the best places on the continent to see the rare, water-loving antelopes called sitatungas. South Luangwa and Lower Zambezi National Parks are good places to see tall and stunningly graceful giraffes, and Zambia has its own subspecies – Thornicroft's giraffe. South Luangwa has its very own subspecies of wildebeest, too – the light-coloured Cookson's wildebeest – but the best place to see these creatures is the Liuwa Plain, a remote grassland area in western Zambia where thousands converge every year for Africa's second-largest wildebeest migration.

These animals naturally attract predators, so most parks contain lions, leopards, hyenas (which you'll probably see) and cheetahs (which you probably won't). Wild dogs were once very rare but are now encountered more frequently. Elephants, another big drawcard, are also found in huge herds in South Luangwa, Lower Zambezi and some other national parks. Zambia's herds of black rhino were killed by poachers in the 1970s and '80s, but reintroduction programs have seen rhino transported to North Luangwa National Park.

Bird lovers will love Zambia, where about 750 species have been recorded. Twitchers used to the 'traditional' Southern African species listed in the *Roberts* and *Newman's* field guides will spend a lot of time identifying unusual species – especially in the north and west. Most notable are the endangered shoebill storks (found in the Bangweulu Wetlands); fish eagles (Zambia's national bird); and the endemic Chaplin's barbets (found mostly around Monze).

Here's one time when you might groan at biological diversity: there are 37 different species of tsetse flies in Kafue National Park. Chewing garlic cloves is said to help keep them away, but heavy-duty insect repellent containing DEET is more effective.

Plants

About 65% of Zambia, mainly plateau areas and escarpments, is covered in miombo woodland, which consists mainly of broadleaved deciduous trees, particularly various species of *Brachystegia* (another name for this type of vegetation is Brachystegia woodland). Some areas are thickly wooded, others are more open, but the trees never form a continuous canopy, allowing grass and other plants to grow between them.

In the drier, hotter valleys and best-known national parks like South Luangwa and Lower Zambezi, much of the vegetation is mopane woodland. Dominant trees are the species *Colophospermum mopane*, usually around 10m high. The baobab tree also grows here. Many legends and stories are associated with the striking and simultaneously grand and grotesque tree. One has it that the gods, upset over the baobabs haughty disdain for inferior-looking flora, thrust them back into the ground, roots upward, to teach them a lesson in humility. You'll see this landscape in Zambia's best-known national parks, Lower Zambezi and South Luangwa.

Zambia has some of the most extensive wetlands in Southern Africa. These include the Bangweulu Wetlands, along the southern and eastern shores of Lake Bangweulu; and the vast plains of the Kafue Flats downstream from Kafue National Park, which is dotted with seasonally flooded marshes, lagoons and oxbow lakes.

Most grassland in Zambia is low, flat and flooded for part of the year, with hardly a tree in sight. The largest flood-plain area is west of the Upper Zambezi – including

Liuwa Plain National Park – where thousands of square kilometres are inundated every year. Another is the Busanga Plains in Kafue National Park.

Along many of Zambia's rivers are riverine forests. Tourists will see a lot of this type of landscape as national park camps are often built on riverbanks, under the shade of huge trees such as ebony, winterthorn and the unmistakable 'sausage tree' (*Kigelia africana*).

Evergreen forest, the 'jungle' of Tarzan films, is found only in isolated pockets in northwest Zambia – a remnant of the larger forests over the border in Angola and the Democratic Republic of the Congo.

National Parks

Zambia boasts 20 national parks and reserves (and 34 Game Management Areas, or GMAs), and some 30% of the land is protected, but after decades of poaching, clearing and general bad management, many are just lines on the map that no longer protect (or even contain) much wildlife. However, some national parks accommodate extremely healthy stocks of wildlife and are among the best in Southern Africa. Privately funded conservation organisations have done much to rehabilitate the condition of some of these.

Admission fees to the parks vary. Each ticket is valid for 24 hours from the time you enter the park.

SURVIVAL GUIDE

❶ Directory A–Z

ACCOMMODATION

Zambia offers an excellent choice of accommodation options to cater for all budgets. National park safari lodges especially provide a memo-

> **❶ SLEEPING PRICE RANGES**
>
> The following price ranges refer to a double room with bathroom in high season (August to October), based on 'international rates'.
>
> **$** less than ZMW500 (US$50)
>
> **$$** ZMW500–1000 (US$50–100)
>
> **$$$** more than ZMW1000 (US$100)

> **BOOK YOUR STAY ONLINE**
>
> For more accommodation reviews by Lonely Planet authors, check out http://lonelyplanet.com/hotels/. You'll find independent reviews, as well as recommendations on the best places to stay. Best of all, you can book online.

rable stay. During shoulder season prices drop, and offer some good deals.

ACTIVITIES

Zambia offers an array of activities for the adventurous traveller. Livingstone (and Victoria Falls town in Zimbabwe) are hubs, with adrenaline-pumping options such as white-water rafting and bungee jumping. At the main national parks you can arrange wildlife drives and walks, though you might prefer to safari on water, canoeing downriver alongside basking hippos.

BUSINESS HOURS

Banks Weekdays from 8am to 3.30pm (or 5pm), and 8am to 11am (or noon) on Saturday.

Government offices From 8am or 9am to 4pm or 5pm weekdays, with a one-hour lunch break between noon and 2pm.

Post offices From 8am or 9am to 4pm or 4.30pm weekdays.

Restaurants Normally open for lunch between 11.30am and 2.30pm and dinner between 6pm and 10.30pm.

Shops Keep the same hours as government offices but also open Saturday.

Supermarkets Normally open from 8am to 8pm weekdays, and 8am to 6pm weekends; some open later at Lusaka's big shopping centres.

CHILDREN

Family-friendly destinations Livingstone, Lusaka, South Luangwa.

High chairs Available at many big-city restaurants.

Nappies Available in major cities, but not elsewhere.

Safaris Wildlife drives are fine, but under 12s aren't allowed on safari walks or canoe trips. Some high-end park lodges do not allow children under 12 years, while others have activities and facilities set up for kids, and offer lower child rates.

ELECTRICITY

Supply is 220V to 240V/50Hz and plugs are of the British three-prong variety.

EMBASSIES & CONSULATES

Most embassies or high commissions are located in Lusaka. The British High Commission looks after the interests of Aussies and Kiwis, as the nearest diplomatic missions for Australia and New Zealand are in Harare (Zimbabwe). Most consulates are open from 8.30am to 5pm Monday to Thursday and from 8.30am to 12.30pm Friday; visas are usually only dealt with in the mornings.

Botswanan High Commission (☑ 0211-250555; 5201 Pandit Nehru Rd; ☺8am-1pm & 2-4pm Mon-Fri)

British High Commission (☑ 0211-423200; www.ukinzambia.fco.gov.uk/en; 5210 Independence Ave; ☺8am-4.30pm Mon-Fri)

Canadian High Commission (☑ 0211-250833; 5119 United Nations Ave; ☺7.45am-5pm Mon-Thu, to 12.15pm Fri)

DRC Embassy (☑ 0211-235679; 1124 Parirenyetwa Rd; ☺8.30am-1pm & 2-4pm Mon-Thu, to noon Fri)

Dutch Embassy (☑ 0211-253819; Swedish Embassy, Haile Selassie Ave; ☺8am-1pm & 2-4pm Mon-Fri)

Finland Embassy (☑ 0211-251988; www.finland.org.zm; Haile Selassie Ave; ☺9am-noon & 2-4pm)

French Embassy (☑ 0977-110020; www.ambafrance-zm.org; 31F Leopards Hill Close; ☺8am 12.30pm & 2-6pm Mon-Thu, 8am-12.30pm Fri)

German Embassy (☑ 0211-250644; www.lusaka.diplo.de; 5219 Haile Selassie Ave; ☺9-11am Mon-Thu)

Irish Embassy (☑ 0211-291298; www.dfa.ie/irish-embassy/zambia; 6663 Katima Mulilo Rd; ☺8am-4.30pm Mon-Thu, to 12.30pm Fri)

Kenyan High Commission (☑ 0211-250722; 5207 United Nations Ave; ☺9am-12.30pm Mon-Fri)

Malawian High Commission (5202 Pandit Nehru Rd; ☺8.30am-noon Mon-Thu, to 11am Fri)

Mozambican Embassy (☑ 0211-220339; 9592 Kacha Rd, Northmead; ☺8am-1pm Mon-Fri)

Namibian High Commission (☑ 0211-260407; 30B Mutende Rd, Woodlands; ☺8am-1pm & 2-4pm Mon-Fri)

South African High Commission (☑ 0211-260999; 26D Cheetah Rd, Kabulonga; ☺8.30am-12.30pm Mon-Thu, to 12.30pm Fri)

Swedish Embassy (☑ 0211-251711; www.swedenabroad.se/lusaka; Haile Selassie Ave; ☺9am-noon & 2-4pm Mon-Fri)

Tanzanian High Commission (☑ 0211-253323; 5200 United Nations Ave; ☺8am-4pm, consular 9am-1pm Mon-Fri)

US Embassy (☑ 0211-357000; https://zm.usembassy.gov; Kabulonga Rd, Ibex Hill)

Zimbabwean High Commission (☑ 0211-254006; 11058 Haile Selassie Ave; ☺8.30am-noon Mon-Thu, to 11am Fri)

INTERNET ACCESS

Wi-fi is available in many lodges across the country, sometimes for a small fee. You can also get online through inexpensive pre-paid sim card internet data bundles; either MTN or Airtel are recommended. For 1GB expect to pay around US$10, which is valid for 30 days. You'll need to bring along your passport to the store to get it activated. Coverage for the most part is fast, but is poor to non-existent within the national parks.

Otherwise there are internet cafes in most large towns.

MONEY

The country's official currency is the Zambian kwacha (ZMW), but US dollars are also widely accepted. Most sizeable towns have ATMs that accept foreign cards. See p721 for exchange rates.

Cash & ATMs

You can obtain cash (kwacha) at ATMs accepting Visa or MasterCard such as Barclays Bank, Stanbic and Standard Chartered banks in the cities and larger towns. Be aware, however, that it's not unheard of for them to be down, so it's always wise to carry an emegerency wad of back-up cash.

In the cities and larger towns, you can also easily change cash (no commission; photo ID required) at branches of Barclays Bank, FNB, Standard Chartered Bank and Zanaco. We've received reports that many banks, including at least one at the airport, won't accept US dollars issued before 2006.

As of 1 January 2013 three zeros were removed from every bank note denomination and the unit of currency changed from ZK to ZMW; eg ZK90,000 is now ZMW90. Note the old currency is no longer accepted as legal tender.

Credit Cards

Some shops, restaurants and better hotels/lodges accept major credit cards. Visa is the most readily recognised, Mastercard less so and Amex even less again. A surcharge of 4% to 7% may be added to your bill if you pay with a credit card.

It's also worth noting that payment by credit card requires a PIN to authorise the transaction.

Moneychangers

The best currencies to take to Zambia (in order of preference) are US dollars, UK pounds, South African rand and euros; most neighbouring countries' currencies are worthless in Zambia, except at the relevant borders. The exception is Botswanan pula, which can be exchanged in Lusaka.

Tipping

Hotels The top-end lodges and camps often provide separate envelopes for staff and guides if guests should wish to tip.

ⓘ EATING PRICE RANGES

The following price ranges refer to a standard main course. Remember that this is a guide only and prices will be considerably more in many lodges and camps in national parks.

$ less than ZMW50 (US$5)

$$ ZMW50–100 (US$5–10)

$$$ more than ZMW100 (US$10)

Restaurants A 10% tip is hugely appreciated for good service, though if restaurants include a 10% service charge, an additional tip isn't required.

Safari Guides & Drivers Around US$5 to US$10 to the driver and guide per day is appropriate, with a higher amount if you're happy with their service, knowledge and guiding skills.

PUBLIC HOLIDAYS

During public holidays, most businesses and government offices are closed.

New Year's Day 1 January

Youth Day 2nd Monday in March

Easter March/April

Labour/Workers' Day 1 May

Africa (Freedom) Day 25 May

Heroes' Day 1st Monday in July

Unity Day 1st Tuesday in July

Farmers' Day 1st Monday in August

Independence Day 24 October

Christmas Day 25 December

SAFE TRAVEL

Zambia is generally very safe, but in the cities and tourist areas there's always a chance of being targeted by muggers or con artists. As always, you can reduce the risk considerably by being sensible.

➔ While civil strife continues in the Democratic Republic of the Congo, avoid areas along the Zambia–Congo border, especially around Lake Mweru.

➔ Due to electricity shortages, load-shedding is now a reality of daily life across the country; however, most tourist lodges will have a back-up generator.

➔ Tsteste flies are an incessant nuisance when driving in many national parks; where problematic, wind the windows up and apply DEET-containing insect repellent.

TELEPHONE

Every landline in Zambia uses the area code system; you only have to dial it if you are calling outside of your area code.

The international access code for dialling outside of Zambia is ☑ 00, followed by the relevant country code. If you're calling Zambia from another country, the country code is ☑ 260, but drop the initial zero of the area code.

Mobile Phones

MTN and Airtel are the most reliable mobile (cell) phone networks. If you own a GSM phone, you can buy a cheap SIM card without a problem (including at the Lusaka or Livingstone Airport). You'll need to bring along your passport to have it activated. You can then purchase credit in whatever denominations you need from the same company as your SIM; scratch cards range from ZMW1 to ZMW100. In Lusaka the best place to buy a cheap mobile phone is around Kalima Towers (corner of Chachacha and Katunjila Rds); a basic model will cost around ZMW80.

Numbers starting with 09 plus another two numbers, eg 0977, are mobile-phone numbers. Mobile-phone reception is getting better all the time; generally, it's very good in urban areas and surprisingly good in some rural parts of the country and patchy or non-existent in others. Don't count on any coverage inside the national parks.

TIME

Zambia is in the Central Africa time zone, which is two hours ahead of Greenwich Mean Time (GMT/UTC). There is no daylight saving.

TOURIST INFORMATION

The regional tourist office in Livingstone is worth visiting for specific enquiries, but the main office in Lusaka is generally of little use.

The official website of Zambia Tourism Agency (www.zambiatourism.com) is pretty useful, though be aware a lot of information is out of date.

VISAS

Visas are generally issued upon arrival.

Tourist visas are available at major borders, airports and ports, but it's important to note that you should have a Zambian visa before arrival if travelling by train or boat from Tanzania. A yellow fever certificate is not required, but it is often requested by immigration officials if you've come from a country with yellow fever.

All foreign visitors – other than Southern African Development Community (SADC) passport holders who are issued visas free of charge – pay US$50 for single entry (up to one month) and US$80 for double entry (up to three months; which is good if you plan on venturing into one of the bordering countries). Applications for multiple-entry visas (US$80) must be made in advance at a Zambian embassy or high commission. If staying less than 24 hours, for example if you are visiting Livingstone from Zimbabwe, you pay only US$20.

In December 2016 the KAZA visa was re-introduced, which allows most visitors to acquire a single 30-day visa (US$50) for both Zambia and Zimbabwe. As long as you remain within these two countries, you can cross the border multiple times (day trips to Botswana at Kazungula will not invalidate the visa). These visas are available at Livingstone and Lusaka airports, as well as at the Victoria Falls and Kazungula crossings.

Payment can be made in US dollars, and sometimes UK pounds. Other currencies such as euros, South African rand, Botswanan pula or Namibian dollars may be accepted at borders, but don't count on it.

Business visas can be obtained from Zambian diplomatic missions abroad, and application forms can be downloaded at www.zambiaimmigration.gov.zm.

VOLUNTEERING

There's a number of opportunities for those looking to volunteer in Zambia. While various international agencies offer roles in a number of fields, you can try the following places based in Zambia:

Chimfunshi Wildlife Orphanage (p604) Offers several roles managing day-to-day affairs at this chimpanzee refuge; get in touch with African Impact (www.africanimpact.com) which coordinates affairs here, as well as other volunteering options in Zambia.

Game Rangers International (☑ 0973 086519, 0973 085358; www.wildzambia.org) This wildlife NGO offers a range of different opportunities through its volunteer program; check its website for upcoming placements.

Habitat for Humanity (☑ 0211-251087; www.habitatzambia.org) Helps to build houses for the nation's poor; over 2700 houses have been built since 1984.

Tikondane Community Centre (p578) A wonderful grassroots organisation assisting with local communities; it accepts volunteers to help out with anything from teaching, agriculture and permaculture to health care. There's a minimum of two weeks and it costs ZMW2000 per week, inclusive of meals and accommodation. It's based in Katate in eastern Zambia, located between Lusaka and South Luangwa National Park.

❶ Getting There & Away

AIR

Given there are very few direct flights into Zambia from outside Africa, many international visitors are likely to transfer to connecting flights in either Johannesburg or Nairobi.

Airports & Airlines

Zambia's main international airport is in Lusaka. An increasing number of international airlines also fly to the airport at Livingstone (for Victoria Falls), and a lesser amount to Mfuwe (for South Luangwa National Park) and Ndola.

LAND

Zambia shares borders with eight countries, so there's a huge number of crossing points. Most are open daily from 6am to 6pm; the border closes at 8pm at Victoria Falls and at 7pm at Chirundu. Before you leave the Zambian side, ensure that you have enough currency of whatever country you're travelling to or South African rand to pay for your visa (if you require one).

If you are crossing borders in your own vehicle, you need a free Temporary Export Permit (TEP), which is obtained at the border – make sure to retain a copy of this form after it's stamped. Before crossing be sure to inform your rental car company in order to guarantee you have all the required documents in order. You'll likely need to purchase insurance, sometimes called COMESA. It can be bought either at the Zambian border crossings or just after you've gone through formalities on the other country's side (for Zimbabwe, it'll cost around ZMW150). For Zimbabwe you also need an Interpol Certificate (good for three months), which can be obtained from the police in Zambia, and a typed 'Permission to Drive' document, which basically states that the vehicle's owner knows you're driving the car.

You also need to request and complete a Temporary Import Permit (TIP), and of course pay for it. Retain the document and payment receipt for when re-entering Zambia.

Heading back into Zambia you might get hassled from Zambians trying to sell you insurance – you don't need this if you're in a Zambian-registered vehicle.

Note also that Zambia charges a carbon tax for non-Zambian registered vehicles; it's usually about ZMW200 per vehicle.

Botswana

Zambia and Botswana share what is probably the world's shortest international boundary: 750m across the Zambezi River at Kazungula. The pontoon ferry (ZMW2 for foot passengers and US$30 for vehicles) across the Zambezi is 65km west of Livingstone and 11km south of the main road between Livingstone and Sesheke. A bridge has long been in the plans to replace what is a fairly dodgy crossing. There are minibuses (ZMW35, one hour) here daily from Livingstone, departing from Nakatindi Rd in the morning.

A quicker and more comfortable (but more expensive) way to reach Botswana from Zambia is to cross from Livingstone to Victoria Falls (in

Zimbabwe), from where shuttle buses head to Kasane.

Buses to Gaborone, via Kasane and Francistown, leave several days a week from Lusaka.

Democratic Republic of the Congo (DRC, Zaïre)

This border is not for the faint hearted. DRC visas are only available to Zambian residents and this rule is strictly enforced unless you can get a letter of invitation from the Congolese government. The most convenient border to use connects Chingola in the Copperbelt with Lubumbashi in Katanga Province, via the border towns of Chililabombwe (Zambia) and Kasumbalesa (DRC). Crossing into the DRC can take a lot of time or money, so it is wise to hook up with some mining consultants or UN workers rather than venturing alone.

Malawi

Most foreigners use the border at Mchinji, 30km southeast of Chipata, because it's along the road between Lusaka and Lilongwe. One figure to keep in mind – it's only 287km from Mfuwe to Lilongwe. Note that visas into Malawi are free for most nationalities.

Further north is another border crossing at Nakonde. Going either way on public transport is extremely difficult; you really need your own wheels.

Mozambique

The main border is between Mlolo (Zambia) and fairly remote Cassacatiza (Mozambique), but most travellers choose to reach Mozambique through Malawi. There is no public transport between the two countries.

Namibia

The only border is at Sesheke (Zambia), on the northern and southern bank of the Zambezi, while the Namibian border is at Wenela near Katima Mulilo. There are bus services to Sesheke from Lusaka and Livingstone respectively; it's 200km west of the latter.

From the Namibian side, it's a 5km walk to Katima Mulilo, from where minibuses depart for other parts of Namibia. Alternatively, cross from Livingstone to Victoria Falls (in Zimbabwe) and travel onwards from there.

South Africa

There is no border between Zambia and South Africa, but several buses travel daily between Johannesburg and Lusaka via Harare and Masvingo in Zimbabwe. Make sure you have a Zimbabwean visa.

Tanzania

The main border by road, and the only crossing by train, is between Nakonde (Zambia) and Tunduma (Tanzania). Bus services run from Lusaka to Nakonde and on to Mbeya. Alternatively, walk across the border from Nakonde, and take a minibus from Tunduma to Mbeya in Tanzania. There is also a crossing at Kasesya, between Mbala and Sumbawanga (Tanzania). At time of research the road was in decent condition and there was daily public transport on both sides of the border.

Although travelling by bus to the Tanzanian border is quicker, the train is a better alternative.

The Tazara railway company usually runs two international trains per week in each direction between Kapiri Mposhi (207km north of Lusaka) and Dar es Salaam (Tanzania). The 'express train' with sleeping compartments leaves Kapiri Mposhi at approximately 4pm on Tuesdays (ZMW334, 42 hours). Kilimanjaro 'ordinary' service dearts 2pm on Fridays (ZMW278, 48 hours). Delays are frequent. A discount of 50% is possible with a student card.

Tickets are available on the spot at the New Kapiri Mposhi (Tazara) train station in Kapiri Mposhi and up to three days in advance from Tazara House in Lusaka. If there are no more seats left at the Lusaka office, don't despair because we've heard from travellers who easily bought tickets at Kapiri Mposhi, and upgraded from one class to another while on board.

It's prudent to get a Tanzanian visa in Lusaka (or elsewhere) before you board the train; at least contact the Tanzanian High Commission in Lusaka about getting a Tanzanian visa on the train or at the border. You can change money on the train, but take care because these guys are sharks.

SEA & LAKE

There is an international port at Mpulungu where you can get the MV *Liemba* ferry along Lake Tanganyika to/from Tanzania.

ⓘ Getting Around

AIR

The main domestic airports are at Lusaka, Livingstone, Ndola, Kitwe, Mfuwe, Kasama and Kalabo. Dozens of minor airstrips, most notably those in the Lower Zambezi National Park (Proflight flies here regularly), Kafue National Park and North Luangwa National Park, cater for chartered planes.

The departure tax for domestic flights is US$8. Proflight tickets include this tax in the price, but for other flights it must be paid at the airport.

Proflight is the only domestic airline offering regularly scheduled flights connecting Lusaka to Livingstone (for Victoria Falls), Lower Zambezi (Jeki and Royal airstrips), Mfuwe (for South Luangwa National Park), Ndola, Kasama and Solwezi. From 2017 they will commence a flight to Kalabo for Liuwa Plain National Park. Charter companies include Proflight, **Corporate Air** (☑ 0965 037434; http://corporateairlimited.

com; Chrismar Hotel, Los Angeles Blvd), **Ngwazi Air Charters** (☑0211-271196; www.ngwaziair charters.com), **Pro Charter** (☑0211-271099, 0974 250110; www.procharter-zambia.com) and **Royal Air Charters** (☑0969 783128; www. royalaircharters.com).

BUS & MINIBUS

Distances are long, buses are often slow and some (but not many these days) roads are badly potholed, so travelling around Zambia by bus and minibus can exhaust even the hardiest of travellers.

All main routes are served by ordinary public buses, which either run on a fill-up-and-go basis or have fixed departures (these are called 'time buses'). 'Express buses' are faster – often terrifyingly so – and stop less, but cost about 15% more. In addition, several private companies run comfortable European-style express buses along the major routes, eg between Lusaka and Livingstone, Lusaka and Chipata, and Lusaka and the Copperbelt region. These fares cost about 25% more than the ordinary bus fares and are well worth the extra kwacha. Tickets for these buses can often be bought the day before. There are also express buses zipping around the country.

A few general tips to keep in mind. Even on buses with air-conditioning – and it very often doesn't work – try to sit on the side of the bus opposite to the sun. Also avoid seats near the speakers, which can be turned up to unbearably high volume. Try to find a seat with a working seatbelt, and avoid bus travel at night.

Many routes are also served by minibuses, which only leave when full – so full that you might lose all feeling in one butt cheek. Fares can be more or less the same as ordinary buses. In remote areas the only public transport is often a truck or pickup.

CAR & MOTORCYCLE

If you're driving into Zambia in a rented or privately owned car or motorcycle, you will need a Carnet de Passage en Douane (CPD); if you don't have one, a free Customs Importation Permit will be issued to you at major borders instead. You'll also be charged a carbon tax if it's a non-Zambian registered vehicle, which just means a bit more paperwork and around ZMW200 at the border, depending on the size of your car.

Compulsory third-party insurance for Zambia is available at major borders (or the nearest large towns). It is strongly advised to carry insurance from your own country on top of your Zambian policy.

While it is certainly possible to get around Zambia by car or motorbike, many sealed roads are in bad condition and the dirt roads can range from shocking to impassable, particularly after the rains. If you haven't driven in Africa before,

this is not the best place to start; particularly when you throw in a herd of angry elephants into the equation. We strongly recommend that you hire a 4WD if driving anywhere outside Lusaka, and certainly if you're heading to any of the national parks or other wilderness areas. Wearing a seat belt in the front seat is compulsory.

Self-drivers should seriously consider purchasing the in-car GPS navigation system Tracks4Africa (www.tracks4africa.co.za), which even shows petrol stations.

Driving Licence

All tourists planning on driving a vehicle in Zambia can drive on their own country's licence for up to three months, so unless you're here long term, you won't need an international driver's licence.

Fuel & Spare Parts

Diesel costs around ZMW11 per litre and petrol ZMW13. Distances between towns with filling stations are great and fuel is not always available, so fill the tank at every opportunity and carry a filled jerry can or two as back-up.

It is advisable to carry at least one spare wheel. If you need spare parts, the easiest (and cheapest) vehicle parts to find are those of Toyota and Nissan.

Hire

Cars can be hired from international and Zambian-owned companies in Lusaka, Livingstone, Kitwe and Ndola. You'll find all the usual chain hire companies at the airport.

Other companies, such as Voyagers (p577), Renmark (p577), **Hemingways** (☑0213 323097; www.hemingwayszambia.com), **4x4 Hire Africa** (☑in South Africa 021-791 3904; www.4x4hire.co.za) and **Limo Car Hire** (☑0977 743145; www.limohire-zambia.com) rent out Toyota Hiluxes and old-school Land Rover vehicles, unequipped or fully decked out with everything you would need for a trip to the bush (including roof-top tents!); prices vary from US$120 to US$250 per day. The best thing about these companies is that vehicles come with unlimited kilometres and you can take them across borders; though read the fine print first.

Most companies insist that drivers be at least 25 years old and have held a licence for at least five years.

Road Conditions

The last few years have seen the conditions of Zambia's roads improve out of sight, with approximately 80% of the major roads tourists use being smooth, sealed tarmac. That said, when the roads are bad they're horrendous, and can involve slow, dusty crawls avoiding pothole after pothole.

ZAMBIA GETTING AROUND

Road Rules

→ Speed limits in and around cities are enforced, but on the open road buses and Land Cruisers fly at speeds of 140kph to 160kph (not advisable if you're behind the wheel!).

→ If you break down, you must place an orange triangle about 6m in front of and behind the vehicle.

→ At police checkposts (which are very common) smile, say good morning/afternoon, be very polite and take off your sunglasses. A little respect makes a huge difference to the way you'll be treated. Mostly you'll be met with a smile, perhaps asked curiously where you're from, and waved through without a problem.

HITCHING

As in any other part of the world, hitching is never entirely safe, and we don't recommend it. Travellers who hitch should understand that they are taking a small but potentially serious risk. Despite this general warning, hitching is a common way to get around Zambia. Some drivers, particularly expats, may offer you free lifts, but you should expect to pay for rides with local drivers (normally about the same as the bus fare, depending on the comfort of the vehicle). In such cases, agree on a price beforehand.

TAXI

Often the most convenient and comfortable way of getting around, especially in the cities. They have no meters, so rates are negotiable; be sure to settle on a price before departure.

TOURS

Tours and safaris around Zambia invariably focus on the national parks. Since many of these parks are hard to visit without a vehicle, joining a tour might be your only option anyway. Budget-priced operators run scheduled trips, or arrange things on the spot (with enough passengers), and can often be booked through a backpackers – try Lusaka Backpackers (p570) in Lusaka or Jollyboys Backpackers (p555) in Livingstone.

African View Safaris (☎ 0213-327271, 0979 374953; www.africanview.it; 10-day safaris from US$1650) This Livingstone-based Italian-run operator offers well-curated safaris across the country. It's also one of Zambia's best for those looking to attend traditional ceremonies or festivals. Motorbike tours were also soon to be on offer.

Barefoot Safaris (☎ in South Africa 073-462 9232; www.barefoot-safaris.com) South African–based operator offering safaris to South Luangwa National Park.

Norman Carr Safaris (☎ 0216-246025; www.normancarrsafaris.com) Zambia's original safari company covers all of South Luangwa, as well as an exclusive concession at Liuwa Plain National Park.

Remote Africa Safaris (☎ 0216-246185; www.remoteafrica.com) Offers remote safaris in South Luangwa National Park.

Robin Pope Safaris (☎ in Malawi 01-794491; www.robinpopesafaris.net) Specialises in walking safaris in South Luangwa.

TRAIN

The Tazara trains between Kapiri Mposhi and Dar es Salaam in Tanzania can also be used for travelling to and from northern Zambia. While the Lusaka–Kitwe service does stop at Kapiri Mposhi, the Lusaka–Kitwe and Tazara trains are not timed to connect with each other, and the domestic and international train terminals are 2km apart.

Zambia's only other railway services are the 'ordinary trains' between Lusaka and Kitwe, via Kapiri Mposhi and Ndola, and the 'express trains' between Lusaka and Livingstone.

Domestic trains are unreliable and ridiculously slow, so buses are always better. Conditions on domestic trains generally range from slightly dilapidated to ready-for-scrap. Most compartments have no lights or locks, so take a torch (flashlight) and something to secure the door at night.

Zimbabwe

☑ 263 / POP 13.1 MILLION

Includes ➡

Harare 619

Mana Pools
National Park 632

Mutare 633

Chimanimani 637

Great Zimbabwe 640

Bulawayo 643

Hwange National
Park 647

Best Places to Eat

➡ Amanzi (p623)

➡ Portuguese Recreation Club (p634)

➡ 26 on Park (p645)

➡ Bulawayo Club (p645)

Best Places to Sleep

➡ Camp Amalinda (p647)

➡ Jacana Gardens Guest Lodge (p621)

➡ Rhino Safari Camp (p631)

➡ Chilo Gorge Safari Lodge (p643)

➡ Heaven Lodge (p638)

Why Go?

While from afar Zimbabwe's plight doesn't paint a rosy picture, the reality is different on the ground for tourists – most insist it's hands down one of the safest, friendliest and most spectacular countries in Africa.

A journey here will take you through an attractive patchwork of landscapes, from highveld, balancing boulders and flaming msasa trees, to laidback towns, lush mountains and lifeblood rivers up north. Here you can spot the Big Five in its national parks, discover World Heritage–listed archaeological sites and stand in awe of one of the natural wonders of the world, Victoria Falls.

Along the way you'll receive a friendly welcome from locals, famous for their politeness and resilience in the face of hardship. After almost two decades of political ruin, violence and economic disaster, Zimbabweans continue to hold on to hope that a new dawn will soon rise upon this embattled nation.

When to Go
Harare

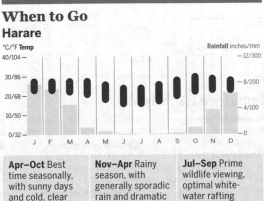

Apr–Oct Best time seasonally, with sunny days and cold, clear nights.

Nov–Apr Rainy season, with generally sporadic rain and dramatic afternoon electrical storms.

Jul–Sep Prime wildlife viewing, optimal white-water rafting and canoeing the Zambezi.

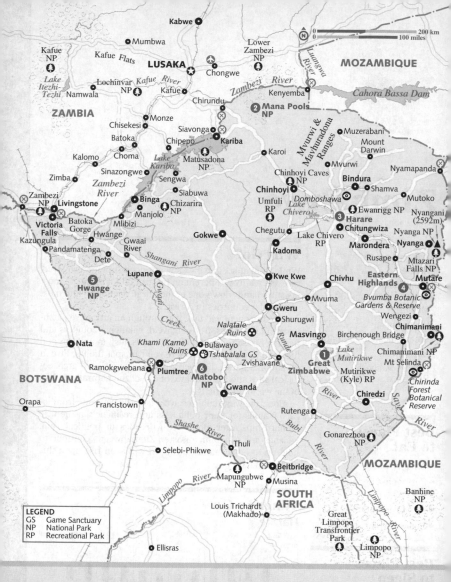

Zimbabwe Highlights

1 Great Zimbabwe (p641)
Exploring the atmospheric 11th-century stone ruins.

2 Mana Pools National Park (p632) Africa's only park (with lions) that allows unguided walking safaris.

3 Harare International Festival of the Arts (p621)

Shopping for crafts in the capital city and going to HIFA.

4 Eastern Highlands (p633) Exchanging arid highveld for cool, lush mountain air.

5 Hwange National Park (p647) Going on safari in Zimbabwe's largest national

park and home to Africa's biggest elephant population.

6 Matobo National Park (p646) Finding the spiritual heart of Zimbabwe, packed with balancing rocks and birdlife.

HARARE

🏷 04 / POP 1.5 MILLION

More attractive than most other Southern African capitals, Harare gets a bad rap and unjustly so. While it's certainly not without its problems, overall it's a safe and laid-back city where wide avenues are lined with dusty red earth, and indigenous plants and blooming jacarandas give it a lovely African summertime feel. While it's tempting to rush off to your safari, it's worth hanging around in Harare to sample its fine dining, museums, craft markets and varied bars.

◉ Sights

Harare has a good variety of sights that make it worthwhile to hang around for a few days. There are some fantastic art galleries, wildlife encounters and a few offbeat sights unique to the city.

★ National Gallery of Zimbabwe GALLERY
(Map p624; 📞 04-704666; www.nationalgallery. co.zw; cnr Julius Nyerere Way & Park Lane; US$1; ⊗ 9am-5pm Tue-Sun) In the southeast corner of **Harare Gardens** (Map p624) FREE, this lovely gallery has multiple spaces exhibiting a mix of contemporary local, African and international artists. Shows change monthly, with a mix of paintings, photography, stone sculptures, masks and carvings. The attached shop is an excellent place to stock up on crafts and books on Zimbabwean art, before coffee and cake in the cafe. There's an open-air Shona sculpture garden outside.

Delta Gallery GALLERY
(Map p620; 📞 04-792135; www.gallerydelta.com; 110 Livingstone Ave; ⊗ 8am-4.30pm Mon-Fri, to 2.30pm Sat) A must for contemporary art lovers is this gallery inside the charming colonial house of eminent Rhodesian painter Robert Paul (1906–79). It showcases wonderful works by contemporary Zimbabwean artists, with shows held monthly.

Wild is Life WILDLIFE RESERVE
(📞 0779 949821; www.wildislife.com; adult/teenager US$95/80; ⊗ 3.30-6.30pm) A wildlife sanctuary with a difference – sip on afternoon tea and champagne while getting a hands-on experience with the injured, rescued or orphaned animals here. Located near the airport (p627). You need to book well in advance and children under 12 are not permitted.

★ National Heroes' Acre MONUMENT
(Map p620; 📞 04-277965; 107 Rotten Row; adult/child museum US$10/5; ⊗ 8am-4.30pm) The grandiose obelisk of Heroes' Acre, overlooking the town, is straight out of Pyongyang, yet lies just 7km from Harare. Designed with the assistance of North Korea, it serves as a sombre memorial to the forces who died during the Second Chimurenga. There's a giant socialist-realism statue of the unknown soldier (actually three soldiers), flanked by bronze friezes depicting stirring war victories. Entrance is free, but there's an admission fee for the interesting museum dedicated to the resistance movement.

Tsoko Gallery GALLERY
(Map p620; 📞 0772 469099; Doon Estate, 5 Harrow Rd, Msasa; ⊗ 10am-4pm Mon-Fri, 9am-2pm Sat) FREE This quality art gallery focuses on mixed media and avant-garde works by cutting-edge Zimbabwean artists; it's in the Doon Estate (p625) complex. Its name translates to 'monkey' in Shona, a reference to the vervet monkeys that run amok in the area.

National Botanic Gardens GARDENS
(Map p620; Alexandra Park, 5th St; adult/child US$2/1; ⊗ 6am-6pm) If you thought Harare couldn't get any more relaxed, you clearly haven't visited its botanical gardens. Spread over 68 hectares, it's an extremely peaceful spot, showcasing 90% of the different ecological habitats found in Zimbabwe. However, it's suffering neglect from recent drought and lack of funding. A bicycle is the ideal way to get around; hire one from It's a Small World (p621). Its restaurant is a pleasant spot for lunch; otherwise pack a picnic to enjoy on the lawns.

Eastgate Centre ARCHITECTURE
(Map p624; Robert Mugabe Rd, btwn 2nd & 3rd sts) ⌀ Inspired by the ruins of Great Zimbabwe, the Eastgate Centre shopping complex is noteworthy for its sustainable design based on a termite mound, which allows for natural cooling and ventilation. Completed in 1996, it uses 10% of the energy of other buildings its size. It was designed by Harare architect Mick Pearce, who's worked on similar eco-buildings around the world.

National Archives of Zimbabwe MUSEUM
(Map p620; 📞 04-792741; www.archives.gov.zw; Ruth Taylor Rd; US$2; ⊗ 8.30am-4pm Mon-Fri) Founded in 1935, this building is the repository for the history of Rhodesia and modern Zimbabwe. It's worth a visit to see artefacts, photos, accounts of early explorers and settlers, and displays about the Second Chimurenga and pre-colonial Zimbabwe. There are original newspaper clippings from significant moments in history, oil paintings

ZIMBABWE HARARE

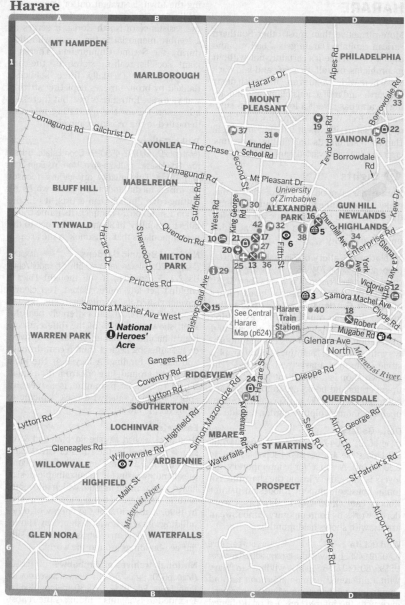

ZIMBABWE HARARE

and the first Union Jack flag raised in Harare (then known as Fort Salisbury) in 1890. To get here, take Churchill Ave off Borrowdale Rd, from where it's signed.

Mukuvisi Woodlands Environmental Centre WILDLIFE RESERVE (Map p620; ☎ 04-747111, 0774 198009; www. mukuvisiwoodland.co.zw; cnr Glenara Ave & Hillside Rd; adult/child US$4/3; ☺8am-5pm) Only 7km from the city, most of the 265 hectares here

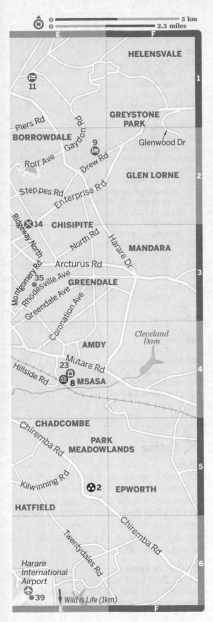

time to visit because you can cycle or walk about without a guide. Birdwatching is excellent ($20 for three hours). Note that there are some depressing animal enclosures.

Tobacco Floor NOTABLE BUILDING
(Map p620; ☑04-666801; www.timb.co.zw; Gleneagles Rd; ☺7.30am-1pm Mon-Fri Feb-Jul) Not quite the NY stock exchange but certainly fast paced. Get among the action on the floors where farmers on one side sell bales of tobacco to brokers on the other. Tobacco used to be one of Zimbabwe's major foreign-exchange earners and the country produced the best leaf in the world. Auctions only take place from around February to July.

🎭 Festivals & Events

**HIFA – Harare International
Festival of Arts** MUSIC
(☑04-300119; www.hifa.co.zw; ☺lateApr/early May) *The* annual event, held over six days, brings international acts to produce a crammed timetable alongside Zimbabwean artists. Performances include Afrobeat, funk, jazz, soul, opera, classical music, theatre and dance. If you're in the region, don't miss it.

🛏 Sleeping

**★It's a Small World
Backpackers Lodge** HOSTEL $
(Map p620; ☑04-335176; www.smallworldlodge. com; 25 Ridge Rd, Avondale; camping US$9, dm US$12, r US$45-65, r with shared bathroom $20-40; ❄️⊗✆) Single-handedly flying the flag for backpackers in Harare, this lodge does a wonderful job catering to the needs of independent travellers with clean rooms, fast and free wi-fi, a communal kitchen, pool table, rooftop deck and a sociable, low-key bar. Bikes are also available for hire (US$5 per day).

★Wavell House GUESTHOUSE $$
(Map p620; ☑04-495263, 0772 236626; www. wavell-house.com; 9 Wavell Rd, Highlands; r incl breakfast US$100-150; ❄️⊗✆) In an attractive renovated colonial house, refined Wavell House is very much an oasis with over a hectare of gardens and a luxurious swimming pool. Rooms vary in size, but are all comfortable, modern and with individual flair; they're excellent value given the rate includes an impressive breakfast spread. The owners are both well-regarded designers, and will make you feel welcome.

★Jacana Gardens Guest Lodge B&B $$
(Map p620; ☑0779 715297; www.jacana-gardens. com; 14 Jacana Dr, Borrowdale; s/d incl breakfast

are natural msasa parkland where zebras, giraffes and antelope species roam free. View from the platform (bring binoculars) or on foot with a safari guide (US$10), or go on a horse safari (adult/child $15/12) at 8.30am, 11am and 3pm. Sundays are a good

Harare

◎ Top Sights
1 National Heroes' Acre B4

◎ Sights
2 Chiremba Balancing Rocks E5
3 Delta Gallery D3
4 Mukuvisi Woodlands
   Environmental Centre D4
5 National Archives of Zimbabwe D3
6 National Botanic Gardens C3
7 Tobacco Floor B5
8 Tsoko Gallery E4

⊜ Sleeping
9 Amanzi Lodges E2
10 It's a Small World Backpackers
   Lodge C3
11 Jacana Gardens Guest Lodge E1
12 Wavel House D3

⊗ Eating
13 40 Cork Road C3
14 Amanzi E2
15 Bakers C4
16 Chang Thai D3
   Dzimbahwe .... (see 13)
17 Fishmonger C3
18 Garwe D4
   Shop Café @ Amanzi .... (see 14)

⊕ Drinking & Nightlife
19 Jam Tree D2
20 Pariah State C3

⊜ Shopping
21 Avondale Flea Market C3

Avondale Shopping Centre .... (see 21)
22 Book Bazaar D2
23 Chapungu Village E4
   Dendera Gallery .... (see 23)
   Doon Estate .... (see 23)
   KwaMambo .... (see 13)
24 Mbare Market C4

ⓘ Information
25 AMI Hospital C3
26 Australian Embassy D2
27 Botswanan Embassy C3
28 French Embassy D3
29 Gays & Lesbians of Zimbabwe C3
30 German Embassy C2
31 Inspiration of Zimbabwe C2
   Internet Cafe .... (see 21)
32 Malawian High Commission C3
33 Namibian Embassy D1
34 Netherlands Embassy D3
35 Nyati Travel E3
36 South African Embassy C3
37 UK Embassy C2
38 Zimbabwe Parks & Wildlife
   Central Reservations Office C3

ⓘ Transport
   Emirates .... (see 27)
39 Europcar E6
   FastJet .... (see 27)
40 Malawian Airlines D4
41 Mbare Musika Bus Terminal C4
42 South African Airways C3
   Zimbabwe Car Hire .... (see 39)

from US$95/130; ❄ 🛜 ≋) Harare does charming guesthouses as well as anywhere in the world, and Jacana is one of its best. The tasteful interior designed by the friendly Dutch owners incorporates Zimbabwean antiques and colourful local paintings. Renowned Zimbabwean architect Mick Pearce designed the award-winning house using the principles of feng shui – natural light pours into open spaces.

★ Amanzi Lodges
LODGE $$$

(Map p620; 🕾0772 367495, 04-499257; www.amanzi.co.zw; 1 Masasa Lane, Kambanji; s/d incl breakfast US$230/280, ste s/d US$280/330; ❄ 🛜 ≋) Set among a tropical, flower-filled garden, this is one of Harare's best choices, offering intimate and classy five-star service. Rooms are individually styled in themes from different African countries; it's worth having a look at a few on its website. There's a gym, pool, tennis court and complimentary coffee and evening snacks at the bar.

✗ Eating

Bakers
PORTUGUESE $

(Map p620; www.facebook.com/bakerschickens; 58 Denbeigh Rd, Belvedere; whole chicken US$7; ⏱10am-9pm Mon, Tue & Thu, 5-9pm Wed, 10am-10pm Fri & Sat) Basic no-frills joint in central Harare known for its delicious peri peri charcoal chicken. It also does steaks and burgers etc. It's 100% halal.

★ 40 Cork Road
CAFE $$

(Map p620; 🕾04-253585; 40 Cork Rd, Belgravia; breakfast/lunch from US$6/10, coffee US$3; ⏱8am-4pm Mon-Fri, to 3pm Sat; 🛜) An attractive house-turned-restaurant with a relaxed garden setting, 40 Cork serves quality breakfasts and lunches, and does one of the best coffees in Harare. Also here is its Tutti Gelati, serving excellent homemade gelato (US$2 a scoop), and the quality KwaMambo (p626) craft shop.

Pointe PORTUGUESE $$
(Map p624; ☑04-703095; 116 Baines Ave; mains from US$10; ⏰9am-10.30pm Sat-Thu, to late Fri) There's no shortage of authentic Portuguese restaurants in Harare, but the Pointe is one of the very best for peri peri charcoal meats. It's in a ramshackle building busy with regulars tucking into classic Portuguese dishes. Friday night (from 9pm) is karaoke time.

Garwe AFRICAN $$
(Map p620; ☑04-778992; bookings@garweres taurant.co.zw; 18637 Donald McDonald Rd, Eastlea; mains from US$5; ⏰11.30am-5pm; ☑) Highly recommended by locals, this restaurant has traditional Zimbabwean cuisine served under a thatched roof around a large roaring fire. Lunch draws a busy crowd filling up on *sadza* (maize-meal porridge) and other dishes, including goat and guinea fowl. Vegetarians are catered for with tasty leaf-vegetable dishes. It's about a US$5 cab ride from town. It can open for dinner if you book ahead, but otherwise it's lunch only.

Shop Café @ Amanzi CAFE $$
(Map p620; 158 Enterprise Rd, Highlands; buffet US$12; ⏰noon-2.30pm Tue-Fri; ☎☑) In a land of carnivores, this vegetarian cafe is a welcome peculiarity. It's moved from its original Doon Estate (p625) locale to set up shop within Amanzi restaurant. It remains as popular as ever for its lunchtime buffets.

Dzimbahwe AFRICAN $$
(Map p620; 72 Cork Rd, Belgravia; mains from US$9; ⏰noon-5pm; ☑) This attractive, relaxed garden restaurant is a good spot to sample traditional Zimbabwean cuisine. You'll get a choice of grilled meats (such as roadrunner chicken or T-bone steaks) to go with white or brown *sadza* (maize-meal porridge) and peanut sauce. Good options for vegetarians, too. It has a handy central location.

★ Amanzi FUSION $$$
(Map p620; ☑04-497768; www.amanzi.co.zw/res taurant.php; 158 Enterprise Rd, Highlands; mains $15-25; ⏰noon-2.30pm Tue-Sat, 6.30-10pm Mon-Sat) Don some nice threads as Amanzi is a class act and still *the* special night out. In a stunning colonial house with African decor, local art (for sale) and an amazing garden, it serves delicious international fusion dishes with a great vibe. The outdoor patio is atmospheric with a nearby garden waterfall and crackling fire brazier. Bookings essential.

Fishmonger SEAFOOD $$$
(Map p620; ☑04-308164; www.fishmonger.biz; 50 East Rd, Avondale; mains US$9-20; ⏰noon-9pm) This atmospheric seafood restaurant in a converted house with a Mediterranean-inspired decor is very popular with locals. The weekly specials are always worth a look, but otherwise expect the likes of grilled Kariba bream, Cajun blackened calamari or good ol' fish and chips, to enjoy indoors or on garden tables. Most of the seafood is imported from nearby Mozambique.

Chang Thai THAI $$$
(Map p620; ☑04-783054; 83 Churchill Ave; mains US$9-22; ⏰noon-3pm & 6-10pm Mon-Sat) With a Thai owner and chef team, it's no wonder this place has locals salivating – and perspiring – at the mention of its name. This is the real deal, with green, red and massaman curries all made from scratch with fresh ingredients; it's some of the most authentic Thai food you'll find outside Bangkok.

🍷 Drinking & Nightlife

Pariah State BAR
(Map p620; www.pariahstate.co.zw; 1 Hilary House, King George Rd, Avondale; beers US$2, cocktails from US$6; ⏰3.30pm-1am) Across the road from Avondale Shopping Centre (p626) is this cool little bar that attracts a mixed, friendly crowd of students and professionals. There's a good choice of drinks, including South African wines and beers. Things get lively Thursday and Friday nights with live bands, while Sundays have DJs playing reggae and hip hop. Also has a few other bars across town.

Jam Tree BEER GARDEN
(Map p620; ☑0778 173286; www.facebook.com/ thejamtreeharare; 40 Bargate Rd, Mt Pleasant; ⏰9am-midnight) One of Harare's current hot spots, the Jam Tree is all about its outdoor garden space, good choice of drinks (including bottled craft beers), tasty food and coffee, and live music. Check its Facebook page for upcoming events.

Jazz 24/7 BAR
(Map p624; www.facebook.com/jazz247zw; 105 Robson Manyika Ave; ⏰9am-3.30am Fri & Sat, to 11.30pm Sun-Thu) Taking over from the long-established Jazz 105, this city pub continues in the same vein with live bands and DJs playing Afro jazz nightly.

☆ Entertainment

Theatre in the Park PERFORMING ARTS
(Map p624; ☑8644 143016; www.theatreinthe park.co.zw; Harare Gardens; tickets from US$3; ⏰from 6pm Wed-Fri) This is a new space in Harare Gardens (p619) for this long-stand-

Central Harare

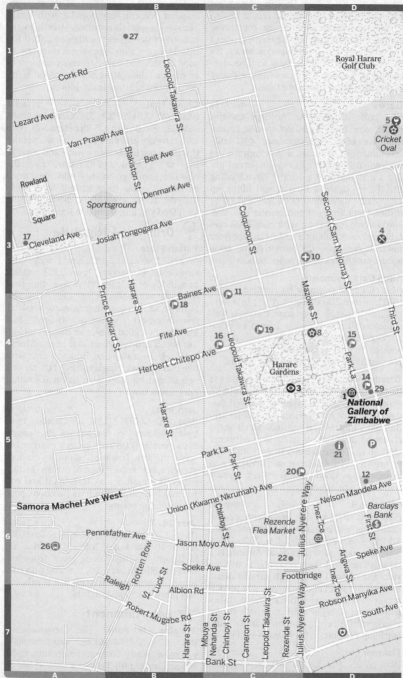

ZIMBABWE

Map labels:
- Royal Harare Golf Club
- Cork Rd
- Leopold Takawira St
- Lezard Ave
- Van Praagh Ave
- Blakiston St
- Beit Ave
- 5
- 7 Cricket Oval
- Denmark Ave
- Rowland Square
- Sportsground
- Colquhoun St
- 4
- 17 Cleveland Ave
- Josiah Tongogara Ave
- Second (Sam Nujoma) St
- 10
- Harare St
- Prince Edward St
- Baines Ave
- 11
- 18
- Mazowe St
- Third St
- Fife Ave
- 16
- 19
- 8
- 15 Park La
- Herbert Chitepo Ave
- Leopold Takawira St
- Harare Gardens
- 14
- 29
- 3
- 1 National Gallery of Zimbabwe
- Harare St
- Park La
- Park St
- 21
- P
- 20
- 12
- Samora Machel Ave West
- Union (Kwame Nkrumah) Ave
- Chinhoyi St
- Nelson Mandela Ave
- Barclays Bank
- Julius Nyerere Way
- Inez Tce
- First St
- 26
- Pennefather Ave
- Rezende Flea Market
- Speke Ave
- Jason Moyo Ave
- Rotten Row
- Luck St
- 22
- Angwa St
- Footbridge
- Raleigh St
- Speke Ave
- Albion Rd
- Inez Tce
- Robson Manyika Ave
- Robert Mugabe Rd
- Harare St
- Mbuya Nehanda St
- Chinhoyi St
- Cameron St
- Leopold Takawira St
- Rezende St
- Julius Nyerere Way
- South Ave
- Bank St

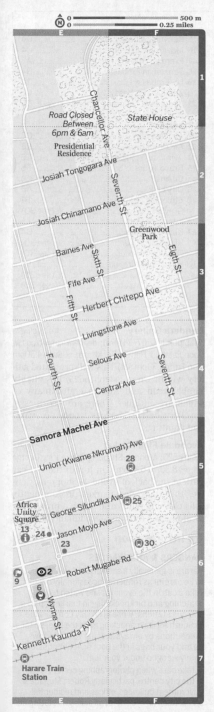

ing theatre company (on hiatus for four years). Plays are held on Wednesday, Thursday and Friday evenings from 6pm – it can be an interesting way to spend an evening. Check the website or its Facebook page for the schedule. In summer there's jazz on Sunday evenings.

Harare Sports Club CRICKET

(Map p624; www.zimcricket.org; cnr Fifth St & Josiah Tongogara Ave) With Zimbabwe regaining its status as a test-playing nation, cricket fans should try to make it to this scenic ground surrounded by jacaranda trees. There's a **pub** (Map p624; www.thecenturion. co.zw; Harare Sports Club, cnr Fifth St & Josiah Tongogara Ave; ⊗8am-late) right behind the bowler's arm, which enhances enjoyment when viewing domestic or international T20s, one-dayers or test matches. See the website for upcoming events.

🔒 Shopping

★ Patrick Mavros JEWELLERY

(📱0772 570533; www.patrickmavros.com; Haslemere Lane, Umwinsidale; ⊗8am-5pm Mon-Fri, to 1pm Sat) His clients may include Bruce Springsteen, Kate Middleton and the king of Spain, but Patrick Mavros' stunning handmade silver jewellery is very affordable. The shop has a spectacular setting, overlooking a picture-perfect valley with wildlife. All silver is from Zimbabwe and you can arrange a behind-the-scenes tour in the workshop.

Doon Estate ARTS & CRAFTS

(Map p620; www.facebook.com/doonestate; 1 Harrow Rd, Msasa; ⊗8am-5pm) A few kilometres east of town, Doon Estate is known for its galleries, cafes and souvenir shops. These days it's a shadow of its former self (many places have closed due to soaring rents), no longer the buzzing complex it once was. It's definitely still worth a visit – especially as it's an initiative that relies on tourists.

Chapungu Village ART

(Map p620; www.facebook.com/doonestate; Doon Estate, 1 Harrow Rd, Msasa; ⊗8am-5pm) Part of the Doon Estate complex, Chapungu has long been one of Harare's best places for Shona sculpture – one of the best things to buy in Zimbabwe. It comprises a collective of 16 artists, each with their own plot to sell their handiwork.

Kikis ARTS & CRAFTS, HOMEWARES

(📱0774 125363; www.kikisgallery.com; 34 Haslemere Lane, Umwinsidale; ⊗9am-5pm Mon-Fri, to 1pm Sat) Set in a homely showroom on a

ZIMBABWE HARARE

Central Harare

⊙ **Top Sights**
1 National Gallery of Zimbabwe............. D5

⊙ **Sights**
2 Eastgate Centre....................................E6
3 Harare Gardens.....................................C4

✪ **Eating**
4 Pointe... D3

◉ **Drinking & Nightlife**
5 Centurion.. D2
6 Jazz 24/7...E6

◉ **Entertainment**
7 Harare Sports Club.............................. D2
8 Theatre in the Park.............................. D4

ℹ **Information**
9 Angolan Embassy..................................E6
10 Avenues Clinic..................................... D3
11 Canadian Embassy................................C3
12 Department of Immigration Control D5
13 Harare Publicity Association.................E6
14 Japanese Embassy................................ D4

15 Kenyan Embassy...................................D4
16 Mozambican Embassy.........................C4
17 Premier Travel & Tours.........................A3
18 Tanzanian Embassy...............................B4
19 US Embassy..C4
20 Zambian Embassy..................................C5
21 Zimbabwe Tourism Authority..............D5

🚍 **Transport**
22 Air Namibia...C6
23 Air Zimbabwe...E6
24 Avis.. E6
25 Bravo Tours.. F5
Citiliner...(see 30)
26 City Link...A6
27 Ethiopian Airlines B1
Greyhound...(see 30)
28 Intercape Pathfinder............................ F5
29 Kenya Airways D4
King Lion ....(see 30)
Pioneer Coaches ....(see 30)
30 Road Port Terminal................................ F6
Tenda ....(see 30)
Zupco ....(see 30)

residential property, this Dutch-owned shop has an attractive range of furniture, art, hand-painted porcelain and Shona wooden stools, 90% of which is produced by local artists. It's located a few doors down from Patrick Mavros (p625).

KwaMambo ARTS & CRAFTS
(Map p620; 40 Cork Rd; ⊗8.30am-4pm Mon-Sat) One of Harare's best spots for crafts, hand-painted ceramics and original paintings by local artists, plus cool clothes and Zimbabwean publications.

Book Bazaar BOOKS
(Map p620; Shop 106, Sam Levy's Village, Borrowdale Rd; ⊗8am-5pm Mon-Fri, 8am-2pm Sat, 9am-1pm Sun) A small bookstore with a good collection of wildlife books, which are worth a look if you're going on safari. It also stocks a decent range of magazines and interesting braai (barbecue) cookbooks.

Mbare Market MARKET
(Map p620) Harare, sleepy? Not in the hectic Mbare area where this infamous market has a heady mix of fresh produce and random goods. It's the curios that bring most tourists here – there's a big collection of Shona sculpture, wooden crafts and basketry. It's in a poor part of town and pickpockets are rife, so leave your valuables at home – best come with a local.

Dendera Gallery ARTS & CRAFTS
(Map p620; ✆0772 114731; dendera@mweb.co.zw; Doon Estate, 1 Harrow Rd, Msasa; ⊗9am-4.30pm Mon-Fri, to 1.30pm Sat) This well-presented gallery within Doon Estate (p625) has quality Zimbabwean and African crafts, many of which are antiques. There are also masks, jewellery, baskets, textiles, wooden carvings and paintings.

Avondale Flea Market MARKET
(Map p620; Avondale Shopping Centre, King George Rd; ⊗8.30am-5.30pm) On top of the old car park at the back of Avondale Shopping Centre, this daily flea market predominantly sells clothing but is also worth a browse for local music, crafts and secondhand books.

ℹ Information

DANGERS & ANNOYANCES

Harare is generally a safe city, but you'll need to be careful as robberies occasionally occur. Take a cab in the evenings and watch for bag snatching and pickpocketing in markets, parks and bus stations. While in no way comparable to South Africa, carjacking is on the rise, so take precautions by always keeping your windows up and your bags in the boot or, if not possible, safely wedged under your feet.

Take care when photographing certain areas in the city centre, particularly Robert Mugabe's government buildings, offices and residential areas. Keep an eye out for street signs stating no photography and avoid snapping anywhere with armed soldiers. Take heed if you're asked to move along as it's not unheard of for tourists clutching cameras to be detained for questioning.

Police Stations
Police (Map p624; ☑ 995; cnr Inez Tce & Kenneth Kaunda Ave)

GAY & LESBIAN TRAVELLERS
Gays & Lesbians of Zimbabwe (Map p620; ☑ 04-740614, 04-741736; http://galz.org; Colenbrander Rd)

INTERNET ACCESS
The town centre, radiating out from First St, has many internet centres. All charge US$1 to US$2 per hour. However, there's free wi-fi internet access at most hotels, restaurants and cafes.

Internet Cafe (Map p620; Avondale Shopping Centre; ⊗ 8am-7pm) Reliable internet; located above Nando's.

MEDICAL SERVICES
Avenues Clinic (Map p624; ☑ 04-251180, 04-251199; www.avenuesclinic.co.zw; cnr Mazowe St & Baines Ave) Hospital recommended by expats.

AMI Hospital (Map p620; ☑ 04-700666; www.ami.co.zw; 15 Lanark Rd; ⊗ 24hr) Also recommended by expats.

MONEY
There were major cash shortages at the time of research, with lengthy waits for most ATMs. Banks accepting international cards include **Barclays** (Map p624; cnr 1st St & Jason Moyo Ave), Stanbic and Standard Chartered. Visa is the preferred card for ATM cash withdrawals, but MasterCard is becoming more common.

POST
Main Post Office (Map p624; ☑ 04-783583; www.zimpost.co.zw; cnr Inez Tce & Jason Moyo Ave; ⊗ 8.30am-4pm Mon-Fri, to 11.30am Sat) Stamp sales and poste-restante facilities are in the arcade, while the parcel office is downstairs.

TOURIST INFORMATION
Department of Immigration Control (Map p624; ☑ 04-791913; www.zimimmigration.gov. zw; 1st fl, Linquenda House, cnr Nelson Mandela Ave & First St; ⊗ 8am-4pm Mon-Fri) To extend your visa, contact this office.

Harare Publicity Association (Map p624; ☑ 04-705085; Africa Unity Sq, cnr Second St & Jason Moyo Ave; ⊗ 7.30am-4pm Mon-Fri, 8am-noon Sat) Supplies a free Harare city map and a few brochures.

Zimbabwe Parks & Wildlife Central Reservations Office (NPWZ; Map p620; ☑ 04-707625, 04-706077; www.zimparks.org; cnr Borrowdale Rd & Sandringham Dr; ⊗ 8am-4pm Mon-Fri) A good source of information and accommoda-

tion-booking assistance for those planning to head into the national parks.

Zimbabwe Tourism Authority (Map p624; ☑ 04-758712; www.zimbabwetourism.net; 55 Samora Machel Ave; ⊗ 8am-4.45pm Mon-Fri) Has a few brochures (but don't expect too much) and an excellent website.

TRAVEL AGENCIES
Experience Africa Safaris (☑ 04-790850; www.xafricasafaris.com) Books tours around Zim and Southern Africa.

Inspiration of Zimbabwe (Map p620; ☑ 04-369447; http://inspirationafrica.travel; Arundel Village, 50 Quorn Ave) Can tailor-make trips to all corners of Zimbabwe, from self-drive safaris to five-star journeys.

Nyati Travel (Map p620; ☑ 04-495804; www.nyati-travel.com; 29 Rhodesville Ave, Greendale) Experienced Dutch-owned company specialising in group and tailor-made tours.

Premier Travel & Tours (Map p624; ☑ 04-704781; www.premier.co.zw; 24 Cleveland Ave, Milton Park) Recommended travel agent.

ⓘ Getting There & Away

AIR
All international and domestic airlines use Harare International Airport (Map p620), located 15km southeast of the city centre. Taxis from the airport cost US$25 into town.

Air Zimbabwe (Map p624; ☑ 04-251836, at airport 04-575111; www.airzimbabwe.aero; cnr Speke Ave & Third St) operates flights to/from Bulawayo (one way/return US$176/342, 45 minutes) and Victoria Falls (one way/return US$215/421).

A more popular option these days to get to Victoria Falls is the low-cost carrier **FastJet** (Map p620; ☑ 086-7700 6061; www.fastjet. com; 9 Phillips Ave, Belgravia; ⊗ 8.30am-4pm Mon-Fri, to noon Sat), with flights starting from as little as US$25.

For international flights, **Emirates** (Map p620; ☑ 04-799999; www.emirates.com; 18 Wakefield Rd, Avondale; ⊗ 8am-4.30pm Mon-Fri, 8.30am-noon Sat), **South African Airways** (Map p620; ☑ 04-702702; 28 Downie Ave, Belgravia; ⊗ 8am-5pm Mon-Fri), FastJet, British Airways, Air Zimbabwe, **Ethiopian Airlines** (Map p624; ☑ 04-790705; www.ethiopianairlines.com; 5 Lezard Ave, Milton Park), **Malawian Airlines** (Map p620; ☑ 04-7043367; www.malawian-airlines.com; CFX Tours & Travel, 5 Londonderry Ave, Eastlea), **Kenya Airways** (Map p624; ☑ 04-731070; www.kenya-airways.com; 1st fl, Social Security Centre Bldg, cnr Julius Nyerere Way & Second St) and **Air Namibia** (Map p624; ☑ 04-751418; www.airnamibia.com.na; 2nd fl, Joina City, cnr Julius Nyerere Way & Jason Moyo Ave) all fly from Harare.

BUS
International

All bus companies servicing international destinations depart from **Road Port Terminal** (Map p624; cnr Robert Mugabe Rd & Fifth St).

Domestic

The best way of getting to/from Harare is via its growing fleet of luxury buses. **Intercape Pathfinder** (Map p624; ☑ 0778 888880; www.intercapepathfinder.com; Cresta Oasis Hotel, 124 Nelson Mandela Ave) is still by far the best company, servicing Bulawayo daily (US$20, six hours), as well as Hwange National Park (US$30, 10 hours) and Victoria Falls (US$35, 12 hours) on Wednesday, Friday and Sunday at 7.30am. Its ticket office is inside Cresta Oasis Hotel, and its buses depart from around the corner. **Bravo Tours** (Map p624; ☑ 0778 888777; www.bravotours.co.zw; 88 George Silundika Ave) and **City Link** (Map p624; ☑ 04-777168; www.citylinkcoaches.co.zw; Rainbow Towers Hotel, 1 Pennefather Ave) are other reputable bus operators, but their buses have varying standards – you may or may not get a seatbelt.

Otherwise you'll need to brave the chaotic **Mbare Musika bus terminal** (Map p620; Ardbennie Rd) for local 'chicken' buses such as **Tenda** (Map p624; ☑ 0772 106954; Road Port Terminal, cnr Robert Mugabe Rd & Fifth St). Be careful of pickpockets at this bus station. There are no schedules, and buses depart when full. Safety records for these buses are questionable, and they are rarely equipped with seatbelts.

The other option popular with intrepid travellers are combis (minibuses); these are inexpensive but they have a poor safety record and are simply not worth the risk.

TRAIN

The **train station** (www.nrz.co.zw; cnr Kenneth Kaunda Ave & Second St) has departures to Bulawayo (sleeper US$15, 11 hours) on Tuesdays, Fridays and Sundays at 8pm, and Mutare (US$7, 8½ hours) at 9.30pm on Wednesdays, Fridays and Sundays. Unfortunately, due to maintenance issues and constant delays, train travel from Harare simply isn't recommended.

ⓘ Getting Around

CAR

Zimbabwe Car Hire (Map p620; ☑ 0783 496253, 09-230306; www.zimbabwecarhire.com; Harare International Airport) gets good reviews for reliable, well-priced vehicle rental. Sedans start at around US$40 a day, and 4WDs from US$80 a day, with discounts for longer rentals. There's also **Avis** (Map p624; ☑ 04-796409; www.avis.co.zw; cnr Third St & Jason Moyo Ave) and **Europcar** (Map p620; ☑ 04-581411; www.europcar.co.zw; Harare International Airport). Mileage is usually around 150km per day, which makes it pricey once outside Harare.

At the time of writing, fuel was freely available at a cost of around US$1.30 per litre for petrol and US$1.20 per litre for diesel.

BUSES FROM HARARE

DESTINATION	COMPANY	FARE (US$)	SCHEDULE	TIME (HR)	TERMINAL
Bulawayo	Intercape Pathfinder	20	7.30am & 2pm	6	Intercape Pathfinder
Bulawayo	Bravo Tours	20-25	7am & 1.30pm	6	Bravo Tours
Bulawayo	City Link	25	7.30am & 2pm	6	Rainbow Towers Hotel
Vic Falls	Intercape Pathfinder	35	7.30am Wed, Fri, Sun	12	Intercape Pathfinder
Vic Falls	Bravo Tours	35	7.30am Wed, Fri, Sun	12	Mbare
Hwange National Park	Intercape Pathfinder	30	7.30am Wed, Fri, Sun	10	Intercape Pathfinder
Masvingo (for Great Zimbabwe)	Local buses & minibuses	8	from 6.30am to early afternoon	4½	Mbare
Mutare (for Eastern Highlands)	Local buses	8	times vary	4½	Mbare
Mutare (for Eastern Highlands)	combis	5-8	regularly	4	4th St Terminal; outside Road Port
Kariba	CAG	10	times vary	6½	Mbare

ROADTRIPPING FROM HARARE TO MUTARE

If you're looking for ideas for day trips from Harare, or are en route to the Eastern Highlands (a highly recommended part of the country), there are a number of very worthwhile options along, or just off, the main Harare–Mutare road.

Chiremba Balancing Rocks (Epworth; Map p620; adult/child with guided tour US$10/5; ☉6am-6pm) While boulders can be found in many places in Zimbabwe, these are probably the most famous, located 13km southeast of Harare, off Chiremba Rd. However, these days the site is a bit neglected and overgrown, and US$10 is steep for entry.

Surrey Pies (Harare–Mutare Rd; pies US$2) Well worth a pit stop en route to Mutare is this Marondera supermarket-bakery that does the best pies in Zimbabwe; go the steak and onion, and grab a bag of its prized biltong for the road.

Bushman Rock Safaris (✆0712-365392, 0734-968172; www.bushmanrock.co.zw; Sellair Rd; 3-course lunch incl wine tasting & game drive US$45, r per person incl half board & game drive US$90; ☉restaurant 10am-3pm) Part winery, part game reserve, part polo field and part boutique lodge: Bushman Rock has a number of faces. The vineyard was established in the 1930s by an Italian immigrant, and today it's one of the few vineyards remaining in what was once Zimbabwe's primary wine-growing region. Wine tasting ($10) is available with prior notice, as are three-course lunches where you taste the estate wines before going on a game drive. It's set on a 650-hectare property, home to wildlife, ancient rock art and horse riding, and is a 40-minute drive from Harare.

Imire: Rhino & Wildlife Conservation (✆2222094, 0772-522201; www.imire.co.zw; Wedza; day visit incl game drive & lunch adult/child US$60/40, walk with rhinos US$30) Located 70km from Marondera, just off the Mutare road (105km east of Harare), this animal sanctuary contributes enormously to the conservation of Zimbabwean wildlife. It's most renowned for its breeding and releasing of black rhinos into Matusadona National Park, as well as for providing orphan elephants and other animals a home/refuge. You can visit on a day trip to do a game drive, walk with the rhinos (both black and white species), go horse riding (per hour US$30) or participate in other activities. Overnight stays are also possible at its popular Sable Lodge. Enquire about its student volunteer program, which offers a range of hands-on activities.

TAXI

Zimbabwe's equivalent to Uber is **GTAXI** (✆8677 200200; www.gtaxi.net), a well-received taxi-booking app that will get you the best prices around Harare.

Taxis are best arranged through your hotel; try **Rixi Taxi** (✆04-753080). Count on around US$50 for day-hire touring of Harare.

NORTHERN ZIMBABWE

Home to some of the most scenic and wild-life-rich parts of the country, the major attraction in this region is the World Heritage–listed Mana Pools National Park (p632). Famous as the only park in Africa where tourists can wander about on foot *without* a guide, wildlife encounters here take on a whole new meaning. Another big lure is Matusadona National Park (p631), one of Zimbabwe's most scenic parks that's characterised by its stunning location overlooking Lake Kariba. As one of the world's largest artificial lakes, the area also serves as Zimbabwe's premier getaway destinations for locals, who flock here for fishing, beers and houseboats.

Kariba Town

✆061 / POP 27,500

This sprawling, sleepy lakeside settlement is spread out along the steep undulating shore of its namesake lake. There are lovely lake views and elephants often come through town. While self-equipped Zimbabwean and South African families flock here to socialise on houseboats and to fish, most foreign tourists are here for a stop en route to their next destination or just to chill out by the lake. It has a much warmer climate compared to other parts of Zimbabwe, so come prepared.

☉ Sights

Most sights in Kariba revolve around the lake and its dam. You have a decent chance to see wildlife, with elephants, zebras, hippos and crocs congregating around the lake.

Church of Santa Barbara   CHURCH

This circular, hilltop, Italian-built church was built in the memory of 86 African and Italian construction workers who lost their lives while building the dam. Of those, 17 bodies remain embedded in the dam wall after flash floods hit during the concreting. It's located on top of the hill (600m) at Kariba Heights, accessed by Heights Dr, off the road heading to the border. There's also an observation tower up here.

Kariba Dam Wall   LANDMARK

Forming the border between Zambia (Siavonga) and Zimbabwe is the Kariba dam wall. It's an impressive engineering feat that you can walk the length across; you'll need to leave your passport or ID with the immigration office. At the time of construction, it was the world's biggest dam and still today remains one of the largest.

Dam Observation Point   VIEWPOINT

FREE Head up to Observation Point for excellent sweeping views of the lake and Kariba Dam. The Kariba Publicity Association is based up here and houses interesting info on the history of the dam's construction. To get here, head towards the border near the dam and take a right at the petrol station.

🏃 Activities

Reel in one of the lake's famous residents, whether it be a tiger fish, Kariba bream or giant vundu. Warthogs Bush Camp can arrange half-/full-day fishing trips.

Natureways Safaris   CANOEING

(☑86-77000309, 0772-348565; www.natureways. com) Based in Kariba, Natureways are well regarded for their mobile tented-camp safaris, often combined with hiking or canoe trails. On the 'shoreline canoe trails', you get a fully licensed guide for safari walks inland and a team to go ahead and set up camp downriver each night – guests are generally flown in for these.

Marineland Harbour   BOATING

(☑0261-2146368;   www.marineland.co.zw; ⊙7.30am-5pm) One of Kariba's major recreational harbours arranges houseboats for hire (starting from US$250 for a minimum of two nights, excluding fuel) and can also supply food, transfers, tours and fishing equipment.

Rhino Rendezvous   BOATING

(☑0772-220831, 04-782809; www.houseboats onkariba.com) Well-established, reputable Kariba-based tour operator with a good variety of houseboats to rent.

🛏 Sleeping

Renting a houseboat allows you to have the whole of beautiful Lake Kariba to yourself while getting close to wildlife and enjoying stellar sunsets over cold drinks.

Most boats here are large vessels that come with a crew and sleep anywhere from 12 to 40 people, making them more suitable for larger groups. Boats cost from US$250 to US$2000. Get in touch with Marineland Harbour or Rhino Rendezvous for details.

★ Warthogs Bush Camp   LODGE $

(☑0775-068406; www.warthogs.co.zw; Kariba; campsite per person US$5, tented camps s/d US$10/15, lodges d US$40, 6-person chalet US$70; 🛜🌀) One of only a handful of places in Zimbabwe catering to the needs of independent budget travellers, Warthogs is doing a fantastic job of it. Accommodation is no-frills, with campsites, domed tents, A-frame huts and thatched cabins, all with piping hot wood-fired showers.

Hornbill Lodge   LODGE $$

(☑0772-348565; www.hornbilllodge.com; 797 Mica Point; r per person incl half board US$115; ❄🛜🌀) A prime spot with a commanding hilltop location, Hornbill has unique open-air design, thatched rondavels with lake views. It's set among landscaped gardens and a small plunge pool.

Caribbea Bay Hotel   RESORT $$$

(☑021-8550395; www.caribbeabayhotel.com; 425 Impala Dr; s/d incl breakfast US$130/170; ❄🛜🌀) While its pink Sardinia-inspired facade is in need of a coat of paint, all up this lakeside resort offers a decent place to stay, in a kitschy Afro-tropicana kinda way. All rooms have views, as does its pool and restaurants, while its nearby beach bar is the perfect spot to order a fruity rum-based cocktail with an umbrella in it.

ⓘ Getting There & Away

The CAG bus has daily departures to **Harare** (US$10, 6½ hours) with the first services from 8am, leaving from Nyamhunga, in Kariba's town centre.

Taxis are the best way to get to Zambia (Siavonga), 10km from Kariba. Expect to pay US$20 to US$25 for a taxi to take you all the way to the Zambia immigration point, including wait time at customs and the journey across the dam. Alternatively, you can get a taxi to the Zimbabwe immigration point for US$15 and make the long, sweaty trek across the dam.

Flying here is also an option for those wanting to charter a flight. Wilderness Air (p660), HAC

TENGENENGE ART COMMUNITY

While the surrounding hills in the Great Dyke region are scarred by years of heavy mining, there's a whole different kind of rock chipping going on at Tengenenge Art Community. Founded in 1966 by former tobacco farmer Tom Bloefield, this harmonious arts village has defied the odds to survive through the hard times and is now home to a population of 120 sculptors, representing three generations.

In a country famous for its sculpture, Tengenenge is the pick of the places to visit. It's a large open-air gallery where you'll meet and see the artists at work, several of whom have exhibited their works overseas. Each has their own plot of land where they both exhibit and work away using serpentine and spring stone, producing world-class, yet affordable, pieces.

Management of the village was in the process of being handed over to Harare's National Gallery, which will likely provide a boost in marketing profile and improve facilities.

Most visitors are day trippers, but it's worth staying overnight in the attractive and well-maintained traditional mud huts for a very off-the-beaten track feel. Visitors are also able to help out at Tengenenge's delightful preschool if they wish. Donations such as kids books and crayons are welcome.

The village is about 150km north of Harare and is around a two-hour drive. Getting here by public transport is more of a challenge, but it can be done. Catch a bus from Mbare station to Guruve (US$5), from where you can get dropped off at Ruyamuro. From here it's a 25km journey to Tengenenge and you have three options: prearrange a lift with the village's pick-up truck (US$5), arrange a taxi (US$20 to US$25) or hitch.

(p660) and **Altair Charters** (📞 0772-515852, 02-7923012; altair@tarazedcharters.com) fly here, among other companies. As of 2016, Air Zimbabwe suspended its scheduled flights to Kariba; double check, however, to see if flights have recommenced.

Matusadona National Park

On the southern shore of Lake Kariba, the beautiful **Matusadona National Park** (📞 0772-143506; www.zimparks.org; per person US$15) is home to the Big Five, including the endangered black rhino. While poaching has hit the park hard in the past decade, there remains an abundance of elephants, lions and outstanding birdwatching. Ghostly dead trees act as roosting places for fish eagles, cormorants and darters. The best time for wildlife viewing is between July and November.

🏃 Activities

You can safari in the area by houseboat, 4WD, canoe or on foot. These activities are included as part of the package offered by lodges. Remarkably the area is rich in dinosaur fossils; **Musango Safari Camp** (📞 0772-307875; www.musangosafaricamp.com) or Rhino Safari Camp can help arrange searches. Note it's illegal to take anything out of the national park.

🛏 Sleeping

Matusadona has some stunning places to stay, most of which look out to waterfront views rich in wildlife. As at Mana Pools, the only downside is the lack of budget accommodation. However, if you have a 4WD, camping at Tashinga campsite is an option.

Tashinga   CAMPGROUND $
(📞 04-706077; www.zimparks.org; campsite per person from US$17, lodge US$138) Run by Zimparks, this national park campsite offers only basic facilities but has a magnificent lakeside location. Accommodation comprises a few tent shelters, a braai stand, showers (including hot water), toilets and firewood; bring plenty of drinking water. There's also a self-catering lodge that sleeps nine. It's only really accessed by 4WD, as there's no boat landing.There's a lot of wildlife about, so take care. Book at the central office (p627) in Harare.

★ Rhino Safari Camp   LODGE $$$
(📞 0772-205000, 0772-400021; www.rhinosafari camp.com; Elephant Point; r per person US$195-340; 📶🐘) One of the best camps in the country, this is remote, wild and everything you want from a safari experience. Its simplicity in design is genius; it blends beautifully into its surrounds, with sandy paths and a rustic charm mixed with subtle luxuries. The thatched, stilted chalets have magnificent views and delightful outdoor bathrooms.

Changa Safari Camp
LODGE $$$

(☎ in Harare 04-498835; www.changasafaricamp.com; Matusadona National Park; per person incl full board & activities US$506; ☎✉) From the same owners as the Hide in Hwange National Park, this is a similarly classy but more rustic affair overlooking Lake Kariba. Its thatched, tented cottages have teak wood furniture and floors and outdoor bathtubs and showers. There's a lovely decking swimming pool and outdoor dining area. Plenty of wildlife passes through, including regular lion sightings.

ℹ️ Getting There & Away

The most common way to arrive to Matusadona is via a speedboat from Kariba (US$70 to US$300 return), which is more economical if you have a group. Depending what lodge you're staying at, the journey takes anywhere from 45 minutes to 1½ hours.

Many visitors fly in with chartered airlines, including Safari Logistics (p660) and Wilderness Air (p660), who offer routes from Harare or Victoria Falls for US$250 to US$290 per person.

Driving is another option, but only if you have a 4WD during the dry season; it's around a 10-hour journey from Harare.

Mana Pools National Park

This magnificent 2200-sq-km **national park** (☎ 63512, 63513; www.zimparks.org/index.php/parks-overview/national/mana-pools; adult/child US$20/15; ⊙ 6am-6pm) is a Unesco World Heritage–listed site and its magic stems from its remoteness and pervading sense of the wild and natural. This is one park in Zimbabwe where you're guaranteed plenty of close encounters with hippos, crocs, zebras and elephants and are *almost* guaranteed to see lions and possibly wild dogs, leopards and cheetahs.

What sets Mana Pools apart from just about any other park in the world is that you're allowed to walk around on foot without a guide. For first-time visitors it's hard to fathom how such an arrangement is possible, especially given the prevalence of roaming wildlife. While incidents are rare, be aware this is about personal responsibility: wild animals are incredibly dangerous – and fast. Walking with a guide is still highly advised.

Game drives and walking safaris (per person, per hour US$30) are the most popular activity in the park. Note you to need to pay a permit (US$15) if you are going to walk without a guide. Canoeing on the Zambezi River provides a breathtaking (read: heart in mouth) experience.

Accommodation options in Mana Pools are limited to either exorbitant all-inclusive luxury lodges or the park lodges and campsites – the latter books out months in advance. Hence it's not the easiest place for independent travellers on a budget. Note that visiting outside the peak season can bring healthy discounts.

Mana Pools National Park is only accessible via 4WD, so it's limited to self-drivers or those on all-inclusive packages. For those self-driving, take note there's no petrol in the park, so come well prepared; Karoi or Makuti are the closest petrol stations (however Makuti often only has diesel). Also be prepared that you need to register at the gate before 3pm. Wet season (November to April) is best avoided as dirt roads turn to sludge and no assisting car service is available. Note that the park mostly closes in the rainy season from January to March.

Charter flights are the other option to get here and popular among many visitors. with Safari Logistics (p660), Wilderness Air (p660) or Altair Charters (p631).

National Parks Camping & Lodges
CAMPGROUND $$

(☎ 706077; www.zimparks.org; campsites US$70, lodges from US$100) The only semibudget option in Mana Pools are these well-equipped lodges and campsites along the Zambezi River at Nyamepi, which offer prime animal viewing. Campsites are inclusive for six people, so it's not great value unless you're in a group (otherwise you can pay per-person rates on arrival).

★ Ruckomechi
TENTED CAMP $$$

(☎ 0772-247155, 43371; www.wilderness-safaris.com/camps/ruckomechi-camp; per person US$995; ⊙ closed mid-Nov–Apr; ✉) One of Mana's best luxury camps, Ruckomechi has a remote location on its private concession in the northwest of the park. All of its tented chalets overlook the Zambezi and beyond to Zambia and the mountainous backdrop.

Kanga Bush Camp
TENTED CAMP $$$

(☎ 09-234307; www.africanbushcamps.com; s/d incl full board & activities US$885/1368; ✉) A very private, permanent but seasonal camp (closed mid-November to April), Kanga Bush Camp's luxury en suite tents are built around the Kanga pan, the only permanent water source in its area. It heaves with wildlife and good predator sightings. It also has its riverfront Zambezi Expeditions lodge, which is a popular option for guests staying on a multinight package.

Mavuradonha Wilderness

📍 091

Little known to many visitors, Mavuradonha is home to some of Zimbabwe's most pristine wilderness, a blend of grey granite with the red serpentine soils of Zimbabwe's Great Dyke Complex. It's the escarpment of the Zambezi Valley, where valleys bisect towering rock faces and grass-covered mountains.

The wilderness area is funded by the Campfire project, which supports local rural communities. A significant portion of its revenue is generated by hunting concessions in the region, a contentious topic that divides conservationists.

Those looking to get deep into the true wilderness should consider the horseback safaris run by **Varden Safaris** (📞0772-908720, 04-861766; www.vardensafaris.com; all-inclusive horseback safaris US$290). Trips run anywhere from weekend journeys to week-long adventures, where you stay in rustic bush camps and eat fresh bush cuisine.

To get to Wildnerness Eco Lodge from Harare, jump on a bus from Mbarae that heads to Muzarabani (US$10, three hours) and ask to be dropped off at the lodge.

Wilderness Eco Lodge　　　　LODGE $
(📞0776-986381, 04-335176; http://smallworld lodge.com/mavuradonha; camping US$9, s/d US$30/35) This lodge run by the team from Small World (p621) backpackers in Harare. It makes for a good rural retreat, off the beaten track in an area famed for its wilderness. Rooms are in simple chalets; there's a self-catering kitchen or staff can arrange basic meals.

EASTERN HIGHLANDS

This narrow strip of mountain country that makes up Manicaland province isn't the Africa that normally crops up in armchair travellers' fantasies. The Eastern Highlands more resembles Great Britain, with verdant hills cloaked in mists, and pine forests and botanical gardens taking the place of the usual arid landscapes and game plains. It's where well-heeled Harare residents used to head away to their weekend holiday homes to fish for trout and sit by the fireplace in between meanders into the countryside.

The region has always had huge tourism potential; during the 1990s it was a backpacker hub, but these days it only gets a fraction of the visitors it deserves. Come to hike in its spectacular national parks – it offers easily the best walks in the country, taking you past tranquil rivers, waterfalls and stunning vistas overlooking Mozambique.

Mutare

📍 020 / POP 262,124

Zimbabwe's fourth largest city, Mutare has a relaxed rural-town atmosphere. It's set in a pretty valley surrounded by hills. There are a few things to see in town, but its real value lies in its proximity to Mozambique, the Bvumba region and Nyanga National Park. It's a nice enough place to break up your trip.

◎ Sights

Cecil Kop Wildlife &
Nature Reserve　　　　WILDLIFE RESERVE
(📞0774 135354; www.cecilkopfriends.com; US$5; ⊙7am-6pm) Only 2km from Mutare, this low-key nature reserve is definitely worth a visit if you're hanging around town. Set over 1500 hectares, it's home to elephants, giraffes, zebras, a variety of antelope and monkeys. A snake park is also planned. There's a good diversity of habitat ranging from forested areas and grasslands to gullies.

Mutare Museum　　　　MUSEUM
(📞020-63630; www.nmmz.co.zw; Aerodrome Rd; adult/child US$10/5; ⊙9am-5pm) Definitely worth popping your head in to see what exhibit is showing at the time. The museum also has a permanent collection of vintage cars, artefacts and displays on anthropology and zoology.

⌁ Sleeping

⭐**Ann Bruce Backpackers**　　　　HOSTEL $
(📞0772 249089, 020-63569; annbruce@zol.co.zw; cnr Fourth St & Sixth Ave; dm US$15, r US$30, r with shared bathroom US$25; 📶) Homely and welcoming, this long-established guesthouse has been catering to budget travellers for years. It's run by the friendly owner Ann Bruce, along with Emma and her extended family, which gives the place a wonderful homestay atmosphere. There's a cosy TV lounge, kitchen for self-caterers, garden gazebo and a mix of dorms and private rooms, but only some have bathrooms.

Gordon's　　　　B&B $$$
(📞020-67200, 0712 231772; www.innsofzimbabwe. co.zw; 125 First St; s/d incl breakfast US$100/160; ❋@📶) Opening its doors in late 2016, this upmarket B&B is run by Gordon Adams, a local identity long involved in the tourist

Mutare

industry. As an experienced hotelier, he knows exactly what makes a place run well. The B&B has comfortable rooms that will suit business travellers and tourists alike, with air-con, wi-fi, filter coffee and TV.

✘ Eating

★ Portuguese Recreation Club   PORTUGUESE $$
(☑020-61518; 5 Hosgood Ave; chicken & chips US$10; ⊙12.45-3pm & 6.30-9pm Tue-Sat, 12.45-3pm Sun) Given this old-school club was set up for the local Portuguese/Mozambique community (with an honor board dating

to the 1950s), it's not surprising the peri peri chicken here is as good as you'll get anywhere. It has an atmospheric front bar, and busy dining area around the back with gingham tablecloths. It's down an industrial street off Simon Mazorodze Rd.

Cafe 1 Eleven   CAFE $$
(☑020-62255; 111 Second St; meals US$6-16; ⊙8am-5pm Mon-Fri, to 9pm Sat) With its inviting open-air deck and outdoor garden, this is a nice place to while away a morning or afternoon with Eastern Highlands coffee, sandwiches, T-bone steaks and other classic Zimbabwean fare.

Mutare

⊙ **Sights**
  1 Mutare Museum B2

🛏 **Sleeping**
  2 Ann Bruce Backpackers D2
  3 Gordon's C2

🍴 **Eating**
  4 Cafe 1 Eleven D1
  5 Portuguese Recreation Club A3

🍷 **Drinking & Nightlife**
  6 Legion's Club B2

ℹ️ **Information**
  7 Barclays C3
  8 Manicaland Publicity Bureau C3
  9 Mozambique Consulate-General A3
  10 Stanbic B4
  11 Standard Chartered Bank C2

🚍 **Transport**
  12 Combis to Mozambique Border B4
    Taxi Stand .... (see 8)
  13 Town Bus Terminal B4

ℹ️ Information

There are a few internet cafes in town, but all lodges have wi-fi.

Barclays (90 Herbert Chitepo St)

Manicaland Publicity Bureau (☎020-64711; www.manicalandpublicity.co.zw; cnr Herbert Chitepo St & Robert Mugabe Rd; ⊙8.30am-12.45pm & 2-4pm Mon-Fri) Has basic tourist info available, but head to Ann Bruce Backpackers (p633) for up-to-date travel info.

Mozambique Consulate-General (☎020-61627; 11 Riverside Ave; ⊙8am-noon & 2-4pm Mon-Fri)

Police Station (Aerodrome Rd)

Stanbic (67 Herbert Chitepo St; ⊙8am-3pm Mon-Fri, to 11.30am Sat)

Standard Chartered Bank (7 Herbert Chitepo St; ⊙8am-3pm Mon-Fri, to 11.30am Sat)

ℹ️ Getting There & Away

Regular local and express buses head to Harare (US$7, four hours) from either the town bus terminal, long-distance bus terminal (Railway Ave) or central bus stand (Sakubva market, Masvingo Rd), 3km south of town. Tenda Bus is the most recommended, but it's essentially a chicken bus.

Regular combis (US$2) head to the Mozambique border (from 6am to 8pm), which is 8km from Mutare. A taxi will cost US$10.

To get to Bvumba, catch a combi (US$3) from the start of Bvumba Rd; they leave when full. Alternatively, Ann Bruce Backpackers (p633) offers a private transfer option and tour (US$40).

Bvumba Mountains

⚑ 020

Just 28km southeast of Mutare, the Bvumba (pronounced, and also often spelled, Vumba) Mountains are characterised by cool, forested highlands and misty valleys. In the language of the Manyika Shona people, Bvumba means 'drizzle' and you'll probably see why. With its meadows, apple orchards, country gardens and teahouses, the area seems akin to the British countryside. While it's beautiful year-round, things can get hazy during August when forest fires commonly burn in the hills.

Bvumba's picturesque green hills are a delight to discover on foot and offer good views; guides can be arranged through your accommodation. Birdwatching is another highlight; **Seldomseen** (☎020-68482; www.seldomseen.co.zw; Nyamheni Rd; per person per hour US$7.50) is the company to get in touch with. Playing golf at Leopard Rock (p636) is also a lovely way to spend time here.

Getting here from Mutare isn't an issue – combis and taxis (US$2 to US$3) depart when full – but getting back is trickier. Your lodge should be able to assist with arranging transport; otherwise a taxi is around US$15 to US$30 to Mutare.

Vumba Botanical Gardens & Reserve GARDENS (☎0717 576442; www.facebook.com/vumbabotanicalgardens; US$10; ⊙7am-5pm) Established in the 1940s, these botanical gardens comprise 64 hectares of indigenous and introduced plants. The lush grounds are a pleasant place to walk among streams, ponds and cycads, proteas and lillies. There's a campground here too.

★ **Hivu** GUESTHOUSE $ (☎0712 207828; http://visitvumba.com; campsite per person US$8, r per person US$15, cottage per person US$20-30) One of Bvumba's best budget traveller picks is this attractive country house (known as Hycroft Cottage) with homely rooms, a calm pastoral setting, picturesque campsite and kitchen for self-catering. There's horse riding (from US$12) and a shop for basic provisions. Rates increase slightly on weekends. Being on the main road it's easy to get transport to/from Mutare (shared taxi US$3).

★ **It's a Small World Lodge Vumba** GUESTHOUSE $ (☎0776 986381, 04-335176; www.smallworldlodge.com; Lot 1, Cloudlands Arusha Estate; camping per person US$8, dm US$12, d from US$40, cottages weekday/weekend US$50/90) This is an attractive guesthouse set in a colonial-style holiday home with an English garden and outlooks to the valley. It's currently undergoing a refurb, but rooms are large and comfy, and there's an inviting lounge with a roaring fireplace in the evenings. There's also a kitchen for self-caterers, and self-contained cottages up the hill.

Inn on the Vumba INN $$
(☑ 020-60722; www.innsofzimbabwe.co.zw/inns/vumba.html; Fernhill Rd; s/d incl breakfast US$60/80, 2-bedroom cottage from US$80; 🛜 🖵)
While only 8km from Mutare, this lodge offers the first glimpse of Bvumba's spectacular views. All the motel-style rooms here look out to a valley with Mozambique in the distance. Its restaurant-bar is one of the best in the Bvumba region with its cosy English B&B ambience.

Leopard Rock Hotel HOTEL $$$
(☑ 0772 100791; www.leopardrockhotel.com; Eggardon Rd; r with half board US$180; ❄ 🛜 🖵)
Once a favourite of English royalty (Room 7 in the turret wing is where Queen Elizabeth II stayed in 1953), Leopard Rock is still the poshest place in the region. Don't expect five-star luxury, however: the appeal is more about its faded colonial charm. There are lounges with fireplaces and an outdoor terrace overlooking the famous **golf course** (☑ 0772 100790; www.leopardrockhotel.com; Leopard Rock Hotel, Eggardon Rd; 9/18 holes US$25/40, club hire US$15/20; ◉ 8am-4pm).

Tony's Coffee Shop DESSERTS $$
(http://tonyscoffeeshop.weebly.com; Bvumba Rd; coffee from US$5, slice of cake US$9-12; ◉10am-5pm Wed-Sun) Yes, US$12 is outrageous for a slice of cake but Tony's can justify it. The white-chocolate cheesecake with edible flowers is divine; enjoy indoors by the fire or on the lawn looking out to orchards. Coffee comes from Chipinge in the Eastern Highlands (US$6 bottomless cup) and there's a selection of 130 different kinds of tea.

Terrace AFRICAN, INTERNATIONAL $$$
(☑ 0772 100791; www.leopardrockhotel.com/facilities/restaurant-bar; Leopard Rock Hotel, Eggardon Rd; mains US$7-22) There are a number of different restaurants, bars and lounges at the Leopard Rock Hotel, but the most scenic spot for lunch is the outdoor Terrace, which overlooks the golf course and grounds. It has international food such as sandwiches, pizza and steaks, as well as traditional Zimbabwean dishes.

Nyanga National Park
☑ 029

The 4700-sq-km **Nyanga National Park** (☑ 0773 500398, 029-8274; www.nyangapark.com; US$10; ◉ 6am-6pm) is a geographically and scenically distinct enclave in the Eastern Highlands. Nyanga is famous not for its wildlife (though it does have antelope and zebras) but rather for its verdant, mountainous scenery, pine forests, crystal-clear streams, and Zim's highest mountain and waterfall. It's also renowned for trout fly-fishing. The main gate is a few kilometres from Nyanga town, close to the Rhodes Nyanga Hotel.

◉ Sights

The flat-topped and myth-shrouded **Nyangani** (2592m) is Zimbabwe's highest mountain. From the car park 14km east of Nyanga Dam, the climb to the summit takes two to three hours. Note that the weather can change abruptly, and when the mists drop the view becomes irrelevant.

Ziwa Ruins ARCHAEOLOGICAL SITE
(adult/child US$10/5) These National Monument ruins of communities who specialised in pottery date to AD 200 and are one of Zimbabwe's more impressive archaeological sites. The terraced hills are from ensuing agricultural communities from the 1500s. There's a museum, along with relics from a fort, furnaces and pit enclosures.

Mtarazi Falls WATERFALL
This is Zim's highest waterfall. Falling from a height of 762m from an impressive escarpment, it trumps Victoria Falls by 300m and is number two in Africa. It's at its peak from February to May.

Rhodes Nyanga Historical Exhibition MUSEUM
(Rhodes Museum; http://ntoz.org/properties/rhodes-nyanga-historical-exhibition; Rhodes Nyanga Hotel; US$2; ◉ 8.30am-5.30pm Wed-Mon) The Nyanga Historical Exhibition is housed in Cecil Rhodes' (1853–1902) former stables in the grounds next door to the Rhodes Nyanga Hotel. It has a wonderful collection of his belongings, as well as some interesting exhibits on the local area, colonial history and stone age relics.

World's View VIEWPOINT
(adult/child US$2/1) A National Trust site, World's View is perched atop the Troutbeck Massif (2000m), with broad views of northern Zimbabwe. There's also a gallery showing

local artists. It's 11km up a winding, steep road from Troutbeck – follow the signposts.

🏃 Activities

Hiking is a big attraction for visitors to the park. While not on the same scale as Vic Falls, Nyanga does have an emerging outdoor adventure scene.

★ Far & Wide   OUTDOORS
(📞0772-469229; www.farandwide.co.zw; Juliasdale) Get the most out of your visit to Nyanga by visiting this outdoor adventure company, which specialises in white-water rafting (per person US$90; November to April), tubing, hiking, abseiling, trout fly fishing and spice-garden tours. It's on the main road in Juliasdale next to the petrol station. It can also arrange accommodation; visit the website for details. The team was also planning supposedly the world's highest zipline, so keep an eye out for that.

🛏 Sleeping & Eating

In keeping with its surrounds, Nyanga's accommodation comprises quaint, atmospheric ye-olde-English B&Bs, lodges and historic hotels. All can arrange local hikes and activities. Far & Wide can arrange a number of cottages and camping options.

Zimparks offers lodges and campsites at Rhodes Dam near the main gate, **Udu Dam** on the western side of the park, and **Mare Dam**, 10km from the main gate.

Pine Tree Inn   INN $$
(📞029-292388, 0776 835481; www.innsofzimbabwe.co.zw/inns/pinetree.html; s/d incl breakfast US$80/120; 🛜) Originally a farmhouse, this quaint English-style inn, in a garden surrounded by fragrant pine forest with a mountainous backdrop, is exactly the reason you should visit Nyanga. Most rooms have fireplaces, porches and claw-foot baths, carpet and flowery curtains. The highlights are its bar, with dark, polished wood and brass finishes, and the cosy reading room.

Inn on Rupurara   INN $$
(📞029-3021; www.innsofzimbabwe.co.zw/inns/rupurara.html; s/d incl breakfast & activities from US$100/135; ❄🛜🏊) A beautifully appointed African-style stone chalet with verandahs, overlooking the valley to Rupurara Mountain (or Bald Man's Head). On its property roam giraffes, zebras, elands and wildebeest, which you can see on a horse safari. There's also a lovely restaurant and wine bar. To get here you'll need a high-clearance vehicle.

Rhodes Nyanga Hotel   HOTEL $$
(📞0782 707837; www.rhodesnyangahotel.com; s/d incl breakfast from US$125/145, ste from US$165; ❄🛜) At the entrance to the national park is the former holiday home of Cecil Rhodes, converted into a hotel in 1933. It features tropical verandahs and English gardens overlooking the Nyanga Dam. There are rondavels as well as rooms, some that have furniture used by the man himself. His actual house is where the restaurant is now, and makes for a good spot for lunch (mains from US$9); it also has the cosy Anglers Inn pub.

National Park Lodge   CAMPGROUND $$
(📞04-707625; www.zimparks.org; campsite per person US$8, d from US$92) While there are three different Zimparks sites within Nyanga, the main lodge is at Rhodes Dam near the main gate, which has self-catering cottages and campsites.

ℹ Information

The **Nyanga Tourist Association** (📞0776 835481) is based at the Claremont Golf Course in Juliasdale, but there's no real information at hand. 'Things to Do in Nyanga' has a good Facebook page of listings in the area, along with upcoming events.

ℹ Getting There & Away

Inter Africa bus runs between Nyanga and Harare's Mbare bus station (US$8, 3½ hours).

Chimanimani
📞026 / POP 2752

Chimanimani, a logging town located 150km south of Mutare, is enclosed by green hills on three sides, and opens on the fourth side to the dramatic wall of the Chimanimani Mountains. It's the gateway town to the national park, offering world-class hiking trails among idyllic surrounds. In the 1990s it was a thriving backpacker centre, and once again eagerly awaits visitors.

◉ Sights

Bridal Veil Falls   WATERFALL
(US$10) The aptly named Bridal Veil Falls drop 50m in a delicate, fanned manner. It's worth a visit for its tranquil sanctuary location where you can swim at the base of the falls. It's 6km northwest of town, just over an hour's walk. Pay the admission fee before you leave at the parks office in town.

Eland Sanctuary   VIEWPOINT
While you'd be very lucky to spot any elands these days, it's still worth the trek up here

ZIMBABWE CHIMANIMANI

Chimanimani & Around

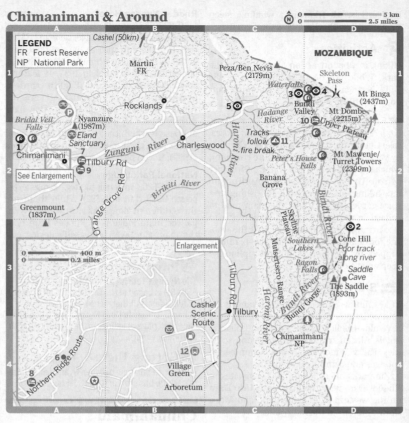

for splendid views of the mountainous surrounds. It's 4km north of town.

🏃 Activities

Almost all visitors are here for hiking in the area and guides can be arranged through the lodges. **African Wilderness Link** (☑026-2436; http://africanwildernesslink.simdif.com; 162a Haynes St; per person from US$15) can organise a number of hikes in the area.

For guided horse-riding trips, get in touch with Tempe at Farmhouse; pony rides are also available for kids.

For cultural events, contact the Chimanimani Tourist Association, which can arrange drumming and *mbira* (thumb piano) performances.

🛌 Sleeping & Eating

Despite being a tiny town, guesthouses are well geared to all the needs of independent travellers, with some of the best budget accommodation in the country. There's a good choice of Western-style dishes on offer at the lodges catering to foreigners. Expect backpacker classics, like wood-fired pizza and burgers at Heaven Lodge, and local produce, such as lamb on the spit, at Farmhouse. While self-catering is an option too, there are only basic groceries in town, so best do all your shopping before you arrive.

⭐ **Heaven Lodge** LODGE **$**
(☑0775 904679, 0772 752752; www.heavenlodge. com; camping per person US$5, dm US$10, d & cottage US$60, d with shared bathroom US$25; 🛜) One of Zimbabwe's original backpackers, Heaven Lodge fell on hard times during the turmoil, but is back as good as ever. It's run by friendly owners, Jacqui and Allen, who are excellent sources of info, and know exactly what backpackers want: cold beer, warm showers and clean rooms. Its common area is a highlight with excellent food, bar and lounge with roaring fireplace.

Chimanimani & Around

⊙ Sights
1 Bridal Veil Falls A2
2 Mt Binga D3
3 North Cave C1
4 Red Wall Cave D1
5 Tessa's Pool C1

✪ Activities, Courses & Tours
6 African Wilderness Link A4

🛏 Sleeping
7 Farmhouse A2
8 Frog & Fern A4
9 Heaven Lodge A2
10 Mountain Hut D1
11 Mutekeswane Base Camp C2

ℹ Information
Ranger's Office .... (see 11)

ℹ Transport
12 Bus Stop B4

Farmhouse
LODGE $

(☎ 0772 101283; www.chimanifarmhouse.com; camping per person US$10, r US$15-60) Run by local farmer Tempe (who has spent her whole life in Chimanimani) and her husband Doug, this 100-year-old homestead is set on a 4-hectare farm. There's a mix of rooms, from tiny bedrooms to cottages and lofts, or the entire house for US$100. It's a good place to arrange your trek, and kids will love the farm animals here.

Frog & Fern
LODGE $

(☎ 0775 920440; www.thefrogandfern.com; camping per person US$10, r from US$35; 🛜) On a hill above town, backing on to the Pork Pie Eland sanctuary, Frog & Fern is Chimanimani's nicest place to stay. There's a choice of stone cabins or rondavel cottages (the double-storey rondavels are architectural masterpieces), all with cooking facilities, fireplaces and garden views. Breakfast is available for US$10, but otherwise it's self-catering.

ℹ Information

There's no ATM in town that accepts international cards, so ensure you bring enough cash. Mutare is the closest town with a bank.

Headed by Jane High from Frog & Fern, the **Chimanimani Tourist Association** (☎ 0775 920440; www.facebook.com/chimanitourism) does a good job of promoting the area. There's no office as such, so call for any info. Also check out www.chimanimani.com for good info.

ℹ Getting There & Away

Transport to Chimanimani is via local buses and combis from either Mutare (US$5, 2½ hours) or Harare (US$15, seven hours); they arrive at/depart from the bus stop in town. For Masvingo, you'll need to catch an early combi to Wengezi (US$4), from where there are buses to Masvingo (US$7) or Great Zimbabwe (US$5).

For self-drivers there's a petrol station in town.

The park entrance for Chimanimani National Park is 15km away. The lodges charge about US$7 to assist with transport to base camp, from where you begin hiking.

Chimanimani National Park

With its pristine wilderness, **Chimanimani National Park** (www.zimparks.org; day fee US$10; ⊙ 6am-6pm) is a hiker's paradise. Sharing a border with Mozambique, the park is still very wild and unspoiled, with stunning mountainous landscapes, evergreen forest, cascading streams and natural swimming holes. Its only downside are unwanted trails created by illegal gold panners who are present in the area. The park is home to eland, sable and bushbuck among other antelope species, and some leopards – but you're unlikely to see much wildlife.

Most people begin their hikes at Mutekeswane Base Camp (p640), 15km from Chimanimani town, where you must sign in and pay park fees. The road ends here and the park is then only accessible on foot.

Hikers need to make sure they're well prepared with plenty of water, food and warm clothing (the weather can change quickly); make sure you let folk know where you're heading. While a guide isn't necessary, it's not a bad idea and can be arranged in Chimanimani town through the lodges or African Wilderness Link.

From the starting point at Mutekeswane Base Camp (p640), where you pay entry fees, **Bailey's Folly** is the shortest and most popular route to the mountain hut (around three hours). Another option is the gentler **Banana Grove Track**. From the mountain hut, it's an easy 40-minute walk to **Skeleton Pass**, a former guerrilla route between Zimbabwe and Mozambique. Go in the late afternoon for an unsurpassed view into Wizard Valley in Mozambique.

The highest point in the Chimanimani Range is the 2437m-high **Mt Binga** on the Mozambican border, a stiff three-hour climb from the hut. Carry plenty of water.

ZIMBABWE CHIMANIMANI NATIONAL PARK

Hadange River Track is a good but challenging exit route that emerges near the Outward Bound School (a children's adventure camp that manages the area) and Tessa's Pool, a lovely swimming hole. Also at Tessa's Pool are San rock art paintings, but drop by the Outward Bound adventure camp first to gain permission, and be sure to take all your rubbish with you. If you exit this way, you'll need to walk back along the road to sign out at base camp.

Bundi Valley is riddled with caves and rock overhangs. The most accessible caves lie near the valley's northern end. North Cave, a 30-minute walk north of the mountain hut, overlooks a waterfall and opens onto views of the highest peaks. Above the waterfall is a pool, perfect for a teeth-chattering dip if you need some refreshment. Red Wall Cave lies 10 minutes further on.

For any info on the park, you're best to get in touch with the Chimanimani Tourist Association (p639) or the Farmhouse (p639). There's also a ranger's office (☑ 0775 475531, 0775 131072) at the base camp and in town.

The park entrance at Mutekeswane Base Camp is 15km from Chimanimani. Unless you have your own vehicle (or you want to walk), it's only reachable by taxi (US$7); you'll need to pre-arrange your return transport with your driver as there's no network signal.

Mountain Hut
HUT $

(www.zimparks.org; per person US$9) At an elevation of 1630m, the mountain hut is a long and steep half-day walk from the base camp. It's a bit grubby but has running water and cooking facilities.

Mutekeswane Base Camp
CAMPGROUND $

(☑ 0775 131072, 0775 475531; www.zimparks.org; campsite per person US$10) At the park's entrance is this well-maintained campsite with showers and toilets. It's a good base from where you can do day hikes.

THE MIDLANDS & SOUTHEASTERN ZIMBABWE

Geographically, the Midlands are known as the highveld, while the warmer, lower-lying southeast is the lowveld. At the transition of the regions is Masvingo and nearby is Great Zimbabwe – one of Southern Africa's more interesting archaeological ruins. The lowveld's finest attraction is the beautiful, often-ignored Gonarezhou National Park.

Masvingo
☑ 039 / POP 73,000

Masvingo is a classic crossroads town that leads to a number of major points. It has a relaxed feel and a few glimpses of charm, but overall offers little for travellers. Most people are here to transfer to Great Zimbabwe, head east to Harare, westwards to Bulawayo or, further south, to the South African border.

The folks at Masvingo Publicity Association (☑ 0773-998028, 262643; masvingopublicity@gmail.com; Robert Mugabe St; ⊙ 8am-4:30pm Mon-Fri) can help with general information and assist with finding accommodation in Masvingo and Great Zimbabwe.

There's no real need to stay overnight as there are much better options around the nearby Great Zimbabwe area. However, if you get stuck there are several large business-style hotels and a very run-down hostel.

Masvingo lacks one central bus station, so you'll have to go to select spots depending on where you're heading. Unfortunately, the chicken buses or combis are your only option here. Regular buses run the gauntlet between Masvingo and Harare (US$8, four hours) and Bulawayo (US$8, four hours) from the corner of Bradburn St and Josiah Tongogara Ave. Buses to Mutare (US$8, four hours) leave from Jason Moyo Ave and Robert Mugabe St; it's a busy road so avoid after late afternoon. To Beitbridge (US$8, four hours), buses stop by the Excel petrol station just south of the Masvingo Publicity Association.

For Great Zimbabwe you can grab a taxi for US$25 or a combi opposite the Pick and Pay supermarket, which heads to Nemanwa (US$2), from where you'll need to walk a further 2½ km.

★ Moira Jane's Blue Bird Cafe
CAFE $

(☑ 0773-272473; 50 Robertson St; meals from US$3; ⊙ 8am-4pm Mon-Fri, 8.30am-2pm Sat; 🤝) A reason to stop by Masvingo is this attractive little cafe that does 10 different kinds of burgers (including some good gourmet varieties), steak rolls and toasted sarnies. They do good coffee from the Eastern Highlands and you can BYO beer. There are picnic tables at the front or try the smart cafe decorated with retro movie posters. Out the back is a second-hand clothing and goods shop to browse.

Great Zimbabwe
☑ 039

The greatest medieval city in sub-Saharan Africa, the World Heritage–listed Great Zimbabwe is one of the nation's most treasured sights. So much so that the country was named after it! These wonderfully preserved ruins of the Bantu civilisation and fabled capital of the Queen of Sheba provide evidence that ancient Africa reached a level of civilisation not suspected by earlier scholars. As a religious and political capital, this city of 10,000 to 20,000 dominated a realm that stretched across eastern Zimbabwe and into modern-day Botswana, Mozambique and South Africa. Trade of gold and ivory was rampant, with goods coming from and going to places as far reaching as Arabia and China.

Located 30km from Masvingo, the ruins make for an essential stop on any visitor's itinerary in Zimbabwe.

History

Great Zimbabwe was first occupied in the 11th century. The settlers probably comprised several scattered groups that recognised there was safety in numbers. Construction of the Hill Complex commenced in the 13th century, while the remainder was built over the next 100 years.

Fuelled by the Swahili gold trade, the city grew into a powerful religious and political capital and became the heart of Rozwi culture. Royal herds increased and coffers overflowed. But Great Zimbabwe likely became

an eventual victim of its own success: by the 15th century the growing human and bovine population, and the associated environmental impacts, had depleted local resources, necessitating emigration to more productive lands. Great Zimbabwe declined rapidly and when the Portuguese arrived in the 16th century the city was virtually deserted.

◉ Sights

Great Zimbabwe ARCHAEOLOGICAL SITE
(☏0776-308755; www.greatzimbabweruins.com; adult/child US$15/8, guide $US3; ⊙6am-6pm) The site is divided into several major ruins with three main areas – Hill Complex, the Valley and the Great Enclosure. It is easily explored by yourself, but for more info, maps and the best routes, duck into the information centre at the site's checkpoint to pick up one of the booklets. If you want to delve even deeper, you can arrange a two-hour guided tour (about US$12 per person) at the checkpoint. The best time to explore (and beat the heat) is dawn and dusk when the sunrise, or sunset, enhances what is already a stunning site. Allow at least three hours to explore.

Great Zimbabwe Museum MUSEUM
(⊙7.45am-4.45pm) FREE Head to the Great Zimbabwe Museum before you start exploring the site to prep yourself and gain some insight through the informative displays

Great Zimbabwe

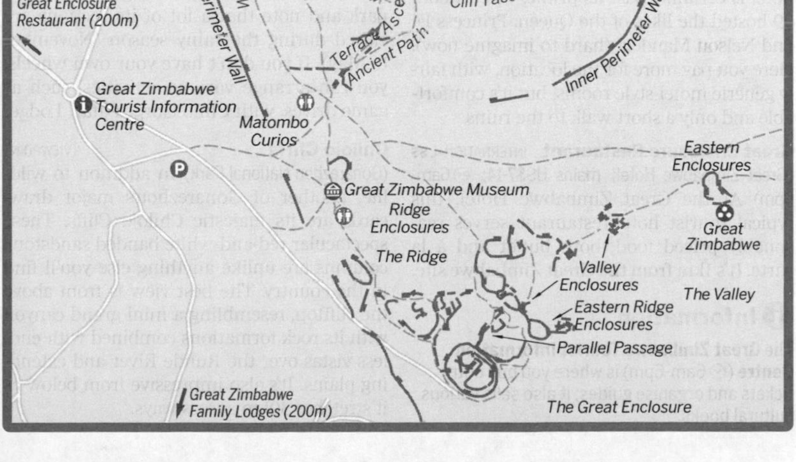

ZIMBABWE GREAT ZIMBABWE

there. They have numerous soapstone bird totems on display, Zimbabwe's national symbol. It's located a short walk within the entry, across from the kiosk.

🛏 Sleeping & Eating

Norma Jeane's Lakeview Resort LODGE $
(📞 0712-220397; normajeanes@yoafrica.com; camping per person US$13, r per person US$30, self-catering lodge per person from US$50, hotel r s/d US$110/175; 🛜) Located 8km from Great Zimbabwe is this wonderful hilltop lodge overlooking Lake Mutirikwi (Lake Kyle). It's set on a sprawling garden property with rooms catering to all budgets, from grassy campsites popular with Overland trucks to basic rooms and fully self-equipped cottages.

Its quaint English-style restaurant is within the former homestead of pioneer Murray McDougal, who engineered the dam at Lake Mutirikwi used for the sugar-cane industry. Don't miss its fantastic roasts.

Great Zimbabwe
Family Lodges CAMPGROUND $
(📞 0775-398917, 0773-456633; camping per person US$7, dm US$10, rondavel s/d with shared bathroom US$20/30, lodge s/d/tr/q from US$30/40/78/80) Inside the main gate and within plain sight of the Great Zimbabwe complex, is this very convenient lodge and campsite. Don't expect too much, but rooms all get the job done and comprise institutional-style dorms, lodges of varying comfort levels (some with TV, kitchen and fridge) and atmospheric rondavels spread out along the hill from reception.

Great Zimbabwe Hotel HOTEL $$$
(📞 039-262274; www.greatzimbabwehotel.com; s/d incl breakfast US$147/177; 🛏) Built in 1905, this hotel is certainly past its prime, when Room 29 hosted the likes of the Queen, Princess Di and Nelson Mandela (hard to imagine now). Here you pay more for the location, with fairly generic motel-style rooms, but it's comfortable and only a short walk to the ruins.

Great Enclosure Restaurant INTERNATIONAL $$
(Great Zimbabwe Hotel; mains US$7-14; ⏱ 6am-9pm) At the Great Zimbabwe Hotel, this typical tourist hotel-restaurant serves reasonably priced food, both buffet and à la carte. It's 1km from the Great Zimbabwe site.

ℹ Information

The **Great Zimbabwe Tourist Information Centre** (⏱ 6am-6pm) is where you buy entry tickets and organise guides; it also sells various cultural books.

ℹ Getting There & Away

Combis runs frequently between Masvingo and Great Zimbabwe (US$2, 30 minutes) and drops off at the Great Zimbabwe Hotel entrance. Walk through the grounds to reach the Great Zimbabwe main gate – about 800m.

Gonarezhou National Park

Hidden in the southeast corner of the country is the stunning **Gonarezhou National Park** (www.zimparks.org; admission US$15; ⏱ 6am-6pm May-Oct), Zimbabwe's second-largest park (5000 sq km) and regarded by many as one of its best-kept secrets. Sharing the border with Mozambique, the park is also virtually an extension of South Africa's Kruger National Park. So, in late 2002, the relevant authorities in Zimbabwe, South Africa and Mozambique created the **Great Limpopo Transfrontier Park**, a 35,000-sq-km park straddling all three countries (with no boundaries). It's one of the Zimbabwe's most scenic parks, with a staggering variation in landscapes, with its iconic sandstone Chilojo Cliffs, major rivers, lowveld scrub and sandveld flood plains, magnificent baobab trees, mopane woodland and tracts of palm-tree forest.

Here you'll find an abundance of elephants, plus giraffes, buffaloes, zebras, lions, leopards, cheetahs, hyenas, wild dogs, nyala (among the usual antelope species) and an impressive 453 different kinds of bird species.

Most people access the park via self-drive 4WD, tour package or charter flight. It's about 300km south of Chimanimani (four hours' drive), along an often pot-holed road, or similar distance from Masvingo on a smooth tarmac through the sugar-cane plantations.

You'll need a 4WD here to get around the park and note that a lot of its sections are closed during the rainy season (November to May). If you don't have your own wheels, you can arrange various activities, such as game drives, with Chilo Gorge Safari Lodge.

Chilojo Cliffs VIEWPOINT
(Gonarezhou National Park) In addition to wildlife, another of Gonarezhou's major drawcards are its majestic Chilojo Cliffs. These spectacular red-and-white banded sandstone columns are unlike anything else you'll find in the country. The best view is from above the clifftop, resembling a mini grand canyon with its rock formations combined with endless vistas over the Runde River and extending plains. It's also impressive from below as it stretches 30km across ways.

National Park Campsites & Lodges
CAMPGROUND, LODGE $$

(www.zimparks.org; campsites US$17-90, tented camps d from US$115, lodges d from US$86) Zimparks offers decent sleeping options at various sites across the park. There's tented camping at the park HQ in Chipinda Pools and lodges at Mabalauta and Swimuwini in the southern sector. Campsites are available but rates are geared towards groups rather than individuals; you can keep costs down if you're OK to risk arriving without a reservation (per person US$17).

★ Chilo Gorge Safari Lodge
LODGE $$$

(☑0774-999059; http://chilogorge.com; per person incl meals & activities US$600; 🛜 ☒) With its stunning elevated location overlooking the Save River, safari lodges really don't get much better than this. All of its luxurious stilted thatched chalets open up to river views, allowing you to spot game from your balcony. The staff is friendly and features a team of crack guides.

WESTERN ZIMBABWE

With no less than three World Heritage–listed sites in the area, out west you'll find some of Zimbabwe's most famous highlights. Its crowning jewel is the mighty Victoria Falls (p559), an awe-inspiring sight that's a feast for the senses. Combined with a world-class outdoor adventure scene, it's clear to see why tourists flock en masse to this resort town.

Only a few hours' drive away is Hwange National Park (p647), one of Africa's best for wild cats and elephants. Further south is Matobo National Park (p646), another Unesco site, characterised by majestic balancing boulders, ancient rock art and a population of wild rhinos. Be sure to leave time to explore Bulawayo, Zimbabwe's 'second', and most beautiful city, with its ornate 19th-century colonial architecture.

Bulawayo

☑ 09 / POP 653,337

Wide tree-lined avenues, parks and charming colonial architecture make Bulawayo, Zimbabwe's second city, an attractive one. It has a lovely historic feel to it, and it's worth spending a night or two, especially given it's a gateway to Matobo National Park, and an ideal staging point for Hwange National Park and Vic Falls.

The city dates back to pre-colonial days, when it was founded in the 1840s by the Nde-bele king, Lobengula Khumalo. Nearly half a century later it was invaded by the British South Africa Company during the Matabele War, and colonised by Cecil Rhodes in 1894. The grand colonial architecture that stands today soon followed, and Bulawayo's claim to fame is that it had electric lighting (switched on in 1897) before London did! The population today remains majority Ndebele.

◉ Sights

★ Bulawayo Railway Museum
MUSEUM

(NRZ Museum; ☑09-36245; www.geoffs-trains.com/museum/museumhome.html; cnr Prospect Ave & Crew Rd; adult/child US$2/1; ⊙8.30am-4.30pm Mon-Fri, from 9am Sat & Sun) Whether you're a train enthusiast or not, Bulawayo's Railway Museum rarely disappoints. Its passionate curator, Gordon Murray, will take you on a tour of the place, where you'll get a fascinating insight into the colonial history of the country through Bulawayo's extensive railway network. There are some wonderful Rhodesian Railways steam engines and carriages to clamber aboard, including the *Jack Tar* (1889), the first train to cross the Victoria Falls Bridge.

★ Natural History Museum
MUSEUM

(☑09-250045; www.naturalhistorymuseumzimbabwe.com; Centenary Park; adult/child US$10/5; ⊙9am-5pm) Zimbabwe's largest and best museum makes for an essential visit. It offers a great overview of the country's natural, anthropological and geological history. Its highlight is its taxidermy display, which includes a monster elephant, shot 160km south from here. There's also an impressive collection of gemstones, showcasing the country's astounding wealth of natural resources. At its centre is a collection of live snakes, including black mambas and cobras.

Khami Ruins
ARCHAEOLOGICAL SITE

(Kame, Kami; adult/child US$10/5; ⊙8am-5pm) Just 22km from Bulawayo, the Unesco World Heritage–listed Khami Ruins may not have the grandeur of Great Zimbabwe, but it's an impressive archaeological site nonetheless. The second largest stone monument built in Zimbabwe, Khami was developed between 1450 and 1650 as the capital of the Torwa dynasty, and abandoned in the 19th century with the arrival of Ndebele. It's spread over a 2km site in a peaceful natural setting overlooking the Khami Dam.

National Art Gallery
GALLERY

(☑09-70721; www.nationalgallerybyo.com; cnr Joshua Nkomo (Main) St & Leopold Takawira Ave; adult/

ZIMBABWE BULAWAYO

Central Bulawayo

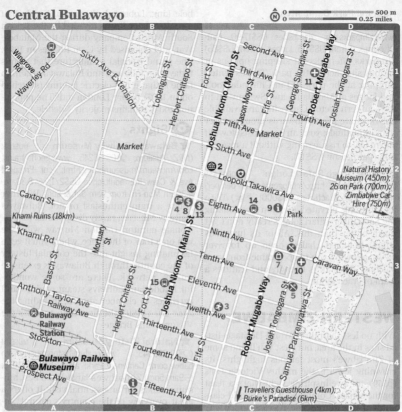

child US$5/3; ☺9am-5pm Tue-Sat) Set in a beautiful 100-year-old, colonial, double-terrace Edwardian building, the National Art Gallery shows temporary and permanent exhibitions of contemporary Zimbabwean sculpture and paintings. A visit here wouldn't be complete without dropping by the studios of the artists in residence, who you can meet at work and buy from directly. There's a quality gallery shop and lovely cafe too.

🏃 Activities

Mike's Bike Shop   CYCLING
(☑0775 195174; cnr Twelfth Ave & Fife St; per day US$15) Offering a handy way to get around town, Mike's mountain bikes come equipped with helmets and repair kits.

👉 Tours

★ Prospector's Pub Crawl   WALKING
(☑0733 781246; hubbardszimtours@gmail.com; half day min 4 people US$65, 1 person US$100) A pub

crawl and history lesson rolled into one: archaeologist, historian and local Paul Hubbard will show you Bulawayo's architectural and pioneer gems. Give 48 hours' notice. There's a range of other themed walks on offer, as well as tours to visit Zimbabwe's ruined cities, from nearby Khami (p643) to further afield.

★ Black Rhino Safaris   OUTDOORS
(☑09-243987, 0712 221284; www.blackrhinossa faris.com) Best known for its rhino tracking tours in Matobo National Park (from US$70 to US$90). It also offers historical tours in Bulawayo (per person US$30) and to Khami Ruins (p643; per person US$40). Tours have a minimum of two people, but you can usually tag along with another tour.

🛏 Sleeping

Burke's Paradise   HOSTEL $
(☑0782 311011, 09-246481; www.burkes-para dise.com; 11 Inverleith Dr, Burnside; campsite per person US$7, dm US$15, s/d with shared bathroom

Central Bulawayo

◎ **Top Sights**
1 Bulawayo Railway Museum A4

◎ **Sights**
2 National Art Gallery C2

◉ **Activities, Courses & Tours**
3 Mike's Bike Shop C3

◉ **Sleeping**
4 Bulawayo Club B2

◉ **Eating**
Bulawayo Club .... (see 4)
5 Dickies C3
6 Indaba Book Cafe C3
Studio Nosh ....(see 2)

◉ **Shopping**
7 Giga & Sons.......................................C3

ⓘ **Information**
8 Barclays Bank....................................B2
9 Bulawayo & District Publicity
   Association......................................C2
10 Galen House Casualty C3
11 Medical Air Rescue Service D1
12 National Parks & Wildlife
   Zimbabwe...D4
13 Stanbic B2

ⓘ **Transport**
14 Combis/Local Bus Terminal C2
15 Intercape Pathfinder.........................B3
16 Renkini Bus Terminal A1

US$25/30; 🛜🏊) Set on a well-maintained, 5-hectare property, Burke's Paradise is hands down Bulawayo's best choice for budget independent travellers. There's a good mix of dorms and private rooms, a lovely pool and an overall relaxed atmosphere. It's on the outskirts of town, but you can catch combis to/from town, or it's a US$10 cab ride.

★ **Bulawayo Club**   HISTORIC HOTEL $$
(☏09-244109, 09-244990; www.bulawayoclub. com; cnr Eighth Ave & Fort St; s/d incl breakfast from US$70/100; 🛜) Founded in 1895, the BC is still the most exclusive address in town. The opportunity to stay in such an elegant historical place at such a reasonable price is hard to pass up. Both its facade and interior are stunning, with period charm and history at every turn. The recently refurbed rooms are lovely, and offer plenty of historical character.

★ **Traveller's Guest House**   GUESTHOUSE $$
(☏09-246059; www.travellerszim.net; 2 Banff Rd, Hillside; s/d from US$45/60, ste d/tr US$90/120;

🛜🏊) Charm oozes from this guesthouse where renovated rooms come with blond-wood floors, stainless-steel bathroom fittings and African art. The suites are the pick of the rooms and worthy of an upgrade. The communal designer kitchen is well-equipped, while the flower-filled garden and pool setting provide a nice spot to kick back in.

✕ Eating

Dickies   AFRICAN $
(cnr Tenth Ave & Josiah Tongogara St; mains US$3-5; ⊙8am-midnight) Try a traditional Zimbabwean meal at this bright and cheery eatery. Follow the locals and plunge your fingers into tasty fish and sticky meat dishes sopped up with filling piles of *sadza* (maize-meal porridge). There are a few branches throughout town. BYO alcohol.

Studio Nosh   CAFE $$
(☏0775 901120; www.facebook.com/studionosh; National Art Gallery, cnr Joshua Nkomo (Main) St & Leopold Takawira Ave; cakes US$3, meals from US$6; ⊙9am-4pm Mon-Sat) Within the National Art Gallery is this quality little cafe doing homemade cakes, burgers and inventive mains such as crocodile-and-eggplant laksa. Otherwise come for its excellent coffee to enjoy on its outdoor terrace next to the artist studios.

Bulawayo Club   INTERNATIONAL $$
(Governors' Restaurant; ☏09-244990; www.bula wayoclub.com; cnr Eighth Ave & Fort St; mains from US$8; ⊙8am-10pm) Chandeliers, silverware, marble pillars and gleaming hardwood floors might have you thinking you need to dust off your blazer. Not to worry chaps: the Bulawayo Club's dining-room surrounds may be decked out for Rhodesian high society, but these days it's welcoming to all. Its retro menu card offers old-world dishes such as pie with gravy, chips and peas, or pavlova for dessert.

Indaba Book Cafe   CAFE $$
(☏09-67068; www.facebook.com/indababook cafe; 92 Josiah Tongogara St; meals from US$7; ⊙8am-4pm Mon-Fri, to 2pm Sat; 🛜) One of downtown's best cafes is this cool little hangout, with books for sale, proper coffee, free wi-fi and quality homemade cakes. The food is also excellent, ranging from double-beef burgers and Asian curries to hearty soups and ever-changing daily specials.

★ **26 on Park**   INTERNATIONAL $$$
(☏09-230399; 26 Park Rd; mains US$13-17; ⊙11am-9pm Wed-Sat, 10am-3pm Sun; 🛜) Housed in a colonial building with sprawling

lawns and a big patio, this casual fine-dining restaurant is one of Bulawayo's best. Its menu changes seasonally, and well-trained chefs cook up the likes of regional Nyanga trout, game venison pie or Zimbabwe dry-aged beef. Its thin-crust pizzas are very popular too, and its cocktail bar makes for a lively drinking spot.

🛍 Shopping

★ Giga & Sons
SHOES

(☎09-62631; 93b Robert Mugabe Way; boots US$140-900; ⏰8.30am-5pm Mon-Fri, 8am-1pm Sat) Established in 1932, this fourth-generation family-run menswear store is most famous for its Courtney Boots – a homegrown shoe, sold worldwide. All of its safari boots are handmade, and are produced from a range of materials, including elephant, hippo, buffalo, kudu, ostrich and crocodile leather. There are also leather bags and a good range of khaki safari wear.

ℹ Information

DANGERS & ANNOYANCES
As with most African cities, avoid walking at night; call a cab instead.

EMERGENCY
Medical Air Rescue Service (MARS; ☎09-60351, 09-78946; 42 Robert Mugabe Way) For ambulance services.

INTERNET ACCESS
Almost all accommodation options and restaurants have wi-fi. Otherwise you shouldn't have trouble finding an internet cafe in town.

MEDICAL SERVICES
Galen House Casualty (☎09-881051; galen@gatorzw.co.uk; cnr Josiah Tongogara St & Ninth Ave) This privately run clinic is better than the central hospital.

MONEY
Barclays Bank (100 Joshua Nkomo (Main) St)
Stanbic (cnr Joshua Nkomo (Main) St & Eighth Ave)

POLICE
Main Police Station (☎09-72516; cnr Leopold Takawira Ave & Fife St)

POST
Main Post Office (☎09-62535; Joshua Nkomo (Main) St; ⏰8am-4pm Mon-Fri, to 11.30am Sat) Between Leopold Takawira and Eighth Aves.

TOURIST INFORMATION
Bulawayo & District Publicity Association (☎09-72969, 09-60867; www.bulawayopublicity.com; btwn Eighth & Leopold Takawira Aves; ⏰8.30am-4.45pm Mon-Fri) In the city hall car park, this is an excellent source of information on accommodation, transport, tours and activities in Bulawayo and around.

National Parks & Wildlife Zimbabwe (☎09-63646; Fifteenth Ave, btwn Fort & Main Sts; ⏰8am-4pm Mon-Fri) Takes accommodation bookings for Matobo National Park.

ℹ Getting There & Away

BUS
Get in touch with the Bulawayo & District Publicity Association for the latest bus and train schedules. Local chicken buses depart from **Renkini Bus Terminal** (Waverley Rd, Thorngrove) heading east, though in terms of safety it's recommended to get one of the luxury buses.

TRAIN
A popular way to get to Victoria Falls is by overnight **train** (☎09-362294; www.nrz.co.zw; ⏰tickets 4-7pm), which departs daily at 7.30pm (1st/2nd class US$12/10). It should arrive around 9am to 11am, but there's been an ongoing issue with delays. The journey takes you through Hwange National Park, a highlight of the trip. First class, comprising a compartment of two beds, is the only way to go. BYO food.

A train to Beitbridge runs Thursdays and Sundays (2nd class US$11), departing 6pm, though it takes nearly 12 hours! Get the bus instead.

The train to Francistown runs Mondays and Fridays (US$4.50), departing 9am.

ℹ Getting Around
The city centre is fairly walkable during the day.

A taxi or **combi** (Eighth Ave, btwn Fife St & Robert Mugabe Way) is the best way to reach the outer limits. Take a taxi for travelling anywhere at night. Try **Proline Taxis** (☎09-886686); agree on a price before setting out.

Zimbabwe Car Hire (☎09-230306; www.zimbabwecarhire.com; 38 Heyman Rd) is a recommended company for those wanting their own wheels for day trips or to head further afield.

Matobo National Park

Home to some of the most majestic granite scenery in the world, the **Matobo National Park** (Matopos; www.zimparks.org; US$15, overnight guests US$8, car US$3; ⏰main gate 24hr, game park 6am-6pm) is one of the unsung highlights of Zimbabwe. This Unesco World Heritage Site is a stunning and otherworldly landscape of balancing rocks known as *kopjes* – giant boulders unfeasibly teetering on top of one another. When you see it, it's easy

ZIMBABWE MATOBO NATIONAL PARK

to understand why Matobo is considered the spiritual home of Zimbabwe.

The national park is separated into two sections – the recreational park and the game park. The recreational area includes World's View and ancient San rock art caves. The widlife park may not have the most prolific animals in Zimbabwe – it's been hard hit by poaching – but it remains one of the best places to see both black and white rhinos (although the black rhinos are difficult to spot).

Just 33km from Bulawayo, Matobo National Park can be done as a day trip, although it's recommended to stay at least one night in this beautiful area. If you don't have transfers prearranged by your accommodation, take a taxi (around US$40).

World's View
(Malindidzimu Hill)   HISTORIC SITE
(adult/child US$10/5) One of Zimbabwe's most breathtaking sites, the aptly named World's View takes in epic 360-degree views of the park. The peacefulness up here is immense, taking on a spiritual quality that makes it clear why it's so sacred to the Ndebele people. It's also the burial spot of Rhodesia's founder, Cecil Rhodes, whose **grave** sits, somewhat controversially, atop between two boulders.

Rock Art Caves   ARCHAEOLOGICAL SITE
(adult/child US$10/5) Dotted around the 425-sq-km Matobo National Park are 3000 officially registered rock-art sites, including one of the best collections in the world of San paintings (estimated to be anywhere from 6000 to 10,000 years old). **White Rhino Shelter**, **Bambata Cave**, **Pomongwe Cave** and **Nswatugi Cave** have some fine examples.

Game Drive   WILDLIFE
The game park is a good spot to try your luck at spying white rhinos; if you're lucky you'll see black rhinos too. Guides can be arranged at the park if you have your own vehicle, otherwise sign up for a tour in Bulawayo or through your lodge.

Maleme Rest Camp   CAMPGROUND $
(☏09-63646; www.zimparks.org; campsite per person US$9, chalet US$40-70, lodge US$86-250) Set around boulders and candclabra cacti, this national park's accommodation offers the best option for budget travellers. While a bit on the shabby side, lodges come with kitchens and bathrooms, while camping is down near the dam. There's no restaurant, but it has a kiosk with basic items.

Farmhouse   GUESTHOUSE $$
(☏0779 544293; www.farmhousematopos.com; s/d incl breakfast US$90/140; 🖥🍴) A charming family-run lodge, Farmhouse is just outside the park with quaintly decked-out thatch-roofed cottages, each with an outdoor braai (barbecue). There's a plunge pool, colonial-style restaurant, plenty of lawn and on-site hiking trails. It's a good place to arrange activities, including mountain-bike hire (US$5), guided walks (US$10), horse safaris (US$20) and game drives (US$20) – all per person.

★Camp Amalinda   LODGE $$$
(☏09-243954; www.campamalinda.com; 45km, Kezi Rd; per person US$255; 🖥🍴) Tucked away in Matobo's granite, the 10 thatched chalets here are carved and seamlessly blended into the boulders and have bulging rocks as in-room features. Each room is unique: some have open bathrooms, claw-foot outdoor baths and even a swing bridge to a private sundeck (room 10). End the day with a sundowner at the stunning lagoon-style pool and bar.

Hwange National Park
☏018

One of the 10 largest national parks in Africa, and the largest in Zimbabwe at 14,651 sq km, **Hwange National Park** (www.zimparks.org; national parks accommodation per day guests/nonguests US$10/20; ⏰main gate 6am-6pm), pronounced 'Wang-ee', has a ridiculous amount of wildlife. Some 400 species of bird and 107 types of animal can be found in the park, including lions, giraffes, leopards, cheetahs, hyenas and wild dogs. But the elephant is what really defines Hwange, being home to one of the world's largest populations of around 40,000 tuskers.

The best time for wildlife viewing is July to October, when animals congregate around the 60 water holes or 'pans' (most of which are artificially filled) and the forest is stripped of its greenery.

Maps and information about the park are available at the rangers offices at **Main Camp** (☏0783 732479, 0773 240235), **Sinamatella Camp** (☏04-706077, 0783 732479; www.zimparks.org; camping US$17, chalet d from US$40, lodge d from US$86) and **Robins Camp** (☏04-706077, 0783 732479; www.zimparks.org; chalet d US$46-229).

◉ Sights

Painted Dog Visitor Centre   WILDLIFE RESERVE
(☏018-710; www.painteddog.org; by donation; ⏰visitor centre 8am-5pm) **FREE** An interesting

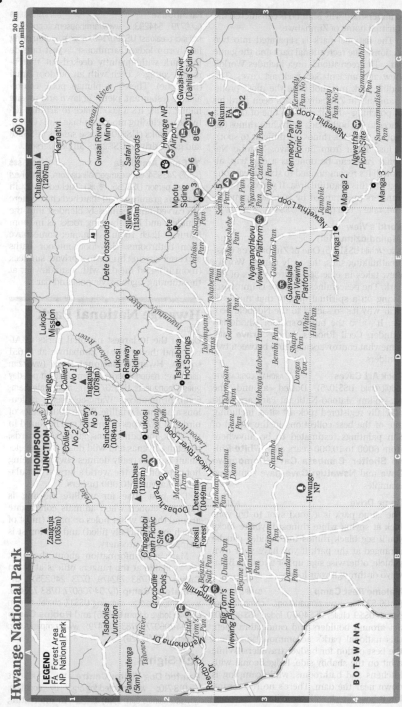

Hwange National Park

LEGEND
FA Forest Area
NP National Park

BOTSWANA

place to visit in-between safaris or en route to the park is this NGO, which works towards the protection of the critically endangered African wild dog. A lot of effort has gone into the place, with detailed, well-presented and personalised accounts of the species and its plight. There is also its rehabilitation centre for injured dogs (with the view of releasing them back into the wild), where you can see the animals, around 1km walk away.

Nyamandhlovu Viewing Platform VIEWPOINT
A driving loop via Main Camp will take you to Nyamandhlovu Pan, with the high-rise Nyamandhlovu Viewing Platform overlooking a water hole popular with animals.

🏃 Activities

If you stay at Hwange Main Camp, you can book guided, three-hour safaris in vehicles (US$45) departing at 7am and 2pm. Guided safari walks (US$10 per person) are also available at Main Camp, as well as Sinamatella and Robins camps.

🛏 Sleeping

Tuskers Campsite CAMPGROUND $
(☑ 09-246430; www.ivorysafarilodge.com/tuskers-camp-site; per person US$15) Tuskers Campsite keeps things real with well-tended sites for those equipped with tents and their own food. There's a food-prep area, fridge, a few power points, hot showers, wood, fire pits and an animal-viewing platform. If you want a proper cooked meal or drink, you can utilise the facilities at Ivory Safari Lodge next door (with enough warning).

Hwange National Park

⊙ Sights
1 Painted Dog Visitor Centre F2

⊜ Sleeping
2 Davison's Camp G3
3 Gwango Heritage Resort F2
4 Hide Safari Camp F2
5 Hwange Main Camp F3
6 Hwange Safari Lodge F2
7 Ivory Safari Lodge F2
8 Khulu Ivory F2
9 Robins Camp A2
10 Sinamatella Camp C2
11 Tuskers Campsite F2

ⓘ Information
Hwange Main Camp
Rangers Office .... (see 5)

Hwange Main Camp CAMPGROUND $
(☑ 018-371, 0783 732479; campsites per person US$17, chalet/cottage/lodge d from US$40/69/86; ⊘ office 6am-6pm; 🛜) At the main park entrance, this attractive camp feels a bit like a village, with its lodges, grocery shop, museum, petrol station and restaurant. More importantly, it's also surrounded by wildlife, and the sounds of predators at night – making it a wonderful spot to stay. There's a good mix of self-catering lodges, cottages with communal kitchens, chalets (without bathroom) and campsites.

Gwango Heritage Resort LODGE $$
(☑ 0783 557773; www.gwango.com; campsite per person US$10, d from US$85, lodge incl full board s/d from US$269/378; 🏊) This relaxed lodge, just off the main highway, is a great new affordable, easily accessible addition to Hwange. There's camping and no-frills A-frame chalets, along with upmarket treetop villas overlooking a pan. The owner has put a lot of thought into the place, which includes an on-site Nambya replica village, complete with interpretive centre and cultural performances.

Khulu Ivory LODGE $$$
(☑ 09-246430, 09-243954; www.accommodationhwange.com; s/d with full board US$575/970) A sister property to **Ivory Safari Lodge** (☑ 09-243954, 09-246430; www.ivorysafarilodge.com; Sikumi FA; s/d with full board US$415/750; 🛜🏊), just down the road, Khulu is both a more wild and luxurious offering. Its spectacular open-air thatched lounge and bar-restaurant looks straight out to the pan where large numbers of elephants regularly congregate, often coming right up for a drink. The chalets all have a rustic safari-chic decor, with outdoor bathtubs overlooking the wilderness.

Davison's Camp TENTED CAMP $$$
(☑ in South Africa +27 11 807 1800; www.wilderness-safaris.com/camps/davisons-camp; Linkwasha Concession; per person incl meals & activities US$605; 🏊) Of the several bush camps run by Wilderness Safaris in this private Linkwasha concession, Davison's is the most popular. Here you've a good chance of spotting all animals in the immediate area. All its luxury tents look out to a water hole, as does the open-air lounge, pool and restaurant.

Hide Safari Camp LODGE $$$
(☑ 04-498835, 0774 724412; www.thehide.com; s/d all-inclusive US$855/1368; 🛜🏊) This is one of the best safari camps in the country. The

spectacular luxury tents here are situated inside the park on the eastern boundary overlooking a water hole. Named after the underground hiding points built to view elephants close up, the Hide has great guides and excellent food.

⊙ Getting There & Away

The park is between Bulawayo and Victoria Falls, 300km and 180km away respectively, making it the most accessible and convenient park for many visitors.

The Intercape Pathfinder (www.intercape. co.za) bus stops at **Hwange Safari Lodge** (⊠ 018-750; www.hwangesafarilodge.com; per person incl breakfast from US$87; ⊛⊠). From here Main Camp (p649) is a further 10km, which you'll need to hitch (never entirely safe and we don't recommend it). A safer option is to arrange a safari drive with Hwange Safari Lodge and get dropped at the Main Camp afterwards.

It's essential to pre-book the bus otherwise it won't make the detour here. Coming from Bulawayo the bus heading to Vic Falls arrives at 6.15pm on Sunday, Monday, Wednesday and Friday; if heading to Bulawayo or Harare the bus arrives at 9.45am from Victoria Falls.

It's an option to fly in, too, by charter plane, arriving at Hwange NP Airport.

⊙ Getting Around

If you're self-driving, most visitors make a few loops starting near the Main Camp. Nyamandhlovu Pan, featuring the high-rise Nyamandhlovu Viewing Platform (p649), overlooks a popular water hole. On the way from the Main Camp, check for wildlife hanging around Dom Pan. South of the Main Camp is Ngwethla Loop, accessible to any vehicle. It passes the magnificent Kennedy Pans, popular with elephants, though the greatest variety of wildlife can be found at the Ngwethla Picnic Site.

There's no private driving after 6pm, so you must leave Robins Camp by 3pm to reach Sinamatella (and vice versa). Robins is 150km west of Hwange Main Camp, so to get there you must depart Robins by noon (and vice versa). Similarly, Sinamatella is 125km northwest of Hwange Main Camp, so you must leave Sinamatella by 2pm.

Access is possible in any sturdy vehicle between May and October, but you'll need a 4WD during the wet season. Consult a ranger (at any of the three camps) about road conditions before heading off too far into the park.

Petrol is available from the Main Camp only, where you'll pay around 10¢ extra a litre than elsewhere.

UNDERSTAND ZIMBABWE

Zimbabwe Today

Zimbabwe continues to dip in and out of international headlines, often creating an unclear but daunting vibe for prospective visitors. Tourists have never been the targets of internal politics and violence, but always check with your embassy or consulate for the latest travel advice.

Despite approaching 93 years of age and plagued by incessant rumours of ongoing health issues, Robert Mugabe shows no intention of relinquishing his grip on the power he's held since 1980. However, in 2016 some cracks were beginning to show as a groundswell of protests spread across the nation in what were the largest antigovernment gatherings in almost a decade. Orchestrated largely through social media, at the forefront was the #ThisFlag movement. Led by activist Pastor Evan Mawarire (who's since fled the country for fear of his safety), Zimbabweans were encouraged to wear the nation's flag as a symbol of peaceful protest, calling for reform and for the return of pride back to the nation. Combined with several 'stay away day' protests by government workers and the war veterans (staunch pro-Mugabe supporters from Zimbabwe's war of independence) denouncing and breaking ties with the government, momentum suggested change was at hand. Predictably, though, Mugable used heavy-handed tactics to shut down the protests. Things remain tense, with none of the demands for change met and cash shortages, rampant corruption, incessant police roadblocks and border trade restrictions remaining in place. Along with the likelihood of the introduction of the bond money, all these factors that will continue to cripple the economy.

With Mugabe's advanced age and heath concerns, talk continues about who his successor will be. If he were to resign due to ill health, current vice president Emmerson Mnangagwa would be the most likely replacement. However, with elections in 2018, there are a few other suitors. Former Zanu PF vice president, Joyce Mujuru (Mugabe's number two for a decade) was stood down in 2014 on grounds of allegedly plotting against him. She has since founded the Zimbabwe People First Party and announced she will run for the presidency in 2018. Ironically, the one key to her removal was Mugabe's wife, Grace – a highly controversial figure in her own right – who was appointed to head of the ZANU-PF Women's League in 2014. Grace Mugabe, married to Robert since 1996, has been the subject of rumours of being groomed to replace her husband. While it's unlikely, the fact she has her foot in the door and apparent influence on decisions has some people concerned. For the opposition, Morgan Tsvangirai remains the other main candidate; however, his diagnosis with bowel cancer in June 2016 has cast doubt upon his future in politics.

History

The Shona Kingdoms & the Portuguese

In the 11th century, the city of Great Zimbabwe was wealthy and powerful from trading gold and ivory for glass, porcelain and cloth from Asia with Swahili traders. By the 15th century, however, its influence was in decline because of overpopulation, overgrazing, political fragmentation and uprisings. During this period, Shona dynasties fractured into autonomous states. In the 16th century Portuguese traders arrived in search of riches and golden cities in the empire of Mwene Mutapa (or 'Monomatapa' to the Europeans). They hoped to find King Solomon's mines and the mysterious land of Ophir.

A new alliance of Shona was formed – the Rozwi State – which covered over half of present-day Zimbabwe, until 1834 when Ndebele (Those Who Carry Long Shields) raiders, under the command of Mzilikazi, invaded from what is now South Africa. They assassinated the Rozwi leader. Upon reaching the Matobo Hills, Mzilikazi established a Ndebele state. After Mzilikazi's death in 1870, his son, Lobengula, ascended the throne and relocated the Ndebele capital to Bulawayo. Lobengula soon came face to face with the British South African Company (BSAC). In 1888 Cecil Rhodes, founder of the company, urged him to sign the Rudd Concession, which granted foreigners mineral rights in exchange for 10,000 rifles, 100,000 rounds of ammunition, a gun-boat and £100 each month.

But a series of misunderstandings followed. Lobengula sent a group of Ndebele raiders to Fort Victoria (near Masvingo) to stop Shona interference between the British and the Ndebele. The British mistook this as aggression and launched an attack on Matabeleland. Lobengula's kraals (hut villages) were destroyed and Bulawayo was burned. A peace offering of gold sent by Lobengula to the BSAC was commandeered by company employees. Ignorant of this gesture, the vengeful British sent the Shangani River Patrol to track down the missing king and finish him off. In the end, Lobengula died in exile of smallpox.

Without their king, the Ndebele continued to resist the BSAC and foreign rule. In the early 1890s they allied themselves with the Shona and guerrilla warfare broke out against the BSAC in the Matobo Hills. When Rhodes suggested a negotiated settlement, the Ndebele, with their depleted numbers, couldn't refuse.

Meanwhile, finding little gold, the colonists appropriated farmlands on the Mashonaland Plateau. By 1895 the new country came to be called Rhodesia, after its founder, and a white legislature was set up. European immigration began in earnest: by 1904 there were some 12,000 settlers in the country, and seven years later the figure had doubled.

Beginnings of Nationalism

Conflicts between blacks and whites came into sharp focus after the 1922 referendum, in which the whites chose to become a self-governing colony rather than join the Union of South Africa. Although Rhodesia's constitution was, in theory, nonracial, suffrage was based on British citizenship and annual income, so few blacks qualified. In 1930 white supremacy was legislated in the form of the Land Apportionment Act, which disallowed black Africans from ownership of the best farmland, and a labour law that excluded them from skilled trades and professions.

Poor wages and conditions eventually led to a rebellion and by the time Southern Rhodesia, Northern Rhodesia and Nyasaland were federated, in 1953, mining and industrial concerns favoured a more racially mixed middle class as a counterweight to the radical elements in the labour force.

Two African parties soon emerged – the Zimbabwe African Peoples' Union (ZAPU), under Joshua Nkomo, and the Zimbabwe African National Union (ZANU), a breakaway group under Ndabaningi Sithole. Following the federation's break-up in 1963 and independence for Northern Rhodesia (Zambia) and Nyasaland (Malawi) – ZAPU and ZANU were banned and their leaders imprisoned.

Ian Smith & the War for Independence

In 1964 Ian Smith took over the Rhodesian presidency and began pressing for independence. British prime minister Harold Wilson argued for conditions to be met before Britain would agree: guarantee of racial equality, course towards majority rule and majority desire for independence. Smith realised the whites would never agree, so in 1965 he made a Unilateral Declaration of Independence.

Britain responded by declaring Smith's action illegal and imposed economic sanctions, which were also adopted by the UN in 1968 (in reality, though, sanctions were ignored by most Western countries and even by some British companies). Meanwhile, ZANU and ZAPU opted for guerrilla warfare. Their raids struck deeper into the country with increasing ferocity and whites, most of whom had been born in Africa and knew no other home, abandoned their properties.

On 11 December 1974, South Africa's John Vorster and Zambia's Kenneth Kaunda persuaded Smith to call a ceasefire and release high-ranking nationalists (namely ZANU and ZAPU party leaders, including Robert Mugabe, who were imprisoned in 1964 during their struggle for majority black rule) and to begin peace negotiations. The talks, however, broke down; ZANU split and Mugabe fled to Mozambique. The following year, ZANU chairman Herbert Chitepo was assassinated in Lusaka by Rhodesian intelligence.

The nationalist groups fragmented and reformed. ZANU and ZAPU created an alliance known as the Patriotic Front (PF) and their military arms – Zipra and Zanla – combined to form the Zimbabwe People's Army.

Smith, facing wholesale white emigration and a collapsing economy, was forced to try an 'internal settlement': Sithole and the leader of the African National Congress (ANC), Abel Muzorewa, joined a so-called 'transitional government' in which whites were guaranteed 28 out of the 100 parliamentary seats; veto over all legislation for 10 years; guarantee of their property and pension rights; and control of the armed forces, police, judiciary and civil service. An amnesty was declared for PF guerrillas.

The effort was a dismal failure. Indeed, the only result was an escalation of the war. To salvage the settlement, Smith entered into secret negotiations with Nkomo, offering to ditch both Sithole and Muzorewa, but Nkomo proved to be intransigent. Finally, Smith was forced to call a general, nonracial election and hand over leadership to Muzorewa, but on much the same conditions as the 'internal settlement'.

Independence

On 10 September 1979, delegations met at Lancaster House, London, to draw up a constitution favourable to both the PF of Nkomo and Mugabe, and the Zimbabwean Rhodesian government of Muzorewa and Smith. Mugabe, who wanted ultimate power, initially refused to make any concessions, but after 14 weeks the Lancaster House Agreement was reached. It guaranteed whites (then 3% of the population) 20 of the 100 parliamentary seats.

In the carefully monitored election of 4 March 1980, Mugabe prevailed by a wide margin and Zimbabwe and its majority-rule government joined the ranks of Africa's independent nations.

Soon after the economy soared, wages increased and basic social programs – notably education and health care – were initiated. However, the initial euphoria, unity and optimism quickly faded: a resurgence of rivalry between ZANU (run mostly by Shona people) and ZAPU (mostly by Ndebele) escalated into armed conflict and the ZAPU leader, Nkomo, was accused of plotting against the government. Guerrilla activity resumed in ZAPU areas of Matabeleland and Mugabe deployed the North Korean–trained Fifth Brigade in early 1983 to quell the disturbances. Villagers were gunned down and prominent members of ZAPU were eliminated in order to root out 'dissidents'. The result was massacres in which tens of thousands of civilians, sometimes entire villages, were slaughtered. A world that was eager to revere Mr Mugabe closed its eyes.

Nkomo, meanwhile, fled to England until Mugabe, as strife threatened to erupt into civil war, publicly relented and guaranteed his safe return. Talks resulted in a ZAPU and ZANU confederation (called ZANU-PF) and amnesty for the dissidents, thereby masterfully sweeping the matter – but not the underlying discontent – under the rug. Zimbabwe's one-party state had begun.

Life as the Opposition

In 1999 thousands attended a Zimbabwe Congress of Trade Unions (ZCTU) rally to launch the Movement for Democratic Change (MDC). Morgan Tsvangirai, the sec-

MONEY – THE SWITCH TO AMERICAN DOLLARS & BACK AGAIN?

Zimbabwe's track record in economic management over the past decade has been nothing short of a total disaster and it's a regular top 20 nominee for the world's most failed states. Unfortunately, in 2016 things seemed as perilous as ever as it underwent another economic crisis, experiencing a major cash shortage. Zimbabwe has effectively run out of US dollars – the main currency used in the country since 2009. This has resulted in the everyday sight of day-long queues for ATMs that snake around the block, as locals wait in hope of being able to withdraw money. The crisis is compounded by 90% unemployment rates and some of the worst droughts experienced in years.

As a solution to the crisis, Zimbabwe's reserve bank introduced its own 'bond' money that was issued in November 2016. Set at parity to the US dollar, initially it was only released in denominations of US$2 and US$5 notes. It was an announcement that sparked outrage across the nation amid fears of returning to dark days of hyperinflation in 2007 to 2008. Back then the Zimbabwean dollar reached 500 billion per cent inflation, resulting in the total collapse of the economy. Supermarket shelves emptied and the country experienced major fuel shortages, forcing many people to relocate abroad, mainly across the border to South Africa or Zambia, of further afield to the UK or Australia.

Hence the concern among locals is that the very currency that single-handedly restored the economy is now soon to disappear. So as the nation waits to see what transpires and whether the bond money will be a permanent or temporary solution, what does this all mean from a traveller's point of view? Mostly, it's strongly advisable to bring enough money with you for the entirety of your trip. While the country is a 'multicurrency' economy – whereby sterling, pula, rand, US dollars and even Chinese yuan are legal tender – the US dollar would remain the most preferable of all these.

retary general, stated he would lead a social democratic party fighting for workers' interests. The arrival of the MDC brought waves of new hope and real opportunity for the end of Mugabe's era.

In 2000 Mugabe's chief propaganda architect, Jonathan Moyo, led the president's campaign for a new constitution. Three months later – and despite the full weight of state media and Treasury – the president's constitution was given the thumbs down by the people. It was Mugabe's first defeat and it notified him of MDC's very real strength at the ballot box. A parliamentary election was due later that year. Ironically, the MDC's greatest success would soon lead to a nasty defeat.

Mugabe responded to the threat of defeat with waves of violence, voter intimidation and a destructive and controversial land-reform program that saw many white farmers lose their land. This resulted in a large exodus of a skilled, educated workforce (it is estimated up to 3 million left the country). Despite this, and the election being damned by the US and EU as 'neither free nor fair', the MDC lost by a mere four seats. Two years later Mugabe's rule was under even greater threat during the country's presidential elections. Again, an election marred by violence and intimidation, backed by a new set of repressive laws, with no independent monitors

and huge numbers of voters turned away, was won by Mugabe.

The next parliamentary election – in 2005 – was not so close. Mugabe and his security and propaganda networks had had five years since 2000 to readjust the playing field. Newspapers were closed (bombed in one case); the state dominated print, radio and TV; voters were offered food (and threatened with no food); the leader of the opposition, Morgan Tsvangirai, went through two treason trials; and up to one million ghost voters were created on the roll. Mugabe won the elections.

Mugabe's toughest ever electoral challenges came in 2008 in the presidential and parliamentary elections. Although the MDC led by Morgan Tsvangirai had been able to campaign in rural areas that were closed to it in previous elections, the 2008 election was again seen as deeply flawed, with areas where the number of votes cast exceeded the number of enrolled voters. Following election day, with growing signs that Mugabe had lost, Mugabe's men took more than a month to 'count' votes. When they were finally announced, Tsvangirai won 47.9% against Mugabe's 43.2%. With neither man having attained 50%, a second round of voting was needed, before which Mugabe's ruling ZANU-PF unleashed waves of violence across the countryside. MDC supporters who had shown their allegiance to the party before the first round of voting were now easily identified. Scores – perhaps hundreds – were killed, many more tortured and thousands fled. In an attempt to stop some of the violence against his supporters, Tsvangirai withdrew from the second round a week before it was scheduled to take place. The second round went ahead anyway and led to yet another victory for Mugabe.

But while South Africa under then president Thabo Mbeki continued to support Mugabe, pressure from other areas was growing. The economy had officially collapsed, Mugabe could not pay his army or civil service, and then came the cholera, which killed more than 4000 people.

In February 2009, Morgan Tsvangirai signed a coalition deal with Zanu-PF, a mutual promise to restore the rule of law and to 'ensure security of tenure to all land holders'. Nonetheless, violence and land grabs continued. While largely tokenistic, the two-party experiment of shared government did, however, provide the most stable political environment in Zimbabwe for the past decade.

The power-sharing government was short-lived, however, with Mugabe's Zanu PF winning the 2013 elections comfortably with 61% of the vote, a result Tsvangirai declared 'null and void' due to alleged vote rigging.

In the meantime a new constitution was introduced to see presidential stints limited to two five-year terms, a timeframe that conveniently shouldn't interfere with 92-year-old Mugabe's ambition to be president for life.

Meanwhile from 2013 to today reports of land grabs and voter intimidation continue, while the diamond watchdog Partnership Africa Canada reports that Mugabe's ruling Zanu-PF party has misappropriated profits from the lucrative diamond industry for its campaign have many concerned. Furthermore, in early 2013 the finance minister announced a paltry US$217 was all that was left in government accounts.

Culture

People of Zimbabwe

Most Zimbabweans are of Bantu origin; 9.8 million belong to various Shona groups and about 2.3 million are Ndebele. The remainder are divided between the Tonga (or Batonga) people of the upper Kariba area, the Shangaan (or Hlengwe) of the lowveld, and the Venda of the far south. Europeans

(18,000), Asians (10,000) and mixed Europeans and Africans (25,000) are scattered around the country.

About 65% of the population lives in rural areas, while around 40% of the population is under 18 years old. The average life expectancy is about 40 years.

The official language of Zimbabwe is English. It's used in government, legal and business proceedings, but is the first language for only about 2% of the population. Most Zimbabweans speak Shona (mainly in the north and east) or Ndebele (in the centre and west). Another dialect, Chilapalapa, is a pidgin version of Ndebele, English, Shona and Afrikaans and isn't overly laden with niceties, so most people prefer you sticking to English.

Way of Life

No matter what their background, Zimbabweans have a stoicism reminiscent of bygone eras. In Zimbabwe, the Southern African expression to 'make a plan' can be defined as 'If it's broke, fix it. If you can't fix it, live with it or change your life' (overnight if need be). This kind of mental strength and generosity, combined with a deep love of Zimbabwe, is the key to their survival.

Sadly, many of Zimbabwe's great gains made since independence – life expectancy, education, health – have been threatened since 1998 (due to gross mismanagement, corruption, and HIV/AIDS).

Certainly, many Zimbabweans experience major difficulties in their day-to-day lives, because basics such as water and electricity are hardly available.

Dollarisation, at the beginning of 2009, temporarily solved many problems for those with access to cash – though, unfortunately, this has dried up as the country again finds itself at a crossroads. Diaspora funding has always buoyed the economy, which avoided collapse for years longer than it should have. It is estimated that 60% of Zimbabweans have someone from the diaspora sending them money. Those who do not – and are in rural areas – remain dangerously below the poverty line.

Somehow, despite the immense hardship for everyday Zimbabweans, crime remains relatively low.

Sport

For a long time Zimbabwe punched well above its weight in football (soccer), constantly upset heavyweights in cricket, produced some cracking tennis and golf players and won Olympic gold. Unfortunately, however, Zimbabwe's sporting teams have followed the same trajectory as the country's economy. Good news for cricket fans is that Zimbabwe was rehanded test status in 2012, but it has a long way to go before it's competitive.

The Arts

Zimbabwe's festivals, fairs and street-side stalls, live music and poetry, dance, art and sculpture are great expressions of its people and a wonderful way for visitors to meet the locals and learn about their lives. Most Zimbabweans are creative in some way: whether they bead, embroider, weave, sculpt or carve.

Sculpture

The word 'Zimbabwe' means 'great stone house', so it is fitting that stone sculpture – also referred to as Shona sculpture – is the art form that most represents the people of Zimbabwe. The exuberance of the work, the vast varieties of stone and the great skill and imagination of the sculptors has led to many major, critically acclaimed exhibitions worldwide over the years.

Literature

Zimbabwe has produced some of the finest African writers. The most contemporary books, *Mukiwa* (A White Boy in Africa) and its sequel, *When a Crocodile Eats the Sun,* by Peter Godwin, are engrossing memoirs. Likewise, *Don't Let's Go to the Dogs Tonight – An African Childhood,* by Alexandra Fuller, is about nature and loss and the unbreakable bond some people have with Africa.

Since independence, Zimbabwean literature has focused on the struggle to build a new society. *Harvest of Thorns,* by Shimmer Chinodya, on the Second War for Independence, won the 1992 Commonwealth Prize for Literature. Another internationally renowned writer, Chenjerai Hove, wrote the war-inspired *Bones,* the tragic *Shadows* and the humorous *Shebeen Tales.*

The country's most famous female writer is the late Yvonne Vera, known for her courageous writing on challenging issues: rape, incest and gender inequality. She won the Commonwealth Prize in 1997 for *Under the Tongue* and the Macmillan book prize for her acclaimed 2002 novel, *The Stone Virgins.*

Environment

The Land

Landlocked Zimbabwe is roughly three times the size of England. It lies within both tropics and consists of middle-veld and highveld plateaus, 900m to 1700m above sea level. A low ridge, running northeast to southwest across the country, marks the divide between the Zambezi and Limpopo–Save River systems.

The northwest is characterised by bushveld dotted with rocky hills. The hot, dry lowveld of southern Zimbabwe slopes gradually towards the Limpopo River.

The mountainous region is in the east, straddling the border with Mozambique. Zimbabwe's highest peak, Nyangani, rises to 2592m.

Wildlife

The Big Five (lions, leopards, buffaloes, elephants and rhinos) are all found in Zimbabwe. There are also cheetahs, hippos, hyenas, wild dogs, giraffes, zebras and a wide range of antelope species such as impala, waterbuck, eland, sable and roan etc. Smaller species include porcupines, jackals, honey badgers, civet cats and the very rarely spotted pangolin and aardvark.

Sadly, poaching – like in most of Southern Africa – remains a major issue. Rhino populations have been decimated, while lions are also heavily targeted. Elephant numbers, however, have been hit the hardest, with some estimating their decline by as much as 40% in the past decade. With that said, elephants are one animal you'll continue to see in great abundance in Zimbabwe, particularly Hwange and Gonarezhou, where elephants appear to be almost at plague proportions.

There are hundreds of bird species found all over the country, including vultures, storks and herons, and Matobo National Park is home to one-third of the world's eagle species.

National Parks

Most of Zimbabwe's national parks are – or contain – Unesco World Heritage sites. Close to 20% of Zimbabwe's surface area is protected, or semiprotected, in national parks, privately protected game parks, nature conservancies and recreational parks.

Park entry fees range from US$5 to US$30 per day. Never enter without paying the fee (which constitutes a permit), as parks are zealously guarded against poaching.

There are different rates for vehicles – none are free – and an average entry fee for a four-seater vehicle is US$5 to US$10, but exact rates should be confirmed when booking. Go to www.zimparks.org for the latest.

Environmental Issues

Zimbabwe is dry for at least nine months of the year and many areas suffer from long-term drought. Poaching, hunting and the destruction of the land has caused serious stress on flora, fauna and the land. Lakes and rivers have also been overfished. These factors have an impact on those whose lives depend on a properly functioning environment. To learn more about Zimbabwe's ecological situation see www.zimwild.org.zw).

SURVIVAL GUIDE

❶ Directory A–Z

ACCOMMODATION

Despite its economic woes, Zimbabwe generally has a good standard of accommodation, from roughing it in dorms to lapping it up in luxury lodges. In larger towns there's usually one or two backpackers, a few boutique guesthouses and some business hotels. National parks, though, are very much geared towards the two ends of the spectrum, from stunning upmarket safari lodges to rudimentary bush camps, with only a few options in between.

ACTIVITIES

It's all about natural features in Zimbabwe: wildlife viewing in national parks, hiking in the Eastern Highlands, canoeing safaris along the Zambezi or fishing on Lake Kariba. Victoria Falls is the epicentre of activities in Southern Africa, where you can whitewater raft, take helicopter rides and bungee jump.

SLEEPING PRICE RANGES

The following price ranges refer to a double room with bathroom in high season.

$ less than US$75

$$ US$75–US$150

$$$ more than US$150

CHILDREN

Zimbabwe is a great place to travel with kids. Wildlife spotting in the national parks and kid-friendly activities in Victoria Falls, such as canoeing and elephant rides, are likely to be the most popular choices. Take note, however, that some lodges in the parks have age limits for safety reasons, so be sure to confirm before booking.

CUSTOMS REGULATIONS

Visitors may import a maximum of US$350 in items not for trade, excluding personal effects. Travellers over 18 years of age can also import up to 5L of alcohol, including 2L of spirits.

While there's no limit on how much you can bring into the country, visitors aren't permitted to take out more than US$1000.

DANGERS & ANNOYANCES

Zimbabwe is nowhere near as dangerous as foreign media makes out and all up it's a very safe country to visit. Although the number of incidents and degree of violence are a far cry from that in South Africa, like anywhere in the world the usual theft and crimes occurs. Don't walk around at night; best option is to take a taxi, which is generally safe. Drivers should take the following precautions: lock all doors, lock all valuables in the boot, keep windows up and avoid stopping at traffic lights at night if it's safe to do so.

Political Sensitivities

There are several things to keep in mind if you're travelling to Zimbabwe while Robert Mugabe is still in power. It is illegal to criticise the government (best to avoid talking about the government at all, avoid antigovernment posts on social media and don't take photographs of 'sensitive' sites, such as government buildings).

Avoid any political gatherings and protests, where clashes with police can occasionally turn violent.

EMBASSIES & CONSULATES

The following embassies and high commissions are based in Harare.

For any embassies or websites not listed here, go to www.embassiesabroad.com/embassies-in/Zimbabwe for addresses and contact details.

Angolan Embassy (Map p624; ☎04-770075; www.angolaembassyzim.com; Doncaster House, 26 Speke Ave; ☺9am-4pm Mon-Fri)

Australian Embassy (Map p620; ☎04-853235; www.zimbabwe.embassy.gov.au; 1 Green Close, Borrowdale; ☺8am-5pm Mon-Thu, to 2pm Fri)

Botswanan Embassy (Map p620; ☎04-794645; www.botswanaembassy.co.zw; 22 Phillips Ave, Belgravia; ☺visas 8am-12.30pm Mon, Wed & Fri, enquiries 8am-12.45pm & 2-4.30pm Mon-Fri)

Canadian Embassy (Map p624; ☎04-252181; www.canadainternational.gc.ca/zimbabwe; 45 Baines Ave; ⊙7.30am-4.30pm Mon-Thu, to noon Fri)

Netherlands Embassy (Map p620; ☎04-776701; http://zimbabwe.nlembassy.org/; 2 Arden Rd, Newlands; ⊙8am-5pm Mon-Thu, to 2pm Fri)

French Embassy (Map p620; ☎04-776118; www.ambafrance-zw.org; 3 Princess Dr, Newlands; ⊙9am-1pm & 2-5pm)

German Embassy (Map p620; ☎04-308655; www.harare.diplo.de; 30 Ceres Rd, Avondale; ⊙9-11am & 2-3pm Mon-Fri)

Japanese Embassy (Map p624; ☎04-250025; www.zw.emb-japan.go.jp; 4th fl, Social Security Centre, cnr Julius Nyerere Way & Second St; ⊙8am-12.45pm & 1.45-5pm Mon-Fri)

Kenyan Embassy (Map p624; ☎04-704820; www.mfa.go.ke/contacts; 95 Park Lane; ⊙8.30am-4.30pm Mon-Thu, to 1pm Fri)

Malawian High Commission (Map p620; ☎04-798584; malahigh@africaonline.co.zw; 9/11 Duthie Rd, Alexandra Park; ⊙visas 9am-noon Mon-Thu)

Mozambican Embassy (Map p624; ☎04-253871; 152 Herbert Chitepo Ave; ⊙visas 8am-noon Mon-Fri)

Namibian Embassy (Map p620, ☎04-885841, secretary@namibianembassy.co.zw; 69 Borrowdale Rd; ⊙8am-5pm Mon-Fri)

South African Embassy (Map p620; ☎04-251843, 04-251845; admin@saembassy.co.zw; 7 Elcombe Ave; ⊙7.30am-4.30pm Mon-Thu, 7.30am-12.30pm Fri)

Tanzanian Embassy (Map p624; ☎04-792714; tanrep@tanrep.co.zw; Ujamaa House, 23 Baines Ave; ⊙9am-1pm Mon-Fri)

UK Embassy (Map p620; ☎04-85855200; www.ukinzimbabwe.fco.gov.uk/en; 3 Norfolk Rd, Mt Pleasant; ⊙8am-4.30pm Mon-Thu, to 1pm Fri)

US Embassy (Map p624; ☎04-250593; http://harare.usembassy.gov; Arax House, 172 Herbert Chitepo Ave; ⊙11am-noon & 1.30-4pm Mon-Thu, 9-11.30am Fri)

Zambian Embassy (Map p624; ☎04-773777; zambians@africaonline.com; Zambia House, 48 Kwame Nkrumah Ave; ⊙9am-1pm Mon-Fri)

EMERGENCY & IMPORTANT NUMBERS

Zimbabwe country code	☎263
International access code	☎00
Ambulance	☎04-771221; 0712-600002; 999
Police	☎995
Fire	☎999, 993

GAY & LESBIAN TRAVELLERS

As in many African nations, homosexual activities for men are illegal and officially punishable by up to five years in jail (although penalties are invariably not nearly as severe), yet lesbianism is not illegal. Contact Gays & Lesbians of Zimbabwe (p627) for information about LGBT clubs and meeting places in Zimbabwe.

INTERNET ACCESS

In the bigger cities, free wi-fi access is widely available in many hotels, restaurants and cafes. It's easy to arrange a local sim card to get data on your phone or a USB dongle for your laptop. Econet and Telecel both have branches at Harare's airport and about town. Otherwise, there are internet centres in all the main cities and towns that charge around US$2 per hour.

MONEY

In late 2016 the Reserve Bank of Zimbabwe controversially released US$10 million worth of bond notes; see p653 for details. It's not accepted as legal tender outside the country, so bear this in mind before departure.

While it remains unclear whether these bond notes will remain long term or are a temporary solution, US dollars will likely remain the most viable currency to carry. South African rand, Botswana pula, pound sterling, euro and Chinese yuan (among a few others) are theoretically also accepted, though to a much lesser extent.

Due to issues in withdrawing cash from banks, as of 2016 it was recommended to carry enough US dollars to last the entirety of your stay; prepay any accommodation or tours to reduce the amount you need to bring in. While new bond coins introduced in 2014 have significantly reduced issues with receiving change at supermarkets, it's still best to take along plenty of small US dollar notes for tips etc.

ATMs

As of result of the cash crisis, many foreign cards were limited to withdrawals of US$100 per day, if any – so it's best not to rely on ATMs and instead bring cash. Check the latest on the situation before departing. Otherwise, ATMs are aplenty across Zimbabwe, but the larger towns are the most reliable. Barclays, Standard Charter and Stanbic are the main banks accepting MasterCard, Visa and Cirrus.

Credit Cards

Credit cards are accepted in top hotels and some upmarket restaurants and shops.

Tipping

Some restaurants automatically add a 10% service charge to the bill; if so, no tip is required. Otherwise, any tip is hugely appreciated.

ℹ PRACTICALITIES

Media Dailies such as the *Herald* and the *Standard* are state-run, while *Daily-News* and *NewsDay* are the independent papers in the country. Overseas several online newspapers (including the *Zimbabwean,* produced in London), offer propaganda-free political reporting. The government controls most TV and radio channels, though most hotels and many lodges have DSTV satellite TV.
Weights & Measures Zimbabwe uses the metric system.

OPENING HOURS
Shops and restaurants are generally open from 8am to 1pm and 2pm to 5pm Monday to Friday, and 8am to noon on Saturday. Very little is open on Sunday.

POST
Most towns in Zimbabwe have post offices where you can send letters internationally to Europe, America and the rest of the world. For sizeable or more valuable items, it's highly advised to use international courier companies such as DHL or FedEx, found in Harare, Bulawayo and Vic Falls.

PUBLIC HOLIDAYS
Most government offices and other businesses are closed during public holidays.

New Year's Day 1 January
Good Friday late March/April
Easter Monday late March/April
Independence Day 18 April
Workers' Day 1 May
Africa Day 25 May
Heroes' Day 11 August
Defence Forces' Day 12 August
National Unity Day 22 December
Christmas Day 25 December
Boxing Day 26 December

SMOKING
Smoking is prohibited indoors at public places and can lead to fines of US$500 or a six-month prison sentence.

TELEPHONE
If calling from overseas, the country code for Zimbabwe is ☏ 263, but drop the initial zero for area codes. The international access code from within Zimbabwe is ☏ 00. International calls can be made from your hotel or lodge.

Mobile Phones
Easily the best option for making calls is to purchase a prepaid SIM card (US$1), available on arrival at the airport; these are cheap and easy to arrange. Econet and Telecel are the main operators and have branches throughout the main towns, as well as at Harare airport. Econet has the best phone and data coverage across the country, but in national parks you won't get network. Be aware that your phone needs to be unlocked to activate the sim. Credit or 'airtime' is widely available from street vendors. Mobile numbers are recognised by the ☏ 07 prefix.

TIME
Zimbabwe is two hours ahead of Greenwich Mean Time (GMT/UTC). No daylight saving.

TOURIST INFORMATION
The Zimbabwe Tourism Authority (p627) has general tourist info. There are publicity associations in Harare, Bulawayo, Victoria Falls, Kariba, Masvingo and Nyanga. Some are very efficient, helpful and have useful information and advice, but others have little more to offer than a smile.

TRAVELLERS WITH DISABILITIES
While many of Zimbabwe's highlights can be accessed by travellers with restricted mobility, it's definitely recommended to travel with the assistance of a companion. In the larger towns and national parks, there's usually a few hotels or lodges that can cater to travellers in wheelchairs.

Though safari vehicles in the parks aren't set up for wheelchair access, travellers can be hoisted into the car with help. The paths leading to outlooks of Victoria Falls are fairly navigable. For the most part, though, when getting around towns and rural areas you'll encounter some uneven surfaces.

VISAS
Single-/double-entry visas cost US$30/45 (and can be issued upon arrival) and multiple-entry visas (valid for six months) cost US$55, but are only issued at Zimbabwean diplomatic missions. British and Irish citizens pay US$55/70 for single/double entry.

In December 2016, the KAZA visa was reintroduced, which allows most visitors to acquire a single 30-day visa (US$50) for both Zimbabwe and Zambia. As long as you remain within these two countries, you can cross the border multiple times (day trips to Botswana at Kazungula will not invalidate the visa). These visas are available at Harare airport, as well as at the Victoria Falls and Kazungula crossings.

For visa extensions, contact the Department of Immigration Control (p627) in Harare.

VOLUNTEERING
There are several volunteering opportunities within the country requiring a broad range of skills and experience. Popular areas include fields working with conservation, teaching or humanitarian efforts.

Imire: Rhino & Wildlife Conservation (p629) is a popular place to volunteer to work with rhinos, elephants and other wildlife.

Getting There & Away

AIR

Several international airlines offer flights into Zimbabwe, arriving in either Harare or Vic Falls.

International flights arriving at Harare International Airport (p627) include the following destinations: Addis Ababa (four hours), Dubai (nine hours, 40 minutes), Johannesburg (1¾ hours), Gaborone (two hours), Windhoek (two hours), Maputo (1½ hours), Lilongwe and Blantyre (1½ hours), Lusaka (50 minutes), Dar es Salaam (2½ hours) and Nairobi (3½ hours).

From Victoria Falls Airport you can fly to/from Johannesburg and Windhoek.

See p627 for airlines with services to/from Zimbabwe:

LAND

Travelling between Zimbabwe's neighbouring Southern African countries by land is fairly hassle free, with visas on arrival issued to many nationalities (but be sure to check this out before you leave). From Harare all buses depart from the Road Port Terminal; there's a US$1 departure tax you'll need to pay at the office.

Botswana

The most popular border crossing into Botswana is from Kazangula near Victoria Falls, which links it to Chobe National Park. The other crossing is at Plumtree, 91km from Bulawayo, heading to Francistown in Botswana. The border posts at Plumtree and Kazungula are open 6am to 6pm.

Zupco (Map p624; ☑04-750571, 0772 666530; www.zupco.co.zw; Road Port Terminal, cnr Robert Mugabe Rd & Fifth St) has buses from Harare to Francistown (US$24) at 4pm.

Malawi

The most direct route between Malawi and Zimbabwe is via Mozambique's Tete Corridor. If travelling through Mozambique to Malawi, you'll need a transit visa (US$25) for Mozambique, which you can arrange in Harare. Alternatively, you'll have to fork out for a visa at the border; enquire with the Mozambique embassy before setting out.

DEPARTURE TAX

Departure tax is usually incorporated into the price of the ticket, with the exception of Air Zimbabwe which charges US$15 for domestic flights and US$50 for international.

Zupco (p659) has buses from Harare to Blantyre (Malawi) daily (except Saturday) at 7.30am (US$25, 12 hours).

Mozambique

There are two border crossings into Mozambique (open from 6am to 8pm). Easily the most popular is from Mutare, which links up to Beira. The other is at Nyamapanda, northeast from Harare, used to get to Malawi.

South Africa

Beitbridge is the somewhat infamous border crossing into South Africa. It's open 24 hours, but always fairly hectic.

Numerous luxury and semiluxury buses ply the route between Harare or Bulawayo to Johannesburg (16 to 20 hours), departing from Road Port Terminal in Harare. It's best to call ahead for departure times.

Buses from Harare:

Intercape Pathfinder (p628) Two daily sleeper buses (US$40 to US$70) at 1pm and 7.30pm.

Greyhound (Map p624; ☑ Bulawayo 09-889078, Harare 04-761463; www.greyhound.co.za; Road Port Terminal, cnr Robert Mugabe Rd & Fifth St) Has an overnight bus departing 8pm Monday to Saturday and 1pm on Sundays (US$37).

Pioneer Coaches (Map p624; ☑ Bulawayo 0783 732721, Harare 0783 732720; www.pioneercoacheszim.co.zw; Road Port Terminal, cnr Robert Mugabe Rd & Fifth St) Has a departure at 2.30pm (US$30).

Citiliner (Map p624; ☑ in South Africa 011 611 8000; www.citiliner.co.za; Road Port Terminal, cnr Robert Mugabe Rd & Fifth St) Daily departures (from US$33).

Buses from Bulawayo:

Intercape Pathfinder (www.intercape.co.za; cnr Joshua Nkomo (Main) St & Eleventh Ave) By far the most recommendable company, with a daily departure at 3.30pm ($US42).

Trains are once again running between Zimbabwe and South Africa. Rovos Rail (p565) runs a three-day/two-night luxury-train journey from Pretoria to Victoria Falls travelling through Zimbabwe via Bulawayo. Prices start from around US$1650 per person, inclusive of meals, alcoholic drinks and excursions.

Zambia

Zimbabwe has three border crossings into Zambia. Victoria Falls (open 6am to 10pm) is by far the most popular. You can also cross via Kariba/Siavonga and Chirundu, which is open 6am to 6pm.

Public transport options from Harare include the following:

Zupco (p659) Two daily buses depart for Lusaka (US$20, nine hours) at 7.30am and a slower bus via Kariba/Siavonga ($20, 10 hours).

King Lion (Map p624; ☏ 0772 635472; www. kinglioncoaches.co.zw; Road Port Terminal, cnr Robert Mugabe Rd & Fifth St) Has a morning and evening bus to Lusaka (US$15, 10 hours) at 7.30am and 7.30pm.

❶ Getting Around

AIR

Air Zimbabwe (p627) has flights from Harare to Bulawayo (45 minutes) and Victoria Falls. New to Zimbabwe is FastJet (p627), a popular budget airline offering cheap flights to Victoria Falls from Harare. There's a domestic departure tax of US$15.

The only way by air from Harare or Vic Falls to Kariba is to charter, which is very expensive. The following companies can arrange charter flights, which will seat four to six people to Kariba, Mana Pools and Matusadona National Park from Harare or Vic Falls:

Altair Charters (☏ 02-7923012, 0772-515852; altair@tarazedcharters.com)

HAC (Halsteds Aviation Corporation; ☏ 0778-750086; www.flyhac.com)

Safari Logistics (☏ 13-46001; www.safari -logistics.com)

Wilderness Air (☏ 13-43371; www.wilder ness-air.com)

BOAT

Kariba Ferries (☏ 0772-236330, 04-614162; www.karibaferries.com; Andora Harbour, Kariba) runs a ferry service between Kariba at the eastern end of the lake and Mlibizi at the western end.

BUS

The express or 'luxury' buses operate according to published timetables. Check carefully, however, as most bus companies have both local ('chicken buses' for locals) and luxury coaches. For example, Pioneer and Zupco have both luxury and chicken buses.

Pathfinder (p628) This luxury '7-star' (it claims to have wi-fi) bus service has started up a daily service linking Harare to Vic Falls, Bulawayo and even Hwange. It has plans for services to Mutare and Kariba.

Bravo (p628) Plies the Harare–Bulawayo–Vic Falls route.

CAR & MOTORCYCLE
Driving Licence

Visitors can use their driving licence from their home country for up to 90 days in Zimbabwe as long as it's written in English. Given the increas-

ing likelihood of police trying to elicit bribes, however, it's best to ensure you also have an international driving licence.

Fuel

As of late 2016, the cost of unleaded petrol was US$1.30 per litre, and US$1.20 for diesel.

Hire

➤ The minimum driving age required by rental companies varies, but it is usually between 23 and 25 years. The maximum age is normally about 65 years.

➤ It's important to note that most collision damage waiver (CDW) insurance policies do not cover 2WD vehicles travelling on rough roads in national parks.

➤ Be sure you have all the relevant papers and your car is fitted with the legally required fire extinguisher (serviced so it's on green), warning triangles and reflectors and a light for the rear number plate. All these are checked routinely at the many roadblocks, with fines issued if any of the above aren't in order.

➤ If you hire a car outside Zimbabwe (particularly South Africa or Zambia) you can expect to be waved down more often at the ubiquitous police roadblocks for revenue-raising safety checks.

Road Hazards

Many residents make a rule of not driving outside the major towns after dark. Police roadblocks are another inevitable pain of driving in Zimbabwe and you can expect to be waved down multiple times for long journeys. As long as you have all the correct papers and safety equipment, a smile and being courteous should see you waved through without any problems. It's important to be courteous at all times in your dealings with police; rude or aggressive behaviour will land you in much more trouble. It's not a bad idea to request and note the force number of the officer. The maximum fine is US$20, but is usually US$10 or less.

LOCAL TRANSPORT

Taxis are safe and reliable and can be booked through your hotel front desk. Most are metered, charging around US$2.50 for 1km at the time of writing. Taxis in cities travel within a 40km radius of the city. Always take a taxi at night.

TRAIN

Connecting Harare, Bulawayo, Mutare and Victoria Falls, all major train services travel at night. The most popular route is from Vic Falls to Bulawayo. Definitely opt for first class, which is good value, comfortable and gets you a sleeping compartment.

Understand Southern Africa

SOUTHERN AFRICA TODAY 662

Southern Africa is dealing with AIDS and a fragile environmental landscape, but it's often doing so with stable governments and strong economies.

HISTORY 664

Embark on a journey that traces human existence to its very beginning. This is where it all started.

CULTURE 671

Southern Africa is a mosaic of African and European cultures, with cohesion and conflict expressed through literature, art, dance and food.

WILDLIFE.................................... 679

From Botswana's world-famous Okavango Delta to the wilds of Zambia's massive protected areas, wildlife is the highlight of the region.

MUSIC IN SOUTHERN AFRICA................ 695

Music, more than any other cultural expression, has best survived the onslaught of Western influences.

ENVIRONMENT.............................. 701

The landscape and its inhabitants are protected through the region's unique reserves and national parks.

Southern Africa Today

Southern Africa's story is as diverse as the nine countries and more than 133 million people that call the region home. In some corners (eg Botswana and Namibia) political stability reigns, in others it looks more like stagnation (eg Zimbabwe and Swaziland). But there are some recurring themes, not least among them a complicated economic and environmental outlook and (finally) a generally positive outlook when it comes to the hitherto catastrophic HIV/AIDS situation.

Best on Film

The Gods Must Be Crazy (1984) Cult comedy starring Botswana's San.
A United Kingdom (2016) Based on the love story of Botswana's first president and his British bride.
Savage Kingdom (2016) Wldlife documentary showing the rivalry between predators in the Savuti region.
Invictus (2009) Covers the historic 1995 Rugby World Cup. Clint Eastwood directs.
Mandela: Long Walk to Freedom (2013) Condensed but enjoyable biography, covering Madiba's journey to South African presidency.

Best in Print

Lost World of the Kalahari (Laurens van der Post; 1958) A 1950s eulogy for San culture.
Cry of the Kalahari (Mark & Delia Owens; 1984) Kalahari wildlife before the tourists arrived.
Don't Let's Go to the Dogs Tonight – An African Childhood (Alexandra Fuller; 2001) A stunning memoir of life and loss and a family's unbreakable bond with Africa.
Disgrace (JM Coetzee; 1999) Booker Prize–winning novel based in post-apartheid South Africa.
The Stone Virgins (Yvonne Vera; 2002) The harrowing, award-winning tale of two sisters caught up in post-independence Zimbabwe.

Political Games

Southern Africa's political map is a snapshot of the continent. There are stunning success stories of the kind that rarely appear in international newspapers – Botswana and Namibia, for example, have stable but relatively open political systems where the ruling parties rarely change but democracy rules. Put simply, both countries may not be perfect but continue to serve as beacons of good governance. Elsewhere, a less robust political situation reigns. South Africa's ruling ANC has been passing through some troubled times under the leadership of Jacob Zuma, while Zambia, Malawi and Mozambique have all seen tumultuous changes of government, albeit, it must be said, without bringing down their democratic systems – of all of these, Mozambique's stability looks the most tenuous. A 2014 coup in Lesotho was a significant black spot for the region. The poorest performers of the region are Swaziland and Zimbabwe, both countries held in a state of stasis for decades, two countries' national lives on hold as their rulers cling to power, seemingly in perpetuity.

AIDS: A Corner Turned?

Nowhere suffered from the horrors of HIV/AIDS quite like Southern Africa. It was a crisis of Biblical proportions, of countless lives cut short and social structures torn asunder. Life expectancy fell to near-apocalyptic levels (life expectancy in Botswana was 35 in 2005), the number of children orphaned by the crisis soared and the impact was felt in every corner of society. The challenges continue – in Swaziland, for example, nearly one-third of the population suffers from HIV/AIDS (28.8%, the highest in the world) and life expectancy at birth is one of the lowest on earth (around 50 years). But there are signs of hope – infection rates are falling across the region, and Botswana (where the government provides antiretrovirals – ARV – treatment free to all of its HIV-positive citizens) has seen mother-to-child transmission plummet from close to 40% to barely 2%. The damage of the epidemic has been incalculable and it will be at least a generation before the health statistics of the region return to pre-HIV/AIDS levels. But finally there are signs that a high watermark may have been reached.

The Economic Outlook

The region's economies vary greatly. Botswana, Namibia and South Africa both rely heavily on their rich underground resources. Despite difficulties in all three national economies, they are difficulties that many other countries in the region would gladly have to deal with: their economic growth rates and per capita incomes are among the highest in Africa. At the other end of the scale, poverty is deeply entrenched and in a different stratosphere to the region's more prosperous economies – the average Botswanan earns US$16,400 per year, while in Malawi/Mozambique the average annual income is US$1100/1200. At this lower end of the spectrum, a combination of factors (not all of which are always present in every country) such as economic mismanagement, poor resource base and a damaging cycle of flood and drought make for a difficult economic future. And the impact of the economic divide is significant, one that has already taken a worrying turn with racial tensions between locals and poorer immigrants in South Africa and Zambia.

A Precarious Environment

The vagaries of rains that never seem to arrive and then arrive so suddenly as to wash everything away is a Southern African specialty. Flood and drought, feast and famine, are the recurring themes of the region's life and they're themes that are reflected in the region's landscapes – the vast deserts of the Kalahari and Namib, the equally vast floodplains of the Okavango and Liuwa, the lush tropical coasts of Mozambique. The extremes that have moulded these lands also produce a slew of environmental travails and challenges – creeping desertification, crippling erosion and widespread water scarcity among them. As for the human population, so too for Southern Africa's wild animals. With wild lands shrinking in the face of growing human populations, numerous species are spiralling dangerously close to extinction as conflict between wildlife and human beings intensifies. National parks and protected areas are important strongholds. But unless things change dramatically, such strongholds will be all that remains in the not-too-distant future.

POPULATION: **133.453 MILLION**

LIFE EXPECTANCY AT BIRTH (YEARS):
  NAMIBIA: **63.6**
  SOUTH AFRICA: **63.1**
  MALAWI: **61.2**
  ZIMBABWE: **58**
  BOTSWANA: **54.5**
  MOZAMBIQUE: **53.3**
  LESOTHO: **53**
  ZAMBIA: **52.5**
  SWAZILAND: **51.6**

PER CAPITA INCOMES (US$):
  BOTSWANA: **16,400**
  SOUTH AFRICA: **13,200**
  NAMIBIA: **11,400**
  SWAZILAND: **8500**
  ZAMBIA: **3900**
  LESOTHO: **3000**
  ZIMBABWE: **2100**
  MOZAMBIQUE: **1200**
  MALAWI: **1100**

belief systems
(% of population)

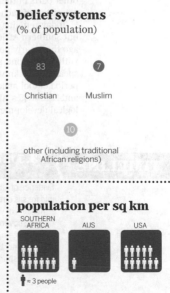

83 Christian

7 Muslim

10 other (including traditional African religions)

population per sq km

SOUTHERN AFRICA · AUS · USA

≈ 3 people

History

The precolonial history of Southern Africa is a compelling, interwoven web of peoples on the move throughout this vast region – the original travellers on our planet. It's also a story of technology and its impact on our early ancestors. Although Southern Africa's history stretches far back into the mists of time, the only records today are intriguing fossil remains and an extraordinary human diary of Stone Age rock art.

The Mists of Time

History of Southern Africa, by JD Omer-Cooper, provides an excellent, highly readable account of the early peoples of Southern Africa, including fascinating cultural detail that differentiates the many Bantu-speaking groups.

The region has revealed many archaeological records of the world's earliest human inhabitants. It's generally agreed among scientists that the first hominids (upright-walking human-like creatures) became established in the savannahs of East and Southern Africa nearly four million years ago, although hominid remains dating to between six and seven million years old have been found further north in Chad.

Sterkfontein in South Africa is regarded as one of the richest places on the planet for early human remains and is a Unesco World Heritage Site. In Malawi, archaeologists have found remains thought to date back as far as 2.5 million years.

It is surmised that about two million years ago several hominid species evolved, with Homo erectus developing basic tool-making abilities and eventually becoming dominant. Later evolving into Homo sapiens (modern humans), these early Africans are believed to have trekked to other parts of the world, where local factors determined the racial characteristics of each group.

Today, remains of temporary camps and stone tools are found throughout Southern Africa, and one site in Namibia suggests that 750,000 years ago these early people were hunting elephants and cutting up carcasses with large stone axes. By 150,000 years ago, people were using lighter spear heads, knives, saws and other tools. Archaeologists classify this period of tool making as the Stone Age, subdivided into the Early, Middle and Late stages, although the term applies to the people's level of technological development, rather than to a specific period.

TIMELINE	c 3.5 million BC	c 2 million BC	c 100,000 BC
	Evidence of early hominid fossils dating back millions of years has been discovered at the Sterkfontein Caves in Gauteng, northwest of Johannesburg, South Africa.	*Homo erectus* becomes the dominant hominid species, later evolving into what we now define as modern humans; sub-Saharan Africa really was the birthplace of humanity.	Zambia's most celebrated early inhabitant, Broken Hill Man, lives and dies. Evidence unearthed by archaeologists suggests Early Stone Age settlements existed along the shore of Lake Malawi at this time.

Early Khoe-San Inhabitants

Thousands of years ago, humans in Southern Africa developed an organised hunting and gathering society. Use of fire was universal, tools became more sophisticated (made from wood and animal products as well as stone), and make-up (natural pigments used for personal adornment) was in fashion. These Boskop people (named after the site in South Africa where their remains were discovered) are believed to be the ancestors of the San people, who still exist in isolated pockets today.

ANCIENT ROCK ART

The magnificent rock art sprinkled around Southern Africa is like a remarkable human diary left by an ancient people, and it's a major highlight for many visitors. There's much speculation about the origins of ancient rock paintings and engravings. Evidence such as tools and animal remains left around major sites, and the kinds of scenes depicted, suggest the artists were the early San people.

A tantalising sliver of Stone Age existence, these sites provide a snapshot of the way the San lived and hunted, and give insight into their spirituality. Unlike works in a museum, rock art remains where it was created, which means you may catch a glimpse of the inspiration that went into these paintings. Although rock art is found all over Southern Africa, the best examples are in Matobo National Park (p646) in Zimbabwe; and Giant's Castle (p432) in South Africa.

Most rock paintings reflect a relationship with nature. Some are stylised representations of the region's people and animals, but the majority are realistic portrayals of hunters, giraffes, elephants, rhinos, lions, antelope and so on, in rich red, yellow, brown and ochre. Common themes include the roles of men and women, hunting scenes and natural medicine. Examples of the lost include trance dancing and spiritual healing using the San life force, known as *nxum*, which was invoked to control aspects of the natural world, including climate and disease. All these elements still feature in San tradition.

Although climatic onslaught means the earliest works have long faded, flaked and eroded into oblivion, the dry climate and sheltered granite overhangs have preserved many of the more recent paintings. Three distinct periods have been identified: the earliest paintings seem to reflect a period of gentle nomadism, during which people were occupied primarily with the hunt; later works, which reveal great artistic improvement, suggest peaceful arrivals by outside groups, perhaps Bantu or Khoekhoen; the final stage indicates a decline in the standard of the paintings – or they may be imitations of earlier works by more recently arrived peoples.

Red pigments were ground mainly from iron oxides, powdered and mixed with animal fat to form an adhesive paste. Whites came from silica, powdered quartz and white clays, and were less adhesive than the red pigments. For this reason, white paintings survive only in sheltered locations. Both pigments were applied to the rock using fingers, sticks and brushes made of animal hair. While admiring rock art, please keep in mind the fragility of the paintings.

c 30,000 BC	c 20,000 BC	c 8000 BC	c 8000 BC
Evidence suggests that the peoples of Southern Africa had developed an organised hunting and gathering lifestyle, made possible by more sophisticated tools and weapons.	The San had made significant technological progress by this time, although it was restricted to stone. This meant increased time for leisure and artistic pursuits, which included rock art.	The San likely began producing pottery around this time, supporting the notion that their progress allowed them increased time away from hunting and gathering food.	The San come under pressure from another group called the Khoekhoen, known in more recent times as Hottentots. These two peoples are thought to share a common ancestry.

Eventually, tools became smaller and better designed, which increased hunting efficiency and allowed time for further innovation, artistic pursuits and admiring the fiery African sunsets. This stage is called the Microlithic Revolution because it was characterised by the working of small stones. The remains of microliths are often found alongside clear evidence of food gathering, shellfish remains and the working of wood, bone and ostrich eggshell.

The artistic traditions of the San are evidenced by pottery and especially by the wonderful paintings that can be seen today in rock shelters and caves all over Southern Africa. The better examples capture the elegance and movement of African wildlife with astonishing clarity. More recent paintings even depict white farmers.

Despite these artistic and technical developments, the San had no knowledge of metal working, and thus remain classified as Stone Age people.

The San and another group called the Khoekhoen (of Khoi-Khoi) are thought to share a common ancestry. Differences between the peoples were slight, based more on habitat and lifestyle than on significant physiological features. The Khoikhoi kept cattle, which were a source of food and transport, and were even trained to charge the enemy in warfare. These two groups also shared a language group, characterised by distinctive 'click' sounds. Today these two peoples are regarded as one, termed Khoe-San or Khoisan, and are mostly found in remote parts of Namibia and Botswana.

In recent times the San have been controversially relocated from their ancestral lands to new government settlements such as New Xade in the central Kalahari in Botswana.

The Bantu Migration

While the Khoe-San were developing, in West Africa another group with larger body types and darker skin was emerging: the Bantu.

Their advanced skills led to improved farming methods and the ability to make unwanted guests of themselves on their neighbours' lands. Over 2000 years ago the Bantu moved into the Congo basin and, over the next thousand years, spread across present-day Uganda, Kenya and Tanzania and migrated south into Zambia, Malawi, Mozambique and other parts of Southern Africa. The term 'migration' here refers to a sporadic spread over many hundreds of years. Typically, a group would move from valley to valley or from one water source to the next. This process inevitably had a knock-on effect, as weaker ethnic groups were constantly being 'moved on' by invaders from other areas.

At first, the Bantu in Southern Africa apparently lived in relative harmony with the original Khoe-San inhabitants, trading goods, language

To learn more about the San, including current issues for survival, see www.kalaharipeoples.org, created by a nonprofit organisation involved with the people of the Kalahari.

Click onto https://networks.h-net.org/h-safrica, and join in with this electronic discussion group on all things pertaining to the history and culture of Southern Africa.

c 2000–500 BC	500–1000 AD	13th century	1498
Iron-skilled Bantu migrate from West Africa through the Congo basin into present-day Zambia and Malawi. Over the centuries they spread into other parts of East and Southern Africa.	Gokomere people and subsequent groups in what is now Zimbabwe develop gold-mining techniques and produce progressively finer-quality ceramics, jewellery, textiles and soapstone carvings.	Construction of Great Zimbabwe commences – the city grows into a powerful religious and political capital, becoming the heart of Rozwi culture and the greatest medieval city in sub-Saharan Africa.	Portuguese explorer Vasco da Gama lands at Mozambique Island. Over the next 200 years, the Portuguese establish coastal trading enclaves and settlements in the interior along the Zambezi Valley.

THE BANTU

The Bantu peoples could more accurately be called 'Bantu-speaking peoples', since the word 'Bantu' actually refers to a language group rather than a specific race. In reality the Bantu ethnic group comprises many subgroups or tribes, each with its own language, customs and traditions, living all over the region. Nevertheless, 'Bantu' has become a convenient term of reference for the black African peoples of Southern and Eastern Africa, even though the grouping is as ill-defined as 'American' or 'Asian'. The Bantu ethnic group comprises many subgroups, each with their own language, customs and traditions.

and culture. As Bantu numbers increased, however, some Khoe-San were conquered or absorbed by this more advanced group of peoples, while the remainder were pushed further and further into inhospitable lands.

Bantu Culture & Early Kingdoms

A feature of Bantu culture was its strong social system, based on extended family or clan loyalties and dependencies, generally centred on the rule of a chief. Some chiefdoms developed into powerful kingdoms, uniting many disparate ethnic groups and covering large geographical areas.

Cattle played an essential role in the lives of Southern Africa's Bantu population. Apart from providing food, skins and a form of capital, cattle were also most essential when it came to bride wealth. Marriage involved the transfer of a woman to the household of her husband. In turn, the cattle from the husband's family were reassigned to the family of the bride's father. A man who had many daughters would one day end up with many cattle.

One of the earliest Bantu kingdoms was Gokomere, in the uplands of Zimbabwe. The Gokomere people are thought to be the first occupants of the Great Zimbabwe site, near present-day Masvingo.

Early Traders

Meanwhile, from the latter half of the 1st millennium, Arabs from the lands around the Red Sea were sailing southwards along the eastern seaboard of Africa. They traded with the local Bantu inhabitants, who by this time had reached the coast, and bought ivory, gold and slaves to take back to Arabia.

Between AD 1000 and 1500, the Arab-influenced Bantu founded several major settlements along the coast, from Mogadishu (in present-day Somalia) to Kilwa (in southern Tanzania), including Lamu (Kenya) and Zanzibar (Tanzania). In Kenya and Tanzania particularly, the

Check out www.southafrica.info/about/history/history.htm for a comprehensive but easily readable overview of South African history. For an overview of the famous figures who have shaped South African history, check out www.sahistory.org.za for a well-presented list of biographies.

1616	17th century	mid-17th century	1750
Portuguese explorer Gaspar Bocarro journeys from Tete (on the Zambezi River) through the Shire Valley to Lake Chilwa, then through the south of Tanzania and back into Mozambique.	Competing European powers begin settling in South Africa, mostly in the Cape. This signals the eventual change of life for the peoples of Southern Africa brought about by European colonialism.	European colonists come into conflict with the San. The early Boers' campaign of land seizures and forced migrations lasts for 200 years and results in the death of up to 200,000 indigenous people.	Dutch elephant hunter Jacobus Coetsee becomes the first European to cross the Orange River, followed by a series of traders, hunters and missionaries.

Bantu people were influenced by the Arabs, and a certain degree of inter-marriage occurred, so that gradually a mixed language and culture was created, called Swahili, which remains intact today.

From southern Tanzania the Swahili-Arabs traded along the coast of present-day Mozambique, establishing bases at Quelimane and Mozambique Island.

From the coast the Swahili-Arabs pushed into the interior, and developed a network of trade routes across much of East and Southern Africa. Ivory and gold continued to be sought-after, but the demand for slaves grew considerably, and reached its zenith in the early 19th century when the Swahili-Arabs and dominant local ethnic groups are reckoned to have either killed or sold into slavery 80,000 to 100,000 Africans per year.

An Introduction to the History of Central Africa – Zambia, Malawi and Zimbabwe, by AJ Wills, provides a comprehensive work on the region and is considered one of the best around.

Later Bantu Kingdoms & People

As early as the 11th century, the inhabitants of Great Zimbabwe had come into contact with Arab-Swahili traders from the coast. Great Zimbabwe became the capital of the wealthiest and most powerful society in Southern Africa – its people the ancestors of today's Shona people – and reached the zenith of its powers around the 14th century, becoming the greatest medieval city in sub-Saharan Africa.

From around the 11th century it appears that more advanced Bantu-speaking Iron Age people migrated to the area, absorbing the earlier immigrants. As they settled they branched out into a number of cultural groups. One of these groups, the Nguni, was distinguished from its neighbours by strict matrimony rules – marriage was forbidden to a partner that could be traced to a common ancestor. The Xhosa were the southernmost of these people. Covering large areas of present-day South

---

LOCAL HISTORIES

➜ *A History of Namibia: From the Beginning to 1990* (2011) by Marion Wallace and John Kinahan

➜ *A Short History of Lesotho: From the Late Stone Age Until the 1993 Elections* (1993) by Stephen J Gill

➜ *A History of Malawi: 1859–1966* (2012) by John McCracken

➜ *A History of Zimbabwe* (2014) by Alois S Mlambo

➜ *Missionary Travels* (1857) by David Livingstone

➜ *Building of a Nation: A History of Botswana from 1800 to 1910* (1996) by Jeff Ramsay, Barry Morton and Part Themba Mgadla

---

1836	1884	19th century	1989
Groups of Boers, dissatisfied with British rule in the Cape Colony, begin a decade of migration known as the Great Trek; increasing numbers abandon their farms and cross the Senqu (Orange) River.	Otto von Bismarck invites other dominant European powers to participate in the Berlin Conference, which officially begins the 'Scramble for Africa', and marks Germany's emergence as an imperial power.	The face of Southern Africa changes significantly as the earlier trickle of European settlers to South Africa becomes widespread colonial settlement, filtering through to many parts of the region.	One of Africa's youngest countries, second only to Eritrea, Namibia officially becomes independent on 1 April after a multiparty peace deal is brokered between Cuba, Angola, South Africa and Namibia's Swapo party.

Africa, Botswana and Lesotho were the Sotho-Setswana, who encouraged intercousin marriage. The Venda, who have a matriarchal culture and are thought to be related to the Shona people of Zimbabwe, occupied the north of Limpopo province in South Africa.

Further north, between the 14th and 16th centuries, another Bantu group called the Maravi (of whom the Chewa became the dominant ethnic group) arrived in Southern Africa from the Congo Basin and founded a powerful kingdom covering southern Malawi and parts of present-day Mozambique and Zambia. Masks made by a men's secret society called Nyau were an integral part of ceremonies for this group. As well as representing cultural ideals with themes such as wisdom, sickness, death and ancestors, masks also caricatured undesirables such as slave-traders, invaders and colonial figures.

At about the same time the Tumbuka and the Phoka groups migrated into the north of Malawi. The Tumbuka are known for their healing practices, which combine traditional medicine and music.

During the 16th and 17th centuries, another Bantu group called the Herero migrated from the Zambezi Valley into present-day Namibia, where they came into conflict with the San and competed with the Khoekhoen for the best grazing lands. Eventually, most indigenous groups submitted to the Herero. Only the Nama people, thought to be descended from early Khoekhoen groups, held out. One of Africa's most traditional cultures, the Himba people in Namibia, are descended from the Herero.

The power of the Bantu kingdoms started to falter in the late 18th and early 19th centuries due to a major dispersal of indigenous ethnic groups called the *difaqane,* and a rapid increase in the number of European settlers.

The Difaqane

The *difaqane* (meaning 'forced migration' in Sotho; *mfeqane,* 'the crushing', in Zulu) was a period of immense upheaval and suffering for the indigenous peoples of Southern Africa. It originated in the early 19th century when the Nguni ethnic groups in modern KwaZulu-Natal (South Africa) changed rapidly from loosely organised collections of chiefdoms to the more centralised Zulu Nation. Based on a highly disciplined and powerful warrior army, the process began under Chief Dingiswayo, and reached its peak under the military commander Shaka Zulu.

Shaka was a ruthless conqueror and his reputation preceded him. Not surprisingly, ethnic groups living in his path chose to flee, in turn displacing neighbours and causing disruption and terror across Southern Africa. Ethnic groups displaced from Zululand include the Matabele, who settled in present-day Zimbabwe, while the Ngoni fled to Malawi

Today's Herero women are distinguished by their extravagant neck to ankle Victorian dresses, petticoats and large hats – a by-product of contact with German missionaries.

The Makololo were uprooted from Zululand during the *difaqane* and moved into southwest Zambia, where they displaced the Tonga people. To this day the dominant language of much of western Zambia remains Makololo.

2006	2006	2008	2010
Botswana's government is reprimanded by the UN's Committee on the Elimination of Racial Discrimination for its resettlement program relocating San from their ancestral lands.	In a highly publicised act mirroring neighbouring Zimbabwe, the Namibian government commences the expropriation of white-owned farms as part of a hotly contested land-reform program.	Long-simmering social discontent boils over and xenophobic rioting breaks out in South Africa, with migrants from neighbouring countries (such as Zimbabwe) targeted; there are more than 60 deaths.	After spending billions upgrading infrastructure, giving a major boost to local employment, South Africa hosts the 2010 FIFA World Cup, which sees new arrivals pour into the region.

and Zambia. Notable survivors were the Swazi and Basotho, who forged powerful kingdoms that became Swaziland and Lesotho.

European Colonisation & Settlement

The Scramble for Africa: White Man's Conquest of the Dark Continent from 1876 to 1912, by Thomas Pakenham, details the colonial history of Southern Africa and the continent in well-written and entertaining prose.

Although there had been a European presence in Southern Africa for several hundred years, in 1820 the British Cape Colony saw a major influx of settlers. Around 5000 were brought from Britain on the promise of fertile farmland around the Great Fish River, near the Shipwreck Coast, Eastern Cape. In reality, the settlers were brought in to form a buffer between the Boers (historic name for the Afrikaner people; to the west of the river) and the Xhosa (amaXhosa; to the east), who competed for territory.

From this point, European settlement rapidly spread from the Cape Colony to Natal and later to the Transvaal – especially after the discovery of gold and diamonds. In many cases Europeans were able to occupy land abandoned by African people following the *difaqane*.

From the 1830s groups of Boers fed up with British rule in the Cape Colony trekked off into the wilds of what is now South Africa, to carve out a living free from British interference. These early trekkers, or Voortrekkers as they were known, went on what is referred to as the Great Trek during a decade of migration.

Over the next 100 to 150 years, an ever-increasing number of Europeans from South Africa settled in areas that became the colonies of Swaziland, Nyasaland (Malawi), Northern and Southern Rhodesia (Zambia and Zimbabwe), Bechuanaland (Botswana), Basotholand (Lesotho), German South West Africa (Namibia) and Portuguese East Africa (Mozambique). With this change, Southern Africans would never again be permitted to follow entirely traditional ways.

2013	2014	2014	2016
The Southern African Development Community (SADC) begins to flex its regional muscle, sending troops to eastern Democratic Republic of Congo (DRC) to oppose rebel forces backed by Rwanda.	Botswana's decision (taken in 2012) to ban commercial or trophy hunting comes into effect.	South Africa holds its fifth general election since the end of apartheid. The ANC wins (with a reduced majority), with 62.1% of the vote, and Jacob Zuma begins a second term as president.	Botswana celebrates 50 years as an independent country.

Culture

Culture in Southern Africa is a fascinating collection of interwoven issues, from the central elements of local life and identity (religion, ethnic group and economic issues) to the region's vibrant artistic endeavours. These include a dynamic music scene, surprising architectural variety, local food in all its infinite manifestations as well as literature, dance and a stirring artistic heritage.

Peoples of Southern Africa

Southern Africa's population consists of Bantu-speaking people (the majority) who migrated from the north and west of the African continent down through the centuries; later-arriving Europeans (including Dutch, British, Portuguese and Germans); Indians (who arrived with the British, brought over to the Cape Colony as labourers); and pockets of the Khoe-San (an ancient Stone Age people who survive in small numbers) in Botswana, Namibia and South Africa.

> If you're offered a gift, don't feel guilty about accepting it. To receive it, accept with both hands and bow slightly.

Multicultural Southern Africa?

Broadly speaking, two societies and cultures (Western and African) run in parallel, and they rarely cross. As you might expect, in a Western situation social customs are similar to those in Europe, although often a touch more formal – but at the same time more friendly – than in other parts of the Western world. For example, Afrikaners will often shake hands and say their name, even if you're only meeting them briefly. While you'll meet locals of European origin and 'Europeanised' black Africans all over the region, especially in urban areas, the societies and cultures are predominantly African.

Southern Africa is very multicultural and surprisingly peaceful given the extraordinary number of ethnic groups. However, integrating European and African populations has been a source of tension for many years in the region, exacerbated by colonial rule, apartheid governments and, in Zimbabwe, a policy of reclaiming white-owned farms in recent years. Disharmony stretches much further back, however, with the destruction and dispersal of the *difaqane* (forced migration), which led to tribal affiliations being disrupted among various Bantu groups in the region. This was exacerbated in South Africa by the Great Trek and the Voortrekkers, who settled into areas they believed were 'vacant'.

Migration from the poorer countries to the wealthier countries in the region has also brought about tensions and hostility. South Africa for example has far more job opportunities than other countries in the region, and this has led to a great number of migrant workers (many illegal) drifting there. Africans who look different or don't speak the local language are often harassed by officialdom and the police. Locals are often suspicious of migrants, too, as there is a perception that they take jobs away from locals and are responsible for crime. Such suspicions spilled over into xenophobic violence targeting immigrants and other foreigners in the South African city of Durban in 2015.

A migrant's money makes a big difference to the local economy back home – Lesotho is a good example, with many travelling to South Africa until the late 1990s to work in mines and sending money back home to their families. It is widely agreed, however, that this type of migration and inter-African mobility has also contributed to the spread of HIV/AIDS.

Daily Life

Southern Africans tend to be conservative, God-fearing peoples whose daily lives revolve around family and other tightly knit social networks. These pillars of society tend to become a little shaky in urban areas, where traditional networks are often less important than economic and other factors. The catastrophe that has been HIV/AIDS has similarly undermined traditional bastions of belonging. Across the region, education is seen as essential to advancement, but many (especially women) still struggle to enjoy the benefits of growing economies.

Many countries within Southern Africa are incredibly ethnically diverse. This is exemplified in South Africa, which has 11 official languages.

Distribution of Wealth

Southern Africa covers an enormous geographical area with an incredibly diverse population, and there is stark wealth differentiation between and within the countries of the region. Therefore, giving a precise impression of daily life for Southern Africans is virtually impossible. Nevertheless, there are some generalisations able to be made that represent very real trends in the region.

Life varies considerably between the 'haves' and the 'have-nots'. Middle-class and wealthy families live in homes reflecting that wealth, and many leafy, wealthy neighbourhoods look just like anywhere else in the Western world. Leisure time is often defined by time spent at upmarket (and in the case of South Africa, heavily guarded) shopping centres, which provide outdoor dining, plenty of retail therapy and a place 'to be seen'.

For the millions of Southern Africans (in fact, the vast majority of the population) who still live in great poverty, however, life is about survival. Simple huts or enclosures house large extended families, and obtaining and preparing food is the focus of daily life.

Famine & Flood

Food shortages and hunger remain critically serious problems in Southern Africa. The region suffers from a seemingly endless cycle of food insecurity.

The simple reason for the food shortage is prolonged dry spells, which lead to crop failure. The reasons behind the region's continued problems in feeding itself, however, are more complex and deeply rooted. The multitude of causes include inadequate agricultural policies, the ripping away of a generation of workers through the HIV/AIDS epidemic, few employment opportunities, bad governance and environmental degradation.

In addition to these problems, floods also wreak havoc, especially in western Zambia, northern Namibia, northern Botswana, Mozambique and (in 2016, for example) South Africa.

HIV/AIDS

The largest problem facing the people of Southern Africa is HIV/AIDS. The sub-Saharan region is the worst-affected region in Africa and, while the statistics are simply dreadful, the socioeconomic effects are overwhelming. In 2013 an estimated 24.7 million people in sub-Saharan Africa were living with HIV – this represents more than two-thirds of the world HIV population. South Africa has the world's largest HIV-positive population (seven million people), and national adult HIV prevalence is above 19% in that country and around the same level in Botswana, Lesotho, Namibia, Zambia and Zimbabwe. Swaziland has a HIV prevalence rate of nearly 29% – the highest ever documented in a country anywhere in the world. It should be noted that both Botswana and Zimbabwe have made progress in recording drops in HIV infection rates, proving that through education change is possible.

Unlike diseases that attack the weak, HIV/AIDS predominantly hits the productive members of a household – young adults. It's particularly rife among those who are highly educated, and have relatively high earnings and mobility. This has an enormous impact on household incomes, with the region facing the loss of a large proportion of a generation in the prime of its life. This has also meant a sharp increase in the number of orphans, of grandparents being pressured into assuming parenting roles of young children, and of children pulled out of school to care for the sick, grow food or earn money. There's still a lot of stigma attached to HIV/AIDS, too, and many locals won't admit to the cause of a loved one's death.

HIV/AIDS has led to a sharp decrease in life expectancy in Southern Africa. Recent projections have put life expectancy at around 50 years across the region – between 1990 and 1995 it peaked at just over 60 years. This fall has hopefully now bottomed out, with new treatments bringing a slight rise in recent years.

Attitudes to Sexuality

All the countries in Southern Africa are conservative in their attitudes towards gay men and lesbians. In traditional African societies, gay sexual relationships are a cultural taboo. In practice, rights for gay citizens contrast strongly between countries. South Africa's progressive constitution, for example, outlaws discrimination on the basis of sexual orientation, and gay couples have won many rights, while Mozambique decriminalised homosexuality in 2015. On the other hand, Namibia and Zimbabwe have strongly condemned homosexuality, with President Mugabe describing homosexuals as 'worse than pigs and dogs' in a 1995 public speech.

South Africa has one of the highest incidences of rape in the world and, as many are too afraid to report the crime, the true extent of the problem is likely much worse than official figures would suggest. Another tragic issue in South Africa is sexual abuse of girls in schools by their teachers; as a result, many girls are reluctant to attend school.

Religion

Religion plays a pivotal role in local life and a person's religion is very often seen as being every bit as important as their ethnic group or nationality. Christianity has the largest number of followers in every country of the region, but there are also significant populations of Muslims, Hindus and others, with traditional African religions still important across the region.

Christianity

Most people in Southern Africa follow Christianity or traditional religion, often combining aspects of both. South Africa, Malawi, Botswana and Namibia have very high Christian populations (between 70% and 80% of the general population), while Mozambique has the lowest (around 56%). All the Western-style Christian churches are represented (Catholic, Protestant, Baptist, Adventist etc), most of which were introduced in colonial times by European missionaries. Their spread across the region reflects their colonial roots – the dominant Christian sect in Namibia is German Lutheranism, while Malawi is dominated by Protestant churches, founded by British missionaries. Mozambique's Portuguese heritage means Roman Catholicism is favoured among that country's Christians.

The influence of missionaries has been beneficial in education, campaigning against the slave trade, and in trying to raise the standard of living in Southern Africa; however, benefits have been tempered by the search for ideological control and disruption to traditional cultures. Missionaries were certainly influential in Malawi, where the country's history and existence was shaped by figures such as Dr Livingstone. He was a famous missionary and explorer whose intrepid travels on foot through

Working to end violence against women and supporting victims of rape, Rape Crisis is based in Cape Town, South Africa. Click onto www.rapecrisis. org.za if you'd like to learn more about its work.

Christianity in Southern Africa is known for its conservatism. Roman Catholic bishops in the region have controversially condemned the use of condoms in the fight against HIV/AIDS.

CULTURE RELIGION

the continent opened up much of Southern Africa to the traders and settlers that followed in his footsteps.

Although Christian denominations in Southern Africa are generally conservative, many churches actively participate in the fight against HIV/AIDS. Organisations such as Churches United Against HIV/AIDS (CUAHA) work with local churches to support families, care for those afflicted by the disease and reduce the stigma associated with HIV/AIDS.

Many indigenous Christian faiths have also been established, ranging from a small congregation meeting in a simple hut to vast organisations with millions of followers, such as the Zion and Apostolic churches in Zimbabwe and South Africa. In South Africa alone the Zion Church claims four million followers (the largest in the country).

South Africa's Archbishop Desmond Tutu said, 'When the missionaries came to Africa, they had the Bible and we had the land. They said, "Let us pray." We closed our eyes. When we opened them, we had the Bible and they had the land.'

Islam, Hinduism & Judaism

Islam is also followed in some areas, predominantly in the north of Malawi and along its lakeshore, and in the northern provinces of Mozambique, where around 20% of the population attest to the Islamic faith, the highest percentage in Southern Africa. There are also Hindus across the region and Jews, particularly in South Africa, but numbers for both communities are small.

Traditional Religions

There are many traditional religions in Southern Africa, but no great temples or written scriptures. For outsiders, beliefs can be complex, as can the rituals and ceremonies that surround them. Most traditional religions are animist – based on the attribution of life or consciousness to natural objects or phenomena – and many accept the existence of a Supreme Being, with whom communication is possible through the intercession of ancestors. Thus, ancestors play a particularly strong role. Their principal function is to protect the tribe or family, and they may on occasion show their pleasure (such as through a good harvest) or displeasure (through a member of the family becoming sick, for example).

Arts

The countries and indigenous peoples of Southern Africa all have their own artistic traditions, often interwoven with culture and beliefs. The story began with the rock art created by the San people since time immemorial and broadens out into local literary, architectural, performance and artistic pursuits. The region's music scene is itself a fascinating story, while the region's culinary delights are also well worth exploring.

WITCHCRAFT

Within many traditional African religions, there is a belief in spells and magic (usually called witchcraft or, in some places, *mutu*). In brief simplistic terms it goes like this: physical or mental illnesses are often ascribed to a spell or curse having been put on the sufferer. Often, a relative or villager is suspected of being the 'witch' who placed the curse, often for reasons of spite or jealousy. A traditional doctor, also called a diviner or witchdoctor, is then required to hunt out the witch and cure the victim. This is done in different ways in various parts of the region, and may involve the use of herbs, divining implements, prayers, chanting, dance or placing the spell in a bottle and casting it into a remote spot (if you find such a bottle in the bush, don't touch it).

Services do not come free of charge, however, and many witchdoctors demand high payments – up to US$20, in countries where an average month's earnings may be little more than this. The 'witches' who are unearthed are frequently those who cannot defend themselves – the sick, the old or the very poorest members of society. There are even reports of witchdoctors accusing very young children of harbouring evil spirits.

Literature

Southern Africa has a strong tradition of oral literature among the various Bantu groups. Traditions and stories were preserved and passed on from generation to generation. In many parts of the region, written language was introduced only by Christian missionaries and assumed more importance in the 20th century. Common forms of literature that have developed include short stories, novels and poetry.

Although writers have focused on themes usually concerning their own country, there are common threads. Nationalism, white minority rule, the struggle for independence and life after colonialism are all themes explored by Southern African writers. In Malawi, oppression and abuse of power were common themes through the Banda years, after independence; Samson Kambalu is a contemporary author who writes about growing up in 1970s and '80s Malawi. Guerrilla poets such as Marcelino dos Santos from Mozambique make fascinating reading. In many countries the growth of literature has paralleled the struggle for independence and freedom.

Works by authors such as Bessie Head from Botswana address African village life and landscape, and Zimbabwean writers include precolonial traditions, myths and folk tales in their writings.

From Malawi, William Kamkwamba (*The Boy Who Harnessed The Wind*; 2009) and Samson Kambalu (*The Jive Talker: or, How to Get a British Passport*; 2008) have written two of Southern Africa's most compelling works of nonfiction.

Stephen Gill has written several historical books on Lesotho and, thanks to him, archives were established and much local history saved.

White South African writers have had considerable overseas success, with literary giants such as Nadine Gordimer and JM Coetzee both awarded Nobel Prizes for Literature. If you want to get a sense of where South Africa has come from and where it's going, delving into its literary roots is a good place to start. Local literature takes you back into the days of apartheid (from both a black and a white perspective) and the realities of building the rainbow nation.

The Penguin Book of Southern African Stories, edited by Stephen Gray, features stories (some thousands of years old) from the region, showing similarities and common threads in various literary traditions.

CULTURE ARTS

Architecture

The greatest indigenous architectural legacy is in the past – in Zimbabwe the ruins of great stone cities such as Great Zimbabwe (p640) and Khami (p643) are rare examples of medieval African architecture in the region. Mapungubwe (p486) in South Africa also contains excellent examples of ancient historical roots from a forgotten kingdom.

Architecturally, the colonial legacy in Southern Africa is dominated by European designs, with South Africa and Namibia containing by far the best examples. Pretoria's stately Union Building (p467) has won much acclaim, while art deco design sprang up in Durban and Cape Town after building booms in the early 20th century. Unique Cape Dutch buildings, especially town houses, can be seen throughout Cape Town.

In Namibia, Germany has left a colonial legacy of late-19th-century-designed places, including art-nouveau design. The most beautiful examples are in Lüderitz, Swakopmund and Windhoek.

Examples of 19th- and 20th-century English architecture (especially Victorian) can be seen in many parts of the region, and at times in the most unlikely of places (such as Livingstonia in Malawi and Shiwa Ng'andu in Zambia). Mozambique Island is an architectural treasure trove and includes the oldest European building in the southern hemisphere.

Safari lodges, such as those in Zimbabwe and Botswana, can be a mix of an English sensibility with African design pieces and environment.

Dance

Dance, along with music, in Southern Africa is often closely linked with, and plays an important role in, social function rather than being mere entertainment. Movement is regarded as an important type of communication in traditional African societies, and dance can be associated with contact between spirits and the living; traditional healers often performed curative dances to rid patients of sickness. Symbolic gestures, mime, props, masks, costumes and body painting can all play a part. If you have the chance to see traditional song and dance while you're in Southern Africa, try not to miss out.

Dance also helps to define culture, and in Swaziland, for example, the Umhlanga (reed) dance plays a very important role in society, drawing the nation together and reinforcing Swazi culture. Mozambicans are on the whole excellent dancers, and Arabic influence is evident in their slow, swaying rhythms.

Images of Power, by D Lewis-Williams and T Dowson, is a fascinating study of the art of the San people, utilising modern scientific techniques and rediscovered records of discussions between the San and early European settlers.

Painting & Sculpture

When travelling around the region, the more popular artworks you'll encounter double as handicrafts. They include: San crafts (particularly in Namibia and Botswana) such as jewellery and leatherwork, bows and arrows, and ostrich shell beads; mohair products such as tapestries and ponchos, especially in Lesotho and South Africa; exquisite palm-woven and African-themed baskets, particularly renowned in Botswana and Zambia; pottery, often highly decorative and, of course, very practical; Shona sculpture (Zimbabwean), renowned worldwide, with recurring themes such as the metamorphosis of man into beast, and Makonde sculpture (Mozambican); glassware and candles (Swazi) in the shape of regional wildlife, and in the case of the former often made from recyclable material. You'll also find wooden carvings, particularly in places where tourists are likely to wander – wildlife carvings such as huge giraffes are popular, and you'll even find earthmovers, aeroplanes and helicopters.

Township art is found throughout the region, and has developed sober themes in an expressive, colourful and usually light-hearted manner. Ranging from complex wire-work toys to prints and paintings, deceptively naive images in township art can embody messages that are far from simple.

In South Africa, the woodcarvers of Limpopo's Venda region have gained international recognition.

Galleries display works from Southern African artists, and include more traditional sculpture and paintings. Painters often interpret the landscape, wildlife and the diverse peoples of the region – Namibia, South Africa, Mozambique and Zambia in particular have galleries that display work from local artists.

Cooking the Southern African Way, by Kari Cornell, includes authentic ethnic foods (even vegetarian ones) from across the region, including a section on holiday and festival food.

Food & Drink

The business of eating tends to be all about survival for most of the population, and much of the day's activity is associated with the preparation of meals. In a region racked by famine, with many countries not able to consistently produce enough food to feed their own population, food is about functionality, not creativity. That said, the variety and quality of food for visitors and well-to-do locals is improving all the time.

The Basics

An urban setting will usually mean more variety for visitors, and the colonial legacy in some countries does mean some intriguing culinary combinations.

South Africa is the best place to eat and certainly has the most variety, an inheritance of its varied African, European and Asian population. Mozambique, too, blends a variety of influences (African, Indian and Portuguese) into its seafood offerings. In Malawi, eating *chambo* (fried fish) by the lake is a highlight.

A favourite for many visitors to Southern Africa is the fruit, and depending on the season you'll find bananas, pineapples, pawpaws (papayas), mangoes and avocados in plentiful supply.

Staples & Specialities

In parts of Southern Africa, especially in South Africa, Namibia and Botswana, meat features as a staple, and anything that can be grilled is grilled – including ostrich, crocodile, warthog and kudu. Meat also features in local celebrations. The braai (barbecue) is a regional obsession.

Takeaway snack food found on the street may include bits of grilled meat, deep-fried potato or cassava chips, roasted corn cobs, boiled eggs, peanuts (called ground nuts locally), biscuits, cakes, fried dough balls (which approximate doughnuts) and miniature green bananas. Prices are always dirt cheap (unfortunately, often with the emphasis on dirt).

For something more substantial, but still inexpensive, the most common meal is the regional staple, boiled maize meal, which is called *mealie pap* in South Africa and Namibia, *sadza* in Zimbabwe, and *nshima* or *nsima* in countries further north. In Botswana, the staple is known as *bogobe*, in which sorghum replaces the maize. When fresh and well cooked, all varieties are both tasty and filling, and are usually eaten with a *relish* (sauce or stew), which is either very simple (eg boiled vegetable leaves) or something more substantial, such as a stew of beef, fish, beans or chicken.

The main meal is at noon, so most cheap eateries are closed in the evening. In the morning you can buy coffee or tea (with or without milk – the latter is cheaper) and bread, sometimes with margarine, or maybe a slightly sweetened breadlike cake.

Up a notch, and popular with tourists, are traditional meals of *mielies* (cobs of maize) and relish, or Western dishes, such as beef or chicken served with rice or chips (fries). More elaborate options, such as steaks, pies, fish dishes, pasta and something that resembles curry over rice are worth trying for a change.

Most cities also have speciality restaurants serving genuine (or at least pretty close to it) Indian, Thai, Chinese, Lebanese, Mexican or ethnic African (such as Ethiopian or West African) cuisine.

Be aware of the source of your seafood: overfishing and inappropriate fishing methods mean that many species are overexploited, and some stocks are running dangerously low. For lists on what to avoid, check out www.wwfsassi.co.za.

FOOD ETIQUETTE

Most travellers will have the opportunity to share an African meal sometime during their stay, and will normally be given royal treatment and a seat of honour. Although concessions are sometimes made for foreigners, to avoid offence be aware that table manners are probably different to those you're accustomed to. The African staple, maize or sorghum meal, is the centre of nearly every meal. It is normally taken with the right hand from a communal pot, rolled into balls, dipped in some sort of *relish* – meat, beans or vegetables – and eaten. As in most societies, it is considered impolite to scoff food, or to hoard it or be stingy with it. If you do, your host may feel that he or she hasn't provided enough. Similarly, if you can't finish your food, don't worry; the host will be pleased that you have been satisfied. Often, containers of water or home-brew beer may be passed around from person to person. It is not customary to share coffee, tea or bottled soft drinks.

TRAVEL YOUR TASTEBUDS

If you're not squeamish about watching wildlife during the day and then sampling it in the evening, meat lovers can try some (nonendangered) local produce: dishes such as warthog stew, buffalo steak and impala sausages go down a treat. They can be hard to find, but wildlife lodges and upmarket restaurants are usually the best bet. In Namibia, kudu or gemsbok or even zebra steaks are much easier to find.

Bunny chow is a South African favourite, also popular in Swaziland. It's basically curry inside a hollowed-out loaf, messy to eat but quite delicious.

African bush tucker varies across the region among Southern Africa's indigenous groups – for example, the San still eat many desert creatures including caterpillar-like mopane worms, prepared in many different ways, such as deep-fried, or just eaten raw. These fat suckers are pulled off mopane trees and fried into little delicacies – they're tasty and a good source of protein; Botswana is a good place to find them.

Vegetarians & Vegans

Vegetarianism isn't widely understood in Africa, and many locals think a meal is incomplete unless at least half of it once lived and breathed. That said, nearly all safari lodges can provide vegetarian options with a little advance notice. Elsewhere, if you're not worried about variety or taste, finding inexpensive vegetarian options isn't that difficult. In the cheapest places, you may have to stick to the *mielies* and greens. A step above that would be eggs and chips (which may be fried in animal fat) with whatever vegetables may be available. Those who eat fish should have even more luck, but note that many places will even serve chicken as a vegetarian dish, on the notion that it's not really meat. Nearly all midrange and upmarket restaurants offer some sort of genuine vegetarian dish, even if it's just a vegetable omelette or pasta and sauce. In larger cities and towns, a growing number of places specialise in light vegetarian cuisine – especially at lunchtime – and of course, Lebanese, Indian and Italian restaurants usually offer various interesting meat-free choices.

The San eat *hoodia*, a prickly, cucumber-like plant, to suppress their appetite on long hunting treks – in the West *hoodia* is used in one of the most popular weight-loss drugs on the market.

Drinks

You can buy tea and coffee in many places, from top-end hotels and restaurants to humble local eating houses.

In bars, hotels and bottle stores you can buy beer and spirits, either imported international brands or locally brewed drinks. South African and Namibian beers (Windhoek brand is excellent) are available throughout the region, and in many areas they dominate local markets. Wonderful South African wines are widely available, as is a growing range of extremely popular spirit coolers.

Traditional beer of the region is made from maize, brewed in the villages and drunk from communal pots with great ceremony on special occasions, and with less ado in everyday situations. This product, known as Chibuku (or *shake-shake*), is commercially brewed in many countries and sold in large blue paper cartons, or by the bucketful. It's definitely an acquired taste, and it does pack a punch.

DOUG MCKINLAY/GETTY IMAGES ©

ve Giraffes, Okavango Delta (p65), Botswana

Wildlife

Southern Africa encompasses diverse habitats ranging from verdant forests to stony deserts and soaring mountains, from lush grasslands to classic African savannahs. It is home to penguins and hippos, great white sharks and elephants, and many more animals that will surprise and amaze visitors. Approximately 15% of the region receives some sort of formal protection. Kruger National Park and Kgalagadi Transfrontier Park include some of the region's largest and most significant protected areas.

Contents
➜ Cats
➜ Primates
➜ Cud-chewing Mammals
➜ Large Mammals
➜ Carnivores
➜ Birds of Prey
➜ Other Birds

1. Lion, Kruger National Park (p476), South Africa 2. Cheetahs, South Africa 3. Leopard, Chobe National Park (p58), Botswana 4. Caracal, Namibia

MARTIN MECNAROWSKI/SHUTTERSTOCK ©

Cats

With excellent vision and keen hearing, the seven cats found in Southern Africa are superb hunters. Experience unforgettable feline scenes, such as big cats making their kills or small cats performing incredible leaps to snatch birds out of the air.

Lion

Those lions sprawled in the shade are actually Africa's most feared predators. With teeth that tear effortlessly through bone and tendon, they can take down an animal as large as a bull giraffe. Each group of adults (a pride) is based around generations of females that do most of the hunting.

Best seen Savuti (p64), Kruger National Park (p476), Etosha National Park (p260)

Cheetah

The cheetah is a world-class sprinter. Although it reaches speeds of 112km/h, it runs out of steam after 300m and must cool down for 30 minutes before hunting again. Adapted for hunting, it lacks the strength to defend its prey from attack by larger predators.

Best seen Kruger National Park (p476), Central Kalahari Game Reserve (p76), Moremi Game Reserve (p74)

Leopard

More common than you realise, the leopard relies on expert camouflage to stay hidden. During the day you might only spot one reclining in a tree after it twitches its tail, but at night there is no mistaking their groans.

Best seen Savuti (p64), Kruger National Park (p476), Nyika National Park (p129)

Caracal

A tawny cat with long, pointy ears, this African version of the European lynx has jacked up hind legs, enabling it to make vertical leaps of 3m and swat birds out of the air.

Best seen Kruger National Park (p476), South Luangwa National Park (p578), Okavango Delta (p65)

Black-footed Cat

This pint-sized predator is one of the smallest cats in the world. Though only 25cm high, this nocturnal cat is a fearsome hunter that can leap six times its height.

Best seen Okavango Delta (p65), Kruger National Park (p476)

Primates

While East Africa is the evolutionary cradle of primate diversity, Southern Africa is a relative newcomer on the scene and home to a mere half-dozen or so species. These versatile, intelligent animals, however, have many fascinating behaviours and complex social systems that can provide hours of entertainment.

Vervet Monkey

Found in well-wooded areas, the vervet spends a lot of time on the ground, but always near to trees where it can escape from predators. Each troop is composed of females, while males fight each other for access to females.

Best seen Moremi Game Reserve (p74), Chobe National Park (p58), Kafue National Park (p590)

Chacma Baboon

Common enough to be overlooked, the Chacma baboon is worth watching because it has complex social dynamics. See if you can spot signs of friendship, deception or deal-making within a troop.

Best seen Bwabwata National Park (p266), Moremi Game Reserve (p74), Mana Pools National Park (p632)

Greater Galago

A cat-sized nocturnal creature with dog-like face, the greater galago (commonly called 'bushbaby') has changed little in 60 million years. They communicate with each other through scent and sound and are rarely seen, except at some safari-lodge feeding stations.

Best seen Liwonde National Park (p144), Okavango Delta (p65), South Luangwa National Park (p578)

Samango Monkey

The Samango monkey is part of a large group of African primates called gentle or blue monkeys. Found exclusively in forests, it lives in peaceful female-based groups.

Best seen iSimangaliso Wetland Park (p423)

1. Vervet monkey, Kruger National Park (p476), South Africa
2. Chacma baboons, Kruger National Park (p476), South Africa
3. Greater Galago, Malawi 4. Samango monkey, South Africa

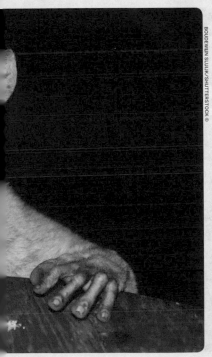

PAULA FRENCH/SHUTTERSTOCK ©

1. Wildebeest, Etosha National Park (p260), Namibia
2. Klipspringer, South Africa **3.** Cape buffalo, Okavango Delta
(p65), Botswana **4.** Impala, Savuti (p63), Botswana

BRAAM COLLINS/SHUTTERSTOCK ©

Cud-chewing Mammals

Many of Africa's ungulates (hoofed mammals) live in groups to protect themselves from the continent's predators.The subgroup of ungulates that ruminate (chew their cud) and have horns are called bovines. Among this family, antelopes are particularly numerous, with more than 20 species in Southern Africa.

Wildebeest

Most wildebeest of Southern Africa are rather sedentary creatures, moving only as the seasons fluctuate. Because it favours expansive views, the wildebeest is in turn easily viewed itself.

Best seen Liuwa Plain National Park (p594), Moremi Game Reserve (p74), Etosha National Park (p260)

Klipspringer

Perpetually walking on tiptoes, the klipspringer finds safety on rocky outcrops in the mountains of central Namibia. Pairs establish permanent territories and communicate with each other by whistling.

Best seen Nyika National Park (p129), Kruger National Park (p476)

African Buffalo (Cape Buffalo)

Imagine a cow on steroids, then add a fearsome set of curling horns. Fortunately it's usually docile, because an angry or injured buffalo is extremely dangerous.

Best seen Moremi Game Reserve (p74), Chobe National Park (p58), Kruger National Park (p476)

Impala

With a prodigious capacity to reproduce, impalas can reach great numbers quickly, outstripping predators' ability to eat them.

Best seen Etosha National Park (p260), Chobe National Park (p58), Hwange National Park (p647)

Sitatunga

The shy aquatic sitatunga antelope will submerge itself in the face of danger, making it hard to find. Listen for its loud barking at night.

Best seen Okavango Delta (p65), Kasanka National Park (p597)

Large Mammals

Other than the giraffe, these ungulates are not ruminants and can be seen over a much broader range of habitats than bovines. At home in Africa for millions of years, they are among the most successful mammals to have ever wandered the continent.

Giraffe

The 5m-tall giraffe does such a good job reaching up to high branches that stretching down to get a simple drink of water is difficult. Though it strolls along casually, a healthy giraffe can outrun most predators.

Best seen Etosha National Park (p260), South Luangwa National Park (p578), Moremi Game Reserve (p74)

African Elephant

Widespread throughout Southern Africa, up to 55,000 elephants congregate in the lush wetlands of Chobe National Park. There are also the unique desert-loving elephants of Namibia.

Best seen Chobe National Park (p58), Hwange National Park (p647), Addo Elephant National Park (p392)

Black Rhinoceros

Once widespread and abundant, the slow-moving rhino has been poached to the brink of extinction. Unfortunately, females may only give birth every five years.

Best seen Etosha National Park (p260), North Luangwa National Park (p584), Damaraland (p269)

Mountain Zebra

The unique mountain zebra of central Namibia and South Africa differs from its savannah relatives in having an unstriped belly and a rusty muzzle.

Best seen Mountain Zebra National Park (p399), Camdeboo National Park (p400)

Hippopotamus

Designed like a big floating sack with tiny legs, the 3000kg hippo spends all its time in or near water. They display a tremendous ferocity and strength when provoked.

Best seen Okavango Delta (p65), Bwabwata National Park (p266), Mana Pools National Park (p632)

MANUEL ROM·RIS/GETTY IMAGES ©

1. Giraffe, Kruger National Park (p476), South Africa 2. Elephants, Chobe National Park (p58), Botswana 3. Black rhinoceros, Etosha National Park (p260), Namibia 4. Zebra, Etosha National Park (p260), Namibia

FRDMR/SHUTTERSTOCK ©

1. Bat-eared fox, Botswana **2.** Spotted hyena, South Luangwa National Park (p578), Zambia **3.** Meerkats, Namibia **4.** Cape fur seal, Namibia

GUALTIERO BOFFI/SHUTTERSTOCK ©

Carnivores

In addition to seven types of cats, Southern Africa is home to a couple of dozen other carnivores, ranging from slinky mongooses to highly social hunting dogs. All are linked in having 'carnassial' (shearing) teeth, and superb hunting prowess.

Bat-Eared Fox

This animal has huge ears that swivel in all directions to pick up the sounds of subterranean food items such as termites. Monogamous pairs of these social foxes will often mingle with others when hunting for food.

Best seen Central Kalahari Game Reserve (p76), Kgalagadi Transfrontier Park (p79), Okavango Delta (p65)

Spotted Hyena

The spotted hyena is one of Southern Africa's most unusual animals. Living in packs ruled by females, this savage fighter uses its bone-crushing jaws to disembowel prey or to do battle with lions.

Best seen Moremi Game Reserve (p74), Liuwa Plain National Park (p594), South Luangwa National Park (p578)

Meerkat

The area's several species of mongoose may be best represented by the meerkat (also known as a suricate). If threatened, they all spit and jump up and down together.

Best seen Makgadikgadi Pans National Park (p55), Kgalagadi Transfrontier Park (p79)

Cape Fur Seal

Several giant breeding colonies of seals can be found along the coastlines of Southern Africa. Forced to gather in dense numbers as protection against marauding hyenas, these colonies are turbulent, noisy and exciting to watch.

Best seen Cape Cross Seal Reserve (p275)

African Wild Dog

Uniquely patterned, hunting dogs run in packs of 20 to 60. Organised in complex hierarchies, these highly social but endangered canids are incredibly efficient hunters.

Best seen Linyanti Marshes (p64), Hluhluwe-iMfolozi Park (p422), Kruger National Park (p476)

Birds of Prey

Southern Africa is home to about 70 species of hawk, eagle, vulture and owl, so you are likely to see an incredible variety of birds of prey. Look for them in trees, soaring high overhead or gathered around a carcass.

Secretary Bird

With the body of an eagle and the legs of a crane, the secretary bird towers 1.3m tall and walks up to 20km a day across the savannah in search of snakes that it kills with lightning speed and agility.

Best seen Central Kalahari Game Reserve (p76), Etosha National Park (p260)

Pale Chanting Goshawk

This grey raptor with red beak and legs is seen perched low on bushes. Look closely because it is probably following some other small hunter, such as a honey badger.

Best seen Kgalagadi Transfrontier Park (p79), Central Kalahari Game Reserve (p76), Hwange National Park (p647)

Bearded Vulture

Around the cliffs of the Drakensberg you may spot one of the world's most sought-after birds of prey – known for its habit of dropping bones onto rocks from great heights to expose the marrow.

Best seen Etosha National Park (p260), Makgadikgadi Pans National Park (p55)

Bateleur

French for 'tightrope walker', the name refers to this bird's low-flying aerial acrobatics. In flight, look for its white wings and tailless appearance; up close look for the bold colour pattern and scarlet face.

Best seen Kgalagadi Transfrontier Park (p79)

African Fish Eagle

With a wingspan over 2m, this eagle hunts for fish, but it is most familiar for its loud ringing vocalisations that have become known as 'the voice of Africa'.

Best seen Okavango Delta (p65), Nkasa Rupara National Park (p267), Lower Zambezi National Park (p585)

1. Secretary bird, South Africa 2. Pale chanting goshawk, South Africa 3. Bearded vulture, South Africa 4. Bateleur, Botswana

ECOPRINT/SHUTTERSTOCK ©

BRAAM COLLINS/SHUTTERSTOCK ©

1. African penguin, Boulders Penguin Colony (p335), South Africa
2. Hamperkop, South Africa **3.** Cape gannets, Namibia **4.** Ostrich,
Etosha National Park (p260), Namibia

Other Birds

Come to Southern Africa prepared to see an astounding number of birds in every shape and colour imaginable. You may find them a pleasant diversion after a couple of days staring at sleeping lions.

African Penguin

The African penguin got its former moniker (jackass penguin) for its donkey-like call, part of the courtship display given by males.

Best seen Simon's Town (p335), South Africa's Western Cape (355)

Hamerkop

The hamerkop is a stork relative with an oddly crested, woodpecker-like head. Nicknamed the 'hammerhead', it hunts frogs and fish at the water's edge. Look for its massive 2m-wide nests in nearby trees.

Best seen Okavango Delta (p65), Nkasa Rupara National Park (p267), Lower Zambezi National Park (p585)

Cape Gannet

This crisply marked seabird gathers by the thousands to catch fish with high-speed dives into the waves.

Best seen Bird Island, Walvis Bay (p283)

Ostrich

Standing 2.7m tall and weighing upwards of 130kg, this flightless bird escapes predators by running away at 70km/h or lying flat on the ground to resemble a pile of dirt.

Best seen Central Kalahari Game Reserve (p76), Etosha National Park (p260), Kgalagadi Transfrontier Park (p79)

Lesser Flamingo

Gathering by the hundreds of thousands on shimmering salt lakes, the rose-pink lesser flamingo creates one of Africa's most dramatic wildlife spectacles.

Best seen Nata Bird Sanctuary (p54), Walvis Bay (p283)

Lilac-Breasted Roller

The gorgeously coloured lilac-breasted roller gets its name from the tendency to 'roll' from side to side in flight to show off its iridescent blues, purples and greens.

Best seen Everywhere!

Music in Southern Africa

Jane Cornwell

Music still marks the important stages of a Southern African person's life. It still enlightens, heals, invokes spirits. It still makes people dance, sing, holler. It does all this regardless of the instrument – whose form can change according to ethnicity, geography, gender of the player and, sometimes, whatever objects are lying around. Expressing oneself through music isn't always easy: think of long-suffering, government-censored Zimbabwe; or Namibia, whose music industry lacks distribution networks and major record labels and is only now slowly addressing the fact; or Mozambique, where most artists don't receive royalties, and promoters frequently don't pay. Regardless, music still pulses in the region like a heartbeat. So remember: just because you can't buy it – or even see or hear it – doesn't mean that it isn't there.

Featuring big-name UK and African live acts and DJs, the award-winning three-day Lake of Stars Music Festival is held on the palm-fringed shores of Lake Malawi each October. It attracts around 1500 locals and travellers; proceeds go to charity.

A Potted History

Early Origins

It's better, initially, to think ethnicity rather than country. Southern Africa is one of the world's oldest inhabited regions, after all, and many of its musical traditions long predate modern African nation-states. The region is so old, in fact, that its earliest music can be traced back some 4000 years to the Stone Age, when groups of hunter-gatherer San played basic flutes and rattles and sang in their click language. Today's San still sound wonderfully ethereal, their singing, clapping trance-dance the stuff of ritual, tourist haunts and left-field record labels. But it's the glorious vocal polyphony of the Bantu-speaking people – the Zulu, Xhosa and Sotho of the present day – that has come to characterise the region; this is the music that attracted Paul Simon before he recorded his seminal 1988 album *Graceland*.

Long before the Christian missionaries and colonialists arrived in the 19th century, there were kingdoms. In Zambia, each king had his own royal musician, just as each kingdom had its own music. Singing often accompanied instrumental music played on horns, percussion, drums and the stringed *babatone* – the inspiration for the contemporary Zambian-style *kalindula*. Elsewhere, herders used flutes and other instruments to help control the movement of cattle. (Oh, and the first major style of South African popular music? None other than penny-whistle jive, later known as *kwela*.) The Bantu of Namibia played gourds, horn trumpets and marimbas, while the various ethnic groups of Malawi travelled widely, spreading musical influences from the Zulu of South Africa and the Islamic Yao people of Tanzania.

European Influence

Colonial rule altered everything. The folk forms of Mozambique, a former Portuguese colony, bear hallmarks of colonial rule – though its main style, *marrabenta*, flourished after independence. Mozambican bands began to play a roots style similar to that heard in Tanzania and Zambia, while musicians in the heart of the country played a style like that of Zimbabwe. The music of southern Mozambique was altered by the influx of workers returning from the South African mines (revolutionary lyrics were delivered over regional melodies), just as the workers who have migrated from Lesotho to the mines and cities of neighbouring South Africa have developed a rich genre of sung oral poetry – or word music – that focuses on the experiences of migrant life. African folk music also became popular in Zambia, as troubadours entertained exhausted miners. In South Africa, Dutch farmers brought a European folk music that became what is known today as *boeremusiek*.

It's no wonder, then, that the banjo, violin, concertina and electric guitar have all had a profound influence on Southern African music. Malawian banjo-and-guitar duos were huge in the 1950s and '60s, after which South African *kwela* took over. The influence of guitar-based *rumba* from Zaïre (now the Democratic Republic of Congo, DRC) was felt right across the region (political upheaval saw many Congolese musicians relocate to Southern Africa); its upstart cousin, *soukous*, has made its presence felt in everything from Zambian *kalindula* to Malawian *kwasa kwasa*. The gospel mega-genre has evolved from the teachings of 19th-century Christian missionaries, which were customised accordingly. Reckon those chord sequences in South African songs are familiar? Blame the Church.

A Political Voice

Numerous musical styles have been born out of oppression, too. Ladysmith Black Mambazo's 'tiptoe' *isicathimiya* music, with its high-kicking, soft-stepping dance, has its origins in the all-male miners' hostels in South Africa's Natal Province (now KwaZulu-Natal) in the 1930s, when workers were at pains not to wake their bosses. *Kwela* music, like most modern South African styles, came out of the townships; *kwela*, meaning 'jump up', was the instruction given to those about to be thrown into police vans during raids. Thomas Mapfumo's *chimurenga* is once again the music of resistance in Zimbabwe, even if – for the majority of Zimbabwean musicians – outspokenness is just not the Zimbabwean way. Even the prolific Oliver 'Tuku' Mtukudzi (whose infectious dance pop, informed by the country's *jit*-jive and *tsava* rhythms, is known simply as 'Tuku music') has never done more than express his great disappointment. Relatively new kids on the block Mokoomba – six Tonga musicians from Victoria Falls – are looking forward with energy and dynamism, their multilingual lyrics rooted in home reality.

In Malawi the intentionally controversial songs of politician and reggae giant Lucius 'Soldier of the Poor Man' Banda has spawned a slew of similarly antsy reggae outfits; there is also a softer reggae led by Black Missionaries and other Malawian Rastafarians. In postapartheid South Africa, freedom of expression is pretty much expected: rap, hip hop and their indigenous sibling *kwaito* are as socially concerned as they are lacking political correctness, depending on who you're listening to. South African jazz remains some of the best in the world; the international success of the likes of Afro-soul/jazz chanteuse Thandiswa and Afro-fusion outfit Freshlyground has new audiences in new countries taking notice.

The popular music of Southern Africa has created itself by mingling local ideas and forms with those from outside the region. And while

Featuring music and interviews by Abdullah Ibrahim, Hugh Masekela and Miriam Makeba among others, Lee Hirsch's documentary *Amandla!! A Revolution in Four Part Harmony* (2002) explores the role of music in the fight against apartheid. Made over nine years, this is a deeply affecting film.

Music Festivals

Cape Town International Jazz Festival

National Arts Festival

Kirstenbosch Summer Sunset Concerts

Joy of Jazz Festival

/Ae//Gams Arts Festival

Lake of Stars Music Festival

Harare International Festival of Art

every country has its own distinctive and constantly evolving array of styles supported by local audiences, that doesn't mean you won't be in one place and hear something from somewhere else.

Musical Instruments

As with most traditional African instruments, the membranophones (drums), chordophones (stringed instruments), aerophones (wind instruments) and idiophones (percussion) of Southern Africa tend to be found in rural areas. Local materials and found objects are often used to musical effect. In Namibia and Zimbabwe dry cocoons are tied together and strapped to dancers' ankles and waists; in Swaziland and South Africa, ankles rattle with dried fruit. Right across the region, everything from seeds, sticks and stalks to horsehair, oryx horns and goat skins are being shaken and blown, plucked and beaten. Some people in Namibia customise their drums by carving human faces into them.

The MaNyungwe people of northeastern Zimbabwe and northwestern Mozambique play *nyanga* music on panpipes, using different interlocking parts and quick bursts of singing in a sort of highly melodic musical round called *hocketting*. The Tonga people of Zambia do a similar thing with animal horns known as *nyele*. Variations on musical themes abound. The people of Sesfontein, Namibia, play reed pipes made from papaya stems. Basotho herding boys fashion their *lekolulo* flutes from sticks, cords and reeds. Everywhere, too, there is men's music and women's music, just as there are men's dances and women's dances. In Lesotho, men use their mouths to play the stringed *setolo-tolo*. Namibian women play the scraped mouth-resonated bow.

Oh, and then there's the voice. Be they roaring Zulu choirs or clicking San, four-part Nama harmonies or ululating Zambian church-goers, the people of Southern Africa really do sing up some glorious polyphonic storms. Keep an ear out.

Drums

There is a huge variety of drums (*ngoma* is the general term in the Bantu language). Stick-struck and hand-struck. Square, round and goblet-shaped. Small cowhide-covered ones for Zulu children. Khetebu 'bush-tom' drums beloved by the South African Tsonga. Namalwa 'lion drums' of Zambia, played by inserting a stick through the drum head and rubbing. High-pitched talking drums (which are more commonly found in West Africa), held tight under the armpit and beaten with hook-shaped sticks; the Chewa people of Zambia call theirs the *vimbuza*. Drum families – mother, father, son, played in sets of three – like the conical drums of the northeast of Namibia. Drums to accompany reed ensembles, a cappella groups and, more often than not, ankle-rattling dances.

Bows

If drums are the region's collective heartbeat, then the bow is its lonely soul. Southern Africa has several kinds of musical bow, many resembling the Brazilian *berimbau*; braced, mouth and/or gourd-resonated bows. There are large hunting bows used as mouth bows; two-stringed bows, played while simultaneously singing and resonating; multiple bows with multiple strings; mouth bows that use palm leaves instead of strings. String instruments abound: the lute (both strummed and bowed) is present in several forms. The Setswana of Botswana sing and strum the violin-like *segeba* (which is a single string attached to a tin). The dance of the Nama of Namibia uses flutes, drums and strings to emulate animal sounds.

For information on music and censorship in Zimbabwe, go to freemuse.org and musicfreedomday.org

Cry of Love (2012) is a musical film starring legendary South African songbird Yvonne Chaka Chaka and award-winning actress Leleti Khumalo. Set in cosmopolitan Johannesburg, it follows the lives of young teens in a performing arts school. Part *Fame*, part *Ubuntu*.

Keyboard & Percussion

The xylophone is also prevalent, and the xylophone music of southern Malawi has influenced contemporary music in both East and Southern Africa. Mallet instruments with wooden keys are the main instrument of the Lozi and Nkoya of western Zambia, who place slats of wood over a long platform and gourds in descending size; up to four people play simultaneously. The marimbas of South Africa feed into the *mbaqanga* (township jive) style. It's an entirely different sound from that of the *mbila* (plural *timbila*) played by the Chopi people of coastal Mozambique, which features resonators made from gourds and a buzzing tone created via a sheet of plastic (formerly an animal skin) over a hole in the ground. The master of *timbila* was the great Venancio Mbande.

Mbiras

But perhaps no instrument is as distinctively Southern African as the *mbira*, a hand-held instrument with small metal keys attached to an amplifying wooden box or calabash; attached shells and/or bottle tops distort and fuzz its sound. There are many traditions of these 'thumb pianos', each with a different name according to its size and origin – for instance, they're called *kankobela* by the Tonga of Zambia. But it is Zimbabwe with which the *mbira* is generally identified: central to the Shona people's marathon religious trance ceremonies known as *bira*, interlocking *mbira* patterns are considered both healing and spiritual. Since independence the *mbira* has been adapted to modern styles, such as the *chimurenga* guitar bands.

Musical Styles

A rich network of musical styles has developed in Southern Africa. And although those of South Africa are probably the best known, the entire region is humming with musical traditions, expressions and textures. In most countries there are polyphonic, repetitive patterns and call-and-response singing. There are styles that reflect ethnic diversity and geography. Cities are dominated by pop, rock, jazz and urban music, much of which combines core African principles with Western influences. Electric guitars fuel genres such as *afroma* in Malawi, *jit*-jive in South Africa and Zam-rock in Zambia. Local sounds keep migrating, metamorphosing. New genres keep forming. The following is a by-no-means definitive round-up of what is being listened to.

Chimurenga

In Zimbabwe in the late 1970s the musician Thomas Mapfumo and the Blacks Unlimited transferred traditional Shona *mbira* patterns to the electric guitar. They sang songs of resistance, using bright, harmonised vocals, against the white-controlled Rhodesian government. *Chimurenga,* meaning 'struggle', became a tool of social activism and, with lyrics in Shona, a secret means of communication. Banned by Zimbabwean state radio then, much of today's *chimurenga* bubbles away underground, and no wonder: high-profile artist and prominent government critic Raymond Majongwe has said in the past that he fears for his life and his work rarely gets an airing inside a country with such tightly controlled media. Apolitical, good-time *sungura* guitar music (the current industry's favoured genre) and bland Shona impersonations of hip hop and ragga (a dance-oriented style of reggae) abound.

Gospel

Gospel music is huge everywhere. In Malawi spiritual songs are sung in church, at school assemblies and political functions, and during everyday tasks. Many of Zambia's Christian churches boast US-style gospel synthe-

Set in the eponymous colourful township, *Katutura* is a film made by Namibians for Namibians. Released in 2016, it underlines the importance of respecting women, children and elders as it celebrates the country's vibrant heritage; including, of course, its music.

Held each July in Selebi-Phikwe, between Gaborone and Francistown, Botswana's National Music Eisteddfod showcases traditional dances and music from around the country, courtesy of its schools, colleges and choirs.

sisers and guitars. The effects of popular influences on church music can be heard in top-sellers Adonai Pentecostal Singers and Ephraim Sekeleti Mutalange. In Botswana, traditional music is present in church singing. Zimbabwe's lucrative gospel market is dominated by Pastor Charles Charamba and his *sungura*-based songs (gospel singers in Zimbabwe are as big as the biggest popular music stars). South Africa is the really commercial holy roller: a megaselling amalgam of European, American, Zulu and other African traditions, neatly divided into traditional and modern styles. Look out for Rebecca Malope, South African Gospel Singers and the 2010 Grammy-winning Soweto Gospel Choir.

Jazz

What Malawi calls 'jazz' began in the late 1960s when, inspired by South African *kwela* music, bands such as Chimvu Jazz featured semirural musicians on acoustic instruments – a tradition that continues today. In Botswana most popular music tends to be labelled 'jazz', but it is probably *gumba-gumba* ('party-party') music – modernised Zulu and Setswana music mixed with traditional jazz – that comes closest to it. Zambia's Zam-rock has its jazzy elements. But if you're after jazz that is structurally, harmonically and melodically distinctive – and is, unequivocally, jazz – then head to South Africa. What was famously an expatriate music representing the suffering of a people is now a thriving, progressive force. The likes of Lira, Thandiswa and the legendary Hugh Masekela are at the vanguard.

Kalindula

The urban dance style known as *kalindula* has its roots in the Bemba traditions of northern Zambia's Luapula Province – where a stringed instrument called the *babatone* swings like a double bass. Inspired (like many Southern African genres) by Congolese rumba, *kalindula* took hold in the mid-1970s in the wake of the presidential decree that 95% of broadcast music should be Zambian. Most *kalindula* bands broke up following the country's economic collapse in the 1990s. Artists such as the Glorious Band tried to revive *kalindula* with moderate success; Kabukulu Mwamba Chimo, whose *kalindula* includes traces of rumba, *sinjonjo* (an upbeat song and type of dance popular in copper-belt mining areas in Zambia and Zimbabwe) and traditional Lamba music, is popular.

Kwaito

Post-1994, *kwaito* (*kway*-to, meaning hot or angry) exploded onto South Africa's dance floors. A rowdy mix of bubblegum, hip hop, R&B, ragga, *mbaqanga*, traditional, jazz, and British and American house music, *kwaito* remains a lifestyle even if its bubble has arguably burst. Chanted or sung in township slang (usually over programmed beats), *kwaito*'s lyrics range from the anodyne to the fiercely political. Given an international lease of life as the soundtrack for the feature film *Tsotsi* (which bagged the 2006 Oscar for Best Foreign Film, and saw *kwaito* star Zola playing a gangster), *kwaito* remains huge across the Southern African region. It's still Lesotho's favourite music style. If you're in Namibia, look out for EES, The Dogg and Gazza. In Zambia, try the *kwaito*-house of Ma Africa. If you're in South Africa, take your pick.

Kwasa Kwasa

Beginning in Zaïre (now DRC) in the mid-1980s and spreading quickly to surrounding areas, *kwasa kwasa* (from the French street slang, *quoi ça?* – 'what's this?') took its cue from Congolese *rumba* and *soukous*. Characterised by an all-important lead guitar and lighter background drumming, *kwasa kwasa* songs typically let guitar and drums set the

Taking place annually on the first Sunday in September, Jazz on the Lake is a free daytime concert and a Jo'burg institution (www.joburg.org.za).

Focus: Music of South Africa (Routledge, 2008), by Carol Ann Muller, is an impressive, scholarly and highly readable tome that takes an in-depth look at the full spectrum of South African music from the past to 2008.

Yfm (www.yfm.
co.za) is South
Africa's most
popular youth
radio station, with
an emphasis on
live podcasting
and blogging and
a 50% self-
imposed local
music quota.

pace before the vocals enter, with an intricate guitar solo somewhere in the middle. Arguments rage over whether *kwasa kwasa* is actually just *rumba*; for others it's simply a dance style. Everyone from politicians to street vendors knows how to do the *kwasa kwasa:* booties wildly gyrating – à la American hip hop – while legs and torsos are kept still.

Marrabenta

Sounding a little like salsa or merengue, *marrabenta* is the best-known urban dance music in Mozambique, and one created from a fusion of imported European music played on improvised materials: oil cans, wooden stakes and fishing lines. Taking its name from the Portuguese word 'to break' (hard-playing musos frequently snap their guitar strings), *marrabenta's* local-language songs of love and social criticism were banned by Portuguese colonialists – ensuring its popularity post-independence. Stalwart *marrabenta* band Ghorwane uses horns, guitars, percussion and strong vocal harmonies; *marrabenta*-meets-dance-music diva Neyma is a megacelebrity.

Rap & Hip Hop

The genre that was born in New York more than three decades ago now has another home in (or has come back to) Africa. In Namibia, writer and skateboarder Ruusa Namupala is mixing township sounds with hip hop. In Botswana, Game 'Zeus' Bantsi is flying the flag for homegrown rap. Young Swaziland rap groups – and indeed, rap groups across Southern Africa – are using the medium to educate listeners about HIV/AIDS. South Africa's rappers are exploring uncharted territory: look out for emerging genres such as Afro-Futurism and township house, and sonic explorers Simphiwe Dana and Spoek Mathambo.

Reggae

In Malawi in particular, you'll hear reggae by the Black Missionaries everywhere; *The Very Best*, a World Music collaboration between Mzuzuborn Esau Mwamwaya and London production duo Radioclit, has had some success internationally.

Environment

Southern Africa's environment is as fragile as elsewhere on the continent, with exploitation and mismanagement the cause of many long-term problems. And the region is where you'll find some of the more complicated issues in wildlife conservation, among them poaching and commercial or trophy hunting. But it's not all bad news – Southern Africa's environment has a wonderful backdrop of stunning landscapes and some of the best wildlife on the planet.

The Land

Southern Africa consists of a plateau rising from 1000m to 2000m, with escarpments on either side. Below the escarpments lies a coastal plain, which is narrowest in Namibia and widest in southern Mozambique.

Deserts

Southern Africa hosts two of Africa's most important deserts: the Kalahari and the Namib. Beyond that, much of western South Africa sees so little rain that shrubs and hardy grasses are the dominant vegetation. Known locally as the Karoo, this area merges with true desert in Namibia. Lack of water keeps larger animals such as zebras and antelopes close to waterholes, but when it rains this habitat explodes with plant and animal life. During the dry season many plants shed their leaves to conserve water.

Great Rift Valley & its Lakes

The most prominent break in the Southern African plateau is the Great Rift Valley – a 6500km-long fissure where tectonic forces have attempted to rip the continent of Africa in two. This enormous fault in the earth's crust runs from the Jordan Valley (between Israel and Jordan) in the north, southward through the Red Sea, where it enters Ethiopia's Danakil Depression. At this point it heads south across Kenya, Tanzania and Malawi, dividing in two at one stage, to form the great lakes of East Africa. Lake Malawi is the third-largest lake in Africa and lies in a trough formed by the valley. This feature has created unique fish life. The lake has more fish species than any inland body of water in the world – there are more than 500, and 350 of these are endemic to the lake. This spreading zone ends at the present site of Lake Kariba, between Zimbabwe and Zambia.

Mountains

The highest part of the region is Lesotho (often called the Kingdom in the Sky) and the neighbouring Drakensberg area, where many peaks rise above 3000m, including Thabana-Ntlenyana (3482m), which is the highest point in Southern Africa. In fact, Lesotho has the fifth-highest average elevation of any country on the planet and is the only independent state in the world whose territory rises entirely above 1000m (3281 ft) in elevation. Its lowest point (1400m, 4593 ft) is also the highest lowest point of any country. And just to prove a point about the region's topographical variety, Botswana is one of the lowest non-island nation states on earth.

Other highland areas include the Nyika Plateau (in northern Malawi and northeastern Zambia), Mt Mulanje (in southern Malawi), the Eastern Highlands (between Zimbabwe and Mozambique) and the Khomas Hochland (Central Namibia).

The longer you spend in Southern Africa, the more you'll appreciate the subtleties of the region, including the delight of spotting some of the less famous species. If you're up for a challenge, the lesser-known Little Five are the rhinoceros beetle, buffalo weaver, elephant shrew, leopard tortoise and ant lion.

These highlands provide jaw-dropping scenery, as well as some of the best-preserved and most distinctive plants, wildlife and ancient rock art in the region. Hiking, climbing and mountain biking are just some of the myriad activities on offer in these often wonderfully preserved patches of African wilderness. Lower and more isolated hills include the characteristic inselbergs of Namibia and South Africa's Karoo, and the lush Zomba Plateau in central Malawi.

Rivers

Several iconic African rivers cut through Southern Africa, none more so than the mighty Zambezi, Africa's fourth-longest river (2693km, 1673 miles). Some 80% of its length passes through Southern African countries (the remainder traverses Angola and a small sliver of Tanzania), with more than 41% of its length within Zambia.

The Zambezi is actually not the longest river to pass through the region – the Chambeshi (or Chambezi) River rises in northeastern Zambia and is considered by some to be the source of the Congo River; it is the most remote headstream of the Congo, although some consider the Lualaba River to be the true source by virtue of its greater water volume.

Other important African rivers:

➡ Orange River (2092km, 1300 miles): South Africa, Namibia, Botswana & Lesotho

➡ Limpopo (1800km, 1118 miles): Mozambique, Zimbabwe, South Africa & Botswana

➡ Okavango (1600km, 994 miles): Angola, Namibia & Botswana

➡ Shire (1200km, 746 miles): Mozambique & Malawi

It's not just the rivers themselves, but rather what they produce, that is so impressive. It is, of course, the waters of the Zambezi that produce one of Africa's greatest natural wonders, Victoria Falls, on the border between Zambia and Zimbabwe. And the Okavango River is what feeds the extraordinary natural spectacle that is the Okavango Delta, one of the world's largest inland river deltas.

Wildlife

Southern Africa contains some of the most accessible and varied wildlife found anywhere on the continent, and it's the major attraction of the area. Countries all over the region provide opportunities for wildlife watching, and each has its highlights. Even the smaller countries such as Swaziland have magnificent wildlife viewing, which can offer great alternatives to better-known parks, but for sheer variety and numbers South Africa and Botswana top the list.

The best times of day for wildlife viewing are early in the morning and in the late afternoon or evening, when many animals are looking for their next meal. Planting yourself at a water hole at these times can be very rewarding. Night safaris provide wonderful wildlife-viewing opportunities, especially to see many nocturnal animals such as genets and bush babies (look in the trees, not just on the ground).

Happily, Southern African parks are some of the best managed in Africa, and the development of the massive transfrontier parks in the region, which link national parks and wildlife migration routes in different countries, should open up even more opportunities for wildlife viewing.

Rhinos aren't named for their colour, but for their lip shape: 'white' comes from *wijde* (wide) – the Boers' term for the fatter-lipped white rhino.

Animals

Nowhere else on the planet is there such a variety and quantity of large mammal species. Southern Africa boasts the world's largest land mammal (the African elephant), as well as the second largest (white rhino) and the third largest (hippopotamus). It's also home to the tallest (giraffe), fastest (cheetah) and smallest (pygmy shrew). You stand a great chance of seeing the Big Five – black rhino, Cape buffalo, elephant, leop-

CLOSE ENCOUNTERS OF THE WILD KIND

Although you'll hear plenty of horror stories, the threat of attack by wild animals in Africa is largely exaggerated and problems are extremely rare. That said, it is important to remember that most African animals are *wild* and that wherever you go on safari, particularly on foot, there is always an element of danger. On organised safaris you should always get advice from your guide. If you're on a self-drive safari, ask authorities of the park you are entering. Some of the advice you will receive – such as not getting between a hippo and its water; and that black rhinos are skittish, as are lone animals such as male elephants and buffaloes – holds true across the region, and you will pick it up easily enough. And a good rule of thumb is, if you're not sure, just don't get too close.

Wildlife viewing requires a bit of common sense, and by following a few simple guidelines you're sure to have a trouble-free experience. Remember that viewing wildlife in its natural habitat may present dangers not found in a zoo, but it's a large part of what makes a visit to Southern Africa so special, and is incomparable to seeing an animal in a cage.

ard and lion – but the region also supports a wonderful array of birds, reptiles, amphibians and even insects (often in less-welcome quantities).

Endangered Species

As a result of years of poaching, the black rhino is the highest-profile entry on Southern Africa's endangered species list, considered to be critically endangered. Other high-profile species considered 'at risk' include elephants, lions, giraffes and African wild dogs. The riverine rabbit is one of Southern Africa's most endangered mammals, and the mountain zebra and hippopotamus are thought to be vulnerable in the wider region. Turtles don't fare well, either, with both the loggerhead and green turtle listed as endangered, while the hawksbill turtle is considered critically endangered.

Elephants

According to the results of the Great Elephant Census (www.greatelephantcensus.com), published in 2016 and the most comprehensive survey of the continent's elephants ever undertaken, 352,271 African savannah elephants survive in 18 countries. These figures represent a 30% fall in Africa's elephant population over the preceding seven years.

The figures confirmed the worst fears of elephant researchers. Every year since 2010, fuelled by a resurgence in demand for ivory products in Asia, poachers have killed an estimated 35,000 elephants across Africa. That's around 7% of Africa's elephant population every year. That's 673 elephants being killed a week, 96 a day. That's four elephants being killed for their tusks every hour. Most worrying of all, a 2014 study found that Africa's elephants had crossed a critical threshold: poachers now kill more African elephants each year than there are elephants being born.

Good places to see elephants include: Chobe National Park (p58; Botswana), Hwange National Park (p647; Zimbabwe), Kruger National Park (p476; South Africa), Nkhotakota Wildlife Reserve (p138; Malawi), Damaraland, Addo Elephant National Park (p392; South Africa) and Gorongosa National Park (p199; Mozambique).

For more information on the battle to save Africa's elephants, contact Save the Elephants (www.savetheelephants.org).

For information on campaigns to save elephants, and the fight against the illegal international trade in wildlife, visit the website of the International Fund for Animal Welfare (www.ifaw.org).

Rhinos

In 2016, Africa's white rhino population estimates stood at between 19,682 and 21,077. With approximately 18,000 white rhinos, South Africa is home to an estimated 90% of the world's population. White rhinos are also present in much smaller populations in Namibia, Botswana, Zimbabwe and Swaziland.

The black rhino is present in Southern Africa in Botswana, Malawi, Mozambique, Namibia, South Africa, Swaziland, Zambia and Zimbabwe, but it very nearly didn't make it. Poaching nearly wiped out the species, reducing the population from 65,000 in 1970, to barely 2300 in 1993. As of 2016, Africa's black rhino population had recovered to between 5042 and 5455 animals. But these figures only tell half the story. In 2003, 22 rhinos were poached in South Africa; in 2015, a staggering 1175 rhinos were poached in South Africa, among 1338 across Africa. Elsewhere in Southern Africa, the numbers are smaller but the trends no less worrying: Namibia lost 80 rhinos in 2015 (a threefold increase from the year before) while poachers killed at least 50 rhinos in Zimbabwe, which was twice the figure from 2014.

The epicentre of the crisis is Kruger National Park in South Africa: in 2014, 827 rhinos were poached from the park. Kruger is officially part of the Great Limpopo Transfrontier Park, which combines Kruger with Limpopo in Mozambique. Many poachers come from Mozambique through the long, porous border between the two parks. In Mozambique, Limpopo's under-resourced and under-capacity antipoaching unit does battle with poaching syndicates that have unlimited resources.

Overwhelmed by the challenge of monitoring the park's huge and largely unattended border with Mozambique, the South African government is embarking upon a massive relocation program. It has moved at least 500 rhinos to safer areas within Kruger and other parks in South Africa and neighbouring countries.

Good places to spot these animals include Hluhluwe-iMfolozi Park (p422; South Africa), Etosha National Park (p260; Namibia), Mkhaya Game Reserve (p543; Swaziland), Kruger National Park (p476; South Africa) and Damaraland (p269).

For more information on the ongoing battle to save the African rhino from extinction, check out www.savetherhino.org and www.stoprhino poaching.com.

The Great Elephant Census in 2016 found 3.2 elephant carcasses for every 10 live elephants spotted in Mozambique, the highest survival rate of any country surveyed. In Zambia's Sioma Ngwezi National Park, the figure was 8.5. per 10 live elephants.

Lions

Scientists such as the peak cat conservation body Panthera (www.panthera.org) estimate that fewer than 20,000 lions remain in Africa (there is a tiny, highly inbred population of Asian lions in the Gir Forest in Gujarat state in India). While that may seem like a lot, the IUCN classifies the lion as Vulnerable, not least because many lions live in small, fragmented and isolated populations that may not be sustainable beyond the short term.

Only six lion populations in Africa – Botswana's Okavango Delta and the broader ecosystem to which it belongs in Namibia, Zambia and Zimbabwe is one of these – are sufficiently protected to hold at least 1000 lions, the conservation gold standard that Panthera applies for guaranteeing the long-term survival of the species.

Like lions elsewhere, lions in Southern Africa are facing threats from poisoning, either in retaliation for killing livestock or encroaching onto farming lands, bushmeat poaching and habitat loss.

Namibia is home to the desert lion along the Skeleton Coast and hinterland; estimates stand at between 180 and 200. They were stars of the show in the recent National Geographic film *Vanishing Kings: Lions of the Namib*. The Desert Lion Conservation Foundation (www.desertlion. org) is the place to go for more information.

The best places to see lions are: Chobe National Park (p58; Botswana), Moremi Game Reserve (p74; Botswana), Etosha National Park (p260; Namibia), Kruger National Park (p476; South Africa), Central Kalahari Game Reserve (p76; Botswana), Kgalagadi Transfrontier Park (p79; Botswana), Kafue National Park (p590; Zambia) and Hwange National Park (p647; Zimbabwe).

FIELD GUIDES
••

Southern Africa's incredible floral and faunal diversity has inspired a large number of field guides for visitors and wildlife enthusiasts. In the UK, an excellent source for wildlife and nature titles is Subbuteo Natural History Books Ltd (www.wildlifebooks.com), while in Australia, check out Andrew Isles Natural History Books (www.andrewisles.com); both accept international mail orders.Field guides, apart from being damned interesting to read, can be invaluable tools for identifying animals while on safari. Our favourites:

➡ *A Field Guide to the Carnivores of the World* (Luke Hunter, 2011) Wonderfully illustrated and filled with fascinating detail.

➡ *The Kingdon Field Guide to African Mammals* (Jonathan Kingdon, 2nd ed, 2015) The latest edition of the classic field guide covering over 1150 species.

➡ *The Behavior Guide to African Mammals* (Richard Despard Estes, 1991) Classic study of the behaviour of mammal species. Estes' follow-up *The Safari Companion: A Guide to Watching African Mammals* (1993) is an excellent, slightly more accessible alternative.

➡ *Field Guide to the Mammals of Southern Africa* (Chris and Mathilde Stuart, 2015) One of the better mammal field guides. Pick up also its companion *Field Guide to Tracks and Signs of Southern, Central and East African Wildlife* (2015).

➡ *Sasol Birds of Southern Africa* (Ian Sinclair et al, 4th ed, 2011) Many birders' pick as the best field guide to the region's birds.

➡ *A Complete Guide to Snakes of Southern Africa* (Johan Marais, 2005) An excellent guide to the region's snakes.

African Wild Dogs
The beautiful African wild dog (also known as the Cape hunting dog) is listed as Endangered by the IUCN. Where once half a million wild dogs are thought to have ranged throughout 39 African countries, today only an estimated 6600 remain in the wild in just 14 countries.

Southern Africa is considered the last stronghold of the species, with populations thought to survive in northern Botswana, western Zimbabwe, eastern and northeastern Namibia, western Zambia, and possibly northern Mozambique, South Africa and Malawi. African wild dogs live in packs of up to 28 animals, which may account for the fact that they have one of the highest hunting success rates (as high as 70%) of all carnivores – that and their maximum speed of 66km/h. Their preferred prey includes impala, red lechwe, wildebeest, steenbok and warthog. Your best chance of sighting them include: Okavango Delta (p65), Linyanti Marshes (p64), Hluhluwe-iMfolozi Park (p422), Kruger National Park (p476), South Luangwa National Park (p578) and Khaudum National Park (p265).

Giraffes
One of the most worrying developments in recent years has been the downgrading of the giraffe's protection status by the IUCN from Least Concern in 2010 to Vulnerable in 2016. The world's tallest land mammal remains widespread across Southern and East Africa, but a precipitous 40% decline (from an estimated 151,702 to 163,452 individuals in 1985, to 97,562 in 2015) has brought the species' fate into sharp focus.

The main threats to the giraffe are illegal hunting, habitat loss, increasing human-wildlife conflict, civil conflict and encroaching human settlements. You'll see giraffes across the region – Lesotho is the only country in Southern Africa without giraffes.

Cheetahs
At the end of 2016, a scientific study confirmed what many conservationists in the field had long feared – the cheetah is in trouble. The latest

estimates suggest that just 7100 cheetahs remain in the wild, all of which live in Africa save for an isolated population of around 50 in the deserts and mountains of central Iran.

Between two-thirds and half of Africa's surviving cheetahs live in Southern Africa, which effectively remains the cheetah's last stronghold. Namibia has the world's largest population, but even there cheetahs live at low densities, and shrinking habitats and human encroachment on former wilderness areas have resulted in increasing conflict between cheetahs and farmers; more than three-quarters of Africa's wild cheetahs live outside protected areas. Elsewhere in the region, in Zimbabwe, the cheetah population has crashed from 1200 to just 170 animals in just 16 years.

Other problems include the smuggling of cheetah cubs out of the continent for sale as pets – baby cheetahs sell for as much as US$10,000 on the black market – with more than 1200 trafficked off the continent over the past decade, 85% of which died in transit.

Organisations such as the Cheetah Conservation Fund (CCF; www. cheetah.org) and AfriCat (www.africat.org) are at the forefront of efforts to mitigate this conflict and are worth contacting to find out more.

THE HUNTING DEBATE

Commercial or trophy hunting in Africa has, until recently, largely operated beneath international attention. That changed in 2015 when a Minnesota dentist, Walter Palmer, shot with a crossbow a much-loved male lion, Cecil, when it strayed outside Hwange National Park in Zimbabwe. The episode cast a spotlight on the industry and one of the most contentious issues in African conservation. Botswana was held up as a shining example of the way forward, thanks to its ban on commercial or trophy hunting in 2014. Namibia, Mozambique, South Africa, Zambia and Zimbabwe all have active hunting industries.

While abhorrent to many conservationists, controlled hunting can, many conservation groups recognise, play an important role in preserving species. According to this argument, tourism revenues have too often failed to reach local communities, reinforcing a perception that wildlife belongs to the government, with little benefit for ordinary forced to live with wildlife that can kill their livestock or trample their crops. Hunting on private concessions, however, generally attracts massive fees (lion licences in Southern Africa can sell for US$20,000), of which, the theory goes, a significant proportion is fed back into local community projects, thereby giving wildlife a tangible economic value for local people.

Hunting, the argument continues, also makes productive use of land that is considered unsuitable for photographic tourism, either because of its remoteness or lack of tourism infrastructure. If controlled strictly – through the use of quotas and killing only a limited number of solitary male lions who are past their prime, for example – hunting can, according to its proponents, play a part in saving species from extinction.

Opponents of hunting argue that the whole debate is premised on the failure of governments and private operators to fairly redistribute their revenues from nonlethal forms of tourism – why, they ask, should we expect that hunting be any different? They also argue that the solution lies in a fairer distribution of tourism revenues and greater community involvement in conservation rather than in killing the very animals upon which tourism depends. And finally, some critics point to the double standards of arresting and imprisoning locals who hunt wildlife (whether for commercial or subsistence reasons), while permitting rich (and usually white) hunters to shoot animals during short visits to the continent.

In early 2014 Namibia's Ministry of Environment and Tourism caused worldwide controversy when it auctioned off a hunting license for a black rhino, a critically endangered species, with a promise that the revenues raised would be channelled back into rhino conservation and antipoaching measures. The winning bidder paid US$350,000 to hunt the animal, although the government claimed that critics of its policy caused an earlier bid of US$1 million to be withdrawn due to negative publicity, thereby costing US$650,000 that could have been used to protect black rhinos. The government also argued that the rhino in question, an older and aggressive bull male, was past breeding age and was considered a serious threat to other rhinos.

Birds

Southern Africa is a fabulous destination for birders, and for sheer abundance and variety, few parts of the world offer as much for the birdwatcher, whether expert or beginner.

Bird Species

Southern Africa is host to nearly 10% of the world's bird species – more than 900 species have been recorded in the region. More than 130 are endemic to Southern Africa or are near-endemic, being found also only in adjoining territories to the north.

Highlights in the region include the world's largest bird (the ostrich) and heaviest flying bird (the kori bustard). Also in abundance are weavers, which share their huge city-like nests (often attached to telephone poles) with pygmy falcons, the world's smallest raptors. Also keep an eye out for majestic birds of prey such as the African fish eagle, bateleur (a serpent eagle), martial eagle, red-necked falcon and chanting goshawk, as well as secretary birds, rollers, vividly coloured bee-eaters, sunbirds and rainbow-flecked kingfishers.

Where to Go Birding

All the region's national parks and reserves are home to a great range of birdlife, but there are some areas that birders prize above all others. Mozambique, for example, has more than half of all bird species identified in southern Africa.

Botswana Okavango Panhandle (p65), Chobe Riverfront (p62), Nata Bird Sanctuary (p54), Central Kalahari Game Reserve (p76)
Lesotho Ts'ehlanyane National Park (p105)
Malawi Liwonde National Park (p144), Nyika National Park (p129), Vwaza Marsh Wildlife Reserve (p130)
Mozambique Bazaruto Archipelago (p194), Gorongosa National Park (p199), Lake Niassa (p217), Maputo Special Reserve (p185)
Namibia Nkasa Rupara National Park (p267), Bwabwata National Park (p266), Walvis Bay (p283), Etosha National Park (p260)
South Africa Kruger National Park (p476), Kgalagadi Transfrontier Park (p501), Hluhluwe-iMfolozi Park (p422), Madikwe Game Reserve (p493)
Swaziland Mkhaya Game Reserve (p543), Hlane Royal National Park (p542)
Zambia Kafue National Park (p590), South Luangwa National Park (p578), Bangweulu Wetlands (p597), Kasanka National Park (p597)
Zimbabwe Mana Pools National Park (p632), Hwange National Park (p647)

When to Go Birding

Birdwatching is excellent year-round across the region, but November is when migratory species begin arriving; they usually remain until March or April. The only problem with this is that these months coincide with the rainy season in many areas, which can make getting around difficult.

Reptiles

Southern Africa's most notable reptile is the Nile crocodile. Once abundant in lakes and rivers across the region, its numbers have been greatly reduced by hunting and habitat destruction. Female crocs lay up to 80 eggs at a time, depositing them in sandy areas above the high-water line. After three months' incubation in the hot sand, the young emerge. Many live up to 70 years.

Southern Africa has a complement of both venomous and harmless snakes, but most of them fear humans and you'll be lucky to even see one. The largest snake – generally harmless to humans – is the python, which grows to more than 5m in length. The puff adder is one of the deadliest and most widespread snakes on the African continent. It inhabits mainly mountain and desert areas, and grows to about 1m long. It's very slow but

ENVIRONMENT WILDLIFE

The status of the world's species is determined by the International Union for the Conservation of Nature (IUCN), which oversees the IUCN Red List of Threatened Species (www. iucnredlist.org). Each species is assessed according to a set of rigorous scientific criteria and classified as Least Concern, Near Threatened, Vulnerable, Endangered, Critically Endangered, Extinct in the Wild or Extinct.

Earthlife Africa (www.earthlife. org.za) is an active environmental group operating in South Africa and Namibia. It's a good contact for anyone wanting to get involved in environmental work.

highly aggressive. Stepping on one, resulting in being bitten, would potentially mean death. The bite of a puff adder is usually a long, slow breakdown of the body if you have no medical attention and is hard to reverse.

Seriously dangerous snakes include the fat and lazy gaboon viper; the black mamba; the boomslang, which lives in trees; the spitting cobra, which needs no introduction; and the zebra snake, which is one of the world's most aggressive serpentine sorts. If you're tramping in snake country, be sure to watch your step.

Lizards are ubiquitous from the hot and dusty Kaokoveld in Namibia to the cool highlands of the Nyika Plateau in Malawi, and from the bathroom ceiling to the kitchen sink. The largest of these is the water monitor, a docile creature that reaches more than 2m in length and is often seen lying around water holes, perhaps dreaming of being a crocodile. Two others frequently seen are chameleons and geckos – the latter often in hotel rooms; they are quite harmless and help to control the bug population.

Plants

The following rundown of major vegetation zones (arranged roughly south to north, and from the coasts to the inland areas) is greatly simplified, but provides a useful overview.

Southern Africa's distinctive *fynbos* (literally 'fine bush'; primarily proteas, heaths and ericas) zone occurs around the Cape Peninsula and along the south coast of South Africa, interspersed with pockets of temperate forest, where you'll find trees such as the large yellowwood, with its characteristic 'peeling' bark.

The west coast of Southern Africa consists largely of desert, which receives less than 100mm of precipitation per year. Vegetation consists of tough grasses, shrubs and euphorbias, plus local specialities, including the bizarre welwitschia (a miniature conifer) and kokerboom (a type of aloe).

TRANSFRONTIER PEACE PARKS

In addition to national parks there are several transfrontier conservation areas at various stages of completion. These mammoth ventures cross national borders and are flagship conservation projects designed to re-establish age-old migration routes.

Malawi and Zambia are setting up the first transfrontier park outside South Africa and secured funding for its establishment in 2012. The area combines the Nyika Plateau on both sides of the border, Malawi's Vwaza Marsh Wildlife Reserve and Kasungu National Park, with Zambian forest reserves, Musalangu Game Management Area and Lukusuzi National Park.

|Ai-|Ais/Richtersveld Transfrontier Park (p504) Africa's grand Fish River Canyon presents one of the most spectacular scenes on the continent and Namibia's most popular hiking track.

Great Limpopo Transfrontier Park (p642) This spreads nearly 100,000 sq km (larger than Portugal) across the borders of South Africa (Kruger National Park), Mozambique (Limpopo National Park) and Zimbabwe (Gonarezhou National Park).

Greater Mapungubwe Transfrontier Conservation Area A conservation area in progress straddling the borders of South Africa, Botswana and Zimbabwe.

Kavango-Zambezi Transfrontier Conservation Area A work in progress situated around the border convergence of Angola, Botswana, Namibia, Zambia and Zimbabwe, and set to become the world's biggest conservation area, taking in the Caprivi Strip in Namibia, Chobe National Park and the Okavango Delta in Botswana, and Victoria Falls in Zambia.

Kgalagadi Transfrontier Park (p79) This park combines Northern Cape's old Kalahari Gemsbok National Park (South Africa) with Botswana's Gemsbok National Park.

Maloti-Drakensberg Transfrontier Project A project that protects the natural and cultural heritage of the Maloti-Drakensberg Mountains in South Africa and Lesotho.

INTRODUCED PLANT SPECIES

Introduced plant species present a real threat to Southern African ecosystems. For example, Australian wattle trees and Mexican mesquite flourish by sinking their roots deeper into the soil than indigenous trees, causing the latter to suffer from lack of nourishment. The Australian hakea shrub was introduced to serve as a hedge, and is now rampant, displacing native trees and killing off smaller plants. Areas such as South Africa's unique Cape *fynbos* floral kingdom are threatened by Australian acacias, which were introduced for their timber products and to stabilise sand dunes.

Along the east coast of Southern Africa, the natural vegetation is coastal bush, a mixture of light woodland and dune forest; high rainfall has also created pockets of subtropical forest. In South Africa's Karoo, typical vegetation includes grasses, bushes and succulents that bloom colourfully after the rains. Much original Karoo vegetation has been destroyed since the introduction of grazing animals and alien plants.

To the east lie the temperate grasslands of the high-veld and to the north, a vast arid savannah, characterised by acacia scrub, which takes in most of central Namibia, much of Botswana and the northern parts of South Africa. To the north and east is the woodland savannah, consisting of mainly broadleaf deciduous trees. Dry woodland, dominated by mopane trees, covers northern Namibia, northern Botswana, the Zimbabwean low-veld and the Zambezi Valley. In wetter areas – central Zimbabwe, northern Mozambique and most of Zambia and Malawi – the dominant vegetation is moist woodland, or miombo. A mix of the two, which occurs in northeastern South Africa and central Mozambique, is known as mixed woodland, or 'bush-veld'.

Small pockets of high ground all over the region have a vegetation zone termed afro-montane, which occurs in highland areas where open grasslands are interspersed with heathland and isolated forests.

There are more than 700 alien plant species in the region, and about 10% of these are classed as invasive aliens – that is, they thrive to the detriment of endemic species.

Environmental Issues

The environmental issues facing Southern Africa are legion, not least among them the risk of desertification, poaching and the rights and wrongs of commercial or trophy hunting. It is not that Southern Africa is uniquely affected by these issues – they are issues for governments and peoples across the continent. Rather, it is here, in a region where wildlife and wilderness areas survive in numbers rarely seen elsewhere, that there may just be a whole lot more to lose.

Desertification

Desertification is caused in part by overgrazing in a region where cattle very often outnumber people. It can result in soil erosion, declining groundwater reserves, reduced soil fertility and deforestation. The related issue of water scarcity is another massive concern, both in terms of the region's agricultural output and in the provision of drinking water to a growing population.

Poaching

Southern Africa is, like the rest of the continent, facing what may amount to a poaching holocaust.

Rhino horn has long been a sought-after commodity in some Asian countries. It is a status symbol and is believed to be a healing agent. By one estimate, rhino horn can sell on the black market in China or Vietnam for US$60,000 per kilo and has been as high as US$100,000. Ivory prices regularly rise above US$2000 per kilo. Both products are now, literally, worth more than their weight in gold.

Trees of Southern Africa, by Keith Coates Palgrave, provides the most thorough coverage of the subcontinent's arboreal richness, illustrated with colour photos and paintings.

From the 1970s various factors (especially the value of ivory) led to an increase in elephant poaching in many parts of Africa. The real money was made not by poachers – often villagers who were paid a pittance for the valuable tusks – but by dealers. The number of elephants in Africa went from 1.3 million to 625,000 between 1979 and 1989, and in East Africa and some Southern African countries – notably Zambia – elephant

SOUTHERN AFRICA'S BEST PARKS & RESERVES

COUNTRY	PARK	FEATURES	ACTIVITIES	BEST TIME TO VISIT
Botswana	Central Kalahari Game Reserve	Kalahari landscapes, one of world's largest protected areas, desert-adapted wildlife	wildlife viewing, walking, visiting San villages	year-round
Botswana	Chobe National Park	grassland, woodland & river, world's largest elephant population	wildlife viewing, birdwatching, fishing	Jun-Oct
Botswana & South Africa	Kgalagadi Transfrontier Park	semi-arid grassland & salt pans	wildlife viewing, birdwatching	year-round
Botswana	Makgadikgadi & Nxai Pans National Parks	largest saltpans in the world, migratory zebra & wildebeest, flamingos	wildlife viewing, trekking with San, quad biking	Mar-Jul
Botswana	Moremi Game Reserve	grassland, flood plains & swamps, huge wildlife density	wildlife viewing, walking, scenic flights	Jun-Oct
Lesotho	Sehlabathebe National Park	high mountain country, prolific birdlife	hiking, birdwatching, horse riding	year-round
Malawi	Liwonde National Park	marshes, mopane (woodland), elephants, rhinos, hippos, crocodile-filled Shire River	wildlife drives, walking safaris, boat safaris, birdwatching, rhino sanctuary	Jun-Oct, Nov-Jan for birdwatching
Malawi	Majete Wildlife Reserve	Miombo (woodland), marshes, elephants, hippos, zebras, buffaloes, lions, rhinos, crocodiles	Wildlife drives, walking safaris, birdwatching, boat safaris	Jun-Oct
Malawi	Nkhotakota Wildlife Reserve	Miombo, bush, nyalas, warthogs, buffaloes, elephants, leopards, crocodiles	croc & elephant spotting, birdwatching, kayaking, fishing	Jul-Nov, Dec & Jan for birdwatching
Malawi	Nyika National Park	sweeping highland grasslands, antelope, zebras, leopards, hyenas, elephants	hiking, mountain biking, wildlife drives, multiday treks, birdwatching	Sep & Oct for mammals, Oct-Apr for birds
Mozambique	Gorongosa National Park	fascinating back story, lions, elephants, prolific birdlife	wildlife safaris, canoeing, walking safaris	Apr-Dec
Namibia	Etosha National Park	semi-arid savannah surrounding a saltpan, 114 mammal species	wildlife viewing, birdwatching, night drives	May-Sep
Namibia & South Africa	|Ai-|Ais Richtersveld Transfrontier Park	Fish River Canyon (Africa's longest), hot springs, mountainous desert, haunting beauty, klipspringers, jackals, zebras, plants, birds	hiking, 4WD adventures	Apr-Nov

populations were reduced by up to 90% in about 15 years. In other Southern African countries, where parks and reserves were well managed, in particular South Africa, Botswana and Namibia, elephant populations were relatively unaffected.

In 1989, in response to the illegal trade and diminishing numbers of elephants, a world body called the Convention on International Trade in

COUNTRY	PARK	FEATURES	ACTIVITIES	BEST TIME TO VISIT
Namibia	Nkasa Rupara National Park	mini-Okavango, 430 bird species, canoe trails through park	wildlife viewing, bird-watching, canoe trips	Sep-Apr
Namibia	Namib-Naukluft Park	Namibia's largest protected area, beautiful sand-dune & mountain landscapes, rare Hartmann's zebras	wildlife viewing, walking	year-round
South Africa	Kruger National Park	savannah, woodlands, thornveld, the Big Five	vehicle safaris, wildlife walks	year-round
South Africa	Addo Elephant National Park	dense bush, grasslands, forested kloofs, elephants, black rhinos, buffaloes	vehicle safaris, walking trails, horse riding	year-round
South Africa	Hluhluwe-iMfolozi Park	lush, subtropical vegetation, savannah, rhinos, giraffes, lions, elephants, birds	wilderness walks, wildlife watching	May-Oct
South Africa	Mkhuze Game Reserve	savannah, woodlands, swamp, rhinos & almost everything else, hundreds of bird species	guided walks, bird walks, vehicle safaris	year-round
South Africa	Khahlamba-Drakensberg Park	awe-inspiring Drakensberg escarpment, fantastic scenery & wilderness areas	hiking	year-round
Swaziland	Mkhaya Game Reserve	rhinos, elephants, birdlife	hiking, wildlife safaris, white-water rafting, caving	year-round
Swaziland	Hlane Royal National Park	elephants, big cats, rhinos, birdlife	bush walking, wildlife drives, mountain biking & cultural tours	year-round
Zambia	Kafue National Park	miombo woodland, open grasslands, Kafue River, red lechwes, leopards, cheetahs, lions	wildlife drives, birdwatching, fishing	May-Oct
Zambia	Lower Zambezi National Park	Zambezi River, sandy flats, mopane woodland, crocs, hippos, elephants, buffaloes, lions	canoeing, boating, birdwatching, wildlife drives	Jun-Sep
Zambia	South Luangwa National Park	mopane & miombo woodland, grasslands, Thornicroft's giraffes, Cookson's wildebeest, lions, leopards, elephants, pukus	day & night wildlife drives, walking safaris	Apr-Oct
Zimbabwe	Mana Pools National Park	hippos, crocs, zebras, elephants, lions, wild dogs, leopards & cheetahs	walking safaris, wildlife safaris	Jun-Oct
Zimbabwe	Hwange National Park	400 bird species, 107 mammal species including lions, giraffes, leopards, cheetahs, hyenas, wild dogs & 40,000 elephants	wildlife safaris	Jul-Oct

NATIONAL PARK ACCOMMODATION

Most parks and reserves contain accommodation, so you can stay overnight and take wildlife drives in the early morning and evening. Accommodation ranges from simple campsites to luxury lodges run by companies that have concessions inside the parks. Prices vary to match the quality of facilities. In some countries you can just turn up and find a place to camp or stay; in other countries reservations are advised (or are essential at busy times).

Endangered Species (CITES) banned the import and export of ivory internationally. It also increased funding for antipoaching measures. When the ban was established, world raw ivory prices plummeted by 90%, and the market for poaching and smuggling was radically reduced.

In 2009, everything changed and poachers again began killing elephants (and rhinos) in great numbers. Perhaps tellingly, a year earlier, in 2008, a number of Southern African countries were allowed to sell their ivory stockpiles to China and Japan, thereby reigniting demand that had shown no signs of growth in decades. Whatever the reason, the killing hasn't stopped since.

> The lure of riches to be made from ivory is staggering. By the late 1980s the price of 1kg of ivory (US$300) was three times the *annual* income of more than 60% of Africa's population.

Governments and park authorities are, of course, fighting back and innovative ways of tracking down poachers are being deployed. These include Shotspotter, a technology usually rolled out in crime-ridden cities in the USA. When a shot is fired, hidden microphones in the bush pick up the sound, triangulate it and feed location information to rangers and police who can respond in real time. But for the moment, the poachers seem to be winning.

National Parks

Southern Africa has some of the finest national parks in Africa, enclosing within their borders landscapes and wilderness areas of singular beauty and home to an astonishing diversity of mammals, birds, reptiles and more.

Practicalities

The term 'national park' is often used in Southern Africa as a catch-all term to include wildlife reserves, forest parks or any government conservation area; there are also several privately owned reserves.

Most parks in Southern Africa conserve habitats and wildlife species and provide recreational facilities for visitors, although park facilities, geography and wildlife-viewing opportunities vary considerably across the region. South African parks are among the best managed in the world, and most of the rest are very good, although Zimbabwean parks have declined, some of Zambia's parks are still recovering from years of neglect, and those in Mozambique are still being developed, with parks such as Gorongosa in the forefront of developments despite many complications along the way.

> See www.peace-parks.org for all the latest news on the transfrontier parks in the region, including progress reports and maps of all the parks.

In most parks and reserves harbouring large (and potentially dangerous) animals, visitors must travel in vehicles or on an organised safari, but several (notably in Zambia and Zimbabwe) do allow hiking or walking with a ranger or safari guide; in Zimbabwe's Mana Pools National Park, you're even allowed to walk *without* a guide or armed escort.

Nearly all parks charge an entrance fee, and in almost all cases foreigners pay substantially more than local residents or citizens. This may rankle some visitors – and some parks are seriously overpriced – but the idea is that residents and citizens pay taxes to the governments that support the parks, and therefore are entitled to discounts.

Survival Guide

DIRECTORY A–Z 714

Accommodation 714

Activities 715

Children 718

Customs
Regulations 718

Electricity 718

Embassies &
Consulates. 718

GLBTI Travellers 719

Insurance. 719

Internet Access. 720

Legal Matters 720

Maps. 720

Money. 720

Opening Hours 722

Post. 722

Public Holidays. 722

Safe Travel. 722

Telephone 723

Time 723

Toilets. 723

Tourist
Information 724

Travellers with
Disabilities. 724

Visas. 724

Volunteering 725

Women Travellers 725

Work 726

TRANSPORT 727

GETTING THERE
& AWAY 727

Entering the Country. . . 727

Air 727

Land 728

Sea 729

Tours. 729

GETTING AROUND 730

Air 730

Bicycle 731

Boat 731

Bus 731

Car & Motorcycle 732

Hitching 735

Local Transport. 735

Train 735

HEALTH 736

Before You Go 736

In Transit 737

In Southern Africa 737

LANGUAGE 741

Directory A–Z

Accommodation

Accommodation in Southern Africa is infinitely varied, from remote and basic campsites, to stunning temples to good taste.

Lodges and tented camps The jewel in Southern Africa's crown, with stunning accommodation in stunning locations.

Camping Ranges from simple, cleared patches of ground to well-resourced campsites with excellent facilities.

Hotels The mainstays for those staying in towns and cities; everything from basic fleapits to business hotels.

B&Bs and Guesthouses Found across the region but at their best in South Africa.

Hostels Common in South Africa but often either rare or uninhabitable elsewhere.

B&Bs & Guesthouses

B&Bs and guesthouses are interchangeable terms in much of Southern Africa. They range from a simple room in someone's house to well-established B&Bs with five-star ratings and deluxe accommodation. B&Bs and guesthouses are most prevalent in South Africa, where the standards are high and features such as antique furniture, private verandah, landscaped gardens and a pool are common. Indeed some of the finest accommodation on the continent is found in B&Bs along the Garden Route. Breakfast is usually included and almost always involves gut-busting quantities of eggs, bacon, toast and other cooked goodies.

Camping

Camping is popular, especially in national parks, in coastal and lakeshore areas, and in more expensive destinations, such as Botswana. Some camping grounds are quite basic, while others have a range of facilities, including hot showers and security fences. 'Wild' or free camping (ie not at an official site) is another option, but security can be a problem and wild animals are always a concern, so choose your tent site with care.

Hostels

Many towns and cities on the main tourist trail have at least one hostel, and in some places, such as South Africa's Garden Route, you'll have a wide choice. The hostels generally mirror small hostels anywhere else in the world and offer camping space, dorms and a few private doubles. Many also have a travel desk where you can book tours and safaris.

Another budget option, albeit dwindling but still available in Malawi and Zambia, are resthouses run by local governments or district councils. These are peppered throughout the region, and many date from colonial times. Some are very cheap and less than appealing; others are well kept and good value.

Hotels

In towns and cities, top-end hotels offer clean, air-conditioned rooms with private bathrooms, while midrange hotels typically offer fans instead of air-con. At the budget end, rooms aren't always clean (and may be downright filthy), and bathrooms are usually shared and may well be in an appalling state. Often, your only source of air will be a hole in the window. Many cheap hotels double as brothels, so if this is your budget level don't be surprised if there's a lot of coming and going during

---

BOOK YOUR STAY ONLINE

For more accommodation reviews by Lonely Planet authors, check out http://lonelyplanet.com/hotels/. You'll find independent reviews, as well as recommendations on the best places to stay. Best of all, you can book online.

the night. Some countries, including Malawi and Botswana, offer little in the way of hotels between budget and top end.

Many hotels offer self-catering facilities, which may mean anything from a fridge and a hotplate in the corner to a full kitchen in every unit. In some cases, guests will have to supply their own cooking implements – and perhaps even water and firewood.

Throughout the region you'll probably encounter hotels and lodges that charge in tiers. That is, overseas visitors are charged international rates (full price), visitors from other Southern African countries pay a regional rate (say around 30% less) and locals get resident rates (often less than half the full rate). Most places also give discounts in the low season. Where possible we quote the international high-season rates, including the value-added tax (VAT), which ranges from 10% to 30%.

Lodges & Tented Camps

Lodges and tented camps are the prestige end of the safari market and it's important to note that 'camp' doesn't necessarily denote a campsite (although it may). A camp sometimes refers to a well-appointed, upmarket option run by a private company. Accommodation is usually in tents or chalets made from natural materials. The contact number for these places will be at their office in a larger town and are for bookings and inquiries only, not for direct contact with the lodge or camp.

In upmarket lodges and camps the rates will typically include accommodation plus full board, activities (wildlife drives, boat trips etc) and perhaps even house wine and beer. It may also include laundry and transfers by air or 4WD (although these are usually extra).

SLEEPING PRICE RANGES

The following price ranges refer to a high-season double room with bathroom, including all taxes, unless otherwise stated.

COUNTRY	$	$$	$$$
Botswana	less than US$75	US$75–150	more than US$150
Lesotho	less than US$50	US$50–100	more than US$100
Malawi	less than US$50	US$50–100	more than US$100
Mozambique	less than US$50	US$50–100	more than US$100
Namibia	less than US$75	US$75–150	more than US$150
South Africa	less than US$50 or less than US$75 depending on area	US$50–100 or US$75–150 depending on area	US$100 or more than US$150 depending on area
Swaziland	less than US$50	US$50–100	more than US$100
Zambia	less than US$50	US$50–100	more than US$100
Zimbabwe	less than US$75	US$75–150	more than US$150

Activities

Besides the staple reasons for visiting – safaris (p31) and birdwatching – there's nothing much you can't do in Southern Africa, from getting the blood running with adrenaline-fuelled craziness in Victoria Falls or Swakopmund to the more sedate pastime of fishing. Dive in!

Adrenaline Activities

Southern Africa is something of a gathering place for adrenaline nuts, and a range of weird and wonderful activities keeps them happily crazed. The top spots for extreme sports are Victoria Falls and Livingstone, while Swakopmund on Namibia's Atlantic Coast covers just about everything else. Otherwise, accessibility and infrastructure make South Africa the easiest destination to scare yourself silly.

➡ Bungee jumping off the Victoria Falls bridge (p551) are hourly occurrences, but the highest bridge bungee jump in the world (allegedly) can be found in South Africa at Bloukrans River Bridge (p382); the bridge is 216m high...

➡ Swakopmund (p279) is the adventure capital of Namibia; sandboarding, skydiving and quad biking through the dunes are popular.

➡ South Africa is also one of the world's top destinations for paragliding, particularly at Cape Town's Table Mountain (p339). The strongest thermals are from November to April.

PRACTICALITIES

Media

The region's media map is varied – the best publications tend to come out of South Africa. Elsewhere, you'll find plenty of local (usually pretty sensationalist) newspapers. News magazines that cover the continent include *Africa Today*, *Business Africa* and *New African*. All are available from newsagents in South Africa and bookshops in capital cities elsewhere.

Smoking

Smoking is banned in public places (the definition of which varies from country to country) in most countries of the region and stiff penalties sometimes apply (from fines to prison sentences!). Malawi and Mozambique lag behind with antismoking legislation and no bans apply in these two countries.

Weights & Measures

All countries in Southern Africa use the metric system.

Canoeing, Kayaking & White-Water Rafting

There are some fabulous opportunities across the region for canoeing and white-water rafting. South Africa and the Zambezi River in Zambia and Zimbabwe in particular are the epicentres for such pursuits. The best rafting months in Victoria Falls/Livingstone are from August to October during the dry season; the lower the Zambezi River is, the better the rapids.

While not really an activity you'll do yourself, sitting in a *mokoro* (wooden dugout canoe) while an expert poler punts through the watery channels of Botswana's Okavango Delta is pleasurable to say the least. And in Mozambique you can try a live-aboard dhow safari, in custom-built traditional wooden dhows.

➡ South Africa has many opportunities for canoeing and kayaking, especially at Garden Route National Park (p374) in the Western Cape, and the Senqu (Orange) River, particularly through Augrabies Falls National Park (p503). There's also some serene canoeing at the iSimangaliso Wetland Park (p423).

➡ In Swaziland, the classic rafting destination is the Great Usutu River (p543).

➡ The Zambezi River (p551) lures white-water rafters from around the globe to tackle its angry churn, and there are plenty of operators in Zimbabwe and Livingstone, Zambia; canoeing is also popular.

➡ Sea kayaking is popular in sporadic locations along the coast, while the lake variety is best experienced in Malawi at Cape Maclear (p140) and Nkhata Bay (p133).

Diving & Snorkelling

Although not ranking among the world's best destinations for diving and snorkelling, there's plenty to pique your interest (including a dazzling array of marine life and hard and soft corals) and, especially in Mozambique, there are few more beautiful places on earth to give it a try. And the chances are you may just have it all to yourself.

➡ The best diving and snorkelling in the region is along the coast of Mozambique, particularly the Bazaruto Archipelago (p195) and Vilankulo (p192), Ponta d'Ouro (p182), Tofo (p188), Pemba (p219) and the Quirimbas Archipelago (p224). Quality equipment, instruction and certification are readily available at most of these locations.

➡ In South Africa, beginners should look to Sodwana Bay (p425) on KwaZulu-Natal's Elephant Coast. Port Elizabeth (p388) is another good choice.

➡ For a freshwater flutter, Lake Malawi offers some of the best lake snorkelling and diving in the world. There are good outfits in Nkhata Bay (p133) and Cape Maclear (p140).

➡ Get your PADI open-water licence, swim among tropical fish or visit a WWI wreck on Lake Tanganyika in Zambia's north; Ndole Bay Lodge (p602) is the place for all equipment etc.

Fishing

Southern Africa's wild and varied coastline and wealth of rivers and lakes make for profitable fishing expeditions.

➡ In Zambia the tigerfish of the Lower Zambezi River (p585) give a good fight, but not as good as the vundu, a catfish weighing upwards of 45kg.

➡ Botswana's Okavango Panhandle is a renowned destination for anglers, with tigerfish, pike, barbel (catfish) and bream all possible.

➡ In South African parks and reserves, anglers fish for introduced trout; there are some particularly good highland streams in the Drakensberg.

➡ Lesotho (p114) is an insider's tip among trout anglers. The nearest fishing area to Maseru is the Makhaleng River. Other places to fish are the Malibamat'so River near Oxbow; the Mokhotlong River in the northeast; and the Thaba-Tseka main dam.

➡ Mozambique's coast is legendary among anglers, particularly in the south between Ponta d'Ouro and Inhassoro. Species you are likely to encounter include marlin, kingfish, tuna, sailfish and more.

➡ Namibia draws anglers from all over Southern Africa. Try the beaches north of Swakopmund, or fly-fishing in the Caprivi region.

Hiking

Across Southern Africa there are many excellent opportunities for hiking, and this is one of the most popular activities in the region. Remember that conditions vary from country to country – in Namibia, most hikes are guided treks only, while independent trekking is more a feature elsewhere.

➡ Namibia's Fish River Canyon (p297) is one of Africa's most spectacular hikes, but proper gear, food, water and experience are musts. Other excellent Namibian trails include those in Waterberg Plateau Park (p257) and Ugab River.

➡ In Malawi you can trek the scenic peaks of Mt Mulanje (p155), the Zomba Plateau (p147) and the Nyika Plateau (p129).

➡ Mozambique boasts beautiful vantage points to trek but little infrastructure, so you'll likely be on your own. A good place to start is the beautiful Chimanimani Mountains (p201), with lovely scenery, a handful of basic campsites and an excellent new eco-camp. Also good is the country around Gurúè.

➡ South Africa's undulating topography offers superb hiking opportunities. Among the best walks are: the

Hoerikwaggo (p340) hiking trails of Table Mountain National Park, the five-day Whale Route in De Hoop Nature Reserve (p365) and the celebrated Otter Trail (p384), a five-day journey along the Garden Route that needs to be booked months in advance. Some other notable South African hikes include the Tsitsikamma Trail, which runs parallel to the Otter Trail, KwaZulu-Natal's Giant's Cup Trail – up to five days in the southern Drakensberg – and Mpumalanga's Blyde River Canyon Hiking Trail (p474).

➡ Zambia's Mutinondo Wilderness (p598) is the pick of the country's hiking options (leaving aside, of course, the walking safaris in the country's national parks).

➡ In Zimbabwe, your best trails are in Chimanimani National Park (p639) and the Bvumba Mountains (p635).

Horse Riding

In South Africa it's easy to find rides for all experience levels. Particularly good are as include the iSimangaliso Wetland Park (p423). Riding is also an option in Zimbabwe's national parks, and on the beach in Mozambique, at Vilankulo and Tofo.

Dedicated horse-riding operations:

Horizon Horseback Adventures (www.ridinginafrica.com) South Africa

Ride Botswana (☏71 671 608, 72 484 354; www.ridebotswana.com) Botswana

Namibia Horse Safari Company (www.namibiahorsesafari.com) Namibia

In the Saddle (☏01299-272 997; www.inthesaddle.com) Safaris across the region

Mountain Biking

It goes without saying that a region so rich in hiking opportunities will have equally rewarding mountain-biking possibilities. Outside South

Africa and the main tourist areas in the region, it's relatively difficult to hire bikes, so you'd need to bring your own, which may deter all but the most dedicated mountain bikers. You can also hire local-style sit-up-and-beg steel roadsters. These are good for getting around towns (especially flat ones) or exploring rural areas at a leisurely pace.

➡ South Africa is littered with excellent biking trails; among the best are those in De Hoop Nature Reserve, with overnight and day trails, and Citrusdal, with a network of trails. Then there's Cape Town, which is something of an unofficial national hub.

➡ In Malawi (p162) great mountain-biking areas include Nyika National Park and the Viphya Plateau. There's even the **Luwawa International Mountain Bike Race** (www.luwawaforestlodge.net/mountain-biking) in June.

Rock Climbing & Abseiling

South Africa is far and away the best place for rock climbers. It's not that other countries don't have excellent climbing venues; rather, it's only in South Africa that you'll find truly professional climbing outfits with all of the necessary equipment and experience.

➡ You'll find the best climbing at Table Mountain, the Cederberg, Montagu, the Drakensberg and Waterval Boven, near Nelspruit in Mpumalanga.

➡ In Malawi you can try abseiling around Manchewe Falls near Livingstonia. There is excellent and challenging climbing on the close-to-sheer faces of the KwaZulu-Natal Drakensberg in South Africa.

➡ Experienced climbers with their own equipment could

also try the Spitzkoppe and the Brandberg in Namibia.

Surfing & Kitesurfing

Any surfer worth their wax is familiar with the legendary waves at J-Bay, better known to nonconverts as Jeffreys Bay (p386). Situated on the Garden Route, the town's choppy surf lures experts and amateurs from around the globe. South Africa also offers myriad less-celebrated alternatives, particularly along the Eastern Cape coast from Port Alfred northwards.

➡ Although undeveloped for surfers, Namibia's Skeleton Coast is famous for rough waves and unspoilt beaches. This stretch is only for the seriously experienced and brave, though, with savage rips, icy water temperatures and the odd great white shark.

➡ Mozambique's best waves are at Ponta d'Ouro (p182) in the far south of the country and (for skilled surfers) at Tofinho (p190) – Mozambique's unofficial surfing capital, just south of Tofo.

➡ Kitesurfing is an increasingly popular pastime in Mozambique, especially in the north at Murrébuè (p223), around 12km south of Pemba, and around Vilankulo (p192).

Children

Southern Africa presents few problems specific to children, and while health concerns are always an issue, food and lodging are mostly quite familiar and manageable. What's more, foreigners with children are usually treated with great kindness, and a widespread local affection for the younger set opens up all sorts of social interaction for travelling families.

In South Africa, away from the coast, many resorts, hotels and national park lodges and camping grounds have a wide range of

facilities for children. Many families hire campervans in South Africa to tour the region. There are fewer child-oriented facilities in the other countries, but here the attractions usually provide entertainment enough: large wild animals in the national parks are a major draw, and even bored teenagers have been known to enjoy Vic Falls and its adrenaline activities. Botswana and Namibia also lend themselves to family camping holidays, and the attractions – such as the wildlife of Etosha National Park or Moermi Game Reserve, or the world's biggest sandbox at Sossusvlei – are entertainment in themselves. Lake Malawi has plenty of child-friendly lodges and the highland areas of Malawi such as the Viphya and Zomba Plateaus are also good for families.

For more advice and anecdotes, see Lonely Planet's *Travel with Children*.

Practicalities

In tourist hotels and lodges, family rooms and chalets are normally available for only a little more than doubles. Otherwise, it's normally easy to arrange more beds in a standard adult double for a minimal extra charge. On public transport children are expected to pay for their seats unless they spend the entire journey on their parents' laps.

In Southern Africa, compared with some other parts of the world, there are few nasty diseases to worry about, and good (if expensive) medical services are often within reach.

Outside cities and major towns in South Africa, do not plan on finding pasteurised milk, formula or disposable nappies. They may be available sporadically (especially in Mozambique, Botswana and Namibia), but this is the exception rather than the rule. Breastfeeding in public is fairly common for locals, but in rural areas it's likely to attract significant unwanted attention for visitors.

Customs Regulations

Customs information varies from country to country in the region.

Electricity

Electricity in Southern Africa is generated at 220V to 240V AC. Most plugs have three prongs (or pins), either round or rectangular ('square') in section. In South Africa, three round-pin plugs are used. Outside South Africa, British-style square three-pin plugs are common, while two-pin European-style plugs are sometimes used. A voltage adaptor is needed for US appliances.

Embassies & Consulates

Embassies are most plentiful in South Africa, where whole suburbs of Pretoria are a Who's Who of global representation. Where home countries have no embassy, often a consul is appointed, who is not a full-time diplomat but has certain

---

EATING PRICE RANGES

The following price ranges refer to a main course.

$ less than US$5

$$ US$5–10

$$$ more than US$10

diplomatic responsibilities. Australia, Canada and New Zealand have few embassies in Southern Africa, but there is limited emergency assistance available from the British High Commission.

It's important to realise what your own embassy can and can't do to help you if you get into trouble. Generally speaking, it won't be much help if whatever trouble you're in is remotely your own fault. Remember that you are bound by the laws of the country you are in. In genuine emergencies you might get some assistance, but only if other channels have been exhausted. If you have all your money and documents stolen, your embassy might assist with getting a new passport, but that's about it.

GLBTI Travellers

Homosexuality is legal in South Africa and was decriminalised in Mozambique in 2015. Everywhere else, male homosexual acts are illegal in all countries of the region; lesbian acts exist in a grey area in some countries.

Countries in the region are extremely conservative in their attitudes towards gay men and lesbians, and homosexuality is rarely discussed in public, not least because in traditional African societies, gay sexual relationships are a cultural taboo. When it does appear as a public issue, it's rarely to express tolerance or solidarity. Zimbabwean president Robert Mugabe has made numerous vociferous diatribes against homosexuals, while back in 2001, then-Namibia president Sam Nujoma famously said, 'Those who are practising homosexuality in Namibia are destroying the nation. Homosexuals must be condemned and rejected in our society.'

Antigay attitudes appear particularly entrenched also in Swaziland, Lesotho, Zambia and Malawi, while things are a little more relaxed in Botswana (where employment laws forbid workplace discrimination or dismissal on the basis of a person's sexual orientation), although homosexual acts remain illegal.

South Africa's constitution is one of the few in Africa that explicitly prohibits discrimination on the grounds of sexual orientation, and there are active gay and lesbian communities and scenes in Cape Town, Jo'burg, Pretoria and Durban. Cape Town is without doubt the focal point, and the most openly gay city on the continent.

Homosexuality has been decriminalised in Mozambique and there is a small but growing gay-and-lesbian scene in Maputo, although cultural attitudes sometimes lag behind the legal situation.

Open displays of affection are generally frowned upon in Southern Africa, whatever your orientation. Please be sensitive to local sensibilities.

ESSENTIAL DOCUMENTS

Travellers with children should be aware of changes regarding the documents you must carry with you while travelling through some countries of the region. The law requires that all parents arriving, transiting and departing South Africa, Namibia and Botswana must produce an unabridged birth certificate for their children, and the birth certificate must state the names of both parents. Families not in possession of these documents will be refused travel.

If one parent is travelling alone with their children, the travelling parent must carry with them an affidavit from the other (ie nontravelling) parent who is listed on the birth certificate granting their consent for the travel to take place in their absence. Where this is not possible, either a court order granting full parental responsibilities and rights, or a death certificate of the other parent, must be produced.

We have travelled across the borders of all three countries with our children on numerous occasions and although we were not always asked for these documents, we were asked for each of them at least once. Travel without them at your peril.

Resources

South African resources:

Exit (www.exit.co.za) South Africa's longest-running gay newspaper.

Gay Pages (www.gaypagessa.co.za) Bimonthly glossy magazine.

OUTright For gay males; available at CNA and other chain bookstores nationwide.

South Africa tourism (www.southafrica.net) Lists gay and lesbian events.

Insurance

All travellers should seriously consider purchasing a travel insurance policy, which will provide some sense of security in the case of a medical emergency or the loss or theft of money or belongings. Travel health-insurance policies can usually be extended to include baggage, flight departure insurance and a range of other options.

Claims on your travel insurance must be accompanied by proof of the value of any items lost or stolen (purchase receipts are the best, so if you buy a new camera for your trip, for example, hang onto the receipt). In the case of medical claims, you'll need detailed medical reports and receipts. If you're claiming on a trip cancelled by circumstances beyond your control (illness, airline bankruptcy, industrial action etc), you'll have to produce all flight tickets purchased, tour agency receipts and itinerary, and proof of whatever glitch caused your trip to be cancelled.

Worldwide travel insurance is available at www.lonelyplanet.com/travel-insurance. You can buy, extend and claim online anytime – even if you're already on the road.

Internet Access

Most capital cities (and some large towns) in the region have at least one internet cafe, and many hotels and backpacker hostels also offer these services. Speed, reliability and hourly rates vary greatly (between about US$1 and US$5). Wireless access is becoming more common everywhere. Rural areas in all countries are essentially devoid of internet access, although some small towns may have an internet centre and lodges and camps increasingly have wireless services. At the same time, many luxury lodges have made a deliberate decision to not provide wi-fi, on the assumption that your need to connect to your surroundings is greater than your need for internet access.

Legal Matters

Although the legal situation varies from country to country, the following guidelines apply across the region:

➡ Drugs are illegal in Southern Africa, penalties are stiff and prisons are deeply unpleasant. Don't think about bringing anything over the borders or buying it while you're here.

➡ Police, military and other officials are generally polite and on their best behaviour. In your dealings with officialdom, you should always make every effort to be patient and polite in return.

➡ Although corruption is rare, petty corruption by local officials and police officers (especially those who pull you over for speeding) does occur.

➡ Always carry your passport with you in a secure location inaccessible to pickpockets and keep a photocopy of the main pages (ie the page with your photo ID and entry stamp or visa) at your hotel.

➡ Homosexual acts are illegal in most countries of the region; South Africa and Mozambique are exceptions.

➡ Avoid taking photos of government buildings, bridges, train stations and other landmarks that suspicious officials may deem to be a security risk.

➡ If you find yourself arrested and in prison, you will most likely be granted a single phone call to your embassy, who may be able to arrange a lawyer.

Maps

The Automobile Association (AA) of South Africa produces a useful map of South Africa (as well as numerous South African area maps), plus others covering Botswana and Namibia. The maps are available from any AA shop in South Africa.

For a useful overview of the region, the best map is the Michelin *Africa: Central & South* (1:4,000,000; Series No 746). Otherwise, pick up a copy of Map Studio's *Southern & Central Africa*, which shows all the countries in Southern Africa. Remember, however, that for navigation you'll need much more detailed maps.

Money

ATMs

ATMs are readily available throughout South Africa and in cities and main urban centres in the rest of the region. If you're planning to travel for lengthy periods of time in rural areas, however, plan ahead: ATMs are still a foreign concept. There are a few ATM scams to be aware of, operating particularly in South Africa and Zimbabwe.

Black Market

In some parts of the world, artificially fixed exchange rates in the bank mean you can get more local money for your hard currency by changing on the so-called black market. Not only is this illegal, it's also potentially dangerous. In most of the region, currency deregulation has eliminated the black market; Zimbabwe is a significant exception. If someone approaches you anywhere in the region offering substantially more than the bank rate, they almost certainly have a well-formulated plan for separating you from your money. If you change money on the black market, always count your money before walking away.

Cash

Most travellers carry a mix of cash and travellers cheques, although cash is more convenient. The best currency to bring is far and away US dollars. British pounds, followed by euros, come a distant second and third.

You'll have no trouble exchanging US cash wherever there are Forex facilities, but try to bring notes (especially US$100) issued from 2006 or later; earlier notes may not be accepted at banks.

The South African rand is also widely recognised

throughout the region, but it's not worth changing your currency into rand before converting it to kwacha, pula or whatever.

It's always wise to have at least an emergency US$20 note tucked somewhere safe in case you find yourself suddenly devoid of all other possessions.

Credit & Debit Cards

Most credit and debit cards can be used in ATMs, which are found all over South Africa, Malawi, Botswana and Namibia. In other countries they're found only in capital cities and larger towns, and aren't always reliable.

Credit cards work for purchases all over South Africa, Namibia and Botswana, and in tourist establishments in other countries. You can also use credit cards to draw cash advances (but even in South Africa this can take several hours, and be wary of high interest charges).

Whatever card you choose to use, it isn't wise to rely totally on plastic, as computer or telephone breakdowns can leave you stranded. Always have some cash or travellers cheques as backup.

Following major cash shortage in Zimbabwe many foreign consulates recommended tourists bring enough US dollars to last the duration of their trip. Zimbabwe's new bond money currency was introduced in late 2016 in hope of easing the money crisis, but time will tell if it's a temporary measure or here to stay.

Currency

The US dollar is the official currency of Zimbabwe, although government-issued bonds were added into the mix in late 2016.

Elsewhere in Southern Africa, many midrange and top-end hotels will quote their room rates (and accept payment) in US dollars.

In all countries it's wise to rely on a variety of methods to fund your trip. Local currency, US dollars and a credit card will cover most bases.

Moneychangers

Throughout the region, you can exchange currency at banks and foreign exchange bureaus, which are normally found near borders, in larger cities and in tourist areas. You can also change money at some shops and hotels (which almost always give very poor rates).

The easiest currencies to exchange are US dollars, followed by euros or British pounds. At border crossings where there is no bank, unofficial moneychangers are usually tolerated by the authorities. It's always important to be alert, though, as these guys can pull all sorts of stunts with poor exchange rates, folded notes and clipped newspaper sandwiched between legitimate notes.

Taxes & Refunds

Throughout the region, quoted prices and tariffs usually include all local taxes, but always ask if you're unsure.

There is no system of sales-tax refunds for tourists who purchase items in most Southern African countries. The exception is South Africa, where the value-added tax (VAT) of 14% can be reclaimed on most goods being taken out of the country by departing foreign visitors.

Tipping

When it comes to tipping, every country is different, but a few general rules apply:

Hotels and restaurants It isn't usually necessary in small local establishments, midrange restaurants, backpackers lodges, hotels or fast-food places, but in any upmarket restaurant that doesn't automatically include a service charge (which isn't obligatory if the service has been poor), it may be appropriate.

Taxis Taxi drivers aren't normally tipped, but may expect about 10% from well-heeled travellers.

EXCHANGE RATES

	AUSTRALIA (A$1)	CANADA (C$1)	EURO (€1)	JAPAN (¥100)	NEW ZEALAND (NZ$1)	UK (£1)	USA (US$1)
Botswana	P8.03	P7.83	P11.62	P10.05	P7.67	P13.05	P10.47
Lesotho	M10.24	M10.53	M14.69	M11.99	M9.79	M17.51	M14.06
Malawi	MK541	MK532	MK783	MK680	MK511	MK515	MK713
Mozambique	Mtc60	Mtc60	Mtc76	Mtc77	Mtc57	Mtc102	Mtc78
Namibia	N$10.46	N$10.50	N$14.95	N$12.60	N$9.92	N$17.63	N$14.17
South Africa	R10.24	R10.53	R14.69	R11.99	R9.79	R17.51	R14.06
Swaziland	E10.24	E10.53	E14.69	E11.99	E9.79	E17.51	E14.06
Zambia	ZMW7.34	ZMW7.44	ZMW10.42	ZMW8.56	ZMW7.04	ZMW12.36	ZMW9.80
Zimbabwe	US$0.76	US$0.75	US$1.10	US$0.95	US$0.72	US$1.22	US$1

For current exchange rates see www.xe.com.

Travellers Cheques

Travellers cheques are becoming increasingly difficult to change and doing so is rarely less than a bureaucratic nightmare.

If you do decide to go with travellers cheques, it's wise to purchase a range of travellers cheque denominations so you don't have to exchange US$100 in a country where you need only half that. When exchanging travellers cheques, many places want to check your purchase receipts (the ones the travellers cheque company told you to always keep separate), but carry them with you only when you want to change money. Just be sure to have photocopies of them, along with the international numbers to call in case of loss or theft.

Be aware that it can be difficult to change travellers cheques in Zambia, Mozambique and Malawi; some banks don't recognise modern purchase receipts (or perhaps don't want to), although US dollars cash in the same institutions is welcomed with open arms.

Opening Hours

Standard opening hours vary from country to country. As a general rule, the working week runs from Monday to Friday; some shops and tourism-related businesses sometimes open on Saturdays, either all day or just in the morning.

Post

The postal system varies from country to country, but, as a general rule, services are slow but reliable. Packages are usually sent from a separate counter or even a different office; note that some will require that you show them the contents of any package so don't seal your box until you're in the office itself.

In some circumstances, international courier companies charge rates that aren't all that much more than government postal rates, and they're usually quicker and more reliable.

Public Holidays

Public holidays vary from one country to the next and usually celebrate country-specific dates commemorating independence and/or historically significant events. Most countries celebrate one or more of the following:

New Year's Day 1 January

Good Friday March or April

Easter Sunday March or April

Easter Monday March or April

Labour or Workers' Day 1 May

Christmas Day 25 December

Boxing Day 26 December

Safe Travel

It is very important not to make sweeping statements about personal safety in Southern Africa. While some areas are undeniably risky, most places are completely safe. Essentially, violent robbery is much more prevalent in cities and towns than in rural or wilderness areas. But even towns can differ; as a general rule, there's more of a danger in those frequented by foreigners than in places off the usual tourist track.

Scams

The main annoyances you'll come across in Southern Africa are the various hustlers, touts, con artists and scam merchants who recognise tourists as easy prey. Although these characters aren't always dangerous, they can part you from your valuables.

Popular scams include young people carrying sign-up sheets, requesting sponsorship for their school, sports team, youth club, grandmother's liver

transplant or other apparently worthwhile causes. The sheets will invariably include the names of 'generous' foreigners who have donated US$100 or more. These are almost invariably a scam; ignore them and politely take your leave. Another scam to look out for is people selling bogus bus tickets in and around bus stations. Always purchase your tickets from official sources, even if that's a hole in the wall with a penned sign above it.

In the major cities of Zimbabwe, South Africa and Mozambique it's advisable to keep your wits about you when using an ATM. There are dozens of scams that involve stealing your cash, your card or your personal identification number (PIN) – usually all three. The ATM scam you're most likely to encounter involves the thief tampering with the machine so your card becomes jammed. By the time you realise this you've entered your PIN. The thief will have seen this, and when you go inside to report that your card has been swallowed, he will take the card and leave your account significantly lighter.

A popular scam in Namibia is when one guy distracts the driver out of the car while another opens up the passenger side, grabbing whatever is lying around and does a runner. Keep your stuff stashed out of sight in the car and be vigilant if someone wanders up to your car window and starts a conversation.

Road Safety

Although vehicle traffic is light on many roads outside of the major towns and cities, the most significant concern for most travellers is road safety. Most Southern African countries have some of the highest per capita accident rates in the world, and drunk and reckless driving are common, as is excessive speed. Never drive at night unless you absolutely have to.

Safety Tips

Some simple precautions will hopefully ensure that you have a trouble-free journey. Travellers who exercise due caution rarely have problems. The precautions suggested in this section are particularly relevant to Johannesburg and parts of Cape Town, but it's worth reading them if you're travelling in other main urban centres as well.

➡ Be discreet with your belongings when on the street. Consider leaving your day-pack and camera in your hotel room if the room is safe.

➡ Don't wear jewellery or watches, however inexpensive they may be. Use a separate wallet for day-to-day purchases, and keep the bulk of your cash out of sight, preferably hidden in a pouch under loose-fitting clothing.

➡ Walk confidently, but not aggressively. Never look like you're lost (even if you are!). Don't obviously refer to a guidebook. Tear out the pages you need, or duck into a shop to have a look at the map to get your bearings.

➡ At night get off the streets and take a taxi – a couple of dollars for the fare could save you a lot of pain and trouble.

➡ Don't fall into the trap of thinking all robbers are on the street. Although most hotels are reputable, some travellers have left money in a safe, only to find that less reputable staff members with a spare key have helped themselves. Often this trick involves taking just a few notes, in the hope that you won't notice. To avoid this, store any valuables in a safe inside a pouch with a lockable zip, or in an envelope you can seal.

Telephone

South Africa in general, and major cities elsewhere in the region, has good telephone facilities. Although local calls are relatively inexpensive, long-distance calls and international calls can be pricey. Aside from public phones, there are also private phone centres where you can pay cash for your call, but at double the rate of public phones.

Mobile Phones

In Southern Africa mobile phones are very popular due, in no small part, to the often dismal state of national landline service providers. Reception varies from country to country, but expect decent coverage in and surrounding most towns, but expect nothing at all out in the bush. Airports in some countries often have a counter where you can rent a mobile phone for the duration of your stay.

Satellite Phones

If you will be out in remote areas for even short periods, it can be worth renting a satellite phone for use in emergencies. 4WD rentals agencies can usually rent you a sat phone, or they'll know someone who does.

Time

In the southern summer, Southern Africa is two hours ahead of UTC (Universal Time Coordinate, formerly called GMT, or Greenwich Mean Time). The only Southern African country with daylight-saving time is Namibia, which turns its clocks forward one hour in September, and back one hour in April.

In the southern winter, however, the region is on the same time as British Summer Time (daylight-saving time).

Toilets

There are two main types of toilet in Africa: the Western style, with a toilet bowl and seat; and the African style, which is a squat toilet with a hole in the floor.

➡ Standards of both types of toilet vary tremendously from pristine to nauseating.

➡ In most tourist hotels, except perhaps those

GOVERNMENT TRAVEL ADVICE

The following government websites offer travel advisories and information for travellers.

Australian Department of Foreign Affairs & Trade (www.smartraveller.gov.au)

Canadian Department of Foreign Affairs & International Trade (www.voyage.gc.ca)

French Ministère des Affaires Étrangères et Européennes (www.diplomatie.gouv.fr/fr/conseils-aux-voyageurs)

Italian Ministero degli Affari Esteri (www.viaggiaresicuri.mae.aci.it)

New Zealand Ministry of Foreign Affairs & Trade (www.safetravel.govt.nz)

UK Foreign & Commonwealth Office (www.gov.uk/foreign-travel-advice)

US Department of State (www.travel.state.gov)

basic places that receive a predominantly African clientele, Western-style toilets are the norm.

➜ In rural areas and campsites, long-drop squat toilets are built over a deep hole in the ground, where waste matter decomposes naturally as long as people avoid depositing rubbish (including tampons or sanitary pads, which should be disposed of separately).

➜ There's also a bizarre hybrid, in which an unplumbed Western toilet is perched over a long-drop hole. As you can imagine, the lack of running water can turn these into an unspeakable horror.

Tourist Information

All countries in Southern Africa have national tourist boards, but their efficiency and benefit range from excellent to little more than a friendly smile to downright uninterested.

South Africa's tourist information centres are prolific and fabulous. Usually staffed by devoted locals, they're a great source of microscopic information for travellers. Tourist offices in Namibia and Botswana are the pick of the rest.

Elsewhere, tourist boards' websites are sometimes useful for preplanning, but offices on the ground rarely provide very much enlightenment.

Travellers with Disabilities

People with mobility limitations will not have an easy time in Southern Africa. Even though there are more disabled people per head of population here than in the West, facilities are few. South Africa stands out from its neighbours with regard to its disabled organisations.

For the imaginative, Zambezi raft trips, *mokoro* (dugout canoe) trips in the Okavango Delta (where at least one mobility-disabled person works as a *mokoro* poler), wildlife drives and cruises, lie-down sandboarding in the Namib dunes (if you can reach the top on a quad bike), and other activities won't be inaccessible. In almost all cases, safari companies – including budget operators – are happy to accommodate travellers with special needs, but they're usually relying more on goodwill than any expertise or infrastructure.

In South Africa, the South African National Parks' website (www.sanparks.org) has a detailed and inspirational overview of accommodation and trail accessibility for the mobility impaired at all its parks, including Kruger.

Most wheelchair users find travel easier with an able-bodied companion, and happily, travel in Southern Africa does offer a few advantages compared with other parts of the developing world:

➜ footpaths and public areas are often surfaced with tar or concrete, rather than with sand, mud or gravel

➜ many buildings (including safari lodges and national park cabins) are single storey, and assistance is usually available on domestic and regional flights

➜ vehicle hire is easy in South Africa, Namibia and Botswana and, with permission, vehicles can be taken to neighbouring countries

For more information and advice, download Lonely Planet's free *Accessible Travel* guide from http://lptravel.to/AccessibleTravel.

Organisations

Mobility International USA (www.miusa.org) In the US, it advises disabled travellers on mobility issues; it primarily runs educational exchange programs, and some include African travel.

Society for Accessible Travel & Hospitality (www.sath.org) In the US; offers assistance and advice.

Access-Able Travel Source (www.access-able.com) Another US-based site providing information on disabled-friendly tours and hotels.

Accessible Travel & Leisure (www.accessibletravel.co.uk) Claims to be the biggest UK travel agent dealing with travel for people with a disability, and encourages independent travel.

Visas

Visa requirements vary according to your nationality. In general, travellers from North America, Commonwealth countries and most of Western Europe don't require visas (or can obtain them on arrival) for much of the region.

At the time of writing, the only place in Mozambique you can reliably get a visa at the border is Cóbuè on Lake Malawi. We strongly advise that you organise your visa beforehand. You can do it in person or via post from the embassy in your home country.

If you're from Asia, Africa, Eastern Europe or Latin America, you should check with the local embassies of the countries you intend to visit, as some may accept only visas issued in your home country.

Useful Documentation

Depending on which countries you're visiting, you may need the following: a vaccination certificate to show you have had all the right jabs; a driver's licence, and perhaps an International Driving Permit (for the rare occasions when it may be required to hire a vehicle, or for insurance purposes if you're buying a vehicle); youth hostel card and a student or youth identity card (such as ISIC), which may be good for accessing discounts on flights, long-distance buses and visits to sites of interest (especially museums). See p719 for documents needed if travelling with children.

Volunteering

Volunteer work is a wonderful way to get to know the region and make a difference in the process. The main areas are teaching or wildlife conservation.

There are some excellent local, grassroots opportunities for travellers wanting to volunteer, but community and conservation projects that exist are sometimes small, focused grassroots projects that simply aren't set up for drop-in volunteers. Approach each on a case-by-case basis.

Organisations

The following international organisations are good places to start gathering information on volunteering, although they won't necessarily always have projects on the go in Southern Africa.

Australian Volunteers International (www.australianvolunteers.com)

Coordinating Committee for International Voluntary Service (http://ccivs.org)

Earthwatch (www.earthwatch.org)

Idealist (www.idealist.org)

International Volunteer Programs Association (www.volunteerinternational.org)

Peace Corps (www.peacecorps.gov)

Step Together Volunteering (www.step-together.org.uk)

UN Volunteers (www.unv.org)

Volunteer Service Abroad (www.vsa.org.nz)

Voluntary Service Overseas (www.vso.org.uk)

Volunteer Abroad (www.goabroad.com/volunteer-abroad)

Worldwide Experience (www.worldwideexperience.com)

Women Travellers

Compared with North Africa and the Middle East, South America and many Western countries, Southern Africa is relatively safe and nonthreatening for women travellers, whether solo or in small groups.

Local Attitudes

Attitudes towards foreign women travellers tend to be fairly liberal, and if travelling solo there are plenty of opportunities to meet people along the way. Southern Africa is one of the few places in the developing world where women can meet and communicate freely with local men – of any race – without automatically being misconstrued. You'll still get questions about what you're doing, and where your husband and children are, but reactions are usually matter-of-fact.

Nightlife is something of an exception and in this sphere both black and white societies in Southern Africa are very much conservative, traditional and male dominated. Some bars are male only (by law of the establishment, or by law of tradition), and even where women are 'allowed', cultural conventions often dictate that women don't enter without a male companion. To avoid attracting unwanted attention, it's best to seek out and follow local female advice on which places are acceptable.

Health & Safety

Stay safe with a bit of common sense and keep your wits about you, ie don't wander around alone anywhere at night, and during the daytime avoid anywhere that's isolated, including streets, beaches and parks. If you go out at night, it's best to go in a group. Additionally, many budget hotels double as brothels, and are best avoided if you're travelling solo.

Never forget that in Africa, HIV/AIDS presents a threat that's unimaginable in the West. Throughout the region, local sex workers are almost always infected. This also means local men may see a foreign woman as a safe alternative.

Tampons and sanitary napkins are sold in pharmacies and supermarkets in major towns, although you're best off bringing your own preferred supply from home. It's also a good idea to pack anti-thrush medication, UTI antibiotics and any other medication you might need.

Resources

Female travellers may like to contact the global organisation called Women Welcome Women World Wide (www.womenwelcomewomen.org.uk), which fosters international friendship by enabling women of different countries to visit one another.

Work

Unemployment in Southern Africa is high and finding work is difficult. There are few opportunities for getting work in the region and those that do exist must be arranged through a company well in advance of your visit to the country. In most cases, to work legally you will not be able to do so on a tourist visa and will instead have to obtain a work visa or permit.

Most opportunities are usually in the fields of aid, conservation and tourism (such as working in a lodge or hotel, as a tour guide, as a diving instructor...); the latter sector is the one most likely to be looking for skilled overseas workers at shorter notice.

Transport

GETTING THERE & AWAY

Southern Africa is well connected to the rest of the world by air, most commonly through Johannesburg. Arriving by land is only possible from Tanzania, while travelling by sea is very much uncharted territory.

Flights, cars and tours can be booked online at lonelyplanet.com/bookings.

Entering the Country

Visitors require a valid passport to enter every country in Southern Africa. To accommodate visas and border stamps, you'll need at least one or two empty pages per country you intend to visit, especially if your itinerary calls for multiple border crossings. If your passport is close to full, get a new one or pick up an insert – but apply for it well in advance. If your passport is due to expire, replace it before you leave home, as some officials won't admit you unless your passport is valid at least three (or even six) months beyond the end of your stay.

Crossing borders with a vehicle considerably increases the time you'll spend completing the formalities and continuing on your way.

Air

Most flights into Southern Africa arrive at Johannesburg (South Africa) and this is usually the cheapest access point for the region. You may find flights that arrive in other Southern African cities – notably Windhoek, Maun, Victoria Falls, Maputo and Lusaka – but options are limited and usually restricted to flights from elsewhere in Africa.

Airports & Airlines

The major air hub for Southern Africa is **OR Tambo International Airport** (Ortia; 011-921 6262; www.airports.co.za) in Johannesburg, which has had a major upgrade. It is now a world-class airport with a full range of shops, restaurants, internet access, ATMs, foreign-exchange bureaus, and mobile-phone and car-rental outlets. It also has a full board of connecting flights to cities across Southern Africa.

Other international airports that serve as minor gateways to the region:

Cape Town International Airport (CPT ; 021-937 1200; www.airports.co.za)

Chief Hosea Kutako (Windhoek) International Airport (WDH; 061-2996602; www.airports.com.na)

Lusaka International Airport (LUN; Kenneth Launda International Airport)

CLIMATE CHANGE & TRAVEL

Every form of transport that relies on carbon-based fuel generates CO_2, the main cause of human-induced climate change. Modern travel is dependent on aeroplanes, which might use less fuel per kilometre per person than most cars but travel much greater distances. The altitude at which aircraft emit gases (including CO_2) and particles also contributes to their climate change impact. Many websites offer 'carbon calculators' that allow people to estimate the carbon emissions generated by their journey and, for those who wish to do so, to offset the impact of the greenhouse gases emitted with contributions to portfolios of climate-friendly initiatives throughout the world. Lonely Planet offsets the carbon footprint of all staff and author travel.

Lilongwe International Airport (Kamuzu International Airport; LLW; ☎0992 991097)

Livingstone Airport (Harry Mwanga Nkumbula International Airport)

Maputo International Airport (☎21-465827/8; www.aeroportos.co.mz)

Maun Airport (MUB; ☎686 1559)

South African Airways (SAA; ☎0860 606 606; www.flysaa.com) has the largest selection of flights into Southern Africa from Africa and elsewhere, but numerous other international airlines fly into Johannesburg from across the globe.

Victoria Falls Airport (VFA)

Departure Tax

Departure tax is included in the price of a ticket.

Land

Unless you're willing to brave Angola and/or Democratic Republic of Congo (DRC), the only way to enter Southern Africa by land is from Tanzania to Zambia, Mozambique or Malawi.

Border Crossings

For a long time, the most frequented routes into Southern Africa were from Tanzania into Malawi at Songwe, and from Tanzania into Zambia at Nakonde. With two bridges now crossing the Rovuma River, it is now straightforward to drive from Tanzania into Mozambique.

TANZANIA-MALAWI

As long as you don't mind taking at least 30 hours to get there, buses connect Lilongwe and Dar es Salaam five times a week; you can also get on/off at Mzuzu.

If your journey involves shorter hops, the towns of Mbeya (southern Tanzania) and Karonga (northern Malawi) serve as gateways to the Songwe border crossing.

TANZANIA-MOZAMBIQUE

There are three land border crossings between Tanzania and Mozambique: Kilambo/Namiranga (130km north of Moçimboa da Praia); Negomano Unity Bridge; and Mtomoni Unity Bridge 2 (120km south of Songea). Moçimboa da Praia (Mozambique) and Palma are sea ports only.

Of these, the main vehicle crossing over the Rovuma is via the Unity Bridge at Negomano, while the main routes with cross-border public transport are Dar-Mtwara-Negomano-Pemba-southwards or via Songea over Unity Bridge 2 to Lichinga. Crossing at Kilango requires an unreliable ferry crossing, while the Palma entry point is for those arriving by dhow or charter flight.

And a word of warning: don't turn up at this border without a visa for both countries already in your passport.

TANZANIA-ZAMBIA

There is a road and train crossing between Nakonde (Zambia) and Tunduma (Tanzania); there are two international rail crossings per week, as well as buses. Once across the border, chances are you'll end up in Kapiri Mposhi (Zambia), which is within easy reach of Lusaka, Livingstone and Victoria Falls.

If you're heading north, it's best if you have a Tanzanian visa in your passport before setting out.

FROM ANGOLA

The situation has improved in Angola since the end of the 27-year war in 2002. Some travellers are crossing to Angola from Namibia, and independent travel is possible although it's recommended only for the intrepid; you need to arrange your visa in advance before entering, and this can take a long time through Angolan embassies in Namibia, as well as ultimately being a frustrating experience. From Angola, the main border crossings into Namibia are at Ruacana, Oshikango and Rundu. Another thing to remember is that Angola can be extremely expensive – Luanda is one of the world's most expensive cities.

A few intrepid travellers are also crossing the border between Angola and Zambia, but this is a very remote crossing and you should research this in advance.

FROM DRC

From DRC, the most convenient crossing connects Chingola in Zambia's Copperbelt with Lubumbashi in Katanga Province, via Chililabombwe (Zambia) and Kasumbalesa (DRC). However, due to safety issues (and because DRC visas are only available to Zambian residents or those with a letter of invitation from the DRC government) few travellers use this option.

Car & Motorcycle

Driving into Southern Africa from Tanzania is relatively straightforward, one of few such sectors on the once-well-worn overland route from Europe to South Africa. The main points to emphasise include the following:

➡ It involves incredibly long distances; expect to take longer than planned thanks to the constant challenge of dealing with police and/or border officials.

➡ Drivers should be mechanically competent and carry a good collection of spares.

➡ You'll need vehicle registration papers, liability insurance, a driver's licence and International Driving Permit, as well as a *carnet de passage*, effectively a passport for the vehicle and temporary waiver of import duty, designed to prevent car-import rackets.

➡ Your home liability insurance won't be valid in many countries, and some require international drivers to purchase expensive (and effectively useless) insurance when crossing borders. In most cases, this is just a racket, and no matter what you spend on local insurance, you'll effectively be travelling uninsured.

OVERLANDING

Although overlanding across Africa from Europe or the Middle East has become quite difficult due to the various 'roadblocks' imposed by unrest, some overland tour operators still take up the challenge. Thanks to troubles across the Sahara and North Africa, most now take the easier option and begin in Kenya. If you're driving these routes, they can represent an epic trip.

The other possibility is as part of an overland tour. While these trips are popular, they're designed mainly for inexperienced travellers who feel uncomfortable striking out on their own or for those who prefer guaranteed social interaction to the uncertainties of the road. If you have the slightest inclination towards independence or would feel confined travelling with the same group of 25 or so people for most of the trip (although quite a few normally drop out along the way), think twice before booking an overland trip.

Sea

For most people, reaching Southern Africa by sea is not a viable option. The days of working your passage on commercial boats have vanished, although a few travellers do manage to hitch rides on private yachts along the east coast of Africa from Mombasa (Kenya) to Mozambique or South Africa.

Alternatively, several cargo-shipping companies sail between Europe and South Africa, with cabins for public passengers. The voyage

between London and Cape Town takes about 16 days.

Tours

If you feel inexperienced, are unsure of travelling by yourself or are just a sucker for constant company, then tours can be a very good option. However, many find the experience quite suffocating and restrictive.

Australia

African Wildlife Safaris (www. africanwildlifesafaris.com) Customised tours and safaris in South Africa and neighbouring countries.

Peregrine (www.peregrine-adventures.com) Guided and independent tours and safaris in South Africa, Swaziland and beyond, including family adventures.

Africa Safari Co (☑02 9541 4199; www.africasafarico.com. au) Uses small lodges and tented camps when planning Southern African itineraries. These include routes such as Cape Town to Vic Falls.

France

Makila Voyages (www.makila.fr) A reputable French outfit offering

tours that cover seven of the region's nine countries.

UK

Explore Worldwide Ltd (☑0845 291 4541; www.exploreworld-wide.com) Organises group tours throughout the region, focusing on adventure and wildlife safaris.

In the Saddle (☑01299-272 997; www.inthesaddle.com) Appeals specifically to horse aficionados, and includes a range of adventurous horse-riding routes.

Naturetrek (☑01962-733051; www.naturetrek.co.uk) This company's aim is to get you to where the animals are. It offers specialised wildlife-viewing itineraries.

Temple World (☑020-8940 4114; www.templeworld.co.uk) This sophisticated and recommended company organises middle- to upper-range tours to the best of the region.

Wildfoot Travel (www.wild foottravel.com) High-end wildlife-focused tours to some of the region's best lodges and wildlife areas.

USA

Africa Adventure Company (☑954-491 8877, 800 882

TOUR TIPS

A few things to remember when considering booking a tour:

➡ Hedge your bets and take a shorter tour – this gives you the option of either taking another tour or striking out on your own, with the benefit of having visited some of the places you may like to spend more time in.

➡ In Europe it's becoming increasingly popular to look for late bookings, which may be advertised in travel sections of weekend newspapers, or even at special late-bookings counters in some international airports.

➡ One of the best places to begin looking for reputable agencies is weekend newspapers or travel magazines, such as *Wanderlust* in the UK and *Outside* or *National Geographic Adventure* in the US.

➡ Speciality magazines for flower, birdwatching, wildlife-viewing, railway and other buffs may also include advertising for tours focusing on their own areas of interest.

9453; www.africa-adventure.
com) These top safari specialists
can organise any sort of Southern Africa itinerary.

Born Free Safaris & Tours
(www.safaris2africa.com) Itineraries covering areas from the
Cape to Swaziland and further
north in Southern Africa.

Bushtracks Expeditions (www.
bushtracks.com) Luxury safaris
and private air charters.

Exodus (☎800 228 8747, 510-
654 1879; www.exodustravels.
com) A travel specialist that
organises budget to midrange
tours and is the US agent for
several overland operators,
including Guerba, Dragoman and
Karibu.

International Expeditions
(☎800 234 9620; www.
ietravel.com) Specialises in
photographic and wildlife-
viewing safaris.

Mountain Travel Sobek (☎888-
831 7526; www.mtsobek.com)
Tours to the big safari destinations across the region.

Premier Tours & Travel (☎800
545 1910; www.premiertours.
com) Premier specialise in
detailed, customised itineraries
all over Southern Africa, including accommodating special
interests.

Wilderness Travel (www.wild
ernesstravel.com) Much-
applauded culture, wildlife and
hiking specialist.

GETTING AROUND

Southern Africa covers a vast
area, so getting around will
usually require you to do the
same. There's a reasonable
road and air network within
the area, but distances are
long, land-based public
transport is inconsistent and
border crossings can slow
things down considerably.

If you're not travelling as
part of an organised tour – an
option taken by many travellers to the region that takes
all the hassle out of arranging
your own transport, albeit
at the cost of much of your

independence – there are two
major options: budget travellers will need to make use
of patchy public transport,
while renting your own 4WD
is extremely popular.

Air

Distances are great in Africa
and, if time is short, regional
flights can considerably wid-
en your options. For example,
after touring South Africa
for a while you could fly
from Cape Town to Victoria
Falls and then tour Zimbabwe or southern Zambia.
Alternatively, fly to Lilongwe,
which is a good staging point
for trips around Malawi or
eastern Zambia, or to Maun,
which opens up northern
Botswana, northern Namibia
and southern Zambia.

Even within a country,
tight schedules can be
accommodated with short
hops by air. Both domestic
and regional flights are usually operated by both state
airlines and private carriers
and, except in Botswana
and Zambia, the competi-
tion generally keeps prices
down to reasonable levels.
Remember, however, to factor in some additional time
to ensure a cancelled flight
doesn't totally ruin your trip.

Sometimes the only prac-
tical way into remote national
parks, reserves and lodges is
by air, and charter flights provide easy access. Although
these are normally for travellers on less restricted budgets, access to the best of the
Okavango Delta and some of
the more remote corners of
Namibia is possible only by
charter flight.

Airlines in Southern Africa

The following list includes regional airlines with domestic
and intra–Southern African
routes.

Air Botswana (☎267-390
5500; www.airbotswana.co.bw)
Domestic Botswana flights and
connections to neighbouring
countries.

Air Namibia (☎264-61-299
6111; www.airnamibia.com)
Connects Windhoek with Johannesburg and other regional
cities.

Air Zimbabwe (☎263-4-
575021; www.airzimbabwe.com)
A handful of regional flights.

Airlink (☎27-11-978 1111; www.
flyairlink.com) Operated by
South African Airways, Airlink
has flights throughout the
region, connecting South Africa
with most other countries including Swaziland.

FastJet (☎010-500 2560;
www.fastjet.com) Low-cost
airline connecting the countries
of the region's east, South Africa
and East Africa.

Linhas Aereas de Moçambique
(☎258-1-426001; www.lam.
co.mz/en) Regional destinations
include Johannesburg and
Harare.

Malawian Airlines (☎265-1-
11734862; www.malawian-air
lines.com) Connects Malawi to
Johannesburg (South Africa),
Lusaka (Zambia) and Harare
(Zimbabwe) from Blantyre and
Lilongwe.

Proflight Zambia (☎260-211
845 944; www.proflight-zambia.
com) Regular flights around
Zambia and between Zambia and
Jo'burg.

SA Express (☎0861 729 227;
www.flyexpress.aero) South
African Airways operated with
good regional links.

Air Passes

The Star Alliance Africa
Airpass allows flexible travel
around sub-Saharan Africa,
including all the countries in
Southern Africa except Swaziland and Lesotho. It covers
more than 30 airports in 23
different countries, and you
can buy between three and
10 coupons (each coupon
representing a single trip, eg
Jo'burg to Windhoek). The
Airpass allows for substantial
savings, and flights are operated by Ethiopian Airlines,
South African Airways and
EgyptAir – see www.staralli
ance.com for more.

Bicycle

Cycling is a cheap, convenient, healthy, environmentally sound and, above all, fun way to travel. It can also be addictive. On a bicycle travellers will often be on an equal footing with locals and will have plenty of opportunities to meet and visit people in small towns and villages along the way. Be aware, however, that cyclists are usually regarded as second-class road users so always be on high alert for cars and trucks.

Aim to travel in cool, dry periods, and carry at least 4L of drinking water. Bikes can easily be carried on buses or trucks – although you'll need to pay an extra luggage fee, and be prepared for some rough handling.

A good source of information may be your national cycling organisation. In Britain, the Cyclists' Touring Club (www.ctc.org.uk) provides cycling advice. In the USA, the International Bicycle Fund (www.ibike.org) organises socially conscious tours and provides information.

You'll normally be able to hire a bike locally, especially in tourist areas. Otherwise, local people in villages and towns are often willing to rent their bikes for the day. Ask at your hotel or track down a bicycle repair shop (every town market has one).

Spare Parts

Outside South Africa, you'll have difficulty buying hi-tech European or American spares, so bring anything essential along with you, and know how to make your own repairs. Plan for frequent punctures, and take lots of spare inner tubes. Because automobile tyres are constantly being repaired, patches and glue are available almost everywhere. However, it may be worth carrying a spare tyre, in case of a really devastating blow-out.

Flying With a Bike

It's quite straightforward to take your bike onto a plane and use the bike to get around on the ground. For air travel, you can dismantle the bike and box it up. Bike boxes are available at airports and most bike shops. If you're willing to risk damage to your bike, it's also possible to deflate the tyres, remove the pedals and turn the handlebars sideways, then just wheel the bike up to the check-in desk (if your bike doesn't hold up to baggage handlers, it probably won't survive Africa!). Some airlines don't charge to carry a bike, and don't even include it in the weight allowance; others charge an extra handling fee of around US$50.

Boat

Options for getting around by boat are limited but there are some possibilities. Boat types and services in the region vary greatly from large ferries and cargo ships to traditional dhows plying the coastline of Mozambique and *mokoros* (dugout canoes) skimming along the Okavango Delta, although the latter is more a form of sightseeing rather than a means of getting from A to B.

Options include the following:

➡ In Malawi and Mozambique, the **Ilala** (✆01-587411; www.malawitourism. com/pages/content/index. asp?PageID=164) ferry chugs passengers and cargo up and down Lake Malawi but only stops at Malawian ports. Malawi–Mozambique connections are made by a newer boat called *MV Chambo*: it links ports on the Mozambican side of Lake Niassa with Malawi, running a twice-weekly northern route from Metangula via Cóbuè to Likoma Island (Malawi) and Nkata Bay (Malawi); and a once-weekly southern route linking Metangula with

Meponda (Mozambique) and Chipoka (Malawi). Full fare Metangula–Chipoka is US$31.

➡ Dhow safaris are possible in Mozambique at Vilankulo (p192) and Pemba (p219).

➡ There is a ferry crossing between Zambia and Botswana, departing from Kazungula, Botswana, which takes vehicles.

➡ Based in South Africa, LBH Africa (www.tallships. co.za) has cargo ships between Durban and various Mozambican ports that sometimes take passengers.

Bus

Long-distance buses operate regularly between most Southern African countries, with most routes covered by fairly basic, cheap and often slow services. From Cape Town and Jo'burg, larger and more comfortable buses run to many destinations in the region including Maseru (Lesotho), Mbabane (Swaziland), Maputo (Mozambique), Gaborone (Botswana) and Windhoek (Namibia).

For bus travellers, border crossings can be tedious while customs officials search through huge amounts of luggage. Minibus services may be more efficient, as fewer passengers will mean less time at the border.

There are also several international bus services especially designed for backpackers and other tourists. These companies normally have pickups/drop offs at main tourist centres and backpackers' hostels. Among these is the **Baz Bus** (www. bazbus.com), which links Cape Town, Jo'burg, Pretoria and Durban.

The following are major bus companies operating throughout the region. They are generally safe and reliable, and standard facilities usually include air-con, video,

AN ALTERNATIVE TO THE BUS – OVERLAND TRUCKS

Lots of companies run overland camping tours in trucks converted to carry passengers. Sometimes the trucks finish a tour, then run straight back to base to start the next one and drivers are often happy to carry 'transit' passengers on their way back. This is not a tour, as such, but can be a comfortable way of transiting between Vic Falls and Jo'burg, or Harare and Nairobi (Kenya), for around US$30 per day, plus food-kitty contributions. Those looking for rides should check around truck stops in well-known tourist areas, such as Cape Town, Jo'burg, Harare, Victoria Falls, Windhoek or Lilongwe or visit backpackers' hostels (where these companies invariably leave stacks of brochures).

sound system, reclining seats and on-board toilet:

Cheetah Express (☑84-244 2103, in South Africa 013-755 1988; cheetahexpressmaputo@ gmail.com; cnr Avenidas Eduardo Mondlane & Julius Nyerere) Maputo–Nelspruit.

Greyhound (☑083 915 9000; www.greyhound.co.za) Jo'burg, Cape Town, Harare, Bulawayo and Maputo.

Intercape Mainliner (☑0861 287 287, 021-380 4400; www. intercape.co.za) Extensive services with destinations including Jo'burg, Cape Town, Maputo, Windhoek, Victoria Falls and Gaborone.

Intercape Pathfinder (Map p624; ☑0778 888880; www. intercapepathfinder.com; Cresta Oasis Hotel, 124 Nelson Mandela Ave) Has a daily service linking Harare to Vic Falls, Bulawayo and even Hwange.

Luciano Luxury Coach (☑84 661 5713, in South Africa 083 993 4897, in South Africa 072-278 1921; Avenida Zedequías Manganhela) Maputo–Durban.

Mahube Express (Map p49; ☑396 0488, 74 236 441; www. mahubeexpress.com) Gaborone–Jo'burg.

Tok Tokkie Shuttle (☑061-300743; www.shuttlesnamibia. com) Windhoek–Gaborone twice weekly.

Translux (☑0861 589 282; www.translux.co.za) Jo'burg, Pretoria, Maputo, Blantyre, Lusaka.

Buying Tickets

In general it's always better to buy tickets in advance, over the phone, on the internet or by dropping into an office in person, although sometimes it may not be necessary. Sample fares include approximately US$30 for Jo'burg to Gaborone, and US$93 for Cape Town to Windhoek (both one way).

Car & Motorcycle

Fuel & Spare Parts

Fuel and spare parts are available across the region, although both have recently been scarce in Zimbabwe. Finding spare parts for newer-model vehicles can be difficult outside the major cities.

Fuel prices vary across the region, but they're roughly comparable to prices in Western countries – for example, in Malawi it's US$1.10 per litre, or US$0.70 per litre in Botswana. Diesel is slightly cheaper than normal petrol.

If you're driving in remote areas, such as Zambia, careful planning is required to ensure you have enough fuel until you reach the next petrol station.

Hire

To rent a car in Southern Africa you must be aged at least 21 (some companies require drivers to be over 25) and have been a licenced driver in your home country for at least two years (sometimes five).

Car rental isn't cheap, but can be a very convenient way to travel, especially if you're short on time or want to visit national parks and other out-of-the-way places. Costs can be mitigated by mustering a group to share the rental and petrol, and will open up all sorts of opportunities.

➡ Check whether you're able to cross borders with a rental vehicle. This is usually allowed by South African companies into Namibia, Botswana, Lesotho, Swaziland, Zambia and Zimbabwe (but not Mozambique). In such cases, they sometimes charge an additional cross-border fee (usually around US$100).

➡ Go for an unlimited-mileage deal. Also, check on the fees for other items such as tax, excess and insurance.

2WD

Generally, South Africa is the cheapest place to hire a car (starting from US$30 per day), although Namibia and Botswana are also pretty good (from US$50 to US$60 per day) and Malawi (US$65) isn't too bad. Zimbabwe is ridiculously expensive and in Zambia and Mozambique you're looking at a minimum of US$80 to US$100 per day to take a 2WD out of the city.

Most companies include insurance and unlimited kilometres in their standard rates, but some require a minimum rental period before they allow unlimited kilometres. Most companies also require a deposit and/or a credit-card imprint.

Additional charges will be levied for dropping off or picking up the car at your hotel (rather than the car-rental office), for dropping off the car at a different office from where you picked it up, and for each additional driver. A 'cleaning fee' (which can amount to US$50!) may be incurred – at the discretion of the rental company – and a 'service fee' may be added.

Most major international car-rental companies have local franchises.

4WD

Prices for 4WD rental range from US$80 to US$250 per day and usually come with unlimited mileage.

TYPES OF 4WD

There are numerous variations on the theme, but the most common vehicle models are two- or four-berth Toyota (Hilux, Land Cruiser or Fortuner), Land Rover (Defender or Discovery, although the former is slowly disappearing) and Ford Ranger, all adapted for camping. This may mean a pop-up roof that has space to sleep two people, rooftop tents and/or ground tents, as well as all camping gear (ie bedding, although some, including Avis, offer blankets instead of sleeping bags), cooking and eating equipment, fridge/freezer and all the mechanical tools necessary to get you out of a tight spot. To be sure of what you're getting, make sure you ask for a full equipment list at the time of your booking.

RENTAL COMPANIES

If you're looking to rent a car for exploring Southern Africa, we recommend booking through companies that offer specialist rental of fully equipped 4WDs with all camping equipment. Most can also arrange for pickups/drop offs in Windhoek as well as Maun, Kasane, Gaborone, Victoria Falls, Harare or Livingstone, but remember that you'll usually pay a fee if you decide to pick up your vehicle in a place away from the company's main office, or

if you drop off your vehicle in a place that's different from where you picked it up – fees range between US$250 and US$500 for either service.

Most 4WD rental agencies have their head offices in South Africa, but have offices across the region. Among the better companies are the following:

Africamper (www.africamper.com)

Avis Safari Rentals (www.avisvanrental.co.za/avis-safari-rental.aspx)

Britz (☑in Jo'burg 27 11 230 5200, in Namibia 264-61-219590; www.britz.co.za)

Bushlore (www.bushlore.com)

If you hire directly through the rental company, you'll get just the vehicle and you'll need to make all of the other travel arrangements on your own. For most travellers, it works out more convenient to book through an operator that can also make campsite and other accommodation bookings, arrange a satellite phone and make any other necessary arrangements. For this, try the following:

Drive Botswana (☑in Palapye 492 3416; www.drivebotswana.com) This excellent operator arranges 4WDs and also organises a complete package itinerary, including maps, trip notes and bookings for campsites. Although Botswana is where it all began, Drive Botswana arranges trips and makes bookings for Mozambique, Namibia, South Africa, Zambia and Zimbabwe.

Safari Drive (www.safaridrive.com) Expensive but professional and upmarket company with its own fleet of recent-model

vehicles. Prices include all equipment, emergency back-up, detailed route preparation and bookings, satellite phone and free tank of fuel.

Self Drive Adventures (☑686 3755; www.selfdriveadventures.com) 4WD rentals and all bookings made on your behalf. Although you do the driving, you'll be accompanied by a support vehicle and a local guide.

Insurance

When hiring a car always check the insurance provisions and any excess that you may be liable to pay in the event of an accident. It's also worth checking if the insurance covers driving into other Southern African countries (depending on where you intend going) and driving on dirt roads for 2WDs.

Some countries, Zambia among them, require you to purchase 3rd-party insurance at the border, regardless of whether you already have it.

Purchase

For visitors, South Africa is the best place to buy a car (other countries place restrictions on foreign ownership, have stiff tax laws, or simply don't have the choice of vehicles). Also, South African–registered vehicles don't need a *carnet de passage* to visit any of the countries in the region. Travelling through Botswana, Lesotho, Namibia and Swaziland is easy, while for Malawi, Mozambique, Zimbabwe and Zambia you'll easily get temporary import permits at the border.

It's usually cheaper to buy privately, but for tourists it is

TRANSPORT CAR & MOTORCYCLE

VEHICLE CHECKS

Whatever kind of vehicle you decide to rent, you should always check the paperwork carefully, and thoroughly examine the vehicle before accepting it. You should also carefully check the condition of your car and never ever compromise if you don't feel totally happy with its state of repair.

often more convenient to go to a dealer. The weekly Cape Ads (www.junkmail.co.za/cape-town) is the best place to look for a private sale. Also try Auto Trader (www.auto-trader.co.za), which advertises thousands of cars around the country.

Although prices tend to be cheaper in Jo'burg, most people do their buying in Cape Town – a much nicer place to spend the week or two that it will likely take for the process. Cape Town's main congregation of used-car dealers is on Voortrekker Rd between Maitland and Belleville metro train stations.

Some dealers might agree to a buy-back arrangement – if you don't trash the car, you can reasonably expect to get a decent percentage of your purchase price back after a three-month trip, but you need to check all aspects of the contract to be sure this deal will stick.

A recommended contact in Cape Town is **Graham Duncan Smith** (📞021 797 3048), who's a Land Rover expert offering consultation,

repairs and sales. He charges a consultation fee.

No matter who you buy from, make sure that the car details correspond accurately with the ownership (registration) papers, that there is a current licence disc on the windscreen and that the vehicle has been checked by the police clearance department. Check the owner's name against their identity document, and check the car's engine and chassis numbers. Consider getting the car tested by a garage.

Cheap cars will often be sold without a roadworthy certificate – required when you register the change-of-ownership form (RLV) and pay tax for a licence disc. Some private garages are now allowed to issue them (a few hundred rand), and some will overlook minor faults.

Registering your car is a bureaucratic headache and will likely take a couple of weeks. The forms you need should be available at vehicle-registration offices, dealers. They include the following:

➡ RLV/NCO5 (notification of change of ownership/sale of motor vehicle)

➡ ANR8 (application and notice in respect of traffic register number).

Next, present yourself at a vehicle-registration office along with the following:

➡ Your passport and a photocopy.

➡ A copy of the seller's ID.

➡ The registration certificate (in the seller's name).

➡ Proof of purchase.

➡ Proof of address (a letter from your accommodation should suffice).

➡ A valid licence.

➡ Your money.

It will help if the seller comes with you and brings their ID. Charges at the time of writing are currently about R500/1000 for a small car/4WD.

Insurance against theft or damage is highly recommended, though not legally required for private-vehicle owners. It can be difficult to arrange by the month. The Automobile Association of South Africa (www.aasa.co.za) is a good contact, and may be willing to negotiate payment for a year's worth of insurance with a pro-rata refund when you sell the car. Insurance agencies include Sansure (www.sansure.com) in Cape Town.

Road Conditions

The good news is that most main roads in Southern Africa are in fair to excellent condition, and are passable for even small compact cars. On lesser roads, standards vary considerably, from relatively smooth highways to dirt tracks.

Other things to remember:

➡ In Malawi, Zambia, Mozambique and elsewhere, you may be slowed down considerably by sealed roads that haven't seen any maintenance for many years and are plagued with bone-

---

DRIVING IN REMOTE AREAS

Careful preparations for any remote trips in Southern Africa are required. You will need a robust 4WD vehicle, and enough supplies to see you through the journey – this includes food and water for the entire trip. You should also consider the following:

➡ Travel in a convoy of at least two vehicles and/or carry with you a satellite phone for use in an emergency.

➡ Carry several spare tyres for each vehicle, a tyre iron, a good puncture-repair kit and a range of vehicle spares, as well as twice as much petrol as the distances would suggest.

➡ For navigation, use a compass, or preferably a global positioning system (GPS). Relevant topographic sheets are also extremely helpful.

➡ Be careful where you camp; always ask permission on private land, and think twice about pitching a tent in shady and inviting riverbeds: large animals often use them as thoroughfares, and they can also be subject to flash floods.

crunching and tyre-bursting potholes.

➤ In Namibia, take special care on the huge network of well-maintained gravel roads that supplement the paved-road network.

Road Hazards

Whatever vehicle you drive, prepare to deal with some of the world's worst, fastest and most arrogant and aggressive drivers. Also be aware of the following:

➤ Tree branches on the road are the local version of warning triangles.

➤ If you come up behind someone on a bicycle, hoot the horn as a warning and offer a friendly wave as you pass.

➤ On rural highways, always be on the lookout for children playing, people selling goods, seeds drying or animals wandering around on the loose. This is particularly the case near roadside settlements.

➤ Livestock is always a concern, and hitting even a small animal can cause vehicle damage, while hitting something large – like a cow or a kudu – can be fatal (for both the driver and the animal).

➤ If you see kids with red flags on the road, it means they're leading a herd of cows.

➤ Potential hazards become much harder to deal with in the dark and many vehicles have faulty lights – or none at all – so avoid driving at night.

➤ In some areas (in northern Botswana, for example), wandering wildlife can also appear unannounced. An elephant encountered in such a manner could wreak havoc with your vehicle.

Road Rules

Traffic officially drives on the left – but that may not always be obvious, so be especially prepared on blind corners and hills.

Hitching

As in any other part of the world, hitching is never entirely safe, and we don't recommend it. Travellers who hitch should understand that they are taking a small but potentially serious risk.

Even so, hitching is a way of life in Southern Africa, and visitors may well have the opportunity to join the throng of locals looking for lifts. While this is a good way to get around places without public transport (or even with public transport), there is a protocol involved. As a visitor, you're likely to take precedence over locals (especially with white drivers), but if other people are hitching, it's still polite to stand further along the road so they'll have the first crack (that is, unless there's a designated hitching spot where everyone waits).

Another option is to wait around petrol stations and try to arrange lifts from drivers who may be going your way. If you do get a lift, be sure to determine what sort of payment is expected before you climb aboard. In most cases, plan on paying just a bit less than the equivalent bus fare.

Local Transport

Within individual countries, public bus services are usually pretty basic.

➤ As well as typically spluttering big buses, many countries also have minibuses.

➤ Minibuses are faster, run more frequently and are usually even more dangerous due to their speed.

➤ Minibuses or combis in Zimbabwe are not recommended to travellers – they break down and constantly have lethal accidents.

➤ In Southern Africa, there's a lack of long-distance shared service taxis (such as the seven-seat Peugeots that are so popular in other parts of Africa).

➤ In rural areas, the frequency of bus services drops dramatically.

➤ Public transport may be limited to the back of a pick-up truck (ute) in rural regions. Everyone pays a fare to the driver, which is normally comparable to the bus fare for a similar distance.

Train

Travelling by train within the various countries is a decent option – and it's almost always fun – but can be a slow way to go. South Africa has the largest and most efficient rail network, with passenger train services also possible in Namibia, Malawi, Mozambique, Zambia and Zimbabwe.

Cross-border services are few and are rarely convenient. For example, for train services between Mozambique and South Africa, the only current route is Maputo–Komatipoort, where you need to disembark at the border and change trains. Trains on the Mozambique side, however, are very bad and slow. It's much better to travel via train on the South Africa side, and then bus or *chapa* (minivan) for the Mozambique stretch (Ressano Garcia to Maputo).

Namibia also has two luxury 'tourist trains' which are effectively chartered for sightseeing on fixed routes that span Namibia and South Africa:

Desert Express (☎061-2982600; www.transnamib.com.na/services/passenger-service)

Shongololo Dune Express (☎in South Africa 27 86 177 7014; www.shongololo.com)

Health

As long as you stay up to date with your vaccinations and take basic preventive measures, you're unlikely to succumb to most health hazards while in Southern Africa. While countries in the region have an impressive selection of tropical diseases on offer, it's more likely you'll get a bout of diarrhoea or a cold than a more exotic malady. The main exception to this is malaria, which is a widespread risk in Southern Africa, and precautions should be taken.

Before You Go

Predeparture Planning

A little predeparture planning will save you trouble later. Get a check-up from your dentist and your doctor if you take any regular medication or have a chronic illness, eg high blood pressure or asthma. You should also organise spare contact lenses and glasses (and take your prescription with you); get a first-aid and medical kit together; and arrange necessary vaccinations.

Travellers can register with the International Association for Medical Assistance to Travellers (www.iamat.org), which provides directories of certified doctors. If you'll be spending much time in remote areas, consider doing a first-aid course (contact

the Red Cross or St John's Ambulance), or attending a remote medicine first-aid course, such as that offered by Wilderness Medical Training (http://wildernessmedi caltraining.co.uk).

If you are bringing medications with you, carry them in their original containers, clearly labelled. A signed and dated letter from your physician describing all medical conditions and medications, including generic names, is also a good idea. If carrying syringes or needles, be sure to have a physician's letter documenting their medical necessity.

Insurance

Find out in advance whether your insurance plan will make payments directly to providers, or will reimburse you later for overseas health expenditures. In most countries in Southern Africa, doctors expect payment upfront in cash. It's vital to ensure that your travel insurance will cover any emergency transport required to get you to a hospital in a major city, or all the way home, by air and with a medical attendant if necessary. Not all insurance covers this, so check the contract carefully. If you need medical assistance, your insurance company might be able to help locate the nearest hospital or clinic, or you can ask at your hotel. In an emergency, contact your embassy or consulate.

Recommended Vaccinations

The World Health Organization (WHO) recommends that all travellers be covered for diphtheria, tetanus, measles, mumps, rubella and polio, as well as for hepatitis B, regardless of their destination. The consequences of these diseases can be severe, and outbreaks do occur.

According to the US Centers for Disease Control & Prevention (www.cdc.gov), the following vaccinations may be recommended for travel in Southern African countries: hepatitis A, hepatitis B, rabies and typhoid, and boosters for tetanus, diphtheria and measles. Yellow fever is not usually a risk in the region, but the certificate is an entry requirement if you're travelling from an infected region. Consult your medical practitioner for the most up-to-date information.

Medical Checklist

It's a very good idea to carry a medical and first-aid kit with you, to help yourself in the case of minor illness or injury. Following is a list of items to consider packing.

➡ antibiotics (prescription only), eg ciprofloxacin (Ciproxin) or norfloxacin (Utinor)

➡ antidiarrhoeal drugs (eg loperamide)

➡ acetaminophen (paracetamol) or aspirin

- anti-inflammatory drugs (eg ibuprofen)
- antihistamines (for hay fever and allergic reactions)
- antibacterial ointment (eg Bactroban) for cuts and abrasions (prescription only)
- antimalaria pills, if you'll be in malarial areas
- bandages, gauze
- scissors, safety pins, tweezers, pocket knife
- DEET-containing insect repellent for the skin
- permethrin-containing insect spray for clothing, tents, and bed nets
- sun block
- oral rehydration salts
- iodine tablets (for water purification)
- sterile needles, syringes and fluids if travelling to remote areas

Websites

There is a wealth of travel-health advice on the internet. The Lonely Planet website at www.lonelyplanet.com is a good place to start. The World Health Organization publishes the helpful *International Travel and Health*, available free at www. who.int/ith/. Other useful websites include MD Travel Health (www.mdtravelhealth. com) and Fit for Travel (www. fitfortravel.scot.nhs.uk). Official government travel health websites:

Australia www.smartraveller.gov. au/guide/all-travellers/health/ Pages/default.aspx

Canada www.hc-sc.gc.ca/ index_e.html

UK www.gov.uk/foreign-travel -advice

USA wwwnc.cdc.gov/travel

Further Reading

- *A Comprehensive Guide to Wilderness and Travel Medicine* (1998) Eric A Weiss
- *The Essential Guide to Travel Health* (2009) Jane Wilson-Howarth
- *Healthy Travel Africa* (2000) Isabelle Young
- *How to Stay Healthy Abroad* (2002) Richard Dawood
- *Travel in Health* (1994) Graham Fry
- *Travel with Children* (2015) Sophie Caupeil et al

In Transit

Deep Vein Thrombosis

Prolonged immobility during flights can cause deep vein thrombosis (DVT) – the formation of blood clots in the legs. The longer the flight, the greater the risk. Though most blood clots are re-absorbed uneventfully, some might break off and travel through the blood vessels to the lungs, where they could cause life-threatening complications. The chief symptom is swelling or pain of the foot, ankle or calf, usually but not always on just one side. When a blood clot travels to the lungs, it may cause chest pain and breathing difficulty. Travellers with any of these symptoms should immediately seek medical attention. To prevent DVT, walk about the cabin, perform isometric compressions of the leg muscles (ie contract the leg muscles while sitting), drink plenty of fluids and avoid alcohol.

Jet Lag

If you're crossing more than five time zones you could suffer jet lag, resulting in insomnia, fatigue, malaise or nausea. To avoid jet lag try drinking plenty of fluids (nonalcoholic) and eating light meals. Upon arrival, get exposure to natural sunlight and readjust your schedule (for meals, sleep etc) as soon as possible.

In Southern Africa

Availability & Cost of Health Care

Good-quality health care is available in the urban areas of many countries in Southern Africa, and private hospitals are generally of a good standard. Public hospitals by contrast are often under-funded and overcrowded; in off-the-beaten-track areas, reliable medical facilities are rare.

Drugs for chronic diseases should be brought from home. In many countries there is a high risk of contracting HIV from infected blood transfusions. The BloodCare Foundation (www. bloodcare.org.uk) is a useful source of safe, screened blood, which can be transported to any part of the world within 24 hours.

Infectious Diseases

With a few basic preventive measures, it's unlikely that you'll succumb to any of the diseases that are found in Southern Africa.

CHOLERA

Cholera is caused by a bacteria, and spread via contaminated drinking water. In South Africa the risk to travellers is very low; you're likely to encounter it only in eastern rural areas, where you should avoid tap water and unpeeled or uncooked fruits and vegetables. The main symptom is profuse watery diarrhoea, which causes debilitation if fluids are not replaced quickly. An oral cholera vaccine is available in the USA, but it is not particularly effective. Most cases of cholera can be avoided by close attention to drinking water and by avoiding potentially contaminated food. Treatment is by fluid replacement (orally or via a drip), but sometimes antibiotics are needed. Self-treatment is not advised.

DENGUE FEVER (BREAK-BONE FEVER)

Dengue fever, spread through the bite of mosquitos, causes a feverish illness with headache and muscle pains similar to those experienced with a bad, prolonged attack of influenza. There might be a rash. Mosquito bites should be avoided whenever possible. Self-treatment: paracetamol and rest. In rare cases in Africa this becomes Severe Dengue Fever, with worsening symptoms including vomiting, rapid breathing and abdominal pain. Seek medical help as this can be fatal.

FILARIASIS

Filariasis is caused by tiny worms migrating in the lymphatic system, and is spread by the bite from an infected mosquito. Symptoms include localised itching and swelling of the legs and/or genitalia. Treatment is available. Self-treatment: none.

HEPATITIS A

Hepatitis A is spread through contaminated food (particularly shellfish) and water. It causes jaundice and, although it is rarely fatal, it can cause prolonged lethargy and delayed recovery. If you've had hepatitis A, you shouldn't drink alcohol for up to six months afterwards, but once you've recovered, there won't be any long-term problems. The first symptoms include dark urine and a yellow colour to the whites of the eyes. Sometimes a fever and abdominal pain might be present. Hepatitis A vaccine (Avaxim, VAQTA, Havrix) is given as an injection: a single dose will give protection for up to a year, and a booster after a year gives 10-year protection. Hepatitis A and typhoid vaccines can also be given as a single-dose vaccine, hepatyrix or viatim. Self-treatment: none.

HEPATITIS B

Hepatitis B is spread through infected blood, contaminated needles and sexual intercourse. It can also be spread from an infected mother to the baby during childbirth. It affects the liver, causing jaundice and occasionally liver failure. Most people recover completely, but some people might be chronic carriers of the virus, which could lead eventually to cirrhosis or liver cancer. Those visiting high-risk areas for long periods or those with increased social or occupational risk should be immunised. Many countries now routinely give hepatitis B as part of the childhood vaccination program. It is given singly or can be given at the same time as hepatitis A (hepatyrix).

A course will give protection for at least five years. It can be given over four weeks or six months. Self-treatment: none.

HIV/AIDS

HIV, the virus that causes AIDS, is an enormous problem across Southern Africa, with a devastating impact on local health systems and community structures. The virus is spread through infected blood and blood products, by sexual intercourse with an infected partner, and from an infected mother to her baby during childbirth and breastfeeding. It can be spread through 'blood to blood' contacts, such as with contaminated instruments during medical, dental, acupuncture and other body-piercing procedures, and through sharing used intravenous needles. At present there is no cure; medication that might keep the disease under control is available, but these drugs are too expensive, or unavailable, for the overwhelming majority of those living in Southern Africa.

If you think you might have been infected with HIV, a blood test is necessary; a three-month gap after exposure and before testing is required to allow antibodies to appear in the blood. Self-treatment: none.

MALARIA

Malaria is a widespread risk in Southern Africa and the risk of catching it should be taken seriously. The disease is caused by a parasite in the bloodstream spread via the bite of the female anopheles mosquito. There are several types of malaria; falciparum malaria is the most dangerous type and the predominant form in South Africa. Infection rates vary with season and climate, so check out the situation before departure. Several different drugs are used to prevent malaria, and new ones are in the pipeline. Up-to-date advice from a travel health clinic is essential as some medication is more suitable for some travellers than others (eg people with epilepsy should avoid mefloquine, and doxycycline should not be taken by pregnant women or children aged under 12).

The early stages of malaria include headaches, fevers, generalised aches and pains, and malaise, which could be mistaken for flu. Other symptoms can include abdominal pain, diarrhoea and a cough. Anyone who develops a fever in a malarial area should assume malarial infection until a blood test proves negative, even if you have been taking antimalarial medication. If not treated, the next stage could develop within 24 hours, particularly if falciparum malaria is the parasite: jaundice, then reduced consciousness and coma (also known as cerebral malaria) followed by death. Treatment in hospital is essential, and the death rate might still be as high as 10% even in the best intensive-care facilities.

Many travellers think that malaria is a mild illness, and that taking antimalarial drugs causes more illness through side effects than actually getting malaria. This is unfortunately not true. If you decide against antimalarial drugs, you must understand the risks, and be obsessive about avoiding mosquito bites. Use nets and insect repellent, and report any fever or flulike symptoms to a doctor as soon as possible. Some people advocate homeopathic preparations against malaria, such as Demal200, but as yet there is no conclusive evidence that this is effective, and many homeopaths do not recommend their use.

Malaria in pregnancy frequently results in miscarriage or premature labour, and the risks to both mother and foetus during pregnancy are considerable. Travel throughout the region when pregnant should be carefully considered. Adults who have survived childhood malaria have developed immunity and usually only develop mild cases of malaria; most Western travellers have no immunity at all. Immunity wanes after 18 months of nonexposure, so even if you have had malaria in the past and used to live in a malaria-prone area, you might no longer be immune.

Antimalarial A to D

➡ A – Awareness of the risk. No medication is totally effective, but protection of up to 95% is achievable with most drugs, as long as other measures have been taken.

➡ B – Bites, to be avoided at all costs. Sleep in a screened room, use a mosquito spray or coils, sleep under a permethrin-impregnated net at night. Cover up at night with long trousers and long sleeves, preferably with permethrin-treated clothing. Apply appropriate repellent to all areas of exposed skin in the evenings.

➡ C – Chemical prevention (ie antimalarial drugs) is usually needed in malarial areas. Expert advice is needed as resistance patterns can change, and new drugs are in development. Not all antimalarial drugs are suitable for everyone. Most antimalarial drugs need to be started at least a week before and continued for four weeks after the last possible exposure to malaria.

➡ D – Diagnosis. If you have a fever or flulike illness within

a year of travel to a malarial area, malaria is a possibility, and immediate medical attention is necessary.

RABIES

Rabies is spread by receiving bites or licks from an infected animal on broken skin. Few human cases are reported in Southern Africa, with the risks highest in rural areas. It is always fatal once the clinical symptoms start (which might be up to several months after an infected bite), so postbite vaccination should be given as soon as possible. Postbite vaccination (whether or not you've been vaccinated before the bite) prevents the virus from spreading to the central nervous system. Animal handlers should be vaccinated, as should those travelling to remote areas where a reliable source of postbite vaccine is not available within 24 hours. Three preventive injections are needed over a month. If you have not been vaccinated you'll need a course of five injections starting 24 hours or as soon as possible after the injury. If you have been vaccinated, you'll need fewer postbite injections, and have more time to seek medical help. Self-treatment: none.

SCHISTOSOMIASIS (BILHARZIA)

This disease is a risk when swimming in freshwater lakes and slow-running rivers – always seek local advice before venturing in. It's spread by flukes (minute worms) that are carried by a species of freshwater snail, which then sheds them into slow-moving or still water. The parasites penetrate human skin during swimming and then migrate to the bladder or bowel. They are excreted via stool or urine and could contaminate fresh water, where the cycle starts again. Swimming in suspect freshwater lakes or slow-running rivers should be avoided. Symptoms range from none to transient fever and rash, and advanced cas-

es might have blood in the stool or in the urine. A blood test can detect antibodies if you might have been exposed, and treatment is readily available. If not treated, the infection can cause kidney failure or permanent bowel damage. It's not possible for you to infect others. Self-treatment: none.

TUBERCULOSIS

Tuberculosis (TB) is spread through close respiratory contact and occasionally through infected milk or milk products. BCG vaccination is recommended if you'll be mixing closely with the local population, especially on long-term stays, although it gives only moderate protection against the disease. TB can be asymptomatic, being picked up only on a routine chest X-ray. Alternatively, it can cause a cough, weight loss or fever, sometimes occurring months or even years after exposure. Self-treatment: none.

TYPHOID

This is spread through food or water contaminated by infected human faeces. The first symptom is usually a fever or a pink rash on the abdomen. Sometimes septicaemia (blood poisoning) can occur. A typhoid vaccine (typhim Vi, typherix) will give protection for three years. In some countries, the oral vaccine Vivotif is also available. Antibiotics are usually given as treatment, and death is rare unless septicaemia occurs. Self-treatment: none.

YELLOW FEVER

Although not a problem within Southern Africa, you'll need to carry a certificate of vaccination if you'll be arriving from an infected country. For a list of countries with a high rate of infection, see the websites of the World Health Organization (www.who.int/en/) or the Centers for Disease Control & Prevention (wwwnc.cdc.gov/travel).

TAP WATER

In most areas of Southern Africa you should stick to bottled water rather than drinking water from the tap, and purify stream water before drinking it.

Traveller's Diarrhoea

This is a common travel-related illness, sometimes simply due to dietary changes. It's possible that you'll succumb, especially if you're spending a lot of time in rural areas or eating at inexpensive local food stalls. To avoid diarrhoea, eat only fresh fruits or vegetables that have been cooked or peeled, and be wary of dairy products that might contain unpasteurised milk. Although freshly cooked food can often be a safe option, plates or serving utensils might be dirty, so be selective when eating food from street vendors (make sure that cooked food is piping hot all the way through). If you develop diarrhoea, be sure to drink plenty of fluids, preferably an oral rehydration solution containing lots of water and some salt and sugar. A few loose stools don't require treatment but, if you start having more than four or five stools a day, you should start taking an antibiotic (usually a quinoline drug, such as ciprofloxacin or norfloxacin) and an antidiarrhoeal agent (such as loperamide) if you're not within easy reach of a toilet. If diarrhoea is bloody, persists for more than 72 hours or is accompanied by fever, shaking chills or severe abdominal pain, you should seek medical attention.

AMOEBIC DYSENTERY

Contracted by eating contaminated food and water, amoebic dysentery causes blood and mucus in the faeces. It can be relatively mild and tends to come on gradually, but seek medical advice if you think you have the illness as it won't clear up without treatment (which is with specific antibiotics).

GIARDIASIS

This, like amoebic dysentery, is also caused by ingesting contaminated food or water. The illness usually appears a week or more after you have been exposed to the offending parasite. Giardiasis might cause only a short-lived bout of typical travellers' diarrhoea, but it can also cause persistent diarrhoea. Ideally, seek medical advice if you suspect you have giardiasis, but if you are in a remote area you could start a course of antibiotics.

Environmental Hazards

HEAT EXHAUSTION

This condition occurs following heavy sweating and excessive fluid loss with inadequate replacement of fluids and salt, and is primarily a risk in hot climates when taking unaccustomed exercise before full acclimatisation. Symptoms include headache, dizziness and tiredness. Dehydration is already happening by the time you feel thirsty – aim to drink sufficient water to produce pale, diluted urine. Self-treatment: fluid replacement with water and/or fruit juice, and cooling by cold water and fans. The treatment of the salt-loss component consists of consuming salty fluids as in soup, and adding a little more table salt to foods than usual.

HEATSTROKE

Heat exhaustion is a precursor to the much more serious condition of heatstroke. In this case there is damage to the sweating mechanism, with an excessive rise in body temperature, irrational and hyperactive behaviour, and eventually loss of consciousness and death. Rapid cooling by spraying the body with water and fanning is ideal. Emergency fluid and electrolyte replacement is usually also required by intravenous drip.

INSECT BITES & STINGS

Mosquitoes might not always carry malaria or dengue fever, but they (and other insects) can cause irritation and infected bites. To avoid these, take the same precautions as you would for avoiding malaria. Bee and wasp stings cause real problems only to those who have a severe allergy to the stings (anaphylaxis), in which case, carry an adrenaline (epinephrine) injection.

Scorpions are found in arid areas. They can cause a painful bite that is sometimes life-threatening. If bitten by a scorpion, take a painkiller. Medical treatment should be sought if collapse occurs.

Ticks are always a risk away from urban areas. If you get bitten, press down around the tick's head with tweezers, grab the head and gently pull upwards. Avoid pulling the rear of the body as this may squeeze the tick's gut contents through the attached mouth parts into the skin, increasing the risk of infection and disease. Smearing chemicals on the tick will not make it let go and is not recommended.

SNAKEBITES

Basically, avoid getting bitten! Don't walk barefoot, or stick your hand into holes or cracks. However, 50% of those bitten by venomous snakes are not actually injected with poison (envenomed). If bitten by a snake, do not panic. Immobilise the bitten limb with a splint (such as a stick) and apply a bandage over the site with firm pressure, similar to bandaging a sprain. Do not apply a tourniquet, or cut or suck the bite. Get medical help as soon as possible.

Language

English is an official language in every Southern African country except Mozambique (where it's Portuguese). Afrikaans is widely used in the region and is the first language of millions of people of diverse ethnic backgrounds. It's also used as a lingua franca in both South Africa and Namibia.

As a first language, most Southern Africans speak either a Bantu or a Khoisan language. Due to common roots, a number of Bantu varieties in the region, including Zulu and Ndebele, as well as Sotho and Tswana, are mutually intelligible. Many native Khoisan speakers also speak at least one Bantu and one other language, usually Afrikaans.

In Mozambique and parts of northern Namibia along the Angola border, Portuguese is the European language of choice. In parts of Namibia, German is also widely spoken, but is the first language of only about 2% of Namibians.

AFRIKAANS

Afrikaans developed from the dialect spoken by the Dutch settlers in South Africa from the 17th century. Until the late 19th century it was considered a Dutch dialect (known as 'Cape Dutch'), and in 1925 it became one of the official languages of South Africa. Today, it has about six million speakers.

If you read our coloured pronunciation guides as if they were English, you should be understood. Note that aw is pronounced as in 'law', eu as the 'u' in 'nurse', ew as the 'ee' in 'see' with rounded lips, oh as the 'o' in 'cold', uh as the 'a' in 'ago', kh as the 'ch' in the Scottish loch, zh as the 's' in 'pleasure', and r is trilled. The stressed syllables are in italics.

WANT MORE?

For in-depth language information and handy phrases, check out Lonely Planet's *Africa Phrasebook*. You'll find it at **shop.lonelyplanet.com**, or you can buy Lonely Planet's iPhone phrasebooks at the Apple App Store.

Basics

Hello.	*Hallo.*	ha·*loh*
Goodbye.	*Totsiens.*	tot·*seens*
Yes.	*Ja.*	yaa
No.	*Nee.*	ney
Please.	*Asseblief.*	a·si·*bleef*
Thank you.	*Dankie.*	*dang*·kee
Sorry.	*Jammer.*	ya·min

How are you?
Hoe gaan dit? — hu khaan dit

Fine, and you?
Goed dankie, en jy? — khut *dang*·kee en yay

What's your name?
Wat's jou naam? — vats yoh naam

My name is ...
My naam is ... — may naam is ...

Do you speak English?
Praat jy Engels? — praat yay *eng*·ils

I don't understand.
Ek verstaan nie. — ek vir·*staan* nee

Eating & Drinking

Can you recommend a ...?	*Kan jy 'n ... aanbeveel?*	kan yay i ... aan·bi·*feyl*
bar	*kroeg*	krukh
dish	*gereg*	khi·*rekh*
place to eat	*eetplek*	*eyt*·plek
I'd like ..., please.	*Ek wil asseblief ... hê.*	ek vil a·si·*bleef* ... he
a table for two	*'n tafel vir twee*	i *taa*·fil fir twey

that dish	daardie gereg	daar·dee khi·rekh
the bill	die rekening	dee rey·ki·ning
the menu	die spyskaart	dee spays·kaart

Emergencies

Help!	Help!	help
Call a doctor!	Kry 'n dokter!	kray i dok·tir
Call the police!	Kry die polisie!	kray dee pu·lee·see

I'm lost.
Ek is verdwaal.   ek is fir·dwaal

Where are the toilets?
Waar is die toilette?   vaar is dee toy·le·ti

I need a doctor.
Ek het 'n dokter nodig.   ek het i dok·tir noo·dikh

Shopping & Services

I'm looking for ...
Ek soek na ...   ek suk naa ...

How much is it?
Hoeveel kos dit?   hu·fil kos dit

What's your lowest price?
Wat is jou laagste prys?   vat is yoh laakh·sti prays

I want to buy a phonecard.
Ek wil asseblief   ek vil a·si·bleef
'n foonkaart koop.   i foon·kaart koop

I'd like to change money.
Ek wil asseblief geld ruil.   ek vil a·si·bleef khelt rayl

I want to use the internet.
Ek wil asseblief die   ek vil a·si·bleef dee
Internet gebruik.   in·tir·net khi·brayk

Transport & Directions

A ... ticket, please.	Een ... kaartjie, asseblief.	eyn ... kaar·kee a·si·bleef
one-way	eenrigting	eyn·rikh·ting
return	retoer	ri·tur

How much is it to ...?
Hoeveel kos dit na ...?   hu·fil kos dit naa ...

Please take me to (this address).
Neem my asseblief na   neym may a·si·bleef naa
(hierdie adres).   (heer·dee a·dres)

Where's the (nearest) ...?
Waar's die (naaste) ...?   vaars dee (naas·ti) ...

Can you show me (on the map)?
Kan jy my   kan yay may
(op die kaart) wys?   (op dee kaart) vays

What's the address?
Wat is die adres?   vat is dee a·dres

CHEWA

Chewa (Chichewa), a Bantu language, is the national language of Malawi and is also a very close relative of Nyanja, spoken in Zambia – the two are mutually intelligible.

Bambo, literally meaning 'father', is a polite way to address any Malawian man. The female equivalent is amai or mai. Mazungu means 'white person', but isn't derogatory.

Chichewa speakers will normally use English for numbers and prices. Similarly, time is nearly always expressed in English.

Hello.	Moni.
Hello, anybody in?	Odi. (when knocking on door or calling at gate)
Come in./Welcome.	Lowani.
Goodbye. (if leaving)	Tsala bwino. (lit: 'stay well')
Goodbye. (if staying)	Pitani bwino. (lit: 'go well')
Good night.	Gonani bwino.
Please.	Chonde.
Thank you./ Excuse me.	Zikomo.
Thank you very much.	Zikomo kwambile/ kwambiri.
Yes.	Inde.
No.	Iyayi.
How are you?	Muli bwanji?
I'm fine.	Ndili bwino.
And you?	Kaya-iwe? (to one person) Kaya inu? (to several people)
Good./Fine./OK.	Chabwino.

NUMBERS: AFRIKAAANS

1	een	eyn
2	twee	twey
3	drie	dree
4	vier	feer
5	vyf	fayf
6	ses	ses
7	sewe	see·vi
8	agt	akht
9	nege	ney·khi
10	tien	teen

DAMARA/NAMA

The Damara and Nama peoples' languages belong to the Khoisan group and, like other Khoisan varieties, they feature several 'click' sounds. The clicks are made by a sucking motion with the tongue against different parts of the mouth to produce different sounds. The clicks represented by ! are a hollow tone, like that when pulling a cork from a bottle. The click represented by / is like the 'tsk!' in English used to indicate disapproval. The sideways click sound, like the sound made when encouraging a horse, is represented by //. However, you'll be forgiven if you just render all the clicks as a 'k' sound.

Good morning.	!Gai//oas.
How are you?	Matisa?
Thank you.	Eio.
Pardon.	Mati.
Yes.	Ii.
Goodbye.	!Gaise hare. (if leaving)
	!Gure. (if staying)
Do you speak English?	Engelsa !goa idu ra?
What's your name?	Mati du/onha?
My name is ...	Ti/ons ge a ...
I'm from ...	Tita ge a ...
How much is this?	No xu o matigo mario ni gan?
Where is the ...?	Maha ... ha?

1	/gui
2	/gam
3	!nona
4	haga
5	goro
6	!nani
7	hu
8	//khaisa
9	khoese
10	disi

HERERO/HIMBA

Herero and Himba, both Bantu languages, are quite similar, and will be especially useful when travelling around Kaokoland and remote areas of north central Namibia, where Afrikaans remains the lingua franca.

Hello.	Tjike.
Good morning, sir.	Wa penduka, mutengua.
Good afternoon, madam.	Wa uhara, serekaze.
Good evening.	Wa tokerua.

Good night.	Ongurova ombua.
Please.	Arikana.
Thank you.	Okuhepa.
How are you?	Kora?
Fine.	Naua.
Well, thank you.	Mbiri naua, okuhepa.
Pardon.	Makuvi.
Yes./No.	Ii./Kako.
Where are you from?	Ove ua za pi?
Do you speak English?	U hungira Otjingirisa?

daughters	ovanatje ovakazona
father	tate
husband	omurumendu ngua kupa
mother	mama
older sibling	erumbi
sons	ovanatje ovazandu
wife	omukazendu ngua kupua
younger sibling	omuangu

caravan park	omasuviro uo zo karavana
game reserve	orumbo ro vipuka
(long/short) hiking trail	okaira ko makaendero uo pehi (okare/okasupi)
river (channel)	omuramba
road	ondjiira
rooms	omatuuo

1	iimue
2	imbari
3	indatu
4	iine
5	indano
6	hamboumue
7	hambomabari
8	hambondatu
9	imuvyu
10	omurongo

!KUNG SAN

The Khoisan languages in Namibia and Botswana are characterised by click sounds. Perhaps the most useful dialect is that of the !Kung people, who are concentrated in eastern Bushmanland in Namibia and around northwestern Botswana.

To simplify matters, in the following phrases all clicks are represented by !k.

Hello.	!Kao.
Good morning.	Tuwa.

Goodbye, go well.	!King se !kau.
What's your name?	!Kang ya tsedia/tsidia? (to a man/woman)
How are you?	!Ka tseya/tsiya? (to a man/woman)
My name is ...	!Kang ya tse/tsi ... (m/f)
Thank you.	!Ka.
Thank you very much.	!Kin!ka.

LOZI

Lozi, a Bantu language, is spoken throughout much of western Zambia and in the Caprivi region of Namibia.

Hello.	Eeni, sha./Lumela.
Good morning.	U zuhile.
Good afternoon/ evening.	Ki manzibuana.
Good night.	Ki busihu.
Goodbye.	Siala foo./Siala hande.
How are you?	U cwang'./W'a pila./ W'a zuha?
I'm fine.	N'i teng'./N'a pila./ N'a zuha.
And you?	Wen'a bo?/Wena u cwang'?
Good./Fine.	Ki hande.
OK.	Ku lukile.
Excuse me.	Ni swalele. (inf) Mu ni swalele. (pol)
Please.	Sha. (only said to people of higher social standing)
Thank you.	N'itumezi.
Thank you very much.	N'i tumezi hahulu.
Yes./No.	Ee./Awa.
Do you speak English?	Wa bulela sikuwa?
How much?	Ki bukai?

1	il'ingw'i
2	z'e peli or bubeli
3	z'e t'alu or bulalu
4	z'e ne or bune
5	z'e keta-lizoho
6	z'e keta-lizoho ka ka li kang'wi
7	supile
10	lishumi
20	mashumi a mabeli likiti

NDEBELE

The language of Zimbabwe's Ndebele people is spoken primarily in Matabeleland in the western and southwestern parts of the country.

It's a Bantu language related to Zulu and is not mutually intelligible with Shona.

The Ndebele of Zimbabwe and that of South Africa (also known as Southern Ndebele) are quite distinct languages.

Hello.	Sawubona./Salibonani.
Hello. (reply)	Yebo.
Good morning.	Livukenjani.
Good afternoon.	Litshonile.
Good evening.	Litshone njani.
How are you?	Linjani?/Kunjani?
I'm well.	Sikona.
Goodbye.	Lisale kuhle. (if staying) Uhambe kuhle. (if leaving)
Yes.	Yebo.
No.	Hayi.
Please.	Uxolo.
Thank you.	Siyabonga kakulu.
What's your name?	Ibizo lakho ngubani?
My name is ...	Elami igama ngingu ...
I'm from ...	Ngivela e ...
sir/madam	umnimzana/inkosikazi
How much?	Yimalini?
Where's the (station)?	Singapi (isiteshi)?

1	okukodwa
2	okubili
3	okutathu
4	okune
5	okuyisihlanu
6	okuyisithupha
7	okuyisikhombisa
8	okuyisitshiyangalo mbila
9	okuyisitshiyangalo lunye
10	okuli tshumi

NORTHERN SOTHO

Northern Sotho (Sepedi) is a Bantu language spoken in South Africa's northeastern provinces.

Hello.	Thobela.
Goodbye.	Sala gabotse.
Yes./No.	Ee./Aowa.
Please.	Ke kgopela.
Thank you.	Ke ya leboga.
What's your name?	Ke mang lebitso la gago?
My name is ...	Lebitso laka ke ...
I come from ...	Ke bowa kwa ...

OWAMBO

A Bantu language, Owambo (Oshiwambo), specifically the Kwanyama dialect, is the first tongue of more Namibians than any other language. It's also spoken as a second or third language by many non-Owambo Namibians of both Bantu and Khoisan origin.

Good morning.	Wa lalapo.
Good evening.	Wa tokelwapo.
How are you?	Owu li po ngiini?
I'm fine.	Ondi li nawa.
Thank you.	Tangi.
Please.	Ombili.
Yes./No.	Eeno./Aawe.
Maybe.	Andiya manga.
Excuse me.	Ombili manga.
I'm sorry.	Onde shi panda.
I don't know.	Ombili mwaa sho.
Do you speak English?	Oho popi Oshiingilisa?
How much is this?	Ingapi tashi kotha?
Can you please help me?	Eto vuluwu pukulule ndje?
I'm lost.	Ombili, onda puka.

Where is the ...?	Openi pu na ...?
bank	ombaanga
hospital	oshipangelo
pharmacy	oaputeka
police station	opolisi
post office	opoosa
telephone	ngodhi
toilet	kandjugo

1	yimwe
2	mbali
3	ndatu
4	ne
5	ntano
6	hamano
7	heyali
8	hetatu
9	omugoyi
10	omulongo

PORTUGUESE

Portuguese is spoken in Mozambique and in parts of northern Namibia. It has nasal vowels (represented in our pronunciation guides by ng after the vowel), which are pronounced 'through the nose', as well as a strongly rolled r (rr in our pronunciation guides). Also note that the symbol zh sounds like the 's' in 'pleasure'. The stressed syllables are in italics.

Basics

Hello.	Olá.	o·laa
Goodbye.	Adeus.	a·de·oosh
How are you?	Como está?	ko·moo shtaa
Fine, and you?	Bem, e você?	beng e vo·se
Excuse me.	Faz favor.	faash fa·vor
Sorry.	Desculpe.	desh·kool·pe
Yes./No.	Sim./Não.	seeng/nowng
Please.	Por favor.	poor fa·vor
Thank you.	Obrigado.	o·bree·gaa·doo (m)
	Obrigada.	o·bree·gaa·da (f)
You're welcome.	De nada.	de naa·da

What's your name?
Qual é o seu nome?   kwaal e oo se·oo no·me

My name is ...
O meu nome é ...   oo me·oo no·me e ...

Do you speak English?
Fala inglês?   faa·la eeng·glesh

I don't understand.
Não entendo.   nowng eng·teng·doo

Eating & Drinking

What would you recommend?
O que é que   oo ke e ke
recomenda?   rre·koo·meng·da

I don't eat ...
Eu não como ...   e·oo nowng ko·moo ...

I'd like (the menu).
Queria (um menu).   ke·ree·a (oong me·noo)

Cheers!
Saúde!   sa·oo·de

NUMBERS IN PORTUGUESE		
1	um	oong
2	dois	doysh
3	três	tresh
4	quatro	kwaa·troo
5	cinco	seeng·koo
6	seis	saysh
7	sete	se·te
8	oito	oy·too
9	nove	no·ve
10	dez	desh

That was delicious.
Isto estava   eesh·too shtaa·va
delicioso.   de·lee·see·o·zoo

Please bring the bill.
Pode-me trazer   po·de·me tra·zer
a conta.   a kong·ta

Emergencies

Help!	*Socorro!*	soo·ko·rroo
Go away!	*Vá-se embora!*	vaa·se eng·bo·ra
Call ...!	*Chame ...!*	shaa·me ...
a doctor	*um médico*	oong me·dee·koo
the police	*a polícia*	a poo·lee·sya

I'm lost.
Estou perdido.   shtoh per·dee·doo (m)
Estou perdida.   shtoh per·dee·da (f)

I'm ill.
Estou doente.   shtoh doo·eng·te

Where is the toilet?
Onde é a casa de   ong·de e a kaa·za de
banho?   ba·nyoo

Shopping & Services

I'd like to buy ...
Queria comprar ...   ke·ree·a kong·praar ...

How much is it?
Quanto custa?   kwang·too koosh·ta

It's too expensive.
Está muito caro.   shtaa mweeng·too kaa·roo

There's a mistake in the bill.
Há um erro na conta.   aa oong e·rroo na kong·ta

Transport & Directions

boat	*barco*	baar·koo
bus	*autocarro*	ow·to·kaa·roo
plane	*avião*	a·vee·owng
train	*comboio*	kong·boy·oo
... ticket	*um bilhete de ...*	oong bee·lye·te de ...
one-way	*ida*	ee·da
return	*ida e volta*	ee·da ee vol·ta

I want to go to ...
Queria ir a ...   ke·ree·a eer a ...

What time does it leave/arrive?
A que horas sai/chega?   a ke o·rash sai/she·ga

Where's (the station)?
Onde é (a estação)?   ong·de e (a shta·sowng)

What's the address?
Qual e o endereço?   kwaal e oo eng·de·re·soo

Could you please write it down?
Podia escrever   poo·dee·a shkre·ver
isso, por favor?   ee·soo poor fa·vor

Can you show me (on the map)?
Pode-me mostrar   po·de·me moosh·traar
(no mapa)?   (noo maa·pa)

SHONA

Shona, a Bantu language, is spoken almost universally in the central and eastern parts of Zimbabwe. The 'high' dialect, used in broadcasts and other media, is Zezuru, which is indigenous to the Harare area.

Where two translations are given for the following phrases, the first is used when speaking to one person; the second, to more than one. Note that dya is pronounced 'jga' (as near to one syllable as possible); tya as 'chka' (said quickly); sv as 's' with the tongue near the roof of the mouth; zv like the 'sv' sound in 'is very', and that m/n before consonants at the start of a word are pronounced as a light 'm' or 'n' humming sound.

Hello.	*Mhoro./Mhoroi.*
Hello. (reply)	*Ahoi.*
Welcome.	*Titambire.*
How are you?	*Makadii?/Makadi-ni?*
I'm well.	*Ndiripo.*
Good morning.	*Mangwanani.*
Good afternoon.	*Masikati.*
Good evening.	*Manheru.*
Goodbye.	*Chisarai zvakanaka.* (if staying) *Fambai zvakanaka.* (if leaving)
Please.	*Ndapota.*
Thank you.	*Ndatenda./Masvita.*
Yes./No.	*Ehe./Aiw.*
What's your name?	*Unonzi ani zita rako?*
My name is ...	*Ndini ...*
I'm from ...	*Ndinobva ku ...*
How much?	*I marii?*

1	*potsi*
2	*piri*
3	*tatu*
4	*ina*
5	*shanu*
6	*tanhatu*
7	*nomwe*
8	*tsere*
9	*pfumbamwe*
10	*gumi*

SOUTHERN SOTHO

Southern Sotho (Sesotho), a Bantu language, is the official language in Lesotho (along with English). It is also spoken by the Basotho people in the Free State, North West and Gauteng provinces in South Africa.

Hello.	Dumela.
Greetings, father.	Lumela ntate.
Greetings, mother.	Lumela 'me.
Greetings, brother.	Lumela abuti.
Greetings, sister.	Lumela ausi.

There are three commonly used ways of saying 'How are you?' (followed by suitable responses). Note that these questions and answers are quite interchangeable.

How are you?	O/Le kae? (sg/pl)
How do you live?	O/Le phela joang? (sg/pl)
How did you get up?	O/Le tsohele joang? (sg/pl)
I'm here.	Ke/Re teng. (sg/pl)
I live well.	Ke/Re phela hantle. (sg/pl)
I got up well.	Ke/Re tsohile hantle. (sg/pl)

When trekking, people always ask Lea kae? or O tsoa kae? (Where are you going?), or the plural Le tsoa kae? (Where have you come from?). When parting, use these expressions:

Stay well.	Sala hantle. (sg)
	Salang hantle. (pl)
Go well.	Tsamaea hantle. (sg)
	Tsamaeang hantle. (pl)

'Thank you' is kea leboha (pronounced 'ke-ya le-bo-wa'). The herd boys often ask for chelete (money) or lipompong (sweets, pronounced 'dee-pom-pong'). To say 'I don't have any', use ha dio.

SWATI

Swati (siSwati) is the official language in Swaziland (along with English). A Bantu language, it's very similar to Zulu, and they are mutually intelligible.

It's the custom to greet everyone you meet. Yebo is often said as a casual greeting. Often you will be asked U ya phi? (Where are you going?).

Hello.	Sawubona. (to one person)
	Sanibona.
	(to more than one person)
How are you?	Kunjani?
I'm fine.	Kulungile.

Goodbye.	Sala kahle. (if leaving)
	Hamba kahle. (if staying)
Please.	Ngicela.
I thank you.	Ngiyabonga.
We thank you.	Siyabonga.
Yes.	Yebo. (also an all-purpose greeting)
No.	Cha.
Sorry.	Lucolo.
What's your name?	Ngubani libito lakho?
My name is ...	Libitolami ningu ...
I'm from ...	Ngingewekubuya e ...
How much?	Malini?

TSONGA

Tsonga (Xitsonga), a Bantu language, is spoken in South Africa (north of Hluhluwe in KwaZulu-Natal) and in parts of Mozambique.

Hello.	Avusheni. (morning)
	Inhelekani. (afternoon)
	Riperile. (evening)
Goodbye.	Salani kahle.
Yes.	Hi swona.
No.	A hi swona.
Please.	Nakombela.
Thank you.	I nkomu.
What's your name?	U mani vito ra wena?
My name is ...	Vito ra mina i ...
I come from ...	Ndzihuma e ...

TSWANA

Tswana (Setswana), a Bantu language, is widely spoken throughout Botswana and in some parts of South Africa (in the eastern areas of Northern Cape, in North West and in western Free State). There are similarities in vocabulary between Tswana and the two Sotho languages, and the speakers of each can generally understand one another.

The letter g is pronounced as the 'ch' in Scottish 'loch'; th is pronounced as a slightly aspirated 't', ie with a puff of air.

The greetings dumela mma, dumela rra and dumelang are considered compliments and Batswana people appreciate their liberal usage. Another useful phrase (usually placed at the end of a sentence or conversation) is go siame, meaning 'all right, no problem'.

Hello.	Dumela mma/rra.
	(to a woman/man)
	Dumelang. (to a group)
Hello!	Ko ko! (on arrival at a gate or house)

Goodbye.	Tsamaya sentle. (if staying)
	Sala sentle. (if leaving)
Yes.	Ee.
No.	Nnyaa.
Please.	Tsweetswee.
Thank you.	Kea leboga.
Excuse me./Sorry.	Intshwarele.
Pardon me.	Ke kopa tsela.
OK./No problem.	Go siame.
How are you?	A o tsogile? (morning)
	O tlhotse jang?
	(afternoon/evening)
Do you speak English?	A o bua Sekgoa?
I don't understand.	Ga ke tlhaloganye.
How much is it?	Ke bokae?
Where is a/the ...?	E ko kae ...?

I'm looking for a/the ...	Ke batla ...
bank	ntlo ya polokelo
guesthouse	matlo a baeng
hotel	hotele
market	mmaraka
post office	poso
public toilet	matlwana a boitiketso
tourist office	ntlo ya bajanala

1	bongwe
2	bobedi
3	borara
4	bone
5	botlhano
6	borataro
7	bosupa
8	boroba bobedi
9	boroba bongwe
10	lesome

VENDA

Venda (Tshivenda), a Bantu language, is spoken in the northeastern region of South Africa's Limpopo province.

Hello.	Ndi matseloni. (morning)
	Ndi masiari. (afternoon)
	Ndi madekwana. (evening)
Goodbye.	Kha vha sale zwavhudi.
Yes.	Ndi zwone.
No.	A si zwone.
Please.	Ndikho u humbela.
Thank you.	Ndo livhuwa.

What's your name?	Zina lavho ndi nnyi?
My name is ...	Zina langa ndi ...
I come from ...	Ndi bva ...

XHOSA

Xhosa (isiXhosa) is the language of the people of the same name. A Bantu language, it's the dominant indigenous variety in Eastern Cape in South Africa, although you'll meet Xhosa speakers throughout the region.

Note that *Bawo* is a term of respect used when addressing an older man.

Hello.	Molo.
Goodbye.	Sala kakuhle.
Goodnight.	Rhonanai.
Please.	Nceda.
Thank you.	Enkosi.
Are you well?	Uphilile na namhlanje?
Yes, I'm well.	Ewe, ndiphilile kanye.
Yes.	Ewe.
No.	Hayi.
Do you speak English?	Uyakwazi ukuthetha siNgesi?
Where are you from?	Uvela phi na okanye ngaphi na?
I'm from ...	Ndivela ...
I'm lost.	Ndilahlekile.
Is this the road to ...?	Yindlela eya ... yini le?
How much is it?	Idla ntoni na?

ZULU

Zulu (isiZulu), a Bantu language, is spoken in South Africa by the people of the same name. As with several other Nguni languages, Zulu uses a variety of clicks. To ask a question, add *-na* to the end of a sentence.

Hello.	Sawubona.
Goodbye.	Sala kahle.
Please.	Jabulisa.
Thank you.	Ngiyabonga.
Yes./No.	Yebo./Cha.
Where does this road go?	Iqondaphi lendlela na?
Which is the road to ...?	Iphi indlela yokuya ku ...?
Is it far?	Kukude yini?
left	ekhohlo
right	ekumene
food	ukudla
water	amanzi

GLOSSARY

Although English is widely spoken in most Southern African countries, native speakers from Australasia, North America and the UK will notice that many words have developed different meanings locally. There are also many unusual terms that have been borrowed from Afrikaans, Portuguese or indigenous languages. This glossary includes some of these particular 'Afro-English' words, as well as some other general terms and abbreviations that may not be understood.

In African English, repetition for emphasis is common: something that burnt you would be 'hot hot'; fields after the rains are 'green green'; a crowded minibus with no more room is 'full full', and so on.

4WD – four-wheel drive; locally called 4x4

apartheid – literally, the state of being apart; a political system in which peoples were officially segregated according to their race

asimilados – Mozambican term for Africans who assimilated to European ways

assegais – spears; used against the colonialists in Zimbabwe

bakkie – pronounced 'bucky'; utility or pick-up truck

barchan dunes – migrating crescent-shaped sand dunes

Basarwa – Batswana name for the San people

Batswana – citizens of Botswana

bemanti – learned Swazi men

Big Five – elephant, lion, rhino, leopard, buffalo

biltong – chewy dried meat that can be anything from beef to kudu or ostrich

bobotie – traditional Malay dish; delicately flavoured curry with a topping of beaten egg baked to a crust, served with stewed fruits and chutney

Boer – farmer in Afrikaans; historic name for the Afrikaner people

boerewors – sausage of varying quality made by Afrikaner farmers

bogobe – sorghum porridge, a staple in Botswana

bojalwa – inexpensive sorghum beer drunk in Botswana that is also brewed commercially

boma – in Zambia, Malawi and some other countries, this is a local word for 'town'; in East Africa the same word means 'fortified stockade'; in Zimbabwe, Botswana, Namibia and much of South Africa, it's normally just a sunken campfire circle; it may be derived from the colonial term BOMA (British Overseas Military Administration), applied to any government building, such as offices or forts

boomslang – dangerous 2m-long tree snake

braai – barbecue; a Southern African institution, particularly among whites

bushveld – flat, grassy plain covered in thorn scrub

camarões – Mozambican term for prawns

camião – truck in Mozambique

campeamento principal – Mozambican term for main entrance

capulanas – colourful sarongs worn by Mozambican women around their waist

capuzinio – mission in Mozambique

casal – room with a double bed, for married couples, in Mozambique

cascata – Mozambican term for waterfall

chapa – word for converted passenger truck or minivan in Mozambique or Malawi

chibuku – local style mass-produced beer, stored in tanks and served in buckets, or available in takeaway cartons (mostly in Zimbabwe and Malawi) and plastic bottles known as *scuds;* it's good for a quick euphoria and a debilitating babalass (hangover)

chiperone – damp misty weather that affects southern Malawi

concession – communal land area designated by the government for use by a given commercial entity for a set amount of time – usually five years; a popular concept in both Namibia and Botswana

coupé – two-person compartment on a train

cuca shops – small shops in northern Namibia; named after the Angolan beer once sold in them

daga hut – traditional African round house consisting of a wooden frame, mud and straw walls, and a thatched roof (mainly in Zimbabwe)

dagga – pronounced da-kha; Southern African term for marijuana

dassies – herbivorous gopher-like mammals of two species: *Procavia capensis,* also called the rock hyrax, and *Dendrohyrax arborea* or tree hyrax; they're in fact not rodents, but are thought to be the closest living relatives of the elephant

dhow – Arabic sailing vessel that dates from ancient times

difaqane – forced migration by several Southern African tribes in the face of Zulu aggression; also known as *mfeqane*

donga – steep-sided gully caused by soil erosion

dorp – small country settlement in South Africa

drift – river ford; most are normally dry

dumpi – 375ml bottle of beer

duplo – term for a room with twin beds used in Mozambique

GLOSSARY

dwalas – bald, knoblike domes of smooth rock

eh – (rhymes with 'hay') all-purpose ending to sentences, even very short ones such as 'Thanks, eh?'

euphorbia – several species of cactuslike succulents; most are poisonous to humans

fly camp – temporary camp set up in the bush away from the main camp

fynbos – literally 'fine bush', primarily proteas, heaths and ericas

galabiyya – men's full-length robe

gap it – make a quick exit; often refers to emigration from troubled African countries

garni – hotel in Namibia that lacks a full dining room, but does offer a simple breakfast

gemütlichkeit – distinctly German appreciation of comfort and hospitality

half-bus – Malawian term for a bus with about 30 seats – to distinguish it from big buses or minibuses

heks – entrance gates, farm gates

high season – in most of Southern Africa, this refers to the dry season, from late June to late September; in South Africa's Cape regions, it refers to the dry season, from late November to early April

highveld – high-altitude grassland

Homelands – formerly self-governing black states (Transkei, Ciskei, Bophuthatswana, Venda etc), which were part of the apartheid regime's plan for a separate black and white South Africa

Incwala – most sacred Swazi ceremony in which the king gives permission to his people to eat the first crops of the new year

inselberg – isolated ranges and hills; literally 'island mountains'

Izzit? – rhetorical question that most closely translates as 'Really?' and is used without regard to gender, person or number of subjects; therefore, it could mean 'Is it?', 'Are you?', 'Is he?', 'Are they?', 'Is she?', 'Are we?' etc; also 'How izzit?' for 'How's it going?'

Jugendstil – German art-nouveau architecture prevalent in Namibia, especially in Swakopmund and parts of Windhoek and Lüderitz

just now – refers to some time in the future but implies a certain degree of imminence; it could be half an hour from now or two days from now

kalindula – rumba-inspired music of Zambia

kampango – catfish in Malawi

kapenta – anchovylike fish (*Limnothrissa mioda*) caught in Lake Kariba and favoured by Zimbabweans

karakul – variety of Central Asian sheep, which produces high-grade wool and pelts; raised in Namibia and parts of Botswana

kgosi – chief in Botswana (Setswana language)

kgotla – village meeting place in Botswana

Khoisan – language grouping taking in all Southern African indigenous languages, including San and Khoikhoi (Nama), as well as the language of the Damara, a Bantu people who speak a Khoikhoi dialect

kizomba – musical style popular in Namibia

kloof – ravine or small valley

kloofing – canyoning into and out of kloofs

kokerboom – quiver tree; grows mainly in southern Namibia and the Northern Cape province of South Africa

konditorei – German pastry shops; found in larger Namibian towns

kopje – pronounced 'koppie'; small hill or rocky outcrop on an otherwise flat plain

kotu – king's court in Zambia

kraal – Afrikaans version of the Portuguese word *curral*; an enclosure for livestock, a fortified village of mud huts, or an Owambo homestead

kwacha – currency in Malawi and Zambia

kwasa kwasa – Congo-style rhumba music

laager – wagon circle

lagosta – crayfish in Mozambique

lapa – large, thatched common area; used for socialising

lekolulo – flutelike instrument played by herd boys in Lesotho

liqhaga – grassware 'bottles'

litunga – king in Zambia

lowveld – see *bushveld*

lupembe – wind instrument made from animal horn

machibombo – large bus in Mozambique

majika – traditional rhythmic sound

makalani – type of palm tree that grows in the Kalahari region; also called *mokolane*

makhosi – Zulu chiefs

malva – apricot pudding of Dutch origin

mapiko – masked dance of the Makonde people

marimba – African xylophone made from strips of resonant wood with various-sized gourds for sound boxes

marrabenta – typical Mo-zambican music, inspired by traditional *majika* rhythms

mataku – watermelon wine

matola – Malawian term for pick-up or van carrying passengers

mbira – thumb piano; it consists of five to 24 narrow

GLOSSARY

iron keys mounted in rows on a wooden sound board

mealie pap – maize porridge, which is a dietary staple throughout the region; also called *mielie pap*

mfeqane – see *difaqane*

mielie pap – see *mealie pap*

mielies – cobs of maize

miombo – dry, open woodland, also called *Brachystegia* woodland; it's composed mainly of mopane and acacia *bushveld*

mojito – Cuban cocktail made of mint, rum, lime juice, sugar and soda

mokolane – see *makalani*

mokoro – dugout canoe used in the Okavango Delta and other riverine areas; the *mokoro* is propelled by a well-balanced poler who stands in the stern

mopane – hardwood tree native to Southern Africa (also called ironwood), highly resistant to drought

mopane worms – the caterpillar of the moth *Gonimbrasiabelina*, eaten as a local delicacy throughout the region

msasa – small, shrubby tree with compound leaves and small, fragrant flowers

multa – a fine in Mozambique

muti – traditional medicine

nalikwanda – huge wooden canoe, painted with black and white stripes, that carries the *litunga*

Nama – popular name for Namibians of Khoikhoi, Topnaar or Baster heritage

não faz mal – 'no problem' in Portuguese; useful in both Mozambique and Angola

!nara – type of melon that grows in desert areas; a dietary staple of the Topnaar people

nartjie – pronounced 'narkie'; South African tangerine

ncheni – lake tiger fish in Malawi

Ngwenyama – the Lion; term given to the king of Swaziland

nshima – filling maize porridgelike substance eaten in Zambia

nxum – the San people's 'life force'

nyama – meat or meat gravy

oke – term for bloke or guy, mainly heard in South Africa

ondjongo – dance performed by Himba cattle owners to demonstrate the care and ownership of their animals

oshana – normally dry river channel in northern Namibia and northwestern Botswana

oshikundu – tasty alcoholic beverage; popular in traditional areas of northern Namibia

otjipirangi (for men) and **outjina** (for women) – Herero dance in which a plank is strapped to one foot in order to deliver a hollow, rhythmic percussion

pan – dry flat area of grassland or salt, often a seasonal lake-bed

participation safari – an inexpensive safari in which clients pitch their own tents, pack the vehicle and share cooking duties

pensão – inexpensive hotel in Mozambique

peri-peri – see *piri-piri*

pint – small bottle of beer or can of oil (or similar), usually around 300mL to 375mL (not necessarily equal to a British or US pint)

piri-piri – very hot pepper sauce of Portuguese Angolan origin; also known as *peri-peri*

potjie – pronounced *poy*-kee; a three-legged pot used to make stew over an open fire; the word also refers to the stew itself, as well as a gathering in which a *potjie* forms the main dish

potjiekos – meat and vegetable stew cooked in a *potjie*

praça – town square in Mozambique

praia – beach in Mozambique

pula – the Botswanan currency; means 'rain' in Setswana

pungwe – all-night drinking and music party in Zimbabwe

relish – sauce of meat, vegetables, beans etc eaten with boiled corn meal (*nshima*, *sadza*, *mealie pap* etc)

rijsttafel – rice with side dishes

Rikki – small, open van; cross between a taxi and a shared taxi

rondavel – round, African-style hut

rooibos – literally 'red bush' in Afrikaans; herbal tea that reputedly has therapeutic qualities

sadza – maize-meal porridge

San – language-based name for indigenous people formerly known as Bushmen

sandveld – dry, sandy belt

sangoma – witch doctor; herbalist

scud – plastic drink bottle

seif dunes – prominent linear sand dunes, as found in the central Namib Desert

shame! – half-hearted expression of commiseration

shebeen – unlicensed township drinking establishment (which may also include a brothel)

sibhaca – type of Swazi dance

Sperrgebiet – forbidden area; alluvial diamond region of southwestern Namibia

Strandlopers – literally 'beach walkers'; term used to describe the ancient inhabitants of the Namib region, who may have been ancestors of the San or Nama peoples; occasionally also refers to the brown desert hyena

sua – salt as in Sua Pan, Botswana

swaartgevaar – Afrikaans for the 'black threat'

thomo – stringed instrument played by women in Lesotho

GLOSSARY

timbila – form of xylophone played by Chope musicians

township – indigenous suburb, typically a high-density black residential area

Trekboers – nomadic pastoralists descended from the Dutch

tufo – traditional dance style from Ilha de Moçambique

tuk-tuk – Asian-style motorised three-wheel vehicle

uitlanders – pronounced 'ait-landers'; foreigners

Umhlanga – reed dance; sacred Swazi ceremony

upshwa – maize- or cassava-based staple in Mozambique

Uri – desert-adapted vehicle produced in Namibia

veld – pronounced 'felt'; open grassland, normally in plateau regions

vlei – pronounced 'flay'; any low, open landscape, sometimes marshy

volkstaal – people's language

Volkstaat – people's state

Voortrekkers – fore-trekkers, pioneers

vundu – Malawian catfish

walende – drink distilled from the *makalani* palm; tastes like vodka

wandelpad – short hiking trail

waterblommetjie bredie – water-flower stew; meat served with the flower of the Cape pondweed

welwitschia – bizarre cone-bearing shrub *(Welwitschia mirabilis)* native to the northern Namib plains

xima – maize- or cassava-based staple in Mozambique, usually served with a sauce of beans, vegetables or fish

Behind the Scenes

SEND US YOUR FEEDBACK

We love to hear from travellers – your comments keep us on our toes and help make our books better. Our well-travelled team reads every word on what you loved or loathed about this book. Although we cannot reply individually to your submissions, we always guarantee that your feedback goes straight to the appropriate authors, in time for the next edition. Each person who sends us information is thanked in the next edition – the most useful submissions are rewarded with a selection of digital PDF chapters.

Visit **lonelyplanet.com/contact** to submit your updates and suggestions or to ask for help. Our award-winning website also features inspirational travel stories, news and discussions.

Note: We may edit, reproduce and incorporate your comments in Lonely Planet products such as guidebooks, websites and digital products, so let us know if you don't want your comments reproduced or your name acknowledged. For a copy of our privacy policy visit lonelyplanet.com/privacy.

OUR READERS

Many thanks to the travellers who used the last edition and wrote to us with helpful hints, useful advice and interesting anecdotes:

Conor Rushby, Daniel Pennings, Danny Hartogs, Elizabeth Keeling, Elsa Drandaki, Gerry Bultendag, Ilya de groot, Jan Prinsen, Kjell Hoegseth, Matthieu Kamerman, Stephen Poovey, Suzanne Fee, Xolile Speelman

WRITER THANKS

Anthony Ham

So many people helped me along the way and brought such wisdom and insight to this book. Special thanks as always to Andy Raggett at Drive Botswana, and to Paul Funston, Lise Hansson, Luke Hunter, Charlotte Pollard, Rob Reid, Eva Meurs, Daan Smit, Jacob Tembo, Induna Mundandwe, Kasia Sliwa, Lara Good, Ying Yi Ho, and to Frank, Juliane, Tim and Ann-Sophie. At Lonely Planet, heartfelt thanks to my editor Matt Phillips – no-one knows Africa like him. And to Marina, Carlota and Valentina – I loved sharing some of my favourite corners of Africa with you.

James Bainbridge

Believe the hype about Malawian friendliness: this really is the Warm Heart of Africa. *Ziko-mo*, then, to pretty much everyone for being

so awesome, and in particular to the many folk, too numerous to mention, in lodges from Mzuzu to Mulanje. My research trip was considerably more fruitful and fun with your local knowledge and sociable bottles of Green.

Lucy Corne

A huge *enkosi* to all who shared their insider tips, including Heather, Ivor, Eben, Terri, Shae, Meruschka, Megan, Scott, Troye, Matt, Sean, Sal, Tanya, Elmar, Ed and Sylvia. Thanks to Matt, Dianne and Dan at LP and great big hugs to my mum and dad for becoming travelling au pairs during research. High five to Kai, the cutest little LP writer-in-training, for being awesome throughout those long road trips. And above all, this one is for Shawn – I absolutely couldn't have done it without you.

Mary Fitzpatrick

Many thanks to all those who helped me during this project, especially to Rafael Holt in Tofo for the excellent background information; to Sidney Bliss in Maputo for updates on the latest Mozambique happenings; and to the staff at Maputo Special Reserve and at Limpopo National Park. My biggest thanks go to Rick, Christopher, Dominic and Gabriel for their company, patience, good humour and support in Mozambique and back home.

Trent Holden

First up thanks to Matt Phillips for commissioning me to go to Zimbabwe, one of my all-time favourite countires in the world, as well as all the production staff for putting this together. A huge thanks to Karl Wright and Jenny Nobes from Rhino Safari Camp for all their assistance in getting around Matusadona and for tips and recommendations across the country – an unbelievable help! Also thanks to the following people for all their time and assistance: the team from Chilo Gorge Lodge, Joy from Victoria Falls and Gordon Addams, Ann Bruce, Tempe, Jane, Jacqui and George from the Eastern Highlands. A huge thanks to James S once again for taking time out to go on a road trip – I had a ball! Finally lots of love to my family, especially my partner Kate who allows me to travel to such far-flung, exotic places.

Brendan Sainsbury

Thanks to all the untold taxi drivers, chefs, hotel receptionists, tour guides and innocent bystanders who helped me during this research. Special thanks to Jasper and Bart in Pemba, the guys at Cinco Portas on Ibo Island, Peter at Pensão Gurûê, and the wonderful staff at Gorongosa National Park.

ACKNOWLEDGEMENTS

Climate map data adapted from Peel MC, Finlayson BL & McMahon TA (2007) 'Updated World Map of the Köppen-Geiger Climate Classification', Hydrology and Earth System Sciences, 11, 163344.

Cover photograph: Two male impalas, Etienne Outram / 500px

THIS BOOK

This 7th edition of Lonely Planet's *Southern Africa* guide was written by Anthony Ham, James Bainbridge, Lucy Corne, Mary Fitzpatrick, Trent Holden and Brendan Sainsbury. David Lukas wrote the text that formed the basis of the Wildlife chapter and Jane Cornwell wrote the Music in Southern Africa chapter. This guidebook was commissioned in Lonely Planet's London office and produced by the following:

Destination Editor Matt Phillips

Product Editors Kate James, Sandie Kestell

Senior Cartographer Diana Von Holdt

Cartographer Rachel Imeson

Book Designers Mike Buick, Gwen Cotter

Assisting Editors Janet Austin, Sarah Bailey, Andrew Bain, Judith Bamber, Michelle Bennett, Melanie Dankel, Andrea Dobbin, Carly Hall, Ali Lemer, Jodie Martire, Rosie Nicholson, Maja Vatrić

Cover Researcher Naomi Parker

Thanks to Megan Eaves, Daniel Fahey, Lauren Keith, Kate Kiely, Anne Mason, Catherine Naghten, Lauren O'Connell, Kirsten Rawlings, Tony Wheeler

Index

ABBREVIATIONS
B   Botswana
GP   Game Park
GR   Game Reserve
L   Lesotho
Mal   Malawi
Moz   Mozambique
N   Namibia
NP   National Park
NR   National Reserve/
        Nature Reserve
S   Swaziland
SA   South Africa
WR   Wildlife Reserve
WS   Wildlife Sanctuary
Zam   Zambia
Zim   Zimbabwe

SYMBOLS
|Ai-|Ais/Richtersveld
  Transfrontier Park (SA)
  504
!Kung San 743-4

A
abseiling 717-18
  Montagu (SA) 368
  Parys (SA) 446
  Semonkong (L) 108
  Storms River (SA) 385
  Table Mountain NP (SA)
    341
  Victoria Falls 551
accommodation 714-15, see
  also individual locations
  Botswana 42, 87-8
  Lesotho 14, 97, 114
  Malawi 118, 162
  Mozambique 169, 233
  South Africa 322, 518, 519
  Swaziland 530, 546

Map Pages 000
Photo Pages 000

Zambia 566, 610
Zimbabwe 617, 656
activities 18, 21-4, 715-18,
  see also individual
  activities, individual
  locations
Addo Elephant NP (SA)
  392-3
African buffalo 685, 684
African fish eagles 690
African penguins 693, 692
African wild dogs 689, 705
Afrikaans language 741-2
Agulhas NP (SA) 367
AIDS 662-3, 672-3, 738
air travel, see also scenic
  flights, individual
  countries
  to/from Southern Africa
    727-8
  within Southern Africa
    730
alcohol 678
Amathole (SA) 396-8
Anglo-Boer wars 507
animals, see wildlife,
  individual animals
antelopes 685
apartheid 455, 508-9
aquariums
  Bayworld (SA) 388
  National Marine Aquarium
    (N) 279
  Stuart M Grant Tropical
    Fish Farm (Mal) 139
  Two Oceans Aquarium
    (SA) 331
  uShaka Marine World
    (SA) 408
archaeological sites, see
  also historic sites,
  rock art
  Dinosaur Footprints
    (L) 110
  Great Zimbabwe (Zim) 15,
    640-2, 641, 15
  Khami Ruins (Zim) 643

Sterkfontein Caves (SA)
  463
Ziwa Ruins (Zim) 636
architecture 675
area codes 17
art galleries, see also
  museums
  Ann Bryant Art Gallery
    (SA) 396
  Art Gallery (Durban,
    SA) 409
  Campbell Collections
    (SA) 409
  Delta Gallery (Zim) 619
  Hester Rupert Art
    Museum (SA) 399
  Johannesburg Art Gallery
    (SA) 451
  National Gallery of
    Zimbabwe (Zim) 619
  Nelson Mandela
    Metropolitan Art
    Museum (SA) 388
  Oliewenhuis Art Museum
    (SA) 442
  Polokwane Art Museum
    (SA) 481-2
  South African National
    Gallery (SA) 327, 330
  Tatham Art Gallery (SA)
    435
  Tsoko Gallery (Zim) 619
  William Humphreys Art
    Gallery (SA) 497
arts 674, see also individual
  countries
ATMs 720
Augrabies Falls NP (SA) 503
Aus (N) 294

B
Bambelela (SA) 485
Banda, Dr Hastings Kamuzu
  159-60
Banda, Joyce 160
Bangweulu Wetlands (Zam)
  597-8

Bantu people 666-9
Barra (Moz) 190
Basotho people 111, 112-13
bat-eared foxes 689, 688
bateleurs 690, 691
bathrooms 723-4
Battlefields (SA) 438-40
Baviaanskloof WA (SA) 384
Bazaruto Archipelago (Moz)
  194-5
beaches 18-19
  Camps Bay (SA) 339
  Cape Vidal (SA) 423
  Chikale Beach (Mal) 133
  Clifton (SA) 339
  Coffee Bay (SA) 403
  Durban (SA) 408
  Jeffreys Bay (SA) 386
  Macaneta Beach (Moz)
    181-2
  Macuti Beach (Moz) 195
  Muizenberg Beach (SA)
    336
  Murrébuè (Moz) 223-4
  Plettenberg Bay (SA) 377
  Port Alfred (SA) 395
  Port Elizabeth (SA) 388
  uMdloti Beach (SA) 419
  Wimbi Beach (Moz) 219,
    221-2
  Xai-Xai (Moz) 186
  Zalala Beach (Moz) 205
bearded vultures 690, 690
Beira (Moz) 195-9, 196
Bela-Bela (SA) 484-6
bicycle travel, see cycling
Bilene (Moz) 184
birds 690-1, 707
Birds of Eden (SA) 377
birdwatching 551, 596, 707
  Bangweulu Wetlands
    (Zam) 597-8
  Boulders Penguin Colony
    (SA) 335
  Bvumba Mountains 635
  De Hoop NR (SA) 365

birdwatching continued
Etosha NP (N) 261
Giant's Castle (SA) 432
Malawi 162
Malolotja NR (S) 541
Maputo Special Reserve (Moz) 185
Mozambique 233
Namibia 309-10
Nata Bird Sanctuary (B) 54
St Lucia (SA) 423
Victoria Falls 551
Walvis Bay (N) 283, 286
black market 720
black-footed cats 681
Blantyre (Mal) 149-54, **150**, **152**
Bloemfontein (SA) 441-6, **444**
Blood River (SA) 439-40
Blyde River Canyon (SA) 473-4
boat travel, see also individual countries
to/from Southern Africa 729
within Southern Africa 731
Bo-Kaap (SA) 323
Bokong NR (L) 105
Bontebok NR (SA) 367
books 662
environment 709
food 676
health 737
history 668
wildlife 705
Boulders Penguin Colony (SA) 335
border crossings 728, see also individual countries
Botswana 38, 42-96, **44**
accommodation 42, 87-8
activities 88-9
business hours 91
climate 42
consulates 89-90
customs regulations 89
disabilities, travellers with 92
embassies 89-90
environment 84-6
food 42, 90
gay travellers 90

Map Pages **000**
Photo Pages **000**

highlights 44
history 82-3
holidays 91
internet access 90
language 743-4, 747-8
lesbian travellers 90
maps 90
money 90-1
national parks 86-7
opening hours 91
people 84
public holidays 91
safe travel 89
telephone services 91-2
time 92
tourist information 92
travel seasons 42
travel to/from 92-4
travel within 95-6
visas 92
weather 42
wildlife 85-6
Boy Who Harnessed the Wind, The 161
Brandberg (N) 270-1
bridge swinging 551
bridge walking 551
budget 17, 715, 718
Botswana 87, 90
Malawi 162, 163
Mozambique 234
South Africa 519
Zambia 610, 612
Zimbabwe 656
buffaloes 581, 685, **684**
Bulawayo (Zim) 643-6, **644**
bungee jumping
Bloukrans Bridge (SA) 382
Orlando Towers (SA) 464
Victoria Falls 551
bus travel 731-2, see also individual countries
bush camps 582
business hours 722
Bvumba Mountains (Zim) 635-6
Bwabwata NP (N) 266-7

C
Cabaceira Grande (Moz) 214-15
Cabaceira Pequena (Moz) 214-15
Cahora Bassa Dam (Moz) 203

Caia (Moz) 203
Camdeboo NP (SA) 400-1
camping 714, see also individual locations
canoeing 551, 716, see also kayaking, mokoro trips, rafting
Augrabies Falls NP (SA) 503
Kariba (Zim) 630
Lake Kariba (Zam) 588
Lower Zambesi NP (Zam) 585
Namibia 312
Noordoewer (N) 301
Maseru (L) 100
Port Alfred (SA) 395
South Africa 518-19
Swaziland 546
Victoria Falls 551
Cape Agulhas (SA) 367
Cape Cross Seal Reserve (N) 275-6
Cape buffalo 685, **684**
Cape fur seals 275, 689, **689**
Cape gannets 693, **692**
Cape Maclear (Mal) 140-4, **142**
Cape of Good Hope (SA) 335, 340
Cape Town (SA) 323-55, **328**, **332**, **336**, **338**, **342**
accommodation 343-7
activities 340-1
drinking 349-51
entertainment 351-2
festivals 340
food 347-9
medical services 353
nightlife 349-51
shopping 352-3
sights 323-39
tourist information 353
tours 327, 341-3
travel to/from 353-4
travel within 354-5
Cape Town Minstrel Carnival (SA) 21, 340
Caprivi Strip (N) 266-8, **266**
car travel 20, see also individual countries
safety 722-3
self-drive safaris 37
to/from Southern Africa 728-9
within Southern Africa 732-5

caracals 681, **681**
castles
Castle of Good Hope (SA) 326
Duwisib Castle (N) 293-4
Heinitzburg Castle (N) 243
Cathedral Peak NR (SA) 431
cathedrals, see churches & cathedrals
cats 680-1
caves
Bathplug Cave (SA) 433
Cango Caves (SA) 369
Chimanimani NP (Zim) 640
Echo Caves (SA) 473-4
Gobholo Cave (S) 543
Main Cave (SA) 432
Makapan's Caves (SA) 484
Stadsaal Caves (SA) 380
Sterkfontein Caves (SA) 463
Cecil Kop Wildlife & NR (Zim) 633
Cederberg Wilderness Area (SA) 380-1
cell phones 16, 723
Central Kalahari GR (B) 76-8, **78**
Central Malawi 136-44, **137**
Central Mozambique 195-206
Chacma baboons 682, **683**
Champagne Valley (SA) 431-2
chapas 241
cheetahs 681, 705-6, **681**
Chewa 742
Chikanka Island Camp (Zam) 589
children, travel with 718, 719
Malawi 163
Mozambique 233
Swaziland 546
Zambia 610
Zimbabwe 656
Chimanimani (Zim) 637-9
Chimanimani Mountains (Moz) 201
Chimanimani NP (Zim) 639-40
Chimanimani NR (Moz) 201
Chimfunshi Wildlife Orphanage (Zam) 604-5

Chimoio (Moz) 199-200
Chimpanzee Eden (SA) 471
chimpanzees 471, 604-5
chimurenga 698
Chingola (Zam) 604
Chintsa (SA) 401-3
Chipata (Zam) 577-8
Chirundu (Zam) 584-5
Chizumulu Island (Mal) 136
Chobe NP (B) 10, 58-65, **59**, **10**
Chobe Riverfront (B) 62-3
Chocas (Moz) 214-15
cholera 737
Choma (Zam) 589-90
Christianity 673-4
churches & cathedrals
    Cathedral of Nossa Senhora da Conceição (Maputo, Moz) 172
    Cathedral of Nossa Senhora de Conceição (Inhambane, Moz) 186
    Cathedral of Nossa Senhora de Fátima (Moz) 206
    Cathedral of St Peter (Mal) 135
    Christuskirche (N) 243
    Church of Santa Barbara (Zim) 630
    Church of the Vow (SA) 436
    Felsenkirche (N) 295
    Igreja da Misericórdia (Moz) 211
    Igreja de Nossa Senhora dos Remedios (Moz) 214-15
    Livingstonia Church (Mal) 128
    Mua Roman Catholic mission (Mal) 140
    St Barbara's Church (N) 259
    St Michael and All Angels Church (Mal) 149
Chuwanga (Moz) 217
cinema, see films
Clanwilliam (SA) 381-2
Clarens (SA) 448-9
climate 16, 21-4, see also individual countries
Cóbuè (Moz) 217-18, 219
Coffee Bay (SA) 403-4
consulates 718-19, see also individual countries
Copperbelt (Zam) 603-5
costs, see budgeting

Cradle of Humankind (SA) 463
crocodiles 707
Cuamba (Moz) 215-16
cultural villages
    Basotho Cultural Village (SA) 447
    Kabwata Cultural Village (Zam) 574
    Mantenga Cultural Village & Nature Reserve 534
    Njobvu Cultural Village (Mal) 144, 146
    Thaba-Bosiu (L) 105-6
culture 19-20, 671-8, see also individual countries
currency 16, 721
cycling 717, 731, see also individual countries

D
da Gama, Vasco 229
Daan Viljoen Game Park (N) 243
Damara language 743
Damaraland (N) 269-72
dance 676
    Gule Wamkulu 160
    Mozambique 231
dangers, see safe travel
De Hoop NR (SA) 365
de Klerk, FW 510
dengue fever 737-8
deserts 701
Devil's Pool (Zam) 554
diarrhoea 740
difaqane 669-70
disabilities, travellers with 724, see also individual countries
diving & snorkelling 716
    Cape Maclear (Mal) 141
    Cape Town (SA) 341
    Bazaruto Archipelago (Moz) 195
    Durban (SA) 412
    Lake Malawi (Mal) 141
    Likoma Island (Mal) 135
    Malawi 39, 162-3
    Margate (SA) 418
    Mossel Bay (SA) 371
    Mozambique 233
    Nkhata Bay (Mal) 133
    Pemba (Moz) 219, 221
    Ponta d'Ouro (Moz) 182
    Port Elizabeth (SA) 389
    Sodwana Bay (SA) 425

Tofo (Moz) 188
Vilankulo (Moz) 192
Dlinza Forest Reserve (SA) 420
dogs, wild 581
dolphins 182
Dorob NP (N) 275
Drakensberg (SA) 11, 427-35, **428**, **11**
Drakenstein Prison (SA) 362
drinking 678
driving, see car travel
driving licences 615
drums 697
Durban (SA) 406-17, **406**, **410**
    accommodation 412-13
    activities 411-12
    drinking 415
    entertainment 415
    food 413-15
    gay travellers 416
    lesbian travellers 416
    medical services 416
    nightlife 415
    safe travel 415-16
    shopping 415
    sights 408-10
    tourist information 416
    tours 412
    travel to/from 416-17
    travel within 417
Duwisib Castle (N) 293-4

E
eagles 690
East London (SA) 396-7
Eastern Cape (SA) 382-404, **383**
Eastern Delta (B) 72-3
Eastern Highlands (SA) 447-9
Eastern Highlands (Zim) 633-40
Eastern Zambia 577-84
economy 663
electricity 718, see also individual countries
Elephant Coast (SA) 421-7
elephants 392, 427, 567, 686, 703, **687**, **694**
Elim (SA) 487
embassies 718-19, see also individual countries
emergencies 17, see also safe travel
environment 663, 701-12, see also individual countries

environmental issues 709-12
Epupa Falls (N) 274
Erindi Private GR (N) 255
Erongo Mountains (N) 253-4
Erongo Mountain Rhino Sanctuary (N) 253
Eshowe (SA) 420-1
Etosha NP (N) 11, 260-4, **262**, **11**
events 21-4
exchange rates 721
Ezulwini Valley (S) 534-7, **535**

F
Falcon Ridge (SA) 431
Featherbed NR (SA) 375
Fernkloof NR (SA) 364
festivals 21-4
Fibwe Hide (Zam) 596
Ficksburg (SA) 449
films 662
Fish River Canyon (N) 10, 297-300, **10**
fishing 716-17
flamingos 286, 693
food 676-8, 718
forts
    Fort Nonqayi Museum Village (SA) 420
    Fort of São João Baptista (Moz) 224
    Fort of São Sebastião (Moz) 211, **13**
    German Fort & Museum (SA) 258
    Ladysmith (SA) 438
    Maputo (Moz) 172
foxes 689
Francistown (B) 50-3, **51**
Franklin GR (SA) 442
Franschhoek (SA) 360-2
Free State (SA) 440-9, **440**
fuel 615

G
Gaborone (B) 43-9, **46**, **49**
    accommodation 43, 46
    festivals 43
    food 47
    medical services 48
    safe travel 47
    shopping 47
    sights 43
    tourist information 48

Gaborone *continued*
  tours 43
  travel to/from 48
  travel within 48-9
Gaborone GR (B) 43
galleries, *see* art galleries, museums
game parks, *see* wildlife reserves & sanctuaries
Garden Route (SA) 371-8
Garden Route East (SA) 382-6
Garden Route NP (SA) 374
  Tsitsikamma section 384-5
Gauteng (SA) 449-71
gay travellers 719, *see also individual countries*
geography 701-2
George (SA) 373-4
Giant's Castle (SA) 432-3
Giant's Cup Trail (SA) 433
giraffes 686, 705, **679**, **686**
GLBTI travellers 719, *see also individual countries*
Goegap NR (SA) 505
Golden Gate Highlands NP (SA) 447-8
golf
  Blantyre (Mal) 149-50
  Bvumba Mountains (Zim) 636
  Durban (SA) 411
  George (SA) 374
  Lilongwe (Mal) 120
  Phalaborwa (SA) 489
Gonarezhou NP (Zim) 642-3
Gondwana Cañon Park (N) 300
Gorongosa NP (Moz) 199
gorge swing 553
goshawks 690, **691**
Graaff-Reinet (SA) 399-400
Grahamstown (SA) 393-5
Graskop (SA) 474-5
Great Rift Valley 701
Great Trek 506
Great Zimbabwe (Zim) 15, 640-2, **641**, **15**
greater galagos 682, **682**
Grootfontein (N) 258-9, **259**

Gule Wamkulu 160
Gurúè (Moz) 205-6
Gweta (B) 55

H
hamerkops 693, **693**
Harare (Zim) 619-29, **620**, **624**
  accommodation 621-2
  drinking 623
  entertainment 623-5
  festivals 621
  food 622-3
  medical services 627
  nightlife 623
  safe travel 626-7
  shopping 625-6
  sights 619-21
  tourist information 627
  travel to/from 627-8
  travel within 628-9
health 736-40
hepatitis 738
Herero language 743
Herero people 305-6
Hermanus (SA) 364-5
Highmoor NR (SA) 434
hiking 20, 37, 717
  Augrabies Falls NP (SA) 503
  Blyde River Canyon (SA) 474
  Botswana 88-9
  Camdeboo NP (SA) 401
  Cape Maclear (Mal) 141
  Cape of Good Hope 340
  Cape Town (SA) 340
  Chimanimani (Zim) 638
  De Hoop NR (SA) 365
  Drakensberg (SA) 427-9
  Fernkloof NR (SA) 364
  Fish River Canyon (N) 298-9
  Garden Route NP (SA) 384
  Giant's Cup Trail (SA) 433
  Golden Gate Highlands NP (SA) 447
  Gurúè (Moz) 206
  Hlane Royal NP (S) 542
  Hluhluwe-iMfolozi Park (SA) 422
  Ibo Island (Moz) 228
  Knysna (SA) 376
  Lake Malawi (Mal) 141
  Lesotho 114, 115
  Malawi 163

Malealea (L) 109
Malolotja NR (S) 541
Montagu (SA) 368
Mossell Bay (SA) 371
Mozambique 233
Mt Mulanje (Mal) 155
Namibia 312
Naukluft Mountains (N) 288-9
Quirimba Island (Moz) 228
Sani Top (L) 108
South Africa 519
Swaziland 546
Ts'ehlanyane NP (L) 105
Victoria Falls 551
Waterberg Plateau Park (N) 257-8
Zomba Plateau (Mal) 149
Himba language 743
Himba people 273, 305-6
Hinduism 674
hippopotamuses 686
historic sites, *see also* archaeological sites, rock art
  Drakenstein prison (SA) 362
  Isandlwana Battlefield (SA) 439
  Magersfontein (SA) 496
  Mgungundlovu (SA) 421
  Ngwenya Iron-Ore Mine (S) 540
  Ondini (SA) 421
  Robben Island (SA) 330-1
  Rorke's Drift Battlefield (SA) 439
  World's View (Malindidzimu Hill, Zim) 647
history 664-70, *see also individual countries*
hitching 735
HIV 662-3, 672-3, 738
Hlane Royal NP (S) 541-2
Hluhluwe-iMfolozi Park (SA) 422-3
Hogsback (SA) 397-8
holidays 722, *see also individual counties*
horse riding 37, 717
  Botswana 89
  iSimangaliso Wetland Park (SA) 423
  Mozambique 193
  Port Alfred (SA) 395
  Royal Natal NP (SA) 430

Swakopmund (N) 280
Swellendam (SA) 366
Victoria Falls 551
hot springs
  Avalon Springs (SA) 368
  Bela-Bela (SA) 484-5
  Ezulwini Valley (S) 534
  Fish River Canyon 299
  Kapishya Hot Springs 599
hunting 308, 706
hunting dogs 689, 705
Hwange NP (Zim) 647-50, **648**
hyenas 689, **689**

I
Ibo Island (Moz) 224-5
Ibo Island coffee 226
Imire: Rhino & Wildlife Conservation (Zim) 629
immigration, *see individual countries*
impalas 685, **685**
Inhaca Island (Moz) 181
Inhambane (Moz) 186-8, **187**
Inkwenkwezi GR (SA) 401
Inner Delta (B) 73-4
insurance 719-20
  health 736
  vehicle 733
internet access 611, 720, *see also individual countries*
internet resources 17
  health 737
  travel advisories 723
Isandlwana (SA) 439
iSimangaliso Wetland Park (SA) 423-7
Islam 674
itineraries 25-30

J
Jeffreys Bay (SA) 386-8
jet boating 551
Johannesburg (SA) 449-64, **450**, **452**, **456**
  accommodation 457-8
  courses 457
  drinking 460-1
  entertainment 461
  food 458-60
  medical services 462
  nightlife 460-1
  safe travel 461-2
  shopping 461

sights 450-5
tourist information 462
tours 455-6
travel to/from 462-3
travel within 463-4
Jonathan, Chief Leabua
112
Judaism 674

K
Kafue NP (Zam) 590-3
Kalahari (B) 76-81
kalindula 699
Kamberg NR (SA) 434
Kamkwamba, William 161
Kaokoveld (N) 272-5
Kapiri Mposhi (Zam) 603
Kariba (Zim) 629-31
Kariba Dam (Zam) 588
Karonga (Mal) 126-8
Karoo (SA) 379, 398-401
Kasama (Zam) 600
Kasane (B) 60-2, **60**
Kasanka NP (Zam) 596-7
Katima Mulilo (N) 267
Katutura (N) 246
kayaking 551, *see also*
  canoeing, *mokoro* trips,
  rafting
  Cape Maclear (Mal) 141
  Cape Town (SA) 340
  Durban (SA) 311-12
  Garden Route NP (SA)
  384
  Knysna (SA) 376
  Lake Malawi (Mal) 141
  Nkhaya Bay (Mal) 133
  South Africa 518-19
  St Lucia (SA) 426
  Victoria Falls 551
  Walvis Bay (N) 284
Kazungula (B) 60
Keetmanshoop (N) 293
Kgalagadi Transfrontier
  Park (B) 12, 79-81, **12**
Kgalagadi Transfrontier
  Park (SA) 12, 501-2,
  502
Khama Rhino Sanctuary
  (B) 50
Khama, Sir Seretse 83
Khaudum NP (N) 265
Khoe-San people 665-6
Khutse GR (B) 79, **78**
Kimberley (SA) 495-9
kitesurfing 193, 718
Kitwe (Zam) 604
klipspringers 685, **685**

Knysna (SA) 374-7, **375**
Kosi Bay (SA) 424
Kruger NP (SA) 11, 476-81,
  478, **11**
Kubu Island (B) 58
Kuomboka ceremony
  (Zam) 595
kwaito 699
kwasa kwasa 699-700
KwaZulu-Natal (SA) 404-
  40, **405**

L
Ladysmith (SA) 438
Lake Kariba (Zam) 588-9
Lake Malawi (Mal) 15,
  140-4, **15**
Lake Malawi (Moz) 217
Lake Niassa (Moz) 217-18,
  219
Lake Sibaya (SA) 424-5
Lake Tanganyika (Zam)
  601-2
languages 16
  !Kung San 743-4
  Afrikaans 741-2
  Chewa 742
  clicking 743
  Damara 743
  Herero 743
  Himba 743
  Lozi 744
  Nama 743
  Ndebele 744
  Northern Sotho (Sepedi)
  744
  Owambo 745
  Portuguese 745-6
  Shona 746
  Southern Sotho
  (Sesotho) 747
  Swati 747
  Tsonga 747
  Tswana 747-8
  Venda 748
  Xhosa 748
  Zulu 748
legal matters 720
leopards 681, **680**
lesbian travellers 719, *see*
  also individual countries
Lesotho 38, 97-117, **98**
  accommodation 14,
  97, 114
  activities 114
  business hours 115
  climate 97
  consulates 115

culture 112-13
embassies 115
environment 113-14
food 97
gay travellers 115
highlights 98
history 111-12
holidays 116
language 747
lesbian travellers 115
literature 113
money 115
national parks 113
opening hours 115
public holidays 116
safe travel 115
telephone services 116
time 116
tourist information 116
transport to/from 116
transport within 116-17
visas 116
weather 97
wildlife 113
women in Lesotho 113
Letaba Valley (SA) 488
Lichinga (Moz) 216
Likoma Island (Mal) 135-6
lilac-breasted rollers 693
Lilayi Elephant Nursery
  (Zam) 567
Lilongwe (Mal) 120-6, **122**
  accommodation 120
  drinking 121
  entertainment 121
  food 121
  information 124
  shopping 121-4
  sights 120
  travel to/from 124-6
  travel within 126
Lilongwe Wildlife Centre
  (Mal) 120
Limbe (Mal) 149-54
Limpopo (SA) 481-9, **482**
Limpopo NP (Moz) 184-6
Linyanti Marshes (B) 64-5
lions 681, 704, **680**
literature, *see* books
Liuwa Plain NP (Zam) 594
Livingstone, David 159
Livingstone (Zam) 554-9,
  556
  accommodation 555-7
  drinking 558
  food 557-8
  immigration 558

information 558
medical services 558
safe travel 558
shopping 558
sights 554
tourist information 558
tours 554-5
travel to/from 558
travel within 559
Livingstonia (Mal) 128-9
Liwonde (Mal) 144-6
Liwonde NP (Mal) 144-6
Liwonde Rhino Sanctuary
  (Mal) 146
Lobamba (S) 537
Lochinvar NP (Zam) 590
Lower Zambezi NP (Zam)
  585-8, **586**
Lozi language 744
Luambe NP (Zam) 583
Lüderitz (N) 294-7, **296**
Lusaka (Zam) 567-77,
  572-3
  accommodation 567-71
  drinking 571-4
  food 571
  immigration 575
  internet access 575
  medical services 575
  money 575
  nightlife 571-4
  safe travel 575
  shopping 574-5
  tourist information 575
  travel to/from 575-7
  travel within 577
Lusaka NP (Zam) 567

M
Macaneta Beach (Moz)
  181-2
Madikwe GR (SA) 493-4
Mafeteng (L) 110
magazines 716
Mahango GR (N) 267
Mahikeng (SA) 494-5
Maitisong Festival 21
Majete WR (Mal) 157-8
Makgadikgadi Pans NP (B)
  55-7, **56**
malaria 738-9
Malawi 39, 118-68, **119**
  accommodation 118, 162
  activities 162, 162-3
  children, travel with 163
  climate 118
  consulates 163

Malawi continued
culture 161
embassies 163
environmental issues 162
food 118, 163
highlights 119
history 158-61
holidays 164
internet access 163
language 742
literature 161
money 163-4
national parks 162
opening hours 163
politics 158
safe travel 164
telephone services 164
time 165
tourist information 165
travel seasons 118
travel to/from 165-7
travel within 167-8
visas 165
volunteering 165
weather 118
Malealea (L) 109-10
Malkerns Valley (S) 537-8
Malolotja NR (S) 541
Mana Pools NP (Zim) 632
Mandela, Nelson 331, 362, 464, 509-13
Manguang Township (SA) 442
Manica (Moz) 200-1
Mantenga Cultural Village NR (S) 534
Manzini (S) 539-40
maps 720
Mapungubwe NP (SA) 486
Maputo (Moz) 172-81, **174-5**
accommodation 173-8
drinking 179
entertainment 179
festivals & events 173
food 178-9
immigration 179
internet access 179
medical services 179
money 179
nightlife 179
safe travel 179-80
shopping 179

sights 172-3
tours 173
travel agencies 180
travel to/from 180
travel within 180-1
Maputo Special Reserve (Moz) 185
Marakele NP (SA) 485
Margate (SA) 418
markets
Avondale Flea Market (Zim) 626
Ezulwini Craft Market (S) 536-7
Joziburg Lane (SA) 455
Lilongwe Craft Market (Mal) 123-4
Lusaka City Market (Zam) 567
Lusaka Sunday Market (Zam) 576-7
Manzini Market (S) 539
Maputo Municipal Market (Moz) 172
Market on Main (SA) 461
Mbare Market (Zim) 626
Nampula Sunday Morning Craft Market (Moz) 208
Neighbourgoods Market (Cape Town, SA) 352-3
Neighbourgoods Market (Johannesburg, SA) 461
Old Breweries Craft Market (N) 251
Route 44 Market (SA) 358
Salaula Clothing Market (Zam) 574
South African Market (SA) 352
V&A Food Market (SA) 348
Victoria Street Market (SA) 415
Marloth NR (SA) 366
marrabenta 231, 700
Marracuene (Moz) 181-2
Maseru (L) 100-3, **102**
Masire, Sir Ketumile 83
Massinga (Moz) 191
Masvingo (Zim) 640
Matemo (Moz) 225
Matobo NP (Zim) 646-7
Matusadona NP (Zim) 631-2
Maun (B) 65-72, **68**

Mavuradonha Wilderness (Zim) 633
Maxixe (Moz) 190-1
Mbabane (S) 532-4, **532**
Mbala (Zam) 600-1
Mbeki, Thabo 512
measures 716
media 716
medical services 737, see also individual countries
Medjumbe (Moz) 225
meerkats 689, **688**
Metangula (Moz) 217
Midlands (SA) 435-8
Midlands (Zim) 640-3
Mkhaya GR (S) 15, 543-4, **15**
Mlawula NR (S) 542-3
Mlilwane WS (S) 539
mobile phones 16, 723
Moçimboa da Praia (Moz) 226-7
Mocuba (Moz) 205
Mohale's Hoek (L) 110
Mokala NP (SA) 499-500
Mokhotlong (L) 107
Mokolodi NR (B) 49-50
Mokopane (SA) 484
mokoro trips 70, 716
money 16, 17, 720-2, see also budgeting, individual countries
moneychangers 721
Mongu (Zam) 593-4
Monkey Bay (Mal) 140
monkeys 682
Monk's Cowl (SA) 431-2
Montagu (SA) 368-9
Montepuez (Moz) 219
Moremi GR (B) 74-6, **75**
Morija (L) 103-4
Morrungulo (Moz) 191
Moshoeshoe the Great 111
Mosi-oa-Tunya NP (Zam) 554, **562**
Mossel Bay (SA) 371-3, **372**
motorcycle travel, see car travel
mountain biking 717
movies, see films
Mozambique 39, 169-241, **170-1**
accommodation 169, 233
activities 233
budgeting 234
business hours 233
children, travel with 233
consulates 234

dance 231
electricity 233
embassies 234
environmental issues 232
food 169, 231
highlights 170-1
history 228-31
holidays 235
internet access 234
language 747
literature 231
money 234-5
music 231
national parks 232
opening hours 233
politics 228
public holidays 235
safe travel 197, 235
telephone services 235-6
time 236
travel seasons 169
travel to/from 236-9
travel within 239-41
visas 236
Mozambique Island (Moz) 13, 210-14, **210**, **13**
Mpika (Zam) 599
Mpulungu (Zam) 601-2
Mpumalanga (SA) 471-6, **470**
Mswati III 544
Mt Mulanje (Mal) 155-7
Mt Namúli (Moz) 206
Mua (Mal) 140
Mueda (Moz) 227
Mugabe, Robert 652-4
Mukuvisi Woodlands Environmental Centre (Zim) 620-1
Mulanje (Mal) 154-7
Murrébuè (Moz) 223-4
museums, see also art galleries
Afrikaans Language Museum (SA) 362
Anglo-Boer War Museum (SA) 442
Apartheid Museum (SA) 455
Bulawayo Railway Museum (Zim) 643
Centenary Centre (SA) 422
Chamare Museum (Mal) 140
Constitution Hill (SA) 454
Copperbelt Museum (Zam) 603

CP Nel Museum (SA) 369

Cultural Village (L) 105-6

Dias Museum Complex (SA) 371

District Six Museum (SA) 337

Drostdy Museum (SA) 366

East London Museum (SA) 396

Fort Nongqayi Museum Village (SA) 420

Geology Museum (Moz) 200-1

German Fort & Museum (N) 258

Great Zimbabwe Museum (Zim) 641-2

Hector Pieterson Museum (SA) 464

Henry Tayali Visual Arts Centre (Zam) 567

Himeville Museum (SA) 434

Independence Memorial Museum (N) 243

International Library of African Music (SA) 394

Iziko Slave Lodge (SA) 326

KwaMuhle Museum (SA) 409

Living Hunter's Museum of the Ju/'Hoansi (N) 269

Lusaka National Museum (Zam) 567

Mafikeng Museum (SA) 494

Masitise Cave House Museum (L) 110-11

McGregor Museum (SA) 497

Michaelis Collection at the Old Town House (SA) 326

Morija Museum & Archives (L) 103

Moto Moto Museum (Zam) 600-1

Msunduzi Museum (SA) 436

Museu de Arte Sacra (Moz) 211

Museu Nacional de Etnografia (Moz) 207

Museum Africa (SA) 454

Museum of Malawi (Mal) 149

Mutare Museum (Zim) 633

Mzuzu Museum (Mal) 131

Namwandwe Gallery (Zam) 567

National Archives of Zimbabwe (Zim) 619-20

National Art Museum (Moz) 172

National English Literary Museum (SA) 394

National Money Museum (Moz) 172-3

National Museum (S) 537

National Museum & Art Gallery (B) 43

National Museum of Namibia (N) 243-6

Natural History Museum (Moz) 173

Natural History Museum (Zim) 643

Natural Science Museum (SA) 408

Nayuma Museum (Zam) 593

Ncome Museum (SA) 440

Observatory Museum (SA) 393-4

Old Courthouse Museum (SA) 409

Outeniqua Transport Museum (SA) 373

Owela Museum (N) 246

Palace & Chapel of São Paulo (Moz) 211

Port Natal Maritime Museum (SA) 409

Pretoria Art Museum (SA) 467

SAB World of Beer (SA) 454

Siege Museum (SA) 438

South African Jewish Museum (SA) 327

South African Museum (SA) 327

Stone House Museum (Mal) 128

Swakopmund Museum (N) 279

Tsumeb Mining Museum (N) 259

Tzaneen Museum (SA) 488

Urquhart House (SA) 399

Whale House Museum (SA) 364

Zeitz MOCAA Museum (SA) 331

music 231, 695-700

festivals 21-4, 696

Musina (SA) 486-7

Musina NR (SA) 486

Mutare (Zim) 633-5, **634**

Mutinondo Wilderness (Zam) 598-9

Mzuzu (Mal) 131-2, **132**

N

Nama language 743

Namakwa (SA) 503-5

Namibia 39, 242-321, **244**

accommodation 242, 311-12

activities 312-13

architecture 307

business hours 316

children, travel with 313

climate 242

consulates 314-15

culture 305-7

customs regulations 313

disabilities, travellers with 317

economy 307

embassies 314-15

environment 307-11

food 242

gay travellers 315

highlights 244

history 301-5

holidays 316

internet access 315

language 743-4, 745

lesbian travellers 315

money 315-16

national parks 310, 311

opening hours 316

postal services 316

public holidays 316

safe travel 313-14

telephone services 316-17

tourist information 317

travel to/from 317-19

travel within 319-21

visas 317

weather 242

wildlife 308-10

women travellers 317

Namib-Naukluft Park (N) 286-92, **288**

NamibRand NR (N) 292

Nampula (Moz) 206-10, **208**

Nata (B) 54-5

Nata Bird Sanctuary (B) 54

National Arts Festival (SA) 23

national parks & nature reserves 710, 712, see also wilderness areas, wildlife reserves & sanctuaries

Addo Elephant NP (SA) 392-3

Agulhas NP (SA) 367

Augrabies Falls NP (SA) 503

Baviaanskloof Wilderness Area (SA) 384

Blyde River Canyon NR (SA) 474

Bokong NR (L) 105

Bontebok NR (SA) 367

Bwabwata NP (N) 266-8

Camdeboo NP (SA) 400-1

Cathedral Peak NR (SA) 431

Cecil Kop Wildlife & NR (Zim) 633

Cederberg Wilderness Area (SA) 380

Chimanimani NR (Moz) 201

Chimanimani NP (Zim) 639-40

Chobe NP (B) 10, 58-65, **59**, **10**

De Hoop NR (SA) 365

Dlinza Forest Reserve (SA) 420

Dorob NP (N) 275

Etosha NP (N) 11, 260-4, **262**, **11**

Featherbed NR (SA) 375

Fernkloof NR (SA) 364

Garden Route NP (SA) 374, 384-5

Goegap NR (SA) 505

Golden Gate Highlands NP (SA) 447-8

Gonarezhou NP (Zim) 642-3

Gondwana Cañon Park (N) 300

Gorongosa NP (Moz) 199

Highmoor NR (SA) 434

Hlane Royal NP (S) 541-2

national parks & nature reserves continued
Hluhluwe-iMfolozi Park (SA) 422-3
Hwange NP (Zim) 647-50, **648**
iSimangaliso Wetland Park (SA) 423-7
Kafue NP (Zam) 590-3
Kamberg NR (SA) 434
Kasanka NP (Zam) 596-7
Khaudum NP (N) 265
Kruger NP (SA) 11, 476-81, **478**, **11**
Limpopo NP (Moz) 184-6
Liuwa Plain NP (Zam) 594
Liwonde NP (Mal) 144-6
Lochinvar NP (Zam) 590
Lower Zambezi NP (Zam) 585-8, **586**
Luambe NP (Zam) 583
Lusaka NP (Zam) 567
Makgadikgadi Pans NP (B) 55-7, **56**
Malolotja NR (S) 541
Mana Pools NP (Zim) 632
Mantenga Cultural Village NR (S) 534
Mapungubwe NP (SA) 486
Maputo Special Reserve (Moz) 185
Marakele NP (SA) 485
Marloth NR (SA) 366
Matobo NP (Zim) 646-7
Matusadona NP (Zim) 631-2
Mlawula NR (S) 542-3
Mokala NP (SA) 499-500
Mokolodi NR (B) 49-50
Mosi-oa-Tunya NP (Zam) 554, **562**
Musina NR (SA) 486
Namib-Naukluft Park (N) 286-92, **288**
NamibRand NR (N) 292
Niassa Reserve (Moz) 218-19
Nkasa Rupara NP (N) 267-8
Nkhotakota WR (Mal) 138-9

North Luangwa NP (Zam) 584
Nsumbu NP (Zam) 602
Nxai Pans NP (B) 57-8, **56**
Nyanga NP (Zim) 636-7
Nyika NP (Mal) 129-30, **130**
Okonjima NR (N) 255-6
Oribi Gorge NR (SA) 418
Phophonyane NR (S) 543
Pilanesberg NP (SA) 492-3
Royal Natal NP (SA) 429-30
Sehlabathebe NP (L) 109
Silvermine NR (SA) 335
South Luangwa NP (Zam) 578-84, **579**
Southern Drakensberg Wilderness Area (SA) 434
Table Mountain NP (SA) 339
Ts'ehlanyane NP (L) 105
uKhahlamba-Drakensberg Park (SA) 11, 427-35, **11**
Victoria Falls NP (Zim) 559
Waterberg Plateau Park (N) 257-8
West Coast NP (SA) 380
Zambezi NP (Zim) 559
Nature's Valley (SA) 382-4
Naukluft Mountains (N) 287-9, **287**
Ndebele language 744
Ndola (Zam) 603-4
Ndumo GR (SA) 427
Nelspruit (Mbombela, SA) 471-3, **472**
newspapers 716
Ngonye Falls (Zam) 595-6
Ngwenya (S) 540
Niassa Reserve (Moz) 218-19
Nkasa Rupara NP (N) 267-8
Nkhata Bay (Mal) 133-5, **134**
Nkhotakota (Mal) 137-9
Nkhotakota WR (Mal) 138-9
Nkwichi Lodge (Moz) 219
Noordoewer (N) 300-1
North Luangwa NP (Zam) 584

North West Province (SA) 489-95
Northern Cape (SA) 495-505, **496**
Northern Malawi 126-36, **127**
Northern Mozambique 206-28
Northern Sotho language 744
Northern Tuli GR (B) 53
Northern Zambia 596-602
Nsumbu NP (Zam) 602-16
Nxai Pans NP (B) 57-8, **56**
Nyae Nyae Conservancy (N) 268-9
Nyanga NP (Zim) 636-7
Nyika NP (Mal) 129-30, **130**

O
Okavango Delta (B) 8, 65-76, 85, **66**, **8**
Okonjima NR (N) 255-6
Oktoberfest (N) 23-4
Omaruru (N) 254-5
opening hours 722
Opuwo (N) 273
Oribi Gorge NR (SA) 418
ostriches 369-70, 693, **693**
Otjiwarongo (N) 256
Oudtshoorn (SA) 369-71
Overberg (SA) 364-7
overlanding 729, 732
Owambo language 745
Owambo people 305
Oxbow (L) 106-7

P
Paarl (SA) 362-3
palaces
Lealui Palace (Zam) 593
Palace & Chapel of Sao Paulo (Moz) 211
pale chanting goshawks 690, **691**
Palma (Moz) 227-8
Palmwag (N) 272
paragliding 340
Parys (SA) 446-7
passports, see individual countries
Pemba (Moz) 219-23, **220**
penguins 693, **692**
Phalaborwa (SA) 488-9
Phophonyane NR (S) 543
Pietermaritzburg (SA) 435-8, **436**

Pilanesberg NP (SA) 492-3
planning
budgeting 17
calendar of events 21-4
health 736-7
internet resources 17
itineraries 25-30
safaris 31-7
Southern Africa basics 16-17
travel seasons 16, 21-4
plants 232, 708-9
Plettenberg Bay (SA) 377-8
poaching 709-10
politics 662, see also individual countries
Polokwane (SA) 481-4
Polokwane GR (SA) 481
Pomene (Moz) 191
Ponta d'Ouro (Moz) 182-4
Ponta Malongane (Moz) 182-4
population 663
Port Alfred (SA) 395-6
Port Elizabeth (SA) 388-92, **390**
Port St Johns (SA) 404
Portuguese 745-6
postal services 722
Pretoria (SA) 465-71, **466**
primates 682
Prince Albert (SA) 379
public holidays 722

Q
quad biking
Clarens (SA) 448
Swakopmund (N) 279
Victoria Falls 551
Quelimane (Moz) 203-5, **204**
Quilaluia (Moz) 226
Quirimba Island (Moz) 226, 228
Quirimbas Archipelago (Moz) 13, 224-6, **13**
Quthing 110-11

R
rabies 739
rafting 716, see also canoeing, kayaking, mokoro trips
Augrabies Falls NP (SA) 503
Clarens (SA) 448
Mkhaya GR (S) 543
Namibia 312

Noordoewer (N) 300-1
Nyanga NP (Zim) 637
Parys (SA) 446
South Africa 518-19
Victoria Falls 551-2
Ramsgate (SA) 418
religion 663, 673-4
rhinoceroses 50, 146, 686, 703-4, **686**
Rhodes, Cecil 636, 651
river cruises 552
Robben Island (SA) 330-1
rock art 665
  Bathplug Cave (SA) 433
  Brandberg (N) 270-1
  Cathedral Peak NR (SA) 431
  Chimanimani NP (Zim) 640
  Chinamapere Rock Paintings (Moz) 200
  Giant's Castle (SA) 432
  Main Cave (SA) 432
  Matobo NP (Zim) 647
  Royal Natal NP (SA) 430
  Sevilla Rock Art Trail (SA) 381
  Twyfelfontein (N) 271
  Wildebeest Kuil Rock Art Centre (SA) 495-6
rock climbing 717-18
Roma (L) 104
Rorke's Drift (SA) 439
Route 62 (SA) 367-71
Royal Natal NP (SA) 429-30
Rundu (N) 264-5, **265**
Rustenburg (SA) 490-1

S
Sabie (SA) 475-6
safaris 18, 31-7, see also individual locations
safe travel 722-3, see also individual locations
samango monkeys 682, **683**
Samfya (Zam) 598
San people 77, 84
Sani Pass (SA) 433-4
Sani Top (L) 107-8
Savuti (B) 63-4
scams 722
scenic flights
  Cape Town (SA) 340
  Okavango Delta (B) 67-8
  Swakopmund (N) 280
  Victoria Falls 552

seals 275, 689, **689**
secretary birds 690, **690**
Sehlabathebe NP (L) 109
Semonkong (L) 108-9
Senanga (Zam) 594-5
Senga Bay (Mal) 139-40
Sepedi language 744
Serenje (Zam) 596
Sesheke (Zam) 596
Sesotho language 747
Sesriem (N) 289-91, **290**
shipwrecks 276
Shiwa Ng'andu (Zam) 599-600
Shona language 746
Siavonga (Zam) 588-9
Silvermine NR (SA) 335
Sinazongwe (Zam) 589
sitatunga antelopes 685
Skeleton Coast (N) 275-7
Skeleton Coast Park (N) 276-7
Skeleton Coast Wilderness Area (N) 277
skiing 106
slavery 158-9
Smith, Ian 652
smoking 716
Smuts, Jan 508
snakes 707-8, 740
snorkelling, see diving & snorkelling
Sobhuza II 537
Sodwana Bay (SA) 425
Solitaire (N) 291-2
Songo (Moz) 203
Sossusvlei (N) 12, 289-91, **290**, **12**
South Africa 39, 322-529, **324**
  accommodation 322, 518, 519
  activities 518-20
  arts 515-16
  business hours 522
  climate 322
  consulates 520-1
  culture 513-16
  customs regulations 520
  economy 513
  embassies 520-1
  emergencies 521
  environment 516-18
  food 322
  gay travellers 521
  highlights 324
  history 506-13
  holidays 522

internet access 521
language 741-2, 744, 747-8
lesbian travellers 521
money 521-2
national parks 517
opening hours 522
peoples 513-15
postal services 522
public holidays 522
religion 515
safe travel 520
telephone services 522
tourist information 522
travel seasons 322
travel to/from 523-5
travel within 525-9
visas 522-3
volunteering 523
weather 322
wildlife 516-17, 520
South Luangwa NP (Zam) 14, 578-84, **579**, **14**
  accommodation 579-82
  food 583
  shopping 583
  travel to/from 583
  travel within 583-4
  wildlife 581
Southbroom (SA) 418
Southern Drakensberg Wilderness Area (SA) 434
Southern Malawi 144-58, **145**
Southern Mozambique 182-95
Southern Sotho language 747
Southern Zambia 584-90
Soweto (SA) 464-5
Spitzkoppe (N) 270
spotted hyenas 689, **689**
Springbok (SA) 504-5
St Lucia (SA) 425-6
steam trains 552-3
Stellenbosch (SA) 355-9, **356**
Storms River (SA) 385-6
Sun City (SA) 491-2
Sunshine Coast (SA) 386-92
surfing 718
  Cape Town (SA) 340
  Jeffreys Bay (SA) 386
  Mossel Bay (SA) 371
  Plettenberg Bay (SA) 378

Port Elizabeth (SA) 388-9
Swakopmund (N) 277-83, **278**
  accommodation 281
  activities 279-81
  food 281-2
  medical services 283
  safe travel 282-3
  shopping 282
  sights 279
  tourist information 283
Swartland (SA) 379-82
Swati language 747
Swazi Candles (S) 538
Swaziland 40, 530-48, **531**
  accommodation 530, 546
  activities 546
  business hours 547
  children, travel with 546
  climate 530
  consulates 546
  economy 545
  embassies 546
  environment 545
  food 530
  gay travellers 547
  highlights 531
  history 544-5
  internet access 547
  language 747
  lesbian travellers 547
  money 547
  opening hours 547
  postal services 547
  safe travel 546
  telephone services 547
  time 547
  tourist information 547-8
  travel seasons 530
  travel to/from 548
  travel within 548
  visas 548
  weather 530
Swellendam (SA) 366-7
swings 553

T
Table Mountain (SA) 326, 339
Table Mountain NP (SA) 339
taxes 721
telephone services 16, 723, see also individual countries

Tembe Elephant Park (SA) 427
Tengenenge Art Community (Zim) 631
Tete (Moz) 201-2
Thaba-Bosiu (L) 104-6
Thokozisa (SA) 431
timbila orchestra 231
time zones 16, 723
tipping 721
Tofinho (Moz) 190
Tofo (Moz) 188-90
toilets 723-4
tourist information 724, see also individual countries
tours 729-30, see also safaris
train travel 552-3, 735, see also individual countries
transfrontier parks 708
|Ai-|Ais/Richtersveld Transfrontier Park (SA) 504
Great Limpopo Transfrontier Park (Zim) 642
Kgalagadi Transfrontier Park (B) 12, 79-81, **12**
Kgalagadi Transfrontier Park (SA) 12, 501-2, **502**
travel advisories 235
travel to/from Southern Africa 727-30
travel within Southern Africa 730-5
travellers cheques 722
trekking, see hiking
trophy hunting 308, 706
Truth & Reconciliation Commission 512
Ts'ehlanyane NP (L) 105
Tsonga 747
tsteste flies 612
Tsumeb (N) 259-60, **260**
Tsumkwe (N) 268-9
Tswana 747-8
Tswana people 84
tuberculosis 739
Tuli Block (B) 53-4
Tutu, Archbishop Desmond 464
Twyfelfontein (N) 271-2
typhoid 739
Tzaneen (SA) 488

U
uKhahlamba-Drakensberg Park (SA) 11, 427-35, **11**
Ulundi (SA) 421
uMdloti Beach (SA) 419
Umgeni River Bird Park (SA) 409
Umhlanga Dance 23
Umhlanga Rocks (SA) 419
uMkhuze GR (SA) 426-7
Upington (SA) 500-1

V
vaccinations 736
Valley of the Olifants (SA) 487-9
vegetarian travellers 678
Venda 748
Venda language (SA) 487
vervet monkeys 485, 682, **682**
Victoria Falls 8, 549-65, **550**, **8**
  access 555
  accommodation 549
  activities 550-3
  food 549
  highlights 550
  travel seasons 549, 552
  Zambia 553-9
  Zimbabwe 559-65
Victoria Falls (Zimbabwe) 559-65, **560**, **562**
Victoria Falls World Heritage National Monument Site (Zam) 554
Vilankulo (Moz) 192-4, **192**
Viphya Plateau (Mal) 136-7
visas 16, 724-5, see also individual countries
visual arts 676
volunteering 725, see also individual countries
Vredefort Dome (SA) 446
vultures 690, **690**
Vwaza Marsh WR (Mal) 130-1

W
walking, see hiking
Walvis Bay (N) 283-6, **284**
water 740
Waterberg (SA) 485
Waterberg Plateau Park (N) 257-8
waterfalls

Augrabies Falls (SA) 503
Bridal Veil Falls (Zim) 637
Epupa Falls (N) 274
Gurúè (Moz) 206
Kalambo Falls (Zam) 602
Ketane Falls (L) 108
Manchewe Falls (Mal) 128
Mtarazi Falls (Zim) 636
Ngonye Falls (Zam) 595-6
Sabie (SA) 475
Victoria Falls NP (Zim) 559
Victoria Falls World Heritage National Monument Site (Zam) 554
weather 16, 21-4, see also individual countries
websites, see internet resources
weights 716
West Coast NP (SA) 380
Western Cape (SA) 355-82
Western Zambia 590-6
Wild is Life (Zim) 619
Wild Coast (SA) 401-4, **402**
wild dogs 581
wildebeest 685, **684**
wilderness areas
  Baviaanskloof Wilderness Area (SA) 384
  Cederberg Wilderness Area (SA) 380
  Mavuradonha Wilderness (Zim) 633
  Mutinondo Wilderness (Zam) 598-9
  Southern Drakensberg Wilderness Area (SA) 434
wildlife 34, 232, 679-94, 702, see also individual species
wildlife reserves & sanctuaries, see also national parks & nature reserves, wilderness areas
  Bambelela (SA) 485
  Birds of Eden (SA) 377
  Boulders Penguin Colony (SA) 335
  Cape Cross Seal Reserve (N) 275-6
  Cecil Kop Wildlife & NR (Zim) 633

Central Kalahari GR (B) 76-8, **78**
Chimfunshi Wildlife Orphanage (Zam) 604-5
Chimpanzee Eden (SA) 471
Daan Viljoen GP (N) 243
Erindi Private GR (N) 255
Erongo Mountain Rhino Sanctuary (N) 253
Falcon Ridge (SA) 431
Franklin GR (SA) 442
Gaborone GR (B) 43
Imire: Rhino & Wildlife Conservation (Zim) 629
Inkwenkwezi GR (SA) 401
Khama Rhino Sanctuary (B) 50
Khutse GR (B) 79, **78**
Lilayi Elephant Nursery (Zam) 567
Lilongwe Wildlife Centre (Mal) 120
Liwonde Rhino Sanctuary (Mal) 146
Madikwe GR (SA) 493-4
Mahango GR (N) 267
Majete WR (Mal) 157-8
Marine Rehabilitation & Education Centre (SA) 388
Mkhaya GR (S) 543-4, **15**
Mlilwane WS (S) 539
Monkeyland (SA) 377
Moremi GR (B) 74-6
Mukuvisi Woodlands Environmental Centre (Zim) 620-1
Nata Bird Sanctuary (B) 54
Ndumo GR (SA) 427
Nkhotakota WR (Mal) 138-9
Northern Tuli GR (B) 53
Polokwane GR (SA) 481
Tembe Elephant Park (SA) 427
Umgeni River Bird Park (SA) 409
uMkhuze GR (SA) 426-7
Vwaza Marsh Wildlife Reserve (Mal) 130-1
Wild is Life (Zim) 619
Windhoek (N) 243-53, **247**, **248**

accommodation 247-9
drinking 251
festivals 246
food 249-50
medical services 252
nightlife 251
safe travel 251-2
shopping 251
sights 243-6
tourist information 252
tours 246
travel to/from 252-3
travel within 253
Winelands (SA) 12, 355-63, **12**
witchcraft 674
white-water rafting, see rafting
women travellers 725-6
work 726

X
Xai-Xai (Moz) 186
Xhosa 748

Y
yellow fever 739

Z
Zalala Beach (Moz) 205
Zambezi NP (Zim) 559
Zambia 40, 566-616, **568-9**
  accommodation 566, 610
  activities 610
  animals 609
  budgeting 610, 612
  business hours 610
  children, travel with 610
  climate 566
  consulates 611
  disabilities, travellers with 658
  electricity 610
  embassies 611
  environmental issues 608
  food 566
  highlights 568-9
  history 605-8
  holidays 612
  internet access 611
  language 742, 744
  money 611-12
  national parks 610
  opening hours 610
  people 608
  plants 609-10
  politics 605
  public holidays 612
  safe travel 612
  telephone services 612
  time 612
  tourist information 612
  tours 616
  travel seasons 566
  travel to/from 613-14
  travel within 614-16
  visas 612-13
  volunteering 613
  weather 566
zebras 581, 686, **687**
Zimbabwe 40, 617-60, **618**
  accommodation 617, 656
  activities 656
  arts 655
  children, travel with 656
  climate 617
  culture 654
  customs regulations 656
  embassies 656-7
  emergencies 657
  environment 655-6
  food 617
  gay travellers 627, 657
  highlights 618
  history 651-4
  holidays 658
  internet access 657
  language 744, 746
  lesbian travellers 627, 657
  money 653, 657
  postal services 658
  public holidays 658
  safe travel 656
  telephone services 658
  time 658
  tourist information 658
  travel seasons 617
  travel to/from 659-60
  travel within 660
  visas 658
  volunteering 658-9
  weather 617
  wildlife 655
ziplining 553
Zomba (Mal) 146-7
Zomba Plateau (Mal) 147-8, **148**
Zulu language 748
Zululand (SA) 419-21
Zuma, Jacob 612

Map Legend

Sights

- Beach
- Bird Sanctuary
- Buddhist
- Castle/Palace
- Christian
- Confucian
- Hindu
- Islamic
- Jain
- Jewish
- Monument
- Museum/Gallery/Historic Building
- Ruin
- Shinto
- Sikh
- Taoist
- Winery/Vineyard
- Zoo/Wildlife Sanctuary
- Other Sight

Activities, Courses & Tours

- Bodysurfing
- Diving
- Canoeing/Kayaking
- Course/Tour
- Sento Hot Baths/Onsen
- Skiing
- Snorkelling
- Surfing
- Swimming/Pool
- Walking
- Windsurfing
- Other Activity

Sleeping

- Sleeping
- Camping

Eating

- Eating

Drinking & Nightlife

- Drinking & Nightlife
- Cafe

Entertainment

- Entertainment

Shopping

- Shopping

Information

- Bank
- Embassy/Consulate
- Hospital/Medical
- Internet
- Police
- Post Office
- Telephone
- Toilet
- Tourist Information
- Other Information

Geographic

- Beach
- Gate
- Hut/Shelter
- Lighthouse
- Lookout
- Mountain/Volcano
- Oasis
- Park
- Pass
- Picnic Area
- Waterfall

Population

- Capital (National)
- Capital (State/Province)
- City/Large Town
- Town/Village

Transport

- Airport
- Border crossing
- Bus
- Cable car/Funicular
- Cycling
- Ferry
- Metro station
- Monorail
- Parking
- Petrol station
- Subway station
- Taxi
- Train station/Railway
- Tram
- Underground station
- Other Transport

Note: Not all symbols displayed above appear on the maps in this book

Routes

- Tollway
- Freeway
- Primary
- Secondary
- Tertiary
- Lane
- Unsealed road
- Road under construction
- Plaza/Mall
- Steps
- Tunnel
- Pedestrian overpass
- Walking Tour
- Walking Tour detour
- Path/Walking Trail

Boundaries

- International
- State/Province
- Disputed
- Regional/Suburb
- Marine Park
- Cliff
- Wall

Hydrography

- River, Creek
- Intermittent River
- Canal
- Water
- Dry/Salt/Intermittent Lake
- Reef

Areas

- Airport/Runway
- Beach/Desert
- Cemetery (Christian)
- Cemetery (Other)
- Glacier
- Mudflat
- Park/Forest
- Sight (Building)
- Sportsground
- Swamp/Mangrove

Mary Fitzpatrick
Maputo, Southern Mozambique Originally from the USA, Mary spent her early years dreaming of how to get across an ocean or two to more exotic locales. Following graduate studies, she set off for Europe. Her fascination with languages and cultures soon led her further south to Africa, where she has spent the past two decades living and working as a professional travel writer all around the continent. She focuses particularly on East and Southern Africa, including Mozambique and Tanzania. Mary has authored and co-authored many guidebooks for Lonely Planet, including *Mozambique; Tanzania; South Africa, Lesotho & Swaziland; East Africa; West Africa;* and *Egypt.*

Trent Holden
Victoria Falls, Zambia, Zimbabwe A writer based in Geelong, just outside Melbourne, Trent has worked for Lonely Planet since 2005. He's covered 30-plus guidebooks across Asia, Africa and Australia. With a penchant for megacities, Trent's in his element when assigned to cover a nation's capital – the more chaotic the better – to unearth cool bars, art, street food and underground subculture. On the flipside he also writes guides to idyllic tropical islands across Asia, in between going on safari to national parks in Africa and the subcontinent. When not travelling, Trent works as a freelance editor and reviewer and spends all his money catching live gigs. You can catch him on Twitter @hombreholden

Brendan Sainsbury
Central Mozambique, Northern Mozambique Born and raised in the UK in a town that never merits a mention in any guidebook (Andover, Hampshire), Brendan spent the holidays of his youth caravanning in the English Lake District and didn't leave Blighty until he was nineteen. Making up for lost time, he's since squeezed 70 countries into a sometimes precarious existence as a writer and professional vagabond. In the last eleven years, he has written over 40 books for Lonely Planet, covering destinations from Castro's Cuba to the canyons of Peru. When not scribbling research notes, Brendan likes partaking in ridiculous 'endurance' races, strumming old Clash songs on the guitar, and experiencing the pain and occasional pleasures of following Southampton Football Club.

OUR STORY

A beat-up old car, a few dollars in the pocket and a sense of adventure. In 1972 that's all Tony and Maureen Wheeler needed for the trip of a lifetime – across Europe and Asia overland to Australia. It took several months, and at the end – broke but inspired – they sat at their kitchen table writing and stapling together their first travel guide, *Across Asia on the Cheap*. Within a week they'd sold 1500 copies. Lonely Planet was born.

Today, Lonely Planet has offices in Franklin, London, Melbourne, Oakland, Dublin, Beijing and Delhi, with more than 600 staff and writers. We share Tony's belief that 'a great guidebook should do three things: inform, educate and amuse'.

OUR WRITERS

Anthony Ham

Botswana, Namibia, Planning, Survival Guide, Health Anthony is a freelance writer and photographer who specialises in Spain, East and Southern Africa, the Arctic and the Middle East. When he's not writing for Lonely Planet, Anthony writes about and photographs Spain, Africa and the Middle East for newspapers and magazines in Australia, the UK and US. In 2001, after years of wandering the world, Anthony finally found his spiritual home when he fell irretrievably in love with Madrid on his first visit to the city. Less than a year later, he arrived there on a one-way ticket, with not a word of Spanish and not knowing a single person in the city. When he finally left Madrid ten years later, Anthony spoke Spanish with a Madrid accent, was married to a local and Madrid had become his second home. Now back in Australia, Anthony continues to travel the world in search of stories.

James Bainbridge

Malawi James is a British travel writer and journalist based in Cape Town, South Africa, from where he roams the globe and contributes to publications world-wide. He has been working on Lonely Planet projects for over a decade, updating dozens of guidebooks and TV hosting everywhere from the African bush to the Great Lakes. He has contributed to several editions of Lonely Planet's *South Africa, Lesotho & Swaziland, Turkey* and *Morocco* guides, and his articles on travel, culture and investment appear in the likes of *BBC Travel,* the UK *Guardian* and *Independent, Condé Nast Traveller* and *Lonely Planet Traveller.*

Lucy Corne

South Africa, Lesotho, Swaziland Lucy left university with a degree in journalism and a pair of perpetually itchy feet. She taught EFL for eight years in Spain, South Korea, Canada, China and India, while writing freelance features for a range of magazines, newspapers and websites. She joined the Lonely Planet team in 2008 and has since worked on a range of titles including *Africa, Canary Islands, South Africa, Lesotho & Swaziland* and several foodie titles. Lucy lives in Cape Town with her husband and young son, where she writes on travel, food and beer. Her popular blog, www.brewmistress.co.za, documents the South African beer scene.

OVER PAGE | MORE WRITERS

Published by Lonely Planet Global Limited
CRN 554153
7th edition – Sep 2017
ISBN 978 1 78657 041 3
© Lonely Planet 2017   Photographs © as indicated 2017
10 9 8 7 6 5 4 3 2
Printed in Singapore